Economics

Goods and services
markets

Economics

Karl E. Case Wellesley College

Ray C. Fair Yale University

Manfred Gärtner University of St Gallen

Ken Heather University of Portsmouth

Prentice Hall Europe

London • New York • Toronto • Sydney • Tokyo

Singapore • Madrid • Mexico City • Munich • Paris

Original fourth edition entitled *Principles of Economics* published by
Prentice Hall Inc
A Simon & Schuster Company
Upper Saddle River
New Jersey, USA
Copyright © 1996 by Prentice Hall Inc

This edition published by Prentice Hall Europe © 1999
Authorized for sale only in Europe, the Middle East and Africa.

Typeset in 10pt Janson Text by
Meridian Colour Repro Ltd, Pangbourne-on-Thames, Berkshire

Printed and bound by Rotolito Lombarda, Italy

British Library Cataloguing in Publication Data

A catalogue record for this book is available from
the British Library

ISBN 0-13-095815-8 (pbk)

1 2 3 4 5 03 02 01 00 99

Brief contents

Part 7
Macroeconomic Analysis and Issues

Part 8
Debates in Macroeconomics and Economic Growth

International Economics

Part 9
The Global Economy

Contents

International Economics

Part 9
The Global Economy

Preface

We live in a rapidly changing world. In the last decade or so the Berlin Wall has fallen and the political map of Eastern Europe has been transformed. Russia remains in deep crisis. Western European integration has moved so rapidly during that time that many Western European countries are embracing a single currency. Many high-growth Asian economies, including Japan, have, in the last year or two, experienced the severest recession since the 1930s and sharp falls in their exchange rates. The US economy has boomed whilst much of Europe has struggled out of a deep recession. What are the forces that shape such events?

We have produced *Economics* specifically for students in Europe. Our aim is not primarily to describe the economic landscape but rather to explain and analyse the processes which will enable students to understand recent events and those which will happen as the early years of the new century unfold. Each chapter deals with an area of economic analysis which is liberally illustrated with relevant examples supported in almost every chapter by applications from other parts of the world.

The result, we hope, is a highly readable first-level text that students will keep on their shelves and use throughout their academic course and beyond.

The plan of the book

The purpose of the book is to introduce the discipline of economics and to provide a basic understanding of how economies function. This requires a blend of economic theory, institutional material, and real-world applications. We have tried to maintain a reasonable balance between these ingredients in every chapter in this book. We have also attempted to present differing theoretical views in an even-handed way.

While we have chosen to present microeconomics first, we have designed the text so that teachers may proceed directly to macroeconomics after teaching the five introductory chapters.

Microeconomics

The organisation of the microeconomic material reflects our belief that the best way to understand how market economies operate – and the best way to understand basic economic theory – is to work through the perfectly competitive model first, including discussions of output *and* input markets and the connections between them, before turning to non-competitive market structures. When students understand how a simple competitive system works, they can start thinking about how the pieces of the economy 'fit together'. We think this is a better approach to teaching economics than some of the more traditional approaches, which encourage students to think of economics as a series of disconnected alternative market models.

We therefore open with a chapter on the methodology of economics and proceed in chapter 2 to explain the nature of the economic problem – scarcity of resources. Then, following a chapter reviewing the European economy today, we explain in chapters 4 and 5 the determination of prices in competitive markets. Chapters 6–11 build on this foundation, examining the behaviour of both consumers and competitive firms in output and resource markets.

Looking at competition first allows students to see the power of the market system. It is impossible to discuss the things that markets do well until students have seen how a simple system determines the allocation of resources.

Chapter 12 is a pivotal chapter that links the world of perfect competition with the imperfect world of non-competitive markets, externalities, imperfect information, and poverty, all of which are subsequently discussed in more detail.

Chapters 13–14 concentrate on market failure due to monopoly power and chapter 15 examines government behaviour towards such power at both the national and European level. Chapter 16 examines more elements of market failure including externatlities, public goods and imperfect information. Markets give rise to an uneven distribution of income and this forms the focus of chapter 17.

In Chapters 18 and 19 students use much of what they have learned in chapters 6–17 to take a closer look at two of the fields of applied microeconomics (the economics of taxation and labour economics).

Macroeconomics

The macroeconomics section opens with three introductory chapters (chapters 20–22). These provide a first, bird's-eye perspective of the macroeconomy. Students are introduced to the tools of macroeconomics, including national income accounting. They are also familiarized with the major concerns of macroeconomics – inflation, income, growth, and unemployment – in the context of European experience.

After these chapters we assemble models – simplified pictures of reality – designed to help us understand, discuss and deal with macroeconomic issues. The crucial choice to be made here is whether to start with an analysis of the long-run features of the macroeconomy, or of its short-run behaviour. We opt for the latter, because this is where the action is: recessions, even major crises may appear small fare when looking back a few decades from now, but they do affect our current lives in dramatic ways.

Chapters 23–27 carve out a first model of the *global economy*. This helps understand the environment within which national economies operate, and has the pedagogical advantage of permitting us to leave out the complications that arise from the international linkages of modern economies.

From chapter 28 onward the focus is the *national economy*. Exports, imports, exchange rates and the balance of payments take centre stage. In chapter 30 we turn to the labour market, where wages are determined. Merging the labour market with the demand-side models of previous chapters displays the macroeconomic interaction between supply and demand. Taking this into account is essential for a full understanding of business cycles and related issues. Chapters 29 and 32 put the models to work: topics addressed there include the European Monetary System, European Monetary Union, inflation, central bank independence, unemployment, oil-price shocks, government budget deficits, the public debt, and budget control mechanisms such as the EU countries' Pact on Stability and Growth.

Chapters 33 and 34 may be skipped without losing track. Chapter 33 shows how to refine the basic model by means of more detailed modelling of firm and household behaviour. Chapter 34 sketches the different schools of thought that have contributed to today's understanding of the macroeconomy. It is emphasized that new directions in theoretical thinking are often triggered by new challenges which reality poses.

Chapter 35 turns to the long-run issues subsumed under the term 'economic growth'. It asks why some countries are rich while others remain poor, and why some countries' incomes grow rapidly while others' don't.

Much of the macroeconomics has been analysed in the context of an open economy but we return in chapter 36 to the underlying basis of international trade and explain more fully the law of comparative advantage first introduced in chapter 2. Chapter 37 deals with the problems of developing economies and their relationships with Europe. Finally, in chapter 38 we consider resource allocation in non-market economies and in those economies which are in transition to a market system.

Key features of the book

A European perspective

The book is truly European. First, we have introduced international economics early in macroeconomics. All European economies are critically dependent upon international trade. Second, the examples in the main text and in the boxes are drawn from all over Europe. In this way students start to understand how the main economic issues affect Europe, and become familiar with the major European currencies and the euro, which is rapidly becoming a key currency in international trading relationships.

Finally, there are many 'Global Perspective' boxes throughout the text. These boxes are designed to illustrate economic logic, with global examples from outside Europe, and to emphasize today's global economy.

The use of mathematics

For those students with a limited mathematical background an appendix to chapter 1 explains the basic quantitative relationships used in the main text. For those with a greater knowledge of mathematics, there are mathematical boxes explaining many of the key economic concepts. These mathematical boxes can be skipped if not required. In this way all economics students can use the text with confidence.

Optional chapters

We have tried to keep uppermost in our minds that time is always tight in an introductory course. For this reason, we have made sure that certain chapters can be skipped without losing the flow of the material. In microeconomics, chapter 11 (on the capital market) can be skipped because chapter 10 (on input markets in general) covers the basics of the capital market. Similarly, the 'topics' chapters in Part Four can be skipped if time is short.

The teaching/learning package

Study Guide

A comprehensive Study Guide has been prepared by Ken Randall of Staffordshire University. Each chapter in the Study Guide corresponds to a chapter in the textbook and contains the following features:

The Chapter in Perspective which introduces the chapter topic, says why it is important, and how it relates to the rest of the material in the textbook.
Reviewing the Chapter which invites students to go through the textbook chapter, reviewing their knowledge of the Key Concepts in it and the crucial tables and diagrams.
Self-Test which lets students check whether they have understood the main ideas.
Structured Notes section which should be completed if the student is still unsure of their grasp of the chapter content. Completing the definitions and answering the questions in this section will create a set of structured notes on the chapter.
Collaborative Learning which suggests ways of working with fellow-students by testing each other's understanding of the topics in the Review section, giving short presentations on key concepts and debating controversial issues.
Answers are provided for the **Self-Test** and the **Structured Notes** sections. These vary from simple answers to explanatory paragraphs, as appropriate

The Study Guide complements the textbook by providing straightforward and flexible help to students who may be finding the chapter content difficult at first reading. On **taught** courses we expect students to use the Study Guide when they are having problems understanding the course, and are unable to get personal help from a tutor. On **open and distance learning courses** we expect the Study Guide to help students to structure their learning around the textbook, and help them to act as their own tutor.

Instructor's Manual

Rebecca Taylor, of the University of Portsmouth, has developed an innovative Instructor's Manual to accompany the text, adapted from the two Instructor's Resource Manuals for *Principles of Microeconomics* and *Principles of Macroeconomics* written by Patricia Euzent of the University of Central Florida.

The manual is designed to equip the instructor with the tools to deliver the text material effectively and to provide students with a valuable learning experience. The manual includes:

■ Detailed chapter outlines with key terminology, teaching notes and lecture suggestions.

■ Specific discussion suggestions to encourage students to relate the concepts being taught to personal and international issues.

■ Global examples which make the learned material more relevant to the students.

■ Extended Applications, which include exercises, activities and experiments to further student understanding of the topics being studied.

■ Solutions to all odd-numbered problems from the text.

CD-ROM

The Instructor's Manual is supported by a CD-ROM containing PowerPoint slides of the key figures from the text, a test item file and the Prentice Hall Custom Test.

The Case, Fair, Gärtner, Heather test item file is a comprehensive test bank of approximately 1500 short-answer, multiple-choice, true/false, and problem set questions. The questions are divided into three levels of difficulty – easy, moderate and difficult. Problem sets (a series of questions based on a graph or scenario) can contain all three levels.

The test item file is designed for use with the Prentice Hall Custom Test, a computer package that allows users to custom design, save and generate classroom tests. The test programme (which runs on DOS and Windows-based computers) permits instructors to edit and add or delete questions from the test item file, to edit existing graphics and create new graphics, and to export files to various word processing programmes, including WordPerfect and Microsoft Word. Graphics capability ensures that all graphs included in the test item file can be printed next to the appropriate questions.

Additional information about the various forms of testing services can be obtained from your Prentice Hall sales representative.

A website to accompany the text is under development. Further details can be found at http://www.prenhall.co.uk

Teaching and learning features

We have attempted to make this text as clear and accessible as possible, catering for those students who have never studied economics before, as well as those with some previous knowledge. The language is lively and engaging and the content is highly topical and up to date. Wherever possible we have chosen examples which relate to students' own experience. The overall structure of the chapters is consistent throughout and the learning features are clearly identified. To familiarise yourself with these features and how they will benefit your study from this text, they are reproduced and described in the 'Guided Tour' following.

Guided Tour

Chapter beginning

Each chapter opens with a brief recap of what the student has learned in the previous chapter.

Key terms

Colour-highlighted within the text in yellow. Definitions are given in the margin.

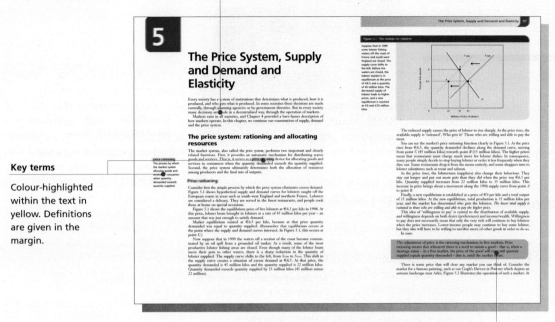

Major principles of economics

These are distinguished from the main text to highlight their importance and to aid revision and review.

Maths boxes

The maths boxes illustrate the main economic concepts, supplementing the explanations in the text.

Application boxes

These bring economic theory to life with topical examples drawn from all over Europe.

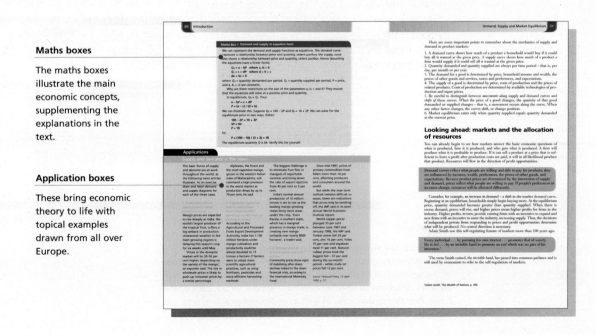

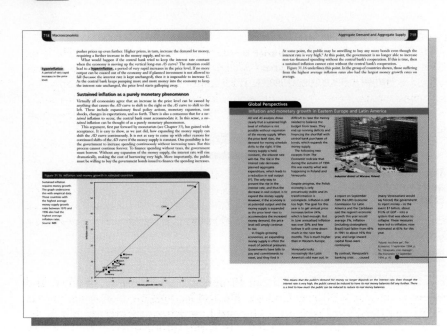

Global Perspective boxes

These illustrative boxes provide economic examples from around the world.

Review terms and concepts

An alphabetical collation of all the key terms in the chapter provides an aid to understanding and a convenient basis for revision.

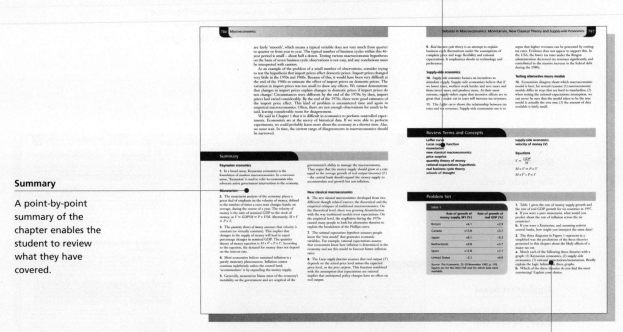

Summary

A point-by-point summary of the chapter enables the student to review what they have covered.

Problem sets

These allow the students to self test, or they can be used as preparations for group discussion. Tasks include graphical analysis or the application of economics to a real world situation or policy decision. Solutions to selected questions appear at the back of the book. Remaining solutions, as well as additional problem sets, are available in the Instructor's Manual.

The Authors

European authors

Manfred Gärtner is Professor of Economics at the University of St Gallen. He is on the editorial board of the *European Journal of Political Economy* and his research has focused on open economy macroeconomics, trade unions and political economy. He has written journal articles and several other books, including *Macroeconomics under Flexible Exchange Rates* (Harvester Wheatsheaf, 1993) and *A Primer in European Macroeconomics* (Prentice Hall, 1997). He has taught macroeconomics at all levels as well as on courses on economic principles and international monetary economics.

Ken Heather is a senior lecturer in economics at the University of Portsmouth. He has taught on a wide range of courses in both macroeconomics and microeconomics. His research interests are primarily in industrial economics. He is the author of *Understanding Economics* (Prentice Hall, 1994, 1997) as well as numerous articles in the area of business economics.

US authors

Karl E. Case is the Marion Butler McLean Professor in the History of Ideas and Professor of Economics at Wellesley College. He also lectures on economics and tax policy in the International Tax Program at Harvard Law School. His research is in the areas of public finance, taxation and housing. He is the author or co-author of four other books, including *Economics and Tax Policy*, as well as numerous articles in professional journals.

Ray C. Fair is Professor of Economics at Yale University and a Fellow of the Econometric Society. Professor Fair's main research is in macroeconomics and econometrics, with particular emphasis on macroeconometric model building. His publications include *Specification, Estimation and Analysis of Macroeconometric Models* (Harvard Press, 1984) and *Testing Macroeconometric Models* (Harvard Press, 1994).

Acknowledgements

We are grateful to those who assisted in this project. The Prentice Hall team did a superb job. Special thanks are due to Monica Balogh, Catherine Newman, Susan Richards and Anne Rix, not only for their professionalism but for their sense of humour, which helped to keep us going.

We also owe a debt of gratitude to those who made comments and suggestions on individual parts of the text. In particular thank you to Celia Armstrong, Con Brewer, Clarissa Gent, Simon Heather, James Heather, Matthius Lutz and Friederike Pohlenz.

Others have contributed to the support materials. A special word of thanks is due to Rebecca Taylor for her fine work on the Instructor's Manual and to Ken Randall for producing such an excellent student workbook.

We welcome comments about the book. Please write to us care of Economics Editor, Prentice Hall, Campus 400, Maylands Avenue, Hemel Hempstead HP2 7EZ, UK.

Credits

Our focus is distinctively European. As a result reference is made throughout the book to many different European countries and their currencies. Some illustrations use the euro, which is planned to be the currency unit in most European countries in the future. The table gives the relative values of all these currencies. Also included in the table are the US dollar and the Japanese yen. Since currency rates change over time these should only be regarded as approximate.

Cross rates enable us to see the value of any currency quoted in the table against any other such currency. If you are not familiar with such tables it is very simple to use. Start with a country and currency of your choice from the first column. Then read across to the column of the country whose relative currency value you wish to know. Take, for example the German mark (DM). Reading across to the column headed FFr enables us to see that one DM is worth about 3.352 French francs. In the UK the currency is the pound sterling. From the table it can be seen that one £ sterling exchanges for about 237 Spanish pesetas. The Dutch florin buys 4.266 Swedish kronor.

The euro is set to become increasingly significant throughout Europe. It can be seen from the table to be worth about 1.597 Swiss francs. It also buys about 1.203 US dollars.

The table can be useful to you as you read the book. Whenever an example or illustration is given in a particular currency, you can discover its approximate worth in any other currency you choose.

Currency cross rates

Country/Currency		BFr	DKr	FFr	DM	I£	L	Fl	NKr	E$	Pta	SKr	SFr	£	US£	Y	€
Belgium	(BFr)	100	18.42	16.24	4.846	1.944	4796	5.465	22.28	497.2	412.1	23.31	3.929	1.739	2.959	354.1	2.480
Denmark	(DKr)	54.28	10	5.815	2.630	1.055	2604	2.967	12.10	269.9	223.7	12.66	2.133	0.944	1.606	192.2	1.335
France	(FFr)	61.56	11.34	10	2.983	1.197	2953	3.364	13.72	306.1	253.7	14.35	2.419	1.071	1.822	216.0	1.514
Germany	(DM)	20.64	3.802	3.352	1	0.401	989.8	1.128	4.599	102.6	85.04	4.811	0.811	0.359	0.611	73.07	0.508
Ireland	(IE)	51.43	9.474	8.355	2.492	1	2467	2.811	11.46	255.7	211.9	11.98	2.021	0.694	1.522	182.1	1.265
Italy	(L)	2.085	0.384	0.339	0.101	0.041	100	0.114	0.465	10.37	6.592	0.486	0.082	0.036	0.062	7.382	0.051
Netherlands	(Fl)	16.30	3.371	2.972	0.587	0.356	877.6	1	4.077	90.98	75.40	4.266	0.719	0.318	0.542	64.79	0.450
Norway	(NKr)	44.88	8.267	7.290	2.175	0.873	2152	2.453	10	223.1	164.9	10.48	1.763	0.780	1.328	158.9	1.104
Portugal	(E$)	20.11	3.705	3.267	0.975	0.391	964.6	1.099	4.482	100	82.88	4.689	0.790	0.350	0.595	71.21	0.495
Spain	(Pta)	24.27	4.470	3.942	1.176	0.472	1184	1.326	5.407	120.7	100	5.657	0.953	0.422	0.718	85.92	0.597
Sweden	(SKr)	42.89	7.902	5.965	2.078	0.834	2057	2.344	9.558	213.3	178.8	10	1.685	0.746	1.269	151.9	1.055
Switzerland	(SFr)	25.45	4.469	4.134	1.233	0.495	1221	1.391	5.871	126.5	104.9	5.934	1	0.443	0.753	90.12	0.626
UK	(£)	57.50	10.59	9.341	2.786	1.118	2758	3.143	12.81	285.9	237.0	13.41	2.259	1	1.702	203.6	1.414
USA	($)	33.79	6.225	5.489	1.637	0.657	1621	1.847	7.530	168.0	139.3	7.878	1.328	0.588	1	119.7	0.831
Japan	(Y)	28.24	5.203	4.588	1.369	0.549	1355	1.543	6.293	140.4	116.4	5.584	1.110	0.491	0.638	100	0.595
Euro	(€)	40.68	7.490	6.605	1.970	0.791	1950	2.222	9.060	202.2	167.5	9.479	1.597	0.707	1.203	144.0	1

Note: The Danish and Norwegian krone, the Swedish krona and the French franc are per 10. The Belgian franc, Italian lira, Portuguese escudo, Spanish peseta and Japanese yen are per 100.

Introduction

1

The Scope and Method of Economics

The study of economics should begin with a sense of wonder. Pause for a moment and consider a typical day in your life. For breakfast you might have sat on a chair made from a tree grown in Sweden, and eaten bread made in a local bakery from wheat grown in the USA and bacon from pigs raised in Denmark packaged in plastic made in the UK. You spill coffee from Colombia on your shirt made in Italy from textiles shipped from India.

Later, you drive with a friend in a Japanese car on a road system that took 20 years and billions of euros' worth of resources to build. You stop for petrol refined in Holland from Saudi Arabian crude oil brought to Europe on a supertanker that took three years to build at a shipyard in Poland.

At night you phone your brother in Sydney. The call travels over fibre optic cable to a powerful antenna that sends it to a transponder on one of over 1000 communications satellites orbiting the earth.

You use or consume tens of thousands of things, both tangible and intangible, every day: buildings, the music of a rock band, the compact disc it is recorded on, telephone services, staples, paper, toothpaste, tweezers, soap, a digital watch, fire protection, indigestion tablets, beer, banks, electricity, eggs, insurance, football fields, computers, buses, rugs, health services, pavements, and so forth. Somebody made each of these things. Somebody decided to organize men and women and materials to produce and distribute each of them. Thousands of decisions went into their completion. Somehow they got to you.

Many millions of people in Europe work at hundreds of thousands of different kinds of jobs producing millions of euros' worth of goods and services every year. Some cannot find work; others choose not to work. Some are rich; others are poor.

Large office buildings go up in central cities. Homes are built in the suburbs. In other places homes are abandoned and boarded up.

Some countries are wealthy. Others are impoverished. Some are growing. Some are stagnating. Some businesses are doing well. Others are going bankrupt.

At any moment in time every society faces constraints imposed by nature and by previous generations. Some societies are handsomely endowed by nature with fertile land, water, sunshine and natural resources. Others have deserts and few mineral resources. Some societies receive much from previous generations – art, music, technical knowledge, beautiful buildings, and productive factories. Others are left with overgrazed, eroded land, cities levelled by war, or polluted natural environments. All societies face limits.

economics
The study of how individuals and societies choose to use the scarce resources that nature and previous generations have provided.

Economics is the study of how individuals and societies choose to use the scarce resources that nature and previous generations have provided. The key word in this definition is *choose*. Economics is a behavioural or social science. In large measure it is the study of how people make choices. The choices that people make, when added up, translate into societal choices.

The purpose of this chapter and the next is to elaborate on this definition and to introduce the subject matter of economics. What is produced? How is it produced? Who gets it? Why do they get it? Is the result good or bad? Can it be improved?

Why study economics?

There are four main reasons to study economics: to learn a way of thinking, to understand society, to understand global affairs, and to be an informed voter.

To learn a way of thinking

Probably the most important reason for studying economics is to learn a way of thinking. A good way to introduce economics is to review three of its most fundamental concepts: opportunity cost, marginalism, and efficient markets. If your study of economics is successful, you will find yourself using these concepts every day in making decisions.

Opportunity cost

What happens in an economy is the outcome of thousands of individual decisions. Households must decide how to divide their incomes among all the goods and services available in the marketplace. People must decide whether to work or not to work, whether to go to university or college, and how much to save. Businesses must decide what to produce, how much to produce, how much to charge, and where to locate. It is not surprising that economic analysis focuses on the process of decision making.

Nearly all decisions involve trade-offs. There are advantages and disadvantages, costs and benefits, associated with every action and every choice. A key concept that recurs again and again in analysing the decision-making process is the notion of **opportunity cost**. The full 'cost' of making a specific choice includes what we give up by not making the alternative choice. What we forgo, or give up, when we make a choice or a decision is called the opportunity cost of that decision.

This concept applies to individuals, businesses and entire societies. The opportunity cost of going to a movie is the value of the other things you could have done with the same money and time. If you decide to take time off from working, the opportunity cost of your leisure is the pay that you would have earned had you worked. Part of the cost of going to university is the income you could have earned by working full time instead of continuing your education. If a firm purchases a new piece of equipment for a given amount of money, it does so because it expects that equipment to generate more profit. There is an opportunity cost, however, because that money could have been deposited in an interest-earning account. To a society, the opportunity cost of using resources to put people into space is the value of the private/civilian goods that could have been produced with the same resources.

Opportunity costs arise because resources are scarce. *Scarce* simply means limited. Consider one of our most important resources – time. There are only 24 hours in a day, and we must live our lives under this constraint. A farmer in rural Brazil must decide whether it is better to continue to farm or to go to the city and look for a job. A hockey player at university must decide whether she will play in the university team or spend more time improving her academic work.

Marginalism and sunk costs

A second key concept used in analysing choices is the notion of marginalism. In weighing the costs and benefits of a decision, it is important to weigh only the costs and benefits that arise from the decision. Suppose, for example, that you live in London and that you are weighing the costs and benefits of visiting your aunt in Rome. If business required that you travel to Geneva, the cost of visiting auntie would be only the additional, or marginal, time and money cost of getting to Rome from Geneva.

Consider the cost of producing this book. Assume that 20,000 copies are produced. The total cost of producing the copies includes the cost of the authors' time in writing the book, the cost of editing, the cost of typesetting, the cost of making the plates for printing, and the cost of the paper and ink. If the total cost were €600,000, then the average cost of one copy would be €30, which is simply €600,000 divided by 20,000.

Although average cost is an important concept, a book publisher must know more than simply the average cost of a book. For example, suppose a second printing is

opportunity cost
What we forgo, or give up, when we make a choice or a decision.

being debated. That is, should another 20,000 copies be produced? In deciding whether to proceed, the costs of writing, editing, typesetting and so forth are irrelevant. Why? Because they have already been incurred – they are **sunk costs**. Sunk costs are costs that cannot be avoided, regardless of what is done in the future, because they have already been incurred. All that matters are the costs associated with the additional, or marginal, books to be printed. Technically, marginal cost is the cost of producing one more unit of output.

sunk costs Costs that cannot be avoided, regardless of what is done in the future, because they have already been incurred.

There are numerous examples in which the concept of marginal cost is useful. For a plane that is about to take off with empty seats, the marginal cost of an extra passenger is effectively zero; the total cost of the trip is essentially unchanged by the addition of an extra passenger. Thus, setting aside a few seats to be sold at big discounts can be profitable even if the fare for those seats is far below the average cost per seat of making the trip. As long as the airline succeeds in filling seats that would otherwise have been empty, doing so is profitable.

Efficient markets – no free lunch

Suppose you are driving on a motorway in France and you come upon a toll gate with six booths. Three toll booths are straight ahead in the three lanes of traffic, and the three other booths are off to the right. Which lane should you choose? It is usually the case that the waiting time is approximately the same no matter what you do. There are usually enough people searching for the shortest queue to make all the queues about the same length. If one queue is much shorter than the others, cars will quickly move into it until the queues are equalized.

As you will see later, the term *profit* in economics has a very precise meaning. Economists, however, often loosely refer to 'good deals' or risk-free ventures as profit opportunities. Using the term loosely, a profit opportunity exists at the toll booths if one queue is shorter than the others. In general, these profit opportunities are rare. At any one time there are many people searching for such opportunities, and as a consequence few exist. At toll booths it is seldom the case that one queue is substantially shorter than the others. Markets like this, where any profit opportunities are eliminated almost instantaneously, are said to be **efficient market**s. (We discuss markets, the institutions through which buyers and sellers interact and engage in exchange, in detail in Chapter 2.)

efficient market A market in which profit opportunities are eliminated almost instantaneously.

The common way of expressing the efficient markets hypothesis is 'There's no such thing as a free lunch'. How should you react when a stockbroker phones you with a hot tip for the stock market? With scepticism. There are thousands of individuals each day looking for hot tips in the market. If a particular tip about a stock is valid there will be an immediate rush to buy the stock, which will quickly drive its price up.

This economists' view that very few profit opportunities exist can, of course, be carried too far. There is a story about two people walking along, one an economist and one not. The non-economist sees a €20 note on the pavement and says 'There's a €20 note on the pavement.' The economist replies 'That's not possible. If there had been a note there, somebody would already have picked it up.'

There are clearly times when profit opportunities exist. Someone has to be first to get the news, and some people have quicker insights than others. Nevertheless, news travels fast, and there are thousands of people with quick insights. The general view that profit opportunities are rare is close to the mark.

> The study of economics teaches us a way of thinking and helps us to make decisions.

To understand society

Another reason for studying economics is to understand society better. You cannot hope to understand how a society functions without a basic knowledge of its economy, and you cannot understand a society's economy without knowing its economic history. Clearly, past and present economic decisions have an enormous influence on the character of life in a society. The current state of the physical environment, the level of material well-being, and the nature and number of jobs are all products of the economic system.

To get a sense of the ways in which economic decisions have shaped our environment, imagine looking out of a top floor window of a high-rise office building in any large city. The work day is about to begin. All around you are other tall glass and steel buildings full of workers. In the distance you see the smoke of factories. Looking down, you see thousands of commuters pouring off trains and buses, and cars backed up at motorway exits. You see trucks carrying goods from one place to another. You also see the face of urban poverty: just beyond the motorway is a large housing estate and, beyond that, burned out and boarded up buildings.

What you see before you is the product of millions of economic decisions made over hundreds of years. People at some point decided to spend time and money building those buildings and factories. Somebody cleared the land, laid the tracks, built the roads and produced the cars and buses.

Not only have economic decisions shaped the physical environment, they have determined the character of society as well. At no time has the impact of economic change on society been more evident than in England during the late eighteenth and early nineteenth centuries, a period that we now call the **Industrial Revolution**. Increases in the productivity of agriculture, new manufacturing technologies, and the development of more efficient forms of transport led to a massive movement of the British population from the countryside to the city. At the beginning of the eighteenth century, approximately two out of three people in Great Britain worked in agriculture. By 1812, only one in three remained in agriculture, and by 1900 the figure was fewer than one in ten. People jammed into overcrowded cities and worked long hours in factories. The world had changed completely in two centuries – a period that, in the run of history, was nothing more than the blink of an eye.

It is not surprising that the discipline of economics began to take shape during this period. Social critics and philosophers looked around them and knew that their philosophies must expand to accommodate the changes. Adam Smith's *Wealth of Nations* appeared in 1776. It was followed by the writings of David Ricardo, Karl Marx, Thomas Malthus and others. Each tried to make sense out of what was happening. Who was building the factories? Why? What determined the level of wages paid to workers or the price of food? What would happen in the future, and what should happen? The people who asked these questions were the first economists.

Similar changes continue to affect the character of life today. While some parts of Europe are growing quickly, others are stagnating. Some people are becoming better off, but the wages of many workers are falling relative to the cost of living. And while some people are paid barely enough to live on, some footballers and rock stars are growing very rich. How do we make sense of all of this? Why do we have unemployment? What forces determine wages? Why is it that some footballers can command such high salaries?

The study of economics is an essential part of the study of society.

To understand global affairs

A third reason for studying economics is to understand global affairs. News headlines are filled with economic stories: the European Union struggles to adopt a common currency. The nations of the former Soviet Union are wrestling with a new phenomenon as they privatize state-owned industries: organized crime. The USA comes under pressure for its record on the environment. Starvation continues in Africa.

All countries are part of a world economy, and understanding international relations begins with a basic knowledge of the economic links between countries. For centuries, countries have attempted to protect their industries and workers from foreign competition by taxing imports and limiting their number. Most economists argue, however,

Industrial Revolution
The period in England during the late eighteenth and early nineteenth centuries in which new manufacturing technologies and improved transport gave rise to the modern factory system and a massive movement of the population from the countryside to the cities.

that unrestricted trade is in the long-run interest of all countries. Just after the Second World War, many countries signed the General Agreement on Tariffs and Trade (GATT), in which they committed themselves to lowering trade barriers. The process continues today. The issue is a passionate one. French farmers, fearing the effects of cheap imports on their livelihood, protested strongly when France undertook to sign the new GATT, now referred to as the World Trade Organization (WTO).

The end of apartheid laws that legally separated the races in South Africa has created a new climate for international investment in that country. Meanwhile, the countries of Eastern Europe are struggling to create, from the ground up, economic and social institutions that took centuries to build in the West.

Another important issue in today's world is the widening gap between rich nations and poor nations. The 75% of the world's population that lives in the less developed countries receives less than 20% of the world's income. In dozens of countries, per capita income is only a few hundred euros a year.

> An understanding of economics is essential to an understanding of global affairs.

To be an informed voter

A knowledge of economics is essential to the informed voter. Probably the most important factor in determining the outcome of an election is the state of the economy.

Most of Europe is emerging only slowly from a recession. How much of the unemployment it has suffered is due to government economic policy? Certainly, some part of it is. Many European governments are taking part in the formation of a single European currency. One condition of being able to do so is that a country's government spending is not much higher than government income. This has meant higher taxes for many people. Lower government spending has led to workers, particularly in the public sector, being put out of jobs. Is it all worth it? Should the electorate of those countries that are not yet members of a single currency vote for politicians wanting to join or for politicians who will concern themselves with full employment?

Another important area of debate is our social security provision. Is high provision of this kind always beneficial? Or does it make people lazy, causing them to choose to remain idle? Are governments who have a minimum wage law helping low income groups? Or are they creating unemployment by making it too expensive for firms to hire them? These are the kinds of economic issues that are usually at the centre of debate during elections.

> When we participate in the political process, we are voting on issues that require a basic understanding of economics.

The scope of economics

Most students taking economics for the first time are surprised by the breadth of what they study. Some think that economics will teach them about the stock market or what to do with their money. Others think that economics deals exclusively with problems like inflation and unemployment. In fact, it deals with all these subjects, but they are pieces of a much larger puzzle.

Economics has deep roots in, and close ties to, social philosophy. An issue of great importance to philosophers, for example, is distributional justice. Why are some people rich and others poor, and whatever the answer, is this fair? A number of nineteenth-century social philosophers wrestled with these questions, and out of their musings economics as a separate discipline was born.

The easiest way to get a feel for the breadth and depth of what you will be studying is to explore briefly the way economics is organized. First of all, there are two major divisions of economics: microeconomics and macroeconomics.

Microeconomics and macroeconomics

microeconomics
The branch of economics that examines the functioning of individual industries and the behaviour of individual decision-making units – that is, business firms and households.

Microeconomics deals with the functioning of individual industries and the behaviour of individual economic decision-making units: business firms and households. Microeconomics explores the decisions that individual businesses and consumers make. Firms' choices about what to produce and how much to charge and households' choices about what and how much to buy help to explain why the economy produces the things it does.

Another big question that microeconomics addresses is: Who gets the things that are produced? Wealthy households get more output than do poor households, and the forces that determine this distribution of output are the province of microeconomics. Why does poverty exist? Who is poor? Why do some jobs pay more than others?

Think again about all the things you consume in a day, and then think back to that view over a big city. Somebody decided to build those factories. Somebody decided to construct the roads, build the housing, produce the cars and smoke the bacon. Why? What is going on in all those buildings? It is easy to see that understanding individual micro decisions is very important to any understanding of society.

macroeconomics
The branch of economics that examines the economic behaviour of aggregates – income, employment, output and so on – on a national scale.

Macroeconomics looks at the economy as a whole. Instead of trying to understand what determines the output of a single firm or industry, or the consumption patterns of a single household or group of households, macroeconomics examines the factors that determine national output, or national product. Microeconomics is concerned with household income; macroeconomics deals with national income.

While microeconomics focuses on individual product prices and relative prices, macroeconomics looks at the overall price level and how quickly (or slowly) it is rising (or falling). Microeconomics questions how many people will be hired (or fired) this year in a particular industry or in a certain geographical area, and the factors that determine how much labour a firm or industry will hire. Macroeconomics deals with aggregate employment and unemployment: How many jobs exist in the economy as a whole, and how many people who are willing to work are not able to find work?

To summarize:

> Microeconomics looks at the individual unit – the household, the firm, the industry. It sees and examines the 'trees'. Macroeconomics looks at the whole, the aggregate. It sees and analyses the 'forest'.

Table 1.1 Examples of microeconomic and macroeconomic concerns

Division of economics	Production	Prices	Income	Employment
Microeconomics	*Production/output in individual industries and businesses*	*Price of individual goods and services*	*Distribution of income and wealth*	*Employment by individual businesses and industries*
	How much steel? How much office space? How many cars?	Price of medical care Price of petrol Food prices Housing rents	Wages in the car industry Minimum wage Executive salaries Poverty	Jobs in the steel industry Number of employees in a firm Number of accountants
Macroeconomics	*National production/output*	*Aggregate price level*	*National income*	*Employment and unemployment in the economy*
	Total industrial output Gross domestic product Growth of output	Consumer prices Producer prices Rate of inflation	Total wages and salaries Total corporate profits	Total number of jobs Unemployment rate

Table 1.1 summarizes these divisions and some of the subjects with which they are concerned.

Applications

The Fields of Economics

A good way to convey the diversity of economics is to describe some of its major fields of study and the issues that economists address.

■ *Industrial organization* looks carefully at the structure and performance of industries and firms within an economy. How do businesses compete? Who gains and who loses?

■ *Urban and regional economics* studies the spatial arrangement of economic activity. Why do we have cities? Why are manufacturing firms locating further and further from the centre of urban areas?

■ *Econometrics* applies statistical techniques and data to economic problems in an effort to test hypotheses and theories. Most schools require students specializing in economics to take at least one course in statistics or econometrics.

■ *Comparative economic systems* examines the ways alternative economic systems function. What are the advantages and disadvantages of different systems? What is the best way to convert the planned economies of the former Soviet Union to market systems?

■ *Economic development* focuses on the problems of poor countries. What can be done to promote development in these nations? Important concerns of development economists include population growth and control, provision for basic needs, and strategies for international trade.

■ *Labour economics* deals with the factors that determine wage rates, employment and unemployment. How do people decide whether to work, how much to work, and at what kind of job? How have the roles of unions and management changed in recent years?

■ *Finance* examines the ways in which households and firms actually pay for, or finance, their purchases. It involves the study of capital markets (including the stock and bond markets), futures and options, capital budgeting and asset valuation.

■ *International economics* studies trade flows among countries and international financial institutions. What are the advantages and disadvantages for a country that allows its citizens to buy and sell freely in world markets? What determines the international value of currencies?

■ *Public economics* examines the role of government in the economy. What are the economic functions of government, and what should they be? How should the government finance the services that it provides? What kinds of government programmes should confront the problems of poverty, unemployment and pollution?

■ *Economic history* traces the development of the modern economy. What economic and political events and scientific advances caused the Industrial Revolution that began in eighteenth-century Britain? What explains the tremendous growth and progress of Japan after the Second World War? What caused the Great Depression of the 1930s?

■ *Law and economics* analyses the economic function of legal rules and institutions. How does the law change the behaviour of individuals and businesses? Do different liability rules make accidents and injuries more, or less, likely? What are the economic costs of crime?

Economics studies many imperfect issues. What are the implications for European economies of increasing international trade? (Reproduced with kind permission of EST trucking.)

■ The history of economic thought, which is grounded in philosophy, studies the development of economic ideas and theories over time, from Adam Smith in the eighteenth century to the works of economists such as Thomas Malthus, Karl Marx and John Maynard Keynes. Because economic theory is constantly developing and changing, studying the history of ideas helps give meaning to modern theory and puts it in perspective.

The diversity and fields of economics

Individual economists focus their research and study in many diverse areas. Many of these specialized fields are reflected in the advanced courses offered at most colleges and universities. Some are concerned with economic history or the history of economic thought. Others focus on international economics or growth in less developed countries. Still others study the economics of cities (urban economics) or the relationship between economics and law. (See 'The Fields of Economics' Application box for more details.)

Economists also differ in the emphasis they place on theory. Some economists specialize in developing new theories, while others spend their time testing the theories of others. Some economists hope to expand the frontiers of knowledge, while others are more interested in applying what is already known to the formulation of public policies.

As you begin your study of economics, look through your prospectus or syllabus and talk to the staff about their interests. You will discover that economics encompasses a broad range of inquiry and is linked to many other disciplines.

The method of economics

positive economics
An approach to economics that seeks to understand behaviour and the operation of systems without making judgements. It describes what exists and how it works.

normative economics
An approach to economics that analyses outcomes of economic behaviour and evaluates them as good or bad, and that may prescribe courses of action. Also called *policy economics*.

Economics asks and attempts to answer two kinds of questions: positive and normative. **Positive economics** attempts to understand behaviour and the operation of economic systems without making judgements about whether the outcomes are good or bad. It strives to describe what exists and how it works. What determines the wage rate for unskilled workers? What would happen if we abolished profits? Who would benefit? Who would lose? The answers to such questions are the subject of positive economics.

In contrast, **normative economics** looks at the outcomes of economic behaviour and asks if they are good or bad and whether they can be made better. Normative economics involves judgements and prescriptions for courses of action. Should the government be involved in regulating the price of petrol? Should income tax be changed to reduce or increase the burden on upper-income families? Should British Airways be allowed to take over other European airlines? Should European governments protect their car industries from other European car producers? Should the European car industry be protected from Japanese car imports?

Of course, most normative questions involve positive questions. To know whether the government should take a particular action, we must know first if it can and second what the consequences are likely to be. For example, if BA takes over other European airlines, will there be higher prices and less competition?

Some claim that positive, value-free economic analysis is impossible. They argue that analysts come to problems with biases that cannot help but influence their work. Furthermore, even in choosing what questions to ask or what problems to analyse, economists are influenced by political, ideological and moral views.

While this argument has some merit, it is nevertheless important to distinguish between analyses that attempt to be positive and those that are intentionally and explicitly normative. Economists who ask explicitly normative questions should be forced to specify their grounds for judging one outcome superior to another. What does it mean to be better? The criteria for such evaluations must be clearly spelled out and thoroughly understood for conclusions to have meaning.

descriptive economics The compilation of data that describe phenomena and facts.

Positive economics is often divided into descriptive economics and economic theory. **Descriptive economics** is simply the compilation of data that describe phenomena and facts.

Descriptive economics and economic theory

Examples of such data can be found in publications by the statistical office of the European Union. One valuable source is *European Economy*, an annual report on many economic variables in Europe but also Japan and the USA. Much information is available on the Internet. A great deal of European data is available on *New Cronos*, published by eurostat.

Of course, there are many series available in book and electronic form for individual countries. These are often published by government agencies. For example, in the UK the government's Office of National Statistics (ONS) produces a wide range of monthly, quarterly and annual data on prices, output, employment and international trade and many other topics in a large range of volumes. Consult your librarian.

economic theory
A statement or set of related statements about cause and effect, action and reaction.

Economic theory attempts to generalize about data and interpret them. An economic theory is a statement or set of related statements about cause and effect, action and reaction. One of the first theories you will encounter in this text is the law of demand, which was most clearly stated by Alfred Marshall in 1890: when the price of a product rises, people tend to buy less of it; when the price of a product falls, they tend to buy more.

inductive reasoning   The process of observing regular patterns from raw data and drawing generalizations from them.

The process of observing regular patterns from raw data and drawing generalizations from them is called **inductive reasoning**. In all sciences, theories begin with inductive reasoning and observed regularities. For example, Aristotle believed that the speed at which objects fall toward the earth depends on their size as well as their weight. But in a series of experiments carried out between 1589 and 1591, Galileo was able to show that bodies of very different sizes seemed to fall at approximately the same speed when dropped from the Leaning Tower of Pisa. Over a century later, Galileo's data led Sir Isaac Newton to formulate the theory of gravity, which eventually became the basis of Albert Einstein's work.

Social scientists, including economists, study human behaviour. They develop and test theories of how human beings, institutions and societies behave. The behaviour of human beings is by its nature not as regular or predictable as the behaviour of electrons, molecules or planets, but there are patterns, regularities and tendencies.

Theories do not always arise out of formal numerical data. All of us have been collecting observations of people's behaviour and their responses to economic stimuli for most of our lives. We may have observed our parents' reaction to a sudden increase – or decrease – in income or to the loss of a job or the acquisition of a new one. We all have seen people standing in a queue waiting for a bargain. And, of course, our own actions and reactions are another important source of data.

Theories and models

model   A formal statement of a theory. Usually a mathematical statement of a presumed relationship between two or more variables.

In many disciplines, including physics, chemistry, meteorology, political science, and economics, theorists build formal models of behaviour. A **model** is a formal statement of a theory. It is usually a mathematical statement of a presumed relationship between two or more variables.

A **variable** is a measure that can change from time to time or from observation to observation. Income is a variable – it has different values for different people, and different values for the same person at different times. The rental price of a film on a videocassette is a variable; it has different values at different shops and at different times. There are countless other examples.

variable   A measure that can change from time to time or from observation to observation.

Because all models simplify reality by stripping part of it away, they are abstractions. Critics of economics often point to abstraction as a weakness. Most economists, however, see abstraction as a real strength.

The easiest way to see how abstraction can be helpful is to think of a map. A map is a representation of reality that is simplified and abstract. A city or state appears on a piece of paper as a series of lines and colours. The amount of reality that the map maker can strip away before the map loses something essential depends on what the map will be used for. If I want to drive from Paris to Rotterdam, I need to know only the major motorways and roads. I lose absolutely nothing and gain clarity by cutting out the local streets. However, if I need to get around in Paris, I may need to see every street and alley.

Most maps are two-dimensional representations of a three-dimensional world; they show where roads and motorways go but do not show hills and valleys along the way. Maps for hikers, however, have 'contour lines' that represent changes in elevation. When you are in a car, changes in elevation matter very little; they would make a map needlessly complex and much more difficult to read. But if you are on foot carrying a 25 kilogram pack, a knowledge of elevation is crucial.

Like maps, economic models are abstractions that strip away detail to expose only those aspects of behaviour that are important to the question being asked. The principle that irrelevant detail should be cut away is called the principle of **Ockham's razor** after the fourteenth-century philosopher William of Ockham.

Ockham's razor
The principle that irrelevant detail should be cut away.

But be careful. Although abstraction is a powerful tool for exposing and analysing specific aspects of behaviour, it is possible to oversimplify. Economic models often strip away a good deal of social and political reality to get at underlying concepts. When an economic theory is used to help formulate actual government or institutional policy, political and social reality must often be reintroduced if the policy is to have a chance of working.

The key here is that the appropriate amount of simplification and abstraction depends upon the use to which the model will be put. To return to the map example: you don't want to walk around Rome with a map made for drivers – there are too many very steep hills!

All else equal: *ceteris paribus*

It is almost always true that whatever you want to explain with a model depends on more than one factor. Suppose, for example, that you want to explain the total number of kilometres driven by car owners in Europe. The distance driven will change from year to year or month to month; it is a variable. The issue, if we want to understand and explain the changes that occur, is what factors cause those changes.

Obviously, many things affect total distance driven. First, more or fewer people may be driving. This, in turn, can be affected by changes in the driving age, by population growth, or by changes in EU laws. Other factors might include the price of petrol, household income, the number and age of children in the household, the distance from home to work, the location of shopping facilities, and the availability and quality of public transport. When any of these variables change, the members of the household may drive more or less. If changes in any of these variables affect large numbers of households across the country, the total number of kilometres driven will change.

Very often we need to isolate or separate out these effects. For example, suppose we want to know the impact on driving of a higher tax on petrol. This change would raise the price of petrol at the pump, but would not (at least in the short run) affect income, workplace location, number of children, and so forth.

ceteris paribus
(all else equal)
A device used to analyse the relationship between two variables while the values of other variables are held unchanged.

To isolate the impact of one single factor, we use the device of **ceteris paribus**, or all else equal. We ask what is the impact of a change in petrol price on driving behaviour, *ceteris paribus* – in other words, assuming that nothing else changes. If petrol prices rise by 10%, how much less driving will there be, assuming no simultaneous change in anything else – that is, assuming that income, number of children, population, laws, and so on all remain constant?

Using the device of *ceteris paribus* is one part of the process of abstraction. In formulating economic theory, the concept helps us simplify reality in order to focus on the relationships that we are interested in.

Expressing models in words, graphs, and equations

Consider the following statements: 'Lower airline ticket prices cause people to fly more frequently.' 'Higher interest rates slow the rate of home sales.' 'When firms produce more output, employment increases.' 'Higher petrol prices cause people to drive less and to buy more fuel-efficient cars.' 'When the Deutschmark falls in value against the value of foreign currencies, firms that export products produced in Germany find their sales increasing.'

Each of these statements expresses a relationship between two variables that can be quantified. In each case there is a stimulus and a response, a cause and an effect. Quantitative relationships can be expressed in a variety of ways. Sometimes words are sufficient to express the essence of a theory, but often it is necessary to be more specific about the nature of a relationship or about the size of a response. The most common method of expressing the quantitative relationship between two variables is to graph that relationship on a two-dimensional plane. In fact, we will use graphical analysis extensively in Chapter 2 and beyond. Because it is essential that you be familiar with the basics of graphing, a careful review of graphing techniques is presented in the appendix to this chapter.

Quantitative relationships between variables can also be presented through equations. For example, suppose we discovered that over time, European households collectively spend, or consume, 90% of their income and save 10% of their income. We could then write:

$$C = 0.90Y \text{ and } S = 0.10Y$$

where C is consumption spending, Y is income and S is saving. Writing explicit algebraic expressions like these helps us understand the nature of the underlying process of decision making. Understanding this process is what economics is all about.

Cautions and pitfalls

In formulating theories and models, it is especially important to avoid two pitfalls: the post hoc fallacy and the fallacy of composition.

■ **The post hoc fallacy** Theories often make statements, or sets of statements, about cause and effect. It can be quite tempting to look at two events that happen in sequence and assume that the first caused the second to happen. Clearly, this is not always the case. This common error is called the **post hoc, ergo propter hoc** (or 'after this, therefore because of this') fallacy.

post hoc, ergo propter hoc
Literally, 'after this (in time), therefore because of this'. A common error made in thinking about causation: if Event A happens before Event B, it is not necessarily true that A caused B.

There are thousands of examples. 'My favourite football team has won seven games in a row. Last night, I went to the match and they lost. I must have 'jinxed' them. They lost because I went to the game.'

Very closely related to the post hoc fallacy is the often erroneous link between correlation and causation. Two variables are said to be correlated if one variable changes when the other variable changes. But correlation does not imply causation. Cities that have high crime rates also have lots of cars, so there is a very high degree of correlation between number of cars and crime rates. Can we argue, then, that cars cause crime? No. The reason for the correlation here may have nothing to do with cause and effect. Big cities have lots of people, lots of people have lots of cars, and therefore big cities have lots of cars. Big cities also have high crime rates for many reasons – crowding, poverty, anonymity, unequal distribution of wealth, and the ready availability of drugs, to mention only a few. But the presence of cars is not one of them.

This caution must also be viewed in reverse. Sometimes events that seem entirely unconnected are actually connected. Some respectable political analysts believe that elections can be decisively affected by the outcome of sporting events. An election immediately following a football World Cup in which the national team has done surprisingly badly may allow some fans to vent their anger on the present government through the ballot box.

fallacy of composition The erroneous belief that what is true for a part is necessarily true for the whole.

■ **The fallacy of composition** To conclude that what is true for a part is necessarily true for the whole is to fall into the **fallacy of composition**. Often, what holds for an individual does not hold for a group or for society as a whole. Suppose that a large number of fishermen fish in the same waters. To an individual fisherman, more fishing means a higher income. But because its capacity is limited, the sea can support only so many fishing boats. If every fisherman increased the number of boats sent out to fish, the sea would become overfished and empty, and everyone's income would fall. In short:

Theories that seem to work well when applied to individuals or households often break down when they are applied to the whole.

Testing theories and models: empirical economics

In science, a theory is rejected when it fails to explain what is observed or when another theory better explains what is observed. Prior to the sixteenth century, almost everyone believed that the earth was the centre of the universe and that the sun and stars rotated around it. The astronomer Ptolemy (AD 127–151) built a model that explained and predicted the movements of the heavenly bodies in a geocentric (earth-centred) universe. Early in the sixteenth century, however, the Polish astronomer Nicholas Copernicus found himself dissatisfied with the Ptolemaic model and proposed an alternative theory or model, placing the sun at the centre of the known universe and relegating the earth to the status of one planet among many. The battle between the competing models was waged, at least in part, with data based on observations – actual measurements of planetary movements. The new model ultimately predicted much better than the old, and in time it came to be accepted.

In the seventeenth century, building on the works of Copernicus and others, Sir Isaac Newton constructed yet another body of theory that seemed to predict planetary motion with still more accuracy. Newtonian physics became the accepted body of theory, relied on for almost 300 years. Then Albert Einstein did his work. The theory of relativity replaced Newtonian physics in some fields because it predicted even better. Relativity was able to explain some things that earlier theories could not.

Economic theories are also confronted with new and often conflicting data from time to time. The collection and use of data to test economic theories is called empirical economics.

empirical economics The collection and use of data to test economic theories.

Numerous large data sets are available to facilitate economic research. For example, economists studying consumer behaviour in the UK can test theories against the actual experiences of thousands of randomly selected people who have been surveyed in the family expenditure survey published annually. Macroeconomists continually monitoring and studying the behaviour of the national economy pass thousands of items of data, collected by both government agencies and private companies, back and forth on diskettes and over the Internet. Housing market analysts analyse data recorded from observations in connection with millions of home sales.

All scientific research needs to isolate and measure the responsiveness of one variable to a change in another variable, *ceteris paribus*. Physical scientists, such as physicists and geologists, can often impose the condition of *ceteris paribus* by conducting controlled experiments. They can, for example, measure the effect of one chemical on another while literally holding all else constant in an environment that they control completely. Social scientists, who study people, rarely have this luxury.

While controlled experiments are difficult in economics and other social sciences, research is still meaningful. Researchers can, to some extent, isolate and measure the effect of one variable on another. There are a number of ways to do this. One way is to observe the behaviour of groups of similar people under different circumstances. For example, suppose you wanted to estimate the effect of the UK government's tax rate reductions in the 1980s and 1990s on the amount that households save, an important tax policy issue. Of course, you could look at household saving before and after the change. But who's to say that what you observe is not due to increases in income that occurred at the same time? To isolate the tax effect, you could look at a set of households whose income did not change. Sophisticated computer programs are now allowing economists to isolate variables more effectively than ever before.

Economic policy

Economic theory helps us understand how the world works, but the formulation of economic policy requires a second step. We must have objectives. What do we want to change? Why? What is good and what is bad about the way the system is operating? Can we make it better?

Such questions force us to be specific about the grounds for judging one outcome superior to another. What does it mean to be better? The following four criteria are frequently applied when judging economic outcomes:

1. Efficiency
2. Equity
3. Growth
4. Stability

Efficiency

In physics 'efficiency' refers to the ratio of useful energy delivered by a system to the energy supplied to it. An efficient car engine, for example, is one that uses up a small amount of fuel per mile for a given level of power.

efficiency In economics, it includes allocative efficiency. An efficient economy is one that produces what people want and does so at the least possible cost.

In economics, **efficiency** includes allocative efficiency. An efficient economy is one that produces what people want at the least possible cost. If the system allocates resources to the production of things that nobody wants, it is inefficient. If all members of a particular society were vegetarian and somehow half of all that society's resources were used to produce meat, the result would be inefficient. It is inefficient when steel beams lie in the rain and rust because somebody made a mistake with a shipping schedule. If a firm could produce its product using 25% less labour and energy without sacrificing quality, it too is inefficient.

The clearest example of an efficient change is a voluntary exchange. If you and I each want something that the other has and we agree to exchange, we are both better off, and no one loses. When a company reorganizes its production or adopts a new technology that enables it to produce more of its product with fewer resources, without sacrificing quality, it has made an efficient change. At least potentially, the resources saved could be used to produce more of something.

Inefficiencies can arise in numerous ways. Sometimes they are caused by government regulations or tax laws that distort otherwise sound economic decisions. Land in Italy is well suited for wine production and land in Scandinavia is well suited for wood production. Clearly, a law that requires Italy to produce only wood and Scandinavia to produce only wine would be inefficient. If firms that cause environmental damage are not held accountable for their actions, the incentive to minimize those damages is lost, and the result is inefficient.

Because most changes that can be made in an economy will leave some people better off and others worse off, we must have a way of comparing the gains and losses that may result. Most often we simply compare their sizes in money terms. A change is efficient if the value of the resulting gains exceeds the value of the resulting losses. In this case the winners can potentially compensate the losers and still be better off.

Equity

equity Fairness.

While efficiency has a fairly precise definition that can be applied with some degree of rigour, **equity** ('fairness') lies in the eye of the beholder. Few people agree on what is fair and what is unfair. To many, fairness implies a more equal distribution of income and wealth. Fairness may imply alleviating poverty, but the extent to which the poor should receive cash benefits from the government is the subject of enormous disagreement. For thousands of years philosophers have wrestled with the principles of justice that should guide social decisions. They will probably wrestle with such questions for thousands of years to come.

Despite the impossibility of defining equity or fairness universally, public policy makers judge the fairness of economic outcomes all the time. Rent control laws operate in some countries because some legislators think that landlords treat low-income tenants unfairly. Certainly, most social welfare programmes are created in the name of equity.

Growth

As the result of technological change, the building of machinery and the acquisition of knowledge, societies learn to produce new things and to produce old things better. When we devise new and better ways of producing the things we use now and develop new products and services, the total amount of production in the economy increases. **Economic growth** is an increase in the total output of an economy. If output grows faster than the population, output per capita rises and standards of living increase. Presumably, when an economy grows there is more of what people want. Rural and agrarian societies become modern industrial societies as a result of economic growth and rising per capita output.

Some policies discourage economic growth and others encourage it. Tax laws, for example, can be designed to encourage the development and application of new production techniques. Research and development in some societies are subsidized by the government. Building roads, highways, bridges and transport systems in developing countries may speed up the process of economic growth. If businesses and wealthy people invest their wealth outside their country rather than in its own industries, growth in their home country may be slowed.

economic growth
An increase in the total output of an economy.

Stability

Economic **stability** refers to the condition in which national output is steady or growing, with low inflation and full employment of resources. An economy may at times be unstable. During the 1950s and 1960s, the European economy experienced a long period of relatively steady growth, stable prices and low unemployment. For example, between 1961 and 1969, consumer prices never rose more than 5% in a single year, and the number of unemployed never exceeded 3% of the labour force. The decades of the 1970s and 1980s, however, were unstable. Europe experienced periods of rapid price inflation (over 10%) and periods of severe unemployment. The first half of the 1990s was another period of instability, with another recession occurring and unemployment in many countries at over 10%, and in Spain over 20%. The causes of instability and the ways in which governments have attempted to stabilize the economy are the subject matter of macroeconomics.

stability
A condition in which output is steady or growing, with low inflation and full employment of resources.

An invitation

This chapter is meant to prepare you for what is to come. The first part of the chapter invited you into an exciting discipline that deals with important issues and questions. You cannot begin to understand how a society functions without knowing something about its economic history and its economic system.

The second part of the chapter introduced the method of reasoning that economics requires and some of the tools that economics uses. We believe that learning to think in this very powerful way will help you better understand the world.

As you proceed, it is important that you keep track of what you've learned in earlier chapters. This book has a plan; it proceeds step by step, each section building on the last. It would be a good idea to look at each chapter's table of contents and flip through each chapter before you read it in detail to be sure you understand where it fits in the big picture.

Summary

1. Economics is the study of how individuals and societies choose to use the scarce resources that nature and previous generations have provided.

Why study economics?

2. There are many reasons to study economics, including (a) to learn a way of thinking, (b) to understand society, (c) to understand global affairs, and (d) to be an informed voter.

3. What we forgo when we make a choice or a decision is the *opportunity cost* of that decision.

The scope of economics

4. *Microeconomics* deals with the functioning of individual markets and industries and with the behaviour of individual decision-making units: firms and households.

5. *Macroeconomics* looks at the economy as a whole. It deals with the economic behaviour of aggregates – national output, national income, the overall price level and the general rate of inflation.

6. Economics is a broad and diverse discipline with many special fields of inquiry. These include economic history, international economics and urban economics.

The method of economics

7. Economics asks and attempts to answer two kinds of questions: positive and normative. *Positive economics* attempts to understand behaviour and the operation of economies without making judgements about whether the outcomes are good or bad. *Normative economics* looks at the results of economic behaviour and asks if they are good or bad and whether they can be improved.

8. Positive economics is often divided into two parts. *Descriptive economics* involves the compilation of data that accurately describe economic facts and events. *Economic theory* attempts to generalize and explain what is observed. It involves statements of cause and effect – of action and reaction.

9. An economic *model* is a formal statement of an economic theory. Models simplify and abstract from reality.

10. It is often useful to isolate the effects of one variable or another while holding 'all else constant'. This is the device of *ceteris paribus*.

11. Models and theories can be expressed in many ways. The most common ways are in words, in graphs and in equations.

12. If one event happens before another, the second event does not necessarily happen as a result of the first. To assume that 'after' implies 'because' is to commit the fallacy of *post hoc, ergo propter hoc*. The erroneous belief that what is true for a part is necessarily true for the whole is the *fallacy of composition*.

13. *Empirical economics* involves the collection and use of data to test economic theories. In principle, the best model is the one that yields the most accurate predictions.

14. To make policy, one must be careful to specify criteria for making judgements. Four specific criteria are used most often in economics: *efficiency*, *equity*, *growth* and *stability*.

Review Terms and Concepts

ceteris paribus
descriptive economics
economic growth
economic theory
economics
efficiency
efficient market
empirical economics
equity
fallacy of composition
inductive reasoning
Industrial Revolution

macroeconomics
microeconomics
model
normative economics
Ockham's razor
opportunity cost
positive economics
post hoc, ergo propter hoc
stability
sunk costs
variable

Problem Set

1. One of the scarce resources that constrain our behaviour is time. Each of us has only 24 hours in a day. How do you go about allocating your time in a given day among competing alternatives? How do you go about weighing the alternatives? Once you choose a most important use of time, why do you not spend all your time on it? Use the notion of opportunity cost in your answer.

2. Which of the following statements are examples of positive economic analysis? Which are examples of 'normative' analysis?
a. Extending the number of countries in the EU to include East European countries such as Poland is likely to increase German car exports.
b. Including Poland in the EU is likely to make the people of Poland better off.
c. Increasing income tax rates for households with high incomes is likely to reduce savings for that group.
d. The higher taxes imposed by the French Government in 1997 are unfair.
e. Raising revenue by increasing taxes on cigarettes is unfair because it will impose larger burdens on lower-income households.
f. Increasing taxes on cigarettes sharply is likely to reduce the amount of cigarettes smoked.

3. Describe one of the major economic issues facing your local or national government. (Hint: You might look at a local newspaper. Most issues that make it into the paper will have an impact on people's lives.) Who will be affected by the resolution of this issue? What alternative actions have been proposed? Who will be the winners? The losers?

4. David signed up with an Internet provider for a fixed fee of €10 per month. For this fee he gets unlimited access to the World Wide Web. During the average month in 1998, he was logged onto the Web for 17 hours. What is the average cost of an hour of Web time to David? What is the marginal cost of an additional hour?

5. Suppose that all of the 10,000 voting-age citizens of Lumpland are required to register to vote every year. Suppose also that the citizens of Lumpland are fully employed and that they each value their time at €10 per hour. In addition, assume that non-voting secondary school students in Lumpland are willing to work for €5 per hour. The government has two choices: (1) it can hire 200 students to work at registration locations for 5 hours per day for 10 days, or (2) it can hire 400 students for 5 hours per day for 10 days. If the government hires 200 students, each of the 10,000 citizens will have to queue for an hour to register. If the government hires 400 students, there will be no waiting time.

Assume that the cost of paying the students is obtained by taxing each citizen equally. The current government is very conservative and has decided to hold taxes down by hiring only 200 students. Do you agree with this decision? Why or why not? Is it efficient? Is it fair?

6. Suppose that a city is considering building a bridge across a river. The bridge will be paid for out of tax, and the city gets its revenues from a sales tax imposed on things sold in the city. The bridge would provide more direct access for commuters and shoppers, and would alleviate the huge traffic jam that currently occurs every morning at a bridge downriver in another city.
a. Who would gain if the bridge were built? Could those gains be measured? How?
b. Who would be hurt? Could those costs be measured? How?
c. How would you determine if it were efficient to build the bridge?

7. Define equity. How would you decide if building the bridge described in Question 6 were fair/equitable?

8. Most European countries have a national lottery. The governments of these countries receive substantial revenue. This can be used to finance schools, repair roads, maintain social programmes, invest in the arts or reduce other taxes.
a. Recall that efficiency means producing what people want at least cost. Can you make an efficiency argument in favour of national lotteries?
b. What costs might be associated with such gambling? Would these costs have an impact on the efficiency argument you made in (a)?
c. Using the concept of equity, argue for or against a national lottery.

9. For each of the following situations, identify the full cost (opportunity costs) involved:
a. A Swedish worker earning an hourly wage of 100 kronor decides to halve working hours in order to attend a course at his local university in Stockholm.
b. Sue decides to drive to Brussels from London to visit her son, who works in a bank there.
c. Tom decides to go to a wild party and stays out all night before his physics exam.
d. Annie spends 2000 French francs on a new dress from Paris.
e. The Confab Company spends 1 million euros to build a new branch plant that will probably be in operation for at least 10 years.
f. Alex's father owns a small grocery shop. Alex works 40 hours a week in the shop but receives no pay.

Appendix to Chapter 1

How to Read and Understand Graphs

Economics is the most quantitative of the social sciences. If you flip through the pages of this or any other economics text, you will see countless tables and graphs. These tables and graphs serve a number of purposes. First, they illustrate important economic relationships. Second, they make difficult problems easier to understand and analyse. Finally, patterns and regularities that may not be discernible in simple lists of numbers can often be seen when those numbers are laid out in a table or on a graph.

A **graph** is a two-dimensional representation of a set of numbers, or data. There are many ways that numbers can be illustrated by a graph.

Time series graphs

It is often useful to see how a single measure or variable changes over time. One way to present this information is to plot the values of the variable on a graph, with each value corresponding to a different time period. A graph of this kind is called a **time series graph**. On a time series graph, time is measured along the horizontal scale and the variable being graphed is measured along the vertical scale. Figures 1A.1 and 1A.2 are time series graphs that present the total income in one particular economy, Germany, for each year between 1987 and 1996.* These graphs are based on the data found in Table 1A.1. By displaying these data graphically, we can see clearly that (1) total personal disposable income has been increasing since

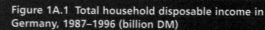

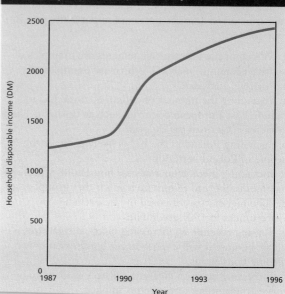

Figure 1A.1 Total household disposable income in Germany, 1987–1996 (billion DM)

Source: OECD Economic Survey, 1997.

1987, and (2) during certain periods, disposable income was increasing at a faster rate than during other periods.

Graphs must be read very carefully. For example, look at Figure 1A.2, which plots the same data that are plotted in Figure 1A.1. Because the values on the vertical axis in Figure 1A.2 start at DM 1000 billion rather than at zero, and because the vertical scales are different, you may be led to believe that income is growing much more rapidly in Figure 1A.2 than in Figure 1A.1. This is not true, of course. The same variable is plotted in both graphs.

Graphing two variables on a Cartesian coordinate system

More important than simple graphs of one variable are graphs that contain information on two variables at the same time. The most common method of graphing two

Table 1A.1 Total household disposable income in Germany, 1987–1996 (billion DM)	
Year	Total household disposable income
1987	1267.6
1988	1323.2
1989	1394.3
1990	1532.7
1991	1871.3
1992	2013.4
1993	2084.4
1994	2154.8
1995	2233.2
1996	2306.6

* *The measure of income presented in Table 1A.1 and in Figures 1A.1 and 1A.2 is household disposable income in billions of deutschemarks. It is an approximation of the total personal income received by all households in Germany added together minus the taxes that they pay.*

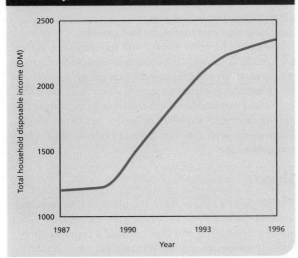

Figure 1A.2 Total household disposable income in Germany, 1987–1996 (billion DM)

Source: OECD Economic Survey, 1997.

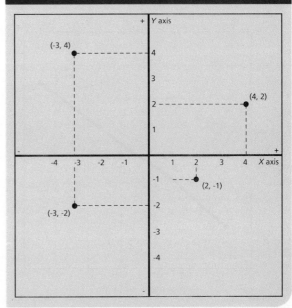

Figure 1A.3 A Cartesian coordinate system

A Cartesian coordinate system is constructed by drawing two perpendicular lines: a vertical axis (the Y-axis) and a horizontal axis (the X-axis). Each axis is a measuring scale.

variables is the **Cartesian coordinate system**. This system is constructed by simply drawing two perpendicular lines: a horizontal line, or **X axis**, and a vertical line, or **Y axis**. The axes contain measurement scales that intersect at 0 (zero). This point is called the **origin**. On the vertical scale, positive numbers lie above the horizontal axis (that is, above the origin) and negative numbers lie below it. On the horizontal scale, positive numbers lie to the right of the vertical axis (to the right of the origin) and negative numbers lie to the left of it. The point at which the graph intersects the Y axis is called the **Y-intercept**, or just 'intercept'.

When two variables are plotted on a single graph, each point represents a *pair* of numbers. The first number is measured on the X axis and the second number is measured on the Y axis. For example, the following points (X, Y) are plotted on the set of axes drawn in Figure 1A.3: (4, 2), (2, –1), (–3, 4), (–3, –2). Most, but not all, of the graphs in this book are plots of two variables where both values are positive numbers, such as (4, 2) in Figure 1A.3. On these graphs, only the upper right-hand quadrant of the coordinate system (that is, the quadrant in which all X and Y values are positive) will be drawn.

Plotting income and consumption data for households

Table 1A.2 presents data collected by the Family Expenditure Survey in the UK. In a survey of about 6,800 households, each household was asked to keep careful track of all its expenditures. The table shows average income and average spending for those households, ranked by income. For example, the average income for the top fifth (20%) of the

households was £659.78 per week, and their average spending was £529.35 per week.

Figure 1A.4 presents the numbers from Table 1A.2 graphically using the Cartesian coordinate system. Along the horizontal scale, the X axis, we measure average income. Along the vertical scale, the Y axis, we measure average consumption spending. Each of the five pairs of numbers from the table is represented by a point on the graph. Because all numbers are positive numbers, we need to show only the upper right quadrant of the coordinate system.

Table 1A.2 Weekly consumption expenditures and income in the UK, 1995 (£)*

	Average income	Average weekly consumption expenditures
Bottom fifth	82.47	103.83
2nd fifth	161.63	182.38
3rd fifth	260.49	270.91
4th fifth	369.70	360.80
Top fifth	659.78	529.35

*Income and consumption data are for households after tax and social security benefits.
Source: Calculated from Family Expenditure Survey, data ONS.

Figure 1A.4 Household consumption and income

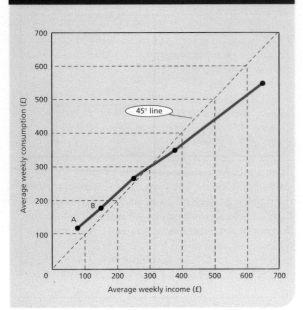

A graph is a simple two-dimensional geometric representation of data. This graph displays the data from Table 1A.2. Along the horizontal scale (X-axis) we measure household income. Along the vertical scale (Y-axis) we measure household consumption. Note: at point A, consumption equals £103.83 and income equals £82.47. At point B, consumption equals £182.38 and income equals £161.63. *Source: Family Expenditure Survey*, UK.

To help you read this graph, there is a dotted line connecting all the points where consumption and income would be equal. *This 45° line does not represent any data.* Rather, it represents the line along which all variables on the X axis correspond exactly to the variables on the Y axis – for example, at the points (1, 1), (2, 2), (3.7, 3.7), etc. The heavy blue line traces out the data; the dotted line is only to help you read the graph.

There are several things to look for when reading a graph. The first thing you should notice is whether the line slopes upwards or downwards as you move from left to right. The line in Figure 1A.4 slopes upwards, indicating that there seems to be a **positive relationship** between income and spending: the higher a household's income, the more a household tends to consume. If we had graphed the percentage of each group receiving welfare payments along the Y axis, the line would presumably slope downwards, indicating that welfare payments are lower at higher income levels. The income level / welfare payment relationship is thus a **negative** one.

Slope

The **slope** of a line or curve is a measure that indicates whether the relationship between the variables is positive or negative and how much of a response there is in Y (the variable on the vertical axis) when X (the variable on the horizontal axis) changes. The slope of a line between two points is the change in the quantity measured on the Y axis divided by the change in the quantity measured on the X axis. We will normally use Δ (the Greek capital letter delta) to refer to a change in a variable. In Figure 1A.5, the slope of the line between points A and B is ΔY divided by ΔX. Sometimes it's easy to remember slope as 'the rise over the run', indicating the vertical change over the horizontal change.

To be precise, ΔX between two points on a graph is simply X_2 minus X_1, where X_2 is the X value for the second point and X_1 is the X value for the first point. Similarly, ΔY is defined as Y_2 minus Y_1, where Y_2 is the Y value for the second point and Y_1 is the Y value for the first point. Slope is equal to:

$$\Delta Y / \Delta X = (Y_2 - Y_1) / (X_2 - X_1)$$

Figure 1A.5 A curve with a positive slope (a), and a curve with a negative slope (b)

A positive slope indicates that increases in X are associated with increases in Y and that decreases in X are associated with decreases in Y. A negative slope indicates the opposite – when X increases, Y decreases; and when X decreases, Y increases.

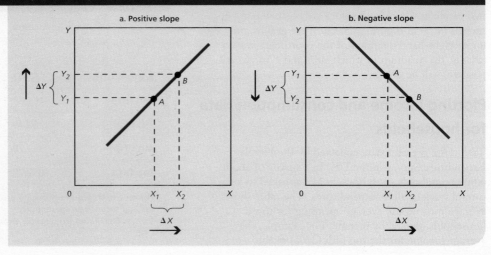

As we move from A to B in Figure 1A.5a, both X and Y increase; the slope is thus a positive number. However, as we move from A to B in Figure 1A.5b, X increases $((X_2 - X_1)$ is a positive number), but Y decreases $((Y_2 - Y_1)$ is a negative number). The slope in Figure 1A.5b is thus a negative number, since a negative number divided by a positive number gives a negative quotient.

To calculate the numerical value of the slope between points A and B in Figure 1A.4, we need to calculate ΔY and ΔX. Because consumption is measured on the Y axis, ΔY is 78.55 $((Y_2 - Y_1) = (182.38 - 103.83))$; and because income is measured along the X axis, ΔX is 79.16 $((X_2 - X_1) = (161.63 - 82.47))$. The slope between A and B is $\Delta Y / \Delta X = 78.5 / 79.16 = + 0.9923$.

Another interesting thing to note about the data graphed in Figure 1A.4 is that all the points lie roughly along a straight line. (If you look very closely, however, you can see that the slope declines as one moves from left to right; the line becomes slightly less steep.) A straight line has a constant slope. That is, if you pick any two points along it and calculate the slope, you will always get the same number. A horizontal line has a zero slope (ΔY is zero); a vertical line has an 'infinite' slope.

Unlike the slope of a straight line, the slope of a *curve* is continually changing. Consider, for example, the curves in Figure 1A.6. Figure 1A.6a shows a curve with a positive slope that decreases as you move from left to right. The easiest way to think about the concept of increasing or decreasing slope is to imagine what it is like walking up a hill from left to right. If the hill is

steep (as it is in the first part of Figure 1A.6a), you are moving a lot in the Y direction for each step you take in the X direction. If the hill is less steep (as it is further along in Figure 1A.6a), you are moving less in the Y direction for every step you take in the X direction. Thus, when the hill is steep, slope ($\Delta Y/\Delta X$) is a larger number than it is when the hill is flatter. The curve in Figure 1A.6b has a positive slope, but its slope *increases* as you move from left to right.

The same analogy holds for curves that have a negative slope. Figure 1A.6c shows a curve with a negative slope that increases (in absolute value)* as you move from left to right. This time, think about skiing down a hill. At first, the descent in Figure 1A.6c is gradual (low slope), but as you proceed down the hill (to the right), you descend more quickly (high slope). Figure 1A.6d shows a curve with a negative slope that *decreases* in absolute value as you move from left to right.

In Figure 1A.6e, the slope goes from positive to negative as X increases. In 1A.6f, the slope goes from negative to positive. At point A in both, the slope is zero. (Remember, slope is defined as $\Delta Y/\Delta X$. At point A, Y is not changing ($\Delta Y = 0$). Therefore slope at point A is zero.)

---

* The absolute value of a number is its value disregarding its sign – that is, disregarding whether it is positive or negative: –7 is bigger in absolute terms than –4, and –9 is bigger in absolute value than +8.

Figure 1A.6

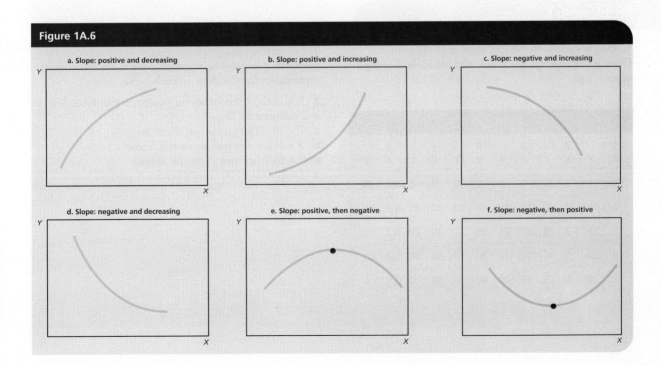

a. Slope: positive and decreasing

b. Slope: positive and increasing

c. Slope: negative and increasing

d. Slope: negative and decreasing

e. Slope: positive, then negative

f. Slope: negative, then positive

Summary

1. A graph is a two-dimensional representation of a set of numbers, or data. A time series graph illustrates how a single variable changes over time.

2. The most common method of graphing two variables on one graph is the Cartesian coordinate system, which includes an X (horizontal) axis and a Y (vertical) axis. The points at which the two axes intersect is called the origin. The point at which a graph intersects the Y axis is called the Y-intercept, or intercept.

3. The slope of a line or curve indicates whether the relationship between the two variables graphed on a Cartesian coordinate system is positive or negative, and how much of a response there is in Y (the variable on the vertical axis) when X (the variable on the horizontal axis) changes. The slope of a line between two points is the change in the quantity measured on the Y axis divided by the change in the quantity measured on the X axis.

Review Terms and Concepts

Cartesian coordinate system A common method of graphing two variables that makes use of two perpendicular lines against which the variables are plotted.
graph A two-dimensional representation of a set of numbers, or data.
negative relationship A relationship between two variables, X and Y, in which a decrease in X is associated with an increase in Y, and an increase in X is associated with a decrease in Y.
origin On a Cartesian coordinate system, the point at which the horizontal and vertical axes intersect.
positive relationship A relationship between two variables, X and Y, in which a decrease in X is associated with a decrease in Y, and an increase in X is associated with an increase in Y.

slope A measurement that indicates whether the relationship between variables is positive or negative and how much of a response there is in Y (the variable on the vertical axis) when X (the variable on the horizontal axis) changes.
times series graph A graph illustrating how a variable changes over time.
X axis On a Cartesian coordinate system, the horizontal line against which a variable is plotted.
Y axis On a Cartesian coordinate system, the vertical line against which a variable is plotted.
Y-intercept The point at which a graph intersects the Y axis.

Problem Set

1. Graph each of the sets of numbers in the table. Draw a line through the points and calculate the slope of each line.

1		2		3		4		5		6	
X	Y	X	Y	X	Y	X	Y	X	Y	X	Y
1	5	1	25	0	0	0	40	0	0	0.1	100
2	10	2	20	10	10	10	30	10	10	0.2	75
3	15	3	15	20	20	20	20	20	20	0.3	50
4	20	4	10	30	30	30	10	30	10	0.4	25
5	25	5	5	40	40	40	0	40	0	0.5	0

2. For each of the graphs in Figure 1, say whether the curve has a positive or negative slope. Give an intuitive explanation for the slope of each curve.

3. For each of the following equations graph the line and calculate its slope.
   a. $P = 10 - 2q_D$ (put q_D on the X axis)
   b. $P = 100 - 4q_D$ (put q_D on the X axis)
   c. $P = 50 + 6q_S$ (put q_S on the X axis)
   d. $I = 10,000 - 500r$ (put I on the X axis)

Figure 1

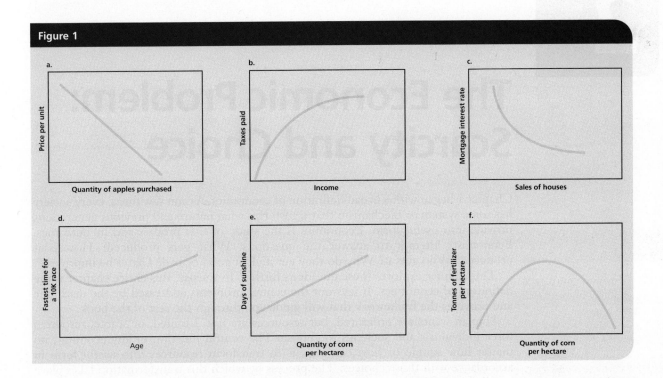

2

The Economic Problem: Scarcity and Choice

Chapter 1 began with a broad definition of economics. As you saw there, every society has some system or mechanism that transforms what nature and previous generations provide into useful form. Economics is the study of that process and its outcomes. Economists attempt to answer the questions: What gets produced? How is it produced? Who gets it? Why do they get it? Is it good or bad? Can it be improved?

This chapter explores these questions further. In a sense, this entire chapter is the definition of economics. It lays out the central problems addressed by the discipline and provides the framework that will guide you through the rest of the book.

Human wants are unlimited, but resources are not. Limited, or scarce, resources force individuals and societies to choose. The central function of any economy, no matter how simple or how complex, is to transform resources into useful form in accordance with those choices. The process by which this transformation takes place is called **production**.

The term **resources** is very broad. Some resources are the product of nature: land, wildlife, minerals, timber, energy, even the rain and the wind. At any given time, the resources, or **inputs**, available to a society also include those things that have been produced by previous generations, such as buildings and equipment. Things that are produced and then used to produce other valuable goods or services later on are called *capital resources*, or simply **capital**. Buildings, machinery, equipment, tables, roads, bridges, desks and so forth are part of a nation's capital stock. *Human resources* – labour, skills and knowledge – are also an important part of a nation's resources.

Producers are those who take resources and transform them into usable products, or **outputs**. Private manufacturing firms purchase resources and produce products for the market. Governments do so as well. National defence, the justice system, and police and fire protection are examples of outputs produced by the government, which in aggregate are sometimes called the *public sector*.

Individual households often produce products for themselves. A household that owns its own home is in essence using land and a structure (capital) to produce 'housing services' that it consumes itself. The Berlin Symphony Orchestra is no less a producer than BMW. An orchestra takes capital resources – a building, musical instruments, lighting fixtures, musical scores and so on – and combines them with land and highly skilled labour to produce performances.

Scarcity, choice and opportunity cost

In the second half of this chapter, we discuss the global economic landscape. But before you can understand the different types of economic systems, it is important to understand the basic economic concepts of scarcity, choice and opportunity cost.

The three basic questions

All societies must answer **three basic questions**:

1. What will be produced?
2. How will it be produced?
3. Who will get what is produced?

production
The process by which resources are transformed into useful forms.

resources *or* inputs Anything provided by nature or previous generations that can be used directly or indirectly to satisfy human wants.

capital Things that have already been produced that are in turn used to produce other goods and services.

producers Those people or groups of people, whether private or public, who transform resources into usable products.

outputs Usable products.

Stated a slightly different way, the economic system must determine the *allocation of scarce resources* among producers, the *mix of output*, and the *distribution of that output* (Figure 2.1).

Scarcity and choice in a one-person economy

The simplest economy is one in which a single person lives alone on an island. Consider David, the survivor of a plane crash, who finds himself cast ashore in such a place. Here, individual and society are one; there is no distinction between social and private. *Nonetheless, nearly all of the basic decisions that characterize complex economies must be made.* That is, although David himself will get whatever he produces, he still must decide how to allocate the resources of the island, what to produce, and how and when to produce it.

First, David must decide what he wants to produce. Notice that the word *needs* does not appear here. Needs are absolute requirements, but beyond just enough water, basic nutrition and shelter to survive, they are very difficult to define. What is an 'absolute necessity' for one person may not be for another. In any case, David must put his wants in some order of priority and make some choices.

Next he must look at the *possibilities*. What can he do to satisfy his wants, given the limits of the island? In every society, no matter how simple or complex, people are constrained in what they can do. In this society of one, David is constrained by time, his physical condition, his knowledge, his skills, and the resources and climate of the island.

Given that resources are limited, David must decide *how* to use them best to satisfy his hierarchy of wants. Food would probably come close to the top of his list. Should he spend his time simply gathering fruits and berries? Should he hunt for game? Should he clear a field and plant seeds? Clearly, the answers to these questions depend on the character of the island, its climate, its flora and fauna (*are* there any fruits and berries?), the extent of his skills and knowledge (does he know anything about farming?), and his preferences (he may be a vegetarian).

Opportunity cost

The concepts of *constrained choice* and *scarcity* are central to the discipline of economics. They can be applied when discussing the behaviour of individuals like David and when analysing the behaviour of large groups of people in complex societies.

Given the scarcity of time and resources, David has less time to gather fruits and berries if he chooses to hunt – he trades more meat for less fruit. There is a trade-off between food and shelter, too. If David likes to be comfortable, he may work on

Figure 2.1 The three basic questions

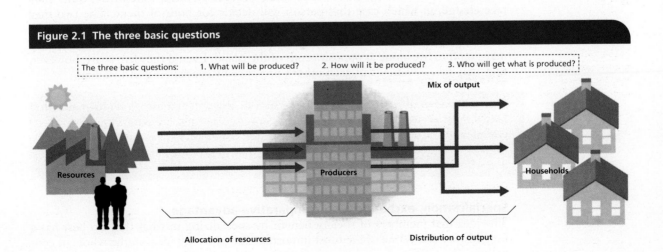

The three basic questions: 1. What will be produced?   2. How will it be produced?   3. Who will get what is produced?

Mix of output

Resources

Producers

Households

Allocation of resources

Distribution of output

building a nice place to live in, but that may require giving up the food he might have produced. As we noted in Chapter 1, what we forgo when we make a choice is the **opportunity cost** of that choice.

opportunity cost
What we give up, or forgo, when we make a choice or a decision.

David may occasionally decide to rest, to lie on the beach and enjoy the sun. In one sense, that benefit is free – he doesn't have to pay for the privilege. In reality, however, it does have a cost – an opportunity cost. Lying in the sun means using time that otherwise could have been spent doing something else. The true cost of that leisure is the value of the other things David could have produced, but did not, during the time he spent on the beach.

Europe, the USA and Russia continue to explore the solar system. To do so requires devoting enormous resources, resources that could be used to produce other things. The opportunity cost of space exploration is the total value of all the other things that those resources could have produced. Among other possibilities, taxes might have been lower. That would have meant more income for us to spend on goods and services. Those same resources could also have been used for medical research, to improve education, to repair roads and bridges, to aid the poor, or to support the arts. Cassini, the module bound for Saturn, is costing Europe and the USA a total of €3.5 billion.

In making everyday decisions it is often helpful to think about opportunity costs. Should I go to the party or not? First, it costs the price of a ticket to get in. When I pay money for anything, I give up the other things that I could have bought with that money. Second, it costs two or three hours. Clearly, time is a valuable commodity for a student. I have exams next week and I need to study. I could go to a film instead of the party. I could go to another party. I could sleep. Just as David must weigh the value of sunning on the beach against more food or better housing, so I must weigh the value of the fun I may have at the party against everything else I might otherwise do with the time and money.

Scarcity and choice in an economy of two or more

Suppose that another survivor of the crash, Anna, appears on the island. Now that David is not alone things are more complex, and some new decisions must be made. David's and Anna's preferences about what things to produce are likely to be different. They will probably not have the same knowledge or skills. Perhaps Anna is very good at tracking animals, while David has a knack for building things. How should they split the work that needs to be done? Once things are produced, they must decide how to divide them. How should their products be distributed?

The mechanism for answering these fundamental questions is clear when David is alone on the island. The 'central plan' is his; he simply decides what he wants and what to do about it. The minute someone else appears, however, a number of decision-making arrangements immediately become possible. One or the other may take charge, in which case that person will decide for both of them. The two may agree to cooperate, with each having an equal say, and come up with a joint plan. Or they may agree to split the planning, as well as the production duties. Finally, they may go off to live alone at opposite ends of the island. Even if they live apart, however, they may take advantage of each other's presence by specializing and trading.

Modern industrial societies must answer exactly the same questions that Anna and David must answer, but the mechanics of larger economies are naturally more complex. Instead of two people living together, countries have populations of many millions. Yet decisions must be made about what to produce, how to produce it, and who gets it.

Specialization, exchange, and comparative advantage

The idea that members of society benefit by specializing in what they do best has a long history and is one of the most important and powerful ideas in the whole of economics. David Ricardo, a major nineteenth-century British economist, formalized the

theory of comparative advantage
Ricardo's theory that specialization and free trade will benefit all trading parties, even those that may be absolutely more efficient producers of all goods.

point precisely. According to Ricardo's **theory of comparative advantage**, specialization and free trade will benefit all trading parties, even when some are 'absolutely' more efficient producers than others. Ricardo's basic point applies just as much to Anna and David as it does to different nations.

To keep things simple, suppose that Anna and David have only two tasks to accomplish each week: gathering food to eat and cutting logs to be used in constructing a house. If Anna could cut more logs than David in one day, and David could gather more nuts and berries than Anna could, specialization would clearly lead to more total production. Both would benefit if Anna only cuts logs and David only gathers nuts and berries. But suppose that David is slow and somewhat clumsy in his nut-gathering and that Anna is better at both cutting logs and gathering food. Ricardo pointed out that it still pays for them to specialize and exchange.

Suppose that Anna can cut 10 logs per day and that David can cut only 5. Also suppose that Anna can gather 10 kilos of food per day and that David can gather only 8. Assume also that David and Anna value kilos of food and logs equally. How then can the two gain from specialization and exchange? Think of opportunity costs. When Anna gives up a day of food production to work on the house, she cuts 10 logs and sacrifices 10 kilos of food. The opportunity cost of 10 logs is thus 10 kilos of food if Anna switches from food to logs. But because David can cut only 5 logs in a day, he has to work for 2 days to cut 10 logs. In 2 days, David could have produced 16 kilos of food (2 days × 8 kilos per day). The opportunity cost of 10 logs is thus 16 kilos of food if David switches from food to logs.

As this example makes clear, even though Anna is *absolutely* more efficient at food production than David, she should specialize in logs and let David specialize in food. This way, the maximum number of logs and kilos are produced. A person or a country is said to have a comparative advantage in producing a good or service if it is *relatively* more efficient than a trading partner at doing so. Anna is relatively more efficient at log production because the opportunity cost of switching from food to logs is lower for her than it is for David.

Looking at the same problem from the standpoint of food production leads to exactly the same conclusion. If Anna were to switch from cutting logs to gathering food, she would sacrifice 10 logs to produce only 10 kilos of food. But if David were to switch from cutting logs to gathering food, he would sacrifice 10 logs to produce a full 16 kilos! Even though Anna has an *absolute advantage* in both cutting logs and producing food, David has a *comparative advantage* producing food because for the same sacrifice of logs, David produces much more food.

The theory of comparative advantage shows that trade and specialization work to raise productivity. But specialization may also lead to the development of skills that enhance productivity even further. By specializing in log cutting, Anna will get even stronger shoulders. By spending more time at gathering food, David will refine his food-finding skills. The same applies to countries that engage in international trade.

The degree of specialization in modern industrial societies is breathtaking. Once again, let your mind wander over the range of products and services available or under development today. As knowledge expands, specialization becomes a necessity. This is true not only for scientists and doctors but also for people in every career, from tree surgeons to divorce lawyers. Understanding specialization and trade will help you to explain much of what goes on in today's global economy.

Weighing present and expected future costs and benefits

Very often we find ourselves weighing benefits available today against benefits available tomorrow. Here too the notion of opportunity cost is helpful.

While alone on the island, David had to choose between cultivating a field and just gathering wild nuts and berries. Gathering nuts and berries provides food now; gathering seeds and clearing a field for planting will yield food tomorrow, if all goes well. Using today's time to farm may well be worth the effort if doing so will yield more food than David would otherwise have in the future. By planting, David is trading present value for future values. Working to gather seeds and clear a field has an opportunity cost – the present leisure he might consume and the value of the berries he might gather if he did not work the field.

The simplest example of trading present for future benefits is the act of saving. When I put income aside today for use in the future, I give up some things that I could have had today in exchange for something tomorrow. The saver must weigh the value of what that income can buy today against what it might be expected to buy later. Since nothing is certain, some judgement about future events and expected values must be made. What are interest rates likely to be? What will my income be in ten years? How long am I likely to live?

We trade off present and future benefits in small ways all the time. If you decide to study rather than go to a party, you are trading present fun for the expected future benefits of higher marks. If you decide to go outside on a very cold day and run eight kilometres, you are trading discomfort in the present for being in better shape later on.

Capital goods and consumer goods

A society trades present for expected future benefits when it devotes a portion of its resources to research and development or to investment in capital. As we said earlier in this chapter, *capital* in its broadest definition is anything that is produced that will be used to produce other valuable goods or services over time.

Building capital means trading present benefits for future ones. David and Anna might trade gathering berries or lying in the sun for cutting logs to build a nicer house in the future. In a modern society, resources used to produce capital goods could have been used to produce **consumer goods** – that is, goods for present consumption. Heavy industrial machinery does not directly satisfy the wants of anyone, but producing it requires resources that could instead have gone into producing things that do satisfy wants directly – food, clothing, toys or golf clubs.

consumer goods
Goods produced for present consumption.

Capital is everywhere. A road is capital. Once it is built, we can drive on it or transport goods and services over it for many years to come. The benefits of producing it will be realized over many years. A house is also capital. When it is built, the builder presumes that it will provide shelter and valuable services for a long time. Before a new manufacturing firm can start up, it must put some capital in place. The buildings, equipment and stocks that it uses are its capital. As it contributes to the production process, this capital yields valuable services through time.

In Chapter 1 we talked about the enormous amount of capital – buildings, factories, housing, cars, trucks, telephone lines and so forth – that you might see. Much of it was put in place by previous generations, yet it continues to provide valuable services today; it is part of this generation's endowment of resources. In order to build every building, every road, every factory, every house, every car or truck, society must forgo using resources to produce consumer goods today. To get an education, I may have to pay tuition and put off joining the workforce for a while.

Capital need not be tangible. When you spend time and resources developing skills or getting an education, you are investing in human capital – your own human capital – that will continue to exist and yield benefits to you for years to come.

investment The process of using resources to produce new capital.

The process of using resources to produce new capital is called **investment**. (In everyday language, the term *investment* is often used to refer to the act of buying a share of stock or a bond, as in 'I invested in some Treasury bonds'. In economics, however, investment always refers to the creation of capital: the purchase or putting in place of buildings, equipment, roads, houses and the like.) A wise investment in capital is one that yields future benefits that are more valuable than the present cost. When you spend money for a house, for example, presumably you value its future benefits. That is, you expect to gain as much or more from living in it than you would from the things you could buy today with the same money.

Because resources are scarce, every investment in capital has an opportunity cost in terms of forgone present consumption.

Applications

Norway seeks to understand family breakdowns

In most European countries, the past thirty years have seen significant changes to the nature of family relationships. A typical pattern was for a wife to stay at home looking after the house and the children, while the male breadwinner went out to work. Now, far more women are in paid employment. The average size of the family has also declined, and the birth rate continues to fall. Furthermore, divorce rates have risen sharply throughout Europe.

In Norway the government is sufficiently concerned about such trends to have established a 'Values Commission'. Norwegian families have been disintegrating more slowly than in some countries but faster than in others. Divorce is four times more common there than 30 years ago, ending half of all marriages. In 1977 only 5% of women aged 20–44 lived with men to whom they were not married. In 1997 the figure was 24%.

Psychologists and sociologists contribute freely to the discussion of such issues. Do economists have any explanation for such trends? Some say yes. An important part of the answer is in the concept of opportunity cost.

Women are now better educated than they were 30 years ago. They can therefore earn more. It is therefore more 'expensive' to stay at home, because the opportunity cost of doing so is higher. They have to forgo a greater salary. Hence many more choose to work. Similarly, it is more expensive to have children. The cost of having children is not only the cost of their food and clothing, but the sacrificed income caring for them. This opportunity cost has increased for many women, so they choose to have fewer children than women 30 years ago.

The argument can be extended to divorce rates too. Since women now are more financially independent than those of the previous generation, they have less to gain from marriage so the divorce rate has increased.

You can decide for yourself how powerful you think the arguments from economists are.

---

production possibility frontier (ppf)

A graph that shows all the combinations of goods and services that can be produced if all of society's resources are used efficiently.

The production possibility frontier

A simple graphical device called the **production possibility frontier (ppf)** illustrates the principles of constrained choice, opportunity cost and scarcity. The ppf is a graph that shows all the combinations of goods and services that can be produced if all of society's resources are used efficiently. Figure 2.2 shows a ppf for a hypothetical economy.

Figure 2.2 Production possibility frontier (ppf)

The ppf illustrates a number of economic concepts. One of the most important is *opportunity cost*. The opportunity cost of producing more capital goods is fewer consumer goods. Moving from E to F, the number of capital goods increases from 550 to 800. But the number of consumer goods decreases from 1300 to 1100.

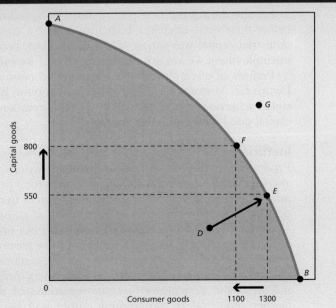

On the Y axis we measure the quantity of capital goods produced, and on the X axis the quantity of consumer goods. All points below and to the left of the curve (the shaded area) represent combinations of capital and consumer goods that are possible for the society given the resources available and existing technology. Points above and to the right of the curve, such as point G, represent combinations that cannot be reached. If an economy were to end up at point A on the graph, it would be producing no consumer goods at all; all resources would be used for the production of capital. If an economy were to end up at point B, it would be devoting all of its resources to the production of consumer goods and none of its resources to the formation of capital.

While all economies produce some of each kind of good, different economies emphasize different things. About 22% of gross output in Germany in 1997 was new capital. In Japan, capital accounted for about 30% of gross output in 1997, while in Sweden the figure was around 16%. Japan is closer to point A on its ppf, Sweden closer to B, and Germany is somewhere in between.

Points that are actually on the ppf are points of both full resource employment and production efficiency. (Recall from Chapter 1 that an efficient economy is one that produces the things that people want at least cost. *Production efficiency* is a state in which a given mix of outputs is produced at least cost.) Resources are not going unused, and there is no waste. Points that lie within the shaded area, but that are not on the frontier, represent either unemployment of resources or production inefficiency. An economy producing at point D in Figure 2.2 can produce more capital goods and more consumption goods, for example, by moving to point E. This is possible only if resources were initially not fully employed or if resources were not being used efficiently.

Economies can often experience periods of prolonged unemployment when millions of workers who are willing to work find themselves without jobs. At the depth of the recession in Europe in the mid-1990s there were 18.5 million people out of a job in the 15 European Union countries. In the middle of 1997, with the French economy still in recession, around three million French workers were unemployed, representing about 12% of the workforce. In Germany there were at that time well over four million out of work, 11.4% of the workforce. Even in countries where the figures have been improving problems remain. For example, in the UK, where the comparable figure is around 6.5%, there are 'pockets' of unemployment. In some cities, 40% of the working population have no employment.

In addition to the hardship that falls on the unemployed themselves, unemployment of labour means unemployment of capital. During a downturn such as that in Europe during the first part of the 1990s, industrial plants were running at well below their total capacity. That meant that a considerable fraction of the nation's industrial capital was sitting idle and, in effect, being wasted. Clearly, when there is unemployment we are not producing all that we can.

Periods of unemployment correspond to points inside the ppf, points like D in Figure 2.2. Moving onto the frontier from a point like D means moving up and to the right, achieving full employment of resources and increasing production of both capital goods and consumer goods.

Inefficiency

Production inefficiency is one way an economy can fail to be efficient. An economy is also inefficient when it is producing at the wrong point on the ppf – that is, when it is producing a combination of goods and services that does not match the wants of its people.

Certainly, a badly managed economy will not produce up to potential and will be inside the ppf. For example, resources in some parts of Europe are best suited for agriculture production and resources in other parts are best suited for industrial production. If European governments force their owners to produce equal amounts of industrial and agricultural output, regardless of the suitability of their resources, neither industrial or agricultural output will be up to potential. The European

Figure 2.3 Inefficiency from misallocation of resources

Society can end up inside its ppf at a point like *A* by using its resources inefficiently. If, for example, governments force resource owners to produce industrial goods when those resources are better suited to agricultural output, society would be at a point such as *A* rather than a point such as *B*.

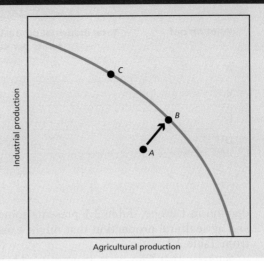

Agricultural production

economy will be at a point like A in Figure 2.3 – inside the frontier. Allowing resources to specialize in producing the goods that may produce best increases the production of both industry and agriculture and moves the economy to a point like B in Figure 2.3.

In extreme cases, a wrong output mix is obvious. Suppose, for example, that a society uses all of its resources to produce beef efficiently, but that everyone in the society is a vegetarian. The result is a total waste of resources (assuming that the society cannot trade beef for vegetables with another society).

Both points *B* and *C* in Figure 2.3 are points of production efficiency and full employment. Whether *B* is more or less efficient than *C*, however, depends on the preferences of the society's members.

Negative slope and opportunity cost

As we've seen, points that lie on the ppf represent points of full resource employment and production efficiency. But society can choose only one point on the curve. Because a society's choices are constrained by available resources and existing technology, when those resources are fully and efficiently employed it can produce more capital goods only by reducing production of consumer goods. The opportunity cost of the additional capital is the forgone production of consumer goods.

The fact that scarcity exists is illustrated by the negative slope of the production possibility frontier. In moving from point *E* to point *F* in Figure 2.2, capital production *increases* by 800 – 550 = 250 units (a positive change), but that increase in capital can be achieved only by shifting resources out of the production of consumer goods. Thus, in moving from point *E* to point *F* in Figure 2.2, consumer good production *decreases* by 1300 – 1100 = 200 units of the consumer good (a negative change). The slope of the curve, the ratio of the change in capital goods to the change in consumer goods, is negative.[1]

The law of increasing opportunity costs

The negative slope of the ppf indicates the trade-off that a society faces between two goods. We can learn something further about the shape of the frontier and the terms of this trade-off. Let us look at the trade-off between industrial and agricultural pro-

---

[1] *The value of the slope of a society's production possibility frontier is called the* marginal rate of transformation (MRT). *In Figure 2.2, the MRT between point* E *and point* F *is simply the ratio of the change in capital goods (a positive number) to the change in consumer goods (a negative number).*

Table 2.1 Production possibility schedule for total industrial and agricultural production in Europe

Point on ppf	Total industrial production (units per year)	Total agricultural production (units per year)
A	700	100
B	650	200
C	510	380
D	400	500
E	300	550

duction in Europe. Table 2.1 presents some hypothetical combinations of industrial and agricultural production that might exist for Europe. Figure 2.4 graphs the data from Table 2.1.

Suppose that Europe is at point *C*. Then suppose that the demand for industrial goods dramatically increases. If this happens, some resources would probably shift from agricultural production to industrial production. Such a shift is represented by a move from point *C* up and to the left along the ppf toward points *A* and *B* in Figure 2.4. As this happens, it becomes more and more difficult to produce additional industrial goods. The best resources for industrial production were presumably in industry, and the best resources for agriculture in agricultural production. As we try to produce more and more industrial output, resources are less and less well suited to that kind of output. And as we take more and more land out of agricultural production, we will be taking increasingly better agriculture-producing resources. All of this is to say that the opportunity cost of more industrial goods, measured in terms of agricultural goods, increases.

Moving from *E* to *D*, we can get 100 extra units of industrial goods (400 – 300) by sacrificing only 50 units of agriculture (550 – 500) – that is, we get two units of

Figure 2.4 Industrial and agricultural production in Europe

The ppf illustrates that the opportunity cost of industrial production increases as we shift resources from agricultural production to industrial production. Moving from *E* to *D*, we get an additional 100 units of industrial output at a cost of 50 units of agricultural output. Moving from *B* to *A*, we get only 50 units of industrial goods at a cost of 100 units of agricultural output. The cost per unit of industrial output – measured in lost agricultural output – has increased.

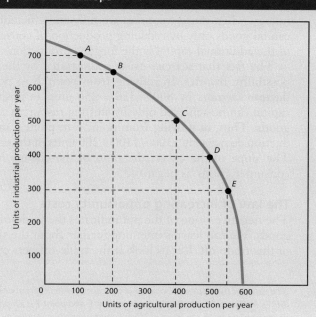

industrial output for every unit of agriculture sacrificed.[2] However, when we are already stretching the ability of resources to produce industrial goods, it becomes more difficult to produce more of them and the opportunity cost goes up. Moving from *B* to *A*, we can get only 50 extra units of industrial goods (700 – 650) by sacrificing 100 units of agricultural output (200 – 100). For every unit of agriculture, we now get only half a unit of industry. On the other hand, if the demand for agricultural goods were to increase substantially and we were to move down and to the right along the ppf, it would become increasingly difficult to produce agricultural products, and the opportunity cost of agriculture, in terms of industry, would rise. This is the law of increasing opportunity cost.

It is important to remember that the ppf represents choices available within the constraints imposed by the current state of agricultural technology. In the long run, technology may improve, and when that happens we have *growth*.

Economic growth

economic growth

An increase in the total output of an economy. It occurs when a society acquires new resources or when it learns to produce more using existing resources.

Economic growth is characterized by an increase in the total output of an economy. It occurs when a society acquires new resources or when society learns to produce more with existing resources. New resources may mean a larger labour force or an increased capital stock. The production and use of new machinery and equipment (capital) increases the productivity of workers. Improved productivity also comes from technological change and innovation, the discovery and application of new, efficient techniques of production.

The last few decades have seen significant increases in productivity in both agriculture and, to a lesser extent, industrial production. Table 2.2 shows that, for example, output per worker in agriculture has increased, on average, by 5½% per year. Such an increase in productivity doubles potential agricultural output in less than 13 years.[3]

These increases are the result of more efficient farming techniques, more and better capital (tractors, combine harvesters and other equipment), and advances in scientific knowledge and technological change (hybrid seeds, fertilizers and so forth). Significant but smaller increases in productivity have been achieved in industrial production. As you can see in Figure 2.5, increases such as these shift the ppf up and to the right.

Table 2.2 Increasing productivity in agricultural and industrial production in Europe,* 1960–1993

	Percentage increase in agricultural output per person	Percentage increase in industrial output per person
1960–73	6.2	5.5
1973–79	4.0	2.9
1979–89	5.0	2.5
1989–93	6.4	1.9
1960–93	5.5	3.7

*15 members of the European Union in 1997.
Source: OECD Historical Statistics, 1995.

[2]*This implies that the marginal rate of transformation is –2 between D and E. Change in industrial goods = +100; change in agricultural production = –50. MRT = + 100 ÷ –50 = –2.*

[3]*This is not to suggest that all output is either agricultural or industrial. The service sector is also important and has achieved substantial productivity gains. We concentrate here on agriculture and industry simply for illustrative purposes.*

Figure 2.5 Economic growth shifts the ppf up and to the right

Productivity increases have enhanced Europe's ability to produce both agriculture and industry. As Table 2.2 shows, productivity increases were more dramatic for agriculture than for industry. The shifts in the ppf were thus not parallel. (Note: the ppf also shifts if there is a change in the amount of resources available. Although we emphasize productivity increases here, the actual shifts between years were in part due to changes in the stock of resources.)

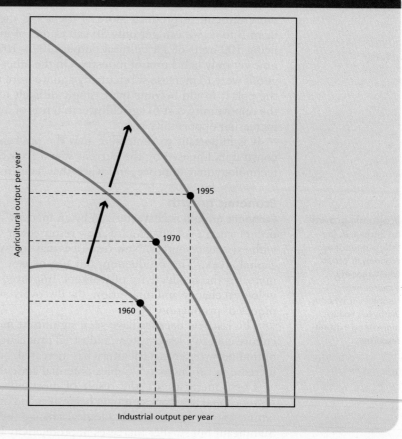

■ **Sources of growth and the dilemma of poor countries** Economic growth arises from many sources, the two most important of which, over the years, have been the accumulation of capital and technological advances. For poor countries, capital is essential; they must build the communication networks and transport systems necessary to develop industries that function efficiently. They also need capital goods to develop their agricultural sectors.

Recall that capital goods are produced only at a sacrifice of consumer goods. The same can be said for technological advances. Technological advances come from research and development that uses resources, and thus they too must be paid for. The resources used to produce capital goods – to build a road, a tractor or a manufacturing plant – *and* to develop new technologies could have been used to produce consumer goods.

When a large part of a country's population is very poor, taking resources out of the production of consumer goods such as food and clothing is very difficult. In addition, in some countries those wealthy enough to invest in domestic industries choose instead to invest abroad because of political turmoil at home. As a result, it often falls to the governments of poor countries to generate revenues for capital production and research out of tax collections.

All these factors have contributed to the growing gap between some poor and rich nations. Figure 2.6 graphs the result, using production possibility frontiers. On the left, the rich country devotes a larger portion of its production to capital, while the poor country produces mostly consumer goods. On the right, you see the result: the ppf of the rich country shifts up and out, further and faster.

Although it exists only as an abstraction, the ppf illustrates a number of very important concepts that we shall use throughout the rest of this book: scarcity,

Figure 2.6 Capital goods and growth in poor and rich countries

Rich countries find it easier than poor countries to devote resources to the production of capital. But the more resources that flow into capital production, the faster the rate of economic growth. Thus the gap between poor and rich countries has grown over time.

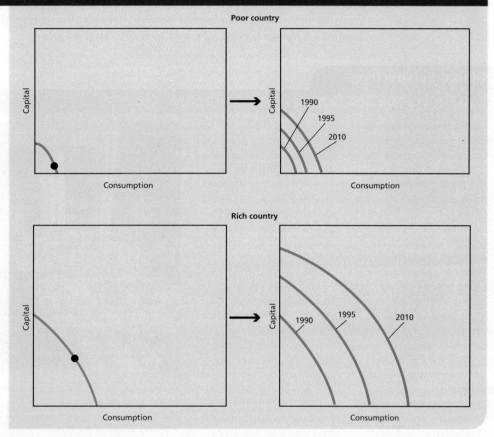

unemployment, inefficiency, opportunity cost, the law of increasing opportunity cost, and economic growth.

The economic problem

Recall the three basic questions facing all economic systems: (1) What will be produced? (2) How will it be produced? (3) Who will get it?

When David was alone on the island, the mechanism for answering these questions was simple: he thought about his own wants and preferences, looked at the constraints imposed by the resources of the island and his own skills and time, and made his decisions. As he set about his work, he allocated available resources quite simply, more or less by dividing up his available time. Distribution of the output was irrelevant. Because David was the society, he got it all.

Introducing even one more person into the economy – in this case, Anna – changed all that. With Anna on the island, resource allocation involves deciding not only how each person spends time but also who does what. Labour must be allocated to the various tasks. And now there are two sets of wants and preferences. And even after two people decide what to produce, they have to decide how to divide it. If David and Anna go off on their own and form two completely separate self-sufficient economies, there will be lost potential. Clearly, two people can do many more things together than one person can do alone. They may use their comparative advantages in different skills to specialize. Cooperation and coordination may give rise to gains that would otherwise not be possible.

When a society consists of millions of people, the problem of coordination and cooperation becomes enormous, but so does the potential for gain. In large, complex economies, specialization can go wild, with people working in jobs as different in their detail as an impressionist painting is from a blank page. The range of products available in a modern industrial society is beyond anything that could have been imagined a hundred years ago, and so is the range of jobs.

Global Perspectives

Eastern Europe and Russia: a mixed progress report

During the late 1980s, the command economies of Eastern Europe collapsed like a row of dominoes. The process began when the Berlin Wall, which had separated the communist East from the capitalist West for nearly 30 years, was torn down. Finally, in 1991, the once mighty Soviet Union disintegrated, ending 75 years of communism and nearly a half century of Cold War with the West.

A decade has passed and the transition to a set of independent economies orientated to the market is progressing. But the road to prosperity has been uneven and quite rocky. Some countries, like Poland, Hungary and the Czech Republic, are doing quite well. Poland was growing at an annual rate of 7.3% in early 1997. However, poorer countries like Albania, Bulgaria and Romania were still waiting for the first signs of growth.

With fading memories of the jubilation at the collapse of communism seven years ago, there is a new divide – some call it the latter-day Iron Curtain – between have and have-not nations of Central and Eastern Europe. Only in the former does the joy remain.

The 1996 economic data showed the division clearly. Foreign investment and rising buyer power have transformed the larger cities of Hungary, the Czech Republic and Poland into places with many of the accoutrements of the West: fast-food restaurants, self-service petrol stations, Benetton stores and apartment complexes complete with fitted satellite dishes.

More than $15 billion in foreign investment has poured into Hungary since 1960. Yet in neighbouring Romania, which has more than twice the population, only $2 billion has come in, and in Bulgaria just $700 million. The average monthly wage in Poland is now well over 330 euros and people have access to adequate and cheap medical care. In chaotic Bulgaria, many hospitals lack even such basics as X-ray film.

The biggest country making the transition was, of course, Russia. While slumping through the early and mid-1990s, Russia finally began to grow in 1997, when aggregate output rose. But deep problems and much uncertainty remain.

The officially recorded economy contracted for eight successive years, leaving it in 1997 at about half its size in 1989 – a steeper fall than in Europe and America at the time of the Great Depression (though the black economy has expanded). Meanwhile,

People who visit planned economies frequently comment on the lack of variety in consumer goods. This problem has substantially decreased in Poland, which began its transition to a free-market economy in the early 1990s.

prices, unemployment and the tally of unpaid wages have been rising. Russia's is now a market economy, whatever its imperfections. Moreover, much of the pain necessary to achieve such an economy may at last be over. In particular, inflation – enemy of the poor and destroyer of social stability – has dropped from 2,505% in 1992 to an annual rate of 15% in April 1997.

Even more notable is the transfer of property into private hands – the biggest in history. In just three years after 1991, 120,000 enterprises changed from state to private ownership. What all this meant was that 22% of Russians – 32 million people – were living below the official poverty line, defined as a minimum subsistence level. Things worsened during 1998 when the value of the rouble fell a further 50%. Among other things, as communists like to point out, this means falling meat and milk consumption: the average salary buys only about two-thirds as much meat as in Soviet days and only about one-third as much milk.

Sources: Jane Perlez, 'New bricks, same old walls for Europe's poor nations', New York Times, 24 January 1997; 'A survey of Russia', The Economist, 12 July 1997, pp. 1–19.

The amount of coordination and cooperation in a modern industrial society is almost impossible to imagine. Yet something seems to drive economic systems, if sometimes clumsily and inefficiently, towards producing the things that people want. Given scarce resources, how, exactly, do large, complex societies go about answering the three basic economic questions? This is the **economic problem**, and this is what this text is about.

Economic systems

Now that you understand the economic problem, we can explore how different economic systems go about answering the three basic questions.

Command economies

In some modern societies, government plays a big role in answering the basic economic questions. In pure **command economies**, a central authority or agency generally draws up a plan that establishes what will be produced and when, sets production goals, and makes rules for distribution. Planners in command economies use complex computer programs to determine the materials, labour and energy inputs required to produce a variety of output targets. The final output targets are then set with an eye towards the same constraint that the single manager of a one-person economy faces – limited resources. Centrally determined income policies then establish how much compensation workers and managers receive for their labours.

Even in pure planned economies, people do exercise some choice. Commodities are sold at prices set by the government, and to the extent that they are able to pay those prices people are free to buy what is available. Sometimes more is demanded than is produced; sometimes goods are left on the shelves. These signals are used in the next plan to adjust output targets.

It is an understatement to say that planned economies have not fared well over the last fifteen years. In fact, the planned economies of Eastern Europe and the former Soviet Union – including the Russian Republic – have completely collapsed. (Another former command economy, that of Poland, is doing somewhat better.) China remains committed to some of the principles of a planned economy, but reforms are moving it away from pure central planning. For further information on the rate of progress in Eastern Europe, see the Global Perspective feature.

Laissez-faire economies: the free market

At the opposite end of the spectrum from the command economy is the **laissez-faire economy**. The term *laissez faire*, which translated literally from French means 'allow [them] to do', implies a complete lack of government involvement in the economy. In this type of economy, individuals and firms pursue their own self-interest without any central direction or regulation; the sum total of millions of individual decisions ultimately determines all basic economic outcomes. The central institution through which a laissez-faire system answers the basic questions is the **market**, a term that is used in economics to mean an institution through which buyers and sellers interact and engage in exchange.

The interactions between buyers and sellers in any market range from simple to complex. In early, simple economies, people engaged in barter. Today, a jewellery maker in Amsterdam may sell gold necklaces to a buyer through a home shopping network that shows the product on television – customers phone in orders and pay with a credit card. Ultimately, funds are transferred through a complicated chain of financial transactions. The result is that a buyer in Scandinavia buys a necklace from an unseen jewellery producer in Amsterdam.

In short:

economic problem
Given scarce resources, how exactly do large, complex societies go about answering the three basic economic questions?

command economy An economy in which a central authority or agency draws up a plan that establishes what will be produced and when, sets production goals, and makes rules for distribution.

laissez-faire economy
Literally from the French: 'allow [them] to do'. An economy in which individual people and firms pursue their own self-interests without any central direction or regulation.

market The means by which buyers and sellers interact and engage in exchange.

Some markets are simple and others are complex, but they all involve buyers and sellers engaging in exchange. The behaviour of buyers and sellers in a laissez-faire economy determines what gets produced, how it is produced, and who gets it.

The following chapters explore market systems in great depth. A quick preview is worthwhile here, however.

Consumer sovereignty

In a free, unregulated market, goods and services are produced and sold only if the supplier can make a profit. In simple terms, making a profit means selling goods or services for more than it costs to produce them. Clearly, you can't make a profit unless someone wants the product that you are selling. This logic leads to the notion of consumer sovereignty: the mix of output found in any free market system is dictated ultimately by the tastes and preferences of consumers who 'vote' by buying or not buying. Businesses rise and fall in response to consumer demands; no central directive or plan is necessary.

> **consumer sovereignty** The idea that consumers ultimately dictate what will be produced (or not produced) by choosing what to purchase (and what not to purchase).

In a free market economy, producers may be small or large. One person who hand paints eggshells may start to sell them as a business; a woman who has been showing her poodle may start handling other people's dogs in the show ring. On a larger scale, a group of furniture designers may put together a large portfolio of sketches and several million euros, and start a bigger business. At the extreme are huge corporations like IBM, Mitsubishi and Shell, each of which sells tens of billions of euros' worth of products every year.

Individual production decisions: free enterprise

Under a free market system, individual producers must also work out how to organize and coordinate the actual production of their products or services. The owner of a small shoe repair shop must buy the equipment and tools that she needs, put up signs, and set prices by herself. In a big corporation, so many people are involved in planning the production process that in many ways corporate planning resembles the planning in a command economy. Whether the firms are large or small, however, production decisions in a market economy are made by separate private organizations acting in what they perceive to be their own interests.

Individuals seeking profits are free to start new businesses. Because new businesses require capital investment before they can begin operation, starting a new business involves risk. Every day, new businesses are born and others fail. A well run business that produces a product for which demand exists will succeed; a poorly run business or one that produces a product for which little demand exists is likely to fail. It is through *free enterprise* that new products and new production techniques find their way into use.

Proponents of free market systems argue that free enterprise leads to more efficient production and better response to diverse and changing consumer preferences. If a producer produces inefficiently, competitors will come along, fight for the business, and eventually take it away. Thus in a free market economy, competition forces producers to use efficient techniques of production. It is competition, then, that ultimately dictates how outputs are produced.

Distribution of output

In a free market system, the distribution of output – who gets what – is also determined in a decentralized way. The amount that any one household gets depends on its income and wealth. *Income* is the amount that a household earns each year. It comes in a number of forms: wages, salaries, interest and the like. *Wealth* is the amount that households have accumulated out of past income through saving or inheritance and have not spent.

To the extent that income comes from working for a wage, it is at least in part determined by individual choice. You will work for the wages available in the market only if those wages (and the things they can buy) are sufficient to compensate you for what you give up by working. Your leisure certainly has a value too. You may also discover that you can increase your income by getting more education or training. You can't increase your income, however, if you acquire a skill that no one wants.

In sum:

> In a free market system, the basic economic questions are answered without the help of a central government plan or directives. This is what the 'free' in free market means – the system is left to operate on its own, with no outside interference. Individuals pursuing their own self-interest will go into business and produce the products and services that people want; people will decide whether to acquire skills or not, whether to work or not, and whether to buy, sell, invest, or save the income that they earn.

Price theory

price The amount for which a unit of a product sells. It reflects what society is willing to pay.

The basic coordinating mechanism in a free market system is price. A **price** is the amount for which a unit of a product sells, and it reflects what society is willing to pay. Prices of inputs – labour, land, capital – determine how much it costs to produce a product. Prices of various kinds of labour, or *wage rates*, determine the rewards for working in different jobs and professions. Many of the independent decisions made in a market economy involve the weighing of prices and costs, so it is not surprising that much of economic theory focuses on the factors that influence and determine prices. This is why microeconomic theory is often simply called *price theory*.

Mixed systems: markets and governments

The differences between command economies and laissez-faire economies in their pure forms are enormous. But these pure forms do not exist in the world; all real systems are in some sense 'mixed'. That is, individual enterprise exists and independent choice is exercised even in economies in which the government plays the major role.

Conversely, no market economies exist without government involvement and government regulation. European countries have a basically free market economy, but government involvement is significant. Governments purchase goods for public consumption and make investments. European governments also redistribute income by means of taxation and social welfare expenditures, and regulate many economic activities.

As you can see from Table 2.3, all this involves a substantial part of total output for most European nations, but it applies to other major economies in the world too. Two things stand out about the table. First, although government spending as a proportion of total output is large in all these economies, there are significant variations. It is around a third in the USA, Japan and Switzerland, and nearly two-thirds in Sweden. The other point to observe is that in most Western economies over recent decades, the extent of government spending as a proportion of output has tended to increase.

One of the major themes in this book, and indeed in economics, is the tension between the advantages of free, unregulated markets and the need for government involvement in the economy. Advocates of free markets argue that such markets work best when left to themselves. Markets produce only what people want; without buyers, sellers go out of business. Competition forces firms to adopt efficient production techniques. Wage differentials lead people to acquire needed skills. Competition also leads to innovation in both production techniques and products. But market systems have problems too.

Even staunch defenders of the free enterprise system recognize that market systems are not perfect. First, they do not always produce what people want at lowest cost – there are inefficiencies. Second, rewards (income) may be unfairly distributed, and

Table 2.3 Government spending as a proportion of total output in selected economies, 1960–1996			
	1960	**1990**	**1996**
Germany	32.4	45.1	49.0
Japan	17.5	31.7	36.2
Netherlands	33.7	54.0	49.9
Norway	29.9	53.8	45.5
Sweden	31.0	59.10	64.7
Switzerland	17.2	33.5	37.6
UK	32.2	39.9	41.9
USA	27.0	33.3	33.3

Source: International Monetary Fund.

some groups may be left out. Third, periods of unemployment and inflation recur with some regularity – market systems can be unstable.

Many people point to these problems as reasons for government involvement. Indeed, for some problems government involvement may be the only solution. But government decisions are made by people who presumably, like the rest of us, act in their own self-interest. While governments may indeed be called upon to improve the functioning of the economy, there is no guarantee that they will do so. Just as markets may fail to produce an allocation of resources that is perfectly efficient and fair, governments may fail to improve matters. We will return to this debate many times throughout the book.

Looking ahead

This chapter has described the economic problem in broad terms. We have outlined the questions that all economic systems must answer. We also discussed very broadly the two kinds of economic systems. In the next chapter we turn from the general to the specific. There we discuss in some detail the institutions of Europe: how the private sector is organized, what the government actually does, and how the international sector operates. Chapters 4 and 5 then begin the task of analysing the way market systems work.

Summary

1. Every society has some system or mechanism for transforming what nature and previous generations have provided into useful form. Economics is the study of that process and its outcomes.

2. *Producers* are those who take resources and transform them into usable products, or *outputs*. Private firms, households and governments all produce something.

Scarcity, choice and opportunity cost

3. All societies must answer *three basic questions*: What will be produced? How will it be produced? Who will

get what is produced? These three questions make up the *economic problem*.

4. One person alone on an island must make the same basic decisions that complex societies make. When society consists of more than one person, questions of distribution, cooperation and specialization arise.

5. Because resources are scarce relative to human wants in all societies, using resources to produce one good or service implies not using them to produce something else. This concept of *opportunity cost* is central to an understanding of economics.

6. Using resources to produce *capital* that will in turn produce benefits in the future implies *not* using those resources to produce consumer goods in the present.

7. Even if one individual or nation is absolutely more efficient at producing all goods than another, all parties will gain if they specialize in producing goods in which they have a *comparative advantage*.

8. A *production possibility frontier* (ppf) is a graph that shows all the combinations of goods and services that can be produced if all of society's resources are used efficiently. The production possibility frontier illustrates a number of important economic concepts: scarcity, unemployment, inefficiency, increasing opportunity cost, and economic growth.

9. *Economic growth* occurs when society produces more, either by acquiring more resources or by learning to produce more with existing resources. Improved productivity may come from additional capital, or from the discovery and application of new, more efficient techniques of production.

Economic systems

10. In some modern societies, government plays a big role in answering the three basic questions. In pure *command economies*, a central authority generally draws up a plan that determines what will be produced, how it will be produced, and who will get it.

11. A *laissez-faire economy* is one in which individuals independently pursuing their own self-interest, without any central direction or regulation, ultimately determine all basic economic outcomes.

12. A *market* is a mechanism by which buyers and sellers interact and engage in exchange. Some markets involve simple face-to-face exchange; others involve a complex series of transactions, often made over great distances or electronically.

13. There are no purely planned economies and no pure laissez-faire economies; all economies are mixed. Individual enterprise, independent choice and relatively free markets exist in centrally planned economies, and there is significant government involvement in market economies such as those of the European Union.

14. One of the great debates in economics revolves around the tension between the advantages of free, unregulated markets and the need for government involvement in the economy. Free markets produce what people want, and competition forces firms to adopt efficient production techniques. The need for government intervention arises because free markets are characterized by inefficiencies and an unequal distribution of income, and experience regular periods of inflation and unemployment.

Review Terms and Concepts

capital
command economy
comparative advantage
consumer goods
consumer sovereignty
economic growth
economic problem
investment
laissez-faire economy

market
opportunity cost
outputs
price
producers
production
production possibility frontier (ppf)
resources or inputs

Problem Set

1. 'Studying economics instead of going to town and partying is like building a boat instead of lying on the beach.' Explain this statement carefully using the concepts of capital and opportunity cost.

2. Define *capital*. What distinguishes land from capital? Is a tree capital?

3. Briefly describe the trade-offs involved in each of the following decisions. Specifically, list some of the opportunity costs associated with the decision, paying particular attention to the trade-offs between present

and future consumption.
a. After a stressful year at school, Eunice decides to take the summer off rather than work before going on to university.
b. Frank is overweight and decides to work out every day and to go on a diet.
c. Mei is very diligent about taking her car in for routine maintenance even though it takes two hours of her time and costs €100 four times each year.
d. Henri is in a big hurry. He drives through a red light on the way to work.

4. Kristen and Anna live in the seaside resort of Cannes. They own a small business in which they make wristbands and potholders and sell them to people on the beach. Kristen can make 15 wristbands per hour, but only 3 potholders. Anna is a bit slower and can make only 12 wristbands or 2 potholders in an hour.

| | Output per hour | |
	Kristen	Anna
Wristbands	15	12
Potholders	3	2

a. For Kristen, what is the opportunity cost of a potholder? What is it for Anna? Who has a comparative advantage in the production of potholders? Explain.
b. Who has a comparative advantage in the production of wristbands? Explain.
c. Assume that Kristen works 20 hours per week in the business. If Kristen were in business on her own, graph the possible combinations of potholders and wristbands that she could produce in a week. Do the same for Anna.
d. If Kristen devoted half of her time (10 out of 20 hours) to wristbands and half of her time to potholders, how many of each would she produce in a week? If Anna did the same thing, how many of each would she produce? How many wristbands and potholders would be produced in total?
e. Suppose that Anna spent all 20 hours of her time on wristbands and Kristen spent 17 hours on potholders and 3 hours on wristbands. How many of each would be produced?
f. Suppose that Kristen and Anna can sell all their wristbands for 1 euro each and all their potholders for €5.50 each. If each of them worked 20 hours per week, how should they split their time between wristbands and potholders? What is their maximum joint revenue?

5. 'If an economy is operating at a point inside its production possibility frontier, it must be that resources are unemployed.' Do you agree or disagree?

6. Suppose that a simple society has an economy with only one resource, labour. Labour can be used to produce only two commodities – X, (food), and Y, (music and merriment). Suppose that the labour force consists of 100 workers. One labourer can produce either 5 units of food per month (by hunting and gathering) or 10 units of music and merriment per month (by writing songs, playing the guitar, dancing and so on).

a. On a graph, draw the economy's production possibility frontier. Where does the ppf intersect the Y axis? Where does it intersect the X axis? What meaning do those points have?
b. Suppose the economy ended up producing at a point *inside* the ppf. Give at least two reasons why this could occur. What could be done to move the economy to a point *on* the ppf?
c. Suppose you succeeded in lifting your economy to a point on its ppf. What point would you choose? How might your small society decide the point at which it wanted to be?
d. Once you have chosen a point on the ppf, you still need to decide how your society's product will be divided up. If you were a dictator, how would you decide? What would happen if you left product distribution to the free market?

7. What progress has been made during the last year in Eastern Europe? Which countries are growing? Which are in decline? What factors seem to have contributed to the differences in success across countries?

8. Match each diagram in the figure with its description. Assume that the economy is producing or attempting to produce at point A, and that most members of society like meat and not fish. Some descriptions apply to more than one diagram and some diagrams have more than one description.

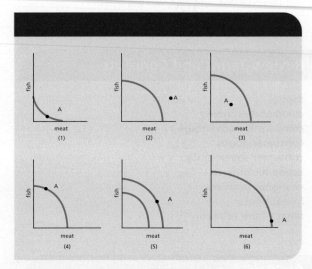

a. Inefficient production of meat and fish.
b. Productive efficiency.
c. An inefficient mix of output.
d. Technological advances in the production of meat and fish.
e. The law of increasing opportunity costs.
f. An impossible combination of meat and fish.

9. A nation with fixed quantities of resources is able to produce any of the following combinations of bread and ovens:

Loaves of bread (millions)	Ovens (thousands)
75	0
60	12
45	22
30	30
15	36

These figures assume that a certain number of previously produced ovens are available in the current period for baking bread.

a. Using the data in the table, graph the production possibilities frontier (with ovens on the vertical axis).

b. Does the principle of 'increasing opportunity cost' hold in this nation? Explain briefly. (*Hint*: What happens to the opportunity cost of bread – measured in number of ovens – as bread production increases?)

c. If this country chooses to produce both ovens and bread, what will happen to the ppf over time? Why?

d. A politician running for national office wants to reallocate resources to produce the maximum possible quantity of bread, with no production of ovens. His slogan is: 'You can't eat ovens!' If this politician is successful, explain what will happen to the production possibilities curve over time. Why?

Now suppose that a new technology is discovered that allows twice as many loaves of bread to be baked in each existing oven.

e. Illustrate (on your original graph) the effect of this new technology on the production possibilities curve.

f. Suppose that before the new technology is introduced, the nation produces 22 ovens. After the new technology is introduced, the nation produces 30 ovens. What is the effect of the new technology on the production of bread? (Give the number of loaves before and after the change.)

3

The Structure and Importance of the European Economy: the Private, Public and International Sectors

The previous chapter described the economic problem. All societies are endowed by nature and by previous generations with resources. However they are scarce relative to wants. The production process combines and transforms these resources into goods and services that are demanded by the members of society.

At the end of Chapter 2, we briefly described the economic systems that exist in the world today. This chapter describes the basic structure of the European economy in more detail, including the main institutions that bind together many European countries into the European Union (EU). Then, because most production is undertaken by private individuals and organizations, we look at the EU's private sector. The **private sector** is made up of independently owned profit making firms, non-profit organizations, and individual households. It includes Volvo Corporation, the Free University of Amsterdam, the Catholic Church, pig farms in Denmark, the local supermarket and the babysitter next door. The private sector is defined by independent ownership and control. In essence, it includes all the decision-making units within the economy that are not part of the government.

Next, we turn to a discussion of the public sector. The **public sector** is government and its agencies. Government employees – tax assessors, state school teachers, post office workers, colonels in the army, judges – work in the public sector. Just as the Volvo Corporation uses land, labour and capital to produce cars, the public sector uses land, labour and capital to produce goods and services such as police and fire protection, education and defence. The public sector also produces some things that are simultaneously produced by the private sector. The post office provides a service that competes directly with similar services provided by private firms. State schools, part of the public sector, directly compete for 'buyers' of their 'product' with schools that provide private education.

Finally, we provide a brief introduction to the **international sector** and discuss the importance of imports and exports to European economies. From any one country's perspective, the international sector consists of the economies of the rest of the world. Most European economies have become more closely integrated in recent years and trade between these countries is becoming increasingly important. However, even an enormous entity, such as the European economy, is not entirely isolated from events in the rest of the world. In a real sense there is only one economy in the world: the world economy.

private sector
Includes all independently owned profit-making firms, non-profit organizations and households; all the decision-making units in the economy that are not part of the government.

public sector
Includes all agencies at all levels of government.

international sector
From any one country's perspective, the economies of the rest of the world.

Recall the distinction drawn in Chapter 1 between descriptive economics and economic theory, and then notice what this chapter is not. We do not analyse behaviour in this chapter. Here we describe institutions only as they exist. We also try very hard to avoid any normative distinctions. We do not talk about proper or improper roles of government in the economy, for example, or the things that governments might do to make the economy more efficient or fair.

In Chapter 4, we begin to analyse behaviour. Before we begin the analysis in Chapter 4, however, it is important to have some sense of the institutional landscape. One purpose for studying economics is to understand the world and what people actually do. This chapter provides some important facts that describe the realities of the European economy.

Europe's place in the world economy

We can divide the world economy into nine regions.[1] They are:

- Western Europe
- North America
- Eastern Europe and the former Soviet Union
- Asian Developing
- Japan
- Latin America
- Middle East and North Africa
- Sub-Saharan Africa, and
- 'Other', which includes Oceania

Of these groupings, Western Europe, North America and the Asian developing economies are the largest producers of goods and services, each item earning about a quarter of the world's income. However, if we focus on income per head of population, a different picture emerges. The developing Asian economies have a huge population, so income per head in this group is much less than in, say, Western Europe. On the other hand, Japan, with only 8% of world income, has a very high income per head. It has far fewer people than the developing Asian economies. The differences in income per head between different parts of the world can be clearly seen in Figure 3.1a. Western European incomes are, on average, very high. Over the last ten years, however, the gap between rich and poor has tended to lessen a little.

The proportion of world income generated within the developing Asian economies has grown more rapidly than elsewhere. In the meantime, its share of world population has grown only very slowly. Figure 3.1b shows the increasing importance of the developing Asian economies. Here is the main reason for the fall in the proportion of world output from Western Europe.

Although the proportion of world income in Western Europe has declined, the absolute level of its income has been rising. Table 3.1 presents figures for the annual percentage growth in incomes, actual and projected, for Western Europe and some other regions.

Incomes in Western Europe have, on average, been growing and are expected to continue to do so. However other regions, notably Asia Developing, saw a more rapid rise until sharp recession in 1997–98. Note the sharply falling incomes in Eastern Europe and former Soviet Union as they restructured in the first half of the 1990s.

[1]*This is a division suggested by the economics section of the Natwest Group's Market Intelligence Department.*

Figure 3.1 (a) Differences in income per head in different parts of the world. (b) The increasing importance of the developing Asian economies

Source: Economic and Financial Outlook. NatWest Group, November, 1997

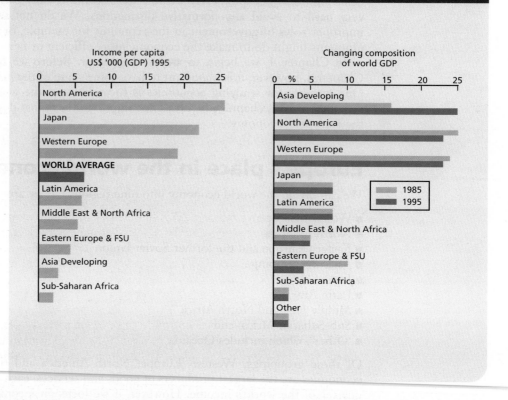

Table 3.1 Economic growth in the world's regions

	1990–1995 (average)	1996	1997 (estimated)	1998–2002 (average)
Western Europe	1.8	1.7	2.5	2.3
North America	1.7	2.7	3.7	2.6
Eastern Europe and former Soviet Union	−7.9	−3.1	0.4	4.0
Asia Developing	8.0	8.0	7.4	6.8
Japan	2.0	3.7	0.7	2.3
Latin America	2.9	3.5	4.9	4.8

Source: NatWest, Economic and Financial Outlook, November 1997.

The European Union: membership and organization

Although all European nations have their own identity, laws and institutions, most countries in Western Europe have become part of the European Union (EU).

Membership of this important organization involves giving up some elements of individual sovereignty and 'pooling' it, so that some decisions are taken at a European level rather than by individual governments. The 15 members of the EU at the beginning of 1998 were: Austria, Belgium, Denmark, Finland, France, Germany, Greece, Ireland, Italy, Luxembourg, The Netherlands, Portugal, Spain, Sweden and the UK.

There are many areas in which the EU states cooperate. Here are the most significant ones. No member state can restrict the flow of goods and services from other member states. For such free trade to take place, there can be no taxes on imports (or tariffs) within the Union. Border controls are being dismantled to make free movement easier. Over time, there is less control on the movement of resources. Capital moves more easily from one country to another. There are also fewer restrictions on the rights of citizens to relocate to other member states.

Common policies are being established on matters relating to health and safety and to the environment.

All EU countries contribute to funds from which sums are paid to assist the EU's poorer countries and regions, providing help with unemployment problems and considerable amounts of agricultural support. Substantial work is also being done so that a single unit of currency, the Euro, can operate between 11 of the 15 EU countries.

We shall consider many of these matters in greater detail in later chapters.

Institutions of the European Union

There are five main EU institutions through which such cooperation takes place. The first is the **European Council**. It consists of heads of state of member governments plus a president. It meets regularly to discuss matters of common concern but has no legislative power.

The **Commission** has 20 commissioners drawn from all EU countries and is, in principle, independent of national governments. It has executive powers within an agreed framework.

The **Council of Ministers** is comprised largely of the foreign ministers of member countries. It makes policy decisions, following proposals from the Commission. For most motions to be passed, they must receive a minimum of 62 of the 87 votes. This is known as Qualified Majority Voting (QMV). Table 3.2 shows how the votes are distributed between the 15 countries. A few matters of major importance require the unanimous approval of the Council.

Members of the **European Parliament** are directly elected by EU citizens. The Maastricht Treaty of 1983 increased the Parliament's power to influence legislation. Indeed, in some areas, its powers are as great as the European Council.

Finally, the **European Court of Justice**, consisting of a judge from each member country, decides whether decisions taken by the other European institutions are consistent with the treaties to which member governments have signed.

Expansion of the European Union

When the European Union first came into being in 1958, it was known as the Common Market. It had just six member countries: Germany, France, Italy, Belgium, The Netherlands and Luxembourg.

Over the last 40 years, the extent of cooperation has increased but so has its membership. The number of member states is expected to grow still further in the next 10 years.

Some European countries who are not members of the EU have special ties with the Union. Liechtenstein, Norway and Iceland have an agreement with the EU not to restrict trade by means of import taxes. These 18 countries form the European Economic Area (EEA). It is possible, but not certain, that these countries may also join the EU at some stage.

Table 3.2 Number of votes in the Council of Ministers per EU member country	
France	10
Germany	10
Italy	10
UK	8
Spain	5
Belgium	5
Greece	5
Netherlands	5
Portugal	5
Austria	4
Sweden	4
Denmark	3
Finland	3
Ireland	3
Luxembourg	2
Total	87

Some countries, such as Turkey, Cyprus and Malta, have agreements on trading with the EU. These countries also may become members.

Some of the countries of the former Soviet Union and its communities are also keen to join. At present, then, the European Union is large enough to be a highly significant organization. It may well become even more so in future.

The private sector: European business and industrial organization

How is business organized in European countries? Let us see first how the law permits *individual firms* to be organized. Then we can talk about the different ways that *industries* are structured. An individual firm's behaviour depends on both its own legal structure and its relationship to other firms in its industry.

The legal organization of firms

Most private sector activity takes place within business firms that exist to make a profit. Some other private sector organizations that exist for reasons other than profit – clubs, cooperatives and non-profit organizations, for example – do produce goods or services. Because these other organizations represent a small fraction of private sector activity, however, we focus here on profit-making firms.

A business set up to make profits may be organized in one of three basic legal forms: (1) a proprietorship, (2) a partnership, or (3) a corporation. A single business may pass through more than one of these forms of organization during its development.

The proprietorship

The least complex and most common form a business can take is the simple **proprietorship**, or sole trader. There is no legal process involved in starting a proprietorship. You simply start operating. You must, however, keep records of revenues and costs, and pay personal income taxes on your profit.

A university lecturer who also does consulting work, for example, receives fees and has costs (computer expenses, research materials and so forth). This consulting business is a proprietorship, even though the proprietor is the only employee and the business is very limited. A large restaurant that employs hundreds of people may also be a proprietorship if it is owned by a single person. Many doctors and lawyers in private practice report their incomes and expenses as proprietors.

In a proprietorship, one person owns the firm. In a sense, that person *is* the firm. If the firm owes money, the proprietor owes the money; if the firm earns a profit, the proprietor earns a profit. There is no limit to the proprietor's responsibility; if the business gets into financial trouble, the proprietor alone is liable. That is, if a business does poorly or ends up in debt, those debts are the proprietor's personal responsibility. There is no wall of protection between a proprietor and her business, as we will see there is between corporations and their owners.

The partnership

A **partnership** is a proprietorship with more than one proprietor. When two or more people agree to share the responsibility for a business, they form a partnership. While no formal legal process is required to start this kind of business, most partnerships are based on agreements, signed by all the partners, that detail who pays what part of the costs and how profits shall be divided. Because profits from partnerships are taxable, accurate records of receipts and expenditures must be kept and each party's profits must be reported to the tax authorities.

In a partnership, as in a proprietorship, there is no limit to the liability of the owners (that is, the partners) for the firm's debts. But with a partnership it can be worse, because each partner is both jointly and separately liable for all the debts of the partnership. If you own one-third of a partnership that goes out of business with a debt of €300,000, you owe your creditors €100,000, and so does each of your partners. But if your partners disappear, you owe the entire €300,000.

The corporation

A **corporation**, or limited company, is a formally established legal entity that exists separately from those who establish it and those who own it. To establish a corporation, a legally defined certificate of incorporation or company charter must be obtained. In most countries this is quite easily accomplished. A lawyer simply fills out the appropriate paperwork and files it along with certain fees. When a corporation is formed, **shares of stock** (certificates of partial ownership) are issued and either sold or assigned. A corporation is owned by its shareholders, who are in a sense partners in the firm's success or failure. Each share of stock entitles the holder to a portion of the corporation's profits. Shareholders differ from simple partners. The liability of shareholders is limited to the amount they paid for the stock. If the company goes out of business or bankrupt, the shareholders may lose what they have invested, but no more than that. They are not liable for the debts of the corporation beyond the amount they invested.

You can get an idea of the distribution of firm sizes in Europe by looking at Table 3.3. Although these figures are rather old eurostat claims that the distribution of firm size changes very slowly over time, so they continue to present an accurate picture of business organization in Europe.

It is clear that small firms play a major part in the economies of Europe. Well over 90% of European enterprises employ fewer than ten people each. Indeed, most are businesses where an individual works for himself or herself and employs no one else at all.

proprietorship
A form of business organization in which a person simply sets up a business to provide goods or services at a profit. In a proprietorship, the proprietor (or owner) is the firm. The assets and liabilities of the firm are the owner's assets and liabilities.

partnership
A form of business organization in which there is more than one proprietor. The owners are responsible jointly and separately for the firm's obligations.

corporation
A form of business organization resting on a legal charter that establishes the corporation as an entity separate from its owners. Owners hold shares and are liable for the firm's debts only up to the limit of their investment, or share, in the firm.

share of stock
A certificate of partial ownership of a corporation that entitles the holder to a portion of the corporation's profits.

Table 3.3 The organization of enterprise in the EU, 1992

Enterprise size (by employees)	Enterprises		Persons employed		Turnover	
	(000)	(%)*	(000)	(%)*	(billion Ecu)	(%)*
Very small (0–9)	14,628	92.9	32,788	32.5	2,966.3	25.4
Small (10–49)	972	6.2	18,992	18.9	2,368.8	20.4
Medium sized (50–249)	146	1.0	15,069	15.0	2,230.2	19.2
Large (250+)	31.5	0.21	34,170.7	33.8	4,070.8	35.0

*Percentages do not sum exactly because of rounding errors.
Source: Enterprises in Europe, Fourth Report, 1996.

However, we should not overstate the importance of these small firms. They employ less than a third of all the workforce and produce only a quarter of European private sector output. The relatively very few large firms employ more people and produce more output than all of the very small firms together.

The distribution of firms' profits

The main purpose of most of these firms is the earning of profits.

Firms' profits are usually divided into three pieces. Some is paid to government in the form of taxes. Some of it is paid out to shareholders as **dividends** (sometimes called *distributed profits*). And some of it usually stays within the corporation to be used for the purchase of capital assets. This part of corporate profits is called **retained earnings**, or *undistributed profits*. Because the firm pays taxes on its profits and individuals pay taxes on the dividends they receive, tax is actually paid twice on profits made.

The internal organization of a firm, whether it is a proprietorship, a partnership or a corporation, affects its behaviour and the behaviour of potential investors. For example, because they are protected by a corporation's limited liability status, potential investors may be more likely to back high-risk but potentially high-paying corporate ventures.

While a firm's internal structure is important, it is equally important to understand the organization of the industry or the market in which the firm competes. For example, whether it is a proprietorship or a corporation, a firm with little or no competition is likely to behave differently from a firm facing stiff competition from many rivals. With this in mind, we now expand our focus from the individual firm to the industry.

The organization of industries

The term **industry** is used loosely to refer to groups of firms that produce similar products. Industries can be defined narrowly or broadly, depending on the issue being discussed. For example, a company that produces and packages cheese is a part of the cheese industry, the dairy products industry, the food products industry and the agricultural products industry.[2]

Whether we define industries broadly or narrowly, how firms within any industry behave depends on how that industry is organized. When we speak of **market organization** we refer to the way an industry is structured: how many firms there are

dividends
The portion of a corporation's profits that the firm pays out each period to shareholders. Also called distributed profits.

retained earnings
The profits that a corporation keeps, usually for the purchase of capital assets. Also called undistributed profits.

industry A group of firms that produce a similar product. The boundaries of a 'product' can be drawn very widely ('agricultural products'), less widely ('dairy products'), or very narrowly ('cheese'). The term *industry* can be used interchangeably with the term *market*.

[2]*Europe conforms to a code system, the Standard Industrial Classification (SIC) system, which defines industries at various levels of detail.*

market organization

The way an industry is structured. Structure is defined by how many firms there are in an industry, whether products are differentiated or are virtually the same, whether or not firms in the industry can control prices or wages, and whether or not competing firms can enter and leave the industry freely.

perfect competition

An industry structure in which there are many firms, each small relative to the industry, producing virtually identical products and in which no firm is large enough to have any control over prices. In perfectly competitive industries, new competitors can freely enter and exit the market.

homogeneous products

Undifferentiated outputs; products that are identical to, or indistinguishable from, one another.

in an industry, whether products are virtually the same or differentiated, whether or not firms in the industry can control prices or wages, whether or not competing firms can freely enter and leave the industry, and so forth. The kind of industry – or *market* – in which a firm operates determines, in large part, how it will behave.

In the discussion that follows, we analyse industries as if their structures fit their definitions precisely. In reality, however, industries are not always easy to categorize. Some industries have some characteristics generally associated with one form of organization and other characteristics associated with a different form of organization. Nonetheless, these categories provide a useful and convenient framework.

Perfect competition

At one end of the market-organization spectrum is the competitive industry in which many relatively small firms produce nearly identical products. **Perfect competition** is a very precisely defined form of industry structure. (The word *perfect* here does not refer to virtue. It simply means 'total' or 'complete'.) In a perfectly competitive industry, no single firm has any control over prices. That is, no single firm is large enough to affect the market price of its product or the prices of the inputs that it buys. This crucial observation follows from two characteristics of competitive industries. First, a competitive industry is composed of many firms, each small relative to the size of the industry. Second, every firm in a perfectly competitive industry produces exactly the same product; the output of one firm cannot be distinguished from the output of the others. Products in a perfectly competitive industry are said to be **homogeneous**.

These characteristics limit the decisions open to competitive firms and simplify the analysis of competitive behaviour. Because all firms in a perfectly competitive industry produce virtually identical products, and because each firm is small relative to the market, perfectly competitive firms have no control over the prices at which they sell their output. Taking prices as a given, then, each firm can decide only how much output to produce and how to produce it.

Consider agriculture, the classic example of a perfectly competitive industry. A European wheat farmer has absolutely no control over the price of wheat. Prices are determined not by the individual farmers but rather by the interaction of many suppliers and many demanders. The only decisions left to the wheat farmer are how much wheat to plant and when and how to produce the crop.

Another mark of perfectly competitive industries is ease of entry. *Ease of entry* means that new firms can easily enter a market and compete for profits. No barriers exist to prevent new firms from competing. New firms can, and do, frequently enter such industries in search of profits, while others go out of business when they suffer losses. For example, suppose a coffee shop opens in a town and business is booming. Good profits are being made. It will attract competition. After all, to sell coffee all you need is a place to do business, a coffee maker – perhaps an espresso machine – and some effort. Entry is easy.

When a firm *exits* an industry, it simply stops producing a product. Sometimes, an exiting firm goes out of business altogether. During the last ten years, for example, thousands of small farmers have gone out of business, sold off their assets, paid what bills they could, and disappeared.

To summarize:

Perfectly competitive industries are made up of many firms, each small relative to the size of the total market. In these industries, individual firms do not distinguish or differentiate their products from those of their competitors. Product prices are determined by market forces and are virtually unaffected by the decisions of any single firm. Entry into and exit from the market are relatively easy.

Monopoly

monopoly An industry structure (or market organization) in which there is only one large firm that produces a product for which there are no close substitutes. Monopolists can set prices but are subject to market discipline. For a monopoly to continue to exist, something must prevent potential competitors from entering the industry and competing for profits.

At the other end of the spectrum is **monopoly**, a market or industry in which only one firm produces a product for which there are no close substitutes.

When there is only one firm in a market, that firm sets the price of its product. This does not mean, however, that monopolies can set any price they please. Even monopolies face the constraint of the market. Even if a firm produces a product that everyone likes, the firm gains nothing if it charges a price so high that no one buys it. The price a monopolist chooses determines the quantity it will be able to sell: it will sell more at lower prices and less at higher prices. Thus, even a monopolist is subject to discipline imposed by the market.

For a monopoly to remain a monopoly, it must find some way to keep other firms from entering its market and competing for profits. Often governments erect such **barriers to entry**. Sometimes they grant an exclusive licence to one producer. In Taiwan, for example, the government licensed only one company to produce beer, and prohibited beer imports until 1987.

barrier to entry Something that prevents new firms from entering and competing in an industry.

In the UK, public utilities – electric power and gas companies, for example, which are privately owned – were once state owned and shielded by the government from competition. Now changes are taking place rapidly. Other firms can purchase gas or electricity and compete on price in selling it to customers. For many years, BT was essentially the exclusive producer of telephone services in Britain, both local and long distance. However, dramatic changes in the UK telecommunications industry in the last few years have made that market much more competitive, with firms such as Mercury and Cable and Wireless offering effective competition.

Sometimes monopolies are specific to a particular time and location. In professional sport, clubs sign exclusive vendor agreements for matches. Sometimes, for example, a single vendor will be responsible for food and beverage sales at a football match. Since some stadiums do not permit you to bring your own food and beverages to the match, the vendor is providing a service for which there is no close substitute, and entry is blocked. Have you ever noticed the price of food and drinks at such matches?

In sum:

> A monopoly is a one-firm industry that produces a product for which there are no close substitutes. Such a firm can set prices, but its pricing behaviour is constrained by its market: It can sell a product only if people are willing to buy it. A monopolist is protected from competition by barriers to entry.

Monopolistic competition

monopolistic competition An industry structure in which many firms compete, producing similar but slightly differentiated products. There are close substitutes for the product of any given firm. Monopolistic competitors have some control over price. Price and quality competition follow from product differentiation. Entry and exit are relatively easy, and success invites new competitors.

Somewhere between monopoly and competition, but much closer to competition, is a very common hybrid market organization called **monopolistic competition**. In a monopolistically competitive industry, many firms compete for essentially the same customers, but each firm produces a slightly different product. If these firms can *differentiate* their products successfully, they establish a *brand loyalty* that allows them to enjoy the benefits of a monopoly. Lever is the only producer of Persil washing powder – it 'monopolizes' the market for Persil – but the soap business is still very competitive because many close substitutes are available. Prentice Hall is the only company that can sell this book, but there are many other economics texts.

While individual firms in perfectly competitive markets have no control over price, monopolistic competitors do exercise some price-setting power. That control is quite limited, however, because of the many close substitutes available. Monopolistically competitive firms are thus subject to a great deal of 'market discipline'.

A good example of monopolistic competition can be found in the music industry. Every rock band has a unique style; each has its own name. Entry is relatively inexpensive; all you need are musicians, instruments, amplifiers and a PA system. Thinking of each band as a small firm, management differentiates the product in an attempt to compete, and the competition is fierce. Very successful groups are more like monopolies, however; there are no 'close' substitutes for The Spice Girls, Oasis or Bon Jovi.

In monopolistically competitive industries, there is both price and quality competition. Firms often enter these industries because they have an idea for a new product that represents a slight variation or improvement on an old one. Perhaps the purest example of a monopolistically competitive market is the restaurant industry. Every major city in the world contains hundreds of restaurants, each producing a slightly differentiated product in a highly competitive way. The cosmetics and clothing industries are also monopolistically competitive. Firms in such industries must decide on output, price, and quality of product.

Free, or at least relatively easy, entry and exit characterize monopolistic competition. When a firm enjoys success in one of its product lines, its profits invite new firms to come into its market with new brands or styles. Many new restaurants are born every year, and many unsuccessful ones quietly expire.

To summarize:

> Monopolistically competitive firms contain large numbers of relatively small firms. Unlike firms in perfectly competitive industries, monopolistically competitive firms differentiate their products. Individual firms produce unique products and thus, despite their small size, exercise some control over price. Entry and exit are relatively easy.

Oligopoly

oligopoly

An industry structure (or market organization) with a small number of (usually) large firms producing products that range from highly differentiated (cars) to standardized (copper). In general, entry of new firms into an oligopolistic industry is difficult but possible.

An industry in which there are only a small number of firms is an **oligopoly**. The car industry in Europe, for example, has only a few firms at most in each country. The industry is dominated by a handful of large producers and a few smaller ones. This is also true of breakfast cereals, cigarettes and steel. Except for the fact that each contains only a few competitors, however, oligopolistic industries have little in common. In some, products are highly differentiated (cars and breakfast cereals, for example); in others, they are not (the steel industry, for example). In some, the industry is dominated by one very large firm; in others, the participating firms are of roughly equal size and have roughly equal power.

Oligopolies behave unpredictably. In markets where two or three large rivals compete head on, the competing firms often execute strategies that anticipate counter-strategies. In setting price, for example, one firm must take into account how its competitors in the oligopoly are likely to react. One firm's action usually triggers a reaction from another, which in turn triggers still another reaction, and so on. The strategies and counter-strategies employed by these firms determine who gets the sales. As a result, oligopolies are characterized by a great deal of uncertainty, and it is difficult to generalize about their behaviour.

Entry into an oligopolistic industry is usually possible, but difficult. Because firms in oligopolies are generally large, a large initial investment is usually required to break in.

In sum:

> Oligopolies are industries with a few large firms, but beyond that it is hard to generalize. In some oligopolies, firms differentiate their products; in others, they do not. Individual firms do exercise control over prices and generally behave 'strategically' with respect to one another.

The four main kinds of market organization in Europe are summarized in Figure 3.2.

Table 3.4 Characteristics of different market organizations

	Number of firms	Products differentiated or homogeneous	Firms have price-setting power	Free entry	Distinguishing characteristics	Examples
Perfect competition	Many	Homogeneous	No	Yes	Price competition only	Wheat farmer Textile firm
Monopolistic competition	Many	Differentiated	Yes, but limited	Yes	Price and quality competition	Restaurants Music industry
Oligopoly	Few	Either	Yes	Limited	Strategic behaviour	Breakfast cereal Steel
Monopoly	One	A unique, single product	Yes	No	Still constrained by market demand	Public utility Beverage vendor at a football ground

Global Perspectives

How competitive is the United States economy?

The United States of America is widely thought of as having a highly competitive economic environment. How correct is this view?

William G. Shepherd provides some evidence. Shepherd defines four market types that correspond roughly to the categories we have defined: (1) pure monopolies, (2) industries with dominant firms, (3) tight oligopolies, and (4) effectively competitive industries.

In Shepherd's classification, monopolies are as we described them: one firm accounts for 100% (or nearly 100%) of an industry's total sales. No close substitutes for its product exist and entry to the market is blocked. Industries with dominant firms are near-monopolies. In such industries, the dominant firm accounts for 50% to 90% of total industry sales, no close rivals exist, and entry to the

market is difficult. Tight oligopolies are industries in which the top four firms account for over 60% of total sales and in which entry barriers are high. Shepherd lumps all other firms together in the 'effectively competitive' category.

The classification 'effectively competitive' signifies more than just perfect competition. It also includes all of what we described as monopolistic competition. In Shepherd's effectively competitive group, the top four firms control less than 40% of the market, and entry barriers are low.

The table shows what happened, according to Shepherd's estimates, to the level of competition in the US economy between 1939 and 1980. Pure monopolies, a category that includes most public utilities and some patented goods, accounted for only 2.5% of total national

Trends in competition in the US economy, 1939–1980: percentage share of national income by industry category.

	1939	1958	1980
Pure monopoly	6.2	3.1	2.5
Dominant firm	5.0	5.0	2.8
Tight oligopoly	36.4	35.6	18.0
Effectively competitive firm	52.4	56.3	76.7
Total	100.0	100.0	100.0

Source: William G. Shepherd, 'Causes of increased competition in the US economy, 1939–1980', *Review of Economics and Statistics*, LXIV (November 1982), 6133–626.

income in 1980. On the other hand, 76.7% of national income originates in sectors that Shepherd classifies as effectively competitive, up from 52.4% in 1939. The estimates indicate that the percentage of national income originating in tight oligopolies has been cut in half since 1958.

The US economy has apparently become

significantly more competitive over the years. A number of factors may have contributed to this change. These factors include increased competition from imports, deregulation (particularly in the trucking, airline and telecommunications industries), and enforcement of anti-monopoly laws.

Table 3.5 Percentage share of income in industrial market economies

Sector	1980	1994
Agriculture	3.1	2.1
Manufacturing industry	24.7	21.5
Non-manufacturing industry	11.8	10.0
Services	60.4	66.4

Source: OECD Economic Surveys.

Structural change

In the last two decades, the breakdown of national income by major product type or industry indicates important changes. First, the percentage of total income accounted for by manufacturing has been continuously shrinking. The decline has been due in part to increased competition from developing Asian economies. We buy a tremendous number of products, including cars, textiles, televisions, VCRs, cameras and machine tools, from countries such as Korea and Taiwan. However, this trend has not been confined to Europe. It has been true generally of industrial market economies, including the USA. This can be seen in Table 3.4.

The fastest growing sector is the service sector. We eat at restaurants, stay at hotels, and consume recreation, entertainment, and personal services at a far greater rate than ever before.

As output changes, so does the need for labour. Table 3.5 shows the average annual changes in employment in different sectors for some selected European economies.

Table 3.6 Growth rates of employment in selected economies (% per annum)

Sector	Germany	France	Italy	UK	Sweden	USA
Agriculture	−2.6	−2.6	−1.2	−1.2	−2.3	−0.2
Mining and quarrying	−2.1	−2.4	n/a	−2.4	−2.3	−0.1
Manufacturing	−0.5	−1.1	−1.5	−1.5	−1.5	−0.2
Electricity, gas and water	0.9	1.1	−1.3	−1.3	0.3	1.7
Construction	−0.7	−1.1	0.5	0.5	−1.5	2.0
Wholesale and retail trade etc.	1.0	0.6	1.9	1.4	−0.1	2.8
Transport and communication	0.8	1.0	1.8	−0.3	0.4	1.2
Finance, insurance and business services	n/a	4.8	n/a	5.0	3.6	7.3
Community, social and personal services	n/a	4.6	n/a	6.2	0.3	3.3
Total industries	0.2	−0.3	0.3	0.3	−0.5	2.3
Government services	2.0	2.4	2.3	0.8	2.8	1.2
Total dependent employment	0.5	0.2	0.6	0.4	0.2	2.1
Self-employment	−0.3	−1.9	0.7	2.5	−0.5	1.3

Source: OECD, Economic Surveys.

We also show the USA for comparison. Notice how for all these economies, its annual average growth of employment in agriculture and in manufacturing is negative. In other words, employment in these sectors has been declining. These figures provide a marked contrast with service sectors such as finance, insurance and business where employment has been rising sharply.

The figures in Table 3.5 conceal substantial variations between countries. The proportion of agricultural employment for the UK is 2.1% and in Belgium it is 2.6%. However, comparable figures for Austria are 7.3%, for Finland 8.3% and for Greece 20.8%.

While some people are deeply concerned over this structural change in Europe, others see it as a natural consequence of continued economic growth and progress. Looking again at Table 3.4, notice that the first category, agriculture, as well as manufacturing, is declining in relative importance. As farmers learn increasingly productive farming methods, the need for farm labour declines, and so do food prices. With lower food prices, people spend their incomes on other things – manufactured goods and services. Because agriculture needs fewer workers, labour is available for employment in the new expanding sectors. Thus as the economy grows, some sectors, such as agriculture, shrink in relative importance and others, such as services, grow in relative importance.

Modern economies are in a continuous state of change. Resources are always moving. Literally thousands of new firms are started every year, and old, tired firms – not to mention young, inefficient ones – go out of business every day. Some firms grow rapidly in size, while others shrink. In the process, the basic industrial structure changes. The purpose of this book is to help you understand this process. Why are new firms formed? Why do others go out of business? Why are some sectors expanding while others are contracting?

Applications

The changing mix of jobs in Europe

There is a widespread view that 'real jobs' are jobs where something is made – the manufacturing of goods. Service jobs, on the other hand, are not real jobs because the worker doesn't make anything. This is economic nonsense. People are employed to produce what people want to buy. If people wish to buy a haircut, the hairdresser's job is a real job producing real (service) output. The disdain for service sector employment is a genuine problem, because this is the part of the European economy that is growing fastest.

Lower paid service-sector jobs are viewed with disdain. Few Europeans believe in the notion of upward mobility, so they are reluctant to take entry-level jobs or temporary work, fearing they will never rise. For instance, Warner Bros. had trouble recruiting for 160 full-time and 1,500 summer positions at its new amusement park in Germany's Ruhr Valley – despite high levels of unemployment from shuttered coal mines in the region. One reason: local unemployment offices discouraged applicants, saying the park did not offer 'real jobs'.

Sometimes it is not just individuals but governments too who believe in the superiority of manufactured goods over service output.

Outmoded regulations stunt the development of the service sector, which could create new employment to offset the loss in manufacturing. For instance, French law protects small shopkeepers from big discounters' competition, so the retail sector remains inefficient. Telecommunications and airlines are just beginning to be deregulated, and financial institutions have yet to experience full competition that would expand the market and create employment.

Nor is it true that service jobs are paid worse than manufacturing jobs. In an information age that values skills, experience and education ever more highly, well paid jobs are being created in areas such as software development and financial services as well as for hamburger flipping and hotel portering.

Source: 'A continent at the breaking point', Business Week, European edition, 24 February 1997.

The public sector: taxes and government spending in Europe

Thus far we have talked only about the sets of decisions facing private firms. But this is only part of the story. While European economies are basically market economies, they also have a public sector that plays a major role in determining the allocation of resources, the mix of output and the distribution of rewards. To understand the workings of any economic system, it is necessary to understand the role of government – the public sector.

How big is this public sector? What does it spend its money on, and where does it get its money?

gross domestic product (GDP)
The total value of all goods and services produced by a national economy within a given time period.

The size of the public sector

An economy's **gross domestic product**, or **GDP**, is the total value of all goods and services produced in the economy in a given period of time – a year, say. The concept of GDP is used extensively in macroeconomics. Here it is enough to say that GDP is used as a measure of a nation's total annual 'output'.

Table 3.7 Government spending as a percentage of GDP

	1870	1913	1920	1937	1960	1980	1990	1996
Austria	–	–	14.7	15.2	35.7	48.1	48.6	51.7
Belgium	–	–	–	21.8	30.3	58.6	54.8	54.3
Canada	–	–	13.3	18.6	28.6	38.8	46.0	44.7
France	12.6	17.0	27.6	29.0	34.6	46.1	49.8	54.5
Germany	10.0	14.8	25.0	42.4	32.4	47.9	45.1	49.0
Italy	11.9	11.1	22.5	24.5	30.1	41.9	53.2	52.9
Japan	8.8	8.3	14.8	25.4	17.5	32.0	31.7	36.2
Netherlands	9.1	0.9	13.5	19.0	33.7	55.2	54.0	49.9
Norway	3.7	8.3	13.7	–	29.9	37.5	53.8	45.5
Spain	–	8.3	9.3	18.4	18.8	32.2	42.0	43.3
Sweden	5.7	6.3	8.1	10.4	31.0	60.1	59.1	64.7
Switzerland	–	2.7	4.6	6.1	17.2	32.8	33.5	37.6
UK	9.4	12.7	26.2	30.0	32.2	43.0	39.9	41.9
USA	3.9	1.8	7.0	8.6	27.0	31.8	33.3	33.3
Average	8.3	9.1	15.4	18.3*	28.5	43.3	46.1	47.1
Australia	–	–	–	–	21.2	31.6	34.7	36.6
Ireland	–	–	–	–	28.0	48.9	41.2	37.6
New Zealand	–	–	–	–	26.9	38.1	41.3	47.1
Average	–	–	–	–	25.4	39.5	39.1	40.4
Total average	8.3	9.1	15.4	20.7	27.9	42.6	44.8	45.9

*Average without Germany, Japan and Spain undergoing war or war preparations at this time
Source: The Economist, 20 September 1997.

As you can see from Table 3.6, the public sector is very large in all economies. Even in those countries that have a relatively small state sector, such as Switzerland and the USA, public sector spending accounts for one-third of national income. In most European economies, the figure is not much under a half and in Sweden it is close to two-thirds.

The other striking feature of the data in Table 3.6 is that the size of the public sector has grown substantially. In every country in the table, government spending takes a considerably larger share of total income than was the case in, say, 1960.

Government spending can be broken into four major categories: purchases of goods and services, transfer payments to households, interest payments, and investment. **Purchases of goods and services** make up that portion of national output that government actually uses, or 'consumes', directly. They include medicines used in state hospitals, and the paper, books and pens produced by private companies that are used by government employees. This category also includes the wages and salaries paid for the services of government employees.

Transfer payments are cash payments made directly to households – social security benefits, unemployment benefits, welfare payments and so forth. The government receives no current services in return for these payments. **Interest payments** are also cash payments, but they are paid to those who have lent money to the government. Governments borrow in a number of different forms, including the issue of government bonds.

We have already said that private firms purchase capital equipment. Buying factories and machinery etc. is called *investment*. However, some investment is done by governments. The building of a motorway and the construction of a new police headquarters are examples of **government investment**.

As you can see from Figure 3.3, the largest category of government spending is that of transfers and subsidies. This has increased substantially since 1960. The only form of government expenditure to have declined as a percentage of GDP for most countries is investment. When governments wish to reduce expenditure it is politically very hard to cut back on transfers, such as unemployment benefit. The easiest option is to cut planned investment expenditures, such as delaying new road building schemes or making the police stay in their old headquarters for a few more years.

Government expenditures in more detail

Each European government is different in the detail of its expenditure and in the way its accounts are presented. However, we take one typical country, Belgium, and look at its government's major expenditure items.

Table 3.7 shows the major transfers to be pensions, health care provision, help for those who have no job and benefits to help those with families. Other transfers are subsidies to help some businesses, and transfers overseas, including foreign aid and

---

government purchases of goods and services

A category of government spending that includes the portion of national output that the government uses, or 'consumes', directly, such as memo pads for teachers and salaries for government employees.

government transfer payments

Cash payments made by the government directly to households for which no current services are received. They include social security benefits, unemployment benefits and welfare payments.

government interest payments

Cash payments made by the government to those who own government debt such as bonds.

government investment

Purchases of capital equipment made by the government. They include expenditure on roads and school buildings.

Figure 3.2 Government spending as a percentage of GDP, 1960 and 1990

Source: The Economist;
IMF.

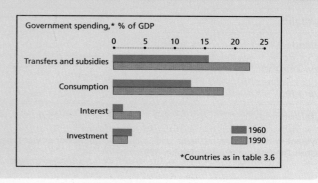

Table 3.8 General government finances of Belgium (Belgian francs)	
Total expenditure before interest charges	3,457
Social security transfers	2,049
of which:	
pensions	726
health care	508
unemployment benefit	179
family allowances	166
Other primary expenditure:	
Employee compensation	761
Net purchases of goods and transfers	177
Business subsidies	160
Transfers overseas	138
Capital expenditure	172
Interest charges	705
Total revenue	3,895
Net financing requirement	−267
% of GDP	−3.2
Outstanding public debt	10,580
% of GDP	127.4

Source: Belgian Ministry of Finance.

payments to the European Union budget. Taken together, these transfers constitute easily the largest item of government expenditure.

Employee compensation is the payment of wages to public service workers. This is part of government purchases of goods and services, because it represents the purchase of its employees' services. You can see that government investment – capital expenditure – is relatively little, though some business subsidies do enable more private sector investment.

In common with almost all governments, Belgium has tended to spend more than it receives in tax revenues etc., so it has built up a significant public debt. It must pay interest charges on this debt. For Belgium, this amount is greater than all its spending on health care.

Note that in 1996 the Belgian government would have spent less than it received in revenue, had it not been for its interest charges. The size of public debt varies as a proportion of GDP substantially between EU countries. Belgium's is one of the largest.

Sources of government revenue

A breakdown of the sources of revenue for one country's government appears in Table 3.8. Again, we choose just one typical country, in this case Ireland.

The biggest source of revenue for the government is the individual income tax, which accounted for over 35% of total revenues in 1996. This includes taxes on wages and salaries, taxes on the income of the self-employed and taxes on income received by individuals in the form of interest and dividends.

Table 3.9 Sources of government revenue in Ireland, 1996 (£ Irish)	
Customs and Excise	2,479
Value added tax	3,105
Income tax	4,562
Corporation tax	1,426
Motor vehicle duties	258
Stamp duties	336
Other tax revenue	354
Total tax revenue	12,520
Non-tax revenue	434
Total revenue	12,954

Source: Central Bank of Ireland, *Quarterly Bulletin*.

corporate income taxes
Taxes levied on the net incomes of corporations.

value added tax
An indirect tax levied at each stage of the production process as a percentage of the 'value added' by a firm (the difference between the cost of its inputs from other firms and the value of its sales).

excise taxes Taxes on specific commodities.

Corporate income taxes are levied on the profits of corporations. They can vary substantially over time, being quite high when companies are doing well but much lower when the economy is performing poorly.

Both forms of tax revenue discussed above are **direct** taxes. They are taxes imposed directly on someone's income. However, governments receive substantial income as indirect tax. These are taxes levied on certain goods or services. The biggest source of **indirect** tax for EU countries is **value added tax** (VAT). A wide range of goods and services bears this tax, although the rate varies between goods and between countries.

VAT is levied at each stage of the production process. The tax rate is a percentage of the 'value added' by a firm – that is, the difference between the cost of the inputs from other firms and the value of its sales.

Excise taxes are taxes on specific commodities, like cigarettes, alcoholic beverages and petrol. They are levied in addition to VAT.

Customs duties are the income to government from tariffs, or import taxes. EU countries do not impose tariffs on imports from other EU members. However, some goods and services purchased from outside of the EU do carry import duties from which governments obtain revenue.

In the long run, the greater the spending of a government, the greater will be the taxes necessary to fund such expenditure, although it can resort to borrowing in the short run.

The international sector: imports and exports in Europe

All economies, regardless of their size, depend to some extent on other economies and are affected by events outside their borders. Ask anyone in France about the impact of foreign trade on farm prices and therefore on the well-being of French farmers. Or ask coal miners in the UK about the effect of cheap German and Australian coal on the economies of the UK's traditional mining areas.

European economies are by no means 'closed'. Thousands of transactions between Europe and virtually every country in the world take place daily.

Table 3.9 indicates the size of these flows for some major European economies. These are monthly averages, expressed in billions of US dollars to make comparisons between countries possible. The figures show the EU countries exporting rather more than they import. Much of Europe, from 1996 to 1998, has been in recession. Lower

Table 3.10 Exports and imports of selected European economies, monthly averages, 1996 (US$ billion)

	Exports	Imports	Balance
Denmark	4.24	3.73	0.51
France*	24.01	22.52	1.49
Germany	43.44	37.98	5.46
Netherlands	16.45	15.05	1.40
Italy	20.90	17.24	3.66
Sweden	7.05	5.56	1.49
UK	21.66	23.92	−2.11
EU 15	176.15	166.02	10.13

*Includes overseas departments.
Source: OECD, Main Economic Indicators.

incomes make people less able to buy imports. Also, firms struggle to sell their goods to domestic consumers during a recession and some turn to export markets instead.

For EU countries, their main markets are with other EU members. This is not surprising. They are near to one another, which makes transport costs less. However, the absence of tariffs between member countries also encourages this trade. Table 3.10 shows just how important member countries find trade with one another. So, for example, of all The Netherlands' exports, 80% go to other EU members.

The composition of European trade

Trade in manufactured goods tends to be very great. A high proportion of domestic manufactured output is exported. *Export intensity* (the ratio of exports to domestic production) for manufacturing is over 30% for most EU countries, over 50% for some and over 70% for The Netherlands and Belgium. The figures for *import penetration* (the ratio of manufactured imports to consumption of domestic goods) are similar.

The comparable figures for services are much lower. Some kinds of services are harder to export. For example, few people will get their car serviced in another country. However, many services can be, and are, traded internationally including banking, insurance and tourism.

Table 3.11 Proportion of international trade with other EU economies, selected countries, 1996

Countries	Exports (%)	Imports (%)
Denmark	63	67
France	63	63
Germany	50	50
Netherlands	80	64
Italy	55	61
Sweden	55	67
UK	58	56

Source: OECD Surveys.

Service export intensity varies from around 5% in Germany to 20% in Belgium. Service import penetration figures are similar.

From institutions to theory

This chapter has sketched the institutional structure of the European economies. As we turn to economic theory, both positive and normative, you should reflect on the basic realities of economic life in Europe presented here. Why is the service sector expanding and the manufacturing sector contracting? Why is the public sector as large as it is? What economic functions does it perform? What determines the level of imports and exports? What effects do cheap foreign products have on the European economies?

One of the most important questions in economics concerns the relative merits of public sector involvement in the economy. Should the government be involved in the economy, or should the market be left to its own devices? Before we can confront these and other important issues, we need to establish a theoretical framework. Our study of the economy and its operation begins in Chapter 4 with the behaviour of suppliers and demanders in private markets.

Summary

1. The *private sector* is made up of privately owned firms that exist to make a profit, non-profit organizations, and individual households. The *public sector* is the government and its agencies at all levels – national and local. The *international sector* is the global economy. From any one country's perspective, the international sector consists of the economies of the rest of the world.

The private sector: European business and industrial organization

2. A *proprietorship* is a firm with a single owner. A *partnership* has two or more owners. Proprietors and partners are fully liable for all the debts of the business. A *corporation* is a formally established legal entity that limits the liability of its owners. The owners are not responsible for the debts of the firm beyond what they invest.

3. The term *industry* is used loosely to refer to groups of firms that produce similar products. Industries can be broadly or narrowly defined. A company that produces cheese belongs to the cheese industry, the dairy industry, the food products industry and the agricultural products industry.

4. In *perfect competition*, no single firm has any control over prices. This follows from two characteristics of this industry structure: (1) perfectly competitive industries are composed of many firms, each small relative to the size of the industry, and (2) each firm in a perfectly competitive industry produces exactly the same product – that is, products are *homogeneous*.

5. A *monopoly* is an industry structure in which only one firm produces a product for which there are no close substitutes. To remain a monopoly in a profitable

industry, a firm must be able to block the entry of competing firms.

6. In *monopolistic competition*, many firms compete, but each firm produces a slightly different product. Although each firm's product is unique, there are many close substitutes. Entry and exit into monopolistically competitive industries are relatively easy.

7. An *oligopoly* is an industry with a small number of firms. In general, entry of new firms into an oligopolistic industry is difficult but possible.

The public sector: taxes and government spending in Europe

8. The public sector in Europe is substantial. In some countries it is one third of GDP in others as high as two thirds. It has increased sharply in the last 30 to 40 years in all of Europe.

9. Most government spending is on transfer payments, such as unemployment benefit, and on the purchase of goods and services. Relatively little is on investment.

10. Tax revenue comes from direct taxes on individuals and companies, and indirect taxes such as VAT and excise duties. Individual income taxes are the largest single item.

The international sector: imports and exports in Europe

11. Thousands of transactions between European countries and virtually every other country in the world take place daily. Most European economies are very open. A large proportion of international trade undertaken by EU members is trade within the EU.

Review Terms and Concepts

barrier to entry	market organization
corporate income taxes	monopolistic competition
corporation	monopoly
dividends	oligopoly
excise taxes	partnership
government interest payments	perfect competition
government investment	private sector
government purchases of goods and services	proprietorship
government transfer payments	public sector
gross domestic product (GDP)	retained earnings
homogeneous products	share of stock
industry	value added tax (VAT)
international sector	

Problem Set

1. Health care continues to be a major issue in the 1990s. Look up the latest figures on health care expenditures as a percentage of GDP for your own country. How does this compare with other forms of expenditure?

2. The European Union has no tariff barriers between its own members but high barriers against many other countries in the world. What groups would be opposed to removing these barriers and who would support their removal? Why?

3. Do a short research project on one of the following large government programmes in your country. What does the programme accomplish or hope to accomplish? What is the basic logic for government involvement? How much was spent on the programme in 1998 compared to 1980?
a. Social security
b. Colleges and universities
c. Student financial aid
d. Motorways

4. Has the public sector in your country expanded relative to the rest of the economy in the last 10 to 20 years? What figures might be quoted in support of this proposition? Do they tell the whole story? Discuss.

5. What are the differences between a proprietorship and a corporation? If you were going to start a small business, which form of organization would you choose? What are the advantages and disadvantages of the two forms of organization?

6. 'Most firms are corporations, but they account for a relatively small portion of total output in Europe.' Do you agree or disagree with this statement? Explain your answer.

7. State whether each of the following industries is essentially competitive, monopolistically competitive, oligopolistic or monopolistic. Your answer should be based on your impressions as a buyer of goods or services, or on what you know about the industry, not on research. Briefly explain your answer.
a. The hotel industry

b. The cable television industry
c. The shampoo industry
d. The airline industry
e. The hamburger industry
f. The higher education (college and university) industry

8. Shareholders directly receive only 30–40% of total corporate profits. What happens to the rest?

9. How is a monopolistically competitive industry like a monopoly? In what ways is it like a perfectly competitive industry?

10. Perfectly competitive industries are made up of large numbers of firms, each small relative to the size of the industry and each producing homogeneous products. What does this imply about an individual firm's ability to influence price? Explain your answer.

11. Of the items that you buy frequently or services that you spend money on, which ones are produced in your country and which are imported? Of the major industries in your home country, which produce products or services that are exported?

12. How is it possible for government spending to increase as a percentage of GDP while taxes and government employment are both decreasing?

13. Why are most European governments spending much more on interest payments now than they were a decade ago? Explain.

14. It is sometimes argued that the government's practice of awarding patents (exclusive rights) to inventors and producers of products creates monopoly power and deprives consumers of the advantages of free competition. The argument surfaces frequently in discussions about the prescription drug market. For example, if a researcher were to discover a cure for AIDS and procure a patent, she would be a monopolist and she'd be able to charge a very high price for her product. Do you agree with this argument? What is the rationale for issuing patents? If you were to obtain a patent on a new formula for a lovely new perfume, would you be a monopoly? Explain your answers.

4

Demand, Supply and Market Equilibrium

Chapters 1 and 2 introduced the discipline, methodology and subject matter of economics. Chapter 3 described the institutional landscape of the European economy – its private, public and international sectors. We now begin the task of analysing how a market economy actually works. This chapter and the next present an overview of the way individual markets work. They introduce some of the concepts needed to understand both microeconomics and macroeconomics.

As we proceed to define terms and make assumptions, it is important to keep in mind what we are doing. In Chapter 1 we explained what economic theory attempts to do. Theories are abstract representations of reality, like a map that represents a city. We believe that the models presented here will help you understand the workings of the economy just as a map helps you find your way around a city. But just as a map presents one view of the world, so too does any given theory of the economy. Alternatives exist to the theory that we present. We believe, however, that the basic model presented here, while sometimes abstract, is useful in gaining an understanding of how the economy works.

In the simple island society discussed in Chapter 2, the economic problem was solved directly. Anna and David allocated their time and used the resources of the island to satisfy their wants. David might be a farmer, Anna a hunter and carpenter. He might be a civil engineer, she a doctor. Exchange occurred, but complex markets were not necessary.

In societies of many people, however, production must satisfy wide-ranging tastes and preferences. Producers therefore specialize. Farmers produce more food than they can eat in order to sell it to buy manufactured goods. Surgeons are paid for specialized services, as are lawyers, building workers and editors. When there is specialization, there must be exchange, and exchange takes place in markets.

This chapter begins to explore the basic forces at work in market systems. The purpose of our discussion is to explain how the individual decisions of households and firms together, without any central planning or direction, answer the three basic questions. What will be produced? How will it be produced? Who will get what is produced? We begin with some definitions.

Firms and households: the basic decision-making units

Throughout this book, we discuss and analyse the behaviour of two fundamental decision-making units: *firms* – the primary producing units in an economy – and *households* – the consuming units in an economy. Both are made up of people performing different functions and playing different roles. In essence, then, what we are developing is a theory of human behaviour.

A **firm** exists when a person or a group of people decides to produce a product or products by transforming *inputs* (that is, resources in the broadest sense) into *outputs* (the products that are sold in the market). Some firms produce goods; others produce services. Some are large, some are small, and some are in between. But all firms exist to transform resources into things that people want. The Berlin Symphony Orchestra

firm An organization that transforms resources (inputs) into products (outputs). Firms are the primary producing units in a market economy.

takes labour, land, a building, musically talented people, electricity and other inputs and combines them to produce concerts. The production process can be extremely complicated. The first flautist in the orchestra, for example, uses training, talent, previous performance experience, a score, an instrument, the conductor's interpretation and her own feelings about the music to produce just one contribution to an overall performance.

Most firms exist to make a profit for their owners, but some do not. Cambridge University, for example, fits the description of a firm: it takes inputs in the form of labour, land, skills, books and buildings and produces a service that we call 'education'. Although it sells that service for a price, it does not exist to make a profit, but rather to provide education of the highest quality possible.

Yet most firms exist to make a profit. They engage in production because they can sell their product for more than it costs to produce it. The analysis of firm behaviour that follows rests on the assumption that *firms make decisions in order to maximize profits*.

An **entrepreneur** is someone who organizes, manages, and assumes the risks of a firm. It is the entrepreneur who takes a new idea or a new product and turns it into a successful business. All firms have implicit in them some element of entrepreneurship. When a new firm is created – whether a proprietorship, a partnership or a corporation – someone must organize the new firm, arrange financing, hire employees and take risks. That person is an entrepreneur. Sometimes existing companies introduce new products, and sometimes new firms develop or improve on an old idea, but at the root of it all is entrepreneurship, which some see as the core of the free enterprise system.

At the root of the debate about the potential of free enterprise in formerly socialist Eastern Europe is the question of entrepreneurship. Does an entrepreneurial spirit exist in that part of the world? If not, can it be developed? Without it the free enterprise system breaks down.

The consuming units in an economy are **households**. A household may consist of any number of people: a single person living alone, a married couple with four children, or 15 unrelated people sharing a house. Household decisions are presumably based on individual tastes and preferences. The household buys what it wants and can afford. In a large, heterogeneous and open society such as the European Union, wildly different tastes find expression in the marketplace. A ten minute walk in any direction on any street in a large city such as Amsterdam or London, or a drive out of a large city into the peace of the surrounding villages, should be enough to convince anyone that it is difficult to generalize about what people like and do not like.

Even though households have wide-ranging preferences, they also have some things in common. All – even the very rich – have ultimately limited incomes, and all must pay in some way for the things they consume. While households may have some control over their incomes – they can choose how much they work – they are also constrained by the availability of jobs, current wages, their own abilities and their accumulated and inherited wealth (or lack of it).

Input markets and output markets: the circular flow

Households and firms interact in two basic kinds of markets: product (or output) markets, and input (or factor) markets. Goods and services that are intended for use by households are exchanged in **product** or **output markets**. In output markets, competing firms *supply* and households *demand*.

To produce goods and services, firms must buy resources in **input** or **factor markets**. Firms buy inputs from households, which supply these inputs. When a firm decides how much to produce (supply) in output markets, it must simultaneously decide how much of each input it needs in order to produce the desired level of output. To produce cars, the Volvo Corporation must use many inputs, including tyres, steel, complicated machinery and many different kinds of labour.

entrepreneur
A person who organizes, manages, and assumes the risks of a firm, taking a new idea or a new product and turning it into a successful business.

households The consuming units in an economy.

product *or* output markets
The markets in which goods and services are exchanged.

input *or* factor markets
The markets in which the resources used to produce products are exchanged.

Figure 4.1 The circular flow of economic activity

Diagrams like this one show the circular flow of economic activity, hence the name *circular flow diagram*. Here, goods and services flow clockwise: labour services supplied by households flow to firms, and goods and services produced by firms flow to households. Money (not pictured here) flows in the opposite (counterclockwise) direction: payment for goods and services flows from households to firms, and payment for labour services flows from firms to households.

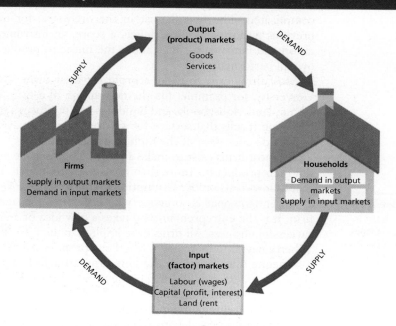

Figure 4.1 shows the *circular flow* of economic activity through a simple market economy. Notice that the flow reflects the direction in which goods and services flow through input and output markets. For example, goods and services flow from firms to households through output markets. Labour services flow from households to firms through input markets. Payment (most often in money form) for goods and services flows in the opposite direction. Payment for goods and services flows from households to firms, and payment for labour services flows from firms to households.

In input markets, households *supply* resources. Most households earn their incomes by working – they supply their labour in the **labour market** to firms that demand labour and pay workers for their time and skills. Households may also loan their accumulated or inherited savings to firms for interest, or exchange those savings for claims to future profits as when a household buys shares of stock in a corporation. In the **capital market**, households supply the funds that firms use to buy capital goods. In exchange, these households receive interest or claims to future profits. Households may also supply land or other real property in exchange for rent in the **land market**.

Inputs into the production process are also called **factors of production**. Land, labour and capital are the three key factors of production. Throughout this text, we use the terms *input* and *factor of production* interchangeably. Thus, input markets and factor markets mean the same thing.

labour market
The input/factor market in which households supply work for wages to firms that demand labour.

capital market
The input/factor market in which households supply their savings, for interest or for claims to future profits, to firms that demand funds in order to buy capital goods.

land market The input/factor market in which households supply land or other real property in exchange for rent.

factors of production
The inputs into the production process. Land, labour and capital are the three key factors of production.

Colour guide
Note that in Figure 4.1 households are depicted in *blue* and firms are depicted in *red*. From now on all diagrams relating to the behaviour of households will be blue or shades of blue, and all diagrams relating to the behaviour of firms will be in red or shades of red.

Early economics texts included entrepreneurship as a type of input, just like land, labour and capital. Treating entrepreneurship as a separate factor of production has fallen out of favour, however, partially because it is unmeasurable. Most economists today implicitly assume that it is in plentiful supply. That is, if profit opportunities exist, it is likely that entrepreneurs will crop up to take advantage of them. This assumption has turned out to be a good predictor of actual economic behaviour and performance.

The supply of inputs and their prices ultimately determine households' income. The amount of income a household earns thus depends on the decisions it makes concerning what types of inputs it chooses to supply. Whether to go to university, how much and what kind of training to get, whether to start a business, how many hours to work, whether to work at all, and how to invest savings are all household decisions that affect income.

As you can see, then:

> Input and output markets are connected through the behaviour of both firms and households. Firms determine the quantities and character of outputs produced and the types of quantities of inputs demanded. Households determine the types and quantities of products demanded and the quantities and types of inputs supplies.[1]

Demand in product/output markets

In real life, households make many decisions at the same time. To see how the forces of demand and supply work, however, let us focus first on the amount of a single product that an individual household decides to consume within some given period of time, such as a month or a year.

A household's decision about what quantity of a particular output, or product, to demand depends upon a number of factors:

- The *price of the product* in question.
- The *income available* to the household.
- The household's *amount of accumulated wealth*.
- The *prices of other products* available to the household.
- The household's *tastes and preferences*.
- The household's *expectations* about future income, wealth and prices.

quantity demanded The amount (number of units) of a product that a household would buy in a given period if it could buy all it wanted at the current market price.

Quantity demanded is the amount (number of units) of a product that a household would buy in a given period *if it could buy all it wanted at the current market price*.

Of course, the amount of a product that households finally purchase depends on the amount of product actually available in the market. But the quantity demanded at any moment may exceed or fall short of the quantity supplied. These differences between the quantity demanded and the quantity supplied are very important. The phrase *if it could buy all it wanted* is critical to the definition of quantity demanded because it allows for the possibility that quantity supplied and quantity demanded are unequal.

Our analysis of demand and supply is leading up to a theory of how market prices are determined. Prices are determined by interaction between demanders and suppliers. To understand this interaction, we first need to know how product prices influence the behaviour of suppliers and demanders *separately*. We therefore begin our discussion of output markets by focusing exclusively on this relationship.

Changes in quantity demanded versus changes in demand

The most important relationship in individual markets is that between market price and quantity demanded. For this reason, we need to begin our discussion by analysing the likely response of households to changes in price using the device of *ceteris paribus*,

---

[1] *Our description of markets begins with the behaviour of firms and households. Modern orthodox economic theory essentially combines two distinct but closely related theories of behaviour. The 'theory of household behaviour', or 'consumer behaviour', has its roots in the works of nineteenth-century utilitarians such as Jeremy Bentham, William Jevons, Carl Menger, Leon Walras, Vilfredo Pareto and F. Y. Edgeworth. The 'theory of the firm' developed out of the earlier classical political economy of Adam Smith, David Ricardo and Thomas Malthus. In 1890 Alfred Marshall published the first of many editions of his Principles of Economics. This book pulled together the main themes of both the classical economists and the utilitarians into what is now called 'neoclassical economics'. While there have been many changes over the years, the basic structure of the model that we build can be found in Marshall's work.*

or 'all else equal'. That is, we will attempt to derive a relationship between the quantity demanded of a good per time period and the price of that good, holding income, wealth, other prices, tastes and expectations constant.

It is very important to distinguish between price changes, which affect the quantity of a good demanded, and changes in other factors (such as income), which change the entire relationship between price and quantity. For example, if a family begins earning a higher income, it might buy more of a good at every possible price. To be sure that we distinguish between changes in price and other changes that affect demand, we will throughout the rest of the text be very precise about terminology. Specifically:

Changes in the price of a product affect the *quantity demanded* per period. Changes in any other factor, such as income or preferences, affect *demand*. Thus we say that an increase in the price of Coca Cola is likely to cause a decrease in the *quantity of Coca Cola* demanded. Similarly, we say that an increase in income is likely to cause an increase in the *demand* for most goods.

Price and quantity demanded: the law of demand

demand schedule
A table showing how much of a given product a household would be willing to buy at different prices.

demand curve
A graph illustrating how much of a given product a household would be willing to buy at different prices.

A **demand schedule** shows the quantities of a product that a household would be willing to buy at different prices. Table 4.1 presents a hypothetical demand schedule for Anna, a student who went off to university in the UK to study economics while her boyfriend went to art school in Paris. If telephone calls were free (a price of zero), Anna would phone her boyfriend every day, or 30 times a month. At a price of 50 pence per call, she makes 25 calls a month. When the price hits £3.50, she cuts back to 7 calls a month. This same information presented graphically is called a **demand curve**. Anna's demand curve is presented in Figure 4.2.

Drawing a smooth curve, as we do in Figure 4.2, suggests that Anna can make a quarter of a phone call or half of a phone call. For example, according to the graph, at a price of £12 per call Anna would make half a call, and at £8 per call about a call and a half. While fractional purchases can be made for goods that are divisible, such as phone calls – you might talk for one minute instead of two minutes – and products sold by weight, they are impossible for large purchases such as cars. We use the term *lumpy* to describe goods that cannot be divided. You would not draw a smooth, downward sloping curve of a household's demand for cars, for example, because there might be only one (or at most two) points, and any points in between would be meaningless. Whenever we draw a smooth demand curve, we are assuming divisibility.

You will notice that in Figure 4.2 *quantity* is measured along the horizontal axis, and *price* is measured along the vertical axis. This is the convention we follow throughout this book.

Table 4.1 Anna's demand schedule for telephone calls

Price per call (£)	Quantity demanded (calls per month)
0.00	30
0.50	25
3.50	7
7.00	3
10.00	1
15.00	0

Figure 4.2 Anna's demand curve

When presented graphically, the relationship between price and quantity demanded is called a demand curve. Normal demand curves have a negative slope, indicating that lower prices cause quantity demanded to increase. Note that Anna's demand curve is blue; demand in product markets is determined by household choice.

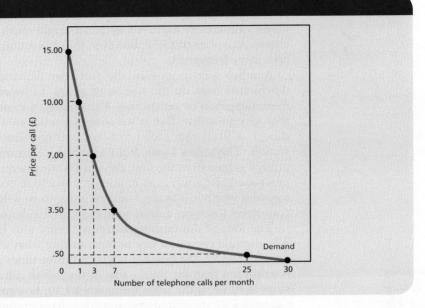

Demand curves slope downwards

The data in Table 4.1 show that at lower prices Anna phones her boyfriend more frequently; at higher prices she calls less frequently. There is thus a *negative, or inverse, relationship between quantity demanded and price*. When price rises, quantity demanded falls, and when price falls, quantity demanded rises. Thus demand curves slope downwards. This negative relationship between price and quantity demanded is often referred to as the **law of demand**, a term first used by economist Alfred Marshall in his 1890 textbook.

law of demand
The negative relationship between price and quantity demanded. As price rises, quantity demanded decreases. As price falls, quantity demanded increases.

Some people are put off by the abstractness of demand curves. Of course, we don't actually draw our own demand curves for products. When we want to make a purchase, we usually face only a single price, and how much we would buy at other prices is irrelevant. But demand curves help analysts understand the kind of behaviour that households are *likely* to exhibit if they are actually faced with a higher or lower price. We know, for example, that if the price of a good rises enough, the quantity demanded must ultimately drop to zero. The demand curve is thus a tool that helps us to explain economic behaviour and predict reactions to possible price changes.

Marshall's definition of a social 'law' captures the idea:

The term 'law' means nothing more than a general proposition or statement of tendencies, more or less certain, more or less definite . . . a social law is a statement of social tendencies; that is, that a certain course of action may be expected from the members of a social group under certain conditions.[2]

It seems reasonable to expect that consumers will demand more of a product at a lower price and less of it at a higher price. Households must divide their incomes over a wide range of goods and services. If the price of a kilo of beef rises while income and the prices of all other products remain the same, the household must sacrifice more of something else in order to buy each kilo of beef. If I spend €4.50 for a kilo of prime beef, I am sacrificing the other things that I might have bought with those €4.50. If the price of prime beef were to jump to €7 per kilo, while chicken breasts remained at €2 (remember *ceteris paribus* – we are holding all else constant), I would have to give

[2]*Alfred Marshall*, Principles of Economics, *8th edn (New York: Macmillan, 1948), p. 33. (The first edition was published in 1890.)*

up more chicken and/or other items in order to buy that kilo of beef. So I would probably eat more chicken and less beef. Anna calls her boyfriend three times when phone calls cost £7 each. A fourth call would mean sacrificing £7 worth of other purchases. At a price of £3.50, however, the opportunity cost of each call is lower, and she calls more frequently.

Another way to explain the fact that demand curves are very likely to slope downwards rests on the notion of *utility*. Economists use the concept of utility to mean happiness or satisfaction. Presumably, we consume goods and services because they give us utility. But as we consume more of a product within a given period of time, it is likely that each additional unit consumed will yield successively less satisfaction. The utility I gain from a second ice cream cone is likely to be less than the utility I gained from the first; the third is worth even less, and so on. This *law of diminishing marginal utility* is an important concept in economics. If each successive unit of a good is worth less to me, I am not going to be willing to pay as much for it. It is thus reasonable to expect a downward slope in the demand curve for that good.

The idea of diminishing marginal utility also helps to explain Anna's behaviour. The demand curve is a way of representing what she is willing to pay per phone call. At a price of £7, she calls her boyfriend three times per month. A fourth call, however, is worth less than the third – that is, the fourth call is worth less than £7 to her, so she stops at three. If the price were only £3.50, however, she would keep on calling. But even at £3.50, she would stop at seven calls per month. This behaviour reveals that the eighth call has less value to Anna than the seventh.

Thinking about the ways that people are affected by price changes also helps us see what is behind the law of demand. Consider this example: Edvard lives and works in Oslo. His elderly mother lives in Copenhagen. Last year, the airlines on this route got into a price war, and the price of flying between Oslo and Copenhagen dropped from 2000 kroner to 1000 kroner. How might Edvard's behaviour change?

First, he is better off. Last year he flew home to Copenhagen three times at a total cost of 6000 kroner. This year he can fly there the same number of times, buy exactly the same combination of other goods and services that he bought last year, and have 3000 kroner left over! Because he is better off – his income can buy more – he may fly home more frequently. Second, the opportunity cost of flying home has changed. Before the price war Edvard had to sacrifice other goods and services worth 2000 kroner each time he flew to Copenhagen. After the price war he must sacrifice only 1000 kroners worth of other goods and services for each trip. The trade-off has changed. Both of these effects are likely to lead to a higher quantity demanded in response to the lower price.[3]

In sum:

> It is reasonable to expect quantity demanded to fall when price rises, *ceteris paribus*, and to expect quantity demanded to rise when price falls, *ceteris paribus*. Demand curves have a negative slope.

Other properties of demand curves

Two additional things are notable about Anna's demand curve. First, it intersects the *Y*, or price, axis. This means that there is a price above which no calls will be made. In this case, Anna simply stops calling when the price reaches £15 per call.

> As long as households have limited incomes and wealth, all demand curves will intersect the price axis. For any commodity, there is always a price above which a household will not, or cannot, pay. Even if the good or service is very important, all households are ultimately 'constrained', or limited, by income and wealth.

[3]*These separate effects are called the 'income' and 'substitution' effects of the price change. They will be formally defined and discussed in later chapters.*

Second, Anna's demand curve intersects the X, or quantity, axis. Even at a zero price, there is a limit to the number of phone calls Anna will make. If telephone calls were free, she would call 30 times a month, but not more.

That demand curves intersect the quantity axis is a matter of common sense. Demands for most goods are limited, if only by time, even at a zero price.

To summarize what we know about the shape of demand curves:

■ They have a negative slope. An increase in price can be expected to lead to a decrease in quantity demanded and a decrease in price can be expected to lead to an increase in quantity demanded.
■ They intersect the quantity (X) axis – a result of diminishing marginal utility.
■ They intersect the price (Y) axis – a result of limited incomes and wealth.

But that's all we can say; it is not possible to generalize further. The actual shape of an individual household demand curve, whether it is steep or flat, whether it is bowed in or bowed out, depends on the unique tastes and preferences of the household and other factors. Some households may be very sensitive to price changes; other households may respond little to a change in price. In some cases plentiful substitutes are available; in other cases they are not. Thus, to fully understand the shape and position of demand curves we must turn to the other determinants of household demand.

Other determinants of household demand

Of the many factors likely to influence a household's demand for a specific product, we have considered only the price of the product itself. Other determining factors include household income and wealth, the prices of other goods and services, tastes and preferences, and expectations.

Income and wealth

Before we proceed, we need to define two terms that are often confused, *income* and *wealth*. A household's **income** is the sum of all the wages, salaries, profits, interest payments, rents and other forms of earnings received by the household *in a given period of time*. Income is thus a flow measure. We must specify a time period for it – income *per month* or *per year*. You can spend or consume more or less than your income in any given period. If you consume less than your income, you save. To consume more than your income in a period, you must either borrow or draw on savings accumulated from previous periods.

Wealth is the total value of what a household owns, less what it owes. Another word for wealth is **net worth** – the amount a household would have left if it sold off all its possessions and paid off all its debts. Wealth is a *stock* measure. It is measured at a given point in time. If, in a given period, you spend less than your income, you save; the amount that you save is added to your wealth. Saving is the flow that affects the stock of wealth. When you spend more than your income, you *dissave* – you reduce your wealth.

Clearly, households with higher incomes and higher accumulated savings or inherited wealth can afford to buy more things. In general, then, we would expect higher demand at higher levels of income/wealth and lower demand at lower levels of income/wealth. Goods for which demand goes up when income is higher and for which demand goes down when income is lower are called **normal goods**. Film tickets, restaurant meals, telephone calls and driving lessons are all normal goods.

But generalization in economics can be hazardous. Sometimes demand for a good falls when household income rises. Consider, for example, the various qualities of meat available. When a household's income rises, it is likely to buy higher quality meats – its demand for fillet steak is likely to rise – but its demand for lower quality

income The sum of all a household's wages, salaries, profits, interest payments, rents and other forms of earnings in a given period of time. It is a flow measure.

wealth *or* net worth The total value of what a household owns, minus what it owes. It is a stock measure.

normal goods Goods for which demand goes up when income is higher and for which demand goes down when income is lower.

meats – chuck steak, for example – is likely to fall. Transport is another example. At higher incomes, people can afford to fly. People who can afford to fly are less likely to use the bus for long distance travel. Thus higher income may reduce the number of times someone catches a bus. Goods for which demand tends to fall when income rises are called inferior goods.

inferior goods
Goods for which demand tends to fall when income rises.

Prices of other goods and services

No consumer decides in isolation on the amount of any one commodity to buy. Rather, each decision is part of a larger set of decisions that are made simultaneously. Households must apportion their incomes over many different goods and services. As a result, the price of any one good can and does affect the demand for other goods.

This is most obviously the case when goods are substitutes for one another. To return to our lonely student: if the price of a telephone call rises to £10, Anna will call her boyfriend only once a month (see Table 4.1). But of course she can get in touch with him in other ways. Presumably she substitutes some other, less costly, form of communication, such as writing more letters, or using the university facilities to e-mail him.

Consider another example. There has been much discussion over many years on the question of Japanese car imports into Europe. In order to protect European car producers, taxes are placed on imported Japanese cars (though not on cars *made* in Europe by Japanese firms), making these cars more expensive to buy. As a result, some European consumers have substituted out of Japanese cars and into European models. The demand for European cars is higher and the quantity of Japanese cars demanded is lower as a result of the (relative) price change.

substitutes
Goods that can serve as replacements for one another; when the price of one increases, demand for the other goes up.

When an *increase* in the price of one good causes demand for another good to *increase* (a positive relationship), we say that the goods are substitutes. A *fall* in the price of a good causes a *decline* in demand for its substitutes. Substitutes are goods that can serve as replacements for one another.

To be substitutes, two products need not be identical. Identical products are called perfect substitutes. Japanese cars are not identical to European cars. Nonetheless, all have four wheels, are capable of carrying people, and run on petrol (or diesel). Thus, significant changes in the price of one country's cars can be expected to influence demand for another country's cars. Compact discs are substitutes for records and tapes, restaurant meals are substitutes for meals eaten at home, and flying from London to Brussels is a substitute for catching the train.

perfect substitutes
Identical products.

complements, complementary goods
Goods that 'go together'; a decrease in the price of one results in an increase in demand for the other, and vice versa.

Often, two products 'go together' – that is, they complement each other. Our lonely letter writer, for example, will find her demand for stamps and stationery rising together as she writes more letters. Bacon and eggs are complementary goods, as are cars and petrol, and cameras and film. In an earlier example of a price war between the airlines when air travel became less expensive, the demand for taxi services to and from airports and for luggage could be expected to increase. When two goods are complements, a *decrease* in the price of one results in *increase* in demand for the other, and vice versa.

Because any one good may have many potential substitutes and complements at the same time, a single price change may affect a household's demands for many goods simultaneously: the demand for some of these products may rise while the demand for others may fall. For example, one of the newer technologies for personal computers is the CD-ROM. Massive amounts of data can now be stored digitally on compact disks that can be read by personal computers with a CD-ROM drive. When these drives first came on to the market they were quite expensive. Now they are much cheaper, and most new personal computers have them built in. As a result, the demand for the CDs (complementary goods) is soaring. One can now purchase an encyclopaedia on CD. As more and more students adopt CD technology and the price of CDs and CD hardware falls, fewer people will be buying things like encyclopaedias printed on paper (substitute goods).

Tastes and preferences

Income, wealth and the prices of things available are the three factors that determine the combinations of things that a household is *able* to buy. You know that you cannot afford to rent a flat at a rate of three times your monthly income. But within these constraints, you are more or less free to choose what to buy. Your final choice depends on your individual tastes and preferences.

Changes in preferences can and do manifest themselves in market behaviour. As the harmful consequences of smoking have become increasingly clear, for example, more and more people have stopped smoking. As a result, the demand for cigarettes has dropped significantly in many countries. Fifteen years ago the major 'big city' marathons drew only a few hundred runners. Now tens of thousands enter and run. The demand for running shoes, running suits, stopwatches and other items has greatly increased.

Within the constraints of prices and incomes, it is preference that shapes the demand curve. But it is difficult to generalize about tastes and preferences. First of all, they are volatile: ten years ago, more people in Europe smoked cigarettes and fewer people had computers. Second, they are idiosyncratic: some people like to talk on the telephone whereas others prefer the written word; some people prefer dogs whereas others like cats; some people like chicken wings whereas others prefer chicken legs. The diversity of individual demands is almost infinite.

Expectations

What you decide to buy today certainly depends on today's prices and your current income and wealth. But you also have expectations about what your position will be in the future. You may have expectations about future changes in prices, too, and these may affect your decisions today.

Examples of the ways expectations affect demand abound. When people buy a house or a car, they often must borrow part of the purchase price and pay it back over a number of years. In deciding what kind of house or car to buy, they presumably must think about their income today, as well as what their income is likely to be in the future.

As another example, consider a medical student in his final year living on a scholarship. Compare him with another person earning a small wage in a full-time job, with no expectation of a significant change in income in the future. The two may have virtually identical incomes. But even if they had the same tastes, the medical student is likely to demand different things, simply because he expects a major increase in income later on.

Increasingly, economic theory has come to recognize the importance of expectations. We will devote a good deal of time to discussing how expectations affect more than just demand. For the time being, however, it is important to understand that demand depends on more than just *current* incomes, prices and tastes.

Shift of demand versus movement along a demand curve

Recall that a demand curve shows the relationship between quantity demanded and the price of a good. Such demand curves are derived while holding income, tastes and other prices constant. If this condition of *ceteris paribus* were relaxed, we would have to derive an entirely new relationship between price and quantity.

Let us return once again to Anna, our UK-based student (Table 4.1 and Figure 4.2). Suppose that when we derived the demand schedule in Table 4.1, Anna had a part-time job that paid £200 per month. Now suppose that her parents inherit some money and begin sending her an additional £200 per month. Assuming that she keeps her job, Anna's income is now £400 per month.

The income from home may affect the amount of time Anna spends working. In the extreme, she may leave her job and her income will remain at £200. In essence, she would be spending the entire £200 on leisure time. Here we assume that she keeps the job and that her income is higher. The point is that since labour supply decisions affect income, they are closely tied to output demand decisions. In a sense, the two decisions are made simultaneously.

Table 4.2 Shift of Anna's demand schedule resulting from an increase in income

Price per call (£)	Schedule D_1 Quantity demanded (calls per month at an income of £200 per month)	Schedule D_2 Quantity demanded (calls per month at an income of £400 per month)
0.00	30	35
0.50	25	33
3.50	7	18
7.00	3	12
10.00	1	7
15.00	0	2
20.00	0	0

With her higher income, Anna would probably call her boyfriend more frequently, regardless of the price of a call. Table 4.2 and Figure 4.3 present Anna's demand schedule at her original income (D_1) and her demand schedule with her increased income (D_2). At 50 pence per call, the frequency of her calls (or the quantity she demands) increases from 25 to 33 calls per month; at £3.50 per call, frequency increases from 7 to 18 calls per month; at £10 per call, frequency increases from 1 to 7 calls per month. (Notice from Figure 4.3 that even if calls are free, Anna's income matters; at zero price, her demand increases. With a higher income, she may visit her boyfriend more, for example, and more visits might mean more phone calls to organize and plan.)

Figure 4.3 Shift of a demand curve following a rise in income

When the price of a good changes, we move along the demand curve for that good. When any other factor that influences demand (income, tastes etc.) changes, the relationship between price and quantity is different; there is a shift of the demand curve, in this case from D_1 to D_2.

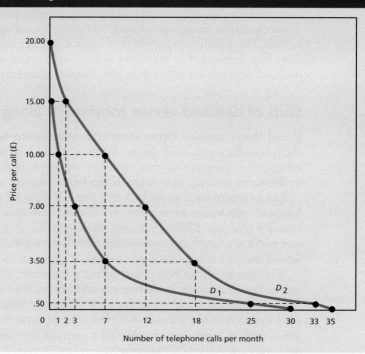

The conditions that were in place at the time we drew the original demand curve have now changed. In other words, a factor that affects Anna's demand for telephone calls (in this case, her income) has changed, and there is now a new relationship between price and quantity demanded. Such a change is referred to as a **shift of the demand curve**.

It is very important to distinguish between a change in quantity demanded – that is, some movement *along* a demand curve – and a shift of demand. Demand schedules and demand curves show the relationship between the price of a good or service and the quantity demanded per period, *ceteris paribus*. If price changes, quantity demanded will change – this is a **movement along the demand curve**. When any of the other factors that influence demand change, however, a new relationship between price and quantity demanded is established – this is a *shift of the demand curve*. The result, then, is a *new* demand curve. Changes in income, preferences, or prices of other goods cause the demand curve to shift:

> Change in *price* of a good or service
> | leads to
> |————————▶ Change in *quantity demanded* (*movement along* the demand curve).
> Change in *income*, *preferences* or *prices of other goods or services*
> | leads to
> |————————▶ Change in *demand* (*shift of* demand curve).

Figure 4.4 illustrates this point. In Figure 4.4a, an increase in household income causes demand for beef mince (an inferior good) to decline, or shift to the left from D_1 to D_2. (Because quantity is measured on the horizontal axis, a decrease means a move to the left.) Demand for steak (a normal good), on the other hand, increases, or shifts to the right, when income rises.

In Figure 4.4b, an increase in the price of beefburgers from €1.49 to €2.49 per pack causes a household to buy fewer beefburgers each month. In other words, the higher price causes the *quantity demanded* to decline from ten packs to five packs per month. This change represents a movement *along* the demand curve for beefburgers. In place of beefburgers, the household buys more chicken. The household's demand for chicken (a substitute for beefburgers) rises – the demand curve shifts to the right. At the same time, the demand for ketchup (a good that complements beefburgers) declines – its demand curve shifts to the left.

From household demand to market demand

Market demand is simply the sum of all the quantities of a good or service demanded per period by all the households buying in the market for that good or service. Figure 4.5 shows the derivation of a market demand curve from three individual demand curves. (Although this market demand curve is derived from the behaviour of only three people, most markets have thousands or even millions of demanders.) As the table in Figure 4.5 shows, when the price of a kilo of coffee is €3.50, both A and C would purchase four kilos per month, while B would buy none; at that price, presumably, B drinks tea. Market demand at €3.50 would thus be a total of four plus four, or eight kilos. At a price of €1.50 per kilo, however, A would purchase eight kilos per month, B three kilos and C nine kilos. Thus, at €1.50 per kilo, market demand would be eight plus three plus nine, or twenty kilos of coffee per month.

The total quantity demanded in the marketplace at a given price, then, is simply the sum of all the quantities demanded by all the individual households shopping in the market *at that price*. A market demand curve shows the total amount of a product that would be sold at each price if households could buy all they wanted at that price. As Figure 4.5 shows, the market demand curve is the sum of all the individual demand

---

shift of the demand curve
The change that takes place in a demand curve when a new relationship between quantity demanded of a good and the price of that good is brought about by a change in the original conditions.

movement along the demand curve
What happens when a change in price causes quantity demanded to change.

market demand
The sum of all the quantities of a good or service demanded per period by all the households buying in the market for that good or service.

Figure 4.4 Shifts versus movement along a demand curve

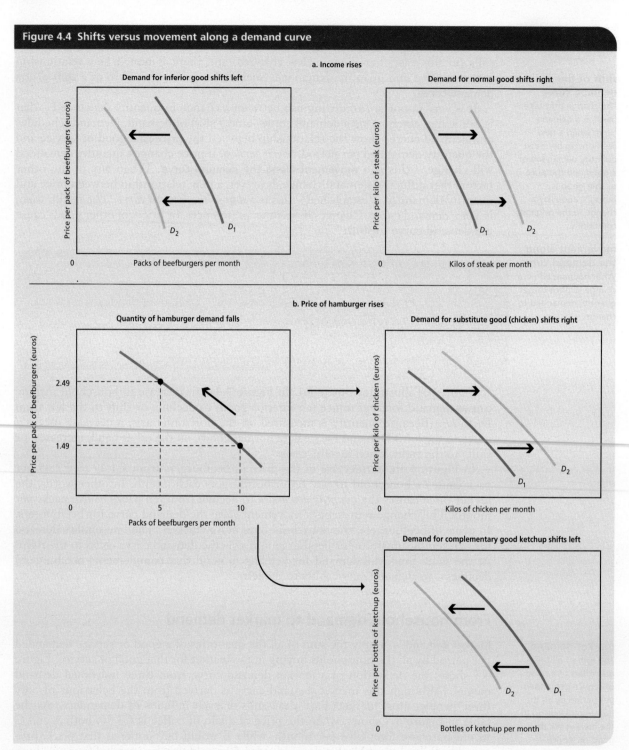

(a) When income increases, the demand for inferior goods *shifts to the left* and the demand for normal goods *shifts to the right*. (b) If the price of beefburgers rises, the quantity of beefburgers demanded declines – this is a movement along the demand curve. The same price would shift the demand for chicken (a substitute for beefburgers) to the right and the demand for ketchup (a complement to beefburgers) to the left.

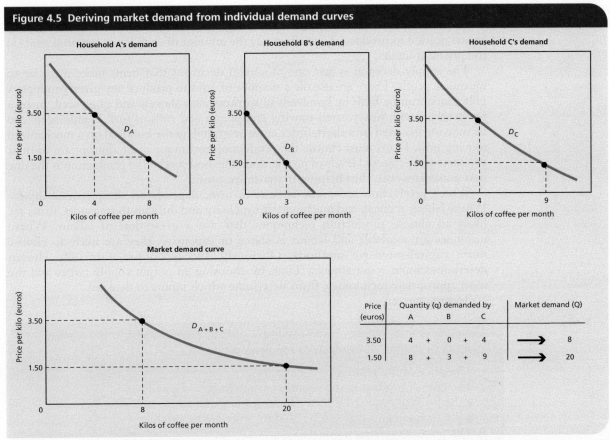

Figure 4.5 Deriving market demand from individual demand curves

Price (euros)	Quantity (q) demanded by A	B	C	Market demand (Q)
3.50	4 +	0 +	4	8
1.50	8 +	3 +	9	20

Total demand in the marketplace is simply the sum of the demands of all the households shopping in a particular market. It is the sum of all the individual demand curves – that is, the sum of all the individual quantities demanded at each price.

curves – that is, the sum of all the individual quantities demanded at each price. The market demand curve thus takes its shape and position from the shapes, positions and number of individual demand curves. If more people decide to shop in a market, more demand curves must be added, and the market demand curve will shift to the right. Market demand curves may also shift as a result of preference changes or income changes.

As a general rule throughout this book, capital letters refer to the entire market and lowercase letters refer to individual households or firms. Thus, in Figure 4.5, Q refers to total quantity demanded in the market, while q refers to the quantity demanded by individual households.

Supply in product/output markets

In addition to dealing with households' demands for outputs, economic theory deals with the behaviour of business firms, which supply in output markets and demand in input markets (see again Figure 4.1). Firms engage in production, and we assume that they do so for profit. Successful firms make profits because they are able to sell their products for more than it costs to produce them.

profit The difference between revenues and costs.

Supply decisions can thus be expected to depend on profit potential. Because **profit** is the simple difference between revenues and costs, supply is likely to react to changes in revenues and changes in production costs. The amount of revenue that a firm earns depends on the price of its product in the market and on how much it sells. Costs of production depend on many factors, the most important of which are (1) the kinds of inputs needed to produce the product, (2) the amount of each input required, and (3) the prices of inputs.

The supply decision is just one of several decisions that firms make in order to maximize profit. There are usually a number of ways to produce any given product. A golf course can be built by hundreds of workers with shovels and grass seed, or by a few workers with heavy earth-moving equipment and rolls of turf. Hamburgers can be individually fried by a short-order cook or grilled by the hundred on a mechanized moving grill. Firms must choose the production technique most appropriate to their products and projected levels of production. The best method of production is the one that minimizes cost, thus helping to maximize profit.

Which production technique is best, in turn, depends on the prices of inputs. Where labour is cheap and machinery is expensive and difficult to transport, firms are likely to choose production techniques that use a great deal of labour. Where machines are available and labour is scarce or expensive, they are likely to choose more capital-intensive methods. Obviously, the technique ultimately chosen determines input requirements. Thus, by choosing an output supply target and the most appropriate technology, firms determine which inputs to demand.

To summarize:

Assuming that its objective is to maximize profits, a firm's decision about what quantity of output, or product, to supply depends on

1. The price of the good or service
2. The cost of producing the product, which in turn depends on
   - the price of required inputs (labour, capital and land), and
   - the technologies that can be used to produce the product
3. The prices of related products

With the caution that no decision exists in a vacuum, let us begin our examination of firm behaviour by focusing on the output supply decision and the relationship between quantity supplied and output price, *ceteris paribus*.

Price and quantity supplied: the law of supply

quantity supplied

The amount of a particular product that a firm would be willing and able to offer for sale at a particular price during a given time period.

Quantity supplied is the amount of a particular product that a firm would be willing and able to offer for sale at a particular price during a given time period. A **supply schedule** shows how much of a product a firm will supply at alternative prices. Table 4.3 itemizes the quantities of wheat that an individual farmer such as Farmer Anders might supply at various prices. If the market paid €1.50 or less for a bushel of wheat, Anders would not supply any wheat. For one thing, it costs more than €1.50 to

supply schedule

A table showing how much of a product firms will supply at different prices.

Table 4.3 Supply schedule for wheat	
Price (euros per bushel)	**Quantity supplied (bushels per year)**
1.50	0
1.75	10,000
2.25	20,000
3.00	30,000
4.00	45,000
5.00	45,000

produce a bushel of wheat; for another, Anders can use his land more profitably to produce something else. At €1.75 per bushel, however, at least some wheat production takes place on Anders' farm, and a price increase from €1.75 to €2.25 per bushel causes the quantity supplied by Anders to increase from 10,000 to 20,000 bushels per year. The higher price may justify shifting land from potato to wheat production or putting previously fallow land into wheat. Or it may lead to more intensive farming of land already in wheat, using expensive fertilizer or equipment that was not cost-justified at the lower price.

Generalizing from Farmer Anders' experience, we can reasonably expect an increase in market price, *ceteris paribus*, to lead to an increase in quantity supplied. In other words, there is a positive relationship between the quantity of a good supplied and price. This statement sums up the **law of supply**.

The information in a supply schedule presented graphically is called a **supply curve**. Supply curves slope upwards. The upward, or positive, slope of Anders' curve in Figure 4.6, for example, reflects this positive relationship between price and quantity supplied.

However, notice from Anders' supply schedule that when price rises above €4 to €5, quantity supplied no longer increases. Often, an individual firm's ability to respond to an increase in price is constrained by its existing scale of operations, or capacity, in the short run. For example, Anders' ability to produce more wheat depends on the size of his farm, the fertility of his soil and the types of equipment he has. The fact that output stays constant at 45,000 bushels per year suggests that he is running up against the limits imposed by the size of his farm, the quality of his soil and his existing technology.

In the longer run, however, Anders may acquire more land, or technology may change, allowing for more wheat production. The terms *short run* and *long run* have very precise meanings in economics; we will discuss them in detail later. Here it is important only to understand that time plays a critical role in supply decisions. When prices change, firms' immediate responses may be different from what they are able to do after a month or a year. Short-run and long-run supply curves are often different.

law of supply
The positive relationship between price and quantity of a good supplied. An increase in market price will lead to an increase in quantity supplied, and a decrease in market price will lead to a decrease in quantity supplied.

supply curve A graph illustrating how much of a product a firm will supply at different prices.

Figure 4.6 Farmer Anders' individual supply curve

A producer will supply more when the price of output is higher. The slope of a supply curve is positive; note that the supply curve is red. Supply is determined by choices made by firms.

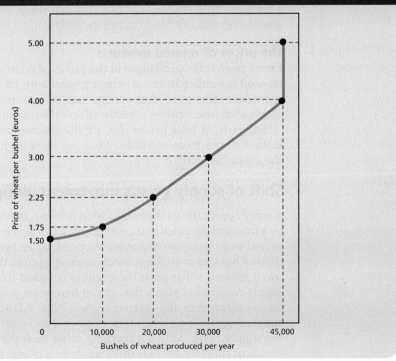

Other determinants of firm supply

Of the factors listed above that are likely to affect the quantity of output supplied by a given firm, we have thus far discussed only the price of output. Other factors that affect supply include the cost of producing the product and the prices of related products.

The cost of production

Regardless of the price that a firm can command for its product, price must exceed the cost of producing the output for the firm to make a profit. Thus, the supply decision is likely to change in response to changes in the cost of production. Cost of production depends on a number of factors, including the available technologies and the price of the inputs needed by the firm (labour, land, capital, energy and so on).

Technological change can have an enormous impact on the cost of production over time. Consider agriculture. The introduction of fertilizers, the development of complex farm machinery, and the use of bioengineering to increase the yield of individual crops have powerfully affected the cost of producing agricultural commodities. Farm productivity in Europe has been increasing dramatically for decades. Since 1960, for example, among the present members of the EU, agricultural output per worker has been increasing at around 5.5% per annum. Put in another way, the average person employed produces five times as much agricultural produce in 1988 as a worker in 1968.

When a technological advance lowers the cost of production, output is likely to increase. When yield per acre increases, individual farmers can and do produce more. The output of the car industry increased substantially after the introduction of assembly line techniques. The production of electronic calculators, and later personal computers, boomed with the development of inexpensive techniques to produce microprocessors.

Cost of production is also affected directly by the price of the factors of production. In recent years, government concern for the environment has led to higher taxes on petrol and diesel fuel to discourage car usage. As a result, taxi drivers face higher petrol prices and transport firms find their costs rising. The result: taxi drivers probably spent less time driving around looking for fares, and transport companies cut a few low-profit routes. The moral of this story: increases in input prices raise costs of production and are likely to reduce supply.

The prices of related products

Firms often react to changes in the prices of related products. For example, if land can be used for either beans or wheat production, an increase in wheat prices may cause individual farmers to shift acreage out of bean production and into wheat. Thus, an increase in wheat prices actually affects the quantity of beans supplied.

Similarly, if beef prices rise, producers may respond by raising more cattle. But leather comes from cowhide. Thus, an increase in beef prices may actually increase the supply of leather.

Shift of supply versus movement along a supply curve

A supply curve shows the relationship between the quantity of a good or service supplied by a firm and the price that good or service brings in the market. Higher prices are likely to lead to an increase in quantity supplied, *ceteris paribus*. Remember: the supply curve is derived holding everything constant except price. When the price of a product changes *ceteris paribus*, a change in the quantity supplied follows – that is, a *movement along* the supply curve takes place. But, as you have seen, supply decisions are also influenced by factors other than the product's price. New relationships between price and quantity supplied come about when factors other than its price change, and the result is a *shift* of the supply curve. When something other than the price of the product causes supply curves to shift, we say that there has been a *change in supply*.

Table 4.4 Shift of supply schedule for wheat following development of a new disease-resistant seed strain

Price (euros per bushel)	Schedule S_1: old seed Quantity supplied (bushels per year)	Schedule S_2: new seed Quantity supplied (bushels per year)
1.50	0	5,000
1.75	10,000	23,000
2.25	20,000	33,000
3.00	30,000	40,000
4.00	45,000	54,000
5.00	45,000	54,000

Recall that the cost of production depends upon the price of inputs and the technologies of production available. Now suppose that a major breakthrough in the production of wheat has occurred: genetic engineering has produced a superstrain of disease- and pest-resistant seed. Such a technological change would enable individual farmers to supply more wheat at any market price. Table 4.4 and Figure 4.7 describe this change. At €3 a bushel, farmers would have produced 30,000 bushels from the old seed (schedule S_1 in Table 4.4); with the lower cost of production and higher yield resulting from the new seed, they produce 40,000 bushels (schedule S_2 in Table 4.4). At €0.75 per bushel, they would have produced 10,000 bushels from the old seed; but with the lower costs and higher yields, output rises to 23,000 bushels.

Increases in input prices may also cause supply curves to shift. Consider, for example, an increase in oil prices. Fertilizers are made in part from petrochemicals, and tractors run on diesel fuel. Farmer Anders then faces higher costs if oil prices rise. Such increases in production cost shift the supply curve to the left – that is, less is produced at any given market price. If Anders' wheat supply curve shifted far enough

Figure 4.7 Shift of supply curve for wheat following development of a new seed strain

When the price of a product changes, we move *along* the supply curve for that product; the quantity supplied rises or falls. When any other factor affecting supply changes, the supply curve *shifts*.

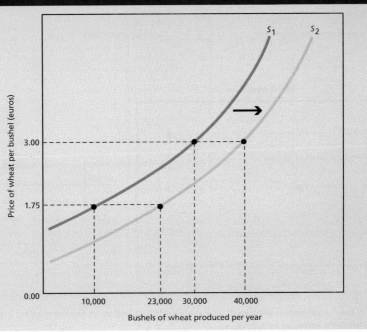

to the left, it would intersect the price axis at a higher point than before, meaning that it would take a higher market price to induce Anders to produce any wheat at all.

As with demand, it is very important to distinguish between *movements along* supply curves (changes in quantity supplied) and *shifts* in supply curves (changes in supply):

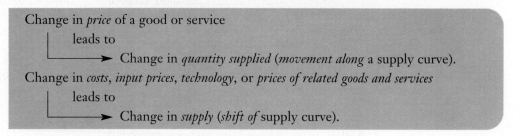

Change in *price* of a good or service

    leads to

       → Change in *quantity supplied* (*movement along* a supply curve).

Change in *costs, input prices, technology,* or *prices of related goods and services*

    leads to

       → Change in *supply* (*shift of* supply curve).

From individual firm supply to market supply

market supply
The sum of all that is supplied each period by all producers of a single product.

Market supply is determined in the same fashion as market demand. It is simply the sum of all that is supplied each period by all producers of a single product. Figure 4.8 derives a market supply curve from the supply curves of three individual firms. (In a market with more firms, total market supply would be the sum of the amounts

Figure 4.8 Deriving market supply from individual firm supply curves

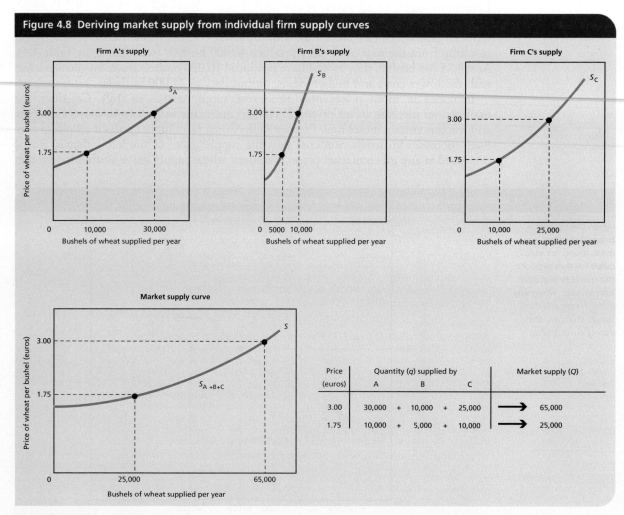

Price	Quantity (q) supplied by			Market supply (Q)
(euros)	A	B	C	
3.00	30,000 +	10,000 +	25,000	65,000
1.75	10,000 +	5,000 +	10,000	25,000

Total supply in the marketplace is the sum of all the amounts supplied by all the firms selling in the market. It is the sum of all the individual quantities supplied at each price.

produced by each of the firms in that market.) As the table in Figure 4.8 shows, at a price of 3 euros farm A supplies 30,000 bushels of wheat, farm B supplies 10,000 bushels, and farm C supplies 25,000 bushels. At this price, the total amount supplied in the market is 30,000 plus 10,000 plus 25,000, or 65,000 bushels. At a price of €1.75, however, the total amount supplied is only 25,000 bushels (10,000 plus 5000 plus 10,000). The market supply curve is thus the simple addition of the individual supply curves of all the firms in a particular market – that is, the horizontal sum of all the individual quantities supplied at each price.

The position and shape of the market supply curve depend on the positions and shapes of the individual firms' supply curves from which it is derived. But it also depends on the number of firms that produce in that market. If firms that produce for a particular market are earning high profits, other firms may be tempted to go into that line of business. When the technology to produce computers for home use became available, literally hundreds of new firms got into the act. When new firms enter an industry, the supply curve shifts to the right. When firms go out of business, or 'exit' the market, the supply curve shifts to the left.

Market equilibrium

So far we have identified a number of factors that influence the amount that households demand and the amount that firms supply in product (output) markets. The discussion has emphasized the role of market price as a determinant both of quantity demanded and quantity supplied. We are now ready to see how supply and demand in the market interact to determine the final market price.

We have been very careful in our discussions thus far to separate household decisions about how much to demand from firm decisions about how much to supply. The operation of the market, however, clearly depends on the interaction between suppliers and demanders. At any moment, one of three conditions prevails in every market: (1) the quantity demanded exceeds the quantity supplied at the current price, a situation called *excess demand*; (2) the quantity supplied exceeds the quantity demanded at the current price, a situation called *excess supply*; or (3) the quantity supplied equals the quantity demanded at the current price, a situation called **equilibrium**. At equilibrium, no tendency for price to change exists.

equilibrium The condition that exists when quantity supplied and quantity demanded are equal. At equilibrium, there is no tendency for price to change.

Excess demand

excess demand *or* **shortage**
The condition that exists when quantity demanded exceeds quantity supplied at the current price.

Excess demand or a **shortage** exists when quantity demanded is greater than quantity supplied at the current price. Figure 4.9, which plots both a supply curve and a demand curve on the same graph, illustrates such a case. As you can see, market demand at €1.75 per bushel (50,000 bushels) exceeds the amount that farmers are currently supplying (25,000 bushels).

When excess demand occurs in an unregulated market, there is a tendency for price to rise as demanders compete against each other for the limited supply. The adjustment mechanisms may differ, but the outcome is always the same. For example, consider the mechanism of a typical auction. In an auction, items are sold directly to the highest bidder. When the auctioneer starts the bidding at a low price, many people bid for the item. At first there is a shortage: quantity demanded exceeds quantity supplied. As would-be buyers offer higher and higher prices, bidders drop out, until the one who offers the most ends up with the item being auctioned. Price rises until quantity demanded and quantity supplied are equal.

At a price of €1.75 (see Figure 4.9 again), farmers produce wheat at a rate of 25,000 bushels per year, but at that price the demand is for 50,000 bushels. Most farm products are sold to local dealers who in turn sell large quantities in major market centres, where bidding would push prices up if quantity demanded exceeded quantity supplied. As price rises above €1.75, two things happen: (1) the quantity demanded falls as buyers drop out of the market and perhaps choose a substitute, and (2) the

Figure 4.9 Excess demand, or shortage

At a price of €1.75 euros per bushel, quantity demanded exceeds quantity supplied. When excess demand arises, there is a tendency for price to rise. When quantity demanded equals quantity supplied, excess demand is eliminated and the market is in equilibrium. Here, the equilibrium price is €2.50 euros and the equilibrium quantity is 35,000 bushels.

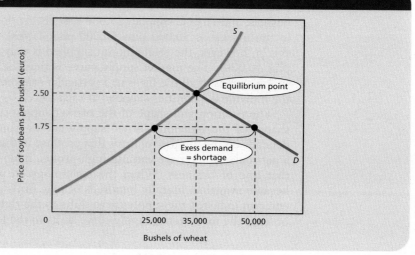

quantity supplied increases as farmers find themselves receiving a higher price for their product and shift additional acres into wheat production.[4]

This process continues until the shortage is eliminated. In Figure 4.9, this occurs at €2.50, where quantity demanded has fallen from 50,000 to 35,000 bushels per year and quantity supplied has increased from 25,000 to 35,000 bushels per year. When quantity demanded and quantity supplied are equal and there is no further bidding, the process has achieved an equilibrium, a situation in which *there is no natural tendency for further adjustment*. Graphically, the point of equilibrium is the point at which the supply curve and the demand curve intersect.

The process through which excess demand leads to higher prices is different in different markets. Consider the market for houses in the hypothetical town of Boomville with a population of 25,000 people, most of whom live in single-family homes. Normally, about 75 homes are sold in the Boomville market each year. But last year a major business opened a plant in town, creating 1,500 new jobs that pay good wages. This attracted new residents to the area, and estate agents now have more buyers than there are properties for sale. Quantity demanded now exceeds quantity supplied. In other words, there is a shortage.

Auctions are not unheard of in the housing market, but they are rare. This market usually works more subtly, but the outcome is the same. Properties are sold very quickly and housing prices begin to rise. Boomville sellers soon learn that there are more buyers than usual, and they begin to hold out for higher offers. As prices for houses in Boomville rise, quantity demanded eventually drops off and quantity supplied increases. Quantity supplied increases in at least two ways: (1) encouraged by the high prices, builders begin constructing new houses, and (2) some people, attracted by the higher prices their homes will fetch, put their houses on the market. Discouraged by higher prices, however, some potential buyers (demanders) may begin to look for housing in neighbouring towns and settle on commuting to Boomville.

[4]*Once farmers have produced in any given season, they cannot change their minds and produce more, of course. When we derived Farmer Anders' supply schedule in Table 4.3, we imagined him reacting to prices that existed at the time he decided how much land to plant in wheat. In Figure 4.9, the upward slope shows that higher prices justify shifting land from other crops. Final price may not be determined until final production figures are in. For our purposes here, however, we have ignored this timing problem. Perhaps the best way to think about it is that demand and supply are flows, or rates, of production – that is, we are talking about the number of bushels produced per production period. Adjustments in the rate of production may take place over a number of production periods.*

Eventually, equilibrium will be re-established, with the quantity of houses demanded just equal to the quantity of houses supplied.

While the mechanics of price adjustment in the housing market differ from the mechanics of an auction, the outcome is exactly the same:

> When quantity demanded exceeds quantity supplied, price tends to rise. When the price in a market rises, quantity demanded falls and quantity supplied rises until an equilibrium is reached at which quantity demanded and quantity supplied are equal.

This process is called *price rationing*. When excess demand exists, some people will be satisfied and some will not. When the market operates without interference, price increases will distribute what is available to those who are willing and able to pay the most. As long as there is a way for buyers and sellers to interact, those who are willing to pay more will make that fact known somehow. (We discuss the nature of the price system as a rationing device in detail in Chapter 5.)

Excess supply

excess supply
or surplus

The condition that exists when quantity supplied exceeds quantity demanded at the current price.

Excess supply, or a surplus, exists when the quantity supplied exceeds the quantity demanded at the current price. As with excess demand, the mechanics of price adjustment in the face of excess supply can differ from market to market. If car dealers find themselves with unsold cars at a time when new models are coming in, for example, you can expect to see price cuts. Sometimes dealers offer discounts to encourage buyers; sometimes buyers themselves simply offer less than the price initially asked. In any event, products do no one any good sitting in dealers' showrooms or on warehouse shelves. The auction metaphor introduced earlier can also be applied here: if the initial asking price is too high, no one bids, and the auctioneer tries a lower price. Think, for example, of your experience of Christmas shopping. Inevitably, certain items do not sell as well as anticipated during the period before Christmas. After Christmas, most shops have big sales during which they lower the prices of overstocked items. Quantities supplied exceeded quantities demanded at the current prices, so retailers cut prices.

Not far from Boomville is Bustville, where a steel plant shuts down its operations and 1,500 people find themselves out of work. With no other prospects for work, many residents decide to pack up and move. They put their houses up for sale, but there are few buyers. The result is an excess supply of houses: the quantity of houses supplied exceeds the quantity demanded at the current prices.

As houses sit unsold on the market for months, sellers start to cut their asking prices. Potential buyers begin offering considerably less than sellers are asking. As prices fall, two things are likely to happen. First, the low housing prices may attract new buyers. People who might have bought in a neighbouring town see that there are housing bargains to be had in Bustville, and quantity demanded rises in response to price decline. Second, some of those who put their houses on the market may be discouraged by the lower prices and decide to stay in Bustville. Developers are most unlikely to be building new housing there. Lower prices thus lead to a decline in quantity supplied as potential sellers take their houses off the market.

This is exactly the kind of situation facing the housing market in a town like Aberdeen in Scotland. Much of the demand for housing in the town comes from oil workers who work on North Sea oil rigs off the coast near Aberdeen. When the market for oil is depressed and oil prices are low, and expected to stay low, fewer oil workers are needed, and the fall in demand for oil workers leads to a fall in the demand for houses. The housing market adjusts price downwards until equilibrium is restored.

Figure 4.10 illustrates another case of excess supply. At a price of €3 per bushel, farmers are supplying wheat at a rate of 40,000 bushels per year, but buyers demand

Figure 4.10 Excess supply or surplus

At a price of €3, quantity supplied exceeds quantity demanded by 18,000 bushels. This excess supply will cause price to fall.

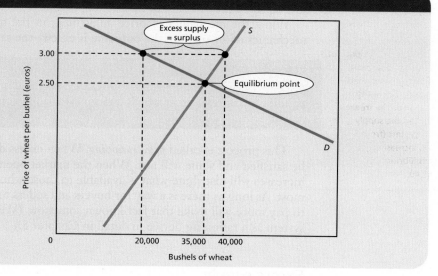

only 22,000. With 18,000 (40,000 minus 22,000) bushels of wheat going unsold, the market price falls. As price falls from €3 to €2.50, quantity supplied decreases from 40,000 bushels per year to 35,000. The lower price causes quantity demanded to rise from 22,000 to 35,000. At €2.50, quantity demanded and quantity supplied are equal. For the data shown here, then, €2.50 and 35,000 bushels are the equilibrium price and quantity.

Although the mechanism by which price is adjusted is different for cars, housing and wheat, the outcome is the same:

> When quantity supplied exceeds quantity demanded at the current price, the price tends to fall. When price falls, quantity supplied is likely to decrease and quantity demanded is likely to increase until an equilibrium price is reached where quantity supplied and quantity demanded are equal.

Changes in equilibrium

When supply and demand curves shift, the equilibrium price and quantity change. The following example will help to illustrate this point.

South America is a major producer of coffee beans. A cold snap there can reduce the coffee harvest enough to affect the world price of coffee beans. In the summer of 1994, a major freeze hit Brazil and Colombia and drove up the price of coffee on world markets to a record $2.40 per pound. (World commodity prices are often quoted in $US.)

Figure 4.11 illustrates how the freeze pushed up coffee prices. Initially, the market was in equilibrium at a price of $1.20. At that price, the quantity demanded was equal to quantity supplied (13.2 billion pounds). At a price of $1.20 and a quantity of 13.2 billion pounds, the demand curve (labelled D) intersected the initial supply curve (labelled S_1). (Remember that equilibrium exists when quantity demanded equals quantity supplied – the point at which the supply and demand curves intersect.)

The freeze caused a decrease in the supply of coffee beans. That is, it caused the supply curve to shift to the left. In Figure 4.11, the new supply curve (the supply curve that shows the relationship between price and quantity supplied after the freeze) is labelled S_2.

Figure 4.11 The coffee market: a shift of supply and subsequent price adjustment

Before the freeze, the coffee market was in equilibrium at a price of $1.20. At that price, quantity demanded equalled quantity supplied. The freeze shifted the supply curve to the left (from S_1 to S_2), increasing equilibrium price to $2.40.

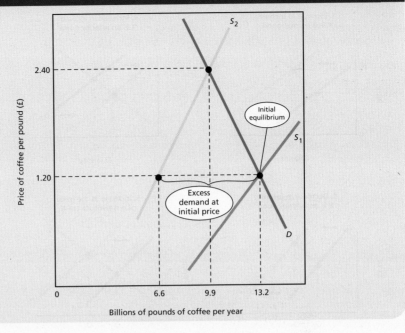

At the initial equilibrium price, $1.20, there is now an excess demand for coffee. If the price were to remain at $1.20, quantity demanded would not change; it would remain at 13.2 billion pounds. But at that price, quantity supplied would drop to 6.6 billion pounds. At a price of $1.20, quantity demanded is greater than quantity supplied.

When excess demand exists in a market, price can be expected to rise, and rise it did. As Figure 4.11 shows, price rose to a new equilibrium at $2.40. At $2.40, quantity demanded is again equal to quantity supplied, this time at 9.9 billion pounds – the point at which the new supply curve (S_2) intersects the demand curve.

Notice that as the price of coffee rose from $1.20 to $2.40, two things happened. First, the quantity demanded declined (a movement along the demand curve) as people shifted to substitutes such as tea. Second, the quantity supplied began to rise, but within the limits imposed by the damage from the freeze. (It might also be that some countries or areas with high costs of production, previously unprofitable, came into production and shipped to the world market at the higher price.) That is, the quantity supplied increased in response to the higher price *along* the new supply curve, which lies to the left of the old supply curve. The final result was a higher price ($2.40), a smaller quantity finally exchanged in the market (9.9 billion pounds), and coffee bought only by those willing to pay $2.40 per pound.

Figure 4.12 presents ten examples of supply and demand shifts and the resulting changes in equilibrium price and quantity. Be sure to go through each graph carefully and ensure that you understand it.

Figure 4.12 Examples of supply and demand shifts for product X

1. Increase in income: X is a normal good

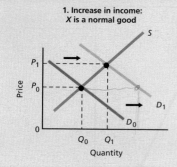

2. Increase in income: X is an inferior good

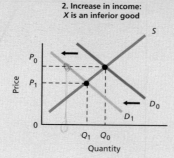

3. Decrease in income: X ia a normal good

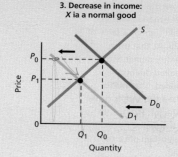

4. Decrease in income: X is an inferior good

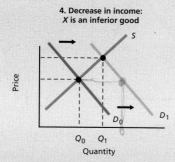

5. Increase in the price of a substitute for X

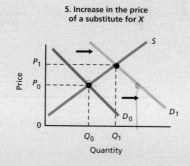

6. Increase in the price of a complement for X

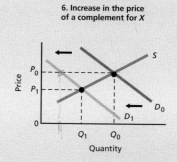

7. Decrease in the price of a substitute for X

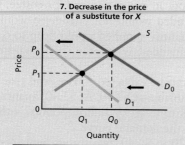

8. Decrease in the price of a complement for X

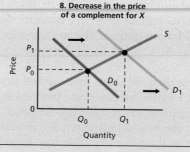

B. SUPPLY SHIFTS

9. Increase in the cost of production of X

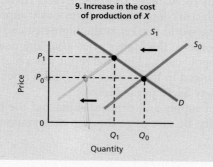

10. Decrease in the cost of production of X

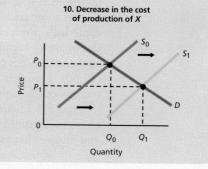

Applications

How could we handle the organ shortage?

All over Europe, people die whose lives could have been saved with an organ transplant. Liver, kidney and heart transplants are now relatively safe and effective but there are not enough of them. Some people are willing to make their own organs available when they die even though they receive no payment for doing so, but the number of organs made available in this way is inadequate to meet the demand.

The situation could be described by Figure 1. The supply curve S_1 shows that because some people are willing to donate their organs on their death, A organs per month become available. More would be supplied if people (or their surviving relatives) were paid. Those who receive a transplant do not pay for the organ, though in some EU countries they pay for the costs of the operation

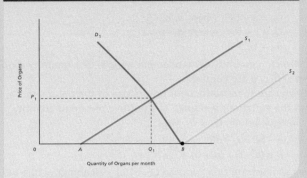

Figure 1 Supply and demand for organs

Price of Organs (vertical axis), *Quantity of Organs per month* (horizontal axis). Curves D_1, S_1, S_2; points P_1, A, Q_1, B.

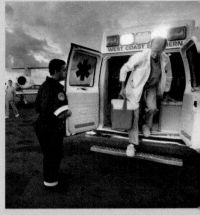

Dr Mark Staples stepping from the ambulance at dawn, returns from a South Florida hospital carrying a cooler containing a harvested donor organ.

itself. At zero price, B organs per month are demanded so there is an excess demand of $B - A$.

Campaigns to encourage people to leave their organs when they die might shift the supply curve to S_2, eliminating the problem. Even without payment there would be no shortage. This is unlikely. Such campaigns have not always been effective in the past. Furthermore, the demand

curve is moving to the right over time as improvements in medical technique mean that more people's lives can be saved by organ transplants.

An alternative solution is to use a price mechanism whereby people pay for organs and where the suppliers receive a price for donating them. On the diagram, given D_1 and S_1 the price would be P_1 and equilibrium quantity at Q_1.

You may have ethical

objections to such a scheme, but remember that under the present system doctors have to make decisions about who receives the limited quantity available. You may have other objectives to this proposal. What are they? What do you think an economist might say to such objections?

Demand and supply in product markets: a review

As you continue your study of economics, you will discover that it is a discipline full of controversy and debate. There is, however, little disagreement about the basic way that the forces of supply and demand operate in free markets. If you hear that a freeze in Spain has destroyed a good portion of the orange crop, you can bet that the price of oranges will rise. If you read that the weather in Europe has been good and a record wheat crop is expected, you can bet that wheat prices will fall. When fishermen in the North Sea go on strike and stop bringing in the daily catch, you can bet that the price of fish will go up. (For additional examples of how the forces of supply and demand work, see the Application feature 'Supply and demand in the news'.)

In economics you have to think twice, however, even about a 'safe' bet. If you bet that the price of frozen orange juice will rise after a freeze, you will lose your money. It turns out that much of the crop that is damaged by a freeze can be used, but for only one thing – to make frozen orange juice. Thus, a freeze actually increases the supply of frozen juice on the market so the price of oranges rises but the price of orange juice will tend to fall!

Maths Box 1 Demand and supply in equation form

We can represent the demand and supply functions as equations. The demand curve expresses a relationship between price and quantity, *ceteris paribus*; the supply curve also shows a relationship between price and quantity, *ceteris paribus*. Hence (assuming the equations have a linear form):

$$Q_d = a - bP \quad \text{where a, b} > 0$$
$$Q_s = c + dP \quad \text{where d} > 0 > c$$
$$da + bc > 0$$

where Q_d = quantity demanded per period, Q_s = quantity supplied per period, P = price, and a, b, c, d are constants.

Why are there restrictions on the size of the parameters a, b, c and d? They ensure that the equations will solve at a positive price and quantity.

In equilibrium, $Q_d = Q_s$. Thus:

$$a - bP = c + dP$$
$$P = (a - c) / (d + b)$$

We can illustrate this. Suppose $Q_d = 100 - 2P$ and $Q_s = 10 + 3P$. We can solve for the equilibrium price in two ways. Either:

$$100 - 2P = 10 + 3P$$
$$5P = 90$$
$$P = 18$$

Or:

$$P = (100 - 10) / (3 + 2) = 18$$

The equilibrium quantity Q is 64. Verify this for yourself.

Applications

Supply and demand in the news

The basic forces of supply and demand are at work throughout the world, as the following news articles illustrate. As an exercise draw and label demand and supply diagrams for each of the three cases.

1. A leftward shift of supply causes a sharp increase in prices.

Mango prices are expected to rise sharply as India, the world's largest producer of the tropical fruit, suffers a big setback in production. Unseasonal weather in the main growing regions is delaying this season's crop for six weeks until May.

'Prices in the domestic market will be 30–50 per cent higher, depending on the variety of the mango', an exporter said. The rise in wholesale prices is likely to push up consumer prices by a similar percentage.

Alphonso, the finest and the most expensive mango, grown in the western Indian state of Maharashtra, will command a high premium in the world market as production drops by up to 70 per cent, he said.

2. A potential rightward shift in supply from improved production techniques could cause an increase in output.

According to the Agricultural and Processed Fruits Export Development Authority, India has 1.136 million hectares under mango cultivation and productivity could be almost doubled to 15 tonnes a hectare if farmers were to adopt more scientific agricultural practices, such as using fertilizers, pesticides and more efficient harvesting methods.

The biggest challenge is to eliminate fruit flies in mangoes of exportable varieties and bring down the rate of export rejection from 40 per cent to 5 per cent.

India's normal annual production of 10 million tonnes is set to rise as the leading mango growing states bring more areas under the crop. 'Even Kerala, a southern state, which has a marginal presence in mango trade, is creating new mango orchards over nearly 8000 hectares', a trader said.

3. A leftward shift in demand causes prices to decline.

Commodity prices show signs of stabilizing after sharp declines linked to the Asian financial crisis, according to the International Monetary Fund.

Since mid-1997, prices of primary commodities have fallen more than 10 per cent, affecting producers and consumers around the world.

But while the near-term outlook remains difficult to assess, there are indications that prices may be levelling off, the IMF said in its semi-annual World Economic Outlook report.

World copper prices plunged 33 per cent between June 1997 and January 1998, the IMF said. Timber prices fell 24 per cent, zinc 16 per cent, hides 15 per cent and soyabean meal 11 per cent. Natural rubber prices took the biggest fall – 37 per cent during the six-month period – while crude oil prices fell 13 per cent.

Source: Financial Times, *15 April 1998, p. 37.*

Here are some important points to remember about the mechanics of supply and demand in product markets:

1. A demand curve shows how much of a product a household would buy if it could buy all it wanted at the given price. A supply curve shows how much of a product a firm would supply if it could sell all it wanted at the given price.

2. Quantity demanded and quantity supplied are always per time period – that is, per day, per month or per year.

3. The demand for a good is determined by price, household income and wealth, the prices of other goods and services, tastes and preferences, and expectations.

4. The supply of a good is determined by price, costs of production and the prices of related products. Costs of production are determined by available technologies of production and input prices.

5. Be careful to distinguish between *movements along* supply and demand curves and *shifts of* these curves. When the price of a good changes, the quantity of that good demanded or supplied changes – that is, a movement occurs along the curve. When any other factor changes, the curves shift, or change position.

6. Market equilibrium exists only when quantity supplied equals quantity demanded at the current price.

Looking ahead: markets and the allocation of resources

You can already begin to see how markets answer the basic economic questions of what is produced, how it is produced, and who gets what is produced. A firm will produce what it is profitable to produce. If it can sell a product at a price that is sufficient to leave a profit after production costs are paid, it will in all likelihood produce that product. Resources will flow in the direction of profit opportunities.

> Demand curves reflect what people are willing and able to pay for products; they are influenced by incomes, wealth, preferences, the prices of other goods, and expectations. Because product prices are determined by the interaction of supply and demand, prices reflect what people are willing to pay. If people's preferences or incomes change, resources will be allocated differently.

Consider, for example, an increase in demand – a shift in the market demand curve. Beginning at an equilibrium, households simply begin buying more. At the equilibrium price, quantity demanded becomes greater than quantity supplied. When there is excess demand, prices will rise, and higher prices mean higher profits for firms in the industry. Higher profits, in turn, provide existing firms with an incentive to expand and new firms with an incentive to enter the industry, increasing supply. Thus, the decisions of independent private firms responding to prices and profit opportunities determine *what* will be produced. No central direction is necessary.

Adam Smith saw this self-regulating feature of markets more than 200 years ago:

> Every individual . . . by pursuing his own interest . . . promotes that of society. He is led . . . by an invisible hand to promote an end which was no part of his intention.[5]

The term Smith coined, the *invisible hand*, has passed into common parlance and is still used by economists to refer to the self-regulation of markets.

[5]*Adam Smith*, The Wealth of Nations, *p. 456.*

Firms in business to make a profit have a good reason to choose the best available technology – lower costs mean higher profits. Thus, individual firms determine *how* to produce their products, again with no central direction.

So far we have barely touched on the question of distribution – *who* gets what is produced? But you can see part of the answer in the simple supply and demand diagrams. When a good is in short supply, price rises. As it does, those who are willing and able to continue buying do so; others stop buying.

The next chapter begins with a more detailed discussion of these topics. How, exactly, is the final allocation of resources (the mix of output and the distribution of output) determined in a market system?

Summary

1. In societies with many people, production must satisfy wide-ranging tastes and preferences, and producers must therefore specialize.

Firms and households: the basic decision-making units

2. A *firm* exists when a person or a group of people decides to produce a product or products by transforming resources, or *inputs*, into *outputs* – the products that are sold in the market. Firms are the primary producing units in a market economy. We assume firms make decisions to maximize profits.

3. *Households* are the primary consuming units in an economy. All households' incomes are subject to constraints.

Input markets and output markets: the circular flow

4. Households and firms interact in two basic kinds of markets: *product* or *output markets* and *input* or *factor markets*. Goods and services intended for use by households are exchanged in output markets. In output markets, competing firms supply and competing households demand. In input markets, competing firms demand and competing households supply.

5. Ultimately, firms determine the quantities and character of outputs produced, the types and quantities of inputs demanded, and the technologies used in production. Households determine the types and quantities of products demanded and the types and quantities of inputs supplied.

Demand in product/output markets

6. The quantity demanded of an individual product by an individual household depends on (1) the price of the product, (2) income, (3) wealth, (4) the prices of other products, (5) tastes and preferences, and (6) expectations about the future.

7. Quantity demanded is the amount of a product that an individual household would buy in a given period if it could buy all it wanted at the current price.

8. A *demand schedule* shows the quantities of a product that a household would buy at different prices. The same information can be presented graphically in a *demand curve*.

9. The *law of demand* states that there is a negative relationship between price and quantity demanded: as price rises, quantity demanded decreases, and vice versa. Demand curves slope downwards.

10. All demand curves eventually intersect the price axis because there is always a price above which a household cannot, or will not, pay. All demand curves also eventually intersect the quantity axis because demand for most goods is limited, if only by time, even at a zero price.

11. When an increase in income causes demand for a good to rise, that good is a *normal good*. When an increase in income causes demand for a good to fall, that good is an *inferior good*.

12. If a rise in the price of good X causes demand for good Y to increase, the goods are *substitutes*. If a rise in the price of X causes demand for Y to fall, the goods are *complements*.

13. Market demand is simply the sum of all the quantities of a good or service demanded per period by all the households buying in the market for that good or service. It is the sum of all the individual quantities demanded at each price.

Supply in product/output markets

14. Quantity supplied by a firm depends on (1) the price of the good or service; (2) the cost of producing the product, which includes the prices of required inputs and the technologies that can be used to produce the product; and (3) the prices of related products.

15. Market supply is the sum of all that is supplied each period by all producers of a single product. It is the sum of all the individual quantities supplied at each price.

16. It is very important to distinguish between *movements along* demand and supply curves and *shifts of* demand and supply curves. The demand curve shows the relationship between price and quantity demanded. The supply curve shows the relationship between price and quantity supplied. A change in price brings a movement along the curve. Changes in tastes, income, wealth, expectations, or prices of other goods and services cause demand curves to shift; changes in costs, input prices, technology, or prices of related goods and services cause supply curves to shift.

Market equilibrium

17. When quantity demanded exceeds quantity supplied at the current price, excess demand (or a shortage) exists and the price tends to rise. When prices in a market rise, quantity demanded falls and quantity supplied rises until an equilibrium is reached at which quantity supplied and quantity demanded are equal. At equilibrium, there is no further tendency for price to change.

18. When quantity supplied exceeds quantity demanded at the current price, excess supply (or a surplus) exists and the price tends to fall. When price falls, quantity supplied decreases and quantity demanded increases until an equilibrium price is reached where quantity supplied and quantity demanded are equal.

Review Terms and Concepts

capital market
complements, complementary goods
demand curve
demand schedule
entrepreneur
equilibrium
excess demand
excess supply
factors of production
firm
households
income
inferior goods
input or factor markets
labour market
land market

law of demand
law of supply
market demand
market supply
movement along a demand curve
normal goods
perfect substitutes
product or output markets
profit
quantity demanded
quantity supplied
shift of a demand curve
substitutes
supply curve
supply schedule
wealth or net worth

Problem Set

1. Illustrate the following with supply and demand curves:
a. Between 1996 and 1997, employment and income in much of Europe fell, creating a decline in the demand for housing and lowering home prices.
b. In 1997, sterling (the UK currency) rose in value on foreign currency markets. One result was that UK exports looked more expensive to foreign buyers. As a result, the demand for UK products decreased.
c. Before economic reforms were implemented in Poland, the price of meat was held substantially below equilibrium by law. When reforms were implemented, prices rose dramatically, the quantity demanded fell, and the quantity supplied rose.
d. Governments impose regulations that sharply decrease the number of trees available for timber production in Scandinavia to protect endangered

species. Illustrate the effects on the timber market and on the housing market.
e. As more and more people bought home computers during the 1990s, the demand for access to the World Wide Web and the Internet increased sharply. At the same time, new companies began to enter the market competing with older more established services. Despite a massive increase in demand, the price of access to the Web actually declined.

2. Do you agree or disagree with each of the following statements? Briefly explain your answers.
a. The price of a good rises causing the demand for another good to fall. Therefore the two goods are substitutes.
b. A shift in supply causes the price of a good to fall. The shift must have been an increase in supply.

c. During 1997–8, disposable incomes rose in some European countries. This change would probably lead to an increase in the prices of both normal and inferior goods in those countries.

d. Two normal goods cannot be substitutes for each other.

e. If demand increases and supply increases at the same time, price will rise.

f. An increase in supply causes the price of good A to fall. This leads to an increase in the price of good B. Therefore A and B are complements.

3. There has been a great debate among housing policy analysts over the best way to increase the number of housing units available to low-income households. One strategy is to focus on demand and to provide people with housing 'vouchers', paid for by the government, that can be used to rent housing supplied by the private market. A second strategy is to concentrate on supply and have the government subsidize housing suppliers or simply to build public housing.

a. Illustrate both supply- and demand-side strategies using supply and demand curves. Which strategy will result in higher rents?

b. Critics of housing vouchers (the demand-side strategy) argue that because the supply of housing to low-income households is limited and will not respond at all to higher rents, demand vouchers will serve only to drive up rents and make landlords better off. Illustrate their point with supply and demand curves.

4. Housing prices in the American towns of Boston and Los Angeles have been on a roller coaster ride. Illustrate each of the following situations with supply and demand curves:

a. In both cities an increase in income combined with expectations of a strong market shifted demand and caused prices to rise rapidly during the mid- to late 1980s.

b. By 1990, the construction industry boomed as more and more developers started new residential projects. But those new projects expanded the supply of housing just as demand was shifting as a result of falling incomes and expectations during the 1990–91 recession.

c. In late 1997, housing markets in higher-income towns in the Boston area were experiencing price increases. At the same time housing markets in lower-income towns, especially in areas hit hard by a decline in manufacturing employment, saw housing prices continue to fall. In part this effect was due to 'trade-up' buyers selling houses in lower-income areas and buying houses in higher-income areas.

d. Despite falling incomes, housing markets in lower-income areas in Los Angeles were actually experiencing some price increases in 1994 and 1995 as immigration of lower-income households continued.

5. The following two sets of statements contain common errors. Identify and explain each.

a. Demand increases, causing prices to rise. Higher prices cause demand to fall. Therefore prices fall back to their original levels.

b. The supply of meat in Russia increases. This causes meat prices to fall. Lower prices mean that Russian households spend more on meat.

6. Think about a large out of town shopping centre near your home. On a Saturday morning a week or two before Christmas the car park is so full that cars are queuing to get in. On a Tuesday morning in February it is only half full and there are no queues. The price of a ticket for a parking space is the same on each occasion.

a. Draw supply and demand curves for parking places on these two occasions. Draw one graph for each time (Hint: supply is fixed. It does not change with price.)

b. Is there a pricing policy that would have filled the car park on Tuesday morning?

c. The price system does not ration car park spaces on the December morning. How do you know? What rationing system operates when price does not do it?

d. Is it a good idea to have a higher priced parking ticket for Saturday morning shopping than for Tuesday morning shopping?

7. Europe administers two programmes that affect the market for cigarettes: cigarette advertising is restricted or banned, and labelling requirements aim to make the public aware of the health dangers of cigarettes. At the same time, the Common Agricultural Policy subsidizes the production of tobacco. Are these two programmes at odds with respect to the goal of reducing cigarette consumption? Explain carefully. As a part of your answer, illustrate graphically the effects of both policies on the market for cigarettes.

8. In the mid-1990s, the scare about BSE (a disease affecting the brain of cattle) reached its peak. Some consumers feared that they could catch this disease by eating affected meat. As a result, the price of pork increased for a time. Illustrate this situation with supply and demand curves (draw diagrams for both markets).

9. Consider the market for pizza. Suppose that the market demand for pizza is given by the equation $Q_d = 300 - 20P$ and the market supply for pizza is given by the equation $Q_s = 20P - 100$, where Q_d = quantity demanded, Q_s = quantity supplied, P = price (per pizza).

a. Graph the supply and demand schedules for pizza using €5 to €15 as the range in P.

b. In equilibrium, how many pizzas would be sold and at what price?

c. What would happen if suppliers set the price of pizza at €15? Explain the market adjustment process.

d. Suppose that the price of hamburgers, a substitute for pizza, doubles. Assume that this leads to a doubling of the demand for pizza (that is, at each price consumers demand twice as much pizza as before). Write the equation for the new market demand for pizza.

e. Find the new equilibrium price and quantity of pizza.

que-ce que tu fais

10. For each of the following, draw a diagram that illustrates the likely effect on the market for eggs. Indicate in each case the impact on equilibrium price and equilibrium quantity.

a. A government health warning declares that high-cholesterol foods cause heart attacks.

b. There is a decrease in the price of bacon, a complementary product.

c. There is an increase in the price of chicken feed.

d. Caesar salads become trendy at dinner parties. (The dressing is made with raw eggs.)

e. A technological innovation reduces egg breakage during packing.

11. Suppose the demand and supply curves for almonds in Europe are given by the following equations:

$Q_d = 100 - 20P$

$Q_s = 10 + 40P$

Price of almonds (euros per tonne)	Quantity demanded (Q_d)	Quantity supplied (Q_s)
0.50		
1.00		
1.50		
2.00		
2.50		

where Q_d = millions of tonnes of almonds Europeans would like to buy each year; Q_s = millions of tonnes of almonds European farms would like to sell each year; P = price per tonne of almonds;

a. Fill in the gaps in the table

b. Use the information in the table to find the equilibrium price and equilibrium quantity.

c. Graph the demand and supply curves, and identify the equilibrium price and quantity.

d. Solve the equilibrium price and quantity algebraically.

12. 'An increase in demand causes an increase in price. But an increase in price causes a decrease in demand. Increases in demand, therefore, largely cancel themselves out.' Comment.

*13. The market demand curve for socks in Hilaria has been estimated at $Q_d = 60 - 3P$, where Q_d = number of pairs of socks per day purchased and P = the price in Hilarian euros.

a. How high does price need to be before quantity demanded is zero?

b. How many pairs of socks could be given away?

*14. Hilarian sock manufacturers advertise their wares and change the demand curve from what it was in Problem 13 to $Q_d = 70 - 2P$.

a. How high does price now need to be before quantity demanded is zero?

b. How many socks could now be given away?

The Price System, Supply and Demand and Elasticity

Every society has a system of institutions that determines what is produced, how it is produced, and who gets what is produced. In some societies these decisions are made centrally, through planning agencies or by government directive. But in every society many decisions are made in a decentralized way, through the operation of markets.

Markets exist in all societies, and Chapter 4 provided a bare-bones description of how markets operate. In this chapter, we continue our examination of supply, demand and the price system.

The price system: rationing and allocating resources

price rationing

The process by which the market system allocates goods and services to consumers when quantity demanded exceeds quantity supplied.

The market system, also called the *price system*, performs two important and closely related functions. First, it provides an automatic mechanism for distributing scarce goods and services. That is, it serves as a price rationing device for allocating goods and services to consumers when the quantity demanded exceeds the quantity supplied. Second, the price system ultimately determines both the allocation of resources among producers and the final mix of outputs.

Price rationing

Consider first the simple process by which the price system eliminates excess demand. Figure 5.1 shows hypothetical supply and demand curves for lobsters caught off the European coasts in areas such as south-west England and northern France. Lobsters are considered a delicacy. They are served in the finest restaurants, and people cook them at home on special occasions.

Figure 5.1 shows the equilibrium price of live lobsters at €6.5 per kilo in 1998. At this price, lobster boats brought in lobsters at a rate of 45 million kilos per year – an amount that was just enough to satisfy demand.

Market equilibrium existed at €6.5 per kilo, because at that price quantity demanded was equal to quantity supplied. (Remember that equilibrium occurs at the point where the supply and demand curves intersect. In Figure 5.1, this occurs at point *C*.)

Now suppose that in 1999 the waters off a section of the coast become contaminated by an oil spill from a grounded oil tanker. As a result, some of the most productive lobster fishing areas are closed. Even though many of the lobster boats move their pots to other waters, there is a sharp reduction in the quantity of lobster supplied. The supply curve shifts to the left, from S_{1998} to S_{1999}. This shift in the supply curve creates a situation of excess demand at €6.5. At that price, the quantity demanded is 45 million kilos and the quantity supplied is 22 million kilos. Quantity demanded exceeds quantity supplied by 23 million kilos (45 million minus 22 million).

Figure 5.1 The market for lobsters

Suppose that in 1999 some lobster fishing waters off the coast of France and south-west England are closed. The supply curve shifts to the left. Before the waters are closed, the lobster market is in equilibrium at the price of €6.5 and a quantity of 45 million kilos. The decreased supply of lobster leads to higher prices, and a new equilibrium is reached at €9 and €35 million kilos.

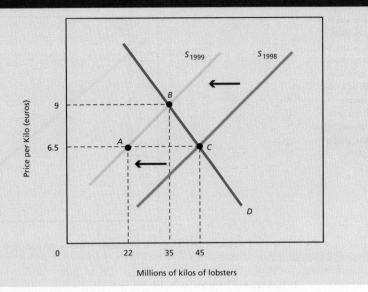

The reduced supply causes the price of lobster to rise sharply. As the price rises, the available supply is 'rationed'. Who gets it? Those who are willing and able to pay the most.

You can see the market's price rationing function clearly in Figure 5.1. As the price rises from €6.5, the quantity demanded declines along the demand curve, moving from point *C* (45 million kilos) towards point *B* (35 million kilos). The higher prices mean that restaurants must charge much more for lobster dishes. In consequence, many people simply decide to stop buying lobster or order it less frequently when they dine out. Some restaurants drop it from the menu entirely, and some shoppers turn to lobster substitutes such as trout and salmon.

As the price rises, the lobstermen (suppliers) also change their behaviour. They stay out longer and put out more pots than they did when the price was €6.5 per kilo. Quantity supplied increases from 22 million kilos to 35 million kilos. This increase in price brings about a movement along the 1996 supply curve from point *A* to point *B*.

Finally, a new equilibrium is established at a price of €9 per kilo and a total output of 35 million kilos. At the new equilibrium, total production is 35 million kilos per year, and the market has determined who gets the lobsters. *The lower total supply is rationed to those who are willing and able to pay the higher price.*

This idea of 'willingness to pay' is central to the distribution of available supply, and willingness depends on both desire (preferences) and income/wealth. Willingness to pay does not necessarily mean that only the very rich will continue to buy lobsters when the price increases. Lower-income people may continue to buy some lobster, but they also will have to be willing to sacrifice more of other goods in order to do so.

In sum:

The adjustment of price is the rationing mechanism in free markets. Price rationing means that whenever there is a need to ration a good – that is, when a shortage exists – in a free market, the price of the good will rise until quantity supplied equals quantity demanded – that is, until the market clears.

There is some price that will clear any market you can think of. Consider the market for a famous painting, such as van Gogh's *Harvest in Provence* which depicts an autumn landscape near Arles. Figure 5.2 illustrates the operation of such a market. At

Figure 5.2 The market for a rare painting

There is some price that will clear any market, even if supply is strictly limited. In an auction for a unique painting, the price (bid) will rise to eliminate excess demand until there is only one bidder willing to purchase the single available painting.

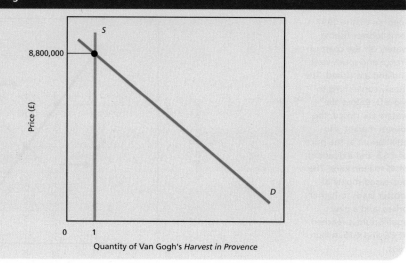

Quantity of Van Gogh's *Harvest in Provence*

a low price, there would be an enormous excess demand for such an important painting. The price would be bid up until there was only one remaining demander. The demander who gets the painting would be the one who is willing and able to pay the most. Presumably, that price would be very high. In fact, van Gogh's *Harvest in Provence* sold for £8.8 million at an auction in London in June 1997. If the quantity of product is in fixed and scarce supply, as a single painting is, its price is said to be *demand determined*; that is, its price is determined solely and exclusively by the amount that the highest bidder or highest bidders are willing to pay.

One might interpret the statement that 'there is some price that will clear any market' to mean 'everything has its price'. But that is not exactly what it means. Suppose you own a small silver bracelet that has been in your family for many generations. It is quite possible that you wouldn't sell it for *any* amount of money. Does this mean that the market is not working, or that quantity supplied and quantity demanded are not equal? Not at all. It means simply that *you* are the highest bidder. By turning down all bids, you are setting your own price, revealing that the bracelet is worth more to you than to those who bid on it. To keep the bracelet, you must be willing to forgo what anybody offers for it.

Constraints on the market, and alternative rationing mechanisms

On occasion, both governments and private firms decide to use some mechanism other than the market system to ration an item for which there is excess demand at the current price. (This was often the case in the former Soviet Union and other Communist nations like China, Poland, East Germany and Cuba.) Policies designed to stop price rationing are commonly justified in a number of ways.

The rationale most often used is fairness. It is not 'fair' to let landlords charge high rents, not 'fair' for oil companies to run up the price of petrol, not 'fair' for insurance companies to charge enormous premiums, and so on. After all, the argument goes, we have no choice but to pay – housing and insurance are necessary, and one needs petrol to get to work. While it is not precisely true that price rationing allocates goods and services solely on the basis of income and wealth, income and wealth do constrain our wants. 'Why should all the petrol or all the tickets to the World Cup Finals go just to the rich?', it is asked.

Various schemes to keep price from rising to equilibrium are based on several perceptions of injustice, among them (1) that rationing by price is bad; (2) that income is unfairly distributed; and (3) that some items are necessities, and everyone should be able to buy them at a 'reasonable' price. Regardless of the rationale, the following examples will make two things clear:

1. Attempts to bypass price rationing in the market and to use alternative rationing devices are much more difficult and costly than they would seem at first glance.
2. Very often, such attempts distribute costs and benefits among households in unintended ways.

Oil, petrol and OPEC

In 1973 and 1974, the Organization of Petroleum Exporting Countries (OPEC) imposed an embargo on shipments of crude oil to the United States. This resulted in a drastic reduction in the quantity of petrol available at local petrol stations in the United States. However, the reduced supply of crude oil also sharply reduced available supplies throughout Europe.

Had the market system been operating freely, refined petrol prices would have increased dramatically until quantity supplied was equal to quantity demanded. Those who were willing and able to pay a very high price would have been the ones to get the petrol. But some governments decided that rationing petrol to only those who were willing and able to pay the most was unfair. Hence, they imposed a **price ceiling**, or maximum price, on petrol. That price ceiling was intended to keep petrol 'affordable', but it also perpetuated the excess demand. At the restricted price, quantity demanded remained greater than quantity supplied, and the available petrol had to be divided up somehow among all potential demanders.

You can see the effects of the price ceiling by looking carefully at Figure 5.3. If the price had been set by the interaction of supply and demand, it would have been

price ceiling
A maximum price that sellers may charge for a good, usually set by government.

Global Perspectives

The market comes to China

Price rationing allocates goods and services to those who are willing and able to pay for them. One of the central premises of communism is that price rationing for basic necessities, such as food, is unfair; everyone should be able to afford such items as food and shelter. But regulating prices to 'fair' levels below equilibrium means that quantity supplied will be less than quantity demanded.

In addition, preventing the price mechanism from operating requires that some device other than price be used to ration the available goods. Before the collapse of communism in the Soviet Union and Eastern Europe, people waited in long queues at state shops, which could not meet the citizens'

demands. Shops were not well stocked, in part because farmers could get a much better price for their goods on the illegal black market.

The biggest problem with regulated prices, however, is that the incentive to produce is lost.

In 1997, China's paramount leader Deng Xiaoping died. Deng, more than any leader in the communist world, understood the importance of market prices as an incentive. In 1978, local officials associated with Deng began to allow poor rural peasants to grow grain on their own individual plots of land. The peasants could not own the land, and a fixed amount of the grain was taken by the state as a tax. But they were permitted to sell all surpluses in private

markets at market prices. This had a dramatic effect on the level of output. As prices increased so did the quantity supplied. Productivity soared, and Chinese agriculture began to grow dramatically.

Deng also knew that the industrial sector could not function without market prices playing a role. From 1997, markets rather than bureaucracies determine the prices of nearly nine-tenths of all finished goods in China.

For the 75% of Chinese who make their living from the land, their average incomes have gone up over 200% since 1978. Industrial incomes have risen even more. China's economy has grown at an average rate of over 9% since 1982. In 1997, it grew at an impressive 10% annual rate.

A farmer on the outskirts of Beijing tills the soil of his vegetable crop on his small plot of land. He will sell the crop to markets in the national capital. China is nurturing more efficient, large-scale farming but the shift may take years because the government will not force farmers to give up tiny plots they won when Beijing disbanded its failed commune system. China must feed one-fifth of the world's population on just 7% of its arable land.

Figure 5.3 Excess demand created by a price ceiling on petrol

In 1974, some countries imposed a ceiling price on petrol. If the price had instead been set by the interaction of supply and demand, it would have increased to P_e. At the price ceiling, the quantity demanded exceeded the quantity supplied. Because the price system was not allowed to function, an alternative rationing system had to be found to distribute the available supply of petrol.

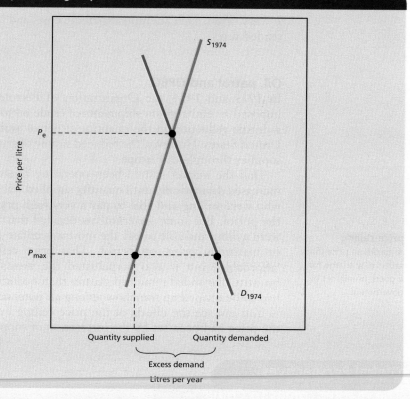

at P_e. Instead, the law made it illegal to sell petrol for more than P_{max}. At that price, quantity demanded exceeded quantity supplied, and a state of excess demand existed. Since the price system was not allowed to function, an alternative rationing system had to be found to distribute the available supply of petrol.

Several devices were tried. The most common of all non-price rationing systems is **queuing**. During 1974 very long queues began to appear at petrol stations, starting as early as 5am. Often people waited for hours to purchase petrol. Under this system, petrol went to those who were willing to pay the most, but the sacrifice was measured in hours and aggravation rather than in money.[1]

A second non-price rationing device used during the petrol crisis was that of **favoured customers**. Many petrol station owners decided not to sell petrol to the general public at all but to reserve their scarce supplies for friends and favoured customers. Not surprisingly, many customers tried to become 'favoured' by offering payments to petrol station owners. Owners also charged high prices for service; by doing so, they increased the real price of petrol but hid it in service overcharges to get around the ceiling.

queuing A non-price rationing mechanism that uses waiting in a queue as a means of distributing goods and services.

favoured customers Those who receive special treatment from dealers during conditions of excess demand.

---

[1]*You can also show formally that the result is inefficient – that there is a resulting net loss of total value to society. First, there is the cost of waiting in the queue. Time has a value. With price rationing, no one has to wait in a queue and the value of that time is saved. Second, there may be additional lost value if the petrol ends up in the hands of someone who places a lower value on it than someone else who gets no petrol. Suppose, for example, that the market price of petrol if unconstrained would rise to €2, but that the government has it fixed at €1. There will be long queues for petrol. Imagine that to motorist A, ten litres of petrol is worth €35 but that she fails to get it because her time is too valuable to wait in a queue. To motorist B, ten litres is worth only €15, but his time is worth much less, so he gets the petrol. Clearly, in the end, A could pay B for the petrol and both could be better off. If A pays B €30 for the petrol, A is €5 better off and B is €15 better off. In addition, A doesn't have to wait in a queue. Thus, the allocation that results from non-price rationing involves a net loss of value. Such losses are called* dead weight losses.

ration coupons
Tickets or coupons that entitle individuals to purchase a certain amount of a given product per month.

Yet another method of dividing up available supply is the use of **ration coupons**. It was suggested in both 1974 and 1979 that families be given ration tickets, or coupons, that would entitle them to purchase a certain number of litres of petrol each month. That way, everyone would get the same amount, regardless of income. Such a system had been employed in Europe during the 1940s, when wartime price ceilings on meat, sugar, butter, tyres, nylon stockings and many other items were imposed.

When ration coupons are used with no prohibition against trading them, however, the result is almost identical to a system of price rationing. Those who are willing and able to pay the most simply buy up the coupons and use them to purchase fuel, chocolate, fresh eggs or anything else that is sold at a restricted price.[2] This means that the price of the restricted good will effectively rise to the market-clearing price. For instance, suppose that you decide not to sell your ration coupon. You are then forgoing what you would have received by selling the coupon. Thus the 'real' price of the good you purchase will be higher (if only in opportunity cost) than the restricted price. Even when trading coupons is declared illegal, it is virtually impossible to stop black markets from developing. In a **black market**, illegal trading takes place at market-determined prices.

black market
A market in which illegal trading takes place at market-determined prices.

The 1998 World Cup

Another way to understand the rationing function of the price system is to look at the ways in which tickets to popular sporting events and concerts are sold and distributed. One of the most interesting recent examples is the 1998 World Cup football tournament.

In the summer of 1998, the World Cup finals went to France. The matches took place in a number of cities, including Paris, Marseilles, Bordeaux and Lyon. A total of 64 matches were played by qualifying teams representing 32 countries. The final itself, between France and Brazil, was played on 12 July in the Stade de France in Paris. (France won 3–0.)

Demand for football tickets was very high. Football is without question the most popular sport in the world, and it is literally true that wars have been fought because of the outcome of matches. With national pride at stake, tens of thousands of people flocked to France. As in previous tournaments, rather than charging market-clearing prices, the event's organizers decided to charge 'fair' prices.

These prices were below equilibrium, and there was excess demand for the tickets from the time that they went on sale. Interestingly, organizers of similar high-interest sporting events (like the Wimbledon tennis tournament and the British Open golf championship) almost always price tickets below the level that would just fill the available seating. Why? In their words, to do otherwise would be 'unfair'; only the 'rich' would be able to attend if prices were set too high.

We have seen, however, that if the price system is not going to be used to allocate the tickets among demanders, another method must be found. One method gives the tickets to certain favoured customers. Over sixty per cent of the tickets for the World Cup in 1998 were committed to French nationals. Many were distributed to corporate sponsors, city officials and other dignitaries. Some were allocated to countries whose teams were taking part.

The distribution of tickets was not really over until the final match was played. Consider the demand for tickets to the final that were distributed months earlier. The organizers did charge more for final tickets – the price of the cheapest ticket was over €40 and the average close to €100. But consider the potential demand! Because the Stade de France stadium holds only 80,000 people, by some estimates the equilibrium ticket price was in the vicinity of €1000!

---

[2] *Of course, if you are assigned a number of tickets, and you sell them, you are better off than you would be with price rationing. Rationing tickets thus serve as a way of redistributing income.*

Figure 5.4 Supply of and demand for 1998 World Cup final tickets

Some tickets for the final of the 1998 World Cup were initially sold for a face price of about €100. The Stade de France near Paris holds 80,000 people, so the supply curve is vertical at 80,000 tickets. At €100, the quantity demanded far exceeded the quantity supplied. The result was enormous excess demand.

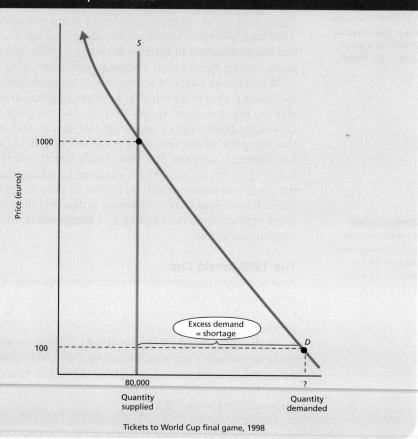

Tickets to World Cup final game, 1998

Figure 5.4 illustrates the situation. The supply curve is vertical at 80,000 tickets – the fixed number of seats available. As the demand curve shows, some people were willing to pay prices far in excess of €100 – and many did. Even before tickets were issued, an extensive and complicated black market had begun operating. Ticket agents ran advertisements in newspapers offering huge sums for good seats in order to resell them at a profit. All this was despite the best efforts of the French authorities to prevent it.

Now consider someone who paid €100 for a final ticket and went to the game. What price did she really pay to go to the match? The answer: a lot more than €100, because she could easily have sold her ticket for many times what she paid for it. The opportunity cost of going to the match was very high. To attend the final she had to give up the opportunity to sell her ticket at a great profit. By not selling her ticket, she revealed that going to the match was worth more to her than all the other things that €1000 could buy.

What, then, can we conclude about alternatives to the price rationing system?

No matter how good the intentions of private organizations and governments, it is very difficult to prevent the price system from operating and to stop willingness to pay from asserting itself. Every time an alternative is tried, the price system seems to sneak in the back door. With favoured customers and black markets, the final distribution may be even more unfair than that which would result from simple price rationing.

Applications

Proposals for extensions of the price system: traffic jams

Very few people have not had the frustrating experience of sitting in traffic. Traffic jams are by no means unique to Europe. Some of the worst traffic congestion in the world can be found in Bangkok in Thailand and Taipei in Taiwan.

Traffic jams are costly. Clearly, time has a value, and the opportunity cost of sitting in traffic for two hours can be significant. Ask yourself how much you would be willing to pay to avoid it. A recent estimate put the cost of the morning rush hour in a major US city at over $13 million.

You can think of congestion as 'excess demand for road space'. That is, at the current price, the quantity demanded exceeds the quantity supplied. The way we currently ration that shortage of space is by queueing in long lines of traffic to use it.

Can we use the price mechanism to help? Although this idea goes back at least 100 years, most give credit to the late Nobel Prize winning economist William Vickrey for promoting an idea whose time may have finally come. The idea is simple: charge people a price to use the roads, a price high enough to keep the traffic flowing. As the price is raised, those who live near public transport and those who might be able to avoid travelling altogether would avoid the congested roads – at least during peak hours. In essence, quantity demanded will drop. Those who must continue to use the roads will pay, but they will not waste time waiting in traffic.

How might such a price be collected? One obvious answer is a toll. Many countries impose tolls for the use of bridges, but most prices are low enough that they have little impact on road use. The City State of Singapore requires car owners to purchase a very expensive licence, to be displayed on the windscreen, if they want to drive on city centre streets during peak hours. Professor Vickrey proposed that every car should be equipped with a radio signal that would register a charge every time the car passed a designated road junction. The charges could be varied according to the time of day and the degree of congestion in the area.

With today's small powerful microprocessors, the necessary technology is already there; it is already being used in some places to speed traffic through toll gates. Some analysts think that the next few years will see a dramatic increase in road prices.

Prices and the allocation of resources

Thinking of the market system as a mechanism for allocating scarce goods and services among competing demanders is very revealing. But the market determines much more than just the distribution of final outputs. It also determines what gets produced and therefore how resources are allocated among competing uses.

Consider a change in consumer preferences that leads to an increase in demand for a specific good or service. In recent decades, for example, people have been going to restaurants much more frequently than before. Researchers think that this trend, which continues today, is partly the result of social changes (such as a dramatic rise in the number of two-earner families) and partly the result of rising incomes. The market responded to this change in demand by shifting resources, both capital and labour, into more and better restaurants.

With the increase in demand for restaurant meals, the price of eating out rose, and the restaurant business became more profitable. The higher profits attracted new businesses and provided old restaurants with an incentive to expand. As new capital, seeking profits, flowed into the restaurant business, so too did labour. New restaurants need chefs. Chefs need training, and the higher wages that came with increased demand provided an incentive for them to get it. In response to the increase in demand for training, new cooking schools opened up and existing schools began to offer courses in the culinary arts.

This story could run on and on, but the point is clear:

Price changes resulting from shifts of demand in output markets cause profits to rise or fall. Profits attract capital; losses lead to disinvestment. Higher wages attract labour and encourage workers to acquire skills. At the core of the system, supply, demand, and prices in input and output markets determine the allocation of resources and the ultimate combinations of things produced.

Supply and demand analysis: the Common Agricultural Policy

The basic logic of supply and demand is a powerful tool of analysis. As an extended example of the power of this logic, we will consider some aspects of the European Union's Common Agricultural Policy (CAP).

All the members of the EU are part of the CAP. It's main purpose is to achieve assured supplies of food by making the EU largely self-sufficient in the production of agricultural commodities. This requires considerable intervention in agricultural markets. Without such intervention, consumers would obtain supplies from the cheapest source, which is often from outside the EU.

The main way in which the CAP achieves its purpose is by raising agricultural prices above market-determined prices, so encouraging EU farmers to grow more and consumers to consume less. The two ways of raising prices are first, import taxes, or tariffs, and second, intervention buying. We will concentrate first on the effect of tariffs.

Simple supply and demand analysis makes the argument for the tariff easier to understand. The first diagram in Figure 5.5 shows the world market for many agricultural foodstuffs in the *absence* of EU tariffs. The world market determines the equilibrium price of a given commodity, shown in Figure 5.5 as P_w.

Figure 5.5b shows the European market. Assume that Europe can buy all that it wants at the world price of P_w. This means that domestic producers cannot get away with charging any more than that price. (Why would anyone pay more for the European product when they can get as much of the foreign commodity as they want at P_w?) The curve labelled *Supply*Europe shows the amount that domestic suppliers will produce at each price level. At a price of P_w (assumed to be €18) production is Q_1. Stated somewhat differently, European producers will produce at point A on the supply curve. The total quantity demanded in Europe is Q_2 per day. This can also be seen in Figure 5.5b. At a price of P_w, the quantity demanded in Europe is at point B on the demand curve, labelled *Demand*Europe.

The difference between the total quantity demanded per day and domestic production per day is total imports per day.

However, the EU imposes a tariff on all imported units of the commodity. What is the size of the tariff? It will normally be expressed as a percentage of the world price, but the percentage figure will vary from one commodity to another. It will also vary from one year to the next for the same commodity. This is necessary if EU farmers are to be assured of a given price level for their crops. If the world price is very low a high tariff is imposed to bring the imported price up to the *intervention price*. A high world price will require a smaller tariff. Hence the tariff is often referred to as a *variable import levy*.

Now suppose that a tax is levied at 33% on this commodity, and let us further suppose that the world price P_w is €18 per unit. The tax will be €6 (or 0.33 × €18). This means that importers in Europe will pay a total of €24 per unit (18 + 6).

This new higher price means that European producers can also charge up to €24 for a unit of output. Note, however, that the tax is paid only on imports. Thus the entire €24 paid for domestic output goes to the domestic producers.

Figure 5.5c shows the result of the tax. First, the higher price leads to a reduction in the quantity demanded to Q_3. This is a movement along the demand curve from point B to point D. At the same time, the quantity supplied by domestic producers increases to Q_4. This is a movement along the supply curve from point A to point C. With an increase in domestic quantity supplied and a decrease in domestic quantity demanded, imports decrease to $Q_4 - Q_3$.

The tax also generates revenues for the EU budget. The total tax revenue collected is equal to the tax per unit (€6) times the number of imported units. Since the quantity imported is $Q_4 - Q_3$, total revenue is $(Q_4 - Q_3) \times €6$ per day. This amount is shown as the shaded area in Figure 5.5c.

Figure 5.5 The world and European markets for agricultural products

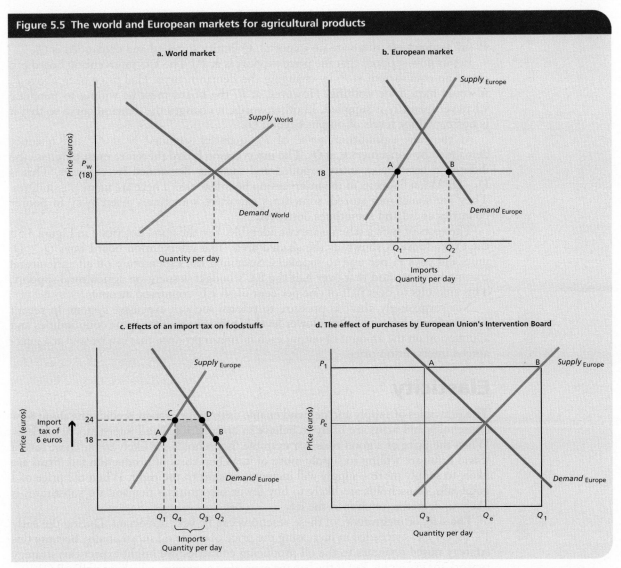

At a world price of €18, domestic production is Q_1 and the total quantity demanded in Europe is Q_2. The difference is total imports. If the government levies a 33% tax on imports, the price rises to €24. The quantity demanded falls to Q_3. At the same time, the quantity supplied by domestic producers increases to Q_4 and the quantity imported falls to $Q_4 – Q_3$. Intervention boards raise the price of foodstuffs by purchasing. This increases demand, raising price to P_1. The board buys $Q_3 – Q_1$ at a total cost to taxpayers of $(Q_3 – Q_1)AB$.

What does all this mean? In the final analysis the tariff will (1) increase domestic production and (2) reduce overall consumption and therefore reduce EU dependence on foreign food supplies. Domestic producers gain from the increased prices at home and the EU budget gets some revenue. However, the news is not all good. Consumers pay higher prices for their food, which is a particularly severe problem for lower-income groups. There is also a problem in that EU countries have less output of other things. Increased domestic production requires increased resources. Those resources have an opportunity cost.

The EU intervenes in other ways too, even in those commodities where Europe is self-sufficient. The EU sometimes wishes its food producers to have a price higher than the equilibrium price that would be determined in the absence of imports. It achieves this by creating an artificial demand for the commodity. We can illustrate the procedure with Figure 5.5d. In the absence of price support the equilibrium price is P_e (by assumption, there are no imports). Quantity supplied and demanded is Q_e.

Let us now suppose that the price support is at P_1. The EU intervention board can create an equilibrium at P_1 by changing the demand curve. Had price been above P_1 it would have done nothing. However, at P_1 the board must be willing to purchase whatever quantity is supplied. In other words, it changes the demand curve so that it is horizontal for levels of output beyond Q_3.

At the new equilibrium price of P_1, quantity supplied is at Q_1 and quantity demanded by consumers is at Q_3. The intervention board therefore must purchase the difference between quantity supplied and quantity demanded *by consumers*. This is $Q_3 - Q_1$. What happens to the intervention board stocks? There are many possibilities. They are sometimes stored, sometimes exported, sometimes given away to poorer countries as aid and sometimes destroyed.

The costs of such a scheme are considerable. For the good described in Figure 5.5d the expenditure is shown as the shaded area. The intervention board buys $Q_3 - Q_1$ units and pays P_1 per unit to suppliers. Summing the expenditure on all agricultural commodities we find that over half the EU's budget is spent on agricultural support. This amounts to over half of one per cent of all EU countries' income.

Not surprisingly, there is pressure to reform such an expensive system. In recent years, reforms have included a lower level of price support for some commodities and a limitation on the amount of output each farm can produce that can be sold at a guaranteed intervention price.

Elasticity

The principles of supply and demand enable us to make certain predictions about how households and firms are likely to behave in both national and international markets. When the price of a good rises, for example, households are likely to purchase less of it and firms are willing to supply more of it. When costs of production fall, firms are likely to supply more – supply will increase, or shift to the right. When the price of a good falls, households are likely to buy fewer substitutes – demand for substitutes is likely to decrease, or shift to the left.

The size, or magnitude, of these reactions can be very important. During the early 1970s, OPEC succeeded in increasing the price of crude oil substantially. Because this strategy raised revenues to the oil producing countries, we might expect this strategy to work for everyone. But if the banana exporting countries, which we will call OBEC, had done the same thing, the strategy would not have worked.

Why? Suppose the banana exporting countries decide to cut production by 30% in order to drive up the world price of bananas. At first, when the quantity of bananas supplied declines, the quantity demanded is greater than the quantity supplied and the world price rises. The issue for OBEC, however, is *how much* the world price will rise. That is, how much will people be willing to pay to continue consuming bananas? Unless the percentage *increase* in price is greater than the percentage *decrease* in output, the OBEC countries will lose revenues. And a little research shows us that the news is not good for OBEC. There are many reasonable substitutes for bananas. As the price of bananas rises, people simply eat fewer bananas and eat more pineapples or oranges. Many people are simply not willing to pay a higher price for bananas. The quantity of bananas demanded declines 30% – to the new quantity supplied – after only a modest price rise, and OBEC fails in its mission; its revenues decrease instead of increase.

The quantity of oil demanded is not nearly as responsive to a change in price because no substitutes for oil are readily available. When the price of crude oil went up in the early 1970s, millions of cars were on the roads consuming petrol. Millions of homes were heated with oil, and industry ran on equipment that used petroleum products. When OPEC cut production, the price of oil rose sharply. Quantity demanded fell somewhat, but price increased by over 400%. What makes the cases of

OPEC and OBEC different is the *magnitude* of the response in the quantity demanded to a change of price.

The importance of actual measurement cannot be overstated. Without the ability to measure and predict how much people are likely to respond to economic changes, all the economic theory in the world would be of little help to policy makers. In fact, most of the research being done in economics today involves the collection and analysis of quantitative data that measure behaviour. This is a dramatic change in the discipline of economics that has taken place only in the last 30 years.

elasticity
A general concept that can be used to quantify the response in one variable when another variable changes.

Economists commonly measure responsiveness using the concept of **elasticity**. Elasticity is a general concept that can be used to quantify the response in one variable when another variable changes. If some variable A changes in response to changes in another variable B the elasticity of A with respect to B is equal to the percentage change in A divided by the percentage change in B:

$$\text{elasticity of } A \text{ with respect to } B = \frac{\%\Delta A}{\%\Delta B}$$

We may speak, for instance, of the elasticity of demand or supply with respect to price, of the elasticity of investment with respect to the interest rate, or of the elasticity of tax payments with respect to income. We begin with a discussion of price elasticity of demand.

Price elasticity of demand

You have already seen the law of demand at work. Recall that, *ceteris paribus*, when prices rise, quantity demanded can be expected to decline. When prices fall, quantity demanded can be expected to rise. The normal negative relationship between price and quantity demanded is reflected in the downward slope of demand curves.

Slope and elasticity

The slope of a demand curve may in a rough way reveal the responsiveness of the quantity demanded to price changes, but slope can be quite misleading. In fact, it is not a good formal measure of responsiveness.

Consider the two identical demand curves for eggs in Figure 5.6. The only difference between the two is that quantity demanded is measured in boxes of eggs in the graph on the left and in eggs in the graph on the right, assuming that eggs are sold in boxes of ten. When we calculate the numerical value of each slope, however, we get very different answers. The curve on the left has a slope of –1/5, and the curve on the right has a slope of –1/50, yet the two curves represent *exactly the same behaviour*. (Review the Appendix to Chapter 1 if you don't understand how these numbers are calculated.)

The problem is that the numerical value of slope depends on the units used to measure the variables on the axes. To correct this problem, we convert the changes in price and quantity to percentages. The price increase in Figure 5.6 leads to a decline of 5 boxes, or 50 eggs, in the quantity of demanded – a decline of 50% from the initial quantity, whether we measure the eggs in boxes or individually.

price elasticity of demand
The ratio of the percentage change in quantity demanded to the percentage change in price; it measures the responsiveness of demand to changes in price.

We define **price elasticity of demand**, then, simply as the ratio of the percentage change in quantity demanded to the percentage change in price. Stated formally:

$$\text{price elasticity of demand} = \frac{\%\text{ change in quantity demanded}}{\%\text{ change in price}}$$

Percentage changes should always carry the sign (plus or minus) of the change. Positive changes, or increases, take a +. Negative changes, or decreases, take a –. The law of demand implies that price elasticity of demand is nearly always a negative number: price increases (+) will lead to decreases in quantity demanded (–), and vice versa. Thus, the numerator and denominator should have opposite signs, resulting in a negative ratio.

Figure 5.6 Slope is not a useful measure of responsiveness

Changing the unit of measure from boxes of eggs to eggs changes the measured slope of the demand curve dramatically. But the behaviour of buyers in the two diagrams is identical.

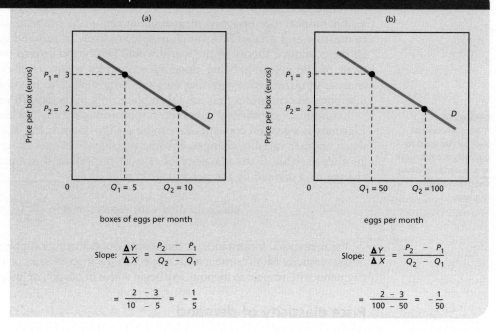

$$\text{Slope:} \quad \frac{\Delta Y}{\Delta X} = \frac{P_2 - P_1}{Q_2 - Q_1}$$

$$= \frac{2 - 3}{10 - 5} = -\frac{1}{5}$$

$$\text{Slope:} \quad \frac{\Delta Y}{\Delta X} = \frac{P_2 - P_1}{Q_2 - Q_1}$$

$$= \frac{2 - 3}{100 - 50} = -\frac{1}{50}$$

Types of elasticity

Table 5.1 gives the hypothetical responses of demanders to a 10% price increase in four markets. Insulin is absolutely necessary to an insulin-dependent diabetic, and the quantity demanded is unlikely to respond to an increase in price. When the quantity demanded does not respond at all to a price change, the percentage change in quantity demanded is zero, and the elasticity is zero. In this case, we say that the demand for the product is **perfectly inelastic**. Figure 5.7a illustrates the perfectly inelastic demand for insulin. Because quantity demanded does not change at all when price changes, the demand curve is simply a vertical line.

Unlike insulin, a basic telephone service is generally considered a necessity, but not an absolute necessity. If a 10% increase in telephone rates results in a 1% decline in the quantity of service demanded, demand elasticity is $(-1 \div 10) = -0.1$.

When the percentage change in quantity demanded is smaller in absolute size than the percentage change in price, as is the case with telephone service, then elasticity is less than one in absolute size.[3] When a product has an elasticity between zero and minus one, we say that demand is **inelastic**. The demand for basic telephone service is

perfectly inelastic demand

Demand in which quantity demanded does not respond at all to a change in price.

inelastic demand

Demand that responds somewhat, but not a great deal, to changes in price. Inelastic demand always has a numerical value between zero and minus one.

Table 5.1 Hypothetical demand elasticities for four products

Product	% change in price (%ΔP)	% change in quantity demanded (%ΔQ_D)	Elasticity (%$\Delta Q_D \div$ %ΔP)
Insulin	+10	0	0 6 ⟶ perfectly inelastic
Basic telephone service	+10	−1	−0.1 6 ⟶ inelastic
Beef	+10	−10	−1.0 6 ⟶ unitarily elastic
Bananas	+10	−30	−3.0 6 ⟶ elastic

[3]*Remember that the term* absolute size *or* absolute value *means ignoring the sign. The absolute value of −4 is 4; the absolute value of −3.8 is greater than the absolute value of 2.*

Figure 5.7 Perfectly inelastic, perfectly elastic and unitary elastic demand curves

Figure 5.7a shows a perfectly inelastic demand curve for insulin. Price elasticity of demand is zero. Quantity demanded is fixed; it does not change at all when price changes. Figure 5.7b shows a perfectly elastic demand curve for one farmer's potatoes. A tiny price increase drives the quantity demanded to zero. In essence, perfectly elastic demand implies that individual producers can sell all they want at the going market price but cannot charge a higher price. Figure 5.7c shows a unit elastic demand curve.

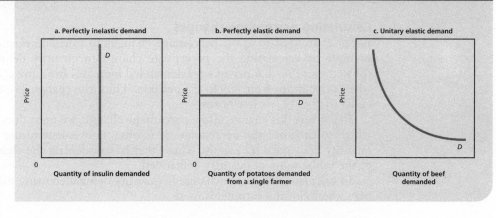

a. Perfectly inelastic demand — Quantity of insulin demanded

b. Perfectly elastic demand — Quantity of potatoes demanded from a single farmer

c. Unitary elastic demand — Quantity of beef demanded

inelastic at –0.1. Stated simply, inelastic demand means that there is some responsiveness of demand, but not a great deal, to a change in price.

A warning: you must be very careful about signs. Because it is generally understood that demand elasticities are negative (demand curves have a negative slope), they are often reported and discussed without the negative sign. For example, a technical paper might report that the demand for housing 'appears to be inelastic with respect to price, or less than one (0.6)'. What the writer means is that the estimated elasticity is –0.6, which is between 0 and –1. Its absolute value is less than one.

Returning to Table 5.1, we see that a 10% increase in beef prices drives down the quantity of beef demanded by 10%. Demand elasticity is thus (–10 ÷ 10) = –1. When the percentage change in quantity of product demanded is the same as the percentage change in price in absolute value, we say that the demand for that product has unitary elasticity. The elasticity of a **unitarily elastic** product is always minus one (–1). As Table 5.1 shows, the demand for beef is assumed to be of unitary elasticity.

When the percentage decrease in quantity demanded is larger than the percentage increase in price, we say that demand is **elastic**. The demand for bananas, for example, is likely to be quite elastic because there are many substitutes for bananas (other fruits, for instance). If a 10% increase in the price of bananas leads to a 30% decrease in the quantity of bananas demanded, the price elasticity of demand for bananas is (–30 ÷ 10) = –3. When the absolute value of elasticity exceeds 1, demand is elastic.

Finally, if a small increase in the price of a product causes the quantity demanded to drop immediately to zero, demand for that product is said to be **perfectly elastic**. Suppose, for example, that you produce a product that can be sold only at a predetermined, fixed price. If you charged even one penny more, no one would buy your product because people would simply buy from another producer who hadn't raised the price. This is very close to reality for many farmers, who cannot charge more for crops such as potatoes than their current market price.

A perfectly elastic demand curve is illustrated in Figure 5.7b. Because the quantity demanded drops to zero above a certain price, the demand curve for a perfectly elastic good is a horizontal line. Perfect elasticity implies that individual producers can sell all they want at a fixed price but cannot charge a higher price.

Calculating elasticities

Elasticities must be calculated cautiously. Return for a moment to the demand curves in Figure 5.6. The fact that these two identical demand curves have dramatically different slopes should be enough to convince you that slope is a poor measure of responsiveness.

The concept of elasticity circumvents the measurement problem posed by the graphs in Figure 5.6 by converting the changes in price and quantity into percentage

unitary elasticity
A demand relationship in which the percentage change in quantity of a product demanded is the same as the percentage change in price in absolute value (a demand elasticity of –1).

elastic demand
A demand relationship in which the percentage change in quantity demanded is larger in absolute value than the percentage change in price (a demand elasticity with an absolute value greater than 1).

perfectly elastic demand
Demand in which quantity demanded drops to zero at the slightest increase in price.

changes. Recall that elasticity of demand is the *percentage* change in quantity demanded divided by the *percentage* change in price.

Calculating percentage changes

Because we need to know percentage changes to calculate elasticity, let's begin our example by calculating the percentage change in quantity demanded. Figure 5.6a showed that the quantity of eggs demanded increases from five (Q_1) to ten boxes (Q_2) when price drops from €3 to €2 per box. Thus, the change in quantity demanded is equal to $Q_2 - Q_1$, or five boxes.

To convert this change into a percentage change, we must decide on a base against which to calculate the percentage. It is often convenient to use the initial value of quantity demanded (Q_1) as the base – that is, to calculate the change as a percentage of the initial value of quantity demanded.

To calculate percentage change in quantity demanded using the initial value as the base, the following formula is used:

$$\% \text{ change in quantity demanded} = \frac{\text{change in quantity demanded}}{Q_1} \times 100$$

$$= \frac{Q_2 - Q_1}{Q_1} \times 100$$

In Figure 5.6, $Q_2 = 10$ and $Q_1 = 5$. Thus:

$$\% \text{ change in quantity demanded} = \frac{10 - 5}{5} \times 100 = \frac{5}{5} \times 100 = 100\%$$

Expressing this equation verbally, we can say that an increase in quantity demanded from five to ten boxes is a 100% increase from five boxes. Note that you arrive at exactly the same result if you use the diagram in Figure 5.6b, in which quantity demanded is measured in individual eggs. An increase from Q_1 (50 eggs) to Q_2 (100 eggs) is a 100% increase.

We can calculate the percentage change in price in a similar way. Once again, let's use the initial value of P (that is, P_1) as the base for calculating the percentage. Using P_1 as the base, the formula for calculating the percentage change in P is simply:

$$\% \text{ change in price} = \frac{\text{change in price}}{P_1} \times 100$$

$$= \frac{P_2 - P_1}{P_1} \times 100$$

In Figure 5.6a, P_2 equals 2, and P_1 equals 3. Thus, the change in P, or ΔP, is a negative number: $P_2 - P_1 = 2 - 3 = -1$. This is true because the change is a decrease in price. Plugging the values of P_1 and P_2 into the equation above, we get:

$$\% \text{ change in price} = \frac{2 - 3}{3} \times 100 = \frac{-1}{3} \times 100 = -33.3\%$$

In other words, decreasing price from €3 to €2 is a 33.3% decline.

Elasticity is a ratio of percentages

Once all the changes in quantity demanded and price have been converted into percentages, calculating elasticity is a matter of simple division. Recall the formal definition of elasticity:

$$\text{price elasticity of demand} = \frac{\text{\% change in quantity demanded}}{\text{\% change in price}}$$

If demand is elastic, the ratio of percentage change in quantity demanded to percentage change in price will have an absolute value greater than one. If demand is inelastic, the ratio will have an absolute value between zero and one. If the two percentages are exactly equal, so that a given percentage change in price causes an equal percentage change in quantity demanded, elasticity is equal to minus one; this is unitary elasticity.

Substituting the percentages calculated above, we see that a 33.3% decrease in price leads to a 100% increase in quantity demanded; thus:

$$\text{price elasticity of demand} = \frac{+100\%}{-33.3\%} = -3.0$$

According to these calculations, the demand for eggs is elastic.

The midpoint formula

Although simple, the use of the initial values of P and Q as the bases for calculating percentage changes can be misleading. Let's return to the example of demand for eggs in Figure 5.6a, where we have a change in quantity demanded of five boxes. Using the initial value Q_1 as the base, we calculated that this change represents a 100% increase over the base. Now suppose that the price of eggs rises back to 3 euros per box, causing the quantity demanded to drop back to five boxes. How much of a percentage decrease in quantity demanded is this? We now have $Q_1 = 10$ and $Q_2 = 5$. Using the same formula we used above, we get:

$$\text{\% change in quantity demanded} = \frac{\text{change in quantity demanded}}{Q_1 \times 100}$$

$$= \frac{Q_2 - Q_1}{Q_1} \times 100$$

$$= \frac{5 - 10}{10} \times 100 = -50\%$$

Thus, an increase from five to ten boxes is a 100% increase (because the initial value used for the base is 5), while a decrease from ten to five boxes is only a 50% decrease (because the initial value used for the base is 10). This does not make much sense because in both cases we are calculating elasticity on the same interval on the demand curve. Changing 'direction' of the calculation should not change the elasticity.

To describe percentage changes more accurately, a simple convention has been adopted. Instead of using the initial values of Q and P as the bases for calculating percentages, we use these values' *midpoints* as the bases. That is, we use the value halfway between P_1 and P_2 for the base in calculating the percentage change in price, and the value halfway between Q_1 and Q_2 as the base for calculating percentage change in quantity demanded.

Thus, the **midpoint formula** for calculating the percentage change in quantity demanded becomes:

$$\text{\% change in quantity demanded} = \frac{\text{change in quantity demanded}}{(Q_1 + Q_2)/2} \times 100$$

$$= \frac{Q_2 - Q_1}{(Q_1 + Q_2)/2} \times 100$$

Substituting the numbers from the original Figure 5.6a we get:

midpoint formula
A more precise way of calculating percentages using the value halfway between P_1 and P_2 for the base in calculating the percentage change in price, and the value halfway between Q_1 and Q_2 as the base for calculating the percentage change in quantity demanded.

$$\% \text{ change in quantity demanded} = \frac{10 - 5}{(5 + 10)/2} \times 100 = \frac{5}{7/5} \times 100 = 66.6\%$$

Using the point halfway between P_1 and P_2 as the base for calculating the percentage change in price, we get:

$$\% \text{ change in price} = \frac{\text{change in price}}{(P_1 + P_2)/2} \times 100$$

$$= \frac{P_2 - P_1}{(P_1 + P_2)/2} \times 100$$

Substituting the numbers from the original Figure 5.6a yields:

$$\% \text{ change in price} = \frac{2 - 3}{(2 + 3)/2} \times 100 = \frac{-1}{2.5} \times 100 = -40.0\%$$

We can thus say that a change from a quantity of 5 to a quantity of 10 is a +66.6% change using the midpoint formula, and a change in price from 3 to 2 euros is a −40% change using the midpoint formula.

Using these percentages to calculate elasticity yields:

$$\text{price elasticity of demand} = \frac{\% \text{ change in quantity demanded}}{\% \text{ change in price}} = \frac{66.6\%}{-40\%} = -1.67$$

Using the midpoint formula in this case gives a lower absolute value of demand elasticity, but the demand remains elastic because the percentage change in quantity demanded is still greater than the percentage change in price in absolute size.

The calculations based on the midpoint approach are summarized in Table 5.2.

Elasticity changes along a straight line demand curve

An interesting and important point is that elasticity changes from point to point along a demand curve even if the slope of that demand curve does not change – that is, even along a straight-line demand curve. Indeed, the differences in elasticity along a demand curve can be quite large.

Table 5.2 Calculating price elasticity with the midpoint formula

First, calculate percentage change in quantity demanded ($\%\Delta Q_D$):

$$\% \text{ change in quantity demanded} = \frac{\text{change in quantity demanded}}{(Q_1 + Q_2)/2} \times 100 = \frac{Q_2 - Q_1}{(Q_1 + Q_2)/2} \times 100$$

Substituting the numbers from Figure 5.6

$$\% \text{ change in quantity demanded} = \frac{10 - 5}{(10 + 5)/2} \times 100 = \frac{5}{7.5} \times 100 = 66.6\%$$

Next, calculate percentage change in price ($\%\Delta P$):

$$\% \text{ change in price} = \frac{\text{change in price}}{(P_1 + P_2)/2} \times 100 = \frac{P_2 - P_1}{(P_1 + P_2)/2} \times 100$$

Substituting the numbers from Figure 5.6:

$$\% \text{ change in price} = \frac{2 - 3}{(3 + 2)/2} \times 100 = \frac{-1}{2.5} \times 100 = -40.0\%$$

Price elasticity compares the percentage change in quantity demanded and the percentage change in price:

$$\frac{\%\Delta Q_D}{\%\Delta P} = -\frac{66.6\%}{40.0\%}$$

$$= -1.67$$

$$= \text{price elasticity of demand}$$

Demand is elastic

Table 5.3 Demand schedule for Commission dining room lunches

Price per lunch (euros)	Quantity demanded (lunches per month)
11	0
10	2
9	4
8	6
7	8
6	10
5	12
4	14
3	16
2	18
1	20
0	22

Consider the demand schedule shown in Table 5.3 and the demand curve in Figure 5.8. Peter works about 22 days per month for the European Commission in Brussels. In the building is a pleasant dining room. If lunch in the dining room costs €10, Peter would eat there only twice a month. If the price of lunch falls to €9, he would eat there four times a month. (Peter would bring his lunch to work on other days.) If lunch were only €1, he would eat there 20 times a month.

Let's calculate price elasticity of demand between points A and B on the demand curve in Figure 5.8. Moving from A to B, the price of a lunch drops from €10 to €9

Figure 5.8 Demand curve for lunch in the European Commission dining room

Between points A and B, demand is quite elastic at −6.4. Between points C and D, demand is quite inelastic at −0.294.

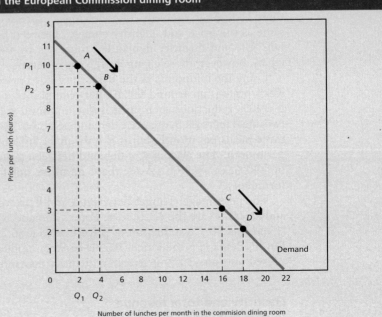

Number of lunches per month in the commision dining room

(a decrease of €1) and the number of dining room lunches that Peter eats per month increases from two to four (an increase of two). We will use the midpoint approach.

First, we calculate the percentage change in quantity demanded:

$$\text{\% change in quantity demanded} = \frac{Q_2 - Q_1}{(Q_1 + Q_2)/2} \times 100$$

Substituting the numbers from Figure 5.8, we get:

$$\text{\% change in quantity demanded} = \frac{4 - 2}{(4 + 2)/2} \times 100 = \frac{2}{3} \times 100 = 66.7\%$$

Next, we calculate the percentage change in price:

$$\text{\% change in price} = \frac{P_2 - P_1}{(P_1 + P_2)/2} \times 100$$

Substituting the numbers from Figure 5.8:

$$\text{\% change in price} = \frac{9 - 10}{(9 + 10)/2} \times 100 = \frac{-1}{9.5} \times 100 = -10.5\%$$

Finally, we calculate elasticity by comparing the two ratios as:

$$\text{elasticity of demand} = \frac{\text{\% change in quantity demanded}}{\text{\% change in price}}$$

$$= \frac{66.7\%}{-10.5\%} = -6.4$$

The percentage change in quantity demanded is 6.4 times larger than the percentage change in price. In other words, Peter's demand between points A and B is quite responsive; his demand between points A and B is elastic.

Now consider a different movement along the same demand curve in Figure 5.8. Moving from point C to point D, the graph indicates that at a price of €3, Peter eats in the Commission dining room 16 times per month. If the price drops to €2, he eats there 18 times per month. These changes expressed in numerical terms are exactly the same as the price and quantity changes between points A and B in the figure – price falls €1, and quantity demanded increases by two meals. Expressed in percentage terms, however, these changes are very different.

Using the midpoints as the base, the 1 euro price decline is only a 10.5% reduction when price is up around €9.50, between points A and B. The same €1 price decline is a 40% reduction when price is down around €2.50, between points C and D. The two-meal increase in quantity demanded is a 66.7% increase when Peter averages only three meals per month, but it is only an 11.76% increase when he averages 17 meals per month. The elasticity of demand between points C and D is thus 11.76% divided by –40%, or –0.294. (Work these numbers out for yourself by using the midpoint formula.)

The percentage changes between A and B are very different from those between C and D, and so are the elasticities. Peter's demand is quite elastic (–6.4) between points A and B; a 10.5% reduction in price caused a 66.7% increase in quantity demanded. But his demand is inelastic (–0.294) between points C and D; a 40% decrease in price caused only an 11.8% increase in quantity demanded.

Elasticity and total revenue

We saw that OPEC increased its revenues in the early 1970s by restricting supply and pushing up the market price of crude oil. We also argued that a similar strategy by

OBEC, the banana exporters, would probably fail. Why? The quantity of oil demanded is not as responsive to a change in price as is the quantity of bananas demanded. In other words, the demand for oil is more inelastic than is the demand for bananas.

We can now use the more formal definition of elasticity to make our argument of why OPEC would succeed and OBEC would fail more precise. In any market, $P \times Q$ is total revenue (TR) received by producers:

$$\text{TR} = P \times Q$$
$$\text{total revenue} = \text{price} \times \text{quantity}$$

OPEC's total revenue is the price per barrel of oil (P) times the number of barrels its participant countries sell (Q). To wheat producers, total revenue is the price per bushel times the number of bushels sold.

As we have seen, when price increases in a market, quantity demanded declines. When price (P) declines, quantity demanded (Q_D) increases. The two factors move in opposite directions:

Effects of price changes $P \uparrow \rightarrow Q_D \downarrow$
on quantity demanded   and
    $P \downarrow \rightarrow Q_D \uparrow$

Because total revenue is the product of P and Q, whether TR rises or falls in response to a price increase depends on which is bigger, the percentage increase in price or the percentage decrease in quantity demanded. If the percentage decrease in quantity demanded is smaller than the percentage increase in price, total revenue will rise. This occurs when demand is *inelastic*. In this case, the percentage price rise simply outweighs the percentage quantity decline, and $P \times Q$ (= TR) rises:

Effect of price increase on $\uparrow P \times Q_D \downarrow = \text{TR} \uparrow$
a product with inelastic demand

If, however, the percentage decline in quantity demanded following a price increase is larger than the percentage increase in price, total revenue will fall. This occurs when demand is *elastic*. The percentage price increase is outweighed by the percentage quantity decline:

Effect of price increase on $\uparrow P \times Q_D \downarrow = \text{TR} \downarrow$
a product with elastic demand

The opposite is true for a price cut. When demand is elastic, a cut in price increases total revenues:

Effect of price cut on $\downarrow P \times Q_D \uparrow = \text{TR} \uparrow$
a product with elastic demand

When demand is inelastic, a cut in price reduces total revenues:

Effect of price cut on $\downarrow P \times Q_D \uparrow = \text{TR} \downarrow$
a product with inelastic demand

Review the logic of these equations to make sure you understand the reasoning thoroughly.

With this knowledge, we can now easily see why OPEC was so effective. The demand for oil is inelastic. Restricting the quantity of oil available led to a huge increase in the price of oil – the percentage increase in the price of oil was larger than the percentage decrease in the quantity of oil demanded. Hence, OPEC's total revenues went up. In contrast, an OBEC cartel would not be effective because the demand for bananas is elastic. A small increase in the price of bananas results in a large decrease in the quantity of bananas demanded and thus causes total revenues to fall.

Maths Box 1 Calculating elasticity of demand at any point on the demand curve

Remember that you will need to have some knowledge in mathematics to follow these boxes. This box requires a basic understanding of calculus. Remember too that these boxes give alternative ways of arriving at a conclusion. You can follow the rest of the text even if you skip these boxes.

Instead of calculating the elasticity of demand at the midpoint of an arc, we can calculate it at any point on the curve we choose, assuming that we know the demand function as represented by the curve.

Elasticity is $\dfrac{dQ}{Q} \div \dfrac{dP}{P}$. We can arrange this to give

$$\frac{dQ}{dP} \times \frac{P}{Q}$$

Thus, at any point on the curve, elasticity can be defined as:

$$\frac{dQ}{dP} \times \frac{P}{Q}$$

Suppose the demand function is $Q = 100 - 2P^2$. Differentiating Q with respect to P gives us

$$\frac{dQ}{dP} = -4P$$

We can now find the elasticity of demand at any point on the curve. What is its value at, say, a price of 3? Q at this point can be found substituting into the demand equation. Hence:

$Q = 100 - 2P^2$
$Q = 100 - 18$
$Q = 82$

At a price of 3: $\dfrac{dQ}{dP} = -4 \times 3 = -12$

Elasticity of demand is: $\dfrac{dQ}{dP} \times \dfrac{P}{Q} = -12 \times \dfrac{3}{82} = -0.44$

At the point on the curve where price is 3 units, demand is inelastic.

For some details on the elasticity experiences of some other businesses, see the Applications box 'London newspapers and European health planners learn about elasticity'.

The determinants of demand elasticity

Elasticity of demand is a way of measuring the responsiveness of consumers' demand to changes in price. As a measure of behaviour, it can be applied to individual households or to market demand as a whole. I love peaches and I would hate to give them up. My demand for peaches is therefore inelastic. But not everyone loves peaches; in fact, the market demand for peaches is relatively elastic. Because no two people have exactly the same preferences, reactions to price changes will be different for different people, and this makes generalizations hazardous. Nonetheless, a few principles do seem to hold.

Availability of substitutes

Perhaps the most obvious factor affecting demand elasticity is the availability of substitutes. When substitute products are easily obtained, the quantity demanded is likely to respond quite readily to changes in price. Consider a number of farm shops in a country district. If every shop sells potatoes of roughly the same type and quality, Westcott Farm will find it very difficult to charge a price much higher than the competition charges because a nearly perfect substitute is available just down the road. The demand for Westcott Farm potatoes is thus likely to be very elastic: an increase in price will lead to a rapid decline in the quantity demanded of Westcott's potatoes.

When substitutes are not readily available, demand is likely to be less elastic. In Table 5.1, we considered one product that has no readily available substitutes, insulin for diabetics. There are many others. Demand for these products is likely to be very inelastic.

The importance of being unimportant

When an item represents a relatively small part of our total budget, we tend to pay little attention to its price. For example, if I pick up a packet of mints once in a while, I might not notice an increase in price from €0.25 to €0.35, yet that is a 40% increase in price. In cases such as these, we are not likely to respond very much to changes in price, and demand is likely to be inelastic.

The time dimension

When the OPEC nations cut output and succeeded in pushing up the price of crude oil in the early 1970s, few substitutes were immediately available. Demand was relatively inelastic, and prices rose substantially. During the last 30 years, however, we have had time to adjust our behaviour in response to the higher price, and the quantity of oil demanded has fallen dramatically. Cars manufactured today get more kilometres per litre, and some drivers have cut down on their driving. Millions have insulated their homes, most have turned down their thermostats, and some have explored alternative energy sources.

All this illustrates a very important point:

> The elasticity of demand in the short run may be very different from the elasticity of demand in the long run. In the longer run, demand is likely to become more elastic, or responsive, simply because households make adjustments over time and producers develop substitute goods.

Applications

London newspapers and European health planners learn about elasticity

Businesses must carefully consider the demand elasticity for their products when adjusting prices. Consider the following two cases.

1. The London *Independent*

Recently, the *Independent*, a daily newspaper printed in London, announced a price cut from 50 p (pence) to 30 p. As a result, its daily circulation increased from 240,000 to 280,000 copies. At first glance, the price cut might seem successful – but look closely at the result.

A price cut from 50 p to 30 p is a 60% reduction (50% using the midpoint formula). The increase in circulation each day is only 16.6% (15.4% using the midpoint formula). Thus, demand is *inelastic*:

$$\text{Elasticity} = \frac{+15.4\%}{-50.0\%} = -0.31$$

When demand is inelastic, a cut in price leads to a reduction in daily revenues.

Before: 50 p × 240,000 copies = 12,000,000 p (£120,000) in revenue

After: 30 p × 280,000 copies = 8,400,000 p (£84,000) in revenue

2. Health care in Europe

In recent years, all European countries have experienced a sharp increase in demand for health care. Like any other service, the provision of health care consumes resources, including hospitals, nurses, respirators, etc. In an important study of European countries, G. Karatzas found that a significant link exists between level of income and the demand for health care. He was also able to quantify the relationship. He discovered that the income elasticity of demand for health care is, at the current level of income, around 0.8–0.9. In other words, if European incomes increase by 1%, health care demand will increase by around 0.9%.

This information is vital for making planning decisions. Over a long period, European incomes have been rising, on average, about 3% per annum. Planners know, then, that if the process continues and there are no other changes affecting health care and demand, resources in this area will have to be increased by over 2½% per annum if European demand for health care is to be met.

Source: G. Karatzas, 'On the effect of income and relative price on the demand for health care – the EC evidence: a comment', Applied Economics, 24, 1992.

Other important elasticities

So far we have been discussing price elasticity of demand, which measures the responsiveness of quantity demanded to changes in price. However, as we noted earlier, elasticity is a perfectly general concept. If B causes a change in A and we can measure the change in both, we can calculate the elasticity of A with respect to B. Let us look briefly at three other important types of elasticity.

Income elasticity of demand

income elasticity of demand
Measures the responsiveness of demand to changes in income.

Income elasticity of demand, which measures the responsiveness of demand with respect to changes in income, is defined as:

$$\text{income elasticity of demand} = \frac{\%\ \text{change in quantity demanded}}{\%\ \text{change in income}}$$

Calculating and measuring income elasticities are important for many reasons. Businesses need to plan ahead, ordering machinery to meet demand over the next few years. Economies are subject to periods of boom and recession. Suppose a boom period is expected. Incomes will be growing. This will increase demand for many firms' products. But *how much* will demand increase? It is the concept of income elasticity that will help to answer the question. So, for example, if the income elasticity of demand for housing is 0.8, then a 10% rise in income is expected to raise the quantity of housing demanded by 8%. Such information is vital to firms in that industry. It enables them to work out the capacity which they will need to have to meet such anticipated demand increases.

Cross-price elasticity of demand

cross-price elasticity of demand
A measure of the response of the quantity of one good demanded to a change in the price of another good.

Cross-price elasticity of demand, which measures the response of quantity of one good demanded to a change in the price of another good, is defined as:

$$\text{cross-price elasticity of demand} = \frac{\%\ \text{change in quantity of } Y \text{ demanded}}{\%\ \text{change in price of } X}$$

Like income elasticity, cross-price elasticity can be either positive or negative. A *positive* cross-price elasticity means that an increase in the price of X causes the demand for Y to rise. This implies that the goods are substitutes. If cross-price elasticity turns out to be *negative*, an increase in the price of X causes a decrease in the demand for Y. This implies that the goods are complements.

Elasticity of supply

elasticity of supply
A measure of the response of quantity of a good supplied to a change in price of that good. Likely to be positive in output markets.

Elasticity of supply, which measures the response of quantity of a good supplied to a change in price of that good, is defined as:

$$\text{elasticity of supply} = \frac{\%\ \text{change in quantity supplied}}{\%\ \text{change in price}}$$

In output markets, the elasticity of supply is likely to be a positive number – that is, a higher price leads to an increase in the quantity supplied, *ceteris paribus*. (Recall our discussion of upward-sloping supply curves in this chapter and the last.)

elasticity of labour supply
A measure of the response of labour supplied to a change in the price of labour.

In input markets, however, some interesting problems crop up. Perhaps the most studied elasticity of all is the **elasticity of labour supply**, which measures the response of labour supplied to a change in the price of labour. Economists have examined household labour supply responses to such government programmes as welfare, social security, the income tax system and unemployment insurance, among others.

In simple terms, the elasticity of labour supply is defined as:

$$\text{elasticity of labour supply} = \frac{\% \text{ change in quantity of labour supplied}}{\% \text{ change in the wage rate}}$$

It seems reasonable at first glance to assume that an increase in wages increases the quantity of labour supplied. That would imply an upward-sloping supply curve and a positive labour supply elasticity. But this is not necessarily so. An increase in wages makes workers better off: they can work the same amount and have higher incomes. One of the things that they might like to 'buy' with that higher income is more leisure time. 'Buying' leisure simply means working fewer hours, and the 'price' of leisure is the lost wages. Thus it is quite possible that an increase in wages to some groups will lead to a reduction in the quantity of labour supplied.

Looking ahead

We have now examined the basic forces of supply and demand and discussed the market/price system. These basic concepts will serve as building blocks for what comes next. Whether you are studying microeconomics or macroeconomics, you will be studying the functions of markets and the behaviour of market participants in more detail in the following chapters.

Since the concepts presented in the first five chapters are so important to your understanding of what is to come, this might be a good point for you to undertake a brief review of Part 1.

Summary

The price system: rationing and allocating resources

1. In a market economy, the market system (or price system) serves two functions. It determines the allocation of resources among producers and the final mix of outputs. It also distributes goods and services on the basis of willingness and ability to pay. In this sense, it serves as a *price rationing* device.

2. Governments sometimes decide not to use the market system to ration an item for which there is an excess demand. Examples of non-price rationing systems include *queuing*, *favoured customers* and *ration coupons*. The most common rationale for policies or practices designed to avoid price rationing is 'fairness'.

3. Attempts to bypass the market and use alternative non-price rationing devices are much more difficult and costly than it would seem at first glance. Schemes that open up opportunities for favoured customers, black markets and side payments often end up less 'fair' than the free market.

Supply and demand analysis: the Common Agricultural Policy

4. The basic logic of supply and demand is a powerful tool for analysis. For example, supply and demand analysis shows that an import tax on agricultural goods will reduce quantity demanded, increase domestic production and generate revenues for the government. However, consumers, particularly in lower-income groups, suffer through higher food prices.

Elasticity

5. *Elasticity* is a general measure of responsiveness that can be used to quantify many different relationships. If one variable A changes in response to changes in another variable B the elasticity of A with respect to B is equal to the percentage change in A divided by the percentage change in B.

6. The slope of a demand curve is an inadequate measure of responsiveness, because its value depends on the units of measurement used. For this reason, elasticities are calculated using percentages.

7. *Price elasticity of demand* is the ratio of the percentage change in quantity demanded of a good to the percentage change in price of that good. *Perfectly inelastic* demand is demand whose quantity demanded does not respond at all to changes in price; its numerical value is zero. *Inelastic* demand is demand whose quantity demanded responds somewhat, but not a great deal, to changes in price; its numerical value is between zero and negative one. *Elastic* demand is demand in which the percentage change in quantity demanded is larger in absolute value than the percentage change in price. Its absolute value is greater than one. *Unitary elasticity* of demand describes a relationship in which the percentage change in the quantity of a product demanded is the same as the percentage change in price; unitary elasticity has a numerical value of minus one. *Perfectly elastic* demand describes a relationship in which a small increase in the price of a product causes the quantity demanded for that product to drop to zero.

8. If demand is elastic, a price increase will reduce the quantity demanded by a larger percentage than the percentage increase in price, and total revenue ($P \times Q$) will fall. If demand is inelastic, a price increase will increase total revenue.

9. If demand is elastic, a price cut will cause quantity demanded to increase by a greater percentage than the percentage decrease in price, and total revenue will rise. If demand is inelastic, a price cut will cause quantity

demanded to increase by a smaller percentage than the percentage decrease in price, and total revenue will fall.

10. The elasticity of demand depends on (1) the availability of substitutes, (2) the importance of the item in individual budgets, and (3) the time frame in question.

11. There are several important elasticities. *Income elasticity of demand* measures the responsiveness of the quantity demanded with respect to changes in income. *Cross-price elasticity of demand* measures the response of quantity of one good demanded to a change in the price of another good. *Elasticity of supply* measures the response of quantity of a good supplied to a change in the price of that good. *The elasticity of labour supply* measures the response of the quantity of labour supplied to a change in the price of labour.

Review Terms and Concepts

black market
cross-price elasticity of demand
elastic demand
elasticity
elasticity of labour supply
elasticity of supply
favoured customers
income elasticity of demand
inelastic demand

midpoint formula
perfectly elastic demand
perfectly inelastic demand
price ceiling
price elasticity of demand
price rationing
queuing
ration coupons
unitary elasticity

Problem Set

1. Illustrate the following with supply and/or demand curves:

a. A situation of excess labour supply (unemployment) caused by a 'minimum wage' law.

b. The effect of a sharp increase in heating oil prices on the demand for insulation material.

2. Many people think that ticket touts are undesirable. However, they may serve a useful function. Do you agree or disagree? Write an essay explaining your answer.

3. Illustrate the following with supply and demand curves:

a. An economy was doing very well in 1997. Income was rising and the stock market hit record highs. As a result, the price of its housing rose.

b. During the 1990s some cows in the UK came down with 'mad cow disease'. As a result, EU countries banned the import of British beef. The result was higher beef prices in continental Europe.

c. In 1999, a survey of garden centres and flower shops indicated that the demand for house plants was rising sharply. At the same time, dozens of low-cost producers

started growing plants for sale. The net result was a decline in the average price of house plants.

4. Suppose the demand and supply schedules for oil in the entire world (including Europe) are as shown in the first table.

Price (euros per barrel)	World quantity demanded (million barrels per day)	World quantity supplied (million barrels per day)
14	80	50
16	70	70
18	60	90
20	50	110
22	40	130

Suppose that the demand and supply schedules for oil in Europe only are as shown in the second table.

Price (euros per barrel)	European quantity demanded (million barrels per day)	European quantity supplied (million barrels per day)
14	16	4
16	15	6
18	14	8
20	13	10
22	12	12

a. On a graph, draw the supply and demand curves for the world and, separately, the supply and demand curves for Europe.
b. What is the world equilibrium price and quantity for oil?
c. With free trade in oil, what price will Europeans pay for their oil? What quantity will Europeans buy? How much of this will be supplied by European producers? How much will be imported? Illustrate total imports on your graph of the European oil market.
d. Suppose Europe imposes a tax of €4 per barrel on imported oil. What total quantity of oil would Europeans buy? How much of this would be supplied by European producers? How much would be imported? How much tax would the government collect?
e. Briefly summarize the impact of an oil-import tax by explaining who is helped and who is hurt among the following groups: domestic oil consumers, domestic oil producers, foreign oil producers, European governments.

5. Use the data in Problem 4 above to answer the following question, but suppose that Europe allows no oil imports.
a. What is the equilibrium price and quantity for oil in Europe?
b. If Europe imposed a price ceiling of 18 euros per barrel on the oil market, would there be an excess supply or an excess demand for oil? How much?
c. Under the price ceiling, quantity supplied and quantity demanded differ. Which of the two will determine how much oil is purchased? Briefly explain why.

6. In an effort to 'support' the price of some agricultural goods, the Common Agricultural Policy (CAP) operates a 'set-aside' policy, which pays farmers a subsidy in cash for every hectare that they leave *unplanted*. Is there any economic justification for this policy?

7. Illustrate the following with supply and/or demand curves:
a. The CAP 'supports' the price of wheat by paying farmers not to plant wheat on some of their land.
b. When the European economy recovers from the recession, incomes rise and expectations about the

future become more positive. As a result, home prices in many parts of the country are rising.
c. The impact of an increase in the price of chicken on the price of beefburgers.
d. Under rent control, rents are held by law to levels below equilibrium. If rent control is discontinued, there will be an impact on housing demand and supply.
e. Incomes rise, shifting the demand for petrol. Crude oil prices rise, shifting the supply of petrol. At the new equilibrium, the quantity of petrol sold is less than it was before. (Crude oil is used to produce petrol.)

8. 'The price of jeans has risen substantially in recent years. Demand for jeans has also been rising. This is hard to explain because the law of demand says that higher prices should lead to lower demand.' Do you agree?

9. Taxi fares in most cities are regulated. Several years ago, taxi drivers in Boston in the USA obtained permission to raise their fares by 10%, and they anticipated that revenues would increase by about 10% as a result. They were disappointed, however. When the commissioner granted the 10% increase, revenues increased by only about 5%.
a. What can you infer about the elasticity of demand for taxicab rides? What were taxicab drivers assuming about the elasticity of demand?

10. A sporting goods shop has estimated the demand curve for Brand A running shoes as a function of price. Use the diagram to answer the questions below:

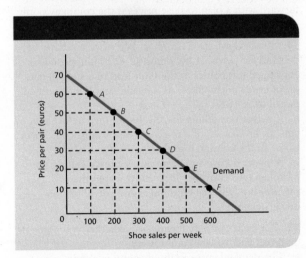

a. Calculate demand elasticity using the midpoint formula between points *A* and *B*, between points *C* and *D*, and between points *E* and *F*.
b. If the store currently charges a price of €50, then increases this price to €60, what happens to total revenue from shoe sales ($P \times Q$)? Repeat the exercise for initial prices of €30 and €10.
c. Explain why the answers to (a) can be used to predict the answers to (b).

11. Using the midpoint formula, calculate the elasticity for each of the following changes in demand by a household:

Demand for	P_1 (euros)	P_2 (euros)	Q_1	Q_2
a. Long-distance telephone service	0.25 per minute	0.15 per minute	300 minutes per month	400 minutes per month
b. Orange juice	1.49 per litre	1.89 per litre	14 litres per month	12 litres per month
c. Big Macs	2.89	1.00	3 per week	6 per week
d. Cooked shrimp	9.00 per kilo	12.00 per kilo	2 kilos per month	1.5 kilos per month

12. Fill in the missing amounts in the following table:

	% change in price	% change in quantity demanded	Elasticity
Demand for Häagen Dazs ice cream	0.1	−12	a
Demand for coffee at football matches	−20	b	− 0.5
Demand for Milan Opera tickets	c	−15	−1.0
Supply of chickens	0.1	d	+1.2
Supply of beef cattle	−15	−10	e

13. Use the table in Problem 12 to defend your answer to the following question:
a. Would you recommend that Häagen Dazs move forward with a plan to raise prices if the company's only goal is to increase revenues?

14. Studies have fixed the short-run price elasticity of demand for petrol at the pump at –0.20. Suppose that continued difficulties in the Gulf lead to a sudden cut-off of crude oil supplies. As a result, supplies of refined petrol drop 10%.
a. If petrol was selling for €1.40 per litre before the cut-off, how much of a price increase would you expect to see in the coming months?
b. Suppose a government imposes a price ceiling on petrol at 1.40 euros per litre. How would the relationship between consumers and petrol station owners change?

15. For each of the following, say whether you agree or disagree, and explain your answer.
a. The demand curve in the diagram is elastic.

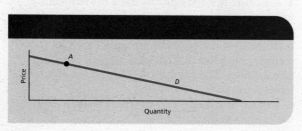

b. If supply were to increase somewhat in the next diagram, prices would fall and firms would earn less revenue.

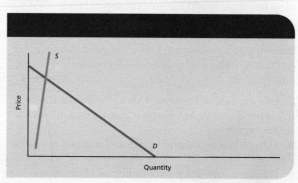

*16. Return to the Hilarian sock manufacturers of questions 13 and 14 of the problem set in Chapter 4. Using calculus, work out the elasticity of demand at €3 per pair both before and after the advertising campaign.

Microeconomics

6

Household Behaviour and Consumer Choice

Now that we have discussed the basic forces of supply and demand, we can explore the underlying behaviour of the two fundamental decision-making units in the economy, households and firms.

Figure 6.1 presents a diagram of a simple competitive economy. The figure is an expanded version of the circular flow diagram first presented in Figure 4.1. It is designed to guide you through Part 2 (Chapters 6–12) of this book. You will see the 'big picture' much more clearly if you follow this diagram closely as you work your way through this part of the book. (For your convenience, the diagram will be repeated several times in the next few chapters.)

Recall that households and firms interact in two kinds of markets: output (product) markets, shown at the top of Figure 6.1, and input (factor) markets, shown at the bottom. Households *demand* outputs and *supply* inputs. In contrast, firms *supply* outputs and *demand* inputs. This chapter explores the behaviour of households, focusing first on household demand for outputs and then on household supply in labour and capital markets.

The remaining chapters in Part 2 focus on firms and the interaction between firms and households. Chapters 7–9 analyse the behaviour of firms in output markets in both the short run and the long run. Chapter 10 focuses on the behaviour of firms in input markets in general, especially the labour and land markets. Chapter 11 discusses the capital market in more detail. Chapter 12 puts all the pieces together and analyses the functioning of a complete market system. Following Chapter 12, Part 3 of the book relaxes many assumptions and analyses market imperfections as well as the potential for, and pitfalls of, government involvement in the economy. The plan for Chapters 6–17 is outlined in Figure 6.2.

Recall that throughout this book, all diagrams that describe the behaviour of households are drawn or highlighted in *blue*. All diagrams that describe the behaviour of firms are drawn or highlighted in *red*. Look carefully at the supply and demand diagrams in Figure 6.1, and notice that in both the labour and capital markets, the supply curves are blue. This is because labour and capital are supplied by households. The demand curves for labour and capital are red because firms demand these inputs for production.

Assumptions

Before we proceed with our discussion of household choice, we need to make a few basic assumptions. The key assumption that we make in Chapters 6–12 is that all markets are perfectly competitive. Recall from Chapter 3 that a *perfectly competitive* market is one in which no single firm is large enough to have any control over the price of its products or the prices of the inputs that it buys. Similarly, no single household in a perfectly competitive market has any control over the prices of the products that it buys or the prices of the inputs (labour and capital) that it sells.

Figure 6.1 Firm and household decisions

Households demand in output markets, and supply labour and capital in input markets. To simplify our analysis, we have not included the government and international sectors in this circular flow diagram. These topics will be discussed in detail later.

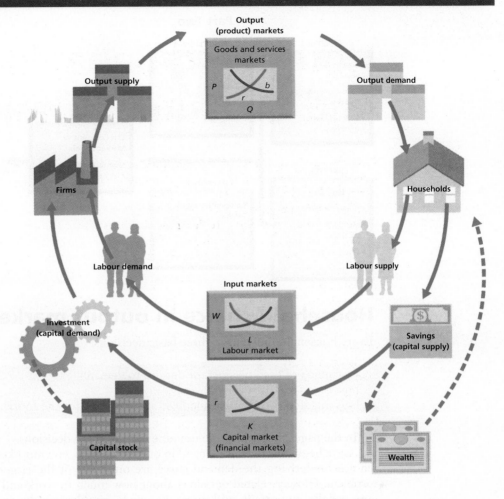

We also assume that households and firms possess all the information they need to make market choices. Specifically, we assume that households possess knowledge of the qualities and prices of everything available in the market. Firms know all that there is to know about wage rates, capital costs and output prices. This assumption is often called the assumption of **perfect knowledge**.

By the end of Chapter 12 we will have a complete picture of an economy, but it will be based on this set of fairly restrictive assumptions. At first, this may seem unrealistic to you. Keep the following in mind, however:

perfect knowledge

The assumption that households possess a knowledge of the qualities and prices of everything available in the market, and that firms have all available information regarding wage rates, capital costs and output prices.

Much of the economic analysis in the chapters that follow applies to all forms of market structure. Indeed, much of the power of economic reasoning is that it is quite general. Because monopolists, oligopolists, monopolistic competitors and perfect competitors share the objective of maximizing profits, it should not be surprising that their behaviour is in many ways similar. We focus here on perfect competition because many of these basic principles are easier to learn in the simplest of cases first.

Figure 6.2 Understanding the microeconomy and the role of government

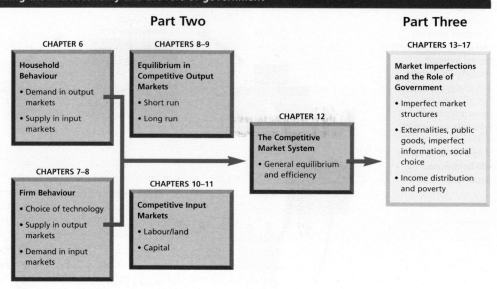

Household choice in output markets

Every household must make three basic decisions:

1. how much of each product, or output, to demand;
2. how much labour to supply; and
3. how much to spend today and how much to save for the future.[1]

In the pages that follow, we examine each of these decisions.

As we begin our look at demand in output markets, you must keep in mind that the choices underlying the demand curve are only part of the larger household-choice problem. Closely related decisions about how much to work and how much to save are equally important and must be made simultaneously with output-demand decisions.

The determinants of household demand

As we saw in Chapter 4:

Several factors influence the quantity of a given good or service demanded by a single household:

■ The price of the product
■ The income available to the household
■ The household's amount of accumulated wealth
■ The prices of other products available to the household
■ The household's tastes and preferences
■ The household's expectations about future income, wealth and prices

Demand schedules and demand curves express the relationship between quantity demanded and price, *ceteris paribus*. A change in price leads to a movement along a demand curve. Changes in income, in other prices or in preferences shift demand

---

[1]*As you will see in Chapters 10 and 11, this decision is of primary importance in the capital market.*

Applications

Do all European consumers have the same tastes?

Hennes and Mauritz is Sweden's fifth largest company. It sells trendy clothes in its shops across Europe. The firm's sales and profits have grown faster over the past decade than those of any clothes retailer in the world. It opened its first shop in Sweden in 1947 and now has almost 500 stores in 12 countries in Europe. Four-fifths of its sales are outside Sweden.

How has H&M managed so well to sell fashion across Europe's internal borders? Only a handful of others – The Gap from America, Zara, a Spanish chain, and perhaps Benetton – have

successfully moved beyond their home markets. Stefan Persson says that H&M has cashed in on a new trend: global fashion. He believes that national tastes are disappearing – a result of feeding the MTV generation from Tokyo to London the same diet of satellite television, movies and music, with the Internet shrinking the world further. To tap that trend almost every H&M store has the same look. Mr Persson rules that the positioning of a V-necked lambswool sweater in its Gothenburg shop should be exactly the same as in Zurich.

This year, the group will open around 60 new stores – 14% more than last year. Eight opened this week alone. Mr Persson says the pace can continue 'for many years to come'. With Switzerland and Sweden saturated, most expansion will be in new markets such as Germany and France. Hot on the heels of this week's launch, H&M will open a second Paris store on March 4 and a third on March 25. Twelve more are planned in the next two years. H&M will also start selling menswear in Britain late this year. Mr Persson sees no limit to H&M's geographical spread – he

says Spain, Italy, America and Japan are all on the cards and that H&M's growth 'may just be starting'.

But there are concerns. The group's move into France will reveal just how international H&M's offering really is. Despite Mr Persson's theories about global taste, H&M's success so far has been in Nordic and Germanic regions where, many argue, tastes and climates are similar across many age groups.

Source: 'Knickers to the market', The Economist, *28 February 1998.*

---

curves to the left or right. We refer to these shifts as 'changes in demand'. But the interrelationship among these variables is more complex than the simple exposition in Chapter 4 might lead you to believe.

The budget constraint

Before we examine the household choice process, we need to discuss exactly what choices are open or not open to households. If you look carefully at the list of items that influence household demand, you will see that the first four actually define the set of options available:

> Information on a household's income and wealth, together with information on product prices, make it possible to distinguish those combinations of goods and services that are affordable from those that are not.[2]

budget constraint
The limits imposed on household choices by income, wealth, and product prices.

Income, wealth and prices thus define what we call a household's **budget constraint**. The budget constraint facing any household results primarily from limits imposed externally by one or more markets. In competitive markets, for example, households cannot control prices; they must buy goods and services at market-determined prices. A household has some control over its income: its members can choose to work or not, and they can sometimes decide how many hours to work and how many jobs to

---

[2]*Remember that we drew the distinction between income and wealth in Chapter 4. Income is the sum of a household's earnings within a given period; it is a flow variable. In contrast, wealth is a stock variable; briefly, it is what a household owns minus what it owes at a given point in time.*

Table 6.1 Possible budget choices of a person earning 40,000 guilders per month after taxes

Bundle	Monthly rent	food	Other expenses	Total	Available?
A	1600	1000	1400	4000	Yes
B	2400	800	800	4000	Yes
C	2800	600	600	4000	Yes
D	4000	400	400	4800	No

hold. But constraints exist in the labour market, too. The amount that household members are paid is limited by current market wage rates. Whether they can get a job is determined by the availability of jobs.

While income does in fact depend, at least in part, on the choices that households make, we will treat it as a given for now. Later on in this chapter we will relax this assumption and explore labour supply choices in more detail.

The income, wealth and price constraints that surround choice are best illustrated with an example. Consider Barbara, a recent university graduate who takes a job as an accounts manager at a public relations firm in Rotterdam. Let's assume that she receives a salary of 4000 guilders per month (after tax), and that she has no wealth and no credit. Barbara's monthly expenditures are limited to her flow of income. Table 6.1 summarizes some of the choices open to her.

A careful search of the housing market reveals four vacant flats. The least expensive is a one-room studio with a small kitchenette; the rent is 1600 guilders per month, including utilities. If she lived there, Barbara could afford to spend 1000 guilders per month on food and still have 1400 guilders left over for other things.

Not far away is a one-bedroom flat with fitted carpets and a larger kitchen. It has much more space, but it is 50% more expensive: the monthly rent is 2400 guilders, including utilities. If Barbara took this flat, she might cut her food expenditures by 200 guilders per month and have only 800 guilders per month left for everything else.

In the same building as the one-bedroom flat is an identical unit on the top floor of the building with a balcony facing west towards the sunset. The balcony and view add 400 guilders to the monthly rent. To live there, Barbara would be left with only 1200 guilders to split between food and other expenses.

Just out of curiosity, Barbara looked at a house in the suburbs whose rent was 4000 guilders per month. Obviously, unless she could get along without eating or doing anything else that costs money, she could not afford it. The combination of the house and any amount of food is outside her budget constraint.

Notice that we have used the information that we have on income and prices to identify different combinations of housing, food and other items that are available to a single-person household with a monthly income of 4000 guilders. We have said nothing about the process of choosing. Rather, we have carved out what is called a **choice set** or **opportunity set**, the set of options that is defined and limited by Barbara's budget constraint.

choice set *or* opportunity set
The set of options that is defined and limited by a budget constraint.

Preferences, tastes, trade-offs and opportunity cost

So far, we have identified only the combinations of goods and services that are available to Barbara and those that are not. Within the constraints imposed by limited incomes and fixed prices, however, households are free to choose what they will buy and what they will not buy. Their ultimate choices are governed by their individual preferences and tastes.

It will help you to think of the household-choice process as a process of allocating income over a large number of available goods and services. A household's final demand for any single product is just one of many outcomes that result from the decision-making process. Think, for example, of a demand curve that shows a household's reaction to a drop in the price of air travel. There are certain times of year when people travel less frequently. During these periods, special fares flood the market and many people decide to take trips that they otherwise would not have taken. The decision to travel is a decision not to do or buy something else. If I live in Zurich and decide to visit my mother in Dublin, the money spent on the air fare will not be available for spending on new clothes, dinners at a restaurant, or a new set of tyres for the car.

A change in the price of a single good changes the constraints within which households choose, and this may change the entire allocation of income. Demand for some goods and services may rise while demand for others falls. A complicated set of trade-offs lies behind the shape and position of a household's demand curve for a single good. Whenever a household makes a choice, it is really weighing the good or service it chooses against all the other things that the same money could buy.

Consider again our young account manager and her options as listed in Table 6.1. Barbara's choice of an apartment from among the three alternatives that lie within her budget constraint depends on her own tastes and preferences. She must make a personal judgement about the relative values that she places on housing, food and other things. If she hates cooking, likes to eat at restaurants, and goes out three nights a week, she will probably trade off some housing for dining out and money to spend on clothes and other things. She will probably rent the studio for 1600 guilders. But she may love to spend long evenings at home reading, listening to classical music and sipping tea while watching the sunset. In that case, she will probably trade off some restaurant meals, evenings out and travel expenses for the added comfort of the larger apartment with the balcony and the view.

Thinking of constraints in this way highlights a very important point:

> As long as a household faces a limited budget – and all households ultimately do – the real cost of any good or service is the value of the other goods and services that could have been purchased with the same amount of money. The real cost of a good or service is its opportunity cost, and opportunity cost is determined by relative prices and income.

The budget constraint more formally

Ann and Tom are struggling graduate economics students at the London School of Economics (LSE). Their tuition is completely paid by graduate fellowships. They live as wardens in an undergraduate hall of residence, in return for which they receive rooms and meals. Their fellowships also give them £200 each month to cover all their other expenses. To simplify things, let's assume that Ann and Tom spend their money on only two things: meals at the local Thai restaurant and nights at the local jazz club, the Hungry Ear. Thai meals cost a fixed price of £20 per couple. Two tickets to the jazz club, including espresso, are £10.

As Figure 6.3 shows, we can graphically depict the choices that are available to our dynamic duo. The axes measure the *quantities* of the two goods that Ann and Tom buy. The horizontal axis measures the number of Thai meals consumed per month, and the vertical axis measures the number of trips to the Hungry Ear. (Note that price is not on the vertical axis here.) Every point in the space between the axes represents some combination of Thai meals and nights at the jazz club. The question is: which of these points can Ann and Tom purchase with a fixed budget of £200 per month? That is, which points are in the opportunity set and which are not?

One possibility is that Ann and Tom don't want to eat their meals with under-graduates: the two graduate students want to avoid the hall dining room at all costs. Thus they might decide to spend all their money on Thai food and none of it on jazz. This decision would be represented by a point *on* the horizontal axis because all the

Figure 6.3 Budget constraint and opportunity set for Ann and Tom

A budget constraint separates those combinations of goods and services that are available, given limited income, from those that are not. The available combinations make up the opportunity set.

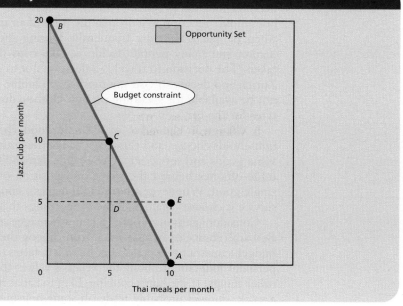

points on that axis are points at which Ann and Tom make no jazz club visits. How many meals can Ann and Tom afford? The answer is simple: if income is £200 and the price of Thai meals is £20, they can afford £200 ÷ £20 = 10 meals. This point is labelled *A* on the budget constraint in Figure 6.3.

Another possibility is that the strain of postgraduate research is getting to Ann and Tom, so they decide to relax at the Hungry Ear to relieve stress. Suppose that they choose to spend all their money on jazz and none of it on Thai food. This decision would be represented by a point *on* the vertical axis because all the points on this are points at which Ann and Tom eat no Thai meals. How many jazz club visits can they afford? Again, the answer is simple: with an income of £200 and with the price of jazz/espresso at £10, they can go to the Hungry Ear £200 ÷ £10 = 20 times. This is the point labelled *B* in Figure 6.3. The line connecting points *A* and *B* is Ann and Tom's budget constraint.

What about all the points between *A* and *B* on the budget constraint? Think about the trade-off between Thai meals and trips to the Ear. Starting from point *B*, suppose Ann and Tom give up trips to the jazz club to buy more Thai meals. Since trips to the jazz club are priced at £10 and Thai meals are priced at £20, each additional Thai meal 'costs' two trips to the Hungry Ear. The opportunity cost of a Thai meal is two jazz club trips.

Point *C* on the budget constraint represents a compromise. Here Ann and Tom go to the club ten times and eat at the Thai restaurant five times. To verify that point *C* is on the budget constraint, price it out. Ten jazz club trips cost a total of £10 × 10 = £100, and five Thai meals cost a total of £20 × 5 = £100. The total is thus £100 + £100 = £200.[3]

The budget constraint divides all the points between the axes into two groups: those that can be purchased for £200 or less (the opportunity set) and those that are

---

[3]*The budget constraint can be written £20X + £10Y = £200, which is the equation of the line in Figure 6.3. This equation simply tells you to multiply the number of units of X consumed by £20, then multiply the number of units of Y consumed by £10; the sum of these two products should equal £200. More generally, the budget constraint in a two-good world is given by $P_X X + P_Y Y = I$, where P_X is the price of X, P_Y is the price of Y, and I is income.*

unavailable. Point D on the diagram costs less than £200; point E costs more than £200. (Verify that this is true.) The opportunity set is the shaded area in Figure 6.3.

Budget constraints change when prices rise or fall

Now suppose that the Thai restaurant offers 'two-for-one' vouchers during the month of November. In effect, this means that the price of Thai meals drops to £10 for Ann and Tom. How would the budget constraint in Figure 6.3 change?

First, point B would not change. If Ann and Tom spend all their money on jazz, the price of Thai meals is irrelevant. Ann and Tom can still afford only 20 trips to the jazz club. What has changed is point A, which moves to point A' in Figure 6.4. At the new lower price of £10, if Ann and Tom spent all their money on Thai meals, they could buy twice as many Thai meals: £200 ÷ £10 = £20. The budget constraint *swivels*, as shown in Figure 6.4.

The new, flatter budget constraint reflects the new trade-off between Thai meals and Hungry Ear visits. Now, after the price of Thai meals drops to £10, the opportunity cost of a Thai meal is only one jazz club visit. Ann and Tom need to sacrifice only one club visit for each meal. The opportunity set has expanded because at the lower price more combinations of Thai meals and jazz are available.

Figure 6.4 thus illustrates a very important point. When the price of a single good changes, more than just the quantity demanded of that good may be affected. The household now faces an entirely different choice problem – the opportunity set has expanded. At the same income of £200, the new lower price means that Ann and Tom might choose more Thai meals, more jazz club visits, or more of both! They are clearly better off.

To summarize:

> The budget constraint is defined by income, wealth, and prices. Within those limits, households are free to choose, and the household's ultimate choice depends on its own likes and dislikes.

The range of goods and services available in a modern society is as vast as consumer tastes are variable, and this makes any generalization about the household choice process hazardous. Nonetheless, the theory of household behaviour that follows is an attempt to derive some logical propositions about the way households make choices.

Figure 6.4 The effect of a decrease in price on Ann's and Tom's budget constraint

When the price of a good decreases, the budget constraint swivels to the right, increasing the opportunities available and expanding choice.

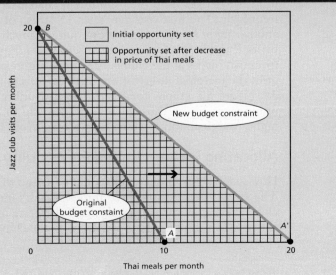

The basis of choice: utility

Somehow, from the millions of things that are available, each of us manages to sort out a set of goods and services to buy. When we make our choices, we make specific judgements about the relative worth of things that are very different.

During the nineteenth century, the weighing of values was formalized into a concept called utility. Whether one item is preferable to another depends upon how much utility, or satisfaction, it yields relative to its alternatives. What is it that enables us to decide on the relative worth of a new puppy or a CD player? A trip to the seaside or a weekend in Paris? Working or not working? As we make our choices, we are effectively weighing the utilities we would receive from all the possible available goods.

Certain problems are implicit in the concept of utility. First, it is impossible to measure utility completely and accurately. Second, it is impossible to compare the utilities of different people – that is, one cannot say whether person A or person B has a higher level of utility. Despite these problems the idea of utility helps us understand the process of choice better, so we will assume for now that we *can* measure utility.

Diminishing marginal utility

In making their choices, most people spread their incomes over many different kinds of goods. One reason people prefer variety is that consuming more and more of any one good reduces the marginal, or extra, satisfaction we get from further consumption of the same good. Formally, marginal utility (MU) is the additional satisfaction gained by the consumption or use of *one more* unit of something.

It is important to distinguish marginal utility from total utility. Total utility is the total amount of satisfaction obtained from consumption of a good or service. Marginal utility comes only from the *last unit* consumed; total utility comes from *all* units consumed.

Suppose that you live next to a shop that sells your favourite home-made ice cream. But even though you get a great deal of pleasure from eating ice cream, you don't spend your entire income on it. The first one of the day tastes heavenly. The second is merely delicious. The third is still very good, but it's clear that the glow is fading. Why? Because the more of any one good we consume in a given period, the less satisfaction, or utility, we get from each additional, or marginal, unit. In 1890 Alfred Marshall called this 'familiar and fundamental tendency of human nature' the law of diminishing marginal utility.[4]

Consider this simple example. Frank, another LSE student, loves live music. A band is playing seven nights a week at a club near his house. Table 6.2 shows how the utility he derives from the band might change as he goes to the club more and more frequently. The first visit generates 12 'utils', or units of utility. If Frank goes again another night he enjoys it, but not quite as much as the first night. The second night by itself yields 10 additional utils. *Marginal utility* is 10, while the *total utility* derived from two nights at the club is 22. Three nights per week at the club provide 28 total utils; the marginal utility of the third night is 6, because total utility rose from 22 to 28. Figure 6.5 graphs total and marginal utility using the data in Table 6.2. Total utility increases up through Frank's fifth trip to the club, but levels off on the sixth night. Marginal utility, which has declined from the beginning, is now at zero.

Allocating income to maximize utility

How many times in one week would Frank go to the club to hear his favourite band? The answer depends on three things: Frank's income, the price of admission to the club, and the alternatives available. If the price of admission were zero and no alternatives existed, he would probably go to the club five nights a week. (Remember, the

utility The satisfaction, or reward, a product yields relative to its alternatives. The basis of choice.

marginal utility (MU) The additional satisfaction gained by the consumption or use of one more unit of something.

total utility The total amount of satisfaction obtained from consumption of a good or service.

law of diminishing marginal utility The more of any one good consumed in a given period, the less satisfaction (utility) generated by consuming each additional (marginal) unit of the same good.

[4]*Alfred Marshall*, Principles of Economics, 8th edn (New York: Macmillan, 1948), p. 93 (1st edn 1890).

Table 6.2 Total utility and marginal utility of trips to the club per week

Trips to club	Total utility	Marginal utility
1	12	12
2	22	10
3	28	6
4	32	4
5	34	2
6	34	0

sixth does not increase his utility, so why should he bother to go?) But Frank is also a film buff. There are many good cinemas nearby, and he can go to one of them six nights a week if he wants to.

Figure 6.5 Graphs of Frank's total and marginal utility

Marginal utility is the additional utility gained by consuming one additional unit of a commodity – in this case, trips to the jazz club. When marginal utility is zero, total utility stops rising.

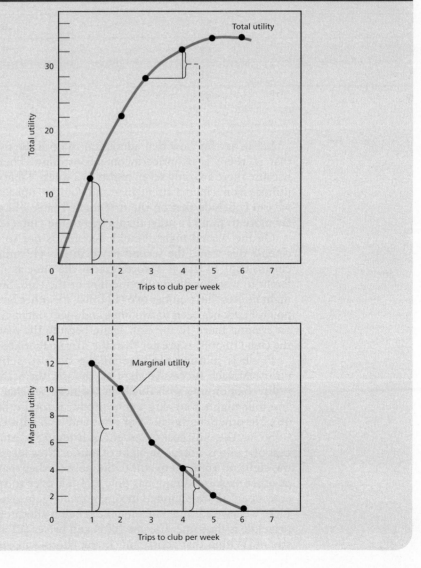

Table 6.3 Allocation of fixed expenditure per week between two alternatives

(1) Trips to club per week	(2) Total utility	(3) Marginal utility (MU)	(4) Price (£) (P)	(5) Marginal utility per £ (MU/£)
1	12	12	3.00	4.0
2	22	10	3.00	3.3
3	28	6	3.00	2.0
4	32	4	3.00	1.3
5	34	2	3.00	0.7
6	34	0	3.00	0

(1) Cinema visits per week	(2) Total utility	(3) Marginal utility (MU)	(4) Price (£) (P)	(5) Marginal utility per £ (MU/£)
1	21	21	6.00	3.5
2	33	12	6.00	2.0
3	42	9	6.00	1.5
4	48	6	6.00	1.0
5	51	3	6.00	.5
6	51	0	6.00	0

Let us say for now that admission to both the music club and the cinema is free – that is, there is no price/income constraint. There is a time constraint, however, because there are only seven nights in a week. Table 6.3 lists Frank's total and marginal utilities from cinema attendance and going to music clubs. From column 3 of the table we can conclude that on the first night Frank will go to a cinema. The film is worth far more to him (21 utils) than a trip to the club (12 utils).

On the second night, Frank's decision is not so easy. Because he has been to one cinema this week, the second is worth less (12 utils, as compared to 21 for the first cinema trip). In fact, it is worth exactly the same as a first trip to the club, so he is indifferent to whether he goes to the film or the club. So he splits the next two nights: one night he sees film number two (12 utils), the other he spends at the club (12 utils). At this point, Frank has been to two films and spent one night at the club. Where will Frank go on evening four? To the club again, because the marginal utility from a second trip to the club (10 utils) is greater than the marginal utility from seeing a third film (9 utils).

Frank is splitting his time among the two activities in order to maximize total utility. At each successive step, he chooses the activity that yields the most marginal utility. Continuing with this logic, you can see that spending three nights at the club and four nights watching a film produces total utility of 76 utils each week (28 plus 48). No other combination of films and club trips can produce as much utility.

So far, the only cost of a night of listening to music is a forgone film, and the only cost of a film is a forgone night of music. Now let's suppose that it costs £3 to get into the club and £6 to go to a film. Suppose further that after paying rent and taking care of other expenses Frank has only £21 left over to spend on entertainment. Typically, consumers allocate limited incomes, or budgets, over a large set of goods and services. Here we have a limited income (£21) being allocated between only two goods, but the principle is the same. Income (£21) and prices (£3 and £6) define Frank's budget constraint. Within that constraint, Frank chooses in order to maximize utility.

Because the two activities now cost different amounts, we need to find the *marginal utility per pound* (or other unit of currency) spent on each activity. If Frank is to spend his money on the combination of activities lying within his budget constraint that gives him the most total utility, each night he must choose the activity that gives him the *most utility per pound spent*. As you can see from column 5 in Table 6.3, Frank gets 4 utils per pound on the first night he goes to the club (12 utils ÷ £3 = 4 utils per pound). On night two he goes to a film and gets 3.5 utils per pound (21 utils ÷ £6 = 3.5 utils per pound). On night three it's back to the club. Then what happens? When all is said and done – work this out for yourself – Frank ends up going to two films and spending three nights at the club. No other combination of activities that £21 will buy yields more utility.

The utility-maximizing rule

In general, a utility-maximizing consumer spreads out his or her expenditures until the following condition holds:

$$\text{Utility-maximizing rule} = \frac{MU_X}{P_X} = \frac{MU_Y}{P_Y} \text{ for all pairs of goods}$$

where MU_X is the marginal utility derived from the last unit of X consumed, MU_Y is the marginal utility derived from the last unit of Y consumed, P_X is the price per unit of X, and P_Y is the price per unit of Y.

To see why this utility-maximizing rule is true, think for a moment about what would happen if it were *not* true. For example, suppose MU_X/P_X were greater than MU_Y/P_Y; that is, suppose that a consumer purchased a bundle of goods so that the marginal utility from the last pound spent on X were greater than the marginal utility from the last pound spent on Y. This would mean that the consumer could increase her or his utility by spending a pound less on Y and a pound more on X. But as a consumer shifts to buying more X and less Y, she runs into diminishing marginal utility. Buying more units of X *decreases* the marginal utility derived from consuming additional units of X. As a result, the marginal utility of another pound spent on X falls. Now *less* is being spent on Y and that means its marginal utility *increases*. This process continues until $MU_X/P_X = MU_Y/P_Y$. When this condition holds, there is no way for the consumer to increase his or her utility by changing the bundle of goods purchased.

You can see how the utility-maximizing rule works in Frank's choice between music and cinemagoing. At each stage, Frank chooses the activity that gives him the most utility per pound. If he goes to a film, the utility he will derive from the next film – marginal utility – falls. If he goes to the club, the utility he will derive from his next visit falls, and so forth.

Diminishing marginal utility and downward-sloping demand

The concept of diminishing marginal utility offers us one reason why people spread their incomes over a variety of goods and services rather than spend them all on one or two items. It also leads us to conclude that demand curves slope downwards.

To see why this is so, let's return to our friends Ann and Tom, the struggling graduate students at the LSE. Recall that they chose between meals at a Thai restaurant and trips to a jazz club. Now think about their demand curve for Thai meals shown in Figure 6.6. When the price of a meal is £40, they decide not to buy any Thai meals. What they are really deciding is that the utility gained from even that first scrumptious meal each month isn't worth the utility that would come from the other things that £40 can buy.

Now consider a price of £25. At this price, Ann and Tom buy five Thai meals. Clearly the first, second, third, fourth and fifth meal each generates enough utility to justify the price. Tom and Ann 'reveal' this by buying five meals. But after the fifth meal, the utility gained from the next meal (the sixth meal) is not worth £25. That is, it does not generate as much utility as the other things that £25 can buy.

Figure 6.6 Diminishing marginal utility and downward-sloping demand

At a price of £40, the utility gained from even the first Thai meal is not worth the price. However, a lower price of £25 lures Ann and Tom into the Thai restaurant five times a month. (The utility from the sixth meal is not worth £25.) If the price is £15, Ann and Tom will eat Thai meals ten times a month – until the marginal utility of a Thai meal drops below the utility they could gain from spending £15 on other goods. At 25 meals a month, they cannot face another Thai meal, even if it is free!

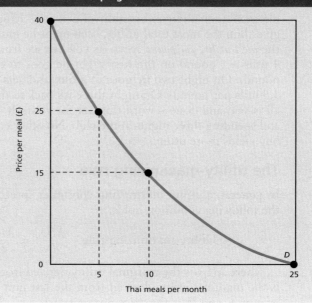

Ultimately, every demand curve hits the quantity axis as a result of diminishing marginal utility – in other words, demand curves slope downwards. How many times will Ann and Tom go to the Thai restaurant if meals are free? Twenty-five times. After 25 times a month, they are so sick of Thai food that they will not eat any more even if it is given away free! That is, marginal utility – the utility gained from the last meal – has dropped to zero. If you think this is unrealistic, ask yourself how much water you drank today.

While the idea of utility is, we believe, a helpful way of thinking about the choice process, there is an explanation for downward-sloping demand curves that does not rely on the concept of utility or the assumption of diminishing marginal utility. This explanation centres on income and substitution effects.

Maths Box 1 Marginal utility analysis: a mathematical approach

We have seen that a consumer's total utility function increases at a decreasing rate as consumption rises. It might be of the form:

$$TU = 100Q - 5Q^2$$

where TU = total utility and Q = quantity consumed per period.
Marginal utility (MU) is the rate of change of TU:

$$MU = \frac{dTU}{dQ} = 100 - 10Q$$

Since a rational consumer maximizes total utility, consumption unconstrained by price or income would be where $MU = 0$.

$$\text{Set } \frac{dTU}{dQ} = 0$$

$$\text{thus } 0 = 100 - 10Q$$

Hence $Q = 10$ where $MU = 0$. In other words, a consumer unconstrained by income would, given the utility function, consume 10 units per period.

Income and substitution effects

Another way of thinking about household choices avoids any direct use of the concept of utility. It also leads us to the conclusion that a negative, or downward-sloping, relationship is very likely to exist between quantity demanded and price.

Keeping in mind that consumers face constrained choices, consider the probable response of a household to a decline in the price of some heavily used product, *ceteris paribus*. How might a household currently consuming many goods be likely to respond to a fall in the price of one of those goods if its income, its preferences and all other prices remained unchanged? Clearly, the household would face a new budget constraint, and its final choice of all goods and services might change. A decline in the price of petrol, for example, may affect not only how much petrol you purchase but also the kind of car you buy, when and how much you travel, where you go, and (not so directly) how many films you see this month and how many projects around the house you get done.

The income effect

Price changes affect households in two ways. First, if we assume that households confine their choices to products that improve their well-being, then a decline in the price of any product, *ceteris paribus*, makes the household unequivocally better off. In other words, if a household continues to buy the exact same amount of every good and service after the price decrease, it will have income left over. That extra income may be spent on the product whose price has declined, hereafter called good X, or on other products. The change in consumption of X due to this improvement in well-being is called the **income effect of a price change**.

income effect of a price change
The change in consumption that results from being better (or worse) off because of a price fall (or rise).

Hans lives in Vienna and three times a year flies to his holiday cottage on the Greek Islands. Last year a return ticket to Greece cost 8000 schillings. This year, however, increased competition among the airlines has led the airlines to offer return tickets for 5000 schillings. Assuming that the price remains at this lower price all year, he is better off this year than last year. He can now fly to his cottage exactly the same number of times, and will have spent 9000 schillings less for airline tickets than he did last year. Now that he is better off, he has additional opportunities. He could fly to his cottage a fourth time this year, leaving 4000 schillings to spend on other things, or he could fly the same number of times as before (three) and spend all of the extra 9000 schillings on other things.

The key idea here is simple:

> When the price of something we buy falls, we are *better off*. When the price of something we buy rises, we are *worse off*.

Look back at Figure 6.4. When the price of Thai meals fell, the opportunity set facing Tom and Ann expanded – they were able to afford more Thai meals, more jazz club trips, or more of both. They were unequivocally better off because of the price decline. In a sense, their 'real' income was higher.

Now recall from Chapter 4 the definition of a normal good. When income rises, demand for normal goods increases. Most goods are normal goods. Because of the price decline, Tom and Ann can afford to buy more; their 'real' income is higher. If Thai food is a normal good, a decline in the price of Thai food should lead to an increase in demand for Thai food.

substitution effect of a price change
The change in consumption that results from a good becoming relatively cheap (or dear) when its price falls (or rises)

The substitution effect

The fact that a price decline leaves households better off is only part of the story. When the price of a product falls, that product also becomes *relatively* cheaper. That is, it becomes more attractive relative to potential substitutes. A fall in the price of product X might cause a household to shift its purchasing pattern away from substitutes towards X. This shift is called the **substitution effect of a price change**.

Earlier, we made the point that the 'real' cost or price of a good is what one must sacrifice in order to consume it. This opportunity cost is determined by relative prices.

To see why this is so, consider again the choice that Hans faces when a return ticket to Greece costs 8000 schillings. Each trip that he takes requires a sacrifice of 8000 schillings' worth of other goods and services. When the price drops to 5000 schillings, the opportunity cost of a ticket has dropped by 3000 schillings. In other words, after the price decline, he has to sacrifice only 5000 (rather than 8000) schillings' worth of other goods and services to his visit cottage.

To clarify the distinction between the income and substitution effects in your mind, imagine how Hans would be affected if two things happened simultaneously. First, the price of return air travel between Vienna and Greece drops from 8000 to 5000 schillings. Second, his income is reduced by 9000 schillings. He is now faced with new relative prices, but – assuming he flew three times last year – he is no better off now than before the price of a ticket declined. The decrease in the price of air travel has exactly offset his decrease in income.

Despite the fact that Hans is no better off than he was before, he is still likely to take more trips to Greece. Why? Because the opportunity cost of a trip to the cottage is now lower, *ceteris paribus* (that is, assuming no change in the prices of other goods and services). A trip to Greece now requires a sacrifice of only 5000 schillings' worth of other goods and services, not the 8000 schillings' worth that it did before. Thus, he will substitute away from other goods towards trips to his Greek cottage.

Everything works in the opposite direction when a price rises, *ceteris paribus*. A price increase makes households worse off. If income and other prices don't change, spending the same amount of money buys less, and households will be forced to buy less. They may purchase less X or cut spending on other things. This is the income effect. In addition, when the price of a product rises, that item becomes more expensive relative to potential substitutes, and the household is likely to substitute other goods for it. This is the substitution effect. (For another example of the income and substitution effects, see the Application box 'The tax laws and the income and substitution effects'.)

What do the income and substitution effects tell us about the demand curve? Quite simply: both the income and substitution effects imply a negative relationship between price and quantity demanded – in other words, downward-sloping demand. When the price of something falls, *ceteris paribus*, we are better off, and we are likely to buy more of that good and other goods (income effect). And because lower price also means 'less expensive relative to substitutes', we are likely to buy more of the good (substitution effect). When the price of something rises, we are worse off, and we will buy less of it (income effect). Higher price also means 'more expensive relative to substitutes', and we are likely to buy less of it and more of other goods (substitution effect).[5]

When the price of an inferior good rises, it is, like any other good, more expensive relative to substitutes, and we are likely to replace it with lower-priced substitutes. However, the price increase leaves us worse off, and when we are worse off we increase our demand for inferior goods. Thus, the income effect could lead us to buy more of the good, partially offsetting the substitution effect.

Even if a good is 'very inferior', demand curves will slope downwards as long as the substitution effect is larger than the income effect. But it is possible, at least in theory, for the income effect to be larger. In such a case, a price increase would actually lead to an increase in quantity demanded. This possibility was pointed out by Alfred Marshall in *Principles of Economics*. Marshall attributes the notion of an upward-sloping demand curve to Sir Robert Giffen, and for this reason the notion is often referred to as Giffen's paradox. Fortunately or unfortunately, no one has ever demonstrated that a Giffen good has ever existed.

Figure 6.7 summarizes the income and substitution effects of a price change.

---

[5]*For some goods the income and substitution effects work in opposite directions. When our income rises, we may buy less of some goods. In Chapter 4, we called such goods inferior goods.*

Applications

The tax laws and the income and substitution effects

Charitable contributions are an important source of revenue for the non-profit sector – organizations such as museums, churches and universities.

Charitable contributions are afforded special treatment in most countries' tax codes. Individuals, families and companies are permitted to deduct their contributions to most non-profit organizations from their taxable income. Thus, for any amount given to such an organization, there is a tax saving. Changes in the tax laws in many countries during the 1980s and 1990s were not favourable to charitable giving, however. To understand how taxes affect charitable giving, the income and substitution effects are critical.

How taxes can affect behaviour

Most people must file a tax return each year, against which they may set certain expenditures. These allowances or deductible expenditures include charitable contributions.

The amount of tax saving from a deduction depends on the taxpayer's tax rate bracket. In the UK in 1979, for example the highest tax bracket was 83 per cent. This meant that if someone in that bracket donated £1000 to the Red Cross, the net cost of that gift to the donor was only £170. Why? Because a tax rate of 83% meant that deducting a gift of £1000 from taxable income saved the donor £830 in taxes, although some of the saving went to the charity not to the donor.

In the late 1990s the highest tax rate was only 40 per cent. Worried non-profit organizations were quick to point out that this tax cut increased the 'cost' of giving substantially. When the top rate decreased from 83% to 40%, the net cost of the £1000 gift rose from £170 to £600.

The predicted effects

How might we expect households to respond to the lower taxes? First,

because tax rates were decreased, some households had more disposable income after the cuts. Assuming that charitable giving is a normal good, this income effect should lead to more giving. But giving to charity is now more expensive relative to other goods. The opportunity cost of a £1000 donation before 1979 was less than in the late 1990s. This substitution effect, which should lead to fewer charitable contributions, is what the non-profit sector worried about.

What are the actual effects of changes?

US economist Charles Clotfelter found that the overall effects of lower tax rates on charitable giving in the USA, where similar income tax changes have occurred, were relatively small over the period he studied, but were generally in line with what theory would predict. For example, he found the largest reductions in giving were among the highest-

income households facing the highest tax brackets. These people had the largest substitution effects. On the other hand, lower-income households actually increased their giving somewhat. This result is exactly what theory would predict. Those in a lower tax bracket had an income effect but a much lower substitution effect. We would expect a strong income effect that is not accompanied by an offsetting substitution effect to lead to increased charitable donations, and this is exactly what happened.

Source: Based on Charles T. Clotfelter, 'The impact of tax reform on charitable giving: A 1989 perspective', Office of Tax Policy Research, Working Paper No. 90-7, School of Business Administration, University of Michigan (Ann Arbor), 1 December 1989.

Figure 6.7 Income and substitution effects of a price change

For normal goods, the income and substitution effects work in the same direction. Higher prices lead to a lower quantity demanded, and lower prices lead to a higher quantity demanded.

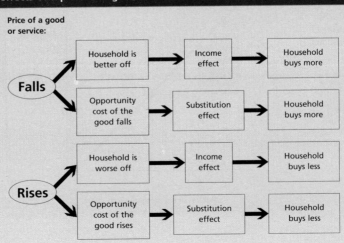

Consumer surplus

The argument, already made several times, that the market forces us to reveal a great deal about our personal preferences is an extremely important one, and it bears repeating at least once more here. If you are free to choose within the constraints imposed by prices and your income and you decide to buy, say, a bottle of wine for 30 Francs, you have 'revealed' that the bottle of wine is worth at least 30 Francs to you. If a consumer decides to buy a hamburger for €2.5, he or she values the hamburger at at least €2.5.

A simple market demand curve such as the one in Figure 6.8a illustrates this point quite clearly. At the current market price of €2.50, European consumers will purchase 7 million hamburgers per month. There is (we shall assume) only one price in the market, and the demand curve tells us how many hamburgers that households would buy if they could purchase all they wanted at the market price of €2.50. Anyone who values a hamburger at €2.50 or more will buy it. Anyone who does not value it that highly will not.

Some people, however, value hamburgers at more than €2.50. As Figure 6.8a shows, even if the price were at €5.00, consumers would still buy one million hamburgers. If these people were able to buy the good at a price of €2.50, they would earn a **consumer surplus**. Consumer surplus is the difference between the maximum amount a person is willing to pay for a good and its current market price. The consumer surplus earned by the people willing to pay €5.00 for a hamburger is approximately equal to the shaded area between point *A* and the price, €2.50.

The second million hamburgers in Figure 6.8a are valued at more than the market price as well, although the consumer surplus gained is slightly less. Point *B* on the simple market demand curve shows the maximum amount that consumers would be willing to pay for the second million hamburgers. The consumer surplus earned by these people is equal to the shaded area between *B* and the price, 2.50 euros. Similarly, for the third million hamburgers, maximum willingness to pay is given by point *C*; consumer surplus is a bit lower than it is at points *A* and *B*, but it is still significant.

The total value of the consumer surplus suggested by the data in Figure 6.8a is roughly equal to the area of the shaded triangle in Figure 6.8b. To understand why

consumer surplus

The difference between the maximum amount a person is willing to pay for a good and its current market price.

Figure 6.8 Market demand, revealed preference and consumer surplus

The difference between the maximum amount that a person is willing to pay for a good and its current market price is the person's consumer surplus. The total consumer surplus suggested by the data in Figure 6.8a is represented by the shaded area in Figure 6.8b.

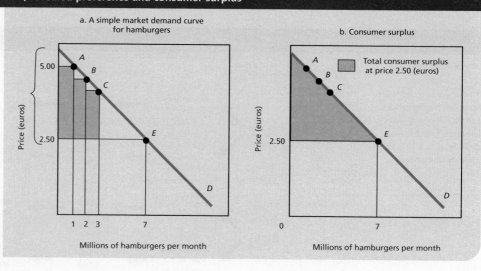

Figure 6.9 The 'value' of water

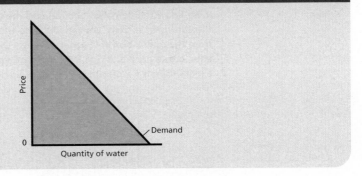

this is so, think about offering hamburgers to consumers at successively lower prices. If the good were actually sold for €2.50, those near point *A* on the demand curve would get a large surplus; those at point *B* would get a smaller surplus. Those at point *E* would get none.

The idea of consumer surplus helps to explain an old paradox that dates back to Plato. Adam Smith wrote about it in 1776:

> The things which have the greatest value in use have frequently little or no value in exchange; and on the contrary, those which have the greatest value in exchange have frequently little or no value in use. Nothing is more useful than water: but it will purchase scarce any thing; scarce anything can be had in exchange for it. A diamond, on the contrary, has scarce any value in use; but a very great quantity of other goods may frequently be had in exchange for it.[6]

diamond/water paradox

A paradox stating that (1) the things with the greatest value in use frequently have little or no value in exchange, and (2) the things with the greatest value in exchange frequently have little or no value in use.

cost-benefit analysis

The formal technique by which the benefits of a project are weighed against its costs.

Although diamonds have arguably more than 'scarce any value in use' today (they are used to cut glass, for example), Smith's **diamond/water paradox** is still instructive, at least where water is concerned.

The low price of water owes much to the fact that it is in plentiful supply. Even at a price of zero we do not consume an infinite amount of water. We consume up to the point where *marginal* utility drops to zero. The *marginal* value of water is zero. Each of us enjoys an enormous consumer surplus when we consume nearly free water. We tend to take water for granted, but imagine what would happen to its price if there were simply not enough for everyone. If water were in very short supply, it would command a high price indeed. As the Figure 6.9 shows, at a price of zero, the 'value' of water is the entire shaded area.

Consumer surplus measurement is a key element in **cost-benefit analysis**, the formal technique by which the benefits of a project are weighed against its costs. If, for example, the Swedish Government is to decide whether to build a new hydroelectric power plant, it needs to know the value, to consumers, of the electricity that it will produce. Just as the value of water to consumers is not just its price times the quantity that people consume, the value of electricity generated is not just the price of electricity times the quantity the new plant will produce. The total value that should be weighed against the costs of the plant includes the consumer surplus that electricity users will enjoy if the plant is built.

[6]*Adam Smith,* The Wealth of Nations, *Modern Library Edition (New York: Random House, 1937), p. 28 (1st edn 1776). The cheapness of water is referred to by Plato in* Euthydemus, *304B.*

Maths Box 2 Calculating the consumer surplus from the demand function

If we know the demand function and the equilibrium price we can calculate the value of the consumer surplus. We can illustrate this by using the supply and demand equations from the maths box in Chapter 4. When $Q_d = 100 - 2P$ and $Q_s = 10 + 3P$, for which the equilibrium price and quantity were shown to be $P = 18$ and $Q = 64$ respectively. Total expenditure is $P \times Q = 18 \times 64 = 1152$. But what is the consumer surplus?

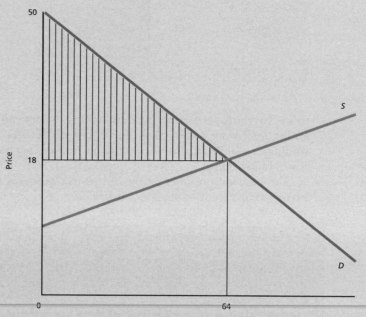

We need to know the size of the shaded triangular area in the figure. The base of the triangle is 64. What is its height? First, find the price at which quantity demanded (Q_d) is zero.

Set $Q_d = 0$
$0 = 100 - 2P$
$P = 50$

thus the height of the triangle is $50 - 18 = 32$. The area of a triangle is (base × height)/2, so the area in the figure is:

$$\frac{(64 \times 32)}{2} = 1024$$

Total utility is expenditure plus consumer surplus:

$TU = 1152 + 1024 = 2176$

Household choice in input markets

So far, we have focused on the decision-making process that lies behind output demand curves. Households with limited incomes allocate those incomes across various combinations of goods and services that are available and affordable. In looking at the factors affecting choices in the output market, we assumed that income was fixed, or given. We noted at the outset, however, that income is in fact partially determined by choices that households make in input markets (look back at Figure 6.1). We now turn to a brief discussion of the two decisions households make in input markets: the labour supply decision and the saving decision.

The labour supply decision

Most income in European countries is wage and salary income paid in compensation for labour. Household members supply labour in exchange for wages or salaries. As in output markets, households face constrained choices in input markets. They must decide:

1. whether to work,
2. how much to work, and
3. what kind of a job to work at.

In essence, household members must decide how much labour to supply. The choices they make are affected by:

1. the availability of jobs,
2. market wage rates, and
3. the skills they possess.

As with decisions in output markets, the labour supply decision involves a set of trade-offs. There are basically two alternatives to working for a wage: (1) not working, and (2) unpaid work. If I don't work, I sacrifice income for the benefits of staying at home and reading, watching TV, going swimming, or sleeping. Another option is to work and produce, but not for a money wage. In this case, I sacrifice money income for the benefits of growing my own food in my garden, bringing up my children or taking care of my house.

As with the trade-offs in output markets, my final choice depends on how I value the alternatives available. If I work, I earn a wage that I can use to buy things. Thus, the trade-off is between the value of the goods and services I can buy with the wages I earn versus the value of things I can produce at home (home-grown food, manageable children, clean clothes, and so on) or the value I place on leisure. This choice is illustrated in Figure 6.10. In general, then:

> The wage rate can be thought of as the price – or the opportunity cost – of the benefits either of unpaid work or of leisure.

Figure 6.10 The trade-off facing households

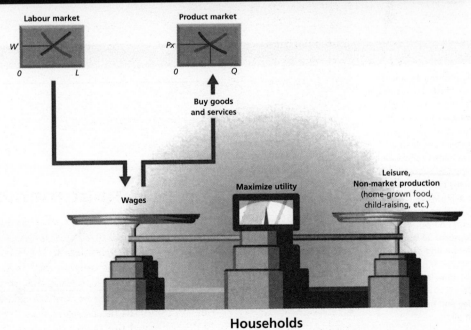

The decision to enter the workforce involves a trade-off between wages (and the goods and services that wages will buy) on the one hand, and leisure and the value of non-market production on the other.

The price of leisure

In our analysis in the early part of this chapter, households had to allocate a limited budget across a set of goods and services. Now they must choose among goods, services and *leisure*.

When we add leisure to the picture, we do so with one important distinction. Trading off one good for another involves buying less of one and more of another, so households simply reallocate *money* from one good to the other. 'Buying' more leisure, however, means reallocating *time* between work and non-work activities.

If we assume that jobs are available, that households have the option of part-time work, that households receive no non-wage income (such as interest, dividends, or gifts from family members), and that there are no taxes, we can draw the budget constraint facing a typical household. Figure 6.11 shows an opportunity set that includes leisure. The quantity of leisure consumed appears on the X axis; on the Y axis is the amount of daily income. Assuming that the primary motive for working is to obtain the things that wages will buy, we can think of the Y axis as a measure of all other goods. Since there is no non-wage income, the only way to get goods and services is by working to earn wages.

If I decide to use all my time for leisure activities, I will earn no income and consume no other goods, the situation indicated by point A on the budget constraint. If I decide to work every hour of the day and night for a wage of €10 per hour, I will earn $24 \times €10 = €240$ per day and be at point B on the budget constraint. If I take a regular job and work eight hours per day, I will earn $8 \times €10 = €80$ per day and consume 16 hours of leisure, point C on the budget constraint. For each hour of leisure that I decide to consume, I give up one hour's wages. Thus the wage rate is the *price of leisure*.

Conditions in the labour market determine the budget constraints and final opportunity sets that face households. The availability of jobs and these jobs' wage rates determine the final combinations of goods and services that a household can afford. The final choice within these constraints depends on each household's unique tastes and preferences. Some people place very little value on leisure, while others place a high value on things like playing tennis or lying on the beach – but everyone needs to put food on the table.

Figure 6.11 The labour/leisure choice

By plotting income on the Y-axis and hours of leisure on the X-axis, the graph shows all combinations of daily income and leisure available to someone who can choose how many hours to work at a given wage rate of €10. If he chose not to work, he would consume 24 hours of leisure and earn no income. If he worked all the time, he would earn $24 \times €10 = €240$ per day and have no leisure at all.

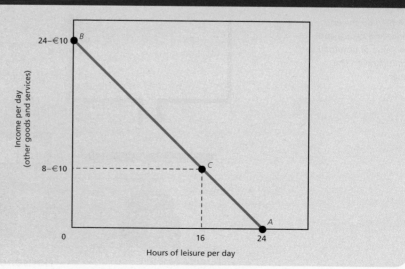

Income and substitution effects of a wage change

A 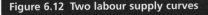 **labour supply curve** shows the quantity of labour supplied as a function of the wage rate. The shape of the labour supply curve depends on how households react to changes in the wage rate.

Consider an increase in wages. First, an increase in wages makes households better off. If they work the same number of hours – that is, if they supply the same amount of labour – they will earn higher incomes and be able to buy more goods and services. But they can also buy more leisure. If leisure is a normal good (that is, a good for which demand increases as income increases), an increase in income will lead to a higher demand for leisure and a lower labour supply. This is the *income effect of a wage increase*.

However, there is also a potential *substitution effect of a wage increase*. A higher wage rate means that leisure is more expensive. If you think of the wage rate as the price of leisure, each individual hour of leisure consumed at a higher wage costs more in forgone wages. As a result, we would expect households to substitute other goods for leisure. This means working more, or a lower demand for leisure and a higher labour supply.

Note that in the labour market the income and substitution effects work in *opposite* directions when leisure is a normal good. The income effect of a wage increase implies buying more leisure and working less; the substitution effect implies buying less leisure and working more. Whether households will supply more labour overall or less labour overall when wages rise depends on the relative strength of both the income and the substitution effects.

Figure 6.12 Two labour supply curves

If we think of leisure as a normal good, an increase in wages that increases income may lead via the income effect to more leisure and less work. When the income effect outweighs the substitution effect, the result may be a 'backward-bending' labour supply curve: lower labour supply at higher wages.

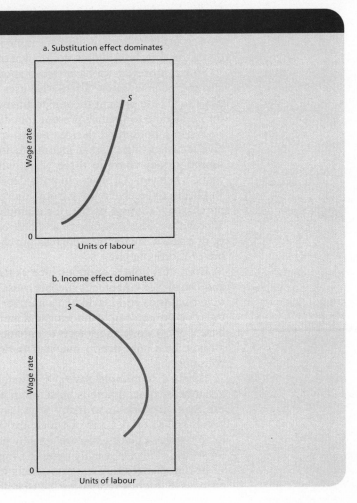

If the substitution effect is greater than the income effect, the wage increase will increase labour supply. This suggests that the labour supply curve slopes upwards, or has a positive slope, like the one in Figure 6.12a. If the income effect outweighs the substitution effect, however, a higher wage will lead to added consumption of leisure, and labour supply will decrease. This implies that the labour supply curve 'bends back', as the one in Figure 6.12b does.

During the early years of the Industrial Revolution in late eighteenth-century Great Britain, the textile industry operated under what was called the 'putting out' system. Spinning and weaving were done in small cottages to supplement the family farm income, hence the term 'cottage industry'. During that period, wages and household incomes rose considerably. Some economic historians claim that this higher income actually led many households to take more leisure and work fewer hours; the empirical evidence suggests a backward-bending labour supply curve.

Just as income and substitution effects helped us to understand household choices in output markets, they now help us to understand household choices in input markets. The point here is simple:

> When leisure is added to the choice set, the line between input and output market decisions becomes blurred. In fact, households decide simultaneously how much of each good to consume and how much leisure to consume.

Saving and borrowing: present versus future consumption

We began this chapter by examining the way households allocate a fixed income over a large number of goods and services. We then pointed out that, at least in part, choices made by households determine income levels. Within the constraints imposed by the market, households decide whether to work and how much to work.

So far, however, we have talked about only the current period – the allocation of current income among alternative uses and the work/leisure choice. But households can also (1) use present income to finance future spending – they can *save* – or (2) use future income to finance present spending – they can *borrow*.

When a household decides not to spend part of its current income but rather to save it, it is using current income to finance future consumption. That future consumption may come in three years, when you use your savings to buy a car; in 10 years, when you sell shares to put a deposit on a house; or in 45 years, when you retire and begin to receive money from your pension. But most people cannot finance large purchases – a house or flat, for example – out of current income and savings. They almost always borrow money and take out a mortgage. When a household borrows, it is, in essence, financing a current purchase with future income. It pays back the loan out of future income.

Even in simple economies such as the two-person desert island economy of Anna and David (see Chapter 2), people must make decisions about *present versus future consumption*. Anna and David had a number of options: They could (1) produce goods for today's consumption by hunting and gathering, (2) consume leisure by sleeping on the beach, or (3) work on projects to enhance future consumption opportunities. Building a house or a boat over a five-year period is trading present consumption for future consumption.

When a household saves, it usually puts the money into something that will generate income. There is no sense in putting money under your mattress when you can make it work in so many ways: savings accounts, money market funds, stocks, bonds and so on – many of which are virtually risk free. When you put your money in any of these places, you are actually lending it out, and the borrower pays you a fee for its use. This fee usually takes the form of *interest*.

Just as changes in wage rates affect household behaviour in the labour market, so changes in interest rates affect household behaviour in capital markets. When interest rates change, they affect both the cost of borrowing *and* the return to saving. Higher interest rates mean that borrowing is more expensive – required monthly payments on a newly purchased house or car will be higher. But higher interest rates also mean that saving will earn a higher return: €1000 invested in a 5% savings account or bond yields €50 per year, but if rates rise to 10% the annual interest rises to €100.

But what impact do interest rates have on saving behaviour? As with the effect of wage changes on labour supply, the effect of changes in interest rates on saving can best be understood in terms of income and substitution effects. Suppose, for example, that I have been saving for a number of years for retirement. Will an increase in interest rates lead to an increase or a decrease in my saving? The answer is not obvious. First, because each part of my income saved will earn a higher rate of return, the 'price' of spending today in terms of forgone future spending is higher. That is, each euro or pound or mark or franc that I spend today (instead of saving) costs me more in terms of future consumption because my saving will now earn a higher return. On this score I will be led to save *more*, and this is the substitution effect at work.

But note that I will also earn more on all the saving that I have done to date, and in this sense I am better off. I will not need to save as much for retirement or future consumption as I did before. Consequently, I will be led to save *less*, and this is the income effect at work. The final impact of a change in interest rates depends on the relative size of the income and substitution effects. Most empirical evidence indicates that saving tends to increase as the interest rate rises. In other words, the substitution effect is larger than the income effect.

Saving and investment decisions involve a huge and complex set of institutions, the financial capital market, in which the suppliers of capital (households that save) and the demand for capital (business firms that want to invest) interact. The amount of capital investment in an economy is constrained in the long run by the saving rate of that economy.[7] You can think of household *saving*, then, as the economy's supply of capital. When a firm borrows to finance a capital acquisition, it is almost as if households have supplied the capital for the fee we call interest. We treat capital markets in detail in Chapter 11.

financial capital market
The complex set of institutions in which suppliers of capital (households that save) and the demand for capital (business firms wanting to invest) interact.

A review: households in output and input markets

In probing the behaviour of households in both input and output markets and examining the nature of constrained choice, we went behind the household demand curve, using the simplifying assumption that income was fixed and given. Income, wealth and prices set the limits, or *constraints*, within which households make their choices in output markets. Within those limits, households make their choices on the basis of personal tastes and preferences.

The notion of *utility* helps to explain the process of choice. The law of *diminishing marginal utility* partly explains why people seem to spread their incomes over many different goods and services and why demand curves have a negative slope. Another important way of explaining the negative relationship between price and quantity demanded lies in *income effects* and *substitution effects*.

As we turned to input markets, we relaxed the assumption that income was fixed and given. In the labour market, households are forced to weigh the value of leisure against the value of goods and services that can be bought with wage income. Once

[7]*Here we are looking at a country as if it were isolated from the rest of the world – as if it were a closed economy. Very often, however, capital investment is financed by funds loaned or provided by foreign citizens or governments. For example, in recent years a substantial amount of Japanese savings has found its way into Europe to buy stocks, bonds and other financial instruments. In part, these flows finance capital investment. Also, Europe and other countries that contribute funds to the World Bank and the International Monetary Fund have provided large sums in outright grants and loans to help developing countries produce capital.*

again, we found household preferences for goods and leisure operating within a set of constraints imposed by the market. Households also face the problem of allocating income and consumption over more than one period of time. They can finance spending in the future with today's income by saving and earning interest, or they can spend tomorrow's income today by borrowing.

We now have a rough sketch of the factors that determine output demand and input supply. (You can review these in Figure 6.1.) In the next three chapters, we turn to firm behaviour and explore in detail the factors that affect output supply and input demand.

Summary

1. In perfectly competitive markets, prices are determined by the forces of supply and demand, and no single household or firm has any control over them. The assumption of a perfectly competitive market underlies all of our discussions through to Chapter 12. Much of what we say in these chapters, however, can be generalized to the other forms of market structure. We also assume that households possess *perfect knowledge* of the qualities and prices of everything available in the market.

Household choice in output markets

2. Every household must make three basic decisions: (1) how much of each product, or output, to demand; (2) how much labour to supply; and (3) how much to spend today and how much to save for the future.

3. Income, wealth, and prices define a household's *budget constraint*. The budget constraint separates those combinations of goods and services that are available from those that are not. All the points below and to the left of a graph of a household's budget constraint make up its *choice set*, or *opportunity set*.

4. It is best to think of the household choice problem as one of allocating income over a large number of goods and services. A change in the price of one good may change the entire allocation. Demand for some goods may rise while demand for others may fall.

5. As long as a household faces a limited income, the real cost of any single good or service is the value of the *other* goods and services that could have been purchased with the same amount of money.

6. Within the constraints of prices, income and wealth, household decisions ultimately depend on preferences.

The basis of choice: utility

7. Whether one item is preferable to another depends on how much utility, or satisfaction, it yields relative to its alternatives.

8. The *law of diminishing marginal utility* says that the more of any good we consume in a given period of time, the less satisfaction, or utility, we get out of each additional, or marginal, unit of that good.

9. Households allocate income among goods and services in order to maximize utility. This implies choosing activities that yield the highest marginal utility per pound, euro or other unit currency. In a two-good world, households will choose so as to equate the marginal utility per unit of currency spent on X with the marginal utility per unit of currency spent on Y. This is the *utility-maximizing rule*.

Income and substitution effects

10. The fact that demand curves slope downwards, or have a negative slope, can be explained in two ways: (1) marginal utility for all goods diminishes, and (2) for most normal goods both the *income* and *substitution effects* of a price decline lead to more consumption of the good.

Consumer surplus

11. When any good is sold at a fixed price, households must 'reveal' whether that good is worth the price being asked. For many people who buy in a given market, the product is worth more than its current price. Those people receive a *consumer surplus*.

Household choice in input markets

12. In the labour market, a trade-off exists between the value of the goods and services that can be bought in the market or produced at home and the value that one places on leisure. The opportunity cost of paid work is leisure and unpaid work. The wage rate is the price, or opportunity cost, of the benefits of either unpaid work or of leisure.

13. The income and substitution effects of a change in the wage rate work in opposite directions. Higher wages mean that (1) leisure is more expensive (probable response: people work *more* – substitution effect); and (2) more income is earned in a given number of hours so some time may be spent on leisure (probable response: people work *less* – income effect).

14. In addition to deciding how to allocate its present income among goods and services, a household may also decide to save or borrow. When a household decides to save part of its current income, it is using current income to finance future spending. When a household borrows, it finances current purchases with future income.

15. A change in interest rates has a positive effect on saving if the substitution effect dominates the income effect, and a negative effect if the income effect dominates the substitution effect. Most empirical evidence shows that the substitution effect dominates here.

Review Terms and Concepts

budget constraint
choice set or opportunity set
consumer surplus
cost-benefit analysis
diamond/water paradox
financial capital market
income effect of a price change

labour supply curve
law of diminishing marginal utility
marginal utility (MU)
perfect knowledge
substitution effect of a price change
total utility
utility

Problem Set

1. Sketch the budget constraints shown in the table (all values are in euros)

	P_X	P_Y	INCOME
a.	20	50	1000
b.	40	50	1000
c.	20	100	1000
d.	20	50	2000
e.	0.25	0.25	7.00
f.	0.25	0.50	7.00
g.	0.50	0.25	7.00

2. Dominique lives in Paris but goes to university in Amsterdam. For the last two years she has made four trips home each year. During 1999, the price of a return ticket from Paris to Amsterdam increased from €350 to €600. As a result she bought five fewer CDs that year and decided not to go with friends to an expensive rock concert.
a. Explain how Dominique's demand for CDs and concert tickets can be affected by an increase in air travel prices.
b. Using this example, explain why both income and substitution effects might be expected to reduce the number of trips home that she takes.

3. On 1 January Professor Coustan made a resolution to lose weight and save some money. He decided that he would strictly budget €100 for lunches each month. For lunch he has only two choices: the senior common room (SCR), where the price of a lunch is €5, and Alice's Restaurant, where a lunch costs €10. Every day that he doesn't eat lunch, he runs five miles.
a. Assuming that Professor Coustan spends the entire €100 each month either at Alice's or in the SCR, sketch his budget constraint. Show actual numbers on the axes.
b. Last month Professor Coustan chose to eat in the SCR ten times and at Alice's five times. Does this choice fit within his budget constraint?
c. Last month Alice ran a half-price lunch special all month. All lunches were reduced to five euros. Show the effect on Professor Smith's budget constraint.
d. During Alice's sale, Professor Coustan continued to eat there only five times but ate in the SCR 15 times. This implies that Alice's meals are 'inferior goods'. Explain why. (*Hint*: use income and substitution effects.)

4. In the United States, reform of the welfare system has been a goal of many administrations, including President Clinton's. The major thrust of welfare reform proposals over the last two decades has been to restore the incentive to work. Because welfare programmes are for low-income families, those who earn income lose their eligibility for welfare. This acts as a stiff 'tax' on working.

In 1981, President Reagan proposed and the Congress approved significant cuts in welfare expenditures. Cutting benefits would make living on welfare less attractive, it was argued, and lead to an expansion of the labour supply. But the way the welfare changes were enacted led to a second effect. Before the cuts, a welfare recipient's benefits were reduced by 50 cents for every dollar he or she earned. For example, someone who earned $200 per month would lose $100 in welfare benefits, so his or her final income would rise by only $100. After the cuts, the implicit tax rate went up to 80%: benefits were reduced by 80 cents for every dollar earned. For example, after the cuts, a person earning $200 would lose $160 in benefits. This meant that final income would rise by only $40.

Using the income and substitution effects, explain how the Reagan cuts could lead to either an increase or a decrease in labour supply.

5. Assume that Mei has €100 per month to divide between dinners at a Chinese restaurant and nights at the Zanzibar, a local pub. Assume that going to the Zanzibar costs €20 and eating at the Chinese restaurant costs €10. Suppose that Mei spends two nights at the Zanzibar and eats six times at the Chinese restaurant.
a. Draw Mei's budget constraint and show that she can afford six meals and two nights at the Zanzibar.
b. Assume that Mei comes into some money and can now spend €200 per month. Draw her new budget constraint.
c. As a result of the increase in income, Mei decides to spend eight nights at the Zanzibar and to eat at the Chinese restaurant four times. What kind of a good is Chinese food? What kind of a good is a night at the Zanzibar?
d. What part of the increase in Zanzibar trips is due to the income effect, and what part is due to the substitution effect? Explain your answer.

6. Sketch the income/leisure budget constraint facing a person with (a) a 24-hour endowment of time daily; (b) €50 in property income per day (received regardless of work effort); (c) a job that requires a minimum of eight hours of work per day and that pays a wage of €10 per hour, plus time-and-a-half for all work over eight hours (1.5 × €10); and (d) no other work opportunities.

Note: All these should be embodied in a single income/leisure budget constraint.

7. For each of the following events, consider how you might react. What things might you consume more of? What things might you consume less of? Would you work more or less? Would you increase or decrease your saving? Are your responses consistent with the discussion of household behaviour in this chapter?

a. Tuition fees at your university are cut by 25%.
b. You receive an award that pays you €300 per month for the next five years.
c. The price of food doubles.
d. A new business opens up nearby offering part-time jobs at €20 per hour.

8. Assume that as a result of two recent hijackings, people's desire to fly diminishes significantly. Describe and graph (using supply and demand curves) how you might expect the air travel market to react. What might happen to the price of airline tickets? Explain consumers' reactions to any price changes in terms of income and substitution effects.

9. Is it possible for a unit of a good to have a negative marginal utility? Can you think of an example? How would consumption of this unit affect total utility? Why would it make no sense to knowingly purchase a good with negative utility?

10. Say whether you agree or disagree with each of the following statements and explain your reason.
a. 'If the income effect of a wage change dominates the substitution effect for a given household, and the household works longer hours following a wage change, wages must have risen.'
b. 'In product markets when a price falls, the substitution effect leads to more consumption, but for normal goods, the income effect leads to less consumption.'

11. For this problem assume that Jo has €80 to spend on books and on going to the cinema each month, and that both goods must be purchased whole (no fractional units). Films cost €8 each, while books cost €20 each. Jo's preferences for films and books are summarized by the information in the table.
a. Fill in the figures for marginal utility and marginal utility per euro for both films and books.
b. Are these preferences consistent with the 'law of diminishing marginal utility'? Explain briefly.
c. Given the budget of €80, what quantity of books and what quantity of films will maximize Jo's level of satisfaction? Explain briefly.
d. Draw the budget constraint (with books on the horizontal axis) and identify the optimal combination of books and films as point A.
e. Now suppose the price of books falls to €10. Which of the columns in the table must be recalculated? Do the required recalculations.
f. After the price change, how many films and how many books will Jo purchase?
g. Draw in the new budget constraint and identify the new optimal combination of books and films as point B.
h. If you calculated correctly, you have found that a decrease in the price of books has caused this person to buy more films as well as more books. How can this be?

Films No. per month	TU	MU	MU/euro	Books No. per month	TU	MU	MU/euro
1	50			1	22		
2	80			2	42		
3	100			3	52		
4	110			4	57		
5	116			5	60		
6	121			6	62		
7	123			7	63		

12. In most countries, an auction has bidders starting at low prices and bidding progressively higher. In The Netherlands, the process is reversed: the auctioneer starts at a high price and bids down. The first person to agree to an announced price will get the good. Which method is more effective at reducing consumer surplus? Why?

13. If leisure is a normal good, would you expect a large inheritance to cause an increase or a decrease in the number of hours a person wants to work? Why? How would a 100% tax rate on a large inheritance affect total desired working hours in the economy?

*14. Marianne's utility function for pizzas is of the form TU = $64Q - 2Q^2$ where Q is the quantity of pizzas demanded per month and TU = total degrees of utility.

a. How many degrees of utility does she derive if she consumes 4 pizzas per month?

b. If she purchases 8 pizzas per month how many degrees of utility does she derive from her consumption?

c. Derive her marginal utility function.

d. Does her marginal utility decline at a constant rate, increasing rate or decreasing rate?

e. At what level of consumption is her marginal utility equal to zero?

*15. Stefan's utility function for petrol is of the form TU = $100Q - 10Q^2 + Q^3$, where Q is the quantity of petrol demanded per year in litres.

a. Derive his marginal utility function for petrol.

b. Does his marginal utility decline at a constant rate, increasing rate or decreasing rate?

Appendix to Chapter 6

Indifference Curves and Goods Characteristics

Early in this chapter, you saw how a consumer choosing between two goods is constrained by the prices of those goods and by his or her income. This appendix analyses the process of choice more formally. (Before we proceed, carefully review 'The budget constraint more formally' subsection of this chapter, in which Ann and Tom trade off jazz club visits against Thai food.)

Assumptions

We base the following analysis on four assumptions:

1. We assume that this analysis is restricted to goods that yield positive marginal utility; or, more simply, that

'more is better'. One way to justify this assumption is to say that if more of something actually makes you worse off, you can simply throw it away at no cost. This is the assumption of free disposal.

2. The **marginal rate of substitution** is defined as MU_X/MU_Y, or the ratio at which a household is willing to substitute Y for X. When MU_X/MU_Y is equal to 4, for example, I would be willing to trade four units of Y for one additional unit of X.

We assume a diminishing marginal rate of substitution. That is, as more of X and less of Y is consumed, MU_X/MU_Y declines. As you consume more of X and less of Y, X becomes less valuable in terms of units of Y, or Y becomes more valuable in terms of X.

This is almost, but not precisely, equivalent to assuming diminishing marginal utility.

3. We assume that consumers have the ability to choose among the combinations of goods and services available. Confronted with the choice between two alternative combinations of goods and services, *A* and *B*, a consumer will respond in one of three ways: (1) she prefers *A* over *B*, (2) she prefers *B* over *A*, or (3) she is indifferent between *A* and *B* – that is, she likes *A* and *B* equally.

4. We assume that consumer choices are consistent with a simple assumption of rationality. If a consumer shows that he prefers *A* to *B* and subsequently shows that he prefers *B* to a third alternative *C*, he should prefer *A* to *C* if confronted with a choice between the two.

Deriving indifference curves

If we accept these four assumptions, we can construct a 'map' of a consumer's preferences. These preference maps are made up of indifference curves. An **indifference curve** is a set of points, each point representing a combination of goods *X* and *Y*, all of which yield the same total utility.

Figure 6A.1 shows how we might go about deriving an indifference curve for a hypothetical consumer. Each point on the diagram represents some amount of *X* and some amount of *Y*. Point *A* in the diagram, for example, represents X_A units of *X* and Y_A units of *Y*. Now suppose that we take some amount of *Y* away from our hypothetical consumer, moving him to *A'*. At *A'* he has the same amount of *X* – that is, X_A units – but less *Y*; he now has only Y_C units of *Y*. Since 'more is better', our consumer is unequivocally worse off at *A'* than he was at *A*.

To compensate for the loss of *Y*, we now begin giving our consumer some more *X*. If we give him just a little,

he will still be worse off than he was at *A*; if we give him lots of *X*, he will be better off. But there must be some quantity of *X* that will just compensate for the loss of *Y*. By giving him that amount, we will have put together a bundle, Y_C and X_C, which yields the exact same total utility as bundle *A*. This is bundle *C* in Figure 6A.1. If confronted with a choice between bundles *A* and *C*, our consumer will say 'Either one. I don't care.' In other words, he is indifferent between *A* and *C*. When confronted with a choice between bundles *C* and *B* (which represents X_B and Y_B units of *X* and *Y*), he is also indifferent. The points along the curve labelled in Figure 6A.1 represent all the combinations of *X* and *Y* that yield the same total utility to our consumer. That curve is thus an indifference curve.

Each consumer has a whole set of indifference curves. Return for a moment to Figure 6A.1. Starting at point *A* again, imagine that we give the consumer a tiny bit more *X* *and* a tiny bit more *Y*. Because more is better, we know that the new bundle will yield a higher level of total utility, and the consumer will be better off. Now, just as we constructed the first indifference curve, we can construct a second one. What we get is an indifference curve that is *higher* and to the *right* of it. Because utility along an indifference curve is constant at all points, every point along the new curve represents a higher level of total utility than every point along the first.

Figure 6A.2 shows a set of four indifference curves. The curve labelled i_4 represents the combinations of *X* and *Y* that yield the highest level of total utility among the four. Many other indifference curves exist between those shown on the diagram; in fact, their number is infinite. Notice that as you move up and to the right, utility increases.

Figure 6A.1 An indifference curve

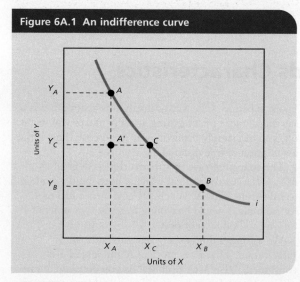

An indifference curve is a set of points, each representing a combination of some amount of good *X* and some amount of good *Y*, that all yield the same amount of total utility. The consumer depicted here is indifferent between bundles *A* and *B*, *B* and *C* and *A* and *C*.

Figure 6A.2 A preference map: a family of indifference curves

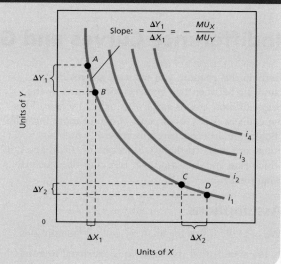

Each consumer has a unique family of indifference curves called a preference map. Higher indifference curves represent higher levels of total utility.

The shapes of the indifference curves depend on the preferences of the consumer, and the whole set of indifference curves is called a **preference map**. Each consumer has a unique preference map.

Properties of indifference curves

The indifference curves shown in Figure 6A.2 are drawn bowing in towards the origin, or zero point, on the axes. In other words, the absolute value of the slope of the indifference curves decreases, or the curves get flatter, as we move down them. Thus, we say that indifference curves are convex towards the origin. This shape follows directly from the assumption of diminishing marginal rate of substitution and makes sense if you remember the law of diminishing marginal utility.

To understand the convex shape, compare the segment of curve i_1 between A and B with the segment of the same curve between C and D. Moving from A to B, the consumer is willing to give up a substantial amount of Y to get a small amount of X. (Remember that total utility is constant along an indifference curve; the consumer is therefore indifferent between A and B.) Moving from C and D, however, the consumer is willing to give up only a small amount of Y to get more X.

This changing trade-off makes complete sense when you remember the law of diminishing marginal utility. Notice that between A and B, a lot of Y is consumed, and the marginal utility derived from a unit of Y is likely to be small. At the same time, though, only a little bit of X is being consumed, so the marginal utility derived from consuming a unit of X is likely to be high.

Suppose, for example, that X is pizza and Y is coffee. Near A and B, a hungry and thirsty footballer who has ten coffees in front of him but only one slice of pizza will trade several coffees for another slice. Down around C and D, however, he has 20 slices of pizza and only a single coffee. Now he will trade several slices of pizza to get an additional coffee.

We can show how the trade-off changes more formally by deriving an expression for the slope of an indifference curve. Let's look at the arc (that is, the section of the curve) between A and B. We know that in moving from A to B, total utility remains constant. That means that the utility lost as a result of consuming less Y must be matched by the utility gained from consuming more X. We can approximate the loss of utility by multiplying the marginal utility of Y (MU_Y) by the number of units by which consumption of Y is curtailed (ΔY). Similarly, we can approximate the utility gained from consuming more X by multiplying the marginal utility of X (MU_X) by the number of additional units of X consumed (ΔX). Remember, because the consumer is indifferent between points A and B, total utility is the same at both points. Thus, these two must be equal in magnitude – that is, the gain in utility from consuming more X must equal the loss in utility from consuming less Y. Since ΔY is a negative number (because consumption of Y decreases from A to B), it follows that:

$$MU_Y \cdot \Delta Y = -(MU_X \cdot \Delta X)$$

If we divide both sides by MU_Y and by ΔX, we obtain:

$$\Delta Y / \Delta X = \left(\frac{MU_X}{MU_Y} \right)$$

Recall that the slope of any line is calculated by dividing the change in Y (that is, ΔY) by the change in X (that is, ΔX). This leads us to conclude that:

> The slope of an indifference curve is the ratio of the marginal utility of X to the marginal utility of Y, and it is negative.

Now let's return to our pizza (X) and coffee (Y) example. As we move down from the A:B area to the C:D area, our footballer is consuming less coffee and more pizza. The marginal utility of pizza (MU_X) is falling and the marginal utility of coffee (MU_Y) is rising. That means that MU_X/MU_Y (**the marginal rate of substitution**) is falling, and the absolute value of the slope of the indifference curve is declining. And, indeed, it does get flatter.

Consumer choice

As you recall, demand depends on income, the prices of goods and services, and preferences or tastes. We are now ready to see how preferences as embodied in indifference curves interact with budget constraints to determine how the final quantities of X and Y will be chosen.

In Figure 6A.3, a set of indifference curves is superimposed on a consumer's budget constraint. Recall that the budget constraint separates those combinations

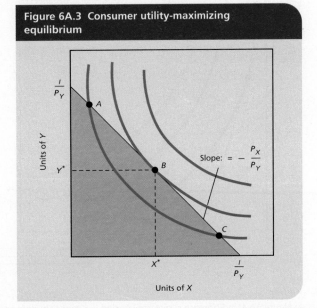

Figure 6A.3 Consumer utility-maximizing equilibrium

Consumers will choose the combination of X and Y that maximizes total utility. Graphically, the consumer will move along the budget constraint until the highest possible indifference curve is reached. At that point, the budget constraint and the indifference curve are tangential. This point of tangency occurs at X^* and Y^* (point B).

of X and Y that are available from those that are not. The constraint simply shows those combinations that can be purchased with an income of I at prices P_X and P_Y. The budget constraint crosses the X axis at I/P_X, or the number of units of X that can be purchased with I if nothing is spent on Y. Similarly, the budget constraint crosses the Y axis at I/P_Y, or the number of units of Y that can be purchased with an income of I if nothing is spent on X. The shaded area is the consumer's opportunity set. The slope of a budget constraint is $-P_X/P_Y$.

Consumers will choose from among available combinations of X and Y the one that maximizes utility. In graphic terms, the consumer will move along the budget constraint until he or she is on the highest possible indifference curve. Utility rises by moving from points such as A or C (which lie on i_1) towards B (which lies on i_2). Any movement away from point B moves the consumer to a lower indifference curve – a lower level of utility. In this case, utility is maximized when our consumer buys X^* units of X and Y^* units of Y. At point B, the budget constraint is just tangent to (that is, just touches) indifference curve i_2.

As long as indifference curves are convex to the origin, utility maximization will take place at that point at which the indifference curve is just tangent to the budget constraint.

The tangency condition has important implications. Where two curves are tangential, they have the same slope, which implies that the slope of the indifference curve is exactly equal to the slope of the budget constraint at the point of tangency:

$$-\frac{MU_X}{MU_Y} = -\frac{P_X}{P_Y}$$

slope of indifference curve = slope of budget constraint

By multiplying both sides by MU_Y and dividing both sides by P_X, we can rewrite this utility-maximizing rule as:

$$\frac{MU_X}{P_X} = \frac{MU_Y}{P_Y}$$

This is the same rule derived in our earlier discussion without using indifference curves. We can describe this rule intuitively by saying that consumers maximize their total utility by equating the marginal utility per money unit spent on X with the marginal utility per money unit spent on Y. If this condition did not hold, utility could be increased by shifting money from one good to the other.

Deriving a demand curve from indifference curves and budget constraints

We now turn to the task of deriving a simple demand curve from indifference curves and budget constraints. A demand curve shows the quantity of a single good, X

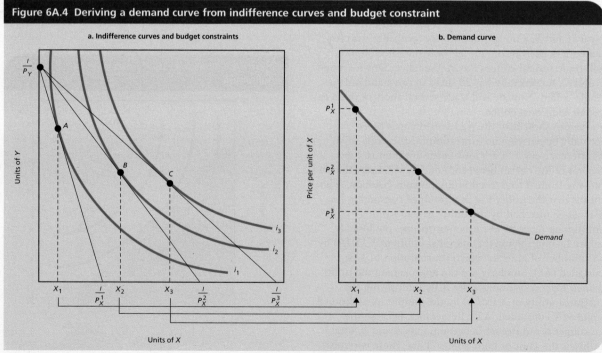

Figure 6A.4 Deriving a demand curve from indifference curves and budget constraint

a. Indifference curves and budget constraints

b. Demand curve

In Figure 6A.4, indifference curves are labelled i_1, i_2 and i_3; budget constraints are shown by the three diagonal lines from I/P_Y to I/P_X^1, I/P_X^2 and I/P_X^3. Lowering the price of X from P_X^1 to P_X^2 and then to P_X^3 shifts the budget constraint to the right. At each price there is a different utility-maximizing combination of X and Y. Utility is maximized at point A on i_1, point B on i_2 and point C on i_3. Plotting the three prices against the quantities of X chosen results in a standard downward-sloping demand curve.

in this case, that a consumer will demand at various prices. To derive the demand curve, we need to confront our consumer with several alternative prices for X while keeping other prices, income and preferences constant.

Figure 6A.4 shows the derivation. We begin with price P_X^1. At that price, the utility-maximizing point is A, where the consumer demands X_1 units of X. Therefore, in the right-hand diagram, we plot P_X^1 against X_1. This is the first point on our demand curve.

Now we lower the price of X to P_X^2. Lowering the price expands the opportunity set, and the budget constraint pivots to the right. Because the price of X has fallen, if our consumer spends all of his income on X, he can buy more of it. He is also better off, since he can move to a higher indifference curve. The new utility-maximizing point is B, where the consumer demands X_2 units of X. Because the consumer demands X_2 units of X at a price of P_X^2 we plot P_X^2 against X_2 in the right-hand diagram. A second price cut to P_X^3 moves our consumer to point C, where he demands X_3 units of X, and so on. Thus, we see how the demand curve can be derived from a consumer's preference map and budget constraint.

Goods characteristics

Kelvin Lancaster has argued that the utility consumers derive from goods comes from those goods' characteristics. When you consider buying a house you will consider not only the prices of possible houses but also their characteristics: size, age, location etc. For a car the characteristics might be comfort, fuel economy, reliability and image. We use Figure 6A.5 to examine Harriet's behaviour with regard to purchasing pairs of tights. The characteristics important to her are sex appeal, measured along the horizontal axis, and durability, measured up the vertical axis. The indifference curves show her preferences. She is prepared to trade some loss of sex appeal against greater durability but she has a diminishing marginal rate of substitution between these two characteristics.

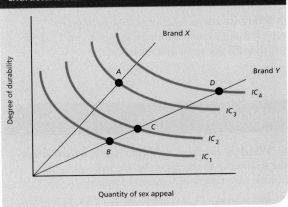

Figure 6A.5 Consumer preference and goods characteristics

The rays from the origin represent different brands of tights. The steeper ray might represent a brand which is quite thick, scoring high on durability and low on sex appeal. We will call it brand X. Brand Y represented by the flatter ray, is much more sheer. It therefore has greater sex appeal but less durability.

Suppose now that for her budget she could buy the combinations of characteristics represented by points A and B. Since A is on the highest indifference curve, she will choose point A and purchase brand X. These tights are not very sexy but they are durable.

Suppose now the price of brand Y falls. Will she switch to that brand? If the price falls only a little way she will be choosing now between, say, points A and C. Since C is still on a lower indifference curve than A, she will stick with her present brand. However, if brand Y falls far enough in price, she will switch. If she can now for the same expenditure choose to be at point A or point D, Harriet will switch brands and buy the sheer tights with the greater sex appeal despite their lack of durability. She will move to point D.

One of the advantages of goods characteristics theory over indifference analysis is that it gives an explanation of consumer decisions to stick with certain brands even if competitors cut price. Only after some critical level of price fall will a switch of brands take place.

Summary

1. An *indifference curve* is a set of points, each point representing a combination of goods X and Y, all of which yield the same total utility. A particular consumer's set of indifference curves is called a *preference map*.

2. The slope of an indifference curve is the ratio of the marginal utility of X to the marginal utility of Y, and it is negative.

3. As long as indifference curves are convex to the origin, utility maximization will take place at that point at which the indifference curve is tangential to (that is, just touches) the budget constraint. The utility-maximizing rule can also be written as $MU_X/P_X = MU_Y/P_Y$.

4. A development of the indifference curve approach is given by *goods characteristics theory*. It emphasizes that goods are purchased for the characteristics that they display.

Review Terms and Concepts

indifference curve A set of points, each point representing a combination of goods X and Y, all of which yield the same total utility.

marginal rate of substitution MU_X/MU_Y; the ratio at which a household is willing to substitute good Y for good X.

preference map A consumer's set of indifference curves.

Problem Set

1. Which of the four assumptions that were made at the beginning of the appendix are violated by the indifference curves in Figure 1? Explain.

2. Assume that a household receives a weekly income of £100. If Figure 2 represents that household's choices as the price of X changes, plot three points of the household's demand curve.

3. If Ann's marginal rate of substitution of Y for X is 5 (that is, $MU_X/MU_Y = 5$), the price of X is £9.00, and the price of Y is £2.00, she is spending too much of her income on Y. Do you agree or disagree? Explain your answer using a graph.

4. Assume that Paul is a rational consumer who consumes only two goods, apples (A) and nuts (N).

Assume that his marginal rate of substitution of apples for nuts is given by the following formula:

$$MRS = MU_N/MU_A = A/N$$

That is, Paul's MRS is simply equal to the ratio of the number of apples consumed to the number of nuts consumed.

a. Assume that Paul's income is £100, the price of nuts is £5 and the price of apples is £10. What quantities of apples and nuts will he consume?

b. Find two additional points on his demand curve for nuts ($P_N = £10$ and $P_N = £2$).

c. Sketch one of the equilibrium points on an indifference curve graph.

Figure 1

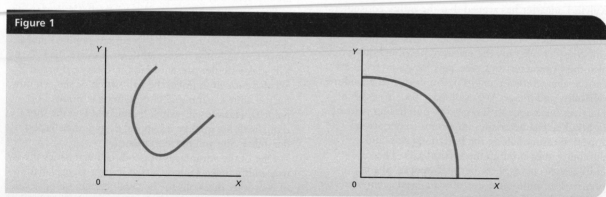

Figure 2

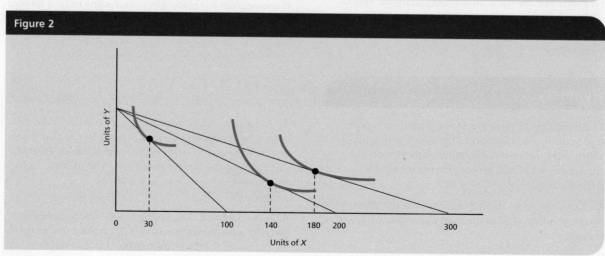

The Behaviour of Profit-maximizing Firms and the Production Process

In Chapter 6, we took a brief look at the household decisions that lie behind supply and demand curves. We spent some time discussing household choices: how much to work and how to choose among the wide range of goods and services available within the constraints of prices and income. We also identified some of the influences on household demand in output markets, as well as some of the influences on household supply behaviour in input markets.

We now turn to the other side of the system and examine the behaviour of firms. Business firms purchase inputs in order to produce and sell outputs. In other words, they *demand* factors of production in input markets and *supply* goods and services in output markets. Figure 7.1 repeats the now familiar circular flow diagram you first encountered in Chapter 6. Here in Chapter 7 we look inside the firm at the production process that transforms inputs into outputs. Chapters 8 and 9 use information on input prices and production technology to discuss cost curves, from which we derive firms' output supply curves. In Chapters 10 and 11, we discuss input markets (specifically, labour, land and capital markets) and derive firms' input demand curves. Chapter 12 puts all the pieces of the system together and analyses how the system as a whole functions.

In Chapters 13–17 we relax some of our assumptions – including the assumption of perfect competition – and examine the role of government in a market economy.

While Chapters 7–12 describe the behaviour of perfectly competitive firms, much of what we say in these chapters also applies to firms that are not perfectly competitive. For example, when we turn to monopoly in Chapter 13, we will be describing firms that are similar to competitive firms in many ways. All firms, whether competitive or not, demand inputs, engage in production and produce outputs. All firms have an incentive to maximize profits and thus to minimize costs.

production The process by which inputs are combined, transformed, and turned into outputs.

Central to our analysis is **production**, the process by which inputs are combined, transformed, and turned into outputs. Firms vary in size and internal organization, but they all take inputs and transform them into things for which there is some demand. An independent accountant, for example, combines labour, paper, telephone service, time, learning and a personal computer to provide help to confused taxpayers. A rock band combines talent, energy, instruments, costumes, amplifiers, lighting and labour to produce music. A car plant uses steel, labour, plastic, electricity, machines and countless other inputs to produce cars. Before we begin our discussion of the production process, however, we need to clarify some of the assumptions on which our analysis is based.

Production is not limited to firms

While our discussions in the next several chapters focus on profit-making business firms, it is important to understand that production and productive activity are not confined to private business firms. Households also engage in transforming factors of production (labour, capital, energy, natural resources etc.) into useful things. When I

Figure 7.1 Firm and household decisions

Firms supply output and demand labour and capital in input markets. This chapter and the next four chapters focus on the left side of this diagram – everything that is highlighted in red.

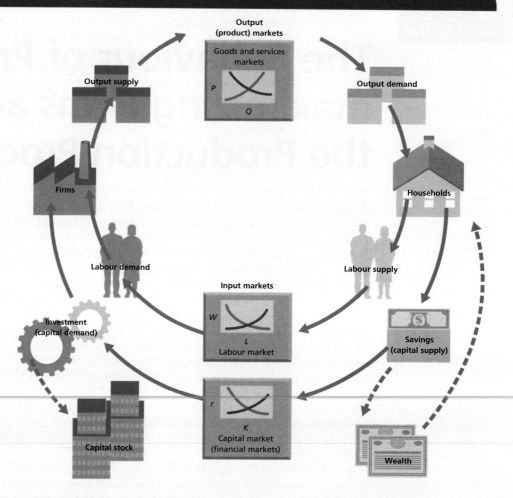

work in my garden, I am combining land, labour, fertilizer, seeds and tools (capital) into the vegetables I eat and the flowers I enjoy. The child-rearing activities of parents transform their young into productive human beings. The government also combines land, labour and capital to produce public services for which demand exists: national defence, police and fire protection and education, to name a few.

Private business firms are set apart from other producers, such as households and government, by their purpose. A **firm** exists when a person or a group of people decides to produce a good or service to meet a perceived demand. In most cases, firms exist to make a profit. They engage in production (that is, they transform inputs into outputs) because they believe that they can sell their products for more than it costs to produce them.

Even among firms that exist to make a profit, however, there are many important differences. A firm's behaviour is likely to depend on how it is organized internally and on its relationship to the firms with which it competes. How many competitors are there? How large are they? How do they compete?

In Chapter 3 we discussed the different ways in which businesses can organize themselves. We also discussed the different forms of industry in European economies – perfect competition, monopolistic competition, oligopoly and monopoly. Before we finish with microeconomics, we will analyse the behaviour of all four of these industry types. But it is logical to start with the simplest. Thus, the next three chapters will deal exclusively with the behaviour of firms in perfectly competitive industries.

firm An organization that comes into being when a person or a group of people decides to produce a good or service to meet a perceived demand. Most firms exist to make a profit.

Perfect competition

perfect competition An industry structure in which there are many firms, each small relative to the industry, producing virtually identical products and in which no firm is large enough to have any control over prices. In perfectly competitive industries, new competitors can freely enter and exit the market.

As you learned in Chapter 3, **perfect competition** exists in an industry that contains many relatively small firms producing identical products. The most important characteristic of a perfectly competitive industry is that no single firm has any control over prices. In other words, an individual firm cannot affect the market price of its product or the prices of the inputs that it buys. This important characteristic follows from two assumptions. First, a competitive industry is composed of many firms, each small relative to the size of the industry. Second, every firm in a perfectly competitive industry produces **homogeneous products**, which means that the output of one firm cannot be distinguished from the output of the others.

These assumptions limit the decisions open to competitive firms and simplify the analysis of competitive behaviour. Firms in perfectly competitive industries do not differentiate their products, nor do they make decisions about price. Rather, each firm takes prices as given – that is, as determined in the market by the laws of supply and demand – and decides only how much to produce and how to produce it.

homogeneous products Undifferentiated products; products that are identical to, or indistinguishable from, one another.

The idea that competitive firms are 'price-takers' is central to our discussion. Of course, we do not mean that firms cannot affix price tags to their merchandise; all firms have this ability. We simply mean that, given the availability of perfect substitutes, any product priced over the market price will not be sold. Thus, to sell any goods, competitive firms must adhere to the market price.

These assumptions also imply that the demand for the product of a competitive firm is perfectly elastic (see Chapter 5). Take, for example, the farmer whose situation is shown in Figure 7.2. The left side of the diagram represents the current conditions in the market. Corn is currently selling for €2.45 per bushel.[1] The right side of the diagram shows the demand for corn as the farmer sees it. If she were to raise her price, she would sell no corn at all; because there are perfect substitutes available, the quantity demanded of her corn would drop to zero. To lower her price would be silly because she can sell all she wants at the current price. (Remember, each farmer's production is very small relative to the entire corn market.)

free entry When there are no barriers to prevent new firms from competing for profits in a profitable industry.

In perfect competition we also assume that firms can freely enter and exit the industry. **Free entry** implies that if firms in an industry are earning high profits, new firms are likely to spring up. There are no barriers that prevent a new firm from

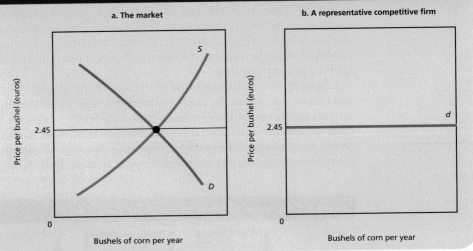

Figure 7.2 Demand facing a single firm in a perfectly competitive market

If a representative firm in a perfectly competitive market raises the price of its output above €2.45, the quantity demanded of *that firm's* output will drop to zero. Each firm faces a perfectly elastic demand curve, *d*.

a. The market

b. A representative competitive firm

[1] *Recall that capital letters refer to the entire market and lower-case letters refer to representative firms. For example, in Figure 7.2, the market demand curve is labelled D and the demand curve facing the firm is labelled d.*

competing. Fast food restaurants are quick to spring up when a new shopping centre opens, and new petrol stations appear when a housing development or a new road is built. Where profit opportunities present themselves, we assume that firms will enter and compete for them.

free exit When firms can easily stop producing their product and leave a market. Firms incur no additional costs by exiting the industry.

Free exit implies that firms can simply stop producing their product and leave a market. Firms incur no additional costs by exiting the industry, hence the term *free exit*. Since the 1970s, for example, one major industry that has been declining is coal. As time has gone on and conditions have changed, fewer and fewer mines have remained in business. Generally speaking, a firm closes down because it is suffering losses or because profits are insufficient. During the last 30 years, large numbers of coal mines have closed in some parts of Europe. This is partly because the demand for other fuel has been increasing. It is also partly because of increased competition from low-cost producers outside Europe, such as Australia and South America.

Agriculture comes close to perfect competition. Although products are differentiated (for example by growing organic produce) no farmer can *brand* his product to distinguish from others. For any given product prices are set by the forces of supply and demand in a huge national market.

The behaviour of profit-maximizing firms

All types of firms must make several basic decisions to achieve what we assume to be their primary objective – maximum profits. Perfectly competitive firms have three basic decisions to make. Actually, *all* firms must make these three decisions, but (as we will see later) non-competitive firms have other decisions to make as well. The three basic decisions (Figure 7.3) that all firms must make are:

1. how much output to supply (quantity of product);
2. how to produce that output (which production technique/technology to use); and
3. how much of each input to demand.

The first and last choices are linked by the second choice. Once a firm has decided how much to produce, the choice of a production method determines the firm's input requirements. If a sweater company decides to produce 5000 sweaters this month, it knows how many production workers it will need, how much electricity it will use, how much raw yarn to purchase and how many sewing machines to run. A grower who sets out to produce and ship 3000 kilos of apples knows how many pickers to hire, how many baskets to have on hand, and so forth.

Similarly, given a technique of production, any set of input quantities determines the amount of output that can be produced. Certainly, the number of machines and workers employed in a sweater factory determines how many sweaters can be produced, and the number of trees and pickers determines the number of kilos of apples a grower can ship.

Changing the *technology* of production will change the relationship between input and output quantities. An apple orchard that uses expensive equipment to lift pickers up into the trees will harvest more fruit with fewer workers in a given period of time than an orchard in which pickers use simple ladders. It is also possible that two different technologies can produce the same quantity of output. For example, a fully computerized textile factory with only a few workers running the machines may

Figure 7.3 The three decisions that all firms must make

| 1. How much output to supply | 2. Which production technology to use | 3. How much of each input to demand |

produce the same number of sweaters as a factory with no sophisticated machines but many workers. A profit-maximizing firm chooses the technology that minimizes its costs for a given level of output.

Remember as we proceed that we are discussing and analysing the behaviour of *perfectly competitive* firms. Thus, we will say nothing about price-setting behaviour, product quality and other characteristics of the product, or choices that lead to product differentiation. In perfect competition, both input and output prices are beyond a firm's control – they are determined in the market and are not the decisions of any individual firm. And remember that all firms in a given industry produce exactly the same product. When we analyse the behaviour of firms in other kinds of markets (in Chapters 13 and 14), the three basic decisions will be expanded to include the setting of prices and the determination of product quality.

Profits and economic costs

We assume that firms are in business to make a profit and that behaviour is guided by the goal of maximizing profits. But what is profit? In simplest terms, **profit** is the difference between total revenues and total costs:

$$\text{Profit} = \text{Total revenue} - \text{Total cost}$$

Revenues are simply receipts from the sale of the product. **Total revenue** is equal to the number of units produced and sold (q) times the price received per unit (P). Costs, however, are more complicated. In economics, the definition of total costs includes more than just out-of-pocket costs. **Economic costs** (which economists use to mean 'total costs') are the *full* costs of production and include (1) a normal rate of return and (2) the opportunity cost of each factor of production.

Normal rate of return

When someone decides to start a firm, he or she must commit resources. To operate a manufacturing firm, you need a plant and some equipment. To start a restaurant, you need to buy grills, ovens, tables, chairs and so on. In other words, you must invest in capital. Such investment requires resources that stay tied up in the firm as long as it operates. Even firms that have been around for a long time must continue to invest. Plant and equipment wear out and must be replaced. Firms that decide to expand must put new capital in place. This is as true of small firms, where the resources usually come directly from the proprietor, as it is of corporations, where the resources needed to make investments usually come from shareholders.

Whenever resources are used to invest in a business, there is an opportunity cost. Instead of opening a sweet shop, I could put my funds into an alternative use such as a certificate of deposit or a government bond, both of which earn interest. Instead of using its retained earnings to build a new plant, a firm could simply earn interest on those funds or pay them out to shareholders.

Why do firms put their funds into the business rather than into the bank or into some other alternative use? When people decide to invest resources in a business, we assume that the decision is based on the expectation of profit. But a firm isn't profitable in a meaningful sense unless it earns more for its investors than what they forgo by not buying a bond or a certificate of deposit. Using resources to invest in a firm thus has an opportunity cost.

A **normal rate of profit** (also called a **normal rate of return**) is the rate that is just sufficient to keep owners or investors satisfied. From the standpoint of a manager, the normal rate of return is the opportunity cost of investment. In other words, it is the rate of profit just equal to the profit rate the firm could make by investing its resources elsewhere. If the rate of return were to fall below normal, it would be difficult or impossible for managers to raise resources needed to purchase new capital. Owners of the firm would be receiving profits that were lower than they could receive elsewhere in the economy.

profit The difference between total revenues and total costs.

revenue, *or* total revenue Receipts from the sale of a product ($P \times q$).

economic costs The full costs of production including (1) a normal rate of return on investment and (2) the opportunity cost of each factor of production.

normal rate of profit, *or* normal rate of return A rate of profit that is just sufficient to keep owners and investors satisfied. For relatively risk-free firms, it should be nearly the same as the interest rate on risk-free government bonds.

If the firm has fairly steady revenues and the future looks secure, the normal profit rate should be very close to the interest rate on risk-free government bonds. I certainly won't keep investors interested in my firm if I don't pay them a rate of return at least as high as they can get from a risk-free government or corporate bond. If my firm is rock solid and the economy is steady, I may not have to pay a much higher rate. But if my firm is in a very speculative industry and the future of the economy is shaky, I may have to pay substantially more to keep my shareholders happy. In exchange for taking such a risk, they will expect a higher return.

A normal profit rate is considered part of the full economic costs of a business. Adding a normal profit rate to costs means that when a firm earns exactly a normal rate of return or profit, it actually earns zero economic profits. **Economic profits**, or **excess profits** are profits over and above normal. In other words, profits are considered economic profits only if they are greater than the opportunity cost of investing in the industry.

economic profits, *or* excess profits
Profits over and above the normal rate of return on investment.

A simple example will illustrate the concepts of a normal profit as part of cost and economic profit as 'profit over and above a normal return to capital'. Suppose that Nicole and Marie decide to start a small business selling belts in Schipol airport in Amsterdam. To get into the business they need to invest in a mobile display unit. The price of a suitable unit is 20,000 guilders with all the displays and attachments built in. Suppose that Nicole and Marie estimate that they will sell 3000 belts annually at 10 guilders each. Further, assume that each belt costs 5 guilders from the supplier. Finally, the display must be staffed by a sales assistant who works for an annual wage of 14,000 guilders. Is this business going to make a profit?

To answer this question, we must determine total revenue and total cost. First, annual revenues are simply 30,000 guilders (3000 belts × 10). Total costs include the costs of the belts – 15,000 guilders (3000 belts × 5) – plus the labour cost of 14,000 guilders, for a total cost of 29,000 guilders. Thus, on the basis of the annual revenue and cost flows, the firm *seems* to be making a profit of 1000 guilders (30,000 – 29,000).

But what about the 20,000 guilder initial investment in the display unit? This investment is *not* a direct part of the cost of Nicole and Marie's firm. If we assume that the unit maintains its value over time, *the only thing that Nicole and Marie are giving up is the interest that they might have earned had they not tied up their funds in the display unit.* That is, the only real 'cost' is the opportunity cost of the investment, which is the forgone interest on the 20,000 guilders.

Now suppose that Nicole and Marie want a minimum return equal to 10% – which is, say, the rate of interest that they could have got by purchasing corporate bonds. This implies a normal return of 10%, or 2000 guilders annually (= 20,000 × 0.10) on the 20,000 guilders investment. But, as we determined above, Nicole and Marie will earn only 1000 guilders annually. This is only a 5% return on their investment. Thus, they are really earning a below normal return. Recall that the opportunity cost of capital must be added to cost in calculating economic profit. Thus, full economic costs in this case are 31,000 guilders (29,000 + 2000 in forgone interest on the investment). Economic profits are negative: 30,000 – 31,000 = –1000 guilders. These calculations are summarized in Table 7.1. Because economic profits are negative, Nicole and Marie are actually earning an *economic loss* on their belt business.

When a firm earns *positive* economic profits, it is earning profit at a rate more than sufficient to retain the interest of investors. In fact, economic profits are likely to attract new firms into an industry and cause existing firms to expand.

When a firm suffers *negative* economic profits – that is, when it incurs economic losses – it is earning at a rate below that required to keep investors happy. Such economic losses may or may not be losses as an accountant would measure them. Even if I earn a positive profit of 10% on my assets, I am earning below normal profits, or making an economic loss, if a normal return for my industry is 15%. In this case, I have a net economic loss of 5% per year, and my investors will be looking to bale out. Economic losses may cause some firms to exit the industry; others will contract in size. Certainly, new investment will not flow into such an industry.

Table 7.1 Calculating total revenue, total cost and profit

Initial investment	20,000 guilders
Market interest rate available	10%
Total revenues (3000 belts × 10 guilders each)	30,000
Costs:	
Belts from supplier	
Labour cost	
Normal return / opportunity cost of capital	
(20,000 guilders × 0.10) =	
15,000	
14,000	
+ 2,000	
Total costs	31,000
Profit = total revenues − total costs	− 1,000

∴ There is an economic loss of 1,000 guilders.

Opportunity costs of all inputs

Economic costs include the opportunity costs of all inputs, not just out-of-pocket costs. If you open a restaurant and work 40 hours a week helping to run it, the cost of running the restaurant includes the cost of your time, even if you do not pay yourself a formal wage. (If you don't pay yourself a wage, your time does not show up on the restaurant's books.) If you could be earning €15 per hour working full-time at a local factory, the opportunity cost of your time helping to run the restaurant is €600 per week (40 hours × €15). In analysing full economic costs, it is important to include both direct out-of-pocket costs *and* opportunity costs.

Short-run versus long-run decisions

The decisions made by a firm – how much to produce, how to produce it and what inputs to demand – all take time into account. If a firm decides that it wants to double or triple its output, it may need time to arrange financing, hire architects and contractors, and build a new plant. Planning for a major expansion can take years. In the meantime, the firm must decide how much to produce within the constraint of its existing plant. If a firm decides to get out of a particular business, it may take time to arrange an orderly exit. There may be contract obligations to fulfil, equipment to sell and so forth. Once again, the firm must decide what to do in the meantime.

A firm's immediate response to a change in the economic environment may differ from its response over time. Consider, for example, a small restaurant with 20 tables that becomes very popular. The immediate problem is getting the most profit within the constraint of the existing restaurant. The owner might consider adding a few tables or speeding up service to squeeze in a few more customers. Some popular restaurants do not accept table reservations, forcing people to wait at the bar, which increases drink revenues and keeps tables full at all times. At the same time, the owner may be thinking of expanding his current facility, moving to a larger facility or opening a second restaurant. In the future, he might buy the building next door and double his capacity. Such decisions might require him to negotiate a lease, buy new equipment and hire more staff. It takes time to make and implement these decisions.

Because the character of immediate response differs from long-run adjustment, it is useful to define two time periods: the short run and the long run. Two assumptions define the **short run**: (1) a fixed scale (or a fixed factor of production) and (2) no entry into or exit from the industry. First, the short run is defined as that period during which existing firms have some *fixed factor of production* – that is, during which some factor locks them into their current scale of operations. Second, new firms cannot enter, and existing firms cannot exit, an industry in the short run. Firms may curtail operations, but they are still locked into some costs, even though they may be in the process of going out of business.

Just which factor or factors of production are fixed in the short run differs from industry to industry. For a manufacturing firm, the size of the physical plant is often the greatest limitation. A factory is built with a given production rate in mind. While that rate can be increased, output cannot increase beyond a certain limit in the short run. For a doctor in general practice, the limit may be her own capacity to see patients; the day has only so many hours. In the long run, she may invite others to join her practice and expand, but for now, in the short run, she is the firm, and her capacity is the firm's capacity. For a farmer, the fixed factor may be land. The capacity of a small farm is limited by the number of hectares being cultivated.

In the **long run**, there are no fixed factors of production. Firms can plan for any output level they find desirable. They can double or triple output, for example. In addition, new firms can start up operations (enter the industry), and existing firms can go out of business (exit the industry).

No hard-and-fast rule specifies how long the short run is. The point is simply that firms make two basic kinds of decisions: those that govern the day-to-day operations

short run The period of time for which two conditions hold: the firm is operating under a fixed scale (fixed factor) of production, and firms can neither enter nor exit an industry.

long run That period of time for which there are no fixed factors of production. Firms can increase or decrease their scale of operation, and new firms can enter and existing firms can exit the industry.

Applications

The small firm sector of an economy can be very important, as Europe is discovering

At a time when Europe's industrial giants continue to shed workers, a raft of small, dynamic companies such as Pujals' are emerging. They are creating jobs and spurring economic regeneration – despite obstacles such as heavy taxes and red tape that have long discouraged the Continent's entrepreneurs. Indeed, Europe's hot growth companies are showing a remarkable ability to take advantage of the Continent's growing trend toward deregulation, its nascent secondary stock markets, and the rapid spread of the Internet, which puts companies in instant touch with new customers.

In industries such as aviation and telecommunications, meanwhile, small-scale growth companies are taking advantage of market openings in the European Union. Regional airlines such as Britain's Cityflyer Express Ltd are taking off now that Europe is allowing full-fledged competition in air travel across the Continent. The trend to outsourcing in the industry is also providing opportunities for small airlines such as Air Atlanta Icelandic. Its sales soared some 20% last year, to more than $100 million, as it expanded its business of providing capacity to other airlines on a temporary basis. Among other gigs, Air Atlanta Icelandic flies groups of pilgrims to Mecca for several carriers. The company has seen its fleet grow to 17 planes and its workforce jump to 700 people since it started 12 years ago.

In telecom, Finland's Elcoteq Network has taken a similar route to success. When 51-year-old CEO Antti Piippo led a management buyout of the struggling flat-panel-display maker in 1991, Elcoteq employed 170 people and had sales of $13.6 million. Spotting an opportunity to apply its expertise to mobile-phone manufacturing, Piippo began supplying Nordic phone giants Nokia Corp. and L. M. Ericsson. Last year, they accounted for 70% of Elcoteq's $303 million in revenues. It now employs 1,800 people.

Many European growth companies are scoring simply by answering consumers' demands for better service. Just four years ago, Euro-Med opened a hotel, fitness centre, beauty spa, and medical clinic near Nuremberg aimed at Europeans who want first-class health and leisure facilities at prices not much higher than those of conventional hospitals. After turning an operating profit of $5 million on sales of $29.5 million in 1997, Euro-Med plans to double its staff of doctors, to 100, by 2000, says President and co-founder Wolf-Michael Wunsche.

Source: 'Startups to the rescue', Business Week, *European edition, 23 March 1998, pp. 14–16.*

of the firm and those that involve longer-term strategic planning. Sometimes, major decisions can be implemented in weeks. Often, however, the process takes years.

The bases of decisions: market price of output, available technology, and input prices

As we said earlier, the three fundamental decisions are made with the objective of maximizing profits. Because profits equal total revenues minus total costs, each firm needs to know how much it costs to produce its product and how much its product can be sold for.

To know how much it costs to produce a good or service, I need to know something about the production techniques that are available and about the prices of the inputs required. To estimate how much it will cost me to operate a service station, for instance, I need to know what equipment I need, how many workers, what kind of building and so on. I also need to know the going wage rates for mechanics and unskilled labourers, the cost of petrol pumps, interest rates, rents per square metre of land on high-traffic corners, and the wholesale price of petrol. And, of course, I need to know how much I can charge customers for petrol and car repairs.

In the language of economics, I need to know three things – the bases of decision making:

1. the market price of output;
2. the techniques of production that are available; and
3. the prices of inputs.

Output price determines potential revenues. The techniques available tell me how much of each input I need, and input prices tell me how much they will cost. Together, the available production techniques and the prices of inputs determine costs.

The rest of this chapter and the whole of the next focus on costs of production. We begin at the heart of the firm, with the production process itself. Faced with a set of input prices, firms must decide on the best, or **optimal, method of production** (Figure 7.4). The optimal method of production is the one that minimizes cost. With cost determined and the market price of output known, a firm will make a final judgement about the quantity to produce and the quantity of each input to demand.

optimal method of production
The production method that minimizes cost.

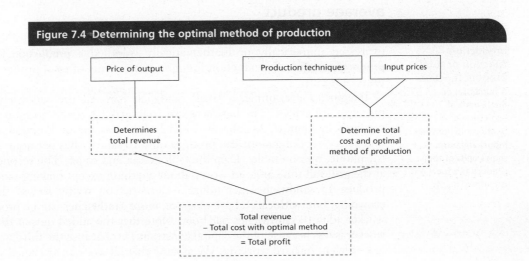

Figure 7.4 Determining the optimal method of production

The production process

production technology
The quantitative relationship between inputs and outputs.

Production is the process through which inputs are combined and transformed into outputs. **Production technology** relates inputs to outputs. Specific quantities of inputs are needed to produce any given service or good. A loaf of bread requires certain amounts of water, flour and yeast, some kneading and shaping, and an oven, gas or electricity. A journey home from the station can be produced with a taxi, 20 minutes of a driver's labour, petrol, and so forth.

Most outputs can be produced by a number of different techniques. You can pull down an old building and clear an area to create a car park in several ways, for example. Five hundred workers with hammers could demolish it and then carry the pieces away by hand; this would be a **labour-intensive technology**. The same park could be produced by two people with a demolition crane, an excavator, a backhoe and a dump truck; this would be a **capital-intensive technology**. Similarly, different inputs can be combined to transport people across a large city. The London Underground and Paris Metro carry thousands of people at a time across their respective cities and use a massive amount of capital relative to labour. Taxi rides of an equivalent distance require much more labour relative to capital; a driver is needed for every few passengers.

labour-intensive technology
Technology that relies heavily on human labour rather than capital.

capital-intensive technology
Technology that relies heavily on capital rather than human labour.

An insurance company needs office space to produce its product, but office space can be assembled in a variety of ways. In suburban locations, business parks are often spacious, with buildings of two or three storeys surrounded by trees and grass. In central cities, offices are stacked on top of one another in glass towers. Thus in the centre of cities a small amount of land is combined with a great deal of capital to produce insurance services. In suburban office developments the same services are produced with more land.

In choosing the most appropriate technology, firms choose the one that minimizes the cost of production. For a firm in an economy with a plentiful supply of inexpensive labour but not much capital, the optimal method of production will involve labour-intensive techniques. For example, the assembly of items like running shoes is done most efficiently by hand. That is why Nike produces virtually all of its shoes in developing countries where labour costs are very low. In contrast, firms in an economy with high wages and high labour costs have an incentive to substitute away from labour and to use more capital-intensive, or labour-saving, techniques. Suburban office developments use more land and have more open space in part because land in the suburbs is more plentiful and less expensive than land in the middle of a big city. Spreading out is cheaper than building a high-rise office tower in the city.

Production functions: total product, marginal product and average product

production function *or* total product function
A numerical or mathematical expression of a relationship between inputs and outputs. It shows units of total product as a function of units of inputs.

The relationship between inputs and outputs (that is, the technology of production) expressed numerically or mathematically is called a **production function** (or **total product function**). A production function shows units of total product as a function of units of inputs.

Imagine, for example, a small sandwich bar. All the sandwiches made on the premises are grilled. The bar owns only one grill, at which no more than two people can work in comfort. As columns 1 and 2 of the production function in Table 7.2 show, one person working alone can produce only 10 sandwiches per hour. He has to answer the phone, wait on tables, keep the tables clean and so on. The second worker can stay at the grill full time and not worry about anything except making sandwiches. She can produce 15 sandwiches per hour. A third person trying to use the grill produces crowding, but, with careful use of space, more sandwiches can be produced. The third worker adds 10 sandwiches per hour. Note that the added output from hiring a third worker is less because of the capital constraint, *not* because the third worker is somehow less efficient or hard working. We assume that all workers are equally capable.

Table 7.2 Production function

(1) Labour units (employees)	(2) Total product (sandwiches per hour)	(3) Marginal product of labour	(4) Average product of labour (total product ÷ labour units)
0	0	–	–
1	10	10	10.0
2	25	15	12.5
3	35	10	11.7
4	40	5	10.0
5	42	2	8.4
6	42	0	7.0

The fourth and fifth workers can work at the grill only while the first three are garnishing and wrapping on the sandwiches they have made. But then the first three must wait to get back to the grill. Worker four adds a net of 5 sandwiches per hour to the total, and worker five adds just 2. Adding a sixth worker adds no output at all: the current maximum capacity of the shop is 42 sandwiches per hour.

Figure 7.5a graphs the total product data from Table 7.2.

Marginal product and the law of diminishing returns

marginal product
The additional output that can be produced by adding one more unit of a specific input, *ceteris paribus*.

Marginal product is the additional output that can be produced by hiring one more unit of a specific input, holding all other inputs constant. As column 3 of Table 7.2 shows, the marginal product of the first unit of labour in the sandwich shop is 10 sandwiches, the marginal product of the second is 15, the third 10, and so on. The marginal product of the sixth worker is 0. Figure 7.5b graphs the marginal product of labour curve from the data in Table 7.2.

Figure 7.5 Production function for sandwiches

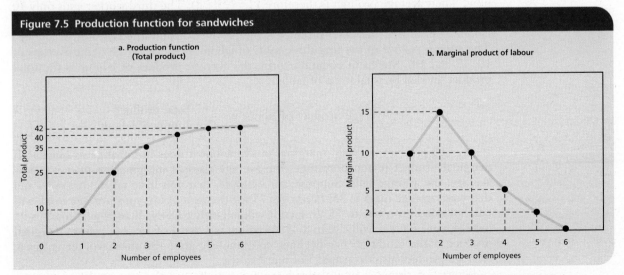

A *production function* is a numerical representation of the relationship between inputs and outputs. In Figure 7.5a, total product (sandwiches) is graphed as a function of labour inputs. The *marginal product* of labour is the additional output that one additional unit of labour produces. Figure 7.5b shows that the marginal product of the second unit of labour at the sandwich shop is 15 units of output; the marginal product of the fourth unit of labour is 5 units of output.

law of diminishing returns

When additional units of a variable input are added to fixed inputs after a certain point, the marginal product of the variable input declines.

The **law of diminishing returns** states that *after a certain point, when additional units of a variable input are added to fixed inputs* (in this case, the building and grill), *the marginal product of the variable input declines.* The British economist David Ricardo first formulated the law of diminishing returns on the basis of his observations of agriculture in nineteenth-century England. Within a given area of land, he noted, successive 'doses' of labour and capital yielded smaller and smaller increases in crop output. The law of diminishing returns is true in agriculture because only so much more can be produced by farming the same land more intensively. In manufacturing, diminishing returns set in when a firm begins to strain the capacity of its existing plant.

At our sandwich bar, diminishing returns set in when the third worker is added. The marginal product of the second worker is actually higher than the first (see Figure 7.5b). The first worker takes care of the phone and the tables, which frees the second worker to concentrate exclusively on sandwich making. But from that point on, the grill gets crowded.

Diminishing returns characterize many productive activities. Consider, for example, an independent accountant who works primarily for private citizens preparing their tax returns. As he adds more and more clients, he must work later and later into the evening. An hour spent working at 1 am after a long day is likely to be less productive than an hour spent working at 10 am. Here the fixed factor of production is the accountant himself. Ultimately, the capacity of his mind and body limit his production, much like the walls of a plant limit production in a factory.

Diminishing returns, or *diminishing marginal product*, begin to show up when more and more units of a variable input are added to a fixed input, such as scale of plant. Recall that we defined the short run as that period in which some fixed factor of production constrains the firm. It follows then, that:

Diminishing returns always apply in the short run, and in the short run every firm will face diminishing returns. This means that every firm finds it progressively more difficult to increase its output as it approaches capacity production.

Marginal product versus average product

average product

The average amount produced by each unit of a variable factor of production.

Average product is the average amount produced by each unit of a variable factor of production. At our sandwich shop with one grill, that variable factor is labour. In Table 7.2, you saw that the first two workers together produce 25 sandwiches per hour. Their average product is therefore 12.5 (25 ÷ 2). The third worker adds only 10 sandwiches per hour to the total. These 10 sandwiches are the *marginal* product of labour. (Recall that marginal product is the product of only the last unit of labour.) The *average product* of the first three units of labour, however, is 11.7 (the average of 10, 15 and 10). Stated in equation form, the average product of labour is the total product divided by total units of labour:

$$\text{Average product of labour} = \frac{\text{Total product}}{\text{Total units of labour}}$$

Average product 'follows' marginal product, but it does not change as quickly. If marginal product is above average, the average rises; if marginal product is below average, the average falls. Suppose, for example, that you have taken six exams and that your average mark is 86. If you get 75 for the next exam, your average mark will fall, but not all the way to 75. In fact, it will fall only to 84.4. If your next mark is 95 instead, your average will rise to 87.3. As columns 3 and 4 of Table 7.2 show, marginal product at the sandwich bar declines continuously after the third worker is hired. Average product also decreases, but more slowly.

Figure 7.6 shows a typical production function, and the marginal and average product curves derived from it. The marginal product curve is a graph of the slope of the total product curve – that is, of the production function. Average product and marginal product start off equal, as they do in Table 7.2. As marginal product climbs, the graph of average product follows it, but more slowly, up to L_1 (point A).

Figure 7.6 Typical production function

Marginal and average product curves can be derived from total product curves. The marginal product of labour is the slope of the total product curve. Average product follows marginal product; it rises when marginal product is above it and falls when marginal product is below it.

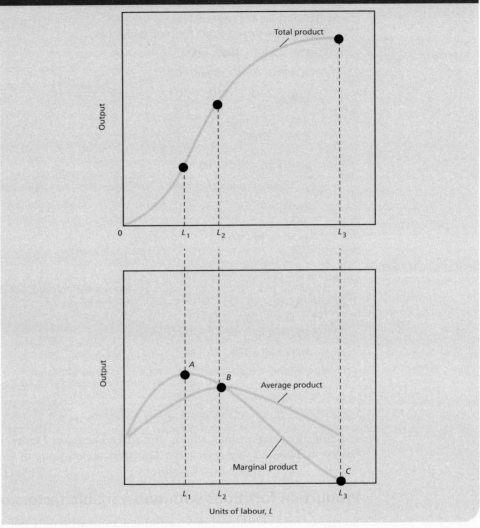

Notice that marginal product starts off by increasing. (Remember that it did so in the sandwich bar as well.) Most production processes are designed to be run well by more than one worker. Take an assembly line, for example. To work efficiently, an assembly line needs a worker at every station; it's a cooperative process. The marginal product of the first workers is low or zero. But as workers are added, the process starts to run and marginal product rises.

At point A (L_1 units of labour), marginal product begins to fall. Because every plant has a finite capacity, efforts to increase production will always run into the limits of that capacity. At point B (L_2 units of labour), marginal product has fallen to equal the average product, which has been increasing. Between points B and C (between L_2 and L_3 units of labour), marginal product falls below average product, and thus average product begins to follow it down. Average product is at its maximum at point B, where it is equal to marginal product.

At L_3, more labour yields no more output and marginal product is zero – the assembly line has no more positions, or the grill is completely congested, or the accountant is so tired that he can't see another client.[2] (If you have trouble under-

[2] In theory, the total product curve could turn downwards beyond L_3. This would imply that more workers would actually get in the way and that output would fall. If this were to happen, marginal product would actually be negative beyond L_3.

Maths Box 1 Using calculus with production functions

We can illustrate the relationships between *TPP*, *APP* and *MPP* using calculus.

Suppose the total product function is given as

$$TPP_L = 20Q_L + 10Q_L^2 - Q_L^3$$

Since $APP_L = TPP_L/Q_L$, then

$$APP_L = \frac{20Q_L}{Q_L} + \frac{10Q_L^2}{Q_L} - \frac{Q_L^3}{Q_L}$$

$$APP_L = 20 + 10Q_L - Q_L^2$$

$$MPP_L = \frac{dTPP_L}{dQ_L}$$

$$MPP_L = 20 + 20Q_L - 3Q_L^2$$

We can now establish that $MPP_L = APP_L$ when APP_L is at its maximum, i.e. where:

$$\frac{dAPP_L}{dQ_L} = 0$$

$$\frac{dAPP_L}{dQ_L} = 10 - 2Q_L$$

Setting this term to zero gives $Q_L = 5$.

So APP_L is maximized when 5 units of labour are employed. Substituting into the APP_L function gives $APP_L = 20 + 50 - 25 = 45$ units of output.

When $Q_L = 5$, what is MPP_L?

Substituting into the MPP_L function gives:

$$MPP_L = 20 + 100 - 75 = 45$$

Where APP_L is maximized, $APP_L = MPP_L = 45$ units of output.

standing the relationships among the three curves in Figure 7.6, review the calculations in Table 7.2 and review the Appendix on graphing in Chapter 1.)

Production functions with two variable factors of production

So far, we have considered production functions with only one variable factor of production. But inputs work together in production. In general, additional capital increases the productivity of labour. Because capital – buildings, machines and so on – is of no use without people to operate it, we say that capital and labour are *complementary inputs*.

A simple example will clarify this point. Consider the sandwich bar again. If the demand for sandwiches began to exceed the bar's capacity to produce them, the owner might decide to expand capacity. This would mean opening up more space and purchasing more capital in the form of a new grill.

A second grill would essentially double the bar's productive capacity. The new higher capacity will mean that the sandwich bar will not run into diminishing returns as quickly. With only one grill, the third and fourth workers are less productive because the single grill gets crowded. With two grills, however, the third and fourth workers could produce 15 sandwiches per hour. In essence, the added capital has raised the *productivity* of labour.

Just as the new grill enhances the productivity of workers in the sandwich bar, new businesses and the capital that they put in place raise the productivity of workers in countries like Malaysia, India and Kenya.

This simple relationship lies at the heart of worries about productivity at the national and international levels. Building new, modern plants and equipment enhances a nation's productivity. Since the 1950s, for example, Japan has accumulated capital (that is, has built plant and equipment) faster than any other country in the world. The result is a very high average quantity of output per worker in Japan.

Choice of technology

As our sandwich bar example shows, inputs (factors of production) are complementary. Capital enhances the productivity of labour. Workers in the sandwich bar are more productive when they are not crowded together while working on a single grill. Similarly, labour enhances the productivity of capital. When more workers are hired at a plant that is operating at 50% of capacity, previously idle machines suddenly become productive.

But inputs can also be substituted for one another. If labour becomes expensive, firms can adopt labour-saving technologies; that is, they can substitute capital for labour. Assembly lines can be automated by replacing human beings with machines, and capital can be substituted for land when land is scarce. (See the Global Perspective box 'Production technologies: robots and skyscrapers around the world'.) If capital becomes relatively expensive, firms can substitute labour for capital. In short, most goods and services can be produced in a number of ways, using alternative technologies. One of the key decisions that all firms must make is which technology to use.

Consider the choices available to a nappy manufacturer in Table 7.3. Five different techniques for producing 100 nappies are available. Technology *A* is the most labour intensive, requiring ten hours of labour and two units of capital to produce 100 nappies. (You can think of units of capital as machine hours.) Technology *E* is the most capital intensive, requiring only two hours of labour but ten hours of machine time.

Global Perspectives

Production technologies: robots and skyscrapers around the world

Most products can be produced with different combinations of inputs; the choice of technique depends on the prices of land, labour and capital, which can change over time and from location to location. The following examples illustrate the importance of technological choice.

Substitution of capital for labour: robotics in manufacturing

The ultimate substitution of capital for labour is robotics. Twenty-five years ago, robots were confined to the world of science fiction. Today, robots are everywhere:

Industrial robots are hard at work in the industrial heartland, spot-welding car bodies on auto assembly lines, placing tiny parts on circuit boards in electronics factories and packing frozen beefburgers into boxes at food-processing plants. And rather than replacing workers in droves, robots are reserved for tasks that either are ill suited to human hand and eye or are so onerous or strenuous that people don't want to do them . . .

. . . Lower cost and greater reliability are the keys, said Steven W. Holland, a robotics specialist at General Motors. Prices today are about half what they were 15 years ago for comparable machines and reliability is four times better, he said.[1]

Substitution of capital for land: office towers in Asia

As you travel into any major city in the world from a distance of 30 miles out, the density of development increases and buildings tend to get taller and taller. Building a tall building is simply the substitution of capital for land in production, and it occurs most frequently where land prices are very high. When available land is scarce and the demand for it is increasing, land prices rise and tall buildings appear.

Frenzied building in the capitals of South-east Asia has long been one of the most visible symbols of the region's spectacular economic boom. In Malaysia, growth averaged nearly 9% for a decade, and buildings in the capital, Kuala Lumpur, went up at a rate to match. The world's tallest building adds 360,000 square metres of space – more than was built in the past two years combined. Although recession struck South-east Asia in the late nineties, office buildings continued to go up at a frenetic pace in mainland Chinese cities like Beijing and Shanghai.[2]

[1]*John Holusha, 'Industrial robots make the grade',* New York Times, *7 September 1994, p. D1.*
[2]*The Economist, 12 April 1997, p. 72.*

Table 7.3 Inputs required to produce 100 nappies using alternative technologies

Technology	Units of capital (K)	Units of labour (L)
A	2	10
B	3	6
C	4	4
D	6	3
E	10	2

To choose a production technique, the firm must look to input markets to find out the current market prices of labour and capital. What is the wage rate (P_L), and what is the cost per hour of capital (P_K)?

Suppose that labour and capital are both available at a price of €1 per unit. Column 4 of Table 7.4 presents the calculations required to determine which technology is the best. The winner is technology C. Assuming that the firm's objective is to maximize profits, it will choose the least-cost technology. Using technology C, the firm can produce 100 nappies for €8. All four of the other technologies produce 100 nappies at a higher cost.

Now suppose that the wage rate (P_L) were to rise sharply, from 1 euro to 5 euros. You might guess that this increase would lead the firm to substitute labour-saving capital for workers, and you'd be right. As column 5 of Table 7.4 shows, the increase in the wage rate means that technology E is now the cost-minimizing choice for the firm. Using ten units of capital and only two units of labour, the firm can produce 100 nappies for €20. All other technologies are now more costly.

To summarize:

Two things determine the cost of production: (1) the technologies that are available and (2) input prices. Profit-maximizing firms will choose the technology that minimizes the cost of production given current market input prices.

So far, we have looked only at a *single* level of output. That is, we have determined how much it will cost to produce 100 nappies using the best available technology when P_K = €1 or €5 and P_L = €1. But the best technique for producing 1000 nappies or 10,000 nappies may be entirely different. The next chapter explores the relationship between cost and the level of output in some detail. One of our main objectives in that chapter will be to determine the amount that a competitive firm will choose to supply during a given time period.

Table 7.4 Cost-minimizing choice among alternative technologies (100 nappies)

(1) Technology	(2) Units of capital (K)	(3) Units of labour (L)	(4) Cost = (L × P_L) + (K × P_K) if P_L = €1 P_K = €1	(5) if P_L = €5 P_K = €1
A	2	10	12	52
B	3	6	9	33
C	4	4	8	24
D	6	3	9	21
E	10	2	12	20

Summary

1. Firms vary in size and internal organization, but they all take inputs and transform them into outputs through a process called *production*.

2. In perfect competition, no single firm has any control over prices. This follows from two assumptions: (1) perfectly competitive industries are composed of many firms, each small relative to the size of the industry; and (2) each firm in a perfectly competitive industry produces *homogeneous products*.

3. The demand curve facing a competitive firm is perfectly elastic. If a single firm raises its price above the market price, it will sell nothing. Because it can sell all it produces at the market price, a firm has no incentive to reduce price.

The behaviour of profit-maximizing firms

4. Profit-maximizing firms in all industries must make three choices: (1) how much output to supply, (2) how to produce that output, and (3) how much of each input to demand.

5. Profit equals *total revenue* minus total cost. Total cost means *economic cost*. It includes (1) a normal return, or profit, to the owners; and (2) the opportunity cost (rather than the money cost) of each factor of production.

6. A *normal rate of return* to capital is included in economic cost because tying up resources in the capital stock has an opportunity cost. If you start a business or buy a share of stock in a company, you do so because you expect a profit. Investors will not invest their money in a business unless they can expect a rate of return similar to or above the rate they can obtain by purchasing risk-free government bonds.

7. *Economic profits* are profits over and above a normal rate of return. A firm earning zero economic profits is a firm earning just exactly a normal rate of return. A firm does not show economic profits unless it is earning above a normal return for its owners.

8. Two assumptions define the *short run*: (1) a fixed scale or fixed factor of production, and (2) no entry to or exit from the industry. In the *long run*, firms can choose any scale of operations they want, and new firms can enter and leave the industry.

9. To make decisions, firms need to know three things: (1) the market price of their output, (2) the production techniques that are available, and (3) the price of inputs.

The production process

10. The relationship between inputs and outputs (the *production technology* expressed numerically or mathematically is called a *production function* or *total product function*).

11. The *marginal product* of a variable input is the additional output that an added unit of that input will produce if all other inputs are held constant. The *law of diminishing returns* states that when additional units of a variable input are added to fixed inputs after a certain point, the marginal product of the variable input will decline.

12. *Average product* is the average amount of product produced by each unit of a variable factor of production. If marginal product is above average product, the average product rises; if marginal product is below average product, the average product falls.

13. Capital and labour are at the same time complementary and substitutable inputs. Capital enhances the productivity of labour, but it can also be substituted for labour.

Choice of technology

14. One of the key decisions that all firms must make is which technology to use. Profit-maximizing firms will choose that combination of inputs that minimizes costs and therefore maximizes profits.

Review Terms and Concepts

average product
capital-intensive technology
economic costs
economic profits, *or* excess profits
firm
free entry
free exit
homogeneous products
labour-intensive technology
law of diminishing returns
long run
marginal product
normal rate of profit, *or* normal rate of return

optimal method of production
perfect competition
production
production function *or* total product function
production technology
profit
revenue, *or* total revenue
short run

Equations

1. Profit = Total revenue – Total cost

2. Average product of labour = $\dfrac{\text{Total product}}{\text{Total units of labour}}$

Problem Set

1. The graph shows the current position in the perfectly competitive market for potatoes in Sweden.

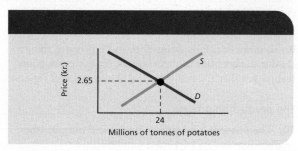

Millions of tonnes of potatoes

a. Graph the demand curve facing a single representative potato farmer.
b. Explain the shape of the individual farmer's demand curve carefully. What specific assumptions lie behind its shape?

2. Suppose that in 1998 Katie became the manager of a small non-profit theatre company. Her playhouse has 120 seats and a small stage. The actors have national reputations, and demand for tickets is enormous relative to the number of seats available; every performance is sold out months in advance. Katie was given the job because she has demonstrated a rare combination: superb acting skills and an ability to raise funds successfully. Describe some of the decisions that Katie must make in the short run. What might she consider to be her 'fixed factor'? What alternative decisions might Katie be able to make in the long run? Explain.

3. Claude runs a small, very stable regional newspaper company in Switzerland. The paper has been in business for 25 years. The total value of the firm's capital stock is 1,000,000 Swiss francs, which Claude owns outright. This year the firm earned a total of 250,000 francs after out-of-pocket expenses. Without taking the opportunity cost of capital into account, this means that Claude is earning a 25% return on his capital. Suppose that risk-free bonds are currently paying a rate of 10% to those who buy them.
a. What is meant by the 'opportunity cost of capital'?
b. Explain why opportunity costs are 'real' costs even though they do not necessarily involve out-of-pocket expenses.
c. What is the opportunity cost of Claude's capital?
d. How much economic profit is Claude earning?

4. The table gives total output or total product as a function of labour units used.
a. Define diminishing returns.
b. Does the table indicate a situation of diminishing returns? Explain your answer.

Labour	Total output
0	0
1	5
2	9
3	12
4	14
5	15

5. A student who lives on the first floor of a hall of residence is assigned to a new room on the seventh floor. She has 11 boxes of books and personal belongings to move. Discuss the alternative combinations of capital and labour that might be used to make the move. How would your answer differ if the move were (1) to another hall 3 km away, or (2) to another university 500 km away?

6. Suppose that widgets can be produced using two alternative technologies, A and B, that employ the combinations of capital (K) and labour (L) shown in the table.

Technology	Number of widgets per hour					
	$Q = 1$		$Q = 2$		$Q = 3$	
	K	L	K	L	K	L
A	2	5	3	10	4	13
B	5	1	8	2	10	3

a. Assume that the price of capital (P_K) is €1 per unit and the price of labour (P_L) is €1 per unit. What is the optimal (least-cost) technology for producing one widget per hour (i.e. $Q = 1$)? Two widgets? Three widgets?
b. Using the optimal technology in each case, what is the cost of producing each of the three levels of output?
c. How much capital in units and how many workers (units of L) would you employ to produce 1 widget per hour? Two widgets? Three widgets?
d. Repeat (a) to (c) above, assuming that $P_L = $ €1 and $P_K = $ €2.

7. During the early phases of industrialization, the number of persons engaged in agriculture usually drops sharply, even as agricultural output is growing. Given what you know about production technology and production functions, can you explain this seeming inconsistency?

8. Since the end of the Second World War, manufacturing firms in Europe and the United States have been moving further and further away from the centre of cities. At the same time, firms in finance, insurance and other parts of the service sector are increasingly concentrated in tall buildings in city-centre business districts. One major reason seems to be that manufacturing firms find it difficult to substitute capital for land, whereas service-sector firms that use office space do not.

a. What kinds of buildings represent substitution of capital for land?

b. Why do you think that manufacturing firms might find it difficult to substitute capital for land?

c. Why is it relatively easier for a law firm or an insurance company to substitute capital for land?

d. Why is the demand for land likely to be very high near the centre of a city?

e. One of the reasons for substituting capital for land near the centre of a city is that land is more expensive near the centre. What is true about the relative supply of land near the centre of a city? (*Hint*: what is the formula for the area of a circle?)

9. The number of repairs produced by a computer repair shop depends on the number of workers, as shown in the table.

Number of workers (per week)	Number of repairs (per week)
0	0
1	8
2	20
3	35
4	45
5	52
6	57
7	60

Assume that all inputs (office, space, telephone, utilities) other than labour are fixed in the short run.

a. Add two additional columns to the table, and enter the marginal product and average product for each number of workers.

b. Over what range of labour input are there increasing returns to labour? Diminishing returns to labour? Negative returns to labour?

c. Over what range of labour input is marginal product greater than average product? What is happening to average product as employment increases over this range?

d. Over what range of labour input is marginal product smaller than average product? What is happening to average product as employment increases over this range?

10. A firm can use three different production technologies, with capital and labour requirements at each level as given in the table.

Daily output	Technology 1		Technology 2		Technology 3	
	K	L	K	L	K	L
100	3	7	4	5	5	4
150	3	10	4	7	5	5
200	4	11	5	8	6	6
250	5	13	6	10	7	8

a. Suppose the firm is operating in a high-wage country, where capital cost is €100 per day and labour cost is €80 per day. For each level of output, which technology is the cheapest?

b. Now suppose the firm is operating in a low-wage country, where capital cost is €100 per day but labour cost is only €40 per unit per day. For each level of output, which technology is the cheapest?

c. Suppose the firms moves from a high-wage to a low-wage country, but that its level of output remains constant at 200 units per day. How will its total employment change?

*11. Given a fixed volume of labour and land, a farmer finds that there is a relationship between his tomato output and the volume of fertilizer he uses of the form:

$$TPP = 64Q_f + 20Q_f^2 - 2Q_f^3$$

where Q_f = tonnes of fertilizer and TPP = output of tomatoes.

a. How much fertilizer maximizes his APP of tomatoes?

b. Confirm that MPP of tomatoes = APP of tomatoes at the quantity of fertilizer used in (a) above.

c. How much fertilizer is required to maximize tomato output? (*Hint*: TPP is maximized where MPP is zero.)

Appendix to Chapter 7

Isoquants and Isocosts

This chapter has shown that the cost structure facing a firm depends on two key pieces of information: (1) input (factor) prices, and (2) technology. This appendix presents a more formal analysis of technology and factor prices and their relationship to cost.

A new look at technology: isoquants

Table 7A.1 is expanded from Table 7.4 to show the various combinations of capital (K) and labour (L) that can be used to produce three different levels of output (q). For example, 100 units of X can be produced with two units of K and ten units of L, or with three units of K and six units of L, or with four units of K and four units of L, and so forth. Similarly, 150 units of X can be produced with three units of K and ten units of L, or with four units of K and seven units of L, and so forth.

A graph that shows all the combinations of capital and labour that can be used to produce a given amount of output is called an **isoquant**. Figure 7A.1 graphs three isoquants, one each for $q_X = 50$, $q_X = 100$, and $q_X = 150$, based on the data in Table 7A.1. If we assume complete divisibility of K and L all the points on the graph can be connected, indicating an infinite number of combinations of labour and capital that can produce each level of output. For example, 100 units of output can also be produced with 3.50 units of labour and 4.75 units of capital. (Verify that this point is on the isoquant labelled $q_X = 100$.)

Figure 7A.1 shows only three isoquants, but there are many more not shown. For example, there are separate isoquants for $q_X = 101$, $q_X = 102$ and so on. If we assume that producing fractions of a unit of output is possible, there must be an isoquant for $q_X = 134.57$, for $q_X = 124.82$ and so on. One could imagine an infinite number of isoquants in Figure 7A.1. The higher the level of output, the further up and to the right the isoquant will lie.

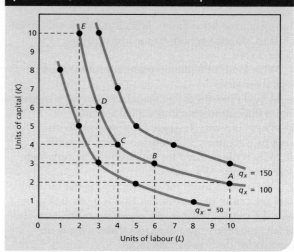

Figure 7A.1 Isoquants showing all combinations of capital and labour that can be used to produce 50, 100 and 150 units of output

Figure 7A.2 derives the slope of an isoquant. Because points A and B are both on the $q_X = 100$ isoquant, the two points represent two different combinations of K and L that can be used to produce 100 units of output. In moving from point A to point B along the curve, less capital is employed but more labour is used. An approximation of the amount of output lost by using less capital is ΔK times the marginal product of capital (MP_K). The marginal product of capital is the number

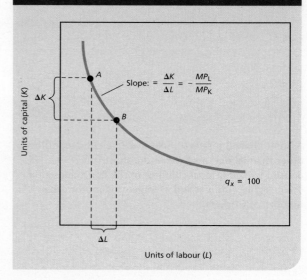

Figure 7A.2 The slope of an isoquant is equal to the ratio of MP_L to MP_K

Table 7A.1 Alternative combinations of capital (K) and labour (L) required to produce 50, 100 and 150 units of output

	$q_X = 50$		$q_X = 100$		$q_X = 150$	
	K	L	K	L	K	L
A	1	8	2	10	3	10
B	2	5	3	6	4	7
C	3	3	4	4	5	5
D	5	2	6	3	7	4
E	8	1	10	2	10	3

of units of output produced by a single marginal unit of capital. Thus, $\Delta K \bullet MP_K$ is the total output lost by using less capital.

But for output to remain constant (as it must, because A and B are on the same isoquant), the loss of output from using less capital must be exactly matched by the added output produced by using more labour. This amount can be approximated by ΔL times the marginal product of labour (MP_L). Since the two must be equal, it follows that:

$$\Delta K \bullet MP_K = -\Delta L \bullet MP_L{*}$$

If we then divide both sides of this equation by ΔL and then by MP_K, we arrive at the following expression for the slope of the isoquant:

$$\text{Slope of isoquant: } \frac{\Delta K}{\Delta L} = -\frac{MP_L}{MP_K}$$

The ratio of MP_L to MP_K is called the **marginal rate of technical substitution**. It is the rate at which a firm can substitute capital for labour and hold output constant.

Factor prices and input combinations: isocosts

A graph that shows all the combinations of capital and labour that are available for a given total cost is called an **isocost line**. (Recall that total cost includes opportunity costs and a normal rate of return.) Just as there are an infinite number of isoquants (one for every possible level of output), there are an infinite number of isocost lines, one for every possible level of total cost.

Figure 7A.3 shows three simple isocost lines that assume that the price of labour (P_L) is €1 per unit and that the price of capital (P_K) is €1 per unit. The lowest isocost line shows all the combinations of K and L that can be purchased for €5. For example, €5 will buy five units of labour and no capital (point A), or three units of labour and two units of capital (point B), or no units of labour and five units of capital (point C).

All these points lie along a straight line. The equation of that straight line is:

$$(P_K \bullet K) + (P_L \bullet L) = TC$$

Substituting our data for the lowest isocost line into this general equation, we get:

$$(1 \bullet K) + (1 \bullet L) = €5, \text{ or } K + L = 5$$

Remember that the X and Y axes are units of labour and units of capital, not euros.

On the same graph are two additional isocosts showing the various combinations of K and L available

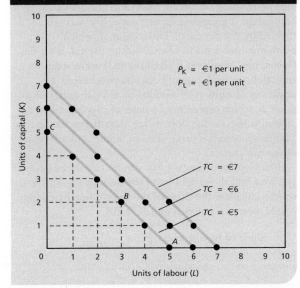

Figure 7A.3 Isocost lines showing the combinations of capital and labour available for €5, €6 and €7

An isocost line shows all the combinations of capital and labour that are available for a given total cost.

for a total cost of €6 and €7 . These are only three of an infinite number of isocosts. At any total cost, there is an isocost that shows all the combinations of K and L available for that amount.

Figure 7A.4 shows another isocost line. This isocost assumes a different set of factor prices, $P_L = €5$ and $P_K = €1$. The diagram shows all the combinations of K and

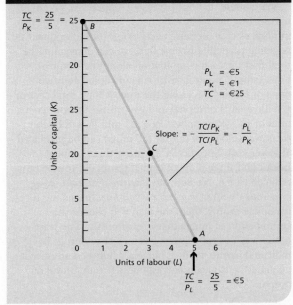

Figure 7A.4 Isocost line showing all combinations of capital and labour available for €25

One way to draw an isocost line is to determine the endpoints of that line and draw a line connecting them.

---

* We need to add the negative sign to ΔL because in moving from point A to point B, ΔK is a negative number and ΔL is a positive number. The minus sign is needed to balance the equation.

L that can be bought for €25. One way to draw the line is to determine the endpoints. For example, if the entire €25 were spent on labour, how much labour could be purchased? The answer is, of course, five units (€25 divided by €5 per unit). Thus, point *A*, which represents five units of labour and no capital, is on the isocost line. Similarly, if all of the €25 were spent on capital, how much capital could be purchased? The answer is 25 units (€25 divided by €1 per unit). Thus, point *B*, which represents 25 units of capital and no labour, is also on the isocost line. Another point on this particular isocost is three units of labour and ten units of capital, point *C*.

The slope of an isocost line can be calculated easily if you first find the endpoints of the line. In Figure 7A.4, we can calculate the slope of the isocost line by taking $\Delta K/\Delta L$ between points *B* and *A*. Thus,

$$\text{Slope of isocost line: } \frac{\Delta K}{\Delta L} = -\frac{TC/P_K}{TC/P_L} = -\frac{P_L}{P_K}$$

Plugging in the endpoints from our example, we get:

$$\text{Slope of line } AB = -\frac{5}{1} = -5$$

Finding the least-cost technology with isoquants and isocosts

Figure 7A.5 superimposes the isoquant for $q_X = 50$ on the isocost lines in Figure 7A.3, which assume that $P_K = €1$ and $P_L = €1$. The question now becomes one of choosing among the combinations of *K* and *L* that can be used to produce 50 units of output. Recall that each point on the isoquant (labelled $q_X = 50$ in Figure 7A.5) represents a different technology – a different combination of *K* and *L*.

We assume that our firm is a competitive, profit-maximizing firm that will choose the combination that minimizes cost. Because every point on the isoquant lies on some particular isocost line, we can determine the total cost for each combination along the isoquant. For example, point *B* (five units of capital and two units of labour) lies along the isocost for a total cost of €7. Five units of capital and two units of labour cost a total of €7. (Remember, $P_K = €1$ and $P_L = €1$.) But the same amount of output (50 units) can be produced at lower cost. Specifically, by using three units of labour and three units of capital (point *A*), total cost is reduced to €6. *No other combination of K and L along isoquant $q_X = 50$ is on a lower isocost line*. In seeking to maximize profits, then, the firm will choose the combination of inputs that is least costly. The least costly way to produce any given level of output is indicated by the point of tangency between an isocost line and the isoquant corresponding to that level of output.[*]

[*]*This assumes that the isoquants are continuous and convex (bowed) towards the origin.*

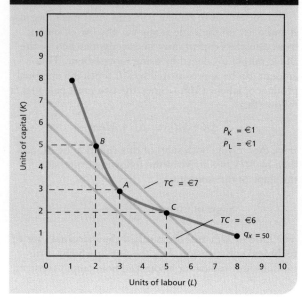

Figure 7A.5 Finding the least-cost combination of capital and labour to produce 50 units of output

Profit-maximizing firms will minimize costs by producing their chosen level of output with the technology represented by the point at which the isoquant is tangential to an isocost line. Here, the cost-minimizing technology – three units of capital and three units of labour – is represented by point *A*.

In Figure 7A.5, the least-cost technology of producing 50 units of output is represented by point *A*, the point at which the $q_X = 50$ isoquant is tangential to (that is, just touches) the isocost line.

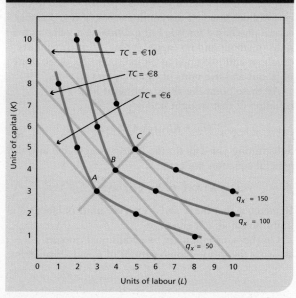

Figure 7A.6 Minimizing cost of production for $q_X = 50$, $q_X = 100$ and $q_X = 150$

Plotting a series of cost-minimizing combinations of inputs – shown in this graph as points *A*, *B* and *C* – on a separate graph results in a cost curve like the one shown in Figure 7A.7.

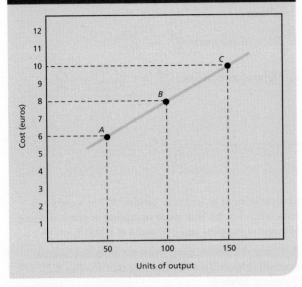

Figure 7A.7 A cost curve shows the *minimum* cost of producing each level of output

an isoquant.) At each point of tangency (such as at points A, B and C in Figure 7A.6), then, the following must be true:

$$\text{Slope of isoquant:} = -\frac{MP_L}{MP_K} = \text{Slope of isocost} = -\frac{P_L}{P_K}$$

Thus:

$$\frac{MP_L}{MP_K} = \frac{P_L}{P_K}$$

Dividing both sides by P_L and multiplying both sides by MP_K we get:

$$\frac{MP_L}{P_L} = \frac{MP_K}{P_K}$$

This is the firm's cost-minimizing equilibrium condition.

This expression makes sense if you think about what it says. The left side of the equation is the marginal product of labour divided by the price of a unit of labour. Thus, it is the product derived from the last euro spent on labour. The right-hand side of the equation is the product derived from the last euro spent on capital. If the product derived from the last euro spent on labour were not equal to the product derived from the last euro spent on capital, the firm could decrease costs by using more labour and less capital or by using more capital and less labour.

Look back to Chapter 6 (especially the appendix) and see if you can find a similar expression and some similar logic in our discussion of household behaviour. In fact, there is great symmetry between the theory of the firm and the theory of household behaviour.

Figure 7A.6 adds the other two isoquants from Figure 7A.1 to Figure 7A.5. Assuming that $P_K = €1$ and $P_L = €1$, the firm will move along each of the three isoquants until it finds the least-cost combination of K and L that can be used to produce each particular level of output. The result is plotted in Figure 7A.7. The minimum cost of producing 50 units of X is €6; the minimum cost of producing 100 units of X is €8; and the minimum cost of producing 150 units of X is €10.

The cost-minimizing equilibrium condition

At the point where a line is tangential to a curve, the two have the same slope. (We have already derived expressions for the slope of an isocost and the slope of

Summary

1. An *isoquant* is a graph that shows all the combinations of capital and labour that can be used to produce a given amount of output. The slope of an isoquant is equal to $-MP_L/MP_K$. The ratio of MP_L to MP_K is the *marginal rate of technical substitution*. It is the rate at which a firm can substitute capital for labour and hold output constant.

2. An *isocost line* is a graph that shows all the combinations of capital and labour that are available for

a given total cost. The slope of an isocost line is equal to $-P_L/P_K$.

3. The least-cost method of producing a given amount of output is found graphically at the point at which an isocost line is tangential to (that is, just touches) the isoquant corresponding to that level of production. The firm's cost-minimizing equilibrium condition is $MP_L/P_L = MP_K/P_K$.

Review Terms and Concepts

isocost line A graph that shows all the combinations of capital and labour available for a given total cost.
isoquant A graph that shows all the combinations of capital and labour that can be used to produce a given amount of output.
marginal rate of technical substitution The rate at which a firm can substitute capital for labour and hold output constant.

Equations

1. Slope of isoquant: $\dfrac{\Delta K}{\Delta L} = -\dfrac{MP_L}{MP_K}$

2. Slope of isocost line: $\dfrac{\Delta K}{\Delta L} = -\dfrac{TC/P_K}{TC/P_L} = -\dfrac{P_L}{P_K}$

Problem Set

 1. Assume that $MP_L = 5$ and $MP_K = 10$. Assume also that $P_L = €2$ and $P_K = €5$. This implies that the firm should substitute capital for labour. Explain why.

2. In the isoquant/isocost diagram (Figure 1), suppose that the firm is producing 1000 units of output at point *A* using 100 units of labour and 200 units of capital. As an outside consultant, what actions would you suggest

to management to improve profits? What would you recommend if the firm were operating at point *B*, using 100 units of capital and 200 units of labour?

3. Using the information from the isoquant/isocost diagram (Figure 2), and assuming that $P_L = P_K = €2$, complete Table 1.

Figure 1

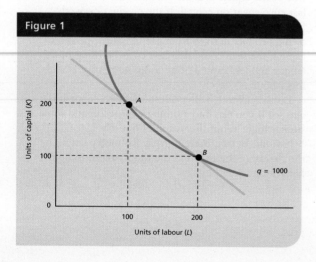

Figure 1

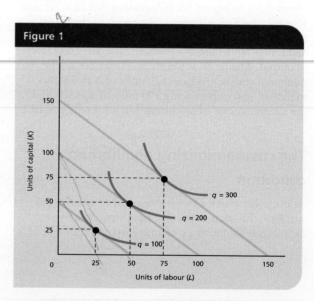

Table 1			
Output units	**Total cost of output**	**Units of labour demanded**	**Units of capital demanded**
100			
200			
300			

8

Short-run Costs and Output Decisions

This chapter continues our examination of the decisions that firms make in their quest for profits. You have seen that firms in perfectly competitive industries make three very specific decisions:

1. how much output to supply;
2. how to produce that output (that is, which production technique/technology to use); and
3. what quantity of each input to demand.

Remember that *all* types of firms make these decisions, not just those in perfectly competitive industries. We continue to use perfectly competitive firms as a teaching device, but much of the material in this chapter applies to firms in non-competitive industries as well.

We have assumed so far that firms are in business to earn profits and that they make choices to maximize those profits. (Remember that *profit* is the difference between revenues and costs.) Because firms in perfectly competitive markets are price-takers in both input and output markets, many decisions depend upon prices over which firms have no control. Like households, firms also face market constraints.

In the last chapter we focused on the production process. This chapter focuses on the *costs* of production. To calculate costs, a firm must know two things: the quantity and combination of inputs it needs to produce its product, and how much those inputs cost. (Don't forget that economic costs include a normal return to capital – the opportunity cost of capital.)

Take a moment to look back at the circular flow diagram in Figure 7.1. There you can see exactly where we are in our study of the competitive market system. The goal of this chapter is to look behind the supply curve in output markets. It is important to understand, however, that producing output implies demanding inputs at the same time. You can also see two of the information sources that firms use in their output supply and input demand decisions: firms look to *output markets* for the price of output and to *input markets* for the prices of capital and labour.

Costs in the short run

Our emphasis in this chapter is on costs *in the short run only*. Recall that the short run is that period during which two conditions hold: (1) existing firms face limits imposed by some fixed factor of production; and (2) new firms cannot enter, and existing firms cannot exit, an industry.

In the short run, all firms (competitive and non-competitive) have costs that they must bear regardless of their output. Some costs, in fact, must be paid even if the firm stops producing (that is, even if output is zero). These kinds of costs are called **fixed cost**s, and firms can do nothing in the short run to avoid them or to change them. In the long run, a firm has no fixed costs, because it can expand, contract, or exit the industry.

fixed cost Any cost that does not depend on the firm's level of output. These costs are incurred even if the firm is producing nothing. There are no fixed costs in the long run.

variable cost A cost that depends on the level of production chosen.

total cost (TC) Fixed costs plus variable costs.

Firms do have certain costs in the short run that depend on the level of output they have chosen. These kinds of costs are called **variable cost**s. Fixed costs and variable costs together make up **total cost**s:

$$TC = TFC + TVC$$

where TC denotes total costs, TFC denotes total fixed costs, and TVC denotes total variable costs. We will return to this equation after discussing fixed costs and variable costs in detail.

Fixed costs

In discussing fixed costs, we must distinguish between total fixed costs and average fixed costs.

Total fixed cost (TFC)

Total fixed cost is sometimes referred to as *overhead*. If you operate a factory, you must heat the building to keep the pipes from freezing in the winter. Even if no production is taking place, you may have to keep the roof from leaking, pay a security firm to protect the building from vandals, and make payments on a long-term lease. There may also be insurance premiums and taxes to pay, as well as contract obligations to workers.

Fixed costs represent a larger portion of total costs for some firms than for others. Water companies, for instance, maintain purification plants and thousands of kilometres of pipes, and so on. In some countries, such plants are financed by issuing bonds to the public (that is, by borrowing). The interest that must be paid on these bonds represents a substantial part of the utilities' operating cost and is a fixed cost in the short run, no matter how much (if any) water is being distributed.

For the purposes of our discussion in this chapter, we will assume that firms use only two inputs: labour and capital.[1] Recall that capital yields services over time in the production of other goods and services. It is the plant and equipment of a manufacturing firm; the computers, desks, chairs, doors and walls of a law office; the boat that David and Anna built on their desert island. It is sometimes assumed that capital is a fixed input in the short run and that labour is the only variable input. To be a bit more realistic, however, we will assume that capital has both a fixed *and* a variable component. After all, some capital can be purchased in the short run.

Consider a small consulting firm that employs several economists, research assistants and secretaries. It rents space in an office building and has a five-year lease. The rent on the office space can be thought of as a fixed cost in the short run. The monthly electricity and heating bills are also essentially fixed (though the amounts may vary slightly from month to month). So are the salaries of the basic administrative staff. Payments on some capital equipment – a large photocopier and the main word processing system – can also be thought of as fixed.

The same firm also has costs that vary with output. When there is a lot of work, the firm hires more employees at both the professional and research assistant level. The capital used by the consulting firm may also vary, even in the short run. Payments on the computer system do not change, but the firm may rent additional computer time when necessary. It can buy additional personal computers, network terminals or databases quickly, if need be. It must pay for the photocopier machine, but the machine costs more when it is running than when it is not.

total fixed costs (TFC) or overhead The total of all costs that do not change with output, even if output is zero.

Total fixed costs (TFC) are those costs that do not change with output, even if output is zero. Column 2 of Table 8.1 presents data on the fixed costs of a hypothetical firm. Fixed costs are €1000 at all levels of output (q). Figure 8.1a shows total fixed costs as

[1]While this may seem unrealistic, virtually everything that we will say about firms using these two factors can easily be generalized to firms that use many factors of production.

Table 8.1 Short-run fixed cost (total and average) of a hypothetical firm

(1) q	(2) TFC (euros)	(3) AFC = (TFC/q) (euros)
0	1000	–
1	1000	1000
2	1000	500
3	1000	333
4	1000	250
5	1000	200

a function of output. Because *TFC* does not change with output, the graph is simply a straight horizontal line at €1000. The important thing to remember here is that:

Firms have no control over fixed costs in the short run. For this reason, fixed costs are sometimes called **sunk costs**.

sunk cost
Another name for fixed costs in the short run, so called because firms have no choice but to pay them.

Average fixed cost (AFC)

Average fixed cost (AFC) is total fixed cost (*TFC*) divided by the number of units of output (*q*):

average fixed cost (AFC)
Total fixed cost divided by the number of units of output; a per unit measure of fixed costs.

$$AFC = \frac{TFC}{q}$$

For example, if the firm in Figure 8.1 produced three units of output, average fixed costs would be €333 (1000 divided by three). If the same firm produced five units of output, average fixed cost would be €200 (1000 divided by five). *Average fixed cost falls as output rises*, because the same total is being spread over, or divided by, a larger

Figure 8.1 Short-run fixed cost (total and average) of a hypothetical firm

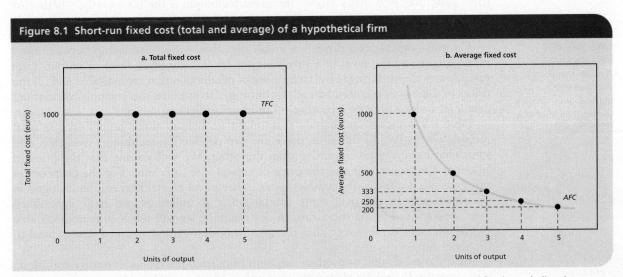

Average fixed cost is simply total fixed cost divided by the quantity of output. As output increases, average fixed cost declines because we are dividing a fixed number (in this case €1000) by a larger and larger quantity.

number of units (see column 3 of Table 8.1). This phenomenon is sometimes called **spreading overhead**.

Graphs of average fixed cost, like that in Figure 8.1b (which presents the average fixed cost data from Table 8.1), are downward-sloping curves. Notice that *AFC* approaches zero as the quantity of output increases. If output were 100,000 units, average fixed cost would equal only €0.01 per unit in our example (1,000 ÷ 100,000 = €0.01). *AFC* never actually reaches zero.

Variable costs

Total variable costs (*TVC*)

Total variable costs (*TVC*) are those costs that depend on or vary with the level of output in the short run. To produce more output, a firm uses more inputs. The cost of additional output depends directly on the additional inputs that are required and how much they cost.

As you saw in Chapter 7, input requirements are determined by technology. Firms generally have a number of production techniques available to them, and the option they choose is assumed to be the one that produces the desired level of output at the least cost. To find out which technology involves the least cost, a firm must compare the total variable costs of producing that level of output using different production techniques.

This is as true of small businesses as it is of large manufacturing firms. Suppose, for example, that you are a small farmer. A certain amount of work has to be done to plant and harvest your 120 hectares. You can get this work done in a number of ways. You might hire four farm workers and divide up the tasks, or you might buy several pieces of complex farm machinery (capital) and do the work single-handedly. Clearly, your final choice depends on a number of things. What machinery is available? What does it do? Will it work on small fields such as yours? How much will it cost to buy each piece of equipment? What wage will you have to pay farm workers? How many workers will you need to get the job done? If machinery is expensive and labour is cheap, you will probably choose the labour-intensive technology. If farm labour is expensive and the local farm equipment dealer is going out of business, you might get a good deal on some machinery and choose the capital-intensive method.

Having compared the costs of alternative production techniques, the firm may be influenced in its choice by the current scale of its operation. Remember, in the short run a firm is locked into a *fixed* scale of operations. A firm currently producing on a small scale may find that a labour-intensive technique is the least costly, whether or not labour is comparatively expensive. The same firm producing on a larger scale might find a capital-intensive technique less costly.

The **total variable cost curve** is a graph that shows the relationship between total variable cost and the level of a firm's output (*q*). At any given level of output, total variable cost depends on (1) the techniques of production that are available and (2) the prices of the inputs required by each technology. To examine this relationship in more detail, let us look at some hypothetical production figures.

Table 8.2 presents an analysis that might lie behind three points on the total variable cost curve. In this case, there are two production techniques available, one somewhat more capital-intensive than the other. We will assume that the price of labour is 1 euro per unit and the price of capital is €2 per unit. For the purposes of this example, we focus on *variable capital* – that is, on capital that can be changed in the short run. In practice, some capital (such as buildings and large specialized machines) is fixed in the short run. In our example, we will use *K* to denote variable capital. Remember, however, that the firm has other capital – capital that is fixed in the short run.

Analysis reveals that to produce one unit of output, the labour-intensive technique is least costly. Technique *A* requires four units of both capital and labour, which would

---

spreading overhead

The process of dividing total fixed costs by more units of output. Average fixed cost declines as *q* rises.

total variable cost (*TVC*)

The total of all costs that depend on or vary with output in the short run.

total variable cost curve

A graph that shows the relationship between total variable cost and the level of a firm's output.

Table 8.2 Derivation of total variable cost schedule from technology and factor prices

To produce	Using technique	Units of input required (production function) K	Units of input required (production function) L	Total variable cost, assuming $P_K = 2$ (euros), $P_L = 1$ (euro) $TVC = (K \times P_K) + (L \times P_L)$
1 Unit of output	A	4	4	$(4 \times 2) + (4 \times 1) = 12$
	B	2	6	$(2 \times 2) + (6 \times 1) = \boxed{10}$
2 Units of output	A	7	6	$(7 \times 2) + (6 \times 1) = 20$
	B	4	10	$(4 \times 2) + (10 \times 1) = \boxed{18}$
3 Units of output	A	9	6	$(9 \times 2) + (6 \times 1) = \boxed{24}$
	B	6	14	$(6 \times 2) + (14 \times 1) = 26$

cost a total of €12. Technique B requires six units of labour but only two units of capital for a total cost of only €10. To maximize profits, the firm would use technique B to produce one unit. The total variable cost of producing one unit of output would thus be €10.

The relatively labour-intensive technique B is also the best method of production for two units of output. Using B, the firm can produce two units for €18. If the firm decides to produce three units of output, however, technique A is the cheaper. Using the least-cost technology (A), the total variable cost of production is €24. The firm will use nine units of capital at €2 each and six units of labour at 1 euro each.

Figure 8.2 graphs the relationship between variable costs and output based on the data in Table 8.2, assuming the firm chooses, for each output, the least-cost technology.

The important point to remember here is that:

The total variable cost curve embodies information about both factor, or input, prices and technology. It shows the cost of production using the best available technique at each output level, given current factor prices.

Figure 8.2 Total variable cost curve

In Table 8.2, total variable cost is derived from production requirements and input prices. A total variable cost curve expresses the relationship between TVC and total output.

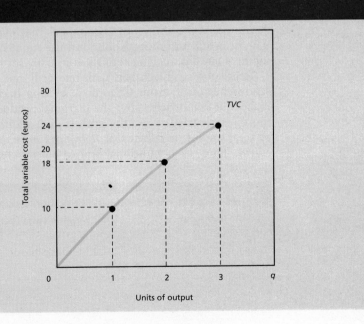

Marginal cost (*MC*)

The most important of all cost concepts is that of **marginal cost (*MC*)**, the increase in total cost that results from the production of one more unit of output. Let us say, for example, that a firm is producing 1000 units of output per period and decides to raise its rate of output to 1001. Producing the extra unit raises costs, and the increase (that is, the cost of producing the 1001st unit) is the marginal cost. Focusing on the 'margin' is one way of looking at variable costs: marginal costs reflect changes in variable costs because they vary when output changes. Fixed costs do not change when output changes.

Table 8.3 shows how marginal cost is derived from total variable cost by simple subtraction. The total variable cost of producing the first unit of output is €10. Raising production from one unit to two units increases total variable cost from 10 to €18; the difference is the marginal cost of the second unit, or €8. Raising output from two to three units increases total variable cost from 18 to €24. The marginal cost of the third unit, therefore, is €6.

It is important to think for a moment about the nature of marginal cost. Specifically, marginal cost is the cost of the added inputs, or resources, needed to produce one additional unit of output. Look back at Table 8.2, and think about the additional capital and labour needed to go from one unit to two units. In other words, think about the added resources needed to produce the second unit of output. Producing one unit of output with technique *B* requires two units of capital and six units of labour; producing two units of output using the same technique requires four units of capital and ten units of labour. Thus, the second unit requires two *additional* units of capital and four *additional* units of labour. What then is the added, or marginal, cost of the second unit? Two units of capital cost €2 each (€4 total) and four units of labour cost 1 euro each (another €4), for a total marginal cost of €8 which is exactly the number we derived in Table 8.3.

While the easiest way to derive marginal cost is to look at total variable cost and subtract, don't lose sight of the fact that when a firm increases its output level, it hires or demands more inputs. *Marginal cost* measures the *additional* cost of inputs required to produce each successive unit of output.

The shape of the marginal cost curve in the short run

The assumption of a fixed factor of production in the short run means that a firm is stuck at its current scale of operation (in our example, the size of the plant). As a firm tries to increase its output, it will eventually find itself trapped by that scale. Thus, our definition of the short run also implies that *marginal cost eventually rises with output*. The firm can hire more labour and use more materials – that is, it can add variable inputs – but diminishing returns eventually set in.

Recall the sandwich bar, with one grill and too many workers trying to prepare sandwiches on it, from Chapter 7. With a fixed grill capacity, more workers could make more sandwiches, but the marginal product of each successive cook declined as more people tried to use the grill. If each additional unit of labour adds less and less to total output, *it follows that it requires more labour to produce each additional unit of output*. Thus, each additional unit of output costs more to produce. In other words,

Table 8.3 Derivation of marginal cost from total variable cost

Units of output	Total variable costs (euros)	Marginal costs (euros)
0	0	0
1	10	10
2	18	8
3	24	6

Figure 8.3 Declining marginal product implies that marginal cost will eventually rise with output

In the short run, every firm is constrained by some fixed factor of production. A fixed input implies diminishing returns (declining marginal product) and a limited capacity to produce. As that limit is approached, marginal costs rise.

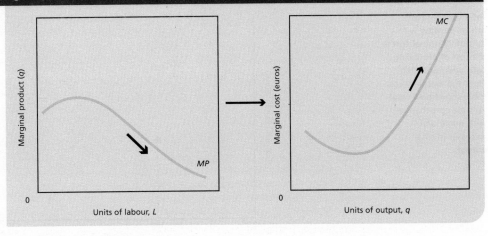

diminishing returns, or decreasing marginal product, implies increasing marginal cost (Figure 8.3).

Recall too the accountant who makes a living by helping people sort out their tax returns. He has an office in his home and works alone. His fixed factor of production is his own time: there are only so many hours in a day, and he has only so much stamina. In the long run, he may decide to hire and train an associate, but in the meantime (the short run) he has to decide how much to produce, and that decision is constrained by his current scale of operations. The fact that he has no trained associate and that each day contains only 24 hours constrains the number of clients that he can take on. The biggest component of the accountant's cost is time. When he works, he gives up leisure and other things that he could do with his time. With more and more clients, he works later and later into the night; as he does so, he becomes less and less productive, and his hours become increasingly valuable for sleep and relaxation. In other words, the marginal cost of doing each successive tax return rises.

To reiterate:

> In the short run, every firm is constrained by some fixed input that (1) leads to diminishing returns to variable inputs and that (2) limits its capacity to produce. As a firm approaches that capacity, it becomes increasingly costly to produce successively higher levels of output. Marginal costs ultimately increase with output in the short run.

Graphing total variable costs and marginal costs

Figure 8.4 shows the total variable cost curve and the marginal cost curve of a typical firm. Notice first that the shape of the marginal cost curve is consistent with short-run diminishing returns. At first MC declines, but eventually the fixed factor of production begins to constrain the firm, and marginal cost rises. Up to 100 units of output, producing each successive unit of output costs slightly less than producing the one before. Beyond 100 units, however, the cost of each successive unit is greater than the one before.

Clearly, more output costs more than less output. Total variable costs (*TVC*), therefore, *always increase* when output increases. Even though the cost of each additional unit changes, *total* variable cost rises when output rises. Thus the *total* variable cost curve always has a positive slope.

You might think of the total variable cost curve as a staircase. Each step takes you out along the quantity axis by a single unit, and the height of each step is the increase in total variable cost. As you climb the stairs, you are always going up, but the steps have different heights. At first, the stairway is steep, but as you climb, the steps get

Figure 8.4 Total variable cost and marginal cost for a typical firm

Total variable costs always increase with output. Marginal cost is the cost of producing each additional unit. Thus, the marginal cost curve shows how total variable cost changes with single unit increases in total output.

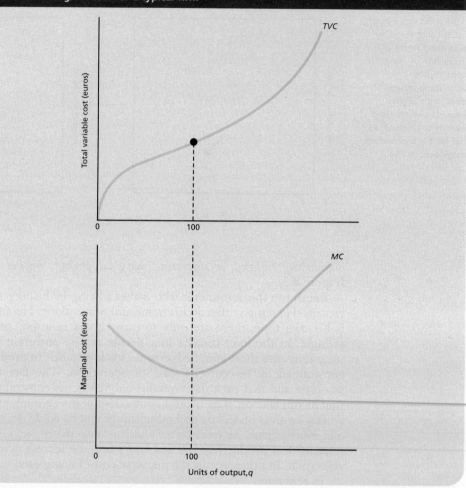

smaller (marginal cost declines). The 100th stair is the smallest. As you continue to walk out beyond 100 units, the steps begin to get larger; the staircase gets steeper (marginal cost increases).

Remember that the slope of a line is equal to the change in the units measured on the Y axis divided by the change in the unit measured on the X axis. The slope of a total variable cost curve is thus the change in total variable cost divided by the change in output ($\Delta TVC/\Delta q$). Since marginal cost is by definition the change in total variable cost resulting from an increase in output of one unit ($\Delta q=1$), *marginal cost is the slope of the total variable cost curve*:

$$\text{Slope of } TVC = \frac{\Delta TVC}{\Delta q} = \frac{\Delta TVC}{1} = \Delta TVC = MC$$

Notice that up to 100 units, marginal cost decreases and the variable cost curve becomes flatter. The slope of the total variable cost curve is declining; that is, total variable cost increases, but at a *decreasing rate*. Beyond 100 units of output, marginal cost increases and the total variable cost curve gets steeper; total variable costs continue to increase, but at an *increasing rate*.

Average variable cost (AVC)

A more complete picture of the costs of a hypothetical firm appears in Table 8.4. Column 2 shows total variable costs – derived from information on input prices and

Table 8.4 Short-run costs (euros) of a hypothetical firm

(1) q	(2) TVC	(3) MC (ΔTVC)	(4) AVC (TVC/q)	(5) TFC	(6) TC (TVC + TFC)	(7) AFC (TFC/q)	(8) ATC (TC/q or AFC + AVC)
0	0	–	–	1000	1000	–	–
1	10	10	10	1000	1010	1000	1010
2	18	8	9	1000	1018	500	509
3	24	6	8	1000	1024	333	341
4	32	8	8	1000	1032	250	258
5	42	10	8.4	1000	1042	200	208.4
–	–	–	–	–	–	–	–
–	–	–	–	–	–	–	–
–	–	–	–	–	–	–	–
500	8000	20	16	1000	9000	2	18

technology. Column 3 derives marginal cost by simple subtraction. For example, raising output from three units to four units increases variable costs from 24 to €32, making the marginal cost of the fourth unit €8 (32 – 24). The marginal cost of the fifth unit is €10, the difference between €32 (*TVC*) for four units and €42 (*TVC*) for five units.

Average variable cost (*AVC*) is total variable cost divided by the number of units of output (*q*):

average variable cost (*AVC*)
Total variable cost divided by the number of units of output.

$$AVC = \frac{TVC}{q}$$

In Table 8.4, we calculate *AVC* in column 4 by dividing the numbers in column 2 (*TVC*) by the numbers in column 1 (*q*). For example, if the total variable cost of producing five units of output is €42, then the average variable cost is 42 ÷ 5 = €8.40.

The important distinction to remember here is as follows:

Marginal cost is the cost of *one additional unit*. Average variable cost is the average variable cost per unit of *all the units* being produced.

Graphing average variable costs and marginal costs

The relationship between average variable cost and marginal cost can be illustrated graphically. When marginal cost is *below* average, average variable cost declines towards it. When marginal cost is *above* average, average variable cost increase towards it. Figure 8.5 duplicates the lower diagram for a typical firm in Figure 8.4 but adds average variable cost. As the graph shows, average variable cost *follows* marginal cost, but lags behind.

As we move from left to right, we are looking at higher and higher levels of output per period. As we increase production, marginal cost – which at low levels of production is above €3.50 per unit – falls as coordination and cooperation begin to play a role. At 100 units of output, marginal cost has fallen to €2.50. Notice that average variable cost falls as well, but not as rapidly as marginal cost.

Maths Box 1 Product and cost curves

We can show the relationships between the product curves and the cost curves more formally. Consider the relationship of average variable costs (*AVC*) to average product (*AP*).

Assume that the only variable input is labour, Q_L, and the price of labour is fixed at *P*. Then:

$$TVC = PQ_L$$

where *P* = price per unit of the variable input, labour.

$$APP = \frac{TP}{Q_L}$$

$$\text{Thus } \frac{Q_L}{TP} = \frac{1}{TP/Q_L} = \frac{1}{AP}$$

$$\text{And } AVC = P_L\left(\frac{Q_L}{TP}\right) = P_L\left(\frac{1}{AP}\right)$$

So the average variable cost is the price of the input multiplied by the reciprocal of average product. You can use the same reasoning to show the relationship of the marginal cost curve to the marginal product curve.

After 100 units of output, we begin to see diminishing returns. Marginal cost begins to increase as higher and higher levels of output are produced. But notice that average cost is still falling until 200 units because marginal cost remains below it. At 100 units of output, marginal cost is €2.50 per unit but the *average* variable cost of production is €3.50. Thus even though marginal cost is rising after 100 units, it is still pulling the average of €3.50 downwards.

At 200 units, however, marginal cost has risen to €3.00 and average cost has fallen to €3.00; marginal and average costs are equal. At this point marginal cost continues to rise with higher output. But from 200 units upward, *MC* is *above AVC*, and thus exerts an *upward* pull on the average variable cost curve. At levels of output below 200 units, marginal cost is below average variable cost, and average variable cost decreases as output increases. At levels of output above 200 units, *MC* is above *AVC*, and *AVC* increases as output increases.

Figure 8.5 More short-run costs

When marginal cost is *below* average cost, average cost is declining. When marginal cost is *above* average cost, average cost is increasing. Rising marginal cost intersects average variable cost at the minimum point of *AVC*.

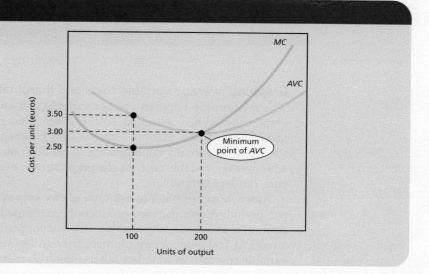

If you follow this logic you will see that:

> Marginal cost intersects average variable cost at the lowest, or minimum, point of *AVC*.

Another example using exam marks should help you to understand the relationship between *MC* and *AVC*. Consider the following sequence of exam marks: 95, 85, 92, 88. The average of these four is 90. Suppose you get 80 for your fifth exam. This score will drag down your average to 88. Now suppose that you get 85 for your sixth exam. This score is higher than 80, but it's still *below* your 88 average. As a result, your average continues to fall (from 88 to 87.5), even though your marginal exam mark rose. But if instead of an 85 you get 89 – just one mark above your average – you've turned your average around; it is now rising.

Total costs

We are now ready to complete the cost picture by adding total fixed costs to total variable costs. Recall that

$$TC = TFC + TVC$$

Total cost is graphed in Figure 8.6, where the same vertical distance (equal to *TFC*, which is constant) is simply added to *TVC* at every level of output. In Table 8.4, column 6 adds the total fixed cost of €1000 to total variable cost to arrive at total cost.

Average total cost (*ATC*)

average total cost (ATC)
Total cost divided by the number of units of output.

Average total cost (ATC) is total cost divided by the number of units of output (*q*):

$$ATC = \frac{TC}{q}$$

Column 8 in Table 8.4 shows the result of dividing the costs in column 6 by the quantities in column 1. For example, at five units of output, *total* cost is €1042; *average* total cost is 1042 ÷ 5 or €208.40. The average total cost of producing 500 units of output is only €18 – that is, €9000 ÷ 500.

Figure 8.6 Total cost equals total fixed cost plus total variable cost

Adding total fixed cost to total variable cost means adding the same amount of total fixed cost to every level of total variable cost. Thus, the total cost curve has the same shape as the total variable cost curve; it is simply higher by an amount equal to *TFC*.

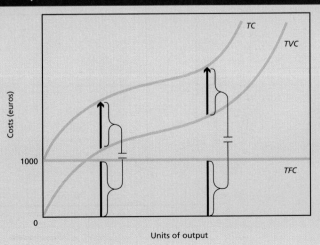

Another, more revealing, way of deriving average total cost is to add average fixed cost and average variable cost together:

$$ATC = AFC + AVC$$

For example, column 8 in Table 8.4 is the sum of columns 4 (AVC) and 7 (AFC).

Figure 8.7 derives average total cost graphically for a typical firm. The bottom part of the figure graphs average fixed cost. At 100 units of output, average fixed cost is $TFC/q = 1000 \div 100 = €10$. At 400 units of output, $AFC = 1000 \div 400 = €2.50$. The top part of Figure 8.7 shows the declining average fixed cost added to AVC at each level of output. Because AFC gets smaller and smaller, ATC gets closer and closer to AVC as output increases, but the two lines never cross.

The relationship between average total cost and marginal cost

The relationship between average *total* cost and marginal cost is exactly the same as the relationship between average *variable* cost and marginal cost. The average total cost curve follows the marginal cost curve, but lags behind because it is an average over all units of output. The average total cost curve lags behind the marginal cost curve even more than the average variable cost curve does, because the cost of each

Figure 8.7 Average total cost = average variable cost + average fixed cost

To get average total cost, we add average fixed and average variable costs at all levels of output. Because average fixed cost falls with output, an ever-declining amount is added to AVC. Thus, AVC and ATC get closer together as output increases, but the two lines never cross.

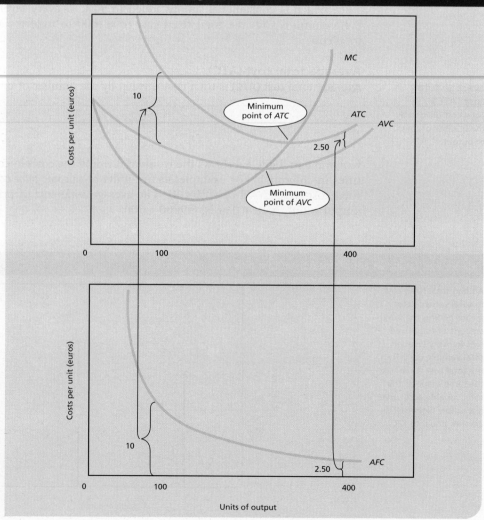

added unit of production is now averaged not only with the variable cost of all previous units produced, but with fixed costs as well.

Fixed costs equal €1000 and are incurred even when the output level is zero. Thus, the first unit of output in the example in Table 8.4 costs €10 in variable cost to produce. The second unit costs only €8 in variable cost to produce. The total cost of two units is €1018; average total cost of the two is (1010 + €8) ÷ 2, or €509. The marginal cost of the third unit is only €6. The total cost of three units is thus €1024, or 1018 + €6, and the average total cost of three units is (1010 + 8 + €6) ÷ 3, or €341.

As you saw with the exam marks example, marginal cost is what drives changes in average total cost:

If marginal cost is *below* average total cost, average total cost will *decline* towards marginal cost; if marginal cost is *above* average total cost, average total cost will *increase*. As a result, marginal cost intersects average *total* cost at *ATC*'s minimum point, for the same reason that it intersects the average *variable* cost curve at its minimum point.

Short-run costs: a review

Let us now pause to review what we learned about the behaviour of firms. We know that firms make three basic choices: how much product or output to produce or supply, how to produce that output, and how much of each input to demand in order to produce what they intend to supply. We assume that these choices are made to maximize profits. Profits are equal to the difference between a firm's revenue from the sale of its product and the costs of producing that product: profit = total revenue minus total cost.

So far, we have looked only at costs, but costs are only one part of the profit equation. To complete the picture, we must turn to the output market and see how these costs compare with the price that a product commands in the market. Before we do so, however, it is important to consolidate what we have said about costs.

Before a firm does anything else, it needs to know the different methods that it can use to produce its product. The technologies available determine the combinations of inputs that are needed to produce each level of output. Firms choose the technique that produces the desired level of output at least cost. The cost curves that result from the analysis of all this information show the cost of producing each level of output using the best available technology.

Remember that so far we have talked only about short-run costs. The curves we have drawn are therefore *short-run cost curves*. The shape of these curves is determined in large measure by the assumptions that we make about the short run, especially the assumption that some fixed factor of production leads to diminishing returns. Given this assumption, marginal costs eventually rise, and average cost curves are likely to be U-shaped.

After gaining a complete knowledge of how to produce a product and how much it will cost to produce it at each level of output, the firm turns to the market to find out what it can sell its product for. It is to the output market that we now turn our attention.

Output decisions: revenues, costs, and profit maximization

To calculate potential profits, firms must combine their cost analyses with information on potential revenues from sales. After all, a firm that can't sell its product for more than it costs to produce it won't be in business long. In contrast, if the market gives the firm a price that is significantly greater than the cost it incurs to produce a unit of its product, the firm may have an incentive to expand output. Large profits might also attract new competitors to the market.

Let us now examine in detail how a firm goes about determining how much output to produce. For the sake of simplicity, we will continue to examine the decisions of a perfectly competitive firm. A perfectly competitive industry, you will recall, has many firms that are small relative to the size of the market. In such an environment, firms have no control over the market price of their products. Product price is determined by the interaction of many suppliers and many demanders.

Figure 8.8 shows a typical firm in a perfectly competitive industry. Price is determined in the market at $P^* = €5$. The individual firm can charge any price that it wants for its product, but if it charges above €5, the quantity demanded falls to zero, and the firm won't sell anything. Many other firms are producing exactly the same product, so why should consumers pay more than the going market price? The firm could also sell its product for less than €5, but there is no reason to do so. If the firm can sell all it wants to sell at the going market price of €5, and we assume that it can, then it would not be sensible to sell it for less.

All this implies that:

> In the short run, a competitive firm faces a demand curve that is simply a horizontal line at the market equilibrium price. In other words, competitive firms face perfectly elastic demand in the short run.

In Figure 8.8, market equilibrium price is $P^* = €5$ and the firm's perfectly elastic demand curve is labelled d.

Total revenue (*TR*) and marginal revenue (*MR*)

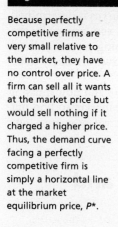

total revenue (TR)
The total amount that a firm takes in from the sale of its product: The price per unit times the quantity of output the firm decides to produce ($P \times q$).

Profit is the difference between total revenue and total cost. **Total revenue** is the total amount that a firm takes in from the sale of its product. A perfectly competitive firm sells each unit of product for the same price, regardless of the output level it has chosen. Therefore, total revenue is simply the price per unit times the quantity of output that the firm decides to produce:

$$\text{Total revenue} = \text{price} \times \text{quantity}$$
$$TR = P \times q$$

Figure 8.8 Demand facing a typical firm in a perfectly competitive market

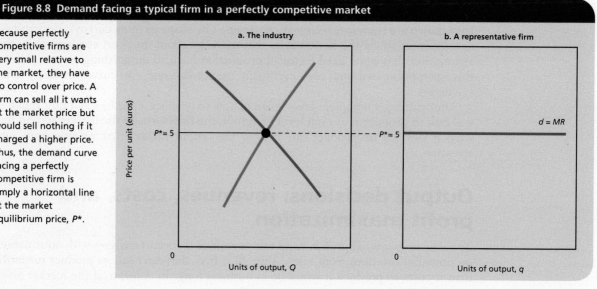

Because perfectly competitive firms are very small relative to the market, they have no control over price. A firm can sell all it wants at the market price but would sell nothing if it charged a higher price. Thus, the demand curve facing a perfectly competitive firm is simply a horizontal line at the market equilibrium price, P^*.

marginal revenue (MR)

The additional revenue that a firm takes in when it increases output by one additional unit. In perfect competition, *P = MR*.

Marginal revenue (MR) is the added revenue that a firm takes in when it increases output by one additional unit. If a firm producing 10,521 units of output per month increases that output to 10,522 units per month, it will take in an additional amount of revenue each month. The revenue associated with the 10,522nd unit is simply the amount that the firm sells that one unit for. Thus, for a competitive firm, marginal revenue is simply equal to the current market price of each additional unit sold. In Figure 8.8, for example, the market price is €5. Thus, if the representative firm raises its output from 10,521 units to 10,522 units, its revenue will increase by €5.

A firm's *marginal revenue curve* shows how much revenue the firm will gain, by raising output by one unit at every level of output. The *marginal revenue curve and the demand curve facing a competitive firm are identical.* The horizontal line in Figure 8.8b can be thought of as both the demand curve facing the firm and its marginal revenue curve: $P^* \equiv d \equiv MR$.

Comparing costs and revenues to maximize profit

The discussion in the next few paragraphs conveys one of the most important concepts in all of microeconomics. As we pursue our analysis, remember that we are working under two assumptions: (1) that the industry we are examining is perfectly competitive, and (2) that firms choose the level of output that yields the maximum total profit.

The profit-maximizing level of output

Look carefully at the diagrams in Figure 8.9. Once again, we have the whole market, or industry, on the left and a single, typical small firm on the right. And again, the current market price is P^*.

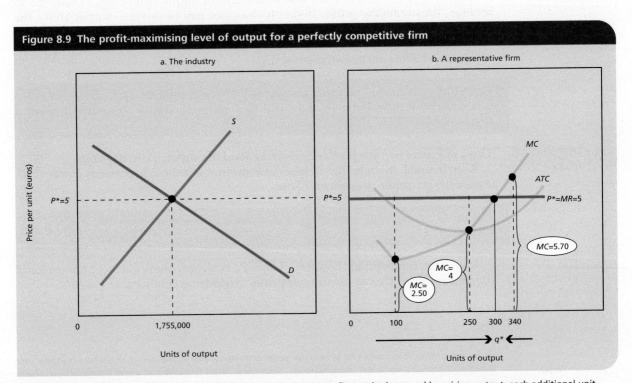

Figure 8.9 The profit-maximising level of output for a perfectly competitive firm

If price is above marginal cost, as it is at 100 and 250 units of output, profits can be increased by raising output; each additional unit increases revenues by more than it costs to produce the additional output. Beyond $q^* = 300$, however, added output will reduce profits. At 340 units of output, an additional unit of output costs more to produce than it will bring in revenue when sold on the market. Profit-maximizing output is thus q^*, the point at which $P^* = MC$.

First, the firm observes market price (Figure 8.9a) and knows that it can sell all that it wants to for $P^* = €5$ per unit. Next, it must decide how much to produce. It might seem reasonable to pick the output level where marginal cost is at its minimum point – in this case, at an output of 100 units. Here the difference between marginal revenue, €5, and marginal cost, €2.50, is the greatest.

But remember that a firm wants to maximize the difference between *total* revenue and *total* cost, not the difference between *marginal* revenue and *marginal* cost. The fact that marginal revenue is greater than marginal cost actually indicates that profit is *not* being maximized! Think about the 101st unit. Adding that single unit to production each period adds €5 to revenues but adds only about €2.50 to cost. Profits each period would be higher by about €2.50. Thus, the optimal (profit-maximizing) level of output is clearly higher than 100 units.

Now look at an output level of 250 units. Here, once again, raising output increases profit. The revenue gained from producing the 251st unit (marginal revenue) is still €5, and the cost of the 251st unit (marginal cost) is only about €4.

This process leads to the conclusion that:

As long as marginal revenue is greater than marginal cost, even though the difference between the two is getting smaller, added output means added profit. Whenever marginal revenue exceeds marginal cost, the revenue gained by increasing output by one unit per period exceeds the cost incurred by doing so.

This logic leads us to 300 units of output. At 300 units, marginal cost has risen to €5. At 300 units of output, $P^* = MR = MC = €5$.

Notice that if the firm were to produce *more* than 300 units, marginal cost rises above marginal revenue. At 340 units of output, for example, the cost of adding the 341st unit is about €5.70 while that added unit of output still brings in only €5 in revenue, thus reducing profit. It simply does not pay to increase output above the point where marginal cost rises above marginal revenue because such increases will *reduce* profit.

The inevitable conclusion, then, is that:

The profit-maximizing perfectly competitive firm will produce up to the point where the price of its output is just equal to short-run marginal cost – the level of output at which $P^* = MC$.[2]

Thus, in Figure 8.9, the profit-maximizing level of output, q^*, is 300 units.

Keep in mind, though, that all types of firms (not just those in perfectly competitive industries) are profit-maximizers. Thus,

The profit-maximizing output level for *all* firms is the output level where $MR = MC$.

In perfect competition, however, $MR = P$, as shown above. Hence, for perfectly competitive firms we can rewrite our profit-maximizing condition as $P = MC$.

[2] *To be very precise, it is possible for price to be equal to marginal cost at two points, one where marginal cost is declining and another where marginal cost is increasing. Profit is maximized where marginal cost crosses price on its way up, as in Figure 8.9b. The marginal costs of the first few units of production are high, because at such a low level of output the firm is not using its plant very efficiently. It would never make sense to produce at these low levels. In fact, to stop at the first point where P = MC would be to minimize profits. Can you work out why?*

Important note: the key idea here is that firms will produce as long as marginal revenue *exceeds* marginal cost. If marginal cost rises smoothly, as it does in Figure 8.9, then the profit-maximizing condition is that *MR* (or *P*) *exactly equals MC*. But if marginal cost moves up in increments, as it does in the following numerical example, marginal revenue or price may never exactly equal marginal cost. The key idea still holds!

A numerical example

Table 8.5 presents some data for a hypothetical German engineering firm. Let's assume that the market has set a 15 deutschemarks (DM) unit price for the firm's product. Total revenue in column 6 is the simple product of $P \times q$ (the numbers in column 1 times 15). The table derives total, marginal and average costs exactly as Table 8.4 did. Here, however, we have included revenues, and we can calculate the profit, which is shown in column 8.

Column 8 shows that a profit-maximizing firm would choose to produce four units of output. At this level, profits are 20 DM; at all other output levels, they are lower. Now let's see if 'marginal' reasoning leads us to the same conclusion.

First, should the firm produce at all? If it produces nothing, it suffers losses equal to 10 DM. If it increases output to one unit, marginal revenue is 15 DM (remember that it sells each unit for 15 DM), and marginal cost is 10 DM. Thus, it gains 5 DM, reducing its loss from 10 DM each period to 5 DM.

Should the firm increase output to two units? The marginal revenue from the second unit is again 15 DM, but the marginal cost is only 5 DM. Thus, by producing the second unit the firm gains 10 DM (15 – 5 DM) and turns a 5 DM loss into a 5 DM profit. The third unit adds 10 DM to profits. Again, marginal revenue is 15 DM and marginal cost is 5 DM, an increase in profit of 10 DM, for a total profit of 15 DM.

The fourth unit offers still more profit. Price is still above marginal cost, which means that producing that fourth unit will increase profits. Price, or marginal revenue, is 15 DM, and marginal cost is just 10 DM. Thus, the fourth unit adds a further 5 DM to profit. At unit number five, however, diminishing returns push marginal cost up above price. The marginal revenue from producing the fifth unit is 15 DM, while marginal cost is now 20 DM. As a result, profit per period drops by 5 DM to 15 DM per period. Clearly, the firm will not produce the fifth unit.

The profit-maximizing level of output is thus four units. The firm produces as long as price (marginal revenue) is greater than marginal cost. (For an in-depth example of profit maximization see the Global Perspective box 'Marginal analysis: an ice cream shop in Ohio'.)

Table 8.5 Profit analysis for a simple firm (DM)							
(1)	(2)	(3)	(4)	(5)	(6) TR	(7) TC	(8) Profit
q	TFC	TVC	MC	P = MR	(P × q)	(TFC + TVC)	(TR – TC)
0	10	0	–	15	0	10	– 10
1	10	10	10	15	15	20	– 5
2	10	15	5	15	30	25	5
3	10	20	5	15	45	30	15
4	10	30	10	15	60	40	20
5	10	50	20	15	75	60	15
6	10	80	30	15	90	90	0

Maths Box 2 Output and profit from the revenue and cost functions

We can work out the profit-maximizing output and maximum profit for our competitive firm if we know the revenue and cost functions.

Suppose $TR = 114Q$ and $TC = 24 + 6Q + Q^3$, where TR = total revenue, TC = total cost (euros) and Q = output per period of time. Let π = total profit. Then:

$$\pi = TR - TC = 114Q - (24 + 6Q + Q^3)$$
$$= -24 + 108Q - Q^3$$

To find the profit-maximizing output, differentiate total profit with respect to output:

$$d\pi/dQ = 108 - 3Q^2$$

Setting $d\pi/dQ$ to zero gives

$$0 = 108 - 3Q^2$$
$$Q = 6$$

The profit-maximizing level of output is 6 units per period of time. To find total profit, substitute into the profit function:

$$\pi = -24 + 648 - 216$$
$$\pi = 408$$

Total profit is €408 per period of time.

The short-run supply curve

Consider how the typical firm shown in Figure 8.9 would behave in response to an increase in price. In Figure 8.10a, assume that something happens that causes demand to increase (shift to the right), driving price from €5 to €6 and finally to €7. When price is €5, a profit-maximizing firm will choose output level 300 in Figure 8.10b. To produce any less, or to raise output above that level, would lead to a lower level of profit. At €6 the same firm would increase output to 350, but it would stop there. Similarly, at €7, the firm would raise output to 400 units of output.

The *MC* curve in Figure 8.10b relates price and quantity supplied. At any market price, the marginal cost curve shows the output level that maximizes profit. A curve that shows how much output a profit-maximizing firm will produce at every price also fits the definition of a supply curve. (Review Chapter 4 if this point is not clear to you.) Therefore, it follows that:

The marginal cost curve of a competitive firm is the firm's short-run supply curve.

However, as you will see there is one important exception to this general rule. There is some price level below which the firm will shut down its operations and simply bear losses equal to fixed costs even if price is above marginal cost. This important point is discussed in Chapter 9.

Figure 8.10 Marginal cost is the supply curve of a perfectly competitive firm

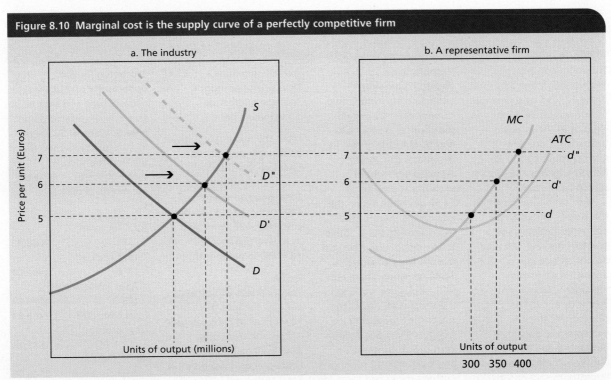

At any market price (except when price is so low that it pays a firm to shut down – a point we will return to in Chapter 9), the marginal cost curve shows the output level that maximizes profit. Thus, the marginal cost curve of a perfectly competitive profit-maximizing firm is the firm's short-run supply curve.

Looking ahead

At the beginning of this chapter we set out to combine information on technology, factor prices and output prices to understand the supply curve of a competitive firm. We have now accomplished that goal.

Because marginal cost is such an important concept in microeconomics, you should carefully review any sections of this chapter that were unclear to you. Above all, keep in mind that the *marginal cost curve* carries information about both *input prices* and *technology*. The firm looks to output markets for information on potential revenues, and the current market price defines the firm's marginal revenue curve. The point where price (which is equal to marginal revenue in perfect competition) is just equal to marginal cost is the perfectly competitive firm's profit-maximizing level of output. Thus, with one important exception discussed in Chapter 9, the marginal cost curve *is* the perfectly competitive firm's supply curve in the short run.

In the next chapter, we turn to the long run. What happens when firms are free to choose their scale of operations without being limited by a fixed factor of production? Without diminishing returns that set in as a result of a fixed scale of production, what determines the shape of cost curves? What happens when new firms can enter industries in which profits are being earned? How do industries adjust when losses are being incurred? How does the structure of an industry evolve over time?

Global Perspectives

Marginal analysis: an ice cream shop in Ohio

The following is a description of the decisions made in 1996 by the owner of a small ice cream shop in Ohio, USA. After being in business for one year, this entrepreneur had to ask herself whether she should stay in business.

The cost figures on which she based her decisions are presented below. These numbers are real, but they do not include one important item: the managerial labour provided by the owner. In her calculations, the entrepreneur did not include a wage for herself, but we will assume an opportunity cost of $30,000 per year ($2,500 per month).

Fixed costs

The fixed components of the shop's monthly costs include the following:

Rent (1,150 square feet)	$2012.50
Electricity	325.00
Debt service (loan payment)	737.50
Maintenance	295.00
Telephone	65.00
Total	$3435.00

Not all of the items on this list are strictly fixed, however. Electricity costs, for example, would be slightly higher if the shop produced more ice cream and stayed open longer, but the added cost would be minimal.

Variable costs

The ice cream shop's variable costs include two components: (1) behind-the-counter labour costs, and (2) the cost of making ice cream. The shop employs high school students at a wage of $4.50 per hour. When the employer's share of the social security tax is added to the wage, the gross cost of each hour of labour is $4.84 per hour. There are two employees working in the shop at all times. The full cost of producing ice cream is $3.27 per gallon. Each gallon contains approximately 12 servings. Customers can add toppings free of charge, and the average cost of the toppings taken by a customer is about 5 cents ($.05):

Gross labour costs	$4.84/hour
Costs of producing one gallon of ice cream (12 servings per gallon)	$3.27
Average cost of added toppings per serving	$0.05

Revenues

The shop sells ice cream cones, sundaes and floats. The average price of a purchase at the shop is $1.45. The shop is open 8 hours per day for 26 days a month, and serves an average of 240 customers per day:

Average purchase	$1.45
Days open per month	26
Average number of customers per day	240

From the information given above, it is possible to calculate the shop's average monthly profit. Total revenue is equal to 240 customers × $1.45 per customer × 26 open days in an average month:
TR = £9048 per month.

Profits

The shop sells 240 servings per day. Because there are 12 servings of ice cream per gallon, the store uses exactly 20 gallons per day (240 servings divided by 12). Total costs are $3.27 × 20, or $65.40, per day for ice cream and $12 per day for toppings (240 × $0.05). The cost of variable labour is $4.84 × 8 hours × 2 workers, or $77.44 per day. Total variable costs are therefore ($65.40 + $12.00 + $77.44) = $154.84 per day. Since the shop is open for 26 days a month, the total variable cost per month is $4025.84 ($154.84 × 26).

Adding fixed costs of $3435 to variable costs of $4025.84, we get total cost of operation of $7460.84 per month. Thus, the firm is averaging a profit of $1587.16 per month ($9048 – 7460.84). *But this is not an 'economic profit' because we haven't* accounted for the opportunity cost of the owner's time and efforts. In fact, when we factor in an implicit wage of $2500 per month for the owner, we see that the shop is suffering *losses* of $912.84 per month ($1587.16 – $2500).

Total revenue (*TR*)	$9048.00
Total fixed cost (*TFC*)	3435.00
+ Total variable cost (*TVC*)	4025.84
Total costs (*TC*)	7460.84
Total profit (*TR* – *TC*)	1587.16
Adjustment for implicit wage	2500.00
Economic profit	–912.84

Should the entrepreneur stay in business? If she wants to make $2500 per month and she thinks that nothing about her business will change, she must shut down in the long run. But two things keep her going: (1) a decision to stay open longer, and (2) hope for more customers in the future.

Opening longer hours: marginal costs and marginal revenues

The shop's normal hours of operation are noon until 8 pm. On an experimental basis, the owner extends its hours until 11 pm for one month. The average number of additional

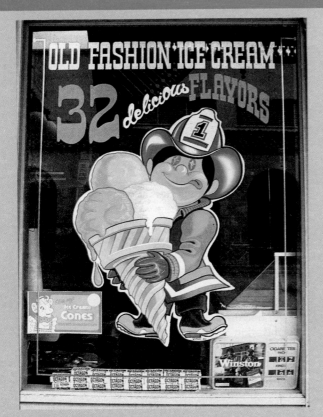

Marginal analysis is as important to the owner of a small ice cream stall as it is to the managers of million-dollar manufacturing operations

customers for each of the added hours is as follows:

Hour	Customers
8–9 pm	41
9–10 pm	20
10–11 pm	8

Assuming that the late customers spend an average of $1.45, we can calculate the marginal revenue and the marginal cost of staying open longer. The marginal cost of one serving of ice cream is $3.27 divided by 12 = $0.27 + 0.05 (for topping) = $0.32 (see the table).

Marginal analysis tells us that the shop should stay open for two additional hours. Each day that the shop stays open from 8 to 9 pm it will make an added profit of $59.45 – $22.80, or $36.65. Staying open from 9 to 10 pm adds $29.00 – $16.08, or $12.92, to profit. Staying open the third hour, however, *decreases*

profits because the marginal revenue generated by staying open from 10 to 11pm is less than the marginal cost. The entrepreneur decides to stay open for two additional hours per day. This adds $49.57 ($36.65 + 12.92) to profits each day, a total of $1288.82 per month.

By adding the two hours, the shop turns an economic loss of $912.84 per month into a $375.98 profit after accounting for the owner's implicit wage of $2500 per month.

The owner decides to stay in business. She now serves over 350 customers per day, and the price of a serving of ice cream has risen to $2.50 while costs have not changed very much. In 1997, she cleared a profit of nearly $10,000 per month!

Hour	Marginal revenue (*MR*)	Marginal cost (*MC*)		Added profit per hour (*MR* – *MC*)
8–9 pm	$1.45 × 41 = $59.45	Ice cream: 0.32 × 41 =	$13.12	$36.65
		Labour: 2 × 4.84 =	9.68	
		Total	$22.80	
9–10 pm	$1.45 × 20 = $29.00	Ice cream: 0.32 × 20 =	£6.40	$12.92
		Labour: 2 × 4.84 =	9.68	
		Total	$16.08	
10–11 pm	$1.45 × 8 = $11.69	Ice cream: 0.32 × 8 =1	$2.56	$ –0.55
		Labour: 2 × 4.84 =	9.68	
		Total	$12.24	

Summary

1. Profit-maximizing firms make decisions in order to maximize profit (total revenue minus total cost).

2. To calculate production costs, firms must know two things: (1) the quantity and combination of inputs they need to produce their product, and (2) how much those inputs cost.

Costs in the short run

3. *Fixed costs* are costs that do not change with the output of a firm. In the short run, firms cannot avoid them or change them, even if production is zero.

4. *Variable costs* are those costs that vary with the level of output chosen. Fixed costs plus variable costs equal *total costs* $(TC = TFC + TVC)$.

5. *Average fixed cost* (AFC) is total fixed cost divided by the quantity of output. As output rises, average fixed cost declines because the same total is being spread over a larger and larger quantity of output. This phenomenon is called *spreading overhead*.

6. Numerous combinations of inputs can be used to produce a given level of output. *Total variable cost* (TVC) is the total of all costs that vary with output in the short run.

7. *Marginal cost* (MC) is the increase in total cost that results from the production of one more unit of output. If a firm is producing 1000 units, the additional cost of increasing output to 1001 units is marginal cost. Marginal cost measures the cost of the additional inputs required to produce each successive unit of output. Because fixed costs do not change when output changes, marginal costs reflect changes in variable costs.

8. In the short run, a firm is limited by a fixed factor of production, or a fixed scale of plant. As a firm increases output, it will eventually find itself trapped by that scale. Because of the fixed scale, marginal cost eventually rises with output.

9. Marginal cost is the slope of the total variable cost curve. The total variable cost curve always has a positive slope, because total costs always rise with output. But increasing marginal cost means that total costs ultimately rise at an increasing rate.

10. *Average variable cost* (AVC) is equal to total variable cost divided by the quantity of output.

11. When marginal cost is above average variable cost, average variable cost is *increasing*. When marginal cost is below average variable cost, average variable cost is *declining*. Marginal cost intersects average variable cost at AVC's minimum point.

12. *Average total cost* (ATC) is equal to total cost divided by the quantity of output. It is also equal to the sum of average fixed cost and average variable cost.

13. If marginal cost is below average total cost, average total cost will decline towards marginal cost. If marginal cost is above average total cost, average total cost will increase. Marginal cost intersects average total cost at ATC's minimum point.

Output decisions: revenues, costs, and profit maximization

14. In the short run, a perfectly competitive firm faces a demand curve that is a horizontal line (in other words, perfectly elastic demand).

15. *Total revenue* (TR) is simply price times the quantity of output that a firm decides to produce and sell. *Marginal revenue* (MR) is the additional revenue that a firm takes in when it increases output by one unit.

16. For a perfectly competitive firm, marginal revenue is equal to the current market price of its product.

17. A profit-maximizing firm in a perfectly competitive industry will produce up to the point at which the price of its output is just equal to short-run marginal cost: $P = MC$. The more general profit-maximizing formula is $MR = MC$ ($P = MR$ in perfect competition). The marginal cost curve of a perfectly competitive firm is the firm's short-run supply curve, with one exception discussed in Chapter 9.

Review Terms and Concepts

average fixed cost (*AFC*)
average total cost (*ATC*)
average variable cost (*AVC*)
fixed cost
marginal cost (*MC*)
marginal revenue (*MR*)
spreading overhead

sunk costs
total cost (*TC*)
total fixed cost (*TFC*), or overhead
total revenue (*TR*)
total variable cost (*TVC*)
total variable cost curve
variable cost

Equations

1. $TC = TFC + TVC$

2. $AFC = TFC/q$

3. Slope of $TVC = MC$

4. $AVC = TVC/q$

5. $ATC = TC/q = AFC + AVC$

6. $TR = P \times q$

7. Profit-maximizing level of output for all firms: $MR = MC$

8. Profit-maximizing level of output for perfectly competitive firms: $P = MC$

Problem Set

1. Table 1 gives capital and labour requirements for ten different levels of production:

Table 1

q	K	L
0	0	0
1	2	5
2	4	9
3	6	12
4	8	15
5	10	19
6	12	24
7	14	30
8	16	37
9	18	45
10	20	54

a. Assuming that the price of labour (P_L) is €5 per unit and the price of capital (P_K) is €10 per unit, compute and graph the total variable cost curve, the marginal cost curve and the average variable cost curve for the firm.

b. Do the curves have the shapes that you might expect? Explain.

c. Using the numbers here, explain the relationship between marginal cost and average variable cost.

d. Using the numbers here, explain the meaning of 'marginal cost' in terms of additional inputs needed to produce a marginal unit of output.

e. If output price was €57, how many units of output would the firm produce? Explain.

2. Do you agree or disagree with each of the following statements? Explain your reasons.

a. If marginal cost is rising, average cost must also be rising.

b. A profit-maximizing firm must minimize cost. Thus firms will always produce the level of output at which average total cost is minimized.

c. Average fixed cost does not change as output changes.

3. A firm's cost curves are given in Table 2.

Table 2

q	TC (£)	TFC (£)	TVC	AVC	ATC	MC
0	100	100				
1	130	100				
2	150	100				
3	160	100				
4	172	100				
5	185	100				
6	210	100				
7	240	100				
8	280	100				
9	330	100				
10	390	100				

a. Complete the table.

b. Graph AVC, ATC and MC on the same graph. What is the relationship between the MC curve and ATC? Between MC and AVC?

c. Suppose that market price is £30. How much will the firm produce in the short run? How much are total profits? Show them on the graph.

d. Suppose that market price is £50. How much will the firm produce in the short run? What are total profits? Show them on the graph.

e. Suppose that market price is £10. How much would the firm produce in the short run? What are total profits? Show them on the graph.

4. A 1998 graduate of a leading Dutch university inherited her mother's printing company. The capital stock of the firm consists of three machines of various vintages, all in excellent condition. All machines can be running at the same time (Table 3).

Table 3		
Machine	**Cost of printing and binding (guilders per book)**	**Maximum total capacity (books per month)**
1	1.00	100
2	2.00	200
3	3.00	500

a. Assume that 'cost of printing and binding' includes *all* labour and materials, including the owner's own wages. Assume further that mother signed a long-term contract (50 years) with a service company to keep the machines in good repair for a fixed fee of 100 guilders per month. (1) Derive the firm's marginal cost curve. (2) Derive the firm's total cost curve.
b. At a price of 2.50 guilders, how many books would the company produce? What would total revenues be? Total costs? Total profits?

5. Figure 1 shows a production function for a firm that uses just one variable factor of production labour. It shows total output, or product, for every level of inputs:

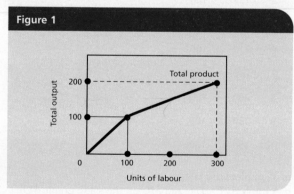

Figure 1

Total output / Units of labour

a. Derive and graph the marginal product curve.
b. Suppose that the wage rate is €4. Derive and graph the firm's marginal cost curve.
c. If output sells for €6, what is the profit-maximizing level of output? How much labour will the firm hire?

6. Petya and Maria move out of Sofia to the Black Sea in Bulgaria. They own a small fishing boat. A crew of four is required to take the boat out fishing. The current wage paid to the four crew members is a total of 5000 leva per day (a lev is the Bulgarian unit of currency; in 1998 the exchange rate was about 2000 leva to the euro). Assume that the cost of operating and maintaining the boat is 1000 leva per day when fishing, and zero otherwise. The schedule in Table 4 gives the appropriate catch for each period during the year.

Table 4	
Period	**Daily catch (kg)**
Prime fishing: 180 days	100
Month 7: 30 days	80
Month 8: 30 days	60
Rest of the year	40

The price of fish in Bulgaria is no longer regulated by the government, and is now determined in competitive markets. Suppose that the price has been stable all year at 80 leva per kilogram.
a. What is the marginal product of a day's worth of fishing during prime fishing season? During month 7? During month 8?
b. What is the marginal cost of a kilogram of fish during prime fishing season? During month 7? During month 8? During the rest of the year?
c. If you were Petya and Maria, how many months per year would you hire the crew and go out fishing? Explain your answer using marginal logic.

7. For each of the following businesses, what is the probable fixed factor of production that defines the short run?
a. A 160-hectare potato farm
b. A Chinese restaurant
c. A dentist in private practice
d. A car dealership
e. A bank

8. A producer of hard disk drives for notebook computers currently has a factory with two disk-pressing machines, which it cannot change in the short run. Each of the machines costs €100 per day (the opportunity cost of the funds used to buy them). Each hired worker costs €50 per day. The relationship between output and the number of workers is shown in Table 5.

Table 5								
Q	**L**	**TFC**	**TVC**	**TC**	**AFC**	**AVC**	**ATC**	**MC**
0	0							
1	10							
2	15							
3	18							
4	22							
5	28							
6	36							
7	48							

a. Fill in the columns for total fixed cost (*TFC*), total variable cost (*TVC*), total cost (*TC*), average fixed cost (*AFC*), average variable cost (*AVC*), average total cost (*ATC*) and marginal cost (*MC*).

b. Verify that the two alternative methods of calculating *ATC* (*TC/q* and *AVC* + *AFC*) give the same answer (except for rounding).

c. Over what range of output are there decreasing marginal costs? Increasing marginal costs? Increasing returns to labour?

d. At which level of output is *AVC* minimized? At which level of output is *ATC* minimized?

e. Suppose this firm operates in a perfectly competitive output market and can sell as many disk drives as it wants for €410 each. In the short run, what is the profit-maximizing level of output for this firm?

f. Does the profit-maximizing output level you found above minimize average total costs? If not, how could the firm be maximizing profits if it is not minimizing costs?

9. Why do self-service newspaper vending machines use a simple technology that allows occasional cheats to remove more than one newspaper, while soft drink machines use a more complicated technology to ensure that each customer gets only one drink? (*Hint*: There are at least two explanations for this phenomenon. One involves the concept of marginal costs; the other relies on the concept of marginal utility.)

*10. A perfectly competitive firm has the following revenue and short-run cost conditions:

$$TR = 104Q$$

$$TC = 10 + 4Q + 2Q^2$$

where Q is quantity of output per day.

a. How much revenue does the firm receive if it makes 20 units of output per day?

b. What are the firm's fixed costs?

c. What are the firm's variable costs at 10 units per day?

d. What are the firm's total costs at 10 units per day?

e. What is the profit-maximizing level of output?

f. What is the total cost per day at that output level?

g. What is the total revenue per day at that output level?

h. What is the total profit per day at that output level?

9

Costs and Output Decisions in the Long Run

The last two chapters discussed the behaviour of profit-maximizing competitive firms in the short run. Recall that all firms must make three fundamental decisions: (1) how much output to produce or supply, (2) how to produce that output, and (3) how much of each input to demand.

Firms use information on input prices, output prices and technology to make the decisions that will lead to the most profit. Because profits equal revenues minus costs, firms must know how much their products will sell for, and how much production will cost using the most efficient technology.

In Chapter 8 we saw how cost curves can be derived from production functions and input prices. Once a firm has a clear picture of its short-run costs, the price at which it sells its output determines the quantity of output that will maximize profit. Specifically, a profit-maximizing perfectly competitive firm will supply output up to the point that price (marginal revenue) equals marginal cost. The marginal cost curve of such a firm is thus the same as its supply curve.

In this chapter, we turn from the short run to the long run. The condition in which firms find themselves in the short run (Are they making profits? Are they incurring losses?) determines what is likely to happen in the long run. Remember that output (supply) decisions in the long run are less constrained than they are in the short run, for two reasons. First, in the long run, the firm has no fixed factor of production that confines its production to a given scale. Second, firms are free to enter industries in order to seek profits and to leave industries in order to avoid losses.

The long run has important implications for the shape of cost curves. As we saw, in the short run a fixed factor of production eventually causes marginal cost to increase along with output. This is not the case in the long run, however. With no fixed scale, the shapes of cost curves become more complex and generalizations are less easy to make. The shapes of long-run cost curves have important implications for the way an industry's structure is likely to evolve over time.

We begin our discussion of the long run by looking at firms in three short-run circumstances: (1) firms earning economic profits, (2) firms suffering economic losses but continuing to operate to reduce or minimize those losses, and (3) firms that decide to shut down and bear losses just equal to fixed costs. We then examine how these firms will alter their decisions in response to these short-run conditions.

Although we continue to focus on perfectly competitive firms, it should be stressed that all firms are subject to the spectrum of short-run profit or loss situations, regardless of market structure. Assuming perfect competition allows us to simplify our analysis and provides us with a strong background for understanding the discussions of imperfectly competitive behaviour in later chapters.

Short-run conditions and long-run directions

Before beginning our examination of firm behaviour, let us review the concept of profit. Recall that a normal rate of profit is included in costs as we measure them in economics. Thus, when we say that a firm is earning profits, we mean that it is earning a profit over and above a normal rate of return to capital. A *normal rate of return* is a profit rate that is just sufficient to keep current investors interested in the industry. Thus, when we speak of profits, we really mean profits above normal. Sometimes, for emphasis, these supranormal profits are called *economic profits* (see Chapter 7).

When we use the term 'profit', then, we are simply taking into account the opportunity cost of capital. By investing in a firm, its owners or lenders are forgoing what they could earn by investing elsewhere. This is why the normal rate of return must be at least equal to the interest rate on 'safe' investments (government bonds, for example). Only when investors earn profits above normal are they earning economic profits. And only when they are earning economic profits are new investors likely to be attracted to the industry.

When we say that a firm is suffering *losses*, we mean that it is earning a profit that is below normal. Such a firm may be suffering losses as an accountant would measure them, or may simply be earning at a very low (that is, below normal) profit rate. Investors in a firm are not going to be happy if they earn a return of only 2% when they can get 6% in government bonds. A firm that is **breaking even**, or earning zero economic profits, is one that is earning exactly a normal profit rate. New investors are not attracted, but current ones are not running away either.

breaking even
The situation in which a firm is earning exactly a normal profit rate.

With these distinctions in mind, then, we can say that for any firm one of three conditions holds at any given moment: (1) The firm is making economic profits, (2) the firm is suffering economic losses, or (3) the firm is just breaking even. Profitable firms will want to maximize their profits in the short run, while firms suffering losses will want to minimize those losses in the short run.

Maximizing profits

When a firm earns revenues in excess of costs (including a normal profit rate), it is earning economic profits. Let us take as an example the Blue Velvet carpet cleaners, that operate in southern England. Suppose that investors have put up £500,000 to purchase vans and all the equipment required to clean carpets. Let's also suppose that investors expect to earn a minimum return of 10% on their investment. If the money to set up the business had been borrowed from the bank instead, the carpet cleaners' owners would have paid a 10% interest rate. In either case, the firm earns an economic profit only after it has paid its investors, or the bank, 10% of £500,000, or £50,000, every year. This normal profit of £50,000 is part of the firm's annual costs.

Our carpet cleaning firm operates for 50 weeks per year and is capable of cleaning up to 800 carpets per week. Whether it is operating or not, there are fixed costs. Those costs include £1000 per week to investors (that is, the £50,000 per year normal profit rate) and £1000 per week in other fixed costs (a basic maintenance contract on the vans, equipment, a long-term lease, and so forth).

When the carpet cleaners is operating, there are also variable costs. Workers must be paid, and materials such as soap and cleaner must be purchased. The wage bill is £1000 per week. Materials, electricity and so on amount to £600 if the firm is at full capacity. If the carpet cleaners is not in operation, there are no variable costs. Table 9.1 summarizes the costs of the Blue Velvet carpet cleaners.

The business is in a quite competitive industry. There are several carpet cleaners of equal quality in the area, and they offer their service at £5. If Blue Velvet wants customers, it cannot charge a price for cleaning a carpet above £5. (Recall the perfectly elastic demand curve facing perfectly competitive firms; review Chapter 8 if necessary.) If we assume that Blue Velvet cleans 800 carpets each week, it takes in revenues of £4000 from operating (800 × £5). Is this total revenue enough to make an economic profit?

The answer is yes. Revenues of £4000 are sufficient to cover both fixed costs of £2000 and variable costs of £1600, leaving an economic profit of £400 per week.

Figure 9.1 graphs the performance of a firm that is earning economic profits in the short run. Figure 9.1a illustrates the industry, or the market, and Figure 9.1b illustrates a representative firm. At present, the market is clearing at a price of £5. Thus,

Table 9.1 Blue Velvet carpet cleaners' weekly costs

Total fixed costs (*TFC*)	
1. Normal return (profit) to investors	£1,000
2. Other fixed costs (maintenance contract, lease, etc.)	£1,000
	£2,000
Total variable costs (*TVC*), 800 washes	
1. Labour	£1,000
2. Materials	£600
	£1,600
Total costs (*TC = FC + TVC*)	£3,600
Total revenue (*TR*) at *P* = £5 (800 × £5)	£4,000
Profit (*TR − TC*)	£400

we assume that the individual firm can sell all it wants at a price of $P^* = £5$, but that it is constrained by its capacity; its marginal cost curve rises in the short run because of a fixed factor. You already know that a perfectly competitive profit-maximizing firm produces up to the point that price equals marginal cost. As long as price (marginal revenue) exceeds marginal cost, firms can push up profits by increasing short-run output. The firm in the diagram, then, will supply $q^* = 300$ units of output (point A, where $P = MC$).

Both revenues and costs are shown graphically. Total revenue (*TR*) is simply the product of price and quantity: $P^* \times q^* = £5 \times 300 = £1500$. On the diagram, total

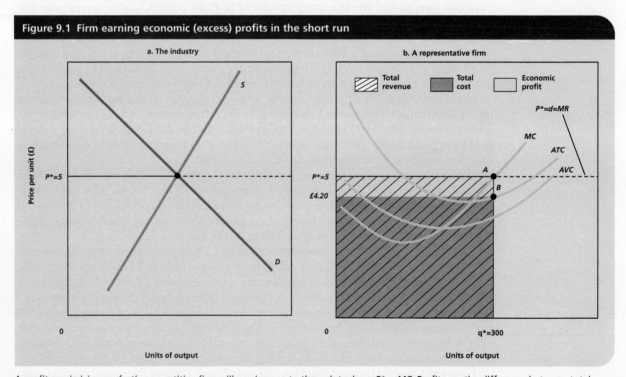

Figure 9.1 Firm earning economic (excess) profits in the short run

A profit-maximizing perfectly competitive firm will produce up to the point where $P^* = MC$. Profits are the difference between total revenue and total costs. At $q^* = 300$, total revenue is £5 × 300 = £1500, total cost is £4.20 × 300 = £1260, and total profit = £1500 − £1260 = £240.

revenue is equal to the area of the rectangle $P*Aq*0$. (The area of a rectangle is equal to its length times its width.) At output $q*$, average total cost is £4.20 (point B). Numerically, it is equal to the length of line segment $q*B$. Because average total cost is derived by dividing total cost by q, we can get back to total cost by *multiplying* average total cost by q. That is,

$$ATC = \frac{TC}{q}$$

and

$$TC = ATC \times q$$

Total cost (TC), then, is £4.20 × 300 = £1260, the area shaded blue in the diagram. Total economic profit is simply the difference between total revenue (TR) and total cost (TC), or £240. This is the area that is shaded pink in the diagram. This firm is earning positive economic profits.

A firm that is earning economic profits in the short run and expects to continue doing so has an incentive to expand its scale of operation in the long run. Those profits also give new firms an incentive to enter and compete in the market.

Minimizing losses

A firm that is not earning economic profit or breaking even is suffering a loss. Firms suffering losses fall into two categories: (1) those that find it advantageous to shut down operations immediately and bear losses equal to fixed costs, and (2) those that continue to operate in the short run to minimize their losses. The most important thing to remember here is that firms cannot exit the industry in the short run. The firm can shut down, but it cannot get rid of its fixed costs by going out of business. Fixed costs must be paid in the short run no matter what the firm does.

Whether a firm suffering losses decides to produce or not to produce in the short run depends on the advantages and disadvantages of continuing production. If a firm shuts down, it earns no revenues and has no variable costs to bear. If it continues to produce, it both earns revenues and incurs variable costs. Because a firm must bear fixed costs *whether or not* it shuts down, its decision depends *solely on whether revenues from operating are sufficient to cover variable costs*. **Operating profit (or loss)** (sometimes called **net operating revenue**) is defined as total revenue (TR) minus total variable cost (TVC). In general:

operating profit (or loss) *or* net operating revenue

Total revenue minus total variable cost ($TR - TVC$).

If revenues exceed variable costs, operating profit is positive and can be used to offset fixed costs and reduce losses, and it will pay the firm to keep operating.

If revenues are smaller than variable costs, the firm suffers operating losses that push total losses above fixed costs. In this case, the firm can minimize its losses by shutting down.

Producing at a loss to offset fixed costs

To return to the carpet cleaning example, suppose that competitive pressure pushes the price per carpet cleaned down to £3. Total revenues for Blue Velvet would fall to £2400 per week (800 cars × £3). If variable costs remained at £1600, total costs would be £3600 (£1600 + £2000 fixed costs), a figure higher than total revenues. The firm would then be suffering economic losses of £3600 – £2400 = £1200.

In the long run, Blue Velvet may want to go out of business, but in the short run it is stuck, and it must decide what to do.

The carpet cleaner has two options: operate or shut down. If it shuts down, it has no variable costs, but it also earns no revenues, and its losses will be equal to its fixed

Table 9.2 A firm will operate if total revenue covers total variable cost

Case 1: Shut down		Case 2: Operate at price = £3	
Total revenue ($q = 0$)	£0	Total revenue (£3 × 800)	£2,400
Fixed costs	£2,000	Fixed costs	£2,000
Variable costs	+ 0	Variable costs	+£1,600
Total costs	£2,000	Total costs	£3,600
Profit/loss ($TR - TC$)	−£2,000	Operating profit/loss ($TR - TVC$)	£800
		Total profit/loss ($TR - TC$)	−£1,200

costs of £2000 (Table 9.2, Case 1). If it decides to stay open (Table 9.2, Case 2), it will make operating profits. Revenues will be £2400, more than sufficient to cover variable costs of £1600. By operating, the firm gains £800 per week operating profits that it can use to offset some of its fixed costs. By operating, then, the firm reduces its losses from £2000 to £1200.

Figure 9.2 graphs a firm suffering economic losses. The market price, set by the forces of supply and demand, is $P^* = £3.50$. If the firm decides to operate, it will do best by producing up to the point where price (marginal revenue) is equal to marginal cost – in this case, at an output of $q^* = 225$ units.

Once again, total revenue (TR) is simply the product of price and quantity ($P^* \times q^*$) = £3.50 × 225 = £787.50, or the area of rectangle P^*Aq^*0. Average total cost at q^* = 225 is £4.10, and it is equal to the length of q^*B. Total cost is the product of average total cost and q^* ($ATC \times q^*$), or £4.10 × 225 = £922.50. Because total cost is greater than total revenue, the firm is suffering economic losses of £135, shown on the graph by the grey shaded rectangle.

Figure 9.2 Firm suffering economic losses but showing an operating profit in the short run

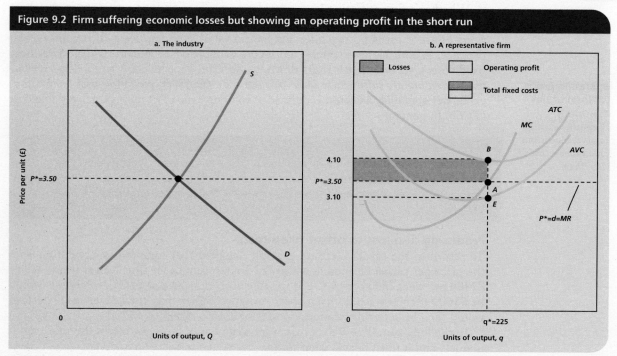

When price is sufficient to cover average variable costs, firms suffering short-run losses will continue to operate rather than shut down. Total revenues ($P^* \times q^*$) cover variable costs, leaving an operating profit of £90 to cover part of fixed costs and reduce losses to £135.

Operating profit – the difference between total revenue and total variable cost – can also be identified. On the graph, total revenue (as we said) is £787.50. *Average variable cost* at q^* is the length of q^*E. Total variable cost is the product of average variable cost and q^*, and is therefore equal to £3.10 × 225 = £697.50. Profit on operation is thus £787.50 − £697.50 = £90, the area of the pink shaded rectangle.

Remember that average total cost is equal to average fixed cost plus average variable cost. This means that at every level of output, average fixed cost is the difference between average total and average variable cost:

$$ATC = AFC + AVC$$

or

$$AFC = ATC - AVC = £4.10 - £3.10 = £1.00$$

In Figure 9.2, therefore, average fixed cost is equal to the length of BE (the difference between ATC and AVC at q^* or £1.00). Because total fixed cost is simply average fixed cost £1.00 times $q^* = £225$, total fixed cost is equal to £225, the entire grey and pink shaded rectangle. Thus, if the firm had shut down, its losses would be equal to £225. By operating, the firm earns an operating profit equal to the pink shaded area (£90), covering some fixed costs and reducing losses to the grey shaded area (£135).

If we think only in averages, it seems logical that a firm in this position will continue to operate:

As long as price (which is equal to average revenue per unit) is sufficient to cover average variable costs, the firm stands to gain by operating rather than by shutting down.

Shutting down to minimize loss

When revenues are insufficient to cover even variable costs, firms suffering losses find it advantageous to shut down, even in the short run.

Suppose, for example, that competition and the availability of sophisticated new machinery pushed the price of cleaning a carpet all the way down to £1.50. Washing 800 cars per week would then yield revenues of only £1200 (Table 9.3). With variable costs at £1600, operating would mean losing an additional £400 over and above fixed costs of £2000. This means that total losses would amount to £2400. Clearly, a profit-maximizing/loss-minimizing carpet cleaning firm would reduce its losses from £2400 to £2000 by shutting down, even in the short run.

Table 9.3 A firm will shut down if total revenue is less than total variable cost

Case 1: Shut down		Case 2: Operate at price = £1.50	
Total revenue ($q = 0$)	£0	Total revenue (£1.50 × 800)	£1,200
Fixed costs	£2,000	Fixed costs	£2,000
Variable costs	+0	Variable costs	+£1,600
Total costs	£2,000	Total costs	£3,600
Profit/Loss ($TR - TC$)	−£2,000	Operating profit/loss ($TR - TVC$)	−£400
		Total profit/loss ($TR - TC$)	−£2,400

From this example, we can generalize that:

Any time that price (average revenue) is below the minimum point on the average variable cost curve, total revenue will be less than total variable cost, and operating profit will be negative (that is, there will be a loss on operation). In other words, when price is below all points on the average variable cost curve, the firm will suffer operating losses at any possible output level the firm could choose.
When this is the case, the firm will stop producing and bear losses equal to fixed costs. This is why the bottom of the average variable cost curve is called the **shut-down point**. At all prices above it, the *MC* curve shows the profit-maximizing level of output. At all prices below it, optimal short-run output is zero.

shut-down point
The lowest point on the average variable cost curve. When price falls below the minimum point on *AVC*, total revenue is insufficient to cover variable costs and the firm will shut down and bear losses equal to fixed costs.

We can now refine our earlier statement that a perfectly competitive firm's marginal cost curve is actually its short-run supply curve. Recall that a profit-maximizing perfectly competitive firm will produce up to the point at which $P = MC$. As we have just seen, though, a firm will shut down when P is less than the minimum point on the *AVC* curve. Also recall that the marginal cost curve intersects the *AVC* curve at *AVC*'s lowest point. It therefore follows that:

The short-run supply curve of a competitive firm is that portion of its marginal cost curve that lies above its average variable cost curve (Figure 9.3).

The short-run industry supply curve

short-run industry supply curve
The sum of marginal cost curves (above *AVC*) of all the firms in an industry.

Supply in a competitive industry is simply the sum of the quantity supplied by the individual firms in the industry at each price level. The **short-run industry supply curve** is the sum of the individual firm supply curves – that is, the marginal cost curves (above *AVC*) of all the firms in the industry. Because quantities are being added (that is, because we are finding the total quantity supplied in the industry at each price level), the curves are added horizontally.

Figure 9.4 shows the supply curve for an industry with just three firms.[1] At a price of £6, firm 1 produces 100 units, the output where $P = MC$. Firm 2 produces 200 units

---

Figure 9.3 Short-run supply curve of a perfectly competitive firm

At prices below average variable cost, it pays a firm to shut down rather than to continue operating. Thus, the short-run supply curve of a competitive firm is the part of its marginal cost curve that lies *above* its average variable cost curve.

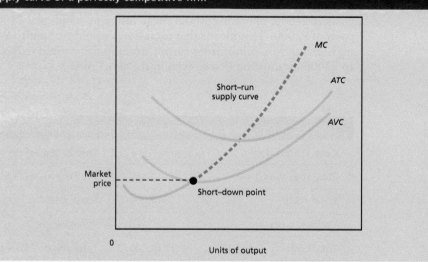

[1]*Perfectly competitive industries are assumed to have many firms. 'Many', of course, means more than three. We use three firms here simply for the purpose of illustration.*

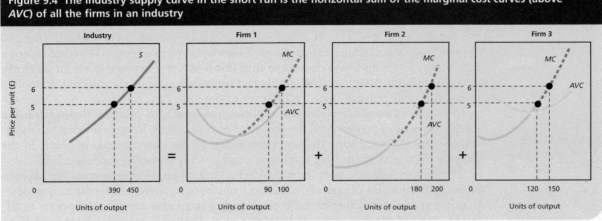

Figure 9.4 The industry supply curve in the short run is the horizontal sum of the marginal cost curves (above AVC) of all the firms in an industry

If there are only three firms in the industry, the industry supply curve is simply the sum of all the products supplied by the three firms at each price. For example, at £6, firm 1 supplies 100 units, firm 2 supplies 200 units and firm 3 supplies 150 units, for a total industry supply of 450.

and firm 3 produces 150 units. The total amount supplied on the market at a price of £6 is thus 450 (100 + 200 + 150). At a price of £5, firm 1 produces 90 units, firm 2 produces 180 units and firm 3 produces 120 units. At a price of £5, the industry thus supplies 390 units (90 + 180 + 120).

Two things can cause the industry supply curve to shift. In the short run, the industry supply curve shifts if something – an increase in the price of some input, for instance – shifts the marginal cost curves of all the individual firms simultaneously. For example, when the cost of producing components of home computers decreased, the marginal cost curves of all computer manufacturers shifted downwards. Such a shift amounted to the same thing as an outward shift in their supply curves. Each firm was willing to supply more computers at each price level because computers were now cheaper to produce.

In the long run, an increase or decrease in the number of firms – and, therefore, in the number of individual firms' supply curves – shifts the total industry supply curve. If new firms enter the industry, the industry supply curve moves to the right; if firms exit the industry, the industry supply curve moves to the left.

We return to shifts in industry supply curves and discuss them further when we take up long-run adjustments later in this chapter.

Long-run directions: a review

Table 9.4 summarizes the different circumstances that perfectly competitive firms may face as they plan for the long run. Profit-making firms will produce up to the point where price and marginal cost are equal in the short run. Because 'profit' means 'economic profit', in the long run there is an incentive for firms to expand their scales of plant, and for new firms to enter the industry.

Table 9.4 Profits, losses and perfectly competitive firms' decisions in the long and short run

	Short-run condition	Short-run decision	Long-run decision
Profits		$P = MC$: operate	Expand: new firms enter
Losses	1. With operating profit ($TR \geq TVC$)	$P = MC$: operate (losses < fixed costs)	Contract: firms exit
	2. With operating losses ($TR < TVC$)	Shut down: losses = fixed costs	Contract: firms exit

Firms suffering losses will produce if, and only if, revenues are sufficient to cover variable costs. If a firm can earn a profit on operations, it can reduce the losses it would suffer if it shut down. Such firms, like profitable firms, will also produce up to the point where $P = MC$. If firms suffering losses cannot cover variable costs by operating, they will shut down and bear losses equal to fixed costs. Whether or not a firm that is suffering losses decides to shut down in the short run, it has an incentive to contract in the long run. The simple fact is that when firms are suffering economic losses, they will generally exit the industry in the long run.

In the short run, a firm's decision about how much to produce depends on the market price of its product and the shapes of its cost curves. Remember that the short-run cost curves show costs that are determined by the current scale of plant. In the long run, however, firms have to choose among many potential scales of plant.

The long-run decisions of individual firms depend on what their costs are likely to be at different scales of operation. Just as firms have to analyse different technologies to arrive at a cost structure in the short run, they must also compare their costs at different scales of plant to arrive at long-run costs. Perhaps a larger scale of operations will reduce production costs and provide an even greater incentive for a profit-making firm to expand. Or perhaps large firms will run into problems that constrain growth. The analysis of long-run possibilities is more complex than the short-run analysis, because more things are variable – scale of plant is not fixed, for example, and there are no fixed costs because firms can exit their industry in the long run. In theory, firms may choose any scale of operation, and so they must analyse many possible options.

Now let us turn to an analysis of cost curves in the long run.

Long-run costs: economies and diseconomies of scale

The shapes of short-run cost curves follow directly from the assumption of a fixed factor of production. As output increases beyond a certain point, the fixed factor (which we usually think of as fixed scale of plant) causes diminishing returns to other factors and thus increasing marginal costs. In the long run, however, there is no fixed factor of production. Firms can choose any scale of production. They can double or triple output or go out of business completely.

The shape of a firm's *long-run* average cost curve depends on how costs vary with scale of operations. For some firms, increased scale, or size, reduces costs. For others, increased scale leads to inefficiency. When an increase in a firm's scale of production leads to lower average costs, we say that there are increasing returns to scale, or economies of scale. When average costs do not change with the scale of production, we say that there are constant returns to scale. Finally, when an increase in a firm's scale of production leads to higher average costs, we say that there are decreasing returns to scale, or diseconomies of scale. Because these economies of scale all are found within the individual firm, they are considered *internal* economies of scale. In the Appendix to this chapter, we talk about *external* economies of scale, which describe economies or diseconomies of scale on an industry-wide basis.

Increasing returns to scale

Technically, the phrase *increasing returns to scale* refers to the relationship between inputs and outputs. When we say that a production function exhibits increasing returns, we mean that a given percentage increase in the production of output requires a smaller percentage increase in the inputs. For example, if a firm were to double output, it would need less than twice as much of each input to produce that output. Stated the other way around, if a firm doubled or tripled inputs, it would more than double or triple output.

When firms can count on fixed input prices – that is, when the prices of inputs do not change with output levels – increasing returns to scale also means that as output

increasing returns to scale, *or* economies of scale

An increase in a firm's scale of production leads to lower costs per unit produced.

constant returns to scale

An increase in a firm's scale of production has no effect on costs per unit produced.

decreasing returns to scale, *or* diseconomies of scale

An increase in a firm's scale of production leads to higher costs per unit produced.

rises, average cost of production falls. The term 'economies of scale' refers directly to the reduction in cost per unit of output that follows from larger-scale production.

The sources of economies of scale

Most of the economies of scale that immediately come to mind are technological in nature. Car production, for example, would be much more costly per unit if a firm were to produce 100 cars per year by hand. Standardized production techniques have increased output volume and have reduced costs per vehicle to make the car available to most people.

Some economies of scale do not result from technology but from sheer size. Very large companies, for instance, can buy inputs in volume at discounted prices. Large firms may also produce some of their own inputs at considerable savings. And they can certainly save in transport costs when items are shipped in bulk.

Economies of scale can be seen all around us. A train that carries 500 people between city centres uses less labour, capital and energy than do 500 different cars driven by 500 people. The cost per passenger (average cost) is lower on the train. People who share a flat are taking advantage of economies of scale. Costs per person for heat, electricity and space are lower when a flat is shared than they would be if each person rented a separate flat.

An example: economies of scale in egg production

Nowhere are economies of scale more visible than in agriculture. Formerly, eggs came mainly from small farmers each producing with only a few hens. Now, much egg production is in the hands of agribusinesses with huge operations. We can compare the cost structures of these two kinds of operation. The large firm, Chicken Licken Eggs, is completely mechanized. Complex machines feed the hens and collect and box the eggs. Large refrigerated vehicles transport the eggs all over the country on a daily basis. In the same district as Chicken Licken, some small farmers still own fewer than 200 hens. These farmers collect the eggs, feed the birds, clean the hen houses by hand, and deliver the eggs to local markets.

Table 9.5 presents some hypothetical cost data for farmer Paul's small operation and for Chicken Licken Eggs. Farmer Paul has his operation working well. He has several hundred hens and spends about 15 hours per week feeding, collecting, delivering and so forth. During the rest of his working week he raises sheep and cattle. We can value Paul's time at €8 per hour, because that is the wage he could earn working at a local manufacturing plant. When we add up all farmer Paul's costs, including a rough estimate of the land and capital costs attributable to egg production, we arrive at €177 per week. Total production on Paul's farm runs at about 200 dozen, or 2400, eggs per week, which means that his average cost comes out to €0.074 per egg.

The costs of the Chicken Licken company are much higher in total; weekly costs are over €30,000. A much higher percentage of costs are capital costs – the firm uses lots of sophisticated machinery that cost millions to put in place. Total output is 1.6 million eggs per week, and the product is shipped all over the country and into neighbouring countries too. The comparatively huge scale of plant has driven average production costs all the way down to €0.019 per egg.

While these numbers are hypothetical, you can see why small farmers find it difficult to compete with large-scale agribusiness concerns that can realize significant economies of scale.

long-run average cost curve (LRAC)
A graph that shows the different scales on which a firm can choose to operate in the long run.

A firm's **long-run average cost curve (LRAC)** shows the different scales on which it can choose to operate in the long run. In other words, a firm's *LRAC* curve traces out the position of all its possible short-run curves, each corresponding to a different scale. At any time, the existing scale of plant determines the position and shape of the firm's short-run cost curve. But the firm must consider in its long-run strategic planning whether to build a plant of a *different* scale. The long-run average cost curve simply shows the positions of the different sets of short-run curves between which the firm must choose. The long-run average cost curve is the 'envelope' of a series of short-

Table 9.5 Weekly costs showing economies of scale in egg production

Paul's farm	Total weekly costs (euros)
15 hours of labour (implicit value 8 euros per hour)	120
Feed, other variable costs	25
Transport costs	15
Land and capital costs attributable to egg production	17
	177
Total output (eggs)	2,400
Average cost per egg (euros)	0.074
Chicken Licken Eggs	**Total weekly costs (euros)**
Labour	5,128
Feed, other variable costs	4,115
Transport costs	2,431
Land and capital costs	19,230
	30,904
Total output (eggs)	1,600,000
Average cost per egg (euros)	0.019

run curves; in other words, it 'wraps around' the set of all possible short-run curves like an envelope. (Later in this chapter, the Applications box 'The Long-run average cost curve: flat or U-shaped?' describes the debate on how the *LRAC* is constructed.)

Figure 9.5 shows short-run and long-run average cost curves for a firm that realizes economies of scale up to about 100,000 units of production and roughly constant returns to scale after that. The diagram shows three potential scales of operation, each

Figure 9.5 A firm exhibiting economies of scale

The long-run average cost curve of a firm shows the different scales on which the firm can choose to operate in the long run. Each scale of operation defines a different short run. Here we see a firm exhibiting economies of scale; moving from Scale 1 to Scale 3 reduces average cost.

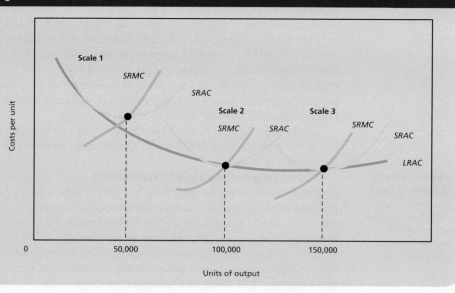

with its own set of short-run cost curves. Each point on the *LRAC* curve represents the minimum cost at which the associated output level can be produced.

Once the firm chooses a scale on which to produce, it becomes locked into one set of cost curves in the short run. If the firm were to settle on Scale 1, it would not realize the major cost advantages of producing on a larger scale. By roughly doubling its scale of operations from 50,000 to 100,000 units (Scale 2), the firm reduces average costs per unit significantly.

Figure 9.5 shows that at every moment firms face two different cost constraints. In the long run, firms can change their scale of operation, and costs may be different as a result. But at any *given* moment, a particular scale of operation exists, constraining the firm's capacity to produce in the short run. Remember that in the short run, a fixed factor of production leads to diminishing returns. That is why we see both short- and long-run curves in the same diagram. The owner of a small restaurant must decide what to do within the walls of her current establishment in the short run; at the same time, she must consider whether or not to expand her capacity in the long run.

Constant returns to scale

Technically, the term *constant returns* means that the quantitative relationship between input and output stays constant, or the same, when output is increased. If a firm doubles inputs, it doubles output; if it triples inputs, it triples output; and so on. Furthermore, if input prices are fixed, constant returns implies that average cost of production does not change with scale. In other words, constant returns to scale means that the firm's long-run average cost curve remains flat.

The firm in Figure 9.5 exhibits roughly constant returns to scale between Scale 2 and Scale 3. The average cost of production is about the same in each. If the firm exhibited constant returns at levels above 150,000 units of output, the *LRAC* would continue as a flat, straight line.

Economists have studied cost data extensively over the years to estimate the extent to which economies of scale exist. Evidence suggests that in most industries firms don't have to be gigantic to realize cost savings from scale economies. For example, car production is accomplished in thousands of separate assembly operations, each with its own economies of scale. Perhaps the best example of efficient production on a small scale is the manufacturing sector in Taiwan. Taiwan has enjoyed very rapid growth based on manufacturing firms that employ fewer than 100 workers!

One simple argument supports the empirical result that most industries seem to exhibit constant returns to scale (a flat *LRAC*) after some level of output. Competition always pushes firms to adopt the least-cost technology and scale. If cost advantages result with larger-scale operations, the firms that shift to that scale will drive the smaller, less efficient firms out of business. A firm that wants to grow when it has reached its 'optimal' size can do so by building another identical plant. It thus seems logical to conclude that most firms face constant returns to scale *as long as* they can replicate their existing plants. Thus, when you look at developed industries, you can expect to see firms of different sizes operating with similar costs. These firms produce using roughly the same scale of plant, but larger firms simply have more plants.

Decreasing returns to scale

When average cost increases with scale of production, a firm faces *decreasing returns to scale*, or *diseconomies of scale*. The most often cited example of a diseconomy of scale is bureaucratic inefficiency. As size increases beyond a certain point, operations tend to become more difficult to manage. You can easily imagine what happens when a firm grows top-heavy with managers who have accumulated seniority and high salaries. The coordination function is more complex for larger firms than for smaller ones, and the chances that it will break down are greater.

A large firm is also more likely than a small firm to find itself facing problems with organized labour. Unions can demand higher wages and more benefits, go on strike,

Figure 9.6 A firm exhibiting economies and diseconomies of scale

Economies of scale push this firm's costs down to q*. Beyond q*, the firm experiences diseconomies of scale; q* is the level of production at lowest average cost, using optimal scale.

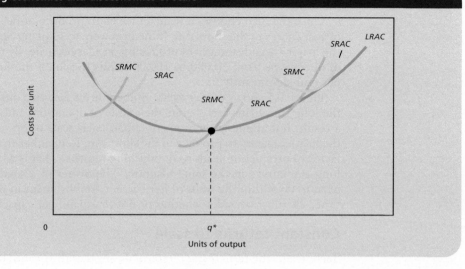

force firms to incur legal expenses, and take other actions that increase production costs. (This does not mean that unions are 'bad', but rather that their activities often increase costs.)

Figure 9.6 describes a firm that exhibits both economies of scale and diseconomies of scale. Average costs decrease with scale of plant up to q* and increase with scale after that. This long-run average cost curve looks very much like the short-run average cost curves we have examined in the last two chapters. But do not confuse the two:

All short-run average cost curves are U-shaped, because we assume a fixed scale of plant that constrains production and drives marginal cost upward as a result of diminishing returns. In the long run, we make no such assumption; rather, we assume that scale of plant can be changed.

The shape of a firm's long-run average cost curve depends on how costs react to changes in scale. Some firms do see economies of scale, and their long-run average cost curves slope downwards. Most firms seem to have flat long-run average cost curves. Still others encounter diseconomies, and their long-run average costs slope upwards. Thus, the same firm can face diminishing returns – a short-run concept – and still have a long-run cost curve that exhibits economies of scale.

Competitive firms will, in the long run, take advantage of economies of scale (if they exist) and avoid diseconomies of scale. The **optimal scale of plant** is the one that minimizes long-run average cost. In fact, as we will see next, competition forces firms to use the optimal scale.

optimal scale of plant

The scale of plant that minimizes long-run average cost.

Long-run adjustments to short-run conditions

We began this chapter by discussing the different short-run positions in which firms may find themselves. Firms can be operating at a profit or suffering economic losses; they can be shut down or producing. The industry is not in equilibrium if firms have an incentive to enter or exit in the long run. Thus, when firms are earning economic profits (profits above normal) or are suffering economic losses (profits below normal, or negative), the industry is not at an equilibrium, and firms will change their

Applications

Economies of scale and European integration

Many European countries have become more integrated in recent years. One potential benefit of this process results from the existence of scale economies. The removal of barriers to trade between countries increases the size of the market to which European firms have access. If they can increase their sales and have not yet exploited all of their scale economies, they can produce more cheaply. Consumers should then benefit in the form of lower prices.

In some markets the advantages of economies of scale will come as there are fewer, much larger producers. These industries would include cars, computers and turbogenerators.[1] In other markets, firms will stay small and exploit scale economies on the basis of a very specialized product range.

This is economies of scale in action. The exploitation of the potential economies of scale does not require huge plants. A single factory in

Ireland, employing just over 200 people, provides sufficient soft drink concentrate to supply over 17 per cent of the global consumption of Coca-Cola products. Two Nordic firms, Nokia and Ericsson, supply about one-third of the $2.0 billion world market for mobile telecommunications equipment, much of it produced in Scandinavia. Sweden accounts for some 40 per cent of the world paperboard market; Swiss-manufactured watches comprise one-third of world exports of watches;

and Italy accounts for over half of world exports of precious metal jewellery. By extending the size of the market, foreign trade gives small producers the opportunity to exploit economies of scale. For small countries, exports provide a means of escape from the limitation of their small size.[2]

[1] 'The economics of 1992', European Economy, *Brussels, March 1988.*

[2] D. McAleese, Economics for Business (Prentice Hall 1997), p. 454.

behaviour. What they are likely to do depends in part on costs in the long run. This is why we have spent a good deal of time discussing economies and diseconomies of scale.

We can now put these two ideas together and discuss the actual long-run adjustments that are likely to take place in response to short-run profits and losses.

Short-run profits: expansion to equilibrium

We begin our analysis of long-run adjustments with a perfectly competitive industry in which firms are earning economic profits. We assume that all firms in the industry are producing with the same technology of production, and that each firm has a long-run average cost curve that is U-shaped. A U-shaped long-run average cost curve implies that there are some economies of scale to be realized in the industry, and that all firms ultimately begin to run into diseconomies at some scale of operation.

Figure 9.7 shows a representative perfectly competitive firm initially producing at Scale 1. Market price is $P_1 = €12$, and individual firms are enjoying economic profits. Total revenue at our representative firm, which is producing 1000 units of output per period, exceeds total cost. Our firm's profit per period is equal to the shaded pink rectangle. (Make sure you understand why the pink rectangle represents profits. Remember that perfectly competitive firms maximize profit by producing at $P = MC$, which is at point A in Figure 9.7.)

At this point, our representative firm has not realized all the economies of scale available to it. By expanding to Scale 2, it will reduce average costs significantly, and unless price drops it will increase profits. As long as firms are enjoying profits and economies of scale exist, firms will expand. Thus, we assume that the firm in Figure 9.7 shifts to Scale 2.

At the same time, the existence of economic profits will attract new entrants to the industry. Both the entrance of new firms and the expansion of existing firms have the same effect on the short-run industry supply curve (Figure 9.7a). Both cause the short-run supply curve to shift to the right, from S to S'. Because the short-run industry supply curve is the sum of all the marginal cost curves (above the minimum point of

Applications

Why does Burger King exist?

We have already seen that the price system is a most important means of allocating scarce resources effectively. Firms combine land, labour, capital etc. to produce output. If they do this efficiently they can hope to sell their product at a price consumers are prepared to pay. This is true of all firms, including Burger King. However, *within* firms, resources are not generally allocated by markets but by management. When you work in a firm, managers do not bargain with you and other employees to find who is willing to do a task at the lowest wage. Management simply allocates the jobs in the way it thinks best.

Why are markets not used to allocate resources *within* firms? The answer is the presence of transactions costs. These are the costs associated with finding someone to do business, reaching agreement about the nature of the exchange, including the price, and ensuring that the parties accept the terms of the agreement.

We have seen that there are technical reasons why

firms can economize on costs. We called them economies of scale. However, firms are able to economize on transactions costs also. For example, offering you a long-term contract with prospects of promotion ensures that you have a stake in performing your tasks well. Management has therefore reduced transactions costs by saving on the time taken to check that you are doing the job properly. We now have a reason why the firm exists and why the task of coordinating resources is not undertaken by markets. Firms economize on transactions costs.

One successful industry in recent years has been the supply of pre-cooked food such as microwaveable dinners. People could organize themselves to buy individual items of food, pay someone to carry it home and someone else to come and cook it. Clearly, however, this involves substantial transactions costs. Many consumers prefer to pay a firm to buy, prepare, cook and package the food for them. Firms in this industry exist because

Firms such as Burger King survive by providing a service that consumers value – they economize on transactions costs.

they economize on such transactions costs.

Burger King and other firms like them have taken the process one step further. They not only provide the cooked food but also somewhere to eat and someone to wash up. If they could not economize on the transactions costs involved, the food they sell would be so expensive that people would make their own arrangements and Burger King would not exist.

What is true for Burger King applies to other firms too. Why do people use travel agents to book a package holiday rather than book travel and hotels separately? Why do people use builders to extend their houses instead of separately hiring labourers, bricklayers, carpenters, plumbers and electricians? Now think of your own examples.

AVC) of all the firms in the industry, it will shift to the right, for two reasons. First, because all firms in the industry are expanding to a larger scale, their individual short-run marginal cost curves shift to the right. Second, with new firms entering the industry, there are more firms and thus more marginal cost curves to add up.

As capital flows into the industry, the supply curve in Figure 9.7a shifts to the right and price falls. The question is, where will the process stop? In general:

Firms will continue to expand as long as there are economies of scale to be realized, and new firms will continue to enter as long as economic profits are being earned.

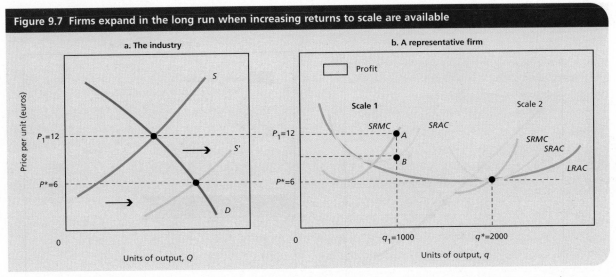

Figure 9.7 Firms expand in the long run when increasing returns to scale are available

When economies of scale can be realized, firms have an incentive to expand. Thus firms will be pushed by competition to produce at their optimal scales. Price will be driven to the minimum point on the *LRAC* curve.

In Figure 9.7a, final equilibrium is achieved only when price falls to $P^* = €6$ and firms have exhausted all the economies of scale available in the industry. At $P^* = €6$, no economic profits are being earned and none can be earned by changing the level of output.

Look carefully at the final equilibrium in Figure 9.7. Each firm will choose the scale of plant that produces its product at minimum long-run average cost. Competition drives firms to adopt not just the most efficient technology in the *short* run, but also the most efficient scale of operation in the *long* run.

In the long run, equilibrium price (P^*) is equal to long-run average cost, short-run marginal cost and short-run average cost. Economic profits are driven to zero:

$$P^* = SRMC = SRAC = LRAC$$

where *SRMC* denotes short-run marginal cost, *SRAC* denotes short-run average cost and *LRAC* denotes long-run average cost. No other price is an equilibrium. Any price above P^* means that there are profits to be made in the industry, and new firms will continue to enter. Any price below P^* means that firms are suffering economic losses, and firms will exit the industry. Only at P^* will economic profits be just equal to zero, and only at P^* will the industry be in equilibrium.

Short-run losses: contraction to equilibrium

Firms that suffer short-run losses have an incentive to leave the industry in the long run, but cannot do so in the short run. As we have seen, some firms incurring losses will choose to shut down and bear losses equal to fixed costs. Others will continue to produce in the short run in an effort to minimize their losses.

Figure 9.8 depicts a firm that will continue to produce $q_1 = 1000$ units of output in the short run, despite its losses. (We are assuming here that the firm is earning losses that are smaller than the firm's fixed costs.) With losses, the long-run picture will change. Firms have an incentive to get out of the industry. As they exit, the industry's short-run supply curve of the industry shifts to the left. As it shifts, the equilibrium price rises, from 8 to €9.

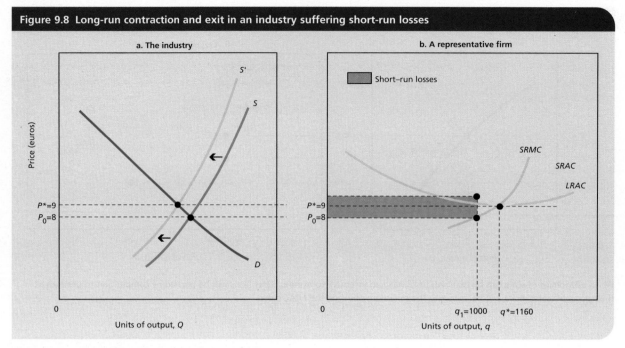

Figure 9.8 Long-run contraction and exit in an industry suffering short-run losses

When firms in an industry suffer losses, there is an incentive for them to exit. As firms exit, the supply curve shifts from S to S', driving price up to P^*. As price rises, losses are gradually eliminated and the industry returns to equilibrium.

Once again the question is: how long will this adjustment process continue? In general:

As long as losses are being sustained in an industry, firms will shut down and leave the industry, thus reducing supply – shifting the supply curve to the left. As this happens, price rises. This gradual price rise reduces losses for firms remaining in the industry until those losses are ultimately eliminated.

In Figure 9.8, equilibrium occurs when price rises to $P^* = €9$. At that point, remaining firms will maximize profits by producing $q^* = 1160$ units of output. Price is just sufficient to cover average costs, and economic profits and losses are zero.

This discussion leads us to conclude that:

Whether we begin with an industry in which firms are earning profits or suffering losses, the final long-run competitive equilibrium condition is the same when we start with losses as it is when we start with profits:

$$P = SRMC = SRAC = LRAC$$

and economic profits are zero. At this point, individual firms are operating at the most efficient scale of plant – that is, at the minimum point on their $LRAC$ curve.

The long-run adjustment mechanism: investment flows towards profit opportunities

The central idea in our discussion of entry, exit, expansion and contraction is this:

In efficient markets, investment capital flows towards profit opportunities. The actual process is complex and varies from industry to industry.

Applications

The long-run average cost curve: flat or U-shaped?

The long-run average cost curve has been a source of controversy in economics for many years. A long-run average cost curve was first drawn as the 'envelope' of a series of short-run curves in a classic article written by Jacob Viner in 1931.[1] In preparing that article, Viner gave his draughtsman the task of drawing the long-run curve through the minimum points of all the short-run average cost curves.

In a supplementary note written in 1950, Viner commented:

the error in Chart IV is left uncorrected so that future teachers and students may share the pleasure of many of their predecessors of pointing out that if I had known what an envelope was, I would not have given my excellent draftsman the technically impossible and economically inappropriate task of drawing an *AC* curve which would pass through the lowest cost points of all the *AC* curves yet not rise above any *AC* curve at any point . . .[2]

While this story is an interesting part of the lore of economics, a more recent debate concentrates on the economic content of this controversy. In 1986, Professor Herbert Simon of Carnegie-Mellon University stated bluntly:

I think the textbooks are a scandal . . . the most widely used textbooks use the old long-run and short-run cost curves to illustrate the

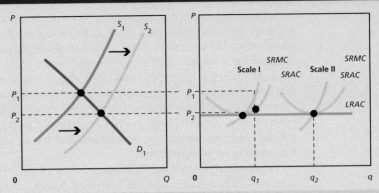

Figure 1 Long-run expansion in an industry with constant returns to scale

theory of the firm . . . [the U-shaped long-run cost curve] postulated that in the long run the size of the firm would increase to a scale associated with the minimum cost on the long-run curve. It was supposed to predict something about the size distribution of firms in the industry. It doesn't do that and there are other problems. Most serious is the fact that most empirical studies show the firm's cost curves not to be U-shaped, but in fact to slope down to the right and then level off, without a clearly defined minimum point.[3]

Professor Simon makes an important point. Suppose that we were to redraw Figure 9.7b with a flat long-run average cost curve. Figure 1 shows a firm earning short-run economic profits using Scale I, but there are no economies of scale to be realized.

Despite the lack of economies of scale, expansion of such an industry would probably take place in much the same way as we have

described. First, existing firms have an incentive to expand because they are making profits. At current prices, a firm that doubles its scale would earn twice the economic profits, even if cost did not fall with expansion. Of course, as long as economic profits persist, new firms have an incentive to enter the industry. Both of these events will shift the short-run industry supply curve to the right, from S_1 to S_2 and price will fall, from P_1 to P_2. Expansion and entry will stop only when price has fallen to *LRAC*. Only then will economic profits be eliminated. At equilibrium, $P = SRMC = SRAC = LRAC$.

This model does not predict the final firm size or the structure of the industry. When the long-run *AC* curve is U-shaped, firms stop expanding at the minimum point on *LRAC* because further expansion means higher costs; thus, optimal firm size is determined technologically. If the *LRAC* curve is flat, however, small firms and large firms have identical average costs.

If this is true, and it seems to be in many industries, the structure of the industry in the long run will depend on whether existing firms expand faster than new firms enter. If new firms enter quickly in response to profit opportunities, the industry will end up with large numbers of small firms. But if existing firms expand more rapidly than new firms enter, the industry may end up with only a few very large firms. There is thus an element of randomness in the way industries expand. In fact, most industries contain some large firms and some small firms, which is exactly what Simon's flat *LRAC* model predicts.

[1]Jacob Viner, 'Cost curves and supply curves', Zeitschrift für Nationalokonomie, *vol. III (1), 1931, pp. 23–46.*

[2]George J. Stigler and Kenneth E. Boulding (eds), AEA Readings in Price Theory, vol. VI (Chicago: Richard D. Irwin, 1952), p. 227.

[3]Interview with Herbert A. Simon. 'The failure of armchair economics', Challenge, November–December, 1986, pp. 23–4.

We talked about efficient markets in Chapter 1. In efficient markets, profit opportunities are quickly eliminated. To illustrate this point, we described driving up to a motorway toll gate and suggested that shorter-than-average queues are quickly eliminated as cars change lanes and move into them. So, too, are profits in competitive industries eliminated as new competing firms move into open slots, or perceived opportunities, in the industry.

In practice, the entry and exit of firms in response to profit opportunities usually involves the financial capital market. In capital markets, people are constantly looking for profits. When firms in an industry do well, capital is likely to flow into that industry in a variety of forms. Entrepreneurs start new firms, and firms producing entirely different products may join the competition in order to break into new markets. It happens all around us. The tremendous success of premium ice cream makers Häagen-Dazs spawned dozens of competitors. When a small ice cream shop opens to rave reviews, long queues, high prices and economic profits, a year later there will be other similar shops, no queues, and lower prices. Magic? No: just the natural functioning of competition.

> **long-run competitive equilibrium**
>
> When $P = SRMC = SRAC = LRAC$ and economic profits are zero.

When there is promise of extraordinary profits, investments are made and output expands. When firms end up suffering losses, firms contract, and some go out of business. It can take quite a while, however, for an industry to achieve **long-run competitive equilibrium**, the point at which $P = SRMC = SRAC = LRAC$ and economic profits are zero. In fact, because costs and tastes are in a constant state of flux, very few industries ever really get there. The economy is always changing. There are always some firms making profits and some firms suffering losses.

This, then, is a story about tendencies:

> Investment, in the form of new firms and expanding old firms, will, over time, tend to favour those industries in which profits are being made. Over time, industries in which firms are suffering losses will gradually contract from disinvestment.

Output markets: a final word

In the last four chapters, we have been building a model of a simple market system under the assumption of perfect competition. Let us provide just one more example to review the actual response of a competitive system to a change in consumer preferences.

Over the past decade, increasing numbers of Europeans have been drinking wine. We know that household demand is constrained by income, wealth and prices, and that income is (at least in part) determined by the choices that households make. Within these constraints, households choose, and, increasingly, they choose – or demand – wine. The demand curve for wine has shifted to the right, causing excess demand which tends to put an upward pressure on price.

With higher prices, wine producers find themselves earning economic profits. This increase in price and consequent rise in profits is the basic signal that leads to a reallocation of society's resources. In the short run, wine producers are constrained by their current scales of operation. There is only a limited number of vineyards and only a limited amount of vat capacity, for example.

In the long run, however, we would expect to see resources flow in to compete for these economic profits, and this is exactly what happens. New firms enter the wine-producing business. New vines are planted and new vats and production equipment are purchased and put in place. In the market for wine, not only European producers such as the Spanish are increasing output but non-European producers such as Chile and Australia are developing and selling their wine into Europe. Overall, more wine is produced to meet the new consumer demand. At the same time, competition, especially from Australia, is forcing firms to operate using the most efficient technology available.

What starts as a shift in preferences thus ends up as a shift in resources. Land is reallocated and labour moves into wine production. All this is accomplished without any central planning or direction.

You have now seen what lies behind the demand curves and supply curves in competitive output markets. The next two chapters take up competitive *input* markets and complete the picture.

Summary

1. For any firm, one of three conditions holds at any given moment: (1) The firm is earning economic profits, (2) the firm is suffering losses, or (3) the firm is just breaking even – that is, earning a normal rate of return and zero economic profits.

Short-run conditions and long-run directions

2. A firm that is earning economic profits in the short run and expects to continue doing so has an incentive to expand in the long run. Profits also provide an incentive for new firms to enter the industry.

3. In the short run, firms suffering losses are stuck in the industry. They can shut down operations ($q = 0$), but they must still bear fixed costs. In the long run, firms suffering losses can exit the industry.

4. A firm's decision about whether to shut down in the short run depends solely on whether its revenues from operating are sufficient to cover its variable costs. If revenues exceed variable costs, the *operating profits* can be used to pay some fixed costs and thus reduce losses.

5. Any time that price is below the minimum point on the average variable cost curve, total revenue will be less than total variable cost, operating profit will be negative, and the firm will shut down. The minimum point on the average variable cost curve (which is also the point where marginal cost and average variable cost intersect) is called the *shut-down point*. At all prices above the shut-down point, the *MC* curve shows the profit-maximizing level of output. At all prices below it, optimal short-run output is zero.

6. The *short-run supply curve* of a firm in a perfectly competitive industry is the portion of its marginal cost curve that lies above its average variable cost curve.

7. Two things can cause the industry supply curve to shift: (1) in the short run, anything that causes marginal costs to change across the industry, such as an increase in the price of a particular input, and (2) in the long run, entry or exit of firms.

Long-run costs: economies and diseconomies of scale

8. When an increase in a firm's scale of production leads to lower average costs, the firm exhibits *increasing returns to scale*, or *economies of scale*. When average costs do not change with the scale of production, the firm exhibits *constant returns to scale*. When an increase in a firm's scale of production leads to higher average costs, the firm exhibits *diseconomies of scale*.

9. A firm's *long-run average cost curve* (*LRAC*) shows the costs associated with different scales on which it can choose to operate in the long run.

Long-run adjustments to short-run conditions

10. When short-run profits exist in an industry, firms will enter and existing firms will expand. These events shift the industry supply curve to the right. When this happens, price falls and ultimately profits are eliminated.

11. When short-run losses are suffered in an industry, some firms exit and some firms reduce scale. These events shift the industry supply curve to the left, raising price and eliminating losses.

12. *Long-run competitive equilibrium* is reached when $P = SRMC = SRAC = LRAC$ and economic profits are zero.

13. In efficient markets, investment capital flows towards profit opportunities.

Review Terms and Concepts

breaking even
constant returns to scale
decreasing returns to scale, or diseconomies of scale
increasing returns to scale, or economies of scale
long-run average cost curve (*LRAC*)
long-run competitive equilibrium
operating profit (or loss) or net operating revenue

optimal scale of plant
short-run industry supply curve
shut-down point

Equation

Long-run competitive equilibrium:
$P = SRMC = SRAC = LRAC$

Problem Set

1. Explain how it is possible that a firm with a production function that exhibits increasing returns to scale can run into diminishing returns at the same time.

2. Which of the following industries do you think are likely to exhibit large economies of scale? Explain why in each case.
a. House building
b. Electricity generation
c. Market gardening
d. Software development
e. Aircraft manufacturing
f. Higher education
g. Accounting services

3. For cases A to F in Table 1, would you (1) operate or shut down in the short run, and (2) expand your plant or exit the industry in the long run?

Table 1						
	A	B	C	D	E	F
Total revenue	1500	2000	2000	5000	5000	5000
Total cost	1500	1500	2500	6000	7000	4000
Total fixed cost	500	500	200	1500	1500	1500

4. Do you agree or disagree with the following statements? Explain why in a sentence or two.
a. A firm will never sell its product for less than it costs to produce it.
b. If the short-run marginal cost curve is U-shaped, the long-run average cost curve is likely to be U-shaped as well.

5. The Alpha pig farm outside Copenhagen produces 25,000 pigs per month. Total cost of production at the Alpha farm is €28,000. In the same locality are two other farms. The Beta farm produces 55,000 pigs a month at a total cost of €50,050. Gamma farm produces 100,000 pigs per month at a total cost of €91,000. These data suggest that there are significant economies of scale in pig production. Do you agree or disagree with this statement? Explain your answer.

6. Indicate whether you agree or disagree with each of the following statements.
a. Firms that exhibit constant returns to scale have U-shaped long-run average cost curves.
b. Firms minimize costs. Thus, a firm earning short-run economic profits will choose to produce at the minimum point on its average total cost function.
c. The supply curve of a competitive firm in the short run is its marginal cost curve above average total cost.

d. A firm suffering losses in the short run will continue to operate as long as total revenue will at least cover fixed costs.

7. You are given the cost data shown in Table 2.

Table 2		
Q	TFC	TVC
0	12	0
1	12	5
2	12	9
3	12	14
4	12	20
5	12	28
6	12	38

If the price output is €7, how many units of output will this firm produce? What is total revenue? What is total cost? Will the firm operate or shut down in the short run? The long run? Briefly explain your answers.

8. The following cost data are for a small airport retail business. The business was started by partners Ann and Sue, who purchased a new mobile display unit with £20,000 of their own money. The unit is located at Heathrow Airport and is used to sell leather belts. Each year, Ann and Sue sell 3000 belts for £10 each. The belts cost them £5 each from their supplier. Staffing the display for 12 hours a day costs them £14,000 in wages per year. If the risk-free interest rate (the normal rate of return) is 10%, how much economic profit are Ann and Sue making?

9. This problem traces the relationship between firm decisions, market supply and market equilibrium in a perfectly competitive market.
a. Complete Table 3 for a single firm in the short run (all values are in euros).
b. Using the information in the table, fill in the supply schedule in Table 4 for this individual firm under perfect competition, and indicate profit (positive or negative) at each output level. (*Hint*: at each hypothetical level price, what is the *MR* of producing one more unit of output? Combine this with the *MC* of another unit to work out the quantity supplied.)
c. Now suppose there are 100 firms in this industry, all with identical cost schedules. In Table 5, fill in the market quantity supplied at each price in this market.
d. Fill in the blanks. From the market supply and demand schedules above, the equilibrium market price for this good is _____ and the equilibrium market

Table 3

Output	TFC	TVC	TC	AVC	ATC	MC
0	300	0				
1		100				
2		150				
3		210				
4		290				
5		400				
6		540				
7		720				
8		950				
9		1240				
10		1600				

Table 4

Price	Quantity supplied	Profit
50		
70		
100		
130		
170		
220		
280		
350		

Table 5

Price	Quantity supplied	Market quantity demanded
50		1000
70		900
100		800
130		700
170		600
220		500
280		400
350		300

quantity is _____. Each firm will produce a quantity of _____ and earn a _____ profit/loss equal to _____.

e. In (d) above, your answers characterize the short-run equilibrium in this market. Do they characterize the long run equilibrium as well? If yes, explain why. If no, explain why not. (That is, what would happen in the long run to change the equilibrium, and why?)

*10. In Chapter 8 we considered a firm with this cost function:

$$TC = 24 + 6Q + Q^3$$

Suppose now it has a different *revenue* function following a fall in the industry price:

$$TR = 18Q$$

a. Find the best positive level of output.
b. Could it do better than the answer given in (a) by closing its operations and producing a zero output?

11. Assume that you are hired as an analyst at a major consulting firm. Your first assignment is to do an industry analysis of the tribble industry. After extensive research, you have obtained the following information. The long-run costs are:

Capital costs   €5 per unit of output
Labour costs   €2 per unit of output

There are no economies or diseconomies of scale, and the industry is currently earning a normal return to capital (economic profit is zero).

The industry is perfectly competitive. Each firm produces the same amount of output, and there are 100 firms. Total industry output is 1.2 million tribbles.

Demand for tribbles is expected to grow rapidly over the next few years to a level twice as high as it is now, but (due to short-run diminishing returns) each of the 100 existing firms is likely to be producing only 50% more.

a. Sketch the long-run cost curve of a representative firm.
b. Show the current conditions by drawing two diagrams, one showing the industry and one showing a representative firm.
c. Sketch the increase in demand and show how the industry is likely to respond in the short run and in the long run.

12. Consider Adam, a baker of apple pies. To make one pie, Adam uses one hour of labour and one kilo of apples. He bakes the pies in an oven that he leases for €100 per day. A (short-run) contract requires him to pay the lease even if he bakes no pies. The hourly wage that Adam pays is €5, and each kilo of apples costs €2. Assume that Adam has only one oven available, and that he can bake a maximum of 50 apple pies in one day.
a. What are Adam's fixed costs (per day)? Variable costs? Total costs? (Express these as a function of q, the number of apple pies.)

b. Determine and graph average variable cost, average fixed cost, average total cost, and marginal cost.

c. Suppose that the market for apple pies is perfectly competitive. Adam can therefore sell all the pies he wants in one day for 8 euros each. How many apple pies

should Adam produce per day in the short run? What will his profits or losses be?

d. At a price of €8, how many pies (per day) should Adam produce in the long run? Explain your answer.

e. What is the minimum price necessary for Adam to operate in the short run? In the long run?

Appendix to Chapter 9

External Economies and Diseconomies and the Long-run Industry Supply Curve

Sometimes, average costs increase or decrease with the size of the industry, in addition to responding to changes in the size of the firm itself. When long-run average costs decrease as a result of industry growth, we say that there are external economies. When average costs increase as a result of industry growth, we say that there are external diseconomies. (Remember the distinction between internal and external economies: *internal economies* of scale are found within firms, while *external economies* occur on an industry-wide basis.)

At present, for example, one of the fastest growing sectors in the European economy is the biotechnology industry. Among many other things, biotech firms produce genetically engineered plants, such as a frost-resistant strawberry and pest-resistant cereals, and complex drugs using bioengineered organisms.

Most biotechnology firms are clustered in one of a few locations. Firms locating near one another can produce potential external economies. As the industry grows, local schools and colleges may begin to train students for jobs in the industry, reducing training expenses for the firms. In addition, people in the industry have easy access to and learn from one another. As an industry grows, suppliers can save money by shipping to just one location rather than to fifteen. Just as the computer producers of a generation earlier found concentration of location brought big cost advantages, so too the biotech industry is likely to reap significant cost advantages as the industry grows and matures.

While the biotechnology industry is an example of one in which external economies are a possibility, the building industry is one in which external diseconomies exist. Recent decades have seen several building booms during which the industry expanded. Expansion affects the price of timber and timber products. Increases in building activity cause the demand for timber products to rise, and this price increase causes the cost of construction to shift upwards for all building firms, especially in countries where timber framed houses are common.

In the building industry, a change in the scale of any individual firm's operations has no impact on the price

of timber, because no one firm has any control over the price. The increase in costs resulting from expansion of the industry are an external diseconomy.

The long-run industry supply curve

Recall that long-run competitive equilibrium is achieved when entering firms responding to profits, or exiting firms fleeing from losses, drive price to a level that just covers long-run average costs. Economic profits are zero, and $P = LRAC = SRAC = SRMC$. At this point, individual firms are operating at the most efficient scale of plant – that is, at the minimum point on their $LRAC$ curve.

As we saw in the chapter text, long-run equilibrium is not easily achieved. But even if a firm or an industry does achieve long-run equilibrium, it will not remain at that point indefinitely. Economies are dynamic. As population and the stock of capital grow, and as preferences and technology change, some sectors will expand and some will contract. How do industries adjust to long-term changes? The answer depends on both internal and external factors.

The extent of *internal* economies (or diseconomies) determines the shape of a firm's long-run average cost curve ($LRAC$). If a firm changes its scale and either expands or contracts, its average costs will increase, decrease or stay the same *along* the $LRAC$ curve. Recall that the $LRAC$ curve shows the relationship between a firm's output (q) and average total cost (ATC). A firm enjoying internal economies will see costs decreasing as it expands its scale; a firm facing internal diseconomies will see costs increasing as it expands its scale.

But *external* economies and diseconomies have nothing to do with the size of *individual* firms in a competitive market. Because individual firms in perfectly competitive industries are very small relative to the market, other firms are affected only minimally when an individual firm changes its output or scale of operation. External economies and diseconomies arise from industry expansions; that is, they arise when many firms increase their output simultaneously or when new

Figure 9A.1 A decreasing-cost industry: external economies

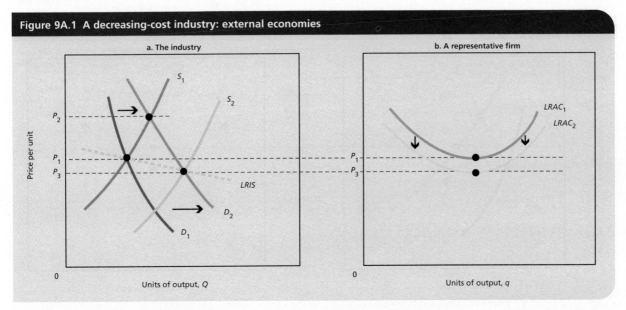

In a decreasing-cost industry, average cost declines as the industry expands. As demand expands from D_1 to D_2, price rises from P_1 to P_2. As new firms enter and existing firms expand, supply shifts from S_1 to S_2, driving price down. If costs decline as a result of the expansion to $LRAC_2$, the final price will be below P_1 at P_3. The long-run industry supply ($LRIS$) curve slopes downwards in a decreasing-cost industry.

firms enter an industry. If industry expansion causes costs to increase (external diseconomies), the $LRAC$ curves facing individual firms shift upwards; costs increase regardless of the level of output finally chosen by the firm. Similarly, if industry expansion causes costs to decrease (external economies), the $LRAC$ curves facing individual firms shift downwards; costs decrease at all potential levels of output.

An example of an expanding industry facing external economies is illustrated in Figure 9A.1. Initially, the industry and the representative firm are in long-run competitive equilibrium at the price P_1 determined by the intersection of the initial demand curve D_1 and the initial supply curve S_1. P_1 is the long-run equilibrium price; it intersects the initial long-run average cost curve ($LRAC_1$) at its minimum point. At this point, economic profits are zero.

Let us assume that as time passes, demand increases – that is, the demand curve shifts to the right from D_1 to D_2. This increase in demand will push price all the way to P_2. Without drawing the short-run cost curves, we know that economic profits now exist and that firms are likely to enter the industry to compete for them. In the absence of external economies or diseconomies, firms would enter the industry, shifting the supply curve to the right and driving price back to the bottom of the long-run average cost curve, where profits are zero. But the industry in Figure 9A.1 enjoys external economies. As firms enter and the industry expands, costs decrease. And as the supply curve shifts to the right from S_1 towards S_2, the long-run average cost curve shifts downwards to $LRAC_2$. Thus, to reach the new long-run equilibrium level of price and output, the supply curve must shift all the way to S_2. Only when the supply curve

reaches S_2 is price driven down to the new equilibrium price of P_3, the minimum point on the new long-run average cost curve.

Presumably, further expansion would lead to even greater savings because the industry encounters external economies. The dashed line in Figure 9A.1a, which traces out price and total output over time as the industry expands, is called the **long-run industry supply curve ($LRIS$)**. When an industry enjoys external economies, its long-run supply curve slopes downwards. Such an industry is called a **decreasing-cost industry.**

In Figure 9A.2, we derive the long-run industry supply curve for an industry that faces external diseconomies. (These were suffered in the building industry, you will recall, when increased house building activity drove up timber prices.) As demand expands from D_1 to D_2, price is driven up from P_1 to P_2. In response to the resulting higher profits, firms enter, shifting the short-run supply schedule to the right and driving price down. But this time, as the industry expands, the long-run average cost curve shifts up to $LRAC_2$ as a result of external diseconomies. Now, price has to fall back only to P_3 (the minimum point on $LRAC_2$), not all the way to P_1, to eliminate economic profits. This type of industry, whose long-run industry supply curve slopes up to the right, is called an **increasing-cost industry**.

It should not surprise you to know that industries in which there are no external economies or diseconomies of scale have flat, or horizontal, long-run industry supply curves. These industries are called **constant-cost industries**.

Figure 9A.2 An increasing-cost industry: external diseconomies

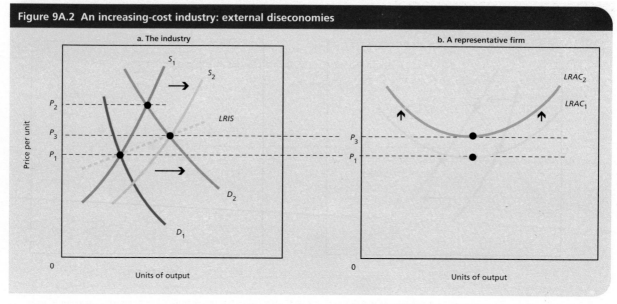

In an increasing-cost industry, average cost increases as the industry expands. As demand shifts from D_1 to D_2, price rises from P_1 to P_2. As new firms enter and existing firms expand output, supply shifts from S_1 to S_2, driving price down. If long-run average costs rise as a result to $LRAC_2$, the final price will be P_3, above P_1. The long-run industry supply curve ($LRIS$) slopes upwards in an increasing-cost industry.

Summary

External Economies and Diseconomies

1. When long-run average costs decrease as a result of industry growth, we say that the industry exhibits *external economies*. When long-run average costs increase as a result of industry growth, we say that the industry exhibits *external diseconomies*.

The long-run industry supply curve

2. The *long-run industry supply curve* (*LRIS*) is a graph that traces out price and total output over time as an industry expands. A *decreasing-cost industry* is one in which average costs fall as the industry expands. It exhibits external economies, and its long-run industry supply curve slopes downwards. An *increasing-cost industry* is one in which average costs rise as the industry expands. It exhibits external diseconomies, and its long-run industry supply curve slopes upwards. A *constant-cost industry* is one that shows no external economies or diseconomies as the industry grows. Its long-run industry supply curve is horizontal, or flat.

Review Terms and Concepts

constant-cost industry An industry that shows no economies or diseconomies of scale as the industry grows. Such industries have flat, or horizontal, long-run supply curves.

decreasing-cost industry An industry that realizes external economies – that is, an industry in which average costs decrease as the industry grows. The long-run supply curve for such an industry has a negative slope.

external economies and diseconomies When industry growth results in a decrease of long-run average costs, there are external economies; when industry growth results in an increase of long-run average costs, there are external diseconomies.

increasing-cost industry An industry that encounters external diseconomies – that is, an industry in which average costs increase as the industry grows. The long-run supply curve for such an industry has a positive slope.

long-run industry supply curve (*LRIS*) A graph that traces out price and total output over time as an industry expands.

Problem Set

1. In deriving the short-run industry supply curve (the sum of firms' marginal cost curves), we assumed that input prices are constant because competitive firms are price-takers. This same assumption holds in the derivation of the long-run industry supply curve. Do you agree or disagree? Explain.

2. Consider an industry that exhibits external diseconomies of scale. Suppose that over the next ten years, demand for that industry's product increases rapidly. Describe in detail the adjustments likely to follow. Use diagrams in your answer.

3. A representative firm producing cloth is earning a short-run profit at a price of €10 per metre. Draw a supply and demand diagram showing equilibrium at this price. Assuming that the industry is a constant-cost industry, use the diagram to show the long-term adjustment of the industry as demand grows over time. Explain the adjustment mechanism.

10

Input Demand: The Labour and Land Markets

As we have seen, all business firms must make three decisions: (1) how much to produce and supply in output markets; (2) how to produce that output (that is, which technology to use); and (3) how much of each input to demand. So far, our discussion of firm behaviour has focused on the first two questions. In Chapters 7 to 9, we explained how profit-maximizing firms choose among alternative technologies and decide how much to supply in output markets.

We now turn to the behaviour of firms in perfectly competitive input markets (highlighted in Figure 10.1), going behind input demand curves in much the same way that we went behind output supply curves in the previous two chapters. When we look behind input demand curves, we discover exactly the same set of decisions that we saw when we analysed output supply curves. In a sense, we have already talked about everything covered in this chapter. It is the perspective that is new.

The three main inputs are labour; land and capital. Transactions in the labour and land markets are fairly straightforward. In the labour market, households sell labour directly to firms in exchange for wages. In the land market, landowners sell or rent land directly to others. The capital market is more complex. To buy a capital asset – a machine, for example – a firm must use funds that it obtains from households. The firm must then pay interest to the households for the use of the funds. In a sense, then, households supply capital, just as they supply labour. This chapter discusses input markets in general, while the next chapter focuses on the capital market in some detail.

Input markets: basic concepts

Before we begin our discussion of input markets, it will be helpful to establish some basic concepts: derived demand, complementary and substitutable inputs, diminishing returns, and marginal revenue.

Demand for inputs: a *derived* demand

derived demand
The demand for resources (inputs) that is dependent on the demand for the outputs those resources can be used to produce.

A firm cannot make a profit unless there is a demand for its product. Households must be willing to pay for the firm's output. The quantity of output that firm produces in both the long run and the short run thus depends on the value placed by the market on the firm's product. This means that demand for inputs depends on the demand for outputs. In other words, input demand is derived from output demand. Inputs are demanded by a firm if, and only if, households demand the good or service produced by that firm.

productivity of an input
The amounts of output produced per unit of that input.

The value attached to a product and the inputs needed to produce that product define the input's productivity. Formally, the productivity of an input is the amount of output produced per unit of that input. When a large amount of output is produced per unit of an input, the input is said to be *highly productive*. When only a small amount of output is produced per unit of the input, the input is said to exhibit *low productivity*.

Figure 10.1 Firm and household decisions

Firms and households interact in both input and output markets. This chapter highlights firm choices in input markets.

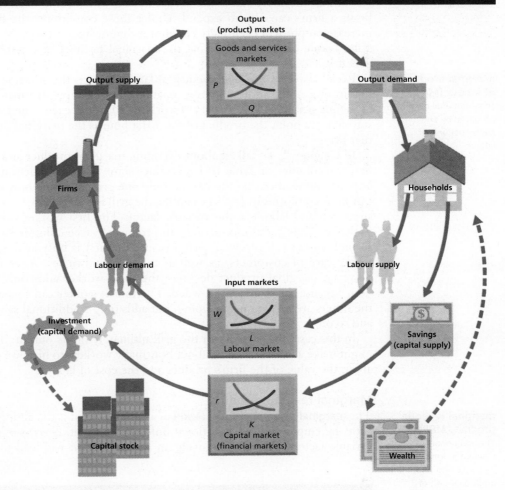

Prices in competitive input markets depend on firms' demand for inputs, households' supply of inputs, and the interaction between the two. In the labour market, for example, households must decide whether to work and how much to work. In Chapter 6 we saw that the opportunity cost of working for a wage is either leisure or the value derived from unpaid labour – working in the garden, for instance, or raising children. In general, firms will demand workers as long as the value of what those workers produce exceeds what they must be paid. Households will supply labour as long as the wage they receive exceeds the value of leisure or the value that they derive from non-paid work.

Inputs: complementary and substitutable

Inputs can be *complementary* or *substitutable*. Two inputs used together may enhance, or complement, each other. For example, a new machine is useless without someone to run it. But machines can also be substituted for labour, or – less often perhaps – labour can be substituted for machines.

All this means that a firm's input demands are tightly linked to one another. An increase or decrease in wages naturally causes the demand for labour to change, but it may also have an effect on the demand for capital or land. If we are to understand the demand for inputs, therefore, we must understand the connections among labour, capital and land.

Diminishing returns

Recall that the short run is the period during which some fixed factor of production limits a firm's capacity to expand. Under these conditions, the firm that decides to increase output will eventually encounter diminishing returns. Stated more formally, a fixed scale of plant means that the marginal product of variable inputs eventually declines.

marginal product of labour (MP_L)
The additional output produced by one additional unit of labour.

Recall also that **marginal product of labour (MP_L)** is the additional output produced if a firm hires one additional unit of labour. For example, if a firm pays for 400 hours of labour per week – 10 workers working 40 hours each – and asks one worker to stay an extra hour, the product of the 401st hour is the marginal product of labour for that firm.

In Chapter 7, we talked about declining marginal product at a sandwich bar. The first two columns of Table 10.1 reproduce some of the production data from that bar. You may remember that the bar has only one grill, at which only two or three people can work comfortably. In this example, the grill is the fixed factor of production in the short run and labour is the variable factor. The first worker can produce 10 sandwiches per hour; and the second can produce 15 (see column 3 of Table 10.1). The second worker can produce more because the first is busy answering the phone and taking care of customers, as well as making sandwiches. After the second worker, however, marginal product declines; the third worker adds only 10 sandwiches per hour because the grill gets crowded. The fourth worker can squeeze in quickly while the others are serving or wrapping, but adds only 5 additional sandwiches each hour, and so on.[1]

In this case, the capacity of the grill ultimately limits output. To see how the firm might make a rational choice about how many workers to hire, we need to know more about the value of the firm's product and the cost of labour.

Marginal revenue product

marginal revenue product (MRP)
The additional revenue a firm earns by employing one additional unit of input, ceteris paribus.

The **marginal revenue product (MRP)** of a variable input is the additional revenue a firm earns by employing one additional unit of that input, *ceteris paribus*. If labour is the variable factor, for example, hiring an additional unit will lead to added output (the

Table 10.1 Marginal revenue product per hour of labour in sandwich production (one grill)

(1) Total labour units (employees)	(2) Total product (sandwiches per hour)	(3) Marginal product of labour (MP_L) (sandwiches per hour)	(4) Price (P_X) (value added per sandwich)*	(5) Marginal revenue product, $MP_L \times P_X$ per hour (euros)
0	0	–	–	–
1	10	10	0.50	5.00
2	25	15	0.50	7.50
3	35	10	0.50	5.00
4	40	5	0.50	2.50
5	42	2	0.50	1.00
6	42	0	0.50	0.00

* The 'price' is essentially profit per sandwich; see discussion in text.

[1] As we said in Chapter 7, we assume that all workers are equally skilled and motivated. The third worker is no less hard working or skilled than the first two. Rather, the grill is getting crowded. Put another way, the capital constraint is binding.

marginal product of labour). The sale of that added output will yield revenue. Marginal revenue product is the revenue produced by selling the good or service that is produced by the marginal unit of labour. In a competitive firm, marginal revenue product is the value of a factor's marginal product.

Using labour as our variable factor, we can state this proposition more formally by saying that if MP_L is the marginal product of labour and P_X is the price of output, then the marginal revenue product of labour is:

$$MRP_L = MP_L \times P_X$$

Figure 10.2 Deriving a marginal revenue product curve from marginal product

The marginal revenue product of labour is the price of output, P_X, times the marginal product of labour, MP_L.

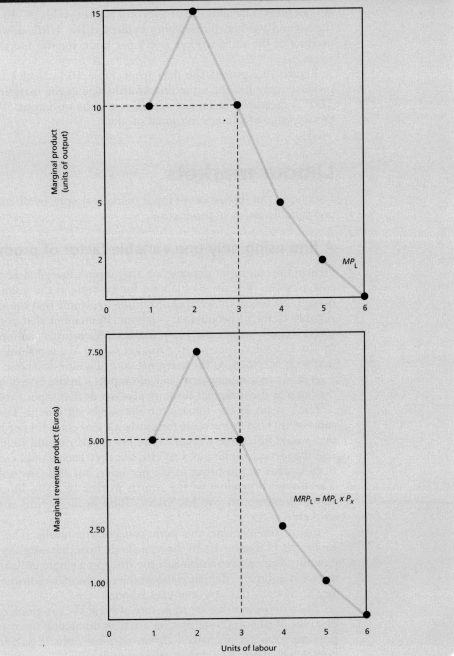

When calculating marginal revenue product, we need to be precise about what is being produced. A sandwich bar, to be sure, sells sandwiches, but it does not produce the bread, meat, cheese, mustard and mayonnaise that go into the sandwiches. What the bar is producing is 'sandwich cooking and assembly services'. The bar is 'adding value' to the meat, bread and other ingredients by preparing and putting them together in ready-to-eat form. With this in mind, let's assume that each finished sandwich in our bar sells for €0.50 over and above the costs of its ingredients. Thus, the *price of the service* the bar is selling is€ 0.50 per sandwich, and the only variable cost of providing that service is that of the labour used to put the sandwiches together. Thus, if X is the product of our bar, $P_X = €50$.

Table 10.1, column 5, calculates the marginal revenue product of each worker if the bar charges €0.50 per sandwich over and above the costs of ingredients. The first worker produces 10 sandwiches per hour which, at €0.50 each, generates revenues of €5 per hour. The addition of a second worker yields €7.50 an hour in revenues. After the second worker, diminishing returns drive MRP_L down. The marginal revenue product of the third worker is €5 per hour, for the fourth worker only €2.50, and so on.

Figure 10.2 graphs the data from Table 10.1. Notice that the marginal revenue product curve has the same downward slope as the marginal product curve, but that MRP is measured in money terms, not units of output. The MRP curve shows the money value of labour's marginal product.

Labour markets

Let's begin our discussion of input markets simply, by discussing a firm that uses only one variable factor of production.

A firm using only one variable factor of production: labour

Demand for an input depends on that input's marginal revenue product and its unit cost, or price. The price of labour, for example, is the wage determined in the labour market. (At this point we are continuing to assume that the sandwich bar uses only one variable factor of production – labour. Remember that competitive firms are price-takers in both output and input markets. Such firms can hire all the labour they want to hire as long as they pay the market wage.) We can think of the hourly wage at the sandwich bar, then, as the marginal cost of a unit of labour.

A profit-maximizing firm will add inputs – in the case of labour, it will hire workers – as long as the marginal revenue product of that input exceeds its market price.

Look again at the figures for the sandwich bar in Table 10.1, column 5. Now suppose that the going wage for sandwich makers is €4 per hour. A profit-maximizing firm would hire three workers. The first worker would yield €5 per hour in revenues, and the second would yield €7.50, but they each would cost only €4 per hour. The third worker would bring in €5 per hour, but still cost only €4 in marginal wages. The marginal product of the fourth worker (€2.50), however, would not bring in enough revenue to pay his salary. Total profit is thus maximized by hiring three workers.

Figure 10.3 presents this same concept graphically. The labour market appears in Figure 10.3a. Figure 10.3b shows a single firm that employs workers. This firm, incidentally, does not represent just the firms in a single industry. Because firms in many different industries demand labour, the representative firm in Figure 10.3b represents any firm in any industry that uses labour.

The firm faces a market wage rate of €10. We can think of this as the marginal cost of a unit of labour. (Note that we are now discussing the margin in units of labour; in previous chapters, we talked about marginal units of *output*.) Given a wage of €10, how much labour would the firm demand?

Figure 10.3 Marginal revenue product and factor demand for a firm using one variable input (labour)

A competitive firm using only one variable factor of production will use that factor as long as its marginal revenue product exceeds its unit cost. A perfectly competitive firm will hire labour as long as MRP_L is greater than the going wage, W^*. The hypothetical firm will demand 210 units of labour.

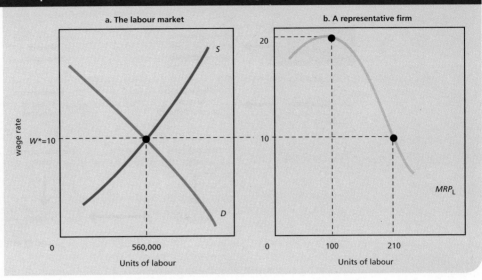

One might think that 100 units would be hired, the point at which the difference between marginal revenue product and wage rate is greatest. But the firm is interested in maximum total profit, not marginal profit. Hiring the 101st unit of labour generates €20 in revenue at a cost of only €10. Because MRP_L is greater than the cost of the input required to produce it, hiring one more unit of labour adds to profit. This will continue to be true as long as MRP_L remains above €10, which is the case all the way to 210 units. At that point, the wage rate is equal to the marginal revenue product of labour, or

$$W^* = MRP_L = 10$$

The firm will not demand labour beyond 210 units, because the cost of hiring the 211th unit of labour would be greater than the value of what that unit produces. (Recall that the fourth sandwich maker can produce only an extra €2.50 an hour in sandwiches, while his salary is €4 per hour.)

Thus the curve in Figure 10.3b tells us how much labour a firm that uses only one variable factor of production will hire at each potential market wage rate. If the market wage falls, the quantity of labour demanded will rise. If the market wage rises, the quantity of labour demanded will fall. This description should sound familiar to you – it is, in fact, the description of a demand curve. Therefore, we can now say that:

> When a firm uses only one variable factor of production, that factor's marginal revenue product curve is the firm's demand curve for that factor in the short run.

For another example of the relevance of marginal revenue product, see the Application box 'Millionaire sportsmen and their marginal revenue product'.

Comparing marginal revenue and marginal cost to maximize profits

In Chapter 8, we saw that a competitive firm's marginal cost curve is the same as its supply curve. That is, at any output price, the marginal cost curve determines how much output a profit-maximizing firm will produce. We came to this conclusion by comparing the marginal revenue that a firm would earn by producing one more unit of output with the marginal cost of producing that unit of output.

There is no difference between the reasoning in Chapter 8 and the reasoning in this chapter. The only difference is that what is being measured at the margin has

Figure 10.4 The two profit-maximizing conditions are simply two views of the same choice process

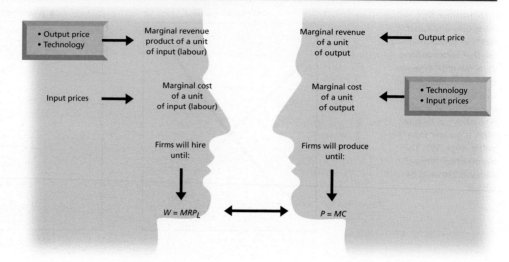

changed. In Chapter 8, the firm was comparing the marginal revenues and costs of producing another unit of output. Here, the firm is comparing the marginal revenues and costs of employing another unit of input. To see this similarity, look at Figure 10.4. If the only variable factor of production is labour, the condition $W^* = MRP_L$ is the same condition as $P = MC$. The two statements say exactly the same thing.

In both cases, the firm is comparing the cost of production with potential revenues from the sale of product *at the margin*. In Chapter 8, the firm compared the price of output (P, which is equal to MR in perfect competition) directly with cost of production (MC), where cost was derived from information on factor prices and technology. (Review the derivation of cost curves in Chapter 8 if this is unclear.) Here, information on output price and technology is contained in the marginal revenue product curve, which is compared with information on input price to determine the optimal level of input to demand.

The assumption of one variable factor of production makes the trade-off facing firms easy to see. Figure 10.5 shows that in essence firms weigh the value of labour as reflected in the market wage against the value of the product of labour as reflected in the price of output.

Assuming that labour is the only variable input, if society values a good more than it costs firms to hire the workers to produce that good, the good will be produced. In general, the same logic also holds for more than one input. Firms weigh the value of outputs as reflected in output price against the value of inputs as reflected in marginal costs.

Deriving input demands

For the small sandwich bar, calculating the marginal product of a variable input (labour) and marginal revenue product was easy. Although it may be more complex, the decision process is essentially the same for large firms.

When an airline hires more cabin crew, for example, it increases the quality of its service to attract more passengers and thus sell more of its product. Flight attendants must be paid a wage, however. In deciding how many to hire, the airline must figure out how much new revenue the extra attendants are likely to generate relative to their wages.

At the sandwich bar, diminishing returns set in at a certain point. The same holds true for a plane. Once a sufficient number of attendants are on a plane, additional attendants add little to the quality of service, and the marginal product of each additional attendant diminishes. Like the grill, the aeroplane has a fixed physical capacity,

Figure 10.5 The trade-off facing firms

Firms weigh the cost of labour, as reflected in wage rates, against the value of labour's marginal product. Assume labour is the only variable factor of production. Then, if society values a good more than it costs firms to hire the workers to produce that good, the good will be produced.

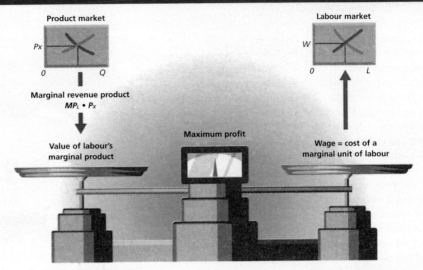

Product market

P_x

0   Q

Marginal revenue product
$MP_L \cdot P_x$

Value of labour's marginal product

Maximum profit

Labour market

W

0   L

Wage = cost of a marginal unit of labour

Firms

and the addition of a variable factor beyond a certain level might even give rise to negative marginal product. Too many attendants could bother the passengers and make it difficult to get to the toilet.

In making your own decisions, you too compare marginal gains with input costs in the presence of diminishing returns. Suppose you grow vegetables in your garden. You do this for a number of reasons. First, you save money at the grocery shop – vegetables are an output with a measurable monetary value. Second, you can plant what you like, and the vegetables taste better fresh from the garden. Third, you simply like to work in the garden – you get sun, exercise and fresh air.

Like the sandwich bar and the airline, you also face diminishing returns. You have only 70 square metres of garden to work with, and with land as a fixed factor in the short run your marginal product will certainly decline. You can work all day and every day, but your limited space will produce only so many beans. The first few hours you spend each week watering, fertilizing and dealing with major weed and pest infestations probably have a high marginal product. But after five or six hours, there is little else you can do to increase yield. Diminishing returns also apply to your sense of satisfaction. The local markets are now full of cheap fresh produce that tastes nearly as good as yours. And once you have been out in the garden for a few hours, the hot sun and hard work start to lose their charm. The earth under your fingernails gives way to the less gritty pleasure of watching a television soap opera.

Although your gardening does not involve a salary (unlike the sandwich bar and the airline, which pay out wages), the labour you supply has a value that must be weighed, even if the cost of your labour is only the value you could derive by using that time doing something else, such as watching television. When the returns from gardening diminish beyond a certain point, you must weigh the value of additional gardening time against leisure and the other options available to you.

It is as true for the sandwich bar as for you that less labour is likely to be employed as the cost of labour rises. If the competitive labour market pushed the daily wage to €6 per hour, the sandwich bar would take on only two workers instead of three (see Table 10.1). If you suddenly became very busy, your time would become more valuable and you would probably devote fewer hours to gardening.

Applications

Millionaire sportsmen and their marginal revenue product

Sporting stars receive huge payments for their services. For example, in 1997, boxing's Evander Holyfield had an income of US$54 millon. In Formula 1 motor racing, Michael Schumacher received $35 million. Tiger Woods's income in golf totalled $26 million, and tennis star Pete Sampras earned $14.5 million. The biggest earner of all was US basketball player Michael Jordan, who earned $78 million.

How in the world could anyone be worth these sums? Why would people be willing to pay so much for a single player? As we've seen in this chapter, profit-maximizing employers will hire workers only as long as their marginal revenue product (MRP_L) is greater than or equal to their wage. Could it then be possible that these people are 'worth it'?

Gerald W. Scully, Professor of Management at the University of Texas at Dallas, produced a statistical estimate of the contribution that baseball players in the USA made to the revenues of their teams during the 1980s. The results may surprise you:

[In 1984] an extra victory was worth $195,653. Now consider the effect on revenues of adding a hitter like Andre Dawson, the National League MVP [most valuable player] of 1987, or a pitcher like Roger Clemens, the Cy Young Award winner in the American League in 1986. Dawson had a slugging average of 0.568 over 621 at bats. Chicago had a team slugging average of 0.432 over 5,583 at bats. Dawson contributed 11.1 per cent of the at bats and 0.63 of the team's slugging

Football stars such as Ronaldo are paid large salaries. However, their wage rates reflect the extra value to their employers – the marginal revenue product.

average. Given the relationship between slugging average and wins, those 63 points were conservatively worth 11 games. The marginal revenue [product] of those 11 games was about $2.2 million. Roger Clemens posted a 24–4 record in Boston in 1986. Assuming that Clemens was the

source of the margin of victory in those net 20 games, his performance was worth $3.9 million [in 1986] . . . By such economic standards such players are not overpaid.[1]

[1]Gerald W. Scully, *The Business of Major League Baseball* (Chicago: University of Chicago Press, 1989), pp. 155–6.

Two variable factors of production in the short and long run

When a firm employs more than one variable factor of production, the analysis of input demand becomes more complicated, but the principles stay the same. We shall now consider a firm that employs variable capital (K) and labour (L) inputs, and thus faces factor prices P_K and P_L.[2] (Recall that *capital* refers to plant, equipment and inventory used in production. We assume that some portion of the firm's capital stock is fixed in the short run, but that some of it is variable – for example, some machinery and equipment can be installed quickly.) Our analysis can be applied to any two factors of production and can easily be generalized to three or more. It can also be applied to the long run, when all factors of production are variable.

You have seen that inputs can be complementary or substitutable. Land, labour and capital are used *together* to produce outputs. The worker who uses a shovel digs a bigger hole than one with no shovel; add a mechanical digger and that worker becomes even more productive. When an expanding firm adds to its stock of capital, it raises the productivity of its labour, and vice versa. Thus, each factor complements the other. At the same time, though, land, labour and capital can also be *substituted* for one another. If labour becomes expensive, some labour-saving technology (robotics, for example) may take its place.

[2]The price of labour, P_L, is the same as the wage rate, W. We will often use the term P_L instead of W to stress the symmetry between labour and capital.

Table 10.2 Response of a firm to an increasing wage rate				
Technology	**Input requirements per unit of output**		**Unit cost (euros) if $P_L = 1$, $P_K = 1$ $(P_L \times L) + (P_K \times K)$**	**Unit cost (euros) if $P_L = 2$, $P_K = 1$ $(P_L \times L) + (P_K \times K)$**
A (capital intensive)	10	5	15	20
B (labour intensive)	3	10	13	23

In firms employing just one variable factor of production, a change in the price of that factor affects only the demand for the factor itself. When more than one factor can vary, however, we must consider the impact of a change in one factor price on the demand for other factors as well.

Substitution and output effects of a change in factor price

Table 10.2 presents data on a hypothetical firm that employs variable capital and labour. Suppose that the firm faces a choice between two available technologies of production technique A, which is capital intensive, and technique B, which is labour intensive. When the market price of labour is 1 euro per unit and the market price of capital is 1 euro per unit, the labour-intensive method of producing output is less costly. Each unit costs only €13 to produce using technique B, while the unit cost of production using technique A is €15. If the price of labour rises to €2 however, technique B is no longer less costly. Labour has become more expensive relative to capital. The unit cost rises to €23 for labour-intensive technique B, but to only €20 for capital-intensive technique A.

Table 10.3 shows the impact of such an increase in the price of labour on both capital and labour demand when a firm produces 100 units of output. When each input factor costs 1euro per unit, the firm chooses technique B and demands 300 units of capital and 1000 units of labour. Total variable cost is €1300. An increase in the price of labour to €2 causes the firm to switch from technique B to technique A. In doing so, it *substitutes* capital for labour. The amount of labour demanded drops from 1000 to 500 units. The amount of capital demanded increases from 300 to 1000 units, while total variable cost increases to €2000.

The tendency of firms to substitute away from a factor whose relative price has risen and towards a factor whose relative price has fallen is called the factor substitution effect. The **factor substitution effect** is part of the reason that *input demand curves slope downwards*. When an input, or factor of production, becomes less expensive, firms tend to substitute it for other factors and thus buy *more* of it. When a particular input becomes more expensive, firms tend to substitute other factors and buy *less* of it. During 1997, the UK government cut the tax on heating fuel in order to make it cheaper for people to heat their homes in winter. Energy is now cheaper relative to insulation. The effect of the tax change may therefore discourage people from purchasing more effective insulation for their homes.

factor substitution effect

The tendency of firms to substitute away from a factor whose price has risen and toward a factor whose price has fallen.

Table 10.3 The substitution effect of an increase in wages on a firm producing 100 units of output			
	To produce 100 units of output		
	Total capital demanded	**Total labour demanded**	**Total variable cost (euros)**
When $P_L = 1$, $P_K = 1$, firm uses technology B	300	1,000	1,300
When $P_L = 2$, $P_K = 1$, firm uses technology A	1,000	500	2,000

The firm described in Tables 10.2 and 10.3 continued to produce 100 units of output after the wage rate doubled. An *increase* in the price of a production factor, however, also means an increase in the costs of production. Notice that total variable cost increased from 1300 to €2000. When a firm faces higher costs, it is likely to produce less in the short run. When a firm decides to cut output, its demand for all factors declines – including, of course, the factor whose price increased in the first place. This is called the **output effect of a factor price increase**.

A *decrease* in the price of a factor of production, in contrast, means lower costs of production. If their output price remains unchanged, firms will increase output. This, in turn, means that demand for all factors of production will increase. This is the **output effect of a factor price decrease**.

The output effect helps explain why input demand curves slope downwards. Output effects and factor substitution effects work in the same direction. Consider, for example, a decline in the wage rate. Lower wages mean that a firm will substitute labour for capital and other inputs. Stated somewhat differently, the factor substitution effect leads to an increase in demand for labour. Lower wages mean lower costs, and lower costs lead to more output. This increase in output means that the firm will hire more of all factors of production, including labour itself. This is the output effect of a factor price decrease. Notice that both effects lead to an increase in the demand for labour when the wage rate falls.

Many labour markets

Although Figure 10.1 depicts the labour market in general, many labour markets exist. There is a market for footballers, for carpenters, for chemists, for university professors and for unskilled workers. Still another market exists for taxi drivers, assembly line workers, secretaries and company executives. Each market has a set of skills associated with it and a relative supply of people with the requisite skills.

Applications

Europe's growing band of temps keep labour costs down

We have been assuming that although firms cannot quickly vary all their capital decisions, they can easily vary their level of labour employment. If firms are to keep costs to a minimum they need to be flexible in their employment decisions. Increasingly, they are doing this by the use of 'temps' – temporary workers.

The rise of the flexible workforce may be a global phenomenon, but nowhere is it more important than in Europe's unbending labour markets. Temporary workers have existed in Europe for years, but mainly as emergency relief. Now, with global competition forcing companies to react quickly to market conditions, temps play a vital role by allowing just-in-time staffing during demand surges. Workers with limited-time contracts represent a huge long-term cost saving over permanent workers, who by law are hard to dismiss.

Europe's temps aren't just doing reception work. Their growing ranks include airline pilots, chemists, nuclear-plant workers, logistics experts, teachers, and engineers.

Many European labour unions vehemently opposed temporary work during the 1980s, arguing that limited-duration contracts exploit workers. Now, as countries experimenting with temp work show big economic benefits, labour leaders are reluctantly acknowledging a role for those contracts. 'When temping began to explode in the 1980s, we had big problems with this trend', says Cor Inja of the FNV, the biggest Dutch trade union. 'But many of our members wanted to work and found jobs only as temps'. Now, The Netherlands has become a glowing example of the benefits of temporary work. Economists link the dramatic growth of temporary and part-time workers – to 10.5% of the total workforce – with the country's sharp decline in unemployment.

Besides fuelling job growth, temporary agencies across Europe have proved effective at putting unemployed workers back into the labour force, funnelling some 30% of their workers annually into full-time jobs.[1]

[1] 'A tidal wave of temps', Business Week, *European edition, 24 November 1997.*

If labour markets are competitive, the wages in those markets are determined by the interaction of supply and demand. As we have seen, firms will hire workers only as long as the value of their product exceeds the relevant market wage. This is true in all competitive labour markets.

Land markets

Unlike labour and capital, land has a special feature that we have not yet considered: it is in strictly fixed (perfectly inelastic) supply in total. The only real questions about land thus centre on how much it is worth and to what use it will be put.

Because land is fixed in supply, we say that its price is **demand determined**. In other words, the price of land is determined exclusively by what households and firms are willing to pay for it. The return to any factor of production in fixed supply is called a **pure rent**.

Thinking of the price of land as demand determined can be confusing because all land is not the same. Some land is clearly more valuable than other land. The value of a plot of land in an attractive London suburb such as Knightsbridge is worth much more than the same sized plot in an unfashionable part of the city such as Whitechapel. The price of a hectare of land in a prime Stockholm location is likely to be several hundred times that of a hectare of land in the snowy wastes in the far north of Sweden.

What lies behind these differences in land values? As with any other factor of production, land will presumably be sold or rented to the user who is willing to pay the most for it. The value of land to a potential user may depend upon the characteristics of the land itself or upon its location. For example, more fertile land should produce more farm products per hectare and thus command a higher price than less fertile land. A piece of property located at the junction of two main roads may be of great value as a site for a petrol station because of the amount of traffic that passes there daily.

A numerical example may help to clarify our discussion. Consider the potential uses of a corner site in a suburb of Bonn. Hans wants to build a clothing shop there. He anticipates that he can earn economic profits of DM 10,000 per year there because of the site's excellent location. Heidi, another person interested in buying the site, believes that she can earn DM 35,000 per year in economic profit if she builds a pharmacy there. Clearly, Heidi will be able to outbid Hans, and the landowner will sell (or rent) to the highest bidder.

Because location is often the key to profits, landowners are frequently able to 'squeeze' their renters. Most European cities have particularly popular locations where the shops and restaurants are full most of the time. Despite this seeming success, many shop and restaurant owners there are not getting rich. Why? Because they must pay very high rents on the location of their premises. A substantial portion of each shop and restaurant's revenues goes to rent the land that (by virtue of its scarcity) is the key to unlocking those same revenues.

Although Figure 10.6 shows that the supply of land is perfectly inelastic (a vertical line), the supply of land in a *given use* may not be perfectly inelastic or fixed. Think, for example, about farmland and land available for housing developments. As a city's population grows, housing developers find themselves willing to pay more and more for land. As land becomes more valuable for development, some farmers sell out, and the supply of land available for development increases. This analysis would lead us to draw an upward-sloping supply curve (not a perfectly inelastic supply curve) for land in the land-for-development category.

Nonetheless, our major point – that land earns a pure rent – is still valid:

The supply of land of a *given quality* at a *given location* is truly fixed in supply, its value is determined exclusively by the amount that the highest bidder is willing to pay for it. Since land cannot be reproduced, supply is perfectly inelastic

---

demand determined price
The price of a good that is in fixed supply; it is determined exclusively by what firms and households are willing to pay for the good.

pure rent   The return to any factor of production that is in fixed supply.

Figure 10.6 The rent on land is demand determined

Because land in general (and each parcel in particular) is in fixed supply, its price is demand determined. Graphically, a fixed supply is represented by a vertical, perfectly inelastic, supply curve. Rent, R_0, depends exclusively on demand – what people are willing to pay.

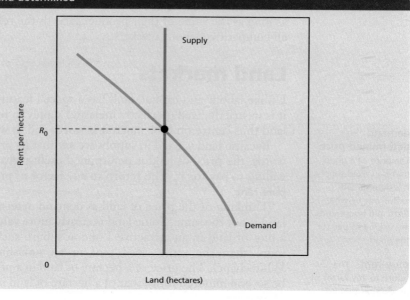

Rent and the value of output produced on land

Because the price of land is demand determined, rent depends on what the potential users of the land are willing to pay for it. As we've seen, land will end up being used by whoever is willing to pay the most for it. But what determines willingness to pay? Let us now connect our discussion of land markets with our earlier discussions of factor markets in general.

As our example of two potential users bidding for a plot of land shows, the bids depend on the land's potential for profit. Hans's plan would generate DM 10,000 a year; Heidi's would generate DM 35,000 a year. But these profits do not just materialize. Rather, they come from producing and selling an output that is valuable to households. Land in a popular city location is expensive because of what can be produced on it. Note that land is needed as an input into the production of nearly all goods and services. A restaurant next door to a popular theatre can charge a premium price because it has a relatively captive clientele. Clearly, the restaurant must produce a good-quality product to stay in business, but the location alone provides a substantial profit opportunity.

It should come as no surprise that the demand for land follows the same rules as the demand for inputs in general. A profit-maximizing firm will employ an additional factor of production as long as its marginal revenue product exceeds its market price. For example, a profit-maximizing firm will hire labour as long as the revenue earned from selling labour's product is sufficient to cover the cost of hiring additional labour–which for perfectly competitive firms equals the wage rate. The same thing is true for land:

A firm will pay for and use land as long as the revenue earned from selling the product produced on that land is sufficient to cover the price of the land. The firm will use land up to the point at which $MRP_A = P_A$, where A is land (area).

Just as the demand curve for labour reflects the value of labour's product as determined in output markets, so the demand for land depends on the value of land's product in output markets. The profitability of the restaurant next door to the theatre results from the fact that the meals produced there command a price in the marketplace.

The allocation of a given plot of land among competing uses thus depends on the trade-off between competing products that can be produced there. Agricultural land is developed when its value in producing housing or manufactured goods or providing space for a shopping complex exceeds its value in producing crops. A corner site in Bonn becomes the site of a chemist's shop rather than a clothing shop because the people in that area have a greater need for a pharmacy.

One final word about land: because land cannot be moved physically, the value of any one parcel depends to a large extent upon the uses to which adjoining parcels are put. A factory belching acrid smoke will probably reduce the value of adjoining land, whereas a new road that increases accessibility may enhance it.

The firm's profit-maximization condition in input markets

Thus far we have discussed the labour and land markets in some detail. Although we will put off a detailed discussion of capital until the next chapter, it is now possible to generalize about competitive demand for factors of production. Every firm has an incentive to use variable inputs as long as the revenue generated by those inputs covers the costs of those inputs at the margin. More formally, firms will employ each input up to the point that its price equals its marginal revenue product. This condition holds for all factors at all levels of output:

> Profit-maximizing condition for the perfectly competitive firm:
>
> $$P_L = MRP_L = (MP_L \times P_X)$$
> $$P_K = MRP_K = (MP_K \times P_X)$$
> $$P_A = MRP_A = (MP_A \times P_X)$$
>
> where L is labour, K is capital, A is land (area), X is output and P_X is the price of that output.

When all these conditions are met, the firm will be using the optimal, or least costly, combination of inputs. If all these conditions hold at the same time, it is possible to rewrite them in another way:

$$\frac{MP_L}{P_L} = \frac{MP_K}{P_K} = \frac{MP_A}{P_A}$$

Your intuition tells you much the same thing that these equations do: the marginal product of the last unit of expenditure on labour must be equal to the marginal product of the last unit of expenditure on capital, which must be equal to the marginal product of the last unit of expenditure on land, and so on. If this were not the case, the firm could produce more with less and reduce cost. Suppose, for example, that $MP_L/P_L > MP_K/P_K$. In this situation, the firm can produce more output by shifting expenditure out of capital and into labour.

Hiring more labour drives down the marginal product of labour, and using less capital increases the marginal product of capital. This means that the ratios come back to equality as the firm shifts out of capital and into labour.

So far, we have used general terms to discuss the nature of input demand by firms in competitive markets, where input prices and output prices are taken as given. The most important point here is that demand for a factor depends on the value that the market places on its marginal product.[3] The rest of this chapter explores the forces that determine the shapes and positions of input demand curves.

---

[3]*If you worked through the appendix to Chapter 7, you saw this same condition derived graphically from an isocost/isoquant diagram. Note: $MP_L/P_L = MP_K/P_K \rightarrow MP_L/MP_K = P_L/P_K$.*

Input demand curves

When we discussed supply and demand in Chapter 5, we spent a good deal of time talking about the factors that influence the responsiveness, or elasticity, of output demand curves. We have not yet talked about *input* demand curves in any detail, however, and we now need to say more about what lies behind them.

Shifts in factor demand curves

Factor (input) demand curves are derived from information on technology (that is, production functions) and output price (see Figure 10.4). A change in the demand for outputs, a change in the quantity of complementary or substitutable inputs, changes in the prices of other inputs, and technological change can all cause factor demand curves to shift. These shifts in demand are important because they directly affect the allocation of resources among alternative uses, as well as the level and distribution of income.

The demand for outputs

A firm will demand an input as long as its marginal revenue product exceeds its market price. Marginal revenue product, which in perfect competition is equal to a factor's marginal product times the price of output, is the value of the factor's marginal product:

$$MRP_L = MP_L \times P_X.$$

The amount that a firm is willing to pay for a factor of production, then, depends directly on the value of the things that the firm produces. It follows that:

If product demand increases, product price will rise and marginal revenue product (factor demand) will increase – the *MRP* curve will shift to the right. If product demand declines, product price will fall and marginal revenue product (factor demand) will decrease – the *MRP* curve will shift to the left.

Go back and raise the price of sandwiches from 0.50 euro to 1 euro in the sandwich bar example examined in Table 10.1 to see that this is so.

The quantity of complementary and substitutable inputs

In our discussion thus far, we have kept coming back to the fact that factors of production complement one another. The productivity of, and thus the demand for, any one factor of production depends upon the quality and quantity of the other factors with which it works.

The effect of capital accumulation on wages is one of the most important themes in all of economics. In general:

The production and use of capital enhances the productivity of labour, and normally increases the demand for labour and drives up wages.

Take transport as an example. In a poor country like Bangladesh, one person with an ox cart can move a small load over bad roads very slowly. By contrast, the stock of capital used by workers in the transport industry in Europe is enormous. A lorry driver in a European country works with a substantial amount of capital. The roads themselves are capital that was put in place by the government. The amount of material that a single driver can now move between distant points in a short time is staggering relative to what it was just 25 years ago. This increase in productivity has resulted directly from the addition of new capital to the industry and is reflected in the wages and incomes of drivers.

The prices of other inputs

When a firm has a choice among alternative technologies, the choice it makes depends to some extent on relative input prices. You saw in Tables 10.2 and 10.3 that an increase in the price of labour substantially increased the demand for capital as the firm switched to a more capital-intensive production technique.

During the 1970s, the large increase in energy prices relative to prices of other factors of production had a number of effects on the demand for those other inputs. Insulation of new buildings, installation of more efficient heating plants and other similar efforts substantially raised the demand for capital as capital was substituted for energy in production. But it has also been argued that the energy crisis led to an increase in demand for labour. According to this argument, if capital and energy are complementary inputs – that is, if technologies that are capital intensive are also energy intensive – then the higher energy prices tended to push firms away from capital-intensive techniques and towards more labour-intensive techniques.[4] A new highly automated technique, for example, might need fewer workers, but it would also require a vast amount of electricity. High electricity prices could lead a firm to reject the new techniques and stick with an old, more labour-intensive, method of production.

Technological change

technological change
The introduction of new methods of production or new products intended to increase the productivity of existing inputs or to raise marginal products.

Closely related to the impact of capital accumulation on factor demand is the potential impact of technological change – that is, the introduction of new methods of production or new products. New technologies usually introduce ways to produce outputs with fewer inputs by increasing the productivity of existing inputs or by raising marginal products. Because marginal revenue product reflects productivity, increases in productivity directly shift input demand curves. If the marginal product of labour rises, for example, the demand for labour shifts to the right (increases).

Technological change can and does have a powerful influence on factor demands. As new products and new techniques of production are born, so are demands for new inputs and new skills. As old products become obsolete, so too do the labour skills and other inputs needed to produce them.

Resource allocation and the mix of output in competitive markets

We now have a complete, but simplified, picture of household and firm making. We have also examined some of the basic forces that determine the allocation of resources and the mix of output in perfectly competitive markets.

In this competitive environment, profit-maximizing firms make three fundamental decisions: (1) how much to produce and supply in output markets, (2) how to produce (which technology to use), and (3) how much of each input to demand. Chapters 7 to 9 looked at these three decisions from the perspective of the output market. We derived the supply curve of a competitive firm in the short run and discussed output market adjustment in the long run. Deriving cost curves, we learned, involves evaluating and choosing among alternative technologies. Finally, we saw how a firm's decision about how much product to supply in output markets implicitly determines input demands. Input demands, we argued, are also derived demands. That is, they are ultimately linked to the demand for output.

To show the connection between output and input markets, this chapter took these same three decisions and examined them from the perspective of input markets. Firms hire up to the point at which each input's marginal revenue product is equal to its price.

---

[4]*The argument was made in a series of papers by Professor Dale Jorgenson of Harvard University.*

The distribution of income

In the last few chapters we have been focusing primarily on the firm. But throughout our study of microeconomics, we have also been building a theory that explains the distribution of income among households. We can now put the pieces of this puzzle together.

As we have seen in this chapter, income is earned by households as payment for the factors of production that household members supply in input markets. Workers receive wages in exchange for their labour, owners of capital receive profits and interest in exchange for supplying capital (saving), and landowners receive rents in exchange for the use of their land. The incomes of workers depend on the wage rates determined in the market. The incomes of capital owners depend on the market price of capital (the amount households are paid for the use of their savings). And the incomes of landowners depend on the rental values of their land.

If markets are competitive, the equilibrium price of each input is equal to its marginal revenue product ($W = MRP_L$, and so forth). In other words, at equilibrium, each factor ends up receiving rewards determined by its productivity as measured by marginal revenue product. This is referred to as the marginal productivity theory of income distribution. We will turn to a more complete analysis of income distribution in Chapter 17.

marginal productivity theory of income distribution

At equilibrium, all factors of production end up receiving rewards determined by their productivity as measured by marginal revenue product.

Looking ahead

We have now completed our discussion of competitive labour and land markets. (More on the labour market and labour unions can be found in Chapter 19.) The next chapter takes up the complexity of what we have been loosely calling the 'capital market'. There we discuss the relationship between the market for physical capital and financial capital markets, and look at some of the ways that firms make investment decisions. When we have examined the nature of overall competitive equilibrium in Chapter 12, we can finally begin relaxing some of the assumptions that have restricted the scope of our inquiry – most importantly, the assumption of perfect competition in input and output markets.

Summary

1. Exactly the same set of decisions that lies behind output supply curves also lies behind input demand curves. It is only the perspective that is different.

Input markets: basic concepts

2. Demand for inputs depends on demand for the outputs that they produce; input demand is thus a *derived demand*. *Productivity* is a measure of the amount of output produced per unit of input.

3. In general, firms will demand workers as long as the value of what those workers produce exceeds what they must be paid. Households will supply labour as long as the wage exceeds the value of leisure or the value that they derive from non-paid work.

4. Inputs are at the same time *complementary* and *substitutable*. For example, capital raises the productivity of labour, and thus it complements labour; at the same time, capital may be substituted for labour.

5. In the short run, some factor of production is fixed. This means that all firms encounter diminishing returns in the short run. Stated somewhat differently, diminishing returns means that all firms encounter declining marginal product in the short run.

6. The *marginal revenue product* (*MRP*) of a variable input is the additional revenue a firm earns by employing one additional unit of the input, *ceteris paribus*. *MRP* is equal to the input's marginal product times the price of output.

Labour markets

7. Demand for an input depends on that input's marginal revenue product. Profit-maximizing perfectly competitive firms will buy an input (for example, hire labour) up to the point where the input's marginal revenue product equals its price. For a firm employing only one variable factor of production, the *MRP* curve is the firm's demand curve for that factor in the short run.

8. For a perfectly competitive firm employing one variable factor of production, labour, the condition $W = MRP_L$ is exactly the same as the condition $P = MC$. Firms weigh the value of outputs as reflected in output price against the value of inputs as reflected in marginal costs.

9. When a firm employs two variable factors of production, a change in factor price has both a *factor substitution effect* and an *output effect*.

10. A wage increase may lead a firm to substitute capital for labour and thus cause the demand for labour to decline. This is the *factor substitution effect of the wage increase*.

11. A wage increase raises cost, and higher cost may lead to lower output and less demand for all inputs, including labour. This is the *output effect of the wage increase*. The effect is the opposite for a wage decrease.

Land markets

12. Because land is in strictly fixed supply, its price is *demand determined* – that is, its price is determined exclusively by what households and firms are willing to pay for it. The return to any factor of production in fixed supply is called a *pure rent*. A firm will pay for and use land as long as the revenue earned from selling the

product produced on that land is sufficient to cover the price of the land. The firm will use land up to the point at which $MRP_A = P_A$, where A is land (area).

13. Every firm has an incentive to use variable inputs as long as the revenue generated by those inputs covers the costs of those inputs at the margin. Therefore, firms will employ each input up to the point at which its price equals its marginal revenue product. This profit-maximizing condition holds for all factors at all levels of output.

Input demand curves

14. A shift in a firm's demand curve for a factor of production can be influenced by the demand for the firm's product, the quantity of complementary and substitutable inputs, the prices of other inputs, and changes in technology.

Resource allocation and the mix of output in competitive markets

15. Because the price of a factor at equilibrium in competitive markets is equal to its marginal revenue product, the distribution of income among households depends in part on the relative productivity of factors. This is the *marginal productivity theory of income distribution*.

Review Terms and Concepts

demand determined price
derived demand
factor substitution effect
marginal product of labour (**MP_L**)
marginal productivity theory of income distribution
marginal revenue product (**MRP**)
productivity of an input

pure rent
technological change

Equations

$MRP_L = MP_L \times P_X$

$W^* = MRP_L$

Problem Set

1. Assume that a Belgian firm that manufactures widgets can produce them with one of three processes, used alone or in combination. Table 1 indicates the

amounts of capital and labour required by each of the three processes to produce one widget.
a. Assuming that capital costs 3 (Belgian) francs per unit and labour costs 1 franc per unit, which process will be employed?
b. Plot the three points on the firm's *TVC* curve corresponding to $q = 10$, $q = 30$ and $q = 50$.
c. At each of the three output levels, how much K and L will be demanded?
d. Repeat problems (a) to (c), assuming the price of capital is 3 francs per unit and that the price of labour has risen to 4 francs per unit.

Table 1		
Process	**Units of labour**	**Units of capital**
1	4	1
2	2	2
3	1	3

2. Table 2 shows the technology of production at the Simone Dufay apple orchard in France for 1998.

Table 2	
Workers	Total no. of apples per hour (kilos)
0	0
1	40
2	70
3	90
4	100
5	105
6	102

If apples sell for 2 francs per kilo and workers can be hired in a competitive labour market for 30 francs per hour, how many workers should be employed? What if workers unionized and the wage rose to 50 francs per hour? (*Hint*: create marginal product and marginal revenue product columns for the table.) Explain your answers clearly.

3. Figure 1 shows the production function for a firm using only one variable factor of production, labour.

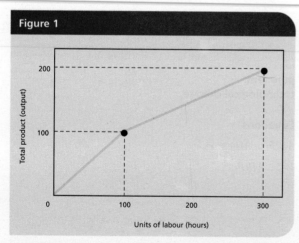

Figure 1

a. Graph the marginal product of labour for the firm as a function of the number of labour units employed.
b. Assuming that the price of output, P_X, is equal to €6, graph the firm's marginal revenue product schedule as a function of the number of labour units employed.
c. If the current equilibrium wage rate is €4 per hour, how many hours of labour would you employ? How much output will you produce?

4. Describe how each of the following events would affect (1) the demand for building workers, and (2) wages in the building sector, in Oslo, Norway. Illustrate with supply and demand curves.

a. A sharp increase in interest rates on new home mortgages reduces the demand for new houses substantially.
b. The economy of the area booms. Office rents rise, creating demand for new office space.
c. A change in the tax laws in 1998 caused three major developers to start planning to build major shopping centres.

5. The demand for land is a derived demand. Think of a popular location near where you live. What determines the demand for land in that area? What outputs are sold by businesses located there? Discuss the relationship between land prices and the prices of those products.

6. Virtually all European countries provide firms with some form of investment subsidy that effectively reduces the price of capital. In theory, these incentives are designed to stimulate new investment and thus create jobs. Critics have argued that if there are strong factor substitution effects, these subsidies could actually *reduce* employment. Explain their arguments.

7. a. Define *marginal revenue product*.
b. At equilibrium in a competitive industry, $W = MRP_L$. Briefly explain why.
c. Suppose that the competitive zump industry employs 50% of the highly trained zump makers in Europe. Suppose also that demand for zumps shifts, driving the price of zumps up by 50%. The wages of people who make zumps are likely to rise. Show why, using a graph.

8. During the 1990s, the UK electricity industry was sold by the government to the private sector. Several years later, some of the people who had been running the industry when it was in government hands were still senior executives. However, their private sector salaries were now several times higher. Is it possible to use the concepts of derived demand and marginal revenue product to justify such enormous salary increases?

9. Jan's farm, near Ostende, has four major fields that he uses to grow potatoes. The productivity of each field is given in Table 3.

Table 3	
Field	Annual yield (hundreds of kilos)
1	10,000
2	8,000
3	5,000
4	3,000

Assume that each field is the same size and that the variable costs of farming are €25,000 per year per field. The variable costs cover labour and machinery time, which is rented. Jan must decide each year how many fields to plant. In 1996, potato farmers received €6.35 per hundred kilos.

How many fields did Jan plant? Explain. By 1998, the price of potatoes had fallen to €4.50 per hundred kilos. How would this price decrease have affected Jan's decision? How would it have affected his demand for labour? What effect will it have had on the value of the land?

10. Assume that you are living in a house with two other people and that the house has a big lawn that has to be mowed. One of your housemates, who hates to work outdoors, suggests that you hire a neighbour's daughter to mow the grass for €20 per week, rather than share the work between yourselves. How would you go about deciding? What factors would you raise when deciding? What are the trade-offs here?

11. Table 4 contains information about a T-shirt manufacturing firm that can sell as many T-shirts as it wants for €3 per shirt.
a. Fill in the blanks in the table.
b. Verify that MRP_L for this firm can be calculated in two ways: (1) the change in TR from adding another worker; or (2) MP_L times the price of output.
c. If this firm must pay a wage rate of €40 per worker per day, how many workers should it hire? Briefly, why?
d. Suppose the wage rate rises to €50 per worker. How many workers should be taken on now? Why?
e. Suppose the firm adopts a new technology that doubles output at each level of employment and that the price of shirts remains at €3. What is the effect of this

Table 4				
Number of workers	Number of shirts produced per day	MP_L	TR	MRP_L
0	0			
1	30			
2	80			
3	110			
4	135			
5		20		
6	170			
7				30
8				15

new technology on MP_L? MRP_L? At a wage of €50, how many workers should the firm hire now?

12. For a given firm, $MRP_L = €50$ and $MRP_K = €100$, while $P_L = €10$ and $P_K = €20$.
a. Is the firm maximizing profits? Why, or why not?
b. Can you identify a specific action that would increase this firm's profits?

11

The Capital Market and the Investment Decision

We saw in Chapter 10 that perfectly competitive firms hire factors of production (inputs) up to the point at which the marginal revenue product of each factor is equal to the price of that factor. The three main factors of production are land, labour and capital. We also saw that factor prices are determined by the interaction of supply and demand in the factor markets. The wage rate is determined in the labour market, the price of land is determined in the land market, and the price of capital is determined in the capital market.

In Chapter 10, we explored the labour and land markets in some detail. In this chapter we consider the demand for capital and the capital market more fully. Transactions between households and firms in the labour and land markets are direct. In the labour market, households offer their labour directly to firms in exchange for wages, and in the land market landowners rent or sell their land directly to firms in exchange for rent or an agreed price. In the capital market, though, households often indirectly supply the financial resources necessary for firms to purchase capital. When households save and add funds to their bank accounts, for example, firms can borrow these funds from the bank to finance their capital purchases.

Earlier, in Chapter 9, we discussed the incentives of new firms entering industries in which profit opportunities exist, and the incentives that existing firms have to leave industries in which they are suffering economic losses. We also described the conditions under which existing firms have an incentive either to expand or to reduce their scales of operation. That chapter was in a preliminary way describing the process of capital allocation. When new firms enter an industry or an existing firm expands, someone pays to put capital (plant, equipment and stocks) in place. Because the future is uncertain, capital investment decisions always involve risk. In market capitalist systems the decision to put capital to use in a particular enterprise is made by private citizens putting their savings at risk in search of private gain. This chapter describes the set of institutions through which such transactions take place.

Capital, investment and depreciation

Before we proceed with our analysis of the capital market, we need to review some basic economic principles and introduce some related concepts.

Capital

capital Those goods produced by the economic system that are used as inputs to produce other goods and services in the future.

One of the most important concepts in all of economics is the concept of **capital**.

Capital goods are those goods produced by the economic system that are used as inputs to produce other goods and services in the future. Capital goods thus yield valuable productive services over time.

Tangible capital

When we think of capital, we generally think of the physical capital employed by business firms. The major categories of **physical**, or **tangible**, capital are (1) non-residential structures (office buildings, power plants, factories, shopping centres, warehouses and docks, for example); (2) durable equipment (machines, lorries, sandwich grills, cars and so on); (3) residential structures; and (4) stocks (inventories) of inputs and outputs that firms hold.

Most firms need tangible capital, along with labour and land, to produce their products. A restaurant's capital requirements include a kitchen, ovens and grills, tables and chairs, silverware, dishes and light fittings. These items must be purchased up front and maintained if the restaurant is to function properly. A manufacturing firm must have a plant, specialized machinery, lorries and stocks of parts. A winery needs casks, vats, piping, temperature-control equipment, and cooking and bottling machinery.

The capital stock of a retail chemists is made up mostly of stocks. Chemists do not produce the aspirin, vitamin tablets and toothbrushes that they sell. Instead, they buy those things from manufacturers and put them on display. The product actually produced and sold by a chemist is convenience. Like any other product, convenience is produced with labour and capital in the form of a shop with lots of products, or stock, displayed on the sales floor and kept in storerooms. The stocks of inputs and outputs that manufacturing firms maintain are also capital. To function smoothly and meet the demands of buyers, for example, a car producer such as Volvo maintains stocks of both car parts (tyres, windscreens etc.) and completed cars.

A block of flats is also capital. Produced by the economic system, it yields valuable services over time, and it is used as an input to produce housing services, which are rented out.

Social capital: infrastructure

Some physical or tangible capital is owned by the public rather than by private firms. **Social capital**, sometimes called **infrastructure**, is capital that provides services to the public. Most social capital takes the form of public works like motorways, roads, bridges, and in most European countries, sewer and water systems. Police stations, fire stations, town halls, law courts and police cars are all forms of social capital that are used as inputs to produce the services that government provides.

All firms use some forms of social capital in producing their outputs. Recent economic research has shown that a country's infrastructure plays a very important role in helping private firms produce their products efficiently. When public capital is not properly cared for – for example, when roads deteriorate or when traffic lights are not modernized to accommodate increasing traffic – private firms that depend on efficient transport networks suffer. When governments are seeking ways to reduce expenditure, they find it politically difficult to cut *current* expenditure – social security and pensions, for example. The temptation is to take the easy, short-term solution and cut spending on infrastructure – such as road and bridge buildings and repairs. In the longer term this can be harmful. Lorries are forced to spend longer in queues and motorway jams, increasing firms' costs and eventually their prices.

Intangible capital

Not all capital is physical. Some things that are **intangible** (non-material) satisfy every part of our definition of capital. When a business firm invests in advertising to establish a brand name, it is producing a form of intangible capital called goodwill. This goodwill yields valuable services to the firm over time.

When a firm establishes a training programme for employees, it is investing in its workers' skills. One can think of such an investment as the production of an intangible form of capital called **human capital**. It is produced with labour (teachers and trainers) and capital (classrooms, computers, projectors and books). Human capital in the form of new or augmented skills is an input – it will yield valuable productive services for the firm in the future.

---

physical *or* tangible capital
Material things used as inputs in the production of future goods and services. The major categories of physical capital are non-residential structures, durable equipment, residential structures, and stocks.

social capital, *or* infrastructure
Capital that provides services to the public. Most social capital takes the form of public works (roads and bridges) and public services (police and fire protection).

intangible capital
Non-material things that contribute to the output of future goods and services.

human capital
A form of intangible capital that includes the skills and other knowledge that workers have or acquire through education and training and that yields valuable services to a firm over time.

When research produces valuable results, such as a new production process that reduces costs or a new formula that creates a new product, the new technology itself can be considered capital. Furthermore, even ideas can be patented and the rights to them can be sold.

The time dimension

The most important dimension of capital is the fact that it exists through time. Labour services are used at the time they are provided. Households consume services and non-durable goods[1] almost immediately after purchase. But capital exists now and into the future. Therefore:

> The value of capital is only as great as the value of the services it will render over time.[2]

Measuring capital

Labour is measured in hours, and land is measured in square metres or hectares. But because capital comes in so many forms, it is virtually impossible to measure it directly in physical terms. The indirect measure generally used is *current market value*. The measure of a firm's **capital stock** is the current market value of its plant, equipment, stocks and intangible assets. Using value as a measuring stick, business managers, accountants and economists can, in a sense, add buildings, barges and bulldozers into a measure of total capital.

capital stock The current market value of a firm's plant, equipment, stocks and intangible assets.

Capital is measured as a stock value. That is, it is measured at a point in time. Although it is measured in terms of money, or value, it is very important to think of the actual capital stock itself:

> When we speak of capital, we refer not to money or to financial assets such as bonds or stocks, but rather to the firm's physical plant, equipment, stocks and intangible assets.

Investment and depreciation

Recall the difference between stock and flow measures discussed in earlier chapters. *Stock measures* are valued at a particular point in time, while *flow measures* are valued over a period of time. The easiest way to think of the difference between a stock and a flow is to think about a bath of water. The volume of water in the bath is measured at a point in time and is a stock. The amount of water that flows into the bath *per hour* and the amount of water that evaporates out of the bath *per day* are flow measures. Flow measures have meaning only when the time dimension is added. Clearly, water flowing into the bath at a rate of five litres per hour is very different from a rate of five litres per year.

Capital stock is affected over time by two flows: investment and depreciation. When a firm produces or puts in place new capital – a new piece of equipment, for

---

[1]Consumer goods are generally divided into two categories: durables and non-durables. Technically, durable goods are goods expected to last for more than one year. Non-durable goods are goods expected to last less than one year.

[2]Conceptually, consumer durable goods, such as cars, washing machines and the like, are capital. They are produced, they yield services over time, and households use them as inputs to produce services such as transport and clean clothes.

Table 11.1 Gross fixed investment in major European economies, 1997

Country	Percentage of GDP
Belgium	17.4
France	19.7
Germany	21.9
Netherlands	19.7*
Ireland	16.8
Italy	17.7
Spain	22.5
Sweden	18.3
UK	17.6

* = 1996

Source: National Accounts.

investment New capital additions to a firm's capital is measured at a given point in time (a stock); investment is measured over a period of time (a flow). The flow of investment increases the stock of capital.

example – it has invested. **Investment** is a flow that increases the stock of capital. Because it has a time dimension, we speak of investment per period (by the month, quarter or year).

As you proceed, be careful to keep in mind that the term *investing* is not used in economics to describe the act of buying a share of stock or a bond. Although people commonly use the term this way ('I invested in some Nestlé stock' or 'He invested in Treasury bonds'), the term *investment* when used correctly refers *only to an increase in capital.*

Table 11.1 presents data on gross investment in some of the European economies in 1997. Typically, around half of the total is in new durable equipment. Almost all the rest is investment in structures, both residential (flats, houses and so forth) and non-residential (factories, shopping malls and so forth). Investment in stocks will always be much smaller.

depreciation The decline in an asset's economic value over time.

Depreciation is the decline in an asset's economic value over time. If you have ever owned a car, you are aware that its resale value falls with age. For Annamari, only a new BMW will fit her image as a beautiful student. She bought a new BMW in 1998 for DM 50,000 and decided to sell it two years and 25,000 miles later. Checking the newspaper and talking to several dealers, she finds out that, given its condition and the mileage, she can expect to get DM 30,000 for it.

The car has depreciated DM 20,000 (DM 50,000 – 30,000) The figures in Table 11.1 relate to gross investment – investment before any allowance for depreciation has been made.

Calculations of the depreciation of investment are rather arbitrary. It is the difference between the value of the capital at the beginning of the period and its value at the end of the period. Since companies will not normally be selling the capital at this stage we cannot be sure what its value is. An estimate must be made. Usually about half of gross investment will be the replacement of worn out capital stock and the other half will be net investment, additions to the stock of capital.

A capital asset can depreciate because it wears out physically or because it becomes obsolete. Take, for example, a computer control system in a factory. If a new, technologically superior system is developed that does the same job for half the price, the old system may be replaced even if it still functions well. The BMW depreciated because of wear and tear and because new models had become available.

Norway's nervousness over North Sea oil investment

Most governments are eager to see high levels of investment in their economies. Occasionally they worry that they may have too much of a good thing. Norwegian investment in North Sea Oil production is an example.

At giant North Sea platforms on the continental shelf off Norway's coast, the oil is surging up from the sea bottom at a record pace. With oil and gas expected to bring in some $25.3 billion in 1997, the country is experiencing an economic boom that most European countries would envy.

Yet Norway, the world's second-largest oil exporter, has grown surprisingly uneasy about its wealth. Worried that the country's 4.3 million population will get hooked on oil money

and that the flow of petrodollars will overheat the economy, some politicians are calling for a cap on oil production at the current level of 3.1 million barrels per day. The reasoning: putting the brakes on production now would slow the rise of the krone, help check inflation, and preserve resources for future generations.

Inevitably, the companies themselves are unenthusiastic about the possible limitations on their activities and are seeking ways around it.

Companies such as Saga are taking precautionary steps. Late last year, Saga surprised the industry by acquiring Santa Fe International Corp., a production and drilling company, from Kuwait for £1.2 billion. By buying Santa Fe, which has substantial reserves in the

British North Sea, Saga seemed to be hedging against actions of its own government. 'As a Norwegian company, it's not good to have all our eggs in one Norwegian basket', Anders Utne, executive vice-president, explains.

Most industry sources doubt the government will push through the production caps. There

could, however, be a slowdown on awards of new acreage for exploration. Even so, production on the continental shelf is expected to grow by 20% over the next 10 years, to more than 4 million barrels.

Source: 'The gusher that's making Norwegians nervous', Business Week, European edn, 10 March 1997.

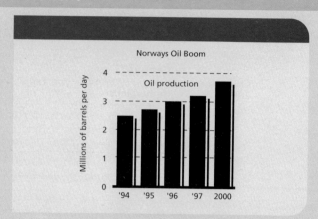

Norways Oil Boom

The capital market

Where does capital come from? How and why is it produced? How much and what kinds of capital are produced? Who pays for it? These questions are answered in the complex set of institutions in which households supply their savings to firms that demand funds in order to buy capital goods. Collectively, these institutions are called the **capital market**.

capital market
The market in which households supply their savings to funds in order to buy capital goods.

Although governments and households make some capital investment decisions, most decisions to produce new capital goods – that is, to invest – are made by firms. However, a firm cannot invest unless it has the funds to do so. Although firms can invest in many ways, it is always the case that:

The funds that firms use to buy capital goods come, directly or indirectly, from households. When a household decides not to consume a portion of its income, it saves. Investment by firms is the *demand for capital*. Saving by households is the *supply of capital*. Various financial institutions facilitate the transfer of households' savings to firms that use them for capital investment.

Let us use a simple example to see how the system works. Suppose that a firm wants to purchase a machine that costs 1000 guilders and that some Dutch household

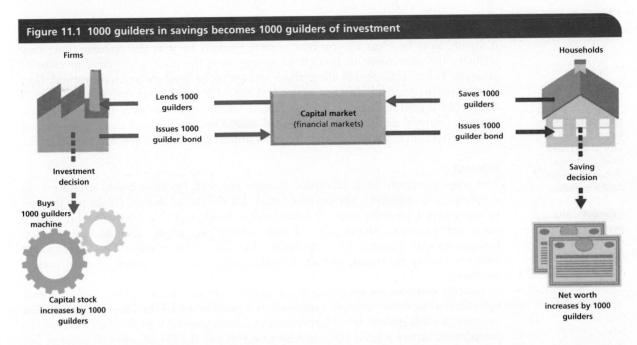

Figure 11.1 1000 guilders in savings becomes 1000 guilders of investment

decides at the same time to save 1000 guilders from its income. Figure 11.1 shows one way in which the household's decision to save might connect with the firm's decision to invest.

Either directly or through a financial intermediary (such as a bank), the household agrees to loan its savings to the firm. In exchange, the firm contracts to pay the household interest at some agreed-upon rate each period. If the household lends directly to the firm, the firm gives the household a **bond**, which is nothing more than a contract that promises to repay the loan at some specific time in the future. The bond also specifies the flow of interest to be paid in the meantime.

The new saving adds to the household's stock of wealth. The household's net worth has increased by the 1000 guilders, which it holds in the form of a bond.[3] The bond represents the firm's promise to repay the 1000 guilders at some future date with interest. The firm uses the 1000 guilders to buy a new machine costing 1000 guilders, which it adds to its capital stock. In essence, the household has supplied the capital demanded by the firm. It's almost as if the household bought the machine and rented it to the firm for an annual fee. Presumably, this investment will generate added profits that will facilitate the payment of interest to the household.

In general, projects are undertaken as long as the profits likely to be realized from the investment are sufficient to cover the interest payments to the household.

Sometimes the transfer of household savings through the capital market into investment occurs without a financial intermediary. Recall from Chapter 4 that an *entrepreneur* is one who organizes, manages, and assumes the risk of a firm. When an entrepreneur starts a new business by buying capital with his own savings, he is both demanding capital and supplying the resources (that is, his savings) needed to purchase that capital; no third party is involved in the transaction. Most investment, however, is accomplished with the help of financial intermediaries (third parties such as banks, insurance companies and pension funds) that stand between the supplier (saver) and the demander (investing firm). The part of the capital market in which savers and investors interact through intermediaries is often called the **financial capital market**.

bond A contract between a borrower and a lender in which the borrower agrees to pay the loan at some time in the future along with interest payments along the way.

financial capital market

The part of the capital market in which savers and investors interact through intermediaries.

[3]Note that it is the act of saving that increases the household's wealth, not the act of buying the bond. Buying the bond simply transforms one financial asset (money) into another (a bond). The household could simply have held on to the money.

Capital income: interest and profits

It should now be clear to you how capital markets fit into the circular flow: they facilitate the movement of household savings into the most productive investment projects. When households allow their savings to be used to purchase capital, they receive payments, and these payments (along with wages and salaries) are part of household incomes. Income that is earned on savings that have been put to use through financial capital markets is called capital income. Capital income is received by households in many forms, the two most important of which are *interest* and *profits*.

capital income
Income earned on savings that have been put to use through financial capital markets.

Interest

The most common form of capital income received by households is interest. In simplest terms, interest is the payment made for the use of money. Banks pay interest to depositors, whose deposits are loaned out to businesses or individuals who want to make investments.[4] Banks also charge interest to those who borrow money. Companies pay interest to households that buy their bonds. The government borrows money by issuing bonds, and the buyers of those bonds receive interest payments.

interest The payments made for the use of money. Interest is almost always expressed as an annual rate.

Interest is almost always expressed as an annual rate. The *interest rate* is the agreed-upon annual interest payment expressed as a percentage of the loan or deposit. For example, a 1000 guilder bond (representing a 1000 guilder loan from a household to a firm) that carries a fixed 10% interest rate will pay the household 100 guilders per year (1000 guilders × 0.10) in interest. A savings account that carries a 5% annual interest rate will pay 50 guilders annually on a balance of 1000 guilders.

The interest rate is usually agreed to at the time a loan or deposit is made. Sometimes, borrowers and lenders agree to adjust periodically the level of interest payments depending on market conditions. These types of loans are called *adjustable* or *floating rate loans*. (*Fixed-rate loans* are loans in which the interest rate never varies.) In recent years there have even been adjustable rates of interest on savings accounts and certificates of deposit.

A loan's interest rate depends on a number of factors. A loan that involves more risk will generally pay a higher interest rate than a loan with less risk. For example, a large corporation such as Shell or BMW will be able to negotiate a loan on more favourable terms than a small firm that has only recently begun trading. A bank will want a higher interest payment from the small firm as compensation for the greater risk it is taking in making the loan.

You may have seen adverts by finance companies offering to loan money 'regardless of credit history'. They are willing to lend to those who pose a relatively high risk of *defaulting*, or not paying off the loan. But be warned. Since their risk is higher they will charge a much higher interest rate.

Most governments would expect to borrow money more cheaply than even the largest firms. This is because most people believe that there is little risk that the government will default on the loans. However, some governments pay more to borrow funds than other governments. If you lend to a government and there is inflation in the economy, the government will be paying you back in the future in currency that has become worth less to you. For this you will want compensation from that government in the form of a higher interest rate. Hence, historically, low-inflation economies such as Switzerland and Germany have governments who can borrow funds more cheaply than those of countries such as Spain and Italy whose inflation record is poorer.

[4]*Although we are focusing on investment by businesses, households can and do make investments too. The most important form of household investment is the construction of a new house, usually financed by borrowing in the form of a mortgage. A household may also borrow to finance the purchase of an existing house, but, when it does so, no new investment is taking place.*

Profits

profit The excess of revenues over cost in a given period

As the term is commonly used, **profit** means any excess of revenues over cost in a given period. Profits can be earned by all forms of business enterprise: proprietorships, partnerships and corporations. Profits are part of the incomes of proprietors and partners. Companies, in contrast, often do not pay out all of their profits to shareholders. As you saw in Chapter 3, corporate profits are divided into three categories: dividends (profits distributed to shareholders), retained earnings (profits not distributed to shareholders), and profit taxes.

Recall that the term *profits*, as used in economics, refers to *economic*, or *excess*, profits – that is, profits over and above a normal return. Economic profit is defined this way because true economic cost includes the opportunity cost of capital. Suppose, for example, that I decide to open a wine shop in France that requires an initial investment of 100,000 francs. Clearly, if I borrow the 100,000 francs from a bank, I am not making a profit until I cover the interest payments on my loan.

Even if I use my own savings or raise the funds I need by selling shares in my business, I am not making a profit until I cover the opportunity cost of using those funds to start my business. Because I always have the option of lending my funds at the current market interest rate, I earn an economic profit only when I earn a rate of return that is higher than the market interest rate. For example, if the market interest rate is 11%, the annual profits my wine shop earns would not be considered economic profits unless they are greater than 11,000 francs. The first 11,000 francs of my profits is actually part of the cost of capital – it is the normal return on a 100,000 franc investment when the interest rate is 11% (100,000 francs × 0.11 = 11,000 francs).

As another example, suppose that the Kauai Lamp Company was started in 1998, and that 100% of the 1 million euros needed to start up the company (to buy the plant and equipment) was raised by selling shares of stock. Now suppose that the company earns a total profit of €200,000 per year, all of which is paid out to shareholders. Because €200,000 is 20% of the company's total capital stock, we could say that the firm is enjoying a 20% rate of profit and that shareholders are earning profits of €200,000. But only a part of that €200,000 is economic profit. If the market interest rate is 10%, then 10% of €1 million (€100,000) is really part of the cost of capital. Not until the firm earns over a 10% rate of return on its investment is it earning economic profits.

Functions of interest and profit

Capital income serves several functions. First, interest and profit may function as incentives to postpone gratification. When you save, you forgo the chance to buy things that you want right now. Rather than spend and consume something today, you decide to spend and consume something in the future, using what you hope will be increased funds. One view of interest and profit holds that they are the rewards for postponing consumption.

Second, interest and profit also serve as rewards for innovation and risk taking. The entrepreneur's goal is to reap rewards in the form of profits from the new enterprise. When a new firm succeeds in a big way, the rewards can be enormous. Successful entrepreneurs have accumulated huge fortunes, for example, Agnelli's Fiat empire in Italy and the Siemens electronics business in Germany. More recently, Margaret Barbour of the Barbour outdoor clothing business has become very wealthy. More recently still, Peter Dawe became one of the first Internet multi-millionaires when he sold his Unipalm business in 1996.

There is now a possibility that Russian citizens may be added to this list. The economy of the former Soviet Union was centrally planned, with social ownership of capital. As such, capital was allocated among the sectors of the economy by plan, and capital markets did not exist. Now Russia has banks, a stock market (although share valuations fluctuate considerably), a bond market, and even a venture capital industry.

Many argue that rewards for innovation and risk taking are the essence of the free enterprise system. The potential for big financial rewards is one factor that motivates innovation, and innovation is good for much of society. Ideas lead to new products and new ways of producing things. Innovation is at the core of economic growth and progress. More efficient production techniques mean that the resources saved can be used to produce new things. There is another side to this story, however: critics of the free enterprise system claim that such large rewards are not justified and that accumulations of great wealth and power are not in society's best interests.

Financial markets in action

As you have seen, when a firm issues a fixed-interest bond, it borrows funds and pays interest at an agreed rate to the person or institution that buys the bond. Many other mechanisms, four of which are illustrated below (and see Figure 11.2), also channel household savings into investment projects. The Global Perspective box 'Rural Credit in Bangladesh and Indonesia' offers additional examples.

Case A: business loans

As Luigi looks around his home town, he sees several ice cream shops doing very well, but thinks that he can make better ice cream than they do. To go into the business, he needs capital: ice cream making equipment, tables, chairs, freezers, signs, and suitable premises. Because he puts up his house as collateral, he is not a big risk, and the bank grants him a loan at a fairly reasonable interest rate. Banks have these funds to lend only because households deposit their savings there.

Case B: venture capital

A scientist at a leading Dutch university develops an inexpensive method of producing a very important family of virus-fighting drugs using micro-organisms created through gene splicing. This is a new process and a new business, and no one really

Figure 11.2 Financial markets link household saving and investment by firms

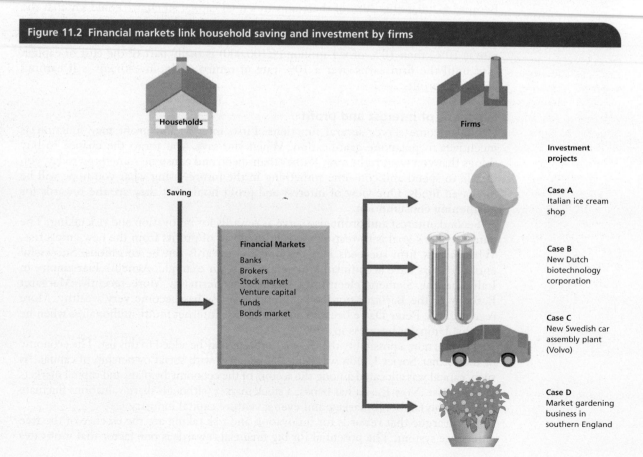

knows whether it will be profitable or not. The business could very well fail within 12 months, but if it succeeds the potential for profit is huge.

Our scientist goes to a *venture capital fund* for financing. Such funds take household savings and put them into high-risk ventures in exchange for a share of the profits if the new businesses succeed. By investing in many different projects, the funds reduce the risk of going broke. Once again, household funds make it possible for firms to undertake investments. If a venture succeeds, those owning shares in the venture capital fund receive substantial profits.

Global Perspectives

Rural Credit in Bangladesh

Recently, the US government established a $382 million fund to expand lending in poor central city and rural areas, where commercial banks find it too risky to lend. The idea was based on a successful rural credit institution in Bangladesh called the Grameen ('Village') Bank.

The Grameen Bank was founded in 1977 by a US-trained economist named Mohammed Yunus. The project was supported by the Bangladesh Bank and seven other government owned commercial banks. Within four years, the Grameen Bank had extended its operations to 433 villages. By 1995, it had loaned money to 1.6 million people in 32,000 villages. The average loan is about $100 and the maximum loan is $1200. A small farmer might borrow money to buy a cow, or a fisherman might borrow to buy materials for a fishing net. The most amazing thing about the Grameen Bank is that 96% of its loans have been paid back in full.

One of the bank's interesting innovations is that it lends to groups. Loans are made to groups of five people of roughly equal socioeconomic status. These groups elect their own leaders and discipline is maintained through peer pressure. The groups must meet weekly and make weekly instalment payments:

Lending to small groups formed by potential borrowers who are collectively responsible for repayment serves several purposes. Small groups . . . generate a sense of belonging and a clear perception that each individual's performance is crucial to the group's overall success or failure. Motivated group members tend to monitor their more lax peers, for no group member can receive further credit until the entire group's debts are repaid.[1]

Grameen Bank's function is exactly the same as the function of Citibank, the stock market, and other financial intermediaries: to collect household saving and make it available to businesses, which pay a fee to use it for the purchase or creation of capital.

A number of small funds supported by foundations have opened in the United States on the Grameen model. Most seem to have very low default rates on loans to very small enterprises in rural or central city areas. But to date, the scale is nothing like it is in Bangladesh.

An institution similar to the Grameen Bank is the Unit Desa ('village unit') of the Bank Rakyat Indonesia, which supplies credit and collects saving in rural Indonesia. A recent report describes two typical loans.[2] One loan of 1.2 million rupiah (about $700) was made to a couple to buy a grinding and milling machine to be used for grinding coffee and milling corn and rice. Before taking the loan, the family was making a living in petty trading. After the loan, the family operated a processing service for the surrounding area and had three full-time employees outside the immediate family. It paid the loan back in full.

Another loan of 3 million rupiah (about $1800) was made to two partners to buy a steam furnace for a bean-curd processing factory. At the time the loan was made, the factory employed four workers and supplied about fifteen beancurd

Bangladeshis harvest potato, a third major food crop after rice and wheat, at a field near capital Dhaka.
Photo: Rafiqur Rahman

peddlers a day. With the steam processor, the output of the factory doubled and four additional full-time workers were hired.

[1] *Jacob Yaron, 'Successful rural finance institutions',* Finance and Development *(March 1994), p. 34.*

[2] *Richard Patton and Jay Rosengard,* Progress with Profits: The Development of Rural Banking in Indonesia *(Cambridge, MA: Harvard Institute for International Development, 1990).*

Case C: retained earnings

Volvo decides that it wants to build a new assembly plant in Sweden, and it discovers that it has enough funds to pay for the new facility. The new investment is thus paid for through internal funds, or *retained earnings*.

The result is exactly the same as if the firm had gone to households via some financial intermediary and borrowed the funds to pay for the new plant. Volvo is owned by its shareholders. When the company earns a profit, that profit really belongs to the shareholders. If Volvo uses its profits to buy new capital, it does so only with the shareholders' implicit consent. When a firm takes its own profit and uses it to buy capital assets instead of paying it out to its shareholders, the total value of the firm goes up, as does the value of the shares held by stockholders. As in the other examples, Volvo's capital stock increases, and so does the net worth of households.

When a household owns a share of stock that *appreciates*, or increases in value, the appreciation is part of the household's income. Unless the household sells the stock and consumes the gain, that gain is part of saving. In essence, when a firm retains earnings for investment purposes, it is actually saving on behalf of its shareholders.

Case D: the stock market

A former government official decides to take early retirement to start a new market gardening business in southern England, and he also decides to raise the funds needed by issuing shares of stock. Households buy the shares with income that they decide not to spend. In exchange, they are entitled to a share of the market garden's profits.

The shares of stock become part of households' net worth. The proceeds from stock sales are used to buy plant equipment and stock. Savings flow into investment, and the firm's capital stock goes up by the same amount as household net worth.

Capital accumulation and allocation

You can see from the preceding examples that various, and sometimes complex, connections between households and firms facilitate the movement of saving into productive investment. The methods may differ, but the results are the same.

Think again about Anna and David, whom we discussed in Chapter 2. They found themselves alone on a deserted island. They had to make choices about how to allocate available resources, including their time. One important choice was how much energy to devote to producing goods and services for present consumption and how much to devote to investment that will bring future enjoyment. By spending long hours working on a house or a boat, Anna and David are saving and investing. First, they are using resources that could be used to produce more immediate rewards – they could gather more food or simply lie in the sun and relax. Second, they are applying those resources to the production of capital and capital accumulation.

Industrialized or agrarian, small or large, simple or complex, all societies exist through time and must allocate resources over time. In simple societies, investment and saving decisions are made by the same people. Anna and David decide whether to forgo present pleasures (consumption) and whether to produce capital goods (a house, a boat). However:

In modern industrial societies, investment decisions (capital production decisions) are made primarily by firms. Households decide how much to save, and in the long run saving limits or constrains the amount of investment that firms can undertake. The capital market exists to direct savings into profitable investment projects.

The demand for new capital, and the investment decision

We saw in Chapter 9 that firms have an incentive to expand in industries that earn economic profits (that is, profits over and above the normal rate of return) and in industries in which economies of scale lead to lower average costs at higher levels of output. We also saw that economic profits in an industry stimulate the entry of new firms. The expansion of existing firms and the creation of new firms both involve investment in new capital.

Even when there are no economic profits in an industry, firms must still do some investing. First, equipment wears out and must be replaced if the firm is to stay in business. Second, firms are constantly changing. A new technology may become available, sales patterns may shift, or the firm may expand or contract its product line.

With these points in mind, we now turn to a discussion of the investment decision process within the individual firm. In the end we will see (just as we did in Chapter 10) that a perfectly competitive firm invests in capital up to the point at which the marginal revenue product of capital is equal to the price of capital. (Because we based much of our discussion in Chapter 10 on the assumption of perfect competition, it makes sense to continue doing so here. Keep in mind, though, that much of what we say here also applies to firms that are not perfectly competitive.)

Forming expectations

We have already said that the most important dimension of capital is time. Capital produces useful services over some *period of time*. In building an office block, a developer makes an investment that will be around for decades. In deciding where to build a branch plant, a manufacturing firm commits a large amount of resources to purchase capital that will be in place for a long time.

It is important to remember, though, that capital goods do not begin to yield benefits until they are used. Often, the decision to build a building or purchase a piece of equipment must be made years before the actual project is completed. While the acquisition of a small business computer may take only days, the planning and building of the Channel Tunnel took many years before it finally opened for business in 1994.

The expected benefits of investments

Decision makers must have expectations about what is going to happen in the future. A new plant will be very valuable – that is, it will produce much profit – if the market for a firm's product grows and the price of that product remains high. The same plant will be worth little if the economy goes into a slump or consumers grow tired of the firm's product. An office block may turn out to be an excellent investment if all the space gets rented at market rents that are as high as, or higher than, rents in other office blocks, but it may be a poor investment if many new office buildings go up at the same time, flooding the office space market, pushing up the vacancy rate, and driving down rents. It follows, then, that:

> The investment process requires that the potential investor evaluate the expected flow of future productive services that an investment project will yield.

Remember that households, business firms and governments all undertake investments. A household must evaluate the future services that a new roof will yield. A firm must evaluate the flow of future revenues that a new plant will generate. Governments must estimate how much benefit society will derive from a new bridge or a war memorial.

It is not easy to evaluate the future flow of revenues that will come from an investment project. Take, for example, the construction of the Channel Tunnel by the Eurotunnel company. The total cost of digging, laying the tracks, ordering the trains and so on came to around £10 billion (90 billion French francs). Would the income from selling journeys through the tunnel justify such a cost? The problems of evaluating the revenue stream from this investment included the following. What would be the total number of cross-channel journeys? By freight companies? By car? By foot passengers? How fast would this market grow? What proportion of the market would

Eurotunnel gain? Would the ferries engage in a price war and cut their prices, forcing Eurotunnel's prices down? Even now, several years after the tunnel opened, it is not clear whether future revenues will be sufficient to justify the original costs of construction.

All firms, not just Eurotunnel, must rely on forecasts to make sensible investment and production decisions, but forecasting is an inexact science because so much depends on events that cannot be foreseen.

The expected costs of investments

The benefits of any investment project take the form of future profits. These profits must be forecast. But costs must also be evaluated. Like households, firms have access to financial markets, both as borrowers and as lenders. If a firm borrows, it must *pay* interest over time; if it lends, it will *earn* interest. If the firm borrows to finance a project, the interest on the loan is part of the cost of the project.

Even if a project is financed with the firm's own funds, rather than by borrowing, there is an opportunity cost involved. A thousand euros put into a capital investment project will generate an expected flow of future profit; the same thousand euros put into the financial market (in essence, loaned to another firm) will yield a flow of interest payments. The project will not be undertaken unless it is expected to yield more than the market interest rate will yield. The cost of an investment project may thus be direct or indirect because:

The ability to lend at the market rate means that there is an opportunity cost associated with every investment project. The evaluation process thus involves not only estimating future benefits, but also comparing them with the possible alternative uses of the funds required to undertake the project. At a minimum, those funds could earn interest in financial markets.

Comparing costs and expected return

Once expectations have been formed, firms must quantify them – that is, they must assign some money value to them. One way to quantify expectations is to calculate an **expected rate of return** on the investment project. For example, if a new computer network that costs €400,000 is likely to save €100,000 per year in data processing costs for ever afterwards, the expected rate of return on that investment is 25% per year. Each year, the firm will save €100,000 as a result of the 400,000 euro investment. The expected rate of return will be less than 25% if the computer network wears out or becomes obsolete after a while and the cost savings cease.

For example, if the network lasts only ten years (with cost savings of €100,000 in each of the ten years), after which time it is worthless and the savings cease, the expected rate of return will be only 21.4 %.[5] The expected rate of return will be even less if the network depreciates gradually during the ten years, resulting in cost savings of less than €100,000 in years two to ten. In short:

The expected rate of return on an investment project depends on the price of the investment, the expected length of time the project provides additional cost savings or revenue, and the expected amount of revenue attributable each year to the project.

Table 11.2 presents a menu of investment choices and expected rates of return that face a hypothetical firm with operations all over Europe. Because expected rates of return are based on forecasts of future profits attributable to the investments, any change in expectations would change all the numbers in column 2.

expected rate of return
The annual rate of return that a firm expects to obtain through a capital investment.

[5] *This 21.4% figure can be computed using the present-value analysis discussed in the appendix to this chapter.*

Table 11.2 Potential investment projects and expected rates of return for a hypothetical firm, based on forecasts of future profits attributable to the investment

Project	(1) Total investment (euros)	(2) Expected rate of return (%)
A. New computer network	400,000	25
B. New branch plant in Sweden	2,600,000	20
C. Another sales office in The Netherlands	1,500,000	15
D. New automated billing system	100,000	12
E. Ten new lorries	400,000	10
F. Advertising campaign in France	1,000,000	7
G. Employee cafeteria	100,000	5

Figure 11.3 graphs the total amount of investment in euros that the firm would undertake at various interest rates. If the interest rate were 24%, the firm would fund only Project A, the new computer network. It can borrow at 24% and invest in a computer that is expected to yield 25%. At 24%, then, the firm's total investment is €400,000. The first vertical orange line in Figure 11.3 shows that at any interest rate above 20% and below 25%, only €400,000 worth of investment (that is, Project A) will be undertaken.

If the interest rate were 18%, the firm would fund projects A and B, and its total investment would rise to €3 million (400,000 + 2,600,000). If the firm could borrow at 18%, the flow of additional profits generated by the new computer and the new plant in Sweden would more than cover the costs of borrowing, but none of the other projects would be justified. At an interest rate of 14%, the firm would undertake projects A, B and C, at a total cost of €4.5 million. Only if the interest rate fell below 5% would the firm fund all seven investment projects.

The investment schedule in Table 11.2 and its graphic depiction in Figure 11.3 describe the firm's demand for new capital, expressed as a function of the market interest rate. If we add the total investment undertaken by all firms at every interest rate, we arrive at the demand for new capital in the economy as a whole. In other

Figure 11.3 Total investment as a function of the market interest rate

The demand for new capital depends on the interest rate. When the interest rate is low, firms are more likely to invest in new plant and equipment than when the interest rate is high. This is because the interest rate determines the direct cost (interest on a loan) or the opportunity cost (alternative investment) of each project.

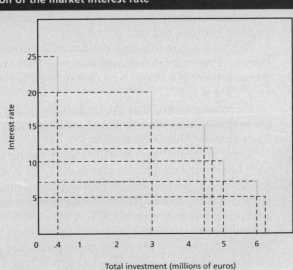

Total investment (millions of euros)

Figure 11.4 Investment demand

Lower interest rates are likely to stimulate investment in the economy as whole, while higher interest rates are likely to slow investment.

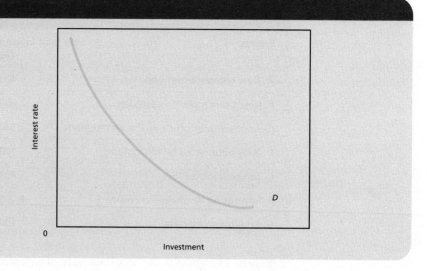

words, the market demand curve for new capital is simply the sum of all the individual demand curves for new capital in the economy (Figure 11.4). In a sense, the investment demand schedule is a ranking of all the investment opportunities in the economy in order of expected yield.

Only those investment projects in the economy that are expected to yield a rate of return higher than the market interest rate will be funded. At lower market interest rates, more investment projects are undertaken.

The most important thing to remember about the investment demand curve is that its shape and position depend critically on the *expectations* of those making the investment decisions. Because many influences affect these expectations, they are usually volatile and subject to frequent change. Thus, while lower interest rates tend to stimulate investment, and higher interest rates tend to slow it, many other hard-to-measure and hard-to-predict factors also affect the level of investment spending. These might include government policy changes, election results, global affairs, inflation, and changes in currency exchange rates.

Coping with risk and uncertainty

Since the future is not guaranteed, the expected return represents the best estimate of what the investment might achieve. How can firms make such estimates? First we distinguish between risk and uncertainty.

Risk means that although the future is unknown, the probability of any outcome *is* known. If you spin an unbiased coin you don't know on which side it will land, but you do know there is a 50 per cent chance of each of the two possible outcomes, heads and tails. That is risk.

Uncertainty means that the probability of any given outcome is also unknown. You know that either outcome *A* or *B* will occur but you do not know if *A* is more or less likely than *B*. That is uncertainty.

There are many ways in which firms can handle risk and uncertainty. We will look very briefly at one or two possibilities. First consider risk. Suppose a firm has an investment project where there is a 50% chance of a 14% rate of return and a 50% chance of a 4% rate of return. It might decide to treat this project as the equivalent of a certain 9% rate of return: (50% × 14) + (50% × 4). If however, it is cautious – that is, it is risk averse – it might prefer another project with a certain 9% rate of return. Now consider uncertainty where the above procedure is impossible because the probabilities are unknown. One possible way of approaching the problem of uncertainty is to use the principle of insufficient reason. This says that we have no sufficient reason for thinking that any one outcome is more or less likely than any other. The procedure is then similar to that for risk where all possible outcomes are treated as being equally likely.

The expected rate of return and the marginal revenue product of capital

The concept of the expected rate of return on investment projects is analogous to the concept of the marginal revenue product of capital (MRP_K). Recall that we defined marginal revenue product as the additional revenue a firm earns by employing one additional unit of an input, *ceteris paribus*. Also recall our earlier discussion of labour demand in a sandwich bar in Chapter 7. If an additional worker can produce 15 sandwiches in one hour (the marginal product of labour: $MP_L = 15$) and each sandwich brings in €0.5 (the price of the service produced by the sandwich shop: $P_X = €0.5$), the marginal revenue product of labour is equal to €7.5 ($MRP_L = MP_L \times P_X = 15 \times 0.5 = €7.5$).

Now think carefully about the return to an additional unit of new capital (the marginal revenue product of capital). Suppose that the expected rate of return on an investment in a new machine is 15%. This means that the investment project yields the same expected return as a bond yielding 15%. If the current interest rate is less than 15%, the investment project will be undertaken because:

A perfectly competitive profit-maximizing firm will keep investing in new capital up to the point at which the expected rate of return is equal to the interest rate. This is analogous to saying that the firm will continue investing up to the point at which the marginal revenue product of capital is equal to the price of capital, or $MRP_K = P_K$, which is what we learned in Chapter 10.

A final word on capital

The concept of capital is one of the central ideas in economics. Capital is produced by the economic system itself. Capital generates services over time, and it is used as an input in the production of goods and services.

The enormous productivity of modern industrial societies is due in part to the tremendous amount of capital that they have accumulated over the years. Some member countries of the European Union have enjoyed significantly higher growth rates than others in recent decades, though EU members have done less well than some non-EU countries. There are many reasons for this disparity. However, part of the explanation is to be found in the higher rates of investment found in some countries compared with others. Between 1980 and 1997, total fixed capital formation averaged just over 17% of GDP in the UK and around 21% in Germany. The comparable figure for Japan, where growth rates have been much higher than the EU average, was just under 30%. These figures, however, include house building and government investment. The differences are smaller if one considers investment in machinery and equipment only.

The bulk of this chapter described the institutions and processes that determine the amount and types of capital produced in a market economy. Existing firms in search of increased profits, potential new entrants to the markets, and entrepreneurs with new ideas all are continuously evaluating potential investment projects. At the same time, households are saving. Each year, households save some portion of their after-tax incomes. This new saving becomes part of their net worth, and they want to earn a return on it. Each year, a good portion of the saving finds its way into the hands of firms that use it to buy new capital goods.

Between households and firms is the financial capital market. Millions of people participate in financial markets every day. There are literally thousands of financial managers, pension funds, mutual funds, brokerage houses, options traders and commercial banks whose sole purpose is to earn the highest possible rate of return on people's saving.

Brokers, bankers and financial managers are continuously scanning the financial horizons for profitable investments. What businesses are doing well? What businesses are doing poorly? Should we lend to an expanding firm? All the analysis done by financial managers seeking to earn a high yield for clients, by managers of firms seeking to earn high profits for their stockholders, and by entrepreneurs seeking profits from innovation, serves to channel capital into its most productive uses. Within firms, the evaluation of individual investment projects involves forecasting costs and benefits and valuing streams of potential income that will be earned only in future years.

We have now completed our discussion of competitive input and output markets. We have looked at household and firm choices in output markets, labour markets, land markets and capital markets.

We now turn to a discussion of the allocative process that we have described. How do all the parts of the economy fit together? Is the result good or bad? Can we improve on it? All this is the subject of Chapter 12.

Summary

Capital, investment and depreciation

1. In market capitalist systems, the decision to put capital to use in a particular enterprise is made by private citizens putting their savings at risk in search of private gain. The set of institutions through which such transactions occur is called the *capital market*.

2. Capital goods are those goods produced by the economic system that are used as inputs to produce other goods and services in the future. Capital goods thus yield valuable productive services over time.

3. The major categories of *physical*, or *tangible*, *capital* are non-residential structures, durable equipment, residential structures, and stocks. *Social capital* is capital that provides services to the public. *Intangible (non-material) capital* includes *human capital* and goodwill.

4. The most important dimension of capital is that it exists through time. Therefore, its value is only as great as the value of the services it will render over time.

5. The most common measure of a firm's *capital stock* is the current market value of its plant, equipment, inventories and intangible assets. However, in thinking about capital it is important to think of the actual capital stock rather than its simple monetary value.

6. In economics, the term *investment* refers to the creation of new capital, not to the purchase of a share of stock or a bond. Investment is a flow that increases the capital stock.

7. *Depreciation* is the decline in an asset's economic value over time. A capital asset can depreciate because it wears out physically or because it becomes obsolete.

The capital market

8. Income that is earned on savings that have been put to use through *financial capital markets* is called *capital income*. The two most important forms of capital income are *interest* and *profits*. Interest is the fee paid by a borrower to a lender. Interest and profits reward households and entrepreneurs for innovation, risk taking and postponing gratification.

9. In modern industrial societies, investment decisions (capital production decisions) are made primarily by firms. Households decide how much to save; and in the long run, saving limits the amount of investment that firms can undertake. The capital market exists to direct savings into profitable investment projects.

The demand for new capital, and the investment decision

10. Before investing, investors must evaluate the expected flow of future productive services that an investment project will yield.

11. The availability of interest to lenders means that there is an opportunity cost associated with every investment project. This cost must be weighed against the stream of earnings that a project is expected to yield.

12. A firm will decide whether to undertake an investment project by comparing costs with expected returns. The *expected rate of return* on an investment project depends on the price of the investment, the expected length of time that the project provides additional cost savings or revenue, and the expected amount of revenue attributable each year to the project.

13. The investment demand curve shows the demand for capital in the economy as a function of the market interest rate. Only those investment projects that are expected to yield a rate of return higher than the market interest rate will be funded. Lower interest rates should stimulate investment.

14. A perfectly competitive, profit-maximizing firm will keep investing in new capital up to the point at which the expected rate of return is equal to the interest rate. This is equivalent to saying that the firm will continue investing up to the point at which the marginal revenue product of capital is equal to the price of capital, or $MRP_K = P_K$.

Review Terms and Concepts

bond
capital
capital income
capital market
capital stock
depreciation
expected rate of return
financial capital market

human capital
intangible capital
interest
investment
physical, or tangible, capital
profit
social capital, or infrastructure

Problem Set

1. Which of the following are capital, and which are not? Explain your answers:
a. A games machine at a local bar
b. A €50 note
c. A university education
d. A Logis de France hotel
e. The shirts on the rack in a department store
f. A government bond
g. The town's main car park
h. A savings account
i. The university library
j. A Hyundai plant in Scotland

2. Jean and 99 other partners are offered the chance to buy a petrol station on the outskirts of Bruges. Each partner would put up 10,000 Belgian francs. The revenues from the operation of the station have been steady at 420,000 francs per year for several years, and are projected to remain steady into the future. The costs (not including opportunity costs) of operating the station (including maintenance and repair, depreciation, salaries, and so forth) have also been steady at 360,000 francs per year. Currently, five-year Treasury bills are yielding 7.5% interest. Would you join in on the deal?

3. During the mid-1990s, many European countries, including Germany, France, Italy, Spain and Ireland, took action to raise interest rates. Rates peaked during 1995 before falling back somewhat in subsequent years. How might this action affect the productive capacity of these economies in the second half of the 1990s?

4. In each of the following, identify who is saving and who is investing. There need not be both actions in every example.

a. Frank sells some Benetton stock to Laura and uses the proceeds to buy ten shares of Reuters stock from Jim.
b. Sarah's income is £20,000 this year. She spent £19,000 and put the rest into Reuters stock.
c. A Paris developer borrows 350 million French francs from a group of banks and builds an office tower.
d. Marie's grandmother earns no income this year. Grandma supports herself by selling DM 5000 worth of bonds to a bond dealer.
e. Peter's income this year was €100,000. He spent €90,000 and put the rest into Luxembourg government bonds. The Luxembourg government used the proceeds to help build a power plant.

Table 1		
Project	Total cost (Singapore $)	Estimated rate of return (%)
Factory in Kuala Lumpur	17,356,400	13
Factory in Bangkok	15,964,200	15
A new company aircraft	10,000,000	12
A factory outlet store	3,500,000	18
A new computer network	2,000,000	20
A cafeteria for workers	1,534,000	7

5. The board of directors of the Quando Company in Singapore was presented with a list of investment projects for implementation in 1998 (Table 1)

Sketch total investment as a function of the interest rate (with the interest rate on the Y axis). Currently, the interest rate in Singapore is 8%. How much investment would you recommend to Quando's board?

6. Give at least three examples of how savings can be channelled into productive investment. Why is investment so important for an economy? What do you sacrifice when you invest today?

7. 'Lower interest rates are discouraging to households, so they are likely to invest less.' Do you agree or disagree with this statement? Explain your answer.

8. Suppose that I decide to start a small business. To raise start-up funds, I sell 1000 shares of stock for €100 each. For the next five years, I take in annual revenues of €50,000. My total annual costs of operating the

business are €20,000. If all of my profits are paid out as dividends to shareholders, how much of my total annual profit can be considered economic profit? Assume that the current interest rate is 10%.

9. Explain what we mean when we say that 'households supply capital and firms demand capital'.

10. When, in 1987, Eurotunnel wished to raise finance to build the Channel Tunnel it issued shares to cover part of the cost. They were bought at £3.50 each. By the middle of 1998, during which time average share prices had increased substantially, Eurotunnel's shares could be purchased for around 60 pence. Why?

11. Describe the capital stock of your college or university. How would you go about measuring its value? Has your college/university made any major investments in recent years? If so, describe them. What does your college/university hope to gain from these investments?

Appendix to Chapter 11

Calculating Present Value

We have seen in this chapter that a firm's major goal in making investment decisions is to evaluate revenue streams that will not materialize until the future. One way for the firm to decide whether or not to undertake an investment project is to compare the expected rate of return from the investment with the current interest rate available in the financial market. This procedure was discussed briefly in the text.

The purpose of this appendix is to present an alternative method of evaluating future revenue streams through present-value analysis.

Present value

Consider the expected flow of profits from the investment shown in Table 11A.1. If such a project cost €1200 to put in place, would the firm undertake it? At first glance, you might answer yes. After all, the total flow of profit is €1600. But this flow of profit is fully realized only after five years have passed. The same €1200 could be put into a money market account, where it would earn interest and perhaps produce a higher yield than if it were invested in the project. You can easily see that the desirability of the investment project will depend on the interest rate that is available in the market.

One way of thinking about interest is to say that it *allows us to buy and sell claims to future euros.* Future euros have prices in the present. That is, a contract for €1 to be delivered in one year, two years or ten years can be purchased today. How? By simply depositing a certain amount in an interest-bearing certificate or account.

Table 11A.1 Expected profits from a €1200 investment project

Year 1	100
Year 2	100
Year 3	400
Year 4	500
Year 5	500
All later years	0
Total	1,600

Using the *present* prices of future euros gives us a way to compare values that will be realized in the future. This method allows us to evaluate investment projects that will yield benefits into the future.

It is not difficult to work out the 'price' today of €1 to be delivered in one year. You must now pay an amount (X) such that when you get X back in one year with interest you will have €1. If r is the interest rate available in the market, r times X, or rX, is the amount of interest that X will earn for you in one year.

Thus, at the end of a year you will have $X + rX$, or $X(1 + r)$, and you want this to be equal to €1. Solving for X algebraically:

$$1 \text{ euro} = X(1 + r), \text{ so } X = \frac{1}{(1 + r)} \text{ euros}$$

We say that X is the **present value (PV)**, or **present discounted value**, of 1 euro one year from now. Actually, X is the current market price of 1 euro to be delivered in one year: it is the amount you have to put aside now if you want to end up with 1 euro a year from now.

Now let's go more than one year into the future and consider more than a single euro. For example, what is the present value of a claim on €100 in two years? Using the same logic as above, let X be the present value, or current market price, of €100 payable in two years. Thus, X plus the interest it would earn compounded for two years is equal to €100.* After one year, you would have $X + rX$, or $X(1 + r)$. After two years, you would have this amount plus another year's interest on the whole amount:

$$X(1 + r) + r[X(1 + r)]$$

or

$$X(1 + r)(1 + r), \text{ which is } X(1 + r)^2$$

Again, solving algebraically for X:

$$€100 = X(1 + r)^2, \text{ so } X = \frac{100}{(1 + r)^2}$$

If the market interest rate were 10%, or 0.10, then the present value of €100 in two years would be:

$$\frac{100}{(1.1)^2} = €82.65$$

If you put €82.65 in a certificate earning 10% per year, you would earn €8.26 in interest after one year, giving you €90.91. Interest in the second year would be €9.09, leaving you with exactly €100 at the end of two years.

In general, the present value, or present discounted value, of R euros t years from now is:

$$PV = \frac{R}{(1 + r)^t}$$

Table 11A.2 calculates the present value of the income stream in Table 11A.1 at an interest rate of 10%.

The total present value turns out to be €1126.06. This tells the firm that it can simply go to the financial market today and buy a contract that pays €100 one

End of:	R (euros)	Divided by $(1 + r)^t$	= Present value (euros)
Year 1	100	(1.1)	90.91
Year 2	100	$(1.1)^2$	82.65
Year 3	400	$(1.1)^3$	300.53
Year 4	500	$(1.1)^4$	341.51
Year 5	500	$(1.1)^5$	310.46
Total present value:			1,126.06

Table 11A.2 Calculation of total present value of a hypothetical investment project (assuming r = 10%)

year from now, another that pays €100 two years from now, still another that pays €400 three years from now, and so on, all for the low price of €1126.06. To put this another way, it could lend out or deposit €1126.06 in an account paying a 10% interest rate, withdraw €100 next year, withdraw €100 in the following year, take another €400 at the end of three years, and so on. When it takes its last €500 at the end of the fifth year, the account will be empty – the balance in the account will be exactly zero. Thus, at *current market interest rates*, the firm has exactly duplicated the income stream that the investment project would have yielded for a total present price of €1126.06. Why then would it pay out €1200 to undertake this investment? The answer, of course, is that it would not. We can restate the point this way:

If the present value of the income stream associated with an investment is less than the full cost of the investment project, the investment should not be undertaken.

It is important to remember here that we are discussing the *demand for new capital*. Business firms must evaluate potential investments in order to decide whether they are worth undertaking. This involves predicting the flow of potential future profits arising from each project, and comparing those future profits with the return available in the financial market at the current interest rate. The present-value method allows firms to calculate how much it would *cost today* to purchase or contract for exactly the same flow of earnings in the financial market.

Lower interest rates, higher present values

Now suppose that interest rates fall from 10% to 5%. With a lower interest rate, the firm will have to *pay more* now to purchase the same number of future dollars. Take, for example, the present value of €100 in two

*Thus far, all our examples have involved simple interest – interest that is computed on principal alone, not on principal plus interest. In the real world, however, many loans involve compound interest – interest that is computed on the basis of principal plus interest. If you deposit funds into an interest-compounding account at a bank and do not withdraw the interest payments as they are added to your account, you will earn interest on your previously earned interest.

years. You saw that if the firm puts aside €82.65 at 10% interest, it will have exactly €100 in two years; at a 10% interest rate, the present discounted value, or current market price, of €100 in two years is €82.65. But €82.65 put aside at a 5% interest rate would generate only €4.13 in interest in the first year and €4.34 in the second year, for a total balance of €91.12 after two years. In order to get €100 in two years, the firm needs to put aside more than €82.65 now. Solving for X as we did before:

$$X = \frac{100}{(1 + r)^2} = \frac{100}{(1.05)^2} = 90.70 \text{ euros}$$

When the interest rate falls from 10% to 5%, the present value of €100 in two years rises by €8.05 (90.70 – 82.65).

Table 11A.3 recalculates the present value of the full stream at the lower interest rate; it shows that a decrease in the interest rate from 10% to 5% causes the total present value to rise to €1334.59. Because the investment project will yield the same stream of earnings for a present price of only €1200, it is now a better deal than the financial markets. Under these conditions, a profit-maximizing firm will make the investment.

The basic rule is:

Table 11A.3 Calculation of total present value of a hypothetical investment project (assuming $r = 5\%$)

End of:	R (euros)	Divided by (1 + r)ᵗ	= Present value (euros)
Year 1	100	(1.05)	95.24
Year 2	100	(1 05)²	90.70
Year 3	400	(1.05)³	345.54
Year 4	500	(1.05)⁴	411.35
Year 5	500	(1.05)⁵	391.76
Total present value:			1,134.59

If the present value of an expected stream of earnings from an investment exceeds the cost of the investment necessary to undertake it, then the investment should be undertaken. But if the present value of an expected stream of earnings falls short of the cost of the investment, then the financial market can generate the same stream of income for a smaller initial investment, and the investment should not be undertaken. When the interest rate or the rate of return offered by the market exceeds the rate of return on a project, the investment is not justified at the current interest rate.

Summary

1. The present value (*PV*) of *R* euros to be paid *t* years in the future is the amount you need to pay today, at current interest rates, to ensure that you end up with *R* euros *t* years from now. It is the current market value of receiving *R* euros in *t* years.

2. If the present value of the income stream associated with an investment is less than the full cost of the investment project, the investment project should not be undertaken. If the present value of an expected stream of income exceeds the cost of the investment necessary to undertake it, then the investment should be undertaken.

Review Terms and Concepts

present value (*PV*), or present discounted value The present discounted value of *R* euros to be paid *t* years in the future is the amount you need to pay today, at current interest rates, to ensure that you end up with *R* euros *t* years from now. It is the current market value of receiving *R* euros in *t* years.

Equation

$$PV = R/(1 + r)^t$$

Problem Set

1. John's Uncle Joe has just died and left €10,000, payable to John when he turns 30 years old. He is now 20. Currently, the annual rate of interest he can obtain by buying ten-year bonds is 6.5%. His brother offers him €6000 cash right now to sign over his inheritance. Should he do it?

2. A special task force has determined that the present discounted value of the benefits from a bridge project in Denmark comes to 23,786,000 kroner. The total construction cost of the bridge is 25,000,000 kroner. This implies that the bridge should be built. Do you agree with this conclusion? Explain your answer. What impact could a substantial decline in Danish interest rates have on your answer?

3. Calculate the present value of the income streams for projects A to E in Table 1 at an 8% interest rate and again at a 10% rate.

Suppose that the investment behind the flow of income in E is a machine that cost €1235 at the beginning of year 1. Would you buy the machine if the interest rate were 8%? If the interest rate were 10%?

4. Determine what someone should be willing to pay for each of the following bonds when the market interest rate for borrowing and lending is 5%.
a. A bond that promises to pay €3000 in a lump-sum payment after 1 year.
b. A bond that promises to pay €3000 in a lump-sum payment after 2 years.

c. A bond that promises to pay €1000 per year for 3 years.

5. What should someone be willing to pay for each of the bonds in problem 4 if the interest rate is 10%?

6. Using your answers to problems 4 and 5, state whether each of the following is true or false.
a. *Ceteris paribus*, the price of a bond increases when the interest rate increases.
b. *Ceteris paribus*, the price of a bond increases when any given amount of money is received sooner rather than later.

Table 1 Income streams (euros) for projects A–E

End of:	A	B	C	D	E
Year 1	80	80	100	100	500
Year 2	80	80	100	100	300
Year 3	80	80	1,100	100	400
Year 4	80	80	0	100	300
Year 5	1,080	80	0	100	0
Year 6	0	80	0	1,100	0
Year 7	0	1,080	0	0	0

12

General Equilibrium and the Efficiency of Perfect Competition

In the last seven chapters, we have built a model of a simple perfectly competitive economy. Our discussion has revolved around the two fundamental decision-making units, *households* and *firms*, which interact in two basic market arenas, *input markets* and *output markets*. (Look again at the circular flow diagram, shown in Figure 12.1.) By limiting our discussion to perfectly competitive firms, we have been able to examine how the basic decision-making units interact in the two basic market arenas.

Households make constrained choices in both input and output markets. In Chapters 4 and 5 we discussed an individual household demand curve for a single good or service. Then in Chapter 6 we went behind the demand curve and saw how income, wealth and prices define the budget constraints within which households exercise their tastes and preferences. We soon discovered, however, that we cannot look at household decisions in output markets without thinking about the decisions made simultaneously in input markets. Household income, for example, depends on choices made in input markets: whether to work, how much to work, what skills to acquire, and so on. Input market choices are constrained by such factors as current wage rates, the availability of jobs, and interest rates.

Firms are the primary producing units in a market economy. Profit-maximizing firms, to which we have limited our discussion, earn their profits by selling products and services for more than it costs to produce them. With firms, as with households, output markets and input markets cannot be analysed separately. All firms make three specific decisions simultaneously: (1) how much output to supply, (2) how to produce that output (that is, which technology to use) and (3) how much of each input to demand.

In Chapters 7 to 9, we explored these three decisions from the viewpoint of output markets. We saw that the portion of the marginal cost curve that lies above a firm's average variable cost curve is the supply curve of a perfectly competitive firm in the short run. Implicit in the marginal cost curve is a choice of technology and a set of input demands. In Chapters 10 and 11, we looked at the perfectly competitive firm's three basic decisions from the viewpoint of input markets.

Output and input markets are connected because firms and households make simultaneous choices in both arenas. But there are other connections among markets as well. Firms buy in both capital and labour markets, for example, and they can substitute capital for labour and vice versa. A change in the price of one factor can easily change the demand for other factors. Buying more *capital*, for instance, usually changes the marginal revenue product of *labour* and shifts the labour demand curve. Similarly, a change in the price of a single good or service usually affects household demand for other goods and services, as when a price decrease makes one good more attractive than other close substitutes. The same change also makes households better off when they find that the same amount of income will buy more. Such additional 'real income' can be spent on any of the other goods and services that the household buys.

Figure 12.1 Firm and household decisions

Firms and households interact in both input and output markets.

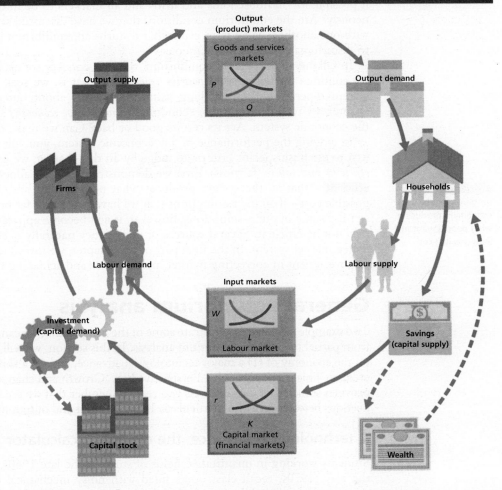

The point here is simple:

> Input and output markets cannot be considered separately or as if they operated independently. While it is important to understand the decisions of individual firms and households and the functioning of individual markets, we now need to 'add it all up', to look at the operation of the system as a whole.

partial equilibrium analysis

The process of examining the equilibrium conditions in individual markets and for households and firms separately.

general equilibrium

The condition that exists when all markets in an economy are in simultaneous equilibrium.

You have seen the concept of equilibrium applied both to markets and to individual decision-making units. In individual markets, supply and demand determine an equilibrium price. Perfectly competitive firms are in short-run equilibrium when price and marginal cost are equal ($P = MC$). In the long run, however, equilibrium in a competitive market is achieved only when economic profits are eliminated. Households are in equilibrium when they have equated the marginal utility per unit of expenditure on each good to the marginal utility per unit of expenditure spent on all goods. This process of examining the equilibrium conditions in individual markets and for individual households and firms separately is called **partial equilibrium analysis**.

A **general equilibrium** exists when all markets in an economy are in simultaneous equilibrium. An event that disturbs the equilibrium in one market may disturb the equilibrium in many other markets as well. The ultimate impact of the event depends on the way *all* markets adjust to it. Thus, partial equilibrium analysis, which looks at adjustments in one isolated market, may be misleading.

Thinking in terms of a general equilibrium leads to some important questions. Is it possible for all households and firms and all markets to be in equilibrium simultaneously? Are the equilibrium conditions that we have discussed separately compatible with one another? Why is an event that disturbs an equilibrium in one market likely to disturb many others simultaneously?

In talking about general equilibrium, the first concept we explore in this chapter, we continue our exercise in *positive economics* – that is, we seek to understand how systems operate without making value judgements about outcomes. Later in the chapter, we turn from positive economics to *normative economics* as we begin to judge the economic system. Are its results good or bad? Can we make them better?

In judging the performance of any economic system, you will recall, it is essential first to establish specific criteria to judge by. In this chapter, we use two such criteria: *efficiency* and *equity* (fairness). First we demonstrate that the allocation of resources is **efficient** – that is, the system produces what people want and does so at the least possible cost – if all the assumptions that we have made thus far hold. When we begin to relax some of our assumptions, however, it will become apparent that free markets may not be efficient. Several sources of inefficiency naturally occur within an unregulated market system. In the final part of this chapter, we introduce the potential role of government in correcting market inefficiencies and achieving fairness.

efficiency The condition in which the economy is producing what people want at least possible cost.

General equilibrium analysis

Two examples will help us illustrate some of the insights that we can gain when we move from partial to general equilibrium analysis. In this section, we will consider the impact on the economy of (1) a major technological advance, and (2) a shift in consumer preferences. This chapter's Global Perspective box, 'Growth and change in global markets', provides some other examples. As you read, remember that we are looking for the connections between markets, particularly between input and output markets.

A technological advance: the electronic calculator

Students working in quantitative fields of study in the late 1960s, and even as late as the early 1970s, recall classrooms filled with noisy mechanical calculators. At that time, a calculator weighed about 20 kilos and was only able to add, subtract, multiply and divide. These machines had no memories, and they took 20 to 25 seconds to solve one multiplication problem.

Large companies had rooms full of accountants with such calculators on their desks, and the sound when 30 or 40 machines were running was deafening. During the 1950s and 1960s, most firms had these machines, but few people had a calculator in their homes because the cost of a single machine was prohibitive. They cost the equivalent of several hundred euros. Some universities, colleges and secondary schools had calculators for accounting classes, but most schoolchildren in Europe had never seen one.

In the 1960s, Wang Laboratories in the USA developed an electronic calculator. Bigger than a modern personal computer, it had several keyboards attached to a single main processor. It could add, subtract, multiply and divide, but it also had a memory. Its main virtue was speed and quiet. It did calculations instantaneously without any noise. The Wang machine sold for around $1500 (€1400).

The beginning of the 1970s saw rapid developments in the industry. First, calculators shrank in size. The early versions could do nothing more than add, subtract, multiply and divide, they had no memories, and they still sold for several hundred dollars. Then, in the early 1970s, a number of technological breakthroughs made it possible to mass produce very small electronic circuits on silicon chips. These circuits in turn, made calculators very inexpensive to produce, not only in the USA but elsewhere, including Europe. It is here that we begin our general equilibrium story. Costs in the calculator industry shifted downwards dramatically (Figure 12.2b). As costs fell, profits increased.

Global Perspectives

Growth and change in global markets

An expanding sector demands labour, attracting workers from other sectors and driving up wages.[1]

In Kentucky, new auto plants – particularly Toyota's sprawling factory in Georgetown – have attracted networks of parts suppliers in recent years, offering thousands of new jobs at $10 an hour or more. They have hired many people who have shifted to the new factory work from lower-paying in construction and tobacco fields.

Demand for Japanese cars contributes to demand for palladium, which interacts with supply

problems and potentially raises the cost of producing electronic goods.[2]

Palladium prices soared yesterday as Western industries grew increasingly desperate for supplies amid questions about the financial health of the world's largest single supplier. Deliveries of new supplies have been at a standstill since December amid labour troubles and political in-fighting in Russia, where the Norilsk nickel mine produces two-thirds of world inventories.

Palladium is used in electronics and computers and is particularly important to the Japanese car sector.

Changes in demand can have major impacts in the labour and capital markets. As a result of soaring demand for steel from automobile and appliance makers, steel mills have been expanded and are working overtime. In addition, the price of steel has increased.

[1]*Louis Uchitelle, 'US job machine absorbing fresh workers', New York Times, 10 July 1997, p. 1.*

[2]*'Prices for palladium surge amid problems on supplies', New York Times, 20 May 1997, p. D17.*

Attracted by economic profits, new firms rapidly entered the market. Instead of one or two firms producing state-of-the-art machines, dozens of firms began turning them out by the thousand. As a result, the industry supply curve shifted out to the right, driving down prices towards the new lower costs (see Figure 12.2a).

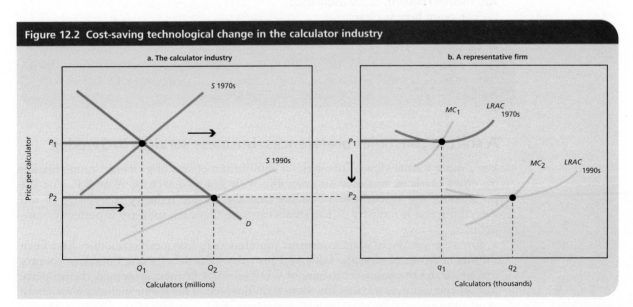

Figure 12.2 Cost-saving technological change in the calculator industry

The 1970s and 1980s brought major technological changes to the calculator industry. In the 1970s, calculators were sold at P_1, which was several hundred euros. As technology made it possible to produce at lower costs, cost curves shifted downwards. As new firms entered the industry and existing firms expanded, output rose and market price dropped. In the 1990s, far more calculators (Q_2) were produced, and they sold at P_2, a price of perhaps €20.

As the price of electronic calculators fell, the market for the old mechanical calculators died a quiet death. With no more demand for their product, producers found themselves suffering losses and got out of the business. As the price of electronic calculators kept falling, thousands of people who had never owned a calculator began to buy them. You can now buy a basic calculator for just a few euros, or even get one free with a magazine subscription.

The rapid decline in the cost of producing calculators led to a rapid expansion of supply and a decline in price. (See Figure 12.2a.) The lower prices increased the quantity demanded to such an extent that most European homes now have at least one calculator, and thousands of people walk around with calculators in their pockets.

This is only a partial equilibrium story, however. The events we have described also had effects on many other markets. In other words, they disturbed the general equilibrium. When mechanical calculators became obsolete, many people who had over the years developed the skills required to produce and repair these complex machines found themselves unemployed. At the same time, demand boomed for workers in the production, distribution and sales of the new electronic calculators. New skills were required, and the expansion of the industry led to an increase in demand for the kinds of labour needed. The new technology thus caused a reallocation of labour across the labour market.

Capital was also reallocated. New firms invested in the plant and equipment needed to produce electronic calculators. Old capital owned by the firms that previously made mechanical calculators became obsolete and depreciated, and it ended up on the scrapheap. The mechanical calculators themselves, once an integral part of the capital stocks of accounting firms, banks and other similar organizations, were scrapped and replaced by the cheaper, more efficient new models.[1]

When a new industry suddenly appears, it earns billions of euros in revenues that might have been spent on other things. Even though the effects of this success on any one other industry were probably small, general equilibrium analysis tells us that in the absence of the new industry and the demand for its product, households will demand other goods and services, and other industries will produce more. In this case, society has benefited a great deal. Everyone can now buy a very useful product at a low price. The new calculators have raised the productivity of certain kinds of labour and reduced costs in many industries.

The point here is clear:

A significant – if not sweeping – technological change in a single industry affects many markets. Households face a different structure of prices and must adjust their consumption of many products. Labour reacts to new skill requirements and is reallocated across markets. Capital is also reallocated.

A shift in consumer preferences: business services in Sweden

For a more formal view of the general equilibrium effects of a change in one market on other markets, consider an economy with just two sectors, X and Y. For the purposes of our discussion, let us say that the service industry is industry X and everything else is industry Y. Let us also assume that each industry is perfectly competitive.

Over the last 20–30 years, consumer preferences in European economies have been shifting in favour of services. Table 12.1 provides some data for one European country that illustrates the point. The share of GDP taken by finance, insurance, the property market and business services has more than doubled. This sector includes a variety of

[1] In recent years, of course, the electronic calculator has increasingly been replaced by the personal computer.

Table 12.1 Relative shares of GDP in Sweden, 1963–1994

Sector	1963	1970	1980	1990	1994
Agriculture	8.0	5.7	3.8	3.7	3.3
Mining and quarrying	1.6	1.3	0.7	0.4	0.5
Manufacturing	35.4	34.9	29.8	28.1	29.3
Construction	11.7	11.6	10.4	9.9	8.0
Electricity, gas and water	3.0	2.5	3.0	3.8	3.6
Wholesale, retail, restaurants and hotels	14.3	15.2	14.5	14.6	14.5
Transport, storage and communication	8.1	8.7	7.2	8.5	8.3
Finance, insurance, property and business services	13.5	15.3	25.2	26.0	27.4
Community, social and personal services	4.6	4.7	5.5	5.0	5.0

Source: OECD Economic Surveys.

business services but for the purposes of our illustration we will call all these kinds of output 'services' and refer to them as industry X. All other output we call industry Y.

Figure 12.3 shows the initial equilibrium in sectors X and Y. We assume that both sectors are initially in long-run competitive equilibrium. Total output in sector X is Q_X^0, the product is selling for a price of P_X^0, and each firm in the industry produces up to where P_X^0 is equal to marginal cost – q_X^0. At that point, price is just equal to average cost, and economic profits are zero. The same condition holds initially in sector Y. The market is in zero profit equilibrium at a price of P_Y^0.

Now assume that a change in consumer preferences (or in the age distribution of the population, or in something else) shifts the demand for X out to the right from D_X^0 to D_X^1. That shift drives price up to P_X^1. If households decide to buy more X, without an increase in income they must buy less of something else. Since everything else is represented by Y in this example, the demand for Y must decline, and the demand curve for Y shifts to the left from D_Y^0 to D_Y^1.

With the shift in demand for X, price rises to P_X^1 and profit-maximizing firms immediately increase output to q_X^1, (the point where $P_X^1 = MC_X$). But now there are economic profits in X, profits over and above a normal rate of return. With the downward shift of demand in Y, price falls to P_X^1. Firms in sector Y cut back to q_Y^1 (the point where $P_X^1 = MC_Y$), and the lower price causes firms producing Y to suffer economic losses.

In the short run, adjustment is simple. Firms in both industries are constrained by their current scales of plant. Firms can neither enter nor exit their respective industries. Each firm in industry X raises output somewhat, from q_X^0 to q_X^1. Firms in industry Y cut back from q_Y^0 to q_Y^1.

In response to the existence of economic profit in sector X, the capital market begins to take notice. In Chapter 9 we saw that new firms are likely to enter an industry in which there are economic profits to be earned. Financial analysts see the economic profits as a signal of future healthy growth, and entrepreneurs may become interested in moving into the industry.

Adding all this together, we would expect to see investment begin to favour sector X. This is indeed the case: capital begins to flow into sector X. As new firms enter, the

Figure 12.3 Adjustment in an economy with two sectors

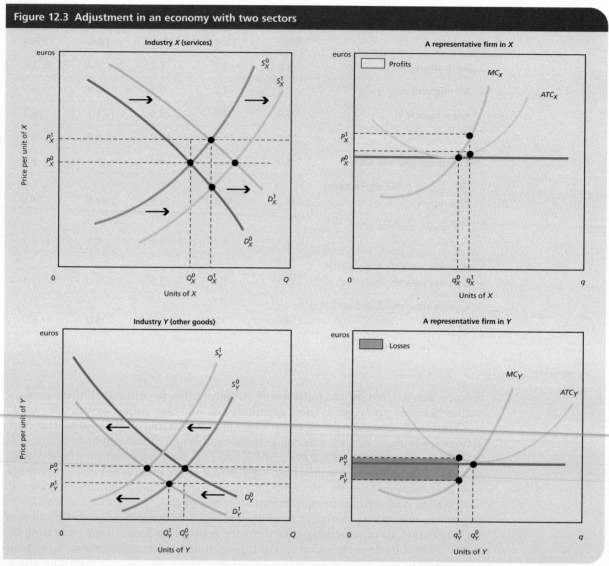

Initially, demand for *X* shifts from D_X^0 to D_X^1. This shift pushes the price of *X* up to P_X^1, creating economic profits. Demand for *Y* shifts down from D_Y^0 to D_Y^1, pushing the price of *Y* down to P_Y^1, and creating economic losses. Firms have an incentive to leave sector *Y* and an incentive to enter sector *X*. Exiting sector *Y* shifts supply in that industry to S_Y^1, raising price and eliminating losses. Entry and expansion shift supply in *X* to S_X^1, thus reducing price and eliminating profits.

short-run supply curve in the industry shifts to the right and continues to do so until all economic profits are eliminated. In the top left diagram in Figure 12.3, the supply curve shifts out from S_X^0 to S_X^1, a shift that drives the price back down to P_X^0.

We would also expect to see a movement out of sector *Y* because of economic losses. Some firms will exit the industry. In the bottom left diagram in Figure 12.3, the supply curve shifts back from S_Y^0 to S_Y^1, a shift that drives the price back up to P_Y^0. At this point all economic losses are eliminated.

Note that a new general equilibrium is not reached until equilibrium is re-established in all markets. If costs of production remain unchanged, as they do in Figure 12.3, this equilibrium occurs at the initial product prices, but with more resources and production in *X* and fewer in *Y*. If, on the other hand, an expansion in *X* drives up the prices of resources used specifically in *X*, the cost curves in *X* will shift upwards and the final post-expansion, zero-profit equilibrium will occur at a higher price. Such an industry is called an increasing-cost industry.

Sector	1963	1970	1980	1990	1994
Agriculture	16.3	10.8	7.8	5.6	5.9
Mining and quarrying	0.7	0.6	0.5	0.3	0.3
Manufacturing	34.4	34.2	35.0	30.8	28.5
Construction	10.7	12.2	10.2	9.9	8.1
Electricity, Gas and Water	0.9	0.9	1.1	1.1	1.1
Wholesale, retail, restaurants and hotels	17.8	19.1	19.8	21.1	21.5
Transport, storage and communication	8.2	8.6	9.4	9.9	10.3
Finance, insurance, property and business services	3.9	5.7	8.1	12.5	13.6
Community, social and personal services	7.0	7.8	8.1	8.8	10.7

Table 12.2 Employment (share of total) in Sweden, 1963–1994

Source: OECD Economic Surveys.

Resources do indeed shift as a result of changes in consumer preference. Table 12.2 focuses on one particular resource, labour. As a result of the shift in consumer preference towards services, the proportion of the labour force now engaged in the production of this kind of output has risen substantially. Sectors such as agriculture and manufacturing have become relatively less heavy employers of labour. The services sector is now of relatively greater importance.

Formal proof of a general competitive equilibrium

Economic theorists have struggled with the question of whether a set of prices that equates supply and demand in all markets simultaneously can actually exist when there are literally thousands and thousands of markets. If such a set of prices were not possible, the result could be continuous cycles of expansion, contraction and instability.

The nineteenth-century French economist Leon Walras struggled with the problem, but he could never provide a formal proof. Using advanced mathematical tools, economists Kenneth Arrow and Gerard Debreu and mathematicians John von Neumann and Abraham Wald have now shown the existence of at least one set of prices that *will* clear all markets in a large system simultaneously.

Allocative efficiency and competitive equilibrium

Chapters 4 to 11 built a complete model of a simple, perfectly competitive economic system. But recall that in Chapters 4 and 5 we made a number of important assumptions. We assumed that both output markets and input markets are perfectly competitive – that is, that no individual household or firm is large enough relative to the market to have any control over price. In other words, we assumed that firms and households are *price-takers*.

We also assumed that households have perfect information on product quality and on all prices available, and that firms have perfect knowledge of technologies and input prices. Finally, we said that decision makers in a competitive system always consider all the costs and benefits of their decisions, that there are no 'external' costs.

If all these assumptions hold, the economy will produce an efficient allocation of resources. As we relax these assumptions one by one, however, you will discover that the allocation of resources is no longer efficient and that a number of sources of inefficiency occur naturally.

Pareto efficiency

In Chapter 1 we introduced several specific criteria used by economists to judge the performance of economic systems and to evaluate alternative economic policies. These criteria are (1) efficiency, (2) equity, (3) growth and (4) stability. In Chapter 1 you also learned that an *efficient* economy is one that produces the things that people want at least cost. The idea behind the efficiency criterion is that the economic system exists to serve the wants and needs of the people. If resources can be somehow reallocated to make the people 'better off', then they should be. We want to use the resources at our disposal to produce maximum well-being. The trick is defining 'maximum well-being'.

For many years, social philosophers wrestled with the problem of 'aggregation'. When we say 'maximum well-being' we mean maximum *for society*. Societies are made up of many people, however, and the problem has always been how to maximize satisfaction, or well-being, for all members of society. What has emerged is the now widely accepted concept of *allocative efficiency*, first developed by the Italian economist Vilfredo Pareto in the nineteenth century. Pareto's very precise definition of efficiency is often referred to as Pareto efficiency or Pareto optimality.

Pareto efficiency *or* Pareto optimality
A condition in which no change is possible that will make some members of society better off without making some other members of society worse off.

Specifically, a change is said to be efficient if it at least potentially makes some members of society better off without making other members of society worse off. An efficient, or *Pareto optimal*, system is one in which no such changes are possible. An example of a change that makes some people better off and nobody worse off is a simple voluntary exchange. I have apples; you have nuts. I like nuts; you like apples. We trade. We both gain, and no one loses.

For such a definition to have any real meaning, we must answer two questions: (1) What do we mean by 'better off'? (2) How do we account for changes that make some people better off and others worse off?

The answer to the first question is simple. People themselves decide what 'better off' and 'worse off' mean. I am the only one who knows whether I'm better off after a change. If you and I exchange one item for another because I like what you have and you like what I have, we both 'reveal' that we are better off after the exchange because we agreed to it voluntarily. If everybody in a town wants a park and they all contribute to a fund to build one, they have consciously changed the allocation of resources, and they all are better off for it.

The answer to the second question is more complex. Nearly every change that one can imagine leaves some people better off and some people worse off. If some gain and some lose as the result of a change, and it can be demonstrated that the value of the gains exceeds the value of the losses, then the change is said to be *potentially efficient*. In practice, however, the distinction between a *potential* and an *actual* efficient change is often ignored, and all such changes are simply called *efficient*.

Example: budget cuts

Suppose, in an effort to reduce a government's spending, the number of clerks dealing with the registration of motor vehicles is cut substantially. Drivers now find themselves waiting in queues for hours when going to register their cars or renew their licenses.

Clearly, drivers and car owners pay a price: standing in a queue, which uses time and energy that could otherwise be used more productively. But before we can make sensible efficiency judgements, we must be able to measure, or at least approximate, the value of both the gains and the losses produced by the budget cut. To approximate the losses to car owners and drivers, we might ask how much people would be willing to pay to avoid standing in those long queues.

Suppose 500 people stand in a queue every day for about one hour each. If each person were willing to pay just €2 to avoid standing in the queue, the damage incurred would be €1000 (500 × €2) per day. If the licensing office were open 250 days per year, the reduction in labour force would create a cost to car owners of €250,000 (250 × €1000) per year.

Now suppose taxpayers save about €80,000 per year by having fewer clerks at that office. If the clerks were reinstated, there would be some gains and some losses. Car owners and drivers would gain, and taxpayers would lose. But because we can show that the value of the gains would substantially exceed the value of the losses, it can be argued that reinstating the clerks would be an efficient change. Note that the only *net* losers would be those taxpayers who don't own a car and don't hold driving licences.[2]

The efficiency of perfect competition

In Chapter 2 we discussed the 'economic problem' of dividing up scarce resources among alternative uses. We also discussed the three basic questions that all societies must answer, and we set out to explain how these three questions are answered in a competitive economy. Here again are the three basic questions:

1. *What will be produced?* What determines the final mix of output?
2. *How will it be produced?* How do capital, labour and land get divided up among firms? In other words, what is the allocation of resources among producers?
3. *Who will get what is produced?* What determines which households get how much? What is the distribution of output among consuming households?

The following discussion of efficiency uses these three questions and their answers to prove informally that perfect competition is efficient. To demonstrate that the perfectly competitive system leads to an efficient, or Pareto optimal, allocation of resources, we need to show that no changes are possible that will make some people better off without making others worse off. Specifically, we will show that under perfect competition (1) resources are allocated among firms efficiently, (2) final products are distributed among households efficiently, and (3) the system produces the things that people want.

Efficient allocation of resources among firms

The simple definition of efficiency holds that firms must produce their products using the best available – that is, lowest cost – technology. Clearly, if more output could be produced with the same amount of inputs, it would be possible to make some people better off without making others worse off.

The perfectly competitive model we have been using rests on several assumptions that assure us that resources in such a system would indeed be efficiently allocated among firms. Most important of these is the assumption that individual firms maximize profits. To maximize profit, a firm must minimize the cost of producing its chosen level of output. With a full knowledge of existing technologies, firms will choose the technology that produces the output they want at least cost.

There is more to this story than meets the eye, however. Inputs must be allocated *across* firms in the best possible way. If we find that it is possible, for example, to take capital from firm A and swap it for labour from firm B and produce more product in both firms, then the original allocation was inefficient. Recall our example from Chapter 2. European producers produce industrial and agricultural output. The

[2]*But, you might ask, aren't there other gainers and losers? What about the clerks themselves? In analyses like this one, it is usually assumed that the citizens who pay lower taxes now spend their added income on other things. The producers of those other things need to expand to meet the new demand, and they hire more labour. Thus, a contraction of 100 jobs in the public sector will open up 100 jobs in the private sector. If the economy is fully employed, the transfer of labour to the private sector is assumed to create no net gains or losses to the workers themselves.*

climate and soil in some parts are best suited to agriculture; the climate and soil in other parts of Europe are best suited to industrial production. A law that forces each region to produce some of each kind of output would result in less of both – an inefficient allocation of resources. But if markets are free and open, resource owners will naturally find a higher return by using their resources in the kind of production to which they are best suited. The free market, then, should lead to an efficient allocation of resources among firms.

The same argument can be made more general. Misallocation of resources among firms is unlikely as long as every single firm faces the same set of prices and trade-offs in input markets. Recall from Chapter 10 that perfectly competitive firms will hire additional factors of production as long as their marginal revenue product exceeds their market price. As long as all firms have access to the *same* factor markets and the *same* factor prices, the last unit of a factor hired will produce the same value in each firm. Certainly, firms will use different technologies and factor combinations, but at the margin, no single profit-maximizing firm can get more value out of a factor than that factor's current market price. If, for example, workers can be hired in the labour market at a wage of €6.50, all firms will hire workers as long as the marginal revenue product produced by the marginal worker (labour's marginal revenue product – MRP_L) remains above €6.50. No firms will hire labour beyond the point at which MRP_L falls below €6.50. Thus, at equilibrium, additional workers are not worth more than €6.50 to any firm, and switching labour from one firm to another will not produce output of any greater value to society. Each firm has hired the profit-maximizing amount of labour. In short:

> The assumptions that factor markets are competitive and open, that all firms pay the same prices for inputs, and that all firms maximize profits, lead to the conclusion that the allocation of resources among firms is efficient.

Efficient distribution of outputs among households

Even if the system is producing the right things, and is doing so efficiently, these things still have to get to the right people. Just as open, competitive factor markets ensure that firms don't end up with the wrong inputs, open, competitive output markets ensure that households don't end up with the wrong goods and services.

Within the constraints imposed by income and wealth, households are free to choose among all the goods and services available in output markets. A household will buy a good as long as that good generates utility, or subjective value, greater than its market price. Utility value is revealed in market behaviour. You don't go out and buy something unless you are willing to pay at least the market price.

Remember that the value you place on any one good depends on what you must give up to have that good. The trade-offs available to you depend on your budget constraint. The trade-offs that are desirable depend on your preferences. If you buy a 400 Euro CD player for your room at university, you may be giving up a trip home. If I buy it, I may be giving up four new tyres for my car. But we've both revealed that the CD player is worth at least as much to us as all the other things that €400 can buy. As long as we are free to choose among all the things that €400 can buy, we will not end up with the wrong things; it's not possible to find a trade that will make us both better off.

This argument is really quite intuitive:

> We all know that people have different tastes and preferences, and that they will buy very different things in very different combinations. But as long as everyone shops freely in the same markets, no redistribution of final outputs among people will make them better off. If you and I buy in the same markets and pay the same prices, and I buy what I want and you buy what you want, neither of us can possibly end up with the wrong combination of things. But free and open markets are essential to this result.

Producing what people want: the efficient mix of output

It does no good to produce things efficiently or to distribute them efficiently if the system produces the wrong things. Will competitive markets produce the things that people want?

If the system is producing the wrong mix of output, we should be able to show that producing more of one good and less of another will make people better off. To show that perfectly competitive markets are efficient, then, we must demonstrate that no such changes in the final mix of output are possible.

The condition that ensures that the right things are produced is $P = MC$. That is, in both the long run and the short run, a perfectly competitive firm will produce at the point where the price of its output is equal to the marginal cost of production. The logic is this: when a firm weighs price and marginal cost, it weighs the value of its product to society *at the margin* against the value of the things that could otherwise be produced with the same resources. Figure 12.4 summarizes this logic.

The argument is quite straightforward. First, price reflects households' willingness to pay. By purchasing a product, individual households reveal that it is worth at least as much as the other things that the same money could buy. Thus, current price reflects the value that households place on a good.

Second, marginal cost reflects the opportunity cost of the resources needed to produce a good. If a firm producing X hires a worker, it must pay the market wage. That wage must be sufficient to attract that worker out of leisure or away from firms producing other products. The same argument holds for capital and land.

Thus, if the price of a good ends up greater than marginal cost, producing more of it will generate benefits to households in excess of opportunity costs, and society gains. Similarly, if the price of a good ends up below marginal cost, resources are being used to produce something that households value less than opportunity costs. Producing less of it creates gains to society.[3]

Society will produce the efficient mix of output if all firms equate price and marginal cost.

Figure 12.5 shows how a simple competitive market system leads individual households and firms to make efficient choices in input and output markets. For

Figure 12.4 The key efficiency condition: price equals marginal cost

The value placed on good X by society through the market, or the social value of a marginal unit of X

$$P_X = MC_X$$

Market-determined value of resources needed to produce a marginal unit of X. MC_X is equal to the opportunity cost of those resources: lost production of other goods or the value of the resources left unemployed (leisure, vacant land, etc.)

If $P_X > MC_X$, society gains value by producing *more X*.
If $P_X < MC_X$, society gains value by producing *less X*.

[3]*It is important to understand that firms do not act consciously to balance social costs and benefits. In fact, the usual assumption is that firms are self-interested, private profit-maximizers. It just works out that in perfectly competitive markets, when firms are weighing private benefits against private costs, they are actually (perhaps without knowing it) weighing the benefits and costs to society as well.*

Figure 12.5 Efficiency in perfect competition follows from a weighing of values by both households and firms

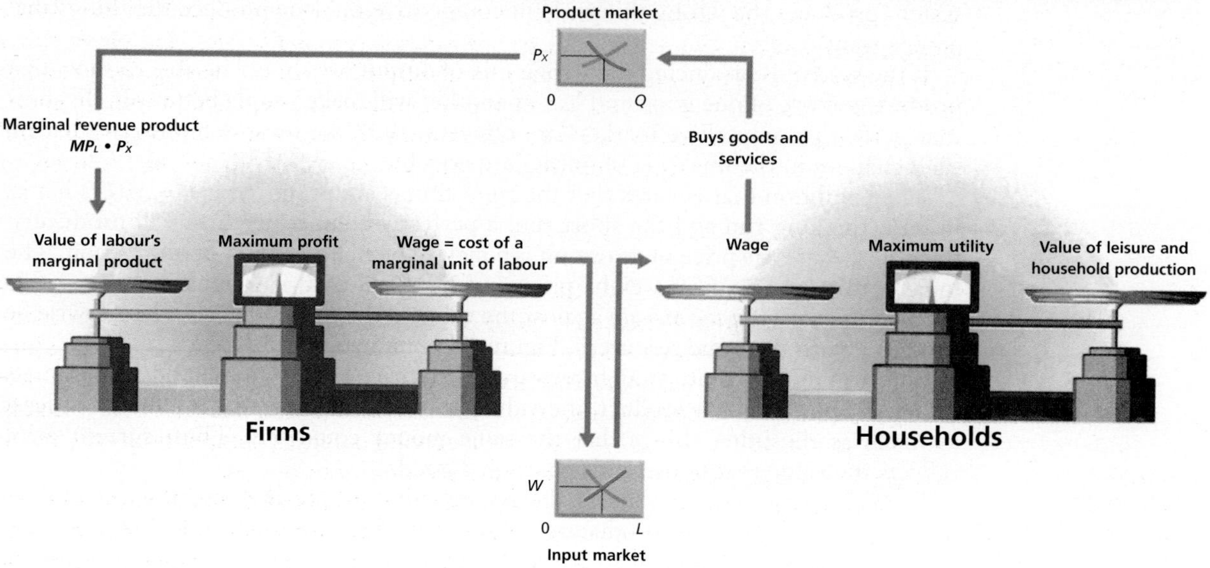

Product market

Marginal revenue product
$MP_L \cdot P_X$

Value of labour's marginal product | Maximum profit | Wage = cost of a marginal unit of labour

Buys goods and services

Wage | Maximum utility | Value of leisure and household production

Firms

Households

Input market

simplicity, the figure assumes only one factor of production, labour. Households weigh the market wage against the value of leisure and time spent in unpaid household production. But the wage is a measure of labour's potential product because firms weigh labour cost (wages) against the value of the product produced and hire up to the point at which $W = MRP_L$. Households use wages to buy market-produced goods. Thus, households implicitly weigh the value of market-produced goods against the value of leisure and household production.

When a firm's scale is balanced, it is earning maximum profit; when a household's scale is balanced, it is maximizing utility. Under these conditions, no changes can improve social welfare.

Perfect competition versus real markets

So far, we have built a model of a perfectly competitive market system that produces an efficient allocation of resources, an efficient mix of output, and an efficient distribution of output. But the perfectly competitive model is built on a set of assumptions, all of which must hold for our conclusions to be fully valid. We have assumed that all firms and households are price-takers in input and output markets, that firms and households have perfect information, and that all firms maximize profits.

But these assumptions do not always hold in real-world markets. When this is the case, the conclusion that free, unregulated markets will produce an efficient outcome breaks down. The remainder of this chapter discusses some inefficiencies that occur naturally in markets and some of the strengths, as well as the weaknesses, of the market mechanism. We also discuss the usefulness of the competitive model for understanding the real economy.

The sources of market failure

In suggesting some of the problems encountered in real markets and some of the possible solutions to these problems, the rest of this chapter previews the next part of this book, which focuses on the economics of market failure and the role of government in the economy.

market failure

Occurs when resources are misallocated, or allocated inefficiently. The result is waste or lost value.

Market failure occurs when resources are misallocated, or allocated inefficiently. The result is waste or lost value. In this section, we briefly describe four important sources of market failure: (1) *imperfect market structure*, or non-competitive behaviour, (2) the existence of *public goods*, (3) the presence of *external costs and benefits*, and (4) *imperfect information*. Each condition results from the failure of one of the assumptions basic to the perfectly competitive model, and each is discussed in more detail in later chapters. Each also points to a potential role for government in the economy. The desirability and extent of actual government involvement in the economy are hotly debated subjects.

Imperfect markets

Until now we have operated on the assumption that the number of buyers and sellers in each market is large. When each buyer and each seller is only one of a great many in the market, no individual buyer or seller can independently influence price. Thus, all economic decision makers are by virtue of their relatively small size forced to take input prices and output prices as given. When this assumption does not hold – that is, when single firms have some control over price and potential competition – the result is **imperfect competition** and an inefficient allocation of resources.

imperfect competition

An industry in which single firms have some control over price and competition. Imperfectly competitive industries give rise to an inefficient allocation of resources.

A Danish pig farmer is probably a 'price-taker', but Microsoft and Toyota most certainly are not. Many firms in many industries do have some control over price. The degree of control that is possible depends on the character of competition in the industry itself.

An industry that consists of just one firm producing a product for which there are no close substitutes is called a **monopoly**. Although a monopoly has no other firms to compete with, it is still constrained by market demand. To be successful, the firm still has to produce something that people want. Essentially, a monopoly must choose both price and quantity of output simultaneously, because the amount that it will be able to sell depends on the price it sets. If the price is too high, it will sell nothing. Presumably, a monopolist sets price in order to maximize profit. That price is generally significantly above average costs, and such a firm usually earns economic profits.

monopoly An industry comprising only one firm that produces a product for which there are no close substitutes and in which significant barriers exist to prevent new firms from entering the industry.

In competition, economic profits will attract the entry of new firms into the industry. A rational monopolist who is not restrained by the government does everything possible to block any such entry in order to preserve economic profits in the long run. As a result, society loses the benefits of more product and lower prices. A number of barriers to entry can be raised. Sometimes a monopoly is actually licensed by government, and entry into its market is prohibited by law. Taiwan has only one beer company; some parts of Europe have only one telephone company and only one electricity distributor. Ownership of a natural resource can also be the source of monopoly power. If I buy up all the coal mines in Europe and I persuade the EU to restrict coal imports, no one can enter the coal industry and compete with me.

Between monopoly and perfect competition are a number of other imperfectly competitive market structures. *Oligopolistic industries* are made up of a small number of firms, each with a degree of price-setting power. *Monopolistically competitive industries* are made up of a large number of firms that acquire price-setting power by differentiating their products or by establishing a brand name. Only Lever can produce Persil, for example, and only Pfizer can produce Viagra.

In all imperfectly competitive industries, output is lower – the product is underproduced – and price is higher than it would be under perfect competition. The equilibrium condition $P = MC$ does not hold, and the system does not produce the most efficient product mix.

In EU countries, many forms of non-competitive behaviour are illegal. A firm that attempts to monopolize an industry or conspires with other firms to reduce competition risks serious penalties. Recently, three industries once thought to be 'natural monopolies' are shifting away from government regulation towards becoming more competitive industries: telephone services, electricity and natural gas. (All of this is discussed in much more detail in Chapters 13, 14 and 15.)

Public goods

A second major source of inefficiency lies in the fact that private producers simply do not find it in their best interest to produce everything that members of society want. More specifically, there is a whole class of goods called **public goods**, or **social goods**, that will be under-produced or not produced at all in a completely unregulated market economy.[4]

> **public goods, *or* social goods**
> Goods or services that bestow collective benefits on members of society. Generally, no one can be excluded from enjoying their benefits. The classic example is national defence.

Public goods are goods or services that bestow collective benefits on society; they are, in a sense, collectively consumed. The classic example is national defence, but there are countless others – police protection, the preservation of 'wilderness' land, and public health, to name a few. These things are 'produced' using land, labour and capital just like any other good. Some public goods, such as national defence, benefit the whole nation. Others, such as clean air, may be limited to smaller areas – the air may be clean in a small, rural Scandinavian town but relatively dirty in a large industrial German city.

Public goods are consumed by everyone, not just by those who pay for them. Once the good is produced, no one can be excluded from enjoying its benefits. Producers of hamburgers and other **private goods** can make a profit because they don't hand over the product to you until you pay for it. Chapters 4–11 centred on the production of private goods.

> **private goods**
> Products produced by firms for sale to individual households.

If the provision of public goods were left to private, profit-seeking producers with no power to force payment, a serious problem would arise. Suppose, for example, that I value some public good, X. If there were a functioning market for X, I would be willing to pay for it. But suppose that I am asked to contribute voluntarily to the production of X. Should I contribute? Perhaps I should on moral grounds, but not on the basis of pure self-interest.

At least two problems can get in the way. First, because I cannot be excluded from using X for not paying, I get the good whether I pay or not. Why should I pay if I don't have to? Second, since public goods that provide collective benefits to large numbers of people are expensive to produce, any one person's contribution is not likely to make much difference to the amount of the good ultimately produced. Would national defence suffer, for example, if you didn't pay your share of the bill? Probably not. Thus, nothing happens if you don't pay; the output of the good doesn't change much, and you get it whether you pay or not.

For these reasons:

> Private provision of public goods fails. A completely laissez-faire market system will not produce everything that all members of a society might want. Citizens must band together to ensure that desired public goods are produced, and this is generally accomplished through government spending financed by taxes. The purpose of government provision of public goods is to correct for a naturally occurring failure of the market to produce everything that consumers want.

Public goods are discussed in Chapter 16.

Externalities

A third major source of inefficiency is the existence of external costs and benefits. An **externality** is a cost or benefit imposed or bestowed on an individual or group that is outside, or external to, the transaction – in other words, something that affects a third party. In a city, external costs are pervasive. The classic example is pollution, but there are thousands of others, such as noise, congestion and painting your house a colour that the neighbours think is hideous.

> **externality** A cost or benefit resulting from some activity or transaction that is imposed or bestowed upon parties outside the activity or transaction.

---

[4]*While they are normally referred to as public goods, many of the things we are talking about are services.*

Not all externalities are negative, however. Housing investment, for example, may yield benefits for neighbours. A farm located near a city provides residents in the area with nice views, fresher air and a less congested environment.

Externalities are a problem only if decision makers do not take them into account. The logic of efficiency presented earlier in this chapter required that firms weigh social benefits against social costs. If a firm in a competitive environment produces a good, it is because the value of that good to society exceeds the social cost of producing it – this is the logic of $P = MC$. If social costs or benefits are overlooked or left out of the calculations, inefficient decisions result.

The market itself has no automatic mechanism that provides decision makers with an incentive to consider external effects. Through government, however, society has established over the years a number of different institutions for dealing with externalities. Tort law, for example, is a body of legal rules that deal with third-party effects. Under certain circumstances, those who impose costs are held strictly liable for them. In other circumstances, liability is assessed only if the cost results from 'negligent' behaviour. Tort law deals with small problems as well as larger ones. If a neighbour sprays her lawn with a powerful chemical and kills your prize shrub, you can take her to court and force her to pay for it. Huge damages were caused when a large oil tanker ran aground off Japan in 1997. Most damage claims resulting from the accident will be settled in court.

The effects of externalities can be enormous. A recent example of an externality with potentially horrifying results is toxic waste dumping. For years, companies piled chemical wastes indiscriminately into dump sites near water supplies and residential areas. In some locations, those wastes seeped into the ground and contaminated the drinking water. In response to the evidence that smoking damages not only the smoker but others as well, governments have increased prohibitions against smoking in public places, and placed restrictions on tobacco advertising.

For years, economists have suggested that a carefully designed set of taxes and subsidies could help to 'internalize' external effects. For example, if a paper mill that pollutes the air and waterways is taxed in proportion to the damage caused by that pollution, it will consider those costs in its decisions.

Sometimes, interaction among and between parties can lead to the proper consideration of externality without government involvement. If someone plays her radio loudly on the fourth floor of your hall of residence, that person imposes an externality on the other residents of the building. The residents, however, can get together and negotiate a set of mutually acceptable rules to govern radio playing.

The key point here is that:

> The market does not always force consideration of all the costs and benefits of decisions. Yet for an economy to achieve an efficient allocation of resources, all costs and benefits must be weighed.

We discuss externalities in detail in Chapter 16.

Imperfect Information

imperfect information
The absence of full knowledge regarding product characteristics, available prices, and so forth.

The fourth major source of inefficiency is **imperfect information** on the part of buyers and sellers:

> The conclusion that markets work efficiently rests heavily on the assumption that consumers and producers have full knowledge of product characteristics, available prices, and so on. The absence of full information can lead to transactions that are ultimately disadvantageous.

Some products are so complex that consumers find it difficult to judge the potential benefits and costs of purchase. Certainly demanders in the market for medical care do not fully understand what they buy. Buyers of life insurance have a very difficult time sorting out the terms of the more complex policies and determining the true 'price' of the product. Consumers of almost any service that requires expertise, such as plumbing or medical care, have a hard time evaluating what is needed, much less how well it is done. It is difficult for a car buyer to discover the true 'quality' of the cars in Honest Joe's Used Cars.

Some forms of misinformation can be corrected with simple rules such as truth-in-advertising regulations. In some cases, the government provides information to citizens; job banks and consumer information services exist for this purpose. In some industries, such as medical care, there is no clear-cut solution to the problem of non-information or misinformation. We discuss all these topics in detail in Chapter 16.

Evaluating the market mechanism

Is the market system good or bad? Should the government be involved in the economy, or should it leave the allocation of resources to the free market? So far, our information is mixed and incomplete. To the extent that the perfectly competitive model reflects the way markets really operate, there seem to be some clear advantages to the market system. But when we relax the assumptions and expand our discussion to include non-competitive behaviour, public goods, externalities and the possibility of imperfect information, we see at least a potential role for government.

The market system does seem to provide most participants with the incentive to weigh costs and benefits and to operate efficiently. Firms can make profits only if a demand for their products exists. If there are no externalities, or if such costs or benefits are properly internalized, firms *will* weigh social benefits and costs in their production decisions. Under these circumstances, the profit motive should provide competitive firms with an incentive to minimize cost and to produce their products using the most efficient technologies. Likewise, competitive input markets should provide households with the incentive to weigh the value of their time against the social value of what they can produce in the labour force.

But markets are far from perfect. Freely functioning markets in the real world do not always produce an efficient allocation of resources, and this provides a potential role for government in the economy. Many have called for government involvement in the economy to correct for market failure – that is, to help markets function more efficiently. As you will see, however, many feel that government involvement in the economy creates more inefficiency than it cures.

In addition, we have thus far discussed only the criterion of efficiency, and economic systems and economic policies must be judged by many other criteria, not the least of which is *equity*, or fairness. Indeed, some contend that the outcome of any free market is ultimately unfair, because some become rich while others remain very poor.

Part Three, which follows, explores the issue of market imperfections and government involvement in the economy in greater depth.

Looking ahead

In this chapter we have wrapped up the perfectly competitive model described in detail in the last seven chapters. In discussing the idea of general equilibrium, we saw how the markets described separately in earlier chapters are all interrelated and how adjustments in any one market can cause subsequent adjustments in many or all of the others. To understand the way an economic system functions and to think properly about public policy issues, it is essential that we consider these interconnections. Partial equilibrium analysis can lead to wrong answers.

We also turned for the first time to normative economics. We began by reviewing the concept of efficiency. Next, we looked at the efficiency of the perfectly competitive system. If all the assumptions of perfect competition hold, the result is efficient. No changes could be made in the allocation of resources among firms, in the mix of output, or in the distribution of output among members of society that would even potentially make some better off without making some worse off.

But the assumptions of perfect competition simply do not hold in the real world. When we relax them in order to describe the world more accurately, we see some of the problems that the unconstrained market does not solve for itself.

Summary

General equilibrium analysis

1. Both firms and households make simultaneous choices in both input and output markets. For example, input prices determine output costs and affect firms' output supply decisions. Wages in the labour market affect labour supply decisions, income, and ultimately how much output households can and do purchase.

2. A *general equilibrium* exists when all markets in an economy are in simultaneous equilibrium. An event that disturbs the equilibrium in one market may disturb the equilibrium in many other markets as well. *Partial equilibrium* analysis can be misleading, because it looks only at adjustments in one isolated market.

Allocative efficiency and competitive equilibrium

3. An *efficient* economy is one that produces the goods and services that people want at least possible cost. A change is said to be efficient if it at least potentially makes some members of society better off without making others worse off. An efficient, or *Pareto optimal*, system is one in which no such changes are possible.

4. If a change makes some people better off and some people worse off, but it can be shown that the value of the gains exceeds the value of the losses, the change is said to be *potentially efficient*, or simply *efficient*.

5. If all the assumptions of perfect competition hold, the result is an efficient, or Pareto optimal, allocation of resources. To prove this statement, it is necessary to show that resources are allocated efficiently among firms, that final products are distributed efficiently among households, and that the system produces what people want.

6. The assumptions that factor markets are competitive and open, that all firms pay the same prices for inputs, and that all firms maximize profits lead to the conclusion that the allocation of resources among firms is efficient.

7. People have different tastes and preferences, and they buy very different things in very different combinations. But as long as everyone shops freely in the same markets, no redistribution of outputs among people will make them better off. This leads to the conclusion that final products are distributed efficiently among households.

8. Because perfectly competitive firms will produce as long as the price of their product is greater than the marginal cost of production, they will continue to produce as long as a gain for society is possible. The market thus guarantees that the right things are produced. In other words, the perfectly competitive system produces what people want.

The sources of market failure

9. When the assumptions of perfect competition do not hold, the conclusion that free, unregulated markets will produce an efficient allocation of resources breaks down.

10. An imperfectly competitive industry is one in which single firms have some control over price and competition. Forms of *imperfect competition* include monopoly, monopolistic competition and oligopoly. In all imperfectly competitive industries, output is lower and price is higher than it would be in competition. Imperfect competition is a major source of market inefficiency.

11. *Public*, or *social*, goods bestow collective benefits on members of society. Because the benefits of social goods are collective, people cannot in most cases be excluded from enjoying them. Thus, private firms usually do not find it profitable to produce public goods. The need for public goods is thus another source of inefficiency.

12. An *externality* is a cost or benefit that is imposed or bestowed on an individual or group that is outside, or external to, the transaction. If such social costs or benefits are overlooked, the decisions of households or firms are likely to be wrong, or inefficient.

13. Market efficiency depends on the assumption that buyers have perfect information on product quality and price and that firms have perfect information on input quality and price. *Imperfect information* can lead to wrong choices and inefficiency.

Evaluating the market mechanism

14. Sources of market failure – such as imperfect markets, social goods, externalities and imperfect information – are considered by many to justify the existence of government and governmental policies that seek to redistribute costs and income on the basis of efficiency, equity, or both.

Review Terms and Concepts

efficiency
externality
general equilibrium
imperfect competition
imperfect information
market failure
monopoly
Pareto efficiency, or Pareto optimality

partial equilibrium analysis
private goods
public goods, or social goods

Equation

Key efficiency condition in perfect competition:

$P_X = MC_X$

Problem Set

1. During the 1990s, cellular (mobile) telephones became very popular. At the same time, new technology made them less expensive to produce. Assuming the technology advance caused cost curves to shift downward at the same time that demand was shifting to the right, draw a diagram or diagrams to show what will happen in the short and long run.

2. A medium-sized bakery has just opened in Slovakia. A loaf of bread is currently selling for 14 koruna (the Slovakian currency) over and above the cost of intermediate goods (flour, etc.). Assuming that labour is the only variable factor of production, the table gives the production function for bread.

Workers	Loaves of bread
0	0
1	15
2	30
3	42
4	52
5	60
6	66
7	70

a. Suppose that the current wage rate in Slovakia is 119 koruna per hour. How many workers will the bakery employ?

b. Suppose that the economy of Slovakia begins to grow, incomes rise and the price of a loaf of bread is pushed up to 20 koruna. Assuming no increase in the price of labour, how many workers will the bakery hire?

c. An increase in the demand for labour pushes up wages to 125 koruna per hour. What impact will this increase in cost have on employment and output in the bakery at the 20 koruna price for bread?

d. If all firms behaved like our bakery, would the allocation of resources in Slovakia be efficient? Explain your answer.

3. Country A has soil that is suited to corn production and yields 135 kilos per hectare. Country B has soil that is not suited for corn and yields only 45 kilos per hectare. Country A has soil that is not suited for soybean production and yields 15 kilos per hectare. Country B has soil that is suited for soybeans and yields 35 kilos per hectare. In 1997, there was no trade between A and B because of high taxes, and both countries together produce high quantities of corn and soybeans, In 1998, taxes were eliminated because of a new trade agreement. What is likely to happen? Can you justify the trade agreement on the basis of Pareto efficiency? Why or why not?

4. Do you agree or disagree with each of the following statements? Explain your answer.
a. 'Housing is a public good and should be produced by the public sector because private markets will fail to produce it efficiently.'
b. 'Monopoly power is inefficient, because large firms will produce too much product, dumping it on the market at artificially low prices.'
c. 'Medical care is an example of a potentially inefficient market because consumers do not have perfect information about the product.'

5. Which of the following are examples of Pareto efficient changes? Explain your answers.

a. Peter trades his laptop computer to Cindy for her old car.

b. Greater competition in the electricity industry causes prices to fall. A study shows that resulting benefits to consumers are larger than the lost monopoly profits.

c. A high tax on woollen sweaters has been deterring buyers. The tax is repealed.

d. A department of the European Commission is reformed. Costs are cut by 25% with no loss of service performed.

6. Suppose that a clerical error means that two passengers both reserve the same – and last available – seat on a train from London to Paris. Two alternatives are proposed: (a) toss a coin, or (b) sell the ticket to the highest bidder. Compare the two from the standpoint of efficiency and equity.

7. Assume that there are two sectors in an economy: goods (*G*) and services (*S*). Both sectors are perfectly competitive, with large numbers of firms and constant returns to scale. As income rises, households spend a larger portion of their incomes on *S* and a smaller portion on *G*. Using supply and demand curves for both sectors and a diagram showing a representative firm in each sector, explain what would happen to output and prices in the short run and the long run in response to an increase in income. (Assume that the increase in income causes demand for *G* to shift to the left and demand for *S* to shift to the right.) In the long run, what would happen to employment in the goods sector? In the service sector? (*Hint*: see Figure 12.3.)

8. Which of the following are actual Pareto efficient changes? Explain briefly.

a. You buy 3 oranges for 1 euro from a street vendor.

b. You are near death from thirst in the desert, and must pay a passing vagabond €10,000 for a glass of water.

c. A mugger steals your wallet.

d. You take a taxi ride during the rush hour.

9. Each instance below is an example of one of the four types of market failure discussed in this chapter. In each case, identify the type of market failure, and defend your choice briefly.

a. A garage convinces you that you need €2000 worth of work on the engine's cylinder head, when all you really need is an oil change.

b. Everyone in a small town would benefit if some derelict land were turned into a park, but no entrepreneur will come forward to finance the transformation.

c. Someone who lives in a block of flats buys an Oasis CD, then plays it at full volume at 3 am.

d. The only two airlines flying direct between Hamburg and Oslo make an agreement to raise their prices.

10. Two factories in the same town take on workers with exactly the same skills. Union agreements require factory A to pay its workers €10 per hour, while factory B must pay €6 per hour. Each factory hires the profit-maximizing number of workers. Is the allocation of labour between these two factories efficient? Explain why or why not?

13

Monopoly

Chapters 6 to 12 built a model of a perfectly competitive economy. To do so, we needed to make some assumptions. In Chapter 12 we began to see what happens when we relax these assumptions.

A number of assumptions, you will recall, underlie the logic of perfect competition. One is that a large number of firms and households interact in each output market. Another is that firms in a given market produce undifferentiated, or homogeneous, products. Together, these two conditions limit firms' choices. With many firms in each market, no single firm has any control over market prices. Single firms may decide how much to produce and how to produce, but the market determines output price. The assumption that new firms are free to enter industries and to compete for profits led us to conclude that opportunities for economic profit are eliminated in the long run as competition drives price to a level equal to the average cost of production.

In the next two chapters, we explore the implications of relaxing these assumptions. In this chapter, we focus on the case of a single firm in an industry – a monopoly.

Imperfect competition and market power: core concepts

imperfectly competitive industry
An industry in which single firms have some control over the price of their output.

A market, or industry, in which individual firms have some control over the price of their output is **imperfectly competitive**. All firms in an imperfectly competitive market have one thing in common: they exercise **market power**, the ability to raise price without losing all demand for their product. Imperfect competition and market power are major sources of inefficiency.

market power
An imperfectly competitive firm's ability to raise price without losing all demand for its product.

Imperfect competition does not mean that *no* competition exists in the market. In some imperfectly competitive markets, competition occurs in *more* arenas than in perfectly competitive markets. Firms can differentiate their products, advertise, improve quality, market aggressively, cut prices and so on.

For a firm to exercise control over the price of its product, it must be able to *limit competition* by erecting barriers to entry. If your firm produces football shirts, and if other firms can enter freely into the industry and produce exactly the same football shirts that you produce, the result will be the outcome that you would expect in a perfectly competitive industry: the supply will increase, the price of football shirts will be driven down to their average cost, and economic profits will be eliminated.

But note that official Manchester United football shirts are more expensive than generic T-shirts. If your firm can prevent other firms from producing exactly the same product, or if it can prevent other firms from entering the market, then it has a chance of preserving its economic profits. Only the Manchester United licensees are allowed to use the official logo.

Defining industry boundaries

A monopoly, you will recall, is an industry with a single firm in which the entry of new firms is blocked. An oligopoly is an industry in which there is a small number of firms, each large enough to have an impact on the market price of its outputs. Firms that differentiate their products in industries that have many producers and free entry are called **monopolistic competitors** (review Figure 3.1). But where do we set the boundary of an industry? Although only one company produces Stella Artois, there are many other brands of lager. In general:

Figure 13.1 The boundary of a market and elasticity

We can define an industry as broadly or as narrowly as we like. The more broadly we define the industry, the fewer substitutes there are, and the less elastic demand for that industry's product is likely to be. A monopoly is an industry with one firm that produces a product for which there are *no close substitutes*. The producer of Brand *X* hamburgers cannot properly be called a monopolist because this producer has no control over market price and there are many substitutes for Brand *X* hamburgers.

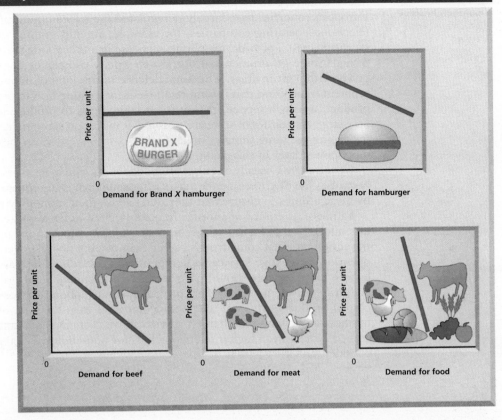

The ease with which consumers can substitute for a product limits the extent to which a monopolist can exercise market power. The more broadly a market is defined, the more difficult it becomes to find substitutes.

Consider hamburgers. A firm that produces Brand *X* hamburgers faces stiff competition from other hamburger sellers, even though it is the only producer of Brand *X*. The Brand *X* firm has little market power because near-perfect substitutes for its hamburgers are available. But if a firm were the only producer of hamburgers (or, better yet, the only producer of beef), it would have more market power, because fewer (or no) alternatives would be available. When fewer substitutes exist, a monopolist has more power to raise price because demand for its product is less elastic, as Figure 13.1 shows. A monopolist that produces all the food in an economy would exercise enormous market power because there are no substitutes at all for food as a category.

To be meaningful, therefore, our definition of a monopolistic industry must be more precise. We define **pure monopoly** as an industry with a single firm (1) that produces a product for which there are no close substitutes, and (2) in which significant barriers to entry prevent other firms from entering the industry to compete for profits.

Barriers to entry

Firms that already have market power can maintain that power either by preventing other firms from producing an exact duplicate of their product or by preventing firms from entering the industry. A number of **barriers to entry** can be erected.

pure monopoly
An industry with a single firm that produces a product for which there are no close substitutes, and in which significant barriers to entry prevent other firms from entering the industry to compete for profits.

barriers to entry
Something that prevents new firms from entering and competing in imperfectly competitive industries.

government franchise

A monopoly by virtue of government directive.

Government franchises

Many firms are monopolies by virtue of government directives. Although some European countries have largely deregulated the telecommunications industry, some telephone-operating companies, for example, are still granted exclusive licences by governments to provide telephone services; in other cases the industry is publicly owned. Some governments also grant electricity companies the sole right to supply power within given areas. The usual defence of this kind of monopoly power by government franchise is that it is more efficient for a single firm to produce the particular product (usually a service) than it is for many firms to produce the same product. If very large economies of scale are possible, it makes no sense to have many small firms producing the same thing at much higher costs. (We discuss these so-called 'natural monopolies' later in this chapter.)

Governments usually regulate monopolies to which they have granted exclusive licences. One of government's major responsibilities is to regulate the prices charged by these utilities to ensure that they don't abuse their monopoly power.

Fairness, or equity, is another frequently cited defence of government-regulated monopoly. Technological progress in the telecommunications industry has reduced the advantages that come from size, for example, but not all governments are ready to open local exchange service to competition. The reason is that some governments believe that everyone should have access to a telephone at affordable rates. In some countries, private households are provided with telephone service at a price below the cost of producing it; local telephone companies earn the bulk of their profits from business users, who are charged a price above cost. Deregulating local service, it is argued, would mean higher telephone bills for households, a change that many would consider 'unfair'.

Global Perspectives

Local telephone service in 1997: still pure monopoly in the USA

One of the last truly 'pure' monopolies in the United States is local telephone service. In nearly all states, the law restricts consumers to a single monopoly provider. This may be changing. In 1996, the US Congress passed the Telecommunications Act, which contained a provision requiring states to open up local service to competition. These provisions, however, were challenged and struck down by the US Court of Appeals for the 8th Circuit on 18 July 1997:

An appeals court struck down key elements of the Federal Communications Commission's rules for opening local telephone markets to competition yesterday, adding yet another obstacle to the already rocky landscape of telecommunications regulation.

The Federal appeals court ruling could further slow the introduction of unbridled competition – and the lower prices expected to result from that competition – in the nation's telecommunications business, because it would allow states to develop different mechanisms for bringing new companies into the market rather than following uniform FCC guidelines.[1]

While the future will see more competition, little had changed by 1997:

Sixteen months after the government opened the $100 billion local phone market to no-holds-barred competition, a new study has found that fewer than half of 1 per cent of Americans receive their residential phone service from a competitor to the monopoly provider.

Moreover, the most likely rivals to the local monopolies – AT&T, MCI, and other long-distance carriers – are entering the residential market only grudgingly, according to the study, which was compiled by the Yankee Group, a telecommunications research firm in Boston.

The report, which is to be released today, is sure to stoke the anger of consumer advocates who argue that the Telecommunications Act of 1996 has failed to deliver on its central promise of fostering competition in the local phone business.[2]

[1]Seth Schiesel, 'Court sets back FCC efforts to open local phone markets', New York Times, 19 July 1997, p. 1.

[2]Mark Lander, 'Monopolies still rule the local phone markets', New York Times, 22 May 1997, p. D1.

Large economies of scale and equity are not the only justifications that governments give for granting monopoly licences, however. Sometimes, government wants to maintain control of an industry, and a monopoly is easier to control than a competitive industry. However, when large economies of scale do not exist in an industry, or when equity is not a concern, the arguments in favour of government-run monopolies are much weaker.

Patents

patent A barrier to entry that grants exclusive use of the patented product or process to the inventor.

Another legal barrier that prevents entry into an industry is a **patent**, which grants exclusive use of the patented product or process to the inventor.

Patents provide an incentive for invention and innovation. New products and new processes are developed through research undertaken by individual inventors and by firms. Research requires resources and time, which have opportunity costs. Without the protection that a patent provides, the results of research would become available to the general public very quickly. If research did not lead to expanded profits, very little research would be done. On the negative side, though, patents do serve as a barrier to competition, and they do keep the benefits of research from flowing through the market to consumers.

To understand a patent's effects on profits, suppose that the industry producing blank videocassettes is competitive and that the full economic cost (including normal profit) of producing videocassettes is €5 each. In a perfectly competitive market, price will be driven to average cost, and consumers will pay €5 per tape.

Now suppose that the BASF company develops a new type of tape material that makes it possible to produce tapes of equal quality for €3. If no patent protection existed, every company in the industry would quickly analyse the new tape material and begin producing tapes at a cost of €3. Soon, competition would drive the price of tapes to €3, and consumers would enjoy the full benefits of the new technology. But this would eliminate BASF's incentive to do research on new materials.

If, however, BASF can protect its new material with a patent, it can produce tapes for €3, charge a price closer to €5, and make significant economic profits. These profits reward the developers of the new material, but they also keep the benefits from consumers.[1]

The expiration of patents after some years represents an attempt to balance the benefits of firms and the benefits of households: on the one hand, it is important to stimulate invention and innovation; on the other hand, invention and innovation do society no good unless their benefits eventually flow to the public.

In recent years, public attention has been focused on the high price of health care. One factor contributing to these costs is the very high price of many prescription drugs. Equipped with newly developed tools of bioengineering, the pharmaceutical industry has been granted thousands of patents for new drugs. When a new drug for a disease is developed, the patent holder can charge a very high price for it. The drug companies argue that these rewards are justified by high research and development costs; others say these profits are simply the result of a monopoly protected by the patent system.

When a patent is granted in connection with a publication, such as this book, it is called a *copyright*. It is illegal for you to copy pages from this textbook and then sell them to your friends. Copyright on a book normally lasts for at least 50 years.

---

[1]*Another alternative is licensing. Suppose BASF licenses the use of its material for 1 euro per tape produced. If other firms use the new material, costs will fall to €4 (€3 per tape plus the licence fee). The price of tapes will fall to €4 and BASF will get a royalty of 1 euro for every tape produced using the new material. Here the new technology is used by all producers, and the inventor splits the benefits with consumers. Because forcing the non-patent-holding producers to use an inefficient technology results in waste, some analysts have proposed adding mandatory licensing to the current patent system.*

Economies of scale and other cost advantages

Some products can be produced efficiently only in big, expensive production facilities. For example, figures published by Eurostat suggest that a washing machine manufacturer has to produce 10% of all the washing machines in Europe to achieve maximum-scale economies. A small entrepreneur is not going to jump into this business in search of economic profit. The need to raise such a large initial investment certainly limits the pool of potential entrants, a situation compounded by the riskiness of the business. Hence, large capital requirements are often a barrier to entry.

Sometimes, large economies of scale are not production related. Breakfast cereal can be produced efficiently on a very small scale, for example; large-scale production does not reduce costs. But the breakfast cereal market is dominated by heavily advertised brand names. To compete, a new firm would need an advertising campaign costing millions of euros. The large 'front-end' investment requirement in the presence of risk is likely to deter would-be entrants to the breakfast cereal market.

Ownership of a scarce factor of production

You can't enter the diamond-producing business unless you own a diamond mine. There are not many diamond mines in the world, and most are already owned by a single firm, the DeBeers Company of South Africa. Once, the Aluminum Company of America (now Alcoa) owned or controlled virtually 100% of the bauxite deposits in the world, and until the 1940s monopolized the production and distribution of aluminium. Obviously, if the production of a product requires a particular input, and one firm owns the entire supply of that input, that firm will control the industry. Ownership alone is a barrier to entry.

Price: the fourth decision variable

To review: a firm has market power when it has some control over the price of its product – raising the price of its product without losing all demand. The exercise of market power requires that the firm be able to limit competition in some way. It does this either by erecting barriers to the entry of new firms or by preventing other firms from producing the same product.

Regardless of the source of market power, the output price is not taken as given by the firm. Rather,

> Price is a decision variable for imperfectly competitive firms. Firms with market power must therefore decide not only (1) how much to produce, (2) how to produce it and (3) how much to demand in each input market (see Figure 7.3), but also (4) *what price to charge for their output.*

This does not mean that 'market power' allows a firm to charge any price it likes. The market demand curve constrains the behaviour even of a pure monopolist. To sell its product successfully, a firm must produce something that people want and sell it at a price they are willing to pay.

Price and output decisions in pure monopoly markets

For the purposes of analysing monopoly behaviour, we make two basic assumptions: (1) that entry to the market is strictly blocked, and (2) that firms act to maximize profits.

Initially, we also assume that our pure monopolist buys in competitive input markets. Even though the firm is the only one producing for its product market, it is only one among many firms buying factors of production in input markets. In some countries, a telephone company will have a monopoly. It will be the only supplier in

Figure 13.2 The demand curve facing a perfectly competitive firm is perfectly elastic; in a monopoly, the market demand curve is the demand curve facing the firm

Perfectly competitive firms are price-takers; they are small relative to the size of the market and thus cannot influence market price. The implication is that the demand curve facing a perfectly competitive firm is perfectly elastic. If the firm raises its price, it sells nothing, and there is no reason for the firm to lower its price if it can sell all it wants at P^* = €5. In a monopoly, the firm is the industry. Thus the market demand curve is the demand curve facing the monopoly, and the total quantity supplied in the market is what the monopoly decides to produce.

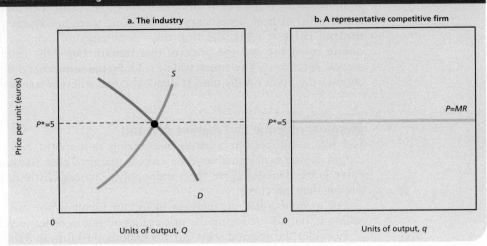

one particular area. However, it must hire labour like any other firm. To attract workers, it must pay the market wage; to buy fibre-optic cable, it must pay the going price. In these input markets, the monopolistic firm is a price-taker.

On the cost side of the profit equation, then, a pure monopolist does not differ one bit from a perfect competitor. Both choose the technology that minimizes the cost of production. The cost curve of each represents the minimum cost of producing each level of output. The difference arises on the revenue, or demand, side of the equation, where we begin our analysis.

Demand in monopoly markets

A competitive firm, you will recall, faces a fixed, market-determined price, and we assume that it can sell all that it wants to sell at that price; it is constrained only by its current capacity in the short run. The demand curve facing a competitive firm is thus a horizontal line (Figure 13.2). Raising the price of its product means losing all demand, because perfect substitutes are available. The competitive firm has no incentive to charge a lower price either.

Because a competitive firm can charge only one price, regardless of the output level chosen, its marginal revenue – the additional revenue that it earns by raising output by one unit – is simply the price of the output, or P^* = €5 in Figure 13.2. Remember that marginal revenue is important, because a profit-maximizing firm will increase output as long as marginal revenue exceeds marginal cost.

The most important distinction between competition and monopoly is that:

With only one firm in a monopoly market, there is no distinction between the firm and the industry. In a monopoly, the firm is the industry. The market demand curve is thus the demand curve facing the firm, and the total quantity supplied in the market is what the firm decides to produce (Figure 13.2a).

To proceed, we need a few more assumptions. First, we assume that a monopolistic firm cannot price discriminate. It sells its product to all demanders at the same price. (Price discrimination means selling to different consumers or groups of consumers at different prices.)

We also assume that the monopoly faces a known demand curve. That is, we assume that the firm has enough information to predict how households will react to different prices. (Many firms use statistical methods to estimate the elasticity of demand for their products. Other firms may use less formal methods, including trial and error, sometimes called 'price searching'. All firms with market power must have some sense of how consumers are likely to react to various prices.) Knowing the demand curve it faces, the firm must simultaneously choose both the quantity of output to supply and the price of that output. Once the firm chooses a price, the market determines how much will be sold. Stated somewhat differently, the monopoly chooses the point on the market demand curve where it wants to be.

Marginal revenue and market demand

Just like a competitor, a profit-maximizing monopolist will continue to produce output as long as marginal revenue exceeds marginal cost. Because the market demand curve is the demand curve for a monopoly, a monopolistic firm faces a downward-sloping demand curve.

For a monopolist, an increase in output involves not just producing more and selling it, but also reducing the price of its output in order to sell it.

Consider the demand schedule of a hypothetical firm in Table 13.1. Column 3 lists the total revenue that the monopoly would take in at different levels of output. If it were to produce one unit, that unit would sell for €10, and total revenue would be €10. Two units would sell for €9 each, in which case total revenue would be €18. As column 4 shows, marginal revenue from the second unit would be €8 (€18 minus €10). Notice that the marginal revenue from increasing output from one unit to two units (€8) is less than the price of the second unit (€9).

Now consider what happens when the firm considers setting production at four units rather than three. The fourth unit would sell for €7, but because the firm can't price discriminate, it must sell *all four* units for €7 each. Had the firm chosen to produce only three units, it could have sold those three units for €8 each. Thus, offsetting the revenue gain of €7 is a revenue loss of €3 – that is, €1 for each of the three units that would have sold at the higher price. The marginal revenue of the fourth unit is €7 minus €3, or €4, which is considerably below the price of €7.

Table 13.1 Marginal revenue facing a monopolist

(1) Quantity	(2) Price (euros)	(3) Total revenue (euros)	(4) Marginal revenue (euros)
0	11	0	0
1	10	10	10
2	9	18	8
3	8	24	6
4	7	28	4
5	6	30	2
6	5	30	0
7	4	28	−2
8	3	24	−4
9	2	18	−6
10	1	10	−8

(Remember, unlike a monopolistic firm, a perfectly competitive firm does not have to charge a lower price to sell more; thus $P = MR$ in competition.)

Marginal revenue can also be derived simply by looking at the change in total revenue. At three units of output, total revenue is €24; at four units of output, total revenue is €28. Marginal revenue is the difference, or €4.

Moving from six to seven units of output actually reduces total revenue for the firm. At seven units, marginal revenue is negative. While it is true that the seventh unit will sell for a positive price (€4), the firm must sell all seven units for €4 each (for a total revenue of €28). If output had been restricted to six units, each would have sold for €5. Thus, offsetting the revenue gain of €4 is a revenue loss of €6 – that is, 1 euro for each of the six units that the firm would have sold at the higher price. Increasing output from six to seven units actually decreases revenue by €2. Figure 13.3 graphs the marginal revenue schedule derived in Table 13.1. Notice that at every level of output except one unit, marginal revenue is below price. Marginal revenue turns from positive to negative after six units of output. When the demand curve is a straight line, the marginal revenue curve bisects the quantity axis between the origin and the point where the demand curve hits the quantity axis (Figure 13.4).

Look carefully at Figure 13.4. What you can see in the diagram is that:

> A monopoly's marginal revenue curve shows the change in total revenue that results as a firm moves along the segment of the demand curve that lies directly above it.

Consider starting at an output of zero units per period in the upper graph of Figure 13.4. At zero units, of course, total revenue (shown in the lower graph) is zero because nothing is sold. To begin selling, the firm must lower the product's price. Marginal revenue is positive, and total revenue begins to increase. To sell increasing quantities of the good, the firm must lower its price more and more. As output increases between zero and Q^* and the firm moves down its demand curve from point A to point B,

---

Figure 13.3 Marginal revenue curve facing a monopolist

At every level of output except one unit, a monopolist's marginal revenue is below price. This is because (1) we assume that the monopolist must sell all its product at a single price (no price discrimination), and (2) to raise output and sell it, the firm must lower the price it charges. Selling the additional output will raise revenue, but this increase is offset somewhat by the lower price charged for all units sold. Therefore, the increase in revenue from increasing output by one (the marginal revenue) is less than price.

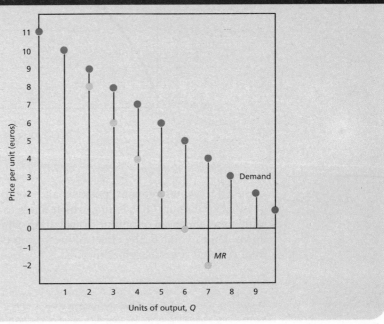

Figure 13.4 Marginal revenue and total revenue

A monopoly's marginal revenue curve bisects the quantity axis between the origin and the point where the demand curve hits the quantity axis: $0Q^* = Q^*C = 0C/2$. A monopoly's *MR* curve shows the change in total revenue that results as a firm moves along the segment of the demand curve that lies exactly above it.

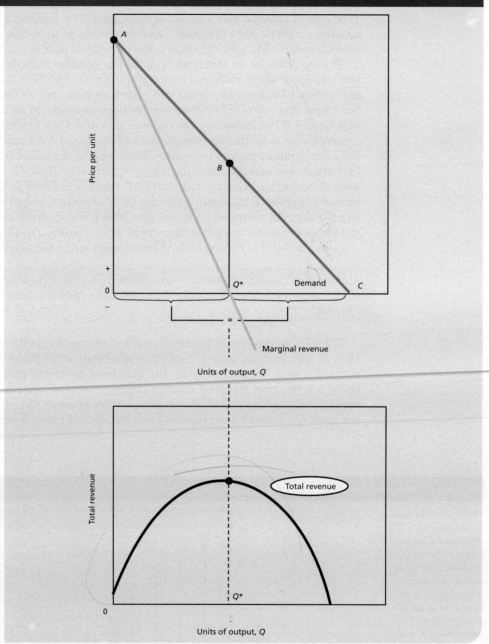

marginal revenue remains positive and total revenue continues to increase. The quantity of output (Q) is rising, which tends to push total revenue ($P \times Q$) up. At the same time, the price of output (P) is falling, which tends to push total revenue ($P \times Q$) down. Up to point B, the effect of increasing Q dominates the effect of falling P, and total revenue rises: marginal revenue is positive (above the quantity axis).[2]

---

[2]*Recall from Chapter 5 that if the percentage change in Q is greater than the percentage change in P as you move along a demand curve, the absolute value of elasticity of demand is greater than one. Thus, as we move along the demand curve in Figure 13.4 between point A and point B, demand is elastic.*

Maths Box 1 Revenue and linear demand

Given a straight line downward-sloping demand curve it is easy to show that the slope of the marginal revenue curve is twice that of the marginal demand curve.

A linear demand curve has the form $P = a - bQ$.

$$TR = P \times Q$$

$$= Q(a - bQ)$$

$$= aQ - bQ^2$$

Dividing TR by Q gives average revenue, AR:

$$AR = a - bQ$$

Differentiating the TR function gives MR, thus:

$$MR = a - 2bQ$$

Hence the slope of $AR = -b$; the slope of $MR = -2b$.

But what happens as we move further along the quantity axis above Q^* – that is, further down the demand curve from point B towards point C? We are still lowering P to sell more output, but above (to the right of) Q^*, marginal revenue is negative and total revenue in the lower graph starts to fall. Beyond Q^*, the effect of cutting price on total revenue is larger than the effect of increasing quantity. As a result, total revenue ($P \times Q$) falls. At point C, revenue once again is at zero, this time because price has dropped to zero![3]

The monopolist's profit-maximizing price and output

We have spent much time in defining and explaining marginal revenue because it is an important factor in the monopolist's choice of profit-maximizing price and output. Figure 13.5 superimposes a demand curve and the marginal revenue curve derived from it over a set of cost curves. In determining price and output, a monopolistic firm must go through the same basic decision process that a competitive firm goes through. As you know, any profit-maximizing firm will raise its production as long as the added revenue from the increase outweighs the added cost. In more specific terms, we can say that:

All firms, including monopolies, raise output as long as marginal revenue is greater than marginal cost. Any positive difference between marginal revenue and marginal cost can be thought of as marginal profit.

The optimal price/output combination for the monopolist in Figure 13.5 is $P_m = €4.00$ and $Q_m = 4000$ units, the quantity at which the marginal revenue curve and the marginal cost curve intersect. At any output below 4000, marginal revenue is greater than marginal cost. At any output above 4000, increasing output would reduce profits, because marginal cost exceeds marginal revenue. This leads us to conclude that:

The profit-maximizing level of output for a monopolist is the one at which marginal revenue equals marginal cost: $MR = MC$.

[3] Beyond Q^*, between points B and C on the demand curve in Figure 13.4, the decline in price must be bigger in percentage terms than the increase in quantity. Thus the absolute value of elasticity beyond point B is less than one: Demand is inelastic. At point B, marginal revenue is zero; the decrease in P exactly offsets the decrease in price, and elasticity is unitary or equal to -1.

Figure 13.5 Price and output choice for a profit-maximizing monopolist

A profit-maximizing monopolist will raise output as long as marginal revenue exceeds marginal cost. Maximum profit is at an output of 4000 units per period and a price of €4. Above 4000 units of output, marginal cost is greater than marginal revenue; increasing output beyond 4000 units would reduce profit.

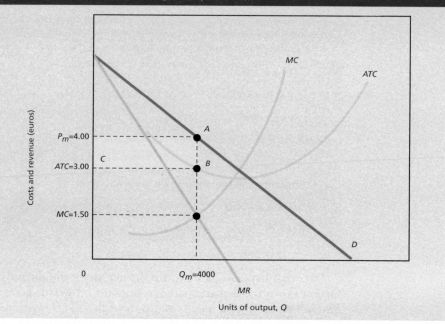

Because marginal revenue for a monopoly lies below the demand curve, the final price chosen by the monopolist will be above marginal cost (P_m = €4.00 is greater than MC = €1.50). At 4000 units of output, price will be fixed at €4 (point A on the demand curve), and total revenue will be $P_m \times Q_m$ = 4 × 4000 = €16,000 (area P_mAQ_m0). Total cost is the product of average total cost and units of output, 3 × 4000 = €12,000 (area CBQ_m0). Total profit is the difference between total revenue and total cost, 16,000 – 12,000 = €4000. In Figure 13.5, total profit is equal to the area of the pink rectangle P_mABC.

Among competitive firms, the presence of economic profits provides an incentive for new firms to enter the industry, thus shifting supply to the right, driving down

Maths Box 2 Maximizing monopoly profit

We can use calculus to confirm that the monopolist maximizes profit where $MC = MR$.
   Suppose the revenue and cost functions are $TR = 40Q - 2Q^2$ and $TC = 10 - 8Q + 2Q^2$. Then:

   $$\pi = TR - TC = 48Q - 4Q^2 - 10$$

The profit maximizing output is where $d\pi/dQ = 0$:

   $$d\pi/dQ = 48 - 8Q$$

Setting this to zero gives $48 - 8Q = 0$, so $Q = 6$ where profits are maximized. This must be where $MC = MR$:

   $$MC = dTC/dQ = -8 + 4Q$$

   $$MR = dTR/dQ = 40 - 4Q$$

   $$40 - 4Q = -8 + 4Q$$

   $$8Q = 48$$

   $$Q = 6$$

where profits are maximized, the level of output at which $MC = MR$.

price and eliminating profits. Remember, however, that for monopolies we assume that barriers to entry have been erected and that profits are protected.

The absence of a supply curve in monopoly

In perfect competition, the supply curve of a firm in the short run is the same as the portion of the firm's marginal cost curve that lies above the average variable cost curve. As the price of the good produced by the firm changes, the perfectly competitive firm simply moves up or down its marginal cost curve in choosing how much output to produce.

As you can see, however, Figure 13.5 contains nothing that we can point to and call a supply curve. The amount of output that a monopolist produces depends on its marginal cost curve and on the shape of the demand curve that it faces. In other words, the amount of output that a monopolist supplies is not independent of the shape of the demand curve.

A monopoly firm has no supply curve that is independent of the demand curve for its product.

To see why, consider what a firm's supply curve means. A supply curve shows the quantity of output the firm is willing to supply at each price. If we ask a monopolist how much output she is willing to supply at a given price, the monopolist will say that her supply behaviour depends not just on marginal cost but also on the marginal revenue associated with that price. And, to know what that marginal revenue would be, the monopolist must know what her demand curve looks like.

Applications

Monopoly power in sports

Considerable monopoly power exists in sport and the cost of watching it is rising.

Money is pouring into sport because viewers are willing to cough up a lot to watch it. They pay for it in different – and mainly indirect – ways: through taxes to finance public-service television; through time spent watching additional advertising during matches broadcast on commercial networks; in subscription fees to cable or satellite channels; or directly, on a pay-per-view basis. But viewers are paying over the odds because sporting authorities are able to use their control over the supply of games to force up the price of TV rights.

BSkyB, which broadcasts via satellite in Britain, is paying the English Premier League £620 m . . . over four seasons for the rights to a fraction of its matches.

In a paper published by Demos, a British think-tank, Julian Le Grand and Bill New, both of the London School of Economics, recommend a government agency to control the prices broadcasters charge viewers. That, in turn, would hold down the fees broadcasters would pay for sports rights. As in other regulated industries, prices could be set to ensure a reasonable return for teams and broadcasters.

This would not be as simple as it sounds. Because viewers pay mainly in indirect ways, the price is difficult to determine, and hence hard to cap. Some broadcasters would surely find clever ways around the rules. Moreover, there is no obvious way to determine the 'right' price. If it is too high, consumers will not benefit. If it is set too low and teams' revenues fall, fans may moan if top stars move abroad to earn higher wages.

Perhaps the solution is competition – among teams. They could be forced to sell broadcasting rights to their home games individually, rather than as a cartel. Boxers already do this. Germany's competition authority recently told German football clubs to do the same for international matches, and is considering applying that rule to domestic ones too.

Roger Noll, an economist at Stanford University in California, believes European sport is becoming more like America's, in which teams are brands rather than sources of local identity. For example, Manchester United, an English football club, has attracted many new fans in recent years, most of whom have no connection with Manchester. That process would speed up, Mr Noll says, if teams could sell their rights individually, because they would gain wider audiences of more fickle television fans. Anti-trust authorities in both Europe and America should try to make sure teams compete as fiercely off the pitch as they do on it.

Sources: 'Tackling monopolies', The Economist, 7 February 1998, p. 110; Fair Game? Tackling Monopoly in Sports Broadcasting (Demos, January 1998).

To summarize: in perfect competition, we can draw a firm's supply curve without knowing anything more than the firm's marginal cost curve. The situation for a monopolist is more complicated:

> A monopolist sets both price and quantity, and the amount of output that it supplies depends on both its marginal cost curve and the demand curve that it faces.

Monopoly in the long and short run

In our analysis of perfectly competitive markets we distinguished between the long run and the short run. In the short run, all firms face some fixed factor of production, and no entry into or exit from the industry is possible. The assumption of a fixed factor of production is the primary reason that marginal cost increases with output in the short run. That is, the short-run marginal cost curve of a typical competitive firm slopes upwards and to the right because of the limitations imposed by the fixed factor. In the long run, however, firms can enter and exit the industry. Long-run equilibrium is established when the entry and exit of firms drives economic profits in the industry to zero.

The distinction between the long and short runs is less important in monopoly markets. In the short run, monopolists are limited by a fixed factor of production, just as competitive firms are. The cost curves in Figure 13.5 reflect the diminishing returns to the monopoly's fixed factor of production (for example, plant size).

What will happen to the monopoly in the long run? If the monopoly is earning economic profits (profits over and above a normal return to capital), nothing will happen. In competition, profits lead to expansion and entry, but in monopoly, entry is blocked. In addition, because we assume that the monopoly is a profit-maximizing firm, it will operate at the most efficient scale of production, and it will neither expand nor contract in the long run. Thus, Figure 13.5 will not change in the long run.

It is possible for a monopoly to find itself suffering economic losses (profits below normal). A monopoly that finds itself unable to cover total costs is illustrated in Figure 13.6. The best that the firm can do is produce $Q_m = 10,000$ units of output (the point at which $MR = MC$) and charge $P_m = €4$ for its output (point E on the demand curve). But at 10,000 units of output per period, total revenue of €40,000 ($P_m \times Q_m$, where $P_m = €4$ and $Q_m = 10,000$), which is equal to the area P_mEQ_m0, is not sufficient to cover total costs of €50,000 ($ATC \times Q_m$, where $ATC = €5$ and $Q_m = 10,000$), which is equal to the area FDQ_m0. The firm thus suffers losses equal to €10,000, the shaded area (rectangle $FDEP_m$). Notice, however, that total revenue is sufficient to cover the level of variable costs, which equals €25,000 ($AVC \times Q_m$, where $AVC = €2.50$ and $Q_m = 10,000$). Thus, operating in the short run generates a profit on operation (total revenue minus total variable costs is greater than zero) that can be used to cover some of the firm's short-run fixed costs. The basis of the monopolist's decision is thus exactly the same as that for a competitive firm:

> If a firm can reduce its losses by operating in the short run, it will do so.

Similarly, in the long run, a firm that cannot generate enough revenue to cover total costs will go out of business, whether it is competitive or monopolistic. Since the demand curve in Figure 13.6 lies completely below the average total cost curve, the monopoly will go out of business in the long run, and its product will not be produced because it is simply not worth the cost of production to buyers.

Perfect competition and monopoly compared

One way to understand monopoly is to compare equilibrium output and price in a perfectly competitive industry with the output and price that would be chosen if the same industry were organized as a monopoly. To make this comparison meaningful,

Figure 13.6 Price and output choice for a monopolist suffering losses in the short run

It is possible for a profit-maximizing monopolist to suffer short-run losses. At 10,000 units of output (the point at which *MR* = *MC*), total revenue is sufficient to cover variable cost but not to cover total cost. Thus, the firm will operate in the short run but, unless demand increases, go out of business in the long run.

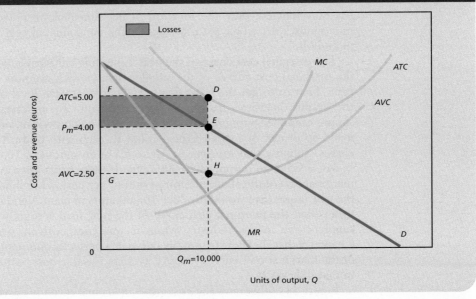

let us exclude from consideration any technological advantage that a single large firm might enjoy.

We begin our comparison, then, with a competitive industry made up of a large number of firms operating with a production technology that exhibits constant returns to scale in the long run. (Recall that constant returns to scale means that average cost is the same whether the firm operates one large plant or many small plants.) Figure 13.7 shows a perfectly competitive industry at long-run equilibrium, a condition in which price is equal to long-run average costs and in which there are no economic profits.

Figure 13.7 A perfectly competitive industry in long-run equilibrium

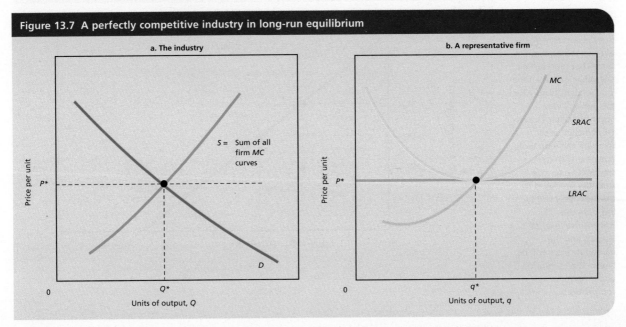

In a perfectly competitive industry in the long run, price will be equal to long-run average cost. The market supply curve is the sum of all the short-run marginal cost curves of the firms in the industry. Here we assume that firms are using a technology that exhibits constant returns to scale: *LRAC* is flat. Big firms enjoy no cost advantage.

Now suppose that the industry were to fall under the control of a single private monopolist. The monopolist now owns one firm with many plants. But technology has not changed; only the location of decision-making power has. To analyse the monopolist's decisions, we must derive the consolidated cost curves now facing the monopoly.

The marginal cost curve of the new monopoly will simply be the horizontal sum of the marginal cost curves of the smaller firms, which are now branches of the larger firm. That is, to get the large firm's *MC* curve, at each level of *MC* we add together the output quantities from each separate plant. To understand why, consider this simple example. Suppose that there is perfect competition and that the industry is made up of just two small firms, A and B, each with upward-sloping marginal cost curves. Suppose that for firm A, $MC = €5$ at an output of 10,000 units, and for firm B, $MC = €5$ at an output of 20,000 units. If these firms were merged, what would the marginal cost of the 30,000th unit of output per period be? The answer is €5, because the new larger firm would produce 10,000 units in plant A and 20,000 in plant B. This means that the marginal cost curve of the new firm is exactly the same curve as the supply curve in the industry when it was competitively organized. (Recall from Chapter 9 that the industry supply curve in a perfectly competitive industry is the sum of the marginal cost curves – above average variable cost – of all the individual firms in that industry.)[4]

Figure 13.8 illustrates the cost curve, marginal revenue curve and demand curve of the consolidated monopoly industry. If the industry were competitively organized, total industry output would have been $Q_c = 4000$ and price would have been $P_c = €3$. These price and output decisions are determined by the intersection of the competitive supply curve, S_c, and the market demand curve.

No longer faced with a price that it cannot influence, however, the monopolist can choose any price/quantity combination along the demand curve. The output level that maximizes profits to the monopolist is $Q_m = 2500$ – the point at which marginal

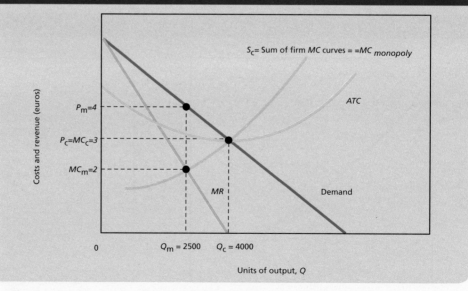

Figure 13.8 Comparison of monopoly and perfectly competitive outcomes for a firm with constant returns to scale

In the newly organized monopoly, the marginal cost curve is exactly the same as the supply curve that represented the behaviour of all the independent firms when the industry was organized competitively. This enables us to compare the monopoly outcome with the competitive outcome. Quantity produced by the monopoly will be less than the competitive level of output, and the monopoly price will be higher than the price under perfect competition.

[4]*The same logic will show that the average cost curve of the consolidated firm is simply the sum of the average cost curves of the individual plants.*

Maths Box 3 Outputs under monopoly and under competition

Using the same cost and revenue functions as before, we can compare the level of output under monopoly with the level of output in a competitive structure.

Given that $TR = 40Q - 2Q^2$ and $TC = 10 - 8Q + 2Q^2$, we showed that the profit-maximizing output for the monopolist was 6.

Under perfect competition, supply, MC = demand (AR)

$$MC = -8 + 4Q$$

$$AR = \frac{TR}{Q} = \frac{40Q}{Q} - \frac{2Q^2}{Q} = 40 - 2Q$$

In perfectly competitive equilibrium,

$$-8 + 4Q = 40 - 2Q$$

$$6Q = 48$$

$$Q = 8$$

Under perfect competition, $Q = 8$, compared to $Q = 6$ under monopoly.

revenue intersects marginal cost. Output will be priced at P_m = €4. To increase output beyond 2500 units or to charge a price below €4 (which represents the amount consumers are willing to pay) would reduce profit. The result:

Relative to a competitively organized industry, a monopolist restricts output, charges higher prices, and earns economic profits.

And remember, all we did was to transfer decision-making power from the individual small firms to a consolidated owner. The new firm gains nothing at all technologically from being big.

Collusion and monopoly compared

collusion The act of working with other producers in an effort to limit competition and increase joint profits.

Suppose now that the industry just discussed above did not become a monopoly. Instead, suppose the individual firm owners simply decide to work together in an effort to limit competition and increase joint profits, behaviour called **collusion**. In this case, the outcome would be exactly the same as the outcome of a monopoly in the industry. Firms certainly have an incentive to collude. When they act independently, they compete away whatever profits they can find. But, as we saw in Figure 13.8, when price increases to €4 across the industry, the monopolistic firm earns economic profits.

Despite the fact that collusion is illegal, it has taken place in some industries. During the mid-1990s, 33 European cement producers were found to have been exchanging information in order to keep prices across Europe uniformly high. At about the same time, European steel producers were found to be operating a cartel in the supply of some steel products used in the construction industry. Fines were imposed on these firms, the biggest being upon British Steel, amounting to Ecu 32 million. Illegal price fixing was also discovered among Italian bread bakeries in New York. (See the Application box, 'Rent-seeking behaviour in the Italian bread market'.)

The social costs of monopoly

So far, we have seen that a monopoly produces less output and charges a higher price than a competitively organized industry, if no large economies of scale exist for the monopoly. You are probably thinking at this point that producing less and charging more to earn economic profits is not likely to be in the best interests of consumers, and you are right.

Inefficiency and consumer loss

In Chapter 12, we argued that price must equal marginal cost ($P = MC$) for markets to produce what people want. This argument rests on two propositions: (1) that price provides a good approximation of the social value of a unit of output, and (2) that marginal cost, in the absence of externalities (costs or benefits to external parties not weighed by firms), provides a good approximation of the product's social opportunity cost. In pure monopoly, price ends up above product's marginal cost. When this happens, the firm is under-producing from society's point of view; society would be better off if the firm produced more and charged a lower price. We can therefore conclude that:

Monopoly leads to an inefficient mix of output.

A slightly simplified version of the monopoly diagram appears in Figure 13.9, which shows how we might make a rough estimate of the size of the loss to social welfare that arises from monopoly. (For the sake of clarity here, we will ignore the short-run cost curves and assume constant returns to scale in the long run.) Under competitive conditions, firms would produce output up to $Q_c = 4000$ units per period, and price would ultimately settle at $P_c = €2$, equal to long-run average cost. Any price above €2 will mean economic profits, which would be eliminated by the entry of new competing firms in the long run. (You should remember all this from Chapter 9.)

A monopoly firm in the same industry, however, would produce only $Q_m = 2000$ units per period and charge a price of $P_m = €4$, since $MR = MC$ at $Q_m = 2000$ units. The monopoly would make a profit equal to total revenue minus total cost, or $P_m \times Q_m$ minus $P_c \times Q_m$. Profit to the monopoly is thus equal to the area P_mACP_c, or €4000 ([4 × 2000] − [2 × 2000] = 8000 − 4000 = €4000. Remember that $P_c = AC$ in this example.)

Now consider the gains and losses associated with increasing price from 2 to €4 and cutting output from 4000 units to 2000 units. As you might guess, the winner will be the monopolist and the loser will be the consumer, but let us see how it works out.

Figure 13.9 Welfare loss from monopoly

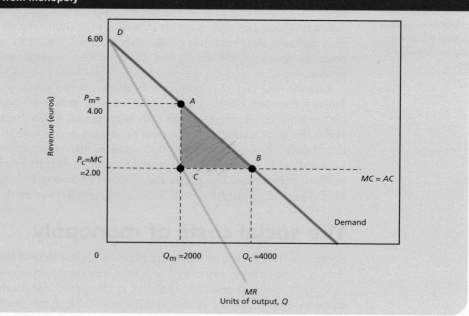

A demand curve shows the amounts that people are willing to pay at each potential level of output. Thus the demand curve can be used to approximate the benefits to the consumer of raising output above 2000 units. *MC* reflects the marginal cost of the resources needed. The triangle *ABC* roughly measures the net social gain of moving from 2000 units to 4000 units per period (or the loss that results when monopoly decreases output from 4000 units to 2000 units per period).

At $P_c = €2$, the price that would be charged under perfect competition, there are no economic profits. Consumers are paying a price of €2, but the demand curve shows that many are willing to pay more than that. For example, a substantial number of people would pay €4. Those people willing to pay more than €2 are receiving what we earlier called a *consumer surplus*. The demand curve shows approximately how much households are willing to pay at each level of output, and thus the area of triangle DBP_c gives us a rough measure of the 'consumer surplus' being enjoyed by households when the price is €2. Consumers willing to pay exactly €4 get a surplus equal to €2. Those who place the highest value on this good – that is, those who are willing to pay €6 – get a surplus equal to DP_c or €4.

Now the industry is reorganized as a monopoly that cuts output to 2000 units and raises price to €4. The big winner is the monopolist, who ends up earning economic profits equal to €4000 each period.

The big losers are the consumers. Their 'surplus' now shrinks from the area of triangle DBP_c to the area of triangle DAP_m. Part of that loss (which is equal to DBP_c minus DAP_m, or the area P_mABP_c) is covered by the monopolist's gain of P_mACP_c, but not all of it. The loss to consumers exceeds the gain to the monopoly by the area of triangle ABC (P_mABP_c minus P_mACP_c), which roughly measures the net loss in social welfare associated with monopoly power in this industry. Since the area of a triangle is half its base times its height, the welfare loss is $^1/_2 \times 2000 \times 2 = €2000$ per period. If we could push price back down to the competitive level and increase output up to 4000 units per period, consumers would gain more than the monopolist would lose, and the gain in social welfare would approximate the area of ABC, or €2000.

In this example, the presence of a monopoly also causes an important change in the distribution of real income. In Figure 13.9, area P_mACP_c is economic profit of €4000 flowing every period to the monopolist. If price were pushed down to €2 by competition or regulation, those excess profits would pass to consumers in the form of lower prices. Society may value this resource transfer on equity grounds in addition to efficiency grounds.

Of course, monopolies may have social costs that do not show up on these diagrams. Monopolies, which are protected from competition by barriers to entry, do not face the same pressures to cut costs and to innovate as competitive firms do. A competitive firm that does not use the most efficient technology will be driven out of business by firms that do. One of the significant arguments against tariffs and quotas to protect such industries as cars and electrical goods from foreign competition is that protection removes the incentive to be efficient and competitive.

Rent-seeking behaviour

In recent years, economists have encountered another serious worry. While triangle ABC in Figure 13.9 represents a real net loss to society, part of rectangle P_mACP_c (the €4000 monopoly profit) may also end up lost. To understand why, we need to think about the incentives facing potential monopolists.

The area of rectangle P_mACP_c is profit over and above a normal return to capital. If entry into the market were free and competition were open, these profits would eventually be competed to zero. Owners of businesses earning economic profits have an incentive to prevent this from happening. In fact, the diagram shows exactly how much they would be willing to pay to prevent it. A rational owner would be willing to pay any amount less than the entire rectangle. Any portion of profits left over after expenses is better than zero, which would be the case if free competition eliminated all profits.

There are many things that a potential monopolist can do to protect his or her profits. One obvious approach is to push the government to impose restrictions on competition. One example is the behaviour of taxi drivers in some large European cities. To operate a taxi legally, you will need a licence. Some cities tightly control the number of licences available. If entry into the taxi business were open, competition would hold down taxi fares to the cost of operating taxis. But taxi drivers in some cities have become a powerful lobbying force and have succeeded in restricting the number of licences issued. This restriction keeps fares high and preserves monopoly profits.

There are countless other examples. Some experts claim that an important function of IATA, the International Air Transport Association, is to restrict competition in the airline industry in order to keep prices and profits high. Lobbyists in other industries may try to persuade politicians to keep or raise tariffs[5] in order to preserve a measure of monopoly profit in their industries.

rent-seeking behaviour
Actions taken by households or firms to preserve extranormal profits

This kind of behaviour, in which households or firms take action to preserve extra-normal profits, is called **rent-seeking behaviour**.[6] Recall from Chapter 10 that rent is the return to a factor of production in strictly limited supply. Rent-seeking behaviour has two important implications.

First, it consumes resources. Lobbying and building barriers to entry are not costless activities. Lobbyists' wages, expenses of the regulatory bureaucracy, and the like must be paid. French farmers periodically drive animals and tractors into Paris to protest about cuts in guaranteed farm prices. This can bring businesses to a standstill and use up police time and resources. Extranormal profits may be completely consumed through rent-seeking behaviour that produces nothing of social value; all it does is help to preserve the current distribution of income.

Second, the frequency of rent-seeking behaviour leads us to another view of government. So far, we have considered only the role that government might play in helping to achieve an efficient allocation of resources in the face of market failure – in this case, failures that arise from imperfect market structure. Later in this chapter and in Chapter 15 we survey the measures government might take to ensure that resources are efficiently allocated when monopoly power arises. But the idea of rent-seeking behaviour introduces the notion of **government failure**, in which the government becomes the tool of the rent seeker, and the allocation of resources is made even less efficient than before.

government failure
Occurs when the government becomes the tool of the rent seeker and the allocation of resources is made even less efficient by the intervention of government.

This idea of government failure is at the centre of **public choice theory**, which holds that governments are made up of people, just as business firms are. These people – politicians and bureaucrats – can be expected to act in their own self-interest, just like owners of firms. We turn to the economics of public choice in Chapter 16.

public choice theory
An economic theory that the public officials who set economic policies and regulate the players act in their own self-interest, just as firms do.

Remedies for Monopoly

It is recognized that monopoly power is not in the public interest, and numerous anti-monopoly laws have been enacted. As we will see in Chapter 15, the government has taken two approaches to limiting monopoly power: (1) breaking up the monopoly into a number of smaller competing firms (restructuring the industry), and (2) allowing the firm to operate as a monopoly, but under strict regulations. One way the government can control monopoly is by setting the price of its output at competitive levels.

Under some, albeit unusual, circumstances, breaking up a monopoly would *not* be in the public interest. Some monopolies may be better left intact. It is to these 'natural monopolies' that we now turn our attention.

[5]A tariff is a tax on imports designed to give a price advantage to domestic producers.

[6]The term 'rent-seeking behaviour' was coined by Anne Krueger in an article published in 1974. Much of the theory dates to earlier work by Gordon Tullock. See Anne O. Krueger, 'The political economy of the rent-seeking society', American Economic Review, 64 (1974), pp. 291–303; and J. Buchanan, R. Tollison and G. Tullock (eds), Toward a Theory of the Rent-Seeking Society (College Station, TX: Texas A & M University Press, 1980).

Applications

Rent seeking behaviour in the Italian bread market

Rent-seeking behaviour refers to actions taken by households or firms to create and protect extranormal profits. The following article from the *New York Times* speaks for itself:

For years, law-enforcement officials heard complaints about a small group of unscrupulous bakers trying to corner the Italian-bread market in much of New York City. Using threats of violence, the authorities were told, the cartel controlled the distribution of fresh Italian bread to small grocery stores in Brooklyn and Staten Island, inflating prices and eliminating competition.

But investigators found that bakers and store owners were reluctant to cooperate. The only way to get to the heart of the Italian-bread racket, they decided, was to open a bakery themselves.

So a team of a half dozen undercover detectives opened a storefront at 327 West 11th Street in Greenwich Village in early 1993 and called it Louis Basile's. Wearing bakers' whites, they pretended to bake several dozen loaves of bread each day, taking turns getting up at 3 am to drive to New Jersey to buy the real stuff, and wrapping the loaves in the customized white paper sleeves that are the signature of authentic, fresh Italian bread.

It was not long after the investigators began trying to sell the bread to neighbourhood grocery stores in Manhattan and Brooklyn that they heard from the Association of Independent Bakers and Distributors of Italian Bread. Over drinks at the White Horse Tavern on Hudson Street, investigators say, a detective posing as a baker was told by two members of the association that violence could come to Basile's and its employees if they did not play by association rules.

The rules involved fixed prices for bread and a system of distribution that forced a store to buy from a single baker, said the Manhattan District Attorney, Robert M. Morgenthau . . .

Daniel J. Castleman, head of investigations in Mr Morgenthau's office, said association members included about 50 bakeries that supplied Italian bread to over 1000 small grocery stores and delicatessens in the city.

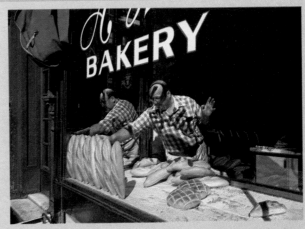

As a result of rent-seeking behaviour, the price of a loaf of Italian bread in New York City was raised ten cents and held to that level. The 1990 price increase cost consumers millions of dollars.

Mr Castleman said the office was unable to estimate what percentage of the city's bread sales were affected by the association's practices, in part because sales in large supermarkets were not involved. But he said the association controlled virtually all of Staten Island and most neighbourhoods in Brooklyn where Italian bread was popular and was expanding into Manhattan, Queens and Westchester and Nassau counties . . .

As an example of the association's activity, Mr Morgenthau cited a decision in 1990 to raise the retail price of bread from 75 to 85 cents. Five cents of the increase went to the bakers and the other five was divided between the bread deliverers and the store owners, he said.

'Because the association had a lock on the market, consumers had no choice but to pay the increase', Mr Morgenthau said . . .

While Mr Morgenthau said he could not estimate how much the association and its members profited from illegal operations, Mr Castleman said the 1990 price increase cost consumers millions of dollars.

Source: Seth Faison, 'Price-fixing plan is charged in New York Italian bakeries', New York Times, 14 July 1994, p. A1.

---

natural monopoly

An industry that realizes such large economies of scale in producing its product that single-firm production of that good or service is most efficient.

Natural monopoly

In comparing monopoly and competition, we assumed that the efficient scale of operation was small. When this is the case, there is no technological reason to have big firms instead of small firms. In some industries, however, there are technological economies of scale so large that it makes sense to have just one firm. Examples are rare, but electricity distribution and water services, for example, are among them. A firm that realizes such large economies of scale is called a **natural monopoly**.

Figure 13.10 A natural monopoly

A natural monopoly is a firm in which the most efficient scale is very large. Here average cost declines until a single firm is producing nearly the entire amount demanded in the market. With one firm producing 500,000 units, average cost is €1 per unit. With five firms each producing 100,000 units, average cost is €5 per unit.

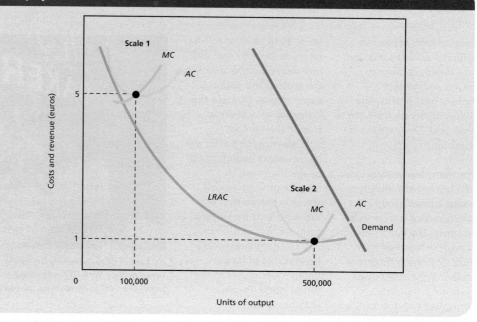

Although Figure 13.10 presents an exaggerated picture, it does serve to illustrate our point. One large-scale plant (Scale 2) can produce 500,000 units of output at an average unit cost of 1 euro. If the industry were restructured into five firms, each producing on a smaller scale (Scale 1), the industry could produce the same amount, but average unit cost would be five times as high (€5). Consumers thus see a considerable gain when economies of scale are realized.

The critical point here is that:

> Economies of scale must be realized at a scale that is close to total demand in the market.

Notice in Figure 13.10 that the long-run average cost curve continues to decline almost until it hits the market demand curve. If at a price of 1 euro market demand is 5 million units of output, there would be no reason to have only one firm in the industry. Ten firms could each produce 500,000 units, and each could reap the full benefits of the available economies of scale.

Do natural monopolies still exist?

The classic examples of natural monopolies over the years have been public utilities: the water company, the telephone company, the electricity company and the gas company. The basic idea was that the huge fixed costs of developing transmission lines and distribution pipes meant large economies of scale. It also made no sense to have five electricity companies all running cables down every street.

Until very recently, many European governments have allowed public utility companies to exist either as nationalized concerns or as monopolies subject to tight regulation of prices. Today everything is changing. The telephone service market is being made more competitive, for example. From 1 January 1998, any telephone company in Europe can offer callers in any other EU country (except Greece, Ireland and Portugal) a local or long-distance service.

In some countries, electricity and natural gas are not far behind. In the UK, for example, gas is a highly competitive industry with many suppliers offering gas to customers. In electricity there has been limited competition among suppliers to sell to large commercial users. Now domestic customers get a choice of supplier. The trick is to force local utilities to allow low-cost suppliers to transmit power over their lines for a fee.

While the trend is clearly away from regulation and towards competition, some governments still fear the consequences of fully deregulated markets. We will return to the subject of regulating natural monopolies in Chapter 15.

Market power in input markets: monopsony

monopsony A market in which there is only one buyer for a good or service.

Up to this point, we have been talking about market power in terms of output, or product, markets. Even monopolies, we assumed, were price-takers in input markets. But it is also possible for a firm to exercise control over prices in input markets. Consider a firm that is the *only buyer* in a market, the company that hires labour in a 'company town'. A market with one buyer is called a **monopsony**.[7]

We have said time and time again that competitive firms are price-takers in input markets as well as output markets. The wage rate, for example, is set by the supply and demand that result when many firms demand labour and many households supply it. An individual competitive firm takes an externally determined wage rate as a given and will demand an input as long as the marginal revenue product of that input exceeds its price. The marginal revenue product of labour, for example, is the added revenue that the firm earns by hiring one additional unit of labour. The unit of labour produces some product – its marginal product – which, when sold, brings in revenue. In making input decisions, the competitive firm compares the marginal gains from hiring each unit of labour (that is, what the product of that unit sells for) against the 'marginal cost' of that unit (that is, the wage rate). (If this sounds unfamiliar, you might want to review Chapter 10.)

When a firm hires labour competitively, it hires all the labour it needs at the current market wage. But suppose that the firm is the only buyer of workers with some particular skill. This means that the firm now faces a market supply curve rather than a market-determined equilibrium wage. The wage rate thus becomes a decision variable for the firm. If the market supply curve of labour slopes upwards, and the monopsony firm needs more labour, it must offer a higher wage to get that labour. The marginal cost of an additional unit of labour is no longer just equal to the wage rate. This leads us to the concept of **marginal factor cost (MFC)**, the additional cost of using one additional unit of a factor of production at the margin.

marginal factor cost (MFC) The additional cost of using one more unit of a given factor of production.

Using the supply schedule in Table 13.2, suppose that a monopsony firm in Holland wants to increase its use of labour from three units to four. The fourth unit of labour will work for a wage of 8 guilders per hour, but because our firm cannot price discriminate, it must pay all workers the higher wage. When the monopsony employed three workers, it had to pay them only 6 guilders per hour each. When the fourth unit of labour is added, those three will each earn an additional 2 guilders per hour. The total cost of increasing labour from three to four units, therefore, is the 8 guilders that goes to the fourth worker plus the 2 guilders to each of the other three. The marginal factor cost is thus 14 guilders. In other words, increasing the use of labour by one unit will cost the firm 14 guilders. The marginal factor cost is higher than the wage rate at every level of labour demand except one worker, because the higher wage needed to attract any additional labour supply goes to all workers, not just to the marginal worker.

---

[7]The terms 'monopoly' and 'monopsony' both derive from Greek root words. In both cases, mon(o) means 'sole' or 'single'. 'Monopoly' adds a form of the Greek verb polein, 'to sell'. 'Monopsony' adds a form of the Greek verb opsonein, 'to buy food'.

Table 13.2 Deriving marginal factor cost for a monopsonist (guilders)

(1) Units of labour supplied	(2) Wage	(3) Total factor cost (TFC)	(4) Marginal factor cost (MFC)
0	0	–	–
1	2	2	–
2	4	8	6
3	6	18	10
4	8	32	14
5	10	50	18
6	12	72	22
7	14	98	26

Figure 13.11 shows a typical marginal factor cost schedule that is above the labour supply schedule facing a monopsonist in a labour market. It is superimposed on the firm's marginal revenue product of labour schedule. Using our now-familiar marginal logic, we can conclude that:

A profit-maximizing firm hires labour as long as its marginal revenue product exceeds its marginal factor cost. Therefore, the profit-maximizing amounts of labour for the monopsonist occurs at the point where $MRP_L = MFC$.

Note that this condition is true for all firms, not just monopsonists. In perfectly competitive labour markets, the wage equals the marginal factor cost. Thus the

Figure 13.11 A monopsonist will hold wages below marginal revenue product, and hire less labour than a perfect competitor

For a monopsonist, the marginal cost of hiring one additional unit of labour is higher than the wage rate, because the firm must increase the wage of all workers to attract the new worker into the labour force. The monopsonist will hire only up to 400,000 hours of labour and pay a wage of 8 guilders per hour.

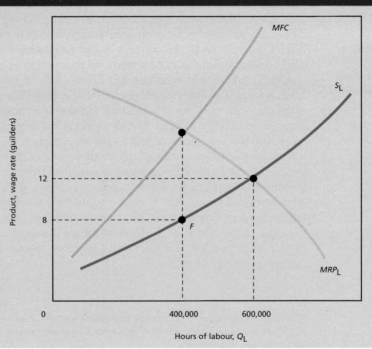

profit-maximizing amount of labour for a perfectly competitive firm can be written as $MRP_L = W$, which is what we learned in Chapter 10.

The monopsonist in Figure 13.11 would hire labour up to 400,000 hours (the point at which MFC and MRP_L intersect) and thus set a wage equal to 8 guilders per hour (point F on the supply curve). In competition, the wage would be 12 guilders per hour, the point at which quantity supplied and quantity demanded (marginal revenue product) are equal, and 600,000 hours of labour would be hired. (Review Chapter 10 if this reasoning is unclear to you.) Thus, much like a monopolist who curtails production and charges a price above the level set by competition, a monopsonist cuts back on the hours of labour hired and pays a wage below the level set by competition.

As you saw in Chapter 12, the condition $W = MRP_L$ ensures that households supply, and that firms hire, the efficient amount of labour. This condition implies that the market wage facing households and affecting their labour-supply behaviour reflects the value of the product of labour. With monopsony, the wage rate is held considerably below MRP_L at competitive equilibrium. Because marginal revenue product is the value of labour's product, keeping the wage lower keeps people out of the workforce who would otherwise be producing output that has a value to society. Thus, monopsony is inefficient.

Imperfect markets: a review and a look ahead

A firm has market power when it exercises some control over the price of its output or the prices of the inputs that it uses. The extreme case of a firm with market power is the pure monopolist. In pure monopoly, a single firm produces a product for which there are no close substitutes in an industry in which all new competitors are barred from entry.

Our focus in this chapter on pure monopoly (which occurs rarely) has served a number of purposes. First, the monopoly model describes a number of industries quite well. Second, the monopoly case illustrates the observation that imperfect competition leads to an inefficient allocation of resources. Finally, the analysis of pure monopoly offers insights into the more commonly encountered market models of monopolistic competition and oligopoly, which we discussed briefly in this chapter and will discuss in detail in the next chapter.

Summary

1. A number of assumptions underlie the logic of pure competition. Among them are: (1) a large number of firms and households are interacting in each market; (2) firms in a given market produce undifferentiated, or homogeneous, products; and (3) new firms are free to enter industries and to compete for profits. The first two imply that firms have no control over input prices or output prices; the third implies that opportunities for economic profit are eliminated in the long run.

Imperfect competition and market power: core concepts

2. A market in which individual firms have some control over price is imperfectly competitive. Such firms exercise *market power*. The three forms of *imperfect*

competition are monopoly, oligopoly and monopolistic competition.

3. A *pure monopoly* is an industry with a single firm that produces a product for which there are no close substitutes and in which there are significant *barriers to entry*.

4. There are many barriers to entry, including government franchises and licences, patents, economies of scale, and ownership of scarce factors of production.

5. Market power means that firms must make four decisions instead of three: (1) how much to produce, (2) how to produce it, (3) how much to demand in each input market, and (4) *what price to charge for their output*.

6. Market power does not imply that a monopolist can charge any price it wants. Monopolies are constrained by market demand. They can sell only what people will buy and only at a price that people are willing to pay.

Price and output decisions in pure monopoly markets

7. In perfect competition, many firms supply homogeneous products. With only one firm in a monopoly market, however, there is no distinction between the firm and the industry – the firm *is* the industry. The market demand curve is thus the firm's demand curve, and the total quantity supplied in the market is what the monopoly firm decides to produce.

8. For a monopolist, an increase in output involves not just producing more and selling it but also reducing the price of its output in order to sell it. Thus marginal revenue, to a monopolist, is not equal to product price, as it is in competition. Rather, marginal revenue is lower than price because to raise output one unit and to be able to sell that one unit, the firm must lower the price it charges to all buyers.

9. A profit-maximizing monopolist will produce up to the point at which marginal revenue is equal to marginal cost ($MR = MC$).

10. Monopolies have no identifiable supply curves. They simply choose a point on the market demand curve. That is, they choose a price and quantity to produce, which depend on both marginal cost and the shape of the demand curve.

11. In the short run, monopolists are limited by a fixed factor of production, just as competitive firms are. Monopolies that do not generate enough revenue to cover costs will go out of business in the long run.

12. Compared to a competitively organized industry, a monopolist restricts output, charges higher prices, and earns economic profits. Because MR always lies below the demand curve for a monopoly, monopolists will always charge a price higher than MC (the price that would be set by perfect competition).

The social costs of monopoly

13. When firms price above marginal cost, the result is an inefficient mix of output. The decrease in consumer surplus is larger than the monopolist's profit, thus causing a net loss in social welfare.

14. Actions that firms take to preserve excess economic profits, such as lobbying for restrictions on competition, are called rent seeking. *Rent-seeking behaviour* consumes resources and adds to social cost, thus reducing social welfare even further.

Natural monopoly

15. When a firm exhibits economies of scale so large that average costs continuously decline with output, it may be efficient to have only one firm in an industry. Such an industry is called a *natural monopoly*.

Market power in input markets: monopsony

16. A market with only one buyer is a *monopsony*. The problems of firms that exercise market power in input markets are similar to the problems of monopoly.

17. *Marginal factor cost* is the additional cost of using one more unit of a given factor of production. A profit-maximizing firm will hire labour as long as its marginal revenue product exceeds its marginal factor cost.

Review Terms and Concepts

barriers to entry
collusion
government failure
government franchise
imperfectly competitive
marginal factor cost (*MFC*)
market power

monopsony
natural monopoly
patent
public choice theory
pure monopoly
rent-seeking behaviour

Problem Set

1. Do you agree or disagree with each of the following statements? Explain your reasoning.
a. For a monopoly, price is equal to marginal revenue because a monopoly has the power to control price.

b. A natural monopoly will produce at an efficient level of output if its price is simply set by the regulatory agency at marginal cost.

c. Because a monopoly is the only firm in an industry, it can charge virtually any price for its product.

2. Explain why the marginal revenue curve facing a competitive firm differs from the marginal revenue curve facing a monopolist.

3. Assume that the snack food industry in Europe in 1997 was competitively structured and in long-run competitive equilibrium; firms were earning a normal rate of return. In 1998 two clever lawyers quietly bought up all the firms and began operations as a monopoly called Zonks. To operate efficiently, Zonks hired a management consulting firm, which estimated long-run costs and demand. These results are presented in Figure 1. (ΣMC_i = the horizontal sum of the marginal cost curves of the individual branches/firms.)

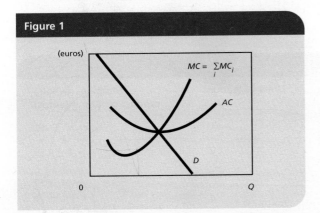

Figure 1

a. Indicate 1998 output and price on the diagram.
b. Assuming that the monopolist is a profit-maximizer, indicate on the graph total revenue, total cost and total profit after the consolidation.
c. Compare the perfectly competitive outcome with the monopoly outcome.
d. The European Commission is concerned that Zonks has monopolized the European snack food industry. Now, suppose the Commission asks you to prepare a brief memo (two or three paragraphs) outlining the issues. In your response, be sure to include (1) the economic justification for action, and (2) a proposal to achieve an efficient market outcome.

4. Jo's Beauty Cream, a product self-tested with great success has come to the market with the demand schedule in Table 1. Calculate marginal revenue over each interval in the schedule (for example, between q = 40 and q = 35). Recall that marginal revenue is the added

revenue from an additional unit of production/ sales, and assume that MR is constant within each interval.

If marginal cost is constant at 20 and fixed cost is 100, what is the profit-maximizing level of output? (Choose one of the specific levels of output from the schedule.) What are economic profits? Explain your answer using marginal cost and marginal revenue. Repeat the exercise for MC = €40.

5. Figure 2 shows the cost structure of a monopoly firm as well as market demand. Identify on the graph and calculate: (a) profit-maximizing output level, (b) optimum price, (c) total revenue, (d) total cost, and (e) total economic profit or loss.

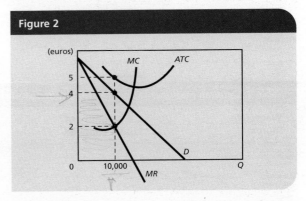

Figure 2

6. Consider a UK monopoly that produces paperback books; fixed costs = £1000, and marginal cost = £1 (and is constant).
a. Draw the average total cost curve and the marginal cost curve on the same graph.
b. Assume that all households have the same demand schedule, given in Figure 3. If there are 400 households in the economy, draw the market demand curve and the marginal revenue schedule facing the monopolist.

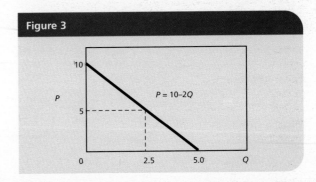

Figure 3

Table 1 Beauty Cream sales									
Price (euros)	20	30	40	50	60	70	80	90	100
Quantity demanded (tubs per month)	40	35	30	25	20	15	10	5	0

c. What is the monopolist's profit-maximizing output? What is the monopolist's price?

d. What is the 'efficient price', assuming no externalities?

e. Suppose that the government 'imposes' the efficient price by setting a ceiling on price at the efficient level. What is the long-run output of the monopoly?

f. Can you suggest an alternative approach for achieving an efficient outcome?

7. Consider the labour supply schedule and production data in Table 2.

a. Calculate marginal factor cost at each level of labour supply.

b. If the firm whose marginal revenue product schedule is given is a monopsonist, how much labour will be demanded? What wage will be paid? Explain your answer.

c. If the *MRP* schedule of labour were the industry demand schedule in a competitive industry, what would the wage rate be? How many units of labour would be employed?

*8. We saw in this chapter that given $TR = 40Q - 2Q^2$ and $TC = 10 - 8Q + 2Q^2$, the monopolist produces 6 units of output per period of time and a perfectly competitive industry produces 8 units.

a. What is the perfectly competitive price?

b. What is the monopolist's price?

c. What is the monopoly profit?

d. What is the size of consumer surplus under perfect competition?

e. What is the size of consumer surplus under monopoly?

f. What is the welfare loss if the industry were to change from a perfectly competitive structure to a monopoly?

fig 13:9 s.310

Table 2 Deriving marginal factor cost for a monopsonist			
Wage rate (euros)	**Quantity of labour supplied**	**Units of labour**	**Marginal revenue product of labour (euros)**
4	1	1	10
5	2	2	9
6	3	3	8
7	4	4	7
8	5	5	6
9	6	6	5
10	7	7	4

14

Monopolistic Competition and Oligopoly

We have now examined two 'pure' market structures. At one extreme is *perfect competition*, a market structure in which many firms, each small relative to the size of the market, produce undifferentiated products and have no market power at all. Each competitive firm takes price as given and faces a perfectly elastic demand for its product. At the other extreme is *pure monopoly*, a market structure in which only one firm is the industry. The monopoly holds the power to set price and is protected against competition by barriers to entry. Its market power would be complete if it did not face the discipline of the market demand curve. Even a monopoly, however, must produce a product that people want and are willing to pay for.

Most industries in Europe fall somewhere between these two extremes. In this chapter, we focus on two types of industries in which firms exercise some market power but at the same time face competition. One type, *monopolistic competition*, differs from perfect competition only in that firms can differentiate their products. Entry to a monopolistically competitive industry is free, and each industry is made up of many firms.

The other type, *oligopoly*, is a broad category that covers many different kinds of firm behaviour and industry structure. An oligopoly is an industry comprising competitors each large enough to have some control over market price, but beyond that the character of competition varies greatly from industry to industry. An oligopoly may have two firms or twenty, and those firms may produce differentiated or undifferentiated products.

Monopolistic competition

A **monopolistically competitive industry** has the following characteristics:

1. a large number of firms
2. no barriers to entry
3. product differentiation

While pure monopoly and perfect competition are rare, monopolistic competition is common throughout Europe. Take, for example, the restaurant business. Each restaurant in a town produces a slightly different product and makes an attempt to distinguish itself in consumers' minds. Entry to the market is certainly not blocked. New restaurants are frequently setting up, while others are going out of business. Although many restaurants fail, small firms can nonetheless compete and survive because economies of scale in the restaurant business are limited.

The feature that distinguishes monopolistic competition from monopoly and oligopoly is that firms that are monopolistically competitive cannot influence market price by virtue of their size. No one restaurant is big enough to affect the market price of a steak dinner even though all restaurants can control their *own* prices. Rather, firms gain control over price in monopolistic competition by *differentiating* their products. You succeed in the restaurant business by producing a product that people want but that others are not producing, and/or by establishing a reputation for good food and good service. By producing a unique product or establishing a particular reputation, a firm becomes, in a sense, a 'monopolist' – that is, no one else can produce exactly the same good.

monopolistic competition

A common form of industry (market) structure in Europe, characterized by a large number of firms, none of which can influence market price by virtue of size alone. Some degree of market power is achieved by firms producing differentiated products. New firms can enter and established firms can exit such an industry with ease.

Table 14.1 Proportion of industry employment and number of establishments accounted for by small firms[1]

| | Hotels and catering | | Trade agents | | Personal services | |
	Small firms' share	Number of units	Small firms' share	Number of units	Small firms' share	Number of units
EU 15	62.1	1,336,999	61.2	323,878	73.4	622,801
Belgium	44.2	53,560	73.8	17,534	56.3	32,978
Denmark	49.3	11,563	44.0	1,156	79.9	6,972
Eire	32.1	692,523	82.0	46,199	74.6	86,792
France	47.2	473,391	30.3	23,005	73.2	81,746
Germany	58.2	232,219	n/a	n/a	59.9	84,693
Italy	73.0	217,628	91.7	106,096	89.9	167,600
Netherlands	46.7	38,060	79.1	1,846	52.4	16,511

Source: Enterprises in Europe, 4th Report, December 1997; Eurostat.

The feature that distinguishes monopolistic competition from pure monopoly is that good substitutes are available in a monopolistically competitive industry. With many restaurants in any given location, there are usually dozens of good Italian, Chinese and French restaurants in most cities. Where the product is similar, so are the prices. The menus in the Chinese restaurants, for example, are nearly identical, and they all charge virtually the same prices. At the other end of the spectrum are those restaurants, with very well established names and prices far above the cost of production, that are always fully booked; this, of course, is the goal of every restaurateur.

Table 14.1 presents data on some of the sectors of the European economy that have the characteristics of monopolistic competition. Each of these sectors includes in each country thousands of individual firms, some of which are larger than others but which are small relative to the industry. In each of the industries in the table, small firms dominate. For example, 73.4% of all EU employees in the personnel services sector work in firms with 9 or less employees. This sector has the smallest average size of all sectors – an average of less than 3 employees for the EU as a whole.

Firms in a monopolistically competitive industry are small relative to the total market. New firms can enter the industry in pursuit of profit, and relatively good substitutes for the firms' products are available. Firms in monopolistically competitive industries try to achieve a degree of market power by differentiating their products – by producing something new, different or better, or by creating a unique identity in the minds of consumers.

Before we go on to discuss the behaviour of such firms, we need to say a few words about advertising and product differentiation.

Product differentiation, advertising and social welfare

product differentiation

A strategy that firms use to achieve market power. Accomplished by producing products that have distinct positive identities in consumers' minds.

Monopolistically competitive firms achieve whatever degree of market power they command through **product differentiation**. To be chosen over competitors, products must have distinct positive identities in consumers' minds. This differentiation is often accomplished through advertising.

[1]*Based on 1992 data.*

Table 14.2 Advertising expenditure by country and medium, 1995

Country	Total advertising expenditure (US$m)	Proportion on			
		Newspapers and magazines	TV	Radio	Other
Austria	1,674.0	61.8	21.2	10.6	6.3
Belgium	1,713.3	50.9	31.4	8.0	9.6
Denmark	1,495.2	77.5	18.0	2.0	2.5
Finland	1,114.6	73.2	20.5	3.4	2.9
France	10,153.3	47.4	33.0	7.4	12.2
Germany	21,966.8	68.9	22.4	4.1	4.5
Ireland	543.7	61.6	33.0	7.8	5.4
Italy	5,280.9	41.1	57.6	1.6	2.6
Netherlands	3,574.8	72.0	19.7	4.6	3.7
Norway	1,063.2	71.5	17.6	8.5	2.3
Sweden	1,847.4	74.9	18.4	1.8	4.9
UK	12.803.2	59.5	32.7	3.3	4.4

Source: European Advertising and Media Yearbook, 1997.

Very large sums are spent on advertising in Europe, as Table 14.2 shows. In each country it is newspapers, magazines and TV that dominate. Notice from Table 14.3 that advertising expenditure per head varies considerably between countries, being over four times higher in Switzerland than Italy.

The effects of product differentiation in general and advertising in particular on the allocation of resources have been hotly debated for years. Advocates claim that these forces give the market system its vitality and power. Critics argue that they cause waste and inefficiency. Before we proceed to the models of monopolistic competition and oligopoly, let's look at this debate.

The case for product differentiation and advertising

The big advantage of product competition is that it provides us with the variety inherent in a steady stream of new products, while ensuring that the quality of those products can satisfy a tremendous variety of tastes and preferences. A walk through several different districts of a big city, or an hour in a modern department store, should convince you that human wants are infinite in their variety.

Free and open competition with differentiated products is the only way to satisfy all of us. Think of the variety of music we listen to – indie, rock, country, folk, rap, classical, jazz. Business firms engage in constant market research to satisfy these wants. What do consumers want? What colours? What styles? What sizes? The only firms that succeed are the ones that answer these questions correctly and thereby satisfy an existing demand.

In recent years, quite a few of us have taken up the sport of running. The market has responded in a big way. Now there are numerous running magazines; hundreds of shoes designed specifically for runners with particular running styles; running suits of every colour, cloth and style; weights for the hands, ankles and shoelaces; tiny radios to slip into your sweatbands; and so on. Even doctors have differentiated their products: sports medicine clinics have diets for runners, therapies for runners, and doctors specializing in shin splints or Morton's toe. There is even a running shoe with

Table 14.3 Per capita advertising by country, 1995		
Country	Per capita expenditure (US$)	Index (Europe = 100)
Switzerland	419.7	205.9
Denmark	286.9	140.8
Germany	269.1	132.0
Norway	243.7	119.6
Netherlands	231.2	113.4
UK	222.7	109.3
Finland	217.9	106.9
Sweden	207.2	101.7
Austria	203.9	100.0
France	174.3	85.5
Belgium	171.2	84.0
Ireland	151.6	74.4
Greece	137.5	67.5
Spain	120.3	59.0
Portugal	107.3	52.6
Italy	96.6	47.4

Source: *European Advertising and Media Yearbook*, 1997.

a small computer built into the heel to monitor a runner's time, distance and calories expended.

The products that satisfy a real demand survive, but the market shows no mercy to products that no one wants. They sit on shelves, are sold at heavy discount prices or not at all, and eventually disappear. Firms making products that don't sell go out of business, the victims of an economic Darwinism in which only the products that can thrive in a competitive environment survive.

The standard of living rises when the technology of production improves – that is, when we learn to produce more with fewer resources. But the standard of living also rises when we have product innovation, when new and better products come on the market. Think of all the things today that didn't exist 10 or 20 years ago: compact disc players, microwave ovens, VCRs, mountain bikes, personal computers . . .

Variety is also important to us psychologically. The astonishing range of products available exists not just because your tastes differ from mine. Human beings get bored easily. We grow tired of things, and diminishing marginal utility sets in. I don't go only to French restaurants; it is nice to eat Greek or Chinese food once in a while too. To satisfy many people with different preferences that change over time, the market must be free to respond with new products.

People who visit planned economies always comment on the lack of variety. Before the Berlin Wall came down in 1989 and East and West Germany were reunited in 1990, those permitted to cross passed from colourful West Berlin into dull and grey East Berlin; variety seemed to vanish. As the Wall came down, thousands of Germans from the East descended on the department stores of the West. Visitors to China since the economic reforms of the mid-1980s claim that the biggest visible sign of change is the increase in the selection of products available to the population.

Proponents of product differentiation also argue that it leads to efficiency. If my product is of higher quality than my competitors' products, my product will sell more and my firm will do better. If I can produce something of high quality more cheaply – that is, more efficiently – than my competitors can, I will force them to do likewise or go out of business. Creating a brand name through advertising also helps to ensure quality. Firms that have spent millions to establish a brand name or a reputation for quality have something of value to protect.

For product differentiation to be successful, consumers must know about product quality and availability. In perfect competition, where all products are alike, we assume that consumers have perfect information; without it, the market fails to produce an efficient allocation of resources. Complete information is even more important when we allow for product differentiation. How do consumers get this information? The answer is, at least in part, through advertising. The basic function of advertising, according to its proponents, is to assist consumers in making informed, rational choices.

Supporters of product differentiation and advertising also claim that these techniques promote competition. New products can compete with old, established brands only if they can get their messages through to consumers. When consumers are informed about a wide variety of potential substitutes, they can more effectively resist the power of monopolies.

The advocates of free and open competition believe that differentiated products and advertising give the market system its vitality and are the basis of its power. They are the only ways to begin to satisfy the enormous range of tastes and preferences in a modern economy. Product differentiation also helps to ensure high quality and efficient production, and advertising provides consumers with the valuable information on product availability, quality and price that they need to make efficient choices in the marketplace.

The case against product differentiation and advertising

Product differentiation and advertising waste society's scarce resources. Critics argue that enormous sums of money are spent to create minute, meaningless differences between products.

Drugs, both prescription and non-prescription, are an example. Companies spend huge amounts to 'hype' brand-name drugs that contain exactly the same compounds as those available under their generic names. The antibiotics erythromycin and erythrocin have the same ingredients, yet the latter is half as expensive as the former. Aspirin is aspirin, yet we pay twice the price for an advertised brand, because the manufacturer has convinced us that there is a tangible – or intangible – difference.

Do we really need 50 different kinds of soap, all of whose prices are inflated substantially by the cost of advertising? For a firm producing a differentiated product, advertising is part of the everyday cost of doing business; its price is built into the average cost curve and thus into the price of the product in the short run and the long run. Thus, consumers pay to finance advertising.

In a way, advertising and product differentiation turn the market system completely around. We have been talking about an economic system that is supposed to meet the needs and satisfy the desires of members of society. Advertising is intended to change people's preferences and to create wants that otherwise would not have existed. From the advertiser's viewpoint, people exist to satisfy the needs of the economy.[2]

Critics also argue that the information content of advertising is minimal at best and deliberately deceptive at worst. It is meant to change our minds, to persuade us, and

[2]This point was made by John Kenneth Galbraith in The Affluent Society (Boston: Houghton Mifflin, 1958).

to create brand 'images'. Try to determine how much real information there is in the next ten advertisements you see on television. To the extent that no information is conveyed, critics argue, advertising creates no real value, and thus a substantial portion of the resources that we devote to advertising is wasted.

Competitive advertising can also easily turn into unproductive warfare. Suppose there are five firms in an industry and that one of these firms begins to advertise heavily. In order to survive, the others respond in kind. If one firm drops out of the race, it will certainly lose out. Advertising of this sort may not increase demand for the product or improve profitability for the industry at all. Instead, it is often a 'zero sum game' – a game that, on balance, no one wins.

Advertising may reduce competition by creating a barrier to the entry of new firms into an industry. One famous case study taught at the Harvard Business School calculates the cost of entering the breakfast cereal market. To be successful, a potential entrant would have to start with millions of dollars in an extensive advertising campaign to establish a brand name recognized by consumers. Entry to the breakfast cereal game is not completely blocked, but such financial requirements make it much more difficult.

Finally, some argue that advertising by its very nature imposes a cost on society. We are continuously bombarded by bothersome jingles and obtrusive images. Driving home from work, we pass 50 advertising hoardings and listen to 15 minutes of news and 20 minutes of advertising on the radio. When we get home, we open and throw away 10 pieces of unsolicited junk mail, glance at a magazine containing 50 pages of writing and 75 pages of advertisements, and perhaps watch a television programme that is interrupted every 15 minutes for a commercial break.

The bottom line, critics of product differentiation and advertising argue, is waste and inefficiency. Enormous sums are spent to create minute, meaningless and possibly non-existent differences among products. Advertising raises the cost of products and frequently contains very little information. Often, it is merely an annoyance. Product differentiation and advertising have turned the system upside down: people exist to satisfy the needs of the economy, not vice versa. Advertising can lead to unproductive warfare and may serve as a barrier to entry, thus reducing real competition.

No right answer

You will see over and over again as you study economics that many questions have no right answers. There are strong arguments on both sides of the advertising debate, and even the empirical evidence leads to conflicting conclusions. Some studies show that advertising leads to concentration and excess profits; others that advertising improves the functioning of the market.[3]

Price and output determination in monopolistic competition

Recall that monopolistically competitive industries are made up of a large number of firms, each small relative to the size of the total market. Thus, no one firm can affect market price by virtue of its size alone. Firms do differentiate their products, however. By doing so, they gain some control over price.

Product differentiation and demand elasticity

Purely competitive firms face a perfectly elastic demand for their product: All firms in a perfectly competitive industry produce exactly the same product. If Firm A tried to

[3]An excellent article discussing these and related issues is 'The Economics of advertising. A re-appraisal', by A, Bearne in Economic Issues, 1 (1), March 1996.

Applications

Selling the product: recent research

Recent research is helping firms to market their goods efficiently. One surprise concerns price cuts. The most common ploy is simply to cut the price for a few weeks. It is an article of faith that they both reward loyal customers and woo new ones.

Now even this is in question. For a start, consumers say they prefer incentives other than price. Price cuts also appear to have little lasting effect on sales volumes. In an unpublished study, a team at Purdue University led by Doug Bowman spend eight years scrutinizing how almost 1600 households in America bought a typical household product such as detergent. The study found that consumers exposed to repeated price cuts learn to ignore the 'usual' price. Instead they wait for the next discount and then stockpile the product.

Neither do most price cuts attract new customers. Andrew Ehrenberg, of Britain's South Bank University, tracked customers' buying habits for 25 established grocery brands in four countries for up to three years. He found that, although sales were higher during a price cut, when it was withdrawn they soon fell back to earlier levels.

The unexpected explanation for this was that almost all the customers buying the discounted product had tried it before. It seems that brands are built in other ways: price cuts are simply a gift to loyal customers. Little wonder that only a third of all promotions pay for themselves.

There are also new ways of using detailed information to target promotions – efficient consumer response (ECR). There are two novelties about ECR. One is the sheer detail of the information that can be gathered about consumers, made possible by the declining cost of computer power. The other is that this detail is not guarded by retailers, but shared across all stages in the supply chain. Ultimately such a system helps suppliers to devise precise promotions and provides the feedback needed to refine them.

Tesco is piloting a software system allowing selected suppliers to monitor sales of any of their products at any time in any store. Thus they can quickly see how a promotion is doing and whether the intended customers are buying it. Joe Galloway, the firm's head of supply-chain systems, reckons that such information can save 30% in promotion costs alone.

Such systems are still in their infancy. But they face two obstacles. First, they will work only if suppliers and retailers give up the habit of a lifetime and start to see each other as allies. A retailer should see itself not merely as a distribution channel for a supplier's brand, but an integral part of marketing that brand. The supplier, meanwhile, must feel confident that retailers will not betray them by handing sensitive product information to competitors or using it to promote an own-branded alternative.

The second risk is that attempts to reach the consumer will begin to seem intrusive. Susan Fournier, of Harvard Business School, has found that consumers are growing irritated and overwhelmed by the personal information being gathered about them in the name of direct marketing. One woman recently cancelled her supermarket loyalty card after she received a personalized letter reminding her that it was time she bought more tampons.

Source: 'Market makers', The Economist, *14 March 1998, p. 88.*

raise price, buyers would go elsewhere and Firm A would sell nothing. When a firm can distinguish its product from all others in the minds of consumers, as we assume it can under monopolistic competition, it probably can raise price without losing all demand. Figure 14.1 shows how product differentiation might make demand somewhat less elastic for a hypothetical firm.

A monopoly is an industry with a single firm that produces a good for which there are no close substitutes. A monopolistically competitive firm is like a monopoly in that it is the only producer of its unique product. Only the brand-owning firm can produce Nutella, or Johnson's Baby Oil, or Levi jeans. But unlike the product in a monopoly market, the product of a monopolistically competitive firm has many close substitutes competing for the consumer's favour.

While the demand curve faced by a monopolistic competitor is likely to be less elastic than the demand curve faced by a perfectly competitive firm, it is likely to be more elastic than the demand curve faced by a monopoly.

Figure 14.1 Product differentiation reduces the elasticity of demand facing a firm

The demand curve faced by a monopolistic competitor is likely to be less elastic than the demand curve faced by a perfectly competitive firm, but more elastic than the demand curve faced by a monopolist, because close substitutes for the products of a monopolistic competitor are available.

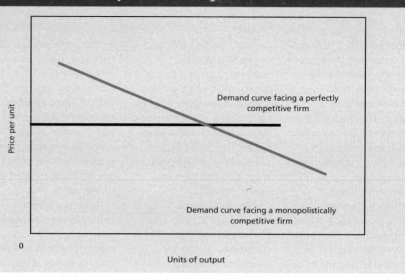

Price/output determination in the short run

Under conditions of monopolistic competition, a profit-maximizing firm behaves much like a monopolist in the short run. First, marginal revenue is not equal to price, because the monopolistically competitive firm has some control over output price. Like a monopolistic firm, a monopolistically competitive firm must lower price to increase output and sell it. The monopolistic competitor's marginal revenue curve thus lies *below* its demand curve, intersecting the quantity axis midway between the origin and the point at which the demand curve intersects it. (If necessary, review Chapter 13 to gain an understanding of this idea.)

The firm chooses the output and price combination that maximizes profit.

To maximize profit, the monopolistically competitive firm will increase production until the marginal revenue from increasing output and selling it no longer exceeds the marginal cost of producing it. This occurs at the point at which marginal revenue equals marginal cost: $MR = MC$.

In Figure 14.2a, the profit-maximizing output is $q_0 = 2000$ units, the point at which marginal revenue equals marginal cost. To sell 2000 units, the firm must charge €6. Total revenue is $P_0 \times q_0 = €12,000$, or the area of P_0Aq_00. Total cost is equal to average total cost times q_0, which is €10,000, or CBq_00. Total profit is equal to the difference, €2000 (the pink shaded area P_0ABC).

Nothing guarantees that a firm in a monopolistically competitive industry will earn economic profits in the short run. Figure 14.2b shows what happens when a firm with similar curves faces a weaker market demand. Even though the firm does have some control over price, market demand is insufficient to make the firm profitable.

As in pure competition, such a firm minimizes its losses by producing up to the point where marginal revenue is equal to marginal cost. Of course, as in pure competition, the price that the firm charges must be sufficient to cover variable costs. Otherwise, the firm will shut down and suffer losses equal to total fixed costs, rather than increase losses by producing more. In other words, the firm must make a profit on operation. In Figure 14.2b, the loss-minimizing level of output is $q_1 = 1000$ at a price of €5. Total revenue is $P_1 \times q_1 = €5000$, or P_1Bq_10. Total cost is $ATC \times q_1 = €6000$, or CAq_10. Because total cost is greater than revenue, the firm suffers a loss of €1000 equal to the blue shaded area, $CABP_1$.

Figure 14.2 Monopolistic competition in the short run

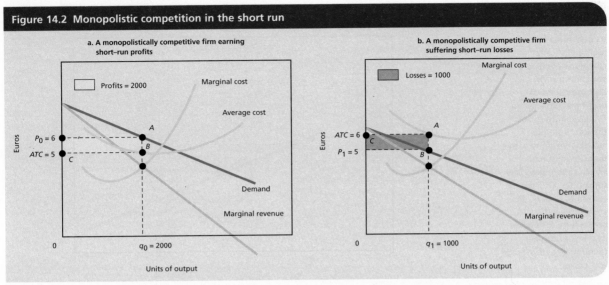

a. A monopolistically competitive firm earning short–run profits

b. A monopolistically competitive firm suffering short–run losses

In the short run, a monopolistically competitive firm will produce up to the point at which $MR = MC$. At $q_0 = 2000$ in graph (a), the firm is earning economic profits equal to $P_0ABC = €2000$. In graph (b), another monopolistically competitive firm with a similar cost structure is shown facing a weaker demand and suffering short-run losses at $q_1 = 1000$ equal to $CABP_1 = €1000$.

Price/output determination in the long run

In analysing monopolistic competition, we assume that entry and exit are free in the long run. Firms can enter an industry when there are profits to be made, and firms suffering losses can go out of business. But entry into an industry of this sort is somewhat different from entry into pure competition, because products are differentiated in monopolistic competition. A firm that enters a monopolistically competitive industry is producing a close substitute for the good in question, *but not the same good.*

Let us begin with a firm earning economic profits in the short run. Those economic profits provide an incentive for new firms to enter the industry. The new firms compete by offering close substitutes, driving down the demand for the product of the firm that was earning economic profits. If several restaurants seem to be doing well in a particular location, others may start up and attract business from them.

New firms will continue to enter the market until excess profits are eliminated. As the new firms enter, the demand curve facing each old firm begins to shift to the left, pushing the marginal revenue curve along with it. (Review Chapter 13 if you are unsure why.) This shift continues until profits are eliminated, which occurs when the demand curve slips down to the average total cost curve. Graphically, this is the point at which the demand curve and the average total cost curve are tangent (the point at which they just touch and have the same slope). Figure 14.3 shows a monopolistically competitive industry in long-run equilibrium. At q^* and P^*, price and average total cost are equal, so there are no economic profits or losses.

Look carefully at this tangency, which in Figure 14.3 is at output level q^*. The tangency occurs at the profit-maximizing level of output. At this point, marginal cost is equal to marginal revenue. At any level of output other than q^*, ATC lies above the demand curve. This means that at any other level of output, ATC is greater than the price that the firm can charge. (Recall that the demand curve shows the price that can be charged at every level of output.) Hence, price equals average cost at q^* and economic profits equal zero.

Figure 14.3 Monopolistically competitive firm at long-run equilibrium

As new firms enter a monopolistically competitive industry in search of profits, the demand curves of profit-making existing firms begin to shift to the left, pushing marginal revenue with them as consumers switch to the new close substitutes. This process continues until profits are eliminated, which occurs for a firm when its demand curve is tangential to its average cost curve.

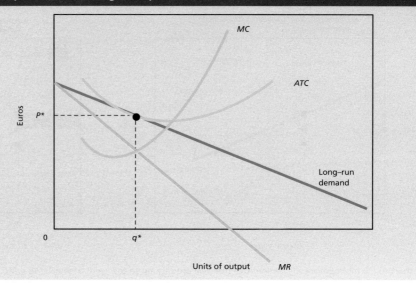

This equilibrium must occur at the point at which the demand curve is *tangential* to the average total cost curve. If the demand curve cut across the average cost curve, intersecting it at two points, the demand curve would be *above* the average cost curve at some levels of output. Producing at those levels of output would mean economic profits. Economic profits would attract entrants, shifting the market demand curve to the left and lowering profits. If the demand curve were always *below* the average cost curve, all levels of output would produce losses for the firm. This would cause firms to exit the industry, thus shifting the market demand curve to the right, and thus increasing profits (or reducing losses) for those firms still in the industry.

> The firm's demand curve must end up tangential to its average total cost curve for economic profits to equal zero. This is the condition for long-run equilibrium in a monopolistically competitive industry.

Even if a monopolistically competitive firm starts with losses, it will arrive at the same long-run equilibrium. (Look back at Figure 14.2b, which shows a firm suffering losses.) Suppose too many restaurants open up in a given small area, for example. If most diners go to one or two of the popular restaurants, business may be slow at the others. Given these circumstances, it seems likely that there will be a 'shake-out' in the near future – that is, one or more of the restaurants suffering losses will decide to drop out of the industry.

When this happens, the firms remaining in the industry will get a larger share of the total business, and their demand curves will shift to the right. Prosperous firms will grow more prosperous, and the firms remaining will still suffer losses but will find those losses reduced by the additional demand. The demand curves of remaining monopolistic competitors will continue to shift until losses are eliminated. Thus, we end up with the same long-run equilibrium as we did when we started out with a firm earning profits. At equilibrium, demand is tangential to average total cost, and there are no economic profits or losses.

Economic efficiency and resource allocation

We have already noted some of the similarities between monopolistic competition and pure competition. Because entry is free and economic profits are eliminated in the long run, we might conclude that the result of monopolistic competition is efficient. There are two problems, however.

First, once a firm achieves any degree of market power by differentiating its product (as is the case in monopolistic competition), its profit-maximizing strategy is to hold down production and charge a price above marginal cost, as you saw in Figures 14.2 and 14.3. Remember from Chapter 12 that price is the value that society places on a good, and marginal cost is the value that society places on the resources needed to produce that good. By holding production down and price above marginal cost, monopolistically competitive firms prevent the efficient use of resources. More product could be produced at a resource cost below the value that consumers place on the product.

Second, as Figure 14.3 shows, the final equilibrium in a monopolistically competitive firm is necessarily to the left of the low point on its average total cost curve. This means that a typical firm in a monopolistically competitive industry will not realize all the economies of scale available. (In pure competition, you will recall, firms are pushed to the bottom of their long-run average cost curves, and the result is an efficient allocation of resources.)

Suppose a number of firms enter an industry and build plants on the basis of initially profitable positions. But as more and more firms compete for those profits, individual firms find themselves with smaller and smaller market shares, and they end up eventually with 'excess capacity'. The firm in Figure 14.3 is not fully using its existing capacity because competition drove its demand curve to the left. Thus, in monopolistic competition we end up with many firms, each producing a slightly different product at a scale that is less than optimal. Would it not be more efficient to have a smaller number of firms, each producing on a slightly larger scale?

The costs of less-than-optimal production, however, need to be balanced against the gains that can accrue from aggressive competition among products. If product differentiation leads to the introduction of new products, improvements in old products and greater variety, then an important gain in economic welfare may counteract (and perhaps outweigh) the loss of efficiency from pricing above marginal cost or not fully realizing all economies of scale.

Most industries that comfortably fit the model of monopolistic competition are very competitive. Price competition coexists with product competition, and firms do not earn very large profits. Nor do they violate any of the competition laws that we discuss in detail in the next chapter.

Monopolistically competitive firms have not been a subject of great concern among economic policy makers. Their behaviour appears to be sufficiently controlled by competitive forces, and no serious attempt has been made to regulate or control them.

Oligopoly

oligopoly A form of industry (market) structure characterized by a few firms, each large enough to influence market price. Products may be homogeneous or differentiated. The behaviour of any one firm in an oligopoly depends to a great extent on the behaviour of others.

An **oligopoly** is an industry dominated by a few firms that, by virtue of their individual sizes, are large enough to influence the market price. Oligopolies exist in many forms. In some oligopoly markets, products are differentiated – the classic example is the car industry. In others, products are nearly homogeneous. In primary copper production, for example, just a few firms produce all the basic metal. Some oligopolies have a very small number of firms, each large enough to influence price. Others have many firms, of which only a few control market price. The other firms tend to take the lead set by the few large dominant firms.

An industry that has a relatively small number of firms that dominate the market is called a concentrated industry. Oligopolies are *concentrated industries*. Table 14.4 contains some data on industries that are relatively concentrated. While the largest firms account for most of the output in each of these industries, some seem to support a large number of smaller firms.

For example, in the motor vehicle industry the manufacture of parts and accessories is increasingly subcontracted and this part of the sector is therefore

Table 14.4 Proportion of industry employment accounted for by large firms* (%)

	Energy and water	Chemicals	Motor vehicles	Banking and finance
EU15	87.7	71.5	86.5	78.1
Belgium	92.7	74.4	89.6	80.8
France	95.7	75.7	87.9	89.7
Germany	90.8	86.7	94.5	74.2
Italy	88.5	60.5	79.3	81.1
Netherlands	88.1	77.1	63.2	n/a
UK	94.3	77.5	77.4	n/a

*Large firms are defined as those with at least 250 employees. Data are for 1992.

Source: *Enterprises in Europe*, 4th report, December 1997; Eurostat.

characterized by a large number of small suppliers. Nevertheless, an average large car manufacturer employs a staff of more than 2500 persons.

The complex interdependence that usually exists among firms in these industries makes oligopoly difficult to analyse. The behaviour of any one firm depends on the reactions it expects of all the others in the industry. Because individual firms make so many decisions – how much output to produce, what price to charge, how much to advertise, whether and when to introduce new product lines, and so forth – industrial strategies are usually complex and it is difficult to generalize about them.

Oligopoly models

Because many different types of oligopolies exist, a number of different oligopoly models have been developed. The following provides a good sample of the alternative approaches to the behaviour (or conduct) of oligopolistic firms. As you will see, all kinds of oligopoly have one thing in common:

The behaviour of any given oligopolistic firm depends on the behaviour of the other firms in the industry comprising the oligopoly.

The collusion model

In Chapter 13, we examined what happens when a perfectly competitive industry falls under the control of a single profit-maximizing firm. In that analysis, we assumed that there were neither technological nor cost advantages to having one firm rather than many. We saw that when many competing firms act independently, they produce more, charge a lower price, and earn less profit than they would have if they had acted as a single unit. If these firms get together and agree to cut production and increase price – that is, if firms can agree not to compete on price – they will have a bigger total-profit pie to carve up. When a group of profit-maximizing oligopolists colludes on price and output, the result is exactly the same as it would be if a monopolist controlled the entire industry:

The colluding oligopoly will face market demand and produce only up to the point at which marginal revenue and marginal cost are equal ($MR = MC$), and price will be set above marginal cost.

Review the subsection 'Collusion and monopoly compared' in Chapter 13 if you are not sure why.

A group of firms that gets together and makes price and output decisions jointly is called a **cartel**. For a cartel to work, a number of conditions must be present. First, demand for the cartel's product must be inelastic. If many substitutes are readily available, the cartel's price increases may become self-defeating as buyers switch to substitutes. Second, the members of the cartel must play by the rules. If a cartel is holding up prices by restricting output, there is a big incentive for members to cheat by increasing output. Breaking ranks can mean very large profits.

Collusion occurs when price- and quantity-fixing agreements are explicit. **Tacit collusion** occurs when firms end up fixing price without a specific agreement, or when such agreements are implicit. A small number of firms with market power may fall into the practice of setting similar prices or following the lead of one firm without ever meeting or setting down formal agreements.

Cartels are generally regarded as bad for consumers. A cartel is often an attempt to set the price that would be charged if the industry were to be monopolistic. As we saw in Chapter 12, monopolistic price and output decisions are thought to be less socially desirable than competitive outcomes.

Not all cartels are bad, however. Recent work by an American economist suggests that the main aim of some real cartels has been to reap economies of scale and cut costs to the benefit of consumers. The idea is that they save by sharing functions such as shipping or order taking.[4]

The cournot model

Perhaps the oldest model of oligopoly behaviour was put forward by Augustin Cournot 150 years ago. The **Cournot model** is based on three assumptions: (1) there are just two firms in an industry – a *duopoly*; (2) that each firm takes the output of the other as given; and (3) that both firms maximize profits.

The story begins with a new firm producing nothing and the existing firm producing everything. The existing firm takes the market demand curve as its own, acting like a monopolist. When the new firm starts operating, it assumes that the existing firm will continue to produce the same level of output and charge the same price as before. The market demand of the new firm, then, is simply market demand less the amount that the existing firm is currently selling. In essence, the new firm assumes that its demand curve is everything on the market demand curve below the price charged by the older firm.

When the new firm starts operating, the existing firm discovers that its demand has eroded because some output is now sold by the new firm. The old firm now assumes that the new firm's output will remain constant, subtracts the new firm's demand from market demand, and produces a new, lower level of output. But that throws the ball back to the new firm, which now finds that the competition is producing *less*.

These adjustments get smaller and smaller, with the new firm raising output in small steps and the other firm lowering output in small steps until the two firms split the market and charge the same price. Like the collusion model:

The Cournot model of oligopoly results in a quantity of output somewhere between the output which would prevail if the market were organized competitively and the output which would be set by a monopoly.

While the Cournot model illustrates the interdependence of decisions in oligopoly, its assumptions about strategic reactions are quite naive. The two firms in the model react only after the fact and never anticipate their competitor's moves.

cartel A group of firms that gets together and makes joint price and output decisions in order to maximize joint profits.

tacit collusion Collusion occurs when price- and quantity-fixing agreements among producers are explicit. Tacit collusion occurs when such agreements are implicit.

Cournot model A model of a two-firm industry (duopoly) in which a series of output-adjustment decisions leads to a final level of output that is between the output that would prevail if the market were organized competitively and the output that would be set by a monopoly.

[4]See Andrew Dick, 'If Cartels were legal would firms fix prices?' Antitrust Division, US Department of Justice, 1997.

The kinked demand curve model

Another common model of oligopolistic behaviour assumes that firms believe that rivals will follow if they *cut* prices but not if they *raise* prices. This **kinked demand curve model** assumes that the elasticity of demand in response to an increase in price is different from the elasticity of demand in response to a price cut. The result is a 'kink' in the demand for a single firm's product.

You can see some of these reactions in the demand curve in Figure 14.4. If the initial price of Firm B's product is P^*, raising its price above P^* would cause Firm X to face an elastic demand curve if its rivals did not also raise their prices (segment d_1 of the demand curve). That is, in response to the price increase, demand for Firm X's product would fall off quickly. The reaction to a price *decrease* would not be as great, however, because rivals would decrease price too. Firm X would lose some of its market share by increasing price, but it would not gain a larger share by decreasing price (segment d_2 of the demand curve).

Recall the very important point that a firm's marginal revenue curve reflects the changes in demand occurring along the demand curve *directly above it*. (Review the derivation of the marginal revenue curve in Chapter 13 if this is not fresh in your mind.) This being the case, MR_1 reflects the changes in P and q along demand curve segment d_1. MR_2 reflects changes in P and q along demand curve segment d_2. Since the demand curve is discontinuous at q^*, the marginal revenue curve is also discontinuous, jumping from point A all the way down to point B.

As always, profit-maximizing firms will produce as long as marginal revenue is greater than marginal cost. If, as in Figure 14.4, the marginal cost curve passes through q^* at any point between A and B, the optimal price is P^* and the optimal output is q^*. To the left of q^*, marginal revenue is greater than marginal cost. To maximize profits, then, the firm should increase output. To the right of q^*, marginal cost is greater than marginal revenue. The firm should not increase output, because producing above q^* will reduce profits.

Notice that this model predicts that price in oligopolistic industries is likely to be more stable than costs. In Figure 14.4, the marginal cost curve can shift up or down by a substantial amount before it becomes advantageous for the firm to change price

Figure 14.4 A kinked demand curve oligopoly model

The kinked demand model assumes that competing firms follow price cuts but not price increases. Thus, if Firm X increases its price, the competition will not, and quantity demanded of Firm X's product will fall off quickly. But if Firm X cuts price, other firms will also cut price and the price cut will not gain as much quantity demanded for Firm X as it would if other firms did not follow. At prices above P^*, demand is relatively elastic. Below P^*, demand is less elastic.

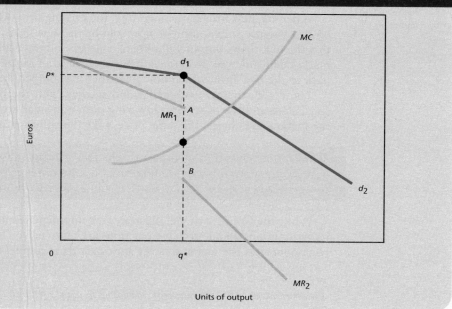

at all. A number of attempts have been made to test whether oligopolistic prices are indeed more stable than costs. While the results do not support the hypothesis of stable prices, the evidence is far from conclusive.[5]

The kinked demand curve model has been criticized. First, it fails to explain why price is at P^* to begin with. Second, the assumption that competing firms will follow price cuts but not price increases is overly simple. Real-world oligopolistic pricing strategies are much more complex.

The price-leadership model

price leadership
A form of oligopoly in which one dominant firm sets prices and all the smaller firms in the industry follow its pricing policy.

In another form of oligopoly, one firm dominates an industry and all the smaller firms follow the leader's pricing policy – hence **price leadership**. If the dominant firm knows that the smaller firms will follow its lead, it will derive its own demand curve simply by subtracting from total market demand the amount of demand that the smaller firms will satisfy at each potential price.

The price-leadership model assumes, first, that the industry is made up of one large firm and a number of smaller competitive firms. Second, it assumes that the dominant firm maximizes profit subject to the constraint of market demand *and* subject to the behaviour of the smaller competitive firms. Finally, the dominant firm allows the smaller firms to sell all they want at the price that the leader has set. The difference between the quantity demanded in the market and the amount supplied by the smaller firms is the amount that the dominant firm will produce.

The final result has the quantity demanded in the market split between the smaller firms and the dominant firm. This result is based entirely on the dominant firm's market power. The only constraint facing a monopoly firm, you will recall, is the behaviour of demanders – that is, the market demand curve. In this case, however, the presence of smaller firms acts to constrain the dominant firm's power. If we were to assume that the smaller firms were out of the way, the dominant firm would face the market demand curve on its own. This means that the dominant firm has a clear incentive to push the smaller firms out of the industry. One way is to lower the price until all of the smaller firms go out of business and then raise the price once the market has been monopolized. The practice of a large, powerful firm driving smaller firms out of the market by temporarily selling at an artificially low price is called *predatory pricing*. As we will see in the next chapter, such behaviour is illegal throughout Western Europe.

As in the other oligopoly models, an oligopoly with a dominant price leader will produce a level of output between the output that would prevail under competition and the output that a monopolist would choose in the same industry. It will also set a price between the monopoly price and the competitive price. Some competition is usually more efficient than none at all.

Game theory

The firms in Cournot's model do not anticipate the moves of the competition. Yet in choosing strategies in an oligopolistic market, real-world firms can and do try to guess what the opposition will do in response.

In 1944, John von Neumann and Oskar Morgenstern published a path-breaking work in which they analysed a set of problems, or *games*, in which two or more people or organizations pursue their own interests and in which no one of them can dictate the outcome.[6] During the last few years, game theory has become an increasingly popular field of study and a fertile area for research. The notions of game theory have

[5]*See, for example, Julian Simon, 'A Further test of the kinky oligopoly demand curve'*, American Economic Review *(December 1969); and George Stigler, 'The kinky oligopoly demand curve and rigid prices'*, Journal of Political Economy, *55 (1947).*

[6]*See J. von Neumann and O. Morgenstern,* Theory of Games and Economic Behaviour *(Princeton NJ: Princeton University Press, 1944).*

been applied to analyses of firm behaviour, politics, international relations and foreign policy.

Game theory goes something like this. In all conflict situations, and thus all games, there are decision makers (or players), rules of the game, and payoffs (or prizes). Players choose strategies without knowing with certainty what strategy the opposition will use. At the same time, though, some information that indicates how their opposition may be 'leaning' may be available to the players.

Figure 14.5 illustrates what is called a payoff matrix for a very simple game. Each of two firms, A and B, must decide whether to mount an expensive advertising campaign. If neither firm decides to advertise, each will earn a profit of €50,000. But if one firm advertises and the other does not, the firm that does will increase its profit by 50% (to €75,000), while driving the competitor into the loss column. If both firms decide to advertise, they will each earn profits of €10,000. They may generate a bit more demand by advertising, but benefit to the firms is more than completely wiped out by the expense of the advertising itself.

If Firms A and B could collude (and we assume that they cannot), their optimal strategy would be to agree not to advertise. That solution maximizes the joint profits to both firms. If neither firm advertises, joint profits are €100,000. If both firms advertise, joint profits are only €20,000. If only one of the firms advertises, joint profits are €75,000 – €25,000 = €50,000.

The strategy that Firm A will actually choose depends on (1) the information available concerning B's likely strategy, and (2) A's preferences for risk. In this case, it is possible to predict behaviour. Consider A's choice of strategy. Regardless of what B does, it pays A to advertise. If B does not advertise, A makes €25,000 more by advertising than by not advertising. Thus, A will advertise. If B does advertise, A must advertise to avoid a loss. The same logic holds for B. Regardless of the strategy pursued by A, it pays B to advertise. A **dominant strategy** is one that is best no matter what the opposition does. In this game, both players have a dominant strategy, and it is likely that both will advertise.

The result of the game in Figure 14.5 is an example of what is called a prisoners' dilemma. The term comes from a game in which two prisoners (call them Yu Min and Emily) are accused or robbing the local bank together, but the evidence is shaky. If they both confess, they each get five years in prison for armed robbery. If neither confesses, they get convicted of a lesser charge, receiving stolen property, and get one year in prison each. The problem is that each of them has been offered a deal independently. If Yu Min confesses and Emily doesn't, Yu Min goes free and Emily gets seven years. If Emily confesses and Yu Min doesn't, Emily goes free and Yu Min gets seven years. The payoff matrix for the prisoners' dilemma is given in Figure 14.6.

game theory
Analyses oligopolistic behaviour as a complex series of strategic moves and reactive countermoves among rival firms. In game theory, firms are assumed to anticipate rival reactions.

dominant strategy
In game theory, a strategy that is best no matter what the opposition does.

Figure 14.5 Payoff matrix for advertising game

	B's STRATEGY	
A's STRATEGY	Don't advertise	Advertise
Don't advertise	A's profit = €50,000 B's profit = €50,000	A's loss = €25,000 B's profit = €75,000
Advertise	A's profit = €75,000 B's loss = €25,000	A's profit = €10,000 B's profit = €10,000

Figure 14.6 The Prisoners' Dilemma

	EMILY	
YU MIN	Don't confess	Confess
Don't confess	Yu Min: 1 year Emily: 1 year	Yu Min = 7 years Emily = free
Confess	Yu Min = free Emily = 7 years	Yu Min = 5 years Emily = 5 years

Looking carefully at the payoffs, you may notice that both Yu Min and Emily have dominant strategies: to confess. That is, Yu Min is better off confessing regardless of what Emily does, and Emily is better off confessing regardless of what Yu Min does. The likely outcome is that both will confess, even though they would be better off if they both kept their mouths shut!

Is there any way out of this dilemma? There may be under circumstances in which the game is played over and over again. Look back at Figure 14.5. The best outcome for both firms is for neither to advertise. Suppose Firm A decided not to advertise for one period to see how Firm B would respond. If Firm B continued to advertise, A would have to resume advertising to survive. But suppose that B's strategy was to play tit for tat. That is, suppose that B decided to simply match A's strategy. In this case, both firms might – with no explicit collusion – end up not advertising after A figures out what B is doing. (For an example of the prisoners' dilemma at work in the airline industry, see the Global Perspective box 'A prisoners' dilemma: price fixing and the US airlines'.)

There are many games in which one player does not have a dominant strategy but in which the outcome is predictable. Consider the game in Figure 14.7a, in which C does not have a dominant strategy. If D plays the left strategy, C will play the top strategy. If D plays the right strategy, C will play the bottom strategy. But what strategy will D choose to play? If C knows the options, she will see that D has a dominant strategy and is likely to play it. D does better playing the right-hand strategy regardless of what C does; he can guarantee himself a €100 win by choosing the right and is guaranteed to win nothing by playing the left. Since D's behaviour is predictable (he will play the right-hand strategy) C will play bottom. When all players are playing their best strategy, given what their competitors are doing, the result is called a **Nash equilibrium**.

Nash equilibrium
In game theory, the result of all players playing their best strategy given what their competitors are doing.

Now suppose that the game in Figure 14.7 is changed. Suppose that all the payoffs are the same, except that if D chooses left and C chooses bottom, C loses €10,000 (Figure 14.7b). While D still has a dominant strategy (playing right), C now stands to lose a great deal by choosing bottom on the off chance that D chooses left instead. When uncertainty and risk are introduced, the game changes. C is likely to play top and guarantee herself a €100 profit rather than to risk losing €10,000 to win €200, even if there is just a small chance of D's choosing left. A **maximin strategy** is one chosen by a player to maximize the minimum gain that it can earn. In essence, one who plays a maximin strategy assumes that the opposition will play the strategy that does the most damage.

maximin strategy
In game theory, a strategy chosen to maximize the minimum gain that can be earned.

When the game theory first appeared in the late 1940s, it seemed that it would in time be able to explain the behaviour of oligopolistic firms in great detail. However,

Figure 14.7 Payoff matrixes for left/right and top/bottom strategies

a. Original Game		
	D's STRATEGY	
C's STRATEGY	Left	Right
Top	C wins €100 D wins 0	C wins €100 D wins €100
Bottom	C loses €100 D wins 0	C wins €200 D wins €100

b. New Game		
	D's STRATEGY	
C's STRATEGY	Left	Right
Top	C wins €100 D wins 0	C wins €100 D wins €100
Bottom	C loses €10,000 D wins 0	C wins €200 D wins €100

when we move from two potential strategies to three or four, and particularly when we move to more than two players, the number of potential outcomes and the properties of the strategy pairings become enormously complex. As a result, it becomes very difficult to predict the strategy (or the combination of strategies) that a firm might choose in any given circumstance.

In the end, game theory leaves us with a greater understanding of the problem of oligopoly but with an incomplete and inconclusive set of propositions about the likely behaviour of oligopolistic firms. Some very interesting conclusions emerge about a fairly small number of specific game circumstances, but game theory doesn't provide much help with an industry of five firms, each simultaneously choosing product, pricing, output and advertising strategies.

About all we are left with is the certainty of interdependence:

> The strategy that an oligopolistic firm chooses is likely to depend on that firm's perception of competing firms' likely responses.

Contestable markets

Before we discuss the performance of oligopolies, we should note one relatively new theory of behaviour that has limited applications but some important implications for understanding imperfectly competitive market behaviour.

perfectly contestable market

A market in which entry and exit are costless.

A market is **perfectly contestable** if entry to it *and* exit from it are costless. That is, a market is perfectly contestable if a firm can move into it in search of excess profits but lose nothing if it fails. To be part of a perfectly contestable market, a firm must have capital that is both mobile and easily transferable from one market to another.

Take an example from the UK. In the 1980s, there were relatively few large banks, but many building societies whose services were restricted to providing mortgages to enable people to finance the purchase of houses. The government then changed the law and allowed the building societies to offer a range of other services such as cheque accounts, previously the preserve of the banks.

From that time on it was easy for the building societies to offer competition to the banks. They already had a substantial network of branches on the high streets. The marginal cost for them to enter the market for cheque accounts was very low. For any building society that subsequently found the process unprofitable it was also relatively costless to exit the market and return to its traditional core business of providing mortgages.

A similar situation may occur when a new industrial complex is built at a fairly remote site and a number of heavy transport companies offer their services. Because the companies' capital stock is mobile, they can move their vehicles somewhere else at no great cost if business is not profitable.

Because entry is cheap, participants in a contestable market are continuously faced with competition or the threat of it. Even if there are only a few firms competing, the openness of the market forces all of them to produce efficiently or be driven out of business. This threat of competition remains high because new firms face little risk in going after a new market. If things don't work out in a crowded market, they don't lose their investment. They can simply transfer their capital to a different place or different use.

> In contestable markets, even large oligopolistic firms end up behaving like perfectly competitive firms. Prices are pushed to long-run average cost by competition, and economic profits do not persist.

We have focused on price determination in oligopolistic markets. However, oligopolists compete on non-price variables too. One such variable is advertising. We can see how the level of advertising varies between industries in Table 14.5, which shows volumes of advertising as proportions of industry sales. Part of the explanation for the variability lies in the nature of the product. Consumers of some products are

Global Perspectives

A prisoners' dilemma: price fixing and the US airlines

During the years 1990, 1991 and 1992 the US airline industry lost a combined total of just under $10 billion. These losses were incurred despite the move to more fuel-efficient planes, falling fuel prices in 1991 and 1992, more passengers and longer average trips. What explains the industry's disastrous performance?

Some economists have argued that part of the explanation may lie in game theory. Consider the following simple game (all numbers are in millions): suppose United Airlines (UA) and American Airlines (AA) are competing for a lucrative route between the coasts. Each may choose independently to cut price or charge a high price. The profits from the route depend on the strategies chosen by both firms and are given in the four boxes.

Notice that if the game is played just once, each

		United Airlines (UA)	
		Price High	**Cut Fares**
American Airlines (AA)	**Price High**	UA's profit = $100 AA's profit = $120	UA's profit = $140 AA's profit = −$200
	Cut Fares	UA's profit = −$200 AA's profit = $150	UA's profit = −$100 AA's profit = −$100

firm has a dominant strategy. That is, AA will choose to cut fares regardless of what UA does and UA will choose to cut fares regardless of what AA does. The outcome is that each loses $100 million. If somehow both were to charge a high price, UA would earn $100 million and AA would earn $120 million. This is a classic prisoners' dilemma. That is, both firms would benefit if they could get together and agree to charge a higher price. But if they are not allowed to collude, they both end up suffering losses.

Recall from the text that one solution to the prisoners' dilemma might be to try a 'tit for tat' strategy in repeated trials in the hopes of signalling the opposition that if it charges a high price you will too. This is exactly what the airlines attempted to do to solve their problem. But the behaviour was noticed by passenger groups and state attorneys-general, who immediately sued the airlines for price fixing.

The following excerpt from the *New York Times* describes part of the settlement made by the airlines:

Major airlines agreed to pay $40 million in discounts to state and local governments to settle a price-fixing lawsuit, a group of 10 state attorneys general said yesterday.

The airlines settled a separate class-action suit last year brought by passengers by agreeing to pay out $458 million in discounts. The airlines earlier this year resolved a Federal anti-trust suit by agreeing not to announce price changes in advance . . .

The price-fixing claims centred on an airline practice of announcing price changes in advance through the reservation systems. If competitors did not go along with the price change, it could be rescinded before it was to take effect.

Source: The Associated Press: 'Suit settled by airlines', New York Times, 12 October 1994, p. D8.

more susceptible to persuasion than consumers of others. However, another part of the explanation is in the structure of the industry. We have already seen that advertising is a feature of monopolistic competition, but firms in oligopoly will also advertise substantially. Shampoos, cereals, washing powders and motor cars are all oligopolistic industries. Firms compete to gain a larger share of the market, not only by price but also by advertising. One of the reasons for such high volumes of advertising is the prisoners' dilemma. Large volumes of advertising may not persuade people to wash their clothes more often – the industry demand curve may not move. However, each oligopolist fears that if it reduces advertising, consumers may switch to rival brands. Under these conditions, total industry advertising volumes are greater than would maximize profits if all firms agreed to reduce advertising simultaneously.

Although advertising is an important example of non-price competition it is not the only one. Others include product differentiation, and research and development (R&D) activity.

Summary

Oligopoly is a market structure that is consistent with a variety of behaviours.

The only necessary condition of oligopoly is that firms are large enough to have some control over price. Oligopolies are concentrated industries. At one extreme is the cartel, in which a few firms get together and jointly maximize profits – in essence, acting as a monopolist. At the other extreme, the firms within the oligopoly vigorously compete for small contestable markets by moving capital quickly in response to observed economic profits. In between are a number of alternative models, all of which stress the interdependence of oligopolistic firms.

Oligopoly and economic performance

How well do oligopolies perform? Should they be regulated or changed? Are they efficient, or do they lead to an inefficient use of resources? On balance, are they good or bad?

Table 14.5 Advertising/sales ratios for selected industries (UK, 1995)

Product	A/S ratio
Indigestion remedies	19.68
Double glazing	76.82
Shampoos	18.39
Cereals	9.03
Washing liquids and powders	11.43
Motor cars, new	2.29
Carpets, floor coverings and tiles	0.19
Men's outerwear	0.11
Hairdressing	0.03
Suntan products	5.22
Cameras	3.23
Trainers	1.07

Source: Advertising Statistics Yearbook, UK, 1997.

With the exception of the contestable-markets model, all the models of oligopoly we have examined lead us to conclude that concentration in a market leads to pricing above marginal cost and output below the efficient level. When price is above marginal cost at equilibrium, consumers are paying more for the good than it costs to produce that good in terms of products forgone in other industries. To increase output would be to create value that exceeds the social cost of the good, but profit-maximizing oligopolists have an incentive not to increase output.

Entry barriers in many oligopolistic industries also prevent new capital and other resources from responding to profit signals. Under competitive conditions or in contestable markets, excess profits would attract new firms and thus increase production. But this does not happen in most oligopolistic industries. The problem is most severe when entry barriers exist and firms explicitly or tacitly collude. The results of collusion are similar to the results of a monopoly. Firms jointly maximize profits by fixing prices at a high level and splitting up the profits.

Product differentiation under oligopoly presents us with the same dilemma that we encountered in monopolistic competition. On the one hand, vigorous product competition among oligopolistic competitors produces variety and leads to innovation in response to the wide variety of consumer tastes and preferences. It can thus be argued that vigorous product competition is efficient. On the other hand, product differentiation may lead to waste and inefficiency. Product differentiation accomplished through advertising may have nothing to do with product quality, and advertising itself may have little or no information content. If it serves as an entry barrier that blocks competition, product differentiation can cause the market allocation mechanism to fail.

Oligopolistic, or concentrated, industries are likely to be inefficient for several reasons. First, profit-maximizing oligopolists are likely to price above marginal cost. When price is above marginal cost, there is underproduction from society's point of view – in other words, resources are not optimally allocated. Second, strategic behaviour can lead to outcomes that are not in society's best interest. Specifically, strategically competitive firms can force themselves into deadlocks that waste resources. Finally, to the extent that oligopolies differentiate their products and advertise, there is the promise of new and exciting products. At the same time, however, there remains a real danger of waste and inefficiency.

Industrial concentration and technological change

One of the major sources of economic growth and progress throughout history has been technological advance. Innovation, both in methods of production and in the creation of new and better products, is one of the engines of economic progress. Much innovation starts with research and development efforts undertaken by firms in search of profit.

Several economists, notably Joseph Schumpeter and John Kenneth Galbraith, argued in works now considered classics that industrial concentration actually increases the rate of technological advance. As Schumpeter put it in 1942:

As soon as we . . . inquire into the individual items in which progress was most conspicuous, the trail leads not to the doors of those firms that work under conditions of comparatively free competition but precisely to the doors of the large concerns . . . and a shocking suspicion dawns upon us that big business may have had more to do with creating that standard of life than keeping it down.[7]

[7]A. Schumpeter, Capitalism, Socialism and Democracy *(New York: Harper, 1942); and J. K. Galbraith,* American Capitalism *(Boston: Houghton Mifflin, 1952).*

This caused the economics profession to pause and take stock of its theories. The conventional wisdom had always been that concentration and barriers to entry insulate firms from competition and lead to sluggish performance and slow growth.

The evidence regarding where innovation comes from is mixed. Certainly, most small businesses do not engage in research and development, and most large firms do. When R&D expenditures are considered as a percentage of sales, firms in industries with high concentration ratios spend more on R&D than firms in industries with low concentration ratios. IBM, which despite its recent problems set the industry standard in personal computers, has certainly introduced as much new technology to the computer industry as any other firm.

However, the 'high-tech revolution' grew out of many tiny start-up operations. Companies such as Apple Computers, Lotus Development Corporation and Intel barely existed only a generation ago. The new biotechnology firms that are just beginning to work miracles with genetic engineering are still tiny operations that started with research done by individual scientists in university laboratories.

As with the debate about product differentiation and advertising, significant ambiguity on this subject remains. Indeed, there may be no right answer. Technological change seems to come in fits and starts, sometimes from small firms and sometimes from large ones.

A role for government?

Certainly, there is much to guard against in the behaviour of large, concentrated industries. Barriers to entry, large size, and product differentiation all lead to market power and to potential inefficiency. Barriers to entry and collusive behaviour stop the market from working towards an efficient allocation of resources.

For several reasons, however, economists no longer attack industry concentration with the same fervour they once did. First, the theory of contestable markets shows that even firms in highly concentrated industries can be pushed to produce efficiently under certain market circumstances. Second, the benefits of product differentiation and product competition are real, at least in part. After all, a constant stream of new products and new variations of old products does come to the market almost daily. Third, the effects of concentration on the rate of R&D spending are, at worst, mixed. It is certainly true that large firms do a substantial amount of the total research. Finally, in some industries, substantial economies of scale simply preclude a completely competitive structure.

In addition to the debate over the desirability of industrial concentration, there is a never-ending debate regarding the role of government in regulating markets. One view is that high levels of concentration lead to inefficiency and that government should act to improve the allocation of resources – to help the market work more efficiently. This logic has been used to justify the laws and other regulations aimed at moderating non-competitive behaviour.

An opposing view holds that the clearest examples of effective barriers to entry are those actually created by government. This view holds that government regulation in past years has been ultimately anti-competitive and has made the allocation of resources less efficient than it would have been with no government involvement. Recall from Chapter 13 that those who earn economic profits have an incentive to spend resources to protect themselves and their profits from competitors. This *rent-seeking* behaviour may include using the power of government.

Complicating the debate further is international competition. Increasingly, firms are faced with competition from foreign firms in domestic markets at the same time that they are competing with other multinational firms for a share of foreign markets. We live in a truly global economy today. Thus, firms that may dominate a domestic market may be fierce competitors in the international arena. This has implications for the proper role of government.

For most individual EU countries, telecommunications and steel are almost monopolistic. However, where international trade is allowed to flourish in such industries they can be regarded as oligopolistic and potentially very competitive.

Summary

Monopolistic competition

1. A monopolistically competitive industry has the following structural characteristics: (1) a large number of firms, (2) no barriers to entry, and (3) *product differentiation*. Relatively good substitutes for a monopolistic competitor's products are available. Thus monopolistic competitors try to achieve a degree of market power by differentiating their products.

2. Advocates of free and open competition believe that differentiated products and advertising give the market system its vitality and are the basis of its power. Critics argue that product differentiation and advertising are wasteful and inefficient.

3. By differentiating their products, firms hope to be able to raise price without losing all quantity demanded. The demand curve facing a monopolistic competitor is less elastic than the demand curve faced by a perfectly competitive firm, but more elastic than the demand curve faced by a monopoly.

4. To maximize profit in the short run, a firm that is monopolistically competitive will produce as long as the marginal revenue from increasing output and selling it exceeds the marginal cost of producing it. This occurs at the point at which $MR = MC$.

5. When firms enter a monopolistically competitive industry, they introduce close substitutes for the goods being produced. This attracts demand away from the firms already in the industry. Demand faced by each firm shifts left, and profits are ultimately eliminated in the long run. This long-run equilibrium occurs at the point where the demand curve is tangential to the average total cost curve.

6. Monopolistically competitive firms end up pricing above marginal cost. This is inefficient, as is the fact that monopolistically competitive firms will not realize all economies of scale available.

Oligopoly

7. An *oligopoly* is an industry dominated by a few firms that, by virtue of their individual sizes, are large enough to influence market price. The behaviour of a single oligopolistic firm depends on the reactions it expects of all the other firms in the industry. Industrial strategies are usually very complicated and difficult to generalize about.

8. When firms collude, either explicitly or tacitly, they jointly maximize profits by charging an agreed-upon price or by setting output limits and splitting profits. The result is exactly the same as it would be if one firm monopolized the industry: The firm will produce up to the point at which $MR = MC$, and price will be set above marginal cost.

9. The *Cournot model* of oligopoly is based on three assumptions: (1) that there are just two firms in an industry – a situation called *duopoly*; (2) that each firm takes the output of the other as a given; and (3) that both firms maximize profits. The model holds that a series of output-adjustment decisions in the duopoly leads to a final level of output between that which would prevail under perfect competition and that which would be set by a monopoly.

10. A firm faces a *kinked demand curve* if competitors follow price cuts but fail to respond to price increases. The kinked demand curve model predicts that in oligopolistic industries price is likely to be more stable than costs.

11. The *price-leadership* model of oligopoly leads to a similar but not identical result as the collusion model. In this organization, the dominant firm in the industry sets a price and allows competing firms to supply all they want at that price. An oligopoly with a dominant price leader will produce a level of output between that which would prevail under competition and that which a monopolist would choose in the same industry. It will also set a price between the monopoly price and the competitive price.

12. *Game theory* analyses the behaviour of firms as if their behaviour were a series of strategic moves and countermoves. It helps us to understand the problem of oligopoly but leaves us with an incomplete and inconclusive set of propositions about the likely behaviour of individual oligopolistic firms.

13. A market is *perfectly contestable* if entry to it and exit from it are costless – that is, if a firm can move into a market in search of excess profits but lose nothing if it fails. Firms in such industries must have mobile capital. In contestable markets, even large oligopolistic firms end up behaving like perfect competitors: prices are pushed to long-run average cost by competition, and economic profits do not persist.

14. The behaviour of oligopolistic firms is likely to lead to an inefficient allocation of resources.

Review Terms and Concepts

cartel
Cournot model
dominant strategy
game theory
kinked demand curve model
maximin strategy
monopolistic competition

Nash equilibrium
oligopoly
perfectly contestable market
price leadership
product differentiation
tacit collusion

Problem Set

1. Which of the following industries would you classify as an oligopoly? Which would you classify as monopolistically competitive? Explain your answer. If you are not sure, what information do you need to know to decide?
a. running shoes
b. rock bands
c. watches
d. aircraft
e. ice cream

2. All over the world in 1998, people were singing. In Japan, Karaoke bars drew millions of patrons who wanted to sing popular songs accompanied by recorded videos and a prompter lighting up the words. In Taiwan, literally tens of thousands of Karaoke (KTV) establishments exist where groups of people can go into small private rooms and sing to each other while being prompted on a video screen. Each establishment is a bit different from the next. Some are upmarket and expensive; others are less expensive, have a smaller selection of songs to choose from, and are not as well maintained. Ten years ago the industry did not exist.
a. Into what industry category does the Taiwanese Karaoke business seem to fall?
b. The first Karaoke establishments in business in Taiwan made lots of money. What do you think has happened to the price of admission and the profits of most KTV establishments in recent years? Use a graph to explain your answer.

3. Write a brief essay explaining each statement:
a. 'A dominant firm price leader in an oligopolistic industry may actually function as a monopolistically competitive firm in the face of international competition in world markets.'
b. 'The Beatles were once a monopolistically competitive firm that became a monopolist.'

4. For each of the following, state whether you agree or disagree. Explain your answer carefully.

a. Successful product differentiation has the effect of increasing the elasticity of demand facing a monopolistically competitive firm.
b. Long-run equilibrium in a monopolistically competitive industry is virtually identical to long-run equilibrium in monopoly.
c. In monopolistically competitive industries, firms are able to exert market power (control prices) by virtue of their size relative to the market.

5. Which of the following markets are likely to be perfectly contestable? Explain your answers.
a. Shipbuilding
b. Road haulage
c. House cleaning services
d. Wine production

6. The matrix in Figure 1 shows payoffs based on the strategies chosen by two firms. If they collude and hold prices at €10, each will earn profits of €5 million. If A cheats on the agreement, lowering its price, but B does not, A will get 75% of the business and earn profits of €8 million and B will lose €2 million. Similarly, if B cheats and A does not, B will earn €8 million and A will lose €2 million. If both cut prices, they will end up with €2 million each in profits.

Which strategy minimizes the maximum potential loss for A? For B? If you were A, which strategy would you choose? Why? If A cheats, what will B do? If B cheats, what will A do? What is the most likely outcome of such a game? Explain.

Figure 1

		B's Strategy	
		Stand by agreement	Cheat
A's strategy	Stand by agreement	A's profit = €5 million B's profit = €5 million	A's profit = –€2 million B's profit = €8 million
	Cheat	A's profit = €8 million B's profit = –€2 million	A's profit = €2 million B's profit = €2 million

7. Assume that you are in the business of building houses in the UK. You have analysed the market carefully, and you know that at a price of £120,000 you will sell 800 houses per year. In addition, you know that at any price above £120,000 no one will buy your houses because other firms provide equal quality houses to anyone who wants one at £120,000. You also know that when you lower your price by £20,000, the quantity that you can sell increases by 200 units. For example, at a price of £100,000 you can sell 1000 houses, at a price of £80,000 you can sell 1200 houses, and so forth.
a. Sketch the demand curve facing your firm.
b. Sketch the effective marginal revenue curve facing your firm.
c. If the marginal cost of building a house is £100,000, how many will you build, and what price will you charge? What if $MC = £85,000$?

8. Examine the short-run graph in Figure 2 for a monopolistically competitive firm.
a. What is the profit-maximizing level of output?
b. What price will be charged in the short run?

c. How much is short-run total revenue? Total cost? Total profit?
d. Describe what will happen to this firm in the long run.

9. Write a position paper on industrial concentration. Is this a problem for your country? For Europe as a whole? What are some of the possible advantages and disadvantages of government actions against concentrated industries?

10. The payoff matrices in Figure 3 show the payoffs for two games. The payoffs are given in parentheses. The number on the left of each pair of numbers refers to the payoff to A, the number on the right to the payoff to B. Hence (2, 25) means a €2 payoff to A and a €25 payoff to B.
a. Is there a dominant strategy in each game for each player?
b. If Game 1 were repeated a large number of times, and you were A and you could change your strategy, what might you do?
c. Which strategy would you play in Game 2? Why?

Figure 2

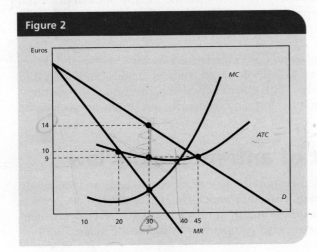

Figure 3

Game 1: Pricing

		Firm B	
		Price High	Price Low
Firm A	Price High	(15, 15)	(2, 25)
	Price Low	(25, 2)	(5, 5)

Game 2: Chicken

		Bob (B)	
		Swerve	Don't Swerve
Ann (A)	Swerve	(5, 5)	(3, 10)
	Don't Swerve	(10, 3)	(−10, −10)

a) MC = MR = 30
b) 14
c) 420,
d) 9·30 = 270, 150
d) hye etableringshinder ⟹ lägre efterfrågan

15

The Control and Regulation of Private Firms

If all the assumptions of perfect competition hold, the allocation of resources in an economy is efficient – the system produces the goods and services that people want, and produces them at lowest cost. No reshuffling of resources or output can improve the welfare of some without reducing the welfare of others. This was the message of Chapter 12.

As we began to relax some of the assumptions of perfect competition, we found several sources of market failure. Chapters 13 and 14 examined the first of these, *imperfect markets*. Firms that are able to achieve some degree of control over their products' price are likely to end up charging more than the socially optimal price and producing less than the socially optimal output. Thus far we have looked carefully at three imperfect market structures that tend to be inefficient: monopoly, monopolistic competition and oligopoly.

When unregulated markets fail to produce efficiently, governments can and do act to improve the allocation of resources. However, government actions can also lead to a less efficient allocation of resources. This chapter discusses government involvement in imperfectly competitive markets, focusing primarily on intervention at the European level.

The development of anti-monopoly law

Historically, governments in market economies have assumed two basic and seemingly contradictory roles with respect to imperfectly competitive industries: (1) They *promote* competition and *restrict* market power, primarily through restrictive practice laws and anti-merger legislation, and (2) they restrict competition by regulating industries.

Regulation of mergers

Most European governments have long been aware of the problems of monopoly power that we examined in Chapter 14. As a result, there are laws preventing large-scale mergers which do not have government sanction. For example, in Germany the Anti-Trust Act, section 24 paragraph 1, prohibits a merger or acquisition:

> if it is anticipated that a merger will result in or strengthen a position of market dominance . . . unless the participating enterprises demonstrate that the merger will also result in improvement to the competitive situation and that these improvements will outweigh the disadvantages of the market dominance.

The body through which this legislation is enforced is the Bundeskartellamt or Federal Cartel Office.

In the UK, the Office of Fair Trading (OFT) can refer large mergers to the Monopolies and Mergers Commission (MMC). The MMC prepares a report advising the government whether it considers the merger to be in 'the public interest'. Usually, but not always, the government will accept these recommendations and act accordingly.

Although each country has its own laws there are also laws at European level for EU countries, enforced through the European Commission. They relate only to very large merger proposals. Specifically there are three criteria by which to judge whether a potential merger should be referred to the Commission:

1. The companies must have a combined world turnover of in excess of 5 billion Ecu.
2. Each company must have a turnover within the EU of 250m Ecu or more.
3. If each company has two-thirds or more of its turnover in one of the EU's member states, a decision on the proposal will be made at the national rather than at EU level.

These criteria mean that less than 50 mergers per year will fall under the EU's auspices. The relationships between EU and national merger control is not always helpful. It is in the interests of all concerned if decisions can be taken promptly and uncertainty removed. But sometimes a proposed merger can be agreed by the Commission and then held up while it is re-examined by an individual government.

Types of merger

There are three major types of merger, each of which raises issues regarding the public interest.

Horizontal mergers

horizontal merger
When two firms join in the same industry at the same stage of production.

A horizontal merger takes place between two (or more) firms in the same industry at the same stage of production. For example, two paper producers may merge.

Such mergers clearly have a potential for the abuse of market power. Increasing the concentration of an industry in this way gives greater power to the merged firm to raise prices and exploit consumers. In Europe, however, there is no presumption that such mergers are harmful to the public interest. There may be significant economies of scale to be gained. These may be passed on to the consumers in the form of *lower* prices.

Vertical mergers

vertical merger
When two firms join in the same industry but at different stages of production.

A vertical merger takes place between firms that are in the same industry but at different stages in production. For example, a paper producer may merge with a timber company. This is *backwards* vertical integration, since the firm is moving backwards towards the raw material supply. Alternatively, a paper firm could merge with an envelope manufacturer or stationery supplier. This is a *forward* vertical merger.

Vertical mergers do not directly increase concentration in an industry. However, they are sometimes scrutinized because they can reduce competition. For example, if the paper producer acquires a substantial amount of timber-producing capacity in an area it may deny supplies to its rivals, forcing other firms to use higher-cost suppliers.

Conglomerate mergers

conglomerate merger
When two firms in different industries join.

These occur when two firms in different industries merge. If the paper producer merges with a brewer or an insurance company this is a conglomerate merger. It is also known as a diversified merger.

Competition authorities rarely examine such mergers because they appear not to raise competition issues. However, conglomerate firms *can* act against the public interest. For example, a conglomerate producer can drive out of business a single-line producer by cutting prices below cost in the short term. It can cross-subsidize its operations from profits in other lines of its business. Then when the single-line producer is forced out of business the conglomerate can use its dominant position in that market to raise price above the socially optimal level.

Market concentration

The focus of concern for government and other regulatory authorities with respect to mergers is that firms should not be able to dominate a market. How can we measure the extent of firm domination? One way is to use the concentration ratio.

The **concentration ratio** (CR) is the proportion of output (or employment) in a given industry accounted for by the largest firms. For example, an industry where the three largest firms produce 60% of the output has a CR_3 (concentration ratio of the three largest firms) of 60%. It would be possible to produce horizontal merger guidelines based on such ratios. We could specify that a merger would not normally be allowed if it raises the CR_3 above, say, 70%.

We have already seen that EU guidelines do not lay down such rules, because it is thought that large-scale mergers might benefit consumers through the achievement of scale economies. However, there are other problems associated with the concentration ratio itself.

Problems with concentration ratios

The first problem is defining the industry's market or product. Suppose a company making potato crisps wants to acquire a company making biscuits. Are these separate products, and is this therefore to be regarded as a diversified merger? Or do we regard the merger as increasing the concentration ratio in the snack foods industry? Now suppose a German biscuit firm wishes to acquire a Dutch biscuit firm. Are they selling in two separate (national) markets, or in one (European) market? From the national viewpoint, the concentration ratios of each of the two markets is unaffected. In the alternative view, however, the European biscuit market will become more concentrated.

Even if there are no ambiguities in defining the market, a concentration ratio is not free of problems as a measure of market power. The choice of the number of firms to consider is arbitrary. Table 15.1 shows the concentration of a number of hypothetical industries. Is Industry A more concentrated than Industry B? The CR_3 shows the answer to be yes. Now suppose we had chosen a four-firm concentration ratio. The CR_4 for Industry A is 95% and for Industry B 100%. Industry B now appears more concentrated than Industry A!

Concentration ratios also tell us little about the distribution of power between firms in a given industry. In Table 15.1, Industries C and D each have a CR_3 of 90%. However, we are interested in the structure of these industries as a guide to their pricing behaviour. Yet price in Industry C is likely to be determined by Firm 1, in much the same way that a monopolist would, with the smaller firms accepting Firm 1 as a price leader. Prices may well be much more competitive in Industry D, where several firms are of equal size.

Finally, under certain circumstances a merger can increase the concentration ratio and *increase* competitive pressures. Suppose Firms 3 and 4 merge in Industry E, increasing the CR_3 from 75% to 90%. It may be that the two firms were too small to provide effective competition to the larger firms. Now they may be large enough to do so. An interesting example of this principle is cross-channel ferries between Calais and Dover. The two largest competitors were once Sealink and P & O Ferries. With the opening of the Channel Tunnel, Eurotunnel became much the largest firm in the

Percentage share of	Firm 1	Firm 2	Firm 3	Firm 4	Firm 5	CR_3
Industry A	60	20	10	5	5	90
Industry B	30	30	25	15	–	85
Industry C	80	5	5	5	5	90
Industry D	30	30	30	10	–	90
Industry E	30	30	15	15	10	75

Table 15.1 Concentration ratios for five hypothetical industries

market, its capacity easily exceeding the combined capacity of the ferry operators. In 1998 the two ferry companies were allowed to merge their cross-channel operations. The decision was based on the view that such a merger could give *more* competition in the market even though market concentration would be higher, because the combined ferry company would provide greater competition to Eurotunnel.

Regulation of mergers in the USA

European merger legislation is designed to give the authorities power to examiner merger proposals and to decide each individual case on its merits. American legislation has much more of a presumption that large mergers, especially of the horizontal kind, are against social welfare. Laws are enforced by the Federal Department of Justice and the Federal Trade Commission.

Clear guidelines laid down for these bodies were drawn up in 1984. These guidelines are not based on concentration ratios. They are based on a measure of market structure called the **Herfindahl–Hirschman Index (HHI)**. The HHI is calculated by expressing the market share of each firm in the industry as a percentage, squaring these figures, and adding. For example, in an industry in which two firms each control 50% of the market, the index is:

$$50^2 + 50^2 = 2500 + 2500 = 5000$$

For an industry in which four firms each control 25% of the market, the index is:

$$25^2 + 25^2 + 25^2 + 25^2 = 625 + 625 + 625 + 625 = 2500$$

Table 15.2 shows HHI calculations for several hypothetical industries. The Justice Department's courses of action, summarized in Figure 15.1, are as follows:

> If the Herfindahl–Hirschman Index is less than 1000, the industry is considered unconcentrated, and any proposed merger will go unchallenged by the Justice Department. If the index is between 1000 and 1800, the department will challenge any merger that would increase the index by over 100 points. HHIs above 1800 mean that the industry is considered concentrated already, and the Justice Department will challenge any merger that pushes the index up more than 50 points.

In 1982 two US breweries, Pabst and Heileman, proposed a merger. At the time, the HHI in the beer industry was about 1772. Before the merger, each firm had about 7.5% of the market. Thus, after a merger, the new firm would have a combined share of 15%. The merger would thus raise the index by 112.5:

$$\underbrace{(15^2)}_{\text{Post-merger}} - \underbrace{(7.5^2 + 7.5^2)}_{\text{Pre-merger}} = 225 - 112.5 = 112.5$$

Herfindahl–Hirschman Index (HHI)
A mathematical calculation that uses market share figures to determine whether or not a proposed merger will be challenged by the government.

Table 15.2 Calculation of a simple Herfindahl–Hirschman Index (HHI) for four hypothetical industries, each with no more than four firms

Percentage share of	Firm 1	Firm 2	Firm 3	Firm 4	HHI
Industry A	50	50	–	–	$50^2 + 50^2 = 5{,}000$
Industry B	80	10	10	–	$80^2 + 10^2 + 10^2 = 6{,}600$
Industry C	25	25	25	25	$25^2 + 25^2 + 25^2 + 25^2 = 2{,}500$
Industry D	40	20	20	20	$40^2 + 20^2 + 20^2 + 20^2 = 2{,}800$

Figure 15.1 Department of Justice merger guidelines (revised 1984)

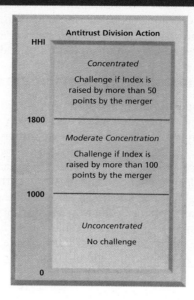

Because the merger increased the index by more than 100 points, it was challenged by the Justice Department.

In 1984 the same two companies reapplied to the Justice Department for permission to merge. This time, Pabst agreed to sell four of its brands – accounting for over one-third of its total production – and one brewery to a third party. The sale was sufficient to bring the merger within the guidelines, and the Antitrust Division dropped its objections. However, the merger never took place. Heileman was bought by an Australian company and in 1991 went bankrupt.

In 1992 the Department of Justice and the FTC issued joint Horizontal Merger Guidelines, updating and expanding the 1984 guidelines. The most interesting part of the new provisions is that the US government will examine each potential merger to determine if it enhances the firms' power to engage in 'coordinated interaction' with other firms in the industry. The guidelines define 'coordinated interaction' as:

actions by a group of firms that are profitable for each of them only as the result of the accommodating reactions of others. This behaviour includes tacit or express collusion, and may or may not be lawful in and of itself.[1]

Clearly, the new guidelines show the increased influence of game theory models of non-cooperative collusion (see Chapter 14).

Laws against restrictive practices

Restrictive practices policy in Europe

In restrictive practices law just as with merger legislation, European governments have long attempted to prevent collusion of various kinds between large firms. The basis of competition policy in the European Union is contained in Articles 85 and 86 of the 1957 Treaty of Rome. Article 85 deals with the joint exercise of market power and outlaws price fixing and agreements to limit production or share markets. A second

---

[1] *US Department of Justice, Federal Trade Commission,* Horizontal Merger Guidelines *(1992), p. 34.*

part of Article 85, however, provides for exemptions from these rules in the case of any agreement 'which contributes to improving production or distribution of goods or to promoting technical or economic progress, while allowing consumers a fair share of the resulting benefit . . .' This provision provides the enforcement authority with great latitude in interpreting agreements. No such clause exists in US antitrust laws.

Article 86 of the Treaty of Rome deals with anti-competitive behaviour on the part of single firms. Among other things it outlaws predatory pricing, tying contracts and unfair trade practices.

Enforcement of the EU's laws in this area is handled by a Directorate General of the European Union Commission. The Commission's powers are considerable. Although it is often difficult to discover whether collusive agreement between firms do exist, the Commission has the power to raid companies and seize documents. Where companies are found guilty of anti-competitive behaviour they can also be fined up to 10% of turnover, and have contracts declared null and void. The Commission has been willing to use these powers. One illustration is European steel. During a recession in the early 1990s, the fall in demand for steel beams did not lead to the expected fall in prices. The European Commission discovered that a cartel of European and Scandinavian producers was preventing competition achieving this and firms were fined. The largest fine, totalling Ecu 132 million, was imposed on British Steel.

Restrictive practices policy in the USA

Two different administrative bodies have the responsibility for initiating actions on behalf of the US government against individuals or companies thought to be in violation of the antitrust laws. These agencies are the **Antitrust Division of the Justice Department** and the Federal Trade Commission (FTC). In addition, private citizens can initiate antitrust actions.

The FTC has established a set of trade regulation rules that make clear what practices it deems unfair and subject to action. One such rule, for example, states that a service station that fails to display octane ratings clearly on its pumps is guilty of an 'unfair or deceptive act or practice'. These rules simplify the process of adjudication by making the standards of conduct clear.

Along with the Antitrust Division, the FTC initiates actions against those who violate antitrust law. The power to impose penalties and remedies formally rests with the courts, but the Antitrust Division decides which cases to prosecute.

The courts are empowered to impose a number of remedies if they find that antitrust law has been violated. Certain civil and criminal penalties can be exacted for past wrongs, and other measures can prevent future wrongs. Specifically, the courts can '(1) forbid the continuation of illegal acts, (2) force the defendant to dispose of the fruits of his or her wrong, and (3) restore competitive conditions'.

Between 75% and 80% of all government-initiated civil suits in the USA are settled with the signing of a consent decree. **Consent decrees** are formal agreements between the prosecuting government and the defendants that must be approved by the courts.

Restrictive practices policy in Japan

Japan has had an antitrust policy since 1947, when it passed the Antimonopoly Law. The law prohibits 'private monopolization, unreasonable restraint of trade and unfair business practices, by preventing the excessive concentration of economic power'.[2] In its basic provisions, the law appears to be similar to the corresponding laws of the USA and the EU.

But in practice, Japanese antitrust policy has been very different. The Japanese Fair Trade Commission (JFTC), empowered to enforce the Antimonopoly Law in Japan,

Antitrust Division (of the Department of Justice)
One of two US federal agencies empowered to act against those in violation of antitrust laws. It initiates action against those who violate antitrust laws and decides which cases to prosecute and against whom to bring criminal charges.

consent decrees
Formal agreements on remedies between all the parties to an antitrust case that must be approved by the courts. Consent decrees can be signed before, during or after a trial.

[2]*Stephen Martin*, Industrial Economics *(New York: Macmillan, 1994), p. 61.*

operates in a society very suspicious of unfettered competition and within a centralized and hierarchical government that has traditionally played a substantial role in protecting and promoting specific industries. The specific goals of the Ministry of Trade and Industry (MITI) include promotion of large-scale industry and strategic mergers to help industries compete internationally. In addition, Japanese law specifically allows legal cartels during periods of hard times. The number of legal cartels in Japan peaked at over 1000 during the mid-1960s, but has dropped steadily since.

While many investigations are conducted by the JFTC, few result in charges being filed, and fines are rare. In fact, when criminal charges were filed in November 1991 against a cartel of wrapping paper manufacturers, it was only the second set of such charges ever filed in Japan.[3]

The restrictive practices enforcement debate

Should governments be more aggressive in prosecuting those who break restrictive practices laws or regulations? Just what level of enforcement activity should we settle for? The issues raised by this debate require further discussion. In the sections that follow we review the economic logic behind these laws before turning to a discussion of recent criticism levelled at enforcement practices.

The case for the enforcement of restrictive practices

In a sense, the first part of this book – particularly Chapters 13 and 14 – has already made the case for antitrust laws. As you have seen, competition has many potential benefits. It drives firms to produce at least cost and provides an incentive to introduce new, efficient production techniques and new products. Thus, the argument goes, the government should step in when anti-competitive behaviour or monopoly power threatens to rob society of the benefits of open competition.

Such laws do more than condemn monopoly; they also restrict certain specific kinds of conduct, whether the industry is monopolistic or not. Most of the specific practices outlawed can result in serious social costs and waste of society's scarce resources. Thus, it is easy to build an economic case for governmental enforcement of prohibitions against unfair and deceptive practices, price fixing, collusion and price discrimination.

Unfair or deceptive practices

For a market economy to work, consumers must have valid information on product availability, quality and price. The variety and complexity of modern life forces the average consumer to consider many products that cannot be fully understood or personally evaluated. Medical care, financial services, insurance, drugs, food products, consumer electronics and products in many other areas are so complicated and specialized that the consumer may well be misinformed about them, if not deliberately deceived. In such cases, it may be reasonable for the government to act on behalf of consumers to prevent unfair and deceptive acts or practices. (We discuss this in Chapter 16.)

Price fixing and collusion

Firms can use price fixing and collusion to protect themselves from competition. Both practices allow firms that would otherwise compete to act together as a monopoly and reap monopoly profits. Competitive markets drive product prices close to the cost of production, and in the long run competitive firms will earn only normal profits. If a monopolist were to gain control of an industry, it would clearly be in his or her interest to cut output, raise price, and do everything possible to prevent competition.

---

[3]*Stephen Martin, ibid., p. 191.*

If firms were permitted to set prices jointly or collude to restrict output and share the market, they would act just like a monopoly, and consumers would lose. Consumers would pay more for the same product than they would pay under competition, and less of the product would be produced. (In Chapter 13 you learned how the size of this net loss to society from the monopolization of an industry is calculated.)

Price discrimination

Suppose that several companies buy rolled steel to make filing cabinets. The largest producer, by virtue of its size and bargaining power, may be able to obtain a very low price from the steel producers, a price not justified by cost savings due to large volume. The bargaining power thus gives the large producer an advantage over its smaller competitors. This can lead to monopoly power in the long run.

Not all forms of this practice of **price discrimination** are inefficient, however. *Third degree price discrimination*, dividing consumers into identifiable groups and charging them different prices, goes on all around us. Airlines, cinemas, public transport and telephone companies all charge different prices for children, senior citizens, students, military personnel and other identifiable groups. Professional and academic journals charge individuals and institutions (libraries) very different subscription fees. Car hire companies offer discounts to members of certain motoring associations, frequent fliers, and employees of certain businesses.

For third degree price discrimination to work, resales must be prevented. Otherwise, the differences in price would be arbitraged. *Arbitrage* occurs when someone buys a good at one price and immediately sells it to someone else at a higher price. Many firms have devised methods that keep arbitrage possibilities to a minimum. This is easily accomplished for services, which must be sold directly to the person consuming them, but is difficult for goods, which can be resold easily.

Assuming that resale cannot occur, is third degree price discrimination inefficient? There is no easy answer. Suppose that Henri and Sarah both like widgets. Henri is willing to pay €3 for a widget, but he will be charged €5 for a widget. Clearly, Henri will not buy. Sarah, however, is able to buy widgets for 1 euro each. She is willing to pay €2 for a widget. The optimal solution, from society's point of view, is for Sarah to buy a widget for 1 euro and then sell it to Henri for €3. But this cannot happen if resale is prevented! Because exchange is blocked, it is likely that society will end up with the wrong distribution of output. Also, when a firm charges more than one price for its product, it is clearly not selling at least some of its product at marginal cost. (Remember, one of the conditions for allocative efficiency is $P = MC$.)

price discrimination

Occurs when a firm charges different buyers different prices for the same product. Such strategies are illegal if they drive out competition.

Applications

Price discrimination in the European car market

Volkswagen, the German car manufacturer, was fined by the European Commission 102m Ecus in 1998 for anti-competitive sales practices. Since prices vary considerably between EU countries for the same model, consumers want to shop across frontiers to get the best deal. VW was accused of preventing their Italian dealers from selling to Austrian and German consumers in order to keep up prices in those countries.

VW said the fine for the behaviour of some its Italian dealers was 'incomprehensible' and 'entirely out of proportion' to the facts. But Karel Van Miert, competition commissioner, said the Commission's decision reflected the duration of VW's misdemeanours, which began in 1987 and escalated after 1993 in spite of two warnings from Brussels. The Commission also took into account VW's bullying behaviour towards the Italian dealers.

Commission investigators uncovered evidence that the company threatened to rip up the contracts of 50 dealers if they were caught selling cars to people from outside Italy. Twelve dealers were penalized in this way.

Under special competition rules that apply to the European car sector, manufacturers are not allowed to refuse to sell to people from other EU countries. 'This was a systematic, covert operation endorsed by the management of the company', said Mr Van Miert.

Source: Emma Tucker and Graham Bowley, Financial Times, 29 January 1998, p. 2.

Ultimately, whether or not third degree price discrimination is in society's best interests depends on the alternative market solution. If the alternative is that the firm will sell all of its product at a single, high, monopoly price, then price discrimination may be preferable. If a firm with market power can expand its output beyond the amount that it would sell at a single fixed price by selling more to certain groups at lower prices, the result will be more efficient and more socially desirable.

Highly concentrated industries

Arguments in favour of action against firms in highly concentrated industries on the basis of industry structure alone are more difficult to make. In theory, a monopoly can be just as efficient as a competitive industry if it does not exercise its power and if it continues to minimize costs and to innovate as if it had rivals. However, those who favour antitrust action on the basis of structure alone argue that such behaviour is extremely unlikely.

Restrictive practices laws as a deterrent

Because we can only speculate about what would have happened without them, we cannot say whether restrictive practices laws have 'worked' or not. Some decisions seem to have produced the desired results. In recent years, substantial fines have been imposed by the European Commission on steel firms, cement producers and carton-board manufacturers, and cartels have been broken up.

But you cannot measure the success of the speed limit laws by looking only at the behaviour of those who get speeding fines; you must also look at how fast most people drive. Proponents of enforcement argue that the real gains of such a policy lie in the cases that never make it to national courts or the European Commission, because such laws and rules serve as a significant deterrent. Without them, they argue, the temptation to fix prices, collude, and engage in deceptive advertising would be irresistible. If no prohibitions existed, can anyone doubt that firms would merge, dominate markets and exploit monopoly power? As you saw in Chapters 13 and 14, the profit incentive for firms to do all these things is compelling.

The case against the enforcement of restrictive practices

Restrictive practices laws are not beyond criticism. While few complain about the laws that make certain kinds of conduct illegal, there is growing concern about remedies aimed at concentrated industries that seem to be performing fairly well. Several themes recur in this recent criticism.

Regulations as the penalty for success?

Critics of regulation contend that the authorities are not concerned with inefficient firms that have not done well; rather, they are interested only in the firms that, in a sense, have done *too well*. If a company produces a better mousetrap and comes to dominate an industry, the government attacks it for being a monopoly!

One example of regulation as the 'penalty for success' occurred in the USA in the early 1960s. Extensive research led the General Motors Corporation (GM) to come up with improvements in the design of intra-city buses. Those improvements were patented, and as a result GM came to dominate the market for intra-city buses.

After a long antitrust battle, the court issued a consent decree forcing GM to give up its patents to the competition. In addition, any further design improvements that GM made through research and development would also have to be made available to its competitors. The result was that GM stopped developing new and better buses, and travellers ended up with worse buses than they might have had.

Many people made the same argument about British Telecom (BT) in the UK. After privatization, this has become an enormously successful private company. No one argued that Telecom had done anything wrong or unethical. Rather, the argument was that competition might lead to an even better result – new products, better service and lower rates. But, the critics cried, the key word was 'might'. And, they added, resorting to familiar and compelling logic, 'If it's not broken, don't fix it!'

The need for big, strong companies to face global competition

If we think of the market for the product as being the domestic national economy we may think that competition between firms in that market is essential. However, markets are becoming more globalized. A firm that dominates, say, the Swedish or Dutch markets may be too small to be competitive in the European market. This has become a strong argument in recent years as trade barriers between EU countries have been reduced. National governments, then, should be thinking less about keeping their own domestic market competitive and more about building up their large firms to be successful in the European or even world market.

Negative effects on research, development and growth

The Schumpeterian hypothesis (Chapter 14) is the foundation for the argument that large firms can devote significant resources to research and development activities, while lower levels of industrial concentration lead to less R&D. But, the evidence is mixed. Larger firms are indeed more likely to have research staffs than smaller firms, but the number of patents procured and the number of important developments over the years do not seem to show any systematic correlation with firm size.

The pharmaceutical industry is one in which large firms are necessary if R&D is to be effective. During 1998, SmithKline Beecham and Glaxo Wellcome proposed a merger. This would have created the world's largest company for their industry, and the second largest for any industry. R&D provides one of the key arguments for such a merger: to supply a new drug to the market takes an average of ten years from research to consumers, and requires many millions of euros. Only very large firms can afford such sums.

Even in such an industry as this, however, the case is not proven. Of the dozen or so large drug mergers and acquisitions over the past 30 years, not one has increase the combined market share of the companies involved.[4] The proposed merger was subsequently abandoned.

Efficient capital flows and relatively contestable markets

Another argument against vigorous enforcement of restrictive practices is that barriers to entry are not as formidable as they once were. Capital markets have become more efficient; investors are always looking for profitable ventures and are now able to mobilize the huge sums necessary to enter almost any industry if there are economic profits to be earned. The efficiency of capital markets serves to make more and more markets contestable. Critics of restrictive practices enforcement argue that both actual entry and the threat of new entry make market power less of a problem.

Distrust of government

Even if it can be shown that such enforcement is a good idea in theory, many people simply do not want to put more power in the hands of government. They feel that government intervention creates more problems than it solves. Bureaucracy is slow and wasteful, the argument goes, and the people in a particular industry clearly know more about what they do than those government employees charged with regulating that industry.

The policy makers' dilemma

One of the lessons that we hope you will take from this book (and from your education as a whole) is that complicated questions have no simple answers. There are strong

[4] *The Economist, 7 February 1988, p. 85.*

arguments for government involvement in the economy. Unchecked monopoly power, collusion and price fixing can be enormously expensive for a society. It is also easy to show that competition provides incentives for efficient production, innovation, and a healthy economy.

It is equally clear, unfortunately, that enforcement of the restrictive practices laws has imposed costs on society. Successful companies have paid a price for their success. Government activities in this area may also have played a part in reducing European firms' ability to compete for international markets.

The role of policy makers is to understand the arguments, weigh the evidence and proceed accordingly. While policy decisions must be made without knowledge of the outcome, enlightened uncertainty is better than ignorance.

Regulation

At the beginning of this chapter we said that the government plays two basic roles that seem contradictory: (1) It *promotes* competition and restricts market power, primarily through merger policy law and restrictive practices laws, and (2) it *restricts* competition by simultaneously regulating and protecting certain industries. So far, we have looked exclusively at the way the government protects competition. Now we turn to government activities that may end up protecting monopoly power.

The government regulates many areas of the economy that have nothing to do with market structure. Some of these areas (environmental protection, for example) are discussed in later chapters. In the section that follows, however, we examine only the regulation of natural monopolies.

The need for regulation: privatization

privatization
The transfer of government business to the private sector.

The last fifteen to twenty years has seen a significant shift of resources out of the state sector and into the private sector. This process we call **privatization**. It has been a particularly strong feature of UK policy. Prior to the 1980s, publicly owned and operated monopolies provided virtually all utility services in the UK. However, during the 1980s and early 1990s the British government privatized all of its utilities (water, gas, electricity, telecommunications and the railway system) by selling them off to private investors.

Many governments around the world, including others in Europe, have followed this policy. What are the reasons? After all, many European cities operate their own public utilities. The railway systems of many countries are run by the government, often quite efficiently. France, for example, operates one of the most efficient and innovative railway networks in the world.

Despite some successful examples of public ownership, however, the prevailing opinion seems to be that the government should stay out of a particular business if the private sector can do the job. The three arguments in favour of privatization are: improved efficiency, greater government revenue, and the benefits of wider share ownership.

The argument for privatization is based partly on cost efficiency. When we talk about cost efficiency, we mean that the firm will produce any given level of output at the lowest possible long-run average cost for *that level of output*. In other words, the firm will be on its cost curve and not above it.

Privatization is often claimed to improve cost efficiency: nationalized industries suffer from low morale, so output is lower than it need be; management has no incentive to reduce waste and improve cost efficiency because it will not be rewarded with increased profits. Only the incentive of improved rewards will reduce costs. Privatization makes that possible. Efficiency can also increase because of access to capital markets. A nationalized concern has to go to government to ask for funds for investment. Whether they will be granted depends not only on the merits of the case itself but also on the wider considerations of the Treasury's finances. In the private sector, industries such as water and electricity will compete for funds on an equal footing. If consumer demand is strong enough to justify investment, the funds will be forthcoming. The industry no longer has to concern itself with the political problems inherent in state intervention, such as when governments are short of cash.

Another apparent advantage of the privatization programme is the revenue that is generated from the sale of the assets. The government may feel that the income generated will enable it to make a better investment. It could use the sales revenue to build more schools or hospitals, for example. However, the increase is more apparent than real. This can be understood if we ask ourselves why anyone is willing to buy these assets from the government. The answer is, of course, because of the expected stream of revenue that will be produced in the form of profits or dividends. As we saw in Chapter 11, the value of the capital will be the discounted value of the expected income stream. Then the government is simply replacing a stream of earnings in the future with a one-off receipt of revenue now. It is not increasing revenue; it is merely altering the timing of its receipts.

The logic of maximizing revenue from the sale of assets requires that the assets should be sold to the highest bidder. But in some countries the government has tended not to do this, and has sold shares to those employed in the industry. This clearly has a claim to be better from an equity point of view, but by severely restricting the market for the shares the likelihood of not achieving the best price for the assets is increased.

The third claimed benefit of the privatization programme is the wider spread of wealth ownership that takes place. This was arguably the UK government's most important aim when the privatization programme was at its height; its long-term objective was to change attitudes to wealth creation through greater individual ownership of capital. It is extremely difficult however, to prove one way or the other whether this has been happening.

Whatever the merits of the arguments, privatization has resulted in the transfer of public sector monopolies into private hands. Attention must therefore be given to the question of control of such industries in order to avoid the exploitation of consumers. And however strong the arguments are for privatization, there has been a sharp increase in the number of industries where firms have the power to exploit consumers. The regulation of these industries would therefore appear to be essential.

Regulation of natural monopoly

In Chapter 13 we introduced you to some of the ways the market fails when market power is unrestrained. Firms that can control price and bar the entry of new firms overprice and underproduce relative to what is best for society. Solutions to this problem are possible, at least in theory. One is to restructure the industry to make it more competitive. A second is to impose some sort of price regulation – a price ceiling at marginal cost, for example. Another is public or government ownership and operation.

The restrictive practices laws that we examined in this chapter are based on the proposition that competition, not regulation or public ownership, is the best way to achieve efficiency in an economy. It has always been argued that not all markets can be, or should be, competitively structured. Most important among these exceptions are firms or industries that can take advantage of very large economies of scale – the natural monopolies mentioned earlier in this chapter and described in Chapter 13.

Figure 15.2 illustrates a natural monopoly. Notice that average total cost is still declining when the demand curve intersects it. To break such a firm into smaller pieces, each producing some fraction of total demand, would mean that each of the small firms would have to produce at a much higher average cost. (All of this is implied by the existence of large economies of scale. If this is not clear, review Chapter 13.)

Most natural monopolies have very high fixed costs and low marginal costs. Take, for example, an electricity company. Building a generating plant and creating a distribution system is costly. Once everything is in place, however, the cost of generating and distributing one additional kilowatt of electricity is low. Part of the reasoning

Figure 15.2 Regulating a natural monopoly

A natural monopoly exists when a firm exhibits very large economies of scale. Here, long-run average costs facing the firm continue to decline with output, even when a single firm is producing all the output demanded in the market. With no regulation, the firm would produce at Q^* and price at P^*. Regulating price to be equal to marginal cost would be efficient but would result in losses. Setting price at P_A means that average cost is covered and that investors earn a normal rate of return.

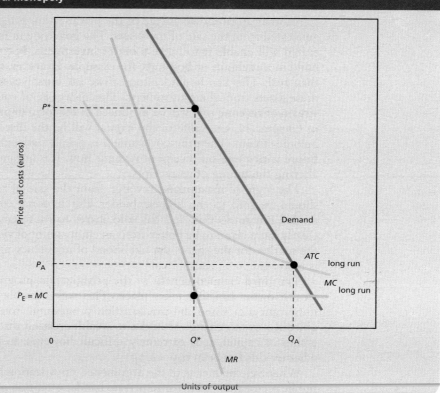

behind the protection of such industries is that having more than one firm undertake the very large initial investment is a waste of resources.

One solution to the natural monopoly problem is to let the firm continue to exist as a monopoly but to regulate its price. If the natural monopoly in Figure 15.2 went unregulated, it would produce Q^* units of output (the point at which $MR = MC$) and charge price P^*, far above marginal costs. But imposing a simple price ceiling at $P_E = MC$ would not work, because at that price marginal cost is below average total cost, and the firm could not make even a normal profit. Remember that price is equal to average revenue, and if average revenue is less than average total cost, total revenue will be less than total cost. This means that a loss is made.

Theory suggests three options for regulation: (1) Set the efficient price ($P = MC$) and provide a subsidy out of general government revenues to the monopoly; (2) set price equal to average cost (P_A), which would allow firms to charge a price that covers all costs, including a normal return on invested capital; or (3) impose a fee on each user of the monopoly's product – a basic service charge as a lump sum, and a price for usage equal to marginal cost. *Any* approach requires that the firm can make a normal return or it will go out of business in the long run.

The problems of regulation

The theory of natural monopoly sounds simple: regulatory bodies set prices that allow regulated monopolies to earn a normal rate of return. A number of problems are inherent in regulation, however, and these will probably always perplex the regulator to some degree.

Gathering and analysing the necessary data

Regulation requires analysing lots of information. The first problem is calculating the base – presumably, some measure of the 'value' of the firm's capital investment – on which a fair return should be allowed.

The regulatory body must also analyse costs. Should all costs be allowed in setting price? Which costs are reasonable? Analysis is a difficult process, subject to differences of opinion and to error.

The UK is the country with more experience of regulating natural monopolies in this way, because more of these industries have been privatized there than in most other countries. Pricing controls must be worked out for each industry separately. Let us take two such examples. First consider British Telecom. The company was privatized but had to work under this pricing formula: each year, BT could raise its charges by the retail price index (RPI), a measure of inflation, less 3%. The view was that technological progress would, over time, move the *LRAC* downwards so that BT could still break even, even with falling prices. Subsequently, the formula was tightened to RPI less 4%, then to RPI less 6.25%, then to RPI less 7.5%.

Second, look at the example of the water industry. This industry was given a price ceiling of RPI *plus*, the size of the plus varying from one water company to another. The idea of allowing these companies to increase water charges in real terms was to enable them to be sufficiently profitable to attract large sums from capital markets. These sums would be needed to engage in major programmes of repairing deteriorating water pipes, and so on.

Notice the difficulty involved in deciding whether the policy is successful. Many would argue that water and electricity companies, among others, have done far better than break even. Recall that *break even* means covering all costs including normal profit; that is, they must make a rate of return on capital comparable to other industries with similar risk. Whether their profits are equal to or greater than that is a matter for debate, but it is clearly difficult to obtain an agreed figure as to what constitutes a normal profit.

Lack of incentives to be efficient

If the return to a regulated natural monopoly is set by a commission, the monopoly may lack the incentive to use efficient production techniques. For example, if a regulatory body fixes the return by setting a rate expressed as a percentage of the utility's assets, the amount of profit depends only on the total value of those assets. Thus, firms may actually have an incentive to over-invest in capital if the allowed return exceeds the cost of capital. This tendency is called the Averch–Johnson Effect, after the scholars who noted the proclivity of regulated firms to build more capital capacity than they need.[5]

Averch–Johnson Effect
The tendency for regulated monopolies to build more capital than they need. Usually occurs when allowed rates of return are set by a regulatory agency at some percentage of fixed capital stocks.

In general, then, we can say that when regulated firms are guaranteed a standard rate of return, they have no incentive to keep costs at a minimum. When profits are not linked to some measure of performance, there is no reason for the firm to perform well, and no severe penalty for weak performance.

A possible way to avoid this problem is simply to set a price ceiling such that any cost savings a firm makes it can keep as enhanced profits. This is not without its problems. BT's price ceiling was lowered a number of times because the company was so successful at reducing costs that its profits were regarded by the regulators as excessive. However, if a company such as BT knows that a decrease in costs and an increase in profits will lead to a tightening of its price ceiling, it may come to the conclusion that efforts to reduce costs are rather pointless. Then the policy will no longer be achieving cost efficiency.

The case for deregulation

Earlier in this chapter we mentioned a key criticism of the privatization process: monopolies, with their power to misallocate resources, are transferred from the public to the private sector. We saw that those privatized companies where substantial

---

[5]*Harvey Averch and Leland Johnson, 'Behaviour of the firm under regulatory constraint'*, American Economic Review, LII (December 1962), pp. 1052–69.

deregulation
The introduction of
competition into an
industry.

monopoly power exists have that power curtailed by a price control. A further technique for controlling monopoly power is that of **deregulation**. Most of the natural monopolies within the public sector have been protected from competition in order to ensure the benefits of economies of scale. This is still true for some industries. For example, the UK Post Office, still publicly owned, has a legally determined monopoly over the delivery of letters (although competition is allowed in parcel deliveries). When an industry is in private hands it can be deregulated. For example, companies such as Mercury have been granted access to BT's cable network, so BT now has some competition. Another example is allowing regional electricity distributors to buy power from whichever source they choose.

Deregulation and privatization are separate but closely related issues. Deregulation is a way of controlling monopoly power in the private sector and encouraging competition to move price/output decisions in industry closer to the social optimum. Is it effective? The most comprehensive attempt to answer this question is provided by Clifford Winston from his collection of researches into the effects of deregulation on American industry.

The results, for those who believe in the power of deregulation, are encouraging. They suggest that substantial welfare gains can be achieved in the form of lower prices and better services (Table 15.3). Notice that this effect is not simply a transfer of welfare from producers to consumers. There are overall gains. Competition improves efficiency. Notice also that, in some cases, consumers and producers both gain. Cost efficiency is improved by competition. Prices fall, but not by as much as costs. Producers increase profits; consumers get lower prices.

The last column in Table 15.3 indicates that, while the process has improved things for society in the USA, prices in those industries do not reflect a welfare optimum. This last column gives an idea of the further benefits available to society if price and output were socially optimal.

The results of the study, then, suggest that deregulation is a powerful way to improve welfare. It is a particularly important means of controlling the monopoly power of privatized industries. All this suggests that the opening up of competition in

Table 15.3 Welfare effects of deregulation, $US billion, 1990

Industry	Consumers	Producers	Total	Additional benefits if deregulation achieves optimality
Airlines	8.8–14.8	4.9	13.7–19.7	4.9
Railroads	7.2–9.7	3.2	10.4–12.9	0.45
Trucking	15.4	−4.8	10.6	0
Telecommunications	0.73–1.6	–	0.73–1.6	11.8
Cable television	0.37–1.3	–	0.37–1.3	0.4–0.8
Brokerage	0.14	−0.14	0	0
Natural gas	–	–	–	4.1
Total	32.6–43.0	3.2	35.8–46.2	21.65–22.05

Note: the additional welfare gains are based on the assumption that regulatory reform actually generates optimal pricing and, where appropriate, optimal service.

Source: C. Winston, 'Economic deregulation: days of reckoning for microeconomists', *Journal of Economic Literature* (September 1993).

electricity, gas, telecommunications and elsewhere does have benefits for consumers. Price controls can also be of benefit to consumers. However, there may be a trade-off between these two means of helping the consumer to achieve better value for money from such industries. Firms are attracted into industries in response to profits, but price controls threaten the very profit that would attract new firms to the market. Hence the denial via price controls of some profit to monopolistic industries may slow the arrival of the competition that deregulation is designed to bring.

Restrictive practices legislation is enforced to *promote* competition. In a way, it is the opposite of market regulation, which nearly always restricts competition.

Summary

The development of anti-monopoly laws

1. Governments have assumed two roles with respect to imperfectly competitive industries: (1) they promote competition and restrict market power, primarily through restrictive practices laws and merger control; and (2) they regulate industries.

2. Large mergers can be prevented by governments or the European Commission where they may result in excessive market power.

3. Mergers can be horizontal, vertical or conglomerate.

4. Market power can be assessed by *concentration ratios*, but these are of only limited value.

5. US merger legislation is more powerful. Currently the Justice Department uses the *Herfindahl–Hirschman Index* to determine whether or not it will challenge a proposed merger.

The enforcement of anti-monopoly laws

6. The European Commission has wide-ranging powers to prevent restrictive practices between large firms. Firms found to be breaking anti-monopoly laws can face heavy fines.

7. Responsibility for the enforcement of US antitrust laws rests primarily with the *Antitrust Division* of the Justice Department and the Federal Trade Commission.

The restrictive practices enforcement debate

8. The case for government intervention in imperfectly competitive industries is well established: unchecked monopoly power, price discrimination, collusion and price fixing can be enormously expensive to society. Proponents of such enforcement say that the real gains are in the cases that never reach the courts because the rules and laws serve as a significant deterrent. Without such laws, the temptation to fix prices, collude, and engage in deceptive advertising would be irresistible.

9. The basic arguments against restrictive practices enforcement are that it penalizes success, that Europe needs strong companies to face foreign competition, that such actions may reduce basic research and development, and that most markets are reasonably competitive.

Regulation

10. When an industry demonstrates large economies of scale, it may be efficient to have only one large firm in that industry, a natural monopoly. If a single-firm industry is protected on the grounds that it is a natural monopoly, it must be regulated to prevent exploitation of its monopoly power.

11. The number of firms subject to regulation has increased in recent years because of the *privatization* process.

12. There are problems with regulation. First, it is difficult to collect and analyse all the data necessary to regulate an industry. Second, firms that are guaranteed a certain rate of return lack incentives to be efficient. This may give rise to the *Averch–Johnson* effect, in which a monopoly tends to build more capital than it needs.

13. The proper role of government in the world of business is hard to define. Doing nothing about non-competitive industries inevitably results in significant social losses. The restrictive practices laws have strengths and weaknesses, but most economists feel they deter behaviour that might cost society too much. Where large economies of scale make it logical to preserve monopoly structure in an industry, regulation can be an appropriate course of action.

14. In some cases *deregulation* may be better than regulation.

Review Terms and Concepts

Antitrust Division (of the Department of Justice)
Averch–Johnson effect
concentration ratio
conglomerate merger
consent decree
deregulation

Herfindahl–Hirschman Index (HHI)
horizontal merger
price discrimination
privatization
vertical merger

Problem Set

1. The leading firms in Europe's domestic appliance market (fridges, freezers, cookers, microwaves, washing machines etc.) are Electrolux (21%), Bosch Siemens (17%), Whirlpool (9%), Miele (7%), Elfi (6%), Candy (5%) and Merloni (5%). Whirlpool is an American firm that purchased the domestic appliance division of Dutch firm Philips in the early 1990s.
a. What is the European CR_3? CR_5?
b. Prices have been falling in this industry during the 1990s. Why do you think this is so?
c. Would you allow a merger to take place between any of the above firms? Why, or why not?

2. When a horizontal merger is allowed between two large firms, trades unions often object because they fear substantial job losses.
a. Why might jobs be lost?
b. Is this good or bad for social welfare?

3. Some foreign-owned companies have opened plants in Europe. Many of these are Japanese owned – Toyota, Nissan and Hyundai are just a few. Does the nationality of the owners matter? What effects for good or ill might foreign companies cause?

4. Suppose the glump industry is made up of five firms, each controlling 15% of the market, and five other firms who each control 5% of the market. If two of the firms that each control 15% of the market propose to merge, do you think the merger would be allowed **a.** in the EU, and **b.** in the USA?

5. Professor Robert H. Bork argues that there is little justification for interfering with the natural operation of a free-market system. Sometimes called 'economic Darwinism', Bork's philosophy is that monopoly or market power are of little concern because they 'will be eroded if not based on superior efficiency'. Write a brief essay either supporting or challenging Professor Bork's position. See Robert Bork, *The Antitrust Paradox* (New York: Basic Books, 1978).

6. What potential problems do you see with governments basing merger decisions based on concentration ratios, and the Herfindahl–Hirschman Index?

7. Explain why restructuring fails as a remedy in the case of a natural monopoly. Illustrate your answer with a graph. What alternatives are there to restructuring in the case of a natural monopoly?

8. Explain, using graphs, why restructuring a monopoly into a number of competing firms can lead to a more efficient allocation of resources.

9. What arguments favour regulation of companies in the telecommunications industry? What arguments favour complete deregulation of that industry?

10. The figure shows marginal cost, average total cost and market demand for a large natural monopoly. On the diagram indicate the following:

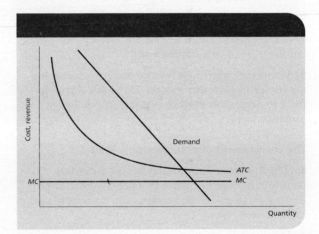

a. Unregulated profit-maximizing price.
b. Total revenue, total cost and economic profit at the price in (a).
c. The efficient price.
d. Total revenue, total cost and economic profit at the price in (c).
e. The price at which demand is satisfied and the firm is allowed to earn a 'normal rate of return'.

11. To what extent would eliminating trade barriers between EU members reduce the need for restrictive practices enforcement?

16

Externalities, Public Goods, Imperfect Information, and Social Choice

In Chapters 6 to 12 we built a complete model of a perfectly competitive economy under a set of assumptions. By Chapter 12, we had demonstrated that the allocation of resources under perfect competition is efficient, and we began to relax some of the assumptions on which the competitive model is based. We introduced the idea of market failure, and in Chapters 13 and 14 we talked about three kinds of imperfect markets: monopoly, oligopoly and monopolistic competition. In Chapter 15 we discussed some of the ways government has responded to the inefficiencies of imperfect markets and to the development of market power.

As we continue our examination of market failure, we look first at *externalities* as a source of inefficiency. Often, when we engage in transactions or make economic decisions, second or third parties suffer consequences that decision makers have no incentive to consider. For example, for many years manufacturing firms and power plants had no reason to worry about the impact of smoke from their operations on the quality of the air we breathe. Now we know that air pollution, an externality, harms people.

Next, we consider a second type of market failure that involves products that private firms find unprofitable to produce even if members of society want them. These products are called *public goods* or *social goods*. Public goods yield collective benefits, and in most societies, governments produce them or arrange to provide them. The process of choosing what social goods to produce is very different from the process of private choice.

A third source of market failure is *imperfect information*. In Chapters 6 to 12, we assumed that households and firms make choices in the presence of perfect information – that households know all that there is to know about product availability, quality and price, and that firms know all there is to know about factor availability, quality and price. When information is imperfect, a misallocation of resources may result.

Finally, while the existence of public goods, externalities and imperfect information are examples of market failure, it is not necessarily true that government involvement will always improve matters. Just as markets can fail, so too can governments. When we look at the incentives facing government decision makers, we find several reasons behind government failure.

Externalities and environmental economics

An externality exists when the actions or decisions of one person or group impose a cost or bestow a benefit on second or third parties. Externalities are sometimes called *spillovers* or *neighbourhood effects*. Inefficient decisions result when decision makers fail to consider social costs and benefits.

The presence of externalities is a significant phenomenon in modern life. Examples are everywhere: air, water, land, sight and sound pollution; traffic congestion and road accidents; abandoned housing; nuclear accidents; and secondhand cigarette smoke are only a few. The study of externalities is a major concern of *environmental economics*.

The opening up of Eastern Europe in 1989 and 1990 revealed that environmental externalities are not limited to free-market economies. Part of the logic of a planned economy is that when economic decisions are made socially (by the government, presumably acting on behalf of the people) rather than privately, planners can and will take all costs – private and social – into account. This has not been the case, however. When East and West Germany were reunited and the borders of Europe were opened, we saw the disastrous condition of the environment in virtually all of Eastern Europe. (See Figure 16.1, and the Global Perspective box 'Transitional economies and environmental issues'.)

As societies become more urbanized, externalities become increasingly important: when we live closer together, our actions are more likely to affect others.

Marginal social cost and marginal-cost pricing

Profit-maximizing perfectly competitive firms will produce output up to the point at which price is equal to marginal cost ($P = MC$). Let us take a moment here to review why this is essential to the proposition that competitive markets produce what people want (an efficient mix of output).

When a firm weighs price and marginal cost and no externalities exist, it is weighing the full benefits to society of additional production against the full costs to society of that production. Those who benefit from the production of a product are the people or households who end up consuming it. The price of a product is a good measure of what an additional unit of that product is 'worth', since those who value it more highly already buy it. People who value it less than the current price are not buying it. If marginal cost includes all costs – that is, all costs *to society* – of producing a marginal unit of a good, then additional production is efficient, provided that P is

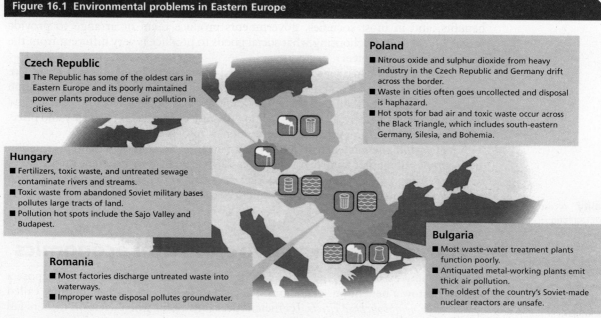

Figure 16.1 Environmental problems in Eastern Europe

Czech Republic
■ The Republic has some of the oldest cars in Eastern Europe and its poorly maintained power plants produce dense air pollution in cities.

Poland
■ Nitrous oxide and sulphur dioxide from heavy industry in the Czech Republic and Germany drift across the border.
■ Waste in cities often goes uncollected and disposal is haphazard.
■ Hot spots for bad air and toxic waste occur across the Black Triangle, which includes south-eastern Germany, Silesia, and Bohemia.

Hungary
■ Fertilizers, toxic waste, and untreated sewage contaminate rivers and streams.
■ Toxic waste from abandoned Soviet military bases pollutes large tracts of land.
■ Pollution hot spots include the Sajo Valley and Budapest.

Bulgaria
■ Most waste-water treatment plants function poorly.
■ Antiquated metal-working plants emit thick air pollution.
■ The oldest of the country's Soviet-made nuclear reactors are unsafe.

Romania
■ Most factories discharge untreated waste into waterways.
■ Improper waste disposal pollutes groundwater.

Source: Marlise Simons, 'East Europe sniffs freedom's air, and gasps', *New York Times*, 3 November 1994, p. A1.

greater than *MC*. Up to the point where *P* = *MC*, each unit of production yields benefits in excess of cost.

Consider a firm in the business of producing washing powder. As long as the price per unit that consumers pay for the washing powder exceeds the cost of the resources needed to produce one marginal unit of it, the firm will continue to produce. Producing up to the point where *P* = *MC* is efficient, because for every unit of detergent produced, consumers derive benefits that exceed the cost of the resources needed to produce it. Producing at a point where *MC* is greater than *P* is inefficient, because marginal cost will rise above the unit price of the washing powder. For every unit produced beyond the level at which *P* = *MC*, society uses up resources that have a value in excess of the benefits that consumers place on washing powder. Figure 16.2a shows a firm and an industry in which no externalities exist.

Figure 16.2 Profit-maximizing competitive firms will produce up to the point that price equals marginal cost (*P* = *MC*)

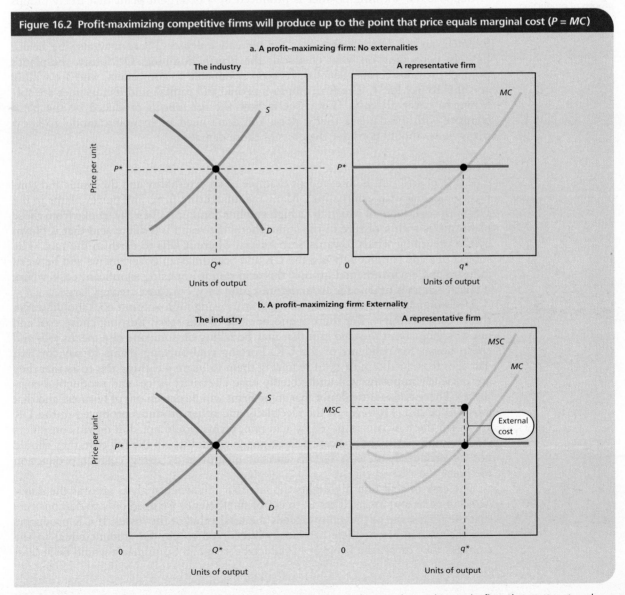

If we assume that the current price reflects what consumers are willing to pay for a product at the margin, firms that create external costs without weighing them in their decisions are likely to produce too much. At *q**, marginal social cost exceeds the price paid by consumers.

But suppose that the production of the firm's product imposes external costs on society as well. If it does not factor those additional costs into its decisions, the firm is likely to overproduce. In Figure 16.2b, a certain measure of external costs is added to the firm's marginal cost curve. We see these external costs in the diagram, but the firm is ignoring them. The curve labelled *MSC* represents the marginal social cost (*MSC*), the simple sum of the marginal costs of producing the product plus the correctly measured damage costs imposed in the process of production.

marginal social cost (*MSC*)

The total cost to society of producing an additional unit of a good or service. *MSC* is equal to the sum of the marginal costs of producing the product and the correctly measured damage costs involved in the process of production.

If the firm does not have to pay for these damage costs, it will produce exactly the same level of output (q^*) as before, and price (P^*) will continue to reflect only the costs that the firm actually pays to produce its product. The firms in this industry will continue to produce, and consumers will continue to consume their product, but the market price takes into account only part of the full cost of producing the good. At equilibrium (q^*), marginal social costs are considerably greater than *price*. (Recall that *price* is a measure of the full value to consumers of a unit of the product at the margin.)

Suppose our washing powder is produced by a detergent plant that freely dumps untreated toxic waste into a river. The waste imposes specific costs on people who live downstream: it kills the fish in the river, it makes the river ugly to look at and rotten to smell, and it destroys the river for recreational use. There may also be health hazards, depending on what chemicals the firm is dumping. Obviously, the plant's product provides certain benefits. Its soap is valuable to consumers, who are willing and able to pay for it. The firm employs people and capital, and its revenues are sufficient to cover all costs. The issue is how the *net benefits* produced by the plant compare with the damage that it does. You don't need an economic model to know that *someone* should consider the costs of those damages.

Acid rain

The case of acid rain is an excellent example of an externality and the issues and conflicts in dealing with externalities. Many manufacturing firms and power plants in the UK burn coal, some of which has a high sulphur content. When the smoke from those plants mixes with moisture in the atmosphere, the result is a dilute acid that is blown by the prevailing winds towards Scandinavia, where it falls to earth in the rain. The subject of some conflict between the UK and Scandinavian governments and between industry and environmental groups, this acid rain is imposing significant costs where it falls. Estimates of damage from deforestation vary, but most are very large.

Decision makers at the manufacturing firms using high-sulphur coal should weigh these costs, of course. But there is another side to this story. Burning cheap coal and not worrying about the acid rain that may be falling on someone else means jobs and cheap power for residents of the UK. Forcing coal-burning plants to pay for past damages from acid rain or even requiring them to begin weighing the costs that they are presently imposing will undoubtedly raise electricity prices and production costs there.[1] There is also little doubt that some firms will be driven out of business and that jobs will be lost. However, if the electricity and other products produced in the UK are worth the full costs imposed by acid rain, plants would not shut down; consumers would simply pay higher prices. If those goods are not worth the full cost, they should not be produced, at least not in current quantities or using current production methods.

The case of acid rain highlights the fact that efficiency analysis ignores the *distribution* of gains and losses. That is, to establish efficiency we need only to demonstrate that the total value of the gains exceeds the total value of the losses. If UK producers and the consumers of their products were forced to pay an amount equal to the damages they cause, the gains from reduced damage in Scandinavia would be at least

---

[1]*Look again at Figure 16.2. If the firm is suddenly forced to pay the full cost of production, it will reduce output. The gains from this output reduction are greater than the value of the goods given up, because marginal social cost is above price.*

Global Perspectives

Transnational economies and environmental issues

In theory, socialist economies are supposed to pay better attention to externalities and social costs than free-market economies, where private firms must often be prodded to consider external effects. The radical changes that have taken place in Eastern Europe over the last few years certainly challenge this once-conventional wisdom, as the following excerpt describes:

Prague: . . .almost five years after the collapse of Communism, the region's environment continues to decay. Chemical works, smelters, coal mines and power plants are still infusing air and water with waste far surpassing international standards and causing severe health problems. Toxic dumps go on poisoning ground water and cities keep on spewing their raw sewage into rivers.

What is more, capitalism is bringing its own problems – more traffic pollution, less public transport, more plastic foam, more clashes between environmentalists and the peddlers of consumerism.

There have been some gains. Factory emissions have dropped, perversely the result of a sputtering economy in which many plants have closed or slowed production. But the enormous task of installing filters, scrubbers and treatment plants has barely begun. And energy still comes largely from highly polluting brown coal . . .

In theory, Communism with its strict central planning had more power than free-wheeling capitalism to avoid or prevent damaging nature. Yet, with its squandering of raw materials and energy, the economic artifice made in Moscow produced exceptional levels of

pollution that maimed the lives of many of its citizens.

In the end, it was this poisoning that provided a rare platform for challenging the state when other forms of protest were not tolerated. The environmental devastation became a powerful catalyst as citizens' groups formed throughout the East, spurring broader protests before the fall of Communism. Almost inevitably, in 1989, the new leaders had to commit themselves to an urgent clean-up . . .

On the cold and high plateaux where the German, Czech and Polish borders meet and tree stumps look as if ravaged by fire, foresters have been planting new and hardy seedlings. Yet few young firs are surviving. In the valleys below, a phalanx of power plants and industries driven by brown coal are still spewing sulphur and soot, as they have done for more than three decades. This region, dubbed the

Pollution and deforestation have been problems in Eastern Europe for years. However they have come much more to the world's attention since the fall of communism.

Black Triangle, is one of the world's biggest makers of acid rain.

Source: Marlize Simons, 'East Europe sniffs freedom's air, and gasps', New York Times, 3 November 1994, p. A1.

as great as costs in the UK. The beneficiaries of forcing UK firms to consider these costs would be the households and firms in Scandinavia.

Other externalities

Other examples of external effects are all around us. When I drive my car into a city centre at rush hour, I contribute to traffic congestion and impose costs (in the form of lost time and exhaust emissions) on others. In fact, one focus of a 1992 world environmental conference called the Earth Summit was the possibility of worldwide climate warming as a result of so-called 'greenhouse emissions' (like carbon dioxide) from industrial plants and vehicles. While potential costs are high, great uncertainty, both in the scientific evidence and in the magnitude of the potential costs, surrounds the issue.

In addition, secondhand cigarette smoke has become a matter of public concern. Smoking has been banned on domestic air carriers, and many countries in the EU have passed laws severely restricting smoking in public places.

The Three Gorges Dam on the Yangtze River in China is under construction and is scheduled for completion in 2009. The dam is the largest hydroelectric project in history, costing an estimated €25 billion. It will create a reservoir of water over 400 miles long. Environmentalists claim that because the Chinese have no plans to deal with the one trillion litres of sewage and industrial waste expected to flow into the reservoir each year, not to mention the thousands of current dump sites that will be flooded, the project is an environmental nightmare.

It is important to keep in mind that not all externalities are negative. For example, an abandoned house in an urban area that is restored and occupied improves the general surroundings and adds value to the neighbours' homes. An inoculation against an infectious disease reduces the chances of other people catching it. These are examples of positive externalities.

Private choices and external effects

To help us to understand externalities, let us use a simple two-person example. Harry lives in a hall of residence at a university, where he is a first-year student. When he started there, his family gave him an expensive stereo system. Unfortunately, the walls of Harry's room are made of thin partitions faced with plasterboard – you can hear people sleeping four rooms away. Harry likes rock music. Because of a hearing loss after an accident on New Year's Eve some years ago, he often fails to notice the volume of the music he plays.

Dan, who lives next door to Harry, isn't much of a music lover, but when he does listen, it's to Brahms' concertos or Mozart. Harry's music bothers Dan.

Let's assume that there are no further external costs or benefits to anyone other than Harry and Dan. Figure 16.3 diagrams the decision process that the two hall residents face. The downward-sloping curve labelled *MB* represents the value of the marginal benefits that Harry derives from listening to his music. Of course, Harry doesn't sit down to draw this curve, any more than anyone else (other than an economics student) sits down to draw actual demand curves. Curves like this are simply

Figure 16.3 Externalities in a hall of residence

The marginal benefits to Harry exceed the marginal costs he must bear to play his stereo for a period of up to eight hours. But when the stereo is playing, a cost is being imposed on Dan. When we add the costs borne by Harry to the damage costs imposed on Dan, we get the full cost of the stereo to the two-person society made up of Harry and Dan. Playing the stereo more than five hours is inefficient, because the benefits to Harry are less than the social cost for every hour above five. If Harry considers only his private costs, he will play the stereo for too long a time from society's point of view.

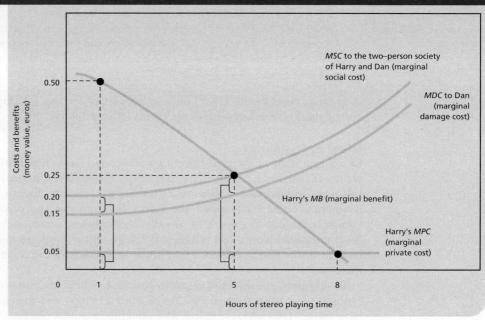

abstract representations of the way people behave. But if you think about it, such a curve must exist. To ask how much an hour of listening to music is worth to you is to ask how much you would be willing to pay to have it. Start at €0.01 and raise the 'price' slowly in your mind. Presumably, you must stop at some point; where you stop depends on your taste for music and your income.

You can think, then, about the benefits Harry derives from listening to rock as the maximum amount of money that he would be willing to pay to listen to his music for an hour. For the first hour, say, the figure for *MB* is €0.50. We assume diminishing marginal utility, of course. The more hours Harry listens, the lower the additional benefits from each successive hour. As the diagram shows, the *MB* curve falls below €0.05 per hour after eight hours of listening time.

We call the costs that Harry must pay for each additional hour of listening to music **marginal private costs**, labelled *MPC* in Figure 16.3. These include the cost of electricity and so on. These costs are constant at €0.05 per hour.

Then there is Dan. Although Harry's music doesn't poison Dan, give him lung cancer, or even cause him to lose money, it damages him nonetheless: he gets a headache, loses sleep and can't concentrate on his work. Dan is harmed, and it is possible (at least conceptually) to measure that harm in terms of the maximum amount that he would be willing to pay to avoid it. The damage, or cost, imposed on Dan is represented in Figure 16.3 by the curve labelled *MDC*. Formally, **marginal damage cost (MDC)** is the additional harm done by increasing the level of an externality-producing activity by one unit. Assuming Dan would be willing to pay some amount of money to avoid the music, it is reasonable to assume the amount increases each successive hour. His headache gets worse with each additional hour during which he is forced to listen to rock.

In the simple two-person society of Dan and Harry, it's easy to add up social benefits and costs. At every level of output (stereo playing time), total social cost is simply the sum of the private costs borne by Harry and the damage costs borne by Dan. In Figure 16.3, *MPC* (constant at €0.05 per hour) is added to *MDC* to get *MSC*.

Consider now what would happen if Harry simply ignored Dan.[2] If Harry decides to play the stereo, Dan will be damaged. As long as Harry gains more in personal benefits from an additional hour of listening to music than he incurs in costs, the stereo will stay on. He will play it for eight hours (the point where Harry's *MB* = *MPC*). This result is inefficient; for every hour of play beyond five, the marginal social cost borne by society (in this case, a society made up of Harry and Dan) exceeds the benefits to Harry (that is, *MSC* is greater than Harry's *MB*).

It is generally true, then, that:

> When economic decisions ignore external costs, whether those costs are borne by one person or by society, those decisions are likely to be inefficient.

We will return to Harry and Dan to see how they deal with their problem. First, we need to discuss the general problem of correcting for externalities.

Internalizing externalities

A number of mechanisms are available to provide decision makers with incentives to weigh the external costs and benefits of their decisions, a process called *internalization*. In some cases, externalities are internalized through bargaining and negotiation without government involvement. In other cases, private bargains fail and the only alternative may be government action of some kind.

---

marginal private cost (MPC)

The amount that a consumer pays to consume an additional unit of a particular good.

marginal damage cost (MDC)

The additional harm done by increasing the level of an externality-producing activity by one unit. If producing product X pollutes the water in a river, *MDC* is the additional cost imposed by the added pollution that results from increasing output by one unit of X per period.

---

[2] *It may actually be easier for people to ignore the social costs imposed by their actions when those costs fall on large numbers of other people whom they do not have to look in the eye or whom they do not know personally. For the moment, however, we assume that Harry takes no account of Dan.*

Five approaches have been taken to solving the problem of externalities: (1) government-imposed taxes and subsidies, (2) private bargaining and negotiation, (3) legal rules and procedures, (4) the sale or auctioning of rights to impose externalities, and (5) direct government regulation. While each is best suited for a different set of circumstances, all five provide decision makers with an incentive to weigh the external effects of their decisions.

Taxes and subsidies

Traditionally, economists have advocated marginal taxes and subsidies as a direct way of forcing firms to consider external costs or benefits. When a firm imposes an external social cost, the reasoning goes, a per unit tax should be imposed equal to the damages of each successive unit of output produced by the firm. The tax should be *exactly equal* to marginal damage costs.[3]

Figure 16.4 repeats the diagram that appears as Figure 16.2b, but this time the damage costs are paid by the firm in the form of a per-unit tax (that is, the tax = MDC). The firm now faces a marginal cost curve that is the same as the marginal social cost curve ($MC' = MSC$). Remember that the industry supply curve is the sum of the marginal cost curves of the individual firms. This means that as a result of the tax the industry supply curve shifts back to the left, driving up price from P_0 to P_1. The efficient level of output is q_1, where $P = MC'$. (Recall our general equilibrium analysis from Chapter 12.)

Because a profit-maximizing firm equates price with marginal cost, the new price to consumers covers both the resource costs of producing the product and the damage costs. The consumer-decision process is now once again efficient at the margin, because marginal social benefit as reflected in market price is equal to the full marginal cost of the product.

Figure 16.4 Tax imposed on a firm equal to marginal damage cost

If a per-unit tax exactly equal to marginal damage costs is imposed on a firm, the firm will weigh the tax, and thus the damage costs, in its decisions. At the new equilibrium price, P_1, consumers will be paying an amount sufficient to cover full resource costs as well as the cost of damage imposed. The efficient level of output for the firm is q_1.

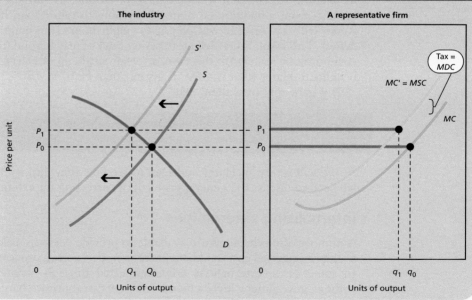

[3]*As we discuss later in this chapter, damage costs are difficult to measure. It is often assumed that they are proportional to the volume of pollutants discharged into the air or water. Instead of taxes, governments often impose effluent charges, which make the cost to polluters proportional to the amount of pollution caused. We will use the term 'tax' to refer both to taxes and effluent charges.*

■ **Measuring damages**   The biggest problem with this approach is that damages must be estimated in financial terms. For the detergent plant polluting the nearby river to be properly taxed, the government must evaluate the damages done to residents downstream in money terms. This is difficult, but not impossible. When legal remedies are pursued, judges are forced to make such estimates as they decide on compensation to be paid. Surveys of 'willingness to pay', studies of property values in affected versus non-affected areas, and sometimes the market value of recreational activities can provide basic data.

The monetary value of damages to health and loss of life is, naturally, much more difficult to estimate, and any measurement of such losses is controversial. But even here, policy makers frequently make judgements that implicitly set values on life and health. Tens of thousands of deaths and millions of serious injuries result from road accidents every year, yet we are unwilling to give up driving or to reduce the speed limit to 40 kilometres per hour – the costs of either course of action would be too high. Indeed, in some EU countries, there is no maximum speed limit on motorways. If most of us are willing to increase the risk of death in exchange for shorter driving times, the value we place on life clearly has its limits.

Be sure to realize that taxing externality-producing activities may not eliminate damages. Taxes on these activities are not designed to eliminate externalities; they are simply meant to force decision makers to consider the full costs of their decisions. Even if we assume that a tax correctly measures all the damage done, the decision maker may find it advantageous to continue causing the damage. The detergent manufacturer may find it most profitable to pay the tax and go on polluting the river. It can continue to pollute because the revenues from selling its product are sufficient to cover the cost of resources used *and to compensate the damaged parties fully*. In such a case, producing the product in spite of the pollution is 'worth it' to society. It would be inefficient for the firm to stop polluting. Only if damage costs were high would it make sense to stop. Thus, you can see the importance of proper measurement of damage costs.

■ **Reducing damages to an efficient level**   Taxes also provide firms with an incentive to use the most efficient technology for dealing with damage. If a tax reflects true damages, and if it is reduced when damages are reduced, firms may choose to avoid or reduce the tax by using a different technology that causes less damage. Suppose our detergent manufacturer is taxed €10,000 per month for polluting the river. If the detergent plant can ship its waste to a disposal site elsewhere at a cost of €7000 per month and thereby avoid the tax, it will do so. If a plant belching sulphides into the air can install smoke 'scrubbers' that eliminate emissions for an amount less than the tax imposed for polluting the air, it will do so.

■ **The incentive to take care and to avoid harm**   You should understand that all externalities involve at least two parties and that it is not always clear which party is 'causing' the damage. Take our friends Harry and Dan. Harry enjoys music; Dan enjoys quiet. If Harry plays his music, he imposes a cost on Dan. If Dan can force Harry to stop listening to music, he imposes a cost on Harry.

Often, the best solution to an externality problem may not involve stopping the externality-generating activity. Suppose Dan and Harry's hall has a third resident, Clarissa. She hates silence and loves rock music. Clarissa and Dan agree to switch rooms. What was once an external cost has been transformed into an external benefit. Everyone is better off. Harry and Clarissa get to listen to music, and Dan gets the silence he craves.

Sometimes, then, the most efficient solution to an externality problem is for the damaged party to avoid the damage. But if full compensation is paid by the damager, damaged parties may have no incentive to do so. Consider a laundry located next to the exhaust fans from the kitchen of a Chinese restaurant. Suppose damages run to €1000 per month because the laundry must use special air filters in its dryers so that the clothes will not smell of Szechuan spices. The laundry looks around and finds a perfectly good alternative location away from the restaurant that costs only €500 per month above its current rent. Without any compensation from the Chinese restaurant, the laundry will move and the total damage will be the €500 per month extra rent that it must pay. But if the restaurant compensates the laundry for damages of €1000 a month, why should the laundry move? Under these conditions, a move is unlikely, even though it would be efficient.

■ **Subsidizing external benefits** Sometimes, activities or decisions generate external benefits instead of costs, as in the case of Harry and Clarissa. Property development provides another example. Investors who revitalize a run-down urban area – an old theatre district in a big city, for example – provide benefits to many people, both in the city and in surrounding areas.

Activities that provide such external social benefits may be subsidized at the margin to give decision makers an incentive to consider them. Just as ignoring social costs can lead to inefficient decisions, so too can ignoring social benefits. Government subsidies for housing and other development, either directly through specific expenditure programmes or indirectly through tax exemptions and abatements, have been justified on such grounds.

Bargaining and negotiation

In a notable article written in 1960, Ronald Coase pointed out that the government need not be involved in every case of externality.[4] Taxes and subsidies would be irrelevant in the case of Harry and Dan, for example. Coase argued that private bargains and negotiations are likely to lead to an efficient solution in many social damage cases without any government involvement at all. This argument is referred to as the **Coase theorem**.

Coase theorem
Under certain conditions, when externalities are present, private parties can arrive at the efficient solution without government involvement.

For Coase's solution to work, three conditions must be satisfied. First, the basic rights at issue must be clearly understood. Either Harry has the right to play his stereo or Dan has the right to silence; these rights will probably be spelled out in hall rules. Second, there must be no impediments to bargaining. Parties must be willing and able to discuss the issues openly and without cost. Third, only a few people can be involved. Serious problems can develop when one of the parties to a bargain is a large group of people, such as all the residents of a large town.

For the sake of our example, let us say that all three of these conditions hold for Harry and Dan and that no room swap with someone like Clarissa is possible. The hall rules establish basic rights in this case by specifying that during certain hours of the day, Harry has the right to play his stereo as loudly as he pleases. Returning to Figure 16.3 and our earlier discussion, suppose that under the rules Harry is free to choose any number of music-playing hours between zero and eight.

Because Harry is under no legal constraint to pay any attention to Dan's wishes, you might be tempted to think that he will ignore Dan and play his stereo for eight hours. (Recall that up to eight hours, the marginal benefits to Harry exceed the marginal costs that he must pay.) However, Dan is willing to pay Harry to play his stereo fewer than eight hours. For the first hour of play, the marginal damage to Dan is €0.15, so Dan would be willing to pay Harry €0.15 in the first hour to have Harry turn off his stereo. The opportunity cost to Harry of playing the first hour is thus €0.15 plus the (constant) marginal private cost of €0.05, or €0.20. Since the marginal gain to Harry in the first hour is €0.50, Harry would not accept the bribe. Likewise, for from two to five hours the marginal benefit to Harry exceeds the bribe that Dan would be willing to pay plus the marginal private cost.

After five hours, however, Dan is willing to pay €0.25 per hour to have Harry turn off his stereo. This means that the opportunity cost to Harry is €0.30. But after five

[4]See Ronald Coase, 'The problem of social cost', Journal of Law and Economics (1960).

hours the marginal benefit to Harry of another hour of listening to his stereo falls below €0.25. Harry will thus accept the bribe not to listen to his music in the sixth hour. Similarly, a bribe of €0.25 per hour is sufficient to have Harry not play the stereo in the seventh and eighth hours, and Dan would be willing to pay such a bribe. Five hours is the efficient amount of playing time. More hours or fewer hours reduces net total benefits to Harry and Dan.

Coase also pointed out that bargaining will bring the contending parties to the right solution regardless of where rights are initially assigned. For example, suppose that the hall rules state that Dan has the right to silence. This being the case, Dan can go to the university authorities and have them enforce the rule. Now when Harry plays the stereo and Dan asks him to turn it off, Harry must comply.

Now the tables are turned. Accepting the hall rules (as he must), Harry knocks on Dan's door. Dan's damages from the first hour are only €0.15. This means that if he were compensated by more than €0.15, he would allow the music to be played. The stage is set for bargaining. Harry gets €0.45 in net benefit from the first hour of playing the stereo (€0.50 minus private cost of €0.05). Thus, he is willing to pay up to €0.45 for the privilege. If there are no impediments to bargaining, money will change hands. Harry will pay Dan some amount between €0.15 and €0.45 and, just as before, the stereo will continue to play. Dan has, in effect, sold his right to have silence to Harry. As before, bargaining between the two parties will lead to five hours of stereo playing. At exactly five hours, Dan will stop taking compensation and tell Harry to turn the stereo off. (Look again at Figure 16.3 to see that this is true.)

In both cases, the offer of compensation might be made in some form other than cash. Dan may offer Harry goodwill, a favour or two, or the use of his motorbike for an hour.

Coase's critics are quick to point out that the conditions required for bargaining to produce the efficient result are not always present. The biggest problem with Coase's system is also a common problem. Very often one party to a bargain is a large group of people, and our reasoning may be subject to a fallacy of composition.

Suppose that a power company is polluting the air. The damaged parties are the 100,000 people who live near the plant. Let's assume the plant has the right to pollute. The Coase theorem predicts that the people who are damaged by the smoke will get together and offer a bribe (as Dan offered a bribe to Harry). If the bribe is sufficient to induce the power plant to stop polluting or to reduce the pollutants with flue gas scrubbers, then it will accept the bribe and cut down on the pollution. If it is not, the pollution will continue, but the firm will have weighed all the costs (just as Harry did when he continued to play the stereo) and the result will be efficient.

But not everyone will contribute to the bribe fund. First, each contribution is so small relative to the whole that no single contribution makes much of a difference. Making a contribution may seem unimportant or unnecessary to some. Second, everyone gets to breathe the cleaner air, whether he or she contributes to the bribe or not. Many people will not participate simply because they are not compelled to, and the private bargain breaks down – the bribe that the group comes up with will be less than the full damages unless everyone participates. (We discuss these two problems – the 'drop-in-the-bucket' and the 'free-rider' – later in this chapter.) When the number of damaged parties is large, government taxes or regulation may be the only avenue to a remedy.

Legal rules and procedures

injunction A court order forbidding the continuation of behaviour that leads to damages.

For bargaining to result in an efficient outcome, the initial assignment of rights must be clear to both parties. When rights are established by law, more often than not some mechanism to protect those rights is also built into the law. In some cases where a nuisance exists, for example, there may be injunctive remedies. In such cases, the victim can go to court and ask for an **injunction** that forbids the damage-producing behaviour from continuing. If the hall rules specifically give Dan the right to silence, Dan's getting the hall manager to speak to Harry is something like getting an injunction.

Injunctive remedies are irrelevant when the damage has already been done. Consider accidents. If your leg has already been broken as the result of a car accident, enjoining the driver of the other car from drinking and driving won't work – it's too late. In these cases, rights must be protected by **liability rules**, rules that require *A* to compensate *B* for damages imposed. In theory, such rules are designed to do exactly the same thing that taxing a polluter is designed to do: provide decision makers with an incentive to weigh all the consequences, actual and potential, of their decisions. Just as taxes do not stop all pollution, liability rules do not stop all accidents.

However, the threat of liability actions does induce people to take more care than they might otherwise. Product liability is a good example. If a person is damaged in some way because a product is defective, the producing company is in most cases held liable for the damages, even if the company took reasonable care when producing the product. Producers have a powerful incentive to be careful. If consumers know they will be generously compensated for any damages, however, they may not have as powerful an incentive to be careful when using the product.

liability rules

Laws that require *A* to compensate *B* for damages imposed.

Selling or auctioning pollution rights

We have already established that not all externality-generating activities should be banned. Around the world, the private car has become the clearest example of an externality-generating activity whose benefits (many believe) outweigh its costs.

Many externalities are imposed when we drive our cars. First, congestion is an externality. When many of us decide to drive into the city during the rush hour, each of us imposes costs on the rest of us. Even though the marginal 'harm' imposed by any one driver is small, the sum total is a serious cost to all who spend hours in traffic jams. Second, most of the air pollution in Europe comes from cars. Finally, driving increases the likelihood of accidents, raising insurance costs to all.

While we do not ignore these costs from the standpoint of public policy, we certainly have not banned driving. This is also true for many other forms of pollution. In many cases we have consciously opted to allow dumping at sea, river pollution and air pollution, within limits.

The right to impose environmental externalities is beneficial to the parties causing the damage. In a sense, the right to dump in a river or pollute the air or the sea is a resource. Thinking of the privilege to dump in this way suggests an alternative mechanism for controlling pollution: selling or auctioning the pollution rights to the highest bidder. In the USA, the Clean Air Act of 1990 takes this approach by strictly limiting the quantity of emissions from the nation's power plants. To minimize the initial cost of compliance and to distribute the burden fairly, each plant is issued tradable pollution rights. These rights can be sold at auction to those plants whose costs of compliance are highest.

Another example of selling externality rights is provided by Singapore, where the right to buy a car is auctioned each year. Despite very high taxes and the need for permits to drive in city centre districts, the roads in Singapore have become quite congested. The government decided to limit the number of new cars on the road because the external costs associated with them (congestion and pollution) have become very high. With these limits imposed, the decision was made to distribute car-ownership rights to those who place the highest value on them. It seems likely that taxi drivers, haulage and bus companies, and travelling salespeople will buy the licences. Some families who drive for convenience instead of taking public transport will find them too expensive.

Congestion and pollution are not the only externalities that Singapore takes seriously. In 1994, the fine for littering was S\$625, for failing to flush a public toilet S\$94, and for eating on a subway S\$312. In addition, 514 people were convicted in 1992 of illegally smoking in public.

Direct regulation of externalities

Taxes, subsidies, legal rules and public auction are all methods of indirect regulation designed to induce firms and households to weigh the social costs of their actions against their benefits. The actual size of the external cost/benefit depends on the reaction of households and firms to the incentives provided by the taxes, subsidies and rules.

For obvious reasons, many externalities are too important to be regulated indirectly. These externalities must be regulated directly. For example, dumping cancer-causing chemicals into the ground near a public water supply is simply illegal, and those who do it can be prosecuted and imprisoned.

Regulation and control of externalities takes place at local, national, European and world levels. Local authorities have laws regulating building on protected sites. Most EU governments have national controls over emissions from chemical plants, oil refineries and waste incinerators. The EU has 'Environmental Action Programmes' setting agreed EU-wide standards in such areas as drinking water quality and the purity of sea water for bathing.

The European Union has attempted to introduce EU taxes on carbon emissions, but resistance by individual governments has so far prevented agreement on the proposal. There have also been worldwide gatherings in recent years aimed at reaching agreement on levels of greenhouse gases. There is so far little evidence that they have managed to persuade governments to implement meaningful policies.

Many criminal penalties and sanctions for violating environmental regulations are like the taxes imposed on polluters. Not all violations and crimes are stopped, but violators and criminals face 'costs'. For the outcome to be efficient, the penalties they expect to pay should reflect the damage their actions impose on society.

Public (social) goods

public goods (or social or collective goods)
Goods or services that bestow collective benefits on members of society. Such goods are non-rival in consumption and their benefits are non-excludable.

Another source of market failure lies in **public goods**, often called **social**, or **collective**, goods. These goods represent a market failure because they have characteristics that make it difficult for the private sector to produce them profitably:

In an unregulated market economy with no government to see that they are produced, public goods would at best be produced in insufficient quantity and at worst not produced at all.

The characteristics of public goods

Public goods are defined by two closely related characteristics: they are non-rival in consumption and/or their benefits are non-excludable.

non-rival in consumption
A characteristic of public goods: one person's enjoyment of the benefits of a public good does not interfere with another's consumption of it.

A good is **non-rival in consumption** when A's consumption of it does not interfere with B's consumption of it. This means that the benefits of the goods are collective – they accrue to everyone. National defence, for instance, benefits us all. The fact that I am protected in no way detracts from the fact that you are protected; every citizen is protected just as much as every other citizen. If the air is cleaned up, my breathing that air does not interfere with your breathing it, nor (under ordinary circumstances) is that air used up as more people breathe it. In contrast, private goods are *rival in consumption*. If I eat a hamburger, you cannot eat it too.

Goods can sometimes generate collective benefits and still be rival in consumption. This happens when crowding occurs. A park or a pool can accommodate many people at the same time, generating collective benefits for everyone. But when too many people crowd in on a hot summer day, they begin to interfere with each other's enjoyment. Beyond a certain level of use, the park or the pool becomes rival in consumption.

non-excludable
A characteristic of most public goods: once a good is produced, no one can be excluded from enjoying its benefits.

Most public goods are also **non-excludable**. Once the good is produced, people cannot be excluded for any reason from enjoying its benefits. Once a national defence system is established, it protects everyone. When the police set up a successful crime-prevention programme, everyone under its protection is less likely to be the victim of a crime.

For a private profit-making firm to produce a good and make a profit, it must be able to withhold that good from those who do not pay. McDonald's can make money by selling chicken sandwiches only because you don't get the chicken sandwich unless you pay for it first. If payment were voluntary, McDonald's would not be in business for long.

Consider an entrepreneur who decides to offer better police protection to the city of Metropolis. Careful (and we assume correct) market research reveals that the citizens of Metropolis want high-quality protection and are willing to pay for it. Not everyone is willing to pay the same amount. Some can afford more, others less, and people have different preferences and different feelings about risk. Our entrepreneur hires a sales force and begins to sell his service. Soon he encounters a problem. Because his is a private company, payment is strictly voluntary. He can't force anyone to pay. Payment for a hamburger is voluntary too, but a hamburger can be withheld for non-payment. The good that our new firm is selling, however, is by nature a public good.

As a potential consumer of a public good, I face a dilemma. I want more police protection, and, let's say, I'm even willing to pay €50 a month for it. But nothing is contingent upon my payment. First, if the good is produced, the crime rate falls and all residents benefit. I get that benefit whether I pay for it or not. I get a free ride! That is why this dilemma is called the **free-rider problem**. Second, my payment is very small relative to the amount that must be collected to provide the service. Thus, the amount of police protection actually produced will not be significantly affected by the amount that I contribute, or whether I contribute at all. This is the **drop-in-the-bucket problem**.

The outcome is clear:

free-rider problem
A problem intrinsic to public goods: because people can enjoy the benefits of public goods whether they pay for them or not, they are usually unwilling to pay for them.

drop-in-the-bucket problem
A problem intrinsic to public goods: the good or service is usually so costly that its provision generally does not depend on whether or not any single person pays.

A consumer acting in his or her own self-interest has no incentive to contribute voluntarily to the production of public goods. Some will feel a moral responsibility or social pressure to contribute, and those people indeed may do so. But the economic incentive is missing, and most people do not find room in their budgets for many voluntary payments.

Income distribution as a public good?

In the next chapter, we add the issues of justice and equity to the matters of economic efficiency that we are considering here. There we explain that the government may wish to change the distribution of income that results from the operation of the unregulated market on the grounds that the distribution is not fair. Before we do so, we need to note that some economists have argued for redistribution of income on grounds that it generates public benefits.

For example, let us say that many members of European society want to eliminate hunger in the EU. Suppose you are willing to give €200 per year in exchange for the knowledge that people are not going to bed hungry. Many private charities use the money they raise to feed the poor. If you want to contribute, you can do so privately, through charity. So why do we need government involvement?

To answer this, we must consider the benefits of eliminating hunger. First, it generates collective psychological benefits; simply knowing that people are not starving helps us sleep better. Second, eliminating hunger may reduce disease, and this has lots of beneficial effects. People who are fit and strong are more likely to remain in higher education and to get and keep jobs. This reduces welfare claims and contributes positively to the economy. If people are less likely to become ill, health insurance costs for everyone will go down. Robberies may decline because fewer people are desperate for money. This means that all of us are less likely to be victims of crime, now and in the future.

These are goals that members of society may very well want to achieve. But just as there is no economic incentive to contribute voluntarily to national defence, so there is no economic incentive to contribute to private causes. If hunger is eliminated, you benefit whether you contributed or not – the free-rider problem! At the same time, poverty is a huge problem and your contribution cannot possibly have much influence on the amount of national hunger – the drop-in-the-bucket problem! Thus, the goals of income redistribution may be more like national defence than like a chicken sandwich from McDonald's.

> If we accept the idea that redistributing income generates a public good, private endeavours may fail to do what we want them to do, and government involvement may be called for.

Public provision of public goods

All societies, past and present, have had to face the problem of providing public goods. When members of society get together to form a government, they do so to provide themselves with goods and services that will not be provided if they act separately. Like any other good or service, a body of laws (or system of justice) is produced with labour, capital and other inputs. Law and the courts yield social benefits, and they must be set up and administered by some sort of collective, cooperative effort.

Notice that we are talking about public *provision*, not public *production*. Once the government decides what service it wants to provide, it often contracts with the private sector to produce the good. Much of the material for national defence is produced by private defence contractors. Motorways, government offices, data processing services and so on are usually produced by private firms.

One of the immediate problems of public provision is that it frequently leads to public dissatisfaction. It is easy to be angry at government. Part, but certainly not all, of the reason for this dissatisfaction lies in the nature of the goods that government provides. Firms that produce or sell private goods post a price – we can choose to buy any quantity we want, or we can walk away without any. It makes no sense to get angry at a shoe shop, because no one can force you to shop there.

You cannot shop for collectively beneficial public goods. When it comes to national defence, the government must choose one and only one kind and quantity of (collective) output to produce. Because none of us can choose how much should be spent or on what, we are all dissatisfied. Even if the government does its job with reasonable efficiency, at any given time about half of us think that we have too much national defence and about half of us think that we have too little.

Optimal provision of public goods

In the early 1950s, Paul Samuelson demonstrated that there exists an *optimal*, or *most efficient*, level of output for every public good.[5] The discussion of the Samuelson solution that follows leads us straight to the thorny problem of how societies, as opposed to individuals, make choices.

Samuelson's theory

An efficient economy produces what people want. Private producers, whether competitors or monopolists, are constrained by the market demand for their products. If they can't sell their products for more than it costs to produce them, they are out of business. But because private goods permit exclusion, firms can withhold their products until households pay. This contingency of delivery upon payment forces households to reveal something about their preferences. No one is forced to buy or

---

[5]*Paul A. Samuelson, 'Diagrammatic exposition of a theory of public expenditure',* Review of Economics and Statistics, *XXXVII (1955).*

not to buy, but if you want a product you must pay for it. Buying a product at a posted price reveals that it is 'worth' at least that amount to you and to everyone who buys it.

Market demand for a private good is the sum of the quantities that each household decides to buy (as measured on the horizontal axis). The diagrams in Figure 16.5 review the derivation of a market demand curve. Assume society consists of two people, A and B. At a price of 1 euro, A demands 9 units of the private good and B demands 13. Market demand at a price of 1 euro is 22 units. If price were to rise to €3, A's demand would drop to 2 units and B's would drop to 9 units; market demand at a price of €3 is thus 2 + 9 = 11 units. The point is that:

> The price mechanism forces people to reveal what they want, and it forces firms to produce only what people are willing to pay for, but it works this way only because exclusion is possible.

People's preferences and demands for public goods are conceptually no different from their preferences and demands for private goods. You may want fire protection and be willing to pay for it in the same way that you want to listen to a CD. To demonstrate that an efficient level of production exists, Samuelson assumes we know people's preferences. Figure 16.6 shows demand curves for buyers A and B. If the public good were available in the private market at a price of €6, A would buy X_1 units. Or, put another way, A is willing to pay €6 per unit to obtain X_1 units of the public good. B is willing to pay only €3 per unit to obtain X_1 units of the public good.

Remember that public goods are non-rival – benefits accrue simultaneously to everyone. One, and only one, quantity can be produced, and that is the amount that everyone gets. If X_1 units are produced, A gets X_1 and B gets X_1. If X_2 units are produced, A gets X_2 and B gets X_2.

To arrive at market demand for public goods, then, we do not sum quantities. Rather, *we add up the amounts that individual households are willing to pay for each potential level of output*. In Figure 16.6, A is willing to pay €6 per unit for X_1 units and B is willing to pay €3 per unit for X_1 units. Thus, if society consists only of A and B, society is willing to pay €9 per unit for X_1 units of public good X. For X_2 units of output, society is willing to pay a total of €4 per unit.

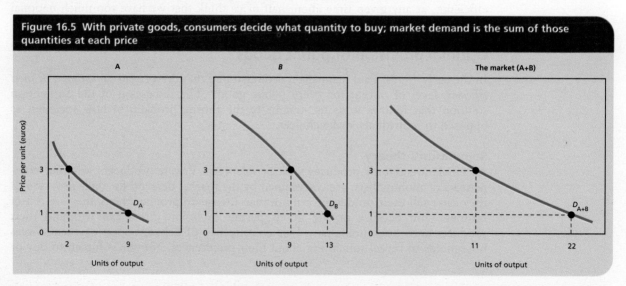

Figure 16.5 With private goods, consumers decide what quantity to buy; market demand is the sum of those quantities at each price

At a price of €3, A buys 2 units and B buys 9 for a total of 11. At a price of €1, A buys 9 units and B buys 13 for a total of 22. We all buy the quantity of each private good that we want. Market demand is the horizontal sum of all individual demand curves.

Figure 16.6 With public goods, there is only one level of output, and consumers are willing to pay different amounts for each level

A is willing to pay €6 per unit for X_1 units of the public good. B is willing to pay only €3 for X_1 units. Society – in this case A and B – is willing to pay a total of €9 for X_1 units of the good. Since only one level of output can be chosen for a public good, we must add A's contribution to B's to determine market demand. This means adding demand curves vertically.

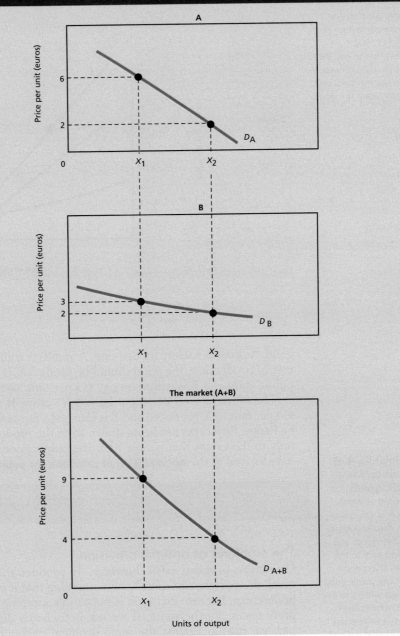

For private goods, market demand is the horizontal sum of individual demand curves – we add the different *quantities* that households consume (as measured on the *horizontal* axis). For public goods, market demand is the vertical sum of individual demand curves – we add the different *amounts* that households are willing to pay to obtain each level of output (as measured on the *vertical* axis).

Samuelson argued that once we know how much society is willing to pay for a public good, we need only compare that amount to the cost of its production. Figure 16.7 reproduces A's and B's demand curves and the total demand curve for the public

Figure 16.7 Optimal production of a public good

Optimal production of a public good means producing as long as society's total willingness to pay per unit (D_{A+B}) is greater than the marginal cost of producing the good.

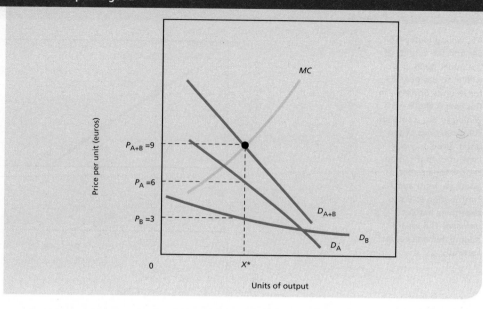

good. As long as society (in this case, A and B) is willing to pay more than the marginal cost of production, the good should be produced. If A is willing to pay €6 per unit of public good and B is willing to pay €3 per unit, society is willing to pay €9.

The efficient level of output here is X^* units. If at that level A is charged a fee of €6 per unit of X produced and B is charged a fee of €3 per unit of X, everyone should be happy. Resources are being drawn from the production of other goods and services only to the extent that people want the public good and are willing to pay for it. We have arrived at the **optimal level of provision for public goods**.

optimal level of provision for public goods

The level at which resources are drawn from the production of other goods and services only to the extent that people want the public good and are willing to pay for it. At this level, society's willingness to pay per unit is equal to the marginal cost of producing the good.

At the optimal level, society's total willingness to pay per unit is equal to the marginal cost of producing the good.

The problems of optimal provision

One major problem exists, however. To produce the optimal amount of each public good, the government must know something that it cannot possibly know – everyone's preferences. Because exclusion is impossible, nothing forces households to reveal their preferences. Furthermore, if we ask households directly about their willingness to pay, we run up against the same problem encountered by our protection-services salesman above. If my actual payment depends on my answer, I have an incentive to hide my true feelings. Knowing that I cannot be excluded from enjoying the benefits of the good and that my payment is not likely to have an appreciable influence on the level of output finally produced, what incentive do I have to tell the truth – or to contribute?

How does society decide which public goods to provide? We assume that members of society want certain public goods. Private producers in the market cannot make a profit by producing these goods, and the government cannot obtain enough information to measure society's demands accurately. No two societies have dealt with this dilemma in the same way. In some countries, dictators simply decide for the people. In others, representative political bodies speak for the people's preferences. In still others, people vote directly. None of these solutions works perfectly. We will return to the problem of social choice at the end of the chapter.

Applications

The UK abandons plans to extend motorway lighting

One kind of output with public goods characteristics is street lighting. It is non-rival in that your consumption of it does not reduce its availability for me. It is also non-excludable, so if motorways are to be lit private companies are unlikely to do it. However, if the government chooses not to allocate resources to street lighting the costs may be high.

Plans to add lighting to 250 miles of busy motorways have been suspended indefinitely.

The decision will leave long stretches of the M1, M6, M4, M2 and M62 unlit.

Road safety campaigners criticized the decision yesterday, claiming that lighting can halve the number of accidents and that the expense would be offset within three years by reducing the costs resulting from accidents. The average cost of a road traffic injury is £61,330 and the cost of a fatality £991,000. The Royal Society for the Prevention of Accidents called on agency officials to overturn their decision, and to expand lighting beyond the 33 per cent of the motorway network that is already lit.

Labour ministers have made clear that widening of motorways is unlikely

other than in exceptional circumstances. Highways Agency officials acknowledge that lighting can reduce the number of accidents by a third but believe that extra lighting is not cost-effective in the short term. 'Widening motorways increases the amount of traffic, but without that we do not expect the same rises so we are reviewing the issue of lighting', a spokesman said.

Among the busiest stretches where lighting plans have been shelved are: the M1 from north of Nottingham to Rotherham; the M62 between Leeds and Pontefract; the M2 from the M25 to Chatham

in Kent; the M6 between Cannock and Newcastle-under-Lyme; and the M4 east of the junction with the M5.

Research in America and Japan suggests that between 40 per cent and 60 per cent of accidents can be avoided by adding lighting. Government figures for last year show that one in four of all motorway accidents happens after dark on lit stretches and one in three on unlit stretches.

Source: 'Motorway lighting plans abandoned after road reviews', The Times (London), 17 April 1998, p. 6.

Local provision of public goods: the Tiebout hypothesis

In 1956 Charles Tiebout made this point: to the extent that local governments are responsible for providing public goods, an efficient market-choice mechanism may exist. Consider a set of towns that are identical except for police protection. Towns that choose to spend a lot of money on police are likely to have a lower crime rate. A lower crime rate will attract households who are risk averse and are willing to pay higher taxes for lower risk of being a crime victim. Those who are willing to bear greater risk may choose to live in the low-tax/high-crime towns. Also, if some town is very efficient at crime prevention, it will attract residents. Given that each town has limited space, property values will be pushed up in the town. The higher house price in this town is the 'price' of the lower crime rate.

Tiebout hypothesis

An efficient mix of public goods is produced when local land/housing prices and taxes come to reflect consumer preferences just as they do in the market for private goods.

According to the **Tiebout hypothesis**, an efficient mix of public goods is produced when local prices (in the form of taxes or higher housing costs) come to reflect consumer preferences just as they do in the market for private goods. What is different in the Tiebout world is that people exercise consumer sovereignty not by 'buying' different combinations of goods in a market, but by 'voting with their feet' (choosing among bundles of public goods and tax rates produced by different towns and participating in local government).

Imperfect information

In Chapters 6 to 12, we assumed households and firms have complete information on products and inputs. To make informed choices among goods and services available in the market, households must have full information on product quality, availability and price. To make sound judgements about what inputs to use, firms must have full information on input availability, quality and price.

The absence of full information can cause households and firms to make mistakes. A voluntary exchange is almost always evidence that both parties benefit. Thus most voluntary exchanges are efficient. But in the presence of imperfect information, not all exchanges are efficient. An obvious example is fraud. Kate sells a bottle of coloured water to Andrew claiming that it will grow hair on Andrew's bald head. Clearly, if Andrew had known what was really in the bottle, he would not have purchased it.

Firms as well as consumers can be the victims of incomplete or inaccurate information. Recall that a profit-maximizing competitive firm will hire workers as long as the marginal revenue product of labour (MRP_L) is greater than the wage rate. But how can a firm judge the *productivity* of a potential hire? Also, suppose that a worker steals from the firm. Clearly, the cost of employing that worker is greater than just the wage that he or she is paid.

Adverse selection

adverse selection

Can occur when a buyer or seller enters into an exchange with another party who has more information.

The problem of **adverse selection** can occur when a buyer or seller enters an exchange with another party who has more information. Suppose there are only two types of workers: lazy workers and hard workers. Each worker knows which she is, but employers cannot tell. If there is only one wage rate, lazy workers will be overpaid relative to their productivity and hard workers will be underpaid. Recall that workers weigh the value of leisure and non-market production against the wage in deciding whether to enter the labour force. Since hard workers will end up underpaid relative to their productivity, fewer hard workers than is optimal will be attracted into the labour force. Similarly, since lazy workers are overpaid relative to their productivity, more of them will be attracted into the labour force than is optimal. Hence, the market has selected among workers adversely.

The classic case of adverse selection is the secondhand car market. Suppose owners (potential sellers) of used cars have all the information about the real quality of their cars. Suppose further that half of all used cars are 'lemons' (bad cars) and that half are 'cherries' (good cars), and that consumers (potential used-car buyers) are willing to pay €6000 for a cherry but only €2000 for a lemon.

If half the cars for sale were lemons and half were cherries, the market price of a car would be about €4000, and consumers would have a 50–50 chance of getting a lemon. But there is an adverse selection problem because of unequal information: used car *sellers* know whether they have a lemon or a cherry but used car *buyers* do not. Lemon owners know they are getting far more than their cars are worth by selling at €4000, while cherry owners know that they are getting far less than their cars are really worth. Thus, more lemon owners are attracted into selling their cars than are cherry owners.

Over time, buyers come to understand that the probability of getting a lemon is greater than the probability of getting a cherry, and the price of used cars drops. This makes matters worse because it provides even less incentive for cherry owners to sell their cars. This process will continue until only lemons are left in the market. Once again, the unequal information leads to an adverse selection.[6]

Adverse selection is also a problem in insurance markets. Insurance companies insure people against risks like health problems or accidents. Individuals know more about their own health than anyone else, even with required medical examinations. If medical insurance rates are set at the same level for everyone, then medical insurance is a better deal for those who are unhealthy than for those who are healthy and likely never to make a claim. This means more unhealthy people will buy insurance, which forces insurance companies to raise premiums. As with used cars, fewer healthy people and more unhealthy people will end up with insurance.

[6]*This discussion is based on a classic article by George Akerlof, 'The market for "lemons": quality, uncertainty, and the market mechanism', Quarterly Journal of Economics, 84 (August 1970), 488–500.*

Moral hazard

moral hazard

Arises when one party to a contract passes the cost of his or her behaviour on to the other party to the contract.

Another information problem that arises in insurance markets is *moral hazard*. Often, people enter into contracts in which the result of the contract at least in part depends on one of the parties' future behaviour. A moral hazard problem arises when one party to a contract passes the cost of his or her behaviour on to the other party to the contract. For example, accident insurance policies are contracts that agree to pay for repairs to your car if it is damaged in an accident. Whether you have an accident or not in part depends on whether you drive carefully. Similarly, property leases may specify that the landlord perform routine maintenance around the house or flat. If you punch the wall every time you get angry, your landlord ultimately pays the repair bill.

Such contracts can lead to inefficient behaviour. The problem is like the externality problem in which firms and households have no incentive to consider the full costs of their behaviour. If my car is fully insured against theft, why should I lock it? If visits to the dentist are free under my dental insurance plan, why not get my teeth cleaned six times a year?

Like adverse selection, the moral hazard problem is an information problem. Contracting parties cannot always determine the future behaviour of the person with whom they are contracting. If all future behaviour could be predicted, contracts could be written to try to eliminate undesirable behaviour. Sometimes this is possible. Life insurance companies do not pay out in the case of suicide. Insurance companies may not issue a fire damage policy unless you have smoke detectors. If you cause unreasonable damage to a rented flat, apartment, your landlord can retain your security deposit.

It is impossible to know everything about behaviour and intentions. If a contract absolves one party of the consequences of his or her action, and people act in their own self-interest, the result is inefficient.

asymmetric information

A situation in which the participants in an economic transaction have different information about the transaction.

One special case of imperfect information is known as asymmetric information, a situation in which the participants in an economic transaction have different information about the transaction. This is a characteristic, for example, of the health care market. Most of us know little about medicine. It takes years of education and on-the-job-training to become a qualified doctor. In addition, the practice of medicine has become increasingly specialized, and the gap between a doctor's knowledge and her patient's knowledge has increased. Virtually all the information on product quality and price rests with the supplier – essentially with the doctor. In a doctor's surgery, hospital or clinic, the services we 'buy' are chosen for us by the person who supplies them to us! Clearly, when suppliers control the information needed to make effective demand decisions, the opportunity for abuse and waste exists.

Market solutions

Imperfect information violates one of the assumptions of perfect competition, but not all information problems are market failures. In fact, information is itself valuable, and there is an incentive for competitive producers to produce it. As with any other good, there is an efficient quantity of information production.

Often, information is produced by consumers and producers themselves. The information-gathering process is called *market research*. When we go shopping for a 'good buy' or for the 'right' jacket, we are collecting the information that we need to make an informed choice. Just as products are produced as long as the marginal benefit from additional output exceeds the marginal cost of production, consumers have an incentive to continue searching out information until the expected marginal benefit from an additional hour of search is equal to the cost of that additional hour. After I've looked in 11 different stores that sell jackets, I know a great deal about the quality and prices available. Continuing to look takes up valuable time and effort that could be used doing other things. In shopping for a house or a car, I may spend much more time and effort searching out information than I might for a jacket, because the potential benefits (or losses) are much greater.

Firms also spend time and resources searching for information. Potential employers ask for letters of reference, resumes, and interviews before offering employment. Market research helps firms respond to consumer preferences. It should come as no surprise to you that the general rule is:

> Like consumers, profit-maximizing firms will gather information as long as the marginal benefits from continued search are greater than the marginal costs of continued search.

Many firms produce information for consumers and businesses. *Which?* is a magazine that tests consumer products and sells the results in the form of a periodical. Credit bureaux keep track of people's credit histories and sell credit reports to firms who need them to evaluate potential credit customers. 'Headhunting' firms collect information and search out applicants for jobs.

Because the market handles many information problems efficiently, we don't need to assume perfect information to arrive at an efficient allocation of resources. However, some information problems are not handled well by the market.

Government solutions

Information is essentially a public good. If a set of test results on the safety of various products is produced, my having access to that information in no way reduces the value of that information to others. In other words, information is non-rival in consumption. When information is very costly for individuals to collect and disperse, it may be cheaper for government to produce it once for everybody.

In many cases, governments require that accurate information reaches the public. Most EU governments regulate advertising, setting standards for claims about the kilometres per litre achieved by cars, for example. There are also laws setting standards of safety for potentially unsafe products. It is generally illegal to sell a pharmaceutical drug that has not been government tested and approved as effective. Producers are obliged to list the contents of packaged food. In many countries governments have 'lemon laws' that grant rights to buyers of cars and other goods if they end up with a troublesome product.

Social choice

One view of government, or the public sector, holds that it exists to provide things that 'society wants'. A society is a collection of individuals, and each has a unique set of preferences. Defining what society wants, therefore, becomes a problem of **social choice** – of somehow adding up, or aggregating, individual preferences.

social choice The problem of deciding what society wants. The process of adding up individual preferences to make a choice for society as a whole.

It is also important to understand that government is made up of individuals – politicians and government workers – whose *own* objectives in part determine what government does. To understand government, we must understand the incentives facing politicians and public servants, as well as the difficulties of aggregating the preferences of the members of a society.

The voting paradox

Democratic societies use ballot procedures to determine aggregate preferences and to make the social decisions that follow from them. If all votes could be unanimous, efficient decisions would be guaranteed. Unfortunately, unanimity is virtually impossible to achieve when hundreds of millions of people, each with his or her own different preferences, are involved.

The most common social decision-making mechanism is majority rule. But this is not perfect. In 1951, Kenneth Arrow proved the **impossibility theorem**.[7] It is impossible to devise a voting scheme that respects individual preferences and gives consistent, non-arbitrary results.

One example of a seemingly irrational result emerging from majority-rule voting is the voting paradox. Suppose that, faced with a decision about the future of the institution, the head of a major university opts to let her three top administrators vote on the following options: should the university (A) increase the number of students and hire more teaching staff, (B) maintain the current size of the staff and student body, or (C) cut back on staff numbers and reduce the student body? Figure 16.8 represents the preferences of the three administrators diagrammatically.

The head of finance (HF) wants growth. He prefers A to B and B to C. The head of development (HD), however, doesn't want to rock the boat. She prefers maintaining the current size of the institution, option B, to either of the others. If the status quo is out of the question, she would prefer option C. The Dean believes in change; he wants to shake the place up, and he doesn't care whether that means increase or decrease. He prefers C to A and A to B.

Table 16.1 shows the results of the vote. When the three vote on A versus B, they vote in favour of A to increase the size of the university rather than keep it the same size. HF and the Dean outvote HD. Voting on B and C produces a victory for option B; two of the three would rather keep things as they are than decrease the size of the institution. After two votes we have the result that A (increase) is preferred to B (no change) and that B (no change) is preferred to C (decrease).

The problem arises when we have the three administrators vote on A against C. Both HD and the Dean vote for C, giving it the victory; C is actually preferred to A. But if A beats B, and B beats C, how can C beat A? The results are inconsistent.

The **voting paradox** illustrates several points. Most important is that when preferences for public goods differ across individuals, any system for adding up, or aggregating, those preferences can lead to inconsistencies. In addition, it illustrates just how much influence the person who sets the agenda has. If a vote had been taken on A and C first, the first two votes might never have occurred. This is why rules committees in parliaments have enormous power; they establish the rules under which, and the order in which, legislation will be considered.

---

impossibility theorem

A proposition demonstrated by Kenneth Arrow showing that no system of aggregating individual preferences into social decisions will always yield consistent, non-arbitrary results.

voting paradox A simple demonstration of how majority-rule voting can lead to seemingly contradictory and inconsistent results. A commonly cited illustration of the kind of inconsistency described in the impossibility theorem.

Figure 16.8 Preferences of three top university officials

HF prefers A to B and B to C. HD prefers B to C and C to A. The Dean prefers C to A and A to B.

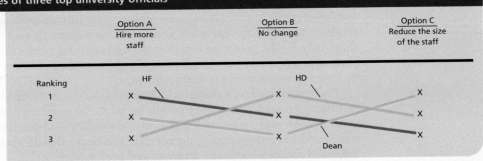

[7]*Kenneth Arrow*, Social Choice and Individual Values *(New York: John Wiley, 1951).*

Table 16.1 Results of voting on the university's plans: the voting paradox

Vote	Votes cast by:			Result*
	HF	HD	Dean	
A versus B	A	B	A	A wins: A > B
B versus C	B	B	C	B wins: B > C
C versus A	A	C	C	C wins: C > A

*Read A > B as 'A is preferred to B'.

logrolling Occurs when representatives trade votes, agreeing to help each other get certain pieces of legislation passed.

Another problem with majority-rule voting is that it leads to **logrolling**. Logrolling occurs when representatives trade votes – D helps get a majority in favour of E's programme, and in exchange E helps D get a majority on her programme. It is not clear whether any bill could get through any legislature without logrolling. Neither is it clear whether logrolling is, on balance, a good thing or a bad thing from the standpoint of efficiency. On the one hand, a programme that benefits one region or group of people might generate enormous net social gains, but because the group of beneficiaries is fairly small, it will not command a majority of delegates. If another bill that is likely to generate large benefits to another area is also awaiting a vote, the trading of support between the two sponsors of the bills should result in the passage of two good pieces of efficient legislation. On the other hand, logrolling can also produce unjustified, inefficient legislation.

A number of other problems also follow from voting as a mechanism for public choice. For one, voters do not have much of an incentive to become well informed. When you go out to buy a car or, on a smaller scale, a CD player, you are the one who suffers the full consequences of a bad choice. Similarly, you are the beneficiary of the gains from a good choice. This is not so in voting. One person's vote is not likely to determine whether a bad choice or a good choice is made. Although many of us feel that we have a civic responsibility to vote, no one really believes that his or her vote will actually determine the outcome of an election. The time and effort it takes just to get to the polls is enough to deter many people. Becoming informed involves even more costs, and it is not surprising that many people do not do it.

Beyond the fact that a single vote is not likely to be decisive is the fact that the costs and benefits of wise and unwise social choices are widely shared. If the member of parliament that I elect makes a bad mistake and wastes a billion euros, I bear only a small fraction of that cost. It may be that the direct consequences of a vote are so widely shared and seem so remote that voters perceive them to be extremely small or even zero. Although the sums involved are large in aggregate, individual voters find little incentive to become informed.

Two additional problems with voting are that choices are almost always limited to *bundles* of publicly provided goods, and we vote infrequently. In private markets, we can look at each item separately and decide how much of each we want. We also can shop daily. In the public sector, though, we vote for a platform or a party that takes a particular position on a whole range of issues. In the public sector it is very difficult, or impossible, for voters to unbundle issues.

There is, of course, a reason why bundling occurs in the sphere of public choice. It is difficult enough to convince people to go to the polls, say, once a year. If we voted separately on every piece of legislation, we would spend our lives at the polls. This is one reason for representative democracy. We elect officials who we hope will become informed and represent our interests and preferences.

Government inefficiency

Recent work in economics has focused not just on the government as an extension of individual preferences but also on government officials as people with their own agendas and objectives. That is, government officials are assumed to maximize their own utility, not the social good. To understand the way government functions, we need to look less at the preferences of individual members of society and more at the incentive structures that exist around public officials. What incentive do these people have to produce a good product and to be efficient? Might such incentives be lacking?

In the private sector, where firms compete for profits, only efficient firms producing goods that consumers will buy survive. If a firm is inefficient – if it is producing at a higher-than-necessary cost – the market will drive it out of business. This is not necessarily so in the public sector. If a government department or agency is producing a necessary service, or one mandated by law, it does not need to worry about customers. No matter how bad the service is at a motor vehicle licensing centre, everyone with a car must buy its product!

The efficiency of a government agency's internal structure depends on the way incentives facing workers and agency heads are structured. If the budget allocation of an agency is based on the last period's spending alone, for example, agency heads have a clear incentive to spend more money, however inefficiently. This point is not lost on government officials, who have experimented with many ways of rewarding agency heads and employees for cost-saving suggestions.

But critics say that such efforts to reward productivity and punish inefficiency are rarely successful. It is difficult to punish, let alone dismiss, a government employee. Elected officials are subject to recall, but it usually takes gross negligence to rouse voters into instituting such a measure. And elected officials are rarely associated with problems of bureaucratic mismanagement, which they decry daily.

Critics of 'the bureaucracy' argue that no set of internal incentives can ever match the discipline of the market, and they point to studies of private versus public refuse collection, airline operations, fire protection, postal services and so on, all of which suggest significantly lower costs in the private sector. One theme of some recent EU administrations has been 'privatization'. If the private sector can possibly provide a service, it is likely to do so more efficiently. The public sector should allow the private sector to take over.

One concern regarding wholesale privatization is the potential effect it may have on distribution. For example, in the UK, much of the stock of public housing has been sold to the private sector. But will the private sector continue to provide housing to poor people? The worry is that it will not, because it may not be profitable to do so.

Like voters, public officials suffer from a lack of incentive to become fully informed and to make tough choices. Consider an elected official. If the real objective of an elected official is to get re-elected, then his or her real incentive must be to provide visible goods for his or her constituency while hiding the costs or spreading them thinly. Self-interest may easily lead to poor decisions and public irresponsibility.

Rent seeking revisited

Another problem with public choice is that special-interest groups can and do spend resources to influence the legislative process. As we said before, individual voters have little incentive to become well informed and to participate fully in the legislative process. But favour-seeking special-interest groups have a great deal of incentive to participate in political decision making. We saw in Chapter 13 that a monopolist would be willing to pay to prevent competition from eroding its economic profits. Many – if not all – industries lobby for favourable treatment, softer regulation or exemption from fair trading legislation. This, as you recall, is *rent seeking*.

Rent seeking extends far beyond those industries that lobby for government help in preserving monopoly powers. Any group that benefits from a government policy has an incentive to use its resources to lobby for that policy. Farmers lobby for continued farm subsidies, and domestic producers lobby for higher EU import taxes.

In the absence of well-informed and active voters, special-interest groups assume an important and perhaps a critical role. But there is another side to this story. Some have argued that favourable legislation is, in effect, for sale in the marketplace. Those willing and able to pay the most are more successful in accomplishing their goals than those with fewer resources.

When firms spend money and effort to influence government policy or to block foreign competition, they are engaging in rent-seeking behaviour. Although most farmers behave as nearly perfect competitors, many have worked hard politically to influence government subsidies and regulations that affect their profits.

> Theory may suggest that unregulated markets fail to produce an efficient allocation of resources. But this should not lead you to the conclusion that government involvement necessarily leads to efficiency. There are reasons to believe that government attempts to produce efficiently the right goods and services in the right quantities may fail.

Government and the market

There is no question that government must be involved in both the provision of public goods and the control of externalities. While the argument is less clear cut, a strong case can also be made for government actions to increase the flow of information. No society has ever existed in which citizens did not get together to protect themselves from the abuses of an unrestrained market and to provide for themselves certain goods and services that the market did not provide. The question is not whether we need government involvement. The question is how much and what kind of government involvement we should have.

Critics of government involvement say correctly that the existence of an 'optimal' level of public-goods production does not guarantee that governments will achieve it. It is easy to show that governments will generally fail to achieve the most efficient level. Nor is there any reason to believe that governments are capable of achieving the 'correct' amount of control over externalities or dispersing the proper information to all who need it. Markets do indeed fail to produce an efficient allocation of resources, but governments also fail for a number of reasons.

1. Measurement of social damages and benefits is difficult and imprecise. For example, estimates of the costs of acid rain range from practically nothing to incalculably high amounts.
2. There is no precise mechanism through which citizens' preferences for public goods can be correctly determined. All voting systems lead to inconsistent results. Samuelson's optimal solution works only if each individual in a society pays in accordance with his or her own preferences. Since this is impossible under our system, we all must be taxed to pay for the mix of public goods that the imperfect voting mechanism provides.
3. Because government agencies are not subject to the discipline of the market, we have little reason to expect they will be efficient producers. The amount of waste, corruption and inefficiency in government is a hotly debated issue. Although government is not subjected to the discipline of the market, it must submit to the discipline of the press, tight budgets and the opinion of the voters.
4. Both elected and appointed officials have needs and preferences of their own, and it is naive to expect them to act selflessly for the good of society (even if they know what would be best for society). Bureaucrats in a defence ministry, for example, have a clear incentive to increase the size of their budgets, and elected officials rely heavily on those same bureaucrats for information.

Just as critics of government involvement concede that the market fails to achieve full efficiency, defenders of government must acknowledge government's failures. Defenders of government involvement respond that we get closer to an efficient allocation of resources by trying to control externalities and by doing our best to produce the public goods (including information) that people want with the imperfect tools we have than we would by leaving everything to the market.

Summary

Externalities and environmental economics

1. Often when we engage in transactions or make economic decisions, second or third parties suffer consequences that decision makers have no incentive to consider. These are called *externalities*. A classic example of an external cost is pollution.

2. When external costs are not considered in economic decisions, we may engage in activities or produce products that are not 'worth it'. When external benefits are not considered, we may fail to do things that are indeed 'worth it'. The result is an inefficient allocation of resources.

3. A number of alternative mechanisms have been used to control externalities: (1) government-imposed taxes and subsidies, (2) private bargaining and negotiation, (3) legal remedies such as *injunctions* and *liability rules*, (4) the sale or auctioning of rights to impose externalities, and (5) direct regulation.

Public (social) goods

4. In a free market, certain goods and services that people want will not be produced in adequate amounts. These *public goods* have characteristics that make it difficult or impossible for the private sector to produce them profitably.

5. Public goods are *non-rival in consumption*; their benefits fall collectively on members of society or on groups of members. Public goods are also *non-excludable*, It is generally impossible to exclude people who have not paid from enjoying the benefits of public goods. An example of a public good is national defence.

6. One of the problems of public provision is that it leads to public dissatisfaction. We can choose any quantity of private goods that we want, or we can walk away without buying any. When it comes to public goods such as national defence, the government must choose one and only one kind and quantity of (collective) output to produce.

7. Theoretically, there exists an *optimal level of provision* for each public good. At this level, society's willingness to pay per unit equals the marginal cost of producing the good. To discover such a level we would need to know the preferences of each individual citizen.

8. According to the *Tiebout hypothesis*, an efficient mix of public goods is produced when local land/housing prices and taxes come to reflect consumer preferences just as they do in the market for private goods.

Imperfect information

9. Choices made in the presence of imperfect information may not be efficient. In the face of incomplete information, consumers and firms may encounter the problem of *adverse selection*. When buyers or sellers enter into market exchanges with other parties who have more information, low-quality goods are exchanged in greater numbers than high-quality goods. *Moral hazard* arises when one party to a contract passes the cost of his or her behaviour on to the other party to the contract. If a contract absolves one party of the consequences of his or her actions, and people act in their own self-interest, the result is inefficient. *Asymmetric information* arises where participants in an economic transaction have different information about the transaction.

10. In many cases, the market provides solutions to information problems. Profit-maximizing firms will continue to gather information as long as the marginal benefits from continued search are greater than the marginal costs of continued search. Consumers will do the same: more time is afforded to the information search for larger decisions. In other cases, government must be called on to collect and disperse information to the public.

Social choice

11. Because we want to know everyone's preferences about public goods, we are forced to rely on imperfect *social choice* mechanisms, such as majority rule.

12. The theory that suggests that free markets do not achieve an efficient allocation of resources should not lead us to conclude that government involvement necessarily leads to efficiency. Governments also fail.

Government and the market

13. Defenders of government involvement in the economy acknowledge its failures but believe we get closer to an efficient allocation of resources with government than without it. By trying to control externalities and by doing our best to provide the public goods that society wants, we do better than we would if we left everything to the market.

Review Terms and Concepts

adverse selection
asymmetric information
Coase theorem
drop-in-the-bucket problem
externality
free-rider problem
impossibility theorem
injunction
liability rules
logrolling
marginal damage cost (*MDC*)

marginal private cost (*MPC*)
marginal social cost (*MSC*)
market failure
moral hazard
non-excludable
non-rival in consumption
optimal level of provision for public goods
public goods (social or collective goods)
social choice
Tiebout hypothesis
voting paradox

Problem Set

1. 'If government imposes on the firms in a polluting industry penalties (taxes) that exceed the actual value of the damages done by the pollution, the result is an inefficient and unfair imposition of costs on those firms and on the consumers of their products.' Discuss. Use a diagram to show how consumers are harmed.

2. Consider the following theories. Briefly explain each theory and how it may be a source of voter anger. Which of the three do you find the most persuasive?
a. *Public goods theory*: Since public goods are collective, the government is constrained to pick a single level of output for all of us. National defence is an example. The government must pick one level of defence expenditure, and some of us will think it's too much, some will think it's too little, and no one is happy.
b. *Problems of social choice*: It is simply impossible to choose collectively in a rational way that satisfies voters/consumers of public goods.
c. *Public choice and public officials*: Once elected or appointed, public officials tend to act in accordance with their own preferences and not out of concern for the public.

3. Two areas of great concern to governments in recent years have been education and health care. Using the concepts of public goods and imperfect information, write a brief essay justifying or criticizing government involvement in these two areas.

4. It has been argued that the following are examples of 'mixed goods'. They are essentially private but partly public. For each, describe the private and public components and discuss briefly why the government should or should not be involved in their provision.
a. Primary and secondary education
b. Higher education

c. Medical care
d. Air traffic control

5. A paper factory dumps polluting chemicals into a major river. Thousands of citizens live along the river, and they bring a suit claiming damages. You are asked by the judge to testify at the trial as an impartial expert. The court is considering the four possible solutions listed below, and you are asked to comment on the potential efficiency and equity of each. Your testimony should be brief.
a. Deny the merits of the case and simply affirm the polluter's right to dump. The parties will achieve the optimal solution without government.
b. Find in favour of the plaintiff. The polluters will be held liable for damages and must fully compensate citizens for all past and future damages imposed.
c. Order an immediate end to the dumping. No damages awarded.
d. Refer the matter to an environmental protection agency, which will impose a tax on the factory equal to the marginal damage costs. Proceeds will not be paid to the damaged parties.

6. Explain why you agree or disagree with each of the following statements:
a. The government should be involved in providing housing for the poor because housing is a 'public good'.
b. From the standpoint of economic efficiency, an unregulated market economy tends to overproduce public goods.

7. Society is made up of two individuals whose demands for public good X are given in Figure 1. Assuming that the public good can be produced at a constant marginal cost of €6, what is the optimal level of output? How much would you charge A? B?

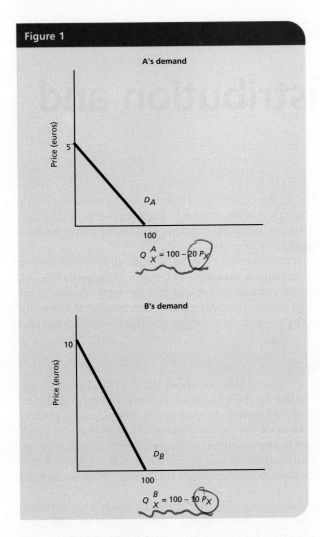

Figure 1

A's demand

Price (euros)

5

D_A

100

$Q_X^A = 100 - 20 P_X$

B's demand

Price (euros)

10

D_B

100

$Q_X^B = 100 - 10 P_X$

8. Government involvement in general scientific research has been justified on the grounds that advances in knowledge are public goods – once produced, information can be shared at virtually no cost. A new production technology in an industry could be made available to all firms, reducing costs of production, driving down price and benefiting the public. The patent system, however, allows private producers of 'new knowledge' to exclude others from enjoying the benefits of that knowledge. Inventors would have little incentive to produce new knowledge if there were no possibility of profiting from their inventions. If one company holds exclusive rights to an advanced production process, it produces at lower cost but can use the exclusion to acquire monopoly power and hold price up.

a. On balance, is the patent system a good or a bad thing?

b. Is government involvement in scientific research a good idea? Discuss.

9. 'The Coase theorem implies that we never need to worry about regulating externalities because the private individuals involved will reach the efficient outcome through negotiations'. Is this statement true or false? Justify your answer and use examples.

10. Explain how imperfect information problems such as adverse selection or moral hazard might affect the following markets or situations:

a. Workers applying for disability benefits from a company.

b. The market for used computers.

c. The market for customized telephone systems for university offices and residences.

d. The market for car insurance.

11. Assume that your economics class has 100 people in it. The lecturer asks you to bring €20 with you next week. You will be asked to split this between two investments, A and B. A is a riskless asset with a zero rate of return. Every euro that you put into A will be returned to you at the end of the lecture. B is a pooled investment with a 50% rate of return. Every euro invested in this pool will be matched by €0.5 by your lecturer. The money in the investment pool, including the 50% bonus, will then be divided *equally among ALL members of the class*. In other words, your share of the Asset B investment pool depends only on the total amount invested in the pool, and not in any way on how much you invested in Asset B. The lecturer has pledged to keep your personal investment split a secret, and the class is not allowed to collude. How much would you invest in A and how much in B? Explain your reasoning. Have you learned anything about the public goods problem?

Income Distribution and Poverty

What role should government play in the economy? Thus far, we have focused only on actions the government might be called upon to take to improve market efficiency. But even if we achieved markets that are perfectly efficient, would the result be fair? We now turn to the question of **equity**, or fairness.

equity Fairness.

Somehow, the goods and services produced in every society get distributed among its citizens. Some citizens end up with palatial mansions in Cannes, ski trips to Gstaad, and Maseratis; others end up without enough to eat and live in shanty towns. This chapter focuses on distribution. Why do some people get more than others? What are the sources of inequality? Should the government change the distribution generated by the market?

The utility possibilities frontier

Ideally, in discussing distribution, we should talk not about the distribution of things but about the distribution of well-being. In the nineteenth century, philosophers used the concept of *utility* as a measure of well-being. As they saw it, people make choices among goods and services on the basis of the utility those goods and services yield. People act to maximize utility. If you prefer a night at a symphony over a rock concert, it is because you expect to get more utility from the symphony. If we extend this thinking, we might argue that if household A gets more total utility than household B, A is better off than B.

Utility is not directly observable or measurable. But thinking about it as if it were can help us understand some of the ideas that underlie debates about distribution. Suppose society consisted of two people, I and J. Next suppose that the line *PP'* in Figure 17.1 represents all the combinations of I's utility and J's utility that are possible, given the resources and technology available in their society. (This is an extension of the production possibilities frontier in Chapter 2.)

utility possibilities frontier

A graphical representation of a two-person world that shows all points at which A's utility can be increased only if B's utility is decreased.

Any point inside *PP'*, or the **utility possibilities frontier**, is inefficient because both I and J could be better off. *A* is one such point. *B* is one of many possible points along *PP'* that society should prefer to *A*, because both members are better off at *B* than they are at *A*.

While point *B* is preferable to point *A* from everyone's point of view, how does point *B* compare with point *C*? Both *B* and *C* are efficient; I cannot be made better off without making J worse off, and vice versa. All the points along *PP'* are efficient, but they may not be equally desirable. If all the assumptions of competitive market theory held, the market system would lead to one of the points along *PP'*. The actual point reached would depend upon I's and J's initial endowments of wealth, skills and so on.

In practice, however, the market solution leaves some people out. The rewards of a market system are linked to productivity, and some people in every society are simply not capable of being very productive. All societies make some provision for the very poor. Most often, public expenditures on behalf of the poor are financed with taxes collected from the rest of society. Society makes a judgement that those who are better off should give up some of their rewards so that those at the bottom can have more than the market system would allocate to them. In a democratic state, such redistribution is presumably undertaken because a majority of the members of that society think it is fair, or just.

Figure 17.1 Utility possibilities frontier

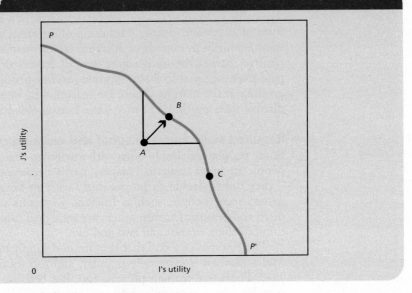

If society were made up of two people, I and J, and all of the assumptions of perfect competition held, the market system would lead to some point along *PP'*. Every point along *PP'* is efficient; it is impossible to make I better off without making J worse off, and vice versa. But which point is best? Is *B* better than *C*?

Early economists drew analogies between social choices among alternative outcomes and consumer choices among alternative outcomes. A consumer chooses on the basis of his or her own unique utility function, or measure of his or her own well-being; a society, they said, chooses on the basis of a social welfare function that embodies the society's ethics.

Such theoretical discussions of fairness and equity focus on the distribution and redistribution of utility. But because utility is neither observable nor measurable, most discussions of social policy centre on the *distribution of income* or the *distribution of wealth* as indirect measures of well-being. It is important that you remember throughout this chapter, however, that income and wealth are imperfect measures of well-being. Someone with a profound love of the outdoors may choose to work in a national park for a low wage rather than to work for a consulting firm in a big city for a high wage. The choice reveals that she is better off, even though her measured income is lower. As another example, think about five people with 1 euro each. Now suppose that one of those people has a magnificent voice, and that the other four give up their euros to hear her sing. The exchange leads to inequality of measured wealth – the singer has €5 and no one else has any, but all are better off than they were before.

While income and wealth are imperfect measures of utility, they have no observable substitutes and are therefore the measures we use throughout this chapter. First, we review the factors that determine the distribution of income in a market setting. Second, we look at the data on income distribution, wealth distribution and poverty in Europe. Third, we talk briefly about some theories of economic justice. Finally, we describe redistributional programmes aimed at reducing income inequalities.

The sources of household income

Why do some people and some families have more income than others? Before we turn to data on the distribution of income, let us review what we already know about the sources of inequality:

Households derive their incomes from three basic sources: (1) from wages or salaries received in exchange for labour; (2) from property (that is, capital, land and so forth); and (3) from government.

Wages and salaries

Typically, about 60–65% of personal income in a European country is received in the form of wages and salaries. Hundreds of different wage rates are paid to employees for their labour in thousands of different labour markets. As you saw in Chapter 10, competitive market theory predicts that all factors of production (including labour) are paid a return equal to their marginal revenue products – the market value of what they produce at the margin. There are reasons why one type of labour might be more productive than another and why some households have higher incomes than others.

Required skills, human capital and working conditions

Some people are simply born with attributes that translate into valuable skills. Some people are great basketball players, partly because they happen to be over 2 metres tall – they didn't decide to go out and invest in height; they were born with the right genes. Some people, such as Luciano Pavarotti and Placido Domingo, have perfect pitch and beautiful voices; others are tone deaf. Some people have quick mathematical minds; others cannot add two and two.

The rewards of a skill that is in limited supply depend on the demand for that skill. Men's football is extremely popular, and top footballers make millions of euros per year. There are women players, too, but because women's football has not become popular, these women's skills go comparatively unrewarded. In tennis, however, people want to see women play, and women therefore earn prize money similar to the money earned by men.

Some people with rare skills can make enormous salaries in a free market economy. Luciano Pavarotti has a voice that millions of people are willing to pay to hear in person and on tapes and CDs. Naomi Campbell and other 'supermodels' earn huge sums for every appearance on a catwalk. Before Pablo Picasso died, he could sell small sketches for vast sums of money. Were they worth it? They were worth exactly what the highest bidder was willing to pay.

Not all skills are inborn. Some people have invested in training and education to improve their knowledge and skills, and therein lies another source of inequality in wages. When we go to school or university, we are investing in **human capital** that we expect to yield dividends, partly in the form of higher wages, later on. Human capital is also produced through on-the-job training. People learn their jobs and acquire 'firm-specific' skills when they are on the job. Thus, in most occupations there is a reward for experience. Pay scales often reflects numbers of years on the job, and those with more experience earn higher wages than those in similar jobs with less experience.

Some jobs are more desirable than others. Entry-level positions in 'glamour' industries such as publishing and television tend to be low-paying. Because talented people are willing to take entry-level jobs in these industries at salaries below what they could earn in other occupations, there must be other, non-wage rewards. It may be that the job itself is more personally rewarding, or that a low-paying apprenticeship is the only way to acquire the human capital necessary to advance. In contrast, less desirable jobs often pay wages that include **compensating differentials**. Of two jobs requiring roughly equal levels of experience and skills that compete for the same workers, the job with the poorer working conditions usually has to pay a slightly higher wage to attract workers away from the job with the better working conditions.

Compensating differentials are also required when a job is very dangerous. Those who take great risks are usually rewarded with high wages. Steeplejacks on high-rise buildings and bridges command premium wages. Firefighters in cities with many old, run-down buildings may be paid more than those in relatively tranquil rural or suburban areas.

Multiple household incomes

Another source of wage inequality among households lies in the fact that many households have more than one earner in the labour force. Second, and even third,

---

human capital

The stock of knowledge, skills and talents that people possess; it can be inborn, or acquired through education and training.

---

compensating differentials

Differences in wages that result from differences in working conditions. Risky jobs usually pay higher wages; highly desirable jobs usually pay lower wages.

Applications

Controversy over comparable worth

One hotly debated issue is 'discrimination' in the workforce. On average, women earn less than men.

There are two views about why these differences exist. One view holds that most wage differentials can be attributed to choices women make about what jobs to take, how many hours to work, and when to enter and leave the labour force. The argument is that labour markets are efficient and that wages reflect productivity. The second view holds that women's choices are not free and that wage differentials cannot be explained by productivity differences. Equal pay should be required by law.

A similar issue is raised because some women are judged more attractive than others and receive better pay. Airline stewardesses, for example, were usually selected for their looks in the past. Now, airlines, under some pressure, have retreated from physical appearance as a job qualification and employ both men and women as flight attendants. Harvard economist Robert Barro comments:

Is it not a good thing if flight attendants are selected by job skills, meaning the ability to serve people well and to carry out safety procedures efficiently, and not at all on physical appearance?

I would say no. I believe the only meaningful measure of productivity is the amount a worker adds to customer satisfaction and to the happiness of co-workers. A worker's physical appearance, to the extent that it is valued by customers and co-workers, is as legitimate a job qualification as intelligence, dexterity, job experience and personality.

Almost everyone can recognize that severing the link between wages and intelligence would reduce efficiency or lower the gross national product because brain power would not be allocated to its most productive uses. Yet outcomes based on intelligence are clearly unfair in the sense that, by and large, smarter people end up richer, and being smart is to a considerable extent a matter of luck. If one wanted the government to redistribute resources from smart people to stupid people, then one would have to believe that the benefits from this redistribution would exceed the resulting losses in national product.

The same reasoning applies to physical appearance. This trait is highly valued in some fields, and reducing its importance to employment and wages would effectively throw away national product. The outcomes are also unfair, in the same sense as they are for intelligence. An interference with the market's valuation of physical appearance is justified only if the benefits from the redistribution of resources from more attractive to less attractive people are greater than the losses in overall product. Thus, it makes no sense to say that basing employment and wages on physical appearance is a form of discrimination, whereas basing them on intelligence is not. The two cases are fundamentally the same.

Most people (and the law) accept this approach to beauty for movie and television personalities and modelling. Obviously, there would be a great loss of national product if the government were to dictate that Cindy Crawford had to be replaced by me in all of her commercials. But the difference between glamour fields and others in terms of the role of physical appearance is merely a matter of degree. If the government stays out, the market will generate a premium for beauty based on the values that customers and co-workers place on physical appearance in various fields. Probably the market will allocate more beauty to movies, television, and modelling than to assembly-line production and economic research. I have no idea how much beauty the unfettered market would allocate to flight-attendant jobs or CEO positions. But whatever the outcomes, are the judgements of government preferable to those of the marketplace?

Source: 'So you want to hire the beautiful. Well, why not?', *Business Week*, 16th March 1998, p. 11.

---

incomes are becoming more the rule than the exception for EU countries. Many of the jobs that have been created in recent years are part-time jobs often taken by women to supplement the family income.

Comparing two-earner and one-earner households highlights another problem of using money income as a measure of well-being. Consider, for example, a family of four with both parents working, and another identical family with only one wage earner. The two-earner family will have a significantly higher money income, but the comparison ignores the value of what the non-wage-earning spouse produces. When one parent stays home, he or she normally provides services that would otherwise have to be purchased. The children are cared for, the house is maintained, food may be grown in the garden. When both parents work, there are expenses for child care, housecleaning, home repairs, and so on.

When one parent stays home voluntarily, that family has revealed that it values the home-produced services more than the income it would otherwise earn. It is better off than it would be if both parents were working, even though it has a lower money income. Again, this means that we must exercise caution when discussing the fairness of the distribution of money income.

Unemployment

Before turning to property income, we need to mention another major cause of inequality that is the subject of much discussion in macroeconomics: *unemployment*.

People earn wages only when they have jobs. In recent years, Europe has been through severe recessions (economic downturns). In early 1998 some countries in the EU were experiencing record levels of unemployment. Germany had 11.6% of its people out of a job, Belgium over 13% and Spain around 20%. These are averages for a whole country. Within each country there are pockets of unemployment where the figure is much higher.

Unemployment hurts primarily those who are out of work, and thus its costs are narrowly distributed. For some workers, the costs of unemployment are lowered by unemployment compensation benefits paid out of government funds.

Income from property

property income
Income from the ownership of real property and financial holdings. It takes the form of profits, interest, dividends, and rents.

Another source of income inequality is that some people have **property income** – income from the ownership of real property and financial holdings – while many others do not. Some people own a great deal of wealth, and some have no assets at all. About 20–25% of personal income in Europe comes from ownership of property. In general:

> The amount of property income that a household earns depends upon (1) how much property it owns, and (2) what kinds of assets it owns. Such income generally takes the form of profits, interest, dividends and rents.

Households come to own assets through saving and through inheritance. Many of today's large fortunes were inherited from previous generations. The Rockefellers and the Kennedys, to name two, still have large holdings of property originally accumulated by previous generations. Thousands of families receive smaller inheritances each year from their parents. (Under tax laws in most EU countries, some wealth can pass from one generation to another free of inheritance taxes.) Most families receive little through inheritance, however, and most of their wealth or property comes from saving.

Often, fortunes accumulate in a single generation when a business becomes successful. *Fortune* magazine estimates that Bill Gates, founder and chief executive officer of Microsoft, is worth over $35 billion. Masatoshi Ito made $5 billion running a supermarket chain in Japan.

Another important component of wealth today is real property. For most people, the biggest asset they will ever own is their home, and the value accumulated in owner-occupied houses is a major source of inequality. A house earns a return just like any other asset, a return that comes in the form of 'housing services' – the owner of the house lives in it rent free.

Income from government: transfer payments

transfer payments
Payments made by government to people who do not supply goods or services in exchange.

Significant amounts of personal income come from governments in the form of **transfer payments**. Transfer payments are payments made by government to people who do not supply goods or services in exchange. Amounts vary substantially between EU countries. Some, but not all, transfer payments (such as unemployment benefits) are made to people with low incomes, precisely because they have low incomes. Transfer payments thus reduce the amount of inequality in the distribution of income.

Not all transfer income goes to the poor, however. Basic state pensions are often paid to all, irrespective of income. Even so, where this is taxed, high-income people will, in effect, receive less pension than poorer people.

Transfer payments are mainly designed to provide income to those in need. They are part of the government's attempts to offset some of the problems of inequality and poverty.

The distribution of income

Despite the many problems associated with using income as a measure of well-being, it is useful to know something about how income is actually distributed. Before we examine these data, however, we should pin down precisely what the data represent.

economic income
The amount of money a household can spend during a given time period without increasing or decreasing its net assets. Wages, salaries, dividends, interest income, transfer payments, rents and so forth are sources of economic income.

Economic income is defined as the amount of money a household can spend during a given period without increasing or decreasing its net assets. Economic income includes anything that enhances your ability to spend – wages, salaries, dividends, interest received, proprietors' income, transfer payments, rents and so forth.

Income inequality in Europe

Table 17.1 presents some estimates of the distribution of income for one country, the UK. The data are presented by 'quintiles'; that is, the total number of households is first ranked by income and then split into five groups of equal size. In 1995 the top quintile earned 50% of total income, while the bottom quintile earned just 2.6%.

In Table 17.1 we can see the extent of income inequality in a number of ways. The first column, equivalized original income, shows the distribution before any adjustments have been made through taxation or transfer payments. However, they have been 'equivalized'. This means that adjustments have been made to allow for different compositions of households. Children have different needs relative to adults. Adults living together in the same household get economies of scale in living. The figures are adjusted to allow for this with larger households moving down the income distribution and smaller ones moving up. Column 2, equivalized gross income, shows income distribution after the payment of cash benefits such as state retirement pensions. Since more of these benefits go to lower-income groups the distribution of income using this measure is less uneven.

The uneven nature of income distribution is further reduced as a result of direct taxes, principally income tax. Higher income groups contribute proportionately more to government revenue. Allowing for this redistribution gives equivalized disposable

Table 17.1 Percentage shares of total original, gross, disposable and post-tax incomes by quintile groups of households, UK, 1995–1996

Quintile group	(1) Equivalized original income	(2) Equivalized gross income	(3) Equivalized disposable income	(4) Equivalized post-tax income
Bottom	2.6	7.4	7.9	6.9
2nd	7	11	12	12
3rd	15	16	17	16
4th	25	23	23	23
Top	50	43	40	43

Note: columns do not sum to 100 because of rounding errors.

Source: Economic Trends, No. 520 (March 1997).

income in column 3. Column 4 allows for the effects on household income of indirect taxes such as VAT. Because such taxes take away a higher proportion of lower incomes the effect of this adjustment is to widen income disparities.

The Lorenz Curve and the Gini coefficient

The distribution of income can be graphed in several ways. The most widely used graph is the **Lorenz Curve**, shown in Figure 17.2. Plotted along the horizontal axis is the percentage of households, and along the vertical axis is the cumulative percentage of income. The curve shown here represents the UK in the year 1995–1996, using data from Table 17.1, equivalized disposable income.

During that year, the bottom 20% of families received only 7.9% of total income. The bottom 40% earned 19.9% (7.9% plus 12.0%), and so forth. If income were distributed equally – that is, if the bottom 20% earned 20% of the income, the bottom 40% earned 40% of the income, and so on – the Lorenz Curve would be a 45-degree line between zero and 100%. More unequal distributions produce Lorenz Curves that are further from the 45-degree line.

The **Gini coefficient** is a commonly used measure of the degree of inequality in a distribution. It is the ratio of the shaded area in Figure 17.2 to the total triangular area below and to the right of the diagonal line 0*A*. For the UK in these years, the Gini coefficient was 0.33. The shaded area represented one-third of the lower triangle.

If income is equally distributed, there is no shaded area (because the Lorenz Curve and the 45-degree line are the same), and the Gini coefficient is zero. The Lorenz Curves for distributions with more inequality are further down to the right, their shaded areas are larger, and their Gini coefficients are higher. The maximum Gini coefficient is one. As the Lorenz Curve shifts down to the right, the shaded area becomes a larger portion of the total triangular area below 0*A*. If one family earned all the income (with no one else receiving anything), the shaded area and the triangle would be the same, and the ratio would equal one.

Lorenz Curve
A widely used graph of the distribution of income, with cumulative percentage of families plotted along the horizontal axis and cumulative percentage of income plotted along the vertical axis.

Gini coefficient
A commonly used measure of inequality of income derived from a Lorenz Curve. It can range from zero to a maximum of one.

Figure 17.2 Lorenz Curve for the UK, 1995–1996

The Lorenz Curve is the most common way of presenting income distribution graphically. The larger the shaded area, the more unequal the distribution. If distribution were equal, the Lorenz Curve would be the 45-degree line 0*A*.

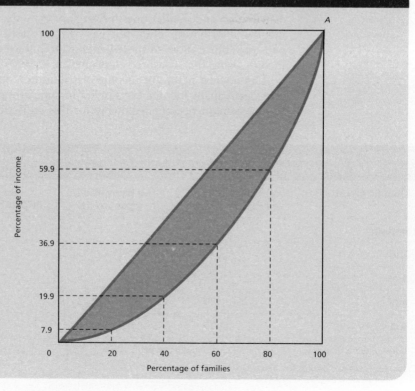

A comparison of income inequalities in Europe

So far, we have concentrated on one country in order to understand what the distribution of income shows us. We can now look at income distribution throughout Europe. However, it is not easy to make comparisons because countries have different methods of collecting and presenting data.

Table 17.2 enables us to see which countries have the most uneven income distribution, by equivalized household disposable income. They are ranked from low to high inequality according to the bottom quintile. Hence Finland has the most even distribution on this basis: 10.8% of Finnish income is received by the poorest 20% of households.

We could also rank by the Gini coefficient. This gives a similar but not identical ranking. The Gini coefficient is a summary measure of the whole distribution. The difference between countries is substantial. Ireland's Gini coefficient is over 13% higher than Finland's.

For comparison we show the USA, whose income is more unevenly distributed than for any of the European countries shown in the table.

Changes in income inequality over time

We have seen that all European countries have a large degree of inequality of income. What is happening over time? Is the inequality increasing or decreasing? There are reasons for expecting it to change. Relative wages may alter with some groups of workers doing better than others. The tax structure may alter. The government may

Table 17.2 Percentage of shares of equivalized disposable income of households, European Union

Country	Bottom	Second	Third	Fourth	Gini coefficient
Finland	10.8	26.4	45.6	68.6	0.207
Luxembourg	10.2	24.8	43.1	66.0	0.238
Belgium	10.2	25.0	43.5	66.4	0.235
Netherlands	10.1	24.5	42.5	65.3	0.268
Germany	9.8	24.2	42.5	65.3	0.250
Norway	9.8	24.9	43.7	66.7	0.234
Sweden	9.5	25.3	44.8	68.2	0.220
France	8.3	21.8	39.1	61.6	0.296
Portugal	8.0	20.9	38.1	60.8	0.310
Italy	8.0	20.7	38.0	61.2	0.310
Switzerland	8.0	21.0	37.8	58.9	0.323
UK	7.5	20.5	38.2	61.8	0.304
Spain	7.4	20.1	37.5	60.2	0.320
Ireland	7.1	19.3	36.3	59.6	0.330
USA	5.7	18.0	35.7	60.2	0.341

Data are from the late 1980s.

Source: A. B. Atkinson, 'Income distribution in Europe and the United States', *Oxford Review of Economic Policy*, 12, 1 (1996).

change the proportion of tax it raises directly compared with indirect taxation. A government may decide to increase or decrease the scale of income support for lower income groups.

There is no consistent pattern across Europe of changes in income over time. Figure 17.3 shows rising inequalities in the UK, Norway, Sweden, The Netherlands, Belgium, Germany (West) and France. However, income has tended to become more evenly distributed in Spain, Portugal, Ireland, Denmark, Finland and Italy. There is increasing inequality in the USA.

Poverty

Most government concern with income distribution and redistribution has focused on poverty. 'Poverty' is a very complicated word to define. In simplest terms, it means the condition of people who have very low incomes. The dictionary defines the term simply as 'lack of money or material possessions'. But how low does your income have to be before you are classified as poor?

The problem of definition

Philosophers and social policy makers have long debated the meaning of 'poverty'. One school of thought argues that poverty should be measured by determining how much it costs to buy the 'basic necessities of life'.

Critics argue that defining bundles of necessities is a hopeless task. While it might be possible to define a minimally adequate diet, what is a 'minimum' housing unit? Is a car a necessity? What about medical care? In reality, low-income families end up using what income they have in an enormous variety of ways.

Some say that poverty is culturally defined and is therefore a relative concept, not an absolute one. Poverty in Bangladesh is very different from poverty in Europe. Even within Europe, urban poverty is very different from rural poverty. If poverty is a relative concept, the definition of it might change significantly as a society accumulates wealth and achieves higher living standards.

Although it is difficult to define precisely, the word 'poverty' is one that we all understand intuitively to some degree. It conveys images of run-down, overcrowded, rat-infested housing, homeless people, untreated illness, and so forth. But it is also a word that we have been forced to define formally for purposes of keeping statistics and administering public programmes.

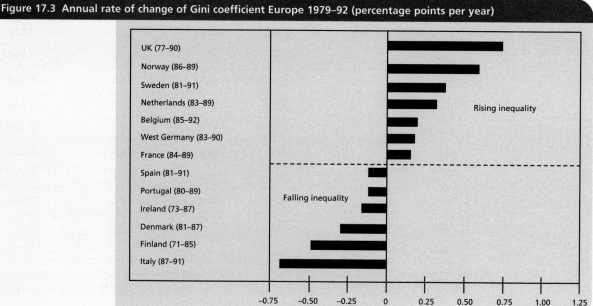

Figure 17.3 Annual rate of change of Gini coefficient Europe 1979–92 (percentage points per year)

Applications

France: the widening gap between haves and have-nots

An article from *Business Week* focuses on some of the problems of a widening income distribution in the French economy.

France's silent masses of unemployed have become a powerful political force. Rallying outside public offices by day and setting bonfires to dramatize night vigils in front of benefits offices, they are riveting international attention on the growing gap between France's rich and poor. The stark reality of 1 million long-term jobless getting a paltry $350 a month in benefits has jolted a nation that prides itself on compassion and a comprehensive social net. 'While the country is getting richer and richer, insecurity is growing wider and wider', says Ahcen Meharga, a 29-year-old social worker in Paris who was laid off last October.

Many of the country's 14.2 million private-sector employees have adapted to flexible work rules and the demands of the global economy, boosting France Inc.'s productivity. Increasingly, qualified young people enter the labour market via temporary jobs – a practice traditionally disdained. Mid-level managers on the way up the career ladder at private French companies often skip the sacred two-hour lunch, work nights and weekends, and are always reachable by cellular phone.

Meanwhile, most of the 5.3 million workers in the heavily unionized public sector, from hospitals to post offices to utilities, cling to the socialist myth of entitlement. They vociferously support a 10% cut in their workweek with no reduction in pay.

Even as corporate profits reached new highs in 1997,

Homeless and jobless shout while demonstrating on the Champs Elysees avenue in Paris Wednesday December 31st 1997.

some 3.5 million unemployed are castaways in a society ill-adapted to the global economy. True, the state's safety net still covers minimal needs. But the widening economic disparity inflames Gallic passion.

Seeing others prosper as economic recovery takes hold is doubly vexing. 'We live sadly. We survive', says Didier Giraud, a 34-year-old industrial technician who

lost his job 18 months ago and can't afford the Nike tennis shoes and toys his 8-year-old son wants.

Says Morgan Stanley, Dean Witter, Discover & Co. senior economist Eric Chaney: 'The paradox is, the protests have erupted as consumption is rising – that exacerbates the contrast.'

Source: 'An economy torn in two', *Business Week*, European edn, 26 January 1998, pp. 24–5.

Absolute and relative poverty

Poverty can be defined in terms of the size of income relative to that of others. This is **relative poverty**. Alternatively we can define poverty as an income below what we might regard as an acceptable amount to meet basic requirements. This is **absolute poverty**.

One measure of relative poverty is that used by the Council of Europe. They suggest that a family is poor if its income is less than 68% of average earnings in the country concerned. This is, of course, arbitrary and other researchers have used different measures. Table 17.3 gives data for the degree of poverty in EU countries based on 50% of equivalized expenditure for the country concerned. Thus, on this basis, Belgium has the least poverty, but even here 8.4% of its citizens are poor.

An alternative measure of relative poverty is the income received by the lowest 40% of households as a proportion of the top quintile. As you can see from Table 17.4, relative poverty varies significantly across the world. It also varies considerably between countries at roughly similar stages of development. Bear in mind that if income were perfectly evenly distributed (a zero Gini coefficient) the ratio of income in the bottom 40% to income in the top 20% would be 2.

In the early 1960s, the US government established an official poverty line. It is based on the fact that poor families tend to spend about one-third of their incomes on food. The official *poverty line* has been set at a figure that is simply three times the cost of the US Department of Agriculture's minimum food budget. This, of course, is a measure of absolute poverty.

relative poverty
The condition of households whose income falls below some defined proportion of that of higher income groups.

absolute poverty
The condition of households whose income falls below some defined amount thought necessary for the purchase of basic necessities.

Table 17.3 The incidence of poverty in Europe

Country	%*	000s
Belgium	8.4	832
Germany (West)	14.3	8,787
Greece	22.4	2,240
Spain	20.8	8,728
France	19.4	10,894
Ireland	19.5	691
Italy	24.2	13,893
Luxembourg	16.0	59
Netherlands	8.5	1,253
Portugal	27.9	2,728
UK	18.7	10,648

* Percentage of people in households below the poverty line – households with expenditure of less than half the national average.

Source: C. Oppenheim and L Harker, *Poverty: The Facts*, 3rd edn (Child Poverty Action Group).

Each year the USDA sets out a nutritionally sound minimum food bundle. For example, a week's food for a woman between 20 and 34 years old includes 4 eggs; 1½ pounds of meat, fish or poultry; 3 pounds of potatoes; 12 ounces of dark green or

Table 17.4 Income shares of poorest 40% relative to richest 20% of households*

Country	Year	Ratio	Income level**
Kenya	1992	0.16	Low income
Nepal	1995–96	0.43	Low income
China	1995	0.32	Low income
Indonesia	1993	0.52	Lower middle income
Ecuador	1994	0.27	Lower middle income
Ukraine	1992	0.66	Lower middle income
South Africa	1993	0.14	Upper middle income
Hungary	1993	0.64	Upper middle income
Chile	1994	0.7	Upper middle income
France	1989	0.42	High income
Germany	1988	0.46	High income
United States	1985	0.37	High income

* After taxes and benefits.

** As defined by the World Bank.

Source: *World Development Report* (World Bank, 1997).

Table 17.5 Mobility of people between income quintiles, USA, 1975–1991					
Income quintile, 1975	Percentage in each quintile, 1991				
	1st	2nd	3rd	4th	5th
5th	0.9	2.8	10.2	23.6	62.5
4th	1.9	9.3	18.8	32.6	37.4
3rd	3.3	19.3	28.3	30.1	19.0
2nd	4.2	23.5	20.3	25.2	26.8
1st	5.1	14.6	21.0	30.3	29.0

Source: Federal Reserve Bank of Dallas, *By Our Own Bootstraps*.

yellow vegetables; 3 pounds of other vegetables; and 8 ounces of fat or oil. In 1994, the department estimated that such a bundle would cost about $97.06 per week for a family of four people. Multiply that by 52 weeks for a total of $5,407 per year; triple that, and you have a poverty line for a family of four set at $15,141. On this basis, 38.1 million people, 14.5% of the total US population, live below the poverty line.

The pervasiveness of poverty

We need to remember, when looking at statistics of poverty, that not all the people who are in the poorest group at any given time are in it some time later. Some, who are poor because they are unemployed, get jobs and become better off.

One study of the US economy has actually tried to measure this movement out of poverty. The data are for the period 1975–91. During this period, the top 20% of families moved from having about seven times that of the bottom 20% to having around eleven times as much. But are we looking at the same people in each case?

Look at Table 17.5. It shows the extent to which people remained in a given quintile of income distribution over that period. Of the poorest 20% of people in 1975 (first quintile), only 5.1% were still in that group by 1991. No less than 80.3% had risen to the middle quintile or above. Now consider Table 17.6. The first (lowest) quintile had an average annual income in 1975 of $1,153 at 1993 prices. By 1991 the people who were in that quintile in 1975 had an average income of $26,475 per year at 1993 prices.

This is not an argument for saying that nothing should be done to help the poor. Poverty is debilitating, even when it persists for a short time. Others do remain in poverty more or less permanently. Nevertheless, it does argue powerfully for a system that enables those on low incomes to increase their income by their own efforts.

Table 17.6 Increases in incomes by quintiles, USA 1975–1991 (US$, at constant [1993] prices)			
Income quintile, 1975	Average income, 1975	Average income, 1991	Absolute gain
5th	45,704	49,678	3,974
4th	22,423	31,292	8,869
3rd	13,030	22,304	9,274
2nd	6,291	28,373	22,080
1st	1,153	26,475	25,322

Source: Federal Reserve Bank of Dallas, *By Our Own Bootstraps*.

Table 17.7 Distribution of wealth in the UK, 1976–1993*

	1976	1981	1986	1991	1993
Marketable wealth					
Percentage of wealth owned by:					
Most wealthy 1%	21	18	18	17	17
Most wealthy 5%	38	36	36	35	36
Most wealthy 10%	50	50	50	47	48
Most wealthy 25%	71	73	73	71	72
Most wealthy 50%	92	92	90	92	93
Total marketable wealth (£ billion)	280	565	955	1,711	1,746

* Estimates are based on the estates of people dying in those years.

** Applies to people aged 18 and over.

Source: UK Inland Revenue.

The distribution of wealth

Data on the distribution of wealth are not as readily available as data on the distribution of income. However, some data are available. We can illustrate the distribution of wealth with reference to the UK; the data are presented in Table 17.7. The richest half of the UK population is estimated to own over 90% of UK marketable wealth.

Clearly, the distribution of wealth is more unequal than the distribution of income. Part of the reason is that wealth is passed from generation to generation and accumulates. Large fortunes also accumulate when small businesses become successful large businesses. Some argue that an unequal distribution of wealth is the natural and inevitable consequence of risk taking in a market economy: it provides the incentive necessary to motivate entrepreneurs and investors. Others believe that too much inequality can undermine democracy and lead to social conflict. Many of the arguments for and against income redistribution, discussed in the next section, apply equally well to wealth redistribution.

The redistribution debate

Debates about the role of government in correcting for inequity in the distribution of income revolve around philosophical and practical issues. *Philosophical* issues deal with the 'ideal'. What should the distribution of income be if we could give it any shape we desired? What is 'fair'? What is 'just'? *Practical* issues deal with what is, and what is not, possible. Suppose we wanted zero poverty. How much would it cost, and what would we sacrifice to achieve it? When we take wealth or income away from higher-income people and give it to lower-income people, do we destroy incentives? What are the effects of this kind of redistribution?

Policy makers must deal with both kinds of issues, but it seems logical to confront the philosophical issues first. If you do not know where you want to go, you cannot talk very well about how to get there or how much it costs to get there. You may find that you do not want to go anywhere at all. Some respected economists and philosophers argue that the government should *not* redistribute income.

Arguments against redistribution

Those who argue against government redistribution believe that the market, when left to operate on its own, is fair. This argument rests on the proposition that 'one is entitled to the fruits of one's efforts'.[1] Remember that if market theory is correct, rewards paid in the market are linked to productivity. In other words, labour and capital are paid in accordance with the value of what they produce.

This view also holds that property income – that is, income from land or capital – is no less justified than labour income. All factors of production have marginal products. Capital owners receive profits or interest because the capital that they own is productive.

The argument against redistribution also rests on the principles behind 'freedom of contract' and the protection of property rights. When I enter into an agreement either to sell my labour or to commit my capital to use, I do so freely. In return I contract to receive payment, which becomes my 'property'. When a government taxes me and gives my income to someone else, that action violates these two basic rights.

The more common arguments against redistribution are not philosophical. Rather, they point to more practical problems. First, it is said that taxation and transfer payments interfere with the basic incentives provided by the market. Taxing higher-income people reduces their incentive to work, save and invest. Taxing the 'winners' of the economic game also discourages risk taking. Furthermore, providing transfers to those at the bottom reduces their incentive to work as well. All of this leads to a reduction in total output that is the 'cost' of redistribution.

Another practical argument against redistribution is that it does not work. Some critics claim that anti-poverty programmes simply drain money without really helping the poor out of poverty. Whether or not these programmes actually help people break out of poverty, the charge of bureaucratic inefficiency in administration always exists. Social programmes must be administered by people who must be paid. Resources allocated to such tasks have an opportunity cost. Some degree of waste and inefficiency is inevitable in any sizeable bureaucracy.

Arguments in favour of redistribution

The argument most often used in favour of redistribution is that a society as wealthy as Europe has a moral obligation to provide all of its members with the basic necessities of life.

Many people, often through no fault of their own, find themselves left out. Some are born with mental or physical problems that severely limit their ability to 'produce'. Then, of course, there are children. Even if some parents can be held accountable for their own low incomes, do we want to punish innocent children for the faults of their parents and thus perpetuate the cycle of poverty? The elderly, without redistribution of income, would have to rely exclusively on savings to survive when they retired, and many conditions can lead to inadequate savings. Should the victims of bad luck be doomed to inevitable poverty? Illness is perhaps the best example. The accumulated savings of very few people can withstand the drain of extraordinary hospital and doctors' bills and the high cost of nursing home care.

Proponents of redistribution refute 'practical' arguments against it by pointing to empirical studies that show little negative effect on the incentives of those who benefit from transfer payment schemes. For many of those people – children, the elderly, the mentally ill – incentives are irrelevant, they say, and providing a basic income to most

[1] *Powerful support for this notion of 'entitlement' can be found in the works of the seventeenth-century English philosophers Thomas Hobbes and John Locke.*

of the unemployed does not discourage them from working when they have the opportunity to do so.[2] We now turn briefly to several more formal arguments.

Utilitarian justice

First put forward by the English thinkers Jeremy Bentham and John Stuart Mill in the late eighteenth and early nineteenth centuries, the essence of the utilitarian argument in favour of redistribution is that 'Money in the hand of a rich person is worth less than money in the hand of a poor person'. The rich spend their marginal income on luxury goods. It is very easy, for example, to spend over €100 per person for a meal in a good restaurant in Paris or Zurich. The poor, in contrast, spend their marginal income on necessities – food, clothing and shelter. If the marginal utility of income declines as income rises, the value of a euro's worth of luxury goods is worth less than a euro's worth of necessity. Thus, redistributing from the rich to the poor increases total utility. To put this notion of utilitarian justice in everyday language: through income redistribution, the rich sacrifice a little and the poor gain a lot.

The utilitarian position is not without its problems, of course. People have very different tastes and preferences. Who is to say that you value income more or less than I do? Because utility is unobservable and unmeasurable, comparisons between individuals cannot be easily made. Nonetheless, many people find the basic logic of the utilitarians persuasive.

Social contract theory: Rawlsian justice

The work of the Harvard philosopher John Rawls has generated a great deal of recent discussion, both within the discipline of economics and between economists and philosophers.[3] In the tradition of Hobbes, Locke and Rousseau, Rawls argues that, as members of society, we have a contract with one another. In the theoretical world that Rawls imagines, an original social contract is drawn up, and all parties agree to it without knowledge of who they are or who they will be in society. This condition is called the 'original position' or the 'state of nature'. With no vested interests to protect, members of society are able to make disinterested choices.

As we approach the contract, everyone has a chance to end up very rich or homeless. On the assumption that we are all 'risk averse', Rawls believes that people will attach great importance to the position of the least fortunate members of society because anyone could end up there. Rawlsian justice, then, is argued from the assumption of risk aversion. Rawls concludes that any contract emerging from the original position would call for an income distribution that would 'maximize the well-being of the worst-off member of society'.

Any society bound by such a contract would allow for inequality, but only if that inequality had the effect of improving the lot of the very poor. If inequality provided an incentive for people to work hard and innovate, for example, those inequalities should be tolerated as long as some of the benefits went to those at the bottom.

The works of Karl Marx

For many decades, a major rivalry existed between the two superpowers, the United States and the Soviet Union. At the heart of this rivalry was a fundamental philosophical difference of opinion about how economic systems work and how they should be managed. At the centre of the debate were the writings of Karl Marx.

Marx did not write very much about socialism or communism. His major work, *Das Kapital* (published in the nineteenth century), was a three-volume analysis and critique of the capitalist system that he saw at work in the world around him. We know what Marx thought was wrong with capitalism, but he was not very clear about what would replace it. In one essay, late in his life, he wrote 'from each according to his ability, to

---

utilitarian justice

The idea that 'a unit of income in the hand of a rich person buys less than a unit of income in the hand of a poor person'. If the marginal utility of income declines with income, transferring income from the rich to the poor will increase total utility.

Rawlsian justice

A theory of distributional justice that concludes that the social contract emerging from the 'original position' would call for an income distribution that would maximize the well-being of the worst-off member of society.

---

[2]For a discussion of the empirical evidence on the effects of transfer programmes and taxation on incentives, see Chapter 19.

[3]See John Rawls, A Theory of Justice (Cambridge, MA: Harvard University Press, 1972).

each according to his needs',[4] but he was not specific about the applications of this principle.

Marx's view of capital income does have important implications for income distribution. In the preceding chapters, we discussed profit as a return to a productive factor: capital, like labour, is productive and has a marginal product. Marx attributed all value to labour and none to capital. According to Marx's **labour theory of value**, the value of any commodity depends only on the amount of labour needed to produce it. The owners of capital are able to extract profit, or 'surplus value', because labour creates more value in a day than it is paid for. Like any other good, labour power is worth only what it takes to 'produce' it. In simple words, this means that under capitalism labour is paid a subsistence wage.

Marx saw profit as an illegitimate expropriation by capitalists of the fruits of labour's efforts. It follows, then, that Marxians see the property income component of income distribution as the primary source of inequality in Europe today. Without capital income, the distribution of income would be much more equal.

Despite the fact that the Soviet Union no longer exists, Marxism remains a powerful force in the world. China, Vietnam, Cuba and a number of other countries remain Communist, and many believe that the Marxian critique of capitalism was correct even though one version of an alternative has failed.

Income distribution as a public good

Those who argue that the unfettered market produces a just income distribution do not believe private charity should be forbidden. Voluntary redistribution does not involve any violation of property rights by the state.

In Chapter 16, however, you saw that there may be a problem with private charity. Suppose that people really do want to end the hunger problem, for example. As they write out their cheques to charity, they encounter the classic public-goods problem. First, there are free riders. If hunger and starvation are eliminated, the benefits – even the merely psychological benefits – flow to everyone, whether they contribute or not. Second, any contribution is a drop in the bucket. One individual contribution is so small that it can have no real effect.

With private charity, as with national defence, nothing depends upon whether I pay or not. Thus, private charity may fail for the same reason that the private sector is likely to fail to produce national defence and other public goods. People will find it in their interest not to contribute. Thus, we turn to government to provide things that we want that will not be provided adequately if we act separately – in this case, help for the poor and hungry.

Redistribution programmes and policies

The role of government in changing the *distribution of income* is hotly debated. The debate involves not only what government programmes are appropriate to fight poverty, but the character of the tax system as well. Unfortunately, the quality of the public debate on the subject is low. Usually it consists of a series of claims and counterclaims about what social programmes do to incentives rather than a serious inquiry into what our distributional goals should be.

In this section, we talk about the tools of redistributional policy in Europe. As we do so, you will have a chance to assess for yourself some of the evidence about their effects.

Financing redistribution programmes: taxes

Redistribution always involves two parties or groups: those who end up with less and those who end up with more. Because redistributional programmes are financed by tax

labour theory of value
Stated most simply, the theory that the value of a commodity depends only on the amount of labour required to produce it.

[4]Karl Marx, 'Critique of the Gotha programme' (May 1875), in Robert Tucker (ed.), The Marx–Engels Reader (New York: W. W. Norton), p. 388.

Table 17.8 Gini coefficients for income distribution at each stage of the tax–benefit system, UK 1995–1996

	Equivalized original income	Equivalized gross income	Equivalized disposable income	Equivalized post-tax income
Gini coefficient	52	36	33	37

Source: *Economic Trends*, No. 520 (March 1997).

payments, it is important to know who the donors and recipients are – that is, who pays the taxes and who receives the benefits of those taxes.

The mainstay of the tax system in most EU countries is the individual income tax. The income tax is always *progressive*. This means that those with higher incomes pay a higher percentage of their incomes in taxes. Even though the tax is subject to many exemptions, deductions and so on that allow some taxpayers to reduce their tax burdens, all studies of income tax show that its burden as a percentage of income rises as income rises.

The effect of direct taxes on the distribution of income for one country can be seen in Table 17.8. (Here we return to the UK data we introduced in Table 17.1.) As you might expect, income is most unevenly distributed (and therefore has the highest Gini coefficient) before taxes and benefits. This is (**equivalized**) original income. Because transfer payments tend to be made to lower income groups, the Gini coefficient for gross income is less than for the original income. Because income tax tends to be progressive, its effect is to lower the Gini coefficient still further (shown as disposable income). The regressive nature of indirect taxes, however, tends to widen income distribution. Hence the Gini coefficient for post-tax distribution is higher than for disposable income.

equivalized income distribution

Income distribution adjusted for the size and age of household members.

Expenditure programmes

Programmes aimed at supporting lower-income groups vary considerably between European countries. We will concentrate on the major kinds of assistance available in most EU member states.

Sickness and invalidity benefit

Many employers will continue to pay employees at least part of their wages or salaries even if they are ill. In most cases this is for a limited period. Lengthy illness can have a dramatic effect on household income, so most countries' governments have schemes whereby part of earnings can be paid to those off work for a long time. This is usually a portion of earnings. Often, however, there is a maximum amount payable. The costs of these programmes are high. Such sickness and invalidity benefits are normally funded partly by contributions paid by each employee when working and partly by the employer.

sickness and invalidity benefits

Cash payments made by the state to those unable to work because of sickness or invalidity.

Unemployment benefits

As we have seen in earlier chapters, changes in demand and in costs change demand for goods and therefore for inputs, including labour. If labour resources are mobile, those who are made redundant by such changes quickly get alternative sources of employment. Sometimes this does not happen. Millions of unemployed people in Europe have been without a job for over a year.

In all EU countries, unemployment benefits are payable to such households. Rules vary widely as to how long you need to be jobless to qualify, how long you can continue to receive benefit, and the level of the benefit payable. On average, EU national governments pay such benefits at around 60% of average earnings.

unemployment benefits

Cash benefits available to unemployed persons who meet certain criteria.

State pensions

We have seen that in a market system each factor, including labour, is paid the value of its marginal product. At retirement, the value of labour's marginal product declines to zero. Many people in Europe have 'occupational' pensions. They and their employers have contributed throughout their working lives to a fund from which they can be paid on retirement.

state pensions
Cash transfers by the state to those who have retired.

Many others have no such pension and rely on the state to provide them with income in retirement. The cost of **state pensions** provision is rising, because in most EU countries the proportion of retired people is rising. Again, this benefit varies greatly between EU countries, but on average such pensions are around 75% of average earnings.

In much of Europe, benefits paid are high, and so are contributions. In other countries, notably the UK, contributions and benefits are much lower.

Other transfers

All the above are cash benefits. Recipients receive the benefit directly as income, which they can spend as they choose. There are other benefits. Some countries pay households additional amounts where there are children, for example. Some transfers, however, are in kind – for example, the provision of subsidized or free medical care, or subsidized or free school education.

How effective are anti-poverty programmes?

We have seen that large numbers of households throughout Europe are poor. Governments do make some attempt to alleviate this poverty. How effective are such efforts?

Some say economic growth is the best way to cure poverty. Poverty programmes are expensive and must be paid for with tax revenues. The high rates of taxation levied to support these programmes, critics say, have eroded the incentive to work, save and invest, slowing the rate of economic growth. In addition, continued poverty in the midst of increasing affluence is cited as evidence that anti-poverty programmes do not work.

The opposite view is that poverty would be much more widespread without anti-poverty measures. Poverty is widespread because insufficient resources are allocated to its removal. Reducing poverty by increased transfers would benefit everyone by increasing social cohesion and by allowing large numbers of people to belong and contribute to, rather than be excluded from, society.

Government or the market? A review

Part 2 (Chapters 6 to 12) introduced you to the behaviour of households and firms in input and output markets. You learned that if all the assumptions of perfect competition held in the real world, the outcome would be perfectly efficient.

But as we began to relax the assumptions of perfect competition in Part 3 (Chapters 13 to 17), we began to see a potential role for government in the economy. Some firms acquire market power and tend to underproduce and overprice. Unregulated markets give private decision makers no incentives to weigh the social costs of externalities. Goods that provide collective benefits may not be produced in sufficient quantities without government involvement. And, as we saw in this chapter, the final distribution of well-being determined by the free market may not be considered equitable by society.

Remember, however, that government is not a cure for all economic woes. There is no guarantee that public sector involvement will improve matters. Many argue that government involvement may bring about even more inequity and inefficiency because bureaucrats are often driven by self-interest, not public interest.

You now have a strong foundation in microeconomic theory. Part 4 of this book – Chapters 18 and 19 – presents two topics in applied economics: public finance, and labour economics. These chapters are meant to provide you with an overview of how the discipline addresses some key issues of our time. They also represent a preview of what you will encounter in more advanced courses in economics.

Summary

1. Even if all markets were perfectly efficient, the result might not be fair. Even in relatively free market economies, governments redistribute income and wealth, usually in the name of fairness, or *equity*.

2. Because utility is neither directly observable nor measurable, most policy discussions deal with the distributions of income and wealth as imperfect substitutes for the concept of 'the distribution of well-being'.

The sources of household income

3. Households derive their incomes from three basic sources: (1) wages or salaries received in exchange for labour, (2) property such as capital and land, and (3) government.

4. Differences in wage and salary incomes across households result from differences in the characteristics of workers (skills, training, education, experience and so on) and from differences in jobs (dangerous, exciting, glamorous, difficult and so forth). Household income also varies with the number of household members in the labour force, and it can decline sharply if members become unemployed.

5. The amount of property income that a household earns depends on the amount and kinds of property it owns. Transfer income from governments flows substantially, but not exclusively, to lower-income households. Except for social security, transfer payments are largely designed to provide income to those in need.

The distribution of income

6. In Europe, the way in which income is distributed varies widely between countries. In all countries, the top quintile of households earns many times that received by the lowest quintile.

7. The *Lorenz Curve* is a commonly used graphical device for describing the distribution of income. The *Gini coefficient* is an index of income inequality that ranges from zero for perfect equality to one for total inequality.

8. Poverty is very difficult to define. It can be defined *absolutely*. Households are absolutely poor if their income falls below the level necessary to purchase necessities. It can be defined *relatively*. A household is relatively poor if its income is less than some defined proportion of that of higher income groups.

9. Income inequality is increasing in some EU countries but is decreasing in others.

10. Data on the distribution of wealth are not as readily available as data on the distribution of income. The distribution of wealth in Europe is more unequal than the distribution of income.

The redistribution debate

11. The basic philosophical argument against government redistribution rests on the proposition that one is entitled to the fruits of one's efforts. It also rests on the principles of freedom of contract and protection of property rights. More common arguments focus on the negative effects of redistribution on incentives to work, save and invest.

12. The basic philosophical argument in favour of redistribution is that a rich modern society has a moral obligation to provide all of its members with the basic necessities of life. More formal arguments can be found in the works of the utilitarians, and Rawls and Marx.

Redistribution programmes and policies

13. In Europe, redistribution is accomplished through taxation and through a number of government transfer systems. The largest of these are sickness and invalidity benefits, state pensions and unemployment benefits.

14. There is some debate over the effectiveness of anti-poverty measures. One view holds that the best way to cure poverty is with economic growth. Poverty programmes are expensive and must be paid for with tax revenues. The high rates of taxation required to support these programmes have eroded the incentive to work, save and invest, thus slowing the rate of economic growth. In addition, the rise in poverty is cited as evidence that anti-poverty measures do not work. The opposite view holds that without anti-poverty programmes, poverty would be much worse.

Review Terms and Concepts

absolute poverty
compensating differentials
economic income
equity
equivalized income distribution

Gini coefficient
human capital
labour theory of value
Lorenz Curve
property income

Rawlsian justice
relative poverty
sickness and invalidity benefits
state pensions

transfer payments
unemployment benefits
utilitarian justice
utility possibilities frontier

Problem Set

1. In the last 10–15 years, most EU governments have cut the marginal rate of tax on high earners. Do you approve? Defend your argument.

2. Women typically earn about three-quarters as much as men. Is there any economic justification for this? Would tougher laws against such discrimination help?

3. Economists call education 'an investment in human capital'. Define 'capital'. In what sense is education capital? Investments are undertaken in order to earn a rate of return. Describe the return to investment in a university education. How would you go about measuring it? How would you decide if it is good enough to warrant the investment?

4. New Ph.D.s in economics entering the job market find that academic jobs (jobs teaching at colleges and universities) pay about 30% less than non-academic jobs such as working at a bank or a consulting firm. Those who take academic jobs are clearly worse off than those who take non-academic jobs. Do you agree? Explain your answer.

5. Using the data in Table 1 plot the Lorenz Curves for each of the three hypothetical countries A, B and C, then answer the following questions.
a. What is the Gini coefficient for Country A?
b. Comment upon the relative income distribution in Countries B and C.
c. Are the following statements true or false? (1) There are more absolutely poor people in Country C than in Country B. (2) Income per head is higher in Country A.

Table 1

	Percentage of income		
	Country A	Country B	Country C
Lowest quintile	20	5	3
2nd	20	10	8
3rd	20	15	18
4th	20	30	34
Highest	20	40	37

(3) Wealth is more concentrated in Country B than in Country C.

6. Should welfare benefits be higher in Germany and Spain than they are in Greece? Defend your answer.

7. Poverty among the elderly has been sharply reduced in the last quarter of a century. How has this been accomplished?

8. Write a memo to your government urging either an increase or a decrease in spending on public housing.

9. 'Income inequality is evidence that our economic system is working well, not poorly.' What arguments might this speaker use to support his opinion of income redistribution policies? How might he respond when racial or gender disparities are brought to his attention?

Public Finance: The Economics of Taxation

An introductory course in economics has several goals. One is to introduce theory about how economies work. The first 17 chapters of this book contain what amounts to the core of microeconomic theory.

Another purpose is to survey the major subfields of the discipline. In Chapter 1 we briefly described a number of these subfields. This chapter is the first of two that expand on those brief descriptions. Because the discipline is so varied, we cannot survey all the areas of economic inquiry. So we limit our discussion to two of the most debated economic issues of the day: public finance (Chapter 18) and labour economics (Chapter 19).

The economics of taxation

The five chapters in Part 3 analysed the potential role of government in the economy. Together, those chapters discuss much of the field of *public economics*. From there it is an easy transition to *public finance*, which begins our survey of applied economics. No matter what functions we end up assigning to government, in order to do anything at all government must first raise revenues. The primary vehicle that government uses to finance itself is taxation.[1]

Remember: taxes are ultimately paid by people, or by households:

> Taxes may be imposed on transactions, institutions, property, meals and other things, but in the final analysis they are paid by individuals or households.

Taxes: basic concepts

tax base The measure or value upon which a tax is levied.

tax rate structure The percentage of a tax base that must be paid in taxes – 25% of income, for example.

To begin our analysis of the tax system, we need to clarify some terms. There are many different kinds of taxes, and tax analysts use a specific language to describe them. Every tax has two parts: a *base* and a *rate structure*. The **tax base** is the measure or value upon which the tax is levied. Taxes are levied on a variety of bases, including income, sales, property and corporate profits. The **tax rate structure** determines the portion of the tax base that must be paid in taxes. A tax rate of 25% on income, for example, means that I pay a tax equal to 25% of my income.

Taxes on stocks versus taxes on flows

Tax bases may be either stock measures or flow measures. A local property tax is a tax on the value of residential, commercial or industrial property. For instance, in many European countries, homeowners are taxed on the current assessed value of their homes. Current value is a stock variable – that is, it is measured or estimated at a point in time.

---

[1]*Before we proceed, you may want to review the discussion of the public sector in Chapter 3. There we describe the basic sources of revenue, as well as the things those revenues are spent on. You will often hear the taxing and spending policies of national governments referred to as 'fiscal policies'. The word fiscal comes from fisc, another word for a government treasury.*

Other taxes are levied on flows. (Review Chapter 4 if the difference between stock and flow variables is unclear to you.) Income is a flow. Most people are paid on a weekly, biweekly or monthly basis, and they have taxes deducted from every pay cheque. Retail sales take place continuously, and a retail sales tax takes a portion of that flow.

Proportional, progressive and regressive taxes

All taxes are ultimately paid out of income. A tax whose burden is a constant proportion of income for all households is a **proportional tax**. A tax of 20% on all forms of income, with no deductions or exclusions, is a proportional tax.

A tax that exacts a higher proportion of income from higher-income households than it does from lower-income households is a **progressive tax**. Because its rate structure increases with income, the individual income tax is generally a progressive tax.

A tax that exacts a lower proportion of income from higher-income families than it does from lower-income families is a **regressive tax**. *Excise taxes* (taxes on specific commodities) are regressive. Value Added Tax (VAT) is also a regressive tax. Suppose VAT in your country is 15%. You might assume that it is a proportional tax because everyone pays 15%. But all people do not spend the same fraction of their income on taxable goods and services. In fact, higher-income households save a larger fraction of their incomes. Even though they spend more on more expensive things and may pay more taxes than lower-income families, they end up paying a smaller *proportion* of their incomes in VAT.

Table 18.1 shows this principle at work in three families. The lowest-income family saves 20% of its 10,000 euro income, leaving €8000 for consumption. With 5% VAT, the household pays €400, or 4% of total income, in VAT. The 50,000 euro family saves 50% of its income, or €25,000, leaving €25,000 for consumption. With 5% VAT, the household pays €1250, only 2.5% of its total income, in tax.

Marginal versus average tax rates

When discussing a specific tax or taxes in general, we should distinguish between average tax rates and marginal tax rates. Your *average tax rate* is the total amount of tax you pay divided by your total income. If you earned a total income of €15,000 and paid income taxes of €1500, your average income tax rate would be 10% (1500 divided by 15,000). If you paid €3000 in taxes, your average rate would be 20% (3000 divided by 15,000).

Your *marginal tax rate* is the tax rate that you pay on any additional income that you earn. If you take a part-time job and pay an additional €280 in tax on the extra €1000 you've earned, your marginal tax rate is 28% (280 divided by 1000).

Marginal and average tax rates are usually different. The individual income tax in most countries shows how and why marginal tax rates can differ. Most people must file a tax return each year. In calculating the total amount of tax that you must pay, you first add up all your income. You are then allowed to subtract certain items from it. Among the things that virtually all taxpayers in Europe can subtract is a *personal*

---

proportional tax

A tax whose burden is the same proportion of income for all households.

progressive tax

A tax whose burden, expressed as a percentage of income, increases as income increases.

regressive tax

A tax whose burden, expressed as a percentage of income, falls as income increases.

Table 18.1 The burden of a hypothetical 5% VAT imposed on three households with different incomes

Household	Income (euros)	Saving rate (%)	Saving (euros)	Consumption (euros)	5% VAT (euros)	VAT as % of income
A	10,000	20	2,000	8,000	400	4.0
B	20,000	40	8,000	12,000	600	3.0
C	50,000	50	25,000	25,000	1,250	2.5

Table 18.2 Individual income tax rates, The Netherlands, 1997

Taxable income (guilders)	Tax rate (%)
0–45,960	37.3
45,960–97,422	50
over 97,422	60
Tax-free allowances (guilders)	
Single person	7,102
Married person (spouse has no income)	14,204

allowance. After everything is subtracted, you are left with *taxable income*. Taxable income is then subject to a set of marginal rates that rise with income. Table 18.2 presents the marginal individual income tax rates for one EU country, The Netherlands.

Different countries in the EU have different rates of income tax which become payable at different levels of income, but these calculations for a Dutch taxpayer illustrate principles common to all countries' personal income tax systems.

Suppose that you are a single taxpayer who earned 120,000 guilders. To calculate your tax you first subtract the tax free allowance (7,102 guilders) from your gross income. This leaves you with a taxable income of 112,898 guilders. To work out the tax payable, you must make several separate calculations. The first 45,960 guilders is taxed at 37.3% (see Table 18.2); the tax on this amount is $0.373 \times 45,960 = 17,143.08$ guilders. The seconds 'slice' of income between 45,960 and 97,422 guilders is taxed at 50%. The difference between 45,960 and 97,422 is 51,462 guilders; the tax on that amount is $0.5 \times 51,462 = 25,731$ guilders. Finally, all additional income is taxed at 60%; so the tax on the last 'slice' of 15,474 guilders is $0.6 \times 15,474 = 9,284.4$ guilders. Your total tax bill is the sum of these three amounts: $17,143.08 + 25,731 + 9,284.4 = 52,158.48$ guilders.

You can now see the difference between average and marginal rates. Your average tax rate is 52,158.4 as a percentage of 120,000, or 43.47%. But any additional income that you might have earned would have been taxed at 60%. These calculations are summarized in Table 18.3.

Table 18.3 Tax calculations for a single taxpayer who earned 120,000 guilders in 1997

Calculations	Results
Total income	120,000
Tax-free allowance	7,102
= Taxable income	112,898
Tax calculation	
0–45,960 at 37.3%: (45,960 × 0.373) =	17,143.08
45,960–97,422 at 50%: (97,422 – 45,960) × 0.5 =	25,731.00
Over 97,422 at 60%: (120,000 – 97,422) × 0.6 =	9,284.40
Total tax: 17,143.08 + 25,731.00 + 9,284.40 =	52,158.48
Average tax rate: 52,158.48 ÷ 120,000 =	43.47%
Marginal tax rate:	60%

Marginal tax rates influence behaviour. Decisions about how much to work depend on how much of the added income you take home. Similarly, a firm's decision about how much to invest depends in part on the additional, or marginal, profits that the investment project would yield after tax.

Tax equity

One of the criteria for evaluating the economy that we defined in Chapter 1 (and returned to in Chapter 17) was fairness, or *equity*. Everyone agrees that tax burdens should be distributed fairly, that all of us should pay our 'fair share' of taxes, but there is endless debate about what constitutes a fair tax system.

One theory of fairness is called the **benefits-received principle**. Dating back to the eighteenth-century economist Adam Smith and earlier writers, the benefits-received principle holds that taxpayers should contribute to government according to the benefits they derive from public expenditures. This principle ties the tax side of the fiscal equation to the expenditure side. For example, the owners and users of cars pay fuel taxes, which are used to build and maintain the road and motorway system. Motoring organizations frequently claim that motorists pay far more taxes than are used for such maintenance. In essence, they argue that the benefits-received principle is being violated.

The difficulty with applying the benefits principle is that the bulk of public expenditures are for public goods – national defence, for example. The benefits of public goods fall collectively on all members of society, and there is no way to determine what value individual taxpayers receive from them.

A different principle, and one that has dominated the formulation of tax policy in most Western societies for decades, is the **ability-to-pay principle**. This principle holds that taxpayers should bear tax burdens in line with their ability to pay. Here the tax side of the fiscal equation is viewed separately from the expenditure side. Under this system, the problem of attributing the benefits of public expenditures to specific taxpayers or groups of taxpayers is avoided.

Horizontal and vertical equity

If we accept the idea that ability to pay should be the basis for the distribution of tax burdens, two principles follow. First, the principle of *horizontal equity* holds that those with equal ability to pay should bear equal tax burdens. Second, the principle of *vertical equity* holds that those with greater ability to pay should pay more.

Although these notions seem appealing, we must have answers to two interdependent questions before they can be meaningful. First, how is ability to pay measured? What is the 'best' tax base? Second, if A has a greater ability to pay than B, *how much* more should A contribute?

What is the 'best' tax base?

The three leading candidates for the best tax base are *income*, *consumption* and *wealth*. Before we consider each as a basis for taxation, let us see what they mean.

Income – to be precise, *economic income* – is anything that enhances one's ability to command resources. The technical definition of economic income is the value of what you consume plus any change in the value of what you own:

$$\text{Economic income} = \text{Consumption} + \text{Change in net worth}$$

Economic income includes all money receipts, whether from employment, profits, or transfers from the government. It also includes the value of benefits not received in money form, such as medical benefits, employer retirement contributions, paid country club memberships, and so on. Increases or decreases in the value of stocks or bonds, whether or not they are 'realized' through sale, are part of economic income.

benefits-received principle
A theory of fairness which holds that taxpayers should contribute to government (in the form of taxes) in proportion to the benefits that they receive from public expenditures.

ability-to-pay principle
A theory of taxation which holds that citizens should bear tax burdens in line with their ability to pay taxes.

For income tax purposes, capital gains count as income only when they are realized, but for purposes of defining economic income, all increases in asset values count, whether they are realized or not.

A few other items that we do not usually think of as income are included in a comprehensive definition of income. If I own my house outright and live in it rent free, income flows from my house just as interest flows from a bond or profit from a share of stock. By owning the house, I enjoy valuable housing benefits that I would otherwise have to pay rent for. I am my own landlord and I am, in essence, earning my own rent. Other components of economic income include any gifts and bequests received and food grown at home.

In economic terms, income is income, regardless of source and use.

Consumption is the total value of things that a household consumes in a given period. It is equal to income minus saving, or:

Consumption = Income – Saving (change in net worth)

Wealth, or *net worth*, is the value of all the things you own after your liabilities are subtracted. If you were to sell off today everything of value you own – stocks, bonds, houses, cars and so forth – at their current market prices and pay off all your debts – loans, mortgages and so forth – you would end up with your net worth.

Net worth = Assets – Liabilities

Remember, income and consumption are *flow* measures. We speak of income per month or per year. Wealth and net worth are *stock* measures at a point in time.

For years, conventional wisdom among economists held that income was the best measure of the ability to pay taxes. Many who feel that consumption is a better measure have recently challenged that assumption. The following arguments are not just arguments about fairness and ability to pay; they are also arguments about the best base for taxation.

Remember as you proceed that the issue under debate is which *base* is the best base, not which tax is the best tax or whether taxes ought to be progressive or regressive. While sales taxes are regressive, it is possible to have a personal consumption tax that is progressive. Under such a system, individuals would report their income as they do now, but all documented saving would be deductible. The difference between income and saving is a measure of personal consumption that could be taxed with progressive rates.

Consumption as the best tax base

The view favouring consumption as the best tax base dates back at least to the seventeenth-century English philosopher Thomas Hobbes, who argued that people should pay taxes in accordance with 'what they actually take out of the common pot, not what they leave in'. The standard of living, the argument goes, depends not on income but on how much income is spent. If we want to redistribute well-being, therefore, the tax base should be consumption, because consumption is the best measure of well-being.

A second argument with a distinguished history dates back to work done by Irving Fisher in the early part of the twentieth century. Fisher and many others have argued that a tax on income discourages saving by taxing savings twice. A story told originally by Fisher illustrates this theory nicely.[2]

---

[2]*Irving Fisher and Herbert Fisher,* Constructive Income Taxation: A Proposal for Reform *(New York: Harper, 1942), Ch. 8, p. 56.*

Suppose Alex builds a house for Frank. For this service, Alex is paid €10,000 and given an orchard containing 100 apple trees. Alex spends the €10,000 today, but he saves the orchard, and presumably he will consume or sell the fruit it bears every year in the future. At year's end the government levies a 10% tax on Alex's total income, which includes the €10,000 and the orchard. First, the government takes 10% of the €10,000, which is 10% of Alex's consumption. Second, it takes 10% of the orchard – 10 trees – which is 10% of Alex's saving. If this is all the government did, there would be no double taxation of saving. If, however, the income tax is also levied in the following year, Alex will be taxed on the income generated by the 90 trees that he still owns. If the income tax is levied in the year after that, Alex will again be taxed on the income generated by his orchard, and so on. The income tax is thus taxing Alex's saving more than once. To tax the orchard fairly, the system should take 10% of the trees or 10% of the fruit going forward, *but not both*. To avoid the double taxation of saving, either the original saving of 100 trees should not be taxed or the income generated from the after-tax number of trees (90) should not be taxed.

The same logic can be applied to cash saving. Suppose the income tax rate is 25% and that you earn €20,000. Out of the €20,000 you consume €16,000 and save €4000. At the end of the year, you owe the government 25% of your total income, or €5000. You can think of this as a tax of 25% on consumption (€4000) and 25% on savings (€1000). Why, then, do we say that the income tax is a double tax on saving? To understand the argument you have to think about the €4000 that is saved.

If you save €4000, you will no doubt put it to some use. Safe possibilities include putting it in an interest-bearing account or buying a bond with it. If you do either of these, you will earn interest that you can consume in future years. In fact, when we save and earn interest we are spreading some of our present earnings over future years of consumption. Just as the orchard yields future fruit, so the bond yields future interest, which is considered income in the year it is earned and is taxed as such. The only way that you can earn that future interest income is if you leave your money tied up in the bond or the account. You can consume the €4000 today or you can have the future flow of interest; you can't have both. Yet both are taxed.

Suppose that the interest rate is 10%. If you save €4000 and put that money into a long-term bond that pays 10% annual interest, you have converted your €4000 into an additional income flow of €400 per year. That flow will be taxed at 25%, or €100 per year. Thus, your saving is taxed both when you earn it and as you consume it in the future. Many people think this is unfair.

It is also inefficient. As you will see later, a tax that distorts economic choices creates *excess burdens*. By double taxing saving, an income tax distorts the choice between consumption and saving, which is really the choice between present consumption and future consumption. Double taxing also tends to reduce the saving rate and the rate of investment – and ultimately the rate of economic growth.

Income as the best tax base

Your ability to pay is your ability to command resources, and many argue that your income is the best measure of your capacity to command resources today. According to proponents of income as a tax base, you should be taxed not on what you actually draw out of the common pot, but rather on the basis of your *ability* to draw from that pot. In other words, your decision to save or consume is no different from your decision to buy apples, to go out for dinner, or to give money to your mother. It is your *income* that enables you to do all these things, and it is income that should be taxed, regardless of its sources and regardless of how you use it. Saving is just another use of income.

If income is the best measure of ability to pay, the double taxation argument doesn't hold water. An income tax taxes savings twice only if consumption is the measure used to gauge a person's ability to pay. It does not do so if income is the measure used. Acquisition of the orchard enhances your ability to pay today; a bountiful crop of fruit enhances your ability to pay when it is produced. Interest income is no different than any other form of income; it too enhances your ability to pay. Taxing both is thus fair.

Wealth as the best tax base

Still others argue that the real power to command resources comes not from any single year's income but from accumulated wealth. Aggregate net worth in Europe is many times larger than aggregate income.

If two people have identical annual incomes of €10,000, but one also has an accumulated net worth of €1 million, is it reasonable to argue that these two people have the same ability to pay, or that they should pay equal taxes? Most people would answer no. Those who favour income taxation, however, argue that net wealth comes from after-tax income that has been saved. An income tax taxes consumption and saving correctly, they say. To subsequently take part of what has been saved would be an unfair second hit – *real* double taxation.

No simple answer

Before the 1970s, most tax economists favoured a comprehensive income base. Today, many economists favour a comprehensive personal consumption tax. Part of the reason for the increasing popularity of consumption taxes is a growing concern with the low saving rates. Compared with, say, many economies in South-east Asia, Europe has had slow productivity growth, and many point to the inadequacy of saving as the culprit. As we saw in earlier chapters, household saving provides resources for firms to invest in capital that raises the productivity of labour. In principle, VAT should help.

VAT is essentially a national sales tax.[3] Most European countries rely very heavily on value-added taxes. The average VAT rate among members of the European Union is around 17%, though rates vary between countries, as does the breadth of coverage.

Opposition to VAT focuses on its inherent regressivity. Recall that a personal consumption tax could be progressive, but that a transaction-based sales tax or VAT is regressive. Some European countries reduce regressivity by exempting items such as food, housing and clothing. In other countries, the rate on such items is much lower.

Tax incidence: who pays?

When a government levies a tax, it writes a law assigning responsibility for payment to specific people or specific organizations. To understand a tax, we must look beyond those named in the law as the initial taxpayers.

First, remember the cardinal principle of tax analysis: the burden of a tax is ultimately borne by individuals or households; institutions have no real taxpaying capacity. Second, the burden of a tax is not always borne by those initially responsible for paying it. Directly or indirectly, tax burdens are often *shifted* to others. When we speak of the **incidence of a tax**, we are referring to the ultimate distribution of its burden.

The simultaneous reactions of many households and/or firms to the presence of a tax may cause relative prices to change, and price changes affect households' well-being. Households may feel the impact of a tax on the sources side or on the uses side of the income equation. (We use the term *income equation* because the amount of income from all *sources* must be exactly equal to the amount of income allocated to all *uses* – including saving – in a given period.) On the **sources side**, a household is hurt if the net wages or profits that it receives fall; on the **uses side**, a household is hurt if the prices of the things that it buys rise. If your wages remain the same but the price of every item that you buy doubles, you are in the same position you would be in if your wages had been cut by 50% and prices hadn't changed.

tax incidence The ultimate distribution of tax's burden.

sources side and uses side
The impact of a tax may be felt on one or the other or on both sides of the income equation. A tax may cause net income to fall (damage on the sources side), or it may cause prices of goods and services to rise so that income buys less (damage on the uses side).

---

[3] *A standard value-added tax (VAT) would be collected from all firms at the same rate based on the value that a firm adds to the product during the production process, hence the term value-added. For example, a car maker would not be taxed on the cost of tyres, because tyres will already have been taxed at the tyre manufacturing firm.*

The imposition of a tax or a change in a tax can change behaviour. Changes in behaviour can affect supply and demand in markets and cause prices to change. When prices change in input or output markets, some households are made better off and some are made worse off. These final changes determine the ultimate burden of the tax.

tax shifting
Occurs when households can alter their behaviour and do something to avoid paying a tax.

Tax shifting takes place when households can alter their behaviour and do something to avoid paying a tax. This is easily accomplished when only certain items are singled out for taxation. For example, suppose a heavy tax were levied on bananas. Initially the tax would make the price of bananas much higher, but there are many potential substitutes for bananas. Consumers can avoid the tax by not buying bananas, and that is what many will do. But, as demand drops, the market price of bananas falls and banana growers lose money. Thus, the tax shifts from consumers to the growers, at least in the short run.

A tax such as VAT, which is levied at the same rate on most consumer goods, is harder to avoid. The only thing that consumers can do to avoid such a tax is to consume less of everything. If consumers do so, saving will increase, but otherwise there are few opportunities for tax avoidance and therefore for tax shifting. The general principle here is that:

> Broad-based taxes are less likely to be shifted and more likely to 'stick' where they are levied than 'partial' taxes are.

The incidence of payroll taxes

A significant part of government taxes comes from social security contributions, also called 'payroll taxes'. The revenues from the various payroll taxes go to support social security, unemployment benefits, and other health and disability benefits for workers. (These are discussed in Chapter 17.) Some of these taxes are levied on employers as a percentage of payroll, and some are levied on workers as a percentage of wages or salaries earned.

Payroll taxes are important to all governments but especially to France, Germany and The Netherlands (Table 18.4). The variation in spread between employee and employer is enormous. In the UK, the contributions paid by employers and employees are about the same; in Italy, most is paid by employees. In The Netherlands and Sweden, well over 80% of all payroll taxes are met by employers.

To analyse the payroll tax, let us take a tax of €T per unit of labour levied on employers and sketch the reactions that are likely to follow. When the tax is first levied, firms find that the price of labour is higher. Before the tax was levied, they paid €W per hour; now they must pay €W + €T. Firms may react in two ways. First, they may substitute capital for the now more expensive labour. Second, higher costs and lower profits may lead to a cut in production. Both reactions mean a lower demand for labour. Lower demand for labour reduces wages, and part of the tax is thus passed on (or *shifted*) to the workers, who end up earning less. The extent to which the tax is shifted to workers depends on how workers react to the lower wages.

We can develop a more formal analysis of this situation with a picture of the market before the tax is levied. Figure 18.1 shows equilibrium in a hypothetical labour market with no payroll tax. Before we proceed, we should review the factors that determine the shapes of the supply and demand curves.

Labour supply and labour demand curves in perfect competition: a review
Recall that the demand for labour in competitive markets depends on its productivity. As you saw in Chapter 10, a competitive, profit-maximizing firm will hire labour up to the point at which the market wage is equal to labour's marginal revenue product. The shape of the demand curve for labour shows how responsive *firms* are to changes in wages. Several factors determine a firm's reactions to changes in wage rates: how

Table 18.4 Payroll taxes as a percentage of government revenue

	Percentage of total tax in social security contributions	Employer contribution	Employee contribution
Austria	30.9	22.9	8.0
Belgium	33.6	20.0	13.6
Denmark	3.3	n/a	–
Finland	32.4	23.9	8.5
France	43.7	26.6	17.1
Germany	40.3	21.9	18.4
Greece	30.7	n/a	–
Ireland	19.2	n/a	–
Italy	32.4	10.7	21.7
Netherlands	41.7	35.0	6.7
Spain	36.7	n/a	–
Sweden	27.4	24.9	2.5
UK	18.9	8.8	10.1

Figures are for 1994, except Ireland which is for 1993.

Source: Economic Trends.

easy it is to substitute capital for labour, whether labour costs are large or small relative to total costs, and how elastic the demand for the firm's product is.[4]

The shape of the labour supply curve shows how responsive *workers* are to changes in wages. As you saw in Chapter 6, lower wages may affect workers' behaviour in two

Figure 18.1 Equilibrium in a competitive labour market: no taxes

With no taxes on wages, the wage that firms pay is the same as the wage that workers take home. At a wage of W_0, the quantity of labour supplied and the quantity of labour demanded are equal.

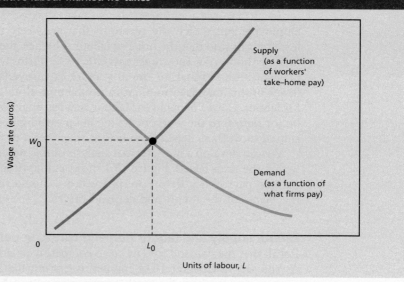

[4]*If demand for output is highly inelastic, increases in costs from a rise in wages generally flow through to consumers in the form of higher prices.*

ways. First, lower wages mean that workers will earn less income for the same amount of effort. They will therefore be able to buy fewer goods and services. They will also buy less leisure by working more. This is the *income effect* of a decrease in wages.

Second, a lower wage means that leisure is less expensive relative to other goods – an additional hour of leisure means an hour of lost wages, and wages are now lower. Workers 'substitute' leisure for other goods by working less and buying less of other goods with the lower income. This is the *substitution effect* of a decrease in wages. An upward-sloping labour supply curve means that, on balance, the substitution effect is stronger than the income effect, and that lower wages lead to less work effort. If the opposite were true, the labour supply curve would bend back.[5]

The labour supply curve represents the reaction of workers to changes in the wage rate. Household behaviour depends on the *after-tax* wage that they actually take home per hour of work. In contrast, labour demand is a function of the full amount that firms must pay per unit of labour, an amount that may include a tax if it is levied directly on payroll, as it is in our example. Such a tax, when present, drives a 'wedge' between the price of labour that firms face and take-home wages.

Imposing a payroll tax: who pays?

In Figure 18.1, there were no taxes, and the wage that firms paid was the same as the wage that workers took home. At a wage of W_0, quantity of labour supplied and quantity of labour demanded were equal, and the labour market was in equilibrium.[6]

But now suppose that employers must pay a tax of €T per unit of labour. Figure 18.2 shows a new supply curve that is parallel to the old supply curve but above it by a distance, T. The new curve, S', shows labour supply as a function of what firms pay. Regardless of how the ultimate burden of the tax is shared, there is a difference between what firms pay and what workers take home.

Figure 18.2 Incidence of a per unit payroll tax in a competitive labour market

With a tax on firms of €T per unit of labour hired, the market will adjust, shifting the tax partially to workers. When the tax is levied, firms must first pay $W_0 + T$. This reduces labour demand to L_d. The result is excess supply, which pushes wages down to W_1 and passes some of the burden of the tax on to workers.

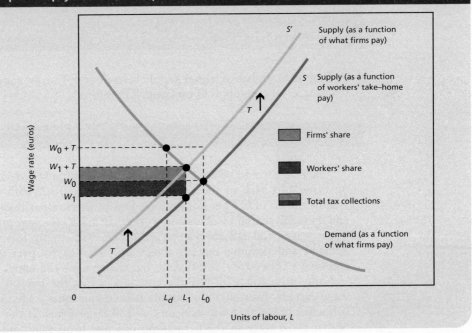

---

[5]*Evidence regarding the relative size of the income and substitution effects is presented in Chapter 19. For more on the backward-bending supply curve, see Figure 6.11 and the accompanying discussion.*

[6]*Although the supply curve has a positive slope, that slope implies nothing about the actual shape of the labour supply curve in Europe.*

If the initial wage is W_0 per hour, firms will face a price of $W_0 + T$ per unit of labour immediately after the tax is levied. Workers still receive only W_0, however. The higher wage rate – that is, the higher price of labour that firms now face – reduces the quantity of labour demanded from L_0 to L_d, and the firms lay off workers. Workers initially still receive W_0, so that amount of labour supplied does not change, and the result is an excess supply of labour equal to $(L_0 - L_d)$.

The excess supply applies downward pressure to the market wage, and wages fall, shifting some of the tax burden onto workers. The issue is: how far will wages fall? Figure 18.2 shows that a new equilibrium is achieved at W_1, with firms paying $W_1 + T$. When workers take home W_1, they will supply L_1 units of labour; if firms must pay $W_1 + T$, they will demand L_1 units of labour, and the market clears.

In this case, then, the burden of the payroll tax is shared by employers and employees. Initially, firms paid W_0; after the tax, they pay $W_1 + T$. Initially, workers received W_0; after the tax, they end up with the lower wage W_1. Total tax collections by the government are equal to $T \times L_1$; geometrically, they are equal to the entire shaded area in Figure 18.2. The workers' share of the tax burden is the lower portion, $(W_0 - W_1) \times L_1$. The firms' share is the upper portion, $[(W_1 + T) - W_0] \times L_1$.

The relative sizes of the firms' share and the workers' share of the total tax burden depend on the shapes of the demand and supply curves. Look at Figure 18.2 and try to imagine what would happen to the size of the worker's shaded rectangle if the supply curve became steeper (more vertical). A more vertical supply curve means that the quantity of labour supplied is relatively inelastic – it does not change very much when net wages change. A more vertical supply curve would mean that the lower shaded rectangle (the workers' share) would be larger and the upper shaded rectangle (the firms' share) would be smaller. A more elastic (horizontal) supply curve would mean that the lower shaded rectangle (workers' share) would be smaller and the upper shaded rectangle (firms' share) would be larger.

> Workers bear the bulk of the burden of a payroll tax if labour supply is relatively inelastic, and firms bear the bulk of the burden of a payroll tax if labour supply is relatively elastic.

Empirical studies of labour supply behaviour in Europe suggest that for most of the workforce, labour supply is inelastic. Therefore:

> Most of the burden of payroll taxes in Europe is probably borne by workers.

The result would be the same if the tax were initially levied on workers rather than on firms. Go back to the equilibrium in Figure 18.2, with wages at W_0. But now assume the tax of €T per hour is levied on workers rather than firms. The burden will end up being shared by firms and workers in *exactly the same proportions*. Initially, take-home wages will fall to $W_0 - T$. Workers will supply less labour, creating excess demand and pushing market wages up. That shifts part of the burden back to employers. The 'story' is different, but the result is the same.

Some economists dispute the conclusion that the payroll tax is borne largely by wage earners. Even if labour supply is inelastic, some wages are set in the process of collective bargaining between unions and large firms. If the payroll tax results in a higher gross wage in the bargaining process, firms may find themselves faced with higher costs. Higher costs either reduce profits to owners or are passed on to consumers in the form of higher product prices.

But as you will see in Chapter 19, a decreasing portion of the labour force is unionized. In spite of arguments to the contrary, then, to the extent that markets are competitive, the burden of the payroll tax does fall heavily on employees.

The incidence of corporate profit taxes

Another tax that requires careful analysis is corporate profit tax. The *corporate profits tax* or *corporation income tax* is a tax on the profits of firms that are organized as corporations. The owners of partnerships and proprietorships do not pay this tax; rather, they report their firms' income directly on their individual income tax returns.

We can think of the corporate tax as a tax on *capital income*, or profits, in one sector of the economy. For simplicity we assume there are only two sectors of the economy – corporate and non-corporate – and only two factors of production – labour and capital. Owners of capital receive profits, and workers (labour) are paid a wage.

As you can see from Table 18.5, taxes paid by corporations on their profits contribute much less to government revenue than social security contributions. The variation in their importance between EU countries is rather less. One possible explanation for this is the relative ease with which large companies can move operations between countries if they feel that corporate taxes are relatively high where they are at present. Governments, then, are relatively powerless to raise corporate taxes sharply.

Like payroll tax, corporation tax may affect households on the sources or the uses side of the income equation. The tax may affect profits earned by owners of capital, wages earned by workers, or prices of corporate and non-corporate products. Once again, the key question is how large these changes are likely to be.

When first imposed, the corporate profit tax initially reduces net (after-tax) profits in the corporate sector. Assuming the economy was in long-run equilibrium before the tax was levied, firms in both the corporate and non-corporate sectors were earning a *normal rate of return*; there was no reason to expect higher profits in one sector than in the other. All of a sudden, firms in the corporate sector become significantly less profitable as a result of the tax.

Table 18.5 Percentage of total taxes paid by corporations in EU countries

Country	%
Austria	3.4
Belgium	6.2
Denmark	5.9
Finland	2.7
France	5.1
Germany	3.2
Greece	8.8
Ireland	n/a*
Italy	8.6
Netherlands	7.4
Spain	n/a*
Sweden	5.0
UK	8.3

* Components of direct taxation were not separately identified.

Figures are for 1994.

Source: Economic Trends.

In response to these lower profits, capital investment begins to favour the non-taxed sector because after-tax profits are higher there. Firms in the taxed sector contract in size or (in some cases) go out of business, while firms in the non-taxed sector expand and new firms enter its various industries. As this happens, the flow of capital from the taxed to the non-taxed sector reduces the profit rate in the non-taxed sector: more competition springs up, and product prices are driven down. Some of the tax burden shifts to capital income earners in the non-corporate sector, who end up earning lower profits.

As capital flows out of the corporate sector in response to lower after-tax profits, the profit rate in that sector rises somewhat because fewer firms means less supply, which means higher prices, and so on. Presumably, capital will continue to favour the non-taxed sector until the after-tax profit rates in the two sectors are equal. Even though the tax is imposed on just one sector, it eventually depresses profits in all sectors equally.

Under these circumstances, the products of corporations will probably become more expensive and products of proprietorships and partnerships will probably become less expensive. But because almost everyone buys both corporate and non-corporate products, these *excise effects* (that is, effects on the prices of products) are likely to have a minimal impact on the distribution of the tax burden; in essence, the price increases in the corporate sector and the price decreases in the non-corporate sector cancel each other out.

Finally, what effect does the imposition of a corporate income tax have on labour? Wages could actually rise or fall, but the effect is not likely to be large. Taxed firms will have an incentive to substitute labour for capital because capital income is now taxed. This could benefit labour by driving up wages. In addition, the contracting sector will use less labour *and* capital, but if the taxed sector is the capital-intensive corporate sector, the bulk of the effect will be felt by capital; its price will fall more than the price of labour.

The burden of corporation tax

The ultimate burden of the corporate profit tax appears to depend on several factors: the relative capital/labour intensity of the two sectors, the ease with which capital and labour can be substituted in the two sectors, and elasticities of demand for the products of each sector. In 1962 Arnold Harberger of the University of Chicago analysed this problem rigorously and concluded:

> Owners of corporations, proprietorships and partnerships all bear the burden of the corporate tax in rough proportion to profits, even though it is directly levied only on corporations.

He also found that wage effects of the corporate tax were small and that excise effects, as we noted, probably cancel each other out.[7]

Although most economists accept Harberger's view of corporate income tax, there are arguments against it. For example, a profits tax on a monopoly firm earning above-normal profits is *not* shifted to other sectors unless the tax drives profits below the competitive level.

You might be tempted to conclude that because monopolists can control market price, they will simply pass on the profits tax in higher prices to consumers of monopoly products. But theory predicts just the opposite: that the tax burden will remain with the monopolist.

Remember that monopolists are constrained by market demand. That is, they choose the combination of price and output that is consistent with market demand and that maximizes profit. If a proportion of that profit is taxed, the choice of price and

---

[7] *Arnold Harberger, 'The incidence of the corporate income tax'*, Journal of Political Economy, LXX (June 1962).

quantity will not change. Why not? Quite simply, if you behave so as to maximize profit, and then I come and take half of your profit, you maximize your half by maximizing the whole, which is exactly what you would do in the absence of the tax. Thus, your price and output do not change, the tax is not shifted, and you end up paying the tax. In the long run, capital will not leave the taxed monopoly sector, as it did in the competitive case. Even with the tax, the monopolist is earning higher profits than are possible elsewhere. To put it another way, the monopolist maximizes profit where $MR = MC$. A tax on profits shifts AC but not MC. Hence, price and output remain the same.

The great debate about whom the corporate tax hurts illustrates the advantage of broad-based direct taxes over narrow-based indirect taxes. Because it is levied on an institution, the corporate tax is indirect, and therefore it is always shifted. Furthermore, it taxes only one factor (capital) in only one part of the economy (the corporate sector). Income tax, in contrast, taxes all forms of income in all sectors of the economy, and it is virtually impossible to shift. It is difficult to argue that a tax is a good tax if we can't be sure who ultimately ends up paying it.

The overall incidence of taxes: empirical evidence

Many researchers have performed complete analyses under varying assumptions about incidence, and in most cases their results are similar. We can draw tentative conclusions for most EU countries:

> Indirect taxes seem as a group to be mildly regressive. Direct taxes, dominated by the individual income tax, are mildly progressive. The overall system is mildly progressive.

Excess burdens and the principle of neutrality

You have seen that when households and firms make decisions in the presence of a tax that differ from those they would make in its absence, the burden of the tax can be shifted from those for whom it was originally intended. Now we can take the same logic one step further:

> When taxes distort economic decisions, they impose burdens on society that in aggregate exceed the revenue collected by the government.

excess burden
The amount by which the burden of a tax exceeds the total revenue collected. Also called dead weight losses.

The amount by which the burden of a tax exceeds the revenue collected by the government is called the **excess burden** of the tax. The *total burden* of a tax is the sum of the revenue collected from the tax and the excess burden created by the tax. Because excess burdens are a form of waste, or lost value, tax policy should be written to minimize them. (Excess burdens are also sometimes called *dead weight losses*.)

The size of the excess burden imposed by a tax depends on the extent to which economic decisions are distorted. The general principle that emerges from the analysis of excess burdens is the **principle of neutrality**.

principle of neutrality
All else equal, taxes that are neutral with respect to economic decisions (that is, taxes that do not distort economic decisions) are generally preferable to taxes that distort economic decisions. Taxes that are not neutral impose excess burdens.

> *Ceteris paribus*, or all else equal,[8] a tax that is neutral with respect to economic decisions is preferred to one that distorts economic decisions.

[8]*The phrase* ceteris paribus *(all else equal) is important. In judging the merits of a tax or a change in tax policy, the degree of neutrality is only one criterion among many, and it often comes into conflict with others. For example, tax A may impose a larger excess burden than tax B, but society may deem B more equitable.*

In practice, all taxes change behaviour and distort economic choices. A product-specific excise tax raises the price of the taxed item, and people can avoid the tax by buying substitutes. An income tax distorts the choice between present and future consumption and between work and leisure. The corporate tax influences investment and production decisions – investment is diverted away from the corporate sector, and firms may be induced to substitute labour for capital.

How do excess burdens arise?

The idea that a tax can impose an extra cost, or excess burden, by distorting choices can be illustrated by example. Consider a competitive industry that produces an output, X, using the technology shown in Figure 18.3. Using technology A, firms can produce one unit of output with seven units of capital (K) and three units of labour (L). Using technology B, the production of one unit of output requires four units of capital and seven units of labour. A is thus the more capital-intensive technology.

If we assume labour and capital each cost €2 per unit, it costs €20 to produce each unit of output with technology A and €22 with technology B. Firms will choose technology A. Because we assume competition, output price will be driven to cost of production, and the price of output will in the long run be driven to €20 per unit.

Now let us narrow our focus to the distortion of technology choice that is brought about by the imposition of a tax. Assume demand for the good in question is perfectly inelastic at 1000 units of output. That is, regardless of price, households will buy 1000 units of product. A price of €20 per unit means consumers pay a total of €20,000 for 1000 units of X.

Now suppose the government levies a tax of 50% on capital. This has the effect of raising the price of capital, P_K, to €3. Figure 18.4 shows what would happen to the unit cost of production after the tax is imposed. With capital now more expensive, the firm switches to the more labour-intensive technology B. With the tax in place, X can be produced at a unit cost of €27 per unit using technology A but for €26 per unit using technology B.

If demand is inelastic, buyers continue to buy 1000 units of X regardless of its price. (We shall ignore any distortions of consumer choices that might result from the imposition of the tax.) Recall that the tax is 50%, or 1 euro per unit of capital used. Because it takes four units of capital to produce each unit of output, firms – which are now using technology B – will pay a total tax to the government of €4 per unit of output produced. With 1000 units of output produced and sold, total tax collections amount to €4000.

But if you look carefully, you will see that the burden of the tax exceeds €4000. After the tax, consumers will be paying €26 per unit for the good; €26 is now the unit cost of producing the good using the best available technology in the presence of the capital tax. Consumers will pay €26,000 for 1000 units of the good. This

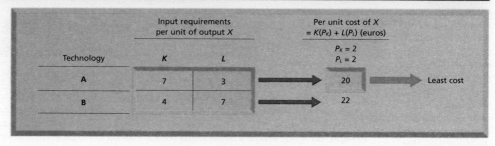

Figure 18.3 Firms choose the technology that minimizes the cost of production

If the industry is competitive, long-run equilibrium price will be €20 per unit of X. If 1000 units of X are sold, consumers will pay a total of €20,000 for X.

Technology	Input requirements per unit of output X		Per unit cost of X = K(P_K) + L(P_L) (euros) $P_K = 2$ $P_L = 2$
	K	L	
A	7	3	20 Least cost
B	4	7	22

Figure 18.4 Imposition of a tax on capital distorts the choice of technology

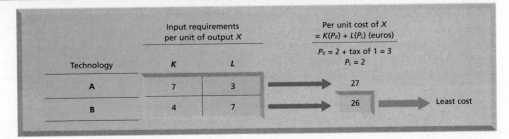

If the industry is competitive, price will be €26 per unit of X when a tax of 1 euro per unit of capital is imposed. If technology B is used, and if we assume that total sales remain at 1000 units, total tax collections will be 1000 × 4 × 1 = €4000. But consumers will pay a total of €26,000 for the good – €6000 more than before the tax. Thus, there is an excess burden of €2000.

represents an increase of €6000 over the previous total of €20,000. The revenue raised from the tax is €4000, but its total burden is €6000. Thus, there is an *excess burden* of €2000.

How did this excess burden arise? Look back at Figure 18.3. You can see that technology B is less efficient than technology A (unit costs of production are €2 per unit higher using technology B). But the tax on capital has caused firms to switch to this less efficient, labour-intensive mode of production. The result is a waste of €2 per unit of output. The total burden of the tax is equal to the revenue collected plus the loss due to the wasteful choice of technology, and the excess burden is €2 per unit times 1000 units, or €2000.

The same principle holds for taxes that distort consumption decisions. Suppose that I prefer to consume bundle X to bundle Y when there is no tax but choose bundle Y when there is a tax in place. Not only do I pay the tax, I also end up with a bundle of goods that is worth less than the bundle I would have chosen had the tax not been levied. Again, we have the burden of an extra cost.

> The larger the distortion that a tax causes in behaviour, the larger the excess burden of the tax. Taxes levied on broad bases tend to distort choices less and impose smaller excess burdens than taxes on more sharply defined bases.

This follows from our discussion earlier in this chapter: the more partial the tax, the easier it is to avoid. A tax that has no excess burden is the so called 'lump sum tax'. Under a lump sum tax, what you pay does not depend on your behaviour or your income or your wealth. Everyone pays the same amount; there is no way to avoid the tax. In 1990, the UK government of Prime Minister Margaret Thatcher replaced the local property tax with a tax that was very similar to a lump sum tax. Such a tax is by its nature highly regressive, and the its perceived unfairness led to its repeal.

The principle of second best

Now that we have established the connection between taxes that distort decisions and excess burdens, we can add more complexity to our earlier discussions. Although it may seem that distorting taxes always create excess burdens, this is not necessarily the case. A distorting tax is sometimes desirable when other distortions already exist in the economy. This is called the **principle of second best**.

principle of second best

The fact that a tax distorts an economic decision does not always imply that such a tax imposes an excess burden. If previously existing distortions exist, such a tax may actually improve efficiency.

> At least two kinds of circumstances favour non-neutral (that is, distorting) taxes: the presence of externalities and the presence of other distorting taxes.

We already examined externalities at some length in Chapter 16. If some activity by a firm or household imposes costs on society that are not considered by decision makers, then firms and households are likely to make economically inefficient choices. Pollution is the classic example of an externality, but there are thousands of others. An

Applications

The Swedish tax system under scrutiny

Swedish citizens pay high levels of tax. An article in the *Financial Times* examines this burden.

Agneta Edberg, a secretary from Gothenburg, could be a typical Swede. From her [Swedish kronor] Skr180,000 ($22,800) annual salary she takes home Skr117,600, after a 34.7 per cent deduction for income tax and state pension contributions. Property tax, sales tax and a cluster of other direct and indirect taxes combine to reduce her real income to Skr82,800, less than half her gross wage.

Ms Ekberg would derive limited benefit from a pay rise to offset the high tax imposition. Anyone earning above Skr209,100 ($26,500) a year is classed as a high income-earner and must pay an additional 5 per cent in marginal income tax. Beyond this point the income tax scale rises sharply, so that someone earning as little as Skr240,000 pays the top marginal rate of 59 per cent.

It is small wonder that Sweden has the second-highest tax burden in the industrialized world, after Denmark. Tax accounted for 49.7 per cent of Swedish gross domestic product in 1995, according to the Organization for Economic Cooperation and Development.

According to the Swedish Taxpayers' Association, the tax burden rose to 53.7 per cent of GDP in 1996. Björn Tarrs-Wahlberg, the association's managing director, says that the weakness of the current system is not the amount of tax paid by the wealthy but the size of the imposition levied on lower income groups.

'We have never had such high taxes on low and middle-income earners in Sweden as now', he says. 'The problem is that welfare provision is over-generous and extends to too wide a range of people.'

The munificence of Sweden's welfare state is well documented. In 1996 the country spent 36 per cent of GDP on welfare as defined by the OECD – more than any other country. Most is funded via Sweden's big public sector: public spending amounted to 63 per cent of GDP in 1996.

Opponents of high taxes blame the current framework for serious structural economic weaknesses. The tax regime, they say, impedes growth among small to medium-sized companies (of which Sweden suffers from a relative dearth) and depresses private consumption, thus acting as a brake on economic growth.

Mr Tarras-Wahlberg argues high taxes have helped entrench high unemployment by reducing incentives to work as well as by inflating labour costs. Employers must pay 33 per cent of employee remuneration into social insurance funds and a further 6–8 per cent to cover costs of complementary pensions.

Prime minister Göran Persson argues tax hikes have been an unavoidable element of the government's budget deficit reduction drive. 'I am not against lower taxes', Mr Persson says. 'But Swedes realize the connection between taxes and quality in the public sector.'

Stefan Fölster, economist at the Research Institute for Industrial Economics in Stockholm, warns Sweden's tax and welfare infrastructure will become unworkable unless reformed. Current rules, he says, fail to address the looming impact of demographic change.

Confronted by a low birth rate and an ageing population, future governments will have to increase spending on pensions and care for the elderly.

Mr Fölster argues this will require repeated tax hikes unless welfare services are privatized and people encouraged to take out private social insurance. 'Even if some people believe the current system is sustainable, it certainly won't be in 20 years', he says.

Source: 'A structure under scrutiny', Financial Times (London), 14 April 1998, 'Survey on Sweden', p. III.

efficient allocation of resources can be restored if a tax is imposed on the externality-generating activity that is exactly equal to the value of the damages caused by it. Such a tax forces the decision maker to consider the full economic cost of the decision.

Because taxing for externalities changes decisions that would otherwise be made, it does in a sense 'distort' economic decisions. But its purpose is to force decision makers to consider real costs that they would otherwise ignore. In the case of pollution, for example, the distortion caused by a tax is desirable. Instead of causing an excess burden, it results in an efficiency gain. (Review Chapter 16 if this is not clear.)

A distorting tax can also improve economic welfare when there are other taxes present that already distort decisions. Suppose that there were only three goods, X, Y and Z. Suppose further that there was a 5% excise tax on both Y and Z. The taxes on Y and Z distort consumer decisions away from those goods and towards X. Imposing a similar tax on X reduces the distortion of the existing system of taxes. When consumers face equal taxes on all goods, they cannot avoid the tax by changing what they buy. The distortion caused by imposing a tax on X corrects for a pre-existing distortion – the taxes on Y and Z.

Let's return to the example described earlier in Figures 18.3 and 18.4. Imposing the tax of 50% on the use of capital generated revenues of €4000 but imposed a burden of €6000 on consumers. A distortion now exists. But what would happen if the government now imposed an additional tax of 50%, or 1 euro per unit, on labour? Such a tax would push our firm back towards the more efficient technology A. In fact, the labour tax will generate a total revenue of €6000, but the burden it imposes on consumers would be only €4000. (It is a good idea for you to work these figures out yourself.)

Optimal taxation

The idea that taxes work together to affect behaviour has led tax theorists to search for optimal taxation systems. Knowing how people will respond to taxes would allow us to design a system that minimized the overall excess burden. For example, if we know the elasticity of demand for all traded goods, we can devise an optimal system of excise taxes that are heaviest on those goods with relatively inelastic demands and lightest on those goods with relatively elastic demands.

Of course, it is impossible to collect all the information required to implement the optimal tax systems that have been suggested. This point brings us full circle, and we end up where we started, with the *principle of neutrality*: all else equal, taxes that are neutral with respect to economic decisions are generally preferable to taxes that distort economic decisions. Taxes that are not neutral impose excess burdens.

Measuring excess burdens

It is possible to measure the size of excess burdens if we know something about how people respond to price changes. Look at the demand curve in Figure 18.5. The product originally sold for a price, P_0, equal to marginal cost (which, for simplicity, we assume is constant). As you recall, when input prices are determined in competitive markets, marginal cost reflects the real value of the resources used in producing the product.

Figure 18.5 The excess burden of a distorting excise tax

A tax that alters economic decisions imposes a burden that exceeds the amount of taxes collected. An excise tax that raises the price of a good above marginal cost drives some consumers to buy less desirable substitutes, reducing consumer surplus.

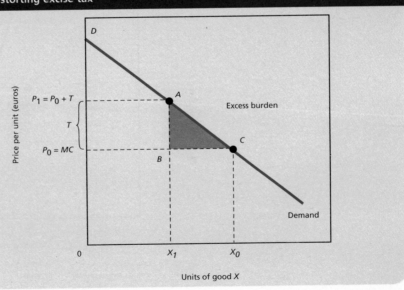

To measure the total burden of the tax we need to recall the notion of consumer surplus from Chapter 6. At any price, some people pay less for a product than it is worth to them. All we reveal when we buy a product is that it is worth *at least* the price being charged. For example, if only one unit of product X were auctioned, someone would pay a price close to D in Figure 18.5. By paying only P_0, that person received a 'surplus' equal to $(D - P_0)$. (For a review of consumer surplus and how it is measured, see Chapter 6.)

Consider what happens when an excise tax raises the price of X from P_0 to $P_1 = P_0 + T$, where T is the tax per unit of X. First, the government collects revenue. The amount of revenue collected is equal to T times the number of units of X purchased (X_1). You can see that $T \times X_1$ is equal to the area of rectangle P_1ABP_0. Second, since consumers now pay a price of P_1, the consumer surplus generated in the market is reduced from the area of triangle DCP_0 to the area of the smaller triangle DAP_1. The excess burden is equal to the original (pre-tax) consumer surplus *minus* the after-tax surplus *minus* the total taxes collected by the government.

In other words, the original value of consumer surplus (triangle DCP_0) has been broken up into three parts: the area of triangle DAP_1 that is still consumer surplus; the area of rectangle P_1ABP_0 that is tax revenue collected by the government; and the area of triangle ACB that is lost. Thus, the area ACB is an approximate measure of the excess burden of the tax. The total burden of the tax is the sum of the revenue collected and the excess burden: the area of P_1ACP_0.

Excess burdens and the degree of distortion

The size of the excess burden that results from a decision-distorting tax depends on the degree to which decisions change in response to that tax. In the case of an excise tax, consumer behaviour is reflected in elasticity of demand:

The more elastic the demand curve, the greater is the distortion caused by any given tax rate.

Figure 18.6 The size of the excess burden of a distorting excise tax depends on the elasticity of demand

The size of the excess burden from a distorting tax depends on the degree to which decisions or behaviours change in response to it.

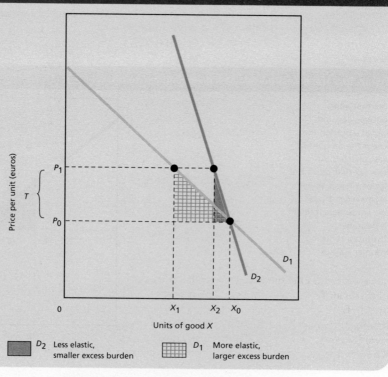

D_2 Less elastic, smaller excess burden

D_1 More elastic, larger excess burden

Figure 18.6 shows how the size of the consumer response determines the size of the excess burden. At price P_0, the quantity demanded by consumers is X_0. Now suppose that the government imposes a tax of T euros per unit of X. The two demand curves (D_1 and D_2) illustrate two possible responses by consumers. The change in quantity demanded along D_1 (from X_0 to X_1) is greater than the change in quantity demanded along D_2 (from X_0 to X_2). In other words, the response of consumers illustrated by D_1 is more elastic than the response of consumers along D_2.

The excess burdens that would result from the tax under the two alternative assumptions about demand elasticity are approximately equal to the areas of the shaded triangles in Figure 18.6. As you can see, where demand is more responsive (more elastic), the excess burden is larger.

If demand were perfectly inelastic, no distortion would occur, and there would be no excess burden. The tax would simply transfer part of the surplus being earned by consumers to the government. That is why some economists favour uniform land taxes over other taxes. Because land is in perfectly inelastic supply, a uniform tax on all land uses distorts economic decisions less than taxes levied on other factors of production that are in variable supply.

Summary

The economics of taxation

1. Public finance is one of the major subfields of applied economics. A major interest within this subfield is the economics of taxation.

2. Taxes are ultimately paid by people. Taxes may be imposed on transactions, institutions, property and all kinds of other things, but in the final analysis, taxes are paid by individuals or households.

3. The *base* of a tax is the measure or value upon which the tax is levied. The *rate structure* of a tax determines the portion of the base that must be paid in tax.

4. A tax whose burden is a constant proportion of income for all households is a *proportional tax*. A tax that exacts a higher proportion of income from higher-income households is a *progressive tax*. A tax that exacts a lower proportion of income from higher-income households is a *regressive tax*. In Europe, income taxes are progressive, and VAT and excise taxes are regressive.

5. Your average tax rate is the total amount of tax you paid divided by your total income. Your marginal tax rate is the tax rate that you pay on any additional income that you've earned. Marginal tax rates have the most influence on behaviour.

6. There is much disagreement over what constitutes a fair tax system. One theory contends that people should bear tax burdens in proportion to the benefits that they receive from government expenditures. This is the *benefits-received principle*. Another contends that people should bear tax burdens in line with their ability to pay. This *ability-to-pay principle* has dominated European tax policy.

7. The three leading candidates for best tax base are income, consumption and wealth.

Tax incidence: who pays?

8. As a result of behavioural changes and market adjustments, tax burdens are often not borne by those initially responsible for paying them. When we speak of the *incidence of a tax*, we are referring to the ultimate distribution of its burden.

9. Taxes change behaviour, and changes in behaviour can affect supply and demand in markets, causing prices to change. When prices change in input markets or in output markets, some people may be made better off and some worse off. These final changes determine the ultimate burden of a tax.

10. *Tax shifting* occurs when households can alter their behaviour and do something to avoid paying a tax. In general, broad-based taxes are less likely to be shifted and more likely to stick where they are levied than partial taxes are.

11. Social security contributions are an important source of government revenue in each EU country, though the proportion of total government income raised by such *payroll taxes* varies between countries.

12. When labour supply is more elastic, firms bear the bulk of a tax imposed on labour. When labour supply is more inelastic, workers bear the bulk of the tax burden. Because labour supply tends to be inelastic in Europe, most economists conclude that most of the payroll tax is probably borne by workers.

13. The ultimate burden of corporate profit tax appears to depend on several factors. One generally accepted study shows that the owners of corporations, proprietorships and partnerships all bear the burden of corporation tax in rough proportion to profits, even though it is directly levied only on corporations; that wage effects are small; and that excise effects are roughly neutral. However, there is still much debate about whom the corporate tax 'hurts'. The burden of corporation tax is progressive, because profits and capital income make up a much bigger part of the incomes of high-income households.

14. In the EU, and under a reasonable set of assumptions about tax shifting, indirect taxes seem as a group to be mildly regressive. Direct taxes, dominated by the individual income tax, are mildly progressive. The overall system is for most EU countries mildly progressive.

Excess burdens and the principle of neutrality

15. When taxes distort economic decisions, they impose burdens that in aggregate exceed the revenue collected by the government. The amount by which the burden of a tax exceeds the revenue collected by the government is called the *excess burden*. The size of excess burdens depends on the degree to which economic decisions are changed by the tax. The *principle of neutrality* holds that the most efficient taxes are broad-based taxes that do not distort economic decisions.

16. The *principle of second best* holds that a tax that distorts economic decisions does not necessarily impose an excess burden. If previously existing distortions or externalities exist, such a tax may actually improve efficiency.

(Optional) Measuring excess burdens

17. The excess burden imposed by a tax is equal to the pre-tax consumer surplus minus the after-tax consumer surplus minus the total taxes collected by the government. The more elastic the demand curve, the greater is the distortion caused by any given tax rate.

Review Terms and Concepts

ability-to-pay principle	regressive tax
benefits-received principle	sources side *and* uses side
excess burden	tax base
principle of neutrality	tax incidence
principle of second best	tax rate structure
progressive tax	tax shifting
proportional tax	

Problem Set

1. Some EU countries have, in recent years, raised less from income tax and more from value-added tax (VAT). Do you favour such a shift? What are the arguments for and against it?

2. Suppose that in 1999 your country passed a new and simple income tax with a flat rate of 25% on all income over €25,000 (no tax is payable on the first €25,000). Assume that the tax is imposed on every individual separately. For each of the following total income levels (in euros) calculate taxes due and compute the average tax rate: 25,000; 35,000; 45,000; 60,000; 80,000; 100,000. Plot the average tax rate on a graph with income along the X axis. Is the tax proportional, progressive or regressive? Explain why.

3. A citizens' group in Europe has the following statement in its charter: 'Our goal is to ensure that large, powerful corporations pay their fair share of taxes in this country.' To implement this goal, the group has recommended and lobbied for an increase in corporation tax and a reduction in individual income tax. Would you support the group's proposal? Explain your logic.

4. 'Taxes imposed on necessities that have low demand elasticities impose large excess burdens because consumers can't avoid buying them.' Do you agree or disagree? Explain.

5. For each of the following, do you agree or disagree? Why?
a. 'Economic theory predicts unequivocally that reductions in social security contributions will increase the supply of labour.'
b. 'Corporation taxes levied on a monopolist are likely to be regressive, because the monopoly can pass on their burden to consumers.'
c. 'All non-neutral taxes are undesirable.'

6. In calculating total staff pay, the administration of Egghead University includes the payroll taxes (social security contributions) it pays as a *benefit* to teaching staff. After all, those tax payments are earning future entitlements for members of staff faculty under social security. However, the Professional Professors' Association has argued that, far from being a benefit, the employer's contribution is simply a tax and that its burden actually falls on staff members, even though it is paid by the university. Discuss both sides of this debate.

7. Developing countries rarely have sophisticated income tax schemes like those in Europe. The primary means of raising revenues in many developing countries is through commodity taxes. What problems do you see with taxing particular goods in these countries? (*Hint*: Think about elasticities of demand.)

8. Suppose a special tax were introduced that used the value of one's car as the tax base. Each person would pay taxes equal to 10% of the value of his or her car. Would the tax be proportional, regressive or progressive? What assumptions do you make in answering this question? What distortions do you think would appear in the economy if such a tax were introduced?

9. You are given the following information on a proposed 'restaurant meals tax' in the Republic of Olympus. Olympus collects no other specific excise taxes, and all other government revenues come from a neutral lump-sum tax. (A lump-sum tax is a tax of a fixed sum paid by all people, regardless of their circumstances.) Assume further that the burden of the tax is fully borne by consumers. Now consider the following data:

- number of meals consumed before the tax: 12 million
- number of meals consumed after the tax: 10 million
- average price per meal: €15 (not including the tax)
- tax rate: 10%

Estimate the size of the excess burden of the tax. What is the excess burden as a percentage of revenues collected from the tax?

10. Suppose an excise tax of €2 a unit is imposed on a good. Sketch the pre-tax and post-tax supply curves. Now assume that instead of the excise tax, VAT is imposed at 20%. Sketch the post-VAT supply curve. Comment on the different effects of the two taxes on industry supply.

19

The Economics of Labour Markets and Trades Unions

Throughout the European Union, millions of people in the civilian labour force hold jobs. Somehow, all these people sorted themselves into thousands of different occupations and jobs, performing an array of tasks in exchange for wages that range from a few euros an hour to millions of euros a year. Some have little or no formal education; others have invested many years in education and training. Some work only part-time; others hold more than one job. Some large employers hire hundreds of people each year into well-defined jobs. Small firms may hire only one or two people every few years for loosely defined jobs. And many people work for themselves.

This chapter addresses a number of important questions. How do people and jobs get matched? How are wage rates determined? Under what circumstances do people get trained? When do firms hire? What happens when people lose their jobs? These questions are answered in what we refer to collectively as 'the labour market', but in fact there are many labour markets. There is a market for professional footballers, a market for lawyers, a market for carpenters and a market for unskilled workers. Each market operates under a different set of rules and through a different set of institutions, but the basic forces that drive all of them are the same.

The importance of the labour market to the economy should not be underestimated. Indeed, perhaps the most dramatic of all the changes currently underway in the republics of the former Soviet Union and Eastern Europe is the introduction of a labour market. Under the central planning systems that dominated Eastern Europe before 1989, national planning agencies determined the economies' staffing needs. Training programmes were then designed to meet those needs, and people were channelled through these programmes into jobs. The introduction of a labour market into these systems means that the responsibility for finding a job is left to workers and the responsibility for finding workers is left to firms. Firms can exercise choice in hiring and firing. Presumably, employment and advancement in the Eastern European economies will begin to depend more on productivity.

Earlier chapters have touched on the economics of labour markets. In Chapter 6, we saw decisions that lie behind the labour supply curve; in Chapter 10, the factors that determine the demand for labour; in Chapter 17, reasons for the inequality of wages. After a quick review, this chapter discusses the workings of labour markets in a more systematic fashion.

In the final part of the chapter, we take up the topic of trades unions. Trades unions have existed for hundreds of years, and their effects are the subject of considerable controversy. Do unions succeed in raising wages? Do they create unemployment? What is their impact on productivity? Almost everyone has a strong opinion about unions. Some say they are responsible for many of our economic woes; others believe that they are the only hope for economic justice.

Competitive labour markets: a review

Here is a brief review of a few key concepts before we begin to examine the theory of labour markets. (You may also wish to review Chapter 10 at this point.)

Marginal revenue product and the demand for labour

Remember that firms make several decisions simultaneously: they decide how much to produce, they choose among alternative techniques of production, and they decide how much of each input to demand. If they have market power, they also decide what price to charge. In making these decisions, they use information from product output markets, from input markets, and from their knowledge of technology.

Marginal revenue product (MRP) is central to an understanding of the demand for labour. The **marginal revenue product of labour (MRP_L)** is the additional revenue that a firm would take in by hiring one additional unit of labour, *ceteris paribus*. Because labour is presumed to be productive, hiring more yields more product. The product produced by one marginal unit of labour is called the *marginal physical product of labour* or simply *marginal product of labour*. To be turned into revenue, that product must be sold. Product prices are determined in output markets, and purely competitive firms take them as given. For perfectly competitive firms the added revenue from hiring one more unit of labour is the marginal product of labour (MP_L) times the price of output: $MP_L \times P_X$.[1]

Figure 19.1 graphs a firm's decision to hire in a competitive labour market. The market-determined wage rate is W^*. The firm can hire all the labour it wants at that wage. We can think of W^* as the marginal cost of a unit of labour. Firms will hire as long as the marginal gains in revenue from hiring additional units of labour (MRP_L) equal or exceed W^*. When labour is the only variable input, the MRP curve is the firm's demand curve for labour. When more than one factor of production can vary, the demand curve is more complicated but essentially the same. (As explained in Chapter 10.)

marginal revenue product of labour (MRP_L)

The additional revenue that a firm will take in by hiring one additional unit of labour, ceteris paribus. For perfectly competitive firms, the marginal revenue product of labour is equal to the marginal physical product of labour times the price of output.

Figure 19.1 Demand for labour in competitive markets depends on labour's productivity

Competitive firms will hire labour as long as marginal revenue product of labour (MRP_L = $MP_L \times P_X$) equals or exceeds the market wage, W^*. When labour is the only variable factor of production, the marginal revenue product curve is the demand curve for labour.

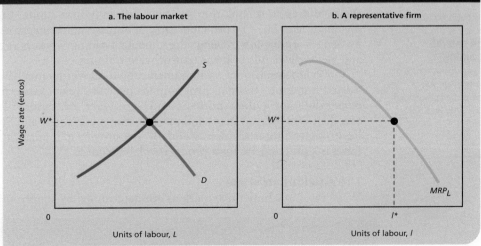

a. The labour market

b. A representative firm

---

[1] *For firms in imperfect markets where output is set by the firm, marginal revenue is equal to marginal physical product times marginal revenue – $MRP_L = MP_L \times MR$. MRP_L is still the revenue gained by hiring an added unit of labour.*

Demand for labour depends on what labour can produce and how much its product sells for in output markets. The *physical* product of labour is technologically determined. Given the state of the technology, machinery and other equipment available, and the level of effort required to produce something, there is a limit to what one unit of labour can produce. The *revenue* product of labour depends on the market value of its product; if no one wants to buy a product, that product has no market value.

The supply of labour

Households supply labour. In any labour market, the supply of labour depends on some factors that households control and some that they do not.

First, each household member must decide whether to work. The alternatives to working for a wage are either working for no pay or enjoying leisure. In this regard, households face a trade-off. Working yields a wage as well as some non-pecuniary rewards and/or costs – you may like your working environment and derive satisfaction from being creative or productive, or you may hate your job because it is dull or dangerous. The opportunity cost of working is either the value of what can be produced using the same time, or the value of leisure. If you are not in the labour force working for a wage, you can redecorate your house, bring up children, or sleep in the sun. All these alternatives have a value that must be weighed in a decision to take a job.

Beyond this basic decision to work or not, there is a more complicated set of choices and constraints. Not everyone can supply his or her labour in every market. Very short people are unlikely to offer themselves as fashion models. A carpenter with no medical training would be breaking the law if she sold herself as a surgeon. Each market requires its own set of skills that workers are either born with or must acquire.

Human capital

human capital
The stock of knowledge, skills and talents that people possess; it can be inborn, or acquired through education and training.

on-the-job training
The principal form of human capital investment, financed primarily by firms.

The stock of knowledge, skills and talents that human beings possess by nature or through education and training is called **human capital**. When people who have special skills or knowledge earn higher wages, a part of their wage can be thought of as a return on human capital.

Both households and firms invest in human capital. The principal form of human capital investment financed mainly by households is education. When parents send their children to school, they are investing in human capital that they hope will pay dividends later on. The principal form of human capital investment financed primarily by firms is **on-the-job training**. Presumably, training workers raises their productivity and yields dividends to firms that provide training.

Governments also invest in human capital. Governments have sponsored and subsidized numerous training programmes over the years. Governments in Europe are responsible for public primary and secondary education. They have also built excellent university systems and provide student financial aid. Some argue that public health expenditures are also essentially investments in human capital. A healthy labour force is a prerequisite for a productive labour force.

The equilibrium wage

Wage rates in competitive markets are determined by supply and demand:

If quantity of labour demanded exceeds quantity of labour supplied, wages should rise until the quantity demanded and the quantity supplied are equal. The resulting higher wages should reduce the quantity of labour demanded and increase the quantity of labour supplied.

Figure 19.2a shows excess demand for labour; as you can see, the initial wage of W_0 rises until the market clears at W^*. When an excess supply of labour exists, we expect

Figure 19.2 Excess demand and supply in labour markets

When excess demand exists, wages will usually rise. When excess supply exists, wages will usually fall.

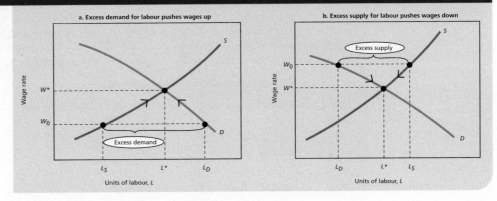

a. Excess demand for labour pushes wages up

b. Excess supply for labour pushes wages down

to see market wages fall. At W_0 in Figure 19.2b, quantity supplied exceeds quantity demanded; this creates a downward pressure on wages. If wages fall, quantity demanded will increase and quantity supplied will fall until equilibrium is restored at W^*.

Disequilibria sometimes persist, however. Minimum wage laws may prevent wages from falling in response to a surplus. Trades union agreements may hold wages above the equilibrium level. Even in competitive markets, some prices are slow to adjust in response to surpluses.

Economic rent and transfer earnings

transfer earnings
Income to a factor of production, such as labour, that covers its opportunity cost.

economic rent
Income to a factor of production, such as labour, in excess of opportunity cost.

In any given labour market all employees receive the same wage. In Figure 19.3 the wage rate paid to all petrol pump attendants is W^*. However, the supply curve for labour shows us that some employees would work for less. For example, if the wage rate W^* is €10,000 per annum, Clarissa is the L_S worker prepared to do the job for €6000, W_0 in Figure 19.3. (W_0 is her **transfer earnings**. Any less and she would transfer to another job, or choose leisure and ride her horses.)

The €6000 is the minimum she would accept to do the job; it is the opportunity cost of doing that job. Clarissa is actually paid €10,000 (the rate sufficient to bring L^* workers into the industry), so she receives €4000 per annum in excess of her transfer earnings. This excess is **economic rent**.

Figure 19.3 Economic rent and transfer earnings of petrol pump attendants

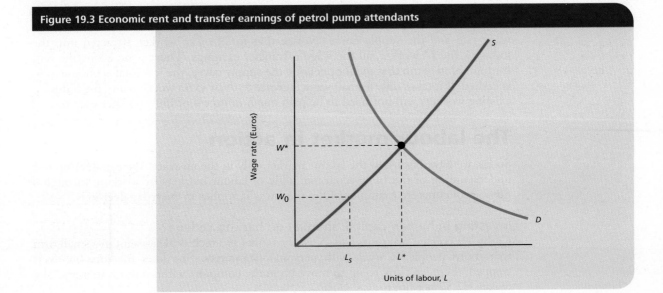

Maths Box 1 Calculating total payments, transfer earnings and economic rent

If we know the supply function for a particular type of labour and we know its price, we can calculate total payments, transfer earnings (*TE*) and economic rent (*ER*). Suppose the supply function for labour is given as $Q_s = -20 + 2W$, where Q_s = quantity of labour supplied per day and W is the wage rate. Now suppose the price of labour is 90 (€) per day:

$Q_s = -20 + 180 = 160$ labour days supplied

Total payments to labour are $Q_s \times W = 160 \times 90 = €14,400$ per day.

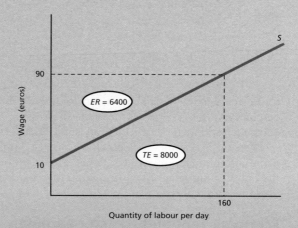

Now find the economic rent. The highest wage at which zero labour is supplied is given as:

$0 = -20 + 2W$

$W = 10$

You can see from the figure that the total economic rent is thus $(80 \times 160)/2 = 6400$. Total transfer earnings are total payments *less* economic rent:

$TE = 14,400 - 6400 = 8000$

For all workers in the industry taken together, transfer earnings is the area under the supply curve to the left of L^*. Economic rent is the triangular area between the wage rate and the supply curve. Notice that for the last worker attracted into the industry, the L^* worker, all the wage is transfer earnings. There is no economic rent for him. Notice too that the more elastic the supply curve, the less total economic rent is earned. If it takes only a small wage increase to draw extra workers into the industry, existing workers will not need to be paid much in excess of their transfer earnings.

The labour market in action

So far, we have discussed the labour market only in the abstract. We can develop our understanding of the basic economic logic of labour markets by working through a number of concrete examples of the theory as it applies in everyday decisions.

Investing in human capital: should I go back to college?

Cathy left college two years ago. Now she works as a technical assistant in a small firm that trains people to work with personal computers. She likes the job, but feels trapped; there isn't any room to move up in the company without more training. She makes €7.50 per hour.

A technical college near Cathy's home is offering a one-year course leading to a certificate of proficiency in two computer languages. With this training, which would move her up a notch in the labour market, she is eligible for a job paying €9.50 per hour. But the college tuition fee is €5000, and students must attend full time. If going to college full time for a year means that Cathy must give up her job, she will incur an opportunity cost of €12,000 in take-home pay (€15,000, less taxes of €3000) in addition to the €5000 tuition fee. If the books and materials that she needs for the course cost another €1000, the full cost of her course is €18,000. Cathy must decide if the investment is worth making.

Cathy is considering an investment in human capital. The training will increase her productivity and her future wages. Figure 19.4 shows some simple calculations. If we assume Cathy works 40 hours per week and 50 weeks per year, her gross wages will increase by €4000 each year when she graduates from college. To determine the *net* return, we must remember to subtract taxes. At her income level, the marginal tax rate (the rate applicable to marginal amounts of income) is, we will assume, 25%.[2] After tax, Cathy's income will be €3000 a year higher if she gets the training.

If these flows continue into the future – that is, if they will stay the same in 'real', or inflation-adjusted, euros – then Cathy's investment will yield 16.7% (3000 ÷ 18,000) per year in real terms. Whether this is a 'good' return depends on the market. In 1998, long-term savings bonds yielded about 6% before taking inflation into account. Cathy's expected return is certainly better than that on a savings account, which pays only about 3 or 4%.

But there is much more to Cathy's case than this. For one, we have counted only costs and benefits measured in actual income. When people make decisions, they usually add other costs and benefits into their calculations. Some people hate college

Figure 19.4 Analysis of a decision to go back to college for one year

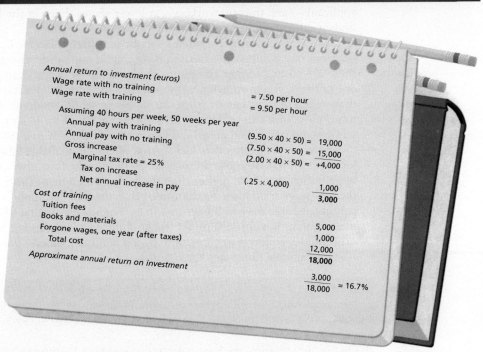

Annual return to investment (euros)	
Wage rate with no training	= 7.50 per hour
Wage rate with training	= 9.50 per hour
Assuming 40 hours per week, 50 weeks per year	
Annual pay with training	(9.50 × 40 × 50) = 19,000
Annual pay with no training	(7.50 × 40 × 50) = 15,000
Gross increase	(2.00 × 40 × 50) = +4,000
Marginal tax rate = 25%	
Tax on increase	(.25 × 4,000) 1,000
Net annual increase in pay	3,000
Cost of training	
Tuition fees	5,000
Books and materials	1,000
Forgone wages, one year (after taxes)	12,000
Total cost	18,000
Approximate annual return on investment	$\frac{3,000}{18,000}$ = 16.7%

[2] *Notice that Cathy's average tax rate is only 20%. She is currently paying a total of €3000 in taxes on an income of €15,000. What matters when we calculate her gains from the new job at the margin is her marginal tax rate, which is 25%. (Review Chapter 18 if you are unsure why this is so.)*

and can't stand studying; this adds to the cost of the investment. At college, however, students might make valuable contacts, and they can use the college careers office to get job interviews. And the higher-paying job might offer intangible psychological rewards and nicer people to work with. All of these benefits would add to the yield of the investment.

Often these 'utility' gains and losses dominate the pecuniary costs and benefits. Someone might decide to pursue a Ph.D. in classics, even if the probability of landing a good university or college teaching position in the field was very low. The yield on such an investment would lie entirely in psychological rewards.

Taxes and financial aid affect the yields of different courses of action and also have an impact on decisions. For example, a 5000 euro scholarship would reduce the cost of Cathy's investment to €13,000. This raises the yield on the investment to 23% (3000 ÷ 13,000), and might well tip the balance in favour of going back to college.

A cut in taxes would have the conflicting effects of increasing the cost of the training while increasing the net benefits. Cathy would sacrifice more take-home pay (higher forgone earnings) to attend college, but she would get to keep more of the 4000 euro annual wage increase in the foreseeable future. The net effect will probably be to increase the return on an investment made now.

What does McDonald's pay?

At two locations a 40 kilometres apart, McDonald's employs workers at very different wage rates. At one franchise, a small sign on the counter reads 'Help wanted, full or part time'. You ask about a job and find that only one part-time opening is available, and that the wage rate offered is the minimum wage.[3] At the other location, a large sign says 'Full-time or part-time positions available, day or night shifts, excellent benefits'. Furthermore, the wage rate offered is much higher. There are six positions available at this second location.

Why would one restaurant pay wages much higher than an identical restaurant with identical jobs in the same region? Simply, because the franchise owner has no applicants – and thus no workers – at lower wages. Even at the higher wage rates, she finds it difficult to keep her positions filled.

The two restaurants are buying labour in different labour markets. If people could get from one point to another at no cost, such wage differences would disappear. But there are costs. Neither restaurant is accessible by public transport. To take a job at one of them, you must live nearby or have a car. Fast food restaurants like McDonald's draw much of their labour from the supply of school students who want to work part time; most don't have cars. The high-wage franchise is some distance from local schools and residential areas; the low-wage franchise is in a town centre.

There are probably other factors that affect the available labour supplies at the two locations as well. Suppose the average income of the four towns surrounding the high-wage franchise is 50% higher than the average income of the four towns surrounding the low-wage franchise. To the extent that the labour supply is made up of students, parents' income may well have an effect. Higher-income families may spend some of their money buying leisure for their children, while many lower-income families expect older children to contribute to the family income.

This example illustrates three points:

First, labour supply depends on a number of factors, including wage rates, non-labour income and wealth. Second, individual firms have very little control over the market wage; firms are forced to pay the wage that is determined by the market. Finally, because people cannot get from one place to another free of charge, and because most people do not reside at their work places – as capital does – there is an important spatial dimension to labour markets.

[3]Most EU countries have a minimum wage although the rate varies between counties.

Different supply and demand conditions can and do prevail at different locations. This is true across regions as well as within cities. Labour markets in different regions of the country are very different. The differences are even greater between countries.

The importance of individual preferences

David was a highly paid young lawyer with a major law firm. Three years ago he was made a partner, and his share of the firm's earnings last year was over €150,000. This year he resigned, sold his house and moved to Norway, where he bought a small restaurant and a cabin near the edge of a fjord. The best he can hope to earn from the restaurant is about €20,000 per year, and even that is optimistic.

Were David's decisions irrational? If we calculate the monetary gains and losses, as we did for Cathy, we can see that David is giving up a great deal. But economic theory in no way suggests that such decisions are irrational. David made his decision to accept a lower income in exchange for things from which he derives utility. The hectic life of a big city may have been a significant cost to him. The beauty of the Norwegian countryside and the pure air may be invaluable benefits. He may like skiing, or he might simply have wanted to buy more leisure time. In other words,

> Preferences play a very important role in the decisions we make about labour supply and in the decisions we make about what to consume.

There are millions of jobholders in Europe. Every one of them has a unique set of talents and preferences. Every one of them has made a different set of decisions about investing in human capital. Some go to college or university and some do not. Some take up apprenticeships and some do not. Those differences help to explain the way people end up being sorted across jobs.

A word of caution

Do not assume that individual preferences and choices makes generalization about labour market behaviour impossible. An enormous amount of empirical work has documented that labour behaves in predictable ways in response to incentives. The manager of McDonald's in the high-wage area got the desired response by raising wages, not by lowering them. People with high non-wage incomes supply less labour than people with low non-wage incomes.

The fact that labour responds to incentives is important for public policy. One of the central themes behind the economic policies pursued in many countries during the 1980s and 1990s was that workers would respond to tax cuts (and therefore higher after-tax wages) by supplying more labour and working harder.

Labour markets and public policy

The government influences the operation of the labour market in a variety of ways. This section examines current public policy issues that affect the labour market. Specifically, we examine the effects of minimum wage legislation, tax policy, welfare schemes and unemployment insurance.

The minimum wage controversy

minimum wage
The lowest wage that firms are permitted to pay workers.

One strategy for reducing poverty that has been used for almost 100 years in many countries is the minimum wage. A **minimum wage** is the lowest wage that firms are permitted to pay workers. The first minimum wage law was adopted in New Zealand in 1894. Now, many European counties have such laws.

The usefulness of the minimum wage laws is controversial. Opponents argue that minimum wage legislation interferes with the smooth functioning of the labour market and creates unemployment. Proponents argue that it has been successful in raising the wages of the poorest workers and alleviating poverty without creating much unemployment.

These arguments can best be understood with a simple supply and demand diagram. Figure 19.5 shows hypothetical demand and supply curves for unskilled labour. The equilibrium wage rate is €3.40. At that wage, the quantity of unskilled labour supplied and the quantity of unskilled labour demanded are equal. Now suppose that a law is passed setting a minimum wage of €4.25. At that wage rate, the quantity of labour supplied increases from the equilibrium level, L^*, to L_S. At the same time, the higher wage reduces the quantity of labour demanded by firms from L^* to L_D. As a result, firms lay off $L^* - L_D$ workers.

It is true that those workers who remain on payrolls receive higher wages. With the minimum wage in effect, unskilled workers receive €4.25 per hour instead of €3.40. But is it worth it? Some gain while others (including those who had been employed at the equilibrium wage) suffer unemployment.

A high unemployment rate among certain groups, such as unskilled or teenage workers, is cited as evidence that the unemployment problem caused by the minimum wage is significant. For example, almost half the under-24s in Spain are out of work; in France and Italy, the figure is over one in four. It is also argued that if 'relativities' are important and skilled workers expect to be paid proportionately more than the unskilled, minimum wages increase costs to some employers but also to those in other industries as their workers press for higher wages to maintain differentials. Proponents of the minimum wage argue that unemployment data are irrelevant, that the demand for unskilled labour is relatively inelastic with respect to the wage rate, and that only a small part of the unemployment problem is due to the minimum wage.

Supporters of a minimum wage also argue that higher wages can increase productivity. If people are paid more and are valued more highly they will work better. In terms of Figure 19.5, a rise in the wage rate is not only a movement along the supply curve; it also shifts the demand curve for labour upwards and to the right. (Remember: the demand curve for labour is the marginal revenue product curve for workers.)

Figure 19.5 Effect of minimum wage legislation

If the equilibrium wage in the market for unskilled labour is below the legislated minimum wage, the result is likely to be unemployment. The higher wage will attract new entrants to the labour force (quantity supplied will increase from L^* to L_S), but firms will hire fewer workers (quantity demanded will drop from L^* to L_D).

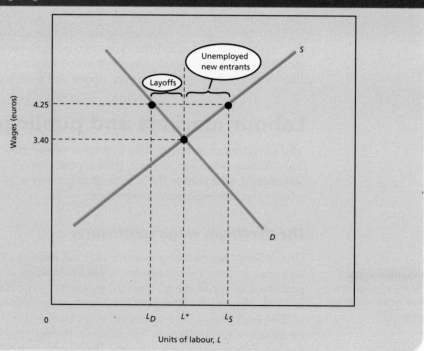

Applications

Who benefits from France's proposed 35-hour week?

Government, employers and unions in France are discussing the introduction of a 35-hour week. *The Economist* reports:

So who really wants Lionel Jospin's 35-hour working week? Certainly not France's employers, who claim it will increase labour costs and reduce their competitiveness. Nor the taxpayer, who suspects he will have to pay higher taxes to finance the scheme. Nor, increasingly, the unions, who fear it will lead to lower wages and fewer workers' rights. Nor even the workers, most of whom expect to continue working as much as before, but with more awkward shifts and unsocial hours. Even the unemployed, the scheme's supposed beneficiaries, are wondering how many jobs, if any, it will actually create.

A revolutionary cut in the working week from 39 to 35 hours 'with no loss of pay' was the star item on the Socialists' election manifesto last summer. It was supposed to create hundreds of jobs, boost productivity and increase leisure time.

How many jobs will be created? Dominique Strauss-Kahn, the finance minister, says perhaps 200,000. Martine Aubry, the employment minister, at first suggested 1m. Sceptics say the scheme will in fact kill jobs.

Nothing in the planned law actually obliges workers to work less, thus making way for the supposed new jobs for France's 3m out of work (12.1% of the new workforce). The bill simply sets a limit (35 hours) beyond which overtime is to be paid. No further mention is made of the reduction in working hours being 'without loss of pay' (which

would have put labour costs up by a hefty 11%). The bill simply states that a cut in wages would be 'undesirable', while the government has begun to talk of the need for 'wage moderation'.

Some ministers, however, talk of making the labour market more flexible, notably by letting employers vary the length of the working week in accordance with seasonal demand, so that the number of hours worked weekly would be calculated as an average over the year. And France's hitherto sacrosanct high minimum wage seems to have been called into question by the plan to introduce two minimums. One would be an hourly rate, rising with inflation and average industrial earnings; the other would be a fixed monthly figure, not subject to indexed hikes.

No wonder the unions are in a tizz. The 35-hour week, hailed only a few months ago by the leader of the Communist-led trade union as 'the most important social advance since 1936', is beginning to look like a Trojan horse. Already some employers are using it as a pretext to dump earlier generous agreements on conditions of work. Other are busy freezing wages, setting up subsidiaries (to escape the 2000 deadline by dividing their workforce into units of less that 20), and even sacking workers in anticipation of the extra costs they fear they will have to face. The great majority claim they have no intention of taking on new workers, 35-hour week or not.

Source: 'Fewer hours, more jobs?', The Economist, 14 April 1998, pp. 46–7.

Taxes and labour supply

One of the beliefs of recent right-wing governments is that high rates of taxation are at the root of the economic problems faced by Europe. High tax rates reduce the incentive to work, save and invest, it is claimed. If tax rates were to go down (increasing take-home pay), more people would go to work, people already working would work harder, and more investment and capital formation would take place. All of this would expand the supply of goods and services.

The European country that has adopted this policy most enthusiastically in the last 20 years is the UK. Although its income tax system is still progressive, its degree of progressiveness is markedly more mild now that the highest marginal tax rate has been cut from 83% to 40%. Some other EU countries have also cut their marginal tax rates for high earners, though the reductions have been much less dramatic than in the UK.

The tax cuts proposed for individuals and families were designed to increase the supply of labour. But economic theory shows that tax cuts could increase or decrease labour supply. Nobody disagrees that reducing taxes on income increases the 'net wage'. The issue is: what is the impact of higher net wages on the supply of labour?

Income and substitution effects of taxes on labour supply

As you recall from Chapter 6, higher wages have both a substitution effect and an income effect. Higher net wages increase the price of leisure. Increasing the price, or opportunity cost, of leisure leads to additional work effort as people find an incentive to substitute other goods, bought with income from working, for leisure. This is the **substitution effect of higher wages**. But higher net wages also make people better off. By working the same number of hours, workers can earn more income. That added income can be spent on any combination of goods, including leisure. Because I have a higher income, I may decide to consume more leisure with the result that I actually work less. This is the **income effect of higher wages**.

The income and substitution effects of higher wages work in opposite directions. If the income effect is larger than the substitution effect, higher net wages will actually reduce the supply of labour.

Wages and elasticity of labour supply

Various studies have attempted to measure the effect of changes in net wages on labour supply, mostly in the USA. One US survey examined 28 studies of the behaviour of adult males and 22 studies of the behaviour of adult females.

Twenty of the 28 studies of men's labour-force behaviour found that the overall elasticity of labour supply with respect to wages is negative but small. A negative wage elasticity means that an increase in wages actually reduces labour supply. Thus, the supply of labour curve for adult males seems to bend back (Figure 6.11b). The negative income effect is therefore larger than the positive substitution effect. All but two of the studies reported positive substitution effects and negative income effects.

Table 19.1 summarizes the results of the general survey. The overall average of wage elasticities for men is –0.06. In other words, a net wage increase of 10% would reduce the supply of male labour by 0.6%. The tax cuts of the 1980s probably had a tiny negative effect on the supply of adult male labour.

The survey showed the opposite effect for women. Of the 22 studies, all but two found a positive overall wage elasticity. This suggests that for women, the substitution effect of a wage increase is greater than the income effect. The average of all 22 studies is 1.94. In other words, an increase in net wages of 10% would increase the supply of adult female labour by a full 9.4%. All but one study of women found a negative income effect, while all the studies that reported substitution elasticities found them to be positive.

Several studies have examined the effects of the sharp drop in marginal tax rates on high UK earners. Flemming and Oppenheimer[4] found no evidence among high income earners of an increased willingness to work when their marginal tax rates were

substitution effect of higher wages

Consuming an additional hour of leisure means sacrificing the wages that would be earned by working. When the wage rate rises, leisure becomes more expensive and households may 'buy' less of it. This means working more.

income effect of higher wages

When wages rise, people are better off. If leisure is a normal good, they may decide to consume more of it and to work less.

Table 19.1 Survey of US labour supply elasticity studies

	Total wage elasticity	Income elasticity	Substitution elasticity
Men (28 studies)	–0.06	–0.16	+0.12
Women (22 studies)	+0.94	–0.17	+0.80
Overall median	+0.10	–0.15	+0.25

Source: Ingemar Hansson and Charles Stuart, 'Tax revenue and the marginal cost of public funds', *Journal of Public Economics* (August 1985).

[4] J. Flemming and P. Oppenheimer, 'Are government spending and taxes too high?' National Institute Economic Review, 157 (July 1996).

reduced. Dilnot and Kell[5] came to broadly the same conclusion. The first significant cut in high-end marginal tax rates was from 83 to 60% in 1979–80. If this were to stimulate effort it would lead to higher earnings and therefore higher income tax revenues. However, the study argued that virtually all of the increase in tax revenues in subsequent years could be explained by factors other than cuts in high earners' marginal tax rates.

Welfare and labour supply

There has always been a concern that, by providing a 'guaranteed' minimum standard of living, welfare schemes available to those at the bottom of the income distribution give potential workers a disincentive to enter the labour force and go to work. Are such worries justified?

When we examined the incentive effects of taxes (Chapter 18), we discovered that income and substitution effects work in opposite directions. Imposing a tax reduces income. If people think of leisure as a good, they will buy less of it and will instead tend to work more when a tax is imposed. But it is also true that imposing a tax or increasing marginal tax rates reduces the opportunity cost, or price, of leisure. With leisure less expensive at the margin, people will tend to buy more of it and work less. Because the two effects counteract each other, theory cannot tell us whether taxes will increase or decrease the supply of labour.

Unlike taxes, however,

Income maintenance programmes produce income and substitution effects that work in the same direction. Theory predicts that both effects will reduce work effort and labour supply. Nearly all income maintenance programmes are targeted on households with low incomes. Because households with higher incomes are ineligible, households that increase their incomes by working will lose some or all of their income maintenance benefits. The system, then, imposes an *implicit tax* on income from labour earned by those who are eligible for welfare.

Income-linked welfare programmes mean that this implicit tax on earnings can be quite high. If you earn €3000 but lose €2000 worth of benefits, your implicit tax rate would be 66%. For some people, the loss of benefits has been estimated at over 100% of marginal income earned.

When we think of loss of benefits as an implicit tax, we conclude that income and substitution effects do not offset each other with an income maintenance programme; labour supply is likely to be lower in the presence of the programme. Income maintenance programmes provide income, some of which is 'spent' on leisure. Withdrawing benefits as income rises also reduces the opportunity cost of leisure. Suppose that for every euro of income I earn, I lose €0.50 in benefits. If the hourly wage available is €4.00, then consuming an extra hour of leisure would cost me only €2.00 (4.00 × 0.50); I give up €4.00 in income but retain €2.00 in benefits. Thus, the substitution effect also leads to a decrease in labour supply.

It seems inevitable, then, that welfare programmes do encourage some people to remain unemployed. This does not, however, provide a conclusive argument for reducing such payments. Once more we have to trade off efficiency against equity. Neither does it mean that equity gains are only available for large efficiency losses. Some have pointed out that the UK's unemployment rates have not been lower than those in other European countries even though its welfare benefits tend to be considerably less. Others have pointed out that in recent years UK unemployment rates have been lower than before, whereas most EU countries seem to be stuck with high levels of unemployment.

[5]A. Dilnot and M. Kell, 'Top-rate tax cuts and incentives: some empirical evidence', Fiscal Studies, 9 (4 November 1988).

Matching jobs and workers: job search

The flow of workers into and out of the labour force is continuous. Some enter higher education, some graduate, others are promoted. As the population ages, some retire. Some people leave jobs, some are dismissed, and some take leave or temporarily drop out of the labour force altogether. At the same time, some firms expand and must hire new workers, changes in technology generate needs for new skills and make others obsolete, and some firms fall on hard times and must lay people off.

This constant flux results in a continuous process of sorting available workers among available jobs. New entrants into the labour force expend time and effort searching for the best possible jobs; firms send recruiters into schools, or 'raid' competing firms, often bringing in candidates from long distances. But no matter how well these systems work:

> The distribution of skills and abilities among the available workforce never corresponds exactly to the skills and abilities currently in demand.

A newspaper can be full of job advertisements at the same time as its headlines lament high unemployment rates! Skills and abilities of available job seekers often do not match firms' needs. Not only do the skills demanded not always match the skills supplied, the location of jobs (labour demand) does not always correspond to the location of job seekers. In 1998, around 20% of the labour force in Spain was out of work, whereas in the UK, the unemployment rate was around 6%.

A person entering the labour force for the first time or considering a job change must carefully sift through the set of jobs that might be available given his or her skills, experience, ability and location. People, even those without highly specialized skills, might have hundreds of possibilities open to them. The problem is finding out about them. Job seeking is a process of gathering data. By making phone calls, applying, being rejected, or perhaps even turning down job offers, job hunters find out what is available and what they can expect. The **job search** is an extended process of information gathering.

job search
The process of gathering information about job availability and job characteristics.

Thinking about the job search as an information-gathering process is revealing. We all want the best available job, the one that matches our abilities and aspirations and pays the highest possible wage. For many people, there are readily available jobs that are not desirable; nearly every university graduate could get a job as a counter assistant at Burger King, but most have higher expectations.

In theory:

> Job hunting by an individual should continue as long as the expected gains from continuing the search exceed the costs of doing so.

The opportunity costs of search are those things that are lost by continuing the search, the most important of which are *forgone earnings* and *time*. Other costs include transport, dressing for interviews, paper, postage and telephone bills. The potential benefits from continuing the search depend on the job seeker's expectations. As the person gathers more and more information, expectations should become more and more accurate.

The government can have a considerable effect on the search process. Consider unemployment benefits. Being laid off, or spending an extended period of time as unemployed – that is, actively looking for a job – can be devastating. During periods of unemployment, suicide rates increase, the crime rate increases and other indicators of 'pain' appear in the economy. To alleviate some of this pain, European countries have an unemployment compensation system that pays benefits to workers who lose their jobs.

Unemployment benefits reduce the cost of job seeking, and some researchers have argued that this results in inefficiency. On average, EU governments make up in unemployment benefit 60% of lost wages. With the costs of looking for a job reduced in this fashion, people have an incentive to prolong the process. Prolonged job search drains tax revenues, artificially increases the unemployment rate, and keeps productive workers out of work – another example of a trade-off between efficiency and equity.

Wage and income differentials

The labour market is not one market – it is made up of many separate, but often closely related, markets, and a general sorting process is always going on. As a result, different occupational groups end up earning different wages, and the distribution of income reflects these differences. Wages differ across jobs for two basic reasons: differences between jobs, and differences between workers.

Some jobs are more desirable than others. Some jobs, like those in coal mining or heavy construction, involve higher levels of risk than others. *Ceteris paribus*, jobs that are more desirable and less risky tend to pay less than jobs that are less desirable and more risky. These wage differences are called compensating differentials.

compensating differentials

Differences in wages that result from differences in working conditions. Risky jobs usually pay higher wages, and highly desirable jobs usually pay lower wages.

In competitive markets, equilibrium wages are equal to the productivity of the marginal worker. And the product of a highly skilled machine operator is clearly worth more than that of an unskilled labourer. An unskilled labourer working on a routine set of tasks adds little to the final value of a product compared to the value added by a skilled machinist working with complex capital equipment. Workers who supply their labour in markets that demand unusual or highly developed skills can expect to earn higher wages, *ceteris paribus*.

But wages are determined by the forces of supply *and* demand. At most major universities, you must have a Ph.D. to be appointed to the humanities staff. The training and skills required are high. But because there are few positions relative to the number of qualified applicants, wages for humanities lecturers have remained low. In contrast, many computing firms have difficulty filling positions. As a result, computer programmers' salaries have increased significantly in recent years.

Earnings differentials

Table 19.2 presents data on wage rate and income differentials in Britain. The price of labour services or wage rates varies considerably between occupations. It also varies between European countries for the same type of labour, though these variations tend to be somewhat smaller. Table 19.2 gives an impression of the huge differences in rewards to different kinds of labour.

If labour mobility were higher, such wage differentials would be much lower between occupations. Because the marginal productivity of labour is much higher for some occupations, the demand curve for that labour is correspondingly greater. *Ceteris paribus*, this would lead to differences in equilibrium wage rates.

However, differences in the demand for labour cannot in and of themselves explain wage rate differentials. After all, if some occupations earn more than others we would expect some people to leave the lower-paid work and seek jobs with better pay. This would reduce labour supply in low-wage occupations and push up pay levels. At the same time, the increase in the supply of labour to better-paid jobs would tend to lower wage rates there. Hence over time we would expect wage rate differentials to be reduced between occupations, notwithstanding big differences in the marginal productivity of labour. Why doesn't this happen?

One reason is that some people do not have sufficient skills and ability. However much a hospital porter may envy a heart surgeon his high salary, the porter may not be capable of doing that work. Some are unable to acquire skills; others are unwilling.

We have also seen that wage rate differentials exist because of non-wage benefits. Such explanations are consistent with efficient markets. However, there are also market inefficiencies and it is to these we now turn.

Table 19.2 Highest and lowest paid occupations, Great Britain, April 1997

Occupation	Average gross weekly pay (£)
Highest paid	
1 General administrators; national government (assistant secretary/Grade 5 and above)	1071.9
2 Treasurers and company financial managers	948.7
3 Medical practitioners	869.8
4 Management consultants, business analysts	775.2
5 Underwriters, claims assessors, common brokers, investment analysts	756.2
6 Organization and methods and work study managers	704.4
7 Police officers (inspector and above)	686.7
8 Solicitors	670.4
9 Education officers, school inspectors	667.0
10 Advertising and public relations managers	666.5
Lowest paid	
1 Kitchen porters, hands	159.4
2 Hairdressers, barbers	163.4
3 Waiters, waitresses	165.3
4 Bar staff	171.8
5 Childcare and related occupations, excluding nursery nurses, playgroup leaders and educational assistants	173.4
6 Counter hands, catering assistants	174.5
7 Petrol pump forecourt assistants	176.4
8 Launderers, dry cleaners, pressers	180.3
9 Retail cash desk and check-out operators	182.9
10 Sewing machinists, menders, darners and embroiderers	184.9

Some occupations are not considered because of small sample size and/or large statistical variation.

Source: Labour Market Trends (November 1997).

Labour market discrimination, crowding and inefficiency

labour market discrimination

Occurs when one group of workers receives inferior treatment from employers because of some characteristic irrelevant to job performance.

Labour market discrimination occurs when one group of workers receives inferior treatment from employers because of some characteristic irrelevant to job performance. Inferior treatment may involve being systematically barred from certain occupations, receiving lower wages, or an inability to win promotion or obtain training.

Suppose women (the same argument can be made for racial and other minorities) were systematically barred from a number of occupations. Let's call those occupations reserved for men sector X, and the rest of the economy sector Y. Since women are excluded from X, the supply of labour in sector X is reduced, and wages are higher than they would otherwise be. At the same time, women must *crowd* into the occupations reserved for them. Such crowding increases the supply of labour in sector Y and pushes wages down. Occupational segregation resulting from discrimination causes a wage differential if the number of restricted jobs is significant.

But there is more to the story than wage differentials. Occupational discrimination also results in a net loss of welfare in the economy. To understand this, you need to recall that the demand for labour depends on the productivity of that labour. When extra workers are crowded into sector Y, wages fall. Because wages are lower, more workers will be hired. (Recall that workers will be hired as long as the value of their product at the margin exceeds the going wage.) With more workers working at a lower wage, the marginal product of workers in Y will end up lower than it otherwise would be.

The opposite occurs in sector X. With fewer workers supplying their labour in the reserved sector, wages remain high. The marginal product of workers in X remains high. What would happen if we transferred one worker at a time from sector Y to sector X? If we assume that the discrimination was unrelated to job qualifications, workers will be moving from a sector in which their productivity was low at the margin to a sector where it is high. The value of the product gained in sector X is greater than the value of the product lost in sector Y. There is thus a net gain in value. *Ending discrimination should increase national income.*

If workers vary in their talents in ways unrelated to gender or race, rules or behaviours that force one group into specific occupations are clearly inefficient.

Critics of discrimination theory argue that competition should put an end to discrimination rather quickly. If women, or any other group that is discriminated against, were more productive than the current wage would suggest, some firms would hire them into the restricted occupations, driving out of business those who persist in their discrimination.

Applications

The Dutch labour market: a model for the rest of Europe?

One country that has managed to have peaceful labour relations and an unemployment rate well below the EU average is The Netherlands, where unemployment is about 6%. *The Economist* analyses their success.

Dutch reform has not only been persistent and far-reaching. It has also occurred with little conflict and without sacrificing a national goal of redistributing money from the rich to the poor.

Consensus lies at the heart of the Dutch success. Since 1983 the government, with the support of employers and unions, has cut public spending as a share of GDP from 60% to 50%. Some of the money saved has been used to reduce employers' social-security contributions to only 7.9% from almost 20% in 1989 to help job-creation. With the same goal, the bottom rate of income tax was halved to 7% in 1994. Top marginal income-tax rates remained at 60%.

In the labour market, the Dutch have tried to combine the flexibility of America with the security of Germany. They have made part-time work easier by permitting part-timers to be paid less than full-timers for the same job. This has helped Dutch companies to adjust their workforce to the demand for labour and has helped unemployed people get back into work. At the same time, centralized wage bargaining has helped build a consensus in favour of wage restraint. Dutch wages in manufacturing have been moderate, compared with Germany and France, where bargaining occurs sector by sector.

Finally, the Dutch have tried to provide incentives to work, because sickness benefits were busting the social-security budget. As long ago as 1985 the value of both unemployment insurance and disability insurance was cut to 70% of final pay from 80%. In 1991 and 1995 the government made it harder to qualify for unemployment; in 1995 it removed the coverage for those who chose to become unemployed. The system has also gradually shifted the burden of supporting the sick onto companies. In 1996, for example, firms became responsible for the benefits paid during the first year of illness.

True, the Dutch performance is not quite as good as it looks. Unemployment is low – but so is employment (at 62% of the economically-active population): many people seem to have dropped out of the workforce altogether. Even so, the employment rate is rising. Such achievements are all the more laudable when set against what has happened elsewhere in Europe.

Source: The Economist, 5 April 1997.

Those who defend the discrimination and crowding theory rejoin that the pure-competition scenario is naive and unrealistic. They argue that the link between productivity and wages is difficult to establish, and that those in positions of power (often white men) have both the incentive and the ability to maintain discriminatory practices over long periods of time.

A lively and emotional debate among labour economists that has ended up in the courts in recent years is the controversy over *comparable worth*. The basic argument is that women are systematically paid less than men for work of equal, or at least comparable, value.

Trades unions

Thus far we have focused on the behaviour of firms and workers in competitive labour markets. There is more to this story, however. For many years, a substantial number of workers have been and still are employed under contracts negotiated between their employers and their trades unions.

Table 19.3 shows that for most European countries the proportion of workers covered by collective bargaining agreements[6] is very high. The UK's figure is much lower, and has been falling for many years. The UK government has been suspicious of trades union power for the last 20 years and has introduced several pieces of legislation that have had the effect of weakening unions. In most of the rest of Europe, collective bargaining is seen as beneficial, and as a way of promoting social solidarity.

The bargaining that takes place between firms' representatives and workers' unions does not necessarily produce the same outcome as the operation of an unregulated, competitive labour market.

Nearly all eligible workers in industries such as cars, mining and steel belong to unions. But workers in other industries (the most significant being the high-tech industries) have lower rates of unionization.

Table 19.3 Collective bargaining coverage in major European countries

Country	Year	Proportion of employees covered by collective agreements (%)
Denmark	1996	55.0
France	1995	90.0
Germany	1996	90.0
Greece	1994	90.0
Ireland	1994	90.0
Netherlands	1996	80.0
Norway	1996	66.0
Spain	1996	82.0
Sweden	1995	85.0
United Kingdom	1994	25.6

Source: World Labour Report, 1997–8.

[6]*Coverage rates are much higher than the proportion of an industry's workers in a union. Unions often bargain for a wage rate for a whole industry or sector; this rate is then set for all employees, whether they are unionized or not.*

Global Perspectives

Trades unions around the world

Union membership in the USA has been on the decline since peaking at over 35% of employed workers during the 1950s. But union membership has not been declining in other parts of the world. Membership is steady or growing in many countries, including Canada, Denmark, Sweden and Germany. Union membership is at its highest in Sweden and Denmark, where only one in ten workers is not in a union.

The roles and functions of trades unions differ from country to country. In the USA, labour unions negotiate contracts and bargain on workers' behalf. Although US unions have historically supported Democratic candidates, their goals are basically economic, not political. As the 1994–95 baseball strike and the 1997 UPS strike showed, the relationship between unions and firms in the USA tends to be adversarial, sometimes violent. Normally, industries rather than individual firms are unionized. The government's role is limited to ensuring that firms and unions 'play by the rules'. The National Labor Relations Board oversees collective bargaining to make sure it is fair.

In other countries, the government is much more involved in union matters, and firms and unions cooperate to a much greater extent. Often, union goals are political as well as economic. For example, in the United Kingdom, where almost half of all wage and salary workers are union members, many unions have strong historical links with the Labour party, and most are actively involved in all aspects of politics.

In Japan, unions and firms are highly cooperative. Large companies like Toyota and Hitachi have what are called *enterprise unions*. Each enterprise union represents only one company's workers, so its loyalty is not divided among different companies. The Japanese tradition of lifelong employment goes some way toward explaining the relationships that exist between firms and unions and their cooperative focus on firms' long-term prosperity.

The system of labour relations in Germany is called *industrial democracy*. German law requires all companies to involve workers in the decision-making process. Works councils are made up of managers and workers who are jointly responsible for work rules and many

German railway employees demonstrate in front of the Deutsche Bahn AG railway company headquarters in Frankfurt, April 30 1998. The workers have threatened to launch a railway strike if employers do not agree to their demands for a pay rise.

operational decisions. In addition, between a third and a half of all boards of directors of German corporations have worker representatives as members, a system known as *codetermination*. Bargaining in Germany is undertaken across industries and, as in Japan, a spirit of cooperation exists between workers and managers.

In Sweden and in Denmark, almost all workers belong to unions. Unions are actually involved in setting wage levels nationally. In Sweden, unions are represented on many governmental commissions, where they represent workers.

Unfortunately, there are signs that the labour relations systems in both Germany and Japan are in danger. Recent recessions in both countries have put pressure on employment practices and are eroding the traditionally close cooperation between management and workers. In Germany, high labour costs and the economic costs of reunification are forcing companies to drive a harder bargain with unions. And in Japan, a closer look at lifetime employment policies shows that they have always been restricted to the largest companies, apply only to men, and end at age 55. Moreover, in recent years companies that have had such policies have been scaling them back.

Economic effects of trades unions

Modern trades unions do not focus exclusively on pay. Much of their concern is for the wider welfare of members, including health and safety, training and other benefits. However, here we focus on trades union attempts to influence pay levels.

One way to analyse union power is to think of a union as a monopolistic seller of labour in a market. If there were many buyers, the union would be similar to a pure monopolist selling in output markets: the union would restrict the supply of labour and charge a wage rate above the competitive equilibrium wage rate. But wages may not be the only concern of unions. Other objectives might include keeping all of their members employed, or improving working conditions.

Unions as monopolies

Let us assume that a union is the only seller of labour in some market. And suppose, as an initial condition, union membership is less than the number of workers that would be employed if the market were competitively organized and that the union's objective is to maximize its members' wages and keep them all employed. In Figure 19.6, if there were 2200 union members, the union would set a wage of €8, corresponding to the relevant point on the demand curve for labour. This is above the competitive wage rate of €6. At €8, 4200 labourers are working or available for work, but firms will hire only 2200 of them. There would be an excess supply of workers, or unemployment, in this market equal to the difference between 4200 and 2200 (= 2000), but the unemployed would all be non-union workers.

For the 8 euro wage to hold, the union would have to restrict membership, because increasing the number of union members would also mean decreasing the wages that union members receive. (This is implied by the downward-sloping demand curve.) Restriction of union membership is common. Some unions simply refuse to admit new members; others have long apprenticeships that must be completed before a worker is admitted.

The distinction between unionized and non-unionized workers is the basis of an **insider–outsider model**. *Insiders* are unionized workers who seek to maximize their own welfare rather than the welfare of the whole workforce. Non-unionized workers are *outsiders*.

According to this view, firms are willing to pay a higher wage rate than equilibrium to insiders rather than replace them with outsiders. Reasons for such behaviour by firms include the costs of having to retrain outsiders. It is cheaper for a firm to pay insiders higher wages than to attempt to replace them with lower-waged outsiders.

insider–outsider model

Union members (insiders) receive higher than equilibrium wages because of the cost to firms of replacing them with non-union members (outsiders)

Figure 19.6 A competitive labour market and a monopoly union

If the union imposes a wage of €8, quantity of labour demanded will be limited to 2200 workers. But there will be a quantity of labour supplied of 4200 workers. Thus, many will not be able to find jobs. But if union membership is 2200, all the unemployed would be non-union workers.

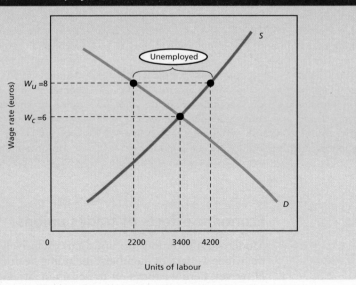

Union power in a competitive labour market is likely to be inefficient. Pushing up wages reduces labour demand and can cause unemployment and restrictions on union membership.

You can see the trade-off in Figure 19.6. If wages were set lower than €8, more workers would be employed. If union membership were greater than 2200, the union leadership would have to make a tough decision. They could get more members into jobs, but only by accepting a lower wage for everyone or by somehow increasing demand for their members' services.

Over the years, unions have shown great concern for keeping members in jobs. The preferred route has been to increase demand for workers rather than to take pay cuts. Unions have used many techniques for shifting the demand curve to the right. Union contracts now include provisions for job security, especially for those with seniority. Some contracts have clauses that preserve jobs even when it is inefficient to do so. This is called **featherbedding**.

featherbedding
The common union practice of preserving jobs even when it is inefficient to do so.

Unions have sought protective trade measures such as tariffs (taxes on imports) and quotas to prevent foreign producers from cutting into the demand for domestic, union-made goods. In the EU there are no such restrictions *between* member countries, only on goods from countries *outside* the EU.

Empirical evidence: do unions raise wages?

The answer to this question, not surprisingly, is yes:

An overwhelming number of studies using very different sets of data and techniques have found that unions have succeeded in raising wages.

Examples of such studies include one by Symon and Walker[7] and another by D Metcalf;[8] these and others agree that unionization raises wage rates. However, they disagree substantially on the size of the impact of unionization. This is not surprising. It is difficult to be sure what a wage rate would have been in the absence of union negotiation.

Do unions decrease or increase productivity?

The picture of unions that has emerged from our discussion so far is not very positive. The monopoly model leads us to the same unflattering conclusions. First, unions raise wages above the competitive level, which leads to unemployment and the under-use of labour. Second, union work rules and featherbedding reduce productivity. Third, unions create inequities by forcing wage differentials between similar workers. And finally, unions may discriminate to limit membership and hold down labour supply.

Another view has recently been put forth by two Harvard economists, Richard Freeman and James Medoff, who argue that unions in fact have a *positive* effect on the allocation of resources. According to Freeman and Medoff, unions actually raise productivity. Union members, they say, have lower resignation rates, remain more loyal to the firm, maintain a higher morale, and are more likely to cooperate on the job. By communicating with management, they help to put efficient policies into effect. They collect information on workers' preferences that leads to more efficient design of benefits packages and better personnel administration.

[7] *E. Symons and I. Walker,* Union/non-union Wage Differentials 1979–84: Evidence from the FES, *mimeo (University of Keele, 1998).*

[8] *D. Metcalf, 'Transformation of British industrial relations: institutions, conduct and outcomes 1980–90', in R. Barrell (ed.),* The UK Labour Market *(Cambridge University Press, 1994).*

Union power versus monopsony power

In Chapter 13, we examined *monopsony*, a market structure in which there is just one buyer. To maximize profits, a single buyer of labour – a monopsonist – that could control part of the labour market would lower wages and hire fewer workers.

In competitive markets, firms can hire all the labour they need at the market-determined wage rate. Since every firm in competition is small relative to the market, no single firm has any control over the wage rate. A profit-maximizing competitive firm will hire labour as long as the marginal revenue product of labour (MRP_L) is equal to or greater than the market wage rate; the equilibrium condition for a competitive firm is $W = MRP_L$. In competition, the market demand curve is the sum of all the marginal revenue product curves of all the firms demanding labour.

In Figure 19.7, the market demand curve for labour is the sum of the firms' MRP_L curves. The equilibrium market wage rate is determined by the interaction of competitive demanders and the supply of labour curve. If the market were organized competitively, the equilibrium wage rate would be W_c.

But suppose instead of many firms demanding labour, there is only one firm demanding labour (a *monopsonist*). This changes our analysis significantly. Under competition, firms can hire all the labour they want at the market wage. But now the large firm faces the *market* labour supply curve. This means that the more labour the firm decides to hire, the higher the wage the firm must pay. At lower wages, less labour is supplied.

The curve in Figure 19.7 is called the *marginal factor cost* curve for labour (MFC_L). (See Chapter 13 for a review.) It represents the added cost of hiring an additional unit of labour. The supply of labour curve (S) shows the wage that must be paid to attract each level of labour supply. Marginal factor cost at every level of output is *higher* than the wage, because to attract added workers at the margin the wage paid to *all* workers must be raised. Suppose that at a wage of €5, six units of labour are supplied, and that at a wage of €6, seven units of labour are supplied. Hiring six units of labour costs €30 (6 units × €5), while hiring seven units of labour costs €42 (7 units × 6). The marginal factor cost of the seventh unit of labour is thus €12 (42 – 30), which is higher than the 6 euro wage rate.

Figure 19.7 A profit-maximizing monopsonist

A profit-maximizing monopsonist would pay a wage, W_m, below the competitive level, W_c.

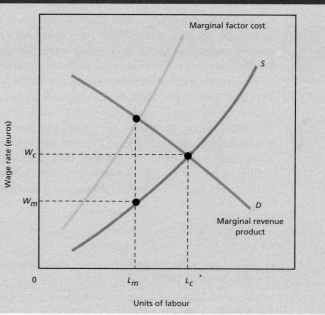

A profit-maximizing firm that is the only buyer of labour in a market (our monopsonist) will hire labour as long as the marginal revenue product of labour (MRP_L) equals or exceeds the marginal factor cost (MFC_L). Thus, in Figure 19.7, the optimal quantity of labour is L_m (the point at which $MRP_L = MFC_L$), and the wage paid to workers is W_m (the lowest wage required to attract L_m units of labour). In essence, monopsony power leads to lower wages and fewer jobs than would be the case under competitive conditions.

When a monopsonist faces a monopolistic *seller* of labour such as a union, the story is different. The union tries to impose a wage rate above the going wage, W_c. The monopsonist wants to pay a wage below W_c. The result depends on the relative bargaining strengths of the union and the firm. In a sense, the union exists to resist and exercise *countervailing power* on the buying side of the labour market. Indeed, many of the most powerfully unionized markets are in concentrated monopsonist-like industries such as steel and cars.

Although union power in a competitive market is likely to be inefficient, unions may actually drive wages closer to their efficient levels in markets where the buying side is highly concentrated.

Summary

Competitive labour markets: a review

1. Demand for labour in competitive markets depends on labour's productivity. Firms will hire labour as long as the *marginal revenue product* equals or exceeds the market wage. The marginal revenue product of labour depends on the market value of its product; if no one wants to buy a product, that product has no market value.

2. Households supply labour. The supply of labour depends on some factors that households control and some that they do not. The alternatives to working for a wage are working for no pay or enjoying one's leisure. Labour supply decisions depend to a large extent on preferences for work and leisure.

3. The stock of knowledge, skills and talents that human beings possess by nature or through education and training is called *human capital*. The principal form of human capital investment financed primarily by households is education. The principal form of human capital investment financed primarily by firms is *on-the-job training*. Governments invest heavily in human capital.

4. Wages in competitive markets are determined by supply and demand. When excess supply exists in a labour market, we can usually expect to see wages fall, but sometimes disequilibria persist.

5. Income to labour consists of *transfer earnings* that cover opportunity cost, and *economic* rent which is income in excess of opportunity cost. The marginal employee's wage is entirely transfer earnings.

The labour market in action

6. Labour supply depends on a number of factors, including wage rates, tax rates, non-labour income and wealth. Individual firms have very little control over the market wage; firms are forced to pay the wage that is determined by the market. Because people cannot get from one point to another free of charge and because most people do not reside at their workplaces – as capital does – there is an important spatial dimension to labour markets.

7. Personal preferences play a big role in the decisions households make about labour supply and in the decisions they make about what to consume.

Labour markets and public policy

8. The *minimum wage* is the lowest wage that firms are permitted to pay workers by law. Opponents argue that minimum wage legislation interferes with the smooth functioning of the labour market and creates unemployment. Proponents argue that the minimum wage has been successful in raising the wages of the poorest workers and alleviating poverty without creating much unemployment.

9. Unlike taxes, income maintenance programmes produce income and substitution effects that work in the same direction. Both effects will reduce work effort and labour supply. Because households receiving welfare benefits lose some or all of their benefits by working, the system imposes an implicit tax on any income that those households earn.

10. The distribution of skills and abilities among the available workforce never corresponds exactly to the skills and abilities currently in demand.

11. *Job searching* is a process of gathering data. In theory, job hunting should continue as long as the expected gains from continuing to search exceed the costs of doing so.

12. Unemployment benefits reduce the cost of the job search. Some have argued that this results in inefficiency. In the EU, unemployment benefits make up on average 60% of lost wages. With the costs of looking for a job reduced in this fashion, people have an incentive to prolong the process. Prolonged job search drains tax revenues, artificially increases the unemployment rate and keeps productive workers out of work.

Wage and income differentials

13. *Ceteris paribus*, jobs that are more desirable and less risky tend to pay less than jobs that are less desirable and more risky. These wage differences are called *compensating differentials*.

14. *Labour market discrimination* occurs when one group of workers receives inferior treatment from employers because of some characteristic irrelevant to job performance. Inferior treatment may involve being systematically barred from certain occupations, receiving lower wages, or being unable to win promotion or obtain training. If workers vary in their talents in ways unrelated to gender or race, rules or behaviour that force one group into specific occupations are inefficient.

Trades unions

15. A high proportion of European labour is covered by collective agreements, though the proportion is much below the average in the UK.

16. Union power in a competitive labour market is likely to be inefficient. Pushing up wages reduces labour demand and can cause unemployment and restrictions on union membership.

17. Insider–outsider models suggest that firms may be willing to pay higher than equilibrium wage rates to unionized workers.

18. An overwhelming number of studies have found that unions have succeeded in raising wages, though there is little agreement about the degree of success.

19. One school of thought holds that unions lead to unemployment, the under-use of labour, lower productivity and artificial wage differentials. Another school argues that unions raise productivity because union members have lower turnover, maintain higher morale, and are more likely to cooperate on the job.

Union versus monopsony power

20. Although union power in a competitive labour market is likely to be inefficient, unions may actually drive wages closer to their efficient levels in markets where the buying side is highly concentrated.

Review Terms and Concepts

compensating differentials
economic rent
featherbedding
human capital
income effect of higher wages
insider–outsider model
job search

labour market discrimination
marginal revenue product of labour (*MRP*$_L$)
minimum wage
on-the-job training
substitution effect of higher wages
transfer earnings

Problem Set

1. If a minimum wage is *below* the average wage, how could the increase lead to unemployment?

2. How could the unemployment rate rise when the number of employed actually increases?

3. Draw a diagram to illustrate each of the following cases:

a. A labour supply curve for a group of households for whom the income effect of a wage increase is stronger than the substitution effect.

b. The effect of a general increase in the productivity of labour (an overall rise in the marginal product of labour).

c. The effect of a union contract that succeeds in raising wage rates above the competitive equilibrium.

d. The effect of a minimum wage above equilibrium in a competitive labour market.

4. Jane is considering returning to university to get an MBA. She currently earns €30,000 a year and pays

€9000 in taxes (30%). Tuition fees at the university of her choice are €15,000 per year, and the course takes two years to complete. She must attend full time and would receive no financial aid.

a. What is the total monetary cost of Jane's MBA?

b. What other information might you need to get a better picture of the full cost of her MBA? (*Hint*: What about summers?)

c. If the degree raises Jane's expected after-tax wage by €5000 per year in real terms for a long time, what is the rate of return on investment for Jane's MBA? What if the increase were €15,000?

d. To make a final decision, what other factors might Jane want to consider?

5. Some people have suggested that government should establish a computerized national and regional job bank to provide people with listings of available jobs. Is this a good idea, or is it an unwarranted intrusion of the government into the private sector? Explain your answer.

6. Explain how the functioning of income-linked schemes such as welfare programmes acts as a tax on the poor that can have an effect on their work effort.

7. Explain how an extension of unemployment benefits could actually lead to unemployment. If evidence were found to support this claim, should we repeal the extension or abandon the unemployment benefits system? Explain.

8. In many developing countries, the government sector pays a higher wage for workers than the private sector does. This has been criticized on the grounds that it creates unemployment as people queue for government jobs, which are concentrated in the cities, rather than stay in the countryside working for market-determined wages. Using supply and demand curves, show how this situation could lead to higher wages and less employment in the private sector job market.

9. The Brotherhood of Widget Makers, a trade union, has 15,000 members. Today, all are employed at €15 per hour. The union is considering a push to raise wages by €1.50 per hour. A union economist says evidence for the industry suggests a labour demand elasticity of –1. What is the potential cost of a new wage contract that accepts the 10% increase? What further contract provisions might you suggest to reduce or eliminate these potential losses?

10. What factors are important in determining a person's wages? Connect these factors to explanations of why some groups (such as women, immigrant workers, teenagers) earn less than others.

11. Sarah had two jobs in 1998. She used her good looks as a receptionist during the day, earning €10 per hour. In the evening she was a waitress at Woods' night club for €17 an hour, including tips. In June, her grandfather left her €400,000. She decided to reduce her waitressing job to two nights a week. Can you say how much of her decrease in hours worked is due to an income effect? A substitution effect?

*12. In a particular European industry the supply of labour is given as $Q_s = -5 + 3W$ and the demand for labour as $Q_d = 20 - 2W$, where W is the wage rate in euros.

a. What is the equilibrium wage rate for the industry?

b. What is the surplus of value to cover capital costs and profit?

c. Calculate the workers' transfer earnings and economic rent.

d. Calculate the total value of the output of the workers.

e. What is the total wage bill?

Macroeconomics

Introduction to Macroeconomics

microeconomics
The branch of economics that deals with the functioning of individual industries and the behaviour of individual decision-making units – business firms and households.

macroeconomics
The branch of economics that deals with the economy as a whole. Macroeconomics focuses on the determinants of total national income, deals with aggregates such as aggregate consumption and investment, and looks at the overall level of prices rather than individual prices.

aggregate behaviour
The behaviour of all households and firms together.

sticky prices Prices that do not always adjust rapidly to maintain equality between quantity supplied and quantity demanded.

microeconomic foundations of macroeconomics
The microeconomic principles underlying macroeconomic analysis.

We now begin our study of macroeconomics. We glimpsed the differences between microeconomics and macroeconomics in Chapter 1. Microeconomics examines the functioning of individual industries and the behaviour of individual decision-making units, typically business firms and households. With a few assumptions about how these units behave (firms maximize profits, households maximize utility), we can derive useful conclusions about how markets work, how resources are allocated, and so forth.

Instead of focusing on the factors that influence the production of particular products and the behaviour of individual industries, macroeconomics focuses on the determinants of total national output. Macroeconomics studies not household income but *national* income, not individual prices but the *overall* price level. It does not analyse the demand for labour in the car industry, but rather total employment in the economy.

Both microeconomics and macroeconomics are concerned with the decisions of households and firms. Microeconomics deals with individual decisions, macroeconomics deals with the sum of these individual decisions. *Aggregate* is used in macroeconomics to refer to sums. When we speak of aggregate behaviour, we mean the behaviour of all households and firms together. We also speak of aggregate consumption and aggregate investment, which refer to total consumption and total investment in the economy.

Since microeconomists and macroeconomists look at the economy from different perspectives, you might expect them to reach somewhat different conclusions about the way the economy behaves. This is true to some extent. Microeconomists generally conclude that markets work well. They see prices as flexible, adjusting to maintain equality between quantity supplied and quantity demanded. Macroeconomists, however, observe that important prices in the economy – for example, the wage rate (or price of labour) – often seem 'sticky'. Sticky prices are prices that do not always adjust rapidly to maintain equality between quantity supplied and quantity demanded. Microeconomists do not expect to see the quantity of apples supplied exceed the quantity of apples demanded, because the price of apples is not sticky. But macroeconomists – who analyse aggregate behaviour – examine periods of high unemployment, where the quantity of labour supplied appears to exceed the quantity of labour demanded. At such times, it appears that wage rates do not adjust fast enough to equate the quantity of labour supplied and the quantity of labour demanded.

In the past, macroeconomists did not try to reconcile their analyses with the postulates and conclusions of microeconomic theory. Today, most agree that microeconomics and macroeconomics cannot lead separate lives. What happens in the macroeconomy must be the result of individual decisions analysed in microeconomics. This is why the search for the microeconomic foundations of macroeconomics ranks high on the research agenda. However, to model all the choices of millions of different people and show how they interact to generate specific macroeconomic outcomes is simply not feasible. Inevitably, at some point along the way we must resort to simplifications, postulating relationships among macroeconomic variables that only *approximate* individual choices but nevertheless work well in explaining many real-world situations.

The roots of macroeconomics

The Great Depression

Great Depression

The period of severe economic contraction and high unemployment that began in 1929 and continued throughout the 1930s.

Economic events of the 1930s, the decade of the **Great Depression**, spurred a great deal of thinking about macroeconomic issues. The 'roaring twenties', as the 1920s are often characterized, had been prosperous years for many industrial countries. Prices were stable (with exceptions!), incomes rose and unemployment was low. But Wall Street's Black Tuesday on 29 October 1929 marked the start of a dramatic turn for the worse. In the USA, within two years unemployment had risen from 3.1% of the labour force in 1929 to 23.5% in 1932. By 1933, income had dropped by 30% compared to 1929 levels.

Many countries in Europe followed the downfall of the US economy. German and British unemployment rose from 5.9% and 7.2% of the labour force in 1929 to 17.2% and 15.3%, respectively, in 1932. During the same period, French incomes fell by 15%. Other European countries had similar though less dramatic experiences.

Classical models

Before the Great Depression, economists applied microeconomic models, sometimes referred to as 'classical models', to economy-wide problems. (The word 'macroeconomics' was not even invented until after the Second World War.) For example, classical supply and demand analysis assumed that an excess supply of labour would drive down wages to a new equilibrium level; as a result, unemployment would not persist.

In other words, classical economists believed that *recessions* (downturns in the economy) were self-correcting. As output falls and the demand for labour shifts to the left, the argument went, the wage rate will decline, thereby raising the quantity of labour demanded by firms who would want to hire more workers at the new lower wage rate. (Graph this movement along the new demand curve yourself.)

But during the Great Depression unemployment levels in most countries remained very high for nearly ten years. In large measure, the failure of simple classical models[1] to explain the prolonged existence of high unemployment provided the impetus for the development of macroeconomics. It is not surprising that what we now call macroeconomics was born during the 1930s.

The Keynesian revolution

One of the most important books in the history of economics, *The General Theory of Employment, Interest and Money*, by the British economist John Maynard Keynes, was published in 1936. Building on what was already understood about markets and their behaviour, Keynes set out to construct a theory that would explain the confusing economic events of his time.

Much of today's macroeconomics has roots in Keynes's work. According to Keynes, it is not prices and wages that determine the level of employment, as classical models had suggested, but rather the level of aggregate demand for goods and services. Keynes believed that governments could intervene in the economy and affect the level of output and employment. The government's role during periods when private demand is low, Keynes argued, is to stimulate aggregate demand and, by so doing, to lift the economy out of recession. (See the Application 'The Great Depression and John Maynard Keynes'.)

---

[1]*Classical models are also sometimes known as 'market clearing' models because they emphasize that prices and wages adjust to ensure that markets always clear – that is, that the quantity supplied is equal to the quantity demanded.*

Recent macroeconomic history

After the Second World War, and especially in the 1950s, Keynes's views began to gain increasing influence over both professional economists and government policy makers. Governments came to believe they could intervene in their economies to attain specific employment and output goals, and they began to use their powers to tax and spend, as well as their ability to affect interest rates and the money supply, for the explicit purpose of controlling the economy's ups and downs. The first country to establish this practice firmly was the one most severely hit by the Great Depression. In the USA, the passage of the Employment Act of 1946 established the Council of Economic Advisers, a group of economists who advise the President on economic issues. It also committed the US federal government to intervening in the economy to prevent large declines in output and employment. The first European consensus with a Keynesian view of the government's role in the macroeconomy is found in Article 114 of the Treaty of Rome in 1957 (which marks the birth of what is now the European Union).

Fine tuning in the 1960s

The notion that the government could, and should, act to stabilize the macroeconomy reached the height of its popularity in the 1960s. During these years, Walter Heller, the chairman of the Council of Economic Advisers under both President Kennedy and President Johnson, alluded to what he called **fine tuning**, the government's role in regulating inflation and unemployment. During the 1960s, many economists believed the government could use the tools available to manipulate unemployment and inflation levels fairly precisely. For example, Germany cured its first postwar recession in 1966/67 with strictly Keynesian medicine. On the legislative level, the so-called *Stabilitätsgesetz* of 1967 obliged the government to steer the economy in pursuit of five macroeconomic goals, including high employment, price stability and adequate growth.

fine tuning The phrase used by Walter Heller to refer to the government's role in regulating inflation and unemployment.

Disillusionment since the 1970s

Since 1970, the world's industrial economies have been through a series of fluctuations in employment, output and inflation. In 1974–75 and again in 1980–82, most countries experienced severe recessions. While not as catastrophic as the Great Depression of the 1930s, these recessions left millions without jobs and resulted in substantial amounts of lost output and income. In 1974–75 and again in 1979–81, many countries experienced inflation in double figures (10% or higher).

Moreover, the 1970s witnessed the birth of **stagflation** (stagnation + inflation). Stagflation occurs when the overall price level rises rapidly (inflation) during periods of recession or high and persistent unemployment (stagnation). Until the 1970s, rapidly rising prices had been observed only in periods when the economy was prospering and unemployment was low (or at least declining). The problem of stagflation was vexing, both for macroeconomic theorists and for policy makers concerned with the health of the economy.

stagflation Occurs when the overall price level rises rapidly (inflation) during periods of recession or high and persistent unemployment (stagnation).

It was clear by 1975 that the macroeconomy was more difficult to control than either Heller's words or textbook theory had led economists to believe. The events of the 1970s and afterwards have had an important influence on macroeconomic theory. Much of the faith in the simple Keynesian model and the 'conventional wisdom' of the 1960s has been lost. New ways of understanding the behaviour of the macroeconomy have been proposed, but as yet there is no consensus as to which explanation is best. It is precisely this flux in macroeconomics, the sense that the discipline is wide open and that many important issues have yet to be resolved, that makes it so exciting to study.

Macroeconomic concerns

Three of the major concerns of macroeconomics are *inflation*, *income* and *unemployment*. Government policy makers would like to have low inflation, high income

Applications

The Great Depression and John Maynard Keynes

Much of the framework of modern macroeconomics comes from the works of John Maynard Keynes, whose *General Theory of Employment, Interest and Money* was published in 1936. The period of the 1930s was a time of deep worldwide recession, with falling output, idle machinery and extremely high unemployment levels. The following excerpt by Robert L. Heilbroner provides some insights into Keynes's life and work.

It was the unemployment that was hardest to bear. The jobless millions were like an embolism in the nation's vital circulation; and while their indisputable existence argued more forcibly than any text that something was wrong with the system, the economists wrung their hands and racked their brains . . . but could offer neither diagnosis nor remedy.

Unemployment – this kind of unemployment – was simply not listed among the possible ills of the system: it was absurd, impossible, unreasonable, and paradoxical. But it was there.

It would seem logical that the man who would seek to solve this impossible paradox of not enough production existing side by side with men fruitlessly seeking work

would be a Left-winger, an economist with strong sympathies for the proletariat, an angry man. Nothing could be further from the fact. The man who tackled it was almost a dilettante with a chip on his shoulder. The simple truth was that his talents inclined in every direction. He had, for example, written a most recondite book on mathematical probability, a book that Bertrand Russell had declared 'impossible to praise too highly'; then he had gone on to match his skill in abstruse logic with a flair for making money – he accumulated a fortune of £500,000 by way of the most treacherous of all roads to riches: dealing in international currencies and commodities. More impressive yet, he had written his mathematics treatise on the side, as it were, while engaged in Government service, and he piled up his private wealth by applying himself for only half an hour a day while still abed.

But this is only a sample of his many-sidedness. He was an economist, of course – a Cambridge don with all the dignity and erudition that go with such an appointment . . . He managed to be simultaneously the darling of the Bloomsbury set, the cluster of Britain's most

avant-garde intellectual brilliants, and also the chairman of a life insurance company, a niche in life rarely noted for its intellectual abandon. He was a pillar of stability in delicate matters of international diplomacy, but his official correctness did not prevent him from acquiring a knowledge of other European politicians that included their . . . neuroses and financial prejudices ... He ran a theatre, and he came to be a Director of the Bank of England. He knew Roosevelt and Churchill and also Bernard Shaw and Pablo Picasso . . .

His name was John Maynard Keynes, an old British name (pronounced to rhyme with 'rains') that could be traced back to one William de Cahagnes and 1066. Keynes was a traditionalist; he liked to think that greatness ran in families, and it is true that his own father was John Neville Keynes, an illustrious enough economist in his own right. But it took more than the ordinary gifts of heritage to account for the son; it was as if the talents that would have sufficed half a dozen men were by happy accident crowded into one person.

By a coincidence he was born in 1883, in the very year that Karl Marx passed away. But the two

John Maynard Keynes

economists who thus touched each other in time, although each was to exert the profoundest influence on the philosophy of the capitalist system, could hardly have differed from one another more. Marx was bitter, at bay, heavy and disappointed; as we know, he was the draftsman of Capitalism Doomed. Keynes loved life and sailed through it buoyant, at ease, and consummately successful to become the architect of Capitalism Viable.

Source: Robert L. Heilbroner, The Worldly Philosophers (New York: Simon & Schuster, 1961).

and growth, and low unemployment. They may not be able to achieve these goals, but the goals themselves are clear. The effectiveness of government policies in pursuing these goals is the subject of later chapters.

We will briefly discuss these three concerns. One troublesome fact should be kept in mind throughout this discussion:

Almost all macroeconomic events are interrelated – making progress on one front often means making conditions worse on another.

For example, some economists believe the only way to cure inflation is to put the economy into a recession (increasing unemployment and lowering output). Not all the good things we want may be compatible with each other. Alas, macroeconomics is rife with trade-offs! One aim of the following chapters is to explore and explain the nature of these trade-offs.

Inflation

inflation

An increase in the overall price level.

Inflation is an increase in the overall price level. The reduction of inflation has long been a goal of government policy. Especially problematic are **hyperinflations**, periods of very rapid increases in the overall price level.

hyperinflation

A period of very rapid increases in the overall price level.

Europe has not seen a hyperinflation for half a century. Events like the German hyperinflation of 1923 or the second Hungarian hyperinflation of 1946 – the last one in Europe, at the peak of which prices tripled daily – are more hearsay than real experience. However, in some countries, people are accustomed to prices rising by the day, by the hour, or even by the minute. During the hyperinflation in Bolivia in 1984 and 1985, the price of an egg rose from 3000 pesos to 10,000 pesos in a week. In 1985, three bottles of aspirin sold for the same price as a luxury car had sold for in 1982. At the same time, the problem of handling money became a burden. Banks stopped counting deposits – a $500 deposit was equivalent to about 32 million pesos, and it just did not make sense to count a huge sack full of banknotes. Bolivia's currency, printed in West Germany and England, was the country's third biggest import in 1984, surpassed only by wheat and mining equipment.

Skyrocketing prices in Bolivia are a small part of the story. When inflation approaches rates of 2000% per year, the economy and the whole organization of a country begin to break down. Workers may go on strike to demand wage increases in line with the high inflation rate, firms find it almost impossible to secure credit, and the economy grinds to a halt. Fortunately, hyperinflations usually end very abruptly. In only a few months, Bolivia's inflation rate went from being the highest in the world to one of the lowest in the Western Hemisphere.

Hyperinflations are rare. Nonetheless, economists have devoted much effort to identifying the costs and consequences of even moderate inflation. Who gains from inflation? Who loses? What costs does inflation impose on society? How severe are they? What causes inflation? What is the best way of stopping it? We will focus on some of these questions in Chapters 22 and 29, where we will see that inflation is a major issue in macroeconomics.

business cycle

The cycle of short-term ups and downs in the economy.

Income and growth

aggregate output or aggregate income

The total quantity of goods and services produced in an economy in a given period.

Economies rarely see incomes grow at a constant rate at all times; instead, they tend to experience short-term ups and downs in their performance. The technical name for these ups and downs is the **business cycle**. The main measure of how an economy is doing is **aggregate output** (or **aggregate income**), the total quantity of goods and services produced in the economy during a given period. When less is produced (in other words, when aggregate output decreases), there are fewer goods and services to go around, and the standard of living declines. When firms cut back on production, they also lay off workers, increasing unemployment.

recession

A period during which aggregate output declines. Conventionally, a period in which aggregate output declines for two consecutive quarters.

Recessions are periods during which real activity weakens. For practical purposes it has become conventional to classify an economic downturn as a 'recession' when aggregate output declines for two consecutive quarters. A prolonged and deep recession is called a **depression**, though economists do not agree on when a recession becomes a depression. The world economic crisis of 1929–32 certainly qualifies as a depression in most countries. Examples of recent recessions are the downturns of 1990–92 in Britain, Finland and Sweden.

depression

A prolonged and deep recession.

In devising explanations for and predicting the business cycle, macroeconomics tries to address certain key questions. Why does the economy fluctuate so much? Why, at times, does it not seem to respond to the simple forces of supply and demand?

There is more to output than its up and down movements during business cycles. The size of the growth rate of output over a long period of time (longer, say, than the typical length of a business cycle) is also of concern to macroeconomists and policy makers. If the growth rate of output is greater than the growth rate of the population, then there is a growing amount of goods and services being produced per person, and on average people are becoming better off. Policy makers are thus concerned not only with smoothing fluctuations in output during a business cycle, but also with policies that might increase the long run growth rate. Long run growth issues are taken up in Chapters 22 and 35.

Unemployment

unemployment rate

The percentage of the labour force that is unemployed.

The **unemployment rate** – the percentage of the labour force unemployed – is a key indicator of the economy's health. High rates in the 1990s indicating poor health are a major concern in most European countries. Because the unemployment rate is usually closely related to the economy's aggregate output, announcements of each month's new figures are followed with great interest by economists, politicians and policy makers.

Although macroeconomists are interested in learning why the unemployment rate has risen or fallen in a given period, they also try to answer a more basic question: why is there any unemployment at all? We do not expect to see zero unemployment. At any time, some firms may go bankrupt due to competition from rivals, bad management or bad luck. Employees of such firms often are not able to find new jobs immediately, and while looking for work, they are unemployed. Also, workers entering the labour market for the first time may require a few weeks, or months, to find a job.

If we base our analysis on supply and demand, as we have in all our discussions so far, we would expect conditions to change in response to the existence of unemployed workers. Specifically, when there is unemployment beyond some minimum amount, there is an excess supply of workers – at the going wage rates, there are people who want to work who cannot find work. In microeconomic theory, the response to excess supply is a decrease in the price of the commodity in question. Demand rises, supply falls, equilibrium is restored. With the quantity supplied equal to the quantity demanded, the market clears.

The existence of unemployment seems to imply that the aggregate labour market is not in equilibrium – that something prevents the quantity supplied and the quantity demanded from equating. But why do labour markets not clear when other markets do? Or is it that labour markets are clearing and the unemployment data reflect something different? The implications of the unemployment data, a major puzzle in macroeconomics, are the focus of Chapters 22, 31 and 32.

The role of government in the macroeconomy

Much of our discussion of macroeconomics concerns the potential role of government in influencing the economy. There are four kinds of policy that governments use to influence the macroeconomy:

1. fiscal policy
2. monetary policy
3. exchange rate policy
4. growth or supply-side policies

Fiscal policy

One way the government affects the economy is through its tax and expenditure decisions, or **fiscal policy**. It collects taxes from households and firms and spends these funds on items ranging from fighter planes to parks to roads. Both the magnitude and composition of these taxes and expenditures have a major effect on the economy.

One of Keynes's main ideas in the 1930s was that fiscal policy could and should be used to stabilize the level of output and employment. Specifically, Keynes believed the government should cut taxes and/or raise spending – called *expansionary fiscal policies* – to get the economy out of a slump. Conversely, he held that the government should raise taxes and/or cut spending – called *contractionary fiscal policies* – to bring the economy out of an inflation.

Monetary policy

Taxes and spending are not the only variables the government controls. Through the central bank,[2] the government can determine the quantity of money in the economy. The effects and proper role of **monetary policy** are among the most hotly debated subjects in macroeconomics. Most economists agree that the quantity of money supplied affects the overall price level, interest rates and exchange rates, the unemployment rate, and the level of output. The main controversies arise in regard to how monetary policy manifests itself and exactly how large its effects are.

Exchange rate policy

A country can leave the determination of its exchange rate – the price of one unit of its currency in terms of some other currency – up to the market. Or it may fix the exchange rate to the level it desires. When the exchange rate is fixed, the government loses control over the money supply. Monetary policy becomes unavailable and is replaced by **exchange rate policy** – the influencing or setting of the exchange rate in order to affect the course of the economy. When the exchange rate changes, our nation's goods become cheaper or more expensive for buyers in other countries. This affects foreign demand for our products and, eventually, our incomes.

Growth policies

Many economists are sceptical about the government's ability to smooth the business cycle with any degree of precision by using monetary and fiscal policy. Their view is that the focus of government policy should be to stimulate aggregate supply to stimulate the growth of aggregate output and income. A host of policies have been aimed at increasing the rate of growth. Many of these are targeted at specific markets and are largely discussed within microeconomics. One major worry of macroeconomists is that government borrowing to finance excesses of spending over tax collections (the 'deficit') is soaking up saving that would otherwise flow to businesses to be used for investment in capital. Another focus of pro-growth government policies has been the tax system. A major goal of tax reforms under way or completed in many European countries is to increase the incentive to work, save and invest by lowering tax rates. These and other pro-growth measures which we will discuss later are sometimes referred to as **supply-side policies**.

The components of the macroeconomy

Macroeconomics focuses on four groups: *households* and *firms* (the private sector), the *government* (the public sector), and the *rest of the world* (the international sector). We provided data on each in Chapter 3. These four groups interact in a variety of ways, many involving either the receipt or payment of income.

---

[2]*The central bank is an arm of the government. However, in most countries it does not always have to do what the government wants it to do. This central bank independence is (or was) high in Germany, Switzerland and the USA, but rather low in Britain, Greece, Italy, Portugal and Spain. The European Central Bank has also been granted considerable independence from governments.*

Figure 20.1 The circular flow of payments

Households receive income from firms and the government, purchase goods and services from firms, and pay taxes to the government. They also purchase foreign-made goods and services (imports). Firms receive payments from households and the government for goods and services; they pay wages, dividends, interest, and rents to households, and taxes to the government. The government receives taxes from both firms and households, pays both firms and households for goods and services – including wages to government workers – and pays interest and transfers to households. Finally, people in other countries purchase goods and services produced domestically (exports). Note: although not shown in this diagram, firms and governments also purchase imports.

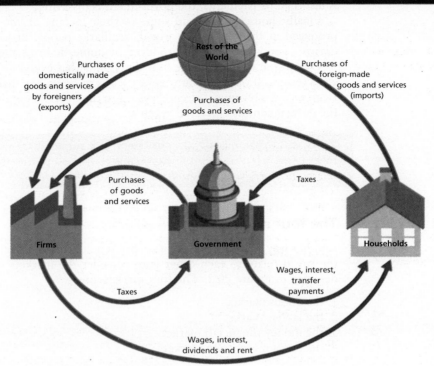

circular flow

A diagram showing the income received and payments made by each sector of the economy.

transfer payments

Cash payments made by the government to people who do not supply goods, services, or labour in exchange for these payments. They include social security benefits, state pensions and welfare payments.

The circular flow diagram

A useful way of seeing the economic interactions among the four sectors in the economy is through a **circular flow** diagram, which shows the income received and payments made by each. A simple circular flow diagram is pictured in Figure 20.1.

Let's walk through the circular flow step by step. Households work for firms and the government, and they receive wages for their work. Our diagram shows a flow of wages to the household sector as payment for supplying work. Households also receive interest on corporate and government bonds and dividends from firms. Many households receive other payments from the government, such as social security benefits, state pensions and welfare payments. Economists call these kinds of payments from the government (for which the recipients do not supply goods, services or labour) **transfer payments**. Together, all these receipts make up the total income received by the households.

Households spend by buying goods and services from firms and by paying taxes to the government. These items make up the total amount paid out by the households. The difference between total receipts and total payments of the households is the amount that the households save or dissave.[3] If households receive more than they spend, they *save* during the period. If they receive less than they spend, they *dissave*. A household can dissave by using up some of its previous savings or by borrowing. In the circular flow diagram, household spending is shown as a flow *out* of the household sector.

Firms sell goods and services to households and the government. These sales earn revenue, which shows up in the circular flow diagram as a flow *into* the firm sector. Firms pay wages, interest and dividends to households, and they pay taxes to the government. These payments are shown flowing *out* of the firm sector.

The government collects taxes from households and firms. The government also makes payments. It buys goods and services from firms, pays wages and interest to

---

[3]*Saving by households is sometimes termed a 'leakage' from the circular flow because it withdraws income, or current purchasing power, from the system.*

households, and makes transfer payments to households. If the government's revenue is less than its payments, the government is dissaving.

Finally, households spend some of their income on *imports* – goods and services produced in the rest of the world. Similarly, people in foreign countries purchase *exports* – goods and services produced by domestic firms and sold to other countries.

One lesson of the circular flow diagram is that everyone's expenditure is someone else's receipt. If you buy your nephew a box of Lego, you make a payment to Lego and Lego receives revenue. If Lego pays tax to the government, it has made a payment and the government has received revenue.

> Everyone's expenditures go somewhere. It is impossible to sell something without there being a buyer, and it is impossible to make a payment without there being a recipient. Every transaction must have two sides.

The four markets

Another way of looking at the ways households, firms, the government and the rest of the world relate to each other is to consider the markets in which they interact, as depicted in Figure 20.2. The four markets are:

1. the goods market
2. the labour market
3. the money (financial) market
4. the foreign exchange market

The goods market

Households and the government purchase goods and services from firms in the *goods and services market*, or *goods market* for short. In this market, firms also purchase goods and services from each other. For example, Benetton buys denim from other firms to make its blue jeans. In addition, firms buy capital goods from other firms. If Citroën needs new robots on its assembly lines, it will probably buy them from another firm rather than make them itself.

Firms *supply* to the goods market. Households, the government and firms *demand* from this market. Finally, the rest of the world both buys from and sells to the goods market. As we mentioned in Chapter 3, European countries import hundreds of

Figure 20.2 The four basic markets

Households, firms, the government, and the rest of the world all interact in the goods, labour, money, and foreign exchange markets.

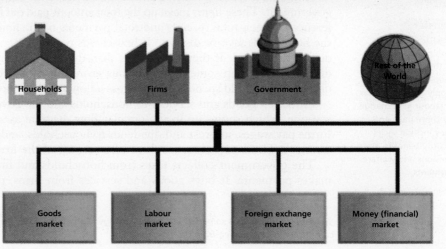

billions of euros' worth of computers, VCRs, oil and other goods from each other and from countries in other parts of the world. At the same time, they export hundreds of billions of euros' worth of cars, aircraft and chemical products.

The labour market

Interaction in the *labour market* takes place when firms and the government purchase labour from households. In this market, households *supply* labour, and firms and the government *demand* labour. In the industrial countries, firms are by far the largest employers of labour, though the government is also a substantial employer. The total supply of labour in the economy depends on the sum of decisions made by households. Individuals must decide whether to enter the labour force (whether to look for a job at all) and how many hours to work.

In principle, labour is also supplied to and demanded from other countries. Particularly after the removal of mobility barriers through the Maastricht Treaty, the European labour market has become an international market comprising all European Union (EU) member countries. For example, London hotels and restaurants would find it very difficult to accommodate and serve millions of tourists if it were not for the labour of migrant workers from Spain and other countries. For years, Turkey (even though it is not a EU member) has provided Germany with 'guest workers' who are willing to take low-paying jobs that more prosperous German workers avoid.

The money market

In the *money market* – sometimes called the *financial market* – households purchase stocks and bonds from firms. Households *supply* funds to this market in the expectation of earning extra income in the form of dividends on stocks and interest on bonds. Households also *demand* (borrow) funds from this market to finance various purchases. Firms borrow to build new facilities in the hope of earning more in the future. The government borrows by issuing bonds. The rest of the world both borrows from and lends to the money market; every morning there are reports on TV and radio about the Japanese and US stock markets. Much of the borrowing and lending of households, firms, the government and the international sector is coordinated by financial institutions – investment firms commercial banks, savings and loan associations, insurance companies, and the like. These institutions take deposits from one group and lend them to others.

When a firm, a household or the government borrows to finance a purchase, it has an obligation to pay back that loan, usually at some specified time in the future. Most loans also involve payment of interest as a fee for the use of the borrowed funds. When a loan is made, the borrower nearly always signs a 'promise to repay', or *promissory note*, and gives it to the lender. When the government borrows, it issues 'promises' called <mark>Treasury bonds</mark>, <mark>notes</mark> or <mark>bills</mark> in exchange for money. Corporations issue <mark>corporate bonds</mark>. A corporate bond might state, for example, that 'Shell agrees to pay €5000 to the holder of this bond on 1 January 2004, and interest thereon at 8.3% annually until that time'.

Instead of issuing bonds to raise funds, firms can also issue shares of stock. A <mark>share of stock</mark> is a financial instrument that gives the holder a share in the firm's ownership and therefore the right to share in the firm's profits. If the firm does well, the value of the stock increases, and the stockholder receives a *capital gain*[4] on the initial purchase. In addition, the stock may pay <mark>dividends</mark> – that is, the firm may choose to return some of its profits directly to its stockholders rather than retain them to buy capital. If the firm does poorly, so does the stockholder. The capital value of the stock may fall, and dividends may not be paid.

Treasury bonds, notes *or* bills
Promissory notes issued by the government when it borrows money.

corporate bonds
Promissory notes issued by corporations when they borrow money.

shares of stock
Financial instruments that give the holder a share in the firm's ownership and therefore the right to share in the firm's profits.

dividends
The portion of a corporation's profits that the firm pays out each period to its shareholders.

---

[4]*A capital gain occurs whenever the value of an asset increases. If you bought a stock for €500 and it is now worth €1000, you have earned a capital gain of €500. A capital gain is 'realized' when you sell the asset. Until you sell, the capital gain is accrued but not realized.*

Stocks and bonds are simply contracts, or agreements, between parties. I agree to loan you a certain amount, and you agree to repay me this amount plus something extra at some future date. Or I agree to buy a part ownership in your firm, and you agree to give me a share of the firm's future profits.

A critical variable in the money market is the *interest rate*. Although we sometimes talk as if there were only one interest rate, there is never just one interest rate at any time. Rather, the interest rate on a given loan reflects the length of the loan and the perceived risk to the lender. A business that is just getting started will have to pay a higher rate than will a well-established company such as Volkswagen. A 30-year mortgage has a different interest rate than a 90-day loan. Nevertheless, interest rates tend to move up and down together, and their movements reflect general conditions in the financial market. (We discuss interest rates in later chapters.)

The foreign exchange market

In the foreign exchange market, people trade one country's currency for the currency of another country. Such transactions are needed whenever households, firms or the government want to acquire something from the rest of the world, something for which they must pay in a currency other than the one in which they receive their revenue. An Amsterdam customer purchasing a pair of Levi jeans wants to pay in euros whereas Levi Strauss insists on payment in US dollars. So the jeans purchase involves euros being offered in the foreign exchange market and US dollars being demanded. In the same way, British pounds need to be bought for euros in the foreign exchange market if a Hamburg businessman decides to use wealth previously kept in a Deutsche Bank savings account to purchase British Midland stocks traded on the London stock exchange.

Finally, the government branch called the central bank may participate in the foreign exchange market, by selling the domestic currency it prints to accumulate foreign exchange reserves, or vice versa.

The methodology of macroeconomics

Macroeconomists build models based on theories, and they test their models using data. In this sense, the methodology of macroeconomics is similar to the methodology of microeconomics.

Connections to microeconomics

How do macroeconomists try to explain aggregate behaviour? One way assumes that the same factors that affect individual behaviour also affect aggregate behaviour. The reason for looking to microeconomics for help in explaining macroeconomic events is simple:

Macroeconomic behaviour is the sum of all the microeconomic decisions made by individual households and firms. If the movements of macroeconomic aggregates, such as total output or total employment, reflect decisions made by individual firms and households, we cannot understand the former without some knowledge of the factors that influence the latter.

Consider unemployment. The unemployment rate is the number of people unemployed as a fraction of the labour force. To be classified as 'in the labour force', a person must either have a job or be actively seeking one. To understand aggregate unemployment, we need to understand individual household behaviour in the labour market. Why do people choose to enter the labour force? Under what circumstances will they drop out? Why does unemployment exist even when the economy seems to be doing very well? A knowledge of microeconomic behaviour is the logical starting point for macroeconomic analysis. Beware, though, of the temptation to jump from microeconomic insights about individual behaviour to macroeconomic conclusions.

For example, if an individual decides to save more, she becomes rich; but if all individuals decide to save more they may well end up poorer than they were before.

Aggregate demand and aggregate supply

A major theme through the next few chapters is the behaviour of aggregate demand and aggregate supply. **Aggregate demand** is the total demand for goods and services. **Aggregate supply** is the total supply of goods and services.

Figure 20.3 shows *aggregate demand* and *aggregate supply* curves. Measured on the horizontal axis is aggregate output. Measured on the vertical axis is the *overall price level*, *not* the price of a particular good or service. (It is very important to keep this in mind.) The economy is in equilibrium at the point where these curves intersect.

As you will discover, aggregate demand and supply curves are much more complicated than the simple demand and supply curves we described in Chapters 4 and 5. The simple logic of supply, demand and equilibrium in individual markets does not explain what is depicted in Figure 20.3. It will take the whole of the next chapter to describe what is meant by 'aggregate output' and the 'overall price level'. Here again, although we will look to the behaviour of households and firms in individual markets for clues about how to analyse aggregate behaviour, there are important differences when we move from the individual to the aggregate level.

Consider, for example, *demand*, one of the most important concepts in economics. When the price of a specific good increases, perhaps the most important determinant of consumer response is the availability of other goods that can be substituted for the good whose price has increased. Part of the reason that an increase in the price of airline tickets causes a decline in the quantity of airline tickets demanded is that a higher price relative to other goods means that the opportunity cost of buying a ticket is higher: the sacrifice required in terms of other goods and services has increased. But when the overall price level changes, there may be no changes at all in relative prices. When analysing the behaviour of aggregate demand, the availability of substitutes is irrelevant.

Microeconomics teaches us that, *ceteris paribus*, the quantity demanded of a good falls when its price rises and rises when its price falls. (This is the microeconomic law of demand.) In other words, individual demand curves and market demand curves slope downwards to the right. The reason the *aggregate* demand curve in Figure 20.3 slopes downwards to the right is more complex. As we will see later, the downward

aggregate demand
The total demand for goods and services in an economy.

aggregate supply
The total supply of goods and services in an economy.

Figure 20.3 The aggregate demand and aggregate supply curves

A major theme in macroeconomics is the behaviour of aggregate demand and aggregate supply. The logic behind the aggregate demand and aggregate supply curves is much more complex than the logic underlying the simple demand and supply curves described in Chapters 4 and 5.

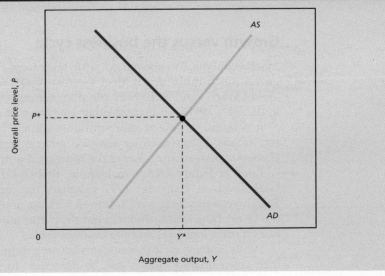

slope of the aggregate demand curve is related to what goes on in the money (financial) market and in the foreign exchange market.

The aggregate supply curve is very different from the supply curve of an individual firm or market. A firm's supply curve is derived under the assumption that all its input prices are fixed. In other words, the firm's input prices are assumed to remain unchanged as the price of the firm's output changes. When we derived Farmer Anders's wheat supply schedule in Chapter 4, we took his input prices as fixed. A change in an input price leads to a shift in Anders's supply curve, not a movement along it. If we are examining changes in the overall price level, however, *all* prices are changing (including input prices), so the aggregate supply curve cannot be based on the assumption of fixed input prices. We will see that the nature of the aggregate supply curve is a major source of controversy in macroeconomics.

Because of the complexity of the aggregate demand and aggregate supply curves, we will need to build our analysis piece by piece. In Chapter 21 we discuss how to measure economic activity and aggregate output. In Chapter 22 we describe the key macro-economic problems of business cycles, inflation and unemployment. Chapters 23 to 29 present the material we need in order to understand the equilibrium levels of aggregate output and the interest rate. In these chapters we discuss the behaviour of households, firms and the government in the goods market, the money market and the foreign exchange market. Chapter 30 brings the labour market into the picture. Later chapters elaborate on this material and discuss a number of macroeconomic policy issues.

Europe's economies in the twentieth century: trends and cycles

As we said earlier, most macroeconomic variables go through ups and downs over time, and the economy as a whole experiences periods of prosperity and periods of recession. One measure of an economy's prosperity is the amount of goods and services it produces during a year, its gross domestic product (GDP, the subject of the next chapter.) Judged by this measure, the general trend in Europe, and in many other parts of the world, has been towards prosperity. What all countries shown in Figure 20.4 have in common is that their economies as measured by GDP have grown steadily. Between 1960 and 1996. Europe's economy grew at an average rate of 3.1% per year. During those years Europe was on average 3.1% richer than it had been the year before.

Of course, Europe's GDP did not really grow by 3.1% every single year. In some years, growth was less than 3.1%, and in some years GDP even fell. In other years, the growth rate was greater than 3.1%. So we need to distinguish between *long-term* or *secular*, *trends* in economic performance and *short-term*, or *cyclical*, *variations*.

Growth versus the business cycle

Macroeconomics is concerned with both long-run trends – Why has Swiss GDP grown much more slowly than German GDP for many decades since the Second World War? – and with short-run fluctuations – Why did Britain's economy contract in the early 1990s while most other European economies were expanding?

It is useful to look at short-run fluctuations, known as *business cycles*, and at long-run trends, referred to as *economic growth*, separately. A closer look at Britain's economic performance during the nineteenth century helps to clarify some concepts.

Look at Figure 20.5, which shows British GDP again. The line connecting the GDP levels of 1900 and 1997 visualizes the long-run trend. This is the path the British economy may have followed without dramatic events like two world wars or the Great Depression, and without short-run movements resulting from phenomena like oil price increases and the business cycle.

While business cycle movements seem unimportant when viewed in historical context, their contemporary impact can be dramatic. To see how macroeconomics separates

Figure 20.4 Real GDP in Europe and the world, 1900–1999

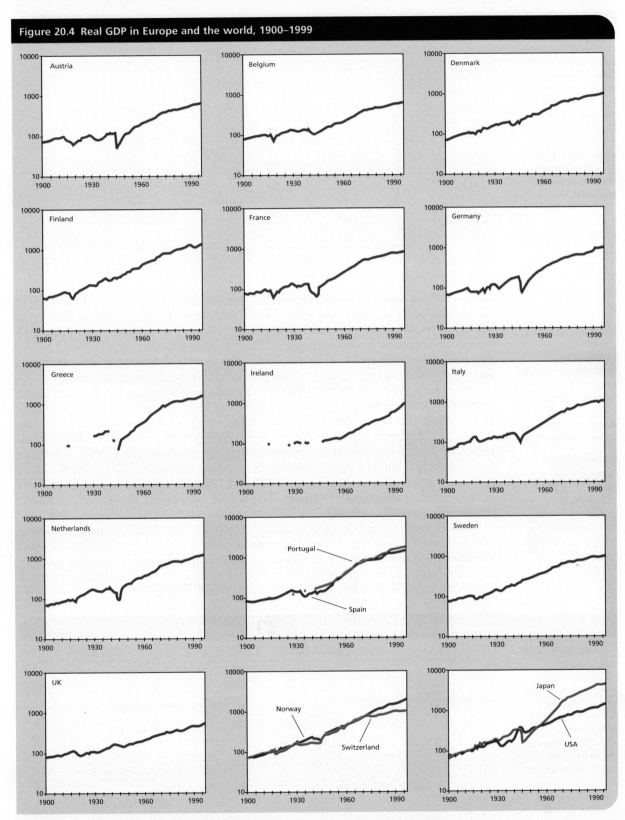

Source: IMF; OECD; Maddison, A. (1995), *Monitoring the World Economy 1820–1992*, Paris: OECD.

Figure 20.5 Actual GDP and trend GDP in Britain, 1900–1999

On a logarithmic scale British GDP in the 20th century follows a steady upward trend depicted by a straight line connecting 1900 and 1999 GDP. Deviations from this trend are usually small. However, large displacements occurred because of the two world wars.

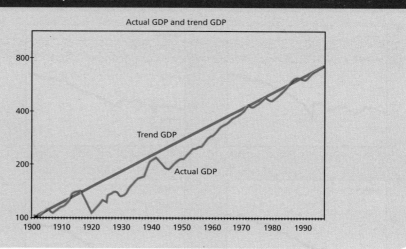

short-run from long-run issues, Figure 20.6 put the last two decades of British GDP movements under a magnifying glass. When economists analyse long-run issues – as when they ask why British income is so much higher than Portugal's, or why did Britain's economy not grow as rapidly between 1975 and 1997 as it did between 1945 and 1974 – they ignore short-run cycles. They only look at the trend line singled out in Figure 20.6b, and try to understand what puts it in this position and what determines its slope.

When economists investigate short-run fluctuations, the slope of the trend line is ignored. The business cycle is isolated from the long-run movement, as in Figure 20.6c. While real-life business cycles are often irregular, due to the many different factors taking turns to influence the economy, Figure 20.6c is as close to the textbook notion of a business cycle as reality gets. Some terminology: the highest point of a business cycle is called a *peak*. The British economy peaked in 1979 and 1989. Low points are *troughs*. These occurred in 1982 and 1992. The period from a trough to a peak is called an **expansion** or a **boom**. The period from a peak to a trough is called a **contraction**, **recession** or **slump**.

Note that the definition of a recession employed here differs from the practical use of the term mentioned earlier. The *practical* definition of the term used in countries like Britain and the USA is that recession is a fall in output for two consecutive quarters. In a *theoretical* context we already speak of a recession when income falls relative to trend. Figure 20.6c applies this definition to the recent British experience.

expansion or boom

The period in the business cycle from a trough up to a peak, during which output and employment rise.

contraction, recession or slump

The period in the business cycle from a peak down to a trough, during which output and employment fall.

Figure 20.6 GDP in Britain: separating the trend from the cycle

Putting a shorter time span under the magnifying glass permits a better view of how an economy's long-run trend is separated from the ups and downs of the business cycle. The latter makes real GDP fluctuate around its trend. Economists study the causes of economic growth along the trend path and the causes of the business cycle separately.

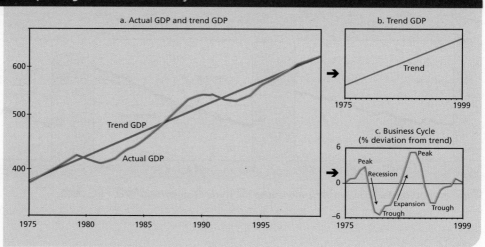

Unemployment, the second key variable in macroeconomics, is shown in Figure 20.7. While the upward movement of European unemployment since the mid-1970s is clearly visible, national experiences display great diversity. In countries like France and

Figure 20.7 Unemployment rates in Europe and the world, 1960–1998

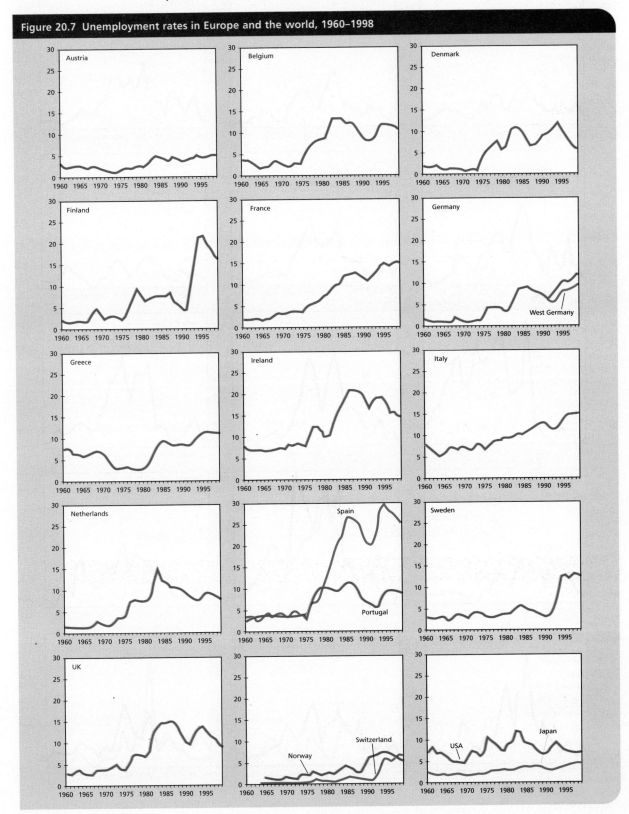

Source: Eurostat, OECD.

Figure 20.8 Inflation in Europe and the world, 1960–1998

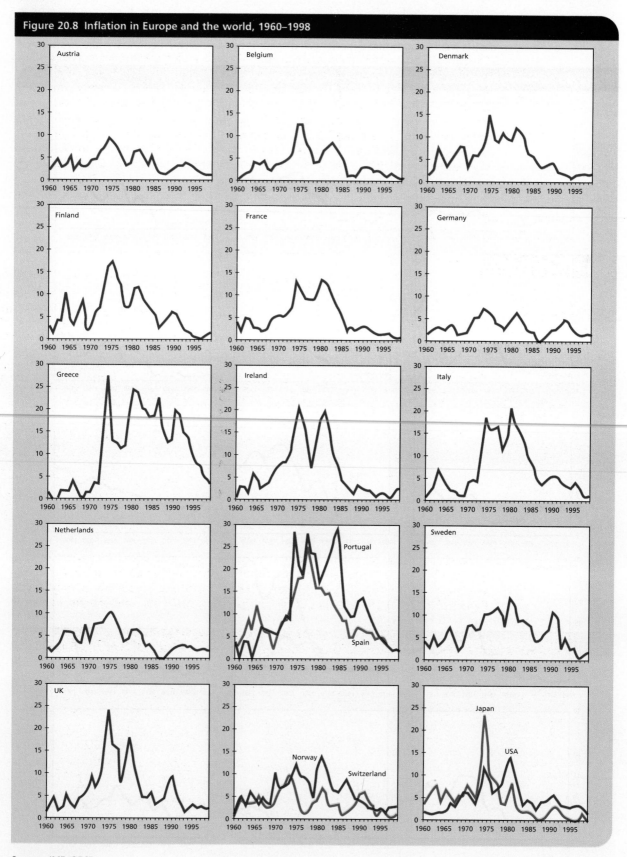

Sources: IMF; OECD.

Italy, the upward drift has been gradual and slow. In others, rapid shifts occurred, resulting in a stepwise increase. Few countries had the success of Britain, Denmark and The Netherlands in turning this trend around and lowering unemployment noticeably.

A final major concern of macroeconomics is *inflation*. Its role is almost a mirror image of what we observed for unemployment (see Figure 20.8). In most countries, inflation was low in the 1960s. But it gradually rose and became the main concern of policy makers and the public in the 1970s. At about the same time as unemployment had started to raise its head, inflation began to fall steadily and almost faded out of the picture of macroeconomic concerns. As EU member countries prepare for European Monetary Union at the close of the twentieth century, a number of commentators are even speculating whether inflation is dead.[5] The chapters to come will discuss what can be done to boost income and stimulate growth to keep unemployment low and inflation in check, and to smooth business cycle fluctuations. (See Application 'Inflation: box office takings over time'.)

Applications

Inflation: box office takings over time

During 1998 Hollywood publicists announced that *Titanic* had taken more money at the box office than any other film in history. This is, strictly speaking, true, but it is also quite misleading. When ticket prices are adjusted for inflation, DiCaprio and Winslet's love story has been nowhere near as commercially successful as some older films.

We can show this as follows. We recalculate the receipts by assuming that audiences of yesteryear all paid for their tickets at today's prices. We can now see the receipts of the leading films at constant (1998) prices in the table (the figures quoted are US box office receipts). *Titanic*'s takings are an estimated total, because the film is still being shown in cinemas.

Film	Year released	Total domestic gross ($ millon at 1998 prices)
Gone With The Wind	1939	1,299.4
Snow White and the Seven Dwarfs	1937	1,034.3
Star Wars	1977	812.0
ET – The Extra Terrestrial	1982	725.4
101 Dalmatians	1961	656.6
Bambi	1961	656.6
Titanic	1997	600
Jaws	1975	590.3
The Sound of Music	1965	565.8
The Ten Commandments	1956	547.6
Return of the Jedi	1983	540.5

Source: *Variety* Magazine.

As a basis for this we will need to develop an understanding of how the economy works. This understanding must cover not only the development of isolated variables as displayed in Figures 20.4, 20.7 and 20.8, but also the interaction among them. Figures 20.9a and 20.9b make this point. In Figure 20.9a the unemployment rate is

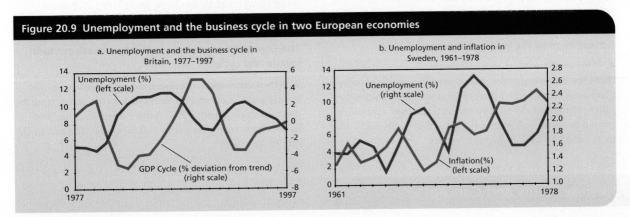

Figure 20.9 Unemployment and the business cycle in two European economies

a. Unemployment and the business cycle in Britain, 1977–1997

b. Unemployment and inflation in Sweden, 1961–1978

Source: IMF, Eurostat, OECD.

[5]See 'Murder, he wrote', The Economist, 13 April 1996.

added to Britain's business cycle experience during the past 20 years. The graphs suggest a clear negative relationship between the two, showing unemployment rising during recessions and falling during booms. Turning to Sweden as another example, Figure 20.9b shows a negative relationship between inflation and unemployment. When inflation goes up unemployment appears to fall, and vice versa.

These examples are hand-picked illustrations. In reality, interactions are too complex always to show up so clearly between one pair of variables alone, without keeping track of what third and fourth variables do.

Summary

1. *Microeconomics* examines the functioning of individual industries and the behaviour of individual decision-making units. *Macroeconomics* is concerned with the sum, or aggregate, of these individual decisions – the consumption of *all* households in the economy, the amount of labour supplied and demanded by *all* individuals and firms, the total amount of *all* goods and services produced.

The roots of macroeconomics

2. Macroeconomics was born out of the effort to explain the *Great Depression* of the 1930s. Since that time, the discipline has evolved, concerning itself with new issues as the problems facing the economy have changed. Through the late 1960s, it was believed that the government could 'fine tune' the economy to keep it running on an even keel at all times. The poor economic performance of the 1970s, however, showed that *fine tuning* does not always work.

Macroeconomic concerns

3. The three topics of primary concern to macroeconomists are increases in the overall price level, or *inflation*; the growth rate as well as the level of aggregate *output*; and the level of *unemployment*.

Government in the macroeconomy

4. Among the tools that governments have available to them for influencing the macroeconomy are *fiscal policy* (decisions on taxes and government spending); *monetary policy* (control of the money supply); *exchange rate policy*; *growth* or *supply-side policies* (policies that focus on increasing the long-run growth rate).

The components of the macroeconomy

5. The *circular flow* diagram shows the flow of income received and payments made by the three sectors of the economy – private, public and international. Everybody's expenditure is someone else's receipt, every transaction must have two sides.

6. Another way of looking at how households, firms, the government and the international sector relate is to consider the markets in which they interact: the goods and services market, the labour market, the money (financial) market and the foreign exchange market.

The methodology of macroeconomics

7. Because macroeconomic behaviour is the sum of all the microeconomic decisions made by individual households and firms, we cannot possibly understand the former without some knowledge of the factors that influence the latter. The movements of macroeconomic aggregates reflect decisions made by individual firms and households.

8. A major theme in macroeconomics is the behaviour of *aggregate demand* and *aggregate supply*. The logic underlying the aggregate demand and supply curves is more complex than the logic underlying individual market demand and supply curves.

The European economies in the twentieth century: trends and cycles

9. Macroeconomics is concerned with both long-run trends and the short-run fluctuations that are part of the business cycle. Since 1970, most European countries have seen several recessions and large fluctuations in the rate of inflation.

Review Terms and Concepts

aggregate behaviour
aggregate demand
aggregate output or aggregate income

aggregate supply
business cycle
circular flow

contraction, recession or slump
corporate bonds
depression
dividends
exchange rate policy
expansion or boom
fine tuning
fiscal policy
Great Depression
hyperinflation
inflation
macroeconomics

microeconomic foundations of macroeconomics
microeconomics
monetary policy
recession
shares of stock
stagflation
sticky prices
supply-side policies
transfer payments
Treasury bonds, notes and bills
unemployment rate

Problem Set

1. Define inflation. Assume that you live in a simple economy in which only three goods are produced and traded: fish, fruit and meat. Suppose that on 1 January 1998 fish sold at €2.50 per kilo, meat at €3.00 per kilo and fruit at €1.50 per kilo. At the end of the year, you discover that the catch was low and that fish prices had increased to €5.00 per pound, but fruit prices stayed at €1.50 and meat prices had actually fallen to €2.00. Can you say what happened to the overall price level? How might you construct a measure of the change in the price level? What additional information might you need to construct your measure?

2. Define unemployment. Should everyone who does not hold a job be considered 'unemployed'? To help with your answer, draw a supply and demand diagram depicting the labour market. What is measured along the demand curve? What factors determine the quantity of labour demanded during a given time period? What is measured along the labour supply curve? What factors determine the quantity of labour supplied by households during a given period? What is the opportunity cost of holding a job?

3. What links the labour market with (a) the market for goods and services; (b) the foreign exchange market? What is the fourth market in a macroeconomy?

4. Consider Marie-Therese, a French database specialist employed by a commercial bank. In what ways will she participate in and/or be affected by the four basic markets of the French macroeconomy?

5. Describe the economy of your country. What is the most recently reported unemployment rate? How fast has the economy grown during the past twelve months? What is the inflation rate? How does your country's performance compare to the other major European economies?

6. Consider the data shown in Figures 20.4, 20.7 and 20.8. Has the macroeconomic performance of the European economies improved or deteriorated during the 1990s as compared to the 1980s? As compared to the 1960s?

7. What were the major macroeconomic issues during the last election campaign in your country? Did the major parties differ in their interpretation of the state of the economy? What types of policies did they propose to improve things?

8. Explain briefly how macroeconomics is different from microeconomics. How can macroeconomists use microeconomic theory to guide them in their work, and why might they wish to do so?

9. Many of the expansionary periods during the twentieth century have occurred during wars. Why do you think this is so?

10. In the USA in the 1940s, you could buy a soda for 5 cents, eat dinner at a restaurant for less than a dollar, and purchase a house for $10,000. From this statement, it follows that US consumers today are worse off than US consumers in the 1940s. Comment.

Measuring National Output and National Income

Macroeconomics relies on data, much of it collected by government. To study the economy, we need data on total output, total income, total consumption, prices, unemployment and the like. One source of these data are the **national income and product accounts**, which describe the components of national income in the economy.

The national income and product accounts do more than convey data about the performance of the economy. They also provide a conceptual framework that macroeconomists use to think about how the pieces of the economy fit together. When an economist thinks about the macroeconomy, the categories and vocabulary he or she uses come from the national income and product accounts.

The national income and product accounts can be compared to the mechanical or wiring diagrams for a car engine. The diagrams do not explain how an engine works, but identify the key parts of an engine and show how they are connected. Trying to understand the macroeconomy without understanding national income accounting is like trying to fix an engine without a mechanical diagram and with no names for the engine parts.

national income and product accounts
Data collected and published by the government describing the various components of national income and output in the economy.

Gross domestic product

The key concept in the national income and product accounts is **gross domestic product**, or **GDP**.

> GDP is the total market value of a country's output. It is the market value of all final goods and services produced within a given period of time by factors of production located within a country.

gross domestic product (GDP)
The total market value of all final goods and services produced within a given period by factors of production located within a country.

GDP in the European Union for 1996 – the value of all the output produced by factors of production in the 15 EU member countries in 1996 – was 5.997 trillion Ecus, or, at 1996 exchange rates, DM 11.442 trillion, £4.869 trillion or US$7.604 trillion. By comparison, US GDP in 1996 was $7.576 trillion.

Final goods and services

Goods and services produced refers to **final goods and services**. Many goods are **intermediate goods**. They are produced by one firm for use in further processing by another firm. For instance, tyres sold to car manufacturers are intermediate goods. The value of intermediate goods is not counted in GDP. Why? Suppose that in producing a car Peugeot pays €600 to Michelin for tyres. Peugeot uses these tyres (among other components) to assemble a car, which it sells for €10,000. The value of the car (including its tyres) is €10,000, not €10,000 + €600. The final price of the car already reflects the value of all its components. To count in GDP both the value of the tyres sold to the car manufacturers and the value of the cars sold to the consumers would result in double counting.

final goods and services
Goods and services produced for final use.

intermediate goods
Goods that are produced by one firm for use in further processing by another firm.

value added
The difference between the value of goods as they leave a stage of production and the cost of the goods as they entered that stage.

Double counting can also be avoided by counting only the value added to a product by each firm in its production process. The **value added** during some stage of production is the difference between the value of goods as they leave that stage of production and the cost of the goods as they entered that stage. Value added is illustrated in Table 21.1. The four stages of the production of a litre of petrol are (1) oil drilling, (2) refining, (3) shipping, and (4) retail sale. In the first stage, value added is the value of sales. In the second stage, the refiner purchases the oil from the driller, refines it into petrol and sells it to the shipper. The refiner pays the driller €0.50 per litre and charges the shipper 0.65 litre. The value added by the refiner is 0.15 per litre. The shipper then sells the petrol to retailers for €0.80. The value added in the third stage of production is thus €0.15. Finally, the retailer sells the petrol to consumers for €1.00. The value added at the fourth stage is €0.20, and the total value added in the production process is €1.00, the same as the value of sales at the retail level. Adding the total values of sales at each stage of production (€0.50 + €0.65 + €0.80 + €1.00 = €2.95) would significantly overestimate the value of the litre of petrol.

> In calculating GDP, we can either sum up the value added at each stage of production or we can take the value of final sales. We do not use the value of total sales in an economy to measure how much output has been produced.

Exclusion of used goods and paper transactions

GDP is concerned only with new, or current, production. Old output is not counted in current GDP because it was already counted back at the time it was produced. It would be double counting to count sales of used goods in current GDP. If someone sells a used car to you, the transaction is not counted in GDP because no new production has taken place. Similarly, a house is counted in GDP only at the time it is built, not each time it is resold. In short:

> GDP ignores all transactions in which money or goods change hands but in which no new goods and services are produced.

Sales of stocks and bonds are not counted in GDP either. These sales are exchanges of paper assets and do not correspond to current production. But what if I sell the stock or bond for more than I originally paid for it? Profits from the stock or bond market have nothing to do with current production, so they are not counted in GDP. However, if I pay a fee to a broker for selling a stock of mine to someone else, this fee is counted in GDP because the broker is performing a service for me. This service is part of current production. Be careful to distinguish between exchanges of stocks and bonds for money (or for other stocks and bonds), which do not involve current production, and fees for performing such exchanges, which do.

Table 21.1 Value added in the production of one litre of petrol (hypothetical numbers)

Stage of production	Value of sales	Value added
(1) Oil drilling	€0.50	€$0.50
(2) Refining	0.65	0.15
(3) Shipping	0.80	0.15
(4) Retail sale	1.00	0.20
Total value added		€1.00

Exclusion of output produced abroad by domestically owned factors of production

> GDP is the value of output produced by factors of production located within a country.

The three basic factors of production are land, labour and capital. The labour of French citizens counts as a domestically owned factor of production for France. The output produced by French citizens abroad (for example, French citizens working in London) is not counted in French GDP because the output is not produced within France. Similarly, profits earned abroad by French companies are not counted in French GDP. However, the output produced by foreigners working in France is counted in French GDP because the output is produced within France. Also, profits earned in France by foreign-owned companies are counted in French GDP.

It is sometimes useful to have a measure of the output produced by factors of production owned by a country's residents regardless of where the output is produced. This measure is called gross national product, or GNP. For most countries, the difference between GDP and GNP is small.[1]

The biggest exception in Europe is Ireland. In 1996 GDP (Irish £42.1 billion) exceeded GNP (£37 billion) by almost 14%. So some 14% of Irish GDP was paid out to foreign-owned factors of production.[2]

The distinction between GDP and GNP can be tricky. Consider the Smart car plant in Hambach, France. The plant is owned by SMH, the Swiss watchmaking company that launched the Swatch, and Daimler-Benz of Germany. Most of the workers employed at the plant are French. Although all of the output of the plant is included in French GDP, only part of it is included in French GNP. The wages paid to French workers are part of French GNP. But profits from the plant are not; profits are counted in Swiss and German GNP because this is output produced by Swiss- and German-owned factors of production (Swiss and German capital in this case). The profits, however, are not counted in Swiss and German GDP because they are not earned in Germany or Switzerland.

The centrality of GDP as a working concept can not be overestimated. Just as an individual firm needs to evaluate the success or failure of its operations each year, so the economy as a whole needs to be assessed. GDP, as a measure of the total production of an economy, provides us with a report on a country's economic condition.

gross national product (GNP)
The total market value of all final goods and services produced within a given period by factors of production owned by a country's citizens, regardless of where the output is produced.

Calculating GDP

GDP can be computed in two ways. One way is to add up the amount spent on all final goods during a given period. This is the expenditure approach to calculating GDP. The other way is to add up the income – wages, rents, interest and profits – received by all factors of production in producing final goods. This is the

expenditure approach
A method of computing GDP that measures the amount spent on all final goods during a given period.

[1] In a few countries, however, there is a large difference between GDP and GNP. For instance, the tiny country of Lesotho (surrounded entirely by South Africa) has an extremely poor and rudimentary domestic economy. Most residents of Lesotho earn their living by working in the mines and industries of neighbouring South Africa. These payments from abroad are not counted in GDP, though they are part of GNP. According to the International Financial Statistics published by the International Monetary Fund, Lesotho's GNP exceeded its GDP by 72% in 1988.

[2] Actually, the figure is probably higher. The 14% is a net percentage, the difference between the share of Irish GDP produced by foreign-owned factors of production and the income generated abroad by Irish-owned factors of production.

income approach
A method of computing GDP that measures the income – wages, rents, interest and profits – received by all factors of production in producing final goods.

income approach to calculating GDP. These two methods lead to the same value for GDP for the reason discussed in the previous chapter: *every payment (expenditure) by a buyer is at the same time a receipt (income) for the seller*. We can measure either income received or expenditures made, and we will end up with the same total output.

Suppose the economy is made up of just one firm and the firm's total output this year sells for €1 million. Because the total amount spent on output this year is €1 million, this year's GDP is €1 million. But *every* one of the €1 million of GDP is either paid to someone or remains with the owners of the firm as profit. Using the income approach, we add up the wages paid to employees of the firm, the interest paid to those who lent money to the firm, and the rents paid to those who leased land, buildings or equipment to the firm. What is left over is profit, which is, of course, income to the owners of the firm. If we add up the incomes of all the factors of production, including profits to the owners, we get a GDP of €1 million.

The expenditure approach

Recall from Chapter 20 the four main groups in the economy: households, firms, the government and the rest of the world. There are also four main categories of expenditure:

- Consumption (*C*) – household spending on consumer goods.
- Investment (*I*) – spending by firms and households on new capital: plant, equipment, inventory and new residential structures.
- Government purchases of goods and services (*G*).
- Net exports (*EX* – *IM*) – net spending by the rest of the world, or exports (*EX*) minus imports (*IM*).

The expenditure approach calculates GDP by adding together these four components of spending. In equation form:

$$GDP = C + I + G + (EX - IM)$$

Table 21.2 shows 1995 GDP and the four components of the expenditure approach for six European countries. The Netherlands, for example, produced output worth 635 billion guilders within its borders.

personal consumption expenditures (*C*)
A major component of GDP: expenditures by consumers on goods and services.

durable goods
Goods that last a relatively long time, such as cars and household appliances.

non-durable goods
Goods that are used up fairly quickly, such as food and clothing.

services The things we buy that do not involve the production of physical things, such as legal and medical services and education.

Consumption (C)

A large part of GDP consists of **personal consumption expenditures (*C*)**. Table 21.2 shows that in 1995 the amount of Dutch personal consumption expenditures accounted for 59.9% of GDP. These are expenditures by consumers on goods and services. Consumption shares in the other countries are in the same range.

There are three main categories of consumer expenditures: durable goods, non-durable goods and services. **Durable goods**, such as cars, furniture and household appliances, last a relatively long time. **Non-durable goods**, such as food, petrol and cigarettes, are used up fairly quickly. Payments for **services** – those things we buy that do not involve the production of physical items – include expenditures for doctors, lawyers and educational institutions.

Investment (*I*)

Investment, as we use it in economics, refers to the purchase of new capital – housing, plants, equipment and inventory. The economic use of the term is in contrast to its everyday use, where *investment* often refers to purchases of stocks, bonds or mutual funds ('He *invested* in some 8% corporate bonds').

Table 21.2 Components of GDP in six countries, 1995: the expenditure approach

	France (billion francs)	Germany (billion DM)	Italy (trillion lire)	Netherlands (billion guilders)	Sweden (billion kronor)	UK (billion £)
Gross Domestic Product (GDP)	7674.8	3457.4	1770.9	635.0	1645.0	698.2
Private consumption (C)	4617.4	1974.7	1087.4	380.5	861.4	444.6
Gross private fixed capital formation (I)	40.6	691.7	270.9	106.5	216.5	97.2
Government expenditure (G)	1724.0	762.1	338.1	107.9	463.2	161.7
Net exports (EX – IM)	182.8	29.0	74.5	40.5	103.9	−5.6
In percentages						
Gross Domestic Product (GDP)	100.0	100.0	100.0	100.0	100.0	100.0
Private consumption (C)	60.2	57.1	61.4	59.9	52.4	63.7
Gross private fixed capital formation (I)	15.0	20.0	15.3	16.7	13.2	14.0
Government expenditure (G)	21.5	21.0	19.1	17.0	28.2	23.2
Net exports (EX – IM)	2.4	0.8	4.2	6.4	6.3	−0.8

Source: Statistical Yearbook 1997 for Foreign Countries, Statistisches Bundesamt; Quarterly National Accounts, OECD; OECD Economic Surveys.

gross private investment (I)

Total investment in capital – that is, the purchase of new housing, plants, equipment and inventory by the private (or non-government) sector.

non-residential investment

Expenditures by firms for machines, tools, plants and so on.

residential investment

Expenditures by households and firms on new houses and residential buildings.

change in business inventories

The amount by which firms' inventories change during a period. Inventories are the goods that firms produce now but intend to sell later.

Total investment in capital by the private sector is called **gross private investment** (*I*). Expenditures by firms for machines, tools, plant and so forth make up **non-residential investment**.[3] Because firms buy investment goods for their own final use, they are part of 'final sales' and counted in GDP. Expenditures for new houses and other residential buildings constitute **residential investment**. The third component of gross private investment, the **change in business inventories**, is the amount by which firms' inventories change during a period. Business inventories can be looked at as the goods that firms produce now but intend to sell later.

■ **Change in business inventories** It is sometimes confusing to students that inventories are counted as capital and that changes in inventory are counted as investment. But conceptually it makes some sense. The inventory a firm owns has a value, and it serves a purpose, or provides a service, to the firm. That it has value is obvious. Think of the inventory of a new car dealer or of a clothing shop, or stocks of newly produced but unsold computers awaiting shipment. All these have value.

But what *service* do inventories provide? Firms keep inventories for a number of reasons. One is to meet unforeseen demand. Firms are never sure how much they will sell from period to period. Sales go up and down. To maintain the goodwill of their customers, firms need to be able to respond to unforeseen increases in sales. The only way to do that is with inventories.

[3] *The distinction between what is considered investment and what is considered consumption is sometimes fairly arbitrary. A firm's purchase of a car or a van is counted as investment, but a household's purchase of a car or a van is counted as consumption of durable goods. In general, expenditures by firms for items that last longer than a year are counted as investment expenditures. Expenditures for items that last less than a year are seen as purchases of intermediate goods.*

Some firms use inventories to provide direct services to customers, the main function of a retail store. A grocer's shop provides a service – convenience. The shop itself doesn't produce any food at all. It simply assembles a wide variety of items and puts them on display so that consumers with varying tastes can come and shop for what they want in one place. The same is true for a clothing or hardware shop. To provide their services, such shops need light fixtures, counters, cash registers, buildings and lots of stock.

Capital stocks are made up of plant, equipment and inventories; inventory accumulations are part of the change in capital stocks, or investment.

Remember: GDP is not the market value of total final sales during a period; it is the market value of total *production*. The relationship between total production and total sales is this: total production (GDP) equals final sales of domestic goods plus the change in business inventories, or:

GDP = Final sales + Change in business inventories.

In 1995, production in The Netherlands exceeded sales by 3.5 billion guilders. Inventories at the end of 1995 were thus 3.5 billion more than they were at the beginning of 1995.

■ **Gross investment versus net investment**　During the process of production, capital (especially machinery and equipment) installed in previous periods gradually wears out. GDP does not give us a true picture of the real production of an economy. GDP includes newly produced capital goods but does not take account of capital goods 'consumed' in the production process.

Capital assets decline in value over time. The reduction in the value of an asset over time is called **depreciation**. A personal computer purchased by a business today may be expected to have a useful life of three years before being worn out or obsolete. Over that period, the computer steadily depreciates.

What is the relationship between gross private investment (I) and depreciation? **Gross investment** is the total value of all newly installed capital goods (plant, equipment, housing and inventory) produced in a given period. It takes no account of the fact that some capital wears out and must be replaced. **Net investment** is equal to gross investment minus depreciation. Net investment is a measure of how much the stock of capital changes during a period. If net investment is positive, the capital stock has increased; if net investment is negative, the capital stock has decreased. Put another way, the capital stock at the end of a period is equal to the capital stock that existed at the beginning of the period plus net investment!

$$\text{Capital}_{\text{end of period}} = \text{Capital}_{\text{beginning of period}} + \text{Net investment}$$

depreciation　The amount by which an asset's value falls in a given period.

gross investment　The total value of all newly produced capital goods (plant, equipment, housing, and inventory) produced in a given period.

net investment　Gross investment minus depreciation.

government purchases of goods and services (G)　Expenditures by national and local governments for final goods and labour.

Government purchases of goods and services (G)

Government purchases of goods and services (G) include expenditures by national and local governments on final goods (tanks, roads, pencils, school buildings) and labour (military salaries, politicians' salaries, schoolteachers' salaries). Government transfer payments (social security benefits, scholarships, etc.) are not included in government purchases of goods and services because these transfers are not purchases of anything currently produced. The payments are not made in exchange for any goods or services. Because interest payments on the government debt are counted as transfers, they are also excluded from GDP on the grounds that they are not payments for current goods or services.

As Table 21.2 shows, government purchases accounted for 107.9 billion guilders, or 17% of Dutch GDP, in 1995. Government expenditure shares in the other five countries are all higher, with Sweden topping the list at 28.2%.

net exports
(EX − IM)

The difference between exports (sales to foreigners of domestically produced goods and services) and imports (domestic purchases of goods and services from abroad). The figure can be positive or negative.

Net exports (EX − IM)

The value of **net exports (EX − IM)** is the difference between exports (sales to foreigners of domestically produced goods and services) and imports (a country's purchases of goods and services from abroad). This figure can be positive or negative. In 1995, The Netherlands exported more than it imported; the level of net exports was 40.5 billion guilders. Four of the other countries are also net exporters. Only Britain imports more than it exports, though the difference is less than 1% of GDP.

The reason for including net exports in the definition of GDP is simple. Consumption, investment and government spending (C, I and G) include expenditures on goods produced both domestically and by foreigners. Therefore, C + I + G overstates domestic production because it contains expenditures on foreign-produced goods – that is, imports (IM), which have to be subtracted from GDP to obtain the correct figure. At the same time, C + I + G understates domestic production because some of what a nation produces is sold abroad. Therefore exports (EX) have to be added in. When a Swedish firm produces buses and sells them in Denmark, the buses are part of Swedish production and should be counted as part of Sweden's GDP.

The income approach

Table 21.3 presents the income approach to calculating GDP, which looks at GDP in terms of who receives it as income rather than who purchases it.

Table 21.3 Components of GDP in six countries, 1995: the income approach

	France (billion francs)	Germany (billion DM)	Italy (trillion lire)	Netherlands (billion guilders)	Sweden (billion kronor)	UK (billion £)
Gross Domestic Product (GDP)	7674.8	3457.4	1770.9	635.0	1645.0	698.2
Factor incomes	5715.7	2632.6	1371.6	491.2	1284.4	531.5
Compensation of employees	3980.5	1877.0	728.4	328.4	936.5	378.1
Property and entrepreneurial income	1735.2	755.6	643.2	162.8	347.9	153.4
Depreciation	985.6	453.0	217.9	73.6	207.6	72.9
Indirect Taxes minus subsidies	973.5	371.8	181.4	70.2	153.0	94.0
In percentages						
Gross Domestic Product (GDP)	100.0	100.0	100.0	100.0	100.0	100.0
Factor incomes	74.5	76.2	77.4	77.3	78.0	76.2
Compensation of employees	51.9	54.3	41.1	51.7	56.9	54.2
Property and entrepreneurial income	21.6	21.9	36.3	25.6	21.1	21.0
Depreciation	12.8	13.1	12.3	11.6	12.6	10.4
Indirect taxes minus subsidies	12.7	10.8	10.2	11.1	9.3	13.5

Source: Statistical Yearbook 1997 for Foreign Countries, Statistisches Bundesamt.

The income approach breaks down GDP into three components: factor incomes, depreciation, and indirect taxes minus subsidies:

$$\text{GDP} = \text{Factor incomes} + \text{Depreciation} + (\text{Indirect taxes} - \text{Subsidies})$$

As we examine each component, keep in mind that total expenditures always equal total income.

Factor incomes

factor incomes
The total income earned by factors of production in a country.

Factor incomes are the total income earned by factors of production in a country. Table 21.3 divides factor incomes into two categories: (1) compensation of employees, and (2) property and entrepreneurial income. Compensation of employees, the larger item by far, includes wages and salaries paid to households by firms and by the government, as well as various supplements to wages and salaries such as contributions that employers make to social security and private pension funds. The other category comprises the income of businesses, the interest paid to business (interest paid by households and by the government is not counted in GDP because it is not assumed to flow from the production of goods and services), and the income received by property owners in the form of rent.

compensation of employees
Includes wages, salaries and various supplements – employer contributions to social security and pension funds, for example – paid to households by firms and by the government.

Depreciation

Recall from our discussion of net versus gross investment that when capital assets wear out or become obsolete, they decline in value. The measure of that decrease in value is called depreciation. This depreciation is part of GDP in the income approach.

It may seem odd that we must *add* depreciation to factor incomes when we calculate GDP by the income approach. But remember that we want a measure of all income, including income that results from the replacement of existing plant and equipment. Because factor incomes do not include depreciation, to get to total income (gross domestic product) we need to add depreciation. In 1995, depreciation accounted for 73.6 billion guilders, or 11.6% of Dutch GDP.

Indirect taxes minus subsidies

indirect taxes
Taxes like sales and value-added taxes, customs duties and licence fees.

In calculating final sales on the expenditures side, indirect taxes – sales and value-added taxes, customs duties and licence fees, for example – are included. These taxes must be accounted for on the income side.

To clarify this, suppose value-added tax is 15% and a firm sells 200 chocolate bars for €100 plus tax. The total sales price is €115, the value of output recorded in the expenditure approach to calculating GDP. Of this €115, €15 goes to pay the tax to the government, some goes to pay wages to the workers in the chocolate factory, and some goes to pay interest. The rest is the firm's profits plus depreciation.

To have the income and expenditure sides match, the value-added tax must be recorded on the income side. If it were not included as part of income, then the basic rule that everyone's expenditure is someone else's income would be violated. Indirect taxes are an expenditure of the households or firms who buy things, but they are not income of firms that sell the products. (Thinking along these lines, indirect taxes can be considered income of the government.) We must add indirect taxes on the income side to make things balance.

subsidies
Payments made by the government for which it receives no goods or services in return.

Subsidies are payments made by the government for which it receives no goods or services in return. These subsidies are subtracted from national income when calculating GDP. (Remember: GDP is national income plus indirect taxes minus subsidies.) For example, farmers receive substantial subsidies from the government. These payments are income to farmers and are thus part of national income, but they do not come from the sale of agricultural products so are not part of GDP. To balance the expenditure side with the income side, these subsidies must be subtracted on the income side.

As you can see from Table 21.3, GDP as calculated by the income approach was the same in 1995 as that calculated using the expenditure approach.

From GDP to national income

Although GDP is the most important concept in national income accounting, some others are also useful to know. Consider Table 21.4. In the first part we see how gross national product GNP is calculated from GDP. Remember that a country's GDP is total production by factors of production located within that country. By contrast, as we already discussed above, GNP is total production by factors of production owned by that country. If we take the Netherlands' 1995 GDP of 635 billion guilders, add to it **net factor payments from the rest of the world** (factor income earned by Dutch citizens abroad minus factor income earned in the Netherlands by foreigners) of 1 billion guilders, we get GNP at 636 billion guilders.

From GNP we can move on to calculate net national product (NNP). Recall that the expenditure approach to GDP (and of GNP) includes gross investment as one of the components. GDP and GNP do not, therefore, account for the fact that some of the nation's capital stock is used up in the process of producing the nation's output. **Net national product (NNP)** is gross national product minus depreciation. In a sense, it is a nation's total production minus (or 'net of') what is required to maintain the current level of the capital stock. Because GDP and GNP do not take into account any depreciation of the capital stock that may have occurred, NNP is sometimes a better measure of how the economy is doing than is GDP or GNP.

net factor payments from the rest of the world
Factor income received from the rest of the world minus factor income paid to the rest of the world.

net national product (NNP)
GNP minus depreciation; a nation's total product minus what is required to maintain the value of its capital stock.

Table 21.4 From GDP to national income in six countries, 1995

	France (billion francs)	Germany (billion DM)	Italy (trillion lire)	Netherlands (billion guilders)	Sweden (billion kronor)	UK (billion £)
Gross Domestic Product (GDP)	7674.8	3457.4	1770.9	635.0	1645.0	698.2
Plus: Net Factor Payments from the Rest of the World	−32.0	−12.6	−24.9	1.0	−66.6	−0.7
Gross National Product (GNP)	7642.8	3444.8	1746.0	636.0	1578.4	697.5
Less: Depreciation	−985.6	−453.0	−217.9	−73.6	−207.6	−72.9
Net National Product (NNP)	6657.2	2991.8	1528.2	562.4	1370.8	624.6
Less: Indirect Taxes Minus Subsidies	−973.5	−371.8	−181.4	−70.2	−153.0	−94.0
National Income	5683.7	2620.0	1346.7	492.2	1217.8	530.6
In percentages						
Gross Domestic Product (GDP)	100.0	100.0	100.0	100.0	100.0	100.0
Plus: Net Factor Payments from the Rest of the World	−0.4	−0.4	−1.4	0.2	−4.0	−0.1
Gross National Product (GNP)	99.6	99.6	98.6	100.2	96.0	99.9
Less: Depreciation	−12.8	−13.1	−12.3	−11.6	−12.6	−10.4
Net National Product (NNP)	86.7	86.5	86.3	88.6	83.3	89.5
Less: Indirect Taxes Minus Subsidies	−12.7	−10.8	−10.2	−11.1	−9.3	−13.5
National Income	74.1	75.8	76.0	77.5	74.0	76.0

Source: Statistical Yearbook 1997 for Foreign Countries, Statistisches Bundesamt.

national income
The total income earned by the factors of production owned by a country's citizens. It equals GNP minus depreciation.

current euros
The current prices that one pays for goods and services.

nominal GDP
Gross domestic product measured in current euros.

To calculate national income, we subtract indirect taxes minus subsidies from NNP. We subtract indirect taxes because they are included in NNP but do not represent payments to factors of production and are thus not part of national income. We add subsidies because they are payments to factors of production but are not included in NNP.

Nominal versus real GDP

So far, we have looked at GDP measured in current euros (or other currencies), or the current prices we pay for things. When a variable is measured in current euros, it is described in *nominal terms*. Nominal GDP is GDP measured in current euros – that is, with all components of GDP valued at their current prices.

In many applications of macroeconomics, nominal GDP is not a desirable measure of production. Why? Assume there is only one good – say, pizza. In year 1 and year 2, 100 units (slices) of pizza were produced. Production thus remained the same for year 1 and year 2. But suppose the price of pizza increased from €1.00 per slice in year 1 to €1.10 per slice in year 2. Nominal GDP in year 1 is €100 (100 units × €1.00 per unit), and nominal GDP in year 2 is €110 (100 units × €1.10 per unit). Nominal GDP has increased by €10, even though no more slices of pizza were produced. If we use nominal GDP to measure growth, we can be misled into thinking production has grown when all that has really happened is a rise in the price level.

If there were only one good in the economy – like pizza – it would be easy to measure production and compare one year's value to another. We would add up all the pizza slices produced each year. In the example, production is 100 in both years. If the number of slices had increased to 105 in year 2, we would say production increased by five slices between year 1 and year 2, which is a 5% increase.

If there were two goods – say, pizza and bicycles – it would not be obvious how to add up pizzas and bicycles to get an overall measure of output. We would certainly want to take into account that baking a slice of pizza is not as important as manufacturing a bicycle. This can be done by assigning different weights to pizzas and bicycles.

index A measure of a variable or group of variables.

index year In computing an index, the year in which the index is assigned a specified value – usually 1 or 100.

Underlying our discussion is the concept of an index. To compute an index for a single variable, we first assign a given value to the index – usually 1 or 100 – in a specified year, called the index year. Then from this index year the index changes by the same percentage as the variable itself changes. For example, if the variable is employment, the index year 1987, and a value of 100 is assigned to the index year, the employment index would be 100 in 1987. If employment then grew by 3.5% in 1988, the employment index in 1988 would be 103.5. Had employment instead fallen by 1.0% in 1988, the employment index in 1988 would be 99.0.

An index, however, need not pertain to just one variable. Suppose we had values for the quantities of apples and oranges produced and for their prices for a number of years. Suppose also that we are not interested in the individual quantities and prices of apples and oranges, but rather in the total quantity of fruit and in the overall price of fruit ('fruit' is taken here to be just apples and oranges). We cannot, as the saying goes, just add up apples and oranges, but we *can* construct fruit indexes. We can construct a fruit *quantity* index to measure the total quantity of fruit, and a fruit *price* index to measure the overall price of fruit. Both quantity and price indexes are explained in detail in the pages that follow: they can be constructed for any number of goods. If *all* goods and services in the economy are included, the quantity index is a quantity index for GDP and the price index is a GDP price index. A quantity index for GDP is an index of the total quantity of all goods and services produced in the economy. It is a measure of total 'real' production, or 'real' GDP.

weight The importance attached to an item within a group of items.

What is a weight? Let's define the term by an example. Suppose in your economics course there are a final exam and two other tests. If the final exam counts for one half of the overall mark and the other two tests for a quarter each, the 'weights' are a half, a quarter and a quarter, respectively. If instead the final exam counts for 80% of the mark and the other two tests for 10% each, the weights are now 0.8, 0.1 and 0.1. The more important an item is in a group, the larger its weight.

Calculating real GDP

real GDP
A measure of GDP that removes the effects of price changes from changes in nominal GDP.

Nominal GDP adjusted for price changes is called **real GDP**. All of the main issues involved in computing real GDP can be discussed using a simple three-good economy and two years. Table 21.5 presents all the data that we will need: price and quantity data for two years and three goods. The goods are labelled A, B and C, and the years are labelled 1 and 2. P denotes price and Q denotes quantity.

The first thing to note from Table 21.5 is that *nominal output* – output in current euros – in year 1 for good A is the price of good A in year 1 (€0.50) times the number of units of good A produced in year 1 (6), which is €3.00. Similarly, nominal output in year 1 is $7 \times 0.30 = €2.10$ for good B and $10 \times 0.70 = €7.00$ for good C. The sum of these three amounts, €12.10 in column 5, is nominal GDP in year 1 in this simple economy. Nominal GDP in year 2 – calculated by using year 2's quantities and year 2's prices – is €19.20 (column 8). Nominal GDP has risen from 12.10 in year 1 to €19.20 in year 2, an increase of 58.7%.

You can see that the price of each good changed between year 1 and year 2 – the price of good A fell (from 0.50 to €0.40) and the prices of goods B and C rose (B from 0.30 to €1.00; C from 0.70 to €0.90). Some of the change in nominal GDP between years 1 and 2 is due to price changes and not production changes. How much can we attribute to price changes and how much to production changes? Here things get tricky. The traditional and still most widespread procedure is to pick a **base year** and use the prices in that base year as weights to calculate real GDP. This is a **fixed-weight procedure** because the weights used, which are the prices, are the same for all years – namely, the prices that prevailed in the base year.

base year The year chosen for the weights in a fixed-weight procedure.

fixed-weight procedure
A procedure that uses weights from a given base year.

A drawback of the fixed-weight procedure is that our pick of the base year can affect the computed growth rate of real GDP. To see this, let year 1 be the base year, which means using year 1 prices as weights. Then in Table 21.5, real GDP in year 1 is €12.10 (column 5), and real GDP in year 2 is €15.10 (column 6). Note that both columns use year 1 prices, and that nominal and real GDP are the same in year 1 since year 1 is the base year. Real GDP has increased from 12.10 to €15.10, an increase of 24.8%.

Let us now see what happens if we use year 2 as the base year, which means using year 2 prices as the weights. In Table 21.5, real GDP in year 1 is €18.40 (column 7), and real GDP in year 2 is €19.20 (column 8). Note that both columns use year 2 prices, and nominal and real GDP are the same in year 2 since year 2 is the base year. Real GDP has increased from 18.40 to €19.20, an increase of 4.3%.

This numerical exercise teaches that growth rates can be sensitive to the choice of the base year – 24.8% using year 1 prices as weights and only 4.3% using year 2 prices as weights. In practice, of course, the dependence of computed growth rates on base year choice is not nearly as dramatic as in our artificial example. To mitigate the problem, base years are changed every so often.

Table 21.5 A three-good economy

	(1)	(2) Production year 2	(3)	(4) Price per unit	(5) GDP in year 1 in year 1 prices	(6) GDP in year 2 in year 1 prices	(7) GDP in year 1 in year 2 prices	(8) GDP in year 2 in year 2 prices
	year 1	year 1	year 2	year 2				
	Q_1	Q_2	P_1	P_2	$P_1 \times Q_1$	$P_1 \times Q_2$	$P_2 \times Q_1$	$P_2 \times Q_2$
Good A	6	11	€0.50	€0.40	€3.00	€5.50	€2.40	€4.40
Good B	7	4	€0.30	€1.00	€2.10	€1.20	€7.00	€4.00
Good C	10	12	€0.70	€0.90	€7.00	€8.40	€9.00	€10.80
Total					€12.10	€15.10	€18.40	€19.20

Calculating the GDP price index

GDP price index
or **GDP deflator**
A price index for GDP.

We now switch from real GDP, a quantity measure, to the **GDP price index** or **GDP deflator**, a price measure. One of economic policy makers' goals is to keep changes in the overall price level small. For this reason, policy makers not only need good measures of how real output is changing but also good measures of how the overall price level in changing. The GDP price index is one measure of the overall price level. We can use the data in Table 21.5 to show how the GDP price index is computed.

Suppose the price of good A fell from €0.50 in year 1 to €0.40 in year 2; the price of good B rose from €0.30 to €1.00; the price of good C rose from €0.70 to €0.90. If we were only interested in how individual prices change, this is all the information we would need. But if we are interested in how the overall price *level* changes, we need to weight the individual prices in some way. The obvious weights to use are the quantities produced, but which quantities – year 1's or year 2's? the same issues arise here for the quantity weights as arose above for the price weights in computing real GDP.

Employing the fixed-weight procedure again, let us first use year 1 as the base year, which means using year 1 quantities as the weights. Then in Table 21.5, the 'bundle' price in year 1 is €12.10 (column 5), and the bundle price in year 2 is €18.40 (column 7). Both columns use year 1 quantities. The bundle price has increased from 12.10 to €18.40, an increase of 52.1%.

Next, let us use year 2 as the base year, which means using year 2 quantities as the weights. Then, the bundle price in year 1 is €15.10 (column 6), and the bundle price in year 2 is €19.20 (column 8). Both columns use year 2 quantities. The bundle price has increased from 15.10 to €19.20, an increase of 27.2%.

As was expected, we have seen that overall price increases can be sensitive to the choice of the base year – 52.1% using year 1 quantities as weights and 27.2% using year 2 quantities as weights. So all the problems and remedies encountered when discussing real GDP growth apply when constructing a GDP price index, usually referred to as the *GDP deflator*.

Limitations of the GDP concept

We generally think of increases in GDP as good. Increasing GDP (or preventing its decrease) is usually considered one of the chief goals of the government's macroeconomic policy. Because some serious problems arise when we try to use GDP as a measure of happiness or well-being, we now point out some of the limitations of the GDP concept as a measure of welfare.

GDP and social welfare

A decrease in crime increases social welfare, but crime levels are not measured in GDP. If crime levels fell, society would be better off, but a decrease in crime is not an increase in output and is not reflected in GDP. Neither is an increase in leisure time. Yet, to the extent that households desire extra leisure time (rather than having it forced on them by a lack of jobs in the economy), an increase in leisure is also an increase in social welfare. Furthermore, some increases in social welfare are associated with a *decrease* in GDP. An increase in leisure during a time of full employment, for example, leads to a decrease in GDP because less time is spent on producing output.

Most non-market and domestic activities, such as housework and child care, are not counted in GDP even though they amount to real production. However, if I decide to send my children to a nursery or employ someone to clean my house or to drive my car for me, GDP increases. The salaries of nursery staff, cleaning people and chauffeurs are counted in GDP, but the time I spend doing the same things is not counted. A mere change of institutional arrangements, even though no more output is being produced, can show up as a change in GDP.

Furthermore, GDP seldom reflects losses or social ills. GDP accounting rules do not adjust for production that pollutes the environment. The more production there is, the larger is GDP, regardless of how much pollution is created in the process.

The correlation between GDP and welfare is far from perfect. One illustration is Denmark, where this was a key issue in their 1998 General Election.

The economy has flourished, GDP has grown by an average of 3% a year, and unemployment has fallen from 12.4% in 1993 to about 7.4% this winter. The general government budget has gone into surplus for the first time in ten years. In purely material terms, it is safe to say, the Danes have never had it so good.

Yet it does not follow that Danes are satisfied with their lot.

The election, it turns out, is about the 'quality of life' – more precisely, the quality of Denmark's vaunted welfare state.

The voters are told gloomy news by one international study after another. Danish schools, it seems, are not much good. Waiting lists for routine hospital operations are irritatingly long, and the newspapers retail many horror stories about the state of the country's hospitals. Statistics show that the average lifespan of almost every other nation in Europe is increasing faster than that of the Danes; nowadays the French and the Swiss both last longer than they do. Parents complain that Europe's highest income taxes require them – both of them – to work too much. So they see too little of their children; 48% of children under the age of two and 80% of those between three and six get parked in day-care centres.

Family life isn't what it used to be.

Unemployment is no longer a great worry, but almost 1m people of working age, well over a fifth of the total, are still in one way or another dependent on welfare for their income. That includes people who have retired early, those on disability pensions, and the beneficiaries of a wide variety of other welfare programmes. The welfare state, you might say, is in that sense working all too well.

The government also has quite an army of employees to support; one Dane out of every eight is tax-financed rather than market-financed. The tax burden is fearsome. But there are few signs of revolt about this. When so many people are tax-financed, trying to cut the tax level is tricky.

Danish voters are also exercised about immigration. There are not many immigrants from countries outside the European Union and Denmark's Nordic neighbours: only about 180,000, out of a total population of 5.3m. But, in a country that until recently was gleamingly homogeneous, that is enough to excite people. The tabloid press encourages the excitement. One story this week claimed that Denmark's 11,000 Somali immigrants, virtually all beneficiaries of the welfare state, have managed to send DKr58 m ($8.4 m) back to Africa over the past nine months. Danish taxpayers are jibbing at that.

Source: The Economist, 7 March 1998, pp. 52–3.

GDP also has nothing to say about the distribution of output among individuals in a society. It does not distinguish, for example, between the case in which most output goes to a few people and the case in which output is evenly divided among all people. We cannot use GDP to measure the effects of redistributive policies (which take income from some people and give income to others). Such policies have no direct impact on GDP. GDP is also neutral about the kinds of goods an economy produces. Symphony performances, guns, cigarettes, football matches, bibles, beer, milk, economics textbooks and comics all get counted, regardless of the values that society might attach to them.

In spite of these limitations, GDP is a highly useful measure of economic activity and well-being. If you doubt this, answer this simple question: would you rather live in your country as it was 200 years ago, when rivers were less polluted and crime rates were probably lower, or in your country as it is today? Most people would say that they prefer the present. Even with all the 'negatives', GDP per person and the average standard of living are much higher today than 200 years ago.

underground economy *or* shadow economy
The part of the economy in which transactions take place and in which income is generated that is unreported and therefore not counted in GDP.

The underground economy

Many transactions are missed in the calculation of GDP, even though in principle they should be counted. Most illegal transactions go unnoticed unless they are 'laundered' into legitimate business. Income that is earned but not reported as income for tax purposes is usually missed, though some adjustments are made in the GDP calculations to take misreported income into account. The part of the economy that should be counted in GDP but is not is sometimes called the **underground economy** or **shadow economy**.

Tax evasion is usually thought to be the major incentive for people to participate in the underground economy. Studies of the size of the US underground economy, for example, have produced estimates ranging from 5% to 30% of GDP. This is comparable to the size of the underground economy in most European countries and is probably much smaller than the size of the underground economy in some Eastern European countries. Estimates of Italy's underground economy range from 10% to 35% of Italian GDP. At the lower end of the scale, estimates for Switzerland range from 3% to 5%.[6]

Why should we care about the underground economy? To the extent that GDP reflects only a part of economic activity rather than a complete measure of what the economy produces, it is misleading. Unemployment rates, for example, may actually be lower than the official measure if people work in the underground economy without reporting this fact to the government. Also, if the size of the underground economy varies between countries – as it does – we can be misled when we compare GDP between countries. For example, Italy's GDP would be much higher if we considered its underground sector as part of the economy, while Switzerland's GDP would change very little.[7]

Per capita GDP or GNP

per capita GDP or GNP

A country's GDP or GNP divided by its population.

GDP and GNP are sometimes expressed in per capita terms. **Per capita GDP** or **GNP** is a country's GDP or GNP divided by the size of its population. It is a better measure of how the average persons well-being developed over time, because it separates the income growth that simply results from a growing population from income growth due to improved productivity. Norway's real GNP rose from 235.06 billion kroner in 1960 to 908.04 billion kroner in 1996. Of course, this does not mean that the average Norwegian was 386.3% better off compared to 1960. Since the population grew from 3.581 million to 4.381 million during that time, per capita GNP increased from 65,640.9 to 207,267.8 kroner. So the material well-being of the average person improved by 315.8% only.

International income comparisons

Often we want to compare how different countries are doing economically. There also, per capita GNP comes in handy, since we would not want to argue that Luxemburg's citizens are worse off than Canadians just because the country is smaller. For international comparisons we need further adjustments, however.

First, per capita GNP needs to be expressed in a common currency. In Table 21.6, the first column following each country showes per capita GNP expressed in US dollars for 1996. Luxemburg has the highest per capita GNP, followed by Switzerland, Japan, Norway, Denmark and Singapore. These six countries plus seven other European countries and the USA had per capita GNP values over $25,000 in that year.

Second, we need to make adjustments for differences in the purchasing power of one dollar in different countries. After all, it is what citizens can buy with their incomes that determines their material well-being, not the numbers written on their pay cheques. $100 spent in Miami do not necessarily buy the same (basket of) goods as $100 (or its euro equivalent) spent in Luxemburg. For example, in 1998 a Big Mac cost about $2.50 in the US but as much as $4.00 in Zurich. A pair of Levi's sold for some $30 in California but easily cost twice as much in Geneva. To correct for such differences, per capita GNP is often not only converted to a common currency, but also adjusted for differences in the purchasing power (that is: in the dollar price level) between countries. Table 21.6 also includes purchasing-power-adjusted per capita incomes. These sometimes give a very different picture. While the Swiss on average made some $16,000 more than Americans in 1996, they could buy even less with their incomes than Americans could.

---

[6] See 'Light on the shadows', *The Economist, 3 May 1997,* for some specific estimates of the size of the underground economy in 17 industrialized countries.

[7] In fact, Italy's official GDP figures are adjusted to take account of activity in the shadow economy. When this was done for the first time in 1987, the Italian economy 'grew' by 18% overnight.

Table 21.6 Per capita GNP for selected countries, 1996

Country	GNP per capita in US dollars	GNP per capita purchasing power adjusted	Country	GNP per capita in US dollars	GNP per capita purchasing power adjusted
Luxemburg	45,360	34,480	Canada	19,020	21,380
Switzerland	44,350	26,340	Ireland	17,110	16,750
Japan	40,940	23,420	Israel	15,870	18,100
Norway	34,510	23,220	New Zealand	15,720	16,500
Denmark	32,100	22,120	Spain	14,350	15,290
Singapore	30,550	26,910	Greece	11,460	12,730
Germany	28,870	21,110	Portugal	10,160	13,450
Austria	28,110	21,650	Chile	4,860	11,700
United States	28,020	28,020	Czech Republic	4,740	10,870
Iceland	26,580	21,710	Mexico	3,670	7,660
Belgium	26,440	22,390	Turkey	2,830	6,060
France	26,270	21,510	Namibia	2,250	5,390
Netherlands	25,940	20,850	Jordan	1,650	3,570
Sweden	25,710	18,770	Jamaica	1,600	3,450
Hong Kong	24,290	24,260	Philippines	1,160	3,550
Finland	23,240	18,260	Egypt	1,080	2,860
Australia	20,090	19,870	Indonesia	1,080	3,310
Italy	19,880	19,890	Bolivia	830	2,860
United Kingdom	19,600	19,960	Mozambique	80	500

Source: The World Bank Atlas, 1998.

Global Perspectives

GDP versus leisure: the choices in Germany and the USA

In 1995, US GDP was 6,737 billion dollars, whereas GDP in Germany was 1,613 billion dollars (adjusted for differences in purchasing power). With populations of 263.0 and 81.6 million respectively, per capita GDP was 25,860 in the USA but only 19,890 in Germany.

Now we may want to consider that a smaller share of the population work in Germany than in the USA, either because they are not active, because they do not want to work, or because they do not find

work. In 1995, employment in Germany was 35.6 million; in the USA it was 128.24 million. This puts output per worker at 52,537 in the USA and 45,331 in Germany. To push the argument further, note that the average German worker works 1,600 hours per year. The average American worker works 1,950 hours. Thus, GDP per hour worked turns out to be 28.3 dollars in Germany, compared to 27.5 dollars' worth of output produced in the USA.

What is the message in this? We started by noting that US per capita GDP exceeds per capita GDP in Germany. Thus a standardized 'family' comprising, say, two adults and two children, earns more dollars in the USA than in Germany. However, fewer persons in the German family work. And those who work do work fewer hours than their US counterparts. So who is better off? The US family, having higher income but little time to spend it? Or

the German family, with ample leisure time but less money to spend? It is your call: since there is an obvious trade-off between income and leisure, it is your preferences that must determine what is right for you or your country. The point is that comparing the welfare of Germans and Americans by looking at per capita GDP only may be just as misleading as comparing it by looking at leisure time alone.

Looking ahead

This chapter has introduced many key variables that macroeconomists are interested in, including GDP and its components. There is much more to be learned regarding the data that macroeconomists use. In the next chapter we discuss the data measuring employment, unemployment and the labour force. In Chapter 26 we discuss the data on money and interest rates. Finally, in Chapter 28 we discuss in more detail the data on the relationship between national economies and the rest of the world.

Summary

1. One source of data on the key variables in the macroeconomy are the national income and product accounts. These accounts provide a conceptual framework that macroeconomists use to think about how the pieces of the economy fit together.

Gross domestic product

2. *Gross domestic product* (*GDP*) is the key concept in national income accounting. GDP is the total market value of all final goods and services produced within a given period by factors of production located within a country. GDP excludes intermediate goods. To include goods both when they are purchased as inputs and when they are sold as final products would be double counting and an overstatement of the value of production.

3. GDP excludes all transactions in which money or goods change hands but in which no new goods and services are produced. For example, Italian GDP includes the income of foreigners working in Italy and the profits earned by foreign companies in Italy, but excludes the income of Italian citizens working abroad and the profits earned by Italian companies in foreign countries.

4. *Gross national product* (*GNP*) is the market value of all final goods and services produced during a given period by factors of production owned by a country's citizens.

Calculating GDP

5. The *expenditure approach* to GDP adds up the amount spent on all final goods and services during a given period. The four main categories of expenditures are *personal consumption expenditures* (*C*), *gross private domestic investment* (*I*), *government purchases of goods and services* (*G*) and *net exports* (*EX – IM*). The sum of these equals GDP.

6. The three main components of personal consumption expenditures (*C*) are *durable goods*, *non-durable goods* and *services*.

7. *Gross private domestic investment* (*I*) is the total investment made by the private sector in a given period. There are three kinds of investment: *non-residential*

investment, *residential investment* and *changes in business inventories*. Gross investment does not take *depreciation* – the decrease in the value of assets – into account. *Net investment* is equal to gross investment minus depreciation.

8. Government purchases of goods and services (*G*) include expenditures by national and local governments for final goods and labour. The value of *net exports* (*EX – IM*) equals the differences between exports (sales to foreigners of home-produced goods and services) and imports (domestic purchases of goods and services from abroad).

9. Because every payment (expenditure) by a buyer is a receipt (income) for the seller, GDP can be computed in terms of who receives it as income, the *income approach* to calculating gross domestic product. The GDP equation using the income approach is GDP = Factor incomes + Depreciation + (Indirect taxes – Subsidies).

10. GNP minus depreciation is *net national product* (NNP). *National income* is the total amount earned by the factors of production in the economy; it is equal to NNP less indirect taxes minus subsidies.

Nominal versus real GDP

11. GDP measured in current euros (the current prices that one pays for goods) is *nominal GDP*. If we use nominal GDP to measure growth, we can be misled into thinking that production has grown when all that has happened is a rise in the price level, or inflation. A better measure of production is *real* GDP, which is nominal GDP adjusted for prices changes.

12. The *GDP price index* (or *deflator*) is a measure of the overall price level.

Limitations of the GDP concept

13. We generally think of increases in GDP as good, but some problems arise when we try to use GDP as a measure of happiness or well-being. The peculiarities of GDP accounting mean that institutional changes can change the value of GDP even if real production has not changed. GDP ignores most social ills, such as pollution or crime. Furthermore, GDP tells us nothing about what kinds of goods are being produced or how income is distributed across the population. GDP also ignores many transactions of the underground economy.

14. *Per capita GDP or GNP* is a country's GDP or GNP divided by the size of its population. Per capita GDP or GNP is a better measure of well-being for the average person than is total GDP or GNP.

Review Terms and Concepts

base year
change in business inventories
compensation of employees
current euros
depreciation
expenditure approach
factor incomes
final goods and services
fixed-weight procedure
GDP price index or GDP deflator
government purchases of goods and services (*G*)
gross domestic product (GDP)
gross investment
gross national product (GNP)
gross private investment (*I*)
income approach
index
index year
indirect taxes
intermediate goods
national income
national income and product accounts
net exports (*EX – IM*)
net factor payments from rest of the world

net investment
net national product
nominal GDP
non-durable goods
non-residential investment
per capita GDP or GNP
personal consumption expenditures (*C*)
real GDP
residential investment
services
subsidies
underground or shadow economy
value added
weight

Equations

Expenditure approach to GDP: $GDP = C + I + G + (EX – IM)$

GDP = Final sales + Change in business inventories

$Net\ investment = Capital_{end\ of\ period} – Capital_{beginning\ of\ period}$

Income approach to GDP: GDP = Factor incomes + Depreciation + (Indirect taxes – Subsidies)

Problem Set

1. From Table 1, calculate the following:
a. Gross private investment
b. Net exports
c. Gross domestic product
d. Gross national product
e. Net national product
f. National income

2. How do we know that calculating GDP by the expenditure approach yields the same answer as calculating GDP by the income approach?

3. Why do we bother to construct real GDP if we already know nominal GDP?

4. Consider the data for the country of Fruitopia shown in Table 2. In each (a) to (d) below, make 1998 the index year and set the index value to 100.
a. Construct values of the fixed-weight quantity index for 1998 and 1999, using 1998 as the base year. What is the percentage change in this quantity index?
b. Construct values of the fixed-weight quantity index for 1998 and 1999, using 1999 as the base year. What is the percentage change in this quantity index?
c. Construct values of the fixed-weight price index for 1998 and 1999, using 1998 as the base year. What is the percentage change in this price index?

Table 1

Transfer payments	15
Subsidies	5
Social insurance payments	35
Depreciation	50
Receipts of factor income from the rest of the world	4
Government purchases	75
Imports	50
Payments of factor income to the rest of the world	5
Personal interest income from government and households	35
Indirect taxes	20
Exports	60
Net private domestic investment	100
Personal taxes	60
Corporate profits	45
Personal consumption expenditures	250
Dividends	4

Table 2

	Production (in number of units)		Production (in units of currency)	
	1998	1999	1998	1999
Apples	10	20	10	10
Oranges	5	8	10	12
Peaches	20	15	5	10

d. Construct values of the fixed-weight price index for 1998 and 1999, using 1999 as the base year. What is the percentage change in this price index?

e. What are some of the problems of fixed-weight indexes? How do (a) to (d) demonstrate them?

5. Explain what double counting is, and discuss why GDP is not equal to total sales.

6. In Swaziland and Lesotho, two small countries in Southern Africa, GNP tends to be substantially bigger than GDP. Given their location, can you offer an explanation as to why this is the case?

7. During 1997, real GDP in Germany rose about 2.9%. During the same period, retail sales in Germany rose only about 1.1% in real terms. What are some possible explanations for retail sales to consumers growing more slowly than GDP? (*Hint*: think of the composition of GDP using the expenditure approach.)

8. Which of the following transactions would not be counted in GDP? Explain your answers.
a. Unilever issues new shares of stock to finance the construction of a plant.
b. Unilever builds a new plant.
c. Company A successfully launches a hostile takeover of Company B, in which it purchases all the assets of Company B.
d. Your grandmother wins €10 million in the lottery.
e. You buy a new copy of this textbook.
f. You buy a used copy of this textbook.
g. The government pays out social security benefits.
h. A public utility installs new anti-pollution equipment.
i. Luigi's Pizza buys 30 kilos of mozzarella cheese, holds it in inventory for a month, and then uses it to make pizza, which it sells.
j. You spend the weekend cleaning your flat.
k. A drug dealer sells €500 worth of illegal drugs.

9. If you buy a new car, the entire purchase is counted as consumption in the year in which you make the transaction. Explain briefly why this is in some sense an 'error' in national income accounting. (*Hint*: how is the purchase of a car different from the purchase of a pizza?) How might you correct this error?

10. Explain why imports are subtracted in the expenditure approach to calculating GDP.

11. GDP calculations do not directly include the economic costs of environmental damage (for example, global warming, acid rain). Do you think these costs should be included in GDP? Why or why not? How could GDP be amended to include environmental damage costs?

Macroeconomic Concerns: Unemployment, Inflation and Growth

In only two decades Spain's unemployment rose from a mere 5.1% in 1977 to 22.3% in 1997. Regions such as Andalusia fare even worse, suffering from unemployment in excess of 35%. Youth unemployment is also over 40% nationwide.

While other European countries were more fortunate, they can hardly consider themselves lucky. Across Western Europe some 20,000,000 people are looking for work, which amounts to about 12% of the labour force.

The hardship of unemployment for individuals and their families can probably only be appreciated by those affected. Their numbers across Europe grew so large in the 1990s that the problem is scaring politicians:

> In 1996 Chancellor Helmut Kohl pledged to halve Germany's unemployment by 2000. The leaders of Sweden's ruling Social Democratic party say they will do the same. Spain's prime minister, Jose Maria Aznar, has promised that 1997 will be 'the year for jobs'. Jacques Chirac was elected president in 1995 partly because he offered to do most to cut French unemployment.[1]

Inflation is not currently an issue in Europe. Average inflation in the European Union fell below 2% in 1997 and is forecast to stay there in the near future. Even Greece's inflation, the highest in Europe for decades, is expected to be below 4% when the millennium ends.

The inflation picture was not always as bright as it currently is. In 1973/74 only two European countries, Austrian and Germany, just managed to keep inflation below 10%. Most countries' inflation rates were between 10% and 20%. For some, including Greece, Ireland, Italy, Portugal and Spain, inflation was higher still, between 20% and 30%.

Does this matter? The effects can be drastic, though they may be different in the long run than in the short run. Suppose the Mullers have a DM 300,000 mortgage on their house. When inflation is, say, 2% and the interest rate is 6%, their annual interest payment is DM 18,000, which is 20% of their annual household income of DM 90,000. Now suppose inflation goes up to 26%, driving the interest rate up to 30%. Interest payments on the family's mortgage jump to DM 90,000, eating up all of their income.

Of course, inflation also drives up income and the nominal value of the house, thus reducing the real value of the mortgage. But before these effects amount to anything the Mullers may already have lost their house.

The 'twin evils' of unemployment and inflation are among the chief concerns of macroeconomists. In this chapter we explore these concerns, describing the periodic ups and downs in the economy that we call the business cycle. Later chapters focus on the likely causes of business cycles and some of the things that government may do to prevent or minimize the damage they create. First, we need to know more about what the business cycle is. What are recessions and depressions? Who is hurt by them? What are the consequences of inflation? Who benefits and who loses when the price level rises rapidly? Why should policy makers in Brussels and national capitals be concerned about the business cycle?

As was also mentioned in Chapter 20, macroeconomists are concerned about the size of the long-run growth rate of output. What are the factors that influence the long-run growth rate? Why do some countries grow faster than others? Can policy makers influence the growth rate? We briefly consider long-run growth issues in this chapter and then return to them in Chapter 35.

Recessions, depressions and unemployment

recession Roughly, a period in which real GDP declines for at least two consecutive quarters. Marked by falling output and rising unemployment.

Recall that, roughly speaking, a **recession** is a period in which real GDP declines for at least two consecutive quarters. Also recall that real GDP is a measure of the actual output of goods and services in the economy during a given period. When real GDP falls, less is being produced. When less output is produced, fewer inputs are used, employment declines, the unemployment rate rises, and a smaller percentage of the capital stock at our disposal is utilized (more plants and equipment are running at less than full capacity). When real output falls, real income declines.

depression A prolonged and deep recession. The precise definitions of prolonged and deep are debatable.

A **depression** is a prolonged and deep recession, though there is disagreement over how severe and how prolonged a recession must be to be called a depression. Nearly everyone agrees that the US economy experienced a depression between 1929 and the late 1930s. And so did Germany. The slowdown in Britain was weaker, however.

Table 22.1 compares the British recession of 1980–82 with how Britain experienced the Great Depression. Between 1929 and 1931, real GDP declined by 5.8%. In other

Table 22.1 Real GDP and unemployment rates in Britain, 1929–1932 and 1979–1982

The early part of the Great Depression, 1929–1933

	Percentage change in real GDP	Unemployment rate
1929	2.9	7.2
1930	−0.7	11.1
1931	−5.1	14.8
1932	0.8	15.3

The Recession of 1980–1982

	Percentage change in real GDP	Unemployment rate	Number of unemployed (millions)	Percentage of firms operating at full capacity
1979	2.8	4.6	1.1	42.3
1980	−2.2	5.6	1.5	26.3
1981	−1.3	8.9	2.3	19.5
1982	1.7	10.3	2.6	23.3

Sources: IMF; Maddison, A. (1991), *Dynamic Forces in Capitalist Development*, Oxford: Oxford University Press.

words, in 1931 Britain produced 5.8% less than in 1929. While only 7.2% of the labour force was unemployed in 1929, 15.3% was unemployed in 1932. By comparison, between 1979 and 1981 real GDP declined by 3.5%. The unemployment rate rose from 4.6% in 1979 to 10.3% in 1982. The percentage of firms operating at full capacity is not available for the 1930s, so we have no point of comparison. However, Table 22.1 shows that this percentage fell from 42.3% in 1979 to 19.5% in 1981. In the light of these numbers, the recession in the early 1980s was a little less severe, but still similar to what happened in Britain during the Great Depression.

Defining and measuring unemployment

In the 1990s, unemployment dwarfs all others macroeconomic concerns in Europe. Talk of remedies is cheap, and it is easy to understand why countries that are performing better than some others should offer their institutions and policies as guiding lights. Unfortunately, unemployment is difficult to measure, let alone compare internationally. Why this is so will become clear after we have defined the concept of unemployment.

Rather than talk in the abstract, Figure 22.1 uses Spanish data to define the unemployment rate and to introduce some labour market vocabulary. In 1994, Spain's population was 39.2 m (million). Out of these, 26.6 m constituted the active population (aged 15–64, according to the OECD definition). The (civilian) **labour force** was 15.7 m, meaning that 10.9 m members of the active population were unwilling to work. Finally, 11.8 m of all men and women willing to work actually did work, thus constituting **employment**.

The labour force in the economy is the sum of employment and unemployment:

Labour force = Employment + Unemployment

This identifies Spain's **unemployment** in 1994 at 15.7 − 11.8 = 3.9 million. The **unemployment rate** is the number of people unemployed relative to the total number of people in the labour force:

$$\text{Unemployment rate} = \frac{\text{Unemployment}}{\text{Employment} + \text{Unemployment}}$$

Thus the Spanish unemployment rate in 1994 was (15.7 − 11.8)/15.7 = 0.251 = 25.1%. A final, useful concept is the **participation rate**, the ratio of the labour force to the active population:

labour force
The number of people employed plus the number of unemployed.

employment
Persons between 15 and 64 years of age working for pay at least one hour per week, or without pay at least 15 hours per week in a family business.

unemployment
Persons between 15 and 64 years of age who are not working, but are available for work, and are actively looking for work.

unemployment rate
The ratio of the number of people unemployed to the total number of people in the labour force.

participation rate
The ratio of the labour force to the active population (aged 15–64).

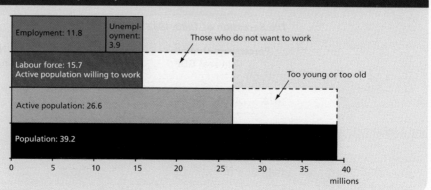

Figure 22.1 Population and labour market concepts in Spain, 1994

Out of Spain's population of 39.2m, 26.6m are 'active', since 12.6m are younger than 15 or older than 64. 10.9m active persons do not want to work, leaving a labour force of 15.7m. 11.8m of these are actually employed, leaving 3.9m unemployed.

$$\text{Participation rate} = \frac{\text{Labour force}}{\text{Active population}}$$

Table 22.2 shows the relationship among these numbers for selected countries in 1994. There is not only quite some variation in the unemployment rate, but also in the participation rate. In Britain and Sweden only a quarter of the active population does not want to work. In Italy the participation rate is much lower at 57.7%.

Although *defining* unemployment as a concept is easy, *measuring* unemployment is quite difficult. Why? Look at Figure 22.1. Obtaining data for population and its active part, the two lower bars, is a straightforward, technical matter. Things get complicated when we close in on the labour force, defined as those 'willing to work'. This willingness is a subjective quality that evades objective measurement. Individuals may misrepresent or fake 'willingness to work' in order to reap benefits or avoid sanctions. And sometimes members of the labour force may conceal from the tax authorities that they are employed.

In view of these problems, the precision and reliability of unemployment data crucially depends on how they are obtained. In the USA, people are simply asked whether they were actively looking for work during some specified period. Most European countries consider persons unemployed who collect unemployment benefits. As Figure 22.1 shows, these methods are not likely to yield comparable results. The OECD goes to great lengths to adjust national data towards a common standard that permits better comparability.

Components of the unemployment rate

The unemployment rate conveys a limited amount of information. To understand unemployment better, we must look at unemployment rates across groups of people, regions and industries.

Table 22.2 Employment, unemployment and the labour force, 1994

	(1) Population (millions)	(2) Population aged 15 – 64 (millions)	(3) Civilian labour force (millions)	(4) Civilian employment (millions)	(5) = (3) – (4) Unemployment (millions)	(6) = (3)/(2) × 100 Labour force participation rate (%)	(7) = (5)/(3) × 100 Unemployment rate (%)
EU 15	371.5	245.6	165.9	147.3	18.6	67.6	11.2
France	57.9	37.9	25.4	21.7	3.6	67.0	14.3
Germany	81.4	55.4	39.6	35.9	3.8	71.5	9.5
Italy	57.2	39.4	22.7	20.0	2.7	57.7	11.9
Netherlands	15.4	10.5	7.2	6.6	0.6	68.4	7.7
Spain	39.2	26.6	15.7	11.8	3.9	59.1	25.1
Sweden	8.8	5.6	4.3	3.9	0.3	76.3	8.0
United Kingdom	58.4	37.8	28.4	25.6	2.9	75.1	10.0

Source: Eurostat, OECD.

Applications

Which country's growth prospects are brightest?

Short term growth prospects are demand led, but if we look to the next 10 years other (supply) factors are the most important.

An economy's long-term growth rate is determined by demographics: the growth in the labour force and how well it is used.

The population of working age can be forecast with more accuracy than any other economic series. All those who will be in it in 2000 to 2010 are alive today and death rates change slowly. Immigration presents the only forecasting problem. Some people of working age are not available to work – the sick or severely disabled, students and those taking early retirement. The labour force is the population of working age multiplied by the proportion available for work (the participation rate).

Some people in the labour force cannot get jobs, so employment is the labour force less the unemployed. The growth in GDP is therefore determined by the growth in the population, less any changes in participation and unemployment rates, which gives the growth in employment, plus productivity – the growth in output per employee.

All countries are ageing but at different rates. Growth in the population of working age, 15 years to 64 years, is slowing down. In Italy, where it is already falling in the 1990s, it will fall faster. In Germany it stops growing and starts shrinking. The German

working-age population falls the fastest between 2000 and 2010, down 0.25 per cent a year. Growth in Britain and Japan is one tenth of one per cent per year. The French working age population increases 0.25 per cent a year between 2000 and 2010, Canada's by 0.5 per cent and America's by 0.75 per cent. American population growth will be boosted by immigration, Japan's won't be, nor probably Europe's. If participation and unemployment rates everywhere are unchanged, America is the favourite in the next decade's growth stakes. Germany is so severely handicapped it could come last.

But if past experience is anything to go by, differences in productivity growth rates will outweigh differences in demography. The best measure of 1990s productivity is GDP growth adjusted for differences in cyclical positions in 1989 and 1999 and divided by labour force growth. Cyclically adjusted GDP growth is likely to be very similar in most countries during the 1990s. All bar Italy and Canada look like achieving two per cent. Italy lags with 1.75 per cent and Canada leads with 2.25 per cent.

When 1990s productivity performance is combined with demographic forecasts for 2000–2010, Britain is the winner, the only economy likely to notch up more than two per cent a year growth. Germany, with good productivity but bad demography, manages a shade below two per cent

Growth in the population of working age is slowing down, but better use of the labour force could solve Europes' ageing problems. Could people be persuaded to retire later – right: a mature baker at work. Source: **Telegraph Colour Library.**

and comes second. France, Canada and Italy are in the middle of the field.

America's worst productivity performance in the 1990s, despite the best demographic prospects after 2000, pushes it in to second to last place, while poor Japan in last place, which scores badly on both, can hope for little more than one per cent a year growth. But these projections assume no change in participation and unemployment rates or productivity growth rates. They provide the handicaps at the start of the race, indicating betting odds, not results. The American performance is likely to be far better than these odds suggest. Its boom is investment-led, not consumption-fed.

Continental Europe suffers low labour participation rates and high unemployment. In America, Japan and Britain three-quarters of the population of working age is in the labour force and

unemployment is low. In Germany and France participation is two-thirds and in Italy less than 60 per cent. Unemployment is twice that in Britain and America and three times its level in Japan. If these differences were eliminated in the next decade, continental Europe's growth could accelerate, German and French to 2.7 per cent, Italian to 3.2 per cent. Italy would then be the top performer.

Better use of the labour force could solve Europe's ageing problem. But there are problems. Can older Germans and Italians be persuaded to retire later? This will require painful changes in pension arrangements. Can young Frenchmen and women be brought back into the labour force? Will lower unemployment lead to faster inflation?

Source: B. Reading 'Productivity explosion can bridge the age gap', The European, 27 April / 3 May 1998, p. 54.

Unemployment rates for different demographic groups

Table 22.3 shows unemployment rates in 1985 and 1995 for six European countries, broken down by sex and age. The key point to note is that there are big differences in unemployment rates across demographic groups. In Italy in 1985, unemployment among women was more than twice as high as among men, and youth unemployment was three times the total unemployment rate. While above-average youth unemployment appears to be a general pattern, with the exception of Germany, unemployment among women is sometimes lower than among men, as is seen in France, Britain and, recently, Sweden.

Another observation is that demographic differences in unemployment are quite robust over time. If total unemployment changes, as in The Netherlands, where it fell from 11.9% in 1985 to 6.8% in 1995, it moves in that direction for all demographic groups. Thus, restating the main point of Table 22.3, the overall unemployment rate is an aggregate measure that hides a great deal of diversity between different segments of the labour market.

> There are large differences in unemployment rates across demographic groups.

Unemployment rates in different regions

Unemployment rates vary by geographical location. For a variety of reasons, even within countries not all states and regions have the same level of unemployment (see Figure 22.2). For one thing, regions have different combinations of industries, which do not all grow and decline at the same time and at the same rate. For another, the labour force is not completely mobile – workers often cannot or do not want to pack up and move to take advantage of job opportunities in other parts of the country, not to speak of other parts of the EU.

> The national unemployment rate does not tell the whole story. A low national rate of unemployment does not mean that the entire nation is growing and producing at the same rate.

Unemployment rates in different industries

Unemployment rates also differ from industry to industry. Table 22.4 shows 1995 unemployment rates in various industries in Denmark and Spain. There are substantial differences within each country, with unemployment in the worst-performing industries being about four times as high as in the best-performing industries. Also, the pattern differs between the two countries. For example, while in Denmark the unemployment rate in hotels is twice as high as in construction, Spain experiences a much higher rate in construction than in hotels.

Table 22.3 Unemployment rates by demographic group in six countries, 1985 and 1995

Country Year	France 1985	France 1995	Germany 1985*	Germany 1995	Italy 1985	Italy 1995	Netherlands 1985	Netherlands 1995	Sweden 1985	Sweden 1995	UK 1985	UK 1995
TOTAL	10.2	11.6	7.9	8.4	9.9	11.9	11.9	6.8	3.1	8	11.1	9.6
Men	12.9	13.9	7.3	7.2	6.5	9.4	10.9	6	3	9.1	13	11.4
Men under 25	21.6	21	9	8.7	28	28.6	23.3	12	5.8	16.7	19.1	17.9
Women	8.3	9.7	8.8	9.9	16.3	16.1	14	8.1	3.3	6.7	8.3	7.3
Women under 25	32.2	30.5	10.7	8.2	40.9	36.5	22.6	13.7	5.7	14	15.9	12.2

* West Germany only.

Source: OECD.

Figure 22.2 Regional differences in unemployment rates, April 1994

The map shows that even within regions as homogeneous as the European Union there is great diversity in unemployment rates. Traditional trouble spots are the very south of Italy and southern Spain, with unemployment rates in excess of 22%. In 1994, the same high rates were found in Spain's Basque region and in the northern part of Finland. At the other extreme, Western Germany, Northern Italy, the south of Sweden, and most of England, Portugal and Greece had unemployment rates below 10%.
Source: Project Gisco, Eurostat.

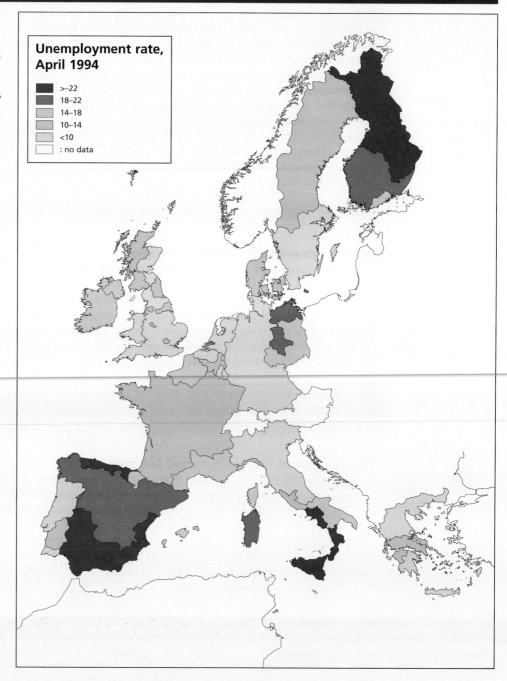

Unemployment rate, April 1994

■	>–22
▨	18–22
▧	14–18
▧	10–14
▧	<10
□	: no data

discouraged-worker effect
The decline in the measured unemployment rate that results when people who want to work but cannot find jobs become discouraged and stop looking, thus dropping out of the ranks of the unemployed and the labour force.

Discouraged-worker effects

Remember: people who stop looking for work are classified as having dropped out of the labour force rather than as being unemployed. During recessions, people may become discouraged about finding a job and stop looking. This lowers the unemployment rate, because those no longer looking for work are no longer counted as unemployed.

To demonstrate how this **discouraged-worker effect** lowers the unemployment rate, suppose there are 10 million unemployed out of a labour force of 100 million. This

Table 22.4 Unemployment in selected industries in Denmark and Spain, 1995

	Denmark	Spain
Agriculture	6.3	18.6
Fishing	4.5	9.9
Mining	3.2	7.2
Manufacturing	7.1	13.6
Construction	6.3	23.0
Hotels	13.5	18.7
Financial intermediation	5.0	5.9
Education	5.9	8.2
Health and Social work	8.0	11.2

List of categories is not comprehensive.

Source: ILO, *Yearbook of Labour Statistics* 1996.

implies an unemployment rate of 10/100 = 0.10 or 10%. If 1 million of these 10 million unemployed people stop looking for work and drop out of the labour force, there would be 9 million unemployed out of a labour force of 99 million. The unemployment rate would then drop to 9/99 = 0.091 or 9.1%.

Surveys provide some evidence on the size of the discouraged-worker effect. Respondents who indicate that they have stopped searching for work are asked why they stopped. If the respondent cites inability to find employment as the sole reason for not searching, that person might be classified as a discouraged worker. Some economists argue that adding the number of discouraged workers to the number who are now classified as unemployed gives a better picture of the unemployment situation.

Duration of unemployment

An unemployment rate of 10% in 1999 may mean that 10% of the labour force was out of work for the entire year, or that each and every man and woman in the labour force was without a job for about five weeks.

Table 22.5 shows that the French, on average, were unemployed about three times as long as Swedes. This ratio was about the same in 1995 as it was in 1975. In both

Table 22.5 Average duration of unemployment, 1975–1995 (weeks)

	France	Sweden
1975	7.6	2.7
1980	14.2	3.0
1985	22.9	3.7
1990	14.5	3.2
1995	15.1	5.4

Sources: Before 1990, R. Layard, S. Nickell and R. Jackman (1991), *Unemployment*, Oxford: Oxford University Press, Table A7. Since 1990, OECD Economic Surveys for France (1997) and Sweden (1997).

countries, average duration doubled during those 20 years. In France, though, most of the increase occurred during the first 10 years. After that, average duration fell again. In Sweden average duration peaked in the 1990s.

The costs of unemployment

In the *Treaty of Rome* of 1957, the six founding members of what is now the European Union laid out the general goals of their economic policy:

Article 104. Each member state shall pursue the economic policy needed to ensure the equ ilibration of its overall balance of payments and to maintain confidence in its currency, while taking care to ensure a high level of employment and a stable level of prices.

On a national level, Germany's 'stability law' of 1967 also requires the government to conduct economic policy so as to achieve a high level of employment (plus three other goals). In the late 1960s, the West German government explicitly defined high employment to mean an unemployment rate of 0.8% (!).

Why should full employment be a policy objective of the government? What costs does unemployment impose on society?

Some unemployment is inevitable

Before discussing the costs of unemployment, we must realize that some unemployment is simply part of the natural workings of the labour market. Remember: to be classified as unemployed, a person must be looking for a job. Every year, thousands of people enter the labour force for the first time. Some have finished mandatory schooling, others have completed apprenticeships or are new university graduates, and still others re-enter after training courses, or after their children have grown up and left home. At the same time, new businesses are starting up and some firms are expanding and creating new jobs, while others are contracting or going out of business.

At any moment, a set of job seekers must be matched with a set of jobs. It is important that the right people end up in the right jobs. The right job for a person will depend on that person's skills, her preferences regarding work environment (large or small firm, formal or informal), where she lives, and her willingness to commute. At the same time, firms want workers who can meet the requirements of the job and grow with the company.

To make a good match, workers must acquire information on job availability, wage rates, location and work environment. Firms must acquire information on worker availability and skills. Information gathering consumes time and resources. The search may involve travel, interviews, the preparation of a CV, telephone calls, and hours going through newspapers or searching the Internet. To the extent that these efforts lead to a better match of workers and jobs, they are well spent. As long as the gains to firms and workers exceed the costs of searching, the result is efficient.

Frictional and structural unemployment

Official unemployment figures include many people who are involved in the normal search for work. Some are either entering the labour force or switching jobs. This unemployment is both natural and beneficial for the economy.

frictional unemployment

The portion of unemployment that results from the normal working of the labour market; used to denote short-run job/skill matching problems.

The portion of unemployment that is due to the normal functioning of the labour market is called **frictional unemployment**. The frictional unemployment rate can never be zero, but it changes over time. As jobs become ever more differentiated and the number of required skills increases, matching skills and jobs becomes more complex, and the frictional unemployment rate may rise.

The concept of frictional unemployment is somewhat abstract because it is hard to know what 'the normal functioning of the labour market' means. The industrial structure of your country's economy is continually changing. Manufacturing, for instance, in most countries has lost part of its share of total employment to services and to finance, insurance and property. Within Europe's manufacturing sector, the steel and textiles industries have contracted sharply, while high-technology sectors, such as electronic components, have expanded.

Although the unemployment that arises from such structural shifts could be classified as frictional, it is usually called **structural unemployment**. The term *frictional unemployment* is used to denote short-run job/skill matching problems, problems that last a few weeks. *Structural unemployment* denotes longer-run adjustment problems – those that tend to last for years.

Although structural unemployment is expected in a dynamic economy, it is painful to the workers who experience it. In some ways, those who lose their jobs because their skills are obsolete are the ones who experience the greatest pain. The fact that structural unemployment is natural and inevitable does not mean that it costs society nothing.

Economists sometimes use the phrase **natural rate of unemployment** to refer to unemployment that occurs as a normal part of the functioning of the economy. This concept is also somewhat vague, because 'natural' is not a precise word. It is probably best to think of the natural rate as the sum of the frictional rate and the structural rate.

Cyclical unemployment and lost output

Although some unemployment is 'natural', there are times when the unemployment rate seems to be above the natural rate. In 1997 this was the case in many European countries. The effect was strongest in France, Germany and Switzerland, where recessions drove unemployment some 2 percentage points above the respective natural rates. By contrast, booming economies drove unemployment rates substantially below natural rates in Denmark, Ireland and the USA. (See the Application 'Structural versus cyclical unemployment' in Chapter 30.) The increase in unemployment that occurs during recessions and depressions is called **cyclical unemployment**.

In one sense, an increase in unemployment during a recession is simply a manifestation of a more fundamental problem. The basic problem is that firms are producing less. Remember that a recession entails a decline in real GDP, or real output. When firms cut back and produce less, they employ fewer workers and less capital. Thus, the first and most direct cost of a recession is the loss of real goods and services that otherwise would have been produced.

Never in the twentieth century was the loss of output in an industrial country more dramatic than in the USA during the Great Depression, when real output fell about 30% between 1929 and 1933. It is, of course, the real output of the economy that matters most – the food we eat, the health care we get, the cars we drive, the films we watch, the new houses that are built, the pots we cook in, and the education we receive. When output falls by 30%, life changes for a lot of people.

In more recent years, Switzerland experienced some of the most severe economic downturns among European countries. From 1974 to the beginning of 1977 output fell by almost 10%. Since 1990, the Swiss economy has more or less stopped growing (1997 income exceeds 1990 income by only 1%). If output had grown each year at 2.0%, as it did on average in the OECD countries, Switzerland's 1997 income would have been 14% higher than it actually was. This is a substantial loss of output.

Actual falls in real GDP have been experienced by many Eastern European countries. As Figure 22.3 shows, incomes in each country shown fell by at least 20% after 1989, before growth set in. In Estonia the drop was close to 40%. Of course, these downturns are the consequences of transforming planned economies to market economies rather than of what we usually mean by the term depression. Also, some think that official statistics overstate the problem because they fail to record what are presumably quite large black (underground) market activities.

---

structural unemployment

The portion of unemployment that results from changes in the structure of the economy that produce a significant loss of jobs in certain industries.

natural rate of unemployment

The unemployment that occurs as a normal part of the functioning of the economy. Sometimes taken as the sum of frictional unemployment and structural unemployment.

cyclical unemployment

The increase in unemployment that occurs during recessions and depressions.

Figure 22.3 GDP in five Eastern European countries, 1989–1998

The experiences of Estonia, Hungary, Poland, Slovenia and the Czech Republic are representative of countries in Eastern Central Europe and other parts of the world that moved from central planning to free enterprise systems. Typically, this transformation hatches several years of falling incomes, often by 20% and more compared to pre-transformation levels. It may take half a decade before income begins to grow again. *Source*: EBRD; IMF (for 1997 and 1998).

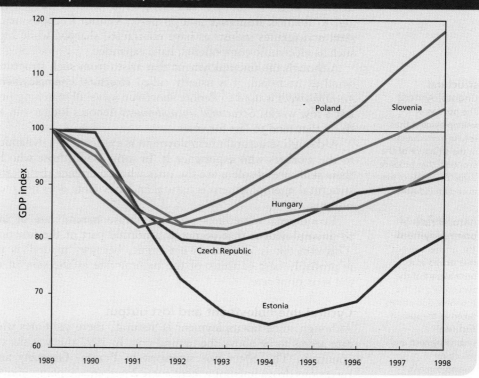

Social consequences

The costs of recessions and depressions are neither evenly distributed across the population nor easily quantifiable. The social consequences of the Depression of the 1930s are perhaps the hardest to comprehend. Most people alive today did not live through the Great Depression and can only read about it in books or hear stories told by parents and grandparents. Few emerged from this period unscathed. At the bottom were the poor and the fully unemployed, about 25% of the labour force. But even those who kept their jobs found themselves working part time. Many people lost all or part of their savings as the stock market crashed and thousands of banks failed.

US Congressional committees heard story after story. In Cincinnati, where the labour force was about 200,000, 48,000 were wholly unemployed, 40,000 more were on short time, and relief payments to the needy averaged $7 to $8 per week:

> Relief is given to a family one week and then they are pushed off for a week in the hope that somehow or other the breadwinner may find some kind of work. We are paying no rent at all. That, of course, is a very difficult problem because we are continually having evictions, and social workers are hard put to find places for people whose furniture has been put out on the street.[2]

From Birmingham, Alabama, in 1932:

[2]*US Senate hearings before a subcommittee of the Committee of Manufacturers, 72nd Congress, first session (1931), p. 239. Cited in Lester Chandler,* America's Greatest Depression, 1929–1941 *(New York: Harper & Row, 1970).*

We have about 108,000 wage and salary workers in my district. Of that number, it is my belief that not exceeding 8000 have their normal incomes. At least 25,000 men are altogether without work. Some of them have not had a stroke of work for more than 12 months. Perhaps 60,000 or 70,000 are working from one to five days a week, and practically all have had serious cuts in wages and many of them do not average over $1.50 per day.[3]

The expansion of the welfare state and mandatory unemployment insurance reduces the economic hardship for today's unemployed. It can do little to ameliorate the non-economic side-effects resulting from long unemployment. In addition to economic hardship, prolonged unemployment may also bring with it social and personal ills: anxiety, depression, a deterioration of physical and psychological health, drug abuse (including alcoholism), and suicide. These appear to be a particular challenge in Europe, where 40% (as compared to 11% in the USA) of the unemployed have been out of work for more than a year.

The benefits of recessions

Do recessions have any benefits? Yes: recessions usually go hand in hand with a falling rate of inflation. While it may not always be clear what is cause and what is effect, one seems to come with the other. Consider Table 22.6, in which are documented two recessions, both following two pronounced surges in Swiss inflation with peaks in 1974 and 1991, respectively. During each of these recessions inflation all but vanished, from a 1974 rate of 9.7% to 1.2% in 1977, and from a 1991 rate of 5.8% to 0.8% in 1994.

While more analysis is needed before we can understand why, the point here is:

Recessions may help to reduce inflation.

Table 22.6 Swiss inflation during two recessions

	GDP growth	Inflation
1973	3.2	8.8
1974	1.2	9.7
1975	−6.7	6.7
1976	−0.9	1.7
1977	2.4	1.2
1990	2.3	5.4
1991	0.0	5.8
1992	−0.1	4.1
1993	−0.5	3.4
1994	0.4	0.8

Source: IMF.

[3]*Ibid.*, p. 47.

Some argue that recessions may increase efficiency by driving the least efficient firms in the economy out of business and by forcing surviving firms to trim waste and manage their resources more competently. As we will discuss in Chapter 28, a recession leads to a decrease in the demand for imports, which improves a nation's balance of payments.

Inflation

Upturns in the business cycle often seem to encourage inflation. Or, as some argue, inflation makes the business cycle go up. In any case, Table 22.7 illustrates that income and inflation often move together. When Swiss inflation accelerated from 1.1% to 6.6% from 1978 to 1981, and from 0.8% to 5.8% from 1986 to 1991, GDP growth was sustained and way above average, with an evident slowdown at the inflation peak.

Why is inflation a problem? If you understand that wages and salaries, as well as other forms of income, increase along with prices during periods of inflation, you will see that this question is more subtle than you might think. If my income doubles and the prices of the things I buy double, am I worse off? I can buy exactly the same things that I bought yesterday, so to the extent that my well-being depends on what I am able to buy, the answer is no.

However, incomes and prices do not all increase at the same rate during inflations. For some people, income increases faster than prices; for others, prices increase faster. Some people benefit from inflations, others are hurt.

The remainder of this chapter focuses on the problem of inflation: its measurement, its costs, and the gains and losses experienced during inflationary periods.

Defining inflation

What is inflation? Not all price increases constitute inflation. Prices of individual goods and services are determined in many ways. In competitive markets, the interaction of many buyers and many sellers – the operation of supply and demand – determines prices. In imperfectly competitive markets, prices are determined by producers' decisions. (This is the core of microeconomic theory.)

Table 22.7 Swiss inflation during two expansions

	GDP growth	Inflation
1978	0.6	1.1
1979	2.4	3.8
1980	4.4	3.9
1981	1.4	6.6
1986	2.9	0.8
1987	2.0	1.5
1988	2.9	1.9
1989	3.9	3.2
1990	2.3	5.4
1991	0.0	5.8

Source: IMF, OECD.

In any economy, prices are continuously changing as markets adjust to changing conditions. A mild winter with little snow may depress tourism in alpine ski resorts, pushing down hotel rates and prices for ski passes. At the same time, OPEC may agree to lower oil production, driving up the price of oil and petroleum products.

When the price of one good rises, that price increase may or may not be part of a larger inflation. Remember: **inflation** is an increase in the overall price level. It happens when many prices increase simultaneously. We measure inflation by looking at a large number of goods and services and calculating the average increase in their prices during some period of time. **Deflation** is a decrease in the overall price level. It occurs when many prices decrease simultaneously.

It is useful to distinguish between a *single* increase in the overall price level and increases in the overall price level that continue over time. For example, the overall price level could rise by 10% in a single month and stop rising, or it could increase steadily over some years. Economists often use *inflation* to refer only to increases in the price level that continue over some significant period. We will refer to such periods as periods of **sustained inflation**.

Price indexes

Price indexes are used to measure overall price levels, and we discussed how these indexes are constructed in the previous chapter. There we encountered the *GDP price index* or price deflator that pertains to all goods and services in the economy. This *GDP deflator* says little about the prices that private households face when they do their spending. This is because the pattern of goods and services *produced* in a country is not likely to match the pattern of goods *bought* by consumers in that country.

The **consumer price index (CPI)** traces the cost of a given bundle of goods, meant to represent the 'shopping basket' purchased every month by a typical consumer. Such a basket may contain, say, a kilo of meat, 4 loaves of bread, 40 bus trips, 40 square metres of living space, 1000 car kilometres, 1 haircut, and much more, all items of a well-defined standard quality. Each month, these quantities are multiplied by their current prices and added up to give *consumer prices*.

Table 22.8 shows recent values in the Greek CPI. These index numbers are used to calculate the percentage changes given on the right. From 1993 to 1994 the CPI increased from 158.4 to 175.7. The percentage change is simply 10.9. So Greece's inflation rate in 1994 (over 1993) was 10.9%.

inflation An increase in the overall price level.

deflation A decrease in the overall price level.

sustained inflation An increase in the overall price level that continues over a significant period.

consumer price index (CPI) A price index computed each month using a bundle of goods and services that consumers typically buy.

Table 22.8 The consumer price index (CPI) and inflation in Greece		
Year	Consumer price index (CPI)	% change in CPI
1990	100	20.3
1991	119.5	19.5
1992	138.4	15.8
1993	158.4	14.5
1994	175.7	10.9
1995	191.4	8.9
1996	207.1	8.2
1997	218.5	5.5
1998	229.2	4.9

Source: IMF, OECD.

Remember from the previous chapter that a fixed-weight price index like the CPI does not account for consumers' substitution away from high-priced goods.

Changes in the CPI somewhat overstate changes in the cost of living.

producer price indexes (PPIs)

Measures of prices that producers receive for products at all stages in the production process.

Other popular price indexes are **producer price indexes (PPIs)**, once called *wholesale price indexes*. These are indexes of prices that producers receive for products at all stages in the production process, not just the final stage. In most countries these indexes are calculated separately for various stages of the production process. The three main categories are *finished goods*, *intermediate materials* and *crude materials*, though there are subcategories within each of these categories.

One advantage of producer price indexes is that they may help detect price increases early in the production process. Because their movements sometimes foreshadow future changes in consumer prices, they are sometimes considered to be **leading indicators** of future consumer prices.

leading indicators

Indices that tend to foreshadow future changes in the economy.

The costs of inflation

If you asked most people why inflation is 'bad', they would tell you that it lowers the overall standard of living by making goods and services more expensive. That is, it cuts into people's purchasing power. People are fond of recalling the days ' . . . when a pretzel cost 7 pfennig. Just think of what we could buy today if prices had not changed!'

What people usually do not think about is what their incomes were in the 'good old days'. The fact that the cost of a pretzel has increased from 7 pfennigs to 75 pfennigs does not mean anything in real terms if a typical hourly wage was 1 DM then but is 25 DM now. Why? The reason is simple:

People's incomes come from wages and salaries, profits, interest and rent. Income from these sources increases during inflations. The wage rate is the price of labour, rent is the price of land, and so on. During inflations, most prices – including input prices – tend to rise together, and input prices determine both the incomes of workers and the incomes of owners of capital and land.

Inflation changes the distribution of income

Whether you gain or lose during a period of inflation depends on whether your income rises faster or slower than the prices of the things you buy. The group most often mentioned in discussing the impact of inflation is people living on fixed incomes. If your income is fixed and prices rise, your ability to purchase goods and services falls proportionately. But who are the fixed-income earners?

Most people think of the elderly. The biggest sources of income for the elderly are pension schemes. These benefits are usually *indexed* to inflation; when prices rise (that is, when the CPI rises) by 5%, social security benefits also increase by 5%. Only to the extent that retired people are receiving unindexed private pensions will inflation reduce their real incomes.

The poor have not fared so well. Welfare benefits, which are often not fully indexed, have in some countries not kept pace with the price level over the last two decades.

Effects on debtors and creditors

It is commonly believed that debtors benefit at the expense of creditors during an inflation. Certainly, if I lend you €100 to be paid back in a year, and prices increase 10% in the meantime, I get back 10% less in real terms than I lent you.

But suppose we had both anticipated prices would rise 10%. I would have taken this into consideration in the deal that I made with you. I would charge you an interest

real interest rate
The difference between the interest rate paid or received in nominal terms and the inflation rate.

rate high enough to cover the decrease in value due to the anticipated inflation. If we agree on a 15% interest rate, then you must pay me €115 at the end of a year. The difference between the interest rate on a loan and the inflation rate is referred to as the real interest rate. In our deal, I will earn a real interest rate of 5%. By charging a 15% interest rate, I have taken into account the anticipated 10% inflation rate. In this sense, I am not hurt by the inflation – I keep pace with inflation and earn a profit on my money too – despite the fact that I am a creditor.

On the other hand, an unanticipated inflation – an inflation that takes people by surprise – can hurt creditors. If the actual inflation rate during the period of my loan to you turns out to be 20%, then I as a creditor will be hurt. I charged you 15% interest, expecting to get a 5% real rate of return, when I needed to charge you 25% to get the same 5% real rate of return. Because inflation turned out to be higher than expected, I got a negative real return of 5%.

Inflation that is higher than expected benefits debtors; inflation that is lower than expected benefits creditors.

Administrative costs and inefficiencies

There are costs associated even with anticipated inflation. One is the administrative cost associated with simply keeping up. Shopkeepers have to recalculate and re-post prices frequently, and this takes time that could be used more efficiently. During the rapid inflation in Israel in the early 1980s, a telephone hotline was set up to give the hourly price index!

More frequent banking transactions may be required. For example, interest rates tend to rise with anticipated inflation. When interest rates are high, the opportunity costs of holding cash outside of banks is high. People therefore hold less cash and need to stop at the bank more often. (We discuss this in more detail in the next part of this book.) In addition, if people are not fully informed, or if they do not understand what is happening to prices in general, they may make mistakes in their business dealings. These mistakes can lead to a misallocation of resources.

Increased risk and slower economic growth

When unanticipated inflation occurs regularly, the degree of risk associated with investments in the economy increases. Increases in uncertainty may make investors reluctant to invest in capital and to make long-term commitments. Because the level of investment may fall, the prospects for long-term economic growth could be lessened.

Global unemployment and inflation

Unemployment and inflation are not just concerns of Europe. Other countries at times experience high unemployment or high inflation (or both). The Great Depression of the 1930s was a worldwide phenomenon, though at its worst in the USA, and most countries experienced high rates of inflation in the 1970s after the OPEC oil price increases.

In 1997 the highest rates of inflation among countries for which we have data were in Bulgaria, Congo, Romania and Turkey. Very high rates of inflation were also seen in other transition economies of Eastern Europe and in developing countries. At the same time, Europe is struggling with high unemployment. Unemployment data for developing countries are difficult to obtain and hard to interpret. (See Table 22.9.)

Output growth

It was pointed out in Chapter 20 that the average growth rate of output in European economies since 1900 has been about 2.7% per year. Some years are better than

Table 22.9 Inflation and unemployment, selected countries, 1997

Country	Rate of inflation (%)	Country	Rate of unemployment (%)
Bulgaria	1,268	Spain	21.3
Congo	544	Belgium	9.5
Romania	175	France	12.5
Turkey	90	Italy	12.0
Venezuela	39	Germany	9.7
Mexico	19	Canada	6.8
Colombia	18	Japan	3.4
Hungary	18	USA	5.4

Source: *The Economist*, 11 October 1997; Eurostat.

others, but on average the rate is 2.7%. The key question in the field of economics called 'growth theory' is: what determines this rate? Why 2.7% and not 2%, or 4%? This question is the subject of Chapter 35, but a few points can be made now.

First, machines (capital) and workers (labour) are needed to produce output. Other things being equal, the more capital and labour there is in a country, the more output can be produced. Second, machines differ in their efficiency and workers differ in their skills. Other things being equal, the more efficient the capital is the more output can be produced per unit of capital, and the more skilled labour is the more output can be produced per worker.

A country's growth rate of output thus depends on (1) how fast its capital stock is growing, (2) how fast the average efficiency of the capital stock is growing, (3) how fast the number of workers (the labour force) is growing, and (4) how fast the average skill level of the labour force is growing. Let us take each of these four in turn.

We saw in Chapter 21 that the capital stock increases when net investment is positive; that is, when the number of new machines produced (gross investment) exceeds the number of machines that wear out (depreciation). Positive net investment is thus good for output growth because it means that the capital stock is increasing, which allows more output to be produced.

When machines are getting more efficient over time, we speak of 'technical progress'. An example of technical progress is the rapid improvement in the speed of personal computers. The more efficient capital is, the more output can be produced per unit of capital. Hence technical progress increases the growth rate of output.

A country's labour force can increase either because the population is growing or because there is an increase in labour force participation (the number of workers as a fraction of the total population). Ignoring the possibility of unemployment, the faster the growth rate of the labour force, the greater will be the growth rate of output.

Finally, if workers are becoming more skilled over time, this will make output grow, since on average workers are becoming more efficient. Workers can acquire skills through education and on-the-job training. A worker's skills are sometimes called 'human capital'. As with physical capital, the more human capital there is, the more output will be produced. Output growth depends in part on the growth of human capital.

Three of the main focuses of growth theory are investment, technical progress and human capital. A related concern is 'productivity', defined as output per worker. If output is growing at 3% and the labour force is growing at 1% (due, say, to population growth), then productivity is growing at 2%. Positive net investment, positive technical progress, and increases in human capital per worker all contribute to an increase in productivity, because all three lead to an increase in output per worker.

Looking ahead

This ends our introduction to the basic concepts and problems of macroeconomics. The first chapter of this part introduced the field, the second discussed the measurement of national product and national income, and this chapter discussed three of macroeconomic's major concerns – unemployment, inflation and income growth.

Thus far, we have said little about what *determines* the level of national output, the number of employed and unemployed workers, and the rate of inflation in an economy. The following chapters provide the background in macroeconomic theory you need to understand *how* these variables are determined and how the macroeconomy functions. With this knowledge, you will be able to understand how government taxing, spending, and monetary policies may affect the economy, how national economies are interrelated, and what current developments in Europe and the world mean in this context.

Summary

Recessions, depressions and unemployment

1. A *recession* is a period in which real GDP declines for at least two consecutive quarters. When less output is produced, employment declines, the unemployment rate rises and a smaller percentage of the capital stock is used. When output falls, real income declines.

2. A *depression* is a prolonged and deep recession, but there is disagreement over how severe and how prolonged a recession must be to be called a depression.

3. The *unemployment* rate is the ratio of the number of unemployed people to the number of people in the labour force. To be considered unemployed and in the labour force, a person must be looking for work.

4. Big differences in rates of unemployment exist across demographic groups, regions and industries. Often, young people experience much higher unemployment rates than older ones.

5. A person who stops looking for work is considered to have dropped out of the labour force and is no longer classified as unemployed. People who stop looking because they are discouraged about ever finding a job are sometimes called *discouraged workers*.

6. Some unemployment is inevitable. Because new workers are continually entering the labour force, because industries and firms are continuously expanding and contracting, and because people switch jobs, there is a constant process of job search as workers and firms try to match the best people to the available jobs. This unemployment is both natural and beneficial for the economy.

7. The unemployment that occurs because of short-run job/skill matching problems is called *frictional unemployment*. The unemployment that occurs because

of longer-run structural changes in the economy is called *structural unemployment*. The *natural rate of unemployment* is the sum of the frictional rate and the structural rate. The increase in unemployment that occurs during recessions and depressions is called *cyclical unemployment*.

8. The major costs associated with recessions and unemployment are decreased real output, the damage done to the people who are unemployed, and lost output in the future. Benefits of recessions are that they may help to reduce inflation and increase efficiency.

Inflation

9. An *inflation* is an increase in the overall price level. It happens when many prices increase simultaneously. Inflation is measured by calculating the average increase in the prices of a large number of goods during some period of time. A *deflation* is a decrease in the overall price level. A *sustained inflation* results from increases in the overall price level that continue over a significant period of time.

10. A number of different indexes are used to measure the overall price level. Among them are the *GDP price index*, *consumer price index (CPI)* and *producer price indexes (PPIs)*.

11. Whether a person gains or loses during a period of inflation depends on whether their income rises faster or slower than the prices of the things they buy. The elderly are more insulated from inflation than most people think, because state pensions are often indexed to inflation. Welfare benefits, which are less often indexed to inflation, may not keep pace with inflation.

12. Inflation that is higher than expected benefits debtors, and inflation that is lower than expected benefits creditors.

Global unemployment rates and inflation

13. Unemployment rates and rates of inflation vary markedly over time and between countries. They can reach quite high levels at times.

Output growth

14. Output growth depends on (1) the growth rate of the capital stock, (2) technical progress, (3) the growth rate of the labour force, and (4) the growth rate of human capital per worker.

Review Terms and Concepts

consumer price index (CPI)
cyclical unemployment
deflation
depression
discouraged-worker effect
employment
frictional unemployment
inflation
leading indicators
labour force
participation rate
natural rate of unemployment
producer price index (PPI)
real interest rate
recession

structural unemployment
sustained inflation
unemployment
unemployment rate

Equations

1. Labour force = Employment + Unemployment

2. Population = Labour force + Not in labour force

3. Unemployment rate = $\dfrac{\text{Unemployment}}{\text{Employment} + \text{Unemployment}}$

4. Participation rate = $\dfrac{\text{Labour force}}{\text{Active population}}$

Problem Set

1. What problems are associated with measuring unemployment?

2. Which groups in an economy are most likely to suffer from high unemployment rates? Can you think of reasons why?

3. 'When an inefficient firm or a firm producing a product that people no longer want goes out of business, people are unemployed, but that's part of the normal process of economic growth and development; the unemployment is part of the natural rate and need not concern policy makers.' Discuss this statement and its relevance to the economy today.

4. What is the unemployment rate in your country today? What was it in 1970, 1975 and 1982? How has your country preformed in relation to other European countries? Do you know, or can you determine, why?

5. Between July and August 1997, total employment in the US economy grew from 129,708,000 to 129,804,000 – an increase of 96,000. At the same time, the unemployment rate rose from 4.8% to 4.9%. How can unemployment rise when the number of employed is also rising?

6. Suppose that all wages, salaries, welfare benefits and other sources of income were indexed to inflation.

Would inflation still be considered a problem? Why or why not?

7. What do the CPI and PPI measure? Why do we need all these price indexes? (Think about what purpose you would use each one for.)

8. Consider an economy with two goods, humbugs and lemon drops. Suppose that, between year 1 and year 2, there is a downward shift in the supply schedule for humbugs and an upward shift in the supply schedule for lemon drops. Explain why the CPI for this two-good economy would overstate the increase in the cost of living.

9. Policy makers talk about the 'capacity' of the economy to grow. What specifically is meant by the 'capacity' of the economy? How might capacity be measured? In what ways is capacity limited by labour constraints? Capital constraints? What are the consequences if demand in the economy exceeds capacity? What signs would you look for?

10. Suppose the stock of capital and the workforce are both increasing at 3% annually in the country of Wholand. At the same time, real output is growing at 6%. How is this possible in the short run? In the long run?

Aggregate Expenditure and Equilibrium Output

We now begin our discussion of macroeconomic theory. We know how to calculate GDP, the measure of a country's output and income, but what factors *determine* it? We know how to define and measure inflation and unemployment, but what circumstances *cause* inflation and unemployment? And what, if anything, can government do to reduce unemployment and inflation or stimulate income?

Analysing the various components of the macroeconomy is a complex undertaking. The level of GDP, the overall price level and the level of employment – three chief concerns of macroeconomists – are influenced by events in four broadly defined 'markets': goods and services markets, money (financial) markets, foreign exchange markets and labour markets. We will explore each market, as well as the links between them, in the chapters that follow.

Macroeconomic markets

Figure 23.1 presents the plan for the next eight chapters, which form the core of macroeconomic theory. Chapters 23 and 24 deal with the market for goods and services, often called the *goods market*. In order not to introduce all complications at once, the perspective taken here and retained through to Chapter 27 is global: we look at the entire world as if it were one economy.[1] This has two advantages: first, it facilitates the discussion, since there are no exports out of and no imports into the global economy. Second, it shows how world income and the world interest rate are determined. Knowing this will come in handy when we move on to look at individual countries and see how their national economies are affected by the state of the world economy that surrounds them.

Figure 23.1 The building blocks of the global and national economies

First insights into the *global economy* obtain from studying the goods and the money market in this and the next four chapters. To understand *national economies* in an international setting, we must also look at the foreign exchange and the labour market. Chapter 31 puts all this together in a national-economy model featuring aggregate demand and aggregate supply.

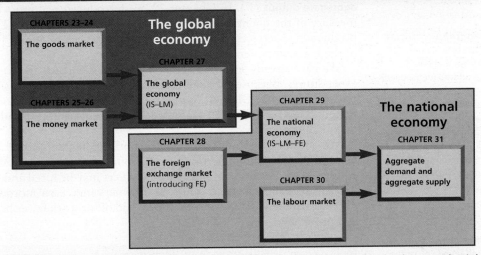

[1] *The model also describes an economy that is 'closed'; that is, it does not interact with other countries. It is therefore often referred to as the closed-economy model. Since this is a rare case in today's integrated world, we refer to it as the global-economy model.*

In Chapters 25 and 26 we focus on the *money market*. We introduce the money market and the banking system, discuss the way central banks such as the European Central Bank or the Bank of England control the money supply, and analyse the demand for money and the way interest rates are determined. Chapter 27 then examines how the goods market and the money market interact to jointly determine income and the interest rate in the global economy.

In Chapter 28 we begin to sharpen our focus to find out what happens in the economy of an individual country that is small compared to the rest of the world. The new features to take into account here are exports and imports of goods and services and the free flow of financial assets across borders. Because Europeans must pay yen for the Japanese TVs they import and US dollars for the Microsoft stocks they buy, Chapter 28 puts the foreign exchange market, where foreign currencies are bought and sold, centre stage. Chapter 29 merges the foreign exchange market with the previously obtained pictures of the goods and the money markets to determine income, the interest rate and other important variables in an individual country.

Chapter 30 discusses the supply of and the demand for labour and the functioning of the *labour market* in the macroeconomy. This material is essential to an understanding of employment and unemployment. It is also used in Chapter 31 to augment the discussion of Chapter 29 for a refined picture of the macroeconomy. After setting up and exploring the aggregate demand and supply curves first mentioned in Chapter 20, we show how the overall price level is determined and how prices and output interact.

Before we begin our discussion of aggregate output and aggregate income, we need to stress that production, consumption and the other activities that we discuss in this and the following chapters are ongoing activities. Nonetheless, it is helpful to think about these activities as if they took place in a series of *production periods*. During each period, some output is produced, income is generated and spending takes place. At the end of each period we can examine the results. Was everything that was produced in the economy sold? What percentage of income was spent? What percentage was saved? Is output (income) likely to rise or fall in the next period? The answers to these questions help us keep track of the economy's performance.

Aggregate output and aggregate income (*Y*)

aggregate output
The total quantity of goods and services produced (or supplied) in an economy in a given period.

aggregate income
The total income received by all factors of production in a given period.

aggregate output (income)
A combined term used to remind you of the exact equality between aggregate output and aggregate income.

Each period, firms produce a quantity of goods and services which we refer to as **aggregate output** (*Y*). In Chapter 22, we introduced real gross domestic product as a measure of the quantity of output produced in the economy, *Y*. Output includes the production of services, consumer goods and investment goods. It is important to think of these as components of 'real' output.

We have already seen that GDP (*Y*) can be calculated in terms of either income or expenditures. Because every euro of expenditure is received by someone as income, we can compute total GDP (*Y*) either by adding up all spending on final goods during a period or by adding up all income – wages, rents, interest and profits – received by factors of production.

We use the variable *Y* to refer to both **aggregate output** and **aggregate income** because they are the same thing, seen from different angles. When output increases, additional income is generated. More workers may be hired and paid; workers may ask for, and be paid for, more hours; and owners may earn more profits. When output decreases, income falls, workers may be laid off or work fewer hours (and be paid less), and profits may fall.

In any given period, there is an exact equality between aggregate output (production) and aggregate income. To remind you of this fact every once in a while we use the combined term **aggregate output (income)**.

Figure 23.2 Saving ≡ Aggregate Income – Consumption

In an economy in which there is no government, all income is either spent on consumption or saved. Thus, $S \equiv Y - C$.

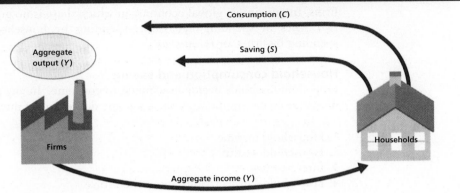

Aggregate output can also be looked on as the aggregate quantity of goods and services supplied, because it is the amount that firms are supplying (producing) during the period. In the discussions that follow, we use the phrase *aggregate output (income)* rather than *aggregate quantity supplied*, but keep in mind that the two are equivalent. Also remember that 'aggregate output' means 'real GDP'.

Think in real terms

From the outset you must think in 'real terms'. For example, when we talk about output (Y), we mean real output, not nominal output. Although we discussed in Chapter 22 that the calculation of real GDP is complicated, you can ignore these complications in the following analysis. To help make things easier to read, we will frequently use euro values for Y, but do not confuse Y with nominal output. The main point is to think of Y as being in real terms – the actual quantities of goods and services produced, not the euros or pounds paid.

Income, consumption and saving (Y, C and S)

Each period (weeks, months, years, etc.), households receive some aggregate amount of income (Y). A household can do two, and only two, things with its income: it can buy goods and services – that is, it can *consume* – or it can save. In practice a household also uses part of its income to pay taxes (T) to the government. To facilitate our first analysis of the world economy, we assume that taxes are zero in this chapter. This assumption is dropped in the next chapter. The part of its income that a household does not consume in a given period is called **saving** (Figure 23.2). Total household saving in the economy (S) is by definition equal to income minus consumption (C):

> Saving ≡ Income – Consumption

$$S \equiv Y - C$$

The triple equal sign means this is an **identity**, or something that is always true.

Remember: saving does *not* refer to the total savings accumulated over time. Saving (without the final s) refers to the portion of a *single period's* income that is not spent in that period. Saving (S) is the amount added to (or subtracted from) *accumulated savings* in any given period. *Saving* is a flow variable; *savings* is a stock variable. (Review Chapter 4 if you are unsure of the difference between stock and flow variables.)

Explaining spending behaviour

So far, we have said nothing about behaviour. We have not described the consumption and saving behaviour of households, nor have we speculated about how much aggregate output firms will decide to produce in a given period. We only have a framework and a set of definitions to work with.

saving (S) The part of its income that a household does not consume in a given period. Distinguished from *savings*, which is the current stock of accumulated saving.

identity Something that is always true.

Macroeconomics, you will recall, is the study of behaviour. To understand the functioning of the macroeconomy, we must understand the behaviour of households and firms. In our simple global economy in which there is no government, there are only two types of spending behaviour: spending by households, or *consumption*; and spending by firms, or *investment*.

Household consumption and saving

How do households decide how much to consume? In any given period, the amount of aggregate consumption in the economy depends on a number of factors, including:

1. Household income
2. Household wealth
3. Interest rates
4. Households' expectations about the future

These factors work together to determine the spending and saving behaviour of households, both individually and in the aggregate. This should come as no surprise. Households with higher income and higher wealth are likely to spend more than households with less income and less wealth. Lower interest rates reduce the cost of borrowing, so lower interest rates are likely to stimulate spending. (Higher interest rates increase the cost of borrowing and are likely to decrease spending.) Finally, positive expectations about the future are likely to increase current spending, while uncertainty about the future is likely to decrease current spending. In 1990, for example, households began consuming less partly because of their uncertainty about the outcome of the conflict in the Gulf.

While all these factors are important, we will concentrate for now on the relationship between income and consumption.[2] In *The General Theory*, Keynes argued that the amount of consumption undertaken by a household is directly related to its income:

> The higher your income is, the higher your consumption is likely to be. People with more income tend to consume more than people with less income.

consumption function

The relationship between consumption and income.

The relationship between consumption and income is called a **consumption function**. Figure 23.3 shows a hypothetical consumption function for an individual household. The curve is labelled $c(y)$, which is read 'c as a function of y', or 'consumption as a function of income'. There are several things you should notice about the curve. First, it has a positive slope. In other words, as y increases, so does c. Second, the curve intersects the c axis above zero. This means that even at an income of zero, consumption is positive. Even if a household found itself with a zero income, it still must consume to survive. It would borrow, or live off its savings, but its consumption could not be zero.

Keep in mind that Figure 23.3 shows the relationship between consumption (c) and income (y) for an individual household. But also remember that macroeconomics is concerned with aggregate consumption. Specifically, macroeconomists want to know how *aggregate* consumption (the total consumption of all households) is likely to respond to changes in *aggregate* income. If all individual households increase their consumption as income increases, and we assume that they do, it is reasonable to assume that a positive relationship exists between aggregate consumption (C) and aggregate income (Y).

[2]*The assumption that consumption is dependent solely on income is, of course, overly simplistic. Nonetheless, many important insights about how the economy works can be obtained through this simplification. In Chapter 33, we relax this assumption and consider the behaviour of households and firms in the macroeconomy in more detail.*

Figure 23.3 A consumption function for a household

A consumption function for an individual household shows the level of consumption at each level of household income.

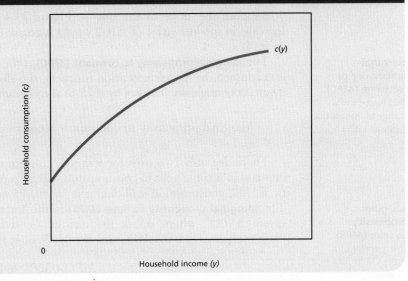

For simplicity, assume that points of aggregate consumption, when plotted against aggregate income, lie along a straight line, as in Figure 23.4. While no major conclusion to be derived is affected by this simplification, it facilitates working with graphs and devising numerical examples. If the aggregate consumption function is a straight line, we can write the following equation to describe it:

$$C = a + bY$$

Y represents aggregate output (income), C is aggregate consumption and a is a constant, the point at which the consumption function intersects the C axis. The letter b is the slope of the line, in this case $\Delta C/\Delta Y$ (since consumption, C, is measured on the vertical axis, and income, Y, is measured on the horizontal axis).[3] Every time income

Figure 23.4 An aggregate consumption function

The consumption function shows the level of consumption at every level of income. The upward slope indicates that higher levels of income lead to higher levels of consumption spending.

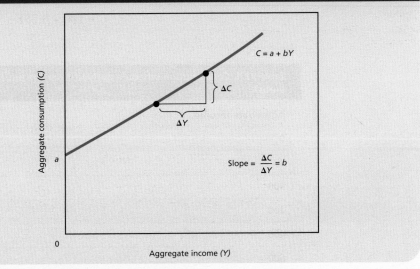

[3]*The Greek letter Δ (delta) means 'change in'. For example, ΔY (read 'delta Y') means the 'change in income'. If income (Y) in 1995 is €100 and income in 1996 is €110, then ΔY for this period is 110 − 100 = €10. For a review of the concept of slope, see the Appendix to Chapter 1.*

increases (say by ΔY), consumption increases by b times ΔY. Thus, $\Delta C = b \times \Delta Y$ and $\Delta C / \Delta Y = b$.

Suppose the slope of the line in Figure 23.4 were 0.75 (that is, $b = 0.75$). An increase in income (ΔY) of €100 would increase consumption by $b\Delta Y = 0.75 \times 100$, or €75.

marginal propensity to consume (MPC)
That fraction of a change in income that is consumed, or spent.

The **marginal propensity to consume (MPC)** is the fraction of a change in income that is consumed. In the consumption function, the slope b is the MPC. An MPC of 0.75 means consumption changes by 0.75 of the change in income.

$$\text{Marginal propensity to consume} = \text{Slope of consumption function} \equiv \frac{\Delta C}{\Delta Y}$$

There are only two uses for income: consumption or saving. If 0.75 of a €1.00 increase in income goes to consumption, €0.25 must go to saving. If income decreases by €1.00, consumption will decrease by €0.75 and saving will decrease by €0.25. The **marginal propensity to save (MPS)** is the fraction of a change in income that is saved: $\Delta S / \Delta Y$, where ΔS is the change in saving. Because everything is either consumed or saved, the MPC and the MPS must add up to one:

marginal propensity to save (MPS)
That fraction of a change in income that is saved.

$$MPC + MPS \equiv 1$$

The marginal propensity to consume (MPC) is the fraction of an increase in income that is consumed (or the fraction of a decrease in income that comes out of consumption). The marginal propensity to save (MPS) is the fraction of an increase in income that is saved (or the fraction of a decrease in income that comes out of saving).

Since C is aggregate consumption and Y is aggregate income, it follows that the MPC is society's marginal propensity to consume out of national income and that the MPS is society's marginal propensity to save out of national income.

Numerical example

The numerical examples used in the rest of this chapter are based on the following consumption function:

$$C = 100 + 0.75Y$$

Table 23.1 Consumption schedule derived from the equation $C = 100 + 0.75Y$ (billions of euros)	
Aggregate income, Y	**Aggregate consumption, C**
0	100
80	160
100	175
200	250
400	400
600	550
800	700
1,000	850

Figure 23.5 An aggregate consumption function derived from the equation C = 100 + 0.75Y

In this simple consumption function, consumption is €100 billion at an income of zero. As income rises, so does consumption. For every €100 billion increase in income, consumption rises by €75 billion. The slope of the line is 0.75.

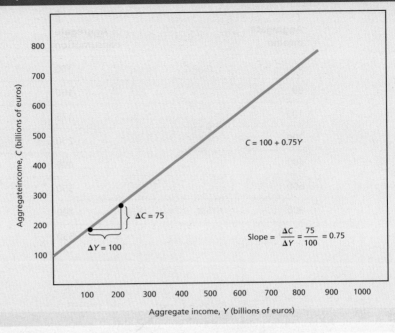

This equation is simply an instance of the generic $C = a + bY$ consumption function we have been discussing. At a national income of zero, consumption is 100 billion (a). As income rises, so does consumption. We will assume that for every €100 billion euro increase in income (ΔY), consumption rises by €75 billion (ΔC). This means that the slope of the consumption function (b) is equal to $\Delta C/\Delta Y$, or 75 billion/ 100 billion = 0.75. The marginal propensity to consume out of national income is therefore 0.75; the marginal propensity to save is 0.25. Some numbers derived from this consumption function appear in Table 23.1 and are graphed in Figure 23.5.

Now consider saving. We already know that $Y \equiv C + S$. Income equals consumption plus saving. Once we know how much consumption will result from a given level of income, we know how much saving there will be.

Recall that saving is everything that is not consumed:

$$S \equiv Y - C$$

From the numbers in Table 23.1, we can easily derive the saving schedule in Table 23.2. At an income of €200 billion, consumption is 250 billion; saving is thus a negative 50 billion ($S \equiv Y - C = 200$ billion $- 250$ billion $= €-50$ billion). At an aggregate income of €400 billion, consumption is exactly 400 billion, and saving is zero. At 800 billion in income, saving is a positive €100 billion.

These numbers are graphed as a saving function in Figure 23.6. The 45° solid black line in the top graph provides a convenient way of comparing C and Y. (All the points along a 45° line are points at which the value on the horizontal axis equals the value on the vertical axis. Thus, the 45° line in Figure 23.6 represents all the points at which aggregate income equals aggregate consumption.) Where the consumption function is *above* the 45° line, consumption exceeds income and saving is negative. Where the consumption function *crosses* the 45° line, consumption is equal to income and saving is zero. Where the consumption function is *below* the 45° line, consumption is less than income and saving is positive. Note that the slope of the saving function is $\Delta S/\Delta Y$, which is equal to the marginal propensity to save (*MPS*).

Table 23.2 Deriving a saving schedule from a consumption schedule (billions of euros)

Y Aggregate income	– C Aggregate consumption	≡ S Aggregate saving
0	100	−100
80	160	−80
100	175	−75
200	250	−50
400	400	0
600	550	50
800	700	100
1,000	850	150

Figure 23.6 Deriving a saving function from a consumption function

Since $S \equiv Y - C$, it is easy to derive a saving function from a consumption function. A 45° line drawn from the origin can be used as a convenient tool to compare consumption and income graphically. At $Y = 200$, consumption is 250. The 45° line shows us that consumption is larger than income by 50. Thus $S \equiv Y - C = -50$. At $Y = 800$, consumption is less than income by 100. Thus, $S = 100$ when $Y = 800$.

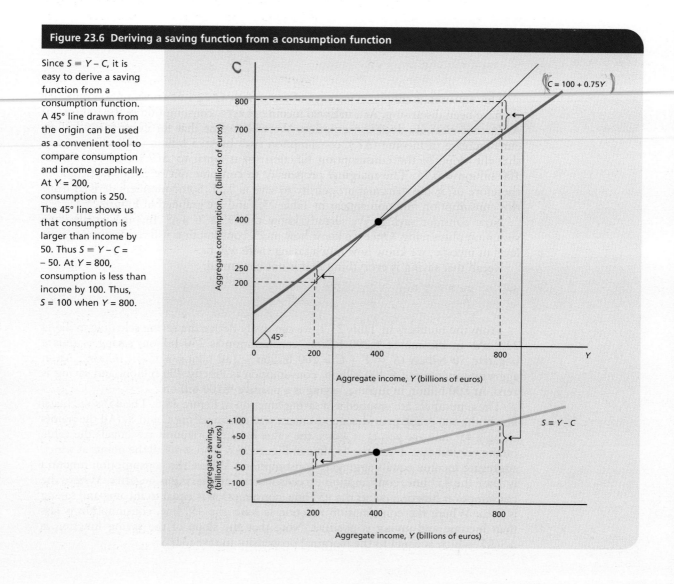

The consumption function and the saving function are mirror images of one another. No information appears in one that does not also appear in the other. These functions tell us how households in the aggregate will divide income between consumption spending and saving at every possible income level. In other words, they embody aggregate household behaviour.

Planned investment (*I*)

Consumption, as we have seen, is the spending by households on goods and services. But what kind of spending do firms engage in? The answer is *investment*.

What is investment?

Let us begin with a brief review of terms and concepts. In everyday language, we use *investment* to refer to what we do with our savings: 'I invested in a mutual fund and some VW stock'. In the language of economics, however, *investment* always refers to the creation of capital stock.

In order not confuse the two uses of the term we call what is referred to in everyday language *financial* investment. When we speak of investment we always mean the second definition: When a firm builds a new plant or adds new machinery to its current stock, it is investing. A restaurant owner who buys tables, chairs, cooking equipment and cutlery is investing. When a university builds a new sports centre, it is investing. From now on, we use **investment** only to refer to purchases by firms of new buildings and equipment and inventories, all of which add to firms' capital stocks.

Recall that inventories are part of the capital stock. When firms add to their inventories, they are investing – they are buying something that creates value in the future. Most of the capital stock of a clothing shop consists of its inventories of unsold clothes in its warehouses and on its racks and display shelves. The service provided by a grocer's or a department store is the convenience of having a large variety of commodities in inventory available for purchase at a single location.

Manufacturing firms generally have two kinds of inventories: *inputs*, or raw materials, and *final products*. Volkswagen has stocks of tyres, rolled steel, engine blocks, valve covers and thousands of other things in inventory, all waiting to be used in producing new cars. In addition, VW has an inventory of finished cars awaiting shipment.

Investment is a flow variable. It represents additions to capital stock in a specific period. A firm's decision on how much to invest each period is determined by many factors. For now, we will focus simply on the effects that given investment levels have on the rest of the economy.

Actual versus planned investment

One of the most important insights of macroeconomics is deceptively simple: a firm may not always end up investing the exact amount that it planned to. The reason is that a firm does not have complete control over its investment decision; some parts of that decision are made by other actors in the economy. (This is not true of consumption, however. Because we assume households have complete control over their consumption, planned consumption is always equal to actual consumption.)

Generally, firms can choose how much new plant and equipment they wish to purchase in any given period. If VW wants to buy a new robot to form car bumpers or McDonald's decides to buy an extra deep fryer, they can usually do so without difficulty. There is, however, another component of investment over which firms have less control – inventory investment.

Suppose VW expects to sell a million cars this quarter and has inventories at a level it considers proper. If the company produces and sells one million cars, it will keep its inventories just where they are now (at the desired level). Now suppose VW produces one million cars but due to a sudden shift of consumer interest it sells only 900,000 cars. By definition, VW's inventories of cars must go up by 100,000 cars. The firm's **change in inventory** is equal to production minus sales. The point here is:

investment
Purchases by firms of new buildings and equipment and additions to inventories, all of which add to firms' capital stock.

change in inventory
Production minus sales.

One component of investment – inventory change – is partly determined by how much households decide to buy, which is not under the complete control of firms. If households do not buy as much as firms expect them to, inventories will be higher than expected, and firms will have made an inventory investment that they did not plan to make.

desired, *or* planned, investment

Those additions to capital stock and inventory that are planned by firms.

actual investment

The actual amount of investment that takes place; it includes items such as unplanned changes in inventories.

Because involuntary inventory adjustments are neither desired nor planned, we need to distinguish between actual investment and **desired**, or **planned**, **investment**. We will use I to refer to desired or planned investment only. In other words, I will refer to planned purchases of plant and equipment and planned inventory changes. **Actual investment**, in contrast, is the actual amount of investment that takes place. If actual inventory investment turns out to be higher than what firms planned, then actual investment is greater than I, planned investment.

For the purposes of this chapter, we will take the amount of investment that firms plan to make each period (I) as fixed at some given level. We assume this level does not vary with income. In the example that follows, $I = €25$ billion, regardless of income. As Figure 23.7 shows, this means that the planned investment function is a horizontal line.

Planned aggregate expenditure (*AE*)

planned aggregate expenditure (*AE*)

The total amount the economy plans to spend in a given period. Equal to consumption plus planned investment: $AE \equiv C + I$.

We define total **planned aggregate expenditure (*AE*)** in the economy as consumption (C) plus planned investment (I). In practice, planned aggregate expenditure on a global level also includes government spending (G): $AE = C + I + G$. In this chapter we are assuming that G is zero. This assumption is relaxed in the next chapter.

Planned aggregate expenditure ≡ Consumption + Planned investment

$$AE \equiv C + I$$

AE is the total amount that the economy plans to spend in a given period. We will now use the concept of planned aggregate expenditure to discuss the economy's equilibrium level of output.

Figure 23.7 The planned investment function

For the time being, we will assume that planned investment is fixed. It does not change when income changes, so its graph is just a horizontal line.

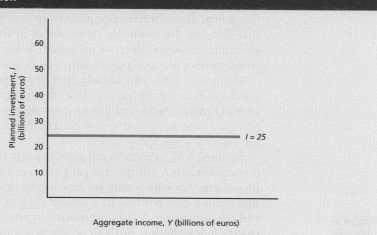

Equilibrium aggregate output (income)

Thus far, we have described the behaviour of firms and households. We now discuss the nature of equilibrium and explain how the economy achieves equilibrium.

A number of definitions of *equilibrium* are used in economics. They all refer to the idea that at equilibrium, there is no tendency for change. In microeconomics, equilibrium is said to exist in a particular market (say, the market for bananas) at the price for which the quantity demanded is equal to the quantity supplied. At this point, both suppliers and demanders are satisfied. The equilibrium price of a good is the price at which suppliers want to furnish the amount that demanders want to buy.

equilibrium Occurs when there is no tendency for change. In the macroeconomic goods market, equilibrium occurs when planned aggregate expenditure is equal to aggregate output.

In macroeconomics, we define **equilibrium** in the goods market as that point at which planned aggregate expenditure is equal to aggregate output:

Aggregate output $\equiv Y$
Planned aggregate expenditure $\equiv AE \equiv C + I$
Equilibrium: $Y \equiv AE$, or $Y \equiv C + I$

This definition of equilibrium can hold if, and only if, planned investment and actual investment are equal. (Remember we are assuming there is no unplanned consumption.)

To understand why, consider Y not equal to AE. First, suppose aggregate output is greater than planned aggregate expenditure:

$$Y > C + I$$
Aggregate output > Planned aggregate expenditure

When output is greater than planned spending, there is unplanned inventory investment. Firms planned to sell more of their goods than they actually sold, and the difference shows up as an unplanned increase in inventories.

Next, suppose planned aggregate expenditure is greater than aggregate output:

$$C + I > Y$$
Planned aggregate expenditure > Aggregate output

When planned spending exceeds output, firms have sold more than they planned to. Inventory investment is smaller than planned. Planned and actual investment are not equal. Only when output is exactly matched by planned spending will there be no unplanned inventory investment.

Equilibrium in the goods market is achieved only when aggregate output (Y) and planned aggregate expenditure ($C + I$) are equal, or when actual and planned investment are equal.

Table 23.3 derives a planned aggregate expenditure schedule and shows the point of equilibrium for our numerical example. (Remember: all our calculations are based on $C = 100 + 0.75Y$.) To determine planned aggregate expenditure, we add consumption spending (C) to planned investment spending (I) at every level of income. Glancing down columns 1 and 4, we see one, and only one, level at which aggregate output and planned aggregate expenditure are equal: $Y = 500$.

Figure 23.8 illustrates the same equilibrium graphically. Figure 23.8a adds planned investment, constant at €25 billion, to consumption at every level of income. Since planned investment is a constant, the planned aggregate expenditure function is simply the consumption function displaced vertically by that constant amount. Figure 23.8b plots the planned aggregate expenditure function with the 45° line. The 45° line, which represents all points on the graph where the variables on the horizontal

Table 23.3 Deriving the planned aggregate expenditure schedule and finding equilibrium (all figures in billions of euros)

(1) Aggregate output (income) Y	(2)* Aggregate consumption C	(3) Planned investment I	(4) Planned aggregate expenditure AE = C + I	(5) Unplanned inventory change Y − (C + I)	(6) Equilibrium? Y = AE?
100	175	25	200	−100	No
200	250	25	275	−75	No
400	400	25	425	−25	No
500	475	25	500	0	Yes
600	550	25	575	+25	No
800	700	25	725	+75	No
1,000	850	25	875	+125	No

* The figures in column 2 are based on the equation $C = 100 + 0.75Y$.

Figure 23.8 Equilibrium aggregate output

Equilibrium occurs when planned aggregate expenditure and aggregate output are equal. Planned aggregate expenditure is the sum of consumption spending and planned investment spending.

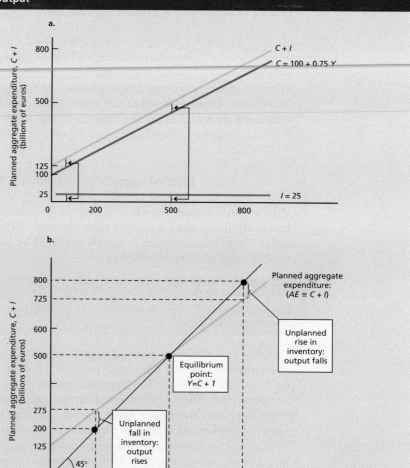

and vertical axes are equal, allows us to compare variables along the two axes. The planned aggregate expenditure function crosses the 45° line at a single point, where $Y = €500$ billion[4] At that point, $Y = C + I$.

Now let us look at some other levels of aggregate output (income). First, consider $Y = €800$ billion. Is this an equilibrium output? Clearly not. At $Y = €800$ billion, planned aggregate expenditure is 725 billion. (See Table 23.3.) This amount is less than aggregate output, which is €800 billion. Because output is greater than planned spending, the difference ends up in inventory as unplanned inventory investment. In this case, unplanned inventory investment is €75 billion.

Next, consider $Y = €200$ billion. Is this an equilibrium output? Again, clearly not. At $Y = 200$ billion, planned aggregate expenditure is €275 billion. Thus, planned spending (AE) is greater than output (Y), and there is unplanned inventory disinvestment of €75 billion.

At $Y = 200$ billion and $Y = €800$ billion, planned investment and actual investment are unequal. There is unplanned investment, and the system is out of balance. Only at $Y = €500$ billion, where planned aggregate expenditure and aggregate output are equal, will planned investment equal actual investment.

Finally, let us find the equilibrium level of output (income) algebraically. Recall that we know the following:

(1) $Y = C + I$ equilibrium
(2) $C = 100 + 0.75Y$ consumption function
(3) $I = 25$ planned investment

Substituting (2) and (3) into (1) we get

$$Y = \underbrace{100 + 0.75Y}_{C} + \underbrace{25}_{I}$$

There is only one value of Y for which this statement is true, and we can find it by rearranging terms:

$$
\begin{aligned}
Y - 0.75Y &= 100 + 25 \\
Y - 0.75Y &= 125 \\
0.25Y &= 125 \\
Y = 125/0.25 &= 500
\end{aligned}
$$

The equilibrium level of output is 500, as we see in Table 23.3 and Figure 23.8.

The saving/investment approach to equilibrium

Because aggregate income must either be saved or spent. By definition, then, $Y \equiv C + S$ – which is an identity. The equilibrium condition is $Y = C + I$, but this is not an identity because it does not hold when we are out of equilibrium.[5] Substituting $C + S$ for Y, the equilibrium condition, we can write:

Saving/investment approach to equilibrium: $C + S = C + I$

Since we can subtract C from both sides of this equation, we are left with $S = I$. Thus, only when planned investment equals saving will there be equilibrium.

---

[4]*This diagram is called the Keynesian cross.*

[5]*It would be an identity if I included unplanned inventory accumulations – in other words, if I were actual investment rather than planned investment.*

Figure 23.9 Planned aggregate expenditure and aggregate output (income)

Saving is a leakage out of the spending stream. If planned investment is exactly equal to saving, then planned aggregate expenditure is exactly equal to aggregate output, and there is equilibrium.

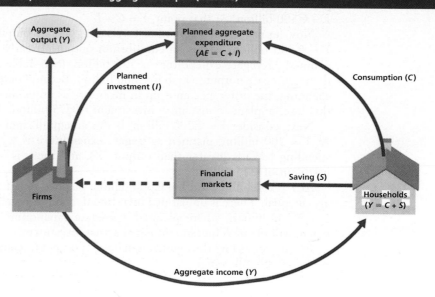

This saving/investment approach to equilibrium intuitively stands to reason if we recall two things: (1) output and income are equal, and (2) saving is income that is not spent. Because it is not spent, saving is like a leakage out of the spending stream. Only if that leakage is counterbalanced by some other component of planned spending can the resulting planned aggregate expenditure equal aggregate output. This other component is planned investment (I).

This counterbalancing effect can be seen in Figure 23.9. Aggregate income flows into households, and consumption and saving flow out. The diagram shows saving flowing from households into the financial market. Firms use this saving to finance investment projects. If the planned investment of firms equals the saving of households, then planned aggregate expenditure ($AE \equiv C + I$) equals aggregate output (income) (Y), and there is equilibrium: the *leakage* out of the spending stream – saving – is matched by an equal *injection* of planned investment spending into the spending stream. For this reason, the saving/investment approach to equilibrium is also called the *leakages/ injections approach* to equilibrium.

Figure 23.10 reproduces the saving schedule derived in Figure 23.6 and the horizontal investment function from Figure 23.7. Notice that $S = I$ at one, and only one, level of aggregate output, $Y = 500$. At $Y = 500$, $C = 475$ and $I = 25$. In other words, $Y = C + I$, and therefore equilibrium exists.

Figure 23.10 The $S = I$ approach to equilibrium

Aggregate output will be equal to planned aggregate expenditure only when saving equals planned investment ($S = I$). Saving and planned investment are equal at $Y = 500$.

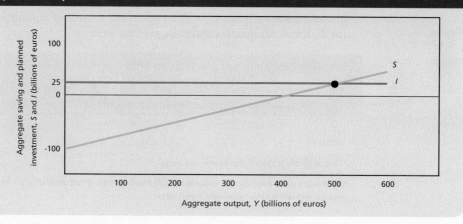

Adjustment to equilibrium

We have defined equilibrium and learned how to find it, but we have said nothing about how firms might react to *disequilibrium*. Let's consider the actions firms might take when planned aggregate expenditure exceeds aggregate output (income).

We already know that the only way firms can sell more than they produce is by selling some inventory. This means that when planned aggregate expenditure exceeds aggregate output, unplanned inventory reductions have occurred. It seems reasonable to assume that firms will respond to unplanned inventory reductions by increasing output. If firms increase output, income must also increase (output and income are two ways of measuring the same thing). As VW builds more cars, it employs more workers (or pays its existing workforce for working more hours), buys more steel, uses more electricity, and so on. These purchases by VW represent income for the producers of labour, steel, electricity, and so on. If VW and all other firms try to keep their inventories intact by increasing production, they will generate more income in the economy as a whole. This will lead to more consumption. Remember that when income rises, consumption also rises.

The adjustment process will continue as long as output (income) is below planned aggregate expenditure. If firms react to unplanned inventory reductions by increasing output, an economy with planned spending greater than output will adjust to equilibrium, with Y higher than before. If planned spending is less than output, there will be unplanned increases in inventories. In this case, firms will respond by reducing output. As output falls, income falls, consumption falls, and so forth, until equilibrium is restored, with Y lower than before.

As Figure 23.8 shows, at any level of output above $Y = 500$, such as $Y = 800$, output will fall until it reaches equilibrium at $Y = 500$, and at any level of output below $Y = 500$, such as $Y = 200$, output will rise until it reaches equilibrium at $Y = 500$.[6]

The multiplier

Now that we know how the equilibrium value of income is determined, we ask: how does the equilibrium level of output change when planned investment changes? If there is a sudden change in planned investment, how will output respond, if it responds at all? As we will see, the change in equilibrium output is *greater* than the initial change in planned investment. Output changes by a multiple of the change in planned investment. This multiple is called the **multiplier**.

The multiplier is defined as the ratio of the change in the equilibrium level of output to a change in some autonomous variable. A variable is **autonomous (or exogenous)** when it is assumed not to depend on the state of the economy – that is, when it is taken as given. In this chapter, we consider planned investment to be autonomous. This simplifies our analysis and provides a foundation for later discussions.

We can ask how much the equilibrium level of output changes when planned investment changes. Remember that we are not trying here to explain *why* planned investment changes; we are simply asking how much the equilibrium level of output

multiplier The ratio of the change in the equilibrium level of output to a change in some autonomous variable.

autonomous (or exogenous) variable
A variable that does not depend on the state of the economy or on other variables. It is taken as given.

[6]*In discussing simple supply and demand equilibrium in Chapters 4 and 5, we saw that when quantity supplied exceeds quantity demanded, the price falls and the quantity supplied declines. Similarly, when quantity demanded exceeds quantity supplied, the price rises and the quantity supplied increases. In the analysis here we are ignoring potential changes in prices or in the price level and focusing on changes in the level of real output (income). Later, after we have introduced money and the price level into the analysis, prices will be very important. At this stage, however, only aggregate output (income) (Y) adjusts when aggregate expenditure exceeds aggregate output (with inventory falling) or when aggregate output exceeds aggregate expenditure (with inventory rising).*

changes when (for whatever reason) planned investment changes. (Beginning in Chapter 27, we will no longer take planned investment as given and will explain how planned investment is determined.)

Consider a sustained increase in planned investment of €25 billion – that is, suppose I increases from €25 billion to €50 billion and stays at €50 billion. If equilibrium existed at I = €25 billion, an increase in planned investment of €25 billion will cause a disequilibrium, with planned aggregate expenditure greater than aggregate output by €25 billion. Firms immediately see unplanned reductions in their inventories, and, as a result, they begin to increase output.

Let us assume the increase in planned investment came from an anticipated increase in travel that leads airlines to purchase more aircraft, car hire companies to increase purchases of cars, and bus companies to purchase more buses. The firms experiencing unplanned inventory declines will therefore be car, bus and aircraft manufacturers – VW, Rover, Scania, Airbus, and so forth. In response to declining inventories of planes, buses and cars, these firms will increase output.

Now suppose these firms raise output by the full €25 billion increase in planned investment. Does this restore equilibrium? No, because when output goes up, people earn more income and a part of that income will be spent. This increases planned aggregate expenditure even further. In other words, an increase in I also leads indirectly to an increase in C. To produce more planes, Airbus has to hire more workers or ask its existing employees to work more hours. It also must buy more engines from Rolls Royce, more tyres from Pirelli, and so forth. Owners of these firms will earn more profits, produce more, take on more workers, and pay out more in wages and salaries.

This added income does not vanish into thin air. It is paid to households that spend some of it and save the rest. The added production leads to added income, which leads to added consumption spending.

If planned investment (I) goes up by €25 billion initially *and is sustained at this higher level*, an increase in output of €25 billion will *not* restore equilibrium, because it generates even more consumption spending (C). People buy more consumer goods. There are unplanned reductions of inventories of basic consumption items – washing machines, food, clothing and so on – and this prompts other firms to increase output. The cycle starts all over again.[7]

Clearly, output and income can rise by much more than the initial increase in planned investment. But how much? How large is the multiplier? This is answered graphically in Figure 23.11. Assume the economy is in equilibrium at point A, where equilibrium output is 500. The increase in I of 25 shifts the $AE = C + I$ curve up by

[7]*Figure 23.9 can help you understand the multiplier effect more clearly. Note in the figure how an increase in planned investment makes its way through the circular flow. Initially, aggregate output is at equilibrium with Y = C + I. That is, every period, aggregate output is produced by firms, and every period, planned aggregate expenditure is just sufficient to take all those goods and services off the market.*

Now note what happens when planned investment spending increases and is sustained at a higher level. Firms experience unplanned declines in inventories and they increase output; more real output is produced in subsequent periods. But the added output means more income; thus we see added income flowing to households. This, in turn, means more spending. Households spend some portion of their added income (equal to the added income times the MPC) on consumer goods.

The higher consumption spending means that even if firms responded fully to the increase in investment spending in the first round, the economy is still out of equilibrium. Follow the added spending back over to firms in Figure 23.9 and you can see that with higher consumption, planned aggregate expenditure will be greater. Firms again see an unplanned decline in inventories and they respond by increasing the output of consumer goods. This sets off yet another round of income and expenditure increases: output rises, and income rises as a result, thus increasing consumption. Higher consumption leads to yet another disequilibrium, inventories fall, and output (income) rises again.

Figure 23.11 The multiplier as seen in the planned aggregate expenditure diagram

At point A, the economy is in equilibrium at $Y = 500$. When I increases by 25, planned aggregate expenditure is initially greater than aggregate output. As output rises in response, additional consumption is generated, pushing equilibrium output up by a multiple of the initial increase in I. The new equilibrium is found at point B, where $Y = 600$. Equilibrium output has increased by 100 (600 – 500), or four times the amount of the increase in planned investment.

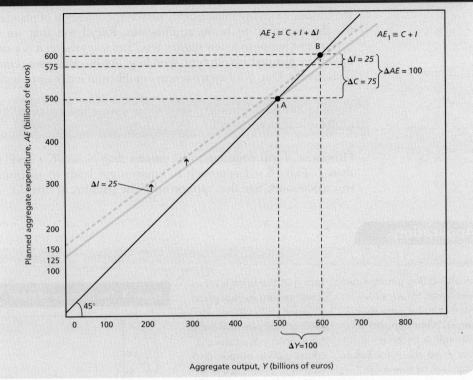

25, because I is higher by 25 at every level of income. The new equilibrium occurs at point B, where the equilibrium level of output is 600. Like point A, point B is on the 45° line and is an equilibrium value. Output (Y) has increased by 100 = 600 – 500, or four times the initial increase in planned investment of 25, between point A and point B. The multiplier in this example is 4. At point B, aggregate spending is also higher by 100. If 25 of this additional 100 is investment (I), as we know it is, the remaining 75 is added consumption (C). From point A to point B then, $\Delta Y = 100$, $\Delta I = 25$ and $\Delta C = 75$.

Why doesn't the multiplier process go on for ever? Because only a fraction of the increase in income is consumed in each round. The other fraction is saved. Successive increases in consumption and income become smaller and smaller in each round of the multiplier process until equilibrium is restored.

The size of the multiplier depends on the slope of the planned aggregate expenditure line. The steeper the slope of this line, the greater the change in output for a given change in investment. When planned investment is fixed, as in our example, the slope of the $AE \equiv C + I$ line is just the marginal propensity to consume ($\Delta C/\Delta Y$). The greater the MPC, the greater the multiplier. This should not be surprising. A large MPC means that consumption increases a lot when income increases, and the more consumption changes, the more output has to change in turn to achieve equilibrium.

The multiplier equation

Is there a way to determine the size of the multiplier without using graphic analysis? Yes, there is.

Assume that the economy is in equilibrium at an income level of $Y = 500$. Now suppose planned investment (I), and thus planned aggregate expenditure (AE), increases and remains higher by €25 billion. Planned aggregate expenditure is greater than output, there is an unplanned inventory reduction, and firms respond by increasing output (income) (Y). This leads to a second round of increases, and so on.

What will restore equilibrium? Look at Figure 23.10 and recall that planned aggregate expenditure ($AE \equiv C + I$) is not equal to aggregate output (Y) unless $S = I$; the leakage of saving must exactly match the injection of planned investment spending for the economy to be in equilibrium. Recall too that we assumed that planned investment jumps to a new higher level and stays there; it is a *sustained* increase of €25 billion in planned investment spending. As income rises, consumption rises and so does saving. Our $S = I$ approach to equilibrium leads us to conclude:

Equilibrium will be restored only when saving has increased by exactly the amount of the initial increase in I.

Otherwise, I will continue to be greater than S, and $C + I$ will continue to be greater than Y. (The $S = I$ approach to equilibrium leads us to an interesting paradox in the macroeconomy. See the Application 'The paradox of thrift'.)

Applications

The paradox of thrift

An interesting paradox can arise when households attempt to increase their saving. What happens if households become concerned about the future and want to save more today to be prepared for hard times tomorrow? If households increase their planned saving, the saving schedule in Figure 1 shifts upward, from S to S'. The plan to save more is a plan to consume less, and the resulting drop in spending leads to a drop in income. Income drops by a multiple of the initial shift in the saving schedule. Before the increase in saving, equilibrium exists at point A, where S = I and Y = €500 billion. Increased saving shifts the equilibrium to point B, the point at which S' = I. New equilibrium output is €300 billion – a €200 billion decrease (ΔY) from the initial equilibrium.

By consuming less, households have actually *caused* the hard times about which they were apprehensive. Worse, the new equilibrium finds

saving at the same level as it was before consumption dropped (€25 billion). In their attempt to save more, households have caused a contraction in output, and thus in income. They end up consuming less, but they have not saved any more.

It should be clear why saving at the new equilibrium is equal to saving at the old equilibrium. Equilibrium requires that saving equal planned investment, and since planned investment is unchanged, saving must remain unchanged for equilibrium to exist. This paradox shows that the interactions among sectors in the economy can be of crucial importance.

This **paradox of thrift** is 'paradoxical' because it contradicts the widely held belief that 'a penny saved is a penny earned'. This may be true for an individual, but when society as a whole saves more, the result is a drop in income but no increased saving.

Does the paradox of thrift always hold? Recall

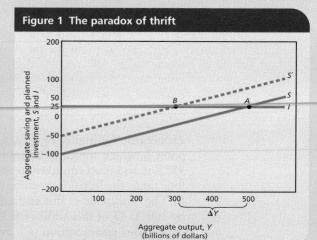

Figure 1 The paradox of thrift

An increase in planned saving from S to S' causes equilibrium output to decrease from €500 billion to €300 billion. The decreased consumption that accompanies increased saving leads to a contraction of the economy and to a reduction of income. But at the new equilibrium, saving is the same as it was at the initial equilibrium. Increased efforts to save have caused a drop in income but no overall change in saving.

our assumption that planned investment is fixed. Let us drop this assumption for a moment. If the extra saving that households want to do to ward off hard times is channelled into additional investment through financial markets, there is a shift upwards in the I schedule. The paradox

could then be averted. If investment increases, a new equilibrium can be achieved at a higher level of saving and income. This result, however, depends critically on the existence of a channel through which additional household saving finances additional investment.

It is possible to calculate how much Y must increase in response to the additional planned investment before equilibrium will be restored. Y will rise, pulling S up with it until the change in saving is exactly equal to the change in planned investment – that is, until S is again equal to I at its new higher level. Since added saving is a *fraction* of added income (the *MPS*), the increase in *income* required to restore equilibrium must be a *multiple* of the increase in planned investment.

Recall that the marginal propensity to save (*MPS*) is the fraction of a change in income that is saved. It is defined as the change in S (ΔS) over the change in income (ΔY):

benägenhet

$$MPS = \frac{\Delta S}{\Delta Y}$$

Since ΔS must be equal to ΔI for equilibrium to be restored, we can substitute ΔI for ΔS and solve:

$$MPS = \frac{\Delta I}{\Delta Y}, \text{ so } \Delta Y = \Delta I \times \frac{1}{MPS}$$

As you can see, the change in equilibrium income (ΔY) is equal to the initial change in planned investment (ΔI) times $1/MPS$. The multiplier is thus $1/MPS$:

$$\text{Multiplier} \equiv \frac{1}{MPS}$$

saving   *consume*

Because $MPS + MPC \equiv 1$, $MPS \equiv 1 - MPC$. It follows that the multiplier is equal to:

$$\text{Multiplier} \equiv \frac{1}{1 - MPC}$$

In our example, the *MPC* is 0.75, so the *MPS* must equal $1 - 0.75$, or 0.25. Thus, the multiplier is 1 divided by 0.25, or 4. The change in the equilibrium level of Y is 4×25 billion, or €100 billion.[8] Also note that the same analysis holds when planned investment is reduced. If planned investment is lowered by a certain amount and is sustained at this lower level, output will fall by a multiple of the reduction in I. As the initial shock is felt and firms cut output, they lay people off. The result: income, and subsequently consumption, falls.

The size of the multiplier in the real world

It would be a mistake to move on from this chapter thinking that national income can be increased by €100 billion simply by increasing planned investment by 25 billion, as a multiplier of 4 suggests. In the real world multipliers are smaller, typically near the lower end of the range between 1.5 and 3. The reason for this discrepancy is not that we plugged an unrealistic number for the *MPC* into the multiplier formula. Rather, when we derived the formula we made some simplifying assumptions that facilitate a first understanding of what the multiplier is, but that exaggerate its size:

1. We assumed that the government levies no taxes. In the more realistic setting to be analysed in Chapter 24, taxes are paid as a share of income. Thus, when income rises not only saving but also taxes do not come back to firms as demand-generating additional income. This additional leakage makes the multiplier effect smaller.

2. We are looking at the global economy, the entire world, with neither imports or exports. In an individual country, a perspective we will begin to employ in Chapter 28,

---

[8] *The multiplier can also be derived algebraically, as the appendix to this chapter demonstrates.*

income spent on imports does not reach domestic firms to generate more income. Again, the effect of this leakage is to make the multiplier smaller.

3. Finally, we ignored the repercussions that demand changes have on financial variables and prices. As demand raises income, prices and interest rates may go up and the exchange rate may appreciate, driving down exports, investment and demand in general. Later chapters look into these effects, and again show that they reduce the multiplier. In the long run they even eliminate the multiplier.

Future refinements will not question the multiplier as an essential concept in macroeconomics. They signal, though, that its magnitude depends on a range of factors. Knowing these factors reveals when (or for what time horizon) it is safe to work with the multiplier model and when it is not.

For now, however, it is enough to point out that:

> In reality, for a time horizon of a few years, the size of the multiplier is between 1.5 and 3. That is, a sustained increase in autonomous spending of €10 billion can be expected to raise real GDP over time by about €15–30 billion. For time horizons beyond five years the multiplier becomes very small.

The multiplier in action: US recovery from the Great Depression

It was in the USA that the Great Depression was at its worst. It began in 1930 and lasted nearly a decade. Real output in 1938 was lower than real output in 1929, and the unemployment rate was always above 14% of the labour force between 1930 and 1940. How did the economy get 'stuck' at such a low level of income and a high level of unemployment? The Keynesian model that we analysed in this chapter can help us answer this question.

If firms do not wish to undertake much investment (I is low) or if consumers decide to increase their saving and cut back on consumption, then planned spending will be low. Firms do not want to produce more because, with many workers unemployed, households do not have the income to buy the extra output that firms might produce. And households, who would purchase more if they had more income, cannot find jobs that would enable them to earn additional income. The economy is caught in a vicious cycle.

How might such a cycle be broken? One way is for planned aggregate expenditure to increase, increasing aggregate output via the multiplier effect. This increase in AE may occur naturally, or it may be caused by a change in government policy.

In the late 1930s, for example, the economy experienced a surge of both residential and non-residential investment. Between 1935 and 1940, total investment spending (in real terms) increased 64% and residential investment more than doubled. There can be no doubt that this increased investment had a multiplier effect. In just five years, employment in the construction industry increased by more than 400,000, employment in manufacturing industries jumped by more than 1 million, and total employment grew by more than 5 million. As more workers were employed, more income was generated, and some of this added income was spent on consumption goods. Inventories declined and firms began to expand output.

Between 1935 and 1940, real output (income) increased by more than a third and the unemployment rate dropped from 20.3% to 14.6%.

But 14.6% is a very high rate of unemployment; the Depression was not yet over. Between 1940 and 1943, the Depression ended, with the unemployment rate dropping to 1.9% in 1943. This recovery was triggered by the mobilization for the Second World War and the significant increase in government purchases of goods and services, which rose from $14 billion in 1940 to $88.6 billion in 1943. In the next chapter, we will explore this *government spending multiplier*, and you'll see how the government can help to stimulate the economy by increasing its spending.

Looking ahead: the government

In this chapter, we took the first step in understanding how the economy works. We described the behaviour of two sectors (household and firm) and discussed how equilibrium is achieved in the market for goods and services. In the next chapter, we will relax some of the assumptions we have made and take into account the roles of government spending in the economy. This will give us a more realistic picture of how our economy works.

Summary

Aggregate output and aggregate income (Y)

1. Each period, firms produce an aggregate quantity of goods and services called *aggregate output* (Y). Because every euro of expenditure is received by someone as income, aggregate output and aggregate income are the same thing.

2. The total amount of aggregate consumption that takes place in any given period depends on factors such as household income, household wealth, interest rates and households' expectations about the future.

3. If taxes are zero, households can do only two things with their income: they can either consume or they can save. C refers to aggregate consumption by households. S refers to aggregate saving by households. By definition, saving equals income minus consumption: $S \equiv Y - C$.

4. The higher someone's income is, the greater his or her consumption will probably be. This is also true for the economy as a whole: there is a positive relationship between aggregate consumption (C) and aggregate income (Y).

5. The *marginal propensity to consume* (MPC) is the fraction of a change in income that is consumed, or spent. *The marginal propensity to save* (MPS) is the fraction of a change in income that is saved. Because all income must be either saved or spent, $MPS + MPC = 1$.

6. The primary form of spending that firms engage in is investment. Strictly speaking, investment refers to the purchase by firms of new buildings and equipment and additions to inventories, all of which add to firms' capital stock.

7. Actual investment can differ from planned investment because changes in firms' inventories are part of actual investment and inventory changes are not under the complete control of firms. Inventory changes are partly determined by how much households decide to buy. I refers to planned investment only.

Equilibrium aggregate output (income)

8. In the global economy with no government, *planned aggregate expenditure* (AE) equals consumption plus planned investment: $AE \equiv C + I$. *Equilibrium* in the goods market is achieved when planned aggregate expenditure equals aggregate output: $C + I = Y$. This holds if, and only if, planned investment and actual investment are equal.

9. Because aggregate income must be saved or spent, the equilibrium condition $Y = C + I$ can be rewritten as $C + S = C + I$, or $S = I$. Only when planned investment equals saving will there be equilibrium. This approach to equilibrium is the *saving/investment* or the *leakages/injections* approach to equilibrium.

10. When aggregate expenditure exceeds aggregate output (*income*), there is an unplanned fall in inventories. Firms will increase output. This increased output leads to increased income and even more consumption. This process will continue as long as output (income) is below planned aggregate expenditure. If firms react to unplanned inventory reductions by increasing output, an economy with planned spending greater than output will adjust to equilibrium, with Y higher than before.

11. Equilibrium output changes by a multiple of the change in planned investment or any other autonomous variable. The multiplier is $1/MPS$.

12. When households increase their planned saving, income decreases and saving does not change. Saving does not increase because in equilibrium saving must equal planned investment and planned investment is fixed. If planned investment also increased, this *paradox of thrift* could be averted and a new equilibrium could be achieved at a higher level of saving and income. This result depends on the existence of a channel through which additional household saving finances additional investment.

Review Terms and Concepts

actual investment
aggregate income
aggregate output
aggregate output (income) (*Y*)
autonomous or exogenous variable
change in inventory
consumption function
desired, or planned, investment (*I*)
equilibrium
identity
investment
marginal propensity to consume (*MPC*)
marginal propensity to save (*MPS*)
multiplier
planned aggregate expenditure (*AE*)
saving (*S*)

Equations

1. $S \equiv Y - C$

2. $MPC \equiv$ slope of consumption function $\equiv \dfrac{\Delta C}{\Delta Y}$

3. $MPC + MPS \equiv 1$

4. $AE \equiv C + I$

5. Equilibrium condition: $Y = AE$ or $Y = C + I$

6. Saving/investment approach to equilibrium: $S = I$

7. Multiplier $\equiv \dfrac{1}{MPS} \equiv \dfrac{1}{1 - MPC}$

Problem Set

1. Briefly define the following pairs of terms and explain the relationship between them:

- *MPC* / multiplier
- Actual investment / planned investment
- Aggregate expenditure / real GDP
- Aggregate output / aggregate income

2. Leading economists in the Republic of Yucklandia estimate real GNP (*Y*) at 200 billion yucks and planned investment spending at 75 billion yucks. Yucklandia is a simple economy with no government, no taxes and no imports or exports. Yucklandians are creatures of habit. They have a rule that everyone saves exactly 25% of their income. Assume that planned investment is fixed and remains at 75 billion yucks.

You are asked by the business editor of *Weird Harold*, the leading financial newspaper, to predict the economic events of the next few months. Using the data above can you make a forecast? What is likely to happen to inventories? What is likely to happen to the level of real GDP? Is the economy at an equilibrium? When will things stop changing?

3. Look at the data in Table 1.
a. Calculate saving at each level of output. Calculate unplanned investment (inventory change) at each level of output.,What is likely to happen to aggregate output if the economy were producing at each of the levels indicated. What is the equilibrium level of output?
b. Over each range of income (2000–2500, 2500–3000 etc.) calculate the marginal propensity to consume. Calculate the marginal propensity to save. What is the multiplier?

Table 1		
Aggregate Output/Income	**Planned**	
	Consumption	**Investment**
2000	2100	300
2500	2500	300
3000	2900	300
3500	3300	300
4000	3700	300
4500	4100	300
5000	4500	300
5500	4900	300

c. Assuming there is no change in the level of the *MPC* and the *MPS*, and planned investment rises by 200 and is sustained at that higher level, recompute the table. What is the new equilibrium level of *Y*? Is this consistent with what you compute using the multiplier?

4. Explain the multiplier intuitively. Why is it that an increase in planned investment of €100 raises equilibrium output by more than €100? Why is the effect on equilibrium output finite? How do we know that the multiplier is 1/*MPS*?

5. Explain how planned investment can differ from actual investment.

6. You are given the following data regarding Freedonia, a legendary country: (1) Consumption function $C = 200 + 0.8Y$; (2) Investment function $I = 100$; (3) $AE \equiv C + I$; (4) $AE = Y$.

a. What is the marginal propensity to consume in Freedonia? The marginal propensity to save?

b. Graph equations (3) and (4) and solve for equilibrium income.

c. Suppose equation (2) were changed to (2'): $I = 110$. What is the new equilibrium level of income? By how much does the increase in planned investment by 10 change equilibrium income? What is the value of the multiplier?

d. Calculate the saving function for Freedonia. Plot this saving function on a graph with equation (2). Explain why the equilibrium income in this graph must be the same as in (b).

7. If I decide to save an extra euro, my saving goes up by that amount. But if everyone decides to save an extra euro, income falls and saving does not rise. Explain.

8. You learned earlier that expenditures and income should always be equal. In this chapter, you've learned that AE and aggregate output (income) can be different. Is there an inconsistency here?

Appendix to Chapter 23

Deriving the Multiplier Algebraically

In addition to deriving the multiplier using the simple substitution we used in the chapter text, we can also derive the formula for the multiplier by using simple algebra.

Recall that our consumption function is

$$C = a + bY$$

where b is the marginal propensity to consume. In equilibrium,

$$Y = C + I$$

We now solve these two equations for Y in terms of I. Substituting the first equation into the second, we get

$$Y = \underbrace{a + bY}_{C} + I$$

This equation can be rearranged to yield

$$Y - bY = a + I$$
$$Y(1 - b) = a + I$$

We can then solve for Y in terms of I by dividing through by $(1 - b)$:

$$Y = (a + I)\left(\frac{1}{1 - b}\right)$$

Now look carefully at this expression and think about increasing I by some amount, ΔI, with a held constant. If I increases by ΔI, income will increase by

$$\Delta Y = \Delta I \times \frac{1}{1 - b}$$

Since $b \equiv MPC$, the expression becomes

$$\Delta Y = \Delta I \times \frac{1}{1 - MPC}$$

The multiplier is thus:

$$\frac{1}{1 - MPC}$$

Finally, since $MPS + MPC = 1$, MPS is equal to $1 - MPC$, making the alternative expression for the multiplier $1/MPS$, just as we saw in the chapter text.

24

The Government and Fiscal Policy

Nothing in macroeconomics or microeconomics arouses as much controversy as the role of government in the economy.

In microeconomics, the active presence of government in regulating competition, providing roads and education, and redistributing income is applauded by those who believe a free market simply does not work well if left to its own devices. Opponents of government intervention say it is the government, not the market, that performs badly. They say bureaucracy and inefficiency could be eliminated or reduced if the government played a smaller role in the economy.

In macroeconomics, the debate over what the government can and should do has a similar flavour, although the issues are somewhat different. At one end of the spectrum are the Keynesians and their intellectual descendants, who believe that the macroeconomy is likely to fluctuate too much if left on its own and that the government should smooth out fluctuations in the business cycle. These ideas can be traced back to Keynes's analysis in *The General Theory*, which suggests that governments can use their taxing and spending powers to increase aggregate expenditure (and thereby stimulate aggregate output) in times of recessions or depressions. At the other end are those who claim that government spending is incapable of stabilizing the economy, or worse, is destabilizing and harmful.

Perhaps the one thing most people can agree on is that, like it or not, governments are important actors in the economies of virtually all countries. For this reason alone, it is worth our while to analyse the way government influences the functioning of the macroeconomy.

While the government has a variety of powers – including regulating firms' entry into and exit from an industry, setting standards for product quality, setting minimum wage levels, and regulating the disclosure of information – in macroeconomics we study a government with general, but limited, powers. Specifically, government can affect the macroeconomy through two channels: fiscal policy and monetary policy. Fiscal policy, the focus of this chapter, refers to the government's spending and taxing behaviour – in other words, its budget policy.[1] Fiscal policy is generally divided into three categories: (1) policies regarding government purchases of goods and labour, (2) policies regarding taxes, and (3) policies regarding transfer payments (such as unemployment and social security benefits, welfare payments and state pensions) to households. Monetary policy, the focus of the next two chapters, refers to the behaviour of the nation's central bank, regarding the nation's money supply.[2]

fiscal policy
The government's spending and taxing policies.

monetary policy
The behaviour of the nation's central bank regarding the nation's money supply.

[1] *The word* fiscal *comes from the root* fisc*, which refers to the 'treasury' of a government.*

[2] *In the national economy to be studied later, monetary policy and exchange rate policy – setting the exchange rate between the national currency and some other country's currency – are closely related. Exchange rate policy is not available for the global economy.*

Government in the economy

Given the scope and power of regional and national governments, there are some matters over which they exert great control and some matters beyond their control. We need to distinguish between variables that a government controls directly and variables that are both a consequence of government decisions and the response of the economy.

For instance, tax rates are controlled by the government. It decides who and what should be taxed and at what rate. Tax *revenue*, on the other hand, is not subject to complete control by the government. Revenue from the personal income tax system depends both on personal tax rates (set by legislators) and on the income of the household sector (which depends on many factors not under direct government control, such as how much households decide to work). Revenue from the corporate profits tax depends both on corporate tax rates and on the size of corporate profits. The government controls corporate tax rates but not the size of corporate profits.

Government spending also depends both on government decisions and on the state of the economy. For example, the unemployment benefits system pays benefits to unemployed people. When the economy goes into a recession, the number of unemployed workers increases and so does the level of government unemployment benefit payments.

Because taxes and expenditures often go up or down in response to changes in the economy rather than as the result of conscious decisions by policy makers, we will occasionally use the term **discretionary fiscal policy** to refer to changes in taxes or spending that are the result of conscious changes in government policy.

discretionary fiscal policy

Changes in taxes or spending that are the result of conscious changes in government policy.

Government purchases (*G*), net taxes (*T*) and disposable income (Y_d)

In the previous chapter, we explored the equilibrium level of aggregate output for a simple economy – no taxes, no government spending, no exports and no imports – to provide you with a general idea of how the macroeconomy operates. This stylized first model will now be refined by adding the government.

To keep things simple, we combine two government activities – the collection of taxes and the payment of transfer payments – into one category we call **net taxes (*T*)**. Specifically, net taxes are equal to the tax payments made to the government by firms and households minus transfer payments made to households by the government. The other variable we consider is government purchases of goods and services (*G*).

net taxes (*T*) Taxes paid by firms and households to the government minus transfer payments made to households by the government.

Our earlier discussions of household consumption omitted taxes. We assumed that all the income generated in the economy was spent or saved by households. When we take into account the role of government, as Figure 24.1 does, we see that as income (*Y*) flows to households, the government takes income from households in the form of net taxes (*T*). The income that ultimately gets to households is called **disposable**, or **after-tax, income (Y_d)**.

disposable, *or* after-tax, income (Y_d)

Total income minus net taxes: *Y – T*.

Disposable income = Total income – Net taxes

$$(Y_d) \equiv Y - T$$

Y_d excludes taxes paid by households and includes transfer payments made to households by the government. For simplicity we are assuming that *T* does not depend on *Y* – that is, net taxes do not depend on income. This assumption, which does not change the main results, is relaxed in Appendix B to this chapter. Taxes that do not depend on income are sometimes called *lump-sum taxes*.

As Figure 24.1 shows, the disposable income (Y_d) of households must end up either as consumption (*C*) or saving (*S*). Thus,

$$Y_d \equiv C + S$$

Figure 24.1 Adding net taxes (T) and government purchases (G) to the circular flow of income

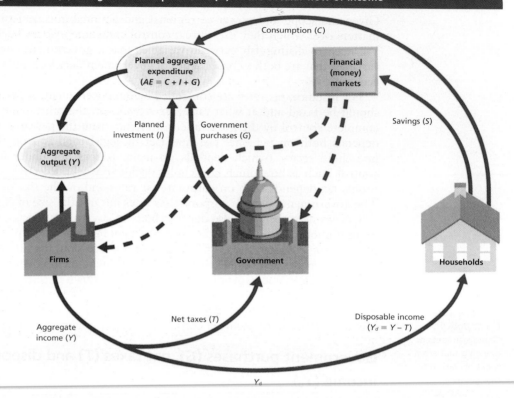

Remember that this equation is an identity, something that is always true.

Because disposable income is simply aggregate income (Y) minus net taxes (T), we can write another identity:

$$Y - T \equiv C + S$$

Adding T to both sides:

$$Y \equiv C + S + T$$

This identity simply says that aggregate income gets cut into three pieces. Government takes a slice (net taxes, T), and then households divide the rest between consumption (C) and saving (S).

Because governments spend money on goods and services, we need to expand our definition of planned aggregate expenditure. Planned aggregate expenditure (AE) is the sum of consumption spending by households (C), planned investment by business firms (I) and government purchases of goods and services (G):[3]

Aggregate expenditure (AE) $\equiv C + I + G$

budget deficit

The difference between what a government spends and what it collects in taxes in a given period: $G - T$.

A government's **budget deficit** is the difference between what it spends (G) and what it collects in net taxes (T) in a given period:

Budget deficit $= G - T$

---

[3]*We are still assuming that net exports (EX – IM) are zero, as it should be in the global economy. When we turn to the national economy in Chapter 28, AE $\equiv$ C + I + G + (EX – IM).*

If G exceeds T, the government must borrow from the public to finance the deficit. It does so by selling government bonds (more on this later). In this case, a part of household saving (S) goes to the government. Observe from the dashed lines in Figure 24.1 that some S goes to firms to finance investment projects and some goes to the government to finance its deficit.[4]

Adding taxes to the consumption function

In Chapter 23 we examined the consumption behaviour of households and noted that aggregate consumption (C) depends on aggregate income (Y): in general, the higher aggregate income is, the higher is aggregate consumption. For the sake of illustration, we used a specific linear consumption function:

$$C = a + bY$$

where a is the amount of consumption that would take place if national income were zero and b is the marginal propensity to consume.

We need to modify this consumption function now that we have added government to the economy. With taxes now a part of the picture, it makes sense to assume that disposable income (Y_d), rather than before-tax income (Y), determines consumption behaviour. If you earn a million euros but have to pay €950,000 in taxes, you have no more disposable income than someone who earns only €50,000 but pays no taxes. Your disposable income is what you have available for spending on current consumption, not your income before taxes.

To modify our aggregate consumption function we replace before-tax income by disposable income. Instead of $C = a + bY$, we write:

$$C = a + bY_d$$

or

$$C = a + b\,(Y - T)$$

Consumption now depends on disposable income rather than on before-tax income.

Investment

What about investment? The government can affect investment behaviour through its tax treatment of depreciation and other tax policies. Investment may also vary with economic conditions and interest rates, as we will see later. For our present purposes, however, we continue to assume that planned investment (I) is fixed.

Equilibrium output: $Y = C + I + G$

We know from Chapter 23 that equilibrium occurs where $Y = AE$ – that is, where aggregate output equals planned aggregate expenditure. Remember, planned aggregate expenditure in an economy with a government is $AE \equiv C + I + G$, so the equilibrium condition is:

Equilibrium condition: $Y = C + I + G$

The equilibrium analysis from Chapter 23 holds here too. If output (Y) exceeds planned aggregate expenditure ($C + I + G$), there will be an unplanned increase in inventories. Actual investment will exceed planned investment. Conversely, if $C + I + G$ exceeds Y, there will be an unplanned decrease in inventories.

[4]*Although it rarely happens these days, governments do sometimes run budget surpluses. A surplus occurs when net taxes are greater than government purchases of goods and services. A surplus is simply a negative deficit.*

An example will illustrate the government's effect on the macroeconomy and on the equilibrium condition. First, our consumption function, which was $C = 100 + 0.75Y$ before we introduced the government sector, now becomes

$$C = 100 + 0.75Y_d$$

or

$$C = 100 + 0.75 (Y - T)$$

Second, we assume that the government is currently purchasing €100 billion of goods and services and collecting net taxes (T) of €100 billion.[5] In other words, the government is running a balanced budget in financing all of its spending with taxes. Third, we assume that planned investment (I) is €100 billion.

Table 24.1 calculates planned aggregate expenditure at several levels of disposable income. For example, at $Y = 500$, disposable income is $Y - T$, or 400. Therefore, $C = 100 + 0.75(400) = 400$. Assuming that I is fixed at €100 billion, and assuming that G is fixed at €100 billion, planned aggregate expenditure is 600 ($C + I + G = 400 + 100 + 100$). Since output ($Y$) is only 500, planned spending is greater than output by 100. As a result, there is an unplanned inventory decrease of 100, giving firms an incentive to raise output. Thus, output of €500 billion is below equilibrium.

If $Y = 1300$, then $Y_d = 1200$, $C = 1000$ and planned aggregate expenditure is 1200. Here, since planned spending is less than output, there will be an unplanned inventory increase of 100, and firms have an incentive to cut back output. Thus, output of €1300 billion is above equilibrium. Only when output is 900 are output and planned aggregate expenditure equal, and only at $Y = 900$ does equilibrium exist.

In Figure 24.2, we derive the same equilibrium level of output graphically. First, the consumption function is drawn, taking into account net taxes of 100. The old function was $C = 100 + 0.75Y$. The new function is $C = 100 + 0.75(Y - T)$ or $C = 100 + 0.75 (Y - 100)$, rewritten as $C = 100 + 1.75Y - 75$, or $C = 25 + 0.75Y$. The marginal propensity to consume has not changed – we assume it remains 0.75. For example,

Table 24.1 Finding equilibrium for I = 100, G = 100 and T = 100 (all figures in billions of euros)

(1) Output (income)	(2) Net taxes	(3) Disposable income	(4) Consumption spending	(5) Saving	(6) Planned investment spending	(7) Government purchases	(8) Planned aggregate expenditure	(9) Unplanned inventory change	(10) Adjustment to equilibrium
Y	T	$Y_d = Y - T$	$C = 100 + 0.75Y_d$	$S = Y_d - C$	I	G	$C + I + G$	$Y - (C + I + G)$	
300	100	200	250	−50	100	100	450	−150	Output ↑
500	100	400	400	0	100	100	600	−100	Output ↑
700	100	600	550	50	100	100	750	−50	Output ↑
900	100	800	700	100	100	100	900	0	Equilibrium
1,100	100	1,000	850	150	100	100	1,050	+50	Output ↓
1,300	100	1,200	1,000	200	100	100	1,200	+100	Output ↓
1,500	100	1,400	1,150	250	100	100	1,350	+150	Output ↓

[5]As we pointed out earlier, the government does not have complete control over tax revenues and transfer payments. We ignore this problem here, however, and set tax revenues minus transfers at a fixed amount. Things will become more realistic later in this chapter and in Appendix B.

Figure 24.2 Finding equilibrium output/income graphically

Since G and I are both fixed at €100 billion, the aggregate expenditure function is the new consumption function displaced upward by $I + G = 200$. Equilibrium occurs at $Y = C + I + G = €900$ billion

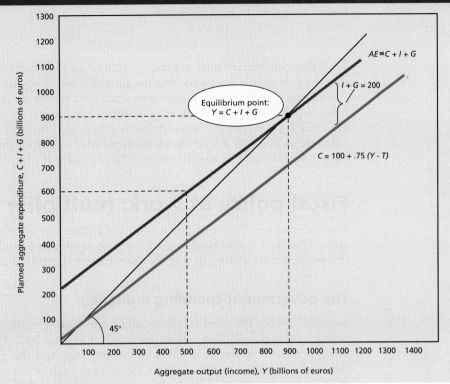

consumption at an income of zero is €25 billion ($C = 25 + 0.75Y = 25 + 0.75(0) = 25$). Note that the consumption function in Figure 24.2 plots the points in columns 1 and 4 of Table 24.1.

Planned aggregate expenditure, recall, adds planned investment to consumption. But now, in addition to 100 in investment, we have government purchases of 100. Because I and G are constant at 100 each at all levels of income, we add $I + G = 200$ to consumption at every level of income. The result is the new AE curve. This curve is just a plot of the points in columns 1 and 8 of Table 24.1. The 45° line helps us find the equilibrium level of real output, which, we already know, is 900. If you examine any level of output above or below 900, you will find a disequilibrium. Look, for example, at $Y = 500$ on the graph. At this level, planned aggregate expenditure is 600, but output is only 500. Inventories will fall below what was planned, and firms will have an incentive to increase output.

The leakages/injections approach to equilibrium

As in the last chapter, we can also examine equilibrium using the leakages/injections approach. Look at the circular flow of income in Figure 24.1. The government takes out net taxes (T) from the flow of income – a leakage – and households save (S) some of their income – also a leakage from the flow of income. The planned spending injections are government purchases (G) and planned investment (I). If leakages ($S + T$) equal planned injections ($I + G$), there is equilibrium:

Leakages/injections approach to equilibrium: $S + T = I + G$

To derive this, we know that in equilibrium, aggregate output (income) (Y) equals planned aggregate expenditure (AE). By definition, AE equals $C + I + G$, and by definition Y equals $C + S + T$. Therefore, in equilibrium

$$C + S + T = C + I + G$$

Subtracting C from both sides leaves

$$S + T = I + G$$

Note that equilibrium does not require that $G = T$ (a balanced government budget) or that $S = I$. It is only necessary that the sum of S and T equals the sum of I and G.

Column 5 of Table 24.1 calculates aggregate saving by subtracting consumption from disposal income at every level of disposable income ($S \equiv Y_d - C$). Since I and G are fixed, $I + G$ equals 200 at every level of income. The table shows that $S + T$ equals 200 only at $Y = 900$. Thus, the equilibrium level of output (income) is 900, the same answer we arrived at through numerical and graphical analysis.

Fiscal policy at work: multiplier effects

You can see from Figure 24.2 that if the government were able to change the levels of either G or T, it would be able to change the equilibrium level of output (income). At this point, we are assuming that the government controls G and T.

The government spending multiplier

Suppose you are the chief economic adviser to your government and the economy is sitting at the equilibrium output pictured in Figure 24.2. Output and income are being produced at a rate of €900 billion per year, and the government is currently buying €100 billion worth of goods and services each year and is financing them with €100 billion in taxes. The budget is balanced. In addition, the private sector is investing (producing capital goods) at a rate of €100 billion per year.

Then your country's President or Prime Minister or Chancellor calls you and says, 'Unemployment is too high. We need to lower unemployment by increasing output and income.' After some research, you determine that an acceptable unemployment rate could be achieved only if aggregate output increased to €1100 billion.

The question you now need to answer is: how can the government use taxing and spending policy – fiscal policy – to increase the equilibrium level of national output? Suppose that the government has announced that taxes will remain at present levels – parliament has just passed a major tax reform package – so adjusting T is out of the question for several years. That leaves you with G. Your only option is to increase government spending while holding taxes constant.

To increase spending without raising taxes (which provides the government with revenue to spend), the government must borrow. When G is bigger than T, the government runs a deficit, and the difference between G and T must be borrowed. For the moment, we will ignore the possible effect of the deficit and focus only on the effect of a higher G with T constant.

The government is awaiting your answer. How much of an increase in spending would be required to generate a €200 billion increase in the equilibrium level of output, pushing it from €900 billion up to €1100 billion and reducing unemployment to the government's acceptable level?

You might be tempted to say that since we need to increase income by 200 (1100 – 900), we should increase government spending by the same amount.[6] But what would happen? The increased government spending will throw the economy out of equilibrium. Since G is a component of aggregate spending, planned aggregate expenditure will increase by 200. Planned spending will be greater than output, inventories will be

---

[6]For the rest of this discussion, we will understand but not state that figures are in billions of euros.

lower than planned, and firms will have an incentive to increase output. Suppose output rises by the desired 200. You might think: 'We increased spending by 200 and output by 200, so equilibrium is restored'.

There is more to the story than this. The moment output rises, the economy is generating more income. This was the desired effect: the creation of more employment. Some of the newly employed workers become consumers and some of their income gets spent. With higher consumption spending, planned spending will be greater than output, inventories will be lower than planned, and firms will raise output, and thus raise income, again. This time firms are responding to the new consumption spending. Already, total income is over 1100.

This story should sound familiar. It is the multiplier in action. Although this time it is government spending (G) that is changed rather than planned investment (I), the effect is the same as the multiplier effect described in Chapter 23. An increase in government spending has the same impact on the equilibrium level of output and income as an increase in planned investment. A euro of extra spending from either G or I is identical with respect to its impact on equilibrium output. The equation for the government spending multiplier is the same as the equation for the multiplier for a change in planned investment.[7]

$$\text{Government spending multiplier} \equiv \frac{1}{MPS}$$

government spending multiplier

The ratio of the change in the equilibrium level of output to a change in government spending.

Formally, the **government spending multiplier** is defined as the ratio of the change in the equilibrium level of output to a change in government spending. This is the same definition we used in the previous chapter, but now the autonomous variable is government spending rather than planned investment.

Remember that we were thinking of increasing government spending (G) by 200. We can use the multiplier analysis to see what the new equilibrium level of Y would be for an increase in G of 200. The multiplier in our example is 4. (Since b – the MPC – is 0.75, the MPS must be $1 - 0.75 = 0.25$. And $1/0.25 = 4$). Thus, Y will increase by 800 (4×200). Since the initial level of Y was 900, the new equilibrium level of Y is 900 + 800 = 1700 when G is increased by 200.

The level of 1700 is much larger than the level of 1100 that we calculated as necessary to lower unemployment to the desired level. Let us step back, then. If we want Y to rise by 200 and if the multiplier is 4, we need to increase G by only 200/4 = 50. If G changes by 50, the equilibrium level of Y will change by 200, and the new value of Y will be 1100 (900 + 200), as desired.

Looking at Table 24.2, we can check our answer to be sure that it is an equilibrium. Look first at the old equilibrium of 900. When government purchases (G) were 100, aggregate output (income) was equal to planned aggregate expenditure ($AE \equiv C + I + G$) at $Y = 900$. But now G has increased to 150. At $Y = 900$, ($C + I + G$) is greater than Y, there's an unplanned fall in inventories and output will rise. But by how much? The multiplier told us that equilibrium income would rise by four times 50, the change in G. Y should rise by $4 \times 50 = 200$, from 900 to 1100 to restore equilibrium. Let's check this. If $Y = 1100$, then consumption is $C = 100 + 0.75Y_d = 100 + 0.75(1000) = 850$. Since I equals 100 and G now equals 100 (the original level of G) + 50 (the additional G brought about by the fiscal policy change) = 150, then $C + I + G = 850 + 100 + 150 = 1100$. Thus, $Y = AE$, and the economy is in equilibrium.

The graphic solution to your government's problem is presented in Figure 24.3. An increase in G of 50 shifts the planned aggregate expenditure function up by 50. The new equilibrium income occurs where the new AE line (AE_2) crosses the 45° line, at $Y = 1100$.

---

[7]*We derive the government spending multiplier algebraically in Appendix A to this chapter.*

Table 24.2 Finding equilibrium after a €50 billion government spending increase (all figures in billions of euros; G has increased from 100 in Table 24.1 to 150 here)

(1) Output (income)	(2) Net taxes	(3) Disposable income	(4) Consumption spending	(5) Saving	(6) Planned investment spending	(7) Government purchases	(8) Planned aggregate expenditure	(9) Unplanned inventory change	(10) Adjustment to equilibrium
Y	T	$Y_d = Y - T$	$C = 100 + 0.75Y_d$	$S = Y_d - C$	I	G	$C + I + G$	$Y - (C + I + G)$	
300	100	200	250	250	100	150	500	−200	Output ↑
500	100	400	400	0	100	150	650	−150	Output ↑
700	100	600	550	50	100	150	800	−100	Output ↑
900	100	800	700	100	100	150	950	−50	Output ↑
1,100	100	1,000	850	150	100	150	1,100	0	Equilibrium
1,300	100	1,200	1,000	200	100	150	1,250	+50	Output ↓
1,500	100	1,400	1,150	250	100	150	1,400	+100	Output ↓

Applications

Keynes, the multiplier and Britain's war time spending

In 1940, John Maynard Keynes discussed the issue of how much leeway Britain had for its war spending without triggering inflation. The reason why his analysis is of interest for us is that it employs the kind of multiplier analysis introduced in this chapter.

Keynes estimates that in 1938, the latest year for which he has data, Britain's production potential (called potential output; a term we will discuss in Chapter 30) is £6.345 billion. In his view, if aggregate demand (or output or income) is driven beyond this level, firms will begin to raise prices, triggering inflation. Since actual income in 1938 is only £5.520 billion, income may raise by £825 million without triggering inflation.

The multiplier tells us by how much income rises after a given increase in government spending: $\Delta Y = $ multiplier $\times \Delta G$. For the question at hand, Keynes reads this equation backwards:

(1) $\Delta G = \dfrac{\Delta Y}{\text{multiplier}}$

This equation tells us what increase in government spending gives a targeted, predetermined increase in income.

Simple analysis

We learned in this chapter that the simple government spending multiplier is 1/MPS. Using this in equation (1), this gives the reverse-multiplier equation

(2) $\Delta G = MPS \times \Delta Y$.

The targeted change in income in income, ΔY, is not to exceed the difference between potential income and actual income:

$\Delta Y = 6.345 - 5.520 = 825$.

Next we make use of $MPS = 1 - MPC$. The marginal propensity to consume may be approximated by the ratio between consumption C and disposable income Y − T, that is $MPC = C/(Y - T)$. Plugging 1938 numbers C = 4,380, T = 770 the Y = 5,520 into this equation gives

$MPC = \dfrac{4,380}{(5,520 - 770)} = 0.92$

This puts the marginal propensity to save at $MPS = 0.08$. Plugging this and $\Delta Y = 825$ into equation (2) gives

$\Delta G = 0.08 \times 825 = 66$.

This result says that though current output falls £825 million short of potential output, the government may raise spending only by £66 million before output exceeds potential output and starts to drive up prices. The reason, of course, is the large multiplier of 1/0.08 = 12.5 that we obtained.

More realistic analysis with income-dependent taxes

In a more realistic setting, taxes depend on income according to T = tY. As the appendix shows, then the multiplier is $1/(1 - MPC + t \times MPC)$. The reverse-multiplier equation then becomes

$\Delta G = [1/(1 - MPC + t \times MPC)]\Delta Y$

Again we must use actual numbers for T and Y to obtain t = 770/5,250 = 0.14. Making use of this along with MPC = 0.92 and $\Delta Y = 825$ gives

$\Delta G = [1/(1 - 0.92 + 0.14 \times 0.92)]\,825 = 173$.

The result is, that in a more realistic scenario the leeway for government spending is much larger due to the smaller multiplier.

Source: J.M. Keynes, How to Pay for the War, pamphlet, 27 February 1940. Reprinted in: The Collected Writings of John Maynard Keynes, Vol. IX, Essays in Persuasion. London: Macmillan, 1971–89.

Figure 24.3 The government spending multiplier

Increasing government spending by €50 billion shifts the AE function up by 50. As Y rises in response, additional consumption is generated. Overall, the equilibrium level of Y increases by 200, from 900 to 1100.

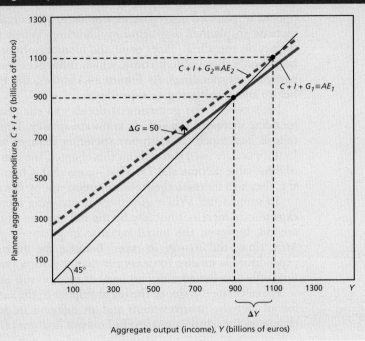

The tax multiplier

Remember that fiscal policy comprises policies regarding government spending *and* policies regarding taxation. To see what effect a change in tax policy has on the economy, imagine the following. You are still chief economic adviser to the government, but now you are instructed to devise a plan to reduce unemployment to an acceptable level *without* increasing the level of government spending. In your plan, instead of increasing government spending (G), you decide to cut taxes and maintain the current level of spending. A tax cut increases disposable income, which is likely to lead to added consumption spending. (Remember our general rule that increased income leads to increased consumption.) Would the decrease in taxes affect aggregate output (income) in the same manner as an increase in G?

Clearly, a decrease in taxes would increase income. The government spends no less than it did before the tax cut, and households find they have a larger after-tax, or disposable, income than they had before. This leads to an increase in consumption. Planned aggregate expenditure will increase, which will lead to lower inventories than planned, which prompts a rise in output. When output rises, more workers are employed and more income is generated, causing a second-round increase in consumption, and so on. Thus, income will increase by a multiple of the decrease in taxes. But beware: there is a catch!

> The multiplier for a change in taxes is *not the same* as the multiplier for a change in government spending.

tax multiplier The ratio of change in the equilibrium level of output to a change in taxes.

Why does the **tax multiplier** – the ratio of a change in the equilibrium level of output to a change in taxes – differ from the spending multiplier? To answer this we need to compare how a tax cut and a spending increase each work their way through the economy.

Look back at Figure 24.1. When the government increases spending, there is an immediate and direct impact on the economy's *total* spending. Because G is a component of planned aggregate expenditure, an increase in G leads to a euro-for-euro increase in planned aggregate expenditure. When taxes are cut, there is no direct impact on spending. Taxes enter the picture only because they have an effect on the household's disposable income, which influences household's consumption (which is part of total spending). As Figure 24.1 shows, the tax cut flows through households before affecting aggregate expenditure.

Let's assume the government decides to cut taxes by €1. By how much would spending increase? We already know the answer. The marginal propensity to consume tells us how much consumption spending changes when disposable income changes. In the example used throughout this chapter, the marginal propensity to consume out of disposable income is 0.75. This means that if households' after-tax incomes rise by €1, they will increase their consumption not by the full €1, but merely by €0.75.[8]

To summarize: When government spending increases by €1, planned aggregate expenditure increases initially by the full amount of the rise in G, or €1. When taxes are cut, however, the initial increase in planned aggregate expenditure is only the *MPC* times the change in taxes. Because the initial increase in planned aggregate expenditure is smaller for a tax cut than it is for a government spending increase, the final effect on the equilibrium level of income will also be smaller.

We calculate the size of the tax multiplier in the same way we derived the multiplier for an increase in investment and an increase in government purchases. The final change in the equilibrium level of output (income) (Y) is:

$$\Delta Y = (\text{initial increase in aggregate expenditure}) \times (\frac{1}{MPS})$$

Since the initial change in aggregate expenditure caused by a tax change of ΔT is $(-\Delta T \times MPC)$, we can solve for the tax multiplier by substitution:

$$\Delta Y = (-\Delta T \times MPC) \times (\frac{1}{MPS}) = -\Delta T \times (\frac{MPC}{MPS})$$

Because a tax cut will cause an *increase* in consumption expenditures and output, and a tax increase will cause a *reduction* in consumption expenditures and output, the tax multiplier is a negative multiplier:

$$\text{Tax multiplier} \equiv -(\frac{MPC}{MPS})$$

We derive the tax multiplier algebraically in Appendix A to this chapter.

If the *MPC* is 0.75, as in our example, the multiplier is –0.75/0.25 = – 3. A tax cut of €100 billion will increase the equilibrium level of output by –€100 × –€3 = €300 billion. This is very different from the effect of our government spending multiplier of 4. Under the same conditions, a €100 billion increase in G will increase the equilibrium level of output by €400 billion (€100 billion × 4).

The balanced-budget multiplier

We have discussed the effects on income that result from (1) changing government spending while leaving taxes unchanged, and from (2) changing taxes leaving gov-

---

[8]*What happens to the other €0.25? Remember that whatever households do not consume is, by definition, saved. The missing €0.25 thus goes to saving.*

ernment spending unchanged. Now the Maastricht Treaty on European Economic and Monetary Union sets narrow restrictions on such policies for aspiring members. A country's budget deficit (which roughly equals $G - T$) must not exceed 3% of GDP – that is $(G - T)/Y \times 0.03$.[9] Once this limit is reached, government spending may rise if taxes increase by the same amount. Such a move would not raise the government's budget deficit any further.

You might think that in this case equal increases in government spending and taxes have no effect on equilibrium income. After all, the extra government spending equals the extra tax revenues collected by the government. But this is not so. Take, for example, a government spending increase of €40 billion. We know from the analysis above that an increase in G of €40 billion, with taxes (T) held constant, should increase the equilibrium level of income by €40 billion times the government spending multiplier. The multiplier is $1/MPS$ or $1/0.25 = 4$. The equilibrium level of income should rise by €160 billion (€40 billion $\times$ 4).

Now suppose that instead of keeping tax revenues constant, we finance the €40 billion increase in government spending with an equal increase in taxes, so as to maintain a balanced budget. What happens to aggregate spending as a result of both the rise in G and the rise in T? There are two initial effects. First, government spending rises by €40 billion. This effect is direct, immediate and positive. But now the government also collects €40 billion more in taxes. The tax increase has a *negative* impact on overall spending in the economy, but it does not fully offset the increase in government spending.

The final impact of a tax increase on aggregate expenditure depends on how households respond to it. The only thing we know about household behaviour so far is that households spend 75% of their added income and save 25%. We know that when disposable income falls, both consumption and saving are reduced. A tax increase of €40 billion reduces disposable income by €40 billion, and that means consumption falls by €40 billion $\times$ MPC. Since $MPC = 0.75$, consumption falls by €30 billion (€40 billion $\times$ 0.75).

The net result in the beginning is that government spending rises by €40 billion and consumption spending falls by €30 billion. Aggregate expenditure increases by €10 billion right after the simultaneous balanced-budget increases in G and T.

So, a balanced-budget increase in G and T will raise output. But by how much? How large is this **balanced-budget multiplier**? The answer may surprise you:

Balanced-budget multiplier = 1

balanced-budget multiplier

The ratio of change in the equilibrium level of output to a change in government spending where the change in government spending is balanced by a change in taxes so as not to create any deficit. The balanced-budget multiplier is equal to one: The change in Y resulting from the change in G and the equal change in T is exactly the same size as the initial change in G or T itself.

Let us combine what we know about the tax multiplier and the government spending multiplier to explain this. To find the final effect of a simultaneous increase in government spending and increase in net taxes, we need to add the multiplier effects of the two. The government spending multiplier is $1/MPS$. The tax multiplier is $-MPC/MPS$. Their sum is $(1/MPS) + (-MPC/MPS) \equiv (1 - MPC)/MPS$. Because $MPC + MPS \equiv 1$, then $1 - MPC \equiv MPS$. This means $(1 - MPC)/MPS \equiv MPS/MPS \equiv 1$.[10]

Back to our example. Using the government spending multiplier, we saw that a €40 billion increase in G would raise equilibrium output by 160 (40 $\times$ the government spending multiplier of 4). Using the tax multiplier, we know that a tax increase of €40 *reduces* the equilibrium level of output by 120 (40 $\times$ the tax multiplier, -3). The net

---

[9]At the 1997 intergovernmental conference in Dublin, governments even spelled out sanctions in the form of fines to ensure that budget deficits are kept in check even after the start of European Monetary Union.

[10]We also derive the balanced-budget multiplier in Appendix A to this chapter.

effect is thus 160 – 120, or 40. It should be clear, then, that the effect on equilibrium Y is equal to the balanced increase in both G and T. In other words, the net increase in the equilibrium level of Y resulting from the equal but opposite changes in G and T is of exactly the same size as the initial change in G or T.

If the government wanted to raise Y by 200 without increasing the deficit, a simultaneous increase in G and T of 200 would do it. To see why, look at the numbers in Table 24.3. In Table 24.1, we saw an equilibrium level of output at 900. With both G and T up by 200, the new equilibrium is 1100 – higher by 200 billion. At no other level of Y do we find $(C + I + G) = Y$.

> An increase in government spending has a direct initial effect on planned aggregate expenditure; a tax increase does not. The initial effect of the tax increase is that households cut consumption by the MPC times the change in taxes. This change in consumption is less than the change in taxes, because the MPC is less than one. The positive stimulus from the government spending increase is thus greater than the negative stimulus from the tax increase. The net effect is that the balanced-budget multiplier is one.

Table 24.4 summarizes everything we have said about fiscal policy multipliers. If anything is still unclear, review the relevant discussions in this chapter.

A warning

Although we have added government to our discussion of the global economy, the story we have told about the multiplier is still incomplete and oversimplified. As noted at the end of the previous chapter, adding more realism to our story has the effect of reducing the size of the multiplier.

One example of this is the case in which taxes depend on income, which is the case in the 'real world'. For simplicity, we have been treating net taxes (T) as a lump-sum, fixed amount. Appendix B to this chapter shows that the size of the multiplier is reduced when we make the more realistic assumption that taxes depend on income. We continue to add more realism to our analysis in Chapter 28, where we look at the national economy.

Table 24.3 Finding equilibrium after a €200 billion balanced-budget increase in G and T (all figures in billions of euros; both G and T have increased from 100 in Table 24.1 to 300 here)

(1) Output (income)	(2) Net taxes	(3) Disposable income	(4) Consumption spending	(5) Saving	(6) Planned investment spending	(7) Government purchases	(8) Planned aggregate expenditure	(9) Unplanned inventory change	(10) Adjustment to equilibrium
Y	T	$Y_d = Y - T$	$C = 100 + 0.75Y_d$	$S = Y_d - C$	I	G	$C + I + G$	$Y - (C + I + G)$	
500	300	200	250		100	300	650	−150	Output ↑
700	300	400	400		100	300	800	−100	Output ↑
900	300	600	550		100	300	950	−50	Output ↑
1,100	300	800	700		100	300	1,100	0	Equilibrium
1,300	300	1,000	850		100	300	1,250	+50	Output ↓
1,500	300	1,200	1,000		100	300	1,400	+100	Output ↓

Table 24.4 Summary of fiscal policy multipliers

	Policy stimulus	Multiplier	Final impact on equilibrium Y
Government-spending multiplier	Increase or decrease in the level of government purchases: ΔG	$\dfrac{1}{MPS}$	$\Delta G \times \dfrac{1}{MPS}$
Tax multiplier	Increase or decrease in the level of net taxes: ΔT	$\dfrac{-MPC}{MPS}$	$\Delta T \times \dfrac{-MPC}{MPS}$
Balanced-budget multiplier	Simultaneous balanced-budget increase or decrease in the level of government purchases and net taxes: $\Delta G = \Delta T$	1	ΔG

The government budget, deficit and debt

Because fiscal policy refers to the manipulation of the many items contained in the government budget, we need to consider those aspects of the budget relevant to our study of macroeconomics. A **government budget** is an enormously complicated document, running to thousands of pages each year. It lists in detail all the things the government plans to spend money on and all the sources of government revenues for the coming year.

government budget
The budget of the central government.

The budget of the Belgian central government

A highly condensed version of Belgium's central government budget is shown in Table 24.5. (Some of this discussion reviews material from Chapter 3, but here we highlight the budget components of particular importance to macroeconomics.) In 1996 the government had total receipts of 3,895.3 billion francs, about a third each from direct taxes (mostly income taxes), indirect taxes such as the value added tax on goods and services, and contributions for social insurance.[11]

Table 24.5 Central government revenues and expenditures in Belgium, 1996 (billions of Belgian francs)

Revenues		Expenditures	
Taxes	3,789.2	Goods and services	937.4
Direct taxes	1,524.2	Subsidies and transfers	2,346.8
Indirect taxes	1,062.6	Interest payments	705.3
Social security contributions	1,202.4		
Other	106.1	Other	172.2
Total	3,895.3	Total	4,161.7
Deficit	266.4		

Source: Banque Nationale de Belgique/Nationale Bank van België

---

[11]*Contributions for social insurance are employer and employee social security taxes.*

Central government expenditures amounted to 4,161.7 billion in 1996. The bulk of this, 2,346.8 billion, represent subsidies and other transfer payments (mostly social security).[12] Government spending on goods and services (including defence spending) (937.4 billion) is the second largest item. Third is interest on the government debt (705.3 billion).

The deficit

The difference between government expenditures and revenues is the budget deficit. Table 24.5 shows that the Belgian government spent more than it took in 1996, as did all other European governments except for Luxemburg, resulting in a deficit of 266.4 billion francs.

The 1996 deficit was nothing new. In fact, Belgium has been running budget deficits for decades. You can see this in Figure 24.4a, where the **deficit ratio** (the deficit as a percentage of GDP) is plotted for the period 1965–1998. As the figure clearly shows, the deficit was positive throughout the entire period. In no year in more than three decades were revenues greater than expenditures. The deficit stayed in the range between 2 and 4% of GDP until the mid-1970s. After that it virtually exploded, with ratios in excess of 10% during the early 1980s. Since then, deficit ratios were gradually brought down. Belgium's successful quest to participate in European Monetary Union brought deficit ratios back to where they had been in the 1960s.

When the government runs a deficit, this must be financed through borrowing. In order to borrow, the government sells government securities (say bonds) to the public. It issues pieces of paper promising to pay a certain amount, with interest, at a future date. In return, it receives funds from the buyers of the paper and uses these funds to pay its bills. This borrowing increases the government (or public) debt, the total amount owed by the government. The **public debt** is the total of all accumulated deficits minus surpluses over time.

Figure 24.4b shows that Belgium is paying a price for the high deficit ratios of the 1980s. The string of large deficits drove up the public debt, which is roughly the sum of all past deficits. Relative to GDP, Belgium's government debt is now the highest in Europe, though on the way down from its peak of 135% in 1993. This record-sized **debt ratio** causes interest payments to eat up a sizeable chunk of government revenues: at 705.3 billion francs they amount to 8.4% of Belgian GDP. To the extent that Belgium's government debt is owned by Belgian citizens, though, these interest payments are simply a transfer from one group within the country (taxpayers) to another (bondholders).

The economy's influence on the deficit

The economic consequences of government debt are discussed in detail in Chapter 32. We conclude this chapter with a discussion of the way the economy affects the deficit.

Tax revenues depend on the state of the economy

As we said earlier, some parts of the government's budget depend on the state of the economy, over which the government has no direct control. Take, for example, the revenue side of the budget. The government passes laws that set tax rates and tax

deficit ratio
The budget deficit as a percentage of GDP.

public debt
The total of all accumulated deficits minus surpluses over time.

debt ratio
The public debt as a percentage of GDP.

[12]*Remember the important difference between transfer payments and government purchases of goods and services. Much of government spending goes to things an economist would classify as transfers (payments that are grants or gifts) rather than purchases of goods and services. It is only the latter that are included in our variable G. Transfers are counted as part of net taxes.*

Figure 24.4 Belgian deficit and debt as a percentage of GDP

The government budget deficit and the public debt are closely related. Belgium's experience illustrates that high budget deficit ratios add to the public debt, making debt ratios increase.

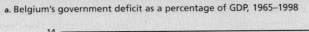

a. Belgium's government deficit as a percentage of GDP, 1965–1998

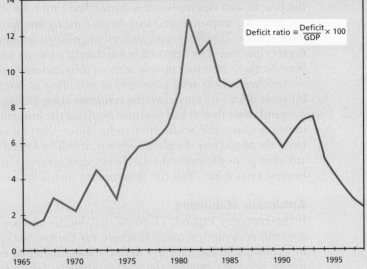

Deficit ratio $\equiv \dfrac{\text{Deficit}}{\text{GDP}} \times 100$

b. Belgium's government debt as a percentage of GDP, 1969–1998

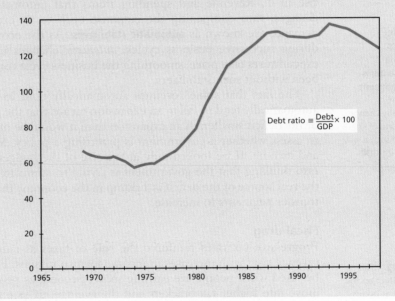

Debt ratio $\equiv \dfrac{\text{Debt}}{\text{GDP}} \times 100$

Source: Eurostat.

brackets. These are clearly variables that the government does control. Tax revenue, on the other hand, depends on taxable income, and income depends on the state of the economy, which the government does *not* control. The government can set a personal income tax rate of 20%, but the tax revenue will depend on the average income earned by households. Clearly, the government will collect much more revenue when average income is €40,000 than it will when average income is €20,000.

Some government expenditures depend on the state of the economy

Some items on the expenditure side of the government budget also depend on the state of the economy. As the economy expands, unemployment falls, and the result is a decrease in unemployment benefits. Welfare payments also decrease somewhat. Some of the people who receive benefits during bad times are able to find jobs when the state of the economy improves, and they begin earning enough income to disqualify themselves from benefit. Transfer payments tend to go down automatically during an expansion, and tax receipts rise. The opposite holds during a slump: transfer payments tend to increase because there are more people without jobs and more poor people generally.

Another reason why government spending is not completely controllable is that inflation often picks up when the economy is expanding. This can force the government to spend more than it had planned. Suppose the government has ordered 20 aircraft and inflation causes the actual price to be higher than expected. If the government decides to go ahead and buy the planes anyway, it will be forced to increase its spending. Finally, any change in the interest rate changes government interest payments. An increase in interest rates means that the government spends more in interest payments.

Automatic stabilizers

If the economy expands (Y rises), say due to an exogenous increase in demand, the government's tax revenue (tY, where t is the tax rate) goes up. This dampens the rise in Y, making it fluctuate less than if t was smaller or even zero. Technically, the multiplier becomes smaller the higher the tax rate t (see Appendix B). Also, as the economy expands unemployment falls. This reduces transfer payments (such as unemployment benefits) and government spending in general, also dampening the rise in Y. Revenue and spending items that automatically change when income changes, thus dampening the response of Y to an exogenous shock to aggregate demand, are known as **automatic stabilizers**. As the economy expands and contracts during successive business cycles, *automatic* changes in government revenues and expenditures take place, smoothing the business cycle compared to what it would have been without such stabilizers.

The fact that some revenues automatically tend to rise and some expenditures automatically tend to fall in an expansion means that the government surplus is larger, or the deficit smaller, in an expansion than it would be otherwise. Suppose we wanted to assess whether a government is practising a policy designed to increase spending and income. If we looked only at the size of the budget deficit, we might be fooled into thinking that the government is trying to stimulate the economy when, in fact, the real source of the deficit is a slump in the economy that caused revenues to fall and transfer payments to increase.

Fiscal drag

Progressive tax rates reinforce the role of taxes as automatic stabilizers. Then tax revenue rises with increases in income for two reasons. First, there is more income to be taxed when people are earning more. Second, as people earn more income, they move into higher tax brackets and the average tax rate that they pay increases. The second type of increase in taxes rates is called **fiscal drag**, because the increase in average tax rates that results when people move into higher brackets acts as a 'drag' on the economy. As the economy expands and income increases, the automatic tax increase mechanism built into the system goes to work. Tax rates go up, reducing after-tax income, and this slows down the expansion.

Full-employment budget

Because the condition of the economy affects the budget deficit, we cannot accurately judge either the intent or the success of fiscal policies just by looking at the deficit. Instead of looking simply at the size of the deficit, economists have developed an alternative way to measure how effective fiscal policy actually is. By examining what the budget would be like if the economy were producing at the full-employment level of output – the so-called **full-employment budget** – we can establish a benchmark for evaluating fiscal policy.

automatic stabilizers
Revenue and expenditure items in the government budget that automatically change with the state of the economy in such a way as to stabilize GDP.

fiscal drag The negative effect on the economy that occurs when average tax rates increase because taxpayers have moved into higher income brackets during an expansion.

full-employment budget
What the government budget would be if the economy were producing at a full-employment level of output.

The distinction between the actual and full-employment deficits is important. Suppose the economy is in a slump and the deficit is €250 billion. If there were full employment, the deficit would fall to €75 billion. This remaining €75 billion deficit would be due to the structure of tax and spending programmes rather than to the state of the economy. This deficit – the deficit that remains at full employment – is sometimes called the **structural deficit**. The structural deficit is equal to the deficit of the full-employment budget. The €175 billion (€250 billion – €75 billion) part of the deficit that is caused by the fact the economy is in a slump is known as the **cyclical deficit**. The size of the cyclical deficit depends on where the economy is in the business cycle, and it vanishes when full employment is reached. By definition, the cyclical deficit of the full-employment budget is zero.

structural deficit
The deficit that remains at full-employment level of income.

cyclical deficit
The deficit that occurs because of a downturn in the business cycle.

Debt and deficits in Europe and beyond

Belgium is not the only country in the world that has a problem with budget deficits and a ballooning public debt. Since the mid-1970s, the majority of industrial countries experienced sizeable budget deficits and saw their public debt rise at a worrying pace. When detailing the plan for a single European currency in the Treaty of Maastricht signed in 1992, governments took into account the threat that large deficits and high debt pose for monetary discipline and price stability (we look into this in Chapter 32) To protect the euro from this danger, countries wishing to participate in the single currency were required to lower the deficit ratio to 3% and drive down the debt ratio towards 60%. As Table 24.6 shows, EU member countries have made serious efforts and been successful beyond expectations regarding the Maastricht Treaty's fiscal policy criterion.

The money market and monetary policy: a preview

We have now seen how the government interacts with households and firms in the goods market, how equilibrium output (income) is determined, and how the government uses fiscal policy to influence the economy. In the following two chapters, we analyse the money market and monetary policy – the government's other major tool for influencing the economy.

Table 24.6 Government deficits and debt as a percentage of nominal GDP in the EU countries, 1997

	Deficit ratio	Debt ratio		Deficit ratio	Debt ratio
Austria	2.5	66.1	Italy	2.7	121.6
Belgium	2.1	122.2	Luxemburg	−1.7	6.7
Denmark	−0.7	65.1	Netherlands	1.4	72.1
Finland	0.9	55.8	Portugal	2.5	62.0
France	3.0	58.0	Spain	2.6	68.8
Germany	2.7	61.3	Sweden	0.8	76.6
Greece	4.0	108.7	United Kingdom	1.9	53.4
Ireland	−0.9	66.3	EU average	2.4	72.1

Source: European Commission Convergence Report, 1998.

Summary

1. The government can affect the macroeconomy through two specific policy channels. Fiscal policy refers to the government's taxing and spending behaviour. *Discretionary fiscal policy* refers to changes in taxes or spending that are the result of conscious changes in government policy. *Monetary policy* refers to the behaviour of the central bank regarding the nation's money supply.

Government participation in the economy

2. The government does not have complete control over tax revenues and those expenditures that depend on the state of the economy.

3. As a participant in the economy, the government makes purchases of goods and services (G), collects taxes, and makes transfer payments to households. Net taxes (T) is equal to tax payments made to the government by firms and households minus transfer payments made to households by the government.

4. *Disposable*, or *after-tax*, income (Y_d) is equal to the amount of income received by households after taxes: $Y_d \equiv Y - T$. After-tax income determines households' consumption behaviour.

5. The *budget deficit* is equal to the difference between what the government spends and what it collects in taxes: $G - T$. When G exceeds T, the government must borrow from the public to finance its deficit.

6. In an economy with a government, planned aggregate expenditure equals consumption spending by households (C) plus planned investment spending by firms (I) plus government spending on goods and services (G): $AE \equiv C + I + G$. Because the condition $Y = AE$ is necessary for the economy to be in equilibrium, it follows that $Y = C + I + G$ is the macroeconomic equilibrium condition. The economy is also in equilibrium when leakages out of the system equal injections into the system. This occurs when savings and net taxes (the leakages) equal planned investment and government purchases (the injections): $S + T = I + G$.

Fiscal policy at work: the multiplier effects

7. Fiscal policy has a multiplier effect on the economy. A change in government budget spending gives rise to a multiplier equal to 1/*MPS*. A change in taxation brings about a multiplier equal to – *MPC/MPS*. A change in government spending and taxes that keeps the budget balanced has a multiplier effect of one.

The government budget

8. Budget deficits in the EU have grown substantially since the 1970s, and with them the public debt. The Maastricht criteria for joining European monetary union have led to a widespread reversal of this trend. Most deficits in Europe are now below 3% of GDP.

9. *Automatic stabilizers* are revenue and expenditure items in the government budget that automatically change with the state of the economy and tend to stabilize GDP. For example, during expansions the government automatically takes in more revenue, because people are making more money that is taxed. Higher income and tax brackets also mean fewer transfer payments.

10. *Fiscal drag* is the negative effect on the economy that occurs when average tax rates increase because taxpayers have moved into higher income brackets during an expansion. These higher taxes reduce disposable income and slow down the expansion.

11. The *full-employment budget* is an economist's construction of what the federal budget would be if the economy were producing at a full-employment level of output. The *structural deficit* is the deficit that remains even at full employment. *Cyclical deficits* occur when there is a downturn in the business cycle.

Review Terms and Concepts

automatic stabilizers
balanced-budget multiplier
budget deficit
cyclical deficit
debt ratio
deficit ratio
discretionary fiscal policy
disposable, or after-tax, income (Y_d)
fiscal drag

fiscal policy
full-employment budget
government budget
government spending multiplier
monetary policy
net taxes (*T*)
public debt
structural deficit
tax multiplier

Equations

1. Disposable income $Y_d \equiv Y - T$

2. $AE \equiv C + I + G$

3. Government budget deficit $\equiv G - T$

4. Equilibrium in an economy with government:
$Y = C + I + G$

5. Leakages/injections approach to equilibrium in an economy with government: $S + T = I + G$

6. Government spending multiplier $\equiv \dfrac{1}{MPS}$

7. Tax multiplier $\equiv -\dfrac{MPC}{MPS}$

8. Balanced-budget multiplier $\equiv 1$

9. Open-economy equilibrium position:
$Y = C + I + G + (EX - IM)$

Problem Set

1. Define *saving and investment*. Data for the simple closed economy of Newt show that in 1998, saving exceeded investment and the government is running a balanced budget. What is likely to happen? What would happen if the government were running a deficit instead, and saving were equal to investment?

2. Leading economists in the Republic of Yuklandia estimate the following: real output/income 1000 billion yuks; government purchases 200 billion yuks; total net taxes 200 billion yuks; and investment spending (planned) 100 billion yuks. Assume that Yuklandians consume 75% of their disposable incomes and that they save 25%.
a. You are asked by the business editor of the *Yuklandian Gazette* to predict the events of the next few months. Using the data above, can you make a forecast? (Assume that investment is constant.)
b. If no changes were made, at what level of GDP (*Y*) would the economy of Yuklandia settle?
c. Some local conservatives blame Yuklandia's problems on the size of the government sector. They suggest cutting government purchases by 25 billion yuks. What effect would such cuts have on the economy? (Be specific.)

3. Does it matter whether increases in government spending go towards infrastructure investments (such as roads or better water supplies) or into higher salaries for public employees?

4. 'A €1 increase in government spending will raise equilibrium income by more than a €1 tax cut, yet both have the same impact on the budget deficit. So if we care about the budget deficit, the best way to stimulate the economy is through increases in spending, not cuts in taxes.' Comment.

5. Assume that in 1998, the following describes the economy of the Republic of Nurd: $Y = 200$, $G = 0$, $C = 160$, $T = 0$, $S = 40$, and I (planned) $= 30$. Households consume 80% of their income, so they save 20% of their income. That is, $C = 0.8Y_d$ and $S = 0.2Y_d$.
a. Is the economy of Nurd in equilibrium? What is Nurd's equilibrium level of income? What is likely to happen in the coming months if the government takes no action?

b. If 200 is the 'full employment' level of Y, what fiscal policy might the government follow if its goal is full employment?
c. If the full-employment level of *Y* is 250, what fiscal policy might the government follow?
d. Suppose that $Y = 200$, $C = 160$, $S = 40$ and $I = 40$. Is Nurd's economy in equilibrium?
e. Starting with the situation in (d), suppose that the government starts spending 30 each year with no taxation and continues to spend 30 in every period. If *I* remains constant, what will happen to the equilibrium level of Nurd's domestic product (*Y*)? What will the new levels of *C* and *S* be?
f. Again starting with the situation in (d), suppose that the government starts taxing the population 30 each year without spending anything, and continues to tax at that rate in every period. If *I* remains constant, what will happen to the equilibrium level of Nurd's domestic product (*Y*)? What will be the new levels of *C* and *S*? How does your answer to (f) differ from your answer to (e)? Why?

6. Suppose that all tax collections are fixed (rather than dependent on income), and that all spending and transfer programmes are also fixed (in the sense that they do not depend on the state of the economy, as, for example, unemployment benefits do). If this were the case, would there be any automatic stabilizers in the government budget? Would there be any distinction between the full-employment deficit and the actual budget deficit? Explain.

7. Answer the following questions:
a. $MPS = 0.4$. What is the government spending multiplier?
b. $MPC = 0.9$. What is the government spending multiplier?
c. $MPS = 0.5$. What is the government spending multiplier?
d. $MPC = 0.75$. What is the tax multiplier?
e. $MPS = 0.1$. What is the tax multiplier?
f. If the government spending multiplier is 6, what is the tax multiplier?
g. If the tax multiplier is 22, what is the government spending multiplier?

h. If government purchases and taxes are both increased by €100 billion simultaneously, what will be the effect on equilibrium output (income)?

8. What is the relationship between the government budget deficit and the government debt? Suppose that a country like France managed to balance its budget in fiscal year 1999. Would there be any effect on the size of the debt?

9. How does the state of the economy affect the budget deficit? If you wanted to compare the *fiscal stance* of two national governments (that is, how profligate they are), what measure would you use?

Appendix A to Chapter 24

Deriving the Fiscal Policy Multipliers

The government spending and tax multipliers

In the chapter text, we noted that the government spending multiplier is equal to $1/MPS$. (This is the same as the investment multiplier.) We can also show that the government spending multiplier is the same as the investment multiplier by using our hypothetical consumption function:

$$C = a + b\,(Y - T)$$

where b is the marginal propensity to consume. As you know, the equilibrium condition is

$$Y = C + I + G$$

Substituting for C, we get

$$Y = a + b(Y - T) + I + G$$
$$Y = a + bY - bT + I + G$$

This equation can be rearranged to yield

$$Y = bY = a + I + G - bT$$
$$Y(1 - b) = a + I + G - bT$$

We can then solve for Y by dividing through by $(1 - b)$:

$$Y = \frac{1}{(1 - b)}\,(a + I + G - bT)$$

We see from this last equation that if G increases by one with the other determinants of Y (a, I and T) remaining constant, Y increases by $1/(1 - b)$. Thus, the multiplier is, as before, simply $1/(1 - b)$, where b is the marginal propensity to consume. And, of course, $1 - b$ equals the marginal propensity to save, so the government spending multiplier is $1/MPS$.

We can also derive the tax multiplier. The last equation above says that when T increases by €1, holding a, I and G constant, income decreases by $b/(1 - b)$ euros. The tax multiplier is thus $-b/(1 - b)$, or $-MPC/(1 - MPC) = -MPC/MPS$. (Remember that we add the negative sign to the tax multiplier because the tax multiplier is a *negative* multiplier.)

The balanced-budget multiplier

It is quite easy to show formally that the balanced-budget multiplier is equal to one. As you know, when taxes and government spending are simultaneously increased by the same amount, there are two effects on planned aggregate expenditure: one positive and one negative. The initial impact of a balanced-budget increase in government spending and taxes on aggregate expenditure would be the *increase* in government purchases (ΔG) minus the *decrease* in consumption (ΔC) caused by the tax increase. The decrease in consumption brought about by the tax increase is equal to $\Delta C = \Delta T(MPC)$.

Increase in spending:	ΔG
– Decrease in spending:	$\Delta C = \Delta T(MPC)$
= Net increase in spending:	$\Delta G - \Delta T(MPC)$

In a balanced-budget increase, $\Delta G = \Delta T$, so we can substitute:

Net initial increase in spending:

$$\Delta G - \Delta G(MPC) = \Delta G(1 - MPC)$$

Since $MPS = (1 - MPC)$, the initial increase in spending is

$$\Delta G(MPS)$$

We can now apply the expenditure multiplier $1/MPS$ to this net initial increase in spending:

$$\Delta Y = \Delta G(MPS)\left(\frac{1}{MPS}\right) = \Delta G$$

Thus, the final total increase in the equilibrium level of Y is just equal to the initial balanced increase in G and T. In other words, the balanced-budget multiplier is one.

Appendix B to Chapter 24

The Case in Which Tax Revenues Depend on Income

In this chapter, we used the simplifying assumption that the government collects taxes in a lump sum. This made our discussion of the multiplier effects somewhat easier to follow. But now suppose that the government collects taxes not solely as a lump sum that is paid regardless of income, but also partly in the form of a proportional levy against income. As we noted earlier, this is clearly a more realistic assumption. Typically, tax collections are either based on income (as with the personal income tax) or they closely follow the ups and downs in the economy (as with sales taxes). Thus, instead of setting taxes equal to some fixed amount, let us say that tax revenues depend on income. If we call the amount of net taxes collected T, we can write: $T = T_0 + tY$.

This equation contains two parts. First, we note that net taxes (T) will be equal to an amount T_0 if income (Y) is zero. Second, the tax rate (t) indicates how much net taxes change as income changes. Suppose that T_0 is equal to -200 and t is $1/3$. The resulting tax function is $T = -200 + 1/3Y$, which is graphed in Figure 24A.1.

Figure 24A.1 The tax function

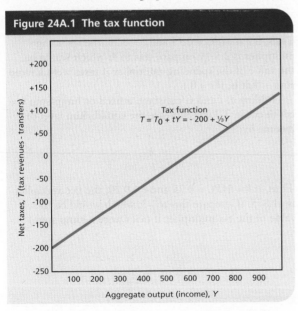

This graph shows net taxes (taxes minus transfer payments) as a function of aggregate income.

Note that when income is zero, the government collects 'negative net taxes', which simply means that it makes transfer payments of 200. As income rises, tax collections increase, because every extra euro of income generates €0.33 in extra revenues for the government.

How do we incorporate this new tax function into our discussion? It is actually quite simple. All we need to do is replace the old value of T (in the example in the chapter, T was set equal to 100) with the new value, $-200 + 1/3Y$. Look first at the consumption equation. Consumption (C) still depends on disposable income, as it did before. Also, disposable income is still $Y - T$, or income minus taxes. Instead of disposable income equalling $Y - 100$, however, the new equation for disposable income is:

$$Y_d \equiv Y - T$$
$$Y_d \equiv Y - (-200 + 1/3Y)$$
$$Y_d \equiv Y + 200 - 1/3Y$$

Since consumption still depends on after-tax income, exactly as it did before, we have:

$$C = 100 + 0.75Y_d$$
$$C = 100 + 0.75 (Y + 200 - 1/3Y)$$

Nothing else needs to be changed. We solve for equilibrium income exactly as before, by setting planned aggregate expenditure equal to aggregate output. Recall that planned aggregate expenditure is $C + I + G$, and aggregate output is Y. If we assume, as before, that $I = 100$ and $G = 100$, the equilibrium is:

$$Y = C + I + G$$
$$Y = \underbrace{100 + 0.75 (Y + 200 - 1/3Y)}_{C} + \underbrace{100}_{I} + \underbrace{100}_{G}$$

This equation may look difficult to solve, but it is not. It simplifies to:

$$Y = 100 + 0.75Y + 150 - 0.25Y + 100 + 100$$
$$Y = 450 + 0.5Y$$
$$0.5Y = 450$$

This means that $Y = 450/0.5 = 900$. The new equilibrium level of income is thus 900.

It is useful to consider the graphic analysis of this equation as shown in Figure 25A.2. The most important thing you should note from Figure 25A.2 is that when we make taxes a function of income (instead of merely a lump-sum amount), the AE function becomes *flatter* than it was before. Why is this so? When tax collections do not depend on income, an increase in income of €1 means that disposable income also increases by a euro. Because taxes are a constant amount, adding more income does not raise the amount of taxes paid. Disposable income therefore changes euro for euro with any change in income.

When taxes depend on income, however, a €1 increase in income does not increase disposable income by a full euro, because some of the additional euro must go to pay extra taxes. In fact, under the modified tax function of Figure 25A.2, an extra euro of income will

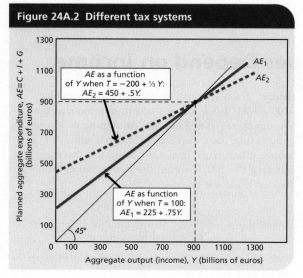

Figure 24A.2 Different tax systems

When taxes are strictly lump sum ($T = 100$) and do not depend on income, the aggregate expenditure function is steeper than when taxes depend on income.

increase disposable income by only €0.67, because €0.33 of the extra euro goes to the government in the form of taxes.

No matter how taxes are calculated, the marginal propensity to consume out of disposable (or after-tax) income is the same – each extra euro of disposable income will increase consumption spending by €0.75. But a €1 change in before-tax income does not have the same effect on disposable income in each case. Suppose we were to increase income by €1. With the lump-sum tax function, disposable income would rise by €1, and consumption would increase by $MPC \times Y_d$, or €0.75. When taxes depend on income, disposable income would rise by only €0.67 from the €1 increase in income, and consumption would rise by only the MPC times the change in disposable income, or €0.75 × 0.67 = €0.50.

Clearly, if a €1 increase in income raises expenditure by €0.75 in one case, and by only €0.50 in the other, the second aggregate expenditure function must be flatter than the first.

The government spending and tax multipliers algebraically

All of this means that if taxes are a function of income, the three multipliers (investment, government spending and tax) are less than they would be if taxes were a lump-sum amount. Using the same linear consumption function we used in the last two chapters, we can derive the multiplier:

$$C = a + b\,(Y - T)$$
$$C = a + b\,(Y - T_0 - tY)$$
$$C = a + bY - bT_0 - btY$$

We know that $Y = C + I + G$. Through substitution we get:

$$Y = \underbrace{a + bY - bT_0 - btY}_{C} + I + G$$

Solving for Y:

$$Y = \frac{1}{(1 - b - bt)}\,(a + I + G - bT_0)$$

This means that a €1 increase in G or I (holding a and T_0 constant) will increase the equilibrium level of Y by:

$$\frac{1}{(1 - b - bt)}$$

Thus, if $b = MPC = 0.75$ and $t = 0.20$, the spending multiplier is 2.5. (Compare this to 4, which would be the value of the spending multiplier if taxes were a lump sum – that is, if $t = 0$.)

Holding a, I and G constant, a fixed or lump-sum tax cut (a cut in T_0) will increase the equilibrium level of income by:

$$\frac{b}{(1 - b - bt)}$$

Thus, if $b = MPC = 0.75$ and $t = 0.20$, the tax multiplier is –1.875. (Compare this to –3, which would be the value of the tax multiplier if taxes were a lump sum.)

The Money Supply and the Central Bank

In the last two chapters, we explored how consumers, firms and the government interact in the goods market. In this chapter and the next we will show how money markets work in the macroeconomy. We begin by examining what money is and the role it plays in the global economy. We then look at the factors that determine the supply of money and show how banks create money. Finally, we discuss the workings of national central banks and the European Central Bank, and the tools at their disposal to control the money supply.

Microeconomics has little to say about money. Microeconomic theories and models are concerned primarily with *real* quantities (apples, oranges, hours of labour) and *relative* prices (the price of apples relative to the price of oranges, the price of labour relative to the prices of other goods). Most of the key ideas in microeconomics do not require us to know anything about money. As we shall see, this is not the case in macroeconomics.

An overview of money

You often hear people say things like 'He makes a lot of money' (in other words, 'He has a high income') or 'She's worth a lot of money' (meaning 'She is very wealthy'). It is true that your employer uses money to pay you your income, and your wealth may be accumulated in the form of money. But *money is not income, and money is not wealth*.

To see that money and income are not the same, think of a €20 note. That note may pass through a thousand hands in a year, yet never be used to pay anyone a salary. Suppose I get a €20 note from an automatic teller machine, and I spend it on dinner. The restaurant deposits that €20 note in a bank the following day. The bank gives it to a woman cashing a cheque the following day; she spends it to watch a film that night. In the end the note has been through many hands, but never as someone's income.

What is money?

Before we propose a formal definition of money, let's start out with the basic idea:

Money is anything that is generally accepted as a means of payment.

Most people take the ability to obtain and use money for granted. When the whole monetary system works well, as it generally does in industrialized countries, the basic mechanics of the system are virtually invisible. People take for granted that they can walk into any shop, restaurant or petrol station and buy whatever they want, as long as they have enough appropriately coloured pieces of paper.

Buying things using money is so natural and obvious that it seems absurd to mention it. But stop and ask yourself: 'How is it that a shop owner is willing to part with a chunk of brie and a loaf of bread that I can eat in exchange for some pieces of paper that are intrinsically worthless?' And why, on the other hand, are there times and places where it takes a shopping basket full of money to purchase a dozen eggs?

The answers to these questions lie in what money is: a means of payment, a store of value, and a unit of account.

Means of payment, or medium of exchange

Money is vital to the working of a market economy. Imagine what life would be like without it. The alternative to a monetary economy is **barter**, people exchanging goods and services for other goods and services directly instead of exchanging via the medium of money.

How does a barter system work? Suppose you want croissants, eggs and orange juice for breakfast. Instead of going to the grocer's and buying these things with money, you would have to find someone who has these items and is willing to trade them. You would also have to have something the baker, the orange juice purveyor and the egg vendor want. Having pencils to trade will do you no good if the baker and the orange juice and egg sellers do not want pencils.

A barter system requires a *double coincidence of wants* for trade to take place. That is, to effect a trade, I not only have to find someone who has what I want, but that person must also want what I have. Where the range of traded goods is small, as it is in relatively unsophisticated economies, it is not difficult to find someone to trade with, and barter is often used. In a complex society with many goods, barter exchanges involve an intolerable amount of effort. Imagine trying to find people who offer for sale all the things you buy in a typical trip to the grocer's, and who are willing to accept goods that you have to offer in exchange for their goods.

Some agreed-upon **medium of exchange** (or **means of payment**) neatly eliminates the double coincidence of wants problem. Under a monetary system, money is exchanged for goods or services when people buy things; goods or services are exchanged for money when people sell things. No one ever has to trade goods for other goods directly. Money is the lubricant in a functioning market economy.

A store of value

Economists have identified other roles for money aside from its primary function as a medium of exchange. Money also serves as a **store of value** – an asset that can be used to transport purchasing power from one period to another. If you raise chicken and at the end of the month sell them for more than you want to consume immediately, you may keep some of your earnings in the form of money until you want to spend it.

There are many other stores of value besides money. You could have decided to hold your 'surplus' earnings by buying such things as antiques, paintings or diamonds, which you could sell later when you want to spend your earnings. Money has several advantages over these other stores of value. First, it comes in convenient denominations and is easily portable. You don't have to worry about the change from a Renoir when you buy 10 litres of petrol. Second, because money is also a means of payment, it is easily exchanged for goods at all times. (A Renoir painting is not easily exchanged for other goods.) These two factors comprise the **liquidity property of money**. Money is easily spent, flowing out of your hands like liquid. Renoirs and ancient Aztec statues are neither convenient nor portable and are not readily accepted as a means of payment.

The main disadvantage of money as a store of value is that the value of money falls when the prices of goods and services rise. If the price of potato crisps rises from €1 per bag to €2 per bag, the value of a euro note in terms of crisps falls from one bag to half a bag. When this happens, it may be better to use crisps (or antiques, or property) as a store of value.

A unit of account

Money also serves as a **unit of account** – a consistent way of quoting prices. All prices are quoted in monetary units. A textbook is quoted as costing €45, not 140 bananas or 4 videotapes, and a banana is quoted at €0.25, not 1.4 apples or 16 pages of a textbook.

---

barter The direct exchange of goods and services for other goods and services.

medium of exchange, *or* **means of payment** What sellers generally accept and buyers generally use to pay for goods and services.

store of value An asset that can be used to transport purchasing power from one time period to another.

liquidity property of money The property of money that makes it a good medium of exchange as well as a store of value: it is portable and readily accepted and thus easily exchanged for goods.

unit of account A standard unit that provides a consistent way of quoting prices.

Obviously, a standard unit of account is extremely useful when quoting prices. This function of money may have escaped your notice – what else would people quote prices in except money?

Commodity and fiat moneys

History is full of stories about items that have been used as money by cultures around the world – huge wheels of carved stone (on the island of Yap in the South Pacific), cowrie shells (in West Africa), beads (among North American Indians), cattle (in southern Africa), cigarettes (in Germany during the first few years after the Second World War) . . . The list goes on. These different kinds of money are generally divided into two groups, commodity moneys and fiat money.

commodity moneys
Items used as money that also have intrinsic value in some other use.

fiat, or token, money
Items decreed as money that are intrinsically worthless.

Commodity moneys are those money items that also have an intrinsic value in other uses. For example, gold represents a form of commodity money. For centuries gold was used directly to buy things, but it also had and has other functions, ranging from jewellery to dental fillings to microchips.

Money today is mostly fiat money. **Fiat money**, sometimes called **token money**, is money that is intrinsically worthless. The actual value of a 5, 10 or 500 euro note is basically zero; what other uses are there for a small piece of paper with some ink on it?

Why would anyone accept worthless scraps of paper as money instead of something that has intrinsic value, such as gold, cigarettes or cattle? If your answer is 'Because the paper money is backed by gold or silver', you are wrong! There was a time when paper money was convertible directly into gold. The government backed each note in circulation by holding a certain amount of gold in its vaults. When the price of gold was $35 per ounce, for example, the US government agreed to sell one ounce of gold for 35 dollars. But dollar bills are no longer backed by any commodity – gold, silver or anything else. Euros are exchangeable only for cents or other euros.

legal tender
Money that a government requires to be accepted in settlement of debts.

The public accepts paper money as a means of payment and a store of value because the government has taken steps to ensure that its money is accepted. The government declares its paper money to be **legal tender**. That is, the government declares that its money must be accepted in settlement of debts. It does this by decree or fiat (hence *fiat money*). It passes laws defining certain pieces of paper printed in certain inks on certain plates to be legal tender. Often, the government can make a start on gaining acceptance for its paper money by requiring that it be used to pay taxes. (Note that you cannot use chickens or Renoir paintings to pay your taxes, only cheques, bank transfers or currency.)

Aside from declaring its currency legal tender, the government usually does one other thing to ensure that paper money will be accepted: it promises the public that it will not print paper money so fast that it loses its value. Expanding the supply of currency so rapidly that it loses much of its value has been a problem throughout history. It is known as **currency debasement**. Debasement of the currency has been a particular problem of governments who lack the strength to take the politically unpopular step of raising taxes. Printing money for government expenditures on goods and services can substitute for tax revenue. Weak governments have often relied on the printing press to finance their expenditures. A recent example is Bulgaria, where the inflation rate hit a record 1,268% in 1997. In later chapters we will thoroughly discuss the links between money and inflation.

currency debasement The decrease in the value of money that occurs when its supply is increased rapidly.

Measuring the supply of money

We now turn to the various kinds of money. Recall that money is used to buy things (a means of payment); as a means of holding wealth (a store of value); and to quote prices (a unit of account). Unfortunately, these characteristics apply to a broad range of assets. It is not at all clear where we should draw the line and say, 'Up to this point it is money, but beyond this it is something else.'

To solve the problem of multiple moneys, economists have given different names to different measures of money. Common measures are M0, the monetary base, M1, transactions money, and broader moneys called M2, M3 and M4.

M0, *or* monetary base

All coins and notes in circulation plus reserves private banks hold at central bank.

M0: the monetary base

M0 or **monetary base** comprises all currency (coins and notes) in circulation plus the reserves that private banks hold at the central bank.

$$M0 \equiv \text{Currency} + \text{Reserves}$$

This measure is very narrow, and clearly an incomplete measure of an economy's liquidity. It derives its importance from the fact that it is under perfect control of the central bank: Only the central bank may print notes to bring into circulation. And it is up to the central bank to determine the reserves that private banks must hold.

M1: transactions money

If M0 is an incomplete measure of liquidity, what should be counted as money? Clearly, currency (a 10 euro note or a 1 pound coin, say) must be counted as money – it fits all the requirements. But what about bank current cheque accounts? Cheques too can be used to buy things and can serve as a store of value. In fact, bankers call cheque accounts *demand deposits*, because depositors have the right to go to the bank and cash in (demand) their entire cheque account (known as current account in Britain) balances at any time. That makes your cheque account virtually equivalent to notes in your wallet, and it should be included as part of the amount of money you hold.

M1, *or* transactions money

Money that can be directly used for transactions.

If we take the value of all currency (including coins) held outside of bank vaults and add to it the value of all demand deposits, we have defined **M1**, or **transactions money**. As its name suggests, this is the money that can be directly used for transactions – to buy things:

$$M1 \equiv \text{Currency} + \text{Demand deposits}$$

To give an idea of magnitudes: at the end of July of 1998, French M1 stood at 1,913 billion francs. M1, like other moneys, is a stock measure; it is measured at a point in time, *on a specific day*. Until now, we have considered supply in the goods market as a flow – a variable with a time dimension: the quantity of wheat supplied *per year*, the quantity of cars supplied to the market *per year*, and so forth.

M2: broad money

Although M1 is a widely used measure of the money supply, there are others. Should savings accounts be considered money? Many of these accounts cannot be used for transactions directly, but it is easy to convert them into cash or to transfer funds from a savings account into a cheque account. And what about money market accounts (which allow only a few cheques per month but pay market-determined interest rates)? These can be used to write cheques and make purchases.

near money

Close substitutes for transactions money, such as savings accounts and money market accounts.

If we add **near money**, close substitutes for transactions money, to M1, we get **M2**, called **broad money** because it includes 'not quite money' moneys such as savings accounts, money market accounts and other near moneys.

$$M2 \equiv M1 + \text{Savings accounts} + \text{Money market accounts} + \text{Other near moneys}$$

M2, *or* broad money

M1 plus savings accounts, money market accounts, and other near monies.

At the end of July 1998, French M2 was 3,670 billion francs, almost twice as large as M1.

M3 and M4

Because a wide variety of financial instruments bear some resemblance to money, some economists have advocated including almost all of them as part of the money supply. Adding private-sector deposits with wholesale banks and building societies gives a very broad and often used measure, called M3 in some countries and M4 in others (including Britain).

Applications

A cashless society: the East versus the West

When Westerners talk of the 'cashless' society it conjures up images of credit cards, debit cards, Internet transactions, electronic bill paying and so forth. But when the Russians talk of the cashless society, they mean there is no money. Since the majority of people still work for the government in Russia, and since the government is broke, millions of workers across the country have been going without cash wages for some time. How do they survive? The firms pay people in kind, and they engage in barter.

The Russian–European Centre for Economic Policy, a monitoring organization sponsored by the European Union, estimated that the proportion of industrial sales in Russian settled by barter rose from about 10% in 1993 to 40% in 1996. One car company is said to pay nine-tenths of its bills with finished cars.

Stories about individual household transactions abound. Siberian workers in 1997 were paid in coffins; workers at a factory in Volgograd were paid in bras. In Altai, Siberia, a local theatre charged 2 eggs for admission, and when eggs ran out, tickets became denominated in empty bottles.

Source: 'The cashless society', The Economist, 15 March 1997.

In recent years, for example, credit cards have come to be used extensively in exchange. Everyone who has a credit card has a credit limit – you can charge only a certain amount against your card before you have to pay it off. Often, we pay our credit card bills with a bank transfer. One of the broadest definitions of money includes the amount of available credit on credit cards (your charge limit minus what you have charged but not paid) as part of the money supply. Note, however, that the majority of credit cards issued in Europe are functionally debit cards. Purchases are charged against your cheque account. Using a debit card instead of writing a cheque has no direct impact on the money supply.

There are no rules for deciding what is money and what is not. This poses problems for economists and those in charge of economic policy. However, *for our purposes here, 'money' will always refer to transactions money, or M1.* For simplicity, we will say that M1 is the sum of two general categories: currency in circulation and deposits. Keep in mind, however, that M1 has *four* specific components: currency held outside banks, demand deposits, travellers' cheques, and other chequeable deposits.

The private banking system

Most of the money used in industrial countries today is 'bank money' of one sort or another. M1 is made up largely of cheque account balances rather than currency, and currency makes up an even smaller part of M2 and other broader definitions of money. Any understanding of money requires some knowledge of the structure of the private banking system.

Banks and other financial intermediaries borrow from individuals or firms with excess funds and lend to those who need funds. For example, commercial banks receive funds in various forms, including deposits in cheque and savings accounts. They take these funds and loan them out in the form of car loans, mortgages, commercial loans and so forth. Banks and bank-like institutions are called **financial intermediaries** because they 'mediate' – that is, act as a link – between people who have funds to lend and those who need to borrow.

financial intermediaries
Other institutions that act as a link between those who have money to lend and those who want to borrow money.

How banks create money

So far, we have described the functions of money and the way the supply of money is measured. But how much money is there available at a given time? Who supplies it, and how does it get into circulation? We are now ready to analyse these questions in detail. In particular, we want to explore a process that many find mysterious: the way banks *create money*.

A historical perspective: goldsmiths

Consider this simplified story of the origins of the modern banking system. In the fifteenth and sixteenth centuries, citizens of many lands used gold as money, particularly for large transactions. Because gold is both inconvenient to carry around and susceptible to theft, people began to place their gold with goldsmiths for safekeeping. Upon receiving the gold, a goldsmith would issue a receipt to the depositor, charging a small fee for looking after the gold. After a time, these receipts themselves, rather than the gold that they represented, began to be traded for goods. The receipts became a form of paper money, making it unnecessary to go to the goldsmith to withdraw gold for a transaction.

At this point, all the receipts issued by goldsmiths were backed 100% by gold. If a goldsmith had 100 ounces of gold in his safe, he would issue receipts for only 100 ounces of gold, and no more. The goldsmiths found, however, that people did not come often to withdraw gold. Why should they, when paper receipts were 'as good as gold'? (In fact, receipts were better than gold – more portable, safer from theft, and so on.) As a result, goldsmiths had a large stock of gold continuously on hand.

Since they had what amounted to 'extra' gold sitting around, goldsmiths realized that they could lend out some of this gold without any fear of running out of gold. Why would they do this? Because instead of just keeping their gold in their vaults, they earned interest on loans. Something subtle, but dramatic, happened at this point. The goldsmiths changed from mere depositories for gold into bank-like institutions that had the power to create money. This transformation occurred as soon as goldsmiths began making loans. Of course, the people who took out a loan didn't want the gold itself, but rather a slip of paper, a receipt, that represents the gold. Without adding any more real gold to the system, the goldsmiths increased the amount of money in circulation by creating additional claims on gold.[1] There were thus more claims than there were ounces of gold.

Goldsmiths-turned-bankers did face certain problems. Once they started making loans, their receipts outstanding (claims on gold) were greater than the amount of gold they had in their vaults at any given moment. If the owners of the now, say, 120 ounces' worth of gold receipts all presented their receipts and demanded their gold at the same time, the goldsmith would be in trouble. With only 100 ounces of gold on hand, everyone could not get their gold at once.

In normal times, people would be happy to hold receipts instead of real gold, and this problem would never arise. If, however, people began to worry about the goldsmith's financial safety, they might begin to have doubts about whether their receipts really were as good as gold. Knowing there were more receipts outstanding than there were ounces of gold in the goldsmith's vault, people might start to demand gold for receipts.

This situation leads to a paradox. It makes perfect sense to hold paper receipts (instead of gold) if you know you can always get gold for your paper. In normal times, goldsmiths could feel perfectly safe in loaning out more gold than they actually had in their possession. But once you (and everyone else) start to doubt the safety of the goldsmith, then you (and everyone else) would be foolish not to demand your gold back from the vault.

run on a bank
When many of those who have claims on a bank (deposits) present them at the same time.

A **run** on a goldsmith (or in our day, a **run on a bank**) occurs when many people present their claims at the same time. These runs tend to feed on themselves. If I see you going to the goldsmith to withdraw your gold, I may become nervous and decide to withdraw my gold as well. It is the *fear* of a run that usually causes the run. Runs on a bank can be triggered by a variety of causes: rumours that an institution may have made loans to borrowers who cannot repay, wars, failures of other institutions that

---

[1] *Remember: these receipts circulated as money, and people used them to make transactions without feeling the need to cash them in – that is, to exchange them for gold itself.*

have borrowed money from the bank, and so on. As you will see later in this chapter, today's bankers differ from goldsmiths, because today's banks are subject to a 'required reserve ratio'. Goldsmiths had no legal reserve requirements, though the amount that they lent out was subject to the restriction imposed on them by their fear of running out of gold.

A modern banking system

To understand how the modern banking system works, you need to be familiar with some basic principles of accounting. Once you are comfortable with the way banks keep their books, the whole process of money creation will seem logical.

A brief review of accounting

Central to accounting practices is the statement that 'the books always balance'. In practice, this means that if we take a snapshot of a firm – any firm, including a bank – at a particular moment in time, then by definition:

> Assets – Liabilities ≡ Capital (or Net Worth), or
> Assets ≡ Liabilities + Capital.

Assets are things a firm owns that are worth something. For a bank, these assets include the bank building, its furniture, its holdings of government securities, cash in its vaults, bonds, stocks and so forth. Most important among a bank's assets, for our purposes at least, are its *loans*. When a bank makes a loan, the borrower gives the bank a promise to repay a certain sum of money on or by a certain date. This promise is an asset of the bank because it is worth something. The bank could (and sometimes does) sell this asset to another bank for cash.

Other bank assets include cash on hand (sometimes called vault cash) and deposits with the central bank. Banking regulations require banks to keep a certain portion of their deposits on hand as vault cash or as deposits with the central bank.

A firm's *liabilities* are its debts – what it owes. A bank's liabilities are the promises to pay, or IOUs, that it has issued. A bank's most important liabilities are its deposits. Deposits are debts owed to the depositors, because when you deposit money in your account, you are in essence making a loan to the bank.

The basic rule of accounting says that if we add up a firm's assets and then subtract the total amount it owes to all those who have lent it funds, the difference is the firm's net worth. *Net worth* represents the value of the firm to its stockholders or owners. How much would you pay for a firm that owns €200,000 of diamonds and had borrowed €150,000 from a bank to pay for them? Clearly, the firm is worth €50,000 – the difference between what it owns and what it owes. If the price of diamonds were to fall, bringing their value down to only €150,000, the firm would be worth nothing.

We keep track of a bank's financial position using a simplified balance sheet called a T account. By convention, the bank's assets are listed on the left side of the T account, and its liabilities and net worth on the right side. By definition, the balance sheet always balances, so that the sum of the item(s) on the left side of the T account is exactly equal to the sum of the item(s) on the right side.

The T account in Figure 25.1 shows a bank having €110 million in *assets*, of which €20 million are **reserves**, the deposits that the bank has made at the central bank and its cash on hand (coins and currency). Reserves are an asset to the bank because it can go to the European Central Bank (ECB) and get cash for them, in just the way you can go to the bank and get cash for the amount in your savings account. Our bank's other asset is its loans, worth €90 million.

Why do banks hold reserves/deposits at the ECB? There are many reasons, but perhaps the most important is the legal requirement that they hold a certain percentage of their deposit liabilities as reserves. The percentage of its deposits that a bank must keep as reserves is known as the **required reserve ratio**. If the reserve ratio

reserves The deposits that a bank has at the central bank plus its cash on hand.

required reserve ratio The percentage of its total deposits that a bank must keep as reserves at the central bank.

Figure 25.1 T account for a typical bank (millions of euros)

The balance sheet of a bank must always balance, so that the sum of assets (reserves and loans) equals the sum of liabilities (deposits and net worth).

	Assets		Liabilities	
Reserves	20		100	Deposits
Loans	90		10	Net worth
Total	110		110	Total

is 20%, then a bank with deposits of €100 million must hold €20 million as reserves, either as cash or as deposits at the ECB. To simplify, we will assume that banks hold all of their reserves in the form of deposits at the ECB.

On the liabilities side of the T account, the bank has taken deposits of €100 million, so it owes this amount to its depositors. This means that the bank has a net worth of €10 million to its owners (€110 million in assets − €100 million in liabilities = €10 million net worth). The net worth of the bank is what 'balances' the balance sheet.

Remember:

> When some item on a bank's balance sheet changes, there must be at least one other change somewhere else to maintain balance.

If a bank's reserves increase by €1, then one of the following must also be true: (1) its other assets (say, loans) decrease by €1; (2) its liabilities (deposits) increase by €1; or (3) its net worth increases by €1. Various combinations of these are also possible.

The creation of money

Like the goldsmiths, today's bankers seek to earn income by lending money out at a higher interest rate than they pay depositors for the use of their money.

In modern times, the chances of a run on a bank are fairly small; and, even if there is a run, the central bank protects private banks in various ways. Therefore:

> Banks usually make loans up to the point where they can no longer do so because of the reserve requirement restriction.

A bank's required amount of reserves is equal to the required reserve ratio times the total deposits in the bank. If a bank has deposits of €100 and the required ratio is 20%, the required amount of reserves is €20. The difference between a bank's actual reserves and its required reserves is its **excess reserves**:

excess reserves
The difference between a bank's actual reserves and its required reserves.

> Excess reserves ≡ Actual reserves − Required reserves

If banks make loans up to the point where they can no longer do so because of the reserve requirement restriction, this means that banks make loans up to the point where their excess reserves are zero.

To see why, note that when a bank has excess reserves, it has credit available, so it can make loans. Actually, a bank can make loans *only* if it has excess reserves. When a bank makes a loan, it creates a demand deposit for the borrower. This creation of a demand deposit causes the bank's excess reserves to fall because the extra deposits created by the loan use up some of the excess reserves the bank has on hand. An example will help.

Assume there is only one private bank in the country, the required reserve ratio is 20%, and the bank starts off with nothing, as shown in Panel 1 of Figure 25.2. Now

Figure 25.2 Balance sheets of a bank in a single-bank economy

Panel 1		Panel 2		Panel 3	
Assets	Liabilities	Assets	Liabilities	Assets	Liabilities
Reserves 0	0 Deposits	Reserves 100	100 Deposits	Reserves 100 Loans 400	500 Deposits

suppose 10-euro notes are in circulation and someone deposits ten of them in the bank. The bank deposits the €100 with the central bank, so it now has €100 in reserves, as shown in Panel 2. The bank now has assets (reserves) of €100 and liabilities (deposits) of €100. If the required reserve ratio is 20%, the bank has excess reserves of €80.

How much can the bank lend and still meet the reserve requirement? For the moment, suppose anyone who gets a loan keeps the entire proceeds in the bank or pays them to someone else who does. Nothing is withdrawn as cash. In this case, the bank can lend €400 and still meet the reserve requirement, as you can see in Panel 3. With €80 of excess reserves, the bank can have up to €400 of additional deposits. The €100 in reserves plus €400 in loans (which are made as deposits) equal €500 in deposits. With €500 in deposits and a required reserve ratio of 20%, the bank must have reserves of €100 (20% of €500) – and it does. The bank can lend no more than €400 because its reserve requirement must not exceed €100. When a bank has no excess reserves and thus can make no more loans, it is said to be *loaned up*.

Remember, the money supply (M1) equals cash in circulation plus deposits. Before the initial deposit, the money supply was €100 (€100 cash and no deposits). After the deposit and the loans, the money supply is €500 (no cash outside of bank vaults and €500 in deposits). It is clear, then, that when cash is converted into deposits, the supply of money can change.

The bank whose T accounts are presented in Figure 25.2 is allowed to make loans of €400 based on the assumption that loans granted *stay in the bank* in the form of deposits. Now suppose I borrow from the bank to buy a personal computer, and I write a cheque to the computer supplier. If the supplier also deposits its money in the bank, my cheque merely results in a reduction in my account balance and an increase in the supplier's account balance within the bank. No cash has left the bank. As long as the system is closed in this way – remember that we have so far assumed that there is only one bank – the bank knows that it will never be called upon to release any of its €100 in reserves. It can expand its loans up to the point where its total deposits are €500.

Of course, there are many banks, a situation depicted in Figure 25.3. As long as the banking system as a whole is closed, it is still possible for an initial deposit of €100 to result in an expansion of the money supply to €500, but more steps are involved when there is more than one bank.

To see why, assume Maria makes an initial deposit of €100 in Bank 1, and that the bank deposits the entire €100 with the ECB (Panel 1 of Figure 25.3). Also assume that all loans that a bank makes are withdrawn from the bank as the individual borrowers write cheques to pay for merchandise. Because of Maria's deposit, Bank 1 can make a loan of up to €80 to Patrick, since it needs to keep only €20 of its €100 deposit as reserves. (We are assuming a 20% required reserve ratio.) In other words, Bank 1 has €80 in excess reserves.

Bank 1's balance sheet at the moment of the loan to Patrick appears in Panel 2 of Fig 25.3. Bank 1 now has loans of €80. It has credited Patrick's account with the €80, so its total deposits are €180 (€80 in loans plus €100 in reserves). Patrick then writes a cheque for €80 to buy replacement parts for his car. Patrick wrote his cheque to Johan's Car Spares, and Johan deposits Patrick's cheque in Bank 2. When the cheque clears, Bank 1 transfers €80 in reserves to Bank 2. Bank 1's balance sheet now looks like the top of Panel 3. Its assets include reserves of €20 and loans of €80; its

Figure 25.3 The creation of money: balance sheets of three banks

	Panel 1		Panel 2		Panel 3	
	Assets	Liabilities	Assets	Liabilities	Assets	Liabilities
Bank 1	Reserves 100	100 Deposits	Reserves 100 Loans 80	180 Deposits	Reserves 20 Loans 80	100 Deposits
Bank 2	Reserves 80	80 Deposits	Reserves 80 Loans 64	144 Deposits	Reserves 16 Loans 64	80 Deposits
Bank 3	Reserves 64	64 Deposits	Reserves 64 Loans 51.20	115.20 Deposits	Reserves 12.80 Loans 51.20	64 Deposits

Summary:	Deposits
Bank 1	100
Bank 2	80
Bank 3	64
Bank 4	51.20
⋮	⋮
Total	500.00

liabilities are €100 in deposits. Both sides of the T account balance: the bank's reserves are 20% of its deposits, as required by law, and it is fully loaned up.

Now look at Bank 2. Since Bank 1 has transferred $80 in reserves to Bank 2, it now has $80 in deposits and $80 in reserves. (See Panel 1, Bank 2.) Since its reserve requirement is also 20%, it has excess reserves of $64 on which it can make loans.

Now assume Bank 2 lends the €64 to Lisa to pay for a textbook and Lisa writes a cheque for €64 payable to the university bookshop. The final position of Bank 2, after it honours Lisa's €64 cheque by transferring €64 in reserves to the bookshop's bank, is reserves of €16, loans of €64 and deposits of €80 (Panel 3, Bank 2).

The university bookshop deposits Lisa's cheque in its account with Bank 3. Bank 3 now has excess reserves, because it has added €64 to its reserves. With a reserve ratio of 20%, Bank 3 can lend out €51.20 (80% of €64, leaving 20% in required reserves to back the €64 deposit).

As the process is repeated over and over again, the total amount of deposits created is €500, the sum of the deposits in each of the banks. Because the banking system can be looked upon as one big bank, the outcome for many banks is the same as the outcome for one bank in Figure 25.2.[2]

The money multiplier

In practice, the banking system is not completely closed – there is some leakage out of the system. Still, the point here is:

An increase in bank reserves leads to a greater than one-for-one increase in the money supply. Economists call the relationship between the final change in deposits and the change in reserves that caused this change the money multiplier. Stated somewhat differently, the **money multiplier** is the multiple by which deposits can increase for every dollar increase in reserves:

money multiplier
The multiple by which deposits can increase for every dollar increase in reserves; equal to one divided by the required reserve ratio.

[2]If banks create money when they make loans, does repaying a loan 'destroy' money? The answer is yes.

$$\text{Deposits} = \text{Money multiplier} \times \text{Reserves}$$

Do not confuse the money multiplier with the spending multipliers we discussed in the last two chapters. While there is a formal similarity, they are not at all the same thing.

In the example we just examined, reserves increased by €100 when the €100 in cash was deposited in a bank, and the value of deposits increased by €500 (€100 from the initial deposit, €400 from the loans made by the various banks from their excess reserves). The money multiplier in this case is €500/€100 = 5. Mathematically, the money multiplier can be defined as:

$$\text{Money multiplier} \equiv \frac{1}{\text{Required reserve ratio}}$$

The required reserve ratio varies between countries, as Table 25.1 shows. Before European Monetary Union the highest ratio was required in Italy, where it was 15% in 1992. This means that an increase in reserves of 1 million lire could cause an increase in deposits of over 6 million if there were no leakage out of the system.

In reality there are leakages. People hold currency, instead of depositing the entire loan obtained in the bank or writing a cheque for a person who will deposit the entire amount in her bank. But in the presence of currency the money supply equals the sum of currency and deposits, which we called M1. The monetary aggregate that the central bank can control is reserves plus currency, which we called the monetary base M0. In this general case the multiplier links the money supply M1 to the monetary base M0 controlled by the central bank:

$$\text{Money supply} = \text{Money multiplier} \times \text{Monetary base}$$

$$(\text{Currency} + \text{Deposits}) = \text{Money multiplier} \times (\text{Currency} + \text{Reserves})$$

Table 25.1 Required reserve ratios in selected countries 1996

	Reserve ratios (%)
Austria	3.0 – 5.0
Belgium	none
France	0.5 – 1.0
Germany	1.5 – 2.0
Italy	15.0
Japan	0.05 – 1.3
Netherlands	variable
Spain	2.0
Sweden	none
Switzerland	2.5
United States	0.35
United Kingdom	3.0 – 10.0

Source: C. Borio, *The Implementation of Monetary Policy in Industrial Countries* (BIS Economic Papers No. 47, July 1997). Bank for International Settlements, Basle.

Maths Box 1 The money multiplier when people hold currency

When people hold currency CU and chequeable deposits D, the money supply is

(1) $M1 = CU + D$

The central bank controls the monetary base:

(2) $M0 = CU + R$

We found that money creation by private banks relates deposits D to reserves R via the required reserve ratio g according to:

(3) $D = \dfrac{1}{g} \times R$

Suppose people hold a fraction f of their deposits as currency:

(4) $CU = f \times D$

Substituting this into equations (1) and (2), and using (3) to get rid of reserves, gives

(1') $M1 = (1 + f) \times D$
(2') $M0 = (g + f) \times D$

Equation (2') may be solved for D to give:

(5) $D = \left(\dfrac{1}{f + g} \right) \times M0$

Substituting (5) into (1') gives

$$M1 = \frac{(1 + f)}{(g + f)} \times M0$$

The fraction $(1 + f)/(g + f)$ is the money multiplier that links the money supply to the monetary base. It is smaller than $1/g$, the money multiplier we obtained for the economy with no currency holding by the public.

Compare this to the multiplier given above for the example with no currency. Since the holding of currency constitutes a leakage out of the system during each round of the money multiplier process, the holding of currency makes the multiplier smaller. Suffice it here to say that it is smaller than 1/ Required reserve ratio (see the box for an algebraic discussion).

The central bank and the money supply

We have now seen how the private banking system creates money by making loans. However, private banks are not free to create money at will. Their ability to create money is controlled by the volume of reserves in the system, which is controlled by the central bank. The central bank, therefore, has the ultimate control over the money supply.

Traditionally, it was the rule for a country to have its own central bank. At the turn of the millennium, in a unprecedented step 11 European countries are transferring the control over their joint money supply to the European Central Bank (ECB). Let's examine the structure of the ECB and the function of the central bank in general.

The European System of Central Banks

The European Central Bank is the central bank of the countries participating in European Monetary Union. It plays the leading part in a complicated institution called the European System of Central Banks (ESCB). The organizational structure of the ESCB is presented in Figure 25.4.

The *Governing Council* is the top executive body of the ESCB. The council consists of the governors of the national central banks of the participating countries and of the members of the *ECB Executive Board*. The Executive Board is formed by the President

Figure 25.4 The European System of Central Banks (ESCB)

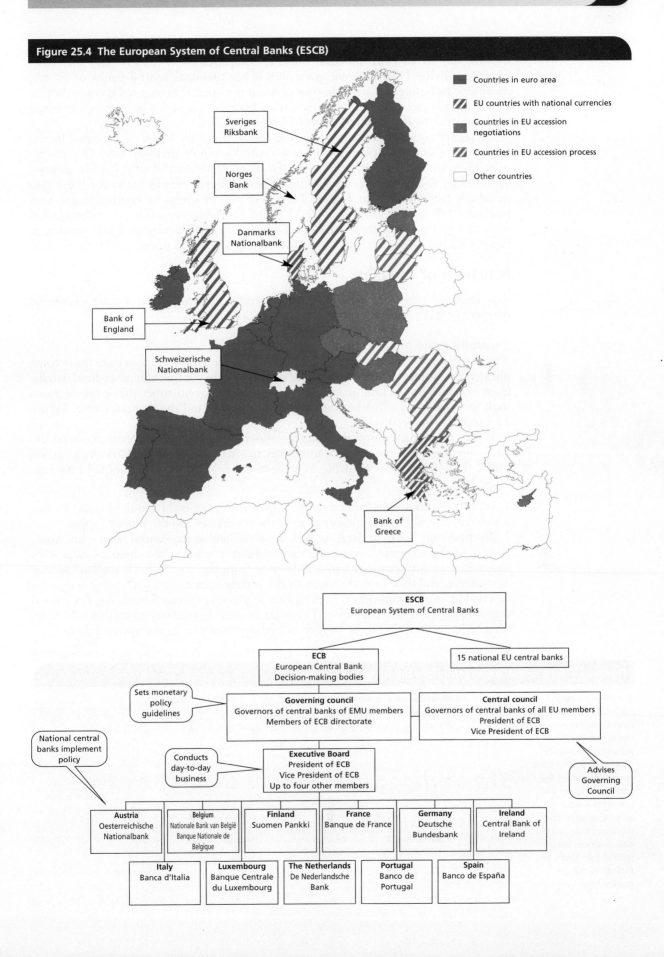

and the Vice-president of the ECB, and four other members. A third body, the *General Council*, has an advisory function only. It comprises the President and the Vice-president of the ECB and the governors of the national central banks of *all* EU members, including those not having adopted the euro. The expanded council's recommendations are likely to be particularly important on decisions such as admitting new countries to European Monetary Union.

Monetary policy guidelines within European Monetary Union are decided by the Governing Council. Most decisions are made by simple majority rule. Day-to-day operations within these guidelines are led by the Executive Board, but are actually executed by the national central banks. These national central banks (of the EMU members marked blue in Figure 25.4) lost the privilege to conduct their own monetary policy on 1 January 1999. Western European central banks still endowed with that privilege are those of EU members not participating in EMU (shown in light blue) and those that remain outside the EU (shown in white).

Functions of the ECB

The ECB, as other central banks, has a variety of tasks. From a macroeconomic perspective its crucial role is to control the money supply.

Controlling the money supply

The details of how modern central banks control the supply of money are quite complicated and display country-specific idiosyncrasies. To cut through procedural details, most of which are of little macroeconomic relevance, remember that a few sections back we established a link between the money supply and the monetary base. Figure 25.5 restates this relationship.

If the central bank wants to raise the money supply it can either try to extend the monetary base, or it can raise the multiplier to affect the lending behaviour of private banks. The instruments available to achieve either of these objectives fall into four categories:

1. We already know what affects the multiplier. The key is the required reserve ratio, which the central bank can lower to raise the multiplier and the money supply.
2. To encourage banks to decrease their reserves held at the central bank – one component of the monetary base – the central bank can lower the discount rate. This makes it more attractive for banks to borrow from the central bank, use that money as a reserve, and then extend its loan to the private sector.
3. The last two instruments are operations to increase currency holdings, the second component of the monetary base. The most frequently used way to do this is by open market operations; that is, by buying and selling securities in the open market.

Figure 25.5 How central banks control the money supply

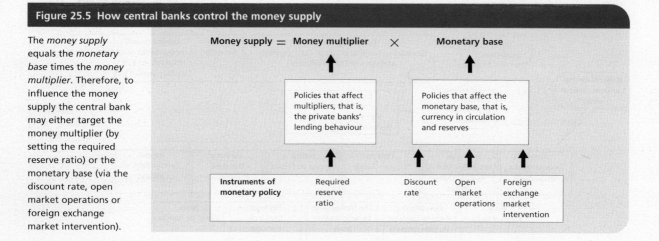

The *money supply* equals the *monetary base* times the *money multiplier*. Therefore, to influence the money supply the central bank may either target the money multiplier (by setting the required reserve ratio) or the monetary base (via the discount rate, open market operations or foreign exchange market intervention).

4. To affect the monetary base, the central bank can also resort to foreign exchange market intervention. This time it buys foreign currency to increase the monetary base.

Global Perspectives

Four central banks in 1998

Most countries have a central bank. While banking systems and financial institutions differ from country to country, the essential function of the central bank is the same: to control the supply of money and to regulate the banking system. As you will see in subsequent chapters, central banks have an impact on the functioning of the economy. Four of the important central banks in the world are described briefly here with a discussion of the major problem each faced during the late 1990s.

The USA: the Federal Feserve system ('the Fed')
The Fed Chairman in 1998 was Alan Greenspan. He was known for his strong anti-inflation views. As you will see in later chapters, excess monetary expansion can lead to inflation. Although no inflation was on the radar screens during 1998, labour markets were very tight and wage inflation was a big worry as the economy continued to expand at a healthy rate. But in the summer of 1998, stock markets around the world came crashing down and that took some of the wind out of the economy. In September Greenspan voiced concern about the growing risk to the US economy from mounting world financial turmoil and signalled the Fed might cut interest rates and thus

expand the money supply if necessary to prevent a recession.

Switzerland: the Swiss National Bank (SNB)
The Swiss economy stopped growing in 1990. In 1997 GDP was a mere 1% higher than in 1990. This stagnation began during a pronounced disinflation engineered by the SNB, lowering inflation from its 1991 peak of 5.8% to 0.8% in 1994. From this coincidence many conclude that the SNB's determination to restore price stability quickly caused the 1990s stagnation. The puzzle remains why growth has not resumed after the disinflation ended. When SNB director Hans Meier took office in 1996 there were signals of a slightly greater concern for the effects of monetary policy on income compared to his predecessors. In 1998 the SNB tried to funnel just enough money into the economy so as not to jeopardize returning growth, but not to rekindle inflation either.

Japan: the Bank of Japan
The Bank of Japan faced one major problem in 1998: recession. GDP had been falling in the first, second and third quarter of this year, making this the longest recession in the post war period. With a key interest rate down to a

Bank officials install an information board with exchange rates outside an exchange booth in downtown Moscow, Thursday, August 13, 1998. As concern grew over the stability of the Russian ruble, the Central Bank imposed new rules on currency trading by commercial banks. (AP Photo/Ivan Sekretarev)

historic low of 0.25%, how monetary policy could possibly become even more expansionary to help the economy out of the recession. It is hardly surprising, therefore, that the government has begun to resort to fiscal policy in the form of a $124 billion stimulus package announced in March. Some suggest that the bank of Japan should drive up inflation, thus possibly producing negative real interest rates and stimulating investment spending.

Russia: the Central Bank of Russia
The Central Bank of Russia has problems dwarfing those of Germany, the USA and Japan. While the list of economic woes in the New

Russia was long, near the top was hyperinflation. In 1992, prices rose about 2000%. By the beginning of 1995, inflation was *down* to about 15% per month. It was still 15% at the beginning of 1998, but was back up to 43% in September. Around that time, both financial panic and political instability sent the stock market and the ruble on downward slides. The new government proposed printing money to pay wages and foreign debt and, to facilitate this, appointed Viktor Gerashchenko as the new head of the central bank. Further increases in inflation is the likely price for attempting to get out of the economic crisis in this fashion.

Table 25.2 Assets and liabilities of the Sveriges Riksbank, 15 January 1998 (millions of kronor)			
Assets		**Liabilities**	
Gold and foreign assets	95,988	Currency	76,192
Government securities and bonds	54,278	Domestic liabilities	19,397
Monetary policy repo	30,978	Capital	32,239
		Balancing account	46,993
Other	2,074	Other	8,356
Total	183,319	Total	183,319

Source: www.riksbank.se.

As a background for a more detailed discussion of the four main instruments for money supply control, let us look at a specific central bank's balance sheet.

The balance sheet of the Sveriges Riksbank

Established in 1668 as the 'Parliament's Bank', Sweden's central bank is the oldest in the world. Although it is a special bank, the Swedish Central Bank (SCB) is in some ways similar to an ordinary commercial bank. Like an ordinary bank, it has a balance sheet that records its asset and liability position at any moment in time, as shown in Table 25.2.

As the asset side of the balance sheet shows, the SCB owns about 96 billion kronor worth of gold and foreign assets. Most of these are securities denominated in foreign currency. This is the SCB's largest asset. Next in size are government securities and bonds, worth about 54 billion kronor. These are obligations of the Swedish government, which the SCB has purchased over the years. The 'monetary policy repo' item represents loans to commercial banks. These loans are an asset just as they would be for a private bank.

The biggest component of the SCB's liabilities is currency in circulation (76 billion kronor). The one-krona note you may carry in your pocket when you go to buy a litre of milk is clearly an asset from your point of view – it is something you own that has value. But since every financial asset is by definition a liability of some other agent in the economy, whose liability is that banknote? Quite simply, that one-krona note is a liability of the SCB. It is, of course, a rather strange liability, because all it can be redeemed for is another note of the same type. The other liabilities worth speaking of are capital (the SCB's net worth) at 32 billion kronor, the balancing account at 47 billion, and domestic liabilities at 19.4 billion.

The required reserve ratio

The simplest way for the ECB to alter the supply of money is to change the required reserve ratio. Table 25.3 shows how. Let us assume the initial required reserve ratio is 20%.

In Panel 1, a simplified version of the ECB's balance sheet (in billions of euros) shows that reserves are €100 billion and currency outstanding is €100 billion. The total value of the ECB's assets is €200 billion, which we assume to be all in government securities. Assuming there are no excess reserves – banks stay fully loaned up – the €100 billion in reserves supports €500 billion in deposits at the commercial banks. (Remember the money multiplier equals (1/required reserve ratio) = 1/0.20 = 5. Thus, €100 billion in reserves can support €500 billion [€100 billion × 5] in deposits when the required reserve ratio is 20%.) The supply of money (M1, or transactions money) is therefore €600 billion made up of €100 billion in currency and €500 billion in (cheque account) deposits at commercial banks.

Now suppose the ECB wants to increase the supply of money to €900 billion. If it lowers the required reserve ratio from 20% to 12.5% (as in Panel 2 of Table 25.3),

Table 25.3 A decrease in the required reserve ratio from 20% to 12.5% increases the supply of money (all figures in billions of euros)

Panel 1: Required reserve ratio = 20%

European Central Bank				Commercial banks			
Assets		Liabilities		Assets		Liabilities	
Government securities	€200	€100	Reserves	Reserves	€100	€500	Deposits
		€100	Currency	Loans	€400		

Note: Money supply (M1) = Currency + Deposits = €600.

Panel 2: Required reserve ratio = 12.5%

European Central Bank				Commercial banks			
Assets		Liabilities		Assets		Liabilities	
Government securities	€200	€100	Reserves	Reserves	€100	€800	Deposits (+€300)
		€100	Currency	Loans (+€300)	€700		

Note: Money supply (M1) = Currency + Deposits = €900.

then the same €100 billion of reserves could support €800 billion in deposits instead of only €500 billion. In this case, the money multiplier is 1/0.125, or 8. At a required reserve ratio of 12.5%, €100 billion in reserves can support €800 billion in deposits. The total money supply would be €800 billion in deposits plus the €100 billion in currency, for a total of €900 billion.[3]

Put another way, with the new lower reserve ratio, banks have excess reserves of €37.5 billion. At a required reserve ratio of 20%, they needed €100 billion in reserves to back their €500 billion in deposits. At the lower required reserve ratio of 12.5%, they need only €62.5 billion of reserves to back their €500 billion of deposits, so the remaining €37.5 billion of the existing €100 billion in reserves are 'extra'. With that €37.5 billion of excess reserves, banks can lend out more money. If we assume that the system loans money and creates deposits to the maximum extent possible, the €37.5 billion of reserves will support an additional €300 billion of deposits (€37.5 billion × the money multiplier of 8 = €300 billion). The change in the required reserve ratio has injected an additional €300 billion into the banking system, at which point the banks will be fully loaned up and unable to increase their deposits further.

In sum:

Decreasing the required reserve ratio allows banks to have more deposits with the existing volume of reserves. As banks create more deposits by making loans, the supply of money (currency + deposits) increases. The reverse is also true: if the ECB wants to restrict the supply of money, it can raise the required reserve ratio, in which case banks will find that they have insufficient reserves and must therefore reduce their deposits by 'calling in' some of their loans.[4] The result is a decrease in the money supply.

[3]To find the maximum volume of deposits (D) that can be supported by an amount of reserves (R), simply divide R by the required reserve ratio. If the required reserve ratio is g, since R = gD, then D = R/g.

[4]In fact, banks never really have to 'call in' loans before they are due in order to reduce the money supply. First, the ECB is almost always expanding the money supply slowly because the real economy grows steadily and, as we shall see, growth brings with it the need for more circulating money. So when we speak of 'contractionary monetary policy', we mean that the ECB is slowing down the rate of money growth, not reducing the money supply. Second, even if the ECB were actually to cut reserves (rather than merely curb their expansion), banks would no doubt be able to comply by reducing the volume of new loans that they make while old ones are coming due.

Most countries' central banks use reserve requirements as a policy instrument. A few don't (see Table 25.1). The ECB has the instrument at its disposal. In July 1998 the Governing Council recommended that it should also use it, applying a reserve ratio between 1.5% and 2.5%.

The discount rate

discount rate

Interest rate that banks pay to the central bank to borrow from it.

Banks may borrow from the ECB. The interest rate they pay is the **discount rate**. When banks increase their borrowing, the money supply increases.

To simplify, assume there is only one bank in the country and the required reserve ratio is 20%. The initial position of the bank and the ECB appear in Panel 1 of Table 25.4, where the money supply (currency + deposits) is €480. In Panel 2, the bank has borrowed €20 from the ECB. By using this €20 as a reserve, the bank can increase its loans by €100, from €320 to €420. (Remember: a required reserve ratio of 20% gives a money multiplier of 5. Excess reserves of €20 allows the bank to create an additional €20 × 5, or €100, in deposits.)

> Bank borrowing from the ECB leads to an increase in the money supply.

Banks that borrow from the ECB must eventually repay, and when they do the money supply goes back down by exactly the amount by which it initially increased.

The ECB can exercise some influence over bank borrowing through the discount rate:

> The higher the discount rate, the higher the cost of borrowing, and the less banks will want to borrow.

If the ECB wants to curtail the growth of the money supply, it can raise the discount rate, which discourages banks from borrowing from it, and thus restrict the growth of reserves (and ultimately deposits).

Changing the discount rate to control the supply of money entails several problems. First, although raising the discount rate does discourage borrowing by banks (and therefore reduces their ability to expand the money supply), it is never

Table 25.4 The effect on the money supply of commercial bank borrowing from the ECB (all figures in billions of euros)

Panel 1: No commercial bank borrowing from the ECB

European Central Bank				Commercial banks			
Assets			Liabilities	Assets			Liabilities
Securities	€160	€80	Reserves	Reserves	€80	€400	Deposits
		€80	Currency	Loans	€320		

Note: Money supply (M1) = Currency + Deposits = €480.

Panel 2: Commercial bank borrowing €20 from the ECB

European Central Bank				Commercial banks			
Assets			Liabilities	Assets			Liabilities
Securities	€160	€100	Reserves (+€20)	Reserves (+€20)	€100	€500	Deposits (+€100)
Loans	€20	€80	Currency	Loans (+€100)	€420	€20	Amount owed to Fed (+€20)

Note: Money supply (M1) = Currency + Deposits = €580.

clear in advance exactly how much of an effect a change in the discount rate will have. If banks are very short of reserves, they may decide to borrow from the central bank even though the discount rate is quite high.

> The discount rate cannot be used to control the money supply with great precision, because its effect on banks' demand for reserves is uncertain.

Second, changes in the discount rate can be largely offset by movements in other interest rates. If the discount rate is set at 10% and the rate paid by Treasury bills is 9%, banks will not borrow from the ECB to purchase Treasury bills. Since they would be paying more in borrowing costs than they would be making in interest revenue, they would lose by borrowing from the ECB. If the Treasury bill rate were to rise to 11%, banks could profitably borrow from the ECB to purchase Treasury bills. So a discount rate that is high enough to discourage borrowing in some circumstances may not be high enough in others.

You may wonder whether the discount rate can ever be below the rate banks charge for loans or below the rate offered on Treasury bills. If this were the case, wouldn't banks borrow enormous quantities from the ECB at the lower rate and lend at the higher rate? In practice, discount rates have at times been lower than the rates that banks charged for their loans, and yet this kind of behaviour is not common. This is because central banks place other constraints on the borrowing behaviour of banks. The central bank practices **moral suasion** to discourage heavy borrowing. Because member banks know that the central bank would look disapprovingly at heavy borrowing, they do not borrow heavily, and the amount that they do borrow responds only slightly to changes in the discount rate.

moral suasion
The pressure exerted by the central bank on member banks to discourage them from borrowing heavily from the central bank.

Open market operations

open market operations
The purchase and sale by the central bank of government securities in the open market; a tool used to expand or contract the amount of reserves in the system and thus the money supply.

A very significant central bank tool for controlling the supply of money is **open market operations**. Open market operations are the sale or purchase of securities by the central bank. Since the central bank does not run commercial risks, it only trades in securities issued by the government or large corporations. If the central bank does not want to or is not permitted to buy government debt (the Bundesbank is an example), it often does so indirectly: it lends to a commercial bank, requiring government bonds as a collateral. To simplify the argument, we only look at the case of direct trade in government securities. When the ECB purchases a government security, it pays for it by writing a cheque which, when cleared, *expands* the quantity of reserves in the system and thus the money supply. When the ECB sells a bond, private citizens or institutions pay for it with a cheque which, when cleared, reduces the quantity of reserves in the system.

Before we look at how open market transactions and reserve controls work, we need to review several key ideas.

Two branches of government deal in government securities

The fact that the ECB is able to buy and sell government securities – bills and bonds – may confuse students. In fact, *two* branches of government deal in financial markets for different reasons, and you must keep the two separate.

First, the Treasury (or ministry of finance) is responsible for collecting taxes and paying the government's bills. Salary cheques paid to government workers, payments to Saab for a new fighter plane, and so on, are all written on accounts maintained by the Treasury. Tax receipts collected are deposited to these accounts. If total government spending exceeds tax receipts, the Treasury must borrow the difference. Recall that the government deficit is $(G - T)$, government purchases minus net taxes. $(G - T)$ is the amount the Treasury must borrow each year to finance the deficit. This means:

> The Treasury cannot print money to finance the deficit.

The Treasury borrows by issuing bills, bonds and notes that pay interest. These government securities are sold to individuals and institutions. Often foreign countries, as well as domestic residents, buy them.

The ECB is not the Treasury. It is an independent agency authorized to buy and sell *outstanding* (pre-existing) government securities on the open market. The bonds and bills initially sold by a national Treasury to finance the deficit are continuously resold and traded among ordinary citizens, firms, banks, pension funds and so forth. The ECB's participation in that trading affects the quantity of reserves in the system, as we will see below.

Because the central bank owns some government securities while being an arm of the government itself, some of what the government owes it owes to itself. Recall that most central banks' largest single asset is government securities. These securities are bills and bonds initially issued by the Treasury to finance the deficit. They were acquired by the central bank over time through direct open market purchases that it made to expand the money supply as the economy grew.

The mechanics of open market operations

How do open market operations affect the money supply? Look again at Table 25.2. As you can see, much of the Swedish Central Bank's assets consist of the government securities we have just been talking about. These will also feature prominently in the ECB's balance sheet.

Suppose the ECB wants to decrease the supply of money. If it can reduce the volume of bank reserves on the liabilities side of its balance sheet, it will force banks in turn to reduce their own deposits (to meet the required reserve ratio). Since these deposits are part of the supply of money, the supply of money will contract.

What will happen if the ECB sells some of its holdings of government securities to the public? The ECB's holdings of government securities must decrease, since the securities it sold will now be owned by someone else. How do the purchasers of securities pay for what they have bought? By writing cheques drawn on their banks and payable to the ECB.

Let's look more carefully at how this works, with the help of Table 25.5. In Panel 1, the ECB initially has €100 billion of government securities. Its liabilities consist of €20 billion of deposits (which are the reserves of commercial banks) and €80 billion of currency. With the required reserve ratio at 20%, the €20 billion of reserves can support €100 billion of deposits in the commercial banks. The commercial banking system is fully loaned up. Panel 1 also shows the financial position of a private citizen, Jane Public. Jane has assets of €5 billion (a large cheque account deposit in the bank) and no debts, so her net worth is €5 billion.

Now imagine that the ECB sells €5 billion in government securities to Jane. Jane pays for the securities by writing a cheque to the ECB, drawn on her bank. The ECB then reduces the reserve account of her bank by €5 billion. The balance sheets of all the participants after this transaction are shown in Panel 2. Note that the supply of money (currency plus deposits) has fallen from €180 billion to €175 billion.

This is not the end of the story. As a result of the ECB's sale of securities, the amount of reserves has fallen from €20 billion to €15 billion, while deposits have fallen from €100 billion to €95 billion. With a required reserve ratio of 20%, banks must have 0.20 × €95 billion, or €19 billion in reserves. Banks are under their required reserve ratio by €4 billion: €19 billion (the amount they should have) minus €15 billion (the amount they do have). To comply with regulations, banks must decrease their loans and their deposits.[5]

The final equilibrium position is shown in Panel 3, where commercial banks have reduced their loans by €20 billion. Notice that the change in deposits from Panel 1 to Panel 3 is €25 billion, which is five times the size of the change in reserves that the ECB

[5]*Once again, banks never really have to call in loans. Loans and deposits would probably be reduced by slowing the rate of new lending as old loans come due and are paid off.*

Table 25.5 Open market operations (numbers in parentheses in panels 2 and 3 are differences between those panels and panel 1; all figures in billions of euros)

Panel 1

European Central Bank		Commercial banks		Jane Public	
Assets	**Liabilities**	**Assets**	**Liabilities**	**Assets**	**Liabilities**
Securities €100	€20 Reserves	Reserves €20	€100 Deposits	Deposits €5	€0 Debts
	€80 Currency	Loans €80			€5 Net Worth

Note: Money supply (M1) = Currency + Deposits = €180.

Panel 2

European Central Bank		Commercial banks		Jane Public	
Assets	**Liabilities**	**Assets**	**Liabilities**	**Assets**	**Liabilities**
Securities €95 (– €5)	€15 Reserves (– €5)	Reserves €15 (– €5)	€95 Deposits (– €5)	Deposits €0 (– €5)	€0 Debts
	€80 Currency.	Loans €80		Securities €5 (+ €5)	€5 Net Worth

Note: Money supply (M1) = Currency + Deposits = €175.

Panel 3

European Central Bank		Commercial banks		Jane Public	
Assets	**Liabilities**	**Assets**	**Liabilities**	**Assets**	**Liabilities**
Securities €95 (– €5)	€15 Reserves (– €5)	Reserves €15 (– €5)	€75 Deposits (– €25)	Deposits €0 (– €5)	€0 Debts
	€80 Currency	Loans €60 (– €20)		Securities €5 (+ €5)	€5 Net Worth

Note: Money supply (M1) = Currency + Deposits = €155.

brought about through its €5 billion open market sale of securities. This corresponds exactly to our earlier analysis of the money multiplier. The change in money (–€25 billion) is equal to the money multiplier (five) times the change in reserves (–€5 billion).

Now consider what happens when the ECB *purchases* a government security. Suppose I hold €100 in Treasury bills, which the ECB buys from me. The ECB writes me a cheque for €100, and I hand over my Treasury bills. I then take the €100 cheque and deposit it in my local bank. This increases the reserves of my bank by €100 and begins a new episode in the money expansion story. With a reserve requirement of 20%, my bank can now lend out €80. If that €80 is spent and ends up back in a bank, that bank can lend €64, and so forth. (Review Figure 25.4.) The ECB can expand the money supply by buying government securities from people who own them, in just the way it reduces the money supply by selling these securities.

We can sum up the effect of these open market operations this way:

■ An open market *purchase* of securities by the central bank results in an increase in reserves and an *increase* in the supply of money by an amount equal to the money multiplier times the change in reserves.
■ An open market *sale* of securities by the central bank results in a *decrease* in reserves and a *decrease* in the supply of money by an amount equal to the money multiplier times the change in reserves.

Open market operations are often a preferred means of controlling the money supply for several reasons. First, open market operations can be used with some precision. If the central bank needs to change the money supply by just a small amount, it can buy or sell a small volume of government securities. If it wants a larger change in the money supply, it can buy or sell a larger amount. Second, open market operations are extremely flexible. If the central bank decides to reverse course, it can easily switch from buying securities to selling them. Finally, open market operations have a fairly predictable effect on the supply of money. Since banks are obliged to meet their reserve requirements, an open market sale of €100 in government securities will reduce reserves by €100, which will reduce the supply of money by €100 times the money multiplier.

Where does the ECB get the money to buy government securities when it wants to expand the money supply? The ECB creates it. In effect, it tells the bank from which it has bought a €100 security that its reserve account (deposit) at the ECB now contains €100 more than it did previously. This is where the power of the ECB, or any central bank, lies. The central bank has the ability to create money at will.

Foreign exchange market intervention

In the global-economy model discussed in these chapters there is only one currency. A foreign exchange market is not necessary, and neither is foreign exchange market intervention. We discuss it here, nevertheless, to assemble a complete list of instruments at the disposal of central banks in the real world.

foreign assets
That part of a bank's assets held in foreign currency.

Literally, foreign exchange market intervention refers to the purchase or sale of foreign currency in exchange for domestic currency. As Table 25.2 exemplifies for Sweden, all central banks hold part of their assets in foreign currency, their **foreign assets**. When the Swiss National Bank holds euros, it would be foolish to actually keep euro bills in its vaults. But let us ignore this for now and see what happens in the SNB's T account if the SNB sells 20 million Swiss francs' worth of euros in exchange for Swiss francs. Doing this has two effects, as shown Table 25.6. First, it reduces the SNB's assets. Foreign assets fall by 20 million. Second, because the francs it receives for the sale of euros are removed from the hands of the public, currency outstanding (and, hence, liabilities) also fall by 20 million. Since the monetary base is made up of currency in circulation plus reserves, this decline in currency constitutes a reduction of the monetary base by 20 million.

The outcome is the same if the SNB really holds French bonds instead of euros. In a first step, the bonds are sold in exchange for euros in which the bonds are denoted. This does not affect the T account yet, where there is only a reshuffling of foreign assets. Foreign bonds fall by 20 million, and foreign currency increases by 20 million. In a second step the transaction is completed by selling the acquired 20 million euros for francs. This reduces the monetary base as described in the previous paragraph.

What if the person buying the SNB's euros pays by cheque written on her Swiss bank account? Well then the SNB deducts the 20 million francs from this bank's reserves held at the SNB. As the T account in Figure 25.7 shows, now the reduction of the SNB's foreign assets by 20 million is matched by a 20 million decline in reserves. This also reduces the monetary base and, hence, the Swiss money supply.

The SNB routinely intervened in the foreign exchange market to control the money supply. The ECB does not plan to use this instrument for this purpose.

Table 25.6 Foreign exchange market intervention using currency	
Swiss National Bank	
Assets	**Liabilities**
Foreign currency −20	Currency −20

Table 25.7 Foreign exchange market intervention using cheques	
Swiss National Bank	
Assets	**Liabilities**
Foreign currency −20	Reserves −20

Table 25.8 Asset structure of selected central banks (percentage of total non-gold assets); various months in 1997

	Belgium	Britain	Denmark	France	Germany	Italy	Switzerland	USA
Foreign assets	79.3	44.5	57.0	67.6	34.9	35.5	87.2	13.5
Loans to banks	11.2	0.1	20.4	18.4	58.7	6.9	9.9	0.0
Government securities	9.6	55.4	8.4	10.2	5.6	57.6	2.9	86.5

Note: Percentages may not add up to 100 due to 'other assets' not shown here.

Source: IMF, IFS, September 1997.

However, all central banks have occasionally intervened in the foreign exchange market *to influence the exchange rate*. But we postpone this aspect until Chapter 29.

The structure of a central bank's assets provides information as to how this central bank prefers to conduct monetary policy. Table 25.8 shows quite diverse patterns.

In the past, only Italy and the USA appear to have purchased government securities on a large scale and thus to have relied on open market operations in a straightforward way. The Bundesbank, by contrast, relied mostly on credit towards commercial banks. In the other countries, foreign exchange market intervention plays the most important role, if not the dominant one as in the case of Switzerland.

Other central bank duties

Clearing interbank payments

Suppose you write a €1000 cheque, drawn on your bank, the Dresdner Bank, to pay for renting a holiday home near Valencia. Your Spanish landlord does not bank at Dresdner, but at Banco de Valencia. How does your money get from your bank to the bank in Spain?

The answer is that the ECB does it. Both Dresdner and Banco de Valencia have accounts at the ECB. When your landlord receives your cheque and deposits it at his bank, the bank submits the cheque to the ECB, asking it to collect the funds from Dresdner. The ECB presents the cheque to Dresdner and is instructed to debit Dresdner's account for the €1000 and to credit the account of Banco de Valencia. Since accounts at the ECB count as reserves, Dresdner loses €1000 in reserves and Banco de Valencia gains €1000 in reserves. The two banks have effectively traded ownerships of their deposits at the ECB. The *total* volume of reserves has not changed, nor has the money supply.

To make EU-wide cross-border payments in euros as safe, reliable and even faster than many national interbank payments, the ECB has developed a new settlement system, called **TARGET** (Trans-European Automated Real-time Gross settlement Express Transfer system). It allows banks to make euro payments almost instantly. All they need to do is send payment orders in the domestic message format they are familiar with. TARGET will take care that the beneficiary participant receives payment within a couple of minutes, if not only a few seconds. In addition to facilitating cross-border payments, TARGET also is to serve the needs of monetary policy conducted within the ESCB in a cross-border setting.

TARGET EU-wide system for euro payments. It comprises fifteen national payments systems which the ECB links to provide a uniform platform for processing cross-border payments.

Further duties of the central bank

Besides facilitating the transfer of funds between banks, the ECB is responsible for many of the regulations governing banking practices and standards in the EMU member countries. Such duties go widely unnoticed during 'normal' times. The need for them is revealed in extraordinary contexts, such as the Barings Bank collapse in 1996, or the 1997 financial crisis in Asia, which forced Japan and other Asian governments to nationalize a substantial number of troubled banks.

Looking ahead

This chapter has discussed only the supply side of the money market. We have seen what money is, how banks create money by making loans, and how the central bank controls the money supply. In the next chapter we turn to the demand side of the money market. We will examine the demand for money and how the supply of, and demand for, money interact to determine the interest rate.

Summary

An overview of money

1. Money has three distinguishing characteristics. It is: (1) a means of payment, or medium of exchange, (2) a store of value, and (3) a unit of account. The alternative to using money is *barter*, in which goods are exchanged directly for other goods. Barter is costly and inefficient in an economy with many different kinds of goods.

2. *Commodity moneys* are items used as money that also have an intrinsic value in some other use (for example, gold and cigarettes). *Fiat moneys* are intrinsically worthless apart from their use as money. To ensure the acceptance of fiat moneys, governments use their power to declare money *legal tender* and promise the public they will not debase the currency by expanding its supply rapidly.

3. There are various definitions of money. M0, the *monetary base*, is the sum of currency and reserves. Currency plus demand deposits comprise M1, or *transactions money* – money that can be used directly to buy things. The addition of savings accounts (*near moneys*) to M1 gives M2, or *broad money*. M3 and M4 are very broad definitions of money, adding private sector deposits with wholesale banks and building societies to M2.

How banks create money

4. The *required reserve ratio* is the percentage of a bank's deposits that must be kept as reserves at the central bank.

5. Banks create money by making loans. When a bank makes a loan to a customer, it creates a deposit in that customer's account. This deposit becomes part of the money supply. Banks can create money only when they have *excess reserves* – reserves in excess of the amount set by the required reserve ratio.

6. The *money multiplier* is the multiple by which the total supply of money can increase for every euro increase in reserves. The money multiplier is equal to 1/Required reserve ratio.

The European system of central banks

7. The ECB's most important function is controlling Europe's money supply. The ECB also performs several other functions: it clears interbank payments and is responsible for many of the regulations governing banking practices and standards.

How the ECB controls the money supply

8. The key to understanding how the ECB controls the money supply is the role of reserves. If the ECB wants to increase the supply of money, it induces banks to hold more reserves, freeing them to create additional deposits. If it wants to decrease the money supply, it makes banks reduce reserves.

9. The central bank has four tools at its disposal to control the money supply: (1) change the required reserve ratio; (2) change the *discount rate* (the interest rate member banks pay when they borrow from the central bank); (3) engage in *open market operations* (the buying and selling of already existing government securities). And (4), to increase the money supply, the central bank can create additional reserves by lowering the discount rate, or by buying government securities or foreign exchange. The central bank can increase the number of deposits that can be created from a given quantity of reserves by lowering the required reserve ratio. To decrease the money supply, the central bank can reduce reserves by raising the discount rate or by selling government securities, or it can raise the required reserve ratio.

Review Terms and Concepts

barter
commodity moneys
currency debasement
discount rate
excess reserves

fiat, or token, money
financial intermediaries
foreign assets
legal tender
liquidity property of money

M0, or the monetary base
M1, or transactions money
M2, or broad money
medium of exchange, or means of payment
money multiplier
moral suasion
near money
open market operations
required reserve ratio
reserves
run on a bank
store of value
TARGET
unit of account

Equations

1. $M0 \equiv$ Currency + Reserves at central bank

2. $M1 \equiv$ Currency held outside banks + Demand deposits + Travellers' cheques + Other chequeable deposits

3. $M2 \equiv M1$ + Savings accounts + Money market accounts + Other near moneys

4. Assets $\equiv$ Liabilities + Capital (or Net Worth)

5. Excess reserves $\equiv$ Actual reserves − Required reserves

6. Money multiplier $\equiv \dfrac{1}{\text{Required reserve ratio}}$

Problem Set

1. Define money. What is meant by the 'store of value' function of money? What is meant by the 'medium of exchange' function of money? Think of your current cash holdings and cheque account balances. How much do you think you have on hand for engaging in transactions (buying things) on a daily basis? How much serves as a store of value? Would you change your cash holdings and your cheque account balance if your local bank started paying 15% interest on three month certificates of deposit? Why, or why not?

2. For each of the following, explain whether it is an asset or a liability in the accounts of a commercial bank. Explain why in each case.
- Cash in the vault
- Demand deposits
- Savings deposits
- Reserves
- Loans
- Deposits at the central bank

3. If the governor of the Bank of Japan wanted to expand the supply of money in 1999, which of the following would do it? Explain your answer.
a. Raising the required reserve ratio.
b. Lowering the required reserve ratio.
c. Increasing the discount rate.
d. Decreasing the discount rate.
e. Buying government securities in the open market.
f. Selling government securities in the open market.

4. In 1997, the US money supply (M1) was $1,077 billion, broken down as follows: $396 billion in currency, $8.6 billion in travellers' cheques, and $672 billion in cheque deposits. Suppose the Fed (the US central bank) has decided to reduce the money supply by increasing the reserve requirement from 10% to 11%. Assuming all banks were initially loaned up (had no excess reserves), and that currency held outside of banks did not change, how large a change in the money supply would have resulted from the change in the reserve requirement?

5. As King of Medivalia, you are constantly short of funds to pay your army. Your chief economic wizard suggests the following plan: 'When you collect your tax payments from your subjects, insist on being paid in gold coins. Take these gold coins, melt them down, and then remint them with an extra 10% of brass thrown in. You will then have 10% more money than you started with.' What do you think of the plan? Will it work?

6. Why is M2 sometimes a more stable measure of money than M1? Explain in your own words, using the definitions of M1 and M2.

7. Do you agree or disagree with each of the following statements? Explain your answers.
a. 'When the UK Treasury issues bonds and sells them to the public to finance the deficit, the money supply remains unchanged because every £ sterling of money taken in by the Treasury goes right back into circulation through government spending. This is not true when the Bank of England sells bonds to the public.'
b. 'The money multiplier depends on the marginal propensity to save.'
c. 'In 1998 the Bank of England moved to raise the discount rate. This move was designed to expand the supply of money in circulation.'

8. When the European Central Bank adds new reserves to the system, some of these new reserves find their way out of the EMU countries into foreign banks or foreign investment funds. In addition, some portion of new reserves ends up in people's pockets and under their mattresses rather than in bank vaults. These 'leakages' reduce the money multiplier and sometimes make it very difficult for the ECB to control the money supply precisely.
a. Explain why this is true.
b. Suppose the reserve requirement is 12%, but 25% of M1 is held as currency. If the ECB buys €1000 worth of securities on the open market, how much will the money supply expand? What is the impact of a 25% leakage on the size of the money multiplier?

Assets		Liabilities	
Reserves	€500	€3500	Deposits
Loans	3000		

9. The table shows a T account for a commercial bank. The required reserve ratio is 10%.

a. How much is the bank required to hold as reserves, given its deposits of 3500?

b. How much are its excess reserves?

c. By how much can the bank increase its loans?

d. Suppose a depositor comes to the bank and withdraws 200 in cash. Show the bank's new balance sheet, assuming that the bank obtains the cash by drawing down its reserves. Does the bank now hold excess reserves? Is it meeting the required reserve ratio? If not, what can it do?

10. What are the major functions of a central bank? Do you think any of these functions could be performed by private banks, or is the central bank the only agent capable of filling these roles? Explain.

Money Demand, the Equilibrium Interest Rate and Monetary Policy

After discussing the *supply* of money in the last chapter, we now turn to the *demand* for money. One goal of this and the previous chapter is to build a theory of how the interest rate is determined in the macroeconomy. Once we have seen how the interest rate is determined, we can examine how the central bank affects the interest rate through monetary policy.

Interest is the fee a borrower pays to a lender for the use of his or her funds. Firms and the government borrow funds by issuing bonds, and they pay interest to the firms and households (the lenders) that purchase those bonds. Households and firms that have borrowed from a bank must pay interest on those loans to the bank. The **interest rate** is the annual interest payment on a loan expressed as a percentage of the loan. A €1000 bond (representing a €1000 loan from a household to a firm) that pays €100 in interest *per year* has an interest rate of 10%. The interest rate is expressed as an *annual* rate. It is the amount of interest received *per year* divided by the amount of the loan.

While there are many different interest rates, we assume there is only one interest rate in the economy. This simplifies our analysis while providing a valuable tool for understanding how the various parts of the macroeconomy relate to one another. Appendix A to this chapter provides a more detailed discussion of the various types of interest rates.

interest The fee that a borrower pays to a lender for the use of his or her funds.

interest rate The annual interest payment on a loan expressed as a percentage of the loan. Equal to the amount of interest received per year divided by the amount of the loan.

The demand for money

The question of what determines the demand for money is a core issue in macroeconomics. As we shall see, the interest rate and the level of national income (Y) are important in determining how much money households and firms wish to hold.

Let us stress one point you may find troublesome. When we speak of the demand for money, we are not asking 'How much cash do you wish you could have?' or 'How much income would you like to earn?' or 'How much wealth would you like?' (The answer to all these questions is presumably 'as much as possible'.) Rather, we are concerned with the question of how much of your financial wealth you want to hold *in the form of money*, which does not earn interest, versus how much you want to hold in interest-bearing assets, such as bonds. We take as given the *total* value of financial wealth; our concern here is how these assets are divided between money and interest-bearing assets.

The transaction motive

The choice of how much money to hold involves a trade-off between the liquidity of money and the interest income offered by other kinds of assets. The main reason for holding money instead of interest-bearing assets is that money is useful for buying

transaction motive

The main reason that people hold money – to buy things.

things. Economists call this rather obvious motive the **transaction motive**. This rationale for holding money is at the heart of the discussion that follows.[1]

Assumptions

To keep our analysis of the demand for money clear, we need to make a few simplifying assumptions. First, we assume that there are only two kinds of assets: bonds and money. By 'bonds' we mean interest-bearing securities of all kinds. By 'money' we mean currency in circulation and deposits, neither of which is assumed to pay interest.[2]

Second, we assume that income for the typical household is bundled. It arrives once a month at the beginning of the month, say. Spending, by contrast, is spread out over time. We assume that spending occurs at a completely uniform rate throughout the month – that is, that the same amount is spent each day (see Figure 26.1). The mismatch between the timing of money inflow and the timing of money outflow is sometimes called the **non-synchronization of income and spending**.

non-synchronization of income and spending

The mismatch between the timing of money inflow to the household and the timing of money outflow for household expenses.

Finally, we assume that spending for the month is exactly equal to income. Because we are focusing on the transactions demand for money and not on its use as a store of value, this assumption is perfectly reasonable.

Money management and the optimal balance

Given these assumptions, how would a rational person (household) decide how much of monthly income to hold as money and how much to hold as interest-bearing bonds? Suppose Martin deposits his entire salary cheque in his cheque account. He earns €1200 per month. The pattern of Martin's bank account balance is illustrated in Figure 26.2. At the beginning of the month, Martin's balance is €1200. As the month rolls by, Martin runs down his balance, writing cheques or withdrawing cash

---

Figure 26.1 The non-synchronization of income and spending

Income arrives only once a month, but spending takes places continuously.

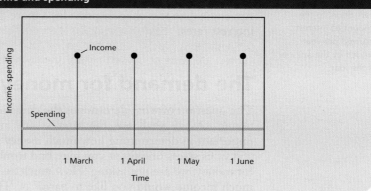

---

[1]The model that we discuss here is known in the economics profession as the Baumol/Tobin model, after the two economists who independently derived it, William Baumol of Princeton University and James Tobin of Yale University.

[2]Remember that the category 'deposits' includes cheque accounts. Many cheque accounts do pay interest. This turns out not to matter for the purposes of our discussion, however. Suppose that bonds pay 10% interest and cheque accounts pay 5%. (Cheque accounts must pay less than bonds. Otherwise, everyone would hold all their wealth in cheque accounts and none in bonds, because cheque accounts are more convenient.) When it comes to choosing whether to hold bonds or money, it is the difference in the interest rates that matters. People are concerned about how much extra interest they will get from holding bonds rather than money. Therefore, in the example above, we could just as well say that bonds pay 5% and money pays 0%, which makes our discussion simpler.

Figure 26.2 Martin's monthly cheque account balances: Strategy 1

Martin could decide to deposit his entire salary (€1200) into his cheque account at the start of the month and run his balance down to zero by the end of the month. In this case, his average balance would be €600.

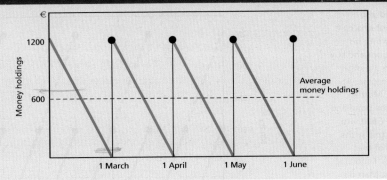

to pay for things he buys. At the end of the month, Martin's bank account balance is down to zero. Just in time, he receives his next month's salary cheque, deposits it, and the process begins again.

One useful statistic we will need to calculate is the *average balance* in Martin's account. Martin spends his money at a constant €40 per day (€40 per day times 30 days per month = €1200). His average balance is just his starting balance (€1200) plus his ending balance (0) divided by 2, or (€1200 + 0)/2 = €600. For the first half of the month Martin has more than his average of €600 on deposit, and for the second half of the month he has less than his average.

Is there anything wrong with Martin's strategy? Yes. Martin is giving up interest on his funds, interest he could earn if he held some of his funds in interest-bearing bonds instead of in his cheque account. How could he manage his funds to give himself more interest?

Instead of depositing his entire salary cheque in his account at the beginning of the month, Martin could put half his salary cheque into his cheque account and buy a bond with the other half. Doing this, he would run out of money in his cheque account halfway through the month. At a spending rate of €40 per day, his initial deposit of €600 would last only 15 days. Martin would have to sell his bond halfway through the month and deposit the €600 from the sale of the bond in his cheque account to pay his bills during the second half of the month.

Martin's money holdings (cheque account balances) using the buy-a-€600-bond strategy are shown in Figure 26.3. He reduces the average amount of money in his cheque account. Comparing the dashed green lines (old strategy) with the solid green lines (buy-a-€600-bond strategy), his average bank balance is exactly half of what it was with the first strategy.[3]

The buy-a-€600-bond strategy seems sensible. The object of this strategy is to keep some funds in bonds, where they could earn interest, instead of as 'idle' money. But why stop there? Another possibility would be for Martin to put only €400 into his account on the first of the month and buy two €400 bonds. The €400 in his account will last for 10 days if he spends €40 per day, so after 10 days he must sell one of the bonds and deposit the €400 from the sale of the bond in his cheque account. This lasts him through the 20th of the month, at which point he sells the second bond and deposit the other €400. He lowers his average money holding (cheque account balance) even further, reducing it to an average of only €200 per month, with correspondingly higher average holdings of interest-earning bonds.

You can imagine Martin going even further. Why not hold all wealth in the form of bonds (where it earns interest) and make transfers from bonds to money for each

---

[3]*Martin's average balance for the first half of the month is (starting balance + ending balance)/2, or (€600 + 0)/2 = €300. His average for the second half of the month is also €300. His average for the month as a whole is thus €300.*

Figure 26.3   Martin's monthly cheque account balances: Strategy 2

Martin could also choose to put one half of his salary into his cheque account and buy a bond with the other half of his income. At mid-month, Martin would sell the bond and deposit the €600 into his account to pay the second half of the month's bills. Following this strategy, Martin's average money holdings would be €300.

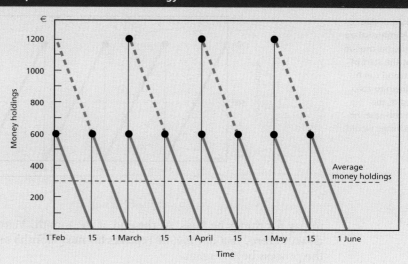

purchase? If selling bonds, transferring funds to cheque accounts and making trips to the bank were without cost, Martin would never hold money for more than an instant. Each time he needed to pay cash for something or write a cheque, he would visit or phone the bank, transfer the exact amount of the transaction to his cheque account, and either withdraw the cash or write the cheque to complete the transaction. Doing this constantly, he would squeeze the most interest possible out of his funds because he would never hold assets that did not earn interest.

In practice, money management of this kind is costly. There are brokerage fees and other costs associated with buying or selling bonds, and time must be spent waiting in a queue at the bank. Yet, it is costly to hold assets in non-interest-bearing form, because they lose potential interest revenue.

We have a trade-off problem of the type that pervades economics. Switching more often from bonds to money raises the interest revenue Martin earns (the more often he switches, the less, on average, he has to hold in his cheque account and the more he can keep in bonds), but this increases his money management costs. Less switching means more interest revenue lost (because average money holdings are higher) but lower money management costs (fewer purchases and sales of bonds, less time spent waiting in bank queues, fewer trips to the bank, and so on).

The optimal balance

There is a level of average money balances that earns Martin the highest profit, taking into account both the interest earned on bonds and the costs paid for switching from bonds to money. This level is his *optimal balance*.

How does the interest rate affect the number of switches Martin makes and thus the average money balance he chooses to hold? It is easy to see why an increase in the interest rate lowers the optimal money balance. If the interest rate is only 2%, it is hardly worthwhile to give up much liquidity by holding bonds instead of cash or cheque balances. But if the interest rate is 30%, the opportunity cost of holding money instead of bonds is high, and people will keep most of their funds in bonds and spend considerable time on managing their money balances. This leads us to conclude:

When interest rates are high, people take advantage of the high return on bonds, so they choose to hold very little money.

Appendix B to this chapter provides a detailed example of this principle.

Figure 26.4 The demand curve for money balances

The quantity of money demanded (the amount of money households and firms wish to hold) is a function of the interest rate. Because the interest rate is the opportunity cost of holding money balances, increases in the interest rate will reduce the quantity of money that firms and households want to hold, and decreases in the interest rate will increase the quantity of money that firms and households want to hold.

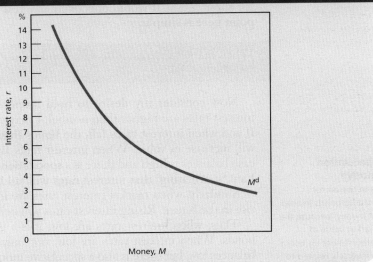

Another way of looking at this is that the interest rate represents the opportunity cost of holding money (and therefore not holding bonds, which pay interest). The higher the interest rate, the higher the opportunity cost of holding money, and the less money people will want to hold.

A demand curve for money, with the interest rate representing the 'price of the money' would look like the curve labelled M^d in Figure 26.4. At higher interest rates, bonds are more attractive than money, so people hold less money because they must make a larger sacrifice in interest forgone for each unit of money they hold. At lower interest rates, the interest earned on bonds is lower, so people hold more money. The curve in Figure 26.4 slopes downwards, just like an ordinary demand curve for, say, oranges or shoes. There is an inverse relationship between the interest rate and the quantity of money demanded.[4]

The speculation motive

A number of theories offer other explanations to why the quantity of money households desire to hold may rise when interest rates fall, and fall when interest rates rise. One involves household expectations and the relationship of interest rates to bond values.

To understand this theory, you need to realize that the market value of most interest-bearing bonds is inversely related to the interest rate. Suppose I bought an 8% bond a year ago for €1000. Now suppose the market interest rate rises to 10%. If I offered to sell my bond for €1000, no one would buy it because anyone can buy a new bond and earn 10% in the market rather than 8% from my bond. But at some lower selling price, my bond becomes attractive to buyers. This is because a lower price increases the actual yield to the buyer of my bond. Suppose I sell you my bond for €500. Since the bond is paying 8% annually on the original €1000 (that is, €80 per year), it is actually paying an annual amount that comes to 16% of your

---

[4]*The theory of money demand presented here assumes that a person knows the exact timing of her or his income and spending path. In practice, both paths have some uncertainty attached to them. For example, some income payments may be unexpectedly delayed a few days or weeks, and some expenditures may arise unexpectedly (such as an unexpected plumbing problem). Because people know that this uncertainty exists, they may choose to hold more money than the strict transactions motive would suggest, as a precaution against unanticipated delays in income receipts or unanticipated expenses. This reason for holding money is sometimes called the precautionary motive.*

investment in the bond (€500 × 0.16 = €80). If you bought that same bond from me for about €800, it would effectively pay you 10% interest (€800 × 0.10 = €80). The point here is simple:

> When market interest rates fall, bond values rise; when market interest rates rise, bond values fall.

Now consider my desire to hold money balances rather than bonds. If market interest rates are higher than normal, I may expect them to come down in the future. If and when interest rates fall, the bonds that I bought when interest rates were high will increase in value. When interest rates are high, the opportunity cost of holding cash balances is high and there is a **speculation motive** for holding bonds in lieu of cash. I am 'speculating' that interest rates will fall in the future.

Similarly, when market interest rates are lower than normal, I may expect them to rise in the future. Rising interest rates will bring about a decline in the value of bonds.

Thus, when interest rates are low, it is a good time to be holding money and not bonds. When interest rates are low, not only is the opportunity cost of holding cash balances low, but there is also a speculative motive for holding a larger amount of money. Why should I put money into bonds now when I expect interest rates to rise in the future? (For more on the interaction between the bond market and the money market, see the Application 'The Bond Market, the Money Market and the Speculation Motive'.)

speculation motive

One reason for holding bonds instead of money: because the market value of interest-bearing bonds is inversely related to the interest rate, investors may wish to hold bonds when interest rates are high with the hope of selling them when interest rates fall.

The total demand for money

So far we have talked only about household demand for cheque account balances. But the total quantity of money demanded in the economy is the sum of the demand for cheque account balances and cash by both households *and firms*.

The trade-off for firms is the same as it was for Martin. Like households, firms must manage their money. They have payrolls to meet and purchases to make; they receive cash and cheques from sales; and many firms that deal with the public must return change – so they need cash in the register. Thus, just like Martin, firms need money to engage in ordinary transactions.

But firms as well as households can hold their assets in interest-earning form. As was true for Martin, holding cash and maintaining cheque account balances has an opportunity cost for firms. Firms manage their assets just as households do, keeping some in cash, some in their cheque accounts and some in bonds. A higher interest rate raises the opportunity cost of money for firms as well as for households and thus reduces the demand for money. A lower interest rate reduces the opportunity cost of holding money and increases the demand for it.

The same trade-off holds for cash. We all walk around with some money in our pockets, for routine transactions. We carry, on average, about what we think we will need. Why not more? Because there are costs – risks of being robbed, and forgone interest.

In sum:

> At any given moment, there is a demand for money – for cash and cheque account balances. Although households and firms need to hold balances for everyday transactions, their demand has a limit. For both households and firms, the quantity of money demanded at this moment depends on the opportunity cost of holding money, a cost determined by the interest rate.

Transactions volume and the price level

The money demand curve in Figure 26.4 is a function of the interest rate. There are other factors besides the interest rate, that influence total desired money holdings. One is the euro value of transactions made during a given period of time.

Applications

The bond market, the money market, and the speculation motive

People are often confused when business-page headlines read 'Bonds Fall, Pushing up Interest Rates' or 'Bonds rise, Driving Yields Down'. Nonetheless, it is true that the current market price or value of all fixed-rate bonds, whether US Treasury Bonds or German corporate bonds, falls in value when interest rates rise, and rises in value when interest rates fall.

To see why, consider Steffi, a German decorator who bought a 10-year German government bond with a fixed rate of 10% for €1000. By buying that bond, Steffi has agreed to accept a return on her money of 10% for ten years. This means a cheque for €100 every year with a promise that her €1000 will be returned at the end of 10 years.

While the German government has no obligation to repay the €1000 before the bond matures in ten years, Steffi may need the money before ten years are up. To get her money back earlier, she can call a bank or broker and sell the bond. In fact, there is a huge market for existing bonds, and their prices are posted in the newspapers every day. To sell the bond, the bank has to find a buyer, and the amount a buyer would be willing to pay depends on the current rate of interest.

Suppose Steffi wants to sell her bond two years after she purchased it. The bond still has eight years left to maturity. Assume that the Bundesbank (the German central bank) has pushed rates for eight-year bonds to 12%. If someone paid €1000 for Steffi's bond today, they would be getting only €100 (10%) interest per year. The same person could be getting interest of €120 per year, or 12%, by buying a newly issued €1000 bond. The result: Steffi's broker will not be able to sell her bond for €1000. Instead, Steffi will have to take a loss because her bond's value has declined.

Do bond values really decline in the real world? Absolutely. When the Federal Reserve raised US interest rates in 1994, the value of outstanding bonds traded in the market fell substantially! Similarly, during Mexico's peso crises in 1995, Mexican interest rates shot up sharply, and Mexican government bonds lost a lot of their value.

Another way to see the same connection between the bond market and the money market is to think of a case in which the demand for bonds increases. Suppose that because of excess demand for bonds in Germany, the value of Steffi's bond goes up to €1100. Someone who is willing to pay €1100 for Steffi's bond *must reveal that he or she is willing to accept an annual yield of less than 10%*. After all, €100 is only 9.1% of €1100. In addition, the buyer who pays €1100 will get back only €1000 when the bond matures. Higher bond prices mean the interest rate that bond buyers are willing to accept is lower than before! If buyers are willing to accept 9% on old bonds, they will accept 9% on new bonds.

Bond prices and interest rates are two sides of the same coin. A 'rally' in the bond market means bond prices have gone up and that interest rates, or bond 'yields', have gone down. Similarly, when the bond market 'drops', interest rates, or yields, have gone up.

These effects have important implications for money demand. Assume households choose only between holding their assets as money (which does not earn interest) or as bonds (which do earn interest). If households and firms believe interest rates are historically high and they are likely to fall, it is a good time to hold bonds. Why? Because a drop in rates means bond values will rise, in a sense earning bondholders a bonus. When interest rates are high and expected to fall, demand for bonds is likely to be high and money demand is likely to be low. Similarly, if people see interest rates as low and expect them to rise, it is not a good time to be holding bonds. Why? Because if interest rates rise, bond holders suffer losses. When interest rates are low, money demand is likely to be high and the demand for bonds is likely to be low. Thus, we have another reason for the negative relationship between interest rates and money demand. As we mentioned in the text, this is the *speculation motive* for holding money.

Suppose Martin's income were to double. Instead of making €1200 in purchases each month, he makes €2400 in purchases. He needs to hold more money. Why? To buy more things, he needs more money.

What is true for Martin is true for the economy as a whole. The total demand for money in the economy depends on the total euro volume of transactions made. The total euro volume of transactions in the economy, in turn, depends on two things: the total *number* of transactions and the average transaction *amount*. While there are no data on the actual number of transactions in the economy, a reasonable indicator is likely to be aggregate output (income) (Y). A rise in aggregate output – real GDP – means there is more economic activity. Firms are producing and selling more output, more people are on payrolls, and household incomes are higher. In short, there are more transactions, and firms and households together will hold more money when they are engaging in more transactions. Thus, an increase in aggregate output (income) increases the demand for money.

Figure 26.5 shows a shift of the money demand curve resulting from an increase in Y:

> For a given interest rate, a higher level of output means an increase in the *number* of transactions and more demand for money. The money demand curve shifts to the right when Y rises. Similarly, a decrease in Y means a decrease in the number of transactions and a lower demand for money. When Y falls the money demand curve shifts to the left.

The amount of money needed by firms and households to facilitate their day-to-day transactions also depends on the average *value* of each transaction. In turn, the average amount of each transaction depends on prices, or rather, on the *price level*. If all prices, including the price of labour (the wage rate) were to double, firms and households would need twice the money balances to carry out their day-to-day transactions – each transaction would require twice as much money. If the price of your lunch increases from €7.00 to €14.00, you will begin carrying more cash. If your end-of-the-month bills are twice as high as they used to be, you will keep more money in your cheque account.

> Increases in the price level shift the money demand curve to the right, and decreases in the price level shift the money demand curve to the left. Even though the number of transactions may not have changed, the quantity of money needed to engage in them has.

The determinants of money demand: a review

Table 26.1 summarizes everything we have said about the demand for money. First, because the interest rate (r) is the opportunity cost of holding money balances for both firms and households, increases in the interest rate decrease the quantity of money

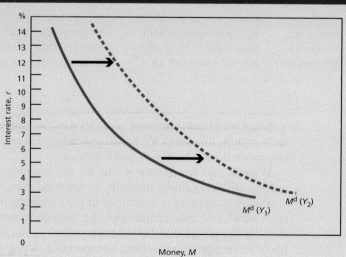

Figure 26.5 An increase in aggregate output (income) (Y) shifts the money demand curve to the right

An increase in Y means that there is more economic activity. Firms are producing and selling more, and households are earning more income and buying more. There are thus more transactions, for which money is needed. As a result, both firms and households are likely to increase their holdings of money balances at a given interest rate.

Table 26.1 Determinants of money demand

1. The interest rate: r (negative effect)
2. The euro volume of transactions (positive effect)
   a. Aggregate output (income): Y (positive effect)
   b. The price level: P (positive effect)

---

demanded; decreases in the interest rate will increase the quantity of money demanded. Thus, the quantity of money demanded is a negative function of the interest rate.

The demand for money also depends on the euro volume of transactions in a given period. The euro volume of transactions depends on both aggregate output (income), Y, and the price level, P. The relationship of money demand to Y and the relationship of money demand to P are both positive. Increases in Y or in P will shift the money demand curve to the right: decreases in Y or P will shift the money demand curve to the left.

Some common pitfalls

We need to consider several pitfalls in thinking about money demand. First, when we spoke in earlier chapters about the demand for goods and services, we were speaking of demand as a *flow variable* – something measured over a period of time. If you say your demand for coffee is three cups, you need to specify whether you are talking about three cups per hour, three cups per day or three cups per week. In macroeconomics, consumption and saving are flow variables. We consume and save continuously, but we express consumption and saving in time-period terms, such as €600 *per month*.

Money demand is *not* a flow measure. It is a *stock variable,* measured at a given point in time. It answers the question: how much money do firms and households desire to hold at a specific point in time, given the current interest rate, volume of economic activity, and price level?

Second, many people think of money demand and saving as roughly the same – they are not. Say that in a given year a household has an income of €50,000 and expenses of €47,000. It saves €3000 during the year. At the beginning of the year the household had no debt and €100,000 in assets. Since the household saved €3000 during the year, it has €103,000 in assets at the end of the year. Some of the €103,000 is held in stocks, some in bonds, some in other forms of securities and some in money. How much the household chooses to hold in the form of money is its demand for money. Depending on the interest rate and the household's transactions, the part of the €103,000 that it chooses to hold in the form of money could range from a few hundred to many thousands of euros. How much of its assets a household holds in the form of money is different from how much of its income it spends during the year.

Finally, recall the difference between a shift in a demand curve and a movement along the curve. The money demand curve in Figure 26.4 shows optimal money balances as a function of the interest rate *ceteris paribus*, all else equal. Changes in the interest rate cause movements along the curve – *changes in the quantity of money demanded*. Changes in real GDP (Y) or in the price level (P) cause shifts of the curve as shown in Figure 26.5 – *changes in demand*.

The equilibrium interest rate

We are now in a position to examine a key question in macroeconomics: how is the interest rate determined in the economy?

Financial markets (what we call the money market) work very well in most industrialized countries. Almost all financial markets clear – that is, almost all reach an equilibrium where quantity demanded equals quantity supplied.

In the money market, the point at which the quantity of money demanded equals the quantity of money supplied determines the equilibrium interest rate in the economy.

This sounds simple but it requires elaboration.

Supply and demand in the money market

We saw in Chapter 25 that the central bank can control the money supply by using one or more of its pertinent instruments. If the ECB wants the money supply to be €900 billion, it can aim for this target by changing the required reserve ratio, by changing the discount rate, or by purchasing or selling securities. In this sense, the supply of money is completely determined by the central bank. If the central bank's money supply target is independent of the interest rate, a plausible assumption, we can draw the money supply curve in Figure 26.6 diagram as a vertical line.

We will see in Chapter 32 that some central banks have indeed been observed to respond to changes in the state of the economy, and perhaps of the interest rate. In such a case the money supply curve would not be vertical. This would not only complicate matters considerably, but also does not seem to be the rule. Many countries have central bank laws that almost bar the central bank from responding to how the economy is doing. The ECB is a particularly strong case in point. So we will assume for now that the money supply curve is vertical. This assumption is relaxed in Chapter 32.

Figure 26.7 superimposes the vertical money supply curve on the downward-sloping money demand curve. Only at interest rate r^* is the quantity of money in circulation (the money supply) equal to the quantity of money demanded. To understand why r^* is an equilibrium, we need to ask what adjustments would take place if the interest rate were not r^*.

To understand the adjustment mechanism, keep in mind that borrowing and lending is a continuous process. The government sells securities (bonds) more or less continuously to finance the deficit. When it does, it is borrowing, and must pay interest to attract bond buyers. Buyers of government bonds, in essence, lend money to the government, just as buyers of corporate bonds lend money to corporations that wish to finance investment projects.

Consider first r_1 in Figure 26.7. At r_1, the quantity of money demanded is M_1^d, and the quantity of money supplied exceeds the quantity of money demanded. This means there is more money in circulation than households and firms want to hold. At r_1, firms and households will attempt to reduce their money holdings by buying bonds.

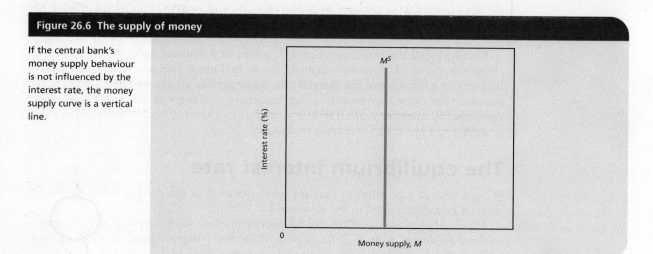

Figure 26.6 The supply of money

If the central bank's money supply behaviour is not influenced by the interest rate, the money supply curve is a vertical line.

M^S

Interest rate (%)

0

Money supply, M

Figure 26.7 Adjustments in the money market

Equilibrium exists in the money market when the supply of money is equal to the demand for money: $M^d = M^s$. At r_1, the quantity of money supplied exceeds the quantity of money demanded, and the interest rate will fall. At r_2, the quantity demanded exceeds the quantity supplied, and the interest rate will rise. Only at r^* is equilibrium achieved.

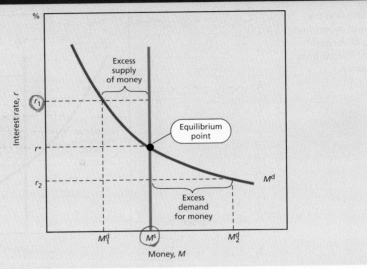

When there is money in circulation looking for a way to earn interest – when demand for bonds is high – those looking to borrow money by selling bonds will find that they can do so at a lower interest rate.

If the interest rate is initially high enough to create an excess supply of money, the interest rate will immediately fall, discouraging people from moving out of money and into bonds.

Now consider r_2, where the quantity of money demanded (M_2^d) exceeds the supply of money currently in circulation – households and firms do not have enough money on hand to facilitate ordinary transactions. They will try to adjust their holdings by shifting assets out of bonds and into their cheque accounts. At the same time, the continuous flow of new bonds being issued must also be absorbed. The government and corporations can sell bonds in an environment where people are adjusting their asset holdings to shift out of bonds only by offering a higher interest rate to the people who buy them.

If the interest rate is initially low enough to create an excess demand for money, the interest rate will immediately rise, discouraging people from moving out of bonds and into money.

Changing the money supply to affect the interest rate

With an understanding of equilibrium in the money market, we can now see how the central bank can affect the interest rate. Suppose, the current interest rate is 13% and the ECB wants to reduce it. To do so, it would expand the money supply, using one of the instruments discussed in Chapter 25: the required reserve rate, the discount rate, open market operations or foreign exchange market intervention. Figure 26.9 shows that such an expansion of the money supply, expansionary **monetary policy**, would shift the initial money supply curve, M_0^s, to the right, to M_1^s.

monetary policy
The behaviour of the central bank regarding the money supply.

At the 13% interest rate, there is an excess supply of money. This immediately puts downward pressure on the interest rate as households and firms try to buy bonds with their money to earn that high interest rate. As this happens, the interest rate falls, until

Figure 26.8 The effect of an increase in the supply of money on the interest rate

An increase in the supply of money from M_0^s to M_1^s lowers the rate of interest from 13% to 7%.

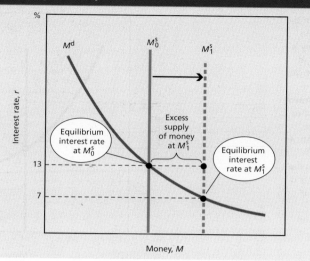

it reaches the new equilibrium interest rate of 7%. At this point, $M_1^s = M^d$, and the market is in equilibrium.

If the central bank wanted to drive the interest rate *up*, it would reduce the money supply. It could do so by increasing the reserve requirement, by raising the discount rate, by selling government securities in the open market, or by selling foreign exchange. Whichever tool it chooses, the result would be a lower supply of money. M_0^s in Figure 26.8 would shift to the left, and the equilibrium interest rate would rise. (As an exercise, draw a graph of this situation.)

Increases in *Y* and shifts in the money demand curve

Changes in the supply of money are not the only factors that influence the equilibrium interest rate. Shifts in money demand can do the same thing.

Recall that the demand for money depends on both the interest rate and the volume of transactions. As a rough measure of the volume of transactions, we use *Y*, the level of aggregate output (income). Remember that the relationship between money demand and *Y* is positive – increases in *Y* mean a higher level of real economic activity. When more is produced, income is higher, and there are more transactions in the economy. Consequently, in the aggregate firms' and households' demand for money is higher.

An increase in *Y* shifts the money demand curve to the right.

Figure 26.9 illustrates such a shift. *Y* increases, causing money demand to shift from M_0^d to M_1^d. The result is an increase in the equilibrium level of the interest rate from 7% to 12%. A decrease in *Y* shifts M^d to the left, and the equilibrium interest rate falls.

The money demand curve also shifts when the price level changes. If the price level rises, the money demand curve shifts to the right, because people need more money for their day-to-day transactions. With the money supply unchanged, however, the interest rate must rise to reduce the quantity of money demanded to the unchanged quantity of money supplied – a movement *along* the money supply curve.

An increase in the price level is like an increase in *Y* in that both events increase the demand for money. The result is an increase in the equilibrium interest rate.

Figure 26.9 The effect of an increase in income on the interest rate

An increase in aggregate output (income) shifts the money demand curve from M_0^d to M_1^d, which raises the equilibrium interest rate from 7% to 12%.

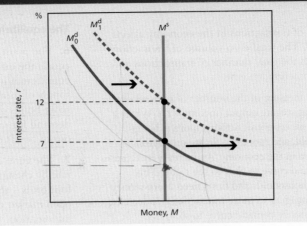

If the price level *falls*, the money demand curve shifts to the left, because people need less money for their transactions. With the money supply fixed, the interest rate must fall to increase the quantity of money demanded to the unchanged quantity of money supplied.

A decrease in the price level leads to a decrease in the equilibrium interest rate.

Looking ahead: the central bank and monetary policy

We now know that the central bank can affect the interest rate by changing the quantity of money supplied. If it increases the quantity of money, the interest rate falls; if it decreases the quantity of money, the interest rate rises.

But we have not yet said *why* the central bank might want to change the interest rate or what happens in the goods market when the interest rate changes. We have hinted at why: a low interest rate stimulates spending, particularly investmen; a high interest rate reduces spending. By changing the interest rate, the central bank can change aggregate output (income). In the next chapter, we will combine our discussions of the goods and money markets and examine how the interest rate affects the equilibrium level of aggregate output (income) (Y) in the goods market.

Summary

1. *Interest* is the fee a borrower pays to a lender for the use of his or her funds. The *interest rate* is the annual interest payment on a loan expressed as a percentage of the loan; it is equal to the amount of interest received per year divided by the amount of the loan. Although there are many different interest rates in the global economy, we assume here that there is only one interest rate. This simplifies our analysis but still provides us

with a tool for understanding how the various parts of the macroeconomy relate to each other.

The demand for money

2. The demand for money depends negatively on the interest rate. The higher the interest rate, the higher the opportunity cost (more interest forgone) of holding money, and the less money people will want to hold. An increase in the interest rate reduces the demand for money, and the money demand curve slopes downwards.

3. The volume of transactions in the economy affects money demand. The total euro volume of transactions depends on both the total number of transactions and the average transaction amount.

4. A reasonable measure of the number of transactions in the economy is aggregate output (income) (Y). When Y rises, there is more economic activity, more is being produced and sold, and more people are on payrolls – more transactions in the economy. An increase in Y causes the money demand curve to shift to the right. This follows because households and firms need more money when they are engaging in more transactions. A decrease in Y causes the money demand curve to shift left.

5. Changes in the price level affect the average euro amount of each transaction. *Increases* in the price level increase the demand for money (shift the money demand curve to the right) because households and firms need more money for their expenditures. *Decreases*

in the price level decrease the demand for money (shift the money demand curve to the left).

The equilibrium interest rate

6. The point at which the quantity of money supplied equals the quantity of money demanded determines the equilibrium interest rate in the economy. An excess supply of money causes households and firms to buy more bonds driving the interest rate down. An excess demand for money causes households and firms to move out of bonds driving the interest rate up.

7. The central bank can affect the equilibrium interest rate by changing the supply of money using one of its four tools – the required reserve ratio, the discount rate, open market operations or foreign exchange market intervention.

8. An increase in the price level is like an increase in Y in that both events cause an increase in money demand. The result is an increase in the equilibrium interest rate. A decrease in the price level leads to reduced money demand and a decrease in the equilibrium interest rate.

Review Terms and Concepts

interest
interest rate
monetary policy

non-synchronization of income and spending
speculation motive
transaction motive

Problem Set

1. A government bond pays €40 in a year.
a. what is the interest rate on the bond if its price today is: (1) €800, (2) €850, (3) €900? .5%, 4,7%, 4.4%
b. What type of relationship between the price of a bond and its return is suggested by your answers to (a)? 1/20
c. How much should the bond be worth today to yield an interest rate of 8%? 500÷

2. At the end of 1998, interest rates in Japan were very low. However, households believed that interest rates were likely to rise eventually. This implies that the quantity of money demanded in Japan at the end of 1998 was quite high. Using the concepts of speculative motive and transaction motive for money, explain why.

3. The spread of automated teller machines has made it easier to convert deposits into cash. What has been the effect on average cash balances held by the public? What has this done to the demand for money as a whole?

4. During the fourth quarter of 1993, real GDP in the United States grew at an annual rate of over 7%. During 1994, the economy continued to expand with modest inflation (Y rose at a rate of 4% and P increased about 3%). At the beginning of 1994, the prime interest

rate (the interest rate that banks offer their best, least risky customers) stood at 6%, where it remained for over a year. By the beginning of 1995, the prime rate had increased to over 8.5%.
a. Using money supply and money demand curves, show the effects of the increase in Y and P on interest rates assuming *no change* in the money supply.
b. On a separate graph, show that the interest rate can rise even if the US Federal Reserve expands the money supply as long as it does so more slowly than money demand is increasing.

5. Illustrate the following situations using supply and demand curves for money:
a. The central bank buys bonds in the open market during a recession.
b. During a period of rapid inflation, the central bank increases the reserve requirement.
c. The central bank acts to hold interest rates constant during a period of high inflation.
d. During a period of no growth in GDP and zero inflation, the central bank lowers the discount rate.
e. During a period of rapid real growth of GDP, the central bank acts to increase the reserve requirement.

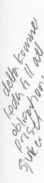

6. During a recession, interest rates may fall even if the central bank takes no action to expand the money supply. Why? Use a graph to explain.

7. The demand for money in a country is given by

$$M^d = 10{,}000 - 10{,}000r + Y$$

where M^d is money demand in local currency units, r is the interest rate (a 10% interest rate means $r = 0.1$), and Y is national income. Assume Y is initially 5000.

a. Graph the amount of money demanded (on the horizontal axis) against the interest rate (on the vertical axis).

b. Suppose the money supply (M^s) is set by the central bank at 10,000. On the same graph you drew for (a), add the money supply curve. What is the equilibrium

rate of interest? Explain how you arrived at your answer.

c. Suppose income rises from $Y = 5000$ to $Y = 7500$. What happens to the money demand curve you drew in (a)? Draw the new curve, if there is one. What happens to the equilibrium interest rate if the central bank doesn't change the supply of money?

d. If the central bank wants to keep the equilibrium interest rate at the same value as it was in (b), by how much should it increase or decrease the supply of money given the new level of national income?

e. Suppose the shift in (b) has occurred, and the money supply remains at 10,000, but there is no observed change in the interest rate. What might have happened that could explain this?

Appendix A to Chapter 26

The Various Interest Rates and How They Are Linked

To simplify the argument, the text speaks of *the* interest rate, pretending there is only one. In reality a spectrum of interest rates exists, depending on whether we lend or borrow, on how trustworthy the borrower is, and on how long the loan is to be extended. What justifies working with only one interest rate in our models is that all the different interest rates that exist in reality tend to move up or down with one another. We first make this point by looking into the relationship between interest rates of different *maturities*, or *terms*. After this we discuss briefly some of the main interest rates in the European economies.

The term structure of interest rates

The *term structure of interest rates* is the relationship between the interest rates offered on securities of different maturities. How are these different rates related? Does a two-year security (that promises to repay principal, plus interest, after two years) pay a lower annual rate than a one-year security (to be repaid, with interest, after one year)? What happens to the rate of interest offered on one-year securities if the rate of interest on two-year securities increases?

Assume you want to invest some money for two years and at the end of the two years you want it back. Assume you want to buy government securities. For this analysis, we restrict your choices to two: (1) you can buy a two-year security today and hold it for two years, at which time you cash it in (we will assume that the interest rate on the two-year security is 9% per year); or (2) you can buy a one-year security today. At the end of one year, you must cash this security in; you can then buy another one-year security. At the end of the second

year, you will cash in the second security. Assume the interest rate on the first one-year security is 8%.

Which would you prefer? Currently, you don't have enough data to answer this question. To consider choice 2 sensibly, you need to know the interest rate on the one-year security that you intend to buy in the second year. This rate, will not be known until the second year. All you know now is the rate on the two-year security and the rate on the current one-year security. To decide what to do, you must form an expectation of the rate on the one-year security a year from now. If you expect the one-year rate (8%) to remain the same in the second year, you should buy the two-year security. You would earn 9% per year on the two-year security but only 8% per year on the two one-year securities. If you expect the one-year rate to rise to 12% a year from now, you should make the second choice. You would earn 8% in the first year, and you expect to earn 12% in the second year. The expected rate of return over the two years is about 10%, which is better than the 9% you can get on the two-year security. If you expected the one-year rate a year from now to be 10%, it would not matter very much which of the two choices you made. The rate of return over the two-year period would be roughly 9% for both choices.

We now alter the focus of our discussion to get to the topic we are really interested in – how the two-year rate is determined. Assume the one-year rate has been set by the central bank and it is 8%. Also assume that people expect the one-year rate a year from now to be 10%. What, is the two-year rate? According to a theory called the *expectations theory of the term structure of interest rates*, the two-year rate is equal to the average of the current one-year rate and the one-year rate expected a year from now. In this example, the two-year rate would be 9% (the average of 8% and 10%).

If the two-year rate were lower than the average of the two one-year rates, people would not be indifferent as to which security they held. They would want to hold only the short-term, one-year securities. To find a buyer for a two-year security, the seller would be forced to increase the interest rate it offers on the two-year security until it is equal to the average of the current one-year rate and the expected one-year rate for next year. The interest rate on the two-year security will continue to rise until people are once again indifferent between one two-year security and two one-year securities.*

Let us now return to central bank behaviour. We know the ECB can affect the short-term interest rate by changing the money supply. But does this also affect long-term interest rates? The answer is 'somewhat'. Since the two-year rate is an average of the current one-year rate and the expected one-year rate a year from now, the ECB influences the two-year rate to the extent that it influences the current one-year rate. The same holds for three-year rates and beyond. The current short-term rate is a means by which the ECB can influence longer-term rates.

In addition, ECB behaviour may directly affect people's expectations of the future short-term rates, which will then affect long-term rates. In recent years, when Alan Greenspan, the chair of the US Federal

Reserve, testified before Congress that he was thinking about raising short-term interest rates, people's expectations of higher future short-term interest rates increased. These expectations then moved up current long-term interest rates.

Types of interest rates

There is some diversity in interest rate categories between countries. This is often due to differences in substance reflecting different institutions. Sometimes it is only a matter of putting different labels on the same thing. The main category are more or less the same, however. For example, the IMF country pages report five groups of interest rates.

■ *Discount rate / bank rate* This is the rate at which the central bank lends or discounts eligible paper for deposit money banks.
■ *Treasury bill rate / money market rate* These are short-term interest rates. The treasury bill rate refers to government securities that mature in less than a year. The money market rate is the rate at which short-term borrowings are effected between financial institutions.
■ *Deposit rates* These rates are offered to customers for demand, time or savings deposits.
■ *Lending rates* These rates apply to short- and medium-term lending to the private sector. Rates are tailored to the creditworthiness of borrowers and objectives of financing.
■ *Government bond rates* Governments securities with terms of one year ore more are called government bonds. Terms vary between one year and 30 years, and different terms have different interest rates. Bonds can be traded before maturity; then yields to maturity are the important factor, not the interest rate.

---

*For longer terms, additional future rates must be averaged in. For a three-year security, for example, the expected one-year rate a year from now and the expected one-year rate two years from now are added to the current one-year rate and averaged.

Appendix B to Chapter 26

The Demand for Money: A Numerical Example

This Appendix presents a numerical example showing how optimal money management behaviour can be derived.

We have seen that the interest rate represents the opportunity cost of holding funds in non-interest-bearing cheque accounts (as opposed to bonds, which yield interest). We have also seen that there are costs involved in switching from bonds to money. Given these costs, our objective is to determine the optimum amount of money for an individual to hold. The optimal average level of money holdings is the amount that maximizes the profits from money management. Interest is earned on average bond holdings, but the cost per switch multiplied by the number of switches

must be subtracted from interest revenue to obtain the net profit from money management.

Suppose the interest rate is 0.05 (5%), that it costs €2 each time a bond is sold, and that the proceeds from the sale are deposited in one's cheque account. Suppose also that the individual's income is €1200 and that this income is spent evenly throughout the period. This situation is depicted in the top half of Table 26A.1. The optimum value for average money holdings is the value that achieves the largest possible profit in column 6 of the table. When the interest rate is 5%, the optimum average money holdings are €150 (which means the individual makes three switches from bonds to money).

Table 26A.1 Optimum money holdings

1 Number of switches[a]	2 Average money holdings[b]	3 Average bond holdings[c]	4 Interest earned[d]	5 Cost of switching[e]	6 Net profit[f]
Assumptions: Interest rate $r = 0.05$. Cost of switching from bonds into money equals €2 per transaction.					
		$r = 5\%$			
0	€600.00	€ 0.00	€ 0.00	€0.00	€0.00
1	300.00	300.00	15.00	2.00	13.00
2	200.00	400.00	20.00	4.00	16.00
3	150.00*	450.00	22.50	6.00	16.50
4	120.00	480.00	24.00	8.00	16.00
Assumptions: Interest rate $r = 0.03$. Cost of switching from bonds into money equals €2 per transaction.					
		$r = 3\%$			
0	€600.00	€ 0.00	€ 0.00	€0.00	€0.00
1	300.00	300.00	9.00	2.00	7.00
2	200.00*	400.00	12.00	4.00	8.00
3	150.00	450.00	13.50	6.00	7.50
4	120.00	480.00	14.40	8.00	6.40

*Optimum money holdings. [a]That is, the number of times you sell a bond. [b]Calculated as 600/(col. 1 + 1). [c]Calculated as 600 – col. 2. [d]Calculated as $r \times$ col. 3, where r is the interest rate. [e]Calculated as $t \times$ col. 1, where t is the cost per switch (€2). [f]Calculated as col. 4 – col. 5.

In the bottom half of Table 26A.1, the same calculations are performed for an interest rate of 3% rather than 5%. In this case, the optimum average money holding is €200 (which means the person/household makes two switches from bonds to money rather than three). The lower interest rate has thus led to an increase in the optimum average money holdings. Under the assumption that people behave optimally, the demand for money is thus a negative function of the interest rate: the lower the rate, the more money on average is held, and the higher the rate, the less money on average is held.

Money, the Interest Rate and Output: Analysis and Policy

goods market

The market in which goods and services are exchanged and in which the equilibrium level of aggregate output is determined.

money market

The market in which financial instruments are exchanged and in which the equilibrium level of the interest rate is determined.

Chapters 23 and 24 discussed the market for goods and services – the **goods market**. Without even mentioning money, the money market or the interest rate we described how the equilibrium level of aggregate output (income) (Y) is determined. For given levels of planned investment spending (I), government spending (G) and net taxes (T), a specific equilibrium level of output in the economy results.

Chapters 25 and 26 discussed the financial market, or **money market**. Without really referring to the goods market we explained how the equilibrium level of the interest rate is determined.

The goods market and the money market are not independent, however. What happens in the money market affects the goods market, and what happens in the goods market affects the money market. Only by analysing the two markets together can we determine the values of aggregate output (income) (Y) and the interest rate (r) that are consistent with the existence of equilibrium in *both* markets.

Looking at both markets together also reveals how fiscal policy reaches over into the money market and how monetary policy reaches over into the goods market. By taking into account the interdependence of the two markets we specifically show how open market purchases of government securities (or other ways to expand the money supply) affect the equilibrium level of national output and income, and how fiscal policy measures (such as tax cuts) affect interest rates and investment spending.

European Monetary Union derives much of its importance from this close interaction between the goods and the money market. Because of this link, the reorientation of monetary policy in Europe in the course of the transition to the euro will not only be felt in financial markets, but in goods markets and movements of national incomes as well.

The links between the goods market and the money market

There are two key *links* between the goods market and the money market.

Link 1: income and the demand for money

The first link between the goods market and the money market exists because the demand for money depends on income. As aggregate output (income) (Y) increases, the number of transactions requiring the use of money increases. (You saw this in Chapter 26.) An increase in output, with the interest rate held constant, leads to an increase in money demand.

Income, which is determined in the goods market, influences the demand for money in the money market.

Link 2: planned investment spending and the interest rate

The second link between the goods market and the money market exists because planned investment spending (I) depends on the interest rate (r). In Chapters 23 and 24 we assumed that planned investment spending is fixed at a certain level, but we did so only to simplify that discussion. In practice, investment is not fixed. Rather, it depends on a number of key economic variables. One is the interest rate. The higher the interest rate, the lower the level of planned investment spending.

> The interest rate, which is determined in the money market, affects planned investment in the goods market.

Investment, the interest rate and the goods market

The relationship between the level of planned investment and the interest rate is a negative one:

> When the interest rate falls, planned investment rises.
> When the interest rate rises, planned investment falls.

To see why, recall that *investment* refers to the purchase of new capital – new machines and plants. Firms undertake investment projects because they expect profits from them in the future. A firm's investment decision depends on whether the expected profits from the project justify its costs. Usually, a major cost factor of an investment project is the interest cost.

Consider a firm opening a new plant, or the investment required to open an ice cream shop. When a manufacturing firm builds a new plant, the contractor must be paid at the time the plant is built. To open a new ice cream shop, the entrepreneur needs freezers, tables, chairs, light fittings and signs. These too must be paid for when they are installed.

The money that pays for such projects is generally borrowed and paid back over an extended period. The real cost of an investment project depends in part on the interest rate – the cost of borrowing. When the interest rate rises, borrowing becomes more expensive, and fewer projects are likely to be undertaken; increasing the interest rate, *ceteris paribus*, is likely to reduce the level of planned investment spending. When the interest rate falls, borrowing becomes less costly, and more investment projects are likely to be undertaken; reducing the interest rate, *ceteris paribus*, is likely to increase the level of planned investment spending.

The relationship between the interest rate and planned investment is illustrated by the downward-sloping demand curve in Figure 27.1. The higher the interest rate, the lower the level of planned investment. At an interest rate of 3%, planned investment is I_0. When the interest rate rises from 3% to 6%, planned investment falls from I_0 to I_1. As the interest rate falls, however, more projects become profitable, so more investment is undertaken.

We can now use the fact that planned investment depends on the interest rate to examine how this relationship affects planned aggregate expenditure (AE). Recall that planned aggregate expenditure in the global economy is the sum of consumption, planned investment and government purchases. That is,

$$AE \equiv C + I + G$$

We just learned that there are many possible levels of I, each corresponding to a different interest rate (as illustrated in Figure 27.1). When the interest rate changes, planned investment changes. Therefore, a change in the interest rate (r) will lead to a change in total planned spending ($C + I + G$) as well.[1]

---

[1] *When we look at household behaviour in the macroeconomy in detail in Chapter 33, you will see that consumption spending (C) may also be stimulated by lower interest rates and discouraged by higher interest rates.*

Figure 27.1 Planned investment schedule

Planned investment spending is a negative function of the interest rate.

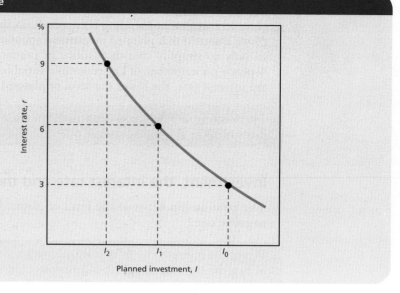

Figure 27.2 shows how planned aggregate expenditure changes when the interest rate rises from 3% to 6%. At the higher interest rate, planned investment is lower; planned aggregate expenditure thus shifts *downwards*. Recall from Chapters 23 and 24: a fall in any component of aggregate spending has an even larger (or 'multiplier') effect on equilibrium income (Y). When the interest rate rises, planned investment (and planned aggregate expenditure) falls, and equilibrium output (income) falls by even more than the fall in planned investment. In Figure 27.2, equilibrium Y falls from Y_0 to Y_1 when the interest rate rises from 3% to 6%.

We can summarize the effects of a change in the interest rate on the equilibrium level of output:

An increase in the interest rate from 3% to 6% lowers planned aggregate expenditure, and thus reduces equilibrium income from Y_0 to Y_1.

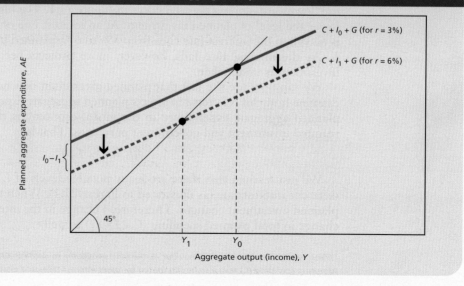

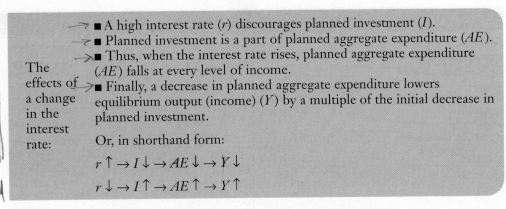

The effects of a change in the interest rate:

- A high interest rate (r) discourages planned investment (I).
- Planned investment is a part of planned aggregate expenditure (AE).
- Thus, when the interest rate rises, planned aggregate expenditure (AE) falls at every level of income.
- Finally, a decrease in planned aggregate expenditure lowers equilibrium output (income) (Y) by a multiple of the initial decrease in planned investment.

Or, in shorthand form:

$$r \uparrow \rightarrow I \downarrow \rightarrow AE \downarrow \rightarrow Y \downarrow$$
$$r \downarrow \rightarrow I \uparrow \rightarrow AE \uparrow \rightarrow Y \uparrow$$

As you can see, the equilibrium level of output (Y) is not determined solely by events in the goods market, as we assumed in our earlier simplified discussions. The reason is that the money market affects the level of the interest rate, which then affects planned investment in the goods market. There is a different equilibrium level of Y for every possible level of the interest rate (r). The final level of equilibrium Y depends on the interest rate resulting from events in the money market.

The *IS* curve

There is another way to graph what we have just learned. We know that in the goods market, there is an equilibrium level of aggregate output (income) (Y) for each value of the interest rate (r). Given a value of r, we can determine the equilibrium value of Y. We also know from Figure 27.2 that the equilibrium value of Y falls when r rises and rises when r falls. There is thus a *negative* relationship between the equilibrium value of Y and r because of the negative relationship between planned investment and the interest rate. When the interest rate rises, planned investment (I) falls, leading to a decrease in the equilibrium value of Y. The negative relationship between the equilibrium value of Y and r is shown in Figure 27.3. This curve is called the **IS curve**.[2] Each point on the *IS* curve represents the equilibrium point in the goods market for a given interest rate.

IS curve A curve illustrating the negative relationship between the equilibrium value of aggregate output (income) (Y) and the interest rate in the goods market.

We also know from our earlier analysis of the goods market that with a constant interest rate, an increase in government purchases (G) raises the equilibrium value of Y. This means the *IS* curve shifts to the right when G increases. With the same value of r and a higher value of G, the equilibrium value of Y is large; when G decreases, the *IS* curve shifts to the left.

Money demand, aggregate output (income) and the money market

We have just seen how the interest rate – which is determined in the money market – influences the level of planned investment spending and thus the goods market. Now we return to the other half of the story: the ways in which the goods market affects the money market.

In Chapter 26 we explored households' and firms' demand for money and why it depends negatively on the interest rate. An increase in the interest rate raises the opportunity cost of holding non-interest-bearing money (as compared to interest-bearing bonds), encouraging people to keep more of their funds in bonds and

---

[2]*The letter I stands for investment, and the letter S stands for saving. IS refers to the fact that in the global economy with no government, equilibrium in the goods market requires planned investment to equal saving.*

Figure 27.3 The *IS* Curve

Each point on the *IS* curve corresponds to the equilibrium point in the goods market for the given interest rate. When government spending (*G*) increases, the *IS* curve shifts to the right, from IS_0 to IS_1.

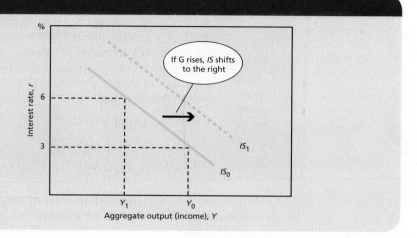

less in checking accounts. The downward-sloping money demand curve (M^d) is shown in Figure 27.4.

We also saw in Chapter 26 that the demand for money depends on the level of income in the economy. More income means more transactions, and an increased volume of transactions implies a greater demand for money. With more people earning higher incomes and buying more goods and services, more money will be demanded to meet the increased volume of transactions. An increase in income therefore shifts the money demand curve to the right. (Review Figure 26.5.)

If, as we are assuming, the central bank's choice of the amount of money to supply does not depend on the interest rate, then the money supply curve is simply a vertical line. The equilibrium interest rate is the point at which the quantity of money demanded equals the quantity of money supplied. This equilibrium is shown at a 6% interest rate in Figure 27.4. If the amount of money demanded by households and firms is less than the amount in circulation as determined by the central bank, as it is at an interest rate of 9% in Figure 27.4, the interest rate will fall. If the amount of money demanded is greater than the amount in circulation, as it is at an interest rate of 3% in Figure 27.4, the interest rate will rise.

Figure 27.4 Equilibrium in the money market

If the interest rate were 9%, the quantity of money in circulation would exceed the amount households and firms want to hold. The excess money balances would cause the interest rate to drop as people try to shift their funds into interest-bearing bonds. At 3% the opposite is true. Excess demand for money balances would push interest rates up. Only at 6% does the amount of money in circulation equal what the economy wants to hold in money balances.

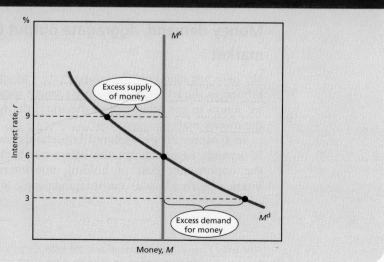

Figure 27.5 The effect of an increase in income (Y) on the interest rate (r)

An increase in income from Y_0 to Y_1 shifts the M^d curve to the right. With the fixed supply of money, there is now an excess demand for money ($M^d > M^s$) at the initial interest rate of 6%. This causes the interest rate to rise. At an interest rate of 9% the money market is again in equilibrium with $M^s = M^d$, but at a higher interest rate than before the increase in income.

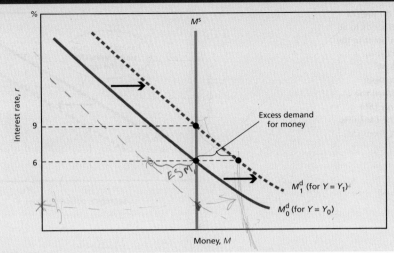

Now consider what happens to the interest rate when there is an increase in aggregate output (income) (Y). This increase in Y causes the money demand curve to shift to the right, as illustrated in Figure 27.5, where an increase in income from Y_0 to Y_1 has shifted the money demand curve from M_0^d to M_1^d. At the initial interest rate of 6%, there is now excess demand for money, and the interest rate rises from 6% to 9%.

The equilibrium level of the interest rate is not determined exclusively in the money market. Changes in aggregate output (income) (Y), which take place in the goods market, shift the money demand curve and cause changes in the interest rate. With a given quantity of money supplied, higher levels of Y will lead to higher equilibrium levels of r. Lower levels of Y will lead to lower equilibrium levels of r: In shorthand form:

$$Y \uparrow \rightarrow M^d \uparrow \rightarrow r \uparrow$$
$$Y \downarrow \rightarrow M^d \downarrow \rightarrow r \downarrow$$

The LM curve

Again, there is an alternative way to graph what we have just learned. In the money market, there is an equilibrium value of the interest rate (r) for every value of aggregate output (income) (Y). The equilibrium value of r is determined at the point where the quantity of money demanded equals the quantity of money supplied. For a given value of Y, we can determine the equilibrium value of r in the money market. We also know from Figure 27.5 that the equilibrium value of r rises when Y rises and falls when Y falls – a *positive* relationship between the equilibrium value of r and Y. The reason for this positive relationship is the positive relationship between the demand for money and Y. When Y rises, the demand for money increases because more money is needed for the greater volume of transactions in the economy. An increase in the demand for money increases the equilibrium value of r – thus the positive relationship between the equilibrium value of r and Y.

The positive relationship between the equilibrium value of r and Y is shown by the **LM curve** in Figure 27.6.[3] Each point on the LM curve represents an equilibrium in the money market for the given value of aggregate output (income).

LM curve A curve illustrating the positive relationship between the equilibrium value of the interest rate and aggregate output (income) (Y) in the money market.

[3]The letter L stands for liquidity, a characteristic of money, and the letter M stands for money.

Figure 27.6 The *LM* curve

Each point on the *LM* curve corresponds to an equilibrium point in the money market for a given value of aggregate output (income). When the money supply (M^s) increases, the *LM* shifts to the right, from LM_0 to LM_1.

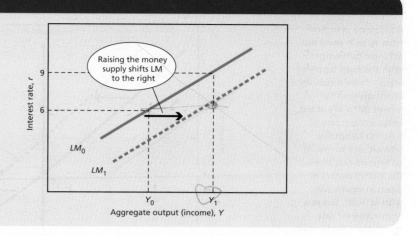

We also know from our analysis of the money market that when the money supply (M^s) increases with a constant level of Y, the equilibrium value of r decreases. As Figure 27.6 shows, this means the *LM* curve shifts to the right when M^s increases. With the same value of Y and a higher value of M^s, the equilibrium value of r is lower. When M^s decreases, the *LM* curve shifts to the left.

Combining the goods market and the money market

Our ultimate goal in this chapter is to find equilibrium levels of Y and r, and to see how monetary or fiscal policy affects them. The separate analyses of the goods and the money market only carry us half way towards this goal. The *IS* curve says what the equilibrium level of income will be for a given interest rate. But what is the interest rate? We do not know yet. The *LM* curve tells us what the equilibrium interest rate will be for given income. But what is income? Again, we do not know yet. Looking back and forth from *IS* to *LM* and *LM* to *IS* leaves us caught in a seemingly unproductive circle. The key is, of course, to look at both markets simultaneously. For the entire economy to be in equilibrium each market must be in equilibrium.

Figure 27.7 projects both the *IS* and *LM* curve into one graph. The point where the two curves intersect is the unique equilibrium of both the goods market and the money market. Because the point is on the *IS* curve there is equilibrium in the goods market. And because the point is on the *LM* curve, there is equilibrium in the money market.

Having established the links between the goods market and the money market, we can now examine the two markets simultaneously. To see how the two markets interact, we consider the effects of changes in fiscal and monetary policy on the economy: what happens to the equilibrium levels of aggregate output (income) (Y) and the interest rate (r) when certain key variables – notably government spending (G), net taxes (T) and the money supply (M^s) – increase or decrease?

Expansionary policy effects

expansionary fiscal policy
An increase in government spending or a reduction in net taxes aimed at increasing aggregate output (income) (Y).

expansionary monetary policy
An increase in the money supply aimed at increasing aggregate output (income) (Y).

Any government policy aimed at stimulating aggregate output (income) (Y) is said to be expansionary. **Expansionary fiscal policy** is an increase in government spending (G) or a reduction in net taxes (T) aimed at increasing aggregate output (income) (Y). **Expansionary monetary policy** is an increase in the money supply aimed at raising aggregate output (income) (Y).

Figure 27.7 The *IS-LM* diagram

The point at which the *IS* and *LM* curves intersect corresponds to the point at which both the goods market and the money market are in equilibrium. The equilibrium values of aggregate output and the interest rate are Y_0 and r_0.

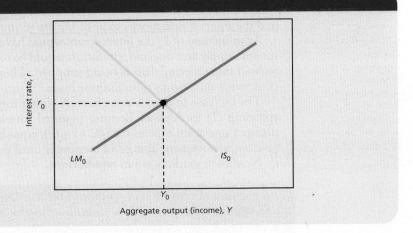

Expansionary fiscal policy: an increase in government purchases (*G*) or a decrease in net taxes (*T*)

As you know from Chapter 24, government purchases (*G*) and net taxes (*T*) are the two tools of government fiscal policy. The government can stimulate the economy – that is, it can increase aggregate output (income) (*Y*) – either by *increasing* government purchases or by *reducing* net taxes. While the impact of a tax cut is somewhat smaller than the impact of an increase in *G*, both have a multiplier effect on the equilibrium level of *Y*, thus shifting *IS* to the right (as shown in Figure 27.8).

Consider an increase in government purchases (*G*) of €10 billion. This increase in expenditure causes firms' inventories to be smaller than planned. Unplanned inventory reductions stimulate production, and firms increase output (*Y*). But because added output means added income, some of which is subsequently spent, consumption spending (*C*) also increases. Again, inventories will be smaller than planned and output will rise even further. At the initial interest rate r_0 the final equilibrium level of output would be higher by a multiple of the initial increase in government purchases.

In our new, refined view this multiplier story is incomplete. Prior to this chapter, we assumed that planned investment (*I*) was fixed. Knowing that planned investment depends on the interest rate we can now discuss what happens to the multiplier when investment responds to repercussions from the money market, which bear on the interest rate.

Figure 27.8 An increase in government purchases (*G*)

When *G* increases, the *IS* curve shifts to the right. This increases the equilibrium value of both *Y* and *r*.

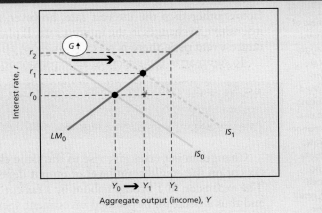

According to the simple fixed investment multiplier story from Chapter 24, income would have risen to Y_2. Now we know better: <u>investment depends on the interest rate, and the interest rate moves so as to equate money demand and money supply.</u>

At an income of Y_2 the interest rate would have to be much higher than r_0 to equate money supply and demand. (In fact, it would have to be at r_2). At r_0 people would want to hold more money than is being supplied. They begin to withdraw deposits, and to counteract this, banks raise interest rates.

The increase in r has a side effect. A higher interest rate causes planned investment spending (I) to decline. Because planned investment spending is a component of planned aggregate expenditure ($C + I + G$), equilibrium income decreases as well. This process, a movement along IS_1, continues until income is at Y_1 and the interest rate is r_1. Now both markets are in equilibrium.

> An increase in government spending (G) increases planned aggregate expenditure and aggregate output. This is partially offset by a decrease in planned investment which reduces aggregate output.

crowding-out effect

The tendency for increases in government spending to cause reductions in private investment spending.

The tendency for increases in government spending to cause reductions in private investment spending is called the **crowding-out effect**. Without an expansion in the money supply to accommodate the rise in income and increased money demand, planned investment spending is partially crowded out by the higher interest rate. The extra spending created by the rise in government purchases is somewhat offset by the fall in planned investment spending. Income still rises, but the multiplier effect of the rise in G is reduced because of the higher interest rate's negative effect on planned investment.

An alternative illustration of the crowding out effect in terms of a more familiar diagram may help. In Figure 27.9 an increase in government purchases from G_0 to G_1 shifts the planned aggregate expenditure curve ($C + I_0 + G_0$) upwards. The increase in (Y) from Y_0 to Y_1 causes the demand for money to rise, which results in a disequilibrium in the money market. The excess demand for money raises the interest rate (r) from r_0 to r_1, causing I to decrease from I_0 to I_1. The fall in I pulls the planned aggregate expenditure curve back down, which lowers the equilibrium level of income to Y^*. (Remember that equilibrium is achieved when $Y = AE$.)

The size of the crowding-out effect, and the ultimate size of the government spending multiplier, depends on several things. First, we assumed the central bank left the money supply unchanged. If, instead, the central bank expanded the quantity of money to accommodate the increase in G, the multiplier would be larger. In this case, the higher demand for money would be satisfied with a higher quantity of money supplied, and the interest rate would not rise. Without a higher interest rate, there would be no crowding out.

interest-sensitivity *or* insensitivity of planned investment

The responsiveness of planned investment spending to changes in the interest rate. Interest sensitivity means that planned investment spending changes a great deal in response to changes in the interest rate; interest insensitivity means little or no change in planned investment as a result of changes in the interest rate.

Second, the crowding-out effect depends on the **interest-sensitivity of planned investment** spending to changes in the interest rate. Crowding out occurs because a higher interest rate reduces planned investment spending. Investment depends on factors other than the interest rate, however, and investment may at times be quite insensitive to changes in the interest rate. If planned investment does not fall when the interest rate rises, there is no crowding-out effect.

To summarize the effects of an expansionary fiscal policy:

Effects of an expansionary fiscal policy:
$$G \uparrow \rightarrow Y \uparrow \rightarrow M^d \uparrow \rightarrow r \uparrow \rightarrow I \downarrow$$
$$\longrightarrow Y \text{ increases less than if } r \text{ did not increase}$$

Changes in net taxes give rise to the same chain of events. The ultimate effect of a tax cut on the equilibrium level of output depends on how the money market reacts. The expansion of Y brought about by a tax cut leads to an increase in the interest rate and thus a decrease in planned investment spending. The ultimate increase in Y will therefore be less than it would be if the interest rate did not rise.

Figure 27.9 The crowding-out effect

An increase in government spending G from G_0 to G_1 shifts the planned aggregate expenditure schedule from 1 to 2. The crowding-out effect of the decrease in planned investment (brought about by the increased interest rate) then shifts the planned aggregate expenditure schedule from 2 to 3.

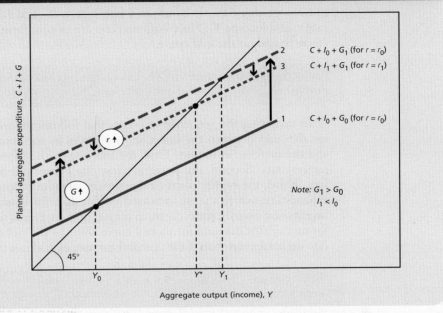

Expansionary monetary policy: an increase in the money supply

We now consider what happens when the central bank increases the supply of money through open market operations. Open market operations inject new reserves into the system and expand the quantity of money supplied. This shifts the LM curve to the right, as shown in Figure 27.10. At the initial interest rate r_0 and the initial income Y_0 the quantity of money supplied is now greater than the amount households want to hold. This causes the interest rate to decline, leading the goods market to respond with the same mechanism at work that we encountered before: planned investment increases as the interest rate falls.

Increased planned investment spending means planned aggregate expenditure is now greater than aggregate output. Firms experience unplanned decreases in inventories, and they raise output (Y). An increase in the money supply decreases the interest rate and increases Y. However, the higher level of Y increases the demand for money (the demand for money curve shifts to the right), and this keeps the interest rate from falling as far as it otherwise would.

Figure 27.10 An increase in the money supply (M^s)

When M^s increases, the LM curve shifts to the right. This increases the equilibrium value of Y and decreases the equilibrium value of r.

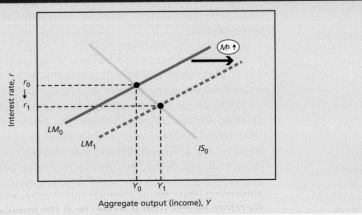

The decrease in the interest rate (originating from the money market), and the concomitant increase in income (the response of the goods market) constitute a movement along IS_0. It comes to a halt where IS_0 and LM_1 intersect, at the interest rate r_1 and income Y_1. Here both markets are in equilibrium, since this point is on the IS curve and on the LM curve.

> An increase in the money supply lowers the interest rate and raises equilibrium output

In reviewing the sequence of events that follows the monetary expansion, you can see the links between the injection of reserves by the central bank into the economy and the increase in output. First, the increase in the money supply pushes down the interest rate. Second, the lower interest rate causes planned investment spending to rise. Third, the higher planned investment spending means more planned aggregate expenditure, which means increased output as firms react to unplanned decreases in inventories. Fourth, the increase in output (income) leads to an increase in the demand for money (the demand for money curve shifts to the right), which means the interest rate decreases less than if the demand for money had not increased. In summary:

> Effects of an expansionary monetary policy:
>
> $$M^s \uparrow \rightarrow r \downarrow \rightarrow I \uparrow \rightarrow Y \uparrow \rightarrow M^d \uparrow$$
>
> $\longrightarrow$ r decreases less than if M^d did not increase.

The power of monetary policy to affect the goods market depends on the size of the reaction at each link in this chain. Perhaps the most critical link is the link between r and I. Monetary policy can be effective *only* if I reacts to changes in r. If firms sharply increase the number of investment projects undertaken when the interest rate falls, expansionary monetary policy works well at stimulating the economy. If, however, firms are reluctant to invest even at low interest rates, expansionary monetary policy will have limited success. In other words, the effectiveness of monetary policy depends on the shape of the investment function. If it is nearly vertical, indicating very low responsiveness of investment to the interest rate, the middle link in this chain is weak, rendering monetary policy ineffective.

Expansionary policy in action: the recessions of 1974–1975, 1980–1982 and 1990–1991

Remember that we are currently looking at the global economy. The individual country that comes closest to the concept of the global economy (with no exports and imports) is the United States, so we can use US examples to illustrate what we have just learned. Since 1970, the United States has experienced three recessions. During two, 1974–1975 and 1980–1982, the government engaged in tax cuts that had the effect of stimulating consumer spending (C). Because C is a component of planned aggregate expenditure, these tax cuts had the effect of increasing aggregate output (income) (Y).

Consider the recession of 1974–1975. The US Tax Reduction Act of 1975 resulted in a 1974 tax rebate of $8 billion. It was paid to consumers in the second quarter of 1975. This rebate and other tax reductions led to increased consumer spending, which helped the economy recover soon after the new tax laws went into effect.

What about the crowding-out effect? Did the 1975 expansionary fiscal policy drive up interest rates and crowd out private spending? In this case, no. At the same time that Congress was cutting taxes to stimulate spending, the Fed (the Federal Reserve, the US central bank) was trying to stimulate the economy by expanding the money supply. Even though the increased output during the expansion caused the *demand* for money to rise, the Fed was simultaneously expanding the *supply* of money,

Figure 27.11 Central bank accommodation of an expansionary fiscal policy

Expansionary fiscal policy (here a tax reduction) shifts the *IS* curve to the right. This would raise both income and interest rate along *LM*₀. To keep the interest rate from rising, the central bank may at the same time increase the money supply. This shifts the *LM* curve to the right. The new equilibrium occurs where *IS₁* and *LM₁* intersect. The interest rate has remained at *r₀* while income rose to *Y₁*.

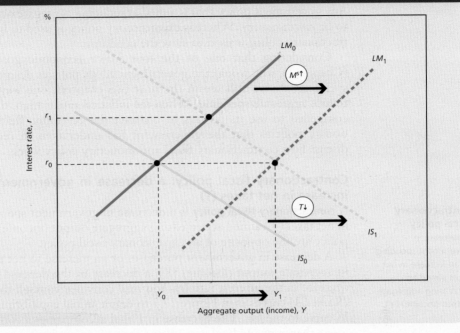

and interest rates did not change very much. This situation mirrors the illustration in Figure 27.11.

A similar sequence of events took place during the recession of 1980–1982. On the recommendation of President Reagan, Congress passed a huge tax cut during the summer of 1981. Like the 1975 tax cut, the 1981 tax cut led to an increase in consumer spending, which helped guide the economy out of the recession.

Recovery from the 1980–1982 recession was also supported by the Fed, which began to increase the supply of money sharply in the spring of 1982. So, even though output and income were expanding by late 1982, thereby increasing the demand for money, interest rates actually *declined* because the supply of money was expanding at the same time. There was no crowding-out effect.

The recession of 1990–1991 began soon after Iraq's invasion of Kuwait in the late summer of 1990. This recession was short-lived and shallow compared to the two previous ones. Real GDP began to rise in the second quarter of 1991. Because productivity was increasing while large firms were trimming payrolls even as output was beginning to expand, the unemployment rate stayed high right into the presidential election of 1992. Therefore this recovery became known as the 'jobless recovery'.

President Bush considered calling for a tax cut to stimulate the economy, but concern with the huge government deficit and pressure from the Fed convinced him to wait. The Fed did push interest rates down in an effort to get the economy moving. Even so, little response was visible by election time.

President Clinton called for some modest fiscal stimulus upon taking office, but Congress balked. Then, in the summer of 1993, Congress passed the Clinton deficit reduction package, which *increased* taxes and *reduced* government spending. In the meantime, monetary policy continued to be expansionary. Eventually, interest rates hit 30-year lows! For much of 1993, the three-month T-bill rate was under 3% for the first time since 1962, and the 30-year bond rate fell below 6% for the first time since the government began selling 30-year bonds.

In late 1994, the slow-growth recovery ended and a lasting expansion began. To the extent that policy was responsible for the expansion, it was monetary (rather than fiscal) policy that finally got things moving.

Contractionary policy effects

Any government policy that is aimed at reducing aggregate output (income) (Y) is said to be *contractionary*. Whereas expansionary policy is used to boost the economy, contractionary policy is used to slow the economy.

Considering that one of the four major economic goals is economic growth (Chapter 1), why would the government adopt policies designed to reduce aggregate spending? As we will see in the next two chapters, one way to fight inflation is to reduce aggregate spending. When the inflation rate is high, the government may feel compelled to use its powers to contract the economy. Before we discuss contractionary policies that the government has undertaken in recent years, we need to discuss how contractionary fiscal and monetary policy work.

Contractionary fiscal policy: a decrease in government spending (G) or an increase in net taxes (T)

> **contractionary fiscal policy**
>
> A decrease in government spending or an increase in net taxes aimed at decreasing aggregate output (income) (Y).

A **contractionary fiscal policy** is a decrease in government spending (G) or an increase in net taxes (T) aimed at decreasing aggregate output (income) (Y). The effects of this policy are the opposite of an expansionary fiscal policy.

A decrease in government purchases or an increase in net taxes leads to a decrease in aggregate output (income) (Y), a decrease in the demand for money (M^d), and a decrease in the interest rate (r). You may convince yourself that this is so by drawing IS and LM curves as in Figure 27.7 to define initial equilibrium, and then shifting the IS curve to the *left*. The decrease in Y that accompanies a contractionary fiscal policy is less than it would be if we omitted the money market because the decrease in r also causes planned investment (I) to increase. This increase in I offsets some of the decrease in planned aggregate expenditure brought about by the decrease in G. Of course, this also means the multiplier effect is smaller than it would be if we did not take the money market into account. The effects of a decrease in G, or an increase in T, can be represented as:

Effects of a contractionary fiscal policy:

$$G \downarrow T \uparrow \rightarrow Y \downarrow \rightarrow M^d \downarrow \rightarrow r \downarrow \rightarrow I \uparrow$$

→ Y decreases less than if r did not decrease.

Contractionary monetary policy: a decrease in the money supply

> **contractionary monetary policy**
>
> A decrease in the money supply aimed at decreasing aggregate output (income) (Y).

A **contractionary monetary policy** is a decrease in the money supply aimed at lowering aggregate output (income) (Y). As you recall, the level of planned investment spending is a negative function of the interest rate: the higher the interest rate, the less planned investment there will be. The less planned investment there is, the lower planned aggregate expenditure, and the lower the equilibrium level of output (income) (Y). The lower equilibrium income results in a decrease in the demand for money, which means that the increase in the interest rate will be less than it would be if we did not take the goods market into account. Representing the effects of a decrease in the money supply:

Effects of a contractionary monetary policy:

$$M^s \downarrow \rightarrow r \uparrow \rightarrow I \downarrow \rightarrow Y \downarrow \rightarrow M^d \downarrow$$

→ r increases less than if M^d did not decrease.

In terms of the *IS–LM* diagram the effects of contractionary monetary policy are revealed after shifting the LM curve to the left.

Contractionary policy in action: 1973–1974, 1979–1980 and 1994

Looking again at the United States, the Fed pursued strong contractionary policies twice during the last two decades: first in 1973–1974 and again in 1979–1980. In both cases, tight monetary policy led to very high interest rates. In 1974, short-term rates exceeded 12%, and in 1981, some short-term rates exceeded 20%! These high interest rates had a negative effect on planned aggregate expenditure and contributed to the recessions that followed. The Fed's purpose in following a tight monetary policy was to slow the inflation rate. (We will learn in Chapter 32 why a contractionary policy may bring the inflation rate down.)

In 1994, worries about inflation surfaced again as the economy began to push towards full employment. Once again, the Fed began to pull on the reins. In February, it announced the first of several increases in the discount rate and the target federal funds rate. By the end of the year, the prime rate had jumped from 6% to 8.5%. Between 1994 and 1997 the Fed made only modest changes in the discount rate.

The macroeconomic policy mix

Although we've been analysing fiscal and monetary policy separately, the examples have shown that they can be used simultaneously. For example, both government purchases (G) and the money supply (M^s) can be increased at the same time, as in the 1974–75 recession. We saw that an increase in G by itself raises both Y and r, while an increase in M^s by itself raises Y but lowers r. Therefore, if the government wanted to increase Y without changing r, it could do so by increasing both G and M^s by the appropriate amounts.

policy mix The combination of monetary and fiscal policies in use at a given time.

Policy mix refers to the combination of monetary and fiscal policies in use at a given time. A policy mix that consists of a decrease in government spending and an increase in the money supply favours investment spending over government spending. This is because both the increased money supply and lower government purchases would cause the interest rate to fall, leading to an increase in planned investment. The opposite is true for a mix that consists of an expansionary fiscal and a contractionary monetary policy. Such a mix favours government spending over investment spending. Tight money and expanded government spending drives the interest rate up and planned investment down.

There is no rule determining what constitutes the 'best' policy mix or the 'best' composition of output. On this, as on many other issues, economists (and others) disagree. In part, someone's preference for a certain composition of output – say, one weighted heavily towards private spending with relatively little government spending – depends on how that person stands on such issues as the proper role of government in the economy.

Figure 27.12 summarizes the effects of various combinations of policies on several important macroeconomic variables. If you can explain the reasoning underlying each of the effects shown in the figure, you have a good understanding of the links between the goods market and the money market.

Figure 27.12 The effects of the macroeconomic policy mix

Income is affected by monetary policy, fiscal policy, or a mix of both. An appropriate policy mix may not only influence Y, but also give the desired *composition* of aggregate demand. Example: Raising *M* raises *Y*, but drives down *r*, *lowering I*. Raising *G* raises *Y*, drives up *r*, *raising I*. Raising *M* and *G* also raises *Y*, but may leave *r* and *I* unchanged.

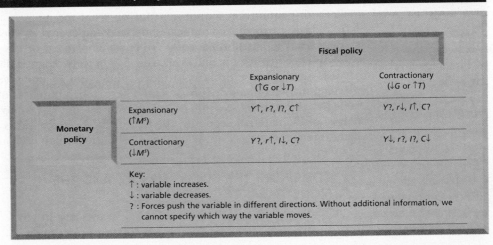

		Fiscal policy	
		Expansionary ($\uparrow G$ or $\downarrow T$)	Contractionary ($\downarrow G$ or $\uparrow T$)
Monetary policy	Expansionary ($\uparrow M^s$)	$Y\uparrow$, $r?$, $I?$, $C\uparrow$	$Y?$, $r\downarrow$, $I\uparrow$, $C?$
	Contractionary ($\downarrow M^s$)	$Y?$, $r\uparrow$, $I\downarrow$, $C?$	$Y\downarrow$, $r?$, $I?$, $C\downarrow$

Key:
$\uparrow$: variable increases.
$\downarrow$: variable decreases.
? : Forces push the variable in different directions. Without additional information, we cannot specify which way the variable moves.

Other determinants of planned investment

We have assumed throughout this chapter that planned investment depends on the interest rate alone. While the interest rate is probably the core factor, planned investment depends on other factors as well. We provide a brief description here, discussing these factors more thoroughly in Chapter 33.

Expectations and animal spirits

Firms' expectations about future sales play an important role in investment decisions. When a firm invests, it adds to its capital stock. Capital, in turn, is used in the production process. If a firm expects increased sales in the future, it may begin to build up its capital stock (that is, to invest) now so that it will be able to produce more in the future when the higher level of sales arrives. Entrepreneurs' optimism or pessimism about the future course of the economy can have important effects on current planned investment. Keynes used the phrase *animal spirits* to describe the feelings of entrepreneurs, arguing that these feelings affect investment decisions.

Capital utilization rates

The degree of utilization of a firm's capital stock is also likely to affect planned investment. If demand for a firm's output has been decreasing and the firm has responded by lowering output, the firm may have a low rate of capital utilization. Once in place it can be costly to get rid of capital quickly. Firms sometimes respond to a fall in output by keeping the capital in place but utilizing it less (for example, by running machines fewer hours per day or at slower speeds). Firms tend to invest less in new capital when their capital utilization rates are low than when they are high.

Relative labour and capital costs

The cost of capital (of which the interest rate is the main component) *relative* to the cost of labour can also affect planned investment. If labour is expensive relative to capital (high wage rates), firms have an incentive to substitute away from labour towards capital. The aim is to hold more capital relative to labour when wage rates are high than when they are low.

Looking ahead: the foreign exchange market and national economy

Our discussion of aggregate output (income) and the interest rate in the goods market and the money market is complete. You should now have a good understanding of how the two markets work together in the global economy. It is time to move on to smaller units: national economies.

In today's national economies, shop and supermarket shelves are filled with products from all parts of the world. To buy a Korean car or US software we (though indirectly) need to acquire and eventually pay in those countries' currencies. Also, we may ask our banks or brokers to move money out of our savings account to buy emerging markets funds or IBM stocks. There, too, a purchase of foreign currency is needed to perform these shifts of wealth into foreign assets. To set the stage for an analysis of the national economy, the task of the next chapter is to study the market where foreign currencies are bought and sold: the foreign exchange market.

Summary

1. The *goods market* and the *money market* do not operate independently. Events in the money market have considerable effects on the goods market, and events in the goods market have considerable effects on the money market.

The links between the goods market and the money market

2. There are two important links between the goods market and the money market: the level of real output (income) (Y), which is determined in the goods market, determines the volume of transactions each period and thus affects the demand for money in the money market. The interest rate (r), which is determined in the money market, affects the level of planned investment spending in the goods market.

3. There is a negative relationship between planned investment and the interest rate because the interest rate determines the cost of investment projects. When the interest rate rises, planned investment will decrease; when the interest rate falls, planned investment will increase.

4. For every value of the interest rate, there is a different level of planned investment spending and a different equilibrium level of output. The final level of equilibrium output depends on what the interest rate turns out to be, which depends on events in the money market.

5. An *IS curve* illustrates the negative relationship between the equilibrium value of aggregate output (income) (Y) and the interest rate in the goods market.

6. For a given money supply the interest rate depends on the demand for money. Money demand depends on the level of output (income) and the interest rate. With a given money supply, then, increases and decreases in Y will affect money demand, which will affect the equilibrium interest rate.

7. An *LM curve* illustrates the positive relationship between the equilibrium value of the interest rate and aggregate output (income) (Y) in the money market.

Combining the goods market and the money market

8. The point at which the *IS* and *LM* curves intersect is the point at which equilibrium exists in both the goods market and the money market.

9. An *expansionary fiscal policy* is an increase in government spending (G) or a reduction in net taxes

(T) aimed at increasing aggregate output (income) (Y). An expansionary fiscal policy based on increases in government spending leads to a *crowding-out effect*: because increased government expenditures mean more transactions in the economy and thus an increased demand for money, the interest rate will rise. The decrease in planned investment spending that accompanies the higher interest rate will then partly offset (crowd out) the increase in aggregate expenditures brought about by the increase in G.

10. The size of the crowding-out effect, which affects the size of the government-spending multiplier, depends on two things: the assumption that the central bank does not change the money supply and the *sensitivity or insensitivity of planned investment* to changes in the interest rate.

11. An *expansionary monetary policy* is an increase in the money supply aimed at increasing aggregate output (income) (Y). An increase in the money supply leads to a lower interest rate, increased planned investment, increased planned aggregate expenditure, and ultimately a higher equilibrium level of aggregate output (income) (Y). Expansionary policies have been used to lift the economy out of recessions.

12. A *contractionary fiscal policy* is a decrease in government spending or an increase in net taxes aimed at decreasing aggregate output (income) (Y). A decrease in government spending or an increase in net taxes leads to a decrease in aggregate output (income) (Y), a decrease in the demand for money, and a decrease in the interest rate. However, the decrease in Y is somewhat offset by the additional planned investment resulting from the lower interest rate.

13. A *contractionary monetary policy* is a decrease in the money supply aimed at decreasing aggregate output (income) (Y). The higher interest rate brought about by the reduced money supply causes a decrease in planned investment spending and a lower level of equilibrium output. However, the lower equilibrium level of output brings about a decrease in the demand for money, which means the increase in the interest rate will be less than it would be if we did not take the goods market into account. Contractionary policies have been used to fight inflation.

14. The *policy mix* is the combination of monetary and fiscal policies in use at a given time. There is no rule about what constitutes the best policy mix or the best composition of output. In part, one's preference for a certain composition of output depends on one's stance regarding such issues as the proper role of government in the economy.

Other determinants of planned investment

15. In addition to the interest rate, the level of planned investment in the economy also depends on expectations, capital utilization rates, and relative capital and labour costs.

Review Terms and Concepts

contractionary fiscal policy
contractionary monetary policy
crowding-out effect
expansionary fiscal policy
expansionary monetary policy
goods market

interest-sensitivity or insensitivity of planned investment
IS curve
LM curve
money market
policy mix

Problem Set

1. On 9 October 1997, the Bundesbank surprised the world by announcing it would take action to raise interest rates. This set off a protest in Germany, where the unemployment rate was above 12%. What impact is an interest rate increase likely to have on the level of unemployment? Explain your answer fully; do not skip steps. What justification might you give for such an action?

2. During the third quarter of 1997, Japanese GDP was falling at an annual rate of over 11%. Many blamed the big increase in Japan's taxes in the spring of 1997 designed to balance the budget. Explain how an increase in taxes with the economy growing slowly could precipitate a recession; again, do not skip steps in your answer. If you were head of the Japanese central bank, how would you respond? What impact would your policy have on the level of investment?

3. Some economists argue that the 'animal spirits' of investors are so important in determining the level of investment in the economy that interest rates do not matter at all. Suppose that this were true – that investment in no way depends on interest rates.
a. How would Figure 27.1 be different?
b. What would happen to the level of planned aggregate expenditures if the interest rate changed?
c. What would be different about the relative effectiveness of monetary and fiscal policy?
d. Can there be any crowding out?

4. Use the *IS–LM* model to predict the changes in output and interest rates for each of the following scenarios:
a. In 1990, the Gulf War led to a sharp drop in consumer confidence. Assume that central banks held the money supply constant.
b. After the 1987 stock market crash, the Bank of England increased the money supply, fearing a

recession. With hindsight, however, the crash did not affect consumption and investment spending.
c. German reunification required large infrastructure investments in former East Germany. At the same time, the Bundesbank left the money supply unchanged.

5. In the United States, the Federal Reserve occasionally sets a policy designed to 'track' the interest rate. This means that the Fed is pursuing policies designed to keep the interest rate constant. If, in fact, the Fed were acting to counter any increases or decreases in the interest rate to keep it constant, what specific actions would you expect to see the Fed take if the following were to occur? (In answering, indicate the effects of each set of events on Y, C, S, I, M^s, M^d and r.)
a. There is an unexpected increase in investor confidence, leading to a sharp increase in orders for new plant and equipment.
b. A major New York bank fails, causing a number of depositors to withdraw a substantial amount of cash from other banks and keep it under their mattresses.

6. Paranoia, the largest country in Central Antarctica, receives word of an imminent penguin attack. The news shakes confidence in future expectations. As a consequence, there is a sharp decline in investment spending plans.
a. Explain in detail the effects of such an event on the economy of Paranoia, assuming no response on the part of the central bank or the Treasury (M^s, T and G all remain constant). Be sure to discuss the adjustments in the goods market and the money market.
b. To counter the fall in investment, the king of Paranoia calls for a proposal to increase government spending. To finance the programme, Paranoia's Chancellor of the Exchequer has proposed three alternative options: (1) Finance the expenditures with an equal increase in taxes. (2) Keep tax revenues constant and borrow the money from the public by issuing new

government bonds. (3) Keep taxes constant and finance the expenditures by printing new money. Consider the three financing options and rank them from most expansionary to least expansionary. Explain your ranking.

7. Why might investment not respond positively to low interest rates during a recession? Why might investment not respond negatively to high interest rates during a boom?

8. The *IS* and *LM* curves in Figure 27.7 divide the diagram into four quadrants. Positions away from either one or both curves correspond to a disequilibrium. These consist of either excess demand or excess supply in the money or goods markets, or both. Define each quadrant in terms of the types of disequilibria (that is, excess supply or excess demand) in the goods and money markets.

9. In the early 1980s, the US Federal Reserve was tightening the money supply to fight inflation at the same time that President Reagan was increasing defence spending and reducing taxes. What would you expect the effects of this policy mix to be?

The Exchange Rate and the Balance of Payments

The last chapters provided an understanding of the global economy as if viewed from a satellite camera in outer space. From that vantage point, international borders and national detail disappear. In this chapter we move closer, zooming in on the individual country as it interacts with the rest of the world.

When analysing a national (as opposed to the global) economy we need not start from scratch. Our newly acquired knowledge of the global economy continues to be useful for two reasons: first, it explains what goes on in the world that surrounds and influences the individual country; second, the global-economy model developed in Chapters 23 to 27 remains an integral part of the national-economy model to be laid out in this and the next chapters.

However, we must refine and augment this picture. As opposed to the world, individual countries sell some of the goods they produce to other countries. In return, goods are imported from abroad and bought by domestic consumers, investors and the government. In addition to constituting injections into and leakages from the circular flow of income, these transactions require the purchase or sale of foreign currency.

> When people in different countries buy from and sell to each other, an exchange of currencies takes place.

French wine exporters, for example, cannot spend dollars obtained from US customers in France – they need euros. Nor can a Swedish timber exporter use euros received from Belgium to pay wages to her workers. Somehow, international exchange must be managed in a way that allows each partner in the transaction to end up with his or her own currency. Currencies are bought and sold in the foreign exchange market. We were able to ignore this market when analysing the global economy, which by definition excludes countries and currencies. The foreign exchange market must be brought into the picture now, and it will take centre stage.

Introductory macroeconomics texts used to (and sometimes still do) spare readers the complications that arise from bringing trade and the exchange rate into the picture. Instead, the global-economy model was also used to analyse the national economy. The justification for this was that exports amounted to only a small fraction of output. Ignoring international trade appeared a small price to pay for keeping the model simple. This escape is no longer available. After dramatic changes known as **globalization** the world's national economies now interact more intensively than ever before.

globalization The recent worldwide expansion of international trade in goods, services and foreign exchange.

This chapter first shows the extent of globalization. We then extend the Keynesian cross and the *IS* curve to include exports and imports, and take a first look at the exchange rate. This perspective is subsequently broadened and refined by looking at the balance of payments, the record of all international transactions of a country.

Globalization

Trade is almost as old as history. Ancient trading routes like the Silk Road linking China and the Mediterranean are evidence that people, even thousands of years ago, were never content with the selection of goods produced in their home country. Also, neither the Swiss bank account nor investment opportunities abroad in general is a recent discovery. Yet while such things were long present, their scale remained small. Little harm was done when macroeconomics ignored international links, settling for the basic global-economy model as a useful description of the national economy as well. But recently, dramatic increases both in the volumes of goods and services traded internationally and of currency bought and sold in the foreign exchange markets have led to a fundamental change, giving rise to the new term *globalization*.

Openness

The global economy discussed in previous chapters is often referred to as a *closed* economy. It neither exports nor imports. By contrast, an economy that exports all it produces and imports all it demands would be a perfectly *open* economy. Thus the ratio of exports to output is a useful measure of an economy's openness or trade inter-action with the rest of the world. Figure 28.1 shows the export ratios for EU members and a few other countries as they were in 1960 and as they are in 1997. The change is dramatic. Not one out of 19 countries is less engaged in international trade than it was in the 1960s. The message is clear. The overwhelming majority of countries are much more open in the mid-1990s than some 35 years earlier. Many, including Austria, France, Ireland, Italy, Spain, Sweden and the USA, have doubled their export share. In other countries the increase is smaller, but nevertheless pronounced. Interestingly and somewhat contrary to Japan's image as the world's most aggressive exporter, the country exports only 13.5% of what it produces. This share is about level with the United States and not much larger than it was back in 1960.

In relation to GDP, European economies export a lot more than Japan, though much of it to each other. Luxemburg's export share is highest at 91%. Most other countries' shares run between 20% and 60%. At the lower end of the spectrum of European countries is Greece, with an export share of only 15.1%.

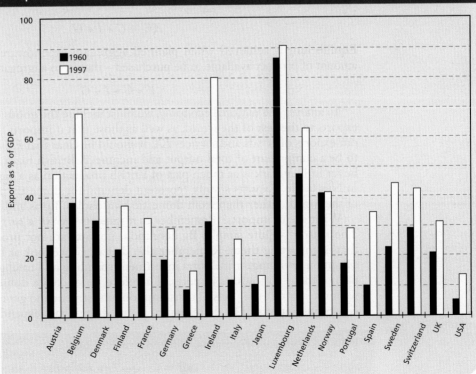

Figure 28.1 International export shares in 1960 and 1997

Export shares measure the openness of an economy, how much it trades with other countries. In the course of globalization, export shares have increased in most countries, and often doubled since 1960. It may surprise you that Japan's export share is only 13%, the lowest among all industrial countries. *Source*: OECD; IMF.

Foreign exchange market transactions

Globalization is not restricted to international trade in goods and services. Another, more comprehensive measure of how intensively the world's economies interact is the volume of transactions in the foreign exchange markets. In these markets people trade dollars in exchange for sterling, or euros for yen. In 1997 currency valued at 1.2 trillion dollars changed hands in the foreign exchange markets on an average trading day. While comprehensive data for worldwide currency trade has only been collected for a few years, data for individual trading centres such as London or New York suggest that today's volume is 10 to 15 times as high as it was in 1980.

Today, most of this trading finances international capital flows rather than trade in goods and services. An indication of these changes is the fact that, between 1970 and 1990, transactions in bonds and equities by US residents across national borders rose from 2.8% to 92.5% of GDP.

Motivated by these numbers, we now generalize the model initially designed to explain the global economy to allow for exports and imports. After that we extend the model to include the foreign exchange market, introducing motives other than trade in goods and services for buying or selling foreign currency.

Equilibrium output (income) in the national economy

We first consider the impact of trade on the economies of the countries involved. To simplify our discussion in this part of the chapter, we assume that exchange rates are fixed. We relax this assumption a little later on.

The international sector and planned aggregate expenditure

Our earlier descriptions of the global-economy multiplier took into account the consumption behaviour of households (C), the planned investment behaviour of firms (I), and the spending of the government (G). We defined the sum of these three components as planned aggregate expenditure (AE):

$$AE \equiv C + I + G$$

Equilibrium is achieved when planned aggregate expenditure is equal to the total amount of product available to be purchased – that is, to aggregate output (income) (Y):

$$Y = C + I + G$$

To analyse the national economy, we must include the goods and services a country exports to the rest of the world, as well as those that it imports from abroad. If we call our exports of goods and services EX, it should be clear that EX is properly considered to be a component of total output and income. A British razor blade that is sold to a buyer in Denmark is as much part of British production as a similar blade that is sold in Newcastle. Exports simply represent demand for domestic products from the rest of the world, rather than from domestic households, firms and the government.

What about imports? Remember that imports are *not a part of domestic output* (Y). The reason is quite simple. By definition, imports are not produced by the country that is importing them. Remember also that when we look at households' total consumption spending, firms' total investment spending and total government spending, part of these go towards imports. Therefore, to calculate domestic output correctly, we must subtract the parts of consumption, investment and government spending that constitute imports. The definition of planned aggregate expenditure becomes:

Planned aggregate expenditure in an open economy:

$$AE \equiv C + I + G + EX - IM$$

Note that if we look at the last two terms ($EX - IM$) together, we have the country's **net exports of goods and services**.

Determining import and export levels

What determines the level of exports and imports in a country? For present purposes, we simply assume that imports are a function of income (Y). The rationale is simple: when Dutch income is higher, Dutch citizens buy more of everything, including Dutch books and TV sets, German cars and Korean steel. Thus, when income rises, imports tend to go up. Algebraically, we can write

$$IM = mY$$

where Y is income and m is some positive number. Recall from Chapter 23 that the marginal propensity to consume (MPC) measures the change in consumption that results from a €1 change in income. Similarly, **the marginal propensity to import**, which we will abbreviate as MPM or m, is the change in imports caused by a €1 change in income. If $m = 0.2$, or 20%, and income is €1000, then imports, IM, are equal to $0.2 \times €1000 = €200$. If income rises by €100 to €1100, then the change in imports will be equal to $m \times$ (the change in income) $= 0.2 \times €100 = €20$.

Regarding exports, note that one country's exports are other countries' imports. If Dutch income (Y) affects Dutch imports from Germany, then the amount of goods and services that Germany imports from The Netherlands (Dutch exports) depend on German income. Generally, if foreign incomes go up, other countries' imports (and thus Dutch exports) increase. For now we assume that foreign income and thus exports (EX) are given.

In Figure 28.2a the assumption that exports are independent of domestic income is represented by a horizontal line. Imports rise as income rises. So their level is represented by a positively sloped line. Net exports $EX - IM$ are simply the vertical distance between the export line and the import line. As panel b indicates, net exports are positive for small levels of income. At income Y_0, exports equal imports. So net exports are zero. When income exceeds Y_0 net exports are negative.

Solving for equilibrium income

With all this in mind we can now determine equilibrium income in the national economy. Figure 28.2c reactivates the Keynesian cross. We start from the blue line which represents $C + I + G$, the demand components that sufficed in the global economy with no exports and imports. To obtain planned aggregate expenditure in the national economy we need to add net exports $EX - IM$ to obtain $AE \equiv C + I + G + EX - IM$, as argued above. The net export line is shown in Figure 28.2b. Adding the indicated values to the $C + I + G$ line in panel c gives the $C + I + G + EX - IM$ line. This red line indicates *planned spending on domestic goods* at different income levels.

Comparing the planned aggregate expenditure lines in the global economy and in the national economy, the important thing to note is that their slopes differ. The slope of the global AE line equals c, the marginal propensity to consume. The reason is that from each unit of additional income a fraction c comes back to domestic producers as additional demand. The slope of the national-economy AE line is only $c - m$. The reason is that when income rises by €1, planned spending rises by c. But at the same time the demand for goods and services produced abroad rises by m. Only the difference between these two, $c - m$, remains in the country as an increase in demand for domestic goods.[1]

---

[1] *Actually, for both c and m we can only be sure that they are between 0 and 1 (values larger than 1 make no sense). So theoretically c – m might be negative, with the AE line sloping down. This case does not occur in real life, though, where c may be taken at about 0.8 and m at, say, 0.2. So we assume 1 > c > m > 0.*

Figure 28.2 Exports and imports in the Keynesian cross

a. Our exports, the goods and services other countries buy from us, do not depend on our income. Therefore, the export line is horizontal. On the other hand, the higher our income, the more we buy from other countries. Thus the import line has a positive slope.

b. At low income we cannot afford to import a lot. Exports exceed imports. Net exports ($NX = EX - IM$) are positive. At high income we import a lot. Imports exceed exports. Net exports are negative. Hence, the net export has a negative slope.

c. At low income the national economy benefits from positive net exports. Aggregate demand is higher than if the economy was closed. At high income the opposite holds. International trade makes the aggregate expenditure line flatter.

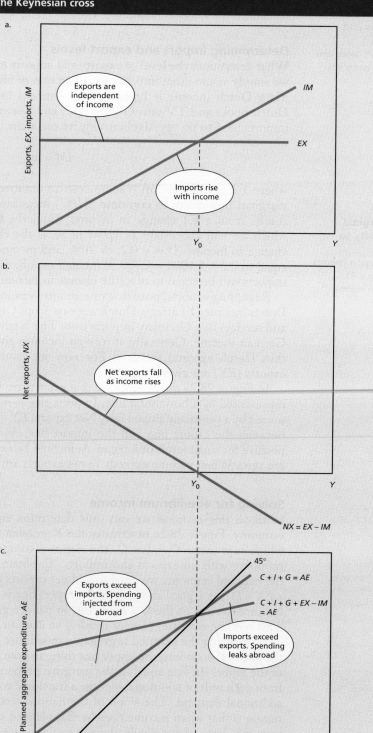

Equilibrium is reached when planned aggregate expenditure on domestic output is equal to aggregate domestic output (income). This is true at only one level of aggregate output, Y_0, in Figure 28.2c, which is where the AE line intersects the 45° line. If Y were below Y_0, planned expenditure would exceed output, inventories would be lower than planned, and output would rise. At levels above Y_0, output would exceed planned expenditure, inventories would be larger than planned, and output would fall.

The national-economy multiplier

The reduced slope of the AE line in the national economy has implications for the size of the multiplier. Recall the multiplier story introduced in Chapter 23, and consider a sustained rise in government purchases (G). Initially, the increase in G causes planned aggregate expenditure to be greater than aggregate output. Domestic firms find their inventories to be lower than planned and thus increase output. But added output means more income. More workers are hired and profits are higher. Some of the added income is saved, and some is spent. The added consumption spending leads to a second round of inventories being lower than planned and rising output. Thus, equilibrium output grows by a multiple of the initial increase in government purchases. This is the multiplier.

In Chapters 23 and 24 we showed that the simple multiplier is equal to $1/(1 - MPC)$, or $1/MPS$. That is, a sustained increase in government purchases equal to ΔG will lead to an increase in aggregate output (income) of $\Delta G[1/(1 - MPC)]$. For example, if the MPC were 0.75 and government purchases rose by €10 billion, equilibrium income would rise by $4 \times$ €10 billion, or €40 billion. The multiplier is $1/(1 - 0.75) = 1/0.25 = 4.0$.

In a national economy, however, some of the increase in income brought about by the increase in G is spent on imports rather than on domestically produced goods and services. The part of income spent on imports does not increase domestic income (Y) because imports are produced by foreigners. Thus, to compute the multiplier we need to know how much of the increased income is used to increase spending on domestic goods. Two opposite effects are at work. First, each unit of additional income raises consumption spending by MPC. If there were no imports, this would all be directed towards domestic goods. But now a share of income equal to the marginal propensity to import (MPM) is directed towards foreign goods, leaving only $MPC - MPM$ as the net increase in the demand for home-produced goods. We may call $MPC - MPM$ the **marginal propensity to demand domestic goods** and write the multiplier for the national economy as:

marginal propensity to demand domestic goods

The fraction of an increase in income that is spent on goods and services produced at home.

$$\text{National-economy multiplier} = \frac{1}{1 - (MPC - MPM)}$$

national-economy multiplier

The multiplier taking into account that countries spend some income abroad.

If the MPC is 0.75 and the MPM is 0.25, then the **national-economy multiplier** is $1/0.5$, or 2.0. Note that this multiplier is smaller than the global-economy multiplier in which imports are not taken into account, which is $1/0.25$, or 4.0.

The major message of the national-economy multiplier model can be put quite succinctly:

The effect of a sustained increase in government spending (or investment) on income – that is, the multiplier – is smaller in a national economy than in the global economy. The reason is simply that when government spending (or investment) increases and income and consumption rise, some of the extra spending that results is on foreign products and not on domestically produced goods and services.

Imports, exports and the exchange rate

So far, we have assumed that imports (and also exports, since they are some other country's imports) depend on income. Somewhat mechanically, a given fraction of income is spent on goods produced abroad. This is a good first approximation when exchange rates are fixed. But it needs to be refined if exchange rates are flexible.

From microeconomics we know that when consumers consider buying a Saab or a Volvo, they note the characteristics of each product, look at the price tag and then make a choice. If one of the two cars becomes cheaper, other things remaining the same, demand for this model increases. In general terms we may state that the demand for Saabs depends on the relative price of Saabs compared to Volvos: P_{Saab}/P_{Volvo}. If this relative price falls, more Saabs are bought.

This reasoning also applies on the international level. Deciding whether to purchase a BMW or a Volvo, Swedes again look at the relative price. The lower it is, the more BMWs are bought and imported to Sweden. Now, for a relative price to be useful, prices must be expressed in a common currency. The price of a BMW made in Germany is given in euros. To obtain the price in kronor, this euro price must be multiplied by the exchange rate. The **exchange rate** states how many units of domestic currency (here, kronor) you need to pay for one unit of foreign currency (here, euros). So the krona price of a BMW relative to the price of a Volvo is:

exchange rate
The price of one country's currency in terms of another country's currency; the ratio at which two currencies are traded for each other.

$$\text{Relative price} = \text{Exchange rate} \times \frac{\text{Price of BMW in euros}}{\text{Price of Volvo in kronor}} = E \times \frac{P_{BMW}}{P_{Volvo}}$$

Applications

Exchange rate terminology

The **nominal exchange rate**, or for short, the exchange rate E, is the price of one unit of foreign currency in terms of domestic currency:

$$\text{Exchange rate } E = \frac{\text{Deutschemarks (DM)}}{\text{French francs}}$$

If the DM/franc exchange rate is 0.25, this means that one French franc costs DM0.25. This common definition has a *counterintuitive implication* that may initially confuse students: if Germany's exchange rate goes up, the mark loses value – it *depreciates*. Germans need more marks to obtain a given number of French francs. A falling exchange rate means that the domestic currency is getting stronger – it *appreciates*.

We only speak of *appreciations* and *depreciations* if the exchange rate is moved by market forces. If governments decide to move the mark up to 0.3 against the French franc in a system of fixed exchange rates, the mark is *devalued*. In the opposite case it is *revalued*.

The nominal exchange rate does not provide any information about the actual buying power of a given amount of currency in different countries. This it can only do in combination with information about individual prices or the general price level. If the Renault Espace sells for 50,000 marks in Germany and for 160,000 francs in France, where is it cheaper? A measure of the relative price level in two countries is the **real exchange rate**:

Real exchange rate

$$R = E \times \frac{P^{World}}{P}$$

$$R = \frac{DM}{\text{francs}} \times \frac{\text{French price}}{\text{German price}}$$

So to purchase an Espace costs 50,000 marks in Germany, but only $0.25 \times 160,000 = \text{DM}40,000$ in France. This also follows from substituting prices and the exchange rate into the above equation. The real exchange rate of $0.25 \times 160,000/50,000 = 0.8$ means that Germans only pay 80% of what the Espace costs on the German market when they buy the car in France.

In this case, or generally whenever the real exchange rate is below one, the DM is said to be **overvalued**. If the exchange rate is higher than one, and DM prices abroad exceed home prices, the mark is **undervalued**.

The exchange rate E^{PPP} that equalizes the domestic and the international purchasing power of a currency is called **purchasing power parity**. It is the nominal exchange rate that sets the real exchange rate to a value of 1, that is,

$$E^{PPP} \times \frac{P^{World}}{P} = 1:$$

Purchasing power parity

$$E^{PPP} = \frac{P}{P^{World}}$$

$$= \frac{\text{German price}}{\text{French price}}$$

In the present numerical example, the purchasing-power-parity exchange rate turns out to be $50,000/160,000 = 0.32$.

Macroeconomists usually look at economy-wide price indexes comprising a representative basket of goods and services rather than prices for individual goods.

This relative price may fall, in which case BMW imports would rise, for three reasons:

1. if the price of Volvos in kronor rises;
2. if the price of BMWs in euros falls;
3. if the krona/euro exchange rate falls.

What we have derived here for one particular pair of goods also holds on the aggregate level. Aggregate imports increase if domestic prices rise, if foreign prices fall, or if the exchange rate falls.

For Swedish exports to Germany (or German imports from Sweden) exactly the opposite holds: they fall if Swedish prices rise, if German prices fall, or if the krona/euro exchange rate falls. Note that if the krona/euro exchange rate falls, the euro/krona exchange rate rises and Germans pay more euros for a Volvo.

Now, since we are currently considering domestic and foreign prices as given, let us set aside the derived price effects for later use and concentrate on how the exchange rate affects equilibrium income.

Equilibrium income and the exchange rate

To carve out the role of the exchange rate in determining equilibrium income, Figure 28.3 first redraws the export, import, net export and *AE* lines from the three panels of Figure 28.2. These lines, shown in grey, are all drawn for a given exchange rate E_0. Now, what happens if the exchange rate rises (that is, depreciates) to E_1. Let us start with panel a. A **depreciation** makes exports cheaper for foreigners. So exports rise and the export line moves up into the red position. Since imports turn more expensive when E goes up, they fall, no matter what the level of income. The import line moves down. The consequence of both these shifts is that net exports are now higher at any level of income, as indicated by the red line in panel b.

With this insight we proceed to panel c. Since planned aggregate expenditure in the national economy is equal to the sum $C + I + G + EX - IM$, the increase in net exports documented in panel b pushes the *AE* line in panel c upwards. This new red *AE* line intersects the 45° line at a higher income level Y_2, which is the new equilibrium income. Therefore

depreciation
A decrease in the value of a currency relative to other currencies; a rising exchange rate.

> A depreciation (an **appreciation**) of the exchange rate raises (lowers) spending on domestic output, which pushes up (down) equilibrium income.

appreciation An increase in the value of a currency relative to other currencies; a falling exchange rate.

The *IS* curve and the exchange rate

In Chapter 27 we introduced the concept of the *IS* curve. The *IS* curve indicates the equilibrium income levels that obtain at different interest rates. In Figure 28.4a, equilibrium income is 600 if the interest rate is 6%. Income rises to 800 if the interest rate falls to 3%, since such a fall stimulates investment spending.

When we talked about how the exchange rate affects income, we assumed the interest rate was constant, without explicitly saying it. We did not really state the exact level at which the interest rate was constant. So the insight that an increase of the exchange rate raises equilibrium income applies at an interest rate of 3%, at an interest rate of 6% or at any other interest rate. No matter at which point on the old blue *IS* curve (which is drawn for a given exchange rate, say E_0) we start, the new equilibrium income obtained after the exchange rate rises to E_1 will be further to the right (Figure 28.4b). So an increase of the exchange rate shifts the *IS* curve to the right, here into the red position.

> An increase of the exchange rate shifts the *IS* curve to the right.

The *IS* curve and domestic and foreign prices

The reason why a rise in the exchange rate shifts the *IS* curve to the right is because it makes foreign goods more expensive (in home currency) relative to domestic goods.

Figure 28.3 Effects of depreciation on exports, imports and equilibrium income.

a. Exchange rate depreciation raises exports and lowers imports at any level of income. Thus the export line moves up and the import line moves down. While net exports were initially zero at Y_0, they are now zero at Y_1.

b. Since a depreciation raises net exports at any level of income, the net export line moves up. It moves up until it intersects the horizontal axis at Y_1.

c. The position of the *AE* line depends on net exports. A depreciation raises net exports. Hence, the *AE* line moves up. This raises equilibrium income from Y_0 to Y_2. *Note*. As you see from looking at panel b, while net exports were zero in the initial equilibrium, they are positive in the new equilibrium that obtains after the depreciation.

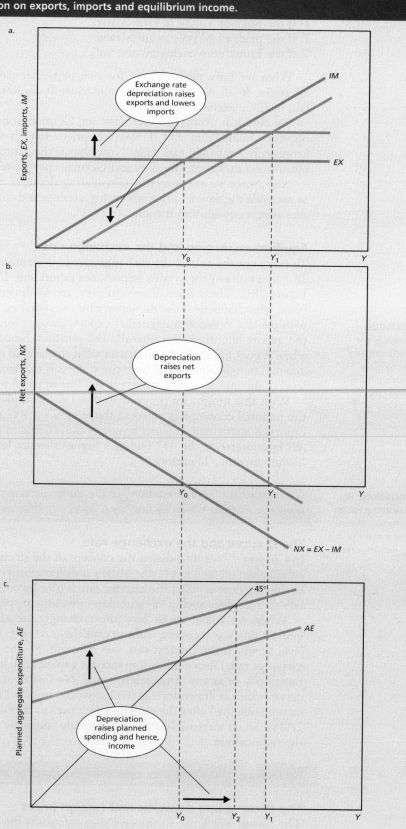

Figure 28.4 The effect of exchange rate depreciation on the *IS* curve

a. The *IS* curve displays equilibrium income levels at different interest rates. The real exchange rate and, hence, goods prices and the nominal exchange rate are considered given.

b. When the exchange rate depreciates, home-produced goods become cheaper on the world market, and imports become more expensive. Hence, net exports rise. This increased demand raises equilibrium income. Since this happens at any interest rate, the *IS* curve shifts to the right.

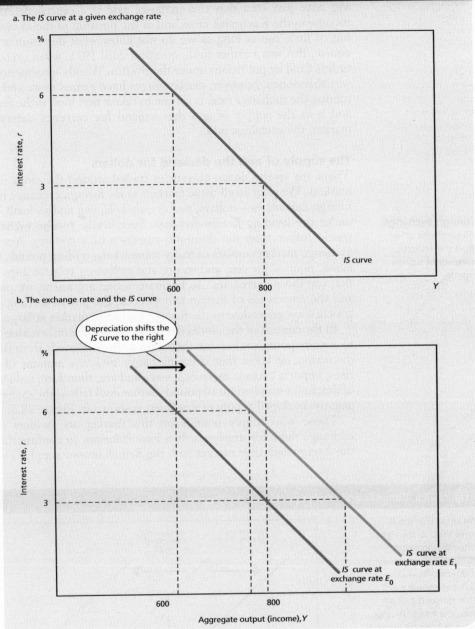

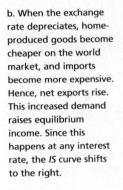

real exchange rate
The price of a (basket of) good(s) abroad, expressed in domestic currency, divided by its price at home.

The effect of E on relative prices (or the **real exchange rate** – see the 'Exchange rate terminology' box) is seen in the equation

$$\text{Relative prices} = E \times \frac{P^W}{P}$$

where $E \times P^W$ transforms foreign prices, represented by P^W, into domestic currency. But then an increase in foreign prices P^W has the same effect as an increase in E. Therefore, an increase in foreign prices also shifts the *IS* curve to the right by making foreign goods more expensive. From the definition of relative prices we further see that an increase in P makes foreign goods more competitive in terms of prices. Thus the demand for domestically produced goods and services falls and the *IS* curve shifts to the left.

A first look at the foreign exchange market

We have just seen that the exchange rate is a crucial determinant of equilibrium income in the Keynesian cross and of the position of the *IS* curve. This is interesting, but of little use as long as we do not know what determines the exchange rate. Of course, this was a rather futile question until 1971, when exchange rates where more or less fixed by politicians under the Bretton Woods agreements. Since this agreement was abandoned, however, market forces have gained more and more weight in determining the exchange rate. It is time to take a first look at the foreign exchange market and how the supply of and the demand for currency determine the price in this market, the exchange rate.

The supply of and the demand for dollars

There are several dozen currencies traded around the clock in the world's currency markets. We refer to all these markets as *the* foreign exchange market. In doing so, all foreign currencies – dollars, roubles, shekels, yen and so forth – are lumped together under the heading *foreign exchange*. Specifically, **foreign exchange** is simply all currencies other than the domestic currency of a country. Actually, Britain's foreign exchange market consists of many submarkets, trading pounds for dollars, pounds for euros, pounds for yen, and so on, and reflecting relationships with all the countries that use those currencies. To facilitate verbal argument, we pick a pair of countries, and the currencies of Britain and Greece, the pound sterling and drachma. But the conclusions generalize to the foreign exchange market at large.

In the context of the model developed so far, the only reason why Greeks may want to acquire pounds is because they want to import goods from Britain. From the above discussion we know that if the exchange rate, the amount of drachmas per pound, rises, imports become more expensive and are, therefore, reduced. Thus, the quantity of drachmas supplied (or of pounds demanded) falls as the exchange rate goes up. This negatively-sloped supply of drachmas is shown in Figure 28.5.

Those who supply pounds on this market are holders of pounds seeking to exchange them for drachmas. It is important not to confuse the supply of pounds on the foreign exchange market with the British money supply. The money supply is the

foreign exchange

All currencies other than the domestic currency of a given country.

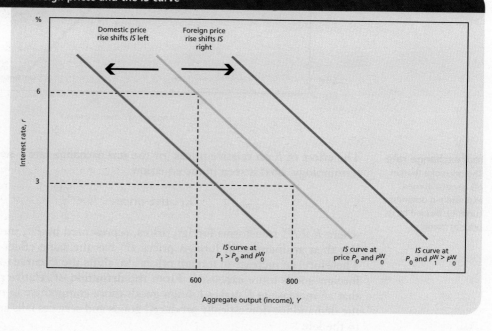

Figure 28.5 Domestic and foreign prices and the *IS* curve

We know that the *IS* curve shifts to the right when the domestic currency depreciates in real terms. The real exchange rate is $E \times P^W/P$. It rises if E or P^W rise, or if P falls. Thus an increase in world prices makes our goods more competitive, raising net exports and shifting *IS* to the right. Rising home prices make domestic goods less competitive, shifting *IS* to the left.

Domestic price rise shifts *IS* left

Foreign price rise shifts *IS* right

IS curve at $P_1 > P_0$ and P^W_0

IS curve at price P_0 and P^W_0

IS curve at P_0 and $P^W_1 > P^W_0$

Interest rate, r

Aggregate output (income), Y

Figure 28.6 Demand, supply and equilibrium in the foreign exchange market

Here foreign currency is only needed to pay for imports. If the drachma (GRD) depreciates, Greeks want less imports from UK. The supply of GRDs in demand for £s falls. The supply curve slopes down. Also, when E goes up, UK imports from Greece rise: So does demand for GRDs. The demand curve slopes up. Where is the equilibrium? At E_1 demand exceeds supply and the GRD/£ rate falls. At E_2 supply exceeds demand. The GRD/£ rate rises. At E_0 the market clears.

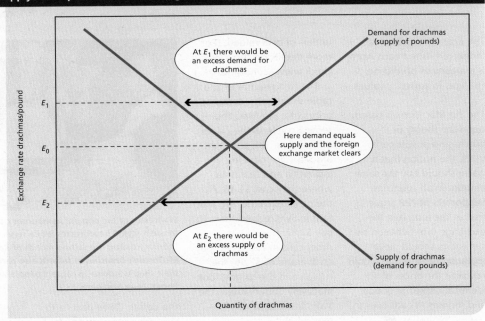

sum of all the money currently in circulation. The supply of pounds on the foreign exchange market is the number of pounds that holders seek to exchange in a given time period for drachmas. Now the only use Britons may have for drachmas is to buy Greek exports. Those become cheaper for Britons if the drachma depreciates; the drachma/pound rate rises, and one pound buys more drachmas than before. But then the demand for drachmas (the supply of pounds) rises as the exchange rate goes up. So the demand curve possesses a positive slope, as the red curve in Figure 28.6 shows.

When exchange rates are flexible they are determined by market forces alone:

The equilibrium exchange rate occurs at the point where the quantity demanded of a foreign currency equals the quantity of that currency supplied.

This is also shown in Figure 28.6. An excess demand for pounds (quantity demanded in excess of quantity supplied) will cause the price of pounds to rise – that is the drachma depreciates with respect to the pound, or the pound appreciates with respect to the drachma. An excess supply of pounds causes the opposite: the drachma appreciates.

Note that the exchange rate that equates supply and demand in our first look at the foreign exchange market also equates imports and exports denoted in a common currency. Now this is not a situation we often encounter in reality. Why is this?

A clue as to why our first look at the foreign exchange market and real life do not seem to conform is provided by two numbers: in 1997, as we already mentioned, 1.2 trillion dollars' worth of currency changed hands in the foreign exchange markets every day. Also in 1997, world trade amounted to 10 trillion dollars over the entire year. But that means that trade – that is, currency purchases to buy exports and imports – only explains 5% of all transactions in the foreign exchange market; 95% of currency transactions must be conducted for other reasons that we have not encountered yet. A modern treatment of exchange rates must include those reasons, since they obviously dominate the foreign exchange market. A natural starting point for their discussion is the balance of payments.

Applications

The Hamburger Standard

The *Economist*'s Big Mac Index, published each April, is a means of predicting changes in currency values:

The Big Mac index is based upon the theory of purchasing-power parity (PPP), the notion that a dollar should buy the same amount in all countries. Supporters of PPP argue that in the long run, the exchange rate between two currencies should move towards the rate that would equalize the prices of an identical basket of goods and services in each country.

Our 'basket' is a McDonald's Big Mac, produced in 110 countries. The Big Mac PPP is the exchange rate that would leave hamburgers costing the same in America as abroad. Comparing actual rates with PPPs signals whether a currency is under- or overvalued. (For more details on the index, check www.economist.com.)

The first column of the table shows local-currency prices of a Big Mac; the second converts the prices into dollars. The cheapest Big Macs are now in Indonesia and Malaysia, where they cost $1.16. At the other extreme, Big Mac fans in Switzerland have to pay $3.87. Given that Americans in four cities pay an average of $2.56, the rupiah and the ringgit look massively undervalued, the Swiss franc massively overvalued.

The third column calculates Big Mac PPPs. For example, dividing the Japanese price by the American price gives the dollar PPP of ¥109. On April 6th, the exchange rate was ¥135, implying that the yen is 19% undervalued against

Waitresses at the popular hamburger chain McDonald's wear Moslem-styled headdresses while serving customers in Jakarta in February during the fasting month of Ramadan. In addition McDonald's branches in Jakarta also partly close the curtains to their shop windows to respect people who fast.
Photo: Enny Nuraheni

the dollar. Three years ago the index suggested that the yen was 100% overvalued against the dollar. Likewise, the D-mark is now only 5% overvalued, against 50% in April 1995.

The most dramatic changes in the index over the past year are in East Asia, where devaluations have left currencies significantly undervalued. This competitive advantage, however, is being eroded by inflation. In Indonesia, the price of a big Mac has more than doubled over the past year. East European currencies also look cheap, with the Hungarian forint 52% undervalued against the dollar. The Big Mac index is not a perfect measure of PPP. Price differences may be distorted by trade barriers on beef, sales taxes, local competition and changes in the cost of non-traded inputs such as rents. But despite its flaws, the Big Mac index produces PPP estimates close to those derived by more sophisticated methods. A currency can deviate from PPP for long periods, but several studies have found that the Big Mac is a useful predictor of future movements – enabling the hungry investor to get rich by putting his money where his mouth is.

The hamburger standard

	Big Mac prices		Implied PPP* of the dollar	Actual $ exchange rate 6/4/98	Under (–)/over (+) valuation against dollar, %
	In local currency	In dollars			
United States**	$2.56	2.56	–	–	–
Belgium	Bfr 109	2.87	42.58	38.00	+12
Britain	£1.84	3.05	1.39_	1.66_	+19
Denmark	Dkr23.8	3.39	9.28	7.02	+32
Germany	DM4.95	2.69	1.93	1.84	+5
Hungary	Forint 259	1.22	101	213	–52
Indonesia	Rupiah 9,900	1.16	3,867	8,500	–55
Japan	¥280	2.08	109	135	–19
Malaysia	M$4.30	1.16	1.68	3.72	–55
Netherlands	Fl5.45	2.63	2.13	2.07	+3
Sweden	SKr24.0	3.00	9.38	8.00	+17
Switzerland	SFr5.90	3.87	2.30	1.52	+51

* Purchasing-power parity: local price divided by price in United States; ** average of New York, Chicago, San Francisco and Atlanta; *** dollars per pound.

Source: McDonald's.

Source: The Economist, *11 April 1998, p. 88.*

The balance of payments

balance of payments

The record of a country's transactions in goods, services, and assets with the rest of the world; also the record of a country's sources (supply) and uses (demand) of foreign exchange.

The **balance of payments** is the record of a country's international transactions. An international transaction always involves the purchase or the sale of foreign currency in exchange for domestic currency. Accounting for any specific transaction in the balance of payments is quite straightforward if you adhere to the following simple rule:[2]

Any transaction that requires a purchase of domestic currency is a credit (positive) item in that country's balance of payments; any transaction that requires a sale of domestic currency is a debit (negative) item.

Since a purchase of domestic currency can only be completed if someone agrees to a sale, the sum of all credit items (purchases) must equal the sum of all debit items (sales). But then the demand for domestic currency always equals the supply of domestic currency, and the foreign exchange market always clears. This is why the conditions that equilibrate the balance of payments also equilibrate the foreign exchange market at the same time.

Before we look at the structure of an actual balance of payments, consider a stylized world with only two countries, Britain and Sweden. Suppose Britain wants to import one Volvo car from Sweden that costs 130,000 kronor. To obtain the 130,000 kronor demanded by the Swedish car maker, the British customer must supply £10,000 at the current exchange rate. In reality, the British buyer only sees and settles the £10,000 price tag. But since Volvo insists on receiving payment in kronor to pay for Swedish workers and steel, someone must offer £10,000 in exchange for 130,000 kronor. Following the rule stated above, the Volvo import shows up as a debit item (that is, with a minus) in Britain's balance of payments (see Figure 28.7). That balance of

---

Figure 28.7 Three ways to finance imports

To pay for imports from Sweden, Britain needs to acquire Swedish kronor. There are three ways to do so:
a. It can export and accept payment in kronor.
b. It can ask Swedes to lend the required amount of kronor and hand over debt titles instead.
c. It can persuade the Bank of England (or the Sveriges Riksbank) to sell kronor for pounds.

a.
Balance of payments

CURRENT ACCOUNT	
Export of CDs	10,000
Import of Volvo	−10,000
Balance	0

Exports raise foreign currency needed to pay for import

All accounts are balanced

b.
Balance of payments

CURRENT ACCOUNT	
Exports	0
Import of Volvo	−10,000
Balance	−10,000

CAPITAL ACCOUNT	
Sale of domestic asset	10,000
Purchase of foreign asset	0
Balance	10,000

Sale of home asset (debt title) to foreigner raises currency needed for import

Capital account surplus covers current account deficit

c.
Balance of payments

CURRENT ACCOUNT	
Exports	0
Import of Volvo	−10,000
Balance	−10,000

OFFICIAL RESERVES	
Purchase of home currency	10,000
Sale of home currency	0
Balance	10,000

Central bank sells foreign currency needed to pay for import

Deterioration of currency reserves covers current account deficit

---

[2]*Bear in mind the distinction between the balance of payments and a balance sheet. A balance sheet for a firm or a country measures that entity's stock of assets and liabilities at a moment in time. The balance of payments, by contrast, measures flows, usually over a period of a month, a quarter or a year. Despite its name, the balance of payments is not a balance sheet.*

current account (CA)

The balance of payments account that records trade in goods and services.

payments account which records trade in goods and services (such as this car import) is called the **current account (CA)**.

Again, and this is important: the Volvo can only be imported if somebody is willing to demand 10,000 pounds in exchange for 130,000 kronor. This may come about in two major ways:

1. There can be another, balancing transaction in the current account (Figure 28.7a). For example, Sweden may import 1000 Elton John CDs costing £10 apiece. To pay the British record company, the Swedish importer must acquire £10,000 in exchange for 130,000 kronor. Since this is exactly the amount the British Volvo importer needs, both transactions, the import and the export, go through as planned. In this case the current account balances. Exports equal imports. Net exports are zero.

Of course, in reality the British importer does not look for a British exporter (or Swedish importer) to buy kronor, but goes to the bank instead. Now the bank needs to find somebody prepared to sell the amount of kronor the bank's customer wants. The bank only serves as a middleman. Leaving it out in our examples does not bear on the substance of the issues.

2. Suppose Swedes want no Elton John CDs but stick with ABBA and Roxette. Then Britain as a whole is unable to pay Volvo in kronor. The only way to import the Volvo would be if Sweden did not insist on payment right now, accepting the promise of payment some time in the future.

Again, reality may be a bit more complicated. Usually, it would not be the British importer who owes Volvo. Instead some British institution, maybe even the government, would go into debt towards some Swedish institution or individual. Suppose in Figure 28.7b that a wealthy Swede buys 10,000 pounds' worth of British Treasury bills (which promise the bearer repayment on some specified date in the future). Because she has to make the payment in pounds, she offers (supplies) 130,000 kronor on the foreign exchange market (in exchange for £10,000). Since this is the amount the British Volvo importer needs, both transactions go through. Purchases and sales of assets such as bonds, stocks and property are recorded in a separate balance of payments account, the **capital account (CP)**. In Figure 28.7b, the item balancing the car import is not recorded in the current account, but in the capital account. The current account records a deficit. The capital account records a surplus of equal size.

capital account (CP)

A separate balance of payments account recording the purchases and sales of assets such as bonds, stocks and property.

Although we have actually exhausted the logical possibilities to finance imports and balance the balance of payments, there is a refinement to the case described in Figure 28.7b. There we assumed that the market, private investors or non-government institutions purchase British assets and supply kronor. Alternatively, this could be done by the government or, more precisely, by the government branch that deals with such matters, the central bank. For example, the Swedish central bank could sell 130,000 kronor in exchange for £10,000. This constitutes a claim on future British output and is usually used to buy British bonds. So net foreign assets of the Swedish central bank rise. As a second possibility, the Bank of England may sell 130,000 kronor' worth of Swedish government bonds it holds, and supply the kronor in the foreign exchange market in exchange for £10,000. In this case, shown in Figure 28.7c, the Bank of England's net foreign assets fall, the private capital account is balanced, and the current account is still in deficit.

The advantage of recording private capital flows and the change in official net foreign assets (mostly covering central bank currency reserves) separately is that it reveals whether foreign exchange market transactions were due to market forces alone, or whether they included the central bank as a buyer or seller. If the capital account only records changes in private net foreign assets, and if central bank involvement in the foreign exchange market is tracked in the **official reserves account (OR)**, we have:

official reserves account (OR)

A separate balance of payments account recording central bank involvement in the foreign exchange market.

Balance of payments (BP) = current account balance (CA) + capital account balance (CP) + official reserves account balance (OR) = 0

But with the balance of payments always zero by definition, is it not a contradiction when commentators speak of a country running a balance of payments deficit or surplus? In a way this terminology is unfortunate. What economists mean by these terms is the nature of official involvement that contributed to this balance. So we can write:

Balance of payments surplus = – official reserves balance = current account balance + capital account balance

In other words, the balance of payments surplus (which may also be negative) indicates the extent to which the central bank intervened in the foreign exchange market, driving a wedge between the usual requirement that the current account and the capital account balances add up to zero. If the central bank stays clear of the foreign exchange market, thus leaving the determination of the exchange rate up to the market, $CA = -CP$ always holds.

A real-world balance of payments

Figure 28.8 shows Germany's balance of payments in real-world numbers for 1996. It consists of the three parts mentioned above: the current account, the capital account and the official reserves account.

Figure 28.8 The German balance of payments in 1996 (billions of marks)

CURRENT ACCOUNT		
Exports of goods	784.3	
Imports of goods	–690.0	
Merchandize trade balance		94.3
Exports of services	130.3	
Imports of services	–182.6	
Services trade balance		–52.3
Income received on investments	115.5	
Income paid on investments	–122.3	
Net investment income		–6.8
Transfer payments from abroad	26.0	
Transfer payments to abroad	–80.9	
Net transfer payments		–54.9
BALANCE ON CURRENT ACCOUNT		–19.7
CAPITAL ACCOUNT		
Change in German holdings of foreign assets		
Change in foreign holdings of German assets		
BALANCE ON CAPITAL ACCOUNT		21.0
(Decrease in private net foreign assets)		
OFFICIAL RESERVES ACCOUNT		
OFFICIAL RESERVES BALANCE		–1.6
(Decrease in Bundesbank net foreign assets)		
STATISTICAL DISCREPANCY		0.3
Balance of payments		0

Labels (left):
- 1000 A class vehicles sold to Sweden
- 10,000 Spice Girls CDs sold in Germany
- Tony Blair flies Lufthansa
- Beckenbauer goes on golf holiday in Marbella
- Munich couple receives dividends on final stocks
- Interest on German government bonds paid to French owner
- Michael Schumacher sends cheque home to mum
- German government contributes to EU budget
- Steffi Graf buys IBM stocks
- Sony builds office tower in Berlin
- Bundesbank buys British T bills

Source: Deutsche Bundesbank, Zahlungsbilanzstatistik.

In the current account, the first two lines record exports and imports of goods. Net exports of goods, called the merchandise trade balance, are traditionally positive in Germany. The year 1996 recorded a surplus of 94.3 billion marks.

Lines 4 and 5 record exports and imports of services. Here the balance is negative at −52.3 billion marks, mainly due to huge amounts spent by Germans travelling abroad.

Lines 7 and 8 show investment income received from abroad and paid to other countries, respectively. The final category records private and government transfer payments to and from other countries. Examples here are German contributions to the EU budget and to the United Nations, foreign aid, and gifts from Turkish families living in Germany to relatives in Turkey.

The sum of all these net payments equals $94.3 − 52.3 − 6.8 − 54.9 = −19.7$. This is the current account. Although traditionally positive, the German current account turned negative upon unification.

The first two lines in the capital account should show the increase in German assets held by foreigners, and the increase in foreign assets held by residents of Germany. Given is only the difference between the two: 21 billion DM. This is the net decrease in Germany's foreign asset holdings, the balance on capital account.

The official reserves account shows that the Bundesbank's holdings of foreign assets increased by 1.6 billion. This measures the Bundesbank's involvement in the foreign exchange market.

In theory, the current account balance, the capital account balance and the official reserves account balance, should add up to zero.

> The overall sum of all entries in the balance of payments must be zero.

statistical discrepancy
A balancing item in balance of payments calculations that compensates for inaccuracies in compiling the data.

As you can see from Figure 28.8, this does not hold in reality. Adding $− 19.7 + 21.0 − 1.6 = −0.3$, which is not zero, primarily due to difficulties of measurement. We thus include a balancing item called the **statistical discrepancy**. If there were no errors in compiling balance of payments data, the statistical discrepancy would be zero.

The exchange rate system and the official reserves account

Two benchmark ways of organizing the foreign exchange market exist: first, a country can choose to fix exchange rates against other currencies. Under such a system of **fixed exchange rates** the exchange rate cannot move to help balance the foreign exchange market (or the balance of payments). Instead, the central bank must intervene in the foreign exchange market to satisfy any excess demand for domestic currency or purchase any excess supply. The extent of these interventions is indicated by the official reserves account balance.

fixed exchange rates
Exchange rates that are fixed against other currencies by the government.

> Under fixed exchange rates the official reserves account is usually not zero. It is a measures of central bank intervention in the foreign exchange market.

flexible exchange rates
Exchange rates that are determined exclusively by the market, without government intervention.

Second, the country may leave the determination of the exchange rate up to the market. Under a pure system of **flexible exchange rates** the central bank has no business in the foreign exchange market. The official reserves account balance is zero by definition. Hence:

> Under flexible exchange rates the capital account balance is the perfect mirror image of the current account balance. The two balances add up to zero.

Current account and capital account balances 1974–1997

Figure 28.9 shows current account and capital account balances in 15 industrial countries for the period 1974 to 1997. In most countries the capital account balance indeed mirrors the current account balance. A positive current account goes with a

Figure 28.9 Current account and capital account in 15 industrial countries, 1974–1997

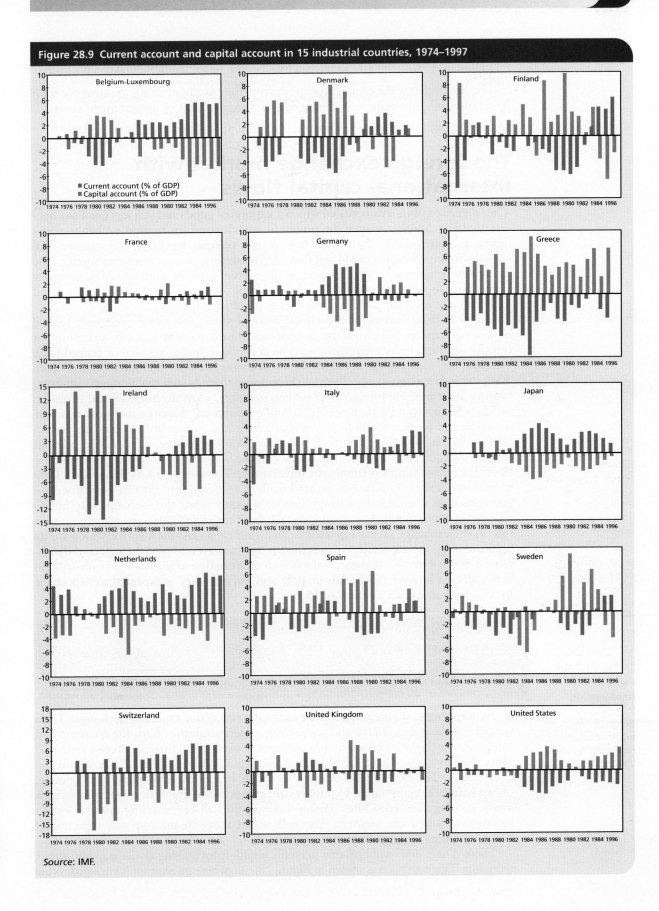

■ Current account (% of GDP)
■ Capital account (% of GDP)

Source: IMF.

negative capital account. We lend to foreign countries so they can buy our exports. In the opposite case we borrow from other countries so we can pay for our high level of imports.

The less perfectly the capital account mirrors the current account, the stronger must be central bank involvement in the foreign exchange market or measurement errors.

The foreign exchange market with international capital flows

The balance of payments revealed why net exports of goods and services need not necessarily be 0. Another source for supply of and demand for foreign exchange is the capital account balance that tracks how people relocate wealth in the international capital markets. If capital could not flow across borders, our previous treatment of the foreign exchange market that focused on the current account alone would be perfectly appropriate. Because capital flows are an integral part of reality, however, these need to be brought into our picture of the foreign exchange market.

Let us start by looking at the capital account alone, just as we previously looked only at net exports (which we use to approximate the current account, assuming net transfers and net investment income to be constants). In the absence of central bank intervention, the capital account shows whether wealth has been shifted from domestic into foreign assets. To simplify, suppose there is only one domestic interest-bearing asset and one foreign interest-bearing asset. How do international investors decide whether to hold their wealth at home or abroad? Suppose investors consider domestic and foreign assets to be perfect substitutes, just as brown eggs are perfect substitutes for white eggs (unless you are colouring Easter eggs). Then all that investors are interested in is which asset yields the highest rate of return. For domestic assets the rate of return is simply the interest rate. For foreign assets things are a little more complicated. The rate of return equals the foreign interest rate only if we are guaranteed an unchanged exchange rate. If we only *expect* the exchange rate not to change, as opposed to being certain, the return is *expected* to equal the foreign interest rate. If the exchange rate is expected to change during, say, the year for which we tie up our money, the expected return is the foreign interest rate plus the expected depreciation of the domestic currency (which is an appreciation of the foreign currency). So if the foreign interest rate stands at 10% and our currency is expected to depreciate by 5%, we may expect a return of 15%.

> **Equilibrium condition in international capital market:**
>
> Rate of return on domestic asset = Expected rate of return on foreign asset
>
> Interest rate = Foreign interest rate + **Expected depreciation**

expected depreciation
Increase of the exchange rate (in %) expected between now and a specified date in the future.

To keep things simple, suppose the exchange rate is not expected to change. Then we can use the terms *returns* and *interest rates* interchangeably, both for domestic and foreign assets. Now investors simply compare domestic and foreign interest rates and move their assets to where the interest rate is highest. Figure 28.10 illustrates this.

In Figure 28.10a, the interest rate abroad is higher than at home. Accordingly, global wealth, as represented by a huge ball, moves out of domestic assets into foreign assets. As long as interest rates remain this way, the ball keeps rolling until all wealth has moved out of the country. The ball would move in the opposite direction if domestic interest rates exceeded those abroad.

There is only one condition that prevents wealth from moving all the way into either direction. This condition is shown in Figure 28.10b, where interest rates are equal. Now

Figure 28.10 International interest rates and the capital balance

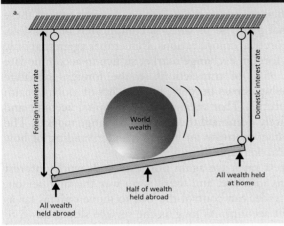

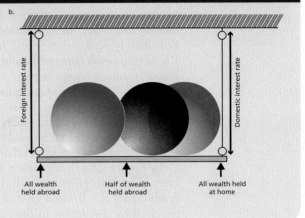

If interest rates abroad exceed domestic interest rates, all international wealth moves abroad.

If foreign and domestic interest rates are equal, investors do not care where they hold wealth. Any position shown in the diagram is acceptable.

international investors have no desire to relocate their assets across borders. They are perfectly fine with the current composition of their portfolio of domestic and foreign assets as indicated by the position of the black ball. What is more, they are just as happy with any other split between domestic and foreign assets such as those indicated by the red or blue balls, since expected returns in both countries are the same. This also means that investors would not resist a change in their international portfolio if this were triggered by some other force. They do not care! Just as you do not bother to open the box in the supermarket to see how many white and brown eggs you have.

To sum up, the capital account can only be in equilibrium if domestic and foreign interest rates (or, more generally, domestic and foreign returns) are equal. If domestic interest rates are higher, everybody wants to shift wealth into domestic assets. To be able to buy them one must first acquire domestic currency. Since no domestic currency is offered, because no one wants to move wealth out of domestic assets, there is an excess demand for domestic currency that drives down the exchange rate (an appreciation of the domestic currency). If interest rates at home are lower than abroad, capital moves out of the country. Everybody wants to get rid of domestic currency, which drives the exchange rate up (a depreciation of the domestic currency).

Simplified equilibrium condition in the international capital market (no depreciation expected):

$$\text{Interest rate} = \text{Foreign interest rate}$$

Merging the capital account and the current account

Now that we understand each of the two non-official balance of payments accounts in isolation, we must merge them for a complete picture of the balance of payments and the foreign exchange market.

Under flexible exchange rates, the balance of payments always balances, and, therefore, the foreign exchange market always clears. Our task is to lay out the macroeconomic conditions that this equilibrium requires.

Logically, a balance of payments equilibrium comes about when the current account and the capital account are each in equilibrium, or with a *CA* surplus and a *CP* deficit of same size, or a *CA* deficit matching a *CP* surplus. To spell out all these combinations and the conditions that give rise to them is complicated but feasible. Fortunately, reality cuts through theoretical complications. Remember again that only 5% of one year's transactions in the foreign exchange market suffice to accommodate global trade. Consequently, some 95% of transactions in the foreign exchange markets reflect shifts of asset ownership across borders, movements of global wealth in search of the highest possible returns. That means that the capital account and international financial investors entirely dominate the foreign exchange market. The analogy suggested in Figure 28.10 may motivate an intuitive understanding of how this characterizes foreign exchange market equilibrium.

In Figure 28.11a, domestic interest rates are again not level with world interest rates. The ball, global wealth, begins to move, and there is no way the tiny person, symbolizing the limited volume of trade, can control the ball to move only as far as required by the deficit in the current account. As long as the surface slopes down to the left, wealth continues to flow in. No equilibrium exists where the person could force the ball to a halt.

In Figure 28.11b the track is level. Interest rates at home and abroad are equal. The ball rests wherever it is pushed to. And, merely by overcoming friction, even the little person can push the ball into any desired location.

The analogy with the balance of payments is that if the exchange rate is, say, higher than the exchange rate that equilibrates the current account, as indicated in Figure 28.6, then the country records a current account surplus that needs to be balanced by a capital account deficit. So wealth must shift from domestic assets into foreign assets. And so it does. Why? Because financial investors do not care in which country they hold assets. Domestic ones are as good as foreign ones. If foreign importers cannot pay immediately but offer debt certificates instead, the international capital market is happy to buy the certificates.

This does not work if domestic and international interest rates differ. In that case, wealth moves in volumes so large that trade imbalances cannot possibly be large enough to neutralize them. Only if the domestic interest rate equals the global one, so that investors do not care where they hold their wealth, is a current account imbalance readily accommodated by the capital account recording the required shift in wealth.

Figure 28.11 Equilibrating the balance of payments: the current account versus the capital balance

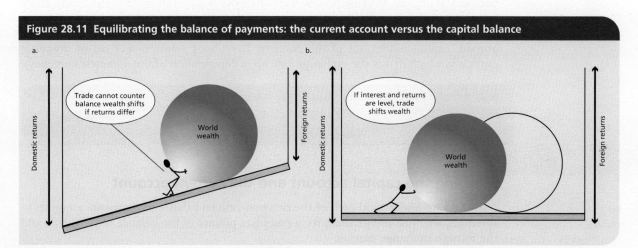

If domestic returns exceed foreign returns, world wealth flows in to an extent that net exports cannot possibly keep in check.

If domestic returns equal foreign returns, investors accept any share of foreign assets in their portfolios. If a current account imbalance requires a shift of wealth across borders, the capital account is happy to comply.

Figure 28.12 The *FE* curve

If international investors dominate the foreign exchange market, home and world interest rates must be equal for the foreign exchange market to clear. If the home interest rate is too high, huge capital inflows result. If it is too low, capital flows out on a grand scale. Since this holds at any level of income, the foreign-exchange-market equilibrium line is horizontal at the world interest rate.

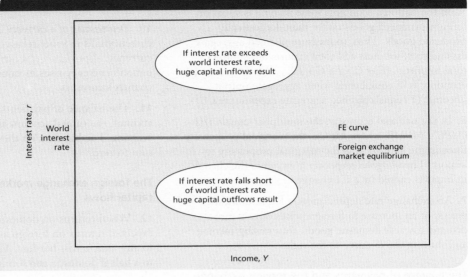

The requirement that the domestic interest rate must equal the foreign interest rate as a precondition for any foreign exchange market equilibrium always applies, no matter what the level of domestic income is. But then we may represent this equilibrium condition in the *i/Y* diagram, previously used to show the *IS* and *LM* curves, by a horizontal line (Figure 28.12). The line cuts the vertical axis at the world interest rate. Since it combines all points that produce a foreign exchange market equilibrium, we call it the *FE* curve.

Looking ahead: the national-economy model

The national economy interacts with other countries' economies. It trades goods and services, but also invests in financial and real assets abroad. All these transactions require the purchase or sale of other countries' currencies. These are traded in the foreign exchange market. This chapter has analysed this market and demonstrated that it is in equilibrium on the horizontal *FE* curve.

The national-economy model comprises the two markets we encountered previously plus this new market. Chapter 29 will discuss how the goods market, the money market and the foreign exchange market interact. We will look at how the presence of the foreign exchange market affects the effectiveness of monetary and fiscal policy, and how the national economy depends on outside developments in the rest of the world.

Summary

1. The main difference between an international transaction and a domestic transaction concerns currency exchange: when people in different countries buy from and sell to each other, an exchange of currencies must also take place.

2. The *exchange rate* is the price of one country's currency in terms of another country's currency.

Globalization

3. Globalization refers to the rapidly increasing interdependence between the world's national economies.

4. The main features of globalization are that more goods and services are traded across borders and more wealth shifts from one country to another than ever before.

Equilibrium income in the national economy

5. In the national economy, some income is spent on foreign-produced goods rather than domestically produced goods. Thus, to measure planned aggregate expenditure, we must add total exports but subtract total imports: $AE \equiv C + I + G + EX - IM$. The national economy is in equilibrium when aggregate output (income) (Y) equals planned aggregate expenditure (AE).

6. In the national economy, the multiplier equals $1/[1 - (MPC - MPM)]$, where MPC is the marginal propensity to consume and MPM is the marginal propensity to import. The *marginal propensity to import* is the change in imports caused by a €1 change in income.

7. An exchange rate depreciation, a fall in domestic prices, or an increase in foreign prices directs more demand towards domestic goods, thus raising income and shifting the *IS* curve to the right.

The balance of payments and the foreign exchange market

8. *Foreign exchange* is simply all currencies other than the domestic currency of a given country. The record of a nation's transactions in goods, services, and assets with the rest of the world is known as its *balance of payments*. The balance of payments is also the record of a country's sources (supply) and uses (demand) of foreign exchange.

9. The equilibrium exchange rate occurs when the quantity demanded of a foreign currency in the foreign exchange market equals the quantity of that currency supplied in the foreign exchange market.

10. *Depreciation of a currency* occurs when a nation's currency falls in value relative to another country's currency. *Appreciation of a currency* occurs when a nation's currency rises in value relative to another country's currency.

11. The balance of payments comprises the current account, the capital account and the official reserves account. The balances on these three accounts always sum to zero.

The foreign exchange market with international capital flows

12. When returns on domestic assets differ from expected returns on foreign assets, huge volumes of wealth shift across borders. Movements may only come to a halt if domestic and foreign returns are equal.

13. Since transactions recorded in the capital account dominate the foreign exchange market, equilibrium only occurs if wealth stops moving. This requires equal returns.

14. Equality of domestic and foreign interest rates (as proxies for returns) is a precondition for foreign exchange market equilibrium at all levels of income. Hence the foreign exchange market equilibrium line is a horizontal line in the interest rate/income diagram. This line is called the *FE* curve.

Review Terms and Concepts

appreciation
balance of payments
capital account (*CP*)
current account (*CA*)
depreciation
exchange rate
expected depreciation
fixed exchange rates
flexible exchange rates

foreign exchange
globalization
marginal propensity to demand domestic goods
marginal propensity to import (*MPM*)
national-economy multiplier
net exports of goods and services (*EX – IM*)
official reserves account (*OR*)
real exchange rate
statistical discrepancy

Problem Set

1. During 1997 and 1998 a series of events rocked the economies of Asia. Describe the effects of each of the following events on: (i) the exchange rate of the euro versus the Japanese yen; (ii) the balance of trade between the EU and Japan; and (iii) the balance of payments between the EU and Japan.
a. European holders of Japanese stocks and bonds become alarmed and sell their holdings, reinvesting the proceeds in European stock and bond markets.

b. Japan finds itself in a recession with GDP falling sharply.
c. The Japanese finance ministry decides to balance the budget and to counteract the contractionary effects by expansionary monetary policy pushing interest rates to under 1%.

2. Suppose that the situation depicted in Figure 1 prevailed on the foreign exchange market in 1998 with flexible exchange rates.

Figure 1

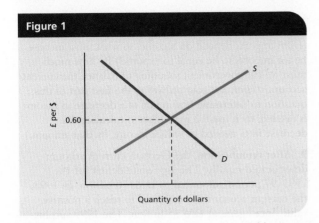

a. Name three phenomena that might shift the demand curve to the right.
b. Which, if any, of these three might cause a simultaneous shift of the supply curve to the left?
c. What effects might the three phenomena have on the balance of payments if the exchange rate floats? And on the balance of trade?

3. List the balance-of-payments account under which each of the following transactions would be classified and explain whether the item represents a credit or debit entry in your country's balance of payments.
a. You go on holiday to Switzerland and spend 300 Swiss francs there on a hotel room, food, transport and so forth.
b. You bring back an oriental carpet that you bought on a trip to the Middle East. The carpet is worth €10,000, but you do not declare it at customs, and no official record of the transaction exists.
c. You buy a new Mazda car (made in Japan) for €15,000.
d. You send your cousin in France a birthday present worth €50.
e. The Volkswagen Group buys a factory in the United States for $100 million.
f. Toyota of Japan buys 10% of all the shares in PSA (the holding company that owns Citroen and Peugeot).
g. You lend your uncle in the United States €5000.
h. Your uncle pays you €500 in interest on the money you previously lent him. He also repays €1000 of the principal.

4. During 1981 and 1982, the President and the Congress of the United States pursued a very expansionary fiscal policy. In 1980 and 1981, the Federal Reserve pursued a very restrictive monetary policy in an attempt to rid the economy of inflation. Ultimately, the economy went into a deep recession, but before it did interest rates went to record levels with the prime rate topping out at over 21%.
a. Explain how this policy mix led to very high interest rates.
b. Show graphically the effect of the high interest rates on the foreign exchange market. What do you think would happen to the value of the dollar under these circumstances?

c. What impact was such a series of events likely to have on the trade balance in Europe and Japan? Explain your answer.

5. What effect will each of the following events have on the balance of payments and the euro exchange rate if (i) the exchange rate is fixed; (ii) if it is flexible?
a. European governments cut taxes, and income rises.
b. The European inflation rate increases, and prices in Europe rise faster than those in the major trading partners.
c. The ECB adopts an expansionary monetary policy. Interest rates fall (and are now lower than those in other countries), and income rises.
d. A 'Buy European' campaign is successful, and European consumers switch from purchasing imported products to those made in Europe.

6. What might be the economic benefits of a 'strong currency'?

7. The exchange rate between the euro and the US dollar is flexible – neither government intervenes in the market for either currency. Suppose a large trade deficit with Japan persuades the European Union to impose quotas on a number of Japanese products imported into the EU and, as a result, the value of these imports falls.
a. The decrease in spending on Japanese products increases spending on European-made goods. Why? What effect will this have on European output and employment? On Japanese output and employment?
b. What happens to European imports from Japan when European output (or income) rises? If the quotas initially reduce imports from Japan by €25 billion, why is the final reduction in imports likely to be less than €25 billion? Explain in terms of the trade feedback effect.
c. Suppose the quotas succeed in reducing imports from Japan by €15 billion. What will happen to the demand for yen? Why?
d. What will happen to the euro–yen exchange rate, and why? (*Hint*: there is an excess supply of yen, or an excess demand for euros.) What effects will the change in the value of each currency have on employment and output in the EU? What about the balance of payments?
e. Considering the macroeconomic effects of a quota on Japanese imports, could a quota actually reduce employment and output in the EU, or have no effect at all? Explain.

8. You are given the following model, which describes the economy of Hypothetica.

■ Consumption function: $C = 100 + 0.8Y_d$
■ Planned investment: $I = 38$
■ Government spending: $G = 75$
■ Exports: $EX = 25$
■ Imports: $IM = 0.05Y_d$
■ Disposable income: $Y_d \equiv Y - T$
■ Taxes: $T = 40$

- Planned aggregate expenditure: $AE \equiv C + I + G + (EX - IM)$
- Definition of equilibrium income: $Y = AE$

a. What is equilibrium income in Hypothetica? What is the government deficit? What is the current account balance?

b. If government spending is increased to $G = 80$, what happens to equilibrium income? Explain, using the government spending multiplier. What happens to imports? Now suppose that the amount of imports is limited to $IM = 40$ by a quota on imports. If government spending is again increased from 75 to 80, what happens to equilibrium income? Explain why the same increase in G has a bigger effect on income in the second case. What is it about the presence of imports that changes the value of the multiplier?

c. If exports are fixed at $EX = 25$, what must income be in order to ensure a current account balance of zero? (*Hint*: imports depend on income, so what must income be for imports to be equal to exports?) By how much must we cut government spending to balance the current account? (*Hint*: use your answer to the first part of this question to determine how much of a decrease in income is needed; then use the multiplier to calculate the decrease in G needed to reduce income by that amount.)

9. After reunification, the German current account deteriorated rapidly. The aggregate deficit for the 1991–97 period amounted to DM170 billion. In 1998, the current account was expected to reach a positive value once again, at DM 25 billion. The 1999 surplus was forecast to reach DM 40 billion. By taking a longer-term perspective, why might one expect such a trend (that is, deficits on the current account) to be followed by surpluses?

Monetary and Fiscal Policy in the National Economy

The previous chapter analysed why and how the national economy differs from the global economy. One difference that stands out is that a country's interest rate is not really free to move. Arbitrage trading by international investors in search of higher returns ties the national interest rate to the rate of return available in the rest of the world. If interest rates were to differ noticeably, huge flows of financial wealth across borders would set in and result in gigantic capital account disequilibria. The volume of exports and imports is too small to possibly compensate for this.

The second important difference is that individual countries trade goods and services with other countries. Exports and imports, among others, depend on the exchange rate, which determines how expensive goods produced at home are relative to goods produced abroad. The exchange rate is determined in the foreign exchange market, where currencies are bought and sold both for the purpose of trading goods and of shifting wealth across borders. This links the two aspects in which the national economy differs from the global economy.

While the previous chapter looked at the foreign exchange market in isolation, we now want to see how it interacts with the money market and the goods market. This chapter begins by describing how equilibrium occurs in the national economy. We will see that the exchange rate system makes a fundamental difference to how equilibrium comes about. Then we take a second look at monetary and fiscal policy. How do these work if they cannot affect the interest rate, as they did in the global economy perspective? After we understand the national economy, we move on to find out how it *interacts* with the rest of the world. Finally, we look at what happens when some countries share a common currency. How does monetary and fiscal policy work in such an arrangement, on which 11 European Union members are now embarking?

exchange rate system

The organisation of the foreign exchange market; focusing on the extent of government interference.

Equilibrium in the national economy

Equilibrium in the national economy obtains when

- the goods market
- the money market, and
- the foreign exchange market

are in equilibrium at the same time.

In terms of our previously employed diagrams, we therefore need to combine the *IS* curve, the *LM* curve and the *FE* curve on one graph.

Three markets combined

Taking account of a third market when proceeding from the global to the national economy introduces a complication. When we dealt with the world economy, only the

Figure 29.1 A situation with no overall equilibrium in the national economy

The national-economy model comprises three markets. In principle, the three market equilibrium lines need not all intersect in the same point. In points 1, 2 and 3 only two markets are in equilibrium, while the third is not. The question is: how does macroeconomic equilibrium (simultaneous equilibrium in all three markets) come about?

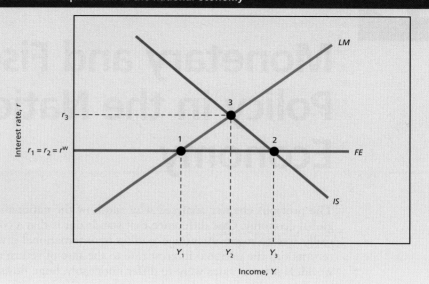

goods market and the money market had to be considered. Equilibrium combinations (of i and Y) for each market could be represented by a straight line. And two straight lines with opposite slopes, here the LM curve and the IS curve, intersect in exactly one point. This point of intersection identifies the interest rate and income level that clear both markets and thus mark a global equilibrium.

The *three* market equilibrium lines that represent the individual country need not intersect in a common point at all. In Figure 29.1 the FE curve and the LM curve intersect at point 1. So at interest rate i_1 and income Y_1 the foreign exchange market and the money market are in equilibrium – but the goods market is *not*.

At point 2, FE and IS intersect; so at i_2 and Y_2 the foreign exchange market and the goods market are in equilibrium. But now the money market is not, because point 2 is not on the LM curve. Finally, at point 3 the goods market and the money market clear. But this constellation throws the foreign exchange market into disequilibrium, because the home interest rate exceeds the expected return on foreign assets.

All this poses the question whether an overall equilibrium in the national economy, in which all three markets clear, is at all feasible (except by pure chance). Fortunately, the answer is yes. The key to understanding how this overall equilibrium is accomplished is the distinction between exogenous variables and endogenous variables.

exogenous variable

A variable that does not depend on the state of the economy, or on other variables. It is taken as given.

We learned in Chapter 23 that an **exogenous (or autonomous) variable** neither depends on nor changes with the state of the economy. It is taken as given. In our model of the global economy we considered government spending and the money supply to be exogenous. An **endogenous variable** is not exogenous; it responds to changes in the state of the economy. We may not take it as given.

endogenous variable

A variable that depends on the state of the economy, or on other variables.

With this distinction between exogenous and endogenous variables in mind, we now take a look at the variables that determine the positions of the FE curve, the LM curve and the IS curve, respectively. Figure 29.2 sums up what we know so far:

■ The position of the LM curve depends on the money supply and on the price level.
■ The position of the FE curve is determined by expected returns on foreign assets (usually taken to equal the foreign interest rate).
■ The position of the IS curve depends on many variables: government spending, income levels in foreign countries, the prices of goods at home and abroad, and the nominal exchange rate.

Which of these positioning variables are exogenous and which are endogenous? This is easy to answer for some: government spending is exogenous, and so is foreign

Figure 29.2 Positioning variables of the *LM* curve, the *FE* curve and the *IS* curve

Y and *r* change as we move along an equilibrium line. Other variables are assumed constant when we draw each line. Most of these 'positioning variables' are exogenous. Those highlighted, the exchange rate and the money supply, may be endogenous, depending on the exchange rate system.

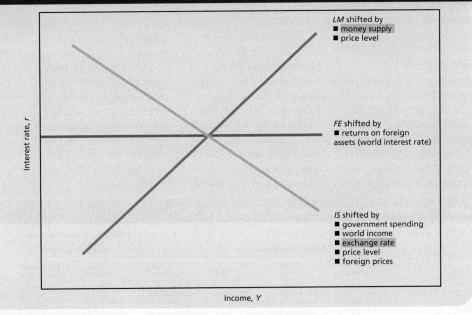

LM shifted by
- money supply
- price level

FE shifted by
- returns on foreign assets (world interest rate)

IS shifted by
- government spending
- world income
- exchange rate
- price level
- foreign prices

income. We currently consider domestic and foreign goods prices as given, and returns on foreign assets too. So what is left is the money supply and the exchange rate. These are highlighted in the graph because they make things tricky. Why? Isn't it clear that exchange rates are endogenous variables determined by supply and demand in the foreign exchange market? And didn't we learn in Chapter 25 that the central bank controls the money supply, making *M* an autonomous variable that is independent of the money supply? Well, yes, under certain conditions. But under others not. These conditions concern the exchange rate system under which a country operates.

The role of the exchange rate system

The world's governments have chosen different exchange rate arrangements for their economies. As you can see from the Global Perspectives box 'Exchange rate arrangements', there is no single dominant form. Although many intermediate forms have been devised and exist in reality, our discussion focuses on two stylized types: flexible exchange rates and fixed exchange rates.

At one extreme, with **flexible exchange rate**s, a country may leave the determination of its exchange rates entirely up to the market. Then its central bank is free to pursue monetary policy as deemed appropriate. The exchange rate is endogenous, determined by market forces that reflect the state of the economy. The money supply is exogenous, set at the discretion of the central bank.

At the other extreme, with **fixed exchange rate**s, a country may fix its exchange rate. For example, Britain might decide unilaterally to fix the price of one euro at one pound sterling. At this price, except for moments of pure chance, one side of the market will not exactly supply what the other side demands. Here the Bank of England must step in. If the market wants to buy more pounds for euros than the market supplies, the Bank of England must supply these extra pounds and accept euros as payment. In terms of the central bank balance sheet discussed in Chapter 25, the Bank of England accumulates foreign currency reserves and puts more domestic currency into circulation. This raises the British money supply. The important thing to note here is that the market *forces* the Bank of England to intervene in the foreign exchange market. The Bank of England has no control over the British money supply, but must supply or purchase any amount of pound sterling the market demands. Control over the money supply is abandoned the moment the exchange rate is fixed.

flexible exchange rate

An exchange rate system that allows the exchange rate to be determined by marked forces alone, without central bank interference.

fixed exchange rate

An exchange rate system in which governments announce an exchange rate at which the central bank is obliged to buy or sell any amount of domestic currency.

Global Perspectives

Exchange rate arrangements

The table shows the diversity of international exchange rate arrangements. Starting on the left (the category 'Currency pegged to'), 66 countries operate under *fixed exchange rates*. Most of them (the 21 in the left column) peg their currencies to the US dollar.

Fourteen former French colonies in Africa fix exchange rates to the French franc. Nine other countries use various currencies, including the mark and the lire. Finally, the 21 countries in columns 4 and 5 do not peg their currencies to some individual currency but to a basket of currencies instead.

The category on the far right of the table (listed as 'More flexible') comprises 99 countries we would classify as having *flexible exchange rates*. From Western Europe this only includes Britain, Sweden and Switzerland.

The category in the middle of the table comprises countries with *hybrid exchange rate systems*. They limit the flexibility of their exchange rates in one way or other, say by means of target zones, but do not strictly fix them. This category mostly contains members of the EMS at that time.

Table 1 Exchange Rate Arrangements (as of March 31, 1997)

Currency pegged to					Flexibility limited in terms of a single currency or group of currencies		More flexible	
US dollar	French franc	Other currency	SDR	Other composite	Single currency	Cooperative arrangements	Other managed floating	Independently floating
Angola	Benin	Bhutan	Libya	Bangladesh	Bahrain	Austria	Algeria	Afghanistan,
Antigua & Barbuda	Burkina Faso	(Indian rupee)	Myanmar	Botswana	Qatar	Belgium	Belarus	Islamic State of
Argentina	Cameroon	Bosnia and		Burundi	Saudi Arabia	Denmark	Brazil	Albania
Bahamas, The	C. African Rep.	Herzegovina		Cape Verde	United Arab	Finland	Cambodia	Armenia
Barbados	Chad	(deutsche mark)		Cyprus	Emirates	France	Chile	Australia
		Brunei Darussalam						Azerbaijan
Belize	Comoros	(Singapore		Czech Republic		Germany	China, PR	
Djibouti	Congo. Rep. of	dollar)		Fiji		Ireland	Colombia	Bolivia
Dominica	Côte d'Ivoire	Estonia		Iceland		Italy	Costa Rica	Bulgaria
Grenada	Equatorial	(deutsche mark)		Jordan		Luxembourg	Croatia	Canada
Iraq	Guinea	Kiribati		Kuwait		Netherlands	Dominican Rep.	Congo, Dem. Rep.
	Gabon	(Australian						Ethiopia
Liberia		dollar)		Malta		Portugal	Ecuador	
Lithuania	Mali			Morocco		Spain	Egypt	Gambia, The
Marshall Islands	Niger	Lesotho		Nepal			El Salvador	Ghana
Micronesia,	Senegal	(South African		Seychelles			Eritrea	Guatemala
Fed. States of	Togo	rand)		Slovak Republic			Georgia	Guinea
Nigeria		Namibia						Guyana
		(South African		Solomon Islands			Greece	
Oman		rand)		Thailand			Guinea-Bissau	Haiti
Panama		San Marino		Tonga			Honduras	India
St. Kitts & Nevis		(Italian lira)		Vanuatu			Hungary	Jamaica
St. Lucia		Swaziland		Western Samoa			Indonesia	Japan
St. Vincent and the		(South African						Kazakhstan
Grenadines		rand)					Iran, IR of	
							Israel	Kenya
Syrian Arab Rep.							Korea	Labanon
							Kyrgyz Rep.	Madagascar
							Lao PD Rep	Malawi
								Mauritania
							Latvia	
							Macedonia,	Mexico
							FYR of	Moldova
							Malaysia	Mongolia
							Maldives	Mozambique
							Mauritius	New Zealand
							Nicaragua	Papua New Guinea
							Norway	Paraguay
							Pakistan	Peru
							Poland	Philippines
							Russia	Romania
							Singapore	Rwanda
							Slovenia	São Tomé and
							Sri Lanka	Principe
							Sudan	Sierra Leone
							Suriname	Somalia
								South Africa
							Tunisia	
							Turkmenistan	Sweden
							Turkey	Switzerland
							Ukraine	Tajikistan, Rep. of
							Uruguay	Tanzania
								Trinidad and
							Uzbekistan	Tobago
							Venezuela	
							Vietnam	Uganda
								United Kingdom
								United States
								Yemen, Republic of
								Zambia
								Zimbabwe

Source: International Financial Statistics Yearbook.

Under *flexible* exchange rates the money supply is an exogenous variable while the exchange rate is endogenous. Under *fixed* exchange rates roles are reversed: the exchange rate is an exogenous variable while the money supply is endogenous.

With our ability to distinguish between exogenous and endogenous variables we return to the question of how overall equilibrium in all three involved markets comes about in the national economy. Since we have learned that the *exchange rate system* determines whether the money supply or the exchange rate are exogenous or endogenous, we look at flexible and fixed exchange rates separately.

Flexible exchange rates

All positioning variables, except the two highlighted in Figure 29.2, are exogenous under any exchange rate system, so the *FE* line is exclusively positioned by the returns on foreign assets. Since these are exogenous, the *FE* curve is where it is, no matter what the markets do.

The *LM* curve is positioned by the price level and the money supply. Under flexible exchange rates the central bank controls the money supply, so once it has decided on the required money supply, the *LM* curve stays put at the implied position, independent of what the market does. As a consequence, the point of intersection between *FE* and *LM*, point *A* in Figure 29.3, determines the interest rate and the output level at which the foreign exchange market and the money market clear, and nothing can change that. What remains open, of course, is what happens when the *IS* curve does not pass through this point. It is important to remember here that the position of the *IS* curve is not only determined by exogenous variables, but also by an endogenous variable: the exchange rate. If the *IS* curve does not pass through *A*, markets make the exchange rate change until *IS* has shifted far enough to pass through *A*. To see how this happens, suppose the economy is initially in point *A* while the *IS* curve is further left, say at position *IS'*. In this situation, the interest rate is i_A and firms produce output

Figure 29.3 Equilibrium in the national economy under flexible exchange rates

The position of the *IS* curve is also determined by the exchange rate. Under flexible exchange rates, the exchange rate adjusts so as to make the *IS* curve pass through point A, where *FE* and *LM* already intersect.

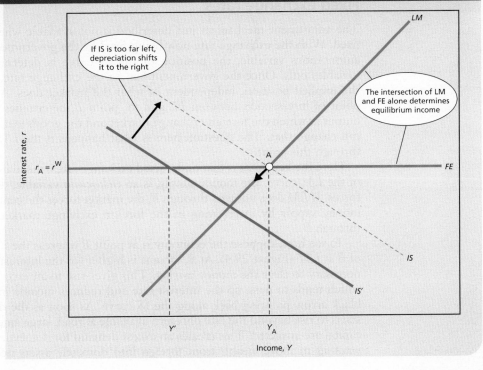

Y_A. But Y_A exceeds the output level Y' at which the goods market would clear. So firms are producing more than is demanded, which sooner or later makes them reduce output.

Lower output also means lower income. At lower incomes, people hold less money. So there is an excess supply of money, which drives down the interest rate as we saw in Chapter 27. In Figure 29.3 the economy begins to move down the LM curve in the direction indicated by the black arrow. But can it really follow the black arrow? Actually, no – at least, not for long: as soon as the interest rate drops below the FE line, the foreign exchange market equilibrium is disturbed. International investors want to get out of their low-paying domestic assets into foreign assets (that promise higher returns). To accomplish this they need to sell domestic currency and buy foreign currency. This generates an excess supply of domestic currency and makes it depreciate.

This depreciation, however, affects the goods market. As we saw in Chapter 28, with a rising exchange rate, domestically produced goods become cheaper relative to foreign goods. Net exports increase, shifting the IS curve to the right. How far? This depends on how much the exchange rate depreciated. If the new IS curve is still to the left of A, however, the situation is qualitatively still the same as before. So depreciation continues, shifting the IS curve until it is in position IS.

If, for some reason, the IS curve initially was to the right of A, the opposite happens of what we just described: there is an excess demand in the goods market. This entices firms to raise output and income. The demand for money goes up, driving up the interest rate. This lures financial investors into domestic currency, driving down the interest rate and shifting the IS curve to the left until it is in position IS.

To summarize:

Under flexible exchange rates, equilibrium income is determined by FE and LM alone. The position of the IS curve is affected by the exchange rate, an endogenous variable. Market forces change the exchange rate until IS passes through the point where FE and LM already intersect.

Fixed exchange rates

The adjustment mechanism just described is not available when exchange rates are fixed. With the exchange rate now being fixed by the government, which makes it an autonomous variable, the position of the IS curve is determined by autonomous variables only. Once the government has set the exchange rate, the IS curve stays at the implied position, independent of what the market does. As a consequence, the point of intersection between FE and IS, point B, determines the interest rate and output at which the foreign exchange market and the goods market clear, and nothing can change that. The question here is what happens if the LM curve does not pass through this point.

Here the key point is that under fixed exchange rates, the main positioning variable of the LM curve, the money supply, is an *endogenous* variable, determined by market forces. If LM does not pass through B, the market forces the central bank to adjust the money supply by intervening in the foreign exchange market until LM does pass through B.

To see how, suppose the economy is at point B whereas the LM curve is to the left of B at LM' (Figure 29.4). At B, income is higher (or the interest rate is lower) than is necessary to clear the money market. This gives rise to an excess demand for money, which tends to push up the interest rate and reduces income in the direction of the black arrow pointing back along the IS curve. As soon as the domestic interest rate starts to rise beyond the rate of return available abroad, large amounts of international capital are attracted. This creates an excess demand for domestic currency: everybody wanting to move wealth from foreign into domestic assets needs first to purchase

Figure 29.4 Equilibrium in the national economy under fixed exchange rates

The position of the *LM* curve is determined by the money supply. Under fixed exchange rates the money supply is endogenous. It adjusts so as to make the *LM* curve pass through point B, where *FE* and *IS* already intersect.

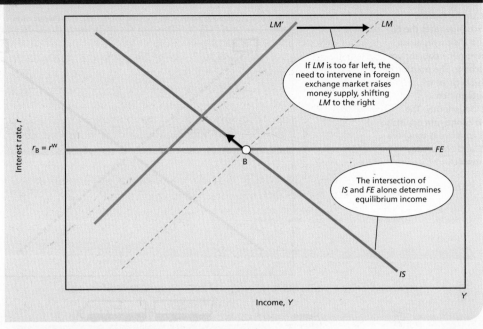

domestic currency to be able to pay for domestic bonds. No sufficient supply of domestic currency is available, because nobody wants to switch into foreign assets.[1] Since the fixing of an exchange rate entails the promise that the central bank buys or sells any amount of domestic currency at this price, the central bank must now sell domestic currency for foreign currency to satisfy the excess demand that initially occurred in the market. This increases currency in circulation and, hence, the domestic money supply. The end result is a shift of the *LM* curve to the right. This mechanism continues to force the central bank to raise the money supply until the *LM* curve passes through *B*.

If for some reason the *LM* curve is positioned to the right of *B*, the process just described works in reverse: there is downward pressure on the interest rate. Mandatory foreign exchange market intervention lowers the money supply, shifting the *LM* curve leftwards until it passes through *B*.

To summarize:

> Under fixed exchange rates, equilibrium income is determined by *FE* and *IS* alone. The position of the *LM* curve is determined by the money supply, an endogenous variable. Market forces change the money supply until *LM* passes through the point where *FE* and *IS* intersect.

Summing up: *IS–LM–FE* under fixed and flexible exchange rates

What we have just learned is very important, so we will restate it in a clear visual form that is easily memorized. Consider Figure 29.5, which shows the *IS–LM–FE* model under flexible exchange rates in (a), and under fixed exchange rates in (b).

---

[1] *The only people who want to buy foreign currency in exchange for domestic currency are importers of foreign goods. In line with the numbers given in Chapter 28, this is bound to be completely insufficient in volume to balance an excess demand for home currency resulting from an inflow of foreign wealth when home interest rates exceed foreign rates of return.*

Figure 29.5 The essentials of the *IS–LM–FE* model under flexible and fixed exchange rates

a. Under flexible exchange rates the *FE* and *LM* curves alone determine equilibrium income. The position of the *IS* curve is determined endogenously. The exchange rate adjusts so as to move *IS* to where *FE* and *LM* already intersect.

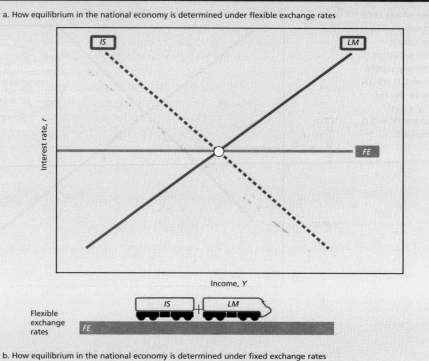

a. How equilibrium in the national economy is determined under flexible exchange rates

b. Under fixed exchange rates the *FE* and *IS* curve alone determine equilibrium income. The position of the *LM* curves is determined endogenously. The money supply adjusts so as to move *LM* to where *FE* and *IS* already intersect.

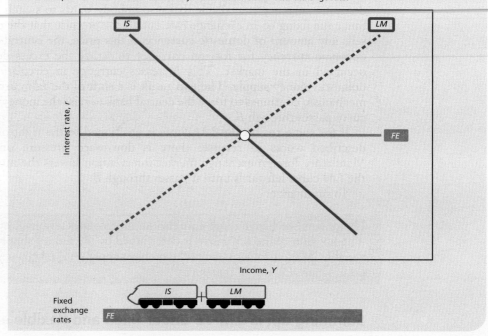

b. How equilibrium in the national economy is determined under fixed exchange rates

Figure 29.5a re-emphasizes that when exchange rates are flexible, the foreign exchange market equilibrium condition *FE* and the money market equilibrium condition *LM* depend on exogenous variables alone and therefore suffice to determine equilibrium income and the equilibrium interest rate. The *IS* curve follows, to wherever the other two lines intersect. It is not really needed to determine equilibrium income and the interest rate, but it tells us what the exchange rate does. The situation is something like a train whose location we want to determine: if we know where the track (the *FE* curve) leads and the position of the powered unit (*LM*), we know the location of the train. We need not pay attention to the second, unpowered unit (*IS*). It is coupled up to the powered unit and will roll to wherever *LM* is on *FE*.

Figure 29.5b shows that under fixed exchange rates the *FE* curve and the *IS* curve depend on exogenous variables alone, and thus suffice to determine equilibrium income and the interest rate. The *LM* curve follows every move of the other two curves and is always where they intersect. Equilibrium income and the interest rate are determined without *LM*, but movements of the money supply can be deduced from what the *LM* curve does. In terms of our train analogy, switching from flexible to fixed exchange rates is like switching the power from the *LM* carriage to the *IS* carriage. Now *IS* is the powered unit and *LM* is unpowered. The train will be wherever *IS* pulls it along the *FE* track. This time, we need pay no attention to *LM*, the unpowered unit in this case. It is coupled to *IS* and ends up wherever the powered *IS* unit is on the *FE* track.

Monetary and fiscal policy in the national economy

Chapter 27 taught us the basics of fiscal and monetary policy. Because the global perspective entertained in that chapter comprises neither trade in goods and services nor a foreign exchange market, we bring these into the picture now. The model we employ is that of the national economy, as represented by the *IS–LM–FE* diagram.

Monetary policy

Monetary policy refers to the control of the money supply. We have just learned that by fixing the exchange rate, the government (or the central bank) hands the control of the money supply over to the market (or to some other central bank, as we will see). The *LM* 'engine' that monetary policy is supposed to move is unpowered. It is being pulled wherever the *IS* curve goes. Thus:

> Monetary policy is unavailable as a policy instrument when exchange rates are fixed. For the central bank to retain control over the money supply, exchange rates must be flexible.

An increase in the money supply

Imagine a national economy under flexible exchange rates that is currently at point *A* in Figure 29.6. All three markets are in equilibrium, since *IS*, *FE* and *LM* all pass through *A*. Now suppose that the government is not happy with the level of income associated with *A*. It asks the central bank to expand the money supply to stimulate aggregate demand and income. What are the consequences of such a move?

Part of what happens echoes what we discussed in Chapter 27, when we analysed the consequences of a money supply increase for the global economy:

First, the *LM* curve shifts to the right, indicating that individuals would only be prepared to hold more money than before if income was higher or the interest rate was lower. In the global economy both happened: the interest rate went down and income went up along the *IS* curve to the new point of intersection between *IS* and *LM* (point *D*). In the national economy, however, the foreign exchange market does not tolerate a drop of the interest rate. As soon as the interest rate begins to fall, assets flow out of the country and the currency depreciates. This stimulates net exports, shifting the goods market equilibrium line *IS* to the right. What this means is that at any interest rate, and thus also at the world interest rate that determines the domestic interest rate, firms must produce more than before to satisfy the higher demand triggered by the more competitive exchange rate. This rightward movement of the *IS* curve continues until the curve passes through *C*, where the *FE* curve and the new *LM* curve intersect. Summing this up:

Figure 29.6 A money supply increase in the national economy, flexible exchange rates

Under flexible exchange rates a money supply increase moves *LM* to the right. If there were no foreign exchange market (as in the global economy) this would move the economy from A towards D. As the interest rate starts to fall, however, investors move assets abroad, selling home currency, making it depreciate. This moves *IS* to the right until it passes through C, the new point of equilibrium.

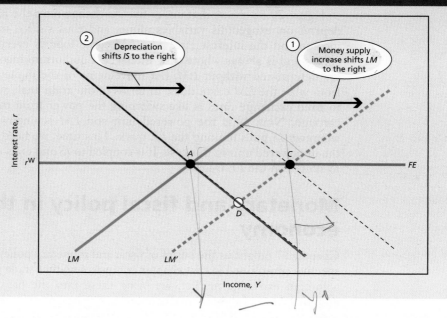

An increase of the money supply under flexible exchange rates raises equilibrium income.

In the global economy, this same effect comes about by a drop in the interest rate that brings the economy to point *D*. In the national economy, the interest rate cannot really fall. But the downward pressure on it makes the domestic currency depreciate and net exports and income rise.

Fiscal policy

Fiscal policy aims to influence aggregate demand, either via government spending or by affecting private spending through taxes. Both these instruments affect the position of the *IS* curve. Remember that when exchange rates are flexible, the *IS* curve endogenously follows where *FE* and *LM* go. So government efforts to control the position of the *IS* curve are nullified by adverse movements of the exchange rate. Hence:

Fiscal policy is ineffective under flexible exchange rates. For fiscal policy to bear on equilibrium income, exchange rates must be fixed.

An increase in government spending under fixed exchange rates

Suppose the economy is initially in equilibrium at point A in Figure 29.7. When the government increases spending, the *IS* curve shifts to the right. Firms, still at point A, experience an excess demand for their products. As a response they raise output and income, which, in turn, raises the demand for money. An excess demand in the money market puts upward pressure on the interest rate. As the interest rate begins to rise, foreign assets start to flow in, and the foreign exchange market experiences an excess demand for domestic currency.

The exchange rate cannot respond to equilibrate supply and demand in the foreign exchange market, because it is fixed. Instead, the central bank must sell the requisite amount of domestic currency, thus increasing the money supply and shifting the *LM* curve to the right. Since all three equilibrium lines must intersect in a common point

Figure 29.7 An increase in government spending under fixed exchange rates

Under fixed exchange rates a rise in government spending moves *IS* right. If there were no foreign exchange market this would move the economy from A towards C. As the interest rate starts to rise, however, investors acquire domestic assets, purchasing domestic currency. The central bank must sell this at the fixed exchange rate, increasing the money supply. This moves *LM* right until it passes through B.

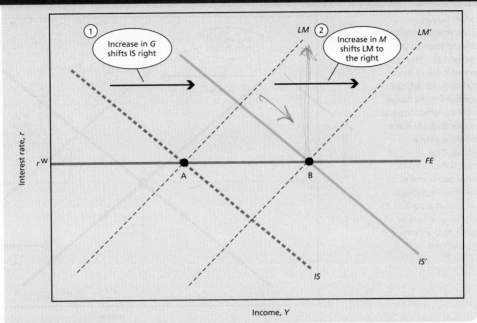

in the new overall equilibrium that obtains after government spending increased, *LM* shifts until it meets the *FE* curve and the new *IS* curve at their new point of intersection *B*. Thus:

An increase in government spending under fixed exchange rates raises equilibrium income.

The mechanism that brings this about is basically the government spending multiplier we encountered far back in Chapter 23. The crowding-out effect observed in the global economy (see Chapter 27) does not occur. The reason is that the government spending increase is reinforced by an expansion of the money supply that the fixed exchange rate forces upon the central bank.

An increase in government spending under flexible exchange rates

crowding out

It occurs when an increase in government spending drives down investment or net exports, thus losing part or all of its effect on income.

The complete **crowding out** of government spending under flexible exchange rates is shown in Figure 29.8. Again, the increase in government spending shifts the IS curve to the right. And, just as described in the previous section, the interest rate inches upwards, and as it starts to do so, an excess demand for domestic currency occurs. This time the exchange rate is flexible, and responds by appreciating. As it does so, net exports fall, aggregate demand falls, and the *IS* curve shifts back to the left. This process continues until it is back in its original position.

Note that aggregate income is the same as before. So fiscal policy does not accomplish anything at this level of aggregation. It does change the *composition* of aggregate demand, though: income equals aggregate demand. Because income has not changed, aggregate demand has not changed. So if one component of aggregate demand rose, other components must have fallen by the same amount. Consumption is unchanged (because *Y* is unchanged). Investment is unchanged (because *i* remained the same). Thus, a rise in *G* of, say, €10 billion must be matched by a 10 billion euro reduction of net exports. *G* increased entirely at the expense of net exports. It does not add anything to aggregate demand or income. There is complete crowding out of government spending under flexible exchange rates.

Figure 29.8 An increase in government spending under flexible exchange rates

An increase in government spending tends to push up the interest rate. This makes domestic assets more attractive, raising the demand for the home currency, which leads to an appreciation if the exchange rate is flexible. The appreciation makes home goods more expensive, moving *IS* left until it is back in its original position. Equilibrium income has not changed.

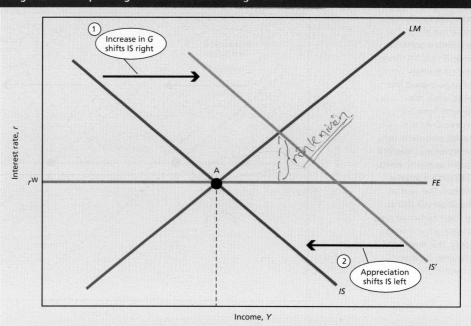

The national economy in a global setting

world interest rate

Here: a weighted average of interest rates in other countries where financial investors may acquire assets.

Our discussions in this and the previous chapter have shown that output in the national economy is affected by outside variables. These are the world interest rate (which determines the position of the *FE* curve) and world income (which, together with other variables, affects the position of the *IS* curve). To the national economy these are exogenous variables that determine its fate in an important way. But they are beyond the control of an individual country. Now, if the world interest rate and world income are exogenous variables from the perspective of each and every one of the world's national economies, how are they determined? Given their importance for national economies, it would be vital to understand where they come from and what makes them change. You may already guess that this is the moment to bring our previous analysis of the global economy back into the picture.

world income

Here: a weighted sum of income levels in the countries with which the national economy trades.

The national economy versus the global economy

All of the world's economies (certainly the European ones) are small relative to the rest of the world. So the model of the global economy remains virtually untouched if we use it to represent the rest of the world as seen from one individual country. To see why this is warranted, consider Germany, one of the world's biggest exporters. At 29.5%, German exports in 1997 constituted a sizeable chunk of German GDP. But from a worldwide perspective, German exports are small fare. German exports, which at the same time are the rest of the world's imports from Germany, are about 2% of world GDP. The world's exports *to* Germany are of the same magnitude.

In representing the rest of the world by the *IS–LM model of the global economy* developed in Chapters 23 to 27, therefore, we only ignore what happens to about 2% of GDP, and for most other countries the figure is even less. This seems fair enough. The national economy – Germany in our example – is represented by the *IS–LM–FE* model assembled in Chapter 28 and the current chapter.

Figure 29.9 shows how the national economy is related to the global economy. The rest of the world, shown in the left panel, functions more or less independently of what goes on in the national economy singled out here and shown on the right. The

Figure 29.9 The national economy and the rest of the world

The global economy, shown on the left, sets the stage for the national economy. In particular, the global economy determines the world interest rate, which sets the position of the *FE* curve for the national economy. The global economy also determines world income, which affects the position of the national economy's *IS* curve.

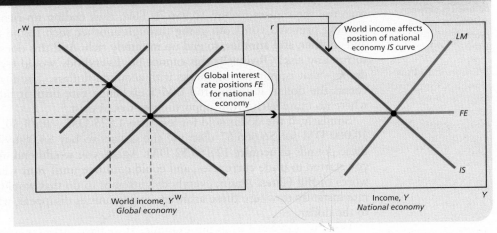

interaction of the global goods market and the global money market determines interest rate and income in the rest of the world. If global monetary policy becomes more expansionary, for example, the *LM* curve shifts to the right, making the global interest rate fall and global income rise.

This sets the stage for the national economy, to which the global (world) interest rate and global (world) income are exogenous variables that cannot be influenced to any significant extent. The global interest rate positions the *FE* curve for the national economy. Global income represents one positioning variable for the national economy's *IS* curve. Together with the national economy's monetary or fiscal policy (depending on the exchange rate system it chooses), this determines aggregate income and the composition of aggregate demand in the national economy.

National economies in an exchange rate system

European Monetary System (EMS)

Arrangement among European countries aimed at reducing exchange rate fluctuations.

In the 1980s and 1990s, those European economies participating in the **European Monetary System (EMS)** were characterized by two distinct features: first, they traded mostly among each other, but very little with the rest of the world; second, and more importantly, their exchange rates were fixed.[2] This second feature poses an interesting question: We just learned that by fixing the exchange rate, a country forfeits control over its money supply. Now, if all countries in the EMS lose control over their money supplies, what mechanism determines the overall money supply in the EMS? It cannot be the money supply in the rest of the world, because exchange rates *vis-à-vis* the pound, the yen, the dollar, the Swiss franc and other currencies are flexible. So the EMS as a whole does have the discretion to steer its aggregate money supply as desired. But, again, who makes that decision?

The *n*th currency

To find the answer to this question, consider the following. On 20 February 1998, the London *Financial Times* reported that it cost $1.632 to buy £1. It also reported that it cost 2.979 DM to buy £1. 'Interesting', you may think, living in Berlin. 'But I'm considering placing an on-line order for a US computer. So what I need to know is how many marks I have to pay for a dollar.' Don't rush back to the library to look up the DM/$ exchange rate. You don't have to. If you consult the *Financial Times* you will find that $1 sold for 1.825 DM. How did I know? There is no magic involved.

[2] *There was some leeway for the exchange rate: ±2.25% in the early days, and ±15% after 1993. But let us ignore this here. Let us also ignore the fact that exchange rates could be and were realigned on occasion.*

The key word is **arbitrage**. If $1 sold for more than 1.825 DM – for 2 DM, say – you could use 10,000 DM to buy £3,356.83, take the pounds to buy $5,478.35, and then use the dollars to buy 10,956.70 DM, thus ending up richer than before. And nothing prevents you from going through another such round of currency trading, and another, and another, to end up infinitely rich. And this doesn't even require you to run any risk! Obviously, this cannot be. Everybody would try to do what you are doing – that is, purchasing marks with acquired dollars. The mark would appreciate versus the dollar, lowering the DM/$ exchange rate until it hit the value of 1.825 where no more such profit opportunities would exist.[3]

Similarly, if the dollar sold for less than 1.825 DM – for 1.50, say – you could sell 10,000 DM for $6,666.67 then use the dollars to buy £4,084.97, and finally use all these pounds to acquire 12,169.12 DM. Again, you would end up richer than before you started to trade currencies, and could continue until your wealth dwarfed the net worth of Bill Gates. Again, everybody's attempt to do that would move the exchange rate instantly to where these arbitrage opportunities disappear, which is at 1.825 DM to the dollar.

What we can learn from this example? If we have three countries, three currencies, and accordingly three exchange rates between each pair of currencies, once two of the exchange rates are determined, the third one is determined as well. This simple insight has important implications for monetary policy. To illustrate, imagine a European Monetary System that comprises three countries only: France, Germany and the Netherlands (Figure 29.10).

The three countries need to agree on three **parity rates**. Let these be 4 FF/DM, 4 FF/guilder and 1 guilder/DM. We know that fixing the exchange rate between the French and the German currency at 4 FF/DM means that the two countries' central

Figure 29.10 A hypothetical European Monetary System with three countries

This hypothetical Monetary System comprises France, Germany and The Netherlands. There are three bilateral exchange rates between three currencies. Fixing two exchange rates fixes the third one as well. Only two central banks need to intervene to defend the two exchange rates (and implicitly the third one). The third central bank may conduct its own monetary policy. This central bank controls the *n*th currency or the anchor currency.

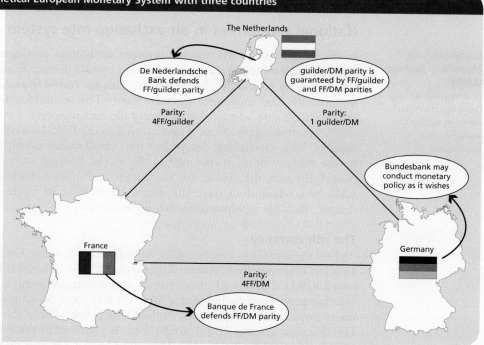

[3]In reality, keeping the exchange rate at precisely 1.825 to rule out riskless profit opportunities is not necessary, because there is a small spread (difference) between the purchase price and the sale price of a currency.

banks are obliged to buy or sell any amount of Francs for marks that the market wants at this price. Actually, it suffices for one of the two central banks to do it. Suppose its the Banque de France.

Let's move on to the guilder/franc parity, set at 4 FF/guilder. Again, we need a central bank prepared to buy or sell francs for guilders as required. The Banque de France can't do it, since it is already busy buying and selling francs to defend the FF/DM parity. So it must be De Nederlandsche Bank that does it.

This leaves the task of defending the guilder/DM parity to the Bundesbank, which is not involved in foreign exchange market intervention otherwise. But wait! Didn't we just learn a moment ago that if you have three exchange rates among three currencies, once two exchange rates are determined, this also determines the third exchange rate? Since the Banque de France is defending the FF/DM parity, and De Nederlandsche Bank is defending the FF/guilder parity, these two central banks implicitly defend the guilder/DM parity. The Bundesbank does not need to act. Its monetary policy is not taken out of its control by the necessity to defend an exchange rate. Rather, the Bundesbank is free to pursue any monetary policy it desires, or, more realistically, any policy on which the members of this imaginary EMS agree.

This insight does not only hold in an exchange rate system comprising three countries and currencies, but also with four countries, with five countries, with twelve countries, and with n countries (where n stands for any number). With three currencies, only two central banks must intervene in the foreign exchange market, and the third one is free to conduct monetary policy at its own discretion. With twelve currencies, eleven central banks must intervene and the twelfth one is free. Or, generally:

> In an exchange rate system comprising n currencies, only $n-1$ central banks are obliged to intervene in the foreign exchange market to defend exchange rate parities. The central bank issuing the **nth currency (_or_ anchor currency)** is free to pursue any monetary policy it likes.

nth currency (_or_ anchor currency)
The currency in a system of fixed exchange rates that is not needed for intervention in the foreign exchange market.

Monetary policy in the EMS

There is an obvious similarity between the relationship between the rest of the world and the individual country (shown in Figure 29.8), and between the country with the nth currency in an exchange rate system and the other member countries. In the global picture, the rest of the world sets the interest rate with which the individual country must live. In an exchange rate system such as the EMS, the nth currency controls monetary policy and the resulting interest rate that the other member countries have to live with in one way or another. Figure 29.11 illustrates what we mean by this.

We focus on three EMS members: France, Germany and Italy. Each country is represented in one of the panels, with Germany in the middle. By mutual accord, the DM is the system's anchor or nth currency, as substantially it has been in the real EMS. Whatever fiscal and monetary policy Germany pursues determines the German interest rate. This, in turn, determines the positions of the FE curves for the other members shown in the left and right panels.

Repercussions of German unification

German unification provides an interesting application of how policy decisions in the anchor country affect other countries in the system.

In Germany, unification resulted in a mix of expansionary fiscal policy and restrictive monetary policy in 1990 and after. A sharp increase in government spending was needed to start rebuilding the public infrastructure in the east of the country, to cushion soaring unemployment, and to provide financial incentives to attract private investment to the former German Democratic Republic. The result was a shift of the German IS curve to the right, as shown in the middle panel.

Concerned that this stimulation of aggregate demand may sooner or later trigger price increases (an issue that we will return to in Chapter 31), the Bundesbank

Figure 29.11 Repercussions from German monetary policy on other EMS members

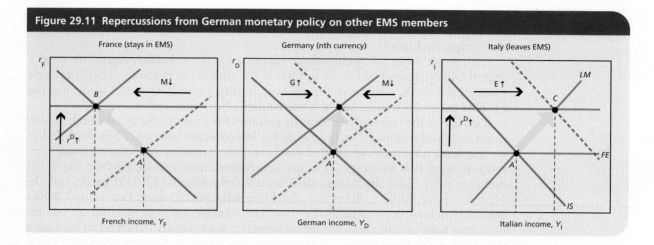

switched to a restrictive monetary policy. This shifted the *LM* curve up to the left. The most striking result from this interplay between fiscal expansion and monetary contraction was a sharp rise in German interest rates, with the money market rate peaking at 9.4% in 1992. A direct consequence for Italy (right panel) and France (left panel) was that their *FE* curves shifted up in line with the German interest rate increase. How did this affect their economies?

In the left panel, with France's economy initially at *A*, French interest rates are way below German rates, and financial investors move their wealth out of the country. At EMS parity an excess demand for DM results, mirrored by an excess supply of francs. The Banque de France must purchase these francs. Taking them out of the market means that France's money supply is reduced and its *LM* curve shifts to the left. By applying what we have already learned in this chapter, we know that *LM* continues to shift left until it passes through *B*, the point where the new *FE* curve and the *IS* curve intersect.[4] The implication is that:

> Under fixed exchange rates, if the anchor currency's or the rest of the world's interest rate rises, the national economy is forced into a recession.

The fall in income forced upon France and other EMS members by staying in the EMS put national governments under enormous political pressure, and some considered alternative options – such as suspending their membership of the EMS. One country that eventually chose that option was Italy.

In the right panel of Figure 29.11, Italy is initially at *A* and interest rates are below German rates. An excess supply of Italian currency results, putting upward pressure on the lira at the EMS parity rate. When Italy suspended EMS membership during the 1992 EMS crisis, the lira was permitted to yield to market pressure and actually depreciate. The resulting price advantage for Italian products stimulated exports and depressed imports, moving the *IS* curve to the right. (The Applications box 'Holidays in Italy before and after 1992' illustrates this point.)

Leaving the determination of exchange rates up to the market, Italy can keep its money supply, and hence the position of its *LM* curve, unchanged. The intersection between *LM* and the new *FE* curve (point *C*) determines equilibrium under flexible exchange rates. Depreciation shifts *IS* to the right until it passes through point *C*. The resulting insight is:

[4]*Remember the rule given above: under fixed exchange rates, the point of intersection between the FE curve and the IS curve determines income and the interest rate. The money supply is forced to adjust to bring the LM curve into the proper position as well.*

Applications

Holidays in Italy before and after 1992

A country's exports largely depend on two variables: the income in the countries to which it exports, and the exchange rates versus those countries' currencies. This does not only apply to a country's aggregate exports, but also to individual export items. Take tourism. Nights spent by foreigners in Italian hotels is an Italian export. Foreigners pay Italy for the privilege of enjoying Italy's culture, food or beaches. When the lira depreciates, holidays in Italy become cheaper and the number of nights booked by tourists from abroad rises. This

effect could be neutralized, though, if foreign incomes fell at the same time.

Incomes usually change slowly, and they often change in different directions in the various countries from which Italy's visitors originate. Therefore, at times when the exchange rate changes dramatically, we may ignore the presumably small effects resulting from income changes. Italy's temporary withdrawal from the EMS in September 1992 is a case in point: the country's effective exchange rate (the

weighted exchange rate versus all its trading partners) depreciated by more than 25% within two years (see the figure).

Note that the effective exchange rate is defined in just the opposite way to our definition of bilateral exchange rates (for which a depreciation means the exchange rate goes up). When the effective exchange rate goes *down*, the lira depreciates!

Just as the theory predicts, when the lira depreciated after 1992, tourism to Italy increased noticeably. The number of

When the lira depreciates, pasta and Pisa become bargains for foreigners, and they flock to Italy in larger numbers.

nights spent rose from 8.6 million in 1992 to 11.8 million in 1996, an increase of 37%. In terms of the *IS* curve this means that it moves to the right when the exchange rate depreciates to make our exports cheaper.

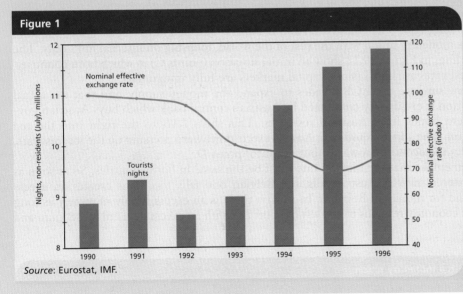

Figure 1

Source: Eurostat, IMF.

Under flexible exchange rates, if the anchor currency's or the rest of the world's interest rate rises, the national economy enjoys an income boom.

One currency, many countries: the advent of the euro

Discussion of the macroeconomics of the national economy would not be complete without a discussion of the most complete and irreversible form of fixing an exchange rate: the introduction of a common currency. A group of countries sharing a single

currency union _or_ monetary union

A group of countries sharing a single currency.

European Monetary Union (EMU)

The currency union set up within the EU.

European Central Bank (ECB)

The institution set up to conduct monetary policy in the European Monetary Union.

currency is called a **currency union** or a **monetary union**. At the turn of the millennium, 11 European countries are embarking on such a project, called the **European Monetary Union (EMU)**. Let us look at how monetary and fiscal policy works within a monetary union.

Monetary policy in a monetary union

We know from Chapter 25 that monetary policy in the EMU is conducted by the **European Central Bank (ECB)**. It is important to realize that the ECB can control the total supply of euros, but it cannot influence the money supply in an individual country.

> In a monetary union, the central bank controls the overall money supply. It has no control over the money supply in any individual member country.

If the total money supply in EMU is M, and M_i denotes the money supply in country i, we have:

$$M = M_A + M_B + M_D + M_E + M_F + M_{FIN} + M_I + M_{IRE} + M_{LUX} + M_{NL} + M_P$$

All that the ECB can control when conducting monetary policy is M, the aggregate. How much of it is supplied (or held) in Austria, in Belgium, in Germany and so on is the result of market forces. The ECB keeps a lid on the total, since the sum of the money supplies in all member countries equals M.

To grasp how monetary policy spills over from one country to another, suppose EMU comprises only countries A and B, Austria and Belgium. Let us ignore the links of this monetary union with the rest of the world, focusing on internal links only. The black lines in Figure 29.12 show an initial situation (points C) in which both countries' interest rates are equal (since capital markets are fully integrated).

Now suppose the ECB decides to expand the money supply, and that the actual operation is exclusively conducted by Austria's central bank which buys Austrian government bonds from Austrian residents. This shifts LM_A to the right into the red position. The added liquidity in Austria exerts downward pressure on the interest rate, moving the economy towards (but not into) point D.

Remember that the interest rate must be the same in both countries. So as soon as the interest rate in Austria falls, the Belgian one falls too. This creates an excess demand for money in Belgium. In Austria there is an excess supply of money as long as the economy remains to the left of point D. With an excess demand in Belgium and

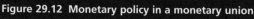

Figure 29.12 Monetary policy in a monetary union

In a monetary union with a common currency a money supply increase spreads to all member states, no matter where the money supply increase originates. Income rises in all countries.

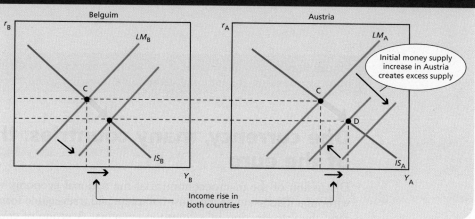

an excess supply in Austria, of course, money moves from Austria into Belgium. This could be euro notes flowing across borders. Or it could be Austrian banks depositing excess reserves in Belgian banks, which can now extend credit to customers. In Figure 29.12 this shifts the Belgian *LM* curve to the right and Austria's *LM* curve back to the left a little. In the end, the money supply has increased in both countries, independently of where the initial money supply increase took place.

> In a monetary union, monetary policy can no longer be targeted at individual member countries. A money supply increase, no matter where it originates, affects all members in a similar way.

As Figure 29.12 shows, a money supply increase raises incomes in all member countries of a monetary union in a similar way.

Fiscal policy in a monetary union

Discipline in fiscal policy was an important test to pass for countries wanting to qualify for membership of EMU; and at the 1996 intergovernmental conference in Dublin, heads of state agreed on a list of sanctions to come into operation if a member country resorted to excessive government spending *after* the start of EMU. Why is there this fear that governments might not be able to resist the temptation to spend excessively? Although a full discussion of deficits and debt must wait until Chapter 32, the model employed here provides a first answer as to why governments dread the idea of other governments spending excessively in a monetary union.

Let Belgium and Austria again be in the equilibrium positions associated with the black curves (Figure 29.13). Now Belgium unilaterally decides to spur income by raising government spending. The multiplier effect shifts Belgium's *IS* curve to the right into the blue position. If Belgium were the world, income and the interest rate would rise and a new equilibrium would obtain at point *C*. Because Belgium is in a monetary union with Austria, however, repercussions are felt in Austria as soon as the Belgian interest rate begins to rise.

Since the Austrian interest rate moves up with Belgium's, income falls, moving the economy leftwards as shown in the right panel of Figure 29.13. The result is an *excess supply* of money in Austria. In Belgium, while the interest rate is still below the value

Figure 29.13 Fiscal policy in a monetary union

In a monetary union national governments may still conduct independent fiscal policy, though with adverse effects in other countries. A fiscal expansion in Belgium pushes Belgian interest rates up. This raises the money supply in Belgium, but reduces it in Austria. As a consequence income rises in Belgium but falls in Austria.

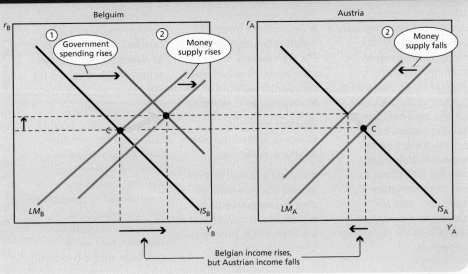

associated with point *C*, there is an *excess demand* for money. In this case, as we encountered before, excess liquidity flows out of Austria into Belgium. So the Belgian *LM* curve shifts to the right and Austria's *LM* curve moves to the left. The new equilibrium obtains on the red *LM* curves, where interest rates are equal.

The result reveals why Austria has no sympathy whatsoever for Belgium's deficit spending:

> In a monetary union, one country can conduct expansionary fiscal policy to spur income at home. However, it will drive incomes in the other member countries down.

EMU member states have signed a 'Pact for stability and growth' (see the Applications box) to guard against the prospect that individual countries in EMU may be tempted to discard fiscal discipline in pursuit of national income gains for which the other members pay a price in the form of recessions.

Looking ahead: the labour market and aggregate supply

This chapter has merged the goods market, the money market and the foreign exchange market to provide an understanding of how the national economy works. These three markets are rooted in the *demand side* of the economy. They help us to understand how the components of aggregate demand are determined, and how they can be affected by fiscal and monetary policy.

Little has been said about the economy's *supply side* so far. Our understanding was that at current prices firms are prepared to produce and sell any volume of goods and services that is demanded. This is a useful assumption in times of idle production capacities. But that is not generally the case, so it is time to refine our approach. The next chapter subjects the economy's supply side, the production and employment decisions of firms, to more serious scrutiny by bringing the labour market into the picture.

Applications

The pact for stability and growth

At the December 1996 Dublin summit and subsequent meetings, EU member states agreed on a 'pact for stability and growth' designed to ensure a long-term orientation of fiscal policy. In essence, the pact aims to prevent members from running excessive budget deficits. Extending the respective Maastricht criterion into phase 3 of European Monetary Union, the pact for stability and growth begins with the following judgement:

■ Government budget deficit ratios smaller than 3% are not excessive.
■ Government budget deficit ratios higher than 3% are normally considered excessive, unless the country suffered a serious economic setback.

Whether a serious economic setback occurred is judged as follows:

■ A decline in real GDP of at least 2% (in a year) is *always* a serious setback.
■ A decline in real GDP of less than 0.75% is *never* a serious setback.

■ A decline in real GDP of between 0.75 and 2% of GDP is evaluated for its seriousness on a case by case basis by the Council of Ministers (or ECOFIN, the supervisory body to be set up).

If a budget deficit is judged excessive, ECOFIN calls upon the member state to take effective measures within four months. Should the member fail to comply with the recommended measures, the Council of Ministers may apply sanctions with a two-thirds

majority vote. These include:

■ An interest-free deposit of 0.2% of GDP to be paid in the first year of excessive spending.
■ In addition, 0.1% of GDP is to be paid as a fine for each percentage point beyond the 3% limit.

The sum of both components is not to exceed 0.5% of GDP annually. If after two years the budget deficit is still excessive, the initial deposit of 0.2% of GDP becomes a fine.

Summary

Equilibrium in the national economy

1. Equilibrium in the national economy obtains when the goods market, the money market and the foreign exchange market are all in equilibrium at the same time. Graphically, this is the case where the *IS* curve, the *LM* curve and the *FE* curve all intersect in one point.

2. Under flexible exchange rates, the intersection between the *FE* curve and the *LM* curve alone determines income and the interest rate. The exchange rate changes so as to make the *IS* curve pass through this point as well.

3. Under fixed exchange rates, the intersection between the *FE* curve and the *IS* curve alone determines income and the interest rate. The money supply changes endogenously so as to make the *LM* curve pass through this point as well.

Monetary and fiscal policy in the national economy

4. The central bank cannot control the money supply when exchange rates are fixed. Monetary policy is only available when exchange rates are flexible.

5. When exchange rates are flexible, an increase in the money supply leads to a depreciation of the exchange rate, increased net exports, increased planned expenditure (a rightward shift of the *IS* curve), and ultimately a higher equilibrium level of income.

6. When exchange rates are fixed, an increase in government spending forces the central bank to increase the money supply, and ultimately yields a higher equilibrium level of income. Just like expansionary monetary policy under flexible exchange rates, it may help an economy out of a recession.

7. When exchange rates are flexible, an increase in government spending makes the exchange rate appreciate. Eventually, this lowers net exports by the same amount by which the government raised spending.

Income remains unchanged. There is complete crowding out. What changes is the composition of aggregate demand: the share of the government is higher and demand from abroad (exports) is lower.

The national economy in a global setting

8. The global economy model (comprising the goods market and the money market only) determines the *world interest rate* and *world income*. The world interest rate determines the position of the *FE* curve and world income affects the position of the *IS* curve for any individual country.

9. In an exchange rate system comprising n countries and currencies, only $n - 1$ central banks are required to intervene in the foreign exchange market to defend parity rates. One central bank is free to conduct monetary policy autonomously. The currency controlled by this nth central bank is called the nth currency (or the anchor currency).

10. In an exchange rate system the nth central bank determines the monetary policy and the interest rate of the other members.

11. In an exchange rate system, if the nth country's monetary policy becomes restrictive and interest rates rise, other members have two options: to remain in the system and be drawn into a recession; or to leave the system and experience a boom.

One currency for many countries: the advent of the euro

12. If the European Central Bank (ECB) raises the money supply, the money supply rises in all member countries. All member countries observe rising incomes.

13. If government spending is increased by one member of EMU, its equilibrium income rises. All other members experience negative repercussions, seeing their incomes fall.

Review Terms and Concepts

arbitrage
crowding out
currency union
endogenous variable
European Central Bank (ECB)
European Monetary System (EMS)
European Monetary Union (EMU)
exchange rate system

exogenous variable
fixed exchange rate
flexible exchange rate
monetary union
nth currency (anchor currency)
parity rate
world income
world interest rate

Problem Set

1. Explain the distinction between the 'domestic demand for goods' and the 'demand for domestic goods'.

2. In mid-1992 the Bundesbank briefly raised the discount rate to 8.75%. Subsequently, it reduced the discount rate in thirteen steps to 2.5% in 1996. The national economy model discussed in the chapter, however, suggests that monetary policy is ineffective in a fixed exchange rate system.
a. How was it possible for the Bundesbank to alter its monetary policy so radically while remaining in the ERM?
b. Use the national economy model to analyse the effect that the above changes in the Bundesbank's monetary policy had on the Dutch economy.
c. Examine the developments in your own country's discount rate (or similar interest rate) during the 1990s. Have they been qualitatively similar to those in Germany?

3. Suppose the government lowers income taxes. What are the effects on income, the interest rate and the exchange rate when (a) the exchange rate is fixed; (b) the exchange rate is flexible? Assume that capital is perfectly mobile internationally.

4. It is often argued that fiscal deficits lead to trade deficits. Contrast the reasons for 'crowding out' in the *global economy* model and in the *national economy* model to explain why.

5. During the first few years after their UK election victory in 1979, the Tory Party under Prime Minister Margaret Thatcher maintained a policy of very tight money. Using the *IS-LM-FE* framework, what do you think happened during that period to (a) the value of Sterling, (b) the trade balance, and (c) output?

6. In May 1998 it was agreed that eleven European countries would join the monetary union. How will this change the relative effectiveness of fiscal and monetary policy?

7. Consider two small economies that operate under flexible exchange rates. Assume the two economies are identical except that country A's total exports and imports make up a larger fraction of GDP than country B's. In which country would an increase in the money supply have a larger effect on output?

8. The European Central Bank decides to increase the supply of euros. What are the consequences for income, the interest rate and the exchange rate when (a) the Fed keeps the US money supply fixed; (b) the Fed also decides to raise the money supply; (c) the Fed decides to lower the money supply?

9. Consider a small country with no capital controls which is ruled by a military dictatorship. After a peaceful revolution, the new democratically elected government reduces military expenditure. Analyse the effects of this policy change on output, interest rate, exchange rate and the trade balance when the spending cuts are due to (a) reduced army salaries; (b) reductions in imported military hardware.

10. Assume that the European Central Bank decides in 2001 to tighten its monetary policy.
a. How would this affect output and the exchange rate in those countries not joining the monetary union (Denmark, Greece, Sweden and the UK)?
b. What could the authorities in the non-member countries do to stabilize output?
c. How would you answers to (a) and (b) change if the non-member countries had fixed their currencies to the euro?

30

The Labour Market and Aggregate Supply

In Chapter 20, we stressed four broadly defined markets in which households, firms, the government and the rest of the world interact: (1) the *goods market*, (2) the *money market*, (3) the *foreign exchange market*, and (4) the labour market. Ten chapters later we have a solid understanding of how the first three of these markets bear on the different demand categories in the economy. Until now, the sum of all demand categories, aggregate demand, determined aggregate output exclusively. Firms were assumed to produce any volume of goods and services that consumers, investors, the government and the rest of the world wanted at current prices. It is now time to subject the production and employment decisions of firms to closer scrutiny by bringing the labour market into the picture.

This certainly doesn't mean that everything we have learned so far becomes useless and that we need to start again from scratch. Even if you never learned another thing about macroeconomics, what you know now would still, in many situations, lead you in the right direction. After all, firms can always raise employment and output to meet a surge in demand. However, they sometimes may not want to. Or initial increases in output may not last.

Addressing this, the two key questions asked in this chapter are:

■ What may keep firms from expanding output when demand increases?
■ If firms do raise output to meet higher demand, why may this not last?

The key to answering these questions is the labour market. Various microeconomic aspects of the labour market were discussed in Chapters 6, 10 and 19. Some of them are reviewed and deepened here and put into a macroeconomic context.

A natural issue to address in a chapter on the labour market is unemployment. After all, unemployment occurs when the labour market does not clear. We discuss reasons why this may be so.

Finally, this chapter starts to relax the assumption of a fixed price level. Here we only look at what a changing price level does to the labour market, employment and aggregate supply. In the next chapter we will also see what it does to the economy's demand side as captured by the national economy model we now have in our tool box.

The labour market: basic concepts

Let's review briefly what the **unemployment rate** measures. The unemployment rate is the number of people unemployed as a percentage of the labour force. To be unemployed, a person must be out of a job and actively looking for work. When a person stops looking for work, he or she is considered *out of the labour force* and is no longer counted as unemployed.

It is useful to distinguish two general types of unemployment. The first is **cyclical unemployment**, the part of unemployment that moves up and down with the business cycle. When the economy contracts, the number of people unemployed and the unemployment rate rise. When the economy expands, unemployment falls.

The second category is **equilibrium or natural unemployment**, the part of unemployment that remains net of the impact of the business cycle, or when the business cycle is in neutral. A major part of Europe's current unemployment rate of 10% plus is equilibrium unemployment.

---

unemployment rate
The ratio of the number of people unemployed to the total number of people in the labour force.

cyclical unemployment
The increase in unemployment that occurs during recessions and depressions.

equilibrium *or* natural unemployment
The part of unemployment that remains net of the impact of the business cycle.

frictional unemployment
The portion of unemployment that is due to the normal working of the labour market; used to denote short-run job/skill matching problems.

structural unemployment
The portion of unemployment that is due to changes in the structure of the economy that result in a significant loss of jobs in certain industries.

Equilibrium or natural unemployment comprises **frictional** and **structural unemployment**, as discussed in Chapter 22. Frictional unemployment occurs because the economy is dynamic; it takes time for people to find the right job in the right place and for employers to match the right workers with the jobs they have. Structural unemployment may be due to changes in the structure of the economy. But it also includes unemployment that results from the specific way in which the labour market operates and is organized in individual countries. Thus,

Unemployment = Cyclical unemployment + Equilibrium unemployment

frictional + structural

The boundaries between the different categories and subcategories of unemployment are not clear cut. Yet categorizing unemployment along these lines helps to organize and guide our thinking.

The classical view of the labour market

The classical view of the labour market has already been discussed in Chapters 10 and 19. We begin by reviewing key concepts and putting them in a wider, macroeconomic perspective.

Classical economists assume that the wage rate adjusts to equate the quantity of labour demanded with the quantity of labour supplied, implying that unemployment cannot exist.

The labour demand curve

labour demand curve
A graph that shows the amount of labour firms want to employ at a particular wage rate.

Each point on the **labour demand curve** represents the amount of labour that firms want to employ at the particular wage rate. A natural starting point for deriving the aggregate labour demand curve (and for discussing the supply side of the macroeconomy) is the aggregate production function. The **aggregate production function** specifies in quantitative terms how an economy's inputs are transformed into aggregate output, as measured by GDP. For the big picture it suffices to classify all inputs into two broad categories: capital, K, and labour, L. Together they produce aggregate output, Y:

aggregate production function
The relationship between the aggregate level of inputs and aggregate output produced in the economy.

$$Y = T \times K^{1/3} \times L^{2/3} \quad \text{production function}$$

Given a production technology T, this production function has the shape of a hill, like the one shown in Figure 30.1. Income increases (you gain altitude) as you walk in the direction of more capital, or more labour, or more of both.

In the short run, the only really flexible one of these two inputs is employment. Capital accumulation (the building of new factories, roads or airports) takes time and

Figure 30.1 The aggregate production function with two inputs

Output Y depends on capital K, labour L and technology. For given technology we may draw a 3D production function (left) showing Y to rise as K or L increases. With K given at K^*, only L remains variable. Raising it moves us up the blue path on the production function 'hill'. This partial production function may be displayed in a two-dimensional Y–L diagram (right).

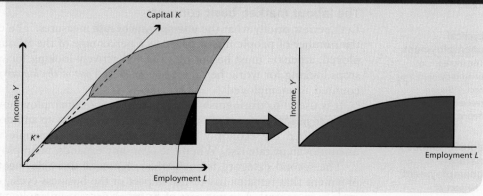

proceeds in small steps only. So does technological change. Therefore, for the short- and medium-run focus of this chapter we may assume that technology T and the capital stock K are both fixed at their current levels.[1]

When employment is the sole flexible variable in the short run, firms can only move along parallels to the L axis. If the capital stock is, say, K^*, the economy's short-run production opportunities can be visualized by placing a vertical cut through the production function parallel to the L axis at capital K^*, and moving that slice out into its own diagram with Y on the vertical axis and L on the horizontal axis. This **partial production function** shows the real output that all firms in the economy produce with only one variable input. Given K^*, it shows which Y is produced at different levels of aggregate employment.

Instead of real income, Y, we may choose to measure *nominal income* (the firms' revenue), $P \times Y$, along the vertical axis. This is called a *partial revenue function*, as shown in the left panel of Figure 30.2. It is proportional to the partial production function shown in the right panel of Figure 30.1. When $P = 1$ the two curves are identical.

The slope of the partial revenue function in Figure 30.2 tells us how much additional revenue firms generate by employing one more unit of labour. This **marginal revenue product of labour (MRPL)** gets smaller and smaller as more and more labour is employed. Therefore, the marginal revenue product of labour curve is a negatively sloped line, as shown in the right panel.

Each firm's decision about how much labour to demand is part of its overall profit-maximizing decision.[2] At a given market wage W_1, workers are hired as long as they generate revenue higher than W_1. This is the case until employment reaches L_1. Beyond that level an additional hour of work costs more than the revenue it creates. So the firm's profits would deteriorate. Since the $MRPL$ schedule indicates how much labour firms can profitably employ at a given wage rate, it also indicates how much labour profit-maximizing firms demand at a given wage rate. The $MRPL$ schedule is therefore the labour demand curve we were looking for.

The labour supply curve

Each point on the **labour supply curve** in Figure 30.3 represents the amount of labour households want to supply at the particular wage rate. A household's decision regarding how much labour to supply is part of the overall consumer choice problem.[3] Each household member looks at the market wage rate, the prices of outputs and the

partial production function

Shows the real output that all firms in the economy produce with only one variable input.

marginal revenue product of labour (MRPL)

The amount of additional revenue that firms generate by employing one more unit of labour.

labour supply curve

A graph that shows the amount of labour households want to supply at a particular wage rate.

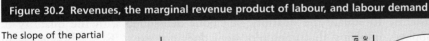

Figure 30.2 Revenues, the marginal revenue product of labour, and labour demand

The slope of the partial revenue function measures the *MRPL*. The right panel shows that the *MRPL* falls when *L* increases. Labour is only employed up to the point where the wage equals the *MRPL*. Beyond that threshold, labour would cost more than the additional revenue it generates.

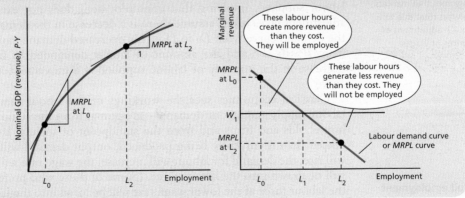

Figure 30.3 The labour supply curve, or the labour force

Deducting those under 15 and over 64 from the population gives the active population. Deducting further those who do not want to work at a given wage rate leaves the labour force (or the labour supply).

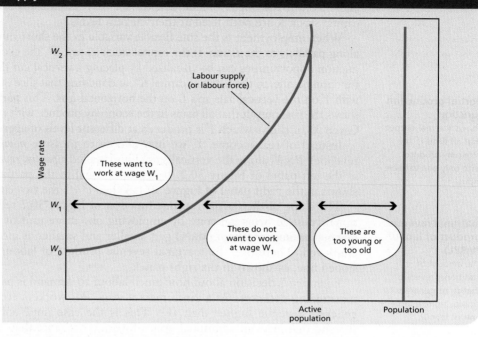

value of leisure time (including the value of staying home and working in the garden or bringing up children) and then chooses the amount of labour to supply (if any). A household member who is not in the labour force is either too young or too old, or decided that their time is more valuably spent on non-market activities.

In Figure 30.3, the *population* and the *active population* are independent of the wage rate and can therefore be represented by vertical lines. Only the active population chooses between work and leisure. This choice depends on the wage rate. At a wage rate of W_0 or below nobody joins the labour force. As the wage rises above W_0, more and more people enter the labour force. At wage W_2 the entire active population wants to work full time.

Figure 30.4 combines the labour supply curve and the labour demand curve in one diagram. **Classical economics** assumes that the wage rate is perfectly flexible, and adjusts instantly to equate the quantity of labour demanded with the quantity of labour supplied, implying that unemployment does not exist. To see how such an adjustment takes place, assume there is a decrease in the demand for labour that shifts the demand curve from D_0 to D_1. This decreased demand causes the wage rate to fall from W_0 to W^* and the amount of labour demanded to fall from L_0 to L^*. The decrease in the quantity of labour supplied is a movement along the labour supply curve.

Classical economics sees the workings of the labour market – the behaviour of labour supply and labour demand – as optimal from the standpoint of both individual households and firms and from the standpoint of society. If households want more output than is currently being produced, output demand will increase, output prices will rise, the demand for labour will increase, the wage rate will rise, and more workers will be drawn into the labour force. (Some of those who preferred not to be a part of the labour force at the lower wage rate will be lured into the labour force at the higher wage rate.) At equilibrium, prices and wages reflect a trade-off between the value that households place on outputs and the value of time spent in leisure and non-market work. At equilibrium, the people who are not working have *chosen* not to work at that market wage. There is always **full employment** in this sense. The classical economists believed that the market would achieve the optimal result if left to its own devices, so there is nothing the government can do to make things better.

Classical economics
assumes that markets always clear due to a quick adjustment of prices or wages.

full employment
In the classical view: all who want to work have found work. In the modern view: the level of employment at the natural rate of unemployment.

Figure 30.4 The classical labour market

Classical economists believe that the labour market always clears. If the demand for labour shifts from D_0 to D_1, the equilibrium wage will fall from W_0 to W^*. Everyone who wants a job at W^* will have one.

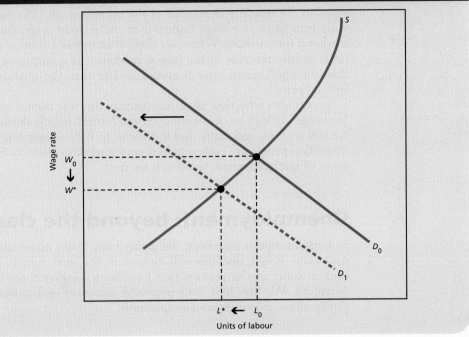

The unemployment rate and the classical view

If, as classical economists assumed, the labour market works well, how can we account for times of high unemployment rates? There seem to be times when millions of people who want jobs at prevailing wage rates cannot find them. How can we reconcile such situations with the classical assumption about the labour market?

Some economists answer by arguing that the unemployment rate is a poor measure of whether the labour market is working well. We know the economy is dynamic. At any given time, some industries are expanding and some are contracting. For example, in many European countries the building industry contracted in recent years. Consider a carpenter who is laid off because of the industry's contraction. This person has probably developed specific skills related to the building industry – skills not necessarily useful for jobs in other industries. If he were earning €30,000 per year as a carpenter, it may be that he could earn only €20,000 per year in another industry. He may eventually work his way back up to a salary of €30,000 in the new industry as he develops new skills, but this will take time. Will the carpenter take a job at €20,000? There are at least two reasons why he may not. First, he may believe the slump in the building industry is temporary so he will soon get his old job back. Second, he may believe he can earn more than €20,000 in another industry and will continue to look for a better job.

If our carpenter decides to continue looking for a job paying more than €20,000 per year, he will be considered unemployed because he is actively looking for work. This does not necessarily mean the labour market is not working properly. The carpenter has *chosen* not to work for a wage of €20,000 per year, but if his value to any firm outside the building industry is truly no more than €20,000 per year, we do not expect him to find a job paying more than €20,000. The unemployment rate as measured by the government is not necessarily an accurate indicator of whether the labour market is working properly in the classical sense.

If the degree to which industries are changing in the economy fluctuates over time, there will be more people like our carpenter at some times than at others. Accordingly, the measured unemployment rate will fluctuate. Some economists argue that the measured unemployment rate may sometimes *seem* high even though the labour market is working well. The quantity of labour supplied at the current wage is equal to the quantity demanded at the current wage. The fact that there are people willing to work at a wage higher than the current wage does not mean the labour market is not working. Whenever there is an upward-sloping supply curve in a market (as is usually the case in the labour market), the quantity supplied at a price higher than the equilibrium price is always greater than the quantity supplied at the equilibrium price.

Economists who view unemployment in this way do not see it as a major problem. Yet images of legions of unemployed and hungry people during the Great Depression are still with us, and many find it difficult to believe everything is optimal when over 20 million people are currently looking for work in Western Europe. There are other views of unemployment, as we will see now.

Unemployment: beyond the classical view

In most European countries, unemployment is the major macroeconomic problem. And many doubt that this will change in the near future. Therefore, we need to explore some of the reasons that have been suggested for the existence of unemployment. We first look into proposed causes of *cyclical unemployment* and then at explanations of *equilibrium unemployment*.

Cyclical unemployment

sticky wages
The downward rigidity of wages as an explanation for the existence of unemployment.

The key explanation for why unemployment increases during the downswing of the business cycle is that wages are 'sticky' on the downward side. That is, the equilibrium wage gets stuck at a particular level and does not fall when the demand for labour declines. The effect of **sticky wages** is illustrated in Figure 30.5, where the equilibrium wage is stuck at W_0 (the original wage) and does not fall to W^* as demand decreases from D_0 to D_1. The result is unemployment of the amount $L_0 - L_1$, where L_0 is the quantity of labour that households want to supply at wage rate W_0 and L_1 is the

Figure 30.5 Sticky wages

If wages 'stick' at W_0 rather than fall to the new equilibrium wage of W^* following a shift of demand from D_0 to D_1, the result will be unemployment equal to $L_0 - L_1$.

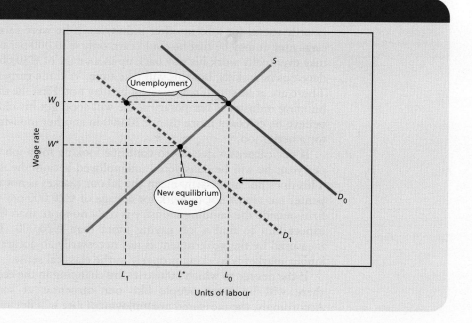

amount of labour that firms want to hire at wage rate W_0. $L_0 - L_1$ is the number of workers who would like to work at W_0 but cannot find jobs.

The sticky-wage explanation of unemployment leads us to ask *why* wages are sticky, if they are, and why wages do not fall to clear the labour market during periods of high unemployment. Many answers have been proposed, but as yet no single answer has been agreed upon. This is one reason why macroeconomics has been in a state of flux for so long. The existence of unemployment continues to be a puzzle. Although we discuss the major theories that have been proposed to explain why wages may not clear the labour market, we can offer no final conclusions. The question remains open.

Social, or implicit, contracts

social, *or* implicit, contracts

Unspoken agreements between workers and firms that firms will not cut wages.

One explanation for downwardly sticky wages is that firms enter into **social**, or **implicit**, **contracts** with workers not to cut wages.

It seems that extreme events – a deep recession, deregulation, or the threat of bankruptcy – are necessary before firms cut wages. Wage cuts did occur during the Great Depression, in the airline industry during the current deregulation of the industry, and again occasionally in other industries during Europe's current spell of unemployment. These are exceptions to the general rule. For reasons that may be more sociological than economic, cutting wages seems to be a taboo.

relative-wage explanation of unemployment

An explanation for sticky wages (and therefore unemployment): if workers are concerned about their wages relative to other workers in other firms and industries, they may be unwilling to accept a wage cut unless they know that all other workers are receiving similar cuts.

A related argument, the **relative-wage explanation of unemployment**, holds that workers are concerned about their wages *relative* to the wages of other workers in other firms and industries. They will not accept wage cuts unless they know other workers are receiving similar cuts. Because it is difficult to reassure any one group of workers that all other workers are in the same situation, workers may resist any cut in their wages. There may be an implicit understanding between firms and workers that firms will not do anything that would make their workers worse off relative to workers in other firms.

Explicit contracts

Many workers' wages are determined by collective agreements between trades unions and employers. Such contracts typically fix wages for a period of one year or longer. Wages set in this way do not fluctuate with economic conditions, either upwards or downwards. If the economy slows down and firms demand fewer workers, the wage will not fall. Instead, some workers will be laid off.

explicit contracts

Employment contracts that stipulate workers' wages, usually for a period of one to three years.

Although **explicit contracts** can explain why some wages are sticky, a deeper question should be considered. When a contract is signed, workers and firms surely know that unforeseen events may cause the wages set by the contract to be too high or too low. Why do firms and workers bind themselves in this way? One explanation is that negotiating wages is costly. Negotiations between unions and firms can take a considerable amount of time – time that could be spent producing output – and it would be very costly to negotiate wages weekly or monthly. Contracts are a way of bearing these costs at no more than one-, two- or three-year intervals. There is a trade-off between the costs of locking workers and firms into contracts for long periods of time and the costs of wage negotiations. From what we observe in practice, the length of contracts that seems to minimize negotiation costs lies between one and three years.

cost of living adjustments (COLAs)

Contract provisions that tie wages to changes in the cost of living. The greater the inflation rate, the more wages are raised.

Some contracts adjust for unforeseen events by **cost of living adjustments (COLAs)** written into the contract. COLAs tie wages to changes in the cost of living: the greater the rate of inflation, the more wages rise. COLAs aim to protect workers from unexpected inflation, though many COLAs adjust wages by a smaller percentage than the percentage increase in prices. The *scala mobile* used in Italy is a well-known example.

Equilibrium unemployment

Figure 30.6 provides a glimpse at Europe's unemployment rates, showing average rates for the time between 1990 and 1998, and the 1998 values. It drives home the point that Europe's high unemployment is hardly a phenomenon that results from a

Figure 30.6 European unemployment in the 1990s

EU unemployment rates average 10% in the 1990s. In most countries unemployment in 1998 does not differ much from the average experience. Exceptions are Germany, Sweden and Switzerland, where it is noticeably higher, and the UK, where it is substantially lower. *Source*: Eurostat, OECD.

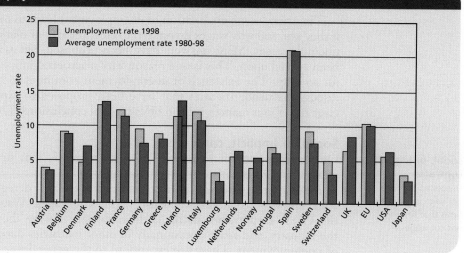

EU unemployment rates average 10% in the 1990s. In most countries unemployment in 1998 does not differ much from the average experience. Exceptions are Germany, Sweden and Switzerland, where it is noticeably higher, and the UK, where it is substantially lower. *Source*: Eurostat, OECD.

short-lived, temporary displacement of the labour market from equilibrium. Such cyclical changes do occur too, and possible reasons were discussed in the last section. Obviously, though, most of Europe's unemployment appears to be a longer-run problem. It shows little tendency to go away by itself, and its magnitude by far exceeds any plausible estimates of unemployment due to natural frictions in the labour market.

Explanations of why *involuntary unemployment* may exist in equilibrium suggest that conditions in the real world may not be as perfect as the classical model assumes. We now discuss some of the imperfections that can keep the labour market from reaching an equilibrium of the type shown in Figure 30.4.

Minimum wage laws

Minimum wage laws may be one source of involuntary unemployment. Such laws set a floor for wage rates – a minimum hourly rate for any kind of labour. Some countries set the minimum wage in absolute terms. For example, in 1998 the federal minimum wage in the USA was $5.15 per hour. Britain introduces a national minimum wage of £3.60 an hour in 1999. Other countries set the minimum wage as a percentage of other wages. As these go up the minimum wage rises too.

minimum wage
A minimum hourly wage rate for any kind of labour.

The effect of a **minimum wage** is straightforward. In terms of Figure 30.5, if the minimum wage is below the market-clearing wage, W^*, the minimum wage has no effect. Firms voluntarily pay the wage rate, W^*, and the labour market clears. However, if the minimum wage rises beyond W^* to, say, W_0, this generates unemployment through two channels. First, employers respond to rising labour costs by reducing labour demand to L_1. Second, workers respond to the prospects of higher pay by expanding the labour supply to L_0. The difference between supply and demand, $L_0 - L_1$, represents involuntary unemployment.

Minimum wage laws may constitute an obstacle to employment when people have little job experience, such as teenagers seeking their first job or women re-entering the labour force after bringing up children. However, they are not likely to be a major culprit in Europe's recent spell of unemployment. First, only six out of 15 EU members have minimum wage laws. Second, in those countries that do, minimum wages have gone down rather than up relative to average wages over the last two decades (see Figure 30.7). And third, Spain, the country with the lowest minimum wage by far, and with the most pronounced *downward* trend, is struggling with the highest unemployment rate.

Monopolistic trade unions

Another institutional feature sets labour markets in Europe and other industrialized countries apart from the ideal classical scenario: wages are set in collective negotiations

Figure 30.7 Minimum wages in Europe

Only six European countries have a history of minimum wage laws. There is no general upward trend in minimum wages (except for France until 1983) that may have driven up unemployment. The UK has decided to implement a national minimum wage rate of £3.60 in April 1999.
Source: Eurostat, OECD.

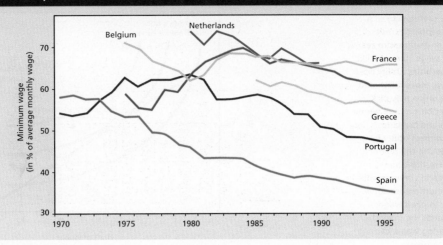

between a trade union and an association of employers (or one large employer). The wage settlement then serves as a minimum wage for individual shops or industries in regions or nationwide. Often (Germany is one example), negotiated wages constitute a minimum wage for non-union workers in the same industry as well.

monopolistic trade unions
Trade unions with the power to dictate any wage rate they want in collective negotiations with employers.

Like a monopolist in the goods market, monopolistic trade unions do not possess the power to set the price *and* the quantity, or here, the wage *and* employment. What they can do is set the wage at their discretion. After that, employers are free to decide how much labour to employ at this wage rate. This choice is always on the labour demand curve, as we saw above. In negotiating, trades unions anticipate the fact that they will end up on the labour demand curve. Having the power to set the wage, they can actually pick any point on the labour demand curve they want. And they pick the one that serves their interest best.

What are the interests of trade unions? In analogy to our discussion of goods-market monopolies in Chapter 13, we assume that the monopolistic trade union maximizes the revenue from selling labour. This revenue is the wage sum, the product of the wage rate W and employment L:

A monopolistic trade union maximizes the wage sum $S = W \times L$.

A given wage sum, say €100, may be generated by a money wage rate of €10 and employment of 10 people, by a wage rate of €5 and employment of 20, and by many other combinations. The wage rate, W, needed to achieve a wage sum of 100 depends on the level of employment according to the equation

$$W = \frac{100}{L}$$

Similarly, those combinations generating a wage sum of €200 must obey the equation

$$W = \frac{200}{L}$$

Figure 30.8 shows these two equations as curved lines (called hyperbolas), together with a third line of $W \times L$ combinations that multiply to 300. Each of these lines represents a *union indifference curve*: for example, on the red curve all points give the same wage sum of €100, so the union interested in the wage sum is indifferent between

Figure 30.8 Monopolistic trades unions

The preferences of a monopolistic trade union that maximizes the wage sum look like hyperbolas. Utility rises as we move north-east. The union may pick any point on the labour demand curve. It maximizes utility by selecting the point where the labour demand curve touches an indifference curve. The implied wage exceeds the market-clearing wage, causing involuntary unemployment.

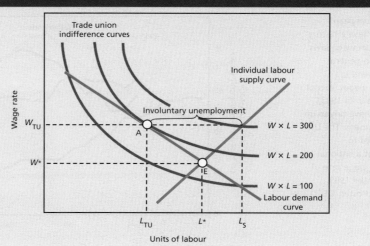

them. But since the trade union wants the wage sum to be as high as possible, it insists on the wage that brings them on the indifference curve furthest to the right. Among all possibilities offered by the firms' labour demand curve (no other combinations are available), point A, the point of tangency between the labour demand curve and a union indifference curve, is the trade union's best choice. No indifference curve with a wage sum exceeding 200 is within reach.

Just like the monopolist in the goods market who sells at a price higher than in competitive equilibrium, a monopolistic trade union pushes the wage above the wage that would clear the labour market in the classical, competitive equilibrium. The wage rate, W_{TU}, generates involuntary unemployment in the same way that a minimum wage does. At this higher wage the demand for labour is only L_{TU}, while the households' supply of labour is L_S. $L_S - L_{TU}$ of these would like to work at the wage rate W_{TU} but cannot find a job.

It is important to note that although the level of unemployment generated by a monopolistic trade union is individually *involuntary*, it is collectively *voluntary*. What we mean by that is the following. Suppose the labour market is dynamic in the sense that firms come and go, forcing workers to look for new jobs, and that there are always workers who enter the market and others who leave. Workers know that at a wage rate W_{TU} there is, say, 5% unemployment. But it is always different people who become unemployed each year, chosen as if a dice had been thrown. Thus each worker every year faces a probability of 5% of being without a job. If union members nevertheless support a wage demand of W_{TU}, they are evidently prepared to accept that risk. From the collective point of view the accompanying unemployment is voluntary. After the smoke clears, those who lost their jobs will individually regret that the wage is so high. But they accept the same gamble the next time around.

Insiders and outsiders

The line of argument in the last paragraph overstates the mobility between employment and unemployment. Finding a job next year when you are unemployed today is often more difficult than keeping your job next year when you have one today. The *insider–outsider theory* elaborates on this theme by defining as **insiders** those who currently work and as **outsiders** those who are looking for work.

Let the economy initially be at point A in Figure 30.9a. As indicated, those who work at this wage are insiders, while those who are unsuccessfully looking for work are outsiders. Now suppose a surge in oil prices shifts the labour demand curve down into the position shown by the broken line. The trade union can't help but accept a dramatic reduction of the wage sum (measured by the blue rectangle $0L_BBW_B$). The

insiders In the insider–outsider theory, those who currently work.

outsiders In the insider–outsider theory, those who are looking for work.

Figure 30.9 The insider–outsider model

a. A surge in oil prices drives the labour demand curve down. Unions respond by moderating wage claims, accepting a reduction in employment. The wage sum shrinks.

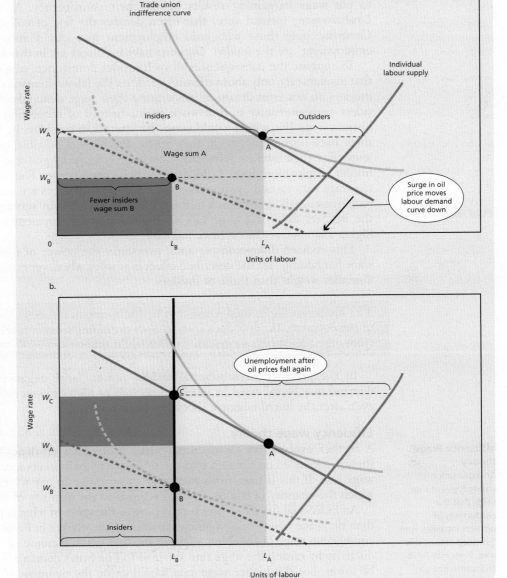

b. When oil prices fall back to their initial level, the labour demand curve moves up to its old position. To maximize the wage sum of insiders and outsiders, unions should go back to point A. If unions are dominated by insiders only wanting to maximize their wage sum, the wage is driven up to W_C at constant employment. Though the oil shock has been reversed, unemployment and the wage rate are now higher; employment and the wage sum are lower.

best it can do for its clients, the original insiders, is accept a reduction of the wage rate to W_B, accompanied by a fall in employment to L_B. The immediate effect is that the number of insiders drops. Whether the number of outsiders (or you might say, unemployment) rises or falls is not clear. This depends on the shapes of the individual labour supply and union indifference curves.

To continue the story, suppose the surge in oil prices was only temporary. After some time, oil prices ease down to their previous level, moving the labour demand curve back into the position shown by the unbroken line. What happens to wages and employment? This depends on who has a say in the trade union's wage decision.

If the current outsiders, including those who lost their jobs when oil prices surged, have the same influence on the union's wage claim as current insiders, then the labour market returns to point A. The detrimental effect of rising oil prices on employment is fully reversed when prices come down again. Unfortunately, reality may not always work like this.

Typically, trades union members who are out of work have little, if any, influence on union wage demands. This is most obvious in situations when union leaders need to put wage bargaining results before their constituency. As exemplified by the *Urabstimmung* (primal vote) that often decides the fate of collective agreements in Germany, only those who hold employment may cast a vote. 'Those who hold employment' are the *insiders*. *Outsiders* have no direct say in the decision.

To appraise the consequences of such insider dominance, suppose in Figure 30.9b that insiders care only about themselves. After the labour demand curve shifts back up, insiders do not even dream of moderating their wage demands in order to give outsiders an opportunity to find work again. Instead of requesting the previous equilibrium wage W_A, which would serve the interest of outsiders by bringing $L_A - L_B$ of them back into employment, they go for the highest possible wage that would not jeopardize their own employment. This wage is found by going up vertically from the insider employment level L_B to the labour demand curve. The wage that maximizes the wage sum earned by insiders is W_C. The consequences are severe. Not only does employment fail to snap back to the pre-shock level, but by serving their own interest the insiders drive the wage rate so high that unemployment is now substantially higher than before the oil price increase.

This stylized discussion certainly overstates the power of insiders in centralized wage bargaining. Yet the described effect is at work whenever outsiders' interests have a smaller weight than those of insiders.

> The insider–outsider model does not by itself explain the existence of unemployment. What it does is show how prevailing market forces are prevented from digesting shocks as quickly as they could otherwise.

In the presence of substantial insider power, large negative shocks to labour demand may be followed by extended periods of high or even rising unemployment, even after the initial negative shock has been reversed.

Efficiency wage theory

efficiency wage theory

An explanation of unemployment that holds that the productivity of workers increases with the wage rate. If this is so, firms may have an incentive to pay wages above the market-clearing rate.

A further explanation for unemployment centres on **efficiency wage theory**. The theory is founded on the idea that the productivity of workers increases with a higher wage rate. If this is true, firms may have an incentive to pay wages *above* the wage at which the quantity of labour supplied is equal to the quantity of labour demanded.

An individual firm hires workers as long as the value of what is produced is greater than the wage rate. Without efficiency effects, the market in Figure 30.4 produces an equilibrium wage of W^*. Now suppose the firm could increase all of its workers' productivity by raising the wage rate above W^*. The firm's demand for labour would not be lower, but the higher wage rate would cause the quantity of labour supplied to increase. The quantity of labour supplied would exceed the quantity of labour demanded at the new higher wage – the *efficiency wage* – and the result is unemployment.

Empirical studies of labour markets have identified several potential benefits to firms from paying workers more than the market-clearing wage. Among them are lower staff turnover, improved morale, and reduced 'shirking' at work.[4] But even though the efficiency wage theory predicts some unemployment, it is unlikely that the behaviour described accounts for much of the observed high levels of unemployment in Europe.

---

[4]*For a good summary, see George Akerlof and Janet Yellen,* Efficiency Wage Models of the Labour Market *(Cambridge: Cambridge University Press, 1986).*

As we have seen, there are many explanations of why the labour market may not clear. The theories are not necessarily mutually exclusive, and they all explain some of today's unemployment – but to different extents in different countries. This is why – apart from the general consensus that Europe's labour markets need more flexibility – solutions also need some tailoring to specific national circumstances.

Applications

Cyclical unemployment and equilibrium unemployment

Economic policy making crucially depends on the proper identification of the nature of current unemployment. Unemployment is the sum of equilibrium unemployment and cyclical unemployment.

Viewed with enough patience, cyclical unemployment may not be considered a problem at all. As the economy moves out of a recession, cyclical unemployment disappears. From a less patient standpoint, if markets are deemed to recover too slowly when left alone, expansionary monetary or fiscal policy may be used to reduce cyclical unemployment more quickly.

Natural (or equilibrium) unemployment needs a different cure, because it reflects various inflexibilities in the labour market rather than a lack of demand in the goods market. To reduce natural unemployment governments could get rid of minimum wages, liberalize job protection laws, cut back on the generosity and duration of unemployment benefits, and curb the power of trades unions.

The figure shows unemployment rates in 1997 and their decomposition into equilibrium and cyclical unemployment. Its main messages are:

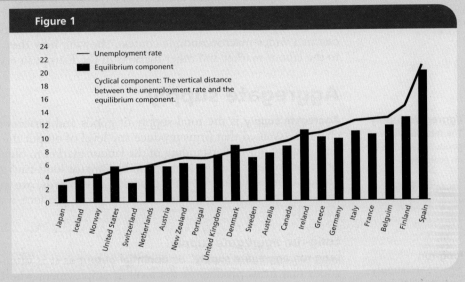

Figure 1

- Unemployment rate
- Equilibrium component
- Cyclical component: The vertical distance between the unemployment rate and the equilibrium component.

Source: OECD.

■ Most of today's unemployment is natural. Only a small part is cyclical.
■ There are big differences in natural unemployment rates. Even within the rather homogeneous European environment, rates vary between about 3% in Switzerland and 20% in Spain.
■ Not all countries appear to be in the same phase of the business cycle. Most of the 11 EMU members were in a recession, which added about 2 percentage points to unemployment rates in France, Germany, Italy and Finland (plus Switzerland as a non-EMU country). The opposite occurred in Denmark and Ireland, where booms temporarily drove unemployment below

natural unemployment.

Which part of unemployment is natural and which part is cyclical is never known for sure, and needs to be estimated. There are two major approaches:

Comparing unemployment and vacancies The idea here is that if we observe unemployment and job openings of the same magnitude, then the cause of this unemployment must be natural. Job searchers and job openings do not match, either with respect to the skills offered and demanded, or with respect to the geographical location.

Using the Phillips curve According to the

Phillips curve (see Chapter 31), inflation increases when the unemployment falls below natural unemployment, and it falls when unemployment rises beyond the natural rate. The unemployment rate that leaves inflation unchanged has been given the name NAIRU (non-accelerating inflation rate of unemployment).

These two approaches do not necessarily give the same results, making the point that there are inherent uncertainties associated with the decomposition of unemployment into natural and cyclical components. This needs to be kept in mind when interpreting and using these indicators.

Simple solutions do not seem to work. Above all, many explanations of unemployment pose new questions: if minimum wages are the problem, why is unemployment highest in Spain where minimum wages are the lowest among those EU members that have them? Similarly, Spain, along with France, has the lowest **unionization rate** in Europe (less than 20%). Yet Spain's and France's unemployment rates are much higher than Denmark's, where unions represent some 90% of the labour force. As regards the big picture, unionization has fallen rather than risen during the last two decades in most European countries. This suggests that if wage legislation and union monopoly power play a major role in Europe's unemployment dilemma, it must be by more complex means than anything measured by aggregate unionization rates.

This will be illustrated in Chapter 31, where the explanations encountered here are cast in a wider macroeconomic context, showing how they may interact with shocks to the labour market and other markets in the European economies.

Aggregate supply

Aggregate supply is the total supply of goods and services in an economy. Previous chapters assumed that firms produce any level of output the market demands; we can now employ our understanding of the labour market to obtain a more refined view of aggregate supply. We first look at equilibrium (or long-run) aggregate supply, the level of output that firms *normally* produce. Afterwards, we turn to short-run supply decisions that may cause firms to temporarily produce more or less than they do normally.

Long-run aggregate supply

Long-run aggregate supply, or **potential output** as it is often called, is the amount of goods that firms produce at the level of employment where the labour market is in equilibrium. Note that this equilibrium of the labour market reflects the institutional characteristics of a country. If the labour market is competitive, as in the classical view, the labour market clears at the point of intersection between the labour demand curve and the labour supply curve, and there is no involuntary unemployment. However, if workers are represented by monopolistic trades unions, or if efficiency wage considerations drive up the wage rate offered by employers, equilibrium in the labour market is accompanied by involuntary unemployment. We start by looking at the classical labour market.

The classical labour market and potential output

Consider the labour market diagram in the lower left panel of Figure 30.10. Suppose demand and supply curves are in their respective black positions, so that the market clears at a wage rate of €20 and employment is 20 (billion) work hours. Given the country's capital stock and current technology, we can read off the partial production function shown in the upper left panel that 20 work hours produce 10 (million) cars (the only good produced in this country). Since 10 cars is what the economy normally produces when the labour market is in equilibrium, this is equilibrium output or **potential output**. The upper right panel maps potential output from the vertical axis to the horizontal axis by means of a 45° line. Finally, the lower right-hand panel notes that 10 cars were produced at the given price level of €20 (thousand) per car.

The price level, potential output, and the long-run aggregate supply curve

Is potential output supplied by firms affected by the price they can charge for their product(s)? One would certainly think so. After all, doesn't a higher price also mean a higher marginal revenue product of labour, making it profitable to employ more labour and thus produce more?

It is true that if the product price goes up from €20 to €30, the marginal revenue product of labour goes up by 50% as well, shifting the labour demand curve from the

---

unionization rate
The percentage of the labour force in trade union membership.

aggregate supply
The total supply of all goods and services in an economy.

long-run aggregate supply *or* potential output
The amount of goods that firms produce at the level of employment where the labour market is in equilibrium.

potential output, *or* potential GDP
The level of aggregate output that firms produce at full employment.

black into the red position. However, this is not the whole story. Remember that workers decide how to allocate available time between leisure and work on the basis of how much *real income* one work hour generates. If prices go up by 50%, nominal wages also need to be 50% higher to buy the same bundle of goods. So in order to supply the same amount of labour as before the price rise, nominal wages need to be 50% higher than before, which shifts the labour supply curve from the black into the red position.

Because in the face of the price increase both the labour demand curve and the labour supply curve have shifted up in proportion to the price increase, the new red supply and demand curves intersect at the same employment level (and the same real wage) as the black curves. But if employment was not affected by the price increase, output was not affected either. So

Potential output (income) is not affected by the price level.

By analogous reasoning, a fall in price to €10 moves the labour demand curve and the labour supply curve down into the blue positions. Again, the real wage, employment and potential output are not affected, as indicated by the blue dot in the lower right-hand panel. Connecting the three dots identified in this panel produces a vertical line.

The vertical line at potential output is the long-run aggregate supply curve. It indicates that potential output is the same at any price level.

Potential income with monopolistic trade unions

We know that the presence of monopolistic trade unions raises the wage rate above the market-clearing level and drives employment below the classical equilibrium. With lower employment, output is lower too, shifting potential output to the left.

Figure 30.10 The long-run AS curve

The south-west panel shows labour demand and supply curves in a diagram with nominal wages on the vertical axis. Since both firms and workers think in terms of real wages, these demand and supply schedules both move up by the same amount when prices rise. They still intersect at the same level of employment. Therefore, in the long run, after the labour market has cleared, employment (and output) does not depend on the price level. Thus the long-run *AS* curve is vertical.

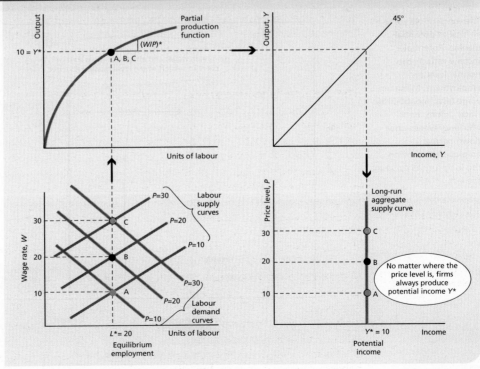

Again, a change in the price level does not affect this monopolistic equilibrium in the labour market: if prices go up, both the labour demand curves and union indifference curves shift up proportionally, leaving the real wage rate and employment unaffected. So, since potential output is lower at all price levels,

> A monopolistic trade union causes the long-run aggregate supply curve to move leftwards.

On this trade-union aggregate supply curve, shown in Figure 30.11, some workers are unemployed involuntarily. Other factors that shift the long-run aggregate supply curve to the left are efficiency wages or minimum wages (if they are defined in real terms).

The discussion of potential output and the long-run aggregate supply curve rests on the assumption that the labour market is in equilibrium. In the classical view, this equilibrium obtains permanently, so aggregate supply is always given by the long-run aggregate supply curve. Under more realistic assumptions, it may take time to restore equilibrium in the labour market after a disturbance. But then the short-run response of aggregate supply may be different from the long-run response. Actual aggregate output may differ from potential output. This requires a separate analysis of the short-run aggregate supply curve.

Short-run aggregate supply

An important feature, which makes labour markets in most countries deviate from the classical notion of constantly adjusting nominal wages, is the presence of long-term wage contracts that make wages sticky. We have already identified sticky wages as a source of cyclical unemployment (which simply reflects cyclical deviations of output from potential output).

Figure 30.11 Trades unions and the long-run *AS* curve

The long-run *AS* curve is vertical at potential income. Potential income reflects the normal level of employment. Minimum wage laws, monopolistic trade unions, or efficiency wages drive down normal employment, moving the long-run *AS* curve to the left.

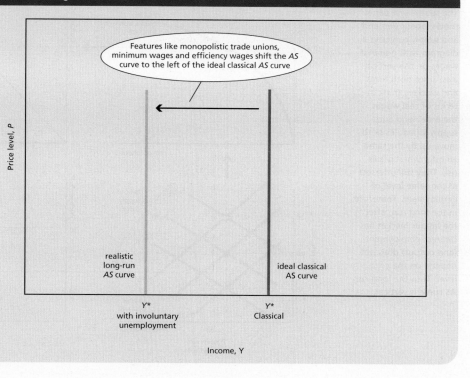

Applications

The simple 'Keynesian' aggregate supply curve

There is a great deal of disagreement regarding the shape of the *AS* curve. One view of the aggregate supply curve, the simple 'Keynesian' view, holds that at any given moment, the economy has a clearly defined capacity, or maximum output. This maximum output, denoted by Y_F, is defined by the existing labour force, the current capital stock and the existing state of technology. If planned aggregate expenditure increases when the economy is producing *below* this maximum capacity, this view holds, inventories will be lower than planned and firms will increase output, but the price level will not change. Firms are operating with underutilized plants (excess capacity) and there is unemployment. Expansion does not exert any upward pressure on prices. However, if planned aggregate expenditure increases when the economy is producing near or at its maximum (Y_F), inventories will be lower than planned, but firms cannot increase their output. The result will be an increase in the price level, or inflation.

This view is illustrated in Figure 1. In the top half of the diagram, aggregate output (income) (Y) and planned aggregate expenditure ($C - I - G \equiv AE$) are initially in equilibrium at AE_1, Y_1 and price level P_1. Now suppose a tax cut or an increase in government spending increases planned aggregate expenditure. If such an increase shifts the AE curve from AE_1 to AE_2 and the corresponding aggregate demand curve (see Chapter 31) from AD_1 to AD_2, the equilibrium level of output will rise from Y_1 to Y_F. (Remember: an expansionary policy shifts the AD curve to the right.) Since we were initially producing below capacity output (Y_1 is lower than Y_F), the price level will be unaffected, remaining at P_1.

But now consider what would happen if AE were to increase even further. Suppose planned aggregate expenditure were to shift from AE_2 to AE_3, with a corresponding shift of AD_2 to AD_3. If the economy were producing below capacity output, the equilibrium level of output would rise to Y_3. But the output of the economy cannot exceed the maximum output of Y_F. As inventories fall below what was planned, firms

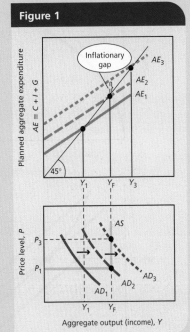

Figure 1

encounter a fully employed labour market and fully utilized plants. Therefore, they cannot increase their output. The result is that the aggregate supply curve becomes vertical at Y_F, and the price level is driven up to P_3.

The difference between planned aggregate expenditure and aggregate output at full capacity is sometimes referred to as an inflationary gap. You can see the inflationary gap in the top half of Figure 1. At Y_F (capacity output), planned aggregate

With planned aggregate expenditure of AE_1 and aggregate demand of AD_1, equilibrium output is Y_1. A shift of planned aggregate expenditure to AE_2, corresponding to a shift of the AD curve to AD_2, causes output to rise but the price level to remain at P_1. If planned aggregate expenditure and aggregate demand exceed Y_F, however, there is an inflationary gap and the price level rises to P_3.

expenditure (shown by AE_3) is greater than Y_F. The price level rises to P_3 until the aggregate quantity supplied and the aggregate quantity demanded are equal.

Despite the fact that the kinked aggregate supply curve provides some insights, most economists find it unrealistic. It does not seem likely that the whole economy suddenly runs into a capacity 'wall' at a specific level of output. As output expands, some firms and industries will hit capacity before others.

The consequence of fixing the nominal wage rate to €20 by contract for, say, a year is that this wage cannot change even if prices rise to erode, or prices fall to enhance, its buying power. Figure 30.12 looks at how aggregate supply responds to price movements in such a constellation.

Suppose the current price level is €20. Trade unions maximize the wage sum by requesting the wage rate $W^* = 20$, at which the real wage W/P is expected to equal 1 and firms are anticipated to employ L^* units of labour. Now, this may happen or it may not, depending on what the price level does during the 12 months for which the collective wage agreement fixes the money wage rate at €20. One of three things may occur.

Figure 30.12 The short-run *AS* curve

At a given nominal wage, firms demand more labour if prices rise, shifting the labour demand curve (in a diagram with nominal wages) to the right. So once the nominal wage is fixed (reflecting the price level expected by unions) employment goes up if prices go up. More output is produced. The south-east panel brings this together: the short-run *AS* curve says that there is a positive relationship between prices and income.

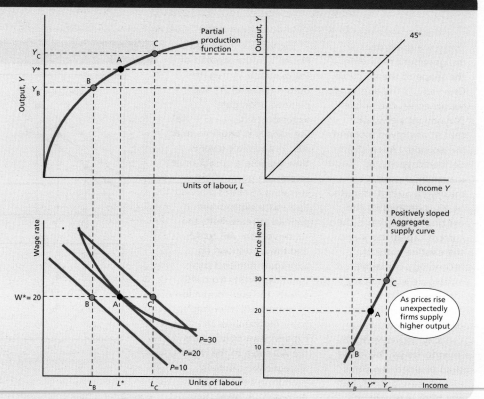

1. The price level stays where it was when the contract was negotiated. Then the labour demand curve stays in the black position. Firms employ *L** work hours, produce output *Y**, and the economy ends up on the long-run aggregate supply curve that applies in the presence of monopolistic trades unions (point *A* in the lower right panel).

2. Immediately after the wage contract is signed, prices drop to €10. This cuts the marginal revenue product of labour in half, moving the labour demand curve down into the green position. Faced with having to pay nominal wage rates of *W**, firms reduce employment to *L*B. Output falls below potential output to *Y*B, as shown in the upper left panel. Transferring this into the lower right panel gives the green dot. What this states is that once nominal wage rates are fixed, output falls below potential output to *Y*B if prices fall from €20 to €10.

3. Immediately after the wage contract was signed, prices rise by 50% to €30. This raises the marginal revenue product of labour as well, moving the labour demand curve up into the blue position. At the negotiated money wage rate of *W**, firms expand employment to *L*C, boosting output to *Y*C . The blue dot in the lower right panel sums up that when prices increase to €30 after money wages were fixed, output rises beyond potential output to *Y*C.

One point needs emphasis here. With rising prices, firms always *want* to employ more labour at the wage rate *W**, yet they can only do so if this labour is also supplied. This would not be the case if the black dot in the labour market diagram marked a classical equilibrium with no involuntary unemployment.[5] Since wage negotiations are

[5]*Then the individual labour supply curve passes through A up to the right. A price rise shifts it up to a position where it intersects the blue labour demand curve at L*. Just as in Figure 30.11, the price rise would have no employment effect. The point is that nobody can force individuals to work at the W* wage rate if they do not want to.*

conducted by a monopolistic trade union, some people who wanted to work at the W^* wage rate and price level of €20 do not find work. Firms can expand employment in the face of fixed nominal wages and rising prices until all who want to work have found work. Figure 30.12 assumes individual labour supply curves to be so far to the right that they do not even show on the graph.

Applications

Is the Internet the end of sticky prices?

Prices don't change every time the oil price moves, holiday prices and standard hotel rates are fixed for months, and doctors seldom alter their fees. Some claim the Internet could change all that. Prices could flick at the click of an computer mouse.

Will the Internet really make prices more flexible? The answer depends on why prices fail to fluctuate with every shift in supply and demand now. Simply put, prices change only when the cost of leaving them unchanged becomes bigger than the expense of adjusting them. In financial markets, prices move all the time because the cost of quoting the 'wrong' price can be huge. If market makers failed to raise prices when they were too low, for instance, they would make hefty losses because they would be obliged to sell unlimited amounts of securities on the cheap. And on a market stall, a fruit trader who didn't lower prices when they were too high would have to throw away unsold produce at the end of the day.

The Internet is unlikely to increase the cost of leaving prices unchanged. It will not make petrol perishable or make it more expensive to sell holidays at less than cost. But it will make it cheaper to change some prices. Digital holiday brochures do not need reprinting. And the Internet makes finding out and comparing prices much easier. Rates for hotel room in Honolulu can now be checked from a laptop in London. That, some argue, will make booking a room more like buying shares, where investors plump for the broker quoting the best price, which changes all the time.

For many goods, they may be right. Most people would buy the latest John Grisham thriller or even their electricity from the supplier with the lowest price; who the retailer is barely matters. In those cases, keener competition may make prices adjust faster to swings in supply and demand. But the Internet is unlikely to make all prices more flexible. Sticky prices are likely to survive in at least three cases: when the quality of a product is hard to assess; when consumers dislike frequent price changes; and when a market is dominated by a few firms.

First, consider firms which compete on quality as well as price. Consumers often find it difficult to judge how good their product is; and making a mistake may be costly. It can be hard to know how good a hotel is until you've stayed there; and a sleepless night in a lousy hotel before a big meeting is best avoided. So customers who have stayed in a hotel they like may return, even if rivals of the same standard are offering cheaper rates – especially as on a repeat visit they may know which side of the hotel is less noisy.

But if prices have risen since their last visit, they may reconsider. This may be why hotels that are nearly full rarely raise their rates for the night, as you might otherwise have expected. And half-empty hotels may be reluctant to cut room prices, because raising them again when demand recovers could drive away repeat customers as well as bargain hunters. That in turn could hurt their reputation – and hence how much new business they are likely to get (they may, of course, have different seasonal or weekend rates).

Firms my also keep prices stable because they are providing insurance to customers who dislike volatile prices, especially when buying expensive things. Customers choosing a holiday do not want prices to change while they are deciding where to go; and they will be loath to book months in advance it the price of their holiday might fall sharply a few days later.

Even when assessing quality is straightforward and consumers have no reason to object to flexible prices, prices may stay sticky if competition is lacking. Take petrol, which is sold by a handful of big companies. As there are only a few providers in the retail market, each will consider its rivals' likely response before changing prices. A petrol company may thus be reluctant to raise prices if it expects its rivals to try to steal a march on it by leaving their prices unchanged. And it may also be wary of cutting prices, because it may gain nothing but earn lower profits if other follow suit. If each firm reasons in this way, prices may change infrequently.

When prices are fixed for too long, of course, supply and demand may get badly out of kilter. In that case, hotels, holiday companies, doctors, petrol retailers and the like will decide to alter their rates, fees and so on. In times of high inflation, too, prices may change more often. But the Internet is unlikely to spell the end for sticky prices.

Source: The Economist, 16 May 1998, p. 98.

short-run aggregate supply curve
A curve that shows how much output all firms produce at any conceivable price level while the money wage rate is fixed. It has a positive slope.

Drawing a line through points A, B and C in the lower right-hand graph gives the **short-run aggregate supply curve**. It simply generalizes what we have just found out:

> The short-run aggregate supply curve shows how much output all firms produce at any conceivable price level while the money wage rate is fixed. It has a positive slope.

Once wages can respond to price changes, the labour market moves back into equilibrium and output moves back to potential output on the long-run aggregate supply curve.

Shifts of the aggregate supply curves

When we drew aggregate supply curves we took certain things as given. We needed those to remain unchanged when drawing the diagrams. As these factors or variables change, the aggregate supply curves shift. Let us first look at factors that shift both the short-run and the long-run aggregate supply curves. We will then look at what may shift the short-run aggregate supply curve alone.[6]

Shifts in the long-run aggregate supply curve

The long-run aggregate supply curve is vertical at potential output. If potential output increases (or falls), the curve shifts to the right (or left). For given trade union preferences, potential output can only change if the production function in the upper left panel changes. This changes what can be produced at any given employment. At the same time, it affects the labour demand curve and, hence, employment.

The partial production function is drawn under the assumption of a given capital stock and given technology. Now suppose technology improves or the capital stock increases. This turns the production function upwards, as shown in Figure 30.13. With better technology or more capital to work with, each work-hour becomes more productive. Thus the labour demand curve turns upwards too. As the point of tangency between this new labour demand curve and a new, higher union indifference curve shows, unions now maximize the wage sum at a higher wage rate and higher employment. The combined effect of higher employment and improved labour productivity leads to an increase of potential output from Y^* to Y^*_1. This shifts the long-run aggregate supply curve to the right into the blue position.

What happens to the short-run aggregate supply (AS) curve? Well, it moves, just as far to the right as the long-run AS curve. Everything that happened before at and around the old potential output now happens at and around the new potential output Y^*_1. If prices do not change after the wage contract is closed, Y^*_1 is produced. If prices rise, output rises beyond Y^*_1. If prices fall, output is driven down below Y^*_1, just as in Figure 30.12.

Shifts in the short-run aggregate supply curve

The short-run AS curve may shift even if potential output remains unchanged. The key to understanding this is that trades unions bargain to maximize the *real* wage sum. So they aspire to a certain *real* wage rate to accompany an expected level of employment. Targeting a real wage is difficult, however, because money wages need to be fixed for a year (or longer) without actual knowledge of the price level that will prevail.

---

[6]*The long-run aggregate supply curve cannot shift alone. When it moves it always pulls the short-run aggregate supply curve along with it.*

Figure 30.13 Shifts in the long-run and the short-run AS curves

If technology improves (or the capital stock rises), the production function turns upward. Being steeper at any level of *L* means that the marginal product of labour has increased at any *L*. The labour demand curve shifts up. It now touches a union indifference curve at a higher level of employment *L**₁. With higher employment and better technology more output is produced. Potential output rises to *Y**₁. This shifts the long-run *AS* curve to the right, and with it the short-run *AS* curves.

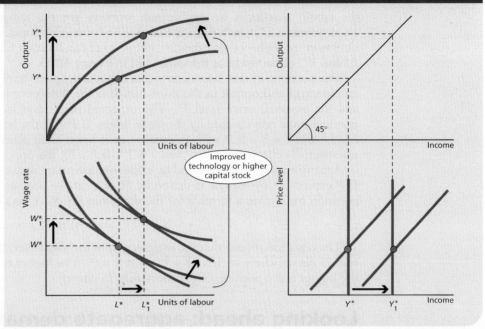

In Figure 30.14 trade unions are aiming for a real wage of 1, as they did in Figure 30.12. They negotiate a nominal wage of 20, for if the price level remained at 20, where it currently is, the real wage W/P would be 1 and employment would be L^*, as desired. This is good if trade unions expect prices to remain at 20, where they currently are.

But what happens if the trade union expects the price level to rise to 30 right after the end of wage negotiations? Then they need to demand the higher wage rate of 30 to ensure the same real wage rate of 1 and employment L^*. The graphical solution is that the union anticipates the labour demand curve to move up to its new position

Figure 30.14 Shifts in the short-run AS curve

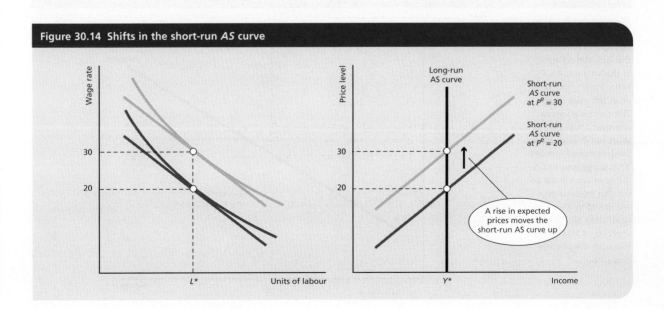

after prices have risen to 30, and the wage sum is maximized where the red indifference curve touches the labour demand curve. If the price level turns out as expected the labour market is in equilibrium: workers get the maximum wage sum, and employment is L^*, which firms use to produce potential output. If the price level turns out lower (or higher) than expected, employment and output fall below (or rise above) L^* and Y^*, respectively, as demonstrated in Figure 30.15.

The outcome of this discussion is that it is not the price level alone that determines employment and output in the short run. It is the difference between the price level and the expected price level P^e. The expected price level is already built into the nominal wage rate claimed by the trade union. If $P = P^e$ the labour market clears and $L = L^*$ and $Y = Y^*$. If $P > P^e$, the real wage is lower than planned – that is, labour is unexpectedly cheap and $L > L^*$ and $Y > Y^*$. If $P < P^e$, the opposite happens.

Approximating what we found by a linear equation we may write $Y = Y^* + b(P - P^e)$. If P exceeds P^e by €10, Y is driven by $10 \times b$ above potential output. Solving this equation for P gives a formula for the short-run AS curve, as shown in Figure 30.15:

$$P = P^e + 1/b(Y - Y^*) \quad \text{Short-run } AS \text{ curve}$$

The equation reveals that the intersection of the short-run AS curve with the long-run AS curve (where we have $Y = Y^*$) is at $P = P^e$. The higher the expected price level, the higher is the position of the short-run AS curve.

Looking ahead: aggregate demand and supply

Chapters 23 to 29 analysed the economy's demand side, comprising the goods market, the money market and the foreign exchange market. We learned how high output would have to be at the given price level to satisfy the spending plans of households, firms, the government and foreigners. We called this level of income a demand-side equilibrium because we assumed that firms would increase output (without raising prices) as long as there was excess demand.

Figure 30.15 An equation for the short-run AS curve

The equation $P = P^e + 1/b\ (Y - Y^*)$ comprises both the short-run and the long-run AS curve. In the long run $P = P^e$. Then $Y = Y^*$, no matter what the price level. The curve is a vertical line over Y^*. In the short run P^e is given, a predetermined number. Y^* is exogenous too. So if P goes up, Y must go up. The two variables are linked by the coefficient $1/b$. The short-run AS curve is a line with the positive slope $1/b$.

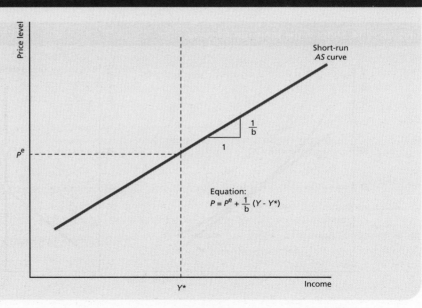

In this chapter we have taken a closer look at the economy's supply side – that is, the production decisions of firms. We saw that at normal employment levels, firms produce a specific level of output (potential output) that is independent of the price level. Temporarily, firms may produce more, but only at higher prices.

The task of the next chapter is to merge the economy's demand side with our newly acquired understanding of the supply side. The tool we will need to derive first is the aggregate demand (*AD*) curve. This counterpart to the *AS* curve shows how demand-side equilibrium income is affected by changes in the price level. When we combine the *AS* curve and the *AD* curve we will see that whenever there is a gap between the demand-side equilibrium and the aggregate supply of firms, the price levels changes to bring these two into line with one another.

Summary

Classical view of the labour market

1. The labour demand curve shows how much labour all firms in an economy demand at different wage rates. This downward-sloping curve is derived from the aggregate production function. It shows the marginal revenue product of labour at each employment level.

2. The labour supply curve shows how much labour all households in an economy offer at different wage rates. This curve is upward sloping. It reflects the optimal balance households strike at each wage rate between leisure time and work time.

3. Classical economists believe that the interaction of supply and demand in the labour market brings about equilibrium at all times. In this equilibrium, no involuntary unemployment exists beyond what occurs as a result of natural frictions and structural changes.

Explaining unemployment: beyond the classical view

4. It is useful to separate unemployment into two components: cyclical unemployment, which reflects the ups and downs of the business cycle, and equilibrium unemployment, which remains unaffected by the business cycle.

5. The main cause of cyclical unemployment is sticky money wages. As a result of implicit or explicit contracts, money wages may not adjust quickly enough to equilibrate supply and demand at all times.

6. *Minimum wage laws*, which set a floor for the wage rate, may contribute to unemployment in low-income segments of the labour market. If the market-clearing wage in this part of the market is below the minimum wage, involuntary unemployment arises.

7. *Monopolistic trade unions* may be thought of as trying to maximize revenue (here, the wage sum) in centralized wage bargaining. In analogy to what a monopolistic firm does in the goods market, this union pushes the wage rate above the market-clearing wage rate. Employment falls below the market-clearing level, and involuntary unemployment results.

8. The insider–outsider model emphasizes that those unemployed (outsiders) have little influence on wage negotiations compared to insiders. As a consequence, negative temporary shocks to labour demand can give rise to lasting unemployment.

9. *Efficiency wage theory* holds that the productivity of workers increases with the wage rate. In this case, firms may have an incentive to pay wages above the market-clearing wage. At all wages above the equilibrium there will be an excess supply of labour and therefore unemployment.

Aggregate supply

10. *Aggregate supply* is the total supply of goods and services in the economy. The aggregate supply curve shows the relationship between the aggregate quantity of output supplied by all firms in an economy and the overall price level. Since output responses to changes in the price level are different in the long run and in the short run, we need to distinguish between long-run and short-run *AS* curves.

11. The *long-run AS curve* is *vertical* at the level of *potential output* (or *potential GDP*). The 'long run' is understood to mean the time required for wage rates to fully adjust to a change in prices.

12. The *short-run AS curve* is a *positively sloped* line. Sticky wages are a major cause for the short-run *AS* curve not to be vertical. Wages are sticky because of explicit long-term wage contracts. Implicit contracts may reinforce this effect.

13. Anything that affects the decisions of firms, and thus potential output, shifts the *AS* curves. Such factors are technological progress; changes in the capital stock due to wars, capital accumulation or natural disasters; or changes in the general quality of the labour force.

14. Relative to a given long-run *AS* curve the position of the short-run *AS* curve is determined by the *expected price level*. The higher the expected price level, the higher is the position of the short-run *AS* curve.

Review Terms and Concepts

aggregate production function
aggregate supply
classical economics
cost of living adjustments (COLAs)
cyclical unemployment
efficiency wage theory
equilibrium or natural unemployment
explicit contracts
frictional unemployment
full employment
insiders
labour demand curve
labour supply curve
long-run aggregate supply or potential output

marginal revenue product of labour (MRPL)
minimum wage
monopolistic trade unions
partial production function
potential output, or potential GDP
outsiders
relative-wage explanation of unemployment
short-run aggregate supply curve
social, or implicit, contracts
sticky wages
structural unemployment
unemployment rate
unionization rate

Problem Set

1. Obtain quarterly data on the unemployment rate and output growth in your country for the last four or five years.
a. What trends do you observe?
b. Plot the data on a graph with the output growth measured on the *X* axis and the unemployment rate on the *Y* axis. Is there evidence of cyclical unemployment?
c. What do you think is the equilibrium level of unemployment in your country?

2. Japan has traditionally had a substantially lower unemployment rate than Europe, at least since the 1960s. Japanese workers rarely move from one city to another and rarely switch employers, staying with one firm for their entire career. How, if at all, do these factors help to explain the difference in unemployment rates between Japan and Europe?

3. In 1998, the country of Ruba was suffering a period of high unemployment. The new president, Wraith Clang, has appointed Laurel Tiedye as his chief economist. Ms Tiedye and her staff estimated the following supply and demand curves for labour from data obtained from the labour minster, Robert Small:

$$Q_D = 100 - 5W$$

$$Q_S = 10W - 20$$

where *Q* is the quantity of labour supplied/demanded in millions of workers and *W* is the wage rate in slugs, the currency of Ruba.

a. Currently, the law in Ruba says that no worker shall be paid less than nine slugs per hour. Estimate the quantity of labour supplied, the number of unemployed, and the unemployment rate.
b. President Clang, ignoring Robert Small's objections, has recommended to parliament that the law be changed to allow the wage rate to be determined in the market. If such a law were passed, and the market adjusted quickly, what would happen to total employment, the size of the labour force, and the unemployment rate? Show the results graphically.
c. Will the Rubanese labour market adjust quickly to such a change in the law? Why or why not?

4. The following policies have at times been advocated to reduce the unemployment rate. Briefly explain how each might work, and explain which type or types of unemployment (frictional, structural or cyclical) each policy is designed to alter. Has your country adopted any of these or similar policies?
a. Lowering the minimum wage for teenagers.
b. Retraining programmes for workers who need to learn new skills in order to find employment.
c. Public employment for people without jobs.
d. Improving information about available jobs and current wage rates.

5. Your boss offers you a wage increase of 10%. Is it possible that you are worse off, even with the wage increase, than you were before?

6. How will the following affect labour-force participation rates, labour supply and unemployment?
a. Because the retired elderly are comprising a larger and larger fraction of the European population, the European Commission convinces national governments to increase social security contributions from individuals in order to continue paying benefits to the elderly.
b. A national child care programme becomes law; it requires employers to provide free child care services.
c. European governments reduce restrictions on immigration into the European Union.
d. The welfare system is eliminated.

7. In 1998, the National Assembly of France voted to reduce the mandatory working week from 39 to 35 hours. Firms with more than 20 employees have to adopt the law by 2000, all other firms by 2002. How might this affect the French unemployment rate?

8. Explain what is meant by *involuntary unemployment* in the case of (a) a high minimum wage; (b) a monopolistic trade union. If the real wage happens to be the same in each case, is there any difference?

9. Can efficiency wage theories explain why it may be in the interest of firms to train their workers?

10. In the text, the short-run aggregate supply curve was given by $P = P^e + 1/b \, (Y - Y^*)$. What is the level of output when expectations are fulfilled?

11. What is the relationship between the following?
a. The slope of the short-run AS curve, and how frequently labour contracts are renegotiated.
b. The rate of inflation, and how frequently labour contracts are renegotiated.
c. On the basis of your previous answers, would you expect a high-inflation country to have a flatter or a steeper short-run AS curve than a country that traditionally has a low rate of inflation?

31

Aggregate Demand and Aggregate Supply

One of the most important issues in macroeconomics is the determination of the overall price level. Recall that inflation – an increase in the overall price level – is one of the key concerns of macroeconomists and government policy makers. Understanding the factors that affect the price level is essential to understanding macroeconomics.

In Chapter 22, we discussed how to measure inflation and the costs of inflation, but made no mention of the *causes* of inflation. For simplicity, our analysis in Chapters 23 to 29 took the price level as fixed. This allowed us to discuss the links between the goods market, the money market and the foreign exchange market without the complication of a changing price level. Knowing how the three markets work, we are now ready to take on flexible prices and how they bear on the economy's demand side.

We begin by discussing the *aggregate demand curve* (*AD* curve). Then the *AD* curve and the *AS* curve derived in the previous chapter are put together so we can discuss how the equilibrium price level is determined in the economy. This analysis allows us to see how the price level affects the economy and how the economy affects the price level. Finally, we reconsider monetary and fiscal policy and changes in the world economy from this more general view.

The aggregate demand curve

Our exploration of the price level begins in the money market. (If you have forgotten the details of how the overall price level is calculated or what it means, review Chapters 21 and 22.) We saw in Chapter 26 that people's demand for money depends on income (Y), the interest rate (r) and the price level (P).

It is easy to understand why the price level affects the demand for money. Suppose you plan to purchase a piece of Roquefort, a baguette and a Snickers bar. If these items cost €2.00, €1.00 and €.50 respectively, you need €3.50 in cash or in your cheque account to make your purchases. Suppose that the price of these goods doubles. To make the same purchases, you need €7.00.

In general, the amount of money required to make a given number of transactions depends directly and proportionately on the price of those transactions. Doubling the price level will double the demand for money. As prices and wages rise, households will want to keep more money in their wallets and in their cheque accounts, firms will need more in their cash drawers, and so forth. If prices and wages are rising at 6% per year, we can expect the demand for money to increase at about 6% per year, *ceteris paribus*.

> Money demand is a function of three variables: the interest rate (r), the level of real income (Y) and the price level (P). (Remember: Y is *real* output, or income. It measures the actual volume of output, without regard to changes in the price level.) Money demand will increase if the real level of output (income) increases, or the price level increases, or the interest rate declines.

Deriving the aggregate demand curve

The channels through which the price level affects aggregate demand are different under different institutional arrangements. We begin by deriving the *AD* curve in the *global economy*. Then we derive the *AD* curve for the *national economy*, first under *flexible exchange rates* and then under *fixed exchange rates*.

The *AD* curve in the global economy

Recall that **aggregate demand** is the total demand for goods and services produced in a country. To derive the aggregate demand curve, we examine what happens to aggregate demand (or income Y) when the price level (P) changes. Does it increase, decrease or remain constant when the price level increases? Our discussions of the goods market and the money market provide the tools to answer this question for the global economy.

The aggregate demand curve is derived assuming the fiscal policy variables – government purchases (G) and net taxes (T) – and the monetary policy variable (M^s) remain unchanged. In other words, we assume that the government does not take any action to affect the economy in response to changes in the price level.

As you know, an increase in the price level increases the demand for money and shifts the money demand curve to the right, as illustrated in Figure 31.1a. At the initial interest rate of 6%, an increase in the price level leads to an excess demand for money. Because of the higher price level, households and firms need to hold larger money balances than before. However, the quantity of money supplied remains the same. (Remember, we are assuming that the central bank takes no action to change the money supply.) The money market is now out of equilibrium. Equilibrium is re-established at a higher interest rate, 9%.

As indicated in Figure 31.1b, with the interest rate now higher, fewer investment projects are desirable, and planned investment spending (I) falls from I_0 to I_1. Lower I means planned aggregate expenditure (AE) is lower, shown in Figure 31.1c as a downward shift of the AE curve. Lower AE means inventories are greater than planned, firms cut back on output, and Y falls from Y_0 to Y_1.

> An increase in the price level causes the level of aggregate output (income) to fall.

Figure 31.1 The impact of an increase in the price level on the economy, assuming no changes in G, T and M^s

An increase in the price level drives down equilibrium income. In the global economy this is because it (1) reduces the real money supply, (2) drives up the interest rate, (3) lowers investment, (4) thus decreasing aggregate demand and income.

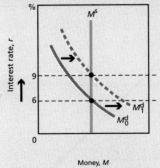

a. An increase in the price level increases the demand for money from M_0^d to M_1^d. With the supply of money unchanged, the interest rate increases from 6% to 9%.

b. The higher interest rate decreases planned investment from I_0 to I_1.

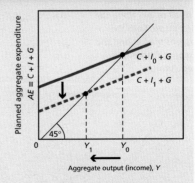

c. Decreased planned investment reduces planned aggregate expenditure and causes equilibrium output (income) to fall from Y_0 to Y_1.

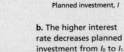

The situation is reversed when the price level declines. A lower price level causes money demand to fall, which leads to a lower interest rate. A lower interest rate stimulates planned investment spending, increasing planned aggregate expenditure, which leads to an increase in Y.

A decrease in the price level causes the level of aggregate output (income) to rise.

This negative relationship between aggregate output (income) and the price level is called the **aggregate demand (AD) curve**, shown in Figure 31.2.

Each point on the aggregate demand curve represents equilibrium in both the goods market *and* the money market. We have derived the AD curve using the analysis from Chapter 27, in which the goods market and the money market were linked together. Therefore,

Each pair of values of P and Y on the aggregate demand curve corresponds to a point at which both the goods market and the money market are in equilibrium.

aggregate demand (AD) curve

A curve that shows the negative relationship between aggregate output (income) and the price level. Each point on the AD curve is a point at which both the goods market and the money market are in equilibrium.

The AD curve in the national economy with flexible exchange rates

The scenario under which the national economy has control over its money supply is that of flexible exchange rates. Let us look at this arrangement first, since the set up is the same as when we derived the AD curve for the global economy.

Again, an increase in the price level raises the demand for money and shifts the money demand curve to the right, as illustrated in Figure 31.3a. Since the central bank keeps the money supply unchanged, an excess demand for money occurs at the initial interest rate of 6%, which begins to push the interest rate up. But here the analogy  with the global economy scenario ends. The national economy's interest rate cannot really rise. In the new equilibrium at the higher price level, the domestic interest rate must still equal the world interest rate of 6% that it equalled initially. Logically, this is only possible if the money demand curve is back in its original position. Since the only two variables that shift the money demand curve are the price level and income, it is clear that in the new equilibrium after the price rise income is lower than before: rising prices shifted the money demand curve to the right; falling income shifted the curve back to the left. How did this happen?

Figure 31.2 The aggregate demand (AD) curve

At all points along the AD curve, both the goods market and the money market are in equilibrium.

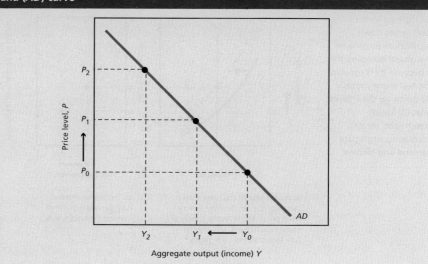

Figure 31.3 The impact of an increase in the price level on the national economy

In the national economy with flexible exchange rates an increase in prices shifts the M^d curve right. Since the interest rate cannot increase, income must fall enough to move the M^d curve back left into its original position. The drop in income is due to an appreciation of the home currency.

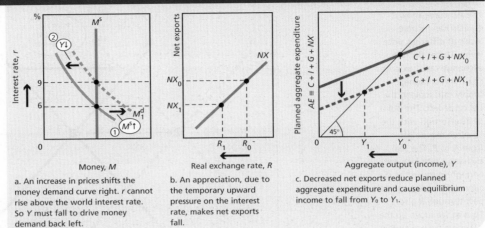

a. An increase in prices shifts the money demand curve right. r cannot rise above the world interest rate. So Y must fall to drive money demand back left.

b. An appreciation, due to the temporary upward pressure on the interest rate, makes net exports fall.

c. Decreased net exports reduce planned aggregate expenditure and cause equilibrium income to fall from Y_0 to Y_1.

As Figure 31.3c indicates, income can only fall from Y_0 to Y_1 if one of the components of planned aggregate expenditure falls. Investment depends on the (unchanged) interest rate, and is therefore constant. So is government spending. Thus the AE line must have shifted down due to a fall in net exports from NX_0 to NX_1. Net exports are a function of the real exchange rate, R, as shown in Figure 31.3b. For net exports to fall, the real exchange rate must have fallen from $R_0 = E_0 P^W / P_0$ to $R_1 = E_1 P^W / P_1$, a real appreciation.

At least part of this fall in R already comes from the rise in P. After all, a rise in domestic prices makes our exports less competitive, reduces net exports and drives down income. In principle, this fall in income might be exactly what was needed to shift the money demand curve back into the original position. Then the nominal exchange rate would not have to change at all. If, however, the fall in income due to the price increase alone is too small to shift the money demand curve back into M_0^D, the real appreciation must be reinforced by an *appreciation of the nominal exchange rate*. Finally, if the fall in income due to the price increase alone shifts the money demand curve too far to the left, this effect must be mellowed by a *depreciation of the nominal exchange rate*.

Qualitatively, our discussion replicated what we found for the global economy:

In a national economy with flexible exchange rates an increase (or decrease) in the price level causes the level of aggregate income to fall (or rise).

This is because rising prices reduce the real money supply, the real exchange rate, net exports and income. The curve looks just like the AD curve shown in Figure 31.2.

Each pair of values of P and Y on the aggregate demand curve of the national economy under flexible exchange rates corresponds to a simultaneous equilibrium of the goods market, the money market and the foreign exchange market.

This suggests that we can also derive the national-economy AD curve from the *IS–LM–FE* model assembled in Chapters 28 and 29.

In Figure 31.4, the economy is initially in equilibrium point A at the price level P_0. Remember that, since exchange rates are flexible, this equilibrium is determined by the positions of the *FE* and *LM* curves alone. The exchange rate always adjusts so as to move the *IS* curve into the proper position as well. Therefore, in order to determine how an increase in the price level affects equilibrium, it suffices to check how the *FE* curve and the *LM* curve are affected.

Prices do not affect the *FE* curve directly. Irrespective of their level, domestic and foreign interest rates must always be the same in equilibrium. This leaves the question of what a price rise does to the *LM* curve, the money market equilibrium line. The

Figure 31.4 From the *IS–LM–FE* model to the *AD* curve under flexible exchange rates

The *AD* curve shows equilibrium income levels at different price levels. Under flexible exchange rates, as prices rise the real money supply falls moving the *LM* curve left. The point of intersection with the *FE* curve moves left from *A* to *B*. The real exchange rate falls just enough to move the *IS* curve left far enough to pass through *B* also. Thus as we move up the *AD* curve from *A* to *B* in the lower panel, the real money supply falls, forcing the real exchange rate to fall as well. The reason why income drops when prices rise is that net exports fall.

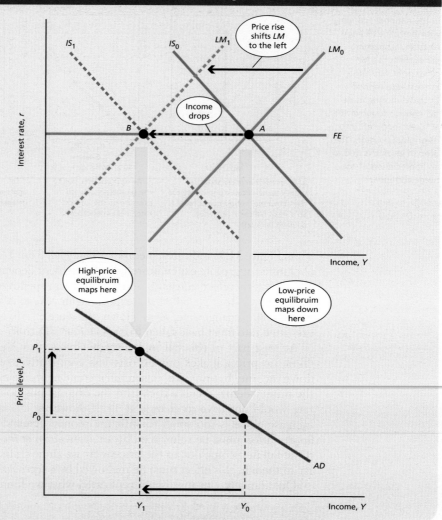

LM curve is always drawn for a given price level, reflecting a specific real money supply *M/P*. This real money supply can change if either *M*, the nominal money supply, changes, or *P* changes. An increase in the real money supply shifts *LM* to the right, and a decrease shifts it to the left (see Chapter 27).

If, while the nominal money supply remains constant prices rise from P_0 to P_1, the real money supply falls, shifting the *LM* curve into LM_1. With *FE* unaffected, the new equilibrium obtains in point *B* at the world interest rate and lower aggregate income Y_1. The *IS* curve follows this move, driven by an appreciating real exchange rate. As in the discussion of Figure 31.3, it remains open what the nominal exchange rate does. The rise in *P* already shifts *IS* to the left. Whether this initial shift falls short of or goes beyond IS_1 determines in what direction the nominal exchange rate needs to move, if at all.

The lower panel of Figure 31.4 maps the result onto a *P/Y* diagram. When prices were low at P_0, income was high at Y_0. This is one demand-side equilibrium point in which the goods market, the money market and the foreign exchange market all clear. When prices rise to P_1, income falls to Y_1: a second equilibrium point. The *AD* curve drawn through these two points has generalized this negative relationship between the price level and demand-side equilibrium income.

Figure 31.5 From the *IS–LM–FE* model to the *AD* curve under fixed exchange rates

The *AD* curve has a negative slope irrespective of the exchange rate system. Under fixed exchange rates, as prices rise the real exchange rate falls moving the *IS* curve left. The point of intersection with the *FE* curve moves from *A* to *B*. The real money supply must fall just enough to move the *LM* curve left far enough to pass through *B* also. Thus as we move up the *AD* curve from *A* to *B* in the lower panel, the real exchange rate falls, forcing the real money supply to fall as well. The reason why income drops when prices rise is that net exports fall.

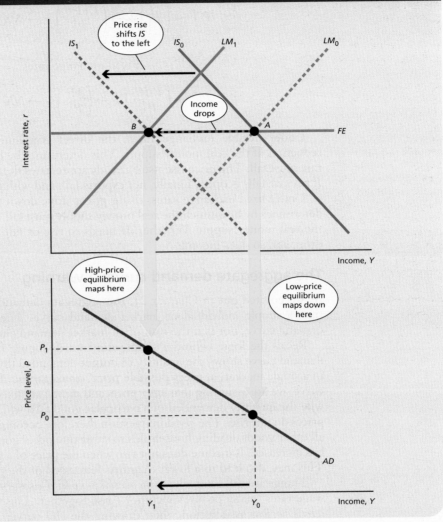

The *AD* curve in the national economy with fixed exchange rates

Remember that under fixed exchange rates the *FE* curve and the *IS* curve alone determine equilibrium income. The central bank must always adjust the money supply so as to move the *LM* curve into the proper position. It therefore suffices here to check how a price increase affects the *FE* curve and the *IS* curve.

In Figure 31.5, point *A* again marks equilibrium at the initial price level P_0. The foreign exchange market equilibrium represented by the *FE* curve is not affected by the price level. But what happens to the goods market equilibrium condition, the *IS* curve? The key positioning variable of the *IS* curve that is affected by the price level is the real exchange rate $R \equiv E \times P^W/P$. With the nominal exchange rate fixed and world prices (P^W) given, an increase in domestic prices lowers the real exchange rate. Domestic goods become more expensive relative to foreign goods. Net exports fall, and the *IS* curve shifts to the left into IS_1. The new equilibrium is obtained in point *B*, which identifies the new, lower equilibrium income Y_1.

The lower panel projects both equilibrium points onto a *P/Y* diagram and uses them to draw the full *AD* curve under fixed exchange rates. It has a negative slope and looks just like the *AD* curve under flexible exchange rates. What differs under both scenarios is the *sequence of events*:

Flexible exchange rates

$$P\uparrow \rightarrow \left(\frac{\bar{M}}{P\uparrow}\right)\downarrow \rightarrow \left(\frac{E?\bar{P}^{W}}{P\uparrow}\right)\downarrow \rightarrow NX\downarrow \rightarrow Y\downarrow$$

Fixed exchange rates

$$P\uparrow \rightarrow \left(\frac{\bar{E}\cdot P^{W}}{P\uparrow}\right)\downarrow \rightarrow \left(\frac{M?}{P\uparrow}\right)\downarrow \rightarrow NX\downarrow \rightarrow Y\downarrow$$

Under flexible exchange rates, the direct consequence of a price rise is the reduction of the real money supply. This determines by how much the real exchange rate must fall. The price rise itself already appreciates the real exchange rate. Whether E rises or falls is open. Finally, net exports fall, and with them income.

Under fixed exchange rates, rising prices drive down the real exchange rate. This determines by how much the real money supply must fall. Rising prices already reduce the real money supply. Whether M needs to rise or fall is open. Finally, net exports drop, and so does income.

The aggregate demand curve: a warning

As we pointed out in Chapter 21, the aggregate demand curve is far more complex than a simple individual or market demand curve. The AD curve is not a market demand curve, nor is it the sum of all market demand curves in the economy.

Recall the logic behind a simple downward-sloping household demand curve. A demand curve shows the quantity of output demanded (by an individual household or in a single market) at every possible price, *ceteris paribus*. In drawing a simple demand curve, we are assuming that *other prices* and *income* are fixed. It follows that one reason why the quantity demanded of a particular good falls when its price rises is that other prices do not rise. The good in question therefore becomes more expensive relative to all other goods, leading households to substitute other goods for the good whose price has increased. If income does not rise when the price of a good does, real income falls. This may also lead to a lower quantity demanded of the good whose price has risen.

Things are different when the *overall price level* rises. Now many prices – including wage rates (many people's income) – rise together. This is why we cannot make the *ceteris paribus* assumption when drawing the AD curve. The logic of why a simple demand curve slopes downwards fails when explaining why the AD curve has a negative slope.

The AD curve is not the sum of all the market demand curves in the economy. It is not a market demand curve.

Aggregate demand falls when prices increase because higher prices cause the demand for money (M^{d}) to rise. With the money supply constant, the interest rate rises in the *global economy* to keep the money market in equilibrium. *It is the higher interest rate that causes aggregate output to fall.*

In the *national economy* under flexible exchange rates, with the money supply constant and the interest rate tied to the world interest rate, income must fall to re-establish equilibrium in the money market. This fall in income is brought about by a fall in the real exchange rate.

Under fixed exchange rates, the real exchange rate is driven down directly by an increase in the price level, driving income down as well.

Other reasons for a downward-sloping aggregate demand curve

In addition to the effects of money supply and money demand on the interest rate, two other factors lie behind the downward slope of the AD curve. These are the consumption link and the real wealth effect.

The consumption link

We noted in Chapter 23 (and elaborate in Chapter 33) that consumption (C) and planned investment (I) depend on the interest rate. Other things being equal, consumption expenditures tend to rise when the interest rate falls and tend to fall when the interest rate rises – just as planned investment does. This tendency is another link between the goods market and the money market. If something happens to change the interest rate in the money market, both consumption and planned investment are affected in the goods market.

The *consumption* link provides another reason for the AD curve's downward slope in the global economy. An increase in the price level increases the demand for money, raising the interest rate, which causes consumption to decrease (as well as planned investment), leading to a decline in aggregate output (income). The initial decrease in consumption (brought about by the increase in the interest rate) contributes to the overall decrease in output.

In the global economy, planned investment is not the sole link from a higher interest rate to a lower level of aggregate output. Decreased consumption brought about by a higher interest rate also contributes to this effect.

The real wealth effect

We also noted in Chapter 23 (and will review in more detail in Chapter 33) that consumption depends on wealth. Other things equal, the wealthier households are, the more they consume. Wealth includes holdings of money, shares, bonds and housing, among other things. If household wealth decreases, say because of a stock market crash, less is consumed now and in the future.

The price level affects the real value of nominal assets. Suppose you are holding €1000 in a cheque account or in a money market fund and the price level rises by 10%. Your holding is now worth 10% less because the prices of the goods that you could buy with your €1000 have all increased by 10%. The purchasing power (or 'real value') of your holding has decreased by 10%.

An increase in the price level lowers the real value of nominal assets.

The fact that the price level lowers the real value of wealth provides another reason for the downward slope of the AD curve. An increase in the price level lowers the real value of wealth; this leads to a decrease in consumption, which leads to a decrease in aggregate output (income), so there is a negative relationship between the price level and output through this **real wealth effect** or **real balance effect**.

**real wealth effect,
or real balance
effect**
The change in
consumption brought
about by a change in
real wealth that
results from a change
in the price level.

Aggregate expenditure and aggregate demand

Throughout our discussion of macroeconomics so far, we have referred to the total planned spending by households (C), firms (I) and the government (G), and net spending from abroad (NX), as planned aggregate expenditure. In equilibrium, planned aggregate expenditure ($AE \equiv C + I + G + NX$) and aggregate output (Y) are equal:[1]

---

[1] In the global economy, the equilibrium condition is $C + I + G = Y$.

Equilibrium condition: $C + I + G + NX = Y$

How does planned aggregate expenditure relate to aggregate demand?

> At every point along the aggregate demand curve, the aggregate quantity demanded is exactly equal to planned aggregate expenditure, $C + I + G + NX$.

We see this in Figures 31.1 and 31.2. When the price level rises, planned aggregate expenditure decreases, moving us up along the aggregate demand curve.

But the aggregate demand curve represents more than just planned aggregate expenditure. Each point on the *AD* curve represents the *particular* level of planned aggregate expenditure that is consistent with equilibrium in the goods market, money market and the foreign exchange market. Notice that the variable on the horizontal axis of the aggregate demand curve in Figure 31.2 is *Y*. At every point along the *AD* curve, $Y = C + I + G + NX$.

Shifts of the aggregate demand curve

The aggregate demand curve shown in Figure 31.2 is drawn with the understanding that the relevant policy variables and all other autonomous variables or parameters are fixed. If any of these variables change, the aggregate demand curve will shift.

Why? Remember that the *AD* curve represents the demand-side equilibrium income as determined in the *IS–LM–FE* model at any particular price level. Therefore, anything that changes equilibrium income in the *IS–LM–FE* model also shifts the *AD* curve. At any given price level, equilibrium income is now different from before. So the *AD* curve must have shifted to a different position.

> All factors that affect equilibrium income in the *IS–LM–FE* model affect the position of the *AD* curve.

Now we merely need to retrieve our insights from Chapter 29. There we learned that the effectiveness of policy instruments and the way our economy responds to changes in the rest of the world depends crucially on international monetary arrangements – that is, the exchange rate system. Taking that into account we also need to distinguish between flexible and fixed exchange rates when asking what shifts the *AD* curve and how it does so.

Flexible exchange rates

Remember that under flexible exchange rates the *FE* and *LM* curves alone determine equilibrium income. So it is only the two variables that shift these two curves which at the same time shift the *AD* curve (see Figure 31.6a). The money supply shifts the *LM* curve to the right, *raising* income along the horizontal *FE* curve. Thus the *AD* curve shifts to the right as well. A rise in the world interest rate pushes the *FE* curve upwards, making income *rise* along the positively sloped *LM* curve. Again, the *AD* curve shifts to the right too.

> Under flexible exchange rates, an increase in the quantity of money supplied or a rise in the world interest rate shift the *AD* curve to the right.

Fixed exchange rates

When exchange rates are fixed, the *FE* and *IS* curves alone determine equilibrium income. The variables that affect the positions of these two curves also move the *AD* curve.

Figure 31.6 Shifting the AD curve

Policy measures or changes in the world economy can shift the AD curve. Which policy measure are at a country's disposal, and how the world economy affects the national economy, depends on whether exchange rates are flexible or fixed.

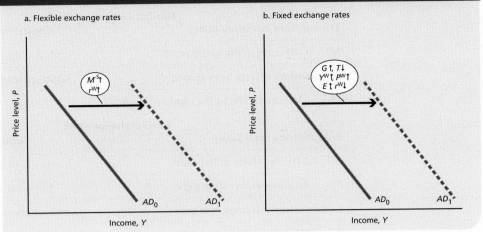

a. Flexible exchange rates

b. Fixed exchange rates

The first is the world interest rate, which moves the FE curve. Note, however, that its effect on income is now reversed. When FE shifts upwards the equilibrium point moves up the negatively sloped IS curve. So income falls. Therefore, the AD curve shifts to the left. It takes a fall in r^w to shift AD to the right.

A whole set of variables can shift the AD curve due to their effect on the IS curve. These variables are: world income, world prices, the exchange rate (now an instrument of **exchange rate policy**), government spending and net taxes. As the first four of these rise or as net taxes fall, aggregate output (income) increases at each possible price level.[2] Therefore, as Figure 31.6a shows:

exchange rate policy
The deliberate use of the exchange rate to achieve policy goals.

> Under fixed exchange rates, an increase in world income, world prices, the exchange rate or government spending, or a fall in the world interest rate or net taxes, shift the AD curve to the right.

Table 31.1 summarizes the ways the aggregate demand curve shifts in response to policy measures or changes in the world economy. To test your understanding of the AD curve, go through the table item by item and explain each of its components.

The equilibrium price level

The *aggregate demand curve* gives aggregate demand at different price levels. Yet if we don't know the price level, we can't determine the level of aggregate demand. The *aggregate supply curve* identifies aggregate supply at different price levels. Again: we can't identify aggregate supply until we know the price level. What helps is that *in equilibrium, aggregate demand must equal aggregate supply*. Therefore the **equilibrium price level** in the economy occurs where the AD curve and the AS curve intersect. But which AS curve, you may ask. Haven't we got two – a short-run AS curve and a long-run AS curve? And these do not necessarily intersect the AD curve at the same point. Do we then have two equilibrium price levels? Yes, exactly. One that applies in the long run and one that applies in the short run. Just as we have one AS curve for each time horizon.

equilibrium price level
The point at which the aggregate demand and aggregate supply curves intersect.

[2]*Doesn't the domestic price level also affect the position of IS and thus equilibrium income? In fact, doesn't it affect LM and thus income under flexible exchange rates? So shouldn't it be listed as a variable shifting the AD curve? The answer is no. The fact that a rising price level drives down income is reflected in the negative slope of the AD curve. As prices rise, we move up the AD curve. It does not shift.*

Table 31.1 Shifts in the aggregate demand curve: a summary

Flexible exchange rates

Expansionary monetary policy	Contractionary monetary policy
$M^s\uparrow \to AD$ curve shifts to the right	$M^s\downarrow \to AD$ curve shifts to the left
Expansionary effects from abroad	**Contractionary effects from abroad**
$r^w\uparrow \to AD$ curve shifts to the right	$r^w\downarrow \to AD$ curve shifts to the left

Fixed exchange rates

Expansionary fiscal policy	Contractionary fiscal policy
$G\uparrow \to AD$ curve shifts to the right	$G\downarrow \to AD$ curve shifts to the left
$T\downarrow \to AD$ curve shifts to the right	$T\uparrow \to AD$ curve shifts to the left
Expansionary exchange rate policy	**Contractionary exchange rate policy**
$E\uparrow \to AD$ curve shifts to the right	$E\downarrow \to AD$ curve shifts to the left
Expansionary effects from abroad	**Contractionary effects from abroad**
$r^w\downarrow \to AD$ curve shifts to the right	$r^w\uparrow \to AD$ curve shifts to the left
$Y^w\uparrow \to AD$ curve shifts to the right	$Y^w\downarrow \to AD$ curve shifts to the left
$P^w\uparrow \to AD$ curve shifts to the right	$P^w\downarrow \to AD$ curve shifts to the left

The price level in the long run

Figure 31.7a shows the AD curve and the long-run AS curve. Remember: each point on the AD curve corresponds to equilibrium in the goods market, the money market and the foreign exchange market. Each point on the long-run AS curve corresponds to long-run equilibrium in the labour market. This means:

> The point where the AD and long-run AS curves intersect corresponds to long-run equilibrium in the labour market and to equilibrium in the goods, the money and the foreign exchange markets.

The equilibrium price level is P^* and the equilibrium level of aggregate output, which is independent of the price level in the long run, is Y^*. Since the plans of all participants have worked out, this is a long-run equilibrium. Unless there is a change

Figure 31.7 The determination of the price level

The intersection between the AS curve and the AD curve determines the price level. The long-run equilibrium price level is determined where $LRAS$ and AD intersect. The short-run equilibrium price level is determined where $SRAS$ and AD intersect.

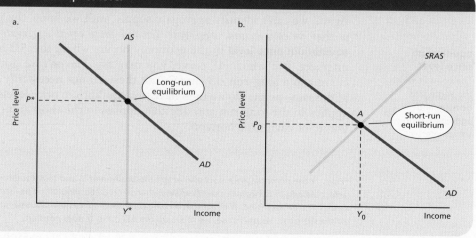

in monetary, fiscal or exchange rate policy, or economic conditions in the rest of the world, the economy will remain in this equilibrium.

The price level in the short run

Figure 31.7b shows the *AD* curve and the short-run *AS* curve. Again, each point on the *AD* curve corresponds to equilibrium in all three demand-side markets. Each point on the short-run *AS* curve corresponds to a current, temporary equilibrium in the labour market. This means that:

> The point where the *AD* and the short-run *AS* curves intersect corresponds to current equilibrium in the labour market and to equilibrium in the goods, the money and the foreign exchange markets.

Now the equilibrium price level is P_0 and aggregate output is Y_0. In this equilibrium all plans work out, except for the trade unions' plans. Depending on whether point *A* is to the right or to the left of the long-run *AS* curve, real wages are lower or higher than what trade unions had aimed for. They are stuck with this, in their view sub-optimal, situation as long as current wage contracts last. When these expire, unions will renegotiate the money wage rate, which changes the current equilibrium.

> If the intersection between the *AD* curve and the short-run *AS* curve is off the long-run *AS* curve, the implied equilibrium is only temporary. It will move over time.

From the short run to the long run

Let's look at how and why the short-run equilibrium price level changes over time and how it is linked to the long-run equilibrium price level. Figure 31.8 shows a short-run equilibrium, but adds a long-run *AS* curve to the diagram.

Figure 31.8 From the short run to the long run

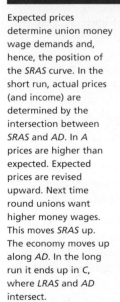

Expected prices determine union money wage demands and, hence, the position of the *SRAS* curve. In the short run, actual prices (and income) are determined by the intersection between *SRAS* and *AD*. In *A* prices are higher than expected. Expected prices are revised upward. Next time round unions want higher money wages. This moves *SRAS* up. The economy moves up along *AD*. In the long run it ends up in *C*, where *LRAS* and *AD* intersect.

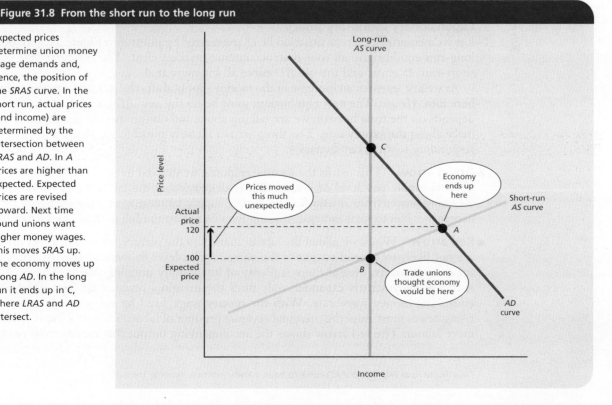

Note that the intersection between the short-run *AS* curve and the long-run *AS* curve always identifies the expected price level. When trade unions signed the current wage contract they expected the price level to be 100. Had prices actually turned out to be 100, the economy would have ended up in point *B* on the long-run *AS* curve.[3]

With the *AD* curve as high as it is, the economy ends up in *A* and prices rise beyond the expected price level to 120. When the next wage negotiations come around, unions will expect a higher price level than they did last time, say 110, and will therefore demand higher money wages. This will shift the short-run *AS* curve up. As long as *AD* remains in the current position, the short-run equilibrium point *A* moves up along *AD*. This process only comes to a halt at point *C*, where *AD* intersects the long-run *AS* curve. Note that this is the long-run equilibrium price level we identified some paragraphs ago.

The indicated gradual movement from *A* towards *C* occurs if unions adapt the price level they expect in the next period to the price level they observe now. In our example, they had expected prices to be 100. After price turned out to be 120, prices expected for the next period were revised upwards to 110, in the direction of actual prices. Expectations formed in this manner are called **adaptive expectations**.

adaptive expectations
Expectations (here, of prices) formed on the basis of the recent history of the variable under consideration.

Policy and external shocks in the *AD–AS* model

We are now ready to use the *AD–AS* framework to examine the effects of various policy measures and changes in the world economy on the national economy.

Monetary policy

Under *flexible exchange rates*, monetary policy is the only instrument with which policy makers can affect the course of the aggregate economy. We first look at the consequences of a monetary expansion in some detail. Then we look at the effects of a monetary contraction, of other policy measures that are available under fixed exchange rates, and of shocks from abroad.

Expansionary monetary policy

Let your country's current situation be characterized by point *A* in Figure 31.9. In this long-run equilibrium, all four macroeconomic markets clear. The *AS* curve, the old short-run *AS* curve and the old *AD* curve all intersect at *A*.

As we just learned, an increase in the money supply shifts the *AD* curve to the right, here into *AD*NEW. The new equilibrium must be on the new *AD* curve. Exactly where depends on the time horizon we are talking about and on the specific assumptions we make about the supply side. The three arrows identify possible supply responses corresponding to different scenarios:

■ **Green arrow**   This marks the income response we derived in the *IS–LM–FE* model. If firms supply any level of output that is demanded at the current price level, the economy moves from *A* into *B*. The money supply increase makes the exchange rate depreciate. Net exports increase, making income rise by the full multiplier effect to Y_B.

■ **Red arrow**   When we added the labour market to the picture, we realized that firms are not likely to expand output at the current price level to meet a surge in demand for their products, even if there is plenty of involuntary unemployment. The reason is that employment is expanded only until the marginal revenue product of labour equals the money wage rate. With the money wage fixed by collective agreement, rising prices must raise the marginal revenue product of labour to induce firms to hire more labour. The red arrow shows the accompanying output that results from rising

---

[3]*This would have required the* AD *curve to be in a lower position, running through B.*

Figure 31.9 The consequences of a monetary expansion

When the *AD* curve shifts to the right, income and/or the price level increases. If firms supply anything that is demanded at unchanged prices (as we assumed up to Chapter 29) only *Y* rises and we move to *B*. Point *C* obtains if *SRAS* determines output supplied. Point *D* obtains in the long run, or if money wages are perfectly flexible.

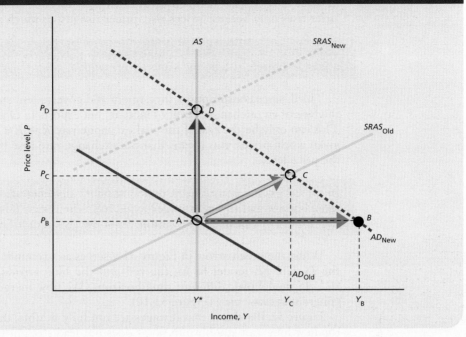

prices. Prices rise until we reach point *C*, where aggregate supply equals aggregate demand Y_C.

Income in this scenario is lower than in the green scenario because of *crowding out*. Aggregate demand is lower than Y_B because rising prices make the exchange rate appreciate, dampening net exports. This moves aggregate demand along the new *AD* curve from Y_B to Y_C.

■ **Blue arrow** While the difference between the green and the red scenarios is due to different views about how firms supply output, the difference between the red and the blue scenarios arises from the different flexibility of money wages (and other input prices). The red arrow shows the economy's response to a money supply increase when nominal wages have *not adjusted at all*, because they are fixed by contract; the blue arrow shows the response when money wages *adjust fully*, as we assumed when discussing the classical labour market in Chapter 30.

The red arrow usually describes the short-run response, and the blue arrow the long-run response. Yet this need not always apply. If money wages are very flexible, say because of the absence of long-term wage contracts or cost-of-living-adjustments clauses, or if the central bank's expansion of the money supply was anticipated, so that trade unions expected prices to rise, the blue response may materialize quite quickly. As a rule, though, it is a benchmark for the *long run*.

It is instructive to pause and think about what happens in the long run, as we move from *A* to *D*.

First, since the interest rate is unchanged at the world interest rate i^W and income is unchanged at potential income Y^*, the real money supply M/P must also be unchanged. This, in turn, requires that the price level rose by the same percentage as the money supply, a very important insight:

All that expansionary monetary policy achieves in the long run is to raise prices, thus creating inflation.

Second, because output and employment have remained the same, nominal wages must have risen just as much as the marginal revenue product of labour. Since the latter rises only because prices rise, prices rise just as much as money wages.

> In the long run, expansionary monetary policy does not affect real wages. Money wages and prices rise by the same percentage.

Third, since consumption, investment and government spending did not change in the face of an unchanged level of income, net exports in *D* are also the same as in *A*.[4] This can only be the case if the real exchange rate $R \equiv E \times P^W/P$ did not change. At given world prices, this means that the exchange rate rose by the same percentage as the price level.

> In the long run, expansionary monetary policy does not affect the real exchange rate. The competitive advantage gained from the rise in *E* is exactly matched by the loss of competitiveness resulting from the rise in domestic prices.

While the green arrow in Figure 31.9 serves as a reminder of how the results from the *IS–LM–FE* model fit in, the red and the blue arrows show the effects in the *AD–AS* model over different time horizons. We now merge these two effects into a coherent *dynamic view* (Figure 31.10).

Figure 31.10a shows that if wages are not fully flexible, the path from the initial to the new long-run equilibrium point does not lead straight upwards. During the first phase after the monetary expansion, both prices and incomes rise. The economy moves towards B. As money wage rates (and the prices of other inputs) begin to respond, the short-run *AS* curve moves up. During this time, short-run equilibrium is always determined by the intersection of the current short-run *AS* curve and *AD*. Therefore, this equilibrium must move up along the *AD* curve. Prices continue to rise, but income falls. The adjustment process comes to a halt when the short-run *AS*, the long-run *AS* and the *AD* curves intersect at point *D*.

There are important lessons to be learned from all this, which partly underline and partly modify previous insights.

Figure 31.10 The dynamic response to a monetary expansion

An increase in aggregate demand, say due to a money supply increase, makes the economy expand from A to B. As nominal wages increase and SRAS moves up, income eases back to its normal level. This movement is reminiscent of the boom phase of the business cycle.

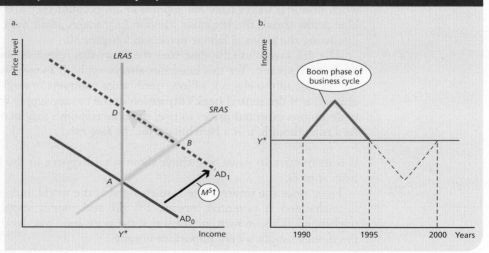

---

[4] *G is autonomous and was not changed by the government. I depends on i, which is unchanged at i^W. And C depends on income which is unchanged at Y*.*

First, the short-run response of income to a money supply increase is similar to, though more modest than, the *IS–LM–FE* model suggested. If the short-run *AS* curve is very flat , the income response is almost like that in the *IS–LM–FE* model. The steeper the short-run *AS*, the more the price level needs to rise to induce firms to produce more output. As the price level rises, it crowds out some aggregate demand.

Second, the income stimulation triggered by the money supply increase does not last. In the long run there is *complete crowding out* by price increases. Empirical work suggests, however, that it usually takes 3–5 years for the income gain to disappear.

Figure 31.10b plots the income response to a money supply increase onto a time line. This graph illustrates that the macroeconomic response to a demand stimulus (in this case expansionary monetary policy) traced here in the *AD–AS* model describes the boom phase of the business cycle quite well.

Contractionary monetary policy

The macroeconomic response to a money supply decrease is the mirror image of what happens after a money supply increase. There is a fall in the price level, both in the short run and in the long run. Income only falls initially. The mechanism here is that, with nominal wages contractually fixed, the falling price level raises the real wage and drives down employment. At a later stage, trade unions settle for lower nominal wage rates, helping to bring real wage rates down again and re-establishing the initial levels of employment and output.

Fiscal policy

Under an arrangement of *fixed exchange rates*, the government may do two things to stimulate the economy. The first is to raise government spending. The second is to devalue the national currency. Both measures shift the *AD* curve to the right, triggering the kind of boom we graphed in Figure 31.10.

In the case of a **devaluation**, the similarity with what happens under flexible exchange rates after a monetary expansion is almost perfect. The only difference is that in the latter case the trigger is an expansion of the nominal and real money supply that forces the real exchange rate to depreciate. Under fixed exchange rates, the trigger is a nominal and real devaluation that forces the real money supply to expand. The common achievement in both cases is a temporary boost of income and a lasting increase in prices.

> Under fixed exchange rates a devaluation raises income for some time. In the long run, income remains unaffected while prices remain higher.

The same diagram results when the government expands spending *G*. There are important differences regarding the *composition* of aggregate demand not visible in the *AD–AS* diagram. Since the government continues to spend more, even in the long run, but income and aggregate demand are unchanged at Y^*, some other category of demand must be lower. This is net exports. In the long run, the rise in government spending crowds out an exactly identical amount of net exports. This can also be read off the circular flow identity we encountered back in Chapter 21:

$$(S - I) + (T - G) + (IM - EX) = 0$$

$$\underbrace{\qquad}_{0} \quad \underbrace{\qquad}_{-} \quad \underbrace{\qquad}_{+}$$

With savings and investment unchanged (because *Y* and *r* remain the same), at unchanged tax revenues the rise in *G* must be matched by an equivalent rise in net imports (or fall in net exports). This reveals a close connection between two deficits that have played a major role in recent policy discussions: *G* – *T* is the **government budget deficit**; *IM* – *EX* = –*NX* is the **trade deficit**. Our analysis of fiscal policy

devaluation
The government (or central bank) raises the exchange rate at which it promises to buy and sell foreign currency.

government budget deficit
The difference between government spending and tax revenues, *G* – *T*.

trade deficit The difference between imports and exports, *IM* – *EX*, equivalent to net imports, –*NX*.

Figure 31.11 The dynamic response to a fiscal contraction

A decrease in aggregate demand, say due to lower government spending, makes the economy contract from *A* to *B*. As nominal wages fall and *SRAS* moves down, income rises back up to its normal level. This movement is reminiscent of a recession.

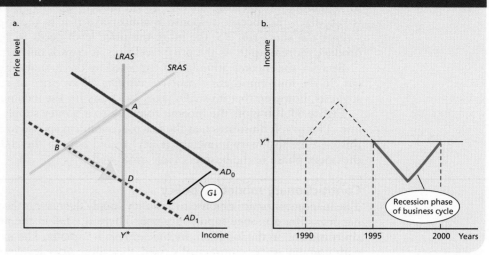

insinuates that both deficits usually come in a package. With $S - I$ more or less constant in the longer run, large government budget deficits are typically accompanied by large trade deficits. The most striking illustration of this link is the US experience of the 1980s, when the so-called **twin deficits** reached record heights.

twin deficits
Term used when budget deficits and trade deficits occur together.

The Maastricht qualification criteria for European Monetary Union forced many countries to cut government spending considerably in the second part of the 1990s. In our current terminology, this amounts to a severely contractionary fiscal policy. The consequences are shown in Figure 31.11, which simply draws out the reverse of what we saw in the case of expansionary monetary policy shown in Figure 31.10. While the left-hand panel shows the temporary fall in income and the long-run reduction in prices, the right-hand panel traces the results through time. The pattern is indicative of the recession segment of the stylized business cycle we encountered back in Chapter 22.

Demand shocks from abroad

We have seen that the *AD–AS* model generates movements in aggregate income in response to policy measures that resemble the ups and downs of the business cycle. In today's national economies the business cycle has a strong international component. Changes in world income, interest rates or prices trigger domestic income responses similar to those encountered previously in this chapter. As we know, the nature and effectiveness of these links is determined by the exchange rate system under which a country operates.

Flexible exchange rates

Flexible exchange rates have the characteristic of *insulating* the domestic economy from much of what happens in the world economy. If world income falls or world prices increase, the exchange rate changes so as to neutralize the consequences of this for domestic income. We discovered this earlier when we saw that Y^W and P^W have no effect on the *AD* curve under flexible exchange rates.

The only link between the national economy and the global economy under flexible exchange rates is the world interest rate. As this rises, the home currency depreciates, causing net exports to surge and moving the *AD* curve to the right. The result is a temporary boost of income which looks like the one shown in Figure 31.10. In the long run, though, rising prices remove all of the competitive advantage gained initially, driving income back to Y^*.

Fixed exchange rates

The link between the national economy and the global economy is different and more complex under fixed exchange rates. Here the rise in the world interest rate forces monetary policy to become contractionary. The real exchange rate cannot change, but investment falls as a result of higher interest rates, hence income drops. In this scenario, the *AD* curve shifts to the left, and economic activity is temporarily depressed, as sketched in Figure 31.11.

Without the insulating buffer of flexible exchange rates, other foreign variables also bear on domestic income. As laid out in Table 31.1, a rise (or fall) in foreign income or prices shifts the *AD* curve to the right (or left) and triggers a dynamic response of the form sketched in Figure 31.10 (or Figure 31.11).

Shocks to aggregate supply

The economy's supply side is also subject to occasional disturbances, both home-made and from abroad. Well-known examples of international supply shocks are the two explosions of crude oil prices in 1973–74 and 1979–80. Let us see how an adverse **supply shock** (the term economists use to describe events such as a sudden surge in the price of oil) affects the national economy.

supply shock

A change in costs that shifts the aggregate supply (*AS*) curve.

When we discussed the labour market and aggregate supply, we paid little attention to the price of inputs other than labour. Let's remedy this somewhat informally by looking at a simple example.

Suppose production does not only require labour as a variable input, but also uses up 0.1 barrels of crude oil per unit of output. The blue curve in Figure 31.12 shows the marginal revenue product of labour (*MRPL*). If no oil is needed in production, or if oil does not cost anything, the *MRPL* curve is the labour demand curve, as we learned in Chapter 30, and trade unions maximize the wage sum in a point such as *A*. Here the hourly wage rate is 20 euros and employment stands at 100 (million) hours. In point *A*, one additional work hour produces 10 units of output. Since each unit of output is priced at €2, the *MRPL* is €20, which, of course, equals the wage rate.

Oil is not free, of course. Assume it costs, say, €10 per barrel. Then the ten units of output produced in point *A* by an additional work hour do not only cost €20 in wages, but an additional €10 in oil. In other words, the *net MRPL*, the part of revenue that firms can actually use to pay wages, is €20 – €10 = €10. This would also apply

Figure 31.12 Oil prices and the labour demand curve

Normally, firms expand the demand for labour until marginal costs (the nominal wage rate) equal the *MRPL*. If labour is used jointly with oil, the *MRPL* must also cover oil costs. Only what is left, the *net MRPL*, can be used to pay labour. Thus firms expand the demand for labour until the wage rate equals the net *MRPL*.

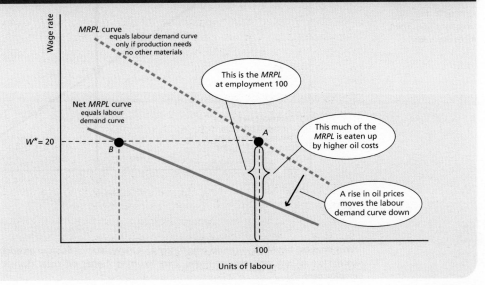

at other employment levels. By deducting the oil costs involved from the *MRPL* curve we obtain the *net MRPL curve*, which is the *labour demand curve*. The higher the price of oil rises, the further the net *MRPL* curve shifts down and the flatter it becomes.[5]

A sudden surge in the price of oil from zero to €10 per barrel moves the labour market from *A* to *B* (the nominal wage is fixed by contract). This also shifts the short-run *AS* curve in Fig. 31.13 to the left. If the surge in oil prices is only temporary, the short-run *AS* curve subsequently moves back to the right and the labour market returns to *A*. If oil prices stay high permanently, real wages need to come down to restore an employment level close to the old one. Real wages may fall because nominal wages fall, or because prices rise and move the labour demand curve up.

> A rise in oil prices (or the price of other input materials) shifts the labour demand curve down. This moves the short-run *AS* curve to the left.

With this knowledge we may now look at the consequences and the problems posed by an adverse supply shock.

In Figure 31.13 the economy is in a long-run equilibrium in point *A* before oil prices increase. A surge in oil prices – like that in 1974, when the price of one barrel of oil more than tripled from $4 to $15 – moves the *AS* curve to the left into the red position. This red curve lists all post-shock aggregate supply options. By moving the *AD* curve up or down, the government and the central bank can achieve any desired price level, and accordingly, any level of income they want.

Figure 31.13 Policy options after an oil price shock

An adverse supply shock shifts the *AS* curve to the left. If policy makers do not respond, prices rise and income falls (point *B*). To prevent inflation, contractionary policy may shift the aggregate demand curve into *AD₂*. Then income falls a lot. To prevent income from falling, expansionary policy may shift the aggregate demand curve into *AD₁*. Then prices rise a lot.

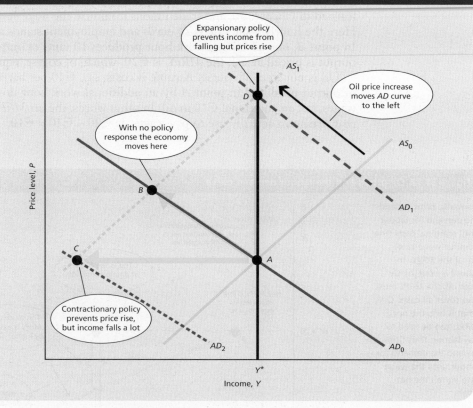

[5]*Why does the net MRPL curve become flatter as it moves down? Because an additional unit of labour is more productive at low employment levels, thus incurring higher oil costs than it would at higher levels of employment.*

One option is not to respond at all, leaving the money supply and government spending at their initial levels. This leaves the *AD* curve in its pre-shock position and brings the economy to the red dot. There is a substantial fall in income, cushioned by a sizeable rise in prices.

If the central bank (or the government) wants to accept neither the fall in income nor the inflationary price surge, it can steer against it through appropriate monetary policies.

If the central bank wants to prevent the price level from rising, it needs to switch to a contractionary monetary policy, shifting the *AD* curve down into the blue position and the economy into point *C*. The obvious price is that income now falls much more than it would have without such a monetary contraction.

At the other extreme, if the central bank wants to prevent income from falling, it must respond with a monetary expansion. The *AD* curve moves up into the green position, and the new equilibrium obtains in point *D*. Income remains where it was before the shock, but at the price of a larger increase in the price level.

When looking at real experiences of the dilemma between stabilizing income and stabilizing prices, *Switzerland* clearly adhered to the latter. Despite the oil price shock, the Swiss National Bank drove the pre-shock 1973 inflation rate of 10% down to 2% in 1976. The price paid was a drop in GDP of almost 10%. *Britain's* income in 1976, on the other hand, was even higher than in 1973. This was achieved by permitting it's pre-shock inflation rate of 10.5% to surge to 20% in 1974, 25% in 1975 and 18% in 1976.

Causes of inflation

We now turn to inflation, and use the *AD–AS* framework to examine its causes.

Inflation versus sustained inflation: a reminder

Recall the distinction we made in Chapter 22. Inflation is an increase in the overall price level. Anything that shifts the *AD* curve to the right or the short-run *AS* curve to the left causes inflation. But it is often useful to distinguish between a *one-time increase* in the price level (a one-time inflation) and an inflation that is sustained. A sustained inflation occurs when the overall price level continues to rise over some fairly long period of time. When we speak of an inflation rate of 7%, for example, we generally mean that the price level has been rising at a rate of 7% per year over a number of years.

We have seen that there are many possible causes of a one-time increase in the price level. But for the price level to continue to increase period after period, most economists believe it must be 'accommodated' by an expanded money supply. This leads to the assertion that a sustained inflation, whatever the initial cause of the increase in the price level, is essentially a monetary phenomenon.

sustained inflation
Occurs when the overall price level continues to rise over a fairly long period.

Demand-pull inflation

Inflation initiated by an increase in aggregate demand is called demand-pull inflation. You can see how demand-pull inflation works by looking at Figure 31.10. The inflation begins with a shift of the aggregate demand schedule from AD_0 to AD_1, which causes the price level to increase along the short-run *AS* curve.

In the long run the initial increase in the price level will cause the *AS* curve to shift to the left as wages respond to the increase in output prices. The increase in wages will shift the short-run *AS* curve to the left until it passes through point *D*, pushing the price level even higher.

demand-pull inflation
Inflation that is initiated by an increase in aggregate demand.

Cost-push inflation

Inflation can also be caused by an increase in costs, referred to as cost-push inflation. As mentioned, twice in the 1970s and 1980s world oil prices increased sharply. Because oil fuels virtually every type of business, costs increased almost ubiquitously.

cost-push inflation
Inflation caused by an increase in costs.

An increase in costs (a cost shock) shifts the *AS* curve to the left, as we saw in Figure 31.13. If we assume the government does not react to this shift in *AS* by changing fiscal or monetary policy, the *AD* curve will not shift. The supply shift will cause the equilibrium price level to rise and the level of aggregate output to decline. Recall from Chapter 20 that **stagflation** occurs when output is falling at the same time as prices are rising – in other words, when the economy is experiencing both a contraction and inflation simultaneously. Figure 31.14 shows that one possible cause of stagflation is an increase in costs.

To return to monetary and fiscal policy for a moment, note that the government can counteract the increase in costs through an expansionary policy (an increase in *G*

stagflation Occurs when output is falling at the same time that prices are rising.

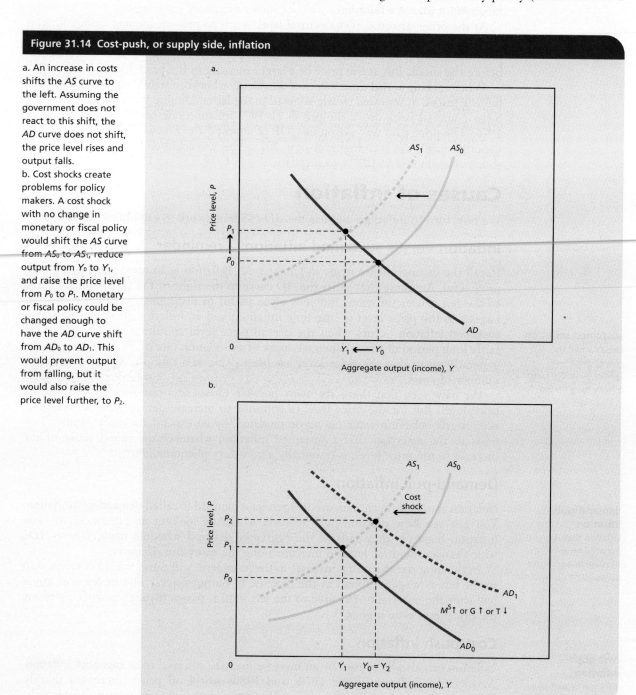

Figure 31.14 Cost-push, or supply side, inflation

a. An increase in costs shifts the *AS* curve to the left. Assuming the government does not react to this shift, the *AD* curve does not shift, the price level rises and output falls.
b. Cost shocks create problems for policy makers. A cost shock with no change in monetary or fiscal policy would shift the *AS* curve from AS_0 to AS_1, reduce output from Y_0 to Y_1, and raise the price level from P_0 to P_1. Monetary or fiscal policy could be changed enough to have the *AD* curve shift from AD_0 to AD_1. This would prevent output from falling, but it would also raise the price level further, to P_2.

or M^s or a decrease in T). This shifts the AD curve to the right, and the new AD curve intersects the new AS curve at a higher level of output. The problem with this policy, however, is that the intersection of the new AS and AD curves takes place at an even higher price level.

Policy makers dislike cost shocks: the only way they can counter the output loss brought about by a cost shock is by letting the price level increase by even more than it would without the policy action.

Money and inflation

We know that an increase in the money supply can lead to an increase in the aggregate price level. This is simply an example of demand-pull inflation.

But the supply of money may also play a role in creating a *sustained inflation*. Consider an initial increase in government spending (G) with the money supply (M^s) unchanged. Because the money supply is unchanged, this increase in G is not 'accommodated' by the central bank. The increase in G shifts the AD curve to the right from AD_0 to AD_1. Its long-run effect is to raise prices from P to P_1 (Figure 31.15).

Remember what happens when the price level increases: higher prices cause the demand for money to increase. With an unchanged money supply and an increase in the quantity of money demanded, the interest rate rises, decreasing planned investment (I) spending. The new equilibrium corresponds to higher G, lower I, a higher interest rate and a higher price level.

Let's go one step further. Suppose the central bank is sympathetic to the expansionary fiscal policy (the increase in G just discussed) and decides to expand the supply of money to keep the interest rate constant. As the higher price level pushes up the demand for money, the central bank expands the supply of money with the goal of keeping the interest rate unchanged, eliminating the crowding-out effect of a higher interest rate.

When the supply of money expands, the AD curve shifts to the right again, from AD_1 to AD_2. This shift of the AD curve, brought about by the increased money supply,

Figure 31.15 Sustained inflation from an initial increase in *G* and central bank accommodation

An increase in *G* with the money supply remaining constant shifts the *AD* curve from AD_0 to AD_1. This leads to an increase in the interest rate and crowding out of planned investment (not shown in this figure). If the central bank tries to keep the interest rate unchanged by increasing the money supply, the *AD* curve will continue to shift further to the right. The result is a sustained inflation, and perhaps even a hyperinflation.

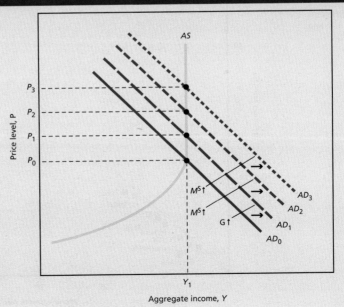

pushes prices up even further. Higher prices, in turn, increase the demand for money, requiring a further increase in the money supply, and so on.

What would happen if the central bank tried to keep the interest rate constant when the economy is moving up the vertical long-run *AS* curve? The situation could lead to a **hyperinflation**, a period of very rapid increases in the price level. If no more output can be coaxed out of the economy and if planned investment is not allowed to fall (because the interest rate is kept unchanged), then it is impossible to increase *G*. As the central bank keeps pumping more and more money into the economy to keep the interest rate unchanged, the price level starts galloping away.

hyperinflation

A period of very rapid increases in the price level.

Sustained inflation as a purely monetary phenomenon

Virtually all economists agree that an increase in the price level can be caused by anything that causes the *AD* curve to shift to the right or the *AS* curve to shift to the left. These include expansionary fiscal policy actions, monetary expansion, cost shocks, changes in expectations, and so forth. There is also a consensus that for a *sustained* inflation to occur, the central bank must accommodate it. In this sense, a *sustained* inflation can be thought of as a purely monetary phenomenon.

This argument, first put forward by monetarists (see Chapter 33), has gained wide acceptance. It is easy to show, as we just did, how expanding the money supply can shift the *AD* curve continuously. It is not as easy to come up with other reasons for continued shifts of the *AD* curve if the money supply is constant. One possibility is for the government to increase spending continuously without increasing taxes. But this process cannot continue forever. To finance spending without taxes, the government must borrow. Without any expansion of the money supply, the interest rate will rise dramatically, making the cost of borrowing very high. More importantly, the public must be willing to buy the government bonds issued to finance the spending increases.

Figure 31.16 Inflation and money growth in selected countries

Sustained inflation requires money growth. The graph underscores this with empirical data. Those countries with the highest average money supply growth rates between 1970 and 1996 also had the highest average inflation rates.
Source: IMF.

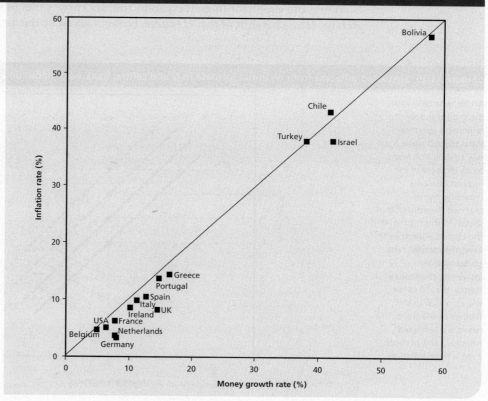

At some point, the public may be unwilling to buy any more bonds even though the interest rate is very high.[6] At this point, the government is no longer able to increase non-tax-financed spending without the central bank's cooperation. If this is true, then a sustained inflation cannot exist without the central bank's cooperation.

Figure 31.16 underlines this point. In the group of countries shown, those suffering from the highest average inflation rates also had the largest money growth rates on average.

Global Perspectives

Inflation and monetary growth in Eastern Europe and Latin America

AD and *AS* analysis shows clearly that a sustained high level of inflation is not possible without expansion of the money supply. When the price level rises, the demand for money schedule shifts to the right. If the money supply is held constant., the interest rate will rise. The rise in the interest rate decreases planned aggregate expenditure, which leads to a reduction in real output (*Y*). The only way to prevent the rise in the interest rate, and thus the decrease in real output, is to expand the money supply. However, if the economy is at potential output and the money supply is expanded as the price level rises to accommodate the increased money demand, the price level will simply continue to rise.

In fragile growing economies, an expanding money supply is often the result of political pressures. Governments have bills to pay and commitments to meet, and they find it difficult to raise the money needed to balance the budget from taxes. They end up running deficits and financing the shortfall with central bank purchases of bonds, which expands the money supply.

The following two excerpts from *The Economist* indicate that during the autumn of 1994 this was exactly what was happening in Poland and Venezuela.

Despite progress, the Polish economy is only precariously stable and its transformation is incomplete. Inflation is still too high. The goal for this year is to get annual price increases below 24%, which is bad enough. But in June annualised inflation was over 30% and few believe it will come down much in the next few months. This is much higher than in Western Europe.

Venezuela looks increasingly like Latin America's odd man out. In

Industrial district of Warsaw, Poland.

a report on September 16th the UN's Economic Commission for Latin America and the Caribbean said the region's economic growth this year would average 3%, inflation (including stratospheric Brazil) had fallen from 49% in 1991 to about 16% this year, and large inward capital flows were continuing.

By contrast, Venezuela's banking crisis . . . caused

(many Venezuelans would say forced) the government to inject money – in the event $7 billion, about 9½% of GDP – into a system that was about to collapse. These measures have led to inflation, now estimated at 65% for this year.

'Poland: not there yet', *The Economist*, 3 September 1994, p. 52; 'Venezuela, crisis manager', *The Economist*, 17 September 1994, p. 42.

[6]*This means that the public's demand for money no longer depends on the interest rate. Even though the interest rate is very high, the public cannot be induced to have its real money balances fall any further. There is a limit to how much the public can be induced to reduce its real money balances.*

The relationship between unemployment and inflation

The *AD–AS* model explains the interaction between income and the price *level*. The previous paragraphs showed that the graphical *AD–AS* model is awkward to work with when there is sustained inflation, because the *AD* curve and the *AS* curve need to shift up period after period. It would be an advantage in such cases to represent *inflation* instead of the price level along the vertical axis.

A second major concern of macroeconomics, in addition to inflation, is *unemployment*. Again, it would be useful if we could trace unemployment explicitly in a diagram. Incidentally, in the 1950s New Zealand economist A.W. Phillips proposed a negative relationship between the inflation rate and the unemployment rate, based on data for the United Kingdom from 1861 to 1957. This relationship, and his claim to fame, became known as the **Phillips curve**.

Phillips curve

A graph illustrating the relationship between inflation and the rate of unemployment.

This section shows that the Phillips curve is closely related to the *AS* curve. As a first step, we show how aggregate supply is related to inflation (instead of the price level). This gives us an *AS* curve in an inflation–income diagram, which will prove valuable in the next chapter. Next, we look at how income is related to unemployment via *Okun's Law*. These two steps link the *AS* curve (drawn in price–income space) to the Phillips curve (drawn in inflation–unemployment space).

Aggregate supply and inflation

Figure 31.17a shows a short-run *AS* curve. A year ago, when the currently valid wage contracts were signed, prices stood at 100. Trade unions expected prices to rise to P^e = 105 this year. What is this year's aggregate supply? We can't tell without knowing this year's price level.

Suppose prices are 105 this year, just as expected. Then firms supply exactly the potential output Y^* (equal to 1000 units). This gives us the information that if prices rose from 100 to 105, or if inflation is 5%, aggregate supply is $Y^* = 1000$. The red dot in Figure 31.17b represents this information in an inflation–income diagram.

Next, suppose prices move higher than expected, say to 110. According to the *AS* curve, this raises aggregate supply to 1100. The same information is represented by the blue dot in the right-hand diagram. At an inflation rate of 10% (prices rose from 100 to 110), aggregate supply is 1100.

If prices rose still higher, to 115, the inflation rate is 15%. So we may say either that aggregate supply equals 1200 if the price level is 115 (Figure 31.17a), or that aggregate supply equals 1200 if the rate of inflation is 15% (Figure 31.17b).

Figure 31.17 From the *AS* curve to the dynamic *AS* curve

The *AS* curve shows aggregate supply at different price levels. The dynamic *AS* curve shows aggregate supply at different inflation rates. Of course, the two are related, since a higher price level means more inflation.

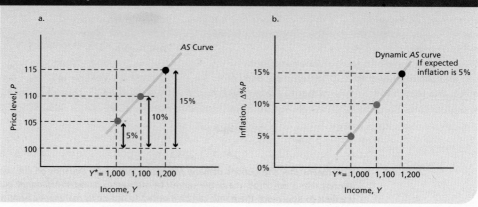

It is important to point out that potential output is not in general equal to 1000 units when inflation is 5%. It only happened here because 5% inflation was expected by the trade unions when negotiating wages. Things go as planned if inflation actually equals 5%, the labour market is in equilibrium at L^* and output produced is Y^*. Things would be different had trade unions expected 10% inflation (or a price level of 110). Then output produced would be Y^* only if actual inflation was 10%.

As a rule, the dynamic AS curve always intersects the vertical line over Y^* if actual **inflation** $\Delta\%P$ equals expected inflation $\Delta\%P^e$. A linear equation for the dynamic AS curve is

inflation The percentage change of the price level:
$$\Delta\%P \equiv \frac{P_1 - P_0}{P_0} \times 100$$

$$\Delta\%P = \Delta\%P^e + b(Y - Y^*) \quad \text{dynamic } AS \text{ curve}$$

> The dynamic AS curve shows how aggregate supply is influenced by the rate of inflation. Different dynamic AS curves obtain at different inflation expectations. The higher the expected inflation, the further up the dynamic AS curve moves.

The relationship between income and unemployment

To bring the second key macroeconomic issue – unemployment – into the picture, we need to establish a link between income and unemployment. From our discussion of aggregate supply in Chapter 30 we know that in equilibrium Y^* is produced, employment is L^*, and the unemployment rate is at its natural level U^*. In the short and medium run – when the capital stock and technology are considered fixed – income may only rise above Y^* if labour in excess of L^* is employed. For a given individual labour supply $N = U + L$, employment L may only rise above L^* if the unemployment rate falls below U^*. We may consolidate this by stating

> When income rises above Y^*, the employment rate falls below U^*:
>
> $$Y - Y^* = a(U^* - U) \quad \text{Okun's law}$$

Okun's Law States that unemployment falls below its normal level if income rises above potential income.

This equation is called **Okun's Law**. The parameter a says that if the unemployment rate drops by one percentage point below U^* (say from $U^* = 7\%$ to 6%), then income rises by a units beyond Y^*. Despite the simple line of argument followed in deriving Okun's Law, the equation receives considerable support from empirical data.

Substituting Okun's Law into the dynamic AS curve we obtain

$$\Delta\%P = \Delta\%P^e - a \times b \left(U - U^* \right)$$

$$\text{Inflation} = \text{expected} - a \times b \left(\begin{array}{c} \text{unemploy-} \\ \text{ment rate} \end{array} - \begin{array}{c} \text{natural} \\ \text{unemploy-} \\ \text{ment rate} \end{array} \right)$$
$$\text{inflation}$$

modern Phillips curve
A graph of the relationship between inflation and the unemployment rate, the position of which is determined by expected inflation.

This is a **modern** version of the **Phillips curve**. It states that for given inflation expectations and natural unemployment, there is a negative relationship between inflation and the unemployment rate. Figure 31.18b shows this negative relationship. Displaying it next to Figure 31.18a emphasizes that the Phillips curve is basically a mirror image of the dynamic AS curve.

If inflation is as expected, unemployment is at its natural level U^*. Unexpectedly high inflation drives unemployment down to, say, U_1. We move up the Phillips curve into the blue point. Note that in this situation trade unions are likely to revise inflation expectations upwards, moving the Phillips curve up for the next period. The negatively sloped Phillips curve is therefore a *short-run Phillips curve*, the position of which is determined by expected inflation. In the long run, expected inflation is the same as actual inflation. Then unemployment is always at its natural rate, regardless of how high inflation is. The long-run Phillips curve is therefore vertical, just as the long-run AS curve is vertical.

Figure 31.18 The Phillips curve and the dynamic *AS* curve

The Phillips curve and the dynamic *AS* curve are mirror images. One shows unemployment rates at different inflation rates. The other shows aggregate supply (income) at different inflation rates. The link between the two is Okun's law. It says that income and unemployment are inversely related.

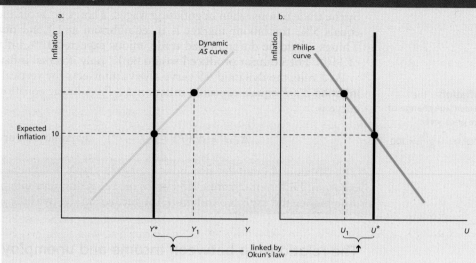

Looking ahead

This chapter concludes our basic analysis of how the macroeconomy works. In the preceding eight chapters, we examined how households and firms behave in the four markets – the goods market, the money market, the foreign exchange market and the labour market. We saw how aggregate output (income), the interest rate, the exchange rate and the price level are determined in the economy, and we examined the relationship between two of the most important macroeconomic variables, the inflation rate and the unemployment rate. In the next chapter, we assemble everything we have learned so far to examine a number of important policy issues.

Summary

The aggregate demand curve

1. Money demand is a function of three variables: (1) the interest rate (r), (2) the level of real income (Y), and (3) the price level (P). Money demand increases if the real level of output (income) rises, the price level expands or the interest rate declines.

2. At a higher price level, households and firms need to hold larger money balances. If, under flexible exchange rates, the money supply remains the same and the interest rate cannot change, then income must fall to keep money demand down. This is achieved by an appreciation of the real exchange rate. An increase in the price level causes the level of aggregate output (income) to fall; a decrease in the price level causes the level of aggregate output (income) to rise.

3. The real exchange rate is determined by three variables: (1) the exchange rate (E), the price level (P), and (3) the world price level (P^W). If the exchange rate

is fixed and world prices are given, the real exchange rate falls if domestic prices rise.

4. Under fixed exchange rates, if prices rise and the real exchange rate falls, net exports decrease. Since the interest rate cannot change, income must fall. An increase in the price level causes the level of aggregate output (income) to fall; a decrease in the price level causes the level of aggregate output (income) to rise.

5. At every point along the aggregate demand curve, the aggregate quantity demanded in the economy is exactly equal to planned aggregate expenditure.

6. Under flexible exchange rates, an increase in the money supply or the world interest rate shifts the aggregate demand curve to the right. Under fixed exchange rates an increase in government spending, world income, world prices or the exchange rate, or a decrease in net taxes or the world interest rate, shift the aggregate demand curve to the right. Movements of these variables in the opposite direction shift the aggregate demand curve to the left.

The equilibrium price level

7. The *long-run equilibrium price level* in the economy is given by the point where the *AD* and the long-run *AS* curves intersect. This intersection corresponds to equilibrium in the goods, money, foreign exchange and labour markets.

8. The *short-run equilibrium price level* in the economy occurs where the *AD* and the short-run *AS* curves intersect. This intersection corresponds to equilibrium in the goods, money and foreign exchange markets. The labour market may be in disequilibrium.

Policy and external shocks in the AD–AS model

9. Expansionary policy measures (or shocks) shift the *AD* curve to the right. Contractionary policy measures (or shocks) move the *AD* curve to the left.

10. Any policy measure or shock moves the *AD* curve horizontally exactly as far as it moved equilibrium in the *IS–LM–FE* model. In the *AD–AS* model, the effect on income resulting in the *IS–LM–FE* model is dampened in the short run by rising prices. The initial effect does not last, since full crowding out occurs in the long run due to rising wages and prices.

11. Expansionary policy or shocks initiate a boom. Contractionary policy or shocks cause a contraction of income.

12. Changes in the price of raw materials used in production alongside labour, such as oil, affect the position of the labour demand curve, and hence the *AS* curve. With sticky wages due to long-term contracts, the short-run shift is much more pronounced than the long-run shift. If the increase in materials prices is only temporary, the shift of the *AS* curve is temporary as well.

13. After an adverse supply shock that shifts the short-run *AS* curve to the left, prices rise and income falls. Expansionary policy may prevent income from falling (as much), at the cost of an even larger price increase. Contractionary policy may keep prices from rising (as much), at the cost of an even larger drop in income.

Causes of inflation

14. *Inflation* is an increase in the overall price level. *Sustained inflation* occurs when the overall price level continues to rise over a fairly long period. Most economists believe that sustained inflations can occur only if the central bank continuously increases the money supply.

15. *Demand-pull inflation* is initiated by an increase in aggregate demand. *Cost-push, or supply-side, inflation* is initiated by an increase in costs. An increase in costs may also lead to *stagflation* – a condition in which the economy is simultaneously experiencing a contraction and inflation.

16. Inflation can become 'built into the system' as a result of expectations. If prices have been rising and people form their expectations on the basis of past pricing behaviour, firms may continue raising prices even if demand is slowing or contracting.

17. When the price level increases, so too does the demand for money. If the economy is operating on the steep part of the *AS* curve and the central bank tries to keep the interest rate constant by increasing the supply of money, a hyperinflation – a period of very rapid increases in the price level – can result.

The relationship between unemployment and inflation

18. The dynamic *AS* curve shows aggregate supply at different inflation rates. Its slope is positive, and its position is determined by the expected rate of inflation.

19. *Okun's Law* states that unemployment falls below its normal level if income rises above potential income.

20. Making use of Okun's Law, the dynamic *AS* curve can be rewritten as a *Phillips curve*. A Phillips curve is a graph illustrating the relationship between inflation and the rate of unemployment.

21. Reflecting the existence of a short-run and a long-run *AS* curve, there also exist short-run and long-run Phillips curves. The long-run Phillips curve is vertical at the natural rate of unemployment. The short-run Phillips curve has negative slope and intersects the long-run Phillips curve at expected inflation.

Review Terms and Concepts

adaptive expectations
aggregate demand
aggregate demand (*AD*) curve
cost-push inflation
demand-pull inflation
devaluation
equilibrium price level
exchange rate policy
government budget deficit
hyperinflation

inflation
modern Phillips curve
Okun's Law
Phillips curve
real wealth, or real balance, effect
stagflation
supply shock
sustained inflation
trade deficit
twin deficits

Problem Set

1. 'The aggregate demand curve slopes downwards because when the price level is lower, people can afford to buy more and aggregate demand rises. When prices rise, people can afford to buy less and aggregate demand falls.' Is this a good explanation of the shape of the *AD* curve? Why or why not?

2. Use the *IS–LM* model to explain what happens to the *AD* curve under flexible exchange rates when (a) the money supply decreases; (b) the world interest rate increases; (c) a major trading partner experiences an economic boom.

3. Use the *IS–LM* model to explain what happens to the *AD* curve under fixed exchange rates when (a) government spending increases; (b) the world interest rate increases; (c) a major trading partner experiences an economic boom.

4. Using aggregate supply and demand curves to illustrate your points, discuss the impacts of the following events on the price level and on equilibrium GDP (*Y*) in the short run: (a) a tax cut holding government purchases constant; (b) an increase in the money supply; (c) an increase in the price of oil caused by a war in the Middle East.

5. During 1997 and 1998, a debate raged over whether the United States was at or above potential GDP. Some economists feared the economy was operating at a level of output above potential GDP and that inflationary pressures were building. They urged the Fed to tighten monetary policy to slow the economy. Others argued that cheap raw materials imports were keeping prices from rising. Using *AS* and *AD* curves, illustrate the following scenarios:

a. Those pushing the Fed to act were right, and prices start to rise more rapidly in 1998 and 1999 due to a high level of aggregate demand. The Fed acts belatedly in 1999 to slow money growth (contract the money supply) and push the economy back to potential GDP.

b. World supplies of raw materials continue to expand more rapidly than demand for them, leading to even lower prices. The result is a falling price level in the United States.

6. The chapter argues that in the long run, inflation is the result of excessive money growth. However, we also learned earlier that monetary policy is ineffective when exchange rates are fixed. What determines the long-run rate of inflation under fixed exchange rates?

7. In country A, all wage contracts are indexed to inflation. That is, each month wages are adjusted to reflect increases in the cost of living as reflected in changes in the price level. In country B, there are no cost-of-living adjustments to wages, but the workforce is completely unionized. Unions negotiate three-year contracts. In which country is an expansionary monetary policy likely to have a larger effect on aggregate output? Explain your answer using *AS* and *AD* curves.

8. In 1998, analysts believed that the economies of Norway and Finland were operating above the natural level of output due to private-sector expenditure booms. Use the *AD–AS* framework to explain how the authorities in the two countries might respond to control inflation. (*Hint*: how are their exchange rates determined?)

9. In an effort to fight inflation in 1974 and 1975, the Swiss government acted with contractionary monetary policy.
a. Using aggregate supply and aggregate demand curves, illustrate the effects that the government expected this policy to have on aggregate output and on the price level.
b. The contractionary monetary policy had the effect of reducing aggregate output; Switzerland experienced a recession in 1975. But although output was reduced, prices continued to increase throughout the recession. Give two alternative explanations for why prices might continue to rise even though output is falling.

10. Draw a graph to illustrate the following.
a. A Phillips curve based on the assumption of a vertical long-run *AS* curve.
b. The effect of accelerating inflationary expectations on a recently stable Phillips curve.

11. Obtain quarterly data on the unemployment rate and output growth for your country over the last 3–5 years.
a. What trends do you observe? Can you explain what you see using *AS* and *AD* curves?
b. Plot the data on a graph with the unemployment rate measured on the *X* axis and the inflation rate on the *Y* axis. Is there any evidence of Okun's Law?

32

Budget Deficits and Central Bank Behaviour

Every day, newspapers carry articles dealing with macroeconomic problems. Issues come and go, but few have been in the headlines as long and as consistently as the convergence process on which EU member countries embarked when they signed the Maastricht Treaty on European Economic and Monetary Union in 1992. Using what we have learned in previous chapters about how the macroeconomy works, we now examine in greater depth the issues that featured prominently in this discussion.

In this chapter, we take up two major issues: (1) the macroeconomic effects of budget deficits and the public debt; and (2) why central banks conduct the monetary policy and thus create the inflation they do. Before we embark on this discussion, we give a brief historical account of European integration.

The European Union and the treaty of Maastricht: a brief history of European integration

The European Union, then called the European Economic Community (EEC), was formally established when Belgium, France, Germany, Italy, Luxemburg and The Netherlands signed the Treaty of Rome in 1957.[1] The time line of European integration shown in Figure 32.1 lists key events that mark the transformation of the European Union from these humble beginnings into the major global player that it is today.

The events above the time line show how membership evolved from the six founding members of the EEC to the current 15. Enlargement usually came in waves, with two or three countries joining at the same time. Only Greece joined alone in 1981. New waves of membership negotiations began in 1998 with Cyprus, the Czech Republic, Estonia, Hungary, Poland and Slovenia, and later with other Central and Eastern European countries. This may well boost membership to 26 countries within the next 10–15 years.

Listed underneath the time line are the major monetary integration efforts and experiences over the period. Efforts to contain exchange rate fluctuations between the currencies of EEC member states began in 1971. Before that, the Bretton Woods system of fixed exchange rates, in operation since the end of the Second World War, had stabilized the exchange rates of member states by pegging currencies to the US dollar. Immediately after the collapse of the Bretton Woods system, the then six EEC members set up the 'snake', the predecessor of the European Monetary System (EMS), agreeing to limit the margin of fluctuation between their currencies to ±2.25% around a central parity rate.

[1]The move drew on the vision of Europeans such as Jean Monnet and Robert Schuman and moved beyond earlier, modest cooperations in coal mining and steel.

Figure 32.1 The time line of European integration

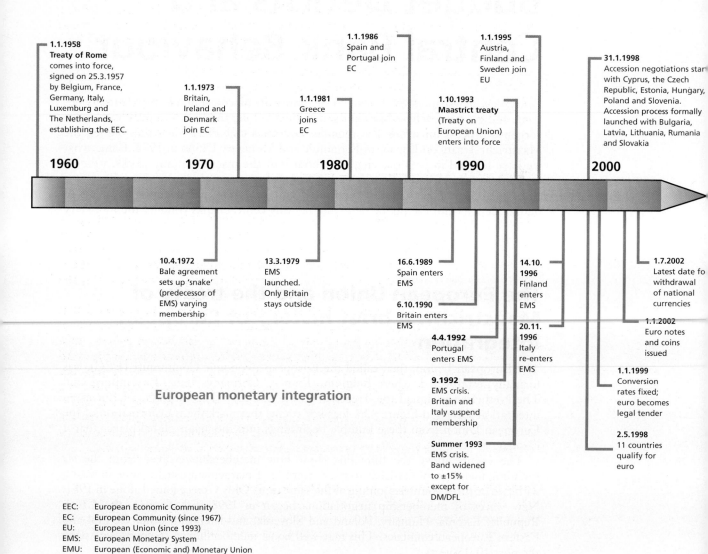

EU membership growth

1.1.1958
Treaty of Rome
comes into force,
signed on 25.3.1957
by Belgium, France,
Germany, Italy,
Luxemburg and
The Netherlands,
establishing the EEC.

1.1.1973
Britain,
Ireland and
Denmark
join EC

1.1.1981
Greece
joins
EC

1.1.1986
Spain and
Portugal join
EC

1.1.1995
Austria,
Finland and
Sweden join
EU

1.10.1993
Maastrict treaty
(Treaty on
European Union)
enters into force

31.1.1998
Accession negotiations star
with Cyprus, the Czech
Republic, Estonia, Hungary,
Poland and Slovenia.
Accession process formally
launched with Bulgaria,
Latvia, Lithuania, Rumania
and Slovakia

1960   1970   1980   1990   2000

10.4.1972
Bale agreement
sets up 'snake'
(predecessor of
EMS) varying
membership

13.3.1979
EMS
launched.
Only Britain
stays outside

16.6.1989
Spain enters
EMS

6.10.1990
Britain enters
EMS

**14.10.
1996**
Finland
enters
EMS

1.7.2002
Latest date fo
withdrawal
of national
currencies

4.4.1992
Portugal
enters EMS

**20.11.
1996**
Italy
re-enters
EMS

1.1.2002
Euro notes
and coins
issued

9.1992
EMS crisis.
Britain and
Italy suspend
membership

1.1.1999
Conversion
rates fixed;
euro becomes
legal tender

European monetary integration

Summer 1993
EMS crisis.
Band widened
to ±15%
except for
DM/DFL

2.5.1998
11 countries
qualify for
euro

EEC: European Economic Community
EC: European Community (since 1967)
EU: European Union (since 1993)
EMS: European Monetary System
EMU: European (Economic and) Monetary Union

The graph's upper part shows how EU membership increased from the initial group of six countries that signed the Treaty of Rome on 25 March 1957, founding the EEC (European Economic Community), to 15 at the turn of the millennium. Membership can be expected to rise to around 25 within a few years. While the EEC and two other Communities [Euratom and the ECSC (European Coal and Steel Community)] were initially referred to as the European Communities, executives were merged and the term European Community (EC) was used for all of them since 1967. The name was changed to European Union (EU) in 1993 when the Maastricht Treaty entered into force.

The lower part shows milestones of European monetary integration. These efforts were spawned (or propelled) by the collapse of the Bretton Woods System of fixed exchange rates around 1971. Starting with the initiative of a handful of countries to stabilize their exchange rates in the 1970s, monetary integration efforts are currently peaking with 11 countries discarding their national currencies in favour of the euro. Of the four EU members that are not participating in European Monetary Union in the first wave, Denmark and Greece are planning to peg their currencies to the euro under EMS II, with margins of fluctuation of ±2.25% and ±15%, respectively. Britain and Sweden do not entertain such plans.

The snake's success was mixed, as documented by constantly varying membership and frequent realignments. In 1979 a redesigned system, the EMS, came into operation, in which all members at that time except Britain participated. After more than a decade of considerable success and stability, the EMS experienced some turmoil in 1992 and 1993, prompting Britain and Italy to suspend membership and later forcing the EU to widen the margins of fluctuation to ±15%. Defying a number of very negative predictions, the EMS returned to stability, seeing the lira re-enter and three more currencies join, and providing the exchange rate stability needed for a smooth transition from national currencies to the euro.

The introduction of the euro began on 1 January 1999 and is to be completed by 1 January 2002. The euro will then be legal tender – that is, a currency that *must* be accepted as payment in all transactions – in all member countries. For a maximum of six months, the respective national currency may remain in use as a parallel currency to provide time for adjusting automatic teller machines (ATMs) and other things.

The Maastricht treaty

The Maastricht Treaty on European Economic and Monetary Union, agreed on 9–10 December 1991 and entered into force on 1 November 1993, is a major stepping stone on the way to further European integration. While the treaty addresses aspects related to the completion of economic and monetary union, it has become famous or notorious for its convergence criteria. The Maastricht convergence criteria spell out five conditions that prospective members must meet before they are allowed into the 'club' of countries adopting the common European currency.

Maastricht convergence criteria

Five conditions that prospective members had to meet before they were allowed into the 'club' of countries adopting the common European currency.

Table 32.1 lists the five criteria. The first two address *fiscal policy*: the first states that the government budget deficit (roughly $G - T$ in our models) must not exceed 3% of GDP; the second says that the public debt, accumulated by past budget deficits, must not exceed 60% of GDP. The remaining criteria address *monetary policy*: the third requires inflation not to exceed the average rate of inflation in the three EU member countries with the lowest inflation rates by more than 1.5 percentage points. In a similar way, the fourth criterion says that a country's interest rate on government bonds must not be more than 2 percentage points above the average interest rates in the three countries with the lowest inflation rates. The final criterion requires membership in the EMS for at least two years without having initiated a devaluation.

Interpreting the Maastricht convergence criteria

The description of the Maastricht convergence criteria suggests a clear link between the criteria and the major policy options we encountered and analysed in the national economy model in earlier chapters. The first two criteria aim at *disciplining fiscal policy*.

Table 32.1 The Maastricht convergence criteria	
Government budget deficit	≤ 3% of GDP
Government debt	≤ 60% of GDP
Inflation	≤ average inflation in the three EU countries with lowest inflation +1.5%
Interest rates	≤ average interest rates in the three EU countries with lowest inflation +2%
Membership in the EMS	≥ 2 years without having initiated a devaluation

deficit criterion
The Maastricht criterion that stipulates the maximum permissible government deficit.

debt criterion   The Maastricht criterion that stipulates the maximum permissible government debt.

European Commission
The institution that serves as executive body for EU policy. It is also charged with upholding treaties and representing the EU's interest to the Council of Ministers.

inflation criterion
The Maastricht criterion that stipulates the maximum permissible rate of inflation.

interest rate criterion
The Maastricht criterion stipulating the maximum permissible interest rate.

EMS membership criterion
The Maastricht criterion requiring a minimum period of EMS membership.

■ **Disciplining fiscal policy**   The **deficit criterion** explicitly prevents the government from embarking on expansionary fiscal policy beyond very narrow limits. Raising government spending G while leaving taxes T unchanged would drive up the budget deficit. So would lowering taxes while leaving the level of spending unchanged.

The **debt criterion** is less directly linked to current fiscal policy. In terms of fiscal discipline it is a record of the sins of the past, for which the current government may or may not share responsibility. These 'sins' may take considerable time to rectify, which may explain why the **European Commission** did not apply this criterion strictly when judging convergence progress in March 1998 and granting qualification for monetary union to 11 countries. This was made possible by a clause in the Treaty of Maastricht stipulating that strict fulfilment of the debt criterion could be waived if sufficient progress was visible.

■ **Disciplining monetary policy**   The remaining three criteria serve the interests of monetary policy discipline, though only the inflation criterion addresses monetary policy directly. As we learned in Chapter 31, for inflation to be more than temporary the money supply needs to increase again and again – either as the direct cause of inflation, or by accommodating other demand or supply shocks. The **inflation criterion** outlaws the operation of an expansionary monetary policy by preventing the government or the central bank from generating inflation beyond narrow limits.

The **interest rate criterion** may sound a little bewildering. After all, didn't we always say that the home interest rate cannot deviate from the world interest rate? We did; but we also noted that this was a simplification that avoided some unimportant complications. The more general condition is that expected returns on financial investments at home and abroad must be the same for the foreign exchange market to be in equilibrium. This leaves some room for international interest rates to differ (see the Application 'Why international interest rates may differ') – either permanently, if inflation rates are not the same, or temporarily, if inflation rates are the same. Since the inflation criterion already calls for a convergence of inflation rates, interest rates could only diverge temporarily, say because one country was in a boom and the other in a recession. Requiring countries to enter monetary union with similar interest rates effectively means that you want them to be in the same phase of the business cycle. This reduces the prospect of conflicts, such as one country requesting the ECB to conduct expansionary monetary policy because it is in a recession, while other countries resist because their economies are in a boom.

The **EMS membership criterion** is somewhat redundant from the perspective of monetary policy. The inflation criterion already forces monetary policy to converge to a common stance. There is little the EMS criterion can add to that. Nevertheless, it may help to stabilize and focus the exchange rate expectations of speculators and other participants in the foreign exchange market and prevent speculative fluctuations of exchange rates in the run-up towards the final fixing of conversion rates between national currencies and the euro.

The success of the Maastricht criteria

Beyond most expectations, the Maastricht convergence criteria turned out to be a considerable success. When data for 1997 became available, it was time to count and compare. It turned out that an unexpectedly high number of 11 countries met the convergence criteria. Of the four countries that didn't join, three would have qualified easily had they been interested – and Greece, the fourth, wouldn't have missed by much and probably made the biggest progress of all. Figure 32.2 illustrates convergence judged by the Maastricht criteria.

It is evident that some criteria posed few problems. These are the EMS membership criterion, which is not shown, and those on inflation and the interest rate. Another, the deficit criterion, looks fine on paper, but many believe that convergence

Applications

Why international interest rates may differ

Through most of this text, the foreign exchange market (or, more precisely, the international asset market) is in equilibrium only when domestic and foreign interest rates are the same. This is a simplification, as we emphasized.

To be more precise: for financial investors to be indifferent between holding assets at home or abroad, domestic and foreign returns (rather than interest rates) must be the same. Suppose you want to invest €10,000 for one year. If you invest them at home, the rate of return equals the domestic interest rate:

Rate of return on domestic assets = (Domestic) interest rate

If you invest the same amount in the USA, your return is made up of two components: the foreign interest rate and the rate of depreciation. To illustrate, suppose the US interest rate is 5% and the exchange rate is 0.50€/US$. Then your €10,000 euros buy $20,000 worth of US assets. After one year these have grown by 5% to $21,000. If the euro has depreciated (meaning the dollar has appreciated) by 10% to 0.55 €/$, this buys you €11,550. Your rate of return equals (11,550 – 10,000)/10,000 = 0.155 = 15.5%. This is half a percent more than the sum of the interest rate of 5% and the rate of depreciation of 10%. The reason is that the appreciation of the dollar does not only make us gain on our investment of 20,000, but also on our interest revenue of $100. This exchange rate gain on the interest payment, 0.5% in this example, is small for realistic interest rates and rates of depreciation. It can be ignored as a first approximation. The rate of return on foreign assets may thus be approximated by

Rate of return on foreign assets = Foreign interest rate + Expected depreciation

Because the two rates of return must be the same, the generalized equilibrium condition for the international asset market reads

Interest rate = Foreign interest rate + Expected depreciation

Our simplifying assumption that domestic and foreign interest rates must be the same is obviously useful when investors do not expect the domestic currency to depreciate. This is often a useful working assumption. But sometimes it is not; to see when, suppose purchasing power parity holds: $P = EP^W$. For the international goods market to be in equilibrium, a given basket of goods must cost the same when we buy it at home as when we buy it abroad. To see what purchasing power parity implies, consider the following examples:

1. If home prices, P, are constant, international prices, P^W, denoted in home currency, EP^W, cannot change. This means if there is inflation in the rest of the world – say, P^W rises by 2% year after year – E must fall by 2% year after year to keep EP^W unchanged.
2. If P^W is unchanged and home inflation is 5% every year, the exchange rate must depreciate by 5% every year to maintain the equation $P = EP^W$.
3. If P rises by 5% every year and P^W rises by 2%, E must rise by 3% to make up for the difference and maintain $P = EP^W$.

These insights can be generalized to the statement that E rises just as fast as P rises relative to P^W:

Depreciation = Inflation (at home) – Inflation abroad

We now know: when there is roughly the same inflation at home and abroad, the equilibrium condition $i = i^W$ is a good working hypothesis. Then the exchange rate does not change, and financial investors have reason not to expect it to change.

The convergence history after the Maastricht treaty illustrates this nicely. The upper right panel in Figure 32.2 shows that inflation in today's EMU countries was still quite diverse during the first half of the 1990s. And so were interest rates, as the panel shows. Those countries with the higher inflation rates had higher interest rates, and reasonably so, since their currencies were expected to depreciate in order to maintain purchasing power parity. When inflation rates converged toward the end of the decade, so did interest rates.

Thus $i = i^W$ can be used when analysing countries with similar inflation rates as the world surrounding them. When inflation rates differ substantially, it becomes mandatory to take inflation or depreciation expectations into account.

in this respect would be less impressive without the 'creative accounting' tricks some of the governments resorted to. The debt criterion was clearly missed by several countries, but progress was considered sufficient by the EU Commission to let all countries pass.

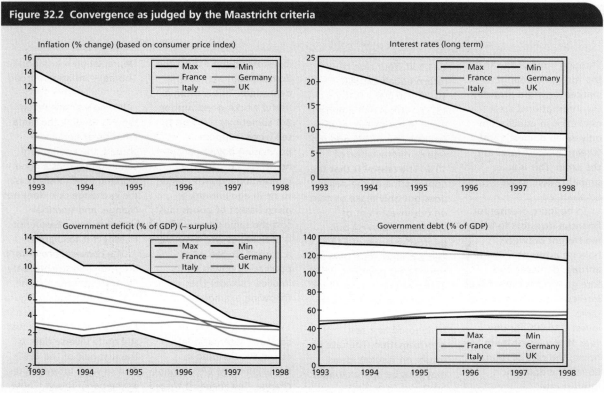

Figure 32.2 Convergence as judged by the Maastricht criteria

Source: European Commission, *Convergence Report*, 1998.

The Maastricht criteria and the national economy model

The Maastricht criteria's focus on disciplining monetary and fiscal policy may seem a little odd in light of what we learned in preceding chapters. Through much of that discussion we focused on demonstrating how expansionary fiscal and monetary policy can stimulate demand to raise income, if only temporarily. So why do governments and central banks not do that consistently? And why would the Maastricht treaty even try to prevent them from doing it, by disciplining monetary and fiscal policy? The answer is that the positive effects of expansionary monetary and fiscal policy on income are not the whole story. There are *negative* effects as well. Some we have already encountered.

Expansionary monetary policy sooner or later leads to inflation. In fact, this is its only outcome in the long run.

Expansionary fiscal policy itself cannot cause sustained inflation. But it may cause the government to put pressure on the central bank to accommodate its expansionary fiscal policy by raising the money supply. Then we end up with inflation again. More importantly, we saw in Chapter 29 that while one country's fiscal expansion boosts its income, in a currency union the price is paid by the other members who are thrown into a recession. Finally, as we shall see in Chapter 35, government deficit spending may hurt long-run growth.

Economic policies in EU member countries' pursuit of the Maastricht criteria reminded many observers of efforts to squeeze the camel through the eye of a needle: while this may be an impressive achievement, who can guarantee that the animal does not grow fat again after it has passed through? This danger worried economists and politicians. The EU has gone to great lengths to ensure that countries also adhere to fiscal and monetary discipline after the start of European Monetary Union. To understand these efforts, which are reflected in the design of the European Central Bank and in the 'stability and growth' pact we encountered in Chapter 29, we now look at fiscal policy and central bank behaviour in more depth and detail.

Central bank behaviour and monetary policy

Suppose exchange rates are flexible. By setting the money supply appropriately, the central bank can move the *AD* curve to any position it wants. In this way it can bring about any price level it wants, because the intersection between the *AD* curve and the short-run and long-run *AS* curves determines prices in the short and long run, respectively. We may actually assume that with appropriate monetary policy the central bank can pick any point on the *AS* curve, and hence any price level it wants, without explicitly drawing the *AD* curve. Of course, if the central bank can pick any point on the *AS* curve (drawn in a price–income diagram) it wants, it can also pick any point on the dynamic *AS* curve (drawn in an inflation–income diagram) it wants. As a short cut, we may then assume that

> The central bank can select any rate of inflation it wants by pursuing appropriate monetary policies.

For now, we need not examine what exactly these policies would be.[2] So if inflation is bad but can be controlled by the central bank, how can inflation ever become a problem? How can there ever be hyperinflations? Why did Britain produce inflation rates in excess of 25% in the 1970s? And why did the Maastricht inflation criterion have to *force* governments to bring inflation down when, technically, it is so easy to do it? The simple answer is:

> In some situations or some institutional environments, governments or central banks do not *want* to reduce or eliminate inflation.

How can this be? How can it be that a central bank, left to act on its own, does not *want* to get rid of inflation that everybody regards as bad? Why does a central bank have to be forced to keep it low? To answer this question we need to look at the **macroeconomic *preferences* of the government** and the central bank. Just as in microeconomics, where we need to know consumers' preferences and the budget constraints under which they operate to understand their choices, to understand why the central bank chooses a particular inflation rate we need to know its preferences and the constraints under which it operates. Let's start by discussing the preferences of governments and policy makers in general.

macroeconomic preferences of the government
How the government rates different states of the economy (expressed in terms of inflation, income or unemployment).

The preferences of policy makers

Like consumers – which they are in one part of their lives – *politicians maximize utility*. This statement is trivial, of course; in fact, it's virtually useless. You cannot use it or prove it wrong unless you're more specific about what yields utility to politicians.[3]

What are the specific things that politicians maximize? Items they appear to be interested in would include: changing the course of their country; a prominent place in history; power, prestige and popularity, and much more. Including all these things would probably yield a highly complex utility function unfit for our macroeconomic model, but a two-step argument produces a simple formulation that can be used in the macroeconomic context:

---

[2]*This is a simplification, of course. In reality, central bank control of the money supply is not perfect, other determinants of demand and supply change constantly, and the economy may respond to monetary policy after a time lag rather than instantly. But, by and large, assuming direct central bank control of the inflation rate is a useful working hypothesis that yields interesting insights.*

[3]*We did the same thing when analysing the behaviour of other actors. For example, to understand the wage bargaining behaviour of monopolistic trade unions in Chapter 30 we postulated that they maximized the wage sum.*

1. Many of the things that politicians are presumably interested in can only be pursued properly when they hold a political office. So being in office may be seen as a simple precondition for achieving objectives such as those listed above. In a democracy, the political system we are dealing with, coming into and remaining in office requires the support of the public. Accordingly, policy makers pay close attention to how policy choices affect *public support*.

2. Public support for governments very much reflects how the economy is performing. When the economy is in poor shape, governments tend to be ousted and the opposition is voted into power. When the state of the economy is good, the government remains in office, free to pursue those things that feature in its utility function. The US presidency provides an excellent example: in 1992 Bill Clinton defeated incumbent George Bush by insisting that the US economy was in the worst recession in decades, summed up in the famous war room slogan 'It's the economy, stupid'. Later, throughout his two terms in office, the extraordinary high-growth, low-inflation performance of the US economy kept an almost unprecedented barrage of scandals, investigations and allegations from affecting the president's popularity.

To evaluate how the economy is performing, the public concentrates on a digestible number of key macroeconomic indicators. Decades of empirical research have indicated that the two most important ones are *inflation* and *unemployment*. The public wants both of these macroeconomic evils to be low. Remember that according to Okun's Law unemployment is low when income is high, and unemployment is high when income is low. We may thus postulate that:

The public likes low inflation and high income.

The nice thing about this is that inflation and income are the very two variables we wrote on the axes of the diagram in which we displayed the dynamic *AS* curve. This proves useful, since we can display the public's preferences on the same diagram (see Figure 32.3).

Figure 32.3 The macroeconomic preferences of the public and the policy maker

Macroeconomic preferences are characterized by two indifference curves – representing 'low' and 'high' utility. If inflation rises at given income (say from *A'* to *B*), utility drops. If income rises at given inflation (say from *A* to *A'*), utility goes up. Indifference curves turn flatter as income rises, meaning that (1) additional income is valued less if income is already high and (2) a hike in inflation hurts more if inflation is already high.

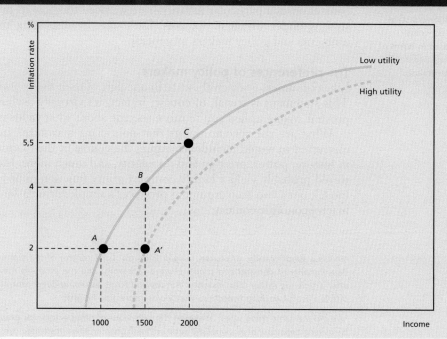

indifference curves

Lines connecting combinations of goods (in microeconomics) or of inflation and income (in macroeconomics) that yield the same utility.

The public's preferences are represented by means of **indifference curves**. Such curves are often used in microeconomics (see Chapter 6). Typically, an indifference curve links all combinations of two goods between which an individual is indifferent. For example, if an individual does not care whether he or she possesses four Ferraris and a house, or two Ferraris and two houses, then this person is *indifferent* between the two combinations. Both yield the same level of utility.

With respect to the economy, the public is interested in two topics: inflation and income. Since income yields utility but inflation yields disutility (negative utility), indifference curves must have a positive slope. To see why, suppose the economy is in point A in Figure 32.3, where income is 1000 and the rate of inflation is 2%. This point yields a level of utility we may call 'low utility'. To uncover the slope of the indifference curve we need to find another inflation/income combination that yields the same level of utility.

Starting from A, let income grow from 1000 to 1500. As long as inflation stays at 2%, this raises the level of utility. Therefore, point A' represents a higher utility level than A. The two points cannot be on the same indifference curve. A different indifference curve must pass through point A', reflecting 'high utility'. To find a point comparable to point A, inflation must rise far enough to drive utility back down from 'high' to 'low'. This is the case in point B, at an inflation rate of 4%. So if income rises from 1000 to 1500 and inflation increases from 2% to 4%, the two effects exactly cancel. Utility stays the same. Therefore, the indifference curve connects and passes through points A and B.

To find a third point on the indifference curve, add another €500 to income, raising it from 1500 to 2000. Now inflation needs to rise by less than two percentage points, from 4% to 5.5%, to keep utility unchanged at the 'low' level. This is the case if 'price stability' – zero inflation – is a normal good with decreasing marginal utility: the more inflation we already have, the more additional inflation hurts. This is why we require less additional inflation to compensate an income gain of €500 when inflation is at 4% than when it is at 2%. The general consequence for the shape of the indifference curve is that it becomes flatter as we move up to the right.

What macroeconomic constellation do policy makers strive to achieve? This can now be read off the utility function as represented by the indifference curves in inflation–income space. The indifference curves do not only represent the preferences of the public, but also appear to follow the preferences of the policy maker too. Why? Remember that in order to stay in power, governments in democracies need to please the public. They very much do what the public wants, acting as though the public's preferences were their own. This is one way of rationalizing why the government's indifference curves look like those in Figures 32.3 and 32.4. A more direct answer is that policy makers are themselves part of the public. If the public wants more income and less inflation, so do policy makers. On this view, even a policy maker who is not subject to re-election or public approval is driven by these kinds of preferences.

Up to now we only know the general preferences of policy makers. Technically, to reach the highest possible utility, he or she wants to end up on an indifference curve as far to the right as possible. This helps as much as knowing that an individual would like to have as many Ferraris and as many houses as possible. With houses and Ferraris, budget constraints permit only part of these desires to be fulfilled. Similarly, policy makers face a constraint, meaning that they cannot move both income *and* inflation at will. When they influence one, the other responds, as described by the national economy model. Let us carve out the restrictions that policy makers face when they try to influence the economy.

The macroeconomic constraint

Using fiscal or monetary policy, the government or the central bank control aggregate demand and, hence, the AD curve; and via the intersection with the AS curve(s), they control the price level and inflation. But they cannot independently control aggregate supply, and hence income; these decisions are made by firms and in the labour market. As summarized by the dynamic AS curve, once money wage rates are fixed, more

---

Figure 32.4 The ordering of the policy maker's indifference curves

Policy makers' and the public's utility increases when we move down to the right. A policy maker who maximizes his or her utility tries to reach an indifference curve as far to the right as possible.

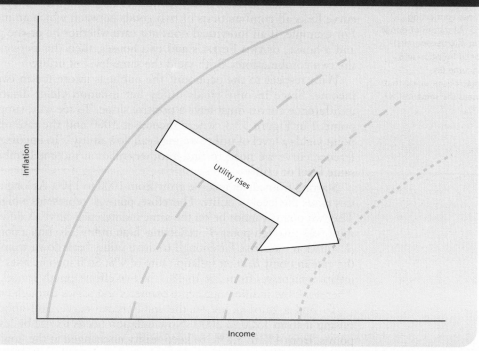

output will only be supplied if inflation goes up. There is nothing the policy maker can do about it. In the long run, when the *AS* curve is vertical, no inflation whatsoever can induce firms to supply more than potential output. Thus the inflation rates and income levels that the policy maker can achieve are limited by the dynamic *AS* curve in the short run, and by the vertical *AS* curve in the long run.

The *AS* curve is the constraint under which policymakers operate.

Why inflation may be higher than most people want

To understand policy choices and macroeconomic outcomes (see Figure 32.5), we can now merge the policy maker's preferences and the macroeconomic constraint she faces into one diagram.

Suppose the economy is in point *A*, operating at potential output with perfect price stability. Trade unions expected zero inflation when money wage rates were negotiated, positioning the aggregate supply curve at DAS_0. If the policymaker maintains price stability, the utility level is 'medium'. But wait, couldn't the policymaker do better? In fact, she could.

The options for the current period (say, a year) are given by DAS_0. By driving up inflation (which, alone, drives utility down), income can be raised (which, alone, raises utility). Up to a certain level, more inflation hurts utility less than what is gained by the accompanying income rise. So there is a net gain in utility. Graphically, by moving 'north-east' from point *A* we encounter indifference curves that are positioned to the right of the red curve, representing higher utility levels.

The highest level of utility is reached at point *B*, where DAS_0 just touches an indifference curve. Driving inflation beyond $\Delta\%P_B$ would move us back onto inferior indifference curves, meaning that inflation costs outweigh income gains. Keeping inflation below $\Delta\%P_B$ also leaves us on an inferior indifference curve. Therefore, any

Figure 32.5 Monetary policy choices and the inflation bias

The policy maker's options when trying for an indifference curve as far to the right as possible are limited by the *DAS* curve in the short run and by the *LRAS* curve in the long run. In the short run, given *DAS₀*, the policy maker can drive inflation up to Δ%*P_B*, and end up in *B* instead of *A*, raising utility from 'medium' to 'high'. If this temptation to create inflation is anticipated by trade unions, the *AS* curve moves up into the red position and the economy ends up in *C*, generating 'low' utility.

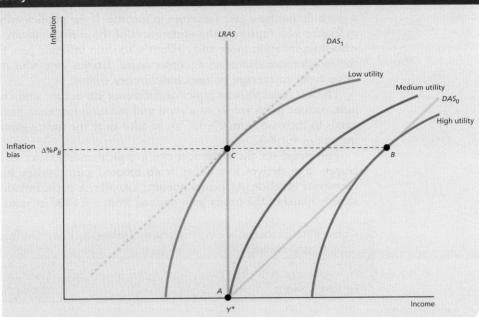

utility-maximizing policy maker will push inflation to Δ%*P_B*, moving the economy from point *A* into point *B*.

We know from what we learned in previous chapters that point *B* is not feasible in the long run. In the next period, trade unions expect higher inflation and demand wage rises accordingly. This moves *DAS* up. If they expect the same inflation rate that they experienced this year, *DAS* moves up into the blue position, maximizing utility (at a lower level) at point *C*. Again, with higher or lower inflation rates, policy makers would end up on an inferior indifference curve.

The described scenario poses a dilemma for monetary policy: by adhering to price stability (point *A*), this period's utility level would have been 'medium'. Policy makers, however, generate 10% inflation, hoping to surprise trade unions, thereby raising income and this period's utility to 'high' (point *B*).

As this pattern becomes evident, however, it fails to work. Anticipating the policy maker's expansionary move, trade unions expect 10% inflation, shifting the *DAS* curve up into the blue position, and the economy ends up in *C* instead of *B*. The irony here is that while the utility function tempts the policymaker to try to do better than point *A*, in the end the policy maker (and the public) fares worse. In point *C*, price stability has been sacrificed without any compensating income gains.

There is no easy way out of this dilemma. You may think that the central bank could simply promise not to inflate. The question is whether such a promise would be credible, whether trade unions would believe it. Suppose they did believe it, expecting zero inflation and setting *DAS* into *DAS₀*. Then the policy maker could steer the economy into point *A*. But she could also do much better by inflating to reach point *B*, which is available once again. Foreseeing this, the trade union does of course not believe the promise of price stability and expects 10% inflation, putting *DAS* into the blue position. The economy ends up in point *C*. This result, that price stability appears to be unavailable and inflation appears to be unavoidable, is called the **inflation bias**.

Having identified the problem of inflation bias, economists and politicians obviously sought ways out of this dilemma. We now discuss those solutions that shaped policy making and the design of institutions in Europe.

inflation bias

The inflation a country apparently cannot get rid of, even though it would be beneficial for society to do so.

Selecting a conservative central banker

Not everyone is equally fond of Ferraris. And not all people are prepared to accept some inflation for a given increase in income. If the public's indifference curves shown in Figure 32.5 represent the preferences of the *average* citizen, there must be citizens who shun inflation more and citizens who shun inflation less. Figure 32.6 shows how the indifference curves of a 'conservative' citizen, one who despises inflation a lot, differ from an average citizen's indifference curves.

The left panel shows a typical indifference curve for a non-conservative citizen. For him, income gains are so important and inflation increases hurt so little that inflation needs to increase from 0% to 3% to take away the utility gained from an increase in income of €1000.

The panel on the right features a typical indifference curve for a conservative citizen. She derives less utility from income gains and/or higher discomfort from increasing inflation. As a consequence, a small rise in the inflation rate from 0% to 1% already matches the utility gain derived from a €1000 increase in income.

> Conservative citizens are very averse to inflation. They display rather flat indifference curves.
>
> Non-conservative citizens are less averse to inflation. Their indifference curves are relatively steep.

Now let's see what difference it makes to a country's inflation bias whether a non-conservative or a conservative citizen heads the central bank, determining monetary policy.

The example given in Figure 32.5 illustrates that the inflationary equilibrium is located on the long-run *AS* curve where the short-run *AS* curve is tangent to an indifference curve (at point *C*, where the *DAS* curve has the same slope as the highest possible indifference curve). Such inflationary equilibria are also constructed in Figures 32.7a and 32.7b.

The left frame shows that when a non-conservative central bank conducts monetary policy, the inflation bias is high (here at 10%). Such a central bank is known to be prepared always to sacrifice a large element of price stability for a small gain in income. Due to the bank's reputation expected inflation is high, the *DAS* curve sits far up, and inflation actually turns out to be high.

Figure 32.6 Average and conservative preferences

Non-conservative citizens who have no particular aversion to inflation have steep indifference curves. Here they are prepared to pay 3% inflation for a €1000 rise in income. Conservative citizens have flat indifference curves. They are prepared to pay only 1% inflation for the €1000 rise in income.

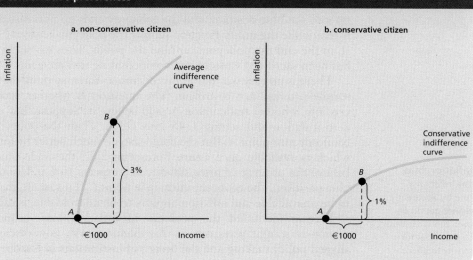

Figure 32.7 How a conservative central banker affects the inflation bias

When a non-conservative central bank conducts monetary policy, a high inflation bias (average inflation rate) results.

If a conservative central bank determines monetary policy, the inflation bias is low.

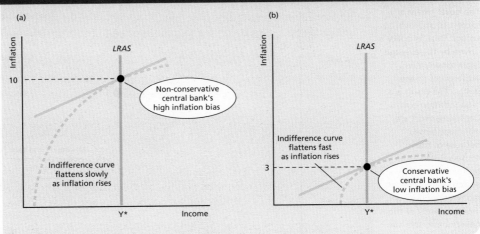

Things are different in the right frame. By construction, the inflationary equilibrium obtains at a much lower rate. The reason is the much flatter indifference curves of the conservative central bank. Its utility losses from higher inflation exceed the utility gains from the accompanying rise in income much earlier. Because of the central bank's reputation for inflation aversion, trade unions expect inflation to be low. The *DAS* curve thus lies fairly far down, and inflation actually turns out to be low.

Appointing a conservative central banker is one way of bringing a country's average inflation rate down. But this will only work under a second condition:

To reduce a country's inflation bias

- a conservative central banker must be appointed, and
- the central bank must be independent from the government.

central bank independence

The shielding of the central bank from political pressure, for example by granting its governors protection from government interference in their appointments, to allow it to conduct monetary policy free from government influence.

The role of central bank independence in reducing the inflation bias is illustrated in Figure 32.8.

A flat indifference curve represents the conservative central bank and gives rise to a low inflation bias. The steep indifference curve is representative of a non-conservative public, and hence of a government whose staying in office depends on public support. If such preferences determine monetary policy, they lead to a high inflation bias.

A country's *actual* inflation bias depends on who runs monetary policy. In some countries, the central bank acts on direct orders from the government. If it refuses to comply, its governors are replaced. With a government-dependent central bank it does not matter much whether the central bank is conservative or not. It is the government's non-conservative preferences that run the show. Monetary policy will have an expansionary slant, and inflation will be high on average.

Other countries have passed laws that prohibit governments from meddling with monetary policy. Central bank governors are shielded from political pressure by granting them terms in office that exceed the time horizon of governments, or by reducing government's say in appointment decisions. Such a central bank is said to be *independent* of the government. It may and will conduct monetary policy in accordance with its own conservative preferences, with the result that inflation will be low on average.

Figure 32.9 shows that the proposed negative relationship between central bank independence and average inflation receives strong backing from empirical data. This is probably one of the most influential results in macroeconomics of recent years.

Figure 32.8 Central bank independence and the inflation bias

The government is subject to approval by voters. Thus its policy is driven by the average (non-conservative) preferences of the public. The result is a high inflation bias. Central bankers are often appointed because of their conservative preferences. If they are permitted to conduct monetary policy independently of the government, this may lower the inflation bias substantially.

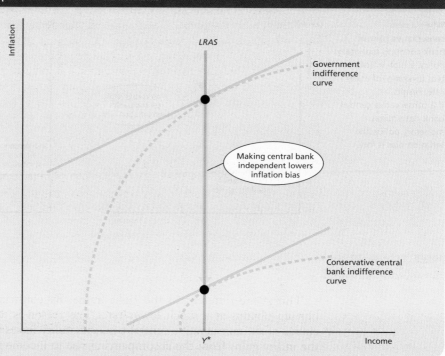

The scatter diagram shows that the countries with the most government-dependent central banks have suffered from the highest inflation rates since the end of the Bretton Woods era of fixed exchange rates. Examples are Greece, Italy and Spain, all with average inflation rates above 10%. On the other end of the spectrum are Germany and Switzerland, commonly thought to have the world's most independent central banks. Here average inflation rates were only between 3 and 4%.

Figure 32.9 Central bank independence and average inflation, 1973–1996

Countries with central banks that are very independent from the government had the lowest inflation rates in recent decades. Central bank independence is not measured easily. Researchers construct Indexes comprising things like who appoints central bankers (parliament or the government) or the length of their terms in office.
Source: IMF; V. Grilli, D. Masciandaro and G. Tabellini (1991).

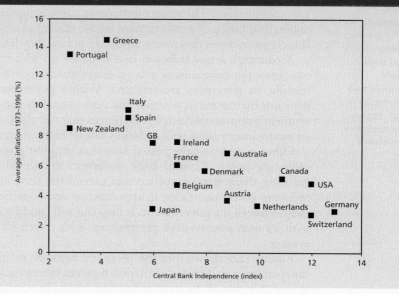

The design of the European Central Bank (ECB)

When drafting the European Central Bank law, EU governments seem to have been very receptive to arguments in favour of central bank independence. On paper, the ECB is better protected from political interference in monetary policy than any other central bank in history. In theory, this is supposed to provide a high degree of stability for the euro. It remains to be seen what will happen in practice, especially in periods of severe macroeconomic strain on incomes and labour markets. The price paid for an independent central bank is that monetary policy becomes unavailable for short-run stimulation. Should this price ever be considered too high, governments may end up revising the central bank law.

Importing a low inflation bias

There is an alternative to bringing down inflation by appointing a conservative central banker. Remember that the central bank (or the government) can only control the money supply if exchange rates are flexible. Only then can it set the inflation rate

Applications

Who wants the euro? The role of past inflation

In the second half of the 1990s, during the advent of the euro, a single European currency was not equally welcome in all 15 EU member states. At one end of the spectrum, 70% of Finland's public welcomed a single European currency and only 15% rejected it. At the other end, only 25% of Danes wanted the euro and a hefty 60% said no. Why this difference? If the public is rational, opinions should reflect the benefits that the euro is expected to bring for the country.

A key accomplishment expected from the introduction of the euro is that it will discipline monetary policy by transferring responsibility for it from the often quite government-dependent national central banks (with a high inflation bias) to the very independent European Central Bank (expected to have a low inflation bias). Who will benefit most from this rearrangement? It must be

those countries who, without the discipline effect of the Maastricht convergence criteria and the euro, had the highest inflation rates (revealing the least discipline in monetary policy) in the past. Their inflation rates will be reduced the most. So we should expect that:

The higher a country's inflation rate in the past, the more its public should welcome the euro.

The figure permits a direct examination of this hypothesis. The horizontal axis measures average inflation between 1980 and 1996 (measuring the monetary discipline produced by national central banks). The vertical axis measures the euro acceptance ratio ('yes' percentage over 'no' percentage).

The data support the above hypothesis. Countries like Italy and Greece, who had very high average

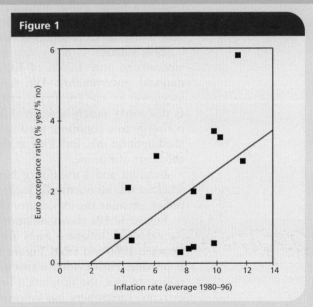

Figure 1

Euro acceptance ratio (% yes/% no) vs Inflation rate (average 1980–96)

inflation rates of about 12%, welcome the euro the most. Acceptance ratios are about 6 and 3, respectively. Austria and Germany, whose central banks were able to control inflation without the single currency, bluntly reject the euro. Acceptance ratios are only 0.5 and 0.6, respectively.

In terms of our discussion of the inflation bias and how it depends on

the independence of the central bank from government, the public in the EU member states seems to know quite well why it does or does not want the euro.

Source: M. Gärtner, 'Who wants the euro – and why? Economic explanations of public attitudes towards a single European currency', Public Choice, 93 (1997), pp. 487–510.

according to its own preferences. This privilege is lost once the exchange rate is fixed. Then the domestic inflation rate by and large follows the world inflation rate. This simple mechanism has facilitated convergence and reduction of inflation rates within the EMS. By fixing exchange rates and permitting Germany's Bundesbank to set the pace of monetary policy, EMS members effectively let the Bundesbank, with its proven record of low inflation and independence, set the inflation rate for the entire system. Other countries were able to import a rate of inflation below what their own governments and central banks could have achieved. Of course, this only works when exchange rates are perfectly fixed. Bands of fluctuation in the EMS, as well as parity realignments in the 1980s and the first half of the 1990s, prevented inflation rates from converging as much as they could have.

We have seen how monetary discipline can be achieved, and how the architects of European Monetary Union (EMU) have attempted to ensure price stability after the transition to the euro. We now turn to a similar discussion of fiscal policy and efforts to discipline government spending.

Deficit reduction and macroeconomic policy

The approach taken to discipline monetary policy in EMU is to hand monetary policy over to a policy maker with conservative preferences – the independent ECB. The ECB will conduct a single monetary policy for all member countries, guaranteeing very much the same inflation rates and leaving no loopholes for individual countries.

This solution is not viable for fiscal policy. Apart from the EU budget (which amounts to only 1.25% of EU GDP), fiscal policy continues to be conducted by national governments. We saw in Chapter 29 that a currency union provides incentives for one country to raise spending and output at the cost of fellow members. Is this worry purely academic? Wouldn't solidarity among members let fiscal policy converge to a common, reasonable stance, similar to that expected for inflation? To shed light on this, let's look at the experience of an actual currency union, right from the heart of Europe.

Belgium and Luxemburg have operated a currency union for decades. To see whether this automatically leads to convergence and discipline in monetary and fiscal policy, examine the experience documented in Figure 32.10.

Figure 32.10a shows inflation in both countries, an indicator of monetary policy. As expected, inflation rates were roughly the same in Belgium and Luxemburg between 1960 and 1998. Figure 32.10b shows budget deficits to indicate fiscal policy. It provides clear evidence that a common currency hardly guarantees common fiscal policy; in fact, the difference between Belgium and Luxemburg could not be more extreme. Luxemburg has followed the most conservative fiscal policy in all of Europe, running budget surpluses regularly. Belgium, by contrast, has been one of Europe's most generous public spenders. Thus specific measures are necessary to encourage fiscal restraint in a currency union.

The interaction between deficits and debt

debt ratio
The public debt as a percentage of GDP.

deficit ratio
The budget deficit as a percentage of GDP.

The Maastricht criteria draw attention to two indicators of fiscal policy performance and use them as disciplining devices: the **deficit ratio** and the **debt ratio**. The *deficit* is the difference between government spending and government revenues. Before now, we have argued that this can be approximated by $G - T$. In the current context we need to be more comprehensive. The government does not only spend on goods and services, G, but it also has to pay interest on its current debt.

This latter spending category, called the *debt service*, equals the debt times the interest rate, $r \times$ debt. The difference $G - T$ is called the *primary deficit*. The total deficit is the sum of the primary deficit and the debt service:

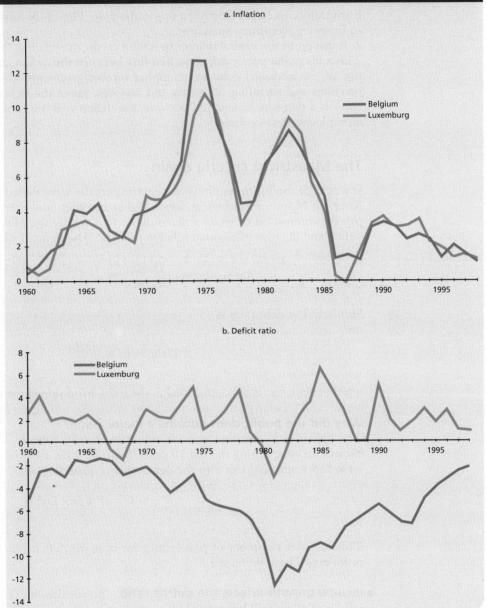

Figure 32.10 Monetary and fiscal policy in the currency union between Belgium and Luxemburg

The currency union between Belgium and Luxemburg teaches two lessons:
(1) Inflation rates are closely linked. So the currency union obviously harmonizes monetary policy.
(2) Government spending behaviour as measured by the deficit ratio could hardly be more different. So the currency union does not harmonize fiscal policy.
Source: IMF, OECD, Eurostat.

a. Inflation

Belgium
Luxemburg

b. Deficit ratio

Belgium
Luxemburg

$$\overbrace{\text{Deficit} \quad = \quad \underbrace{(G - T)}_{\substack{\text{Primary} \\ \text{deficit}}} \quad + \quad \underbrace{(r \times \text{Debt})}_{\substack{\text{Debt} \\ \text{service}}}}^{\text{Deficit adds to debt}}$$

Deficit adds to debt

Debt adds to deficit

The equation reveals the links between deficits and the debt. The deficit is that part of total government outlays, $G + (r \times \text{Debt})$, not covered by revenue, T. To deal with a deficit, there are only two things the government can do:

1. The government can ask the central bank for money to pay for excess spending. But since this raises the money supply, it leads to inflation. Governments, including European ones, have resorted to this in the past. The ECB, however, is not permitted to finance government spending.

2. It can go to the capital market to obtain credit in exchange for government bonds. This adds to the public debt, our first link between the deficit and the debt. But that's not all: an increased debt means higher interest payments which, at unchanged tax revenues and spending on goods and services, raises the deficit, the other link. So there is a two-way interaction between the deficit and the debt that may give rise to an explosive development.

The Maastricht criteria again

It would be foolish to require France to respect the same deficit limits as Luxemburg. After all, bigger economies generate higher incomes, and therefore find it easier to pay the interest on or repay a given debt. This is why the Maastricht criteria define deficit and debt limits as *ratios* relative to GDP. The deficit ratio is

$$\text{Deficit ratio} = \frac{\text{Deficit}}{\text{Income}} \equiv \frac{G - T + (r \times \text{Debt})}{Y}$$

Similarly, the debt ratio is

$$\text{Debt ratio} \equiv \frac{\text{Debt}}{Y}$$

which, as you see, is also embedded in the right-hand side of the deficit ratio equation.

Why did the public debt become a major issue?

The deficit ratio equation provides clues as to why concern about the public debt became an issue during the last 30 years. Suppose taxes are proportional to income: $T = t \times Y$. Substituting this into the deficit ratio equation gives:

$$\text{Deficit ratio} = \frac{G - tY + (r \times \text{Debt})}{Y}$$

This suggests a number of possibilities for how the deficit ratio, and hence the debt ratio, might have increased.

■ **Income growth affects the deficit ratio**   To see this, let $G = 40$, $r \times \text{Debt} = 10$, $t = 0.3$ and $Y = 100$. This gives a deficit ratio of

$$\frac{40 - (0.3 \times 100) + 10}{100} = 0.2 = 20\%$$

Now suppose income grows by 10% to 110. With all other factors unchanged, the deficit ratio drops to

$$\frac{40 - (0.3 \times 110) + 10}{110} \approx 0.15 = 15\%$$

This is just a simple exercise, playing with numbers. In the real world, other factors will not remain constant. For example, G usually rises as income rises. But what the numerical exercise demonstrates is that if income growth is reduced, this tends to drive up deficit ratios and, eventually, debt ratios. This is exactly the change that

European economies experienced. While average growth during the 1960s was 4.5%, it dropped to 3.0% in the 1970s, 2.2% in the 1980s and 2.1% in the 1990s.

■ **The interest rate affects the debt ratio** This can be seen directly from the deficit equation. As r goes up, interest payments on the existing debt go up. If all other factors remain the same, the deficit ratio goes up, feeding the debt ratio. Table 32.2 shows that EU countries were affected by such a change, with interest rates in the 1980s clearly higher than in the 1960s.

■ **Government spending on goods and services affects the debt ratio** If $G - T$, the primary deficit, rises, the deficit ratio goes up and the debt ratio eventually rises. There is no upward trend in the primary deficits run by European governments since the 1960s. While G has been rising in most cases, net taxes T kept pace, neutralizing the effect on the deficit.

From all this we can conclude that the dramatic surge in debt ratios experienced in many European countries during the 1980s and early 1990s must primarily be attributed to unfavourable changes in the economic environment: rising real interest rates and weakening growth. Higher deficit spending on goods and services was not a major source of debt explosions.

The EMU remedy: the pact for stability and growth

When they were still free to act at their own discretion, Europe's national governments did not appear to be moving towards a desirable degree of fiscal discipline. The Treaty of Maastricht *forced* prospective EMU members to strive for more discipline in pursuit of the criteria on deficit and debt. The thresholds enshrined in the treaty – 3% for the deficit ratio and 60% for the debt ratio – are certainly arbitrary. Yet almost everyone agrees that more discipline in government spending was a step in the right direction.

Table 32.2 Real interest rates in Europe between 1960 and 1997

Country	1970–79	1980–89	1990–97
Austria	2.32	4.35	4.11
Belgium	1.13	5.69	5.35
Denmark	3.44	6.82	5.78
France	−0.06	4.37	5.47
Germany	3.07	4.62	4.00
Ireland	−0.14	3.81	5.94
Italy	−1.42	3.26	6.34
Luxemburg	0.57	4.05	4.25
Netherlands	1.20	5.38	4.81
Norway	−1.23	4.07	5.25
Sweden	−0.03	4.10	4.55
Switzerland	0.12	1.42	1.96
UK	−0.70	3.74	4.66

Note: Real interest rates are the difference between government bond yields and inflation.

Source: IMF.

This view is based on similar arguments to the inflation bias phenomenon encountered previously in this chapter: The government is always willing to accept some loss of price stability (that is an inflation rate higher than 0%) in exchange for a boost of income beyond potential income Y^*. The dynamic AS curve provides this option. An increase in G boosts demand and income. G cannot rise indefinitely, as the money supply could, but government spending can be driven beyond what is deemed optimal for society. Where the inflation bias called for measures to discipline monetary policy, a *government spending bias* requires measures disciplining fiscal policy. Bringing down inefficiently high government spending frees income for better use. As we will see in Chapter 35 on economic growth, in these situations more fiscal discipline can raise potential income, Y^*.

To ensure that the progress achieved under the Maastricht deficit criterion does not vanish after entering EMU, the EU has agreed on a **pact for stability and growth**. As described in Chapter 29, the pact tries to move the 3% deficit criterion over to EMU by threatening to impose fines and other sanctions on countries that exceed this threshold.

The pros and cons of disciplining fiscal policy

Achieving fiscal discipline is an issue not unique to European countries. Since the mid-1980s, the USA has witnessed similar legislative action, including balanced budget amendments to the constitution. International organizations such as the World Bank and the International Monetary Fund routinely tie requirements of fiscal discipline to loans and other aid granted to countries in need. Let's now take stock of the benefits and the costs of disciplining fiscal policy.

The pros of fiscal discipline

■ **Reduced risk of inflation** An increase in government spending on goods and services raises the price level, but it cannot account for sustained inflation. As we have learned, sustained inflation requires a constantly growing money supply. However, public deficits may cause inflation indirectly. As we know, a deficit can be financed either by going into debt or by printing money. If the government wants to avoid running up its debt still further, it may pressure the central bank to accommodate the government deficit with a monetary expansion. Part of the purpose of the EMU pact on stability and growth is to prevent this from happening.

■ **Lower interest rates** If the government participates as a borrower in the capital market, it is likely to drive up interest rates. The experience of Belgium and Luxemburg lends some support to this. The more the Belgian deficit ratio exceeded that of Luxemburg, the more Belgian interest rates exceeded Luxemburg's (see Figures 32.10b and 32.11). In a currency union, such gaps can only open if financial investors consider loans to the Belgian government more risky than loans to Luxemburg. Otherwise Belgian interest rates would pull up Luxemburg's as well. To prevent this from happening, the Maastricht treaty includes a **no-bailout clause**, stating that neither the EU nor national governments are allowed to rescue a country from going bankrupt.

■ **Higher potential income** When a government deficit is financed by lending from the public, it is likely to crowd out some private investment. This is particularly clear from a global-economy perspective. There, the government's lending desires compete directly for household saving with firms needing funds to finance investment projects. Given a level of saving, private investment goes down when the government deficit goes up. With lower investment the country has to make do with a smaller capital stock, and hence with lower output, even when all factors of production are employed. We will look at this in more detail in Chapter 35.

---

pact for stability and growth
An agreement between EU member states made at the December 1996 Dublin summit and subsequent meetings, designed to ensure a long-term orientation of fiscal policy. In essence, the pact aims to prevent members from running excessive budget deficits.

no-bailout clause
A clause in the Maastricht treaty preventing the EU and national governments from rescuing a member country from bankruptcy.

Figure 32.11 National interest rates in a currency union: Belgium and Luxemburg, 1960–1998

According to the experience of Belgium and Luxemburg interest rates in a currency union move together, but need not be exactly the same. Comparing this graph with Belgium's budget deficit shown in Figure 32.10b, it appears that in times of extreme deficits the Belgian interest rate was driven above Luxemburg's.
Source: IMF.

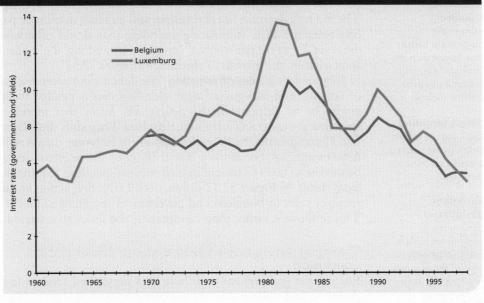

The cons of fiscal discipline

■ **Income losses during adjustment**   To bring a deficit ratio of, say, 9.5%, as Italy still had in 1993, in line with the Maastricht requirements, government spending needs to be reduced or taxes must be raised. We saw in Chapter 31 that such contractionary fiscal policy throws the country into a recession. Although this is only a temporary effect, it is particularly unwelcome in times of lacklustre growth and high unemployment, a common experience for EU members in the 1990s.

■ **Fiscal policy lost as stabilization tool**   In a world with no deficit targeting, the government makes decisions each year about how much to spend and how much to tax. The deficit is both the result of these decisions and of the state of the economy. With a 3% ceiling or a **balanced budget rule** the roles are reversed. The size of the deficit is set (or limited) in advance. Taxes and government spending must be adjusted to produce this deficit.

balanced budget rule
Requiring the government by law to balance the budget – either each year or on average over two or three years.

What difference does it make whether the Maastricht treaty chooses a target deficit, forcing the government to adjusts spending and taxes, or instead governments decide how much to spend and tax, letting the deficit adjust itself? The difference may be substantial. Consider a leftward shift of the *AD* curve caused by a negative demand shock, or a leftward shift of the *AS* curve caused by a rise in oil prices. Usually, governments decide in such cases to raise government spending to lessen the income drop. A balanced budget rule does not permit countercyclical fiscal policy aimed at income stabilization. The Maastricht 3% ceiling may leave a little leeway. If the government runs a surplus or a balanced budget during normal times, it may be able to raise spending somewhat when a recession hits.

■ **Loss of automatic stabilization**   The cost of fixing the deficit ratio goes beyond even the loss of fiscal policy as a stabilization instrument. Consider again a negative demand shock. The leftward shift of the *AD* curve lowers aggregate output (income), which causes the deficit ratio to increase twofold: first, because tax revenue drops and transfer payments rise; second, because income is lower.

automatic stabilizer

Items in the government budget that change with the state of the economy in such a way as to stabilize income.

deficit targeting

Requiring the budget deficit (ratio) not to exceed a specified threshold.

automatic destabilizer

Items in the government budget that change with the state of the economy in such a way as to destabilize income.

In a world without deficit targeting, the increase in the deficit during contractions provides an **automatic stabilizer** for the economy. (Review Chapter 24 if this is hazy.) The induced decrease in tax revenues and increase in transfer payments tends to boost consumer incomes, stimulating spending that would otherwise be weak. Thus, the decrease in aggregate output (income) caused by the negative shock is lessened somewhat by the growth of the deficit (Figure 32.12).

In a world with **deficit targeting**, the deficit ratio must not rise. Some combination of tax increases and government spending cuts is needed to offset what would otherwise be an increase in the deficit. We know that increases in taxes or cuts in spending are contractionary in themselves. They shift the *AD* curve still further to the left. Consequently, the drop in income will be larger than it would have been without deficit targeting, because the initial effect of the negative demand shock is worsened by the rise in taxes or the cut in government spending required to keep the deficit ratio from rising. As Figure 32.12 shows, deficit targeting acts as an **automatic destabilizer**. It requires taxes to be raised and government spending to be cut during a contraction. This reinforces, rather than counteracts, the shock that started the contraction.

Conclusion

Forcing the government to adhere to a prescribed level of fiscal discipline has both desirable and undesirable macroeconomic consequences. Nonetheless, the EU has decided that fixed ceilings, as initially laid down in the Treaty of Maastricht, provide the only way to induce governments to keep the deficit in check. If this is true, there is clearly a trade-off. We can have the discipline and bear the macroeconomic costs, or not have the discipline and not bear the costs. This trade-off is part of the debate regarding the Maastricht criteria and EMU's pact on stability and growth.

Figure 32.12 Deficit targeting as an automatic destabilizer

Deficit targeting changes the way the economy responds to negative demand shocks because it does not allow the deficit to increase. The result is a smaller deficit, but a larger decline in income than would otherwise have occurred.

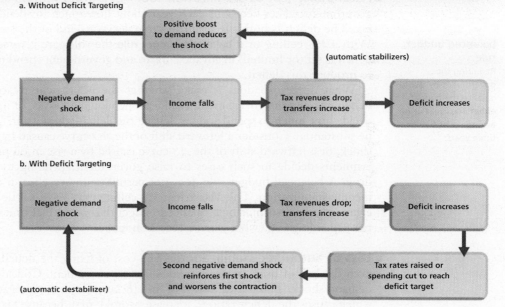

Summary

The european union and the treaty of maastricht: a brief history of european integration

1. The key dates in the history of European integration are the founding of the EEC in 1958, the installation of the EMS in 1979, the treaty of Maastricht on European Economic and Monetary Union in 1993, and the move to a single currency starting in 1999.

The Maastricht treaty

2. The biggest impact of the Maastricht treaty came from its convergence criteria. These forced prospective EMU members to reduce budget deficits and the public debt, lower inflation and interest rates, and to maintain EMS membership prior to EMU for a minimum of two years. The thrust of these criteria aimed at disciplining monetary and fiscal policy. All 11 aspiring members met the criteria in 1997.

3. The 'Pact for stability and growth' aims to ensure that EMU members do not run deficits in excess of 3% of GDP after the transition to a common currency. Violations are only tolerated in the case of severe recessions. Otherwise, sanctions may be levied on countries that do not comply.

Central bank behaviour and monetary policy

4. A compact way to represent the macroeconomic preferences of the public and of policy makers is by stating that they *like income and dislike inflation*. These preferences can be represented by indifference curves in an inflation–income diagram.

5. Monetary policy can always control inflation when exchange rates are flexible. But policy makers may not want to bring inflation down to zero, leaving the economy stuck with an inflation bias.

6. Ways to reduce an economy's inflation bias are (1) to select a conservative central banker and make them independent of the government, or (2) to fix the exchange rate to the currency of a country with a proven record of maintaining price stability.

Deficit reduction and macroeconomic policy

7. There is a dynamic interaction between the government deficit and the public debt: high deficits add to the debt; high debt calls for high interest payments, raising the deficit.

8. In most European countries, the deficit and the debt rose in the 1980s not because of higher government spending on goods and services, but because of a change in the macroeconomic environment.

9. By analogy to the inflation bias in monetary policy, policy makers' preferences may give rise to a spending bias.

10. The 'Pact for stability and growth' uses guidelines and sanctions to discipline government spending after the start of European Monetary Union.

Review Terms and Concepts

automatic destabilizer
automatic stabilizer
balanced budget rule
central bank independence
debt criterion
debt ratio
deficit criterion
deficit ratio
deficit targeting
EMS membership criterion

European Commission
indifference curves
inflation bias
inflation criterion
interest rate criterion
Maastricht convergence criteria
macroeconomic preferences of the government
no-bailout clause
pact for stability and growth

Problem Set

1. Some people argue that the national debt is not a problem because the country 'owes the debt to itself'. Who actually owns the national debt? Does this mean that the debt is not a problem?

2. List the Maastricht criteria. Explain carefully the rationale for each of them. Does the country you live in satisfy each of them? If your country participates in the monetary union, which criterion was the most difficult to satisfy? If your country does not participate, which criterion would it find most difficult to satisfy?

3. You are given the following information about the economy of Macary in 1996 (all amounts are in billions of macs):

Consumption function: $C = 100 + 0.8\,Y_d$
Taxes: $T = -150 + 0.25Y$
Investment function: $I = 60$
Disposable income: $Y_d = Y - T$
Government spending: $G = 80$
Equilibrium: $Y = C + I + G$

Hint: the deficit is given by $D = G - T = G - (-150 + 0.25Y)$.

a. Find equilibrium income. Show that the government budget deficit (the difference between government spending and tax revenues) is 5 billion.
b. The Macarian parliament passes a law that requires that the deficit be zero this year. If the budget adopted by parliament has a deficit that is larger than zero, the deficit target must be met by cutting spending. Suppose spending is cut by 5 billion (to 75 billion). What is the new value for equilibrium GDP? What is the new deficit? Explain carefully why the deficit is not zero.
c. Suppose that the new law is not in effect and that planned investment falls to $I = 55$. What is the new value of GDP? What is the new government budget deficit? What happens to GDP if the law is in effect and spending is cut to reach the deficit target? (*Hint*: spending must be cut by 21.666 billion to balance the budget.)

4. Some people argue that governments should be required always to balance their budgets. Would this be stabilizing or destabilizing?

5. How do the slopes of the policy makers' indifference curves change as a result of the following shifts in voters' preferences?
a. Fighting inflation yields less political support than increasing output.

b. The public is entirely indifferent towards inflation.

6. Between 1997 and 1998, Ireland and Finland were growing at 10.5% and 6%, respectively. Commentators feared that their economies were seriously overheating, leading to higher inflation in the future.
a. What types of policies could their governments use to slow the economies? Why?
b. Both countries were also running budget surpluses in 1998. Why might this make it difficult to implement the policies advocated in problem (a)?
c. What type of monetary policy would the Irish and Finnish governments want the European Central Bank to adopt? Explain.

7. The text describes two ways by which a country can reduce the inflation bias.
a. Has your country adopted one of them?
b. Are there any costs associated with a reduction in the inflation bias?

8. Figure 32.9 showed a negative correlation between the degree of central bank independence and average inflation. The chapter suggests that the causality runs from central bank behaviour to inflation. Can you think of any reasons why the causality might run the other way – that is, from inflation to the degree of central bank independence?

9. During 1997, stock markets in Asia collapsed. Hong Kong was down nearly 30%, Thailand down 62%, Malaysia down 60%. Big drops were also experienced in Japan and Korea.
a. What impacts would these events have on the economies of the countries themselves? Explain your answer.
b. In what ways would you have expected these events to influence the European economies?
c. How might the spending of Asians on European goods be affected?
d. What is the effect on Europeans who have invested in these Asian countries?

33

Household and Firm Behaviour in the Macroeconomy

In Chapters 23 to 30, we considered the interactions of households, firms, the government and the rest of the world in the goods, money, foreign exchange and labour markets. The macroeconomy is complicated, and there is a lot to learn about these interactions. To keep our discussions as uncomplicated and transparent as possible, we assumed simple behaviour for households and firms – the two basic decision-making units in the economy. We assumed that household consumption (C) depends only on income and that firms' planned investment (I) depends only on the interest rate. We considered neither the simultaneity of household consumption and labour supply decisions nor the simultaneity of firms' investment and employment decisions.

Now that we understand the basic interactions in the economy, we can relax these assumptions. In the first section of this chapter, we present a more realistic picture of the influences on households' consumption and labour supply decisions. In the second section, we present a more detailed and realistic picture of the influences on firms' investment and employment decisions. We then use what we have learned to analyse further macroeconomic issues.

Households: consumption and labour supply decisions

In discussing household behaviour earlier, we assumed that consumption depends on current income alone. Although this idea, originating in Keynes's *General Theory of Employment, Interest and Money*, is a useful starting point, it is far from complete as a description of the consumption decision. We need to consider other theories of consumption.

The life-cycle theory of consumption

life-cycle theory of consumption

A theory of household consumption: households make lifetime consumption decisions based on their expectations of lifetime income.

The **life-cycle theory of consumption** is an extension of Keynes's theory. The basic idea of the life-cycle theory is that people make lifetime consumption plans. Realizing that they are likely to earn more in their prime working years than they earn earlier or later, they make consumption decisions based on their expectations of lifetime income. People tend to consume less than they earn during their main working years – they *save* during those years – and they tend to consume more than they earn during their early and later years – they *dissave*, or use up savings, during those years. Medical students generally have very low current incomes, for example, though few live in the poverty those incomes might predict. Instead, they borrow now and plan to pay back when their incomes improve.

The lifetime income and consumption pattern of a representative individual is shown in Figure 33.1. This person has a low income during the first part of her life, high income in the middle, and low income in retirement. Her income in retirement is not zero because she has income from sources other than her own labour – state pensions and other benefits, interest and dividends, and the like.

Figure 33.1 Life-cycle theory of consumption

In their early working years, people consume more than they earn. This is also true in the retirement years. In between, people save (consume less than they earn) to pay off debts from borrowing and to accumulate savings for retirement.

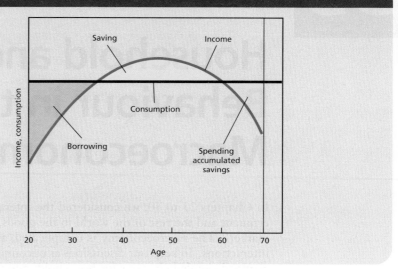

The consumption path as drawn in Figure 33.1 is constant over the person's life. This is an extreme assumption, but it illustrates the point that the path of consumption over a lifetime is likely to be much more stable than the path of income. We consume more than we earn early in our working careers. We do this by borrowing against future income, by taking out a car loan, or a mortgage to buy a house. This debt is repaid once our incomes have risen enough to pay off past borrowing without substantially lowering our consumption. The reverse is true for our retirement years. Here, too, our incomes are low. But because we consume less than we earn during our prime working years, we can save up a 'nest egg' allowing us to maintain an acceptable standard of living during retirement.

Fluctuations in wealth are also an important component of the life-cycle story. Many young households borrow in anticipation of higher income in the future. Some households actually have *negative wealth* – the value of their assets is less than the debts they owe. A household in its prime working years saves to pay off debts and to build up assets for its later years, when income typically goes down. Such households, whose assets are greater than the debts they owe, have *positive wealth*. With its wage earners retired, a household consumes its accumulated wealth. Generally speaking, wealth is negative to start with, then turns positive, and then approaches zero near the end of life. Wealth, therefore, is intimately linked to the cumulative saving and dissaving behaviour of households.

The key difference from the Keynesian theory of consumption is that the life-cycle theory suggests consumption and saving decisions are based not just on current income but on expectations of future income as well. The consumption behaviour of households immediately after the Second World War clearly supports the life-cycle story. Just after the war ended, income fell as wage earners moved out of war-related work. However, consumption spending did not fall commensurately, as Keynesian theory would predict. People expected to find jobs in other sectors, so they did not adjust their consumption spending to the temporarily lower incomes they were earning in the meantime.

The phrase **permanent income** is sometimes used to refer to the average level of your expected future income stream. If you expect your income to be high in the future (even though it may not be high now), your permanent income is said to be high. With this concept, we can sum up the life-cycle theory by saying that current consumption decisions are likely to be based on permanent income rather than on

permanent income

The average level of one's expected future income stream.

current income.[1] This means that policy changes such as tax-rate changes may have more of an effect on household behaviour if they are considered as permanent rather than temporary.

Although this insight enriches our understanding of the consumption behaviour of households, the analysis still lacks the other main household decision: the labour supply decision.

The labour supply decision

The size of an economy's labour force is of obvious importance. A growing labour force is one way in which national income/output can expand, and the larger the proportion of people who work, the higher is potential output per capita.

So far, we have said little about what determines the size of the labour force. Of course, demographics are a key; the number of children born between 1998 and 2000 will go a long way towards determining the potential number of workers between 20 and 22 years of age in 2018. In addition, immigration, both legal and illegal, plays a role.

But so does behaviour. Households make decisions about whether to work and how much to work. These decisions are closely tied to consumption decisions, because most households rely on wages and salaries to finance spending.

> Households make consumption and labour supply decisions simultaneously. Consumption cannot be considered separately from labour supply, because it is by selling labour that you earn income to pay for your consumption.

As we discussed in Chapter 4, the alternative to supplying your labour in exchange for a wage or salary is leisure or other non-market activities. Non-market activities include bringing up children, going to university, looking after the home, or working as a subsistence farmer.

But what determines the quantity of labour supplied by a household? Among the list of factors are the wage rate, prices, wealth and non-labour income.

The wage rate

A changing wage rate can affect labour supply, but whether the effect is positive or negative is ambiguous.

For example, an increase in the wage rate affects a household in two ways. First, work becomes more attractive relative to leisure and other non-market activities. Because every hour spent in leisure now requires giving up a higher wage, the opportunity cost of leisure is higher. As a result, a higher wage leads to a larger labour supply – a larger workforce. This is called the *substitution effect of a wage rate increase*.

On the other hand, households who work are better off after a wage rate increase. By working the same number of hours as before, they earn more income. As long as leisure is a normal good, people with higher income will spend some of it on leisure by working less. This is the *income effect of a wage rate increase*.

When wage rates rise, the substitution effect suggests that people will work more, while the income effect suggests that they will work less. The net effect depends on which separate effect is more powerful. The data seem to favour the substitution effect. That is, higher wages lead to a larger labour supply, while lower wage rates usually lower the labour supply. This is what we assumed in Chapter 31 when we introduced the labour supply.

---

[1] *The pioneering work on this topic drew on Milton Friedman,* A Theory of the Consumption Function *(Princeton, NJ: Princeton University Press, 1957). In the mid-1960s, Franco Modigliani did closely related work, including the formulation of the life-cycle theory.*

Prices

Prices also play a major role in the consumption/labour supply decision. In our discussions of the possible effects of an increase in the wage rate, we have been implicitly assuming that the prices of goods and services do not rise at the same time. If the wage rate and all other prices rise simultaneously, the story is different. Things become clearer when we need to distinguish between the nominal wage rate and the real wage rate.

The **nominal wage rate** is the wage rate in current euros or pounds, or whatever the currency. When we adjust the nominal wage rate for changes in the price level, we obtain the **real wage rate**. The real wage rate measures what wages can buy in terms of goods and services. Workers do not care about their nominal wage; they care about the purchasing power of this wage – the real wage.

Suppose skilled workers in Manchester were paid a wage rate of £10 per hour in 1998. Now suppose their wage rate rose to £12 per hour in 1999, a 20% increase. If the prices of goods and services were exactly the same in 1999 as in 1998, the real wage rate would have increased by 20%. An hour of work in 1999 (£12) would have bought 20% more than an hour of work in 1998 (£10).

But what if the prices of all goods and services also increased by 20% between 1998 and 1999? The purchasing power of an hour's wages would not have changed. The real wage rate would not have increased at all. Twelve pounds in 1999 bought the same quantity of goods and services that £10 bought in 1998.

To measure the real wage rate, we use a price index to adjust the nominal wage rate. Chapter 22 presented several such indexes, including the consumer price index and the GDP price index.[2]

We can now apply the life-cycle theory to our wage/price story. According to life-cycle theory, people look ahead when making their decisions. In relation to real wage rates, this means that:

> Households look at expected future real wage rates as well as the current real wage rate when making their current consumption and labour supply decisions.

Consider the medical student who expects a high future income. This expectation obviously has an effect on current decisions about what to consume and whether or not to take a part-time job.

Wealth and non-labour income

Life-cycle theory says that wealth fluctuates over the life cycle. Households accumulate wealth during their working years to pay off debts accumulated when they were young and to support themselves in retirement. This role of wealth is clear, but the existence of wealth itself poses another question. Consider two households that are at the same stage in their life cycles and have pretty much the same expectations about future wage rates, prices and so on. They have identical life expectancies and both plan to bequeath the same amount. They differ merely in their wealth. As a result of a past inheritance, Household 1 has more wealth than Household 2. Which household is likely to have a higher consumption path for the rest of its life? Household 1, because it has more wealth to spread out over the rest of its life.

> Holding everything else constant (including the stage in the life cycle), the more wealth a household holds, the more it will consume, both now and in the future.

nominal wage rate

The wage rate in current euros or other applicable currency.

real wage rate

The amount that the nominal wage rate can buy in terms of goods and services.

[2]To calculate the real wage rate, we divide the nominal wage rate by the price index. Suppose the wage rate rose from £5 per hour in 1984 to £9 per hour in 1994 and the price level rose 50% during the same period. Using 1984 as the base year, the price index would be 1.00 in 1984 and 1.50 in 1994. The real wage rate is W/P, where W is the nominal wage rate and P is the price level. The real wage rate is £5 in 1984 (£5/£1) and £6 in 1994 (£9/£1.50), using 1984 as the base year.

Now consider a household that has a sudden unexpected increase in wealth, perhaps after an inheritance from a distant relative. How is the household's consumption pattern affected? The household will increase its consumption, both now and in the future, allocating the inheritance over the course of the rest of its life.

An increase in wealth can also be looked upon as an increase in non-labour income. **Non-labour, or non-wage, income** is income from sources other than working – inheritances, interest, dividends, and transfer payments such as welfare and social security payments. As with wealth:

> An unexpected increase in non-labour income will have a positive effect on a household's consumption.

non-labour, *or* non-wage, income
Any income received from sources other than working – inheritances, interest, dividends, transfer payments, and so on.

What about the effect of an increase in wealth or non-labour income on labour supply? We know that an increase in income results in an increase in the consumption of normal goods, including leisure. Therefore, an unexpected increase in wealth or non-labour income results in both an increase in consumption and an increase in leisure. With leisure increasing, labour supply must fall, so:

> An unexpected increase in wealth or non-labour income leads to a decrease in labour supply.

This point should be obvious. If I win a million euros in the national lottery, I will probably work less in the future than I otherwise would have done.

Interest rate effects on consumption

Recall that the interest rate influences a firm's investment decision. A higher interest rate leads to a low level of planned investment, and vice versa. This was a key link between the money market and the goods market, and it was the channel through which monetary policy had an impact on planned aggregate expenditure.

We can now expand on this link: the interest rate also affects household behaviour. Consider the effect of a fall in the interest rate on consumption. A fall in the interest rate lowers the reward to saving. When the interest rate falls from 10% to 5%, I earn 5 pence, say, instead of 10 pence per year on every pound saved. This means that the opportunity cost of spending a euro today (instead of saving to consume it plus the interest income a year from now) has fallen. I will substitute towards current consumption and away from future consumption when the interest rate falls: I consume more today and save less. A rise in the interest rate leads me to consume less today and save more. This effect is called the *substitution effect*.

There is also an *income effect* of an interest rate change on consumption. If a household has positive wealth and is earning interest on that wealth, a fall in the interest rate lowers interest income. This is a decrease in non-labour income, which, as we just saw, has a negative effect on consumption. For households with positive wealth, the income effect works in the opposite direction from the substitution effect. By contrast, if a household is a debtor paying interest on its debt, a fall in the interest rate leads to a fall in interest payments. Debtor households are better off and will consume more. In this case, the income and substitution effects work in the same direction. Typically, the total household sector has positive wealth, and so in the aggregate the income and substitution effects work in opposite directions.

On balance, the data suggest that the substitution effect dominates the income effect, so that the interest rate has a negative net effect on consumption. There is also some evidence, however, that the income effect is getting larger over time. In most countries, households own most of the national government's debt, and in most countries the size of this debt has increased dramatically in the last 20 years. Changes in government interest payments, and thus changes in household interest income, are now larger at a given interest rate than before. This leads to a larger income effect for a given change in interest rates.

Government effects on consumption and labour supply: taxes and transfers

The government influences household behaviour primarily through tax rates and transfer payments. When the government raises tax rates, after-tax real wages decrease, reducing consumption. When the government lowers tax rates, after-tax real wages increase, increasing consumption.

A change in tax rates also affects labour supply. If the substitution effect dominates, as we are assuming, then an increase in tax rates, which lowers after-tax wages, will lower labour supply. A decrease in tax rates will increase labour supply.

Transfer payments are payments such as social security benefits, state pensions and welfare benefits. An increase in transfer payments is an increase in non-labour income, which has a positive effect on consumption and a negative effect on labour supply. Decreases in transfer payments reduce consumption and increase labour supply. Figure 33.2 summarizes these results.

A possible employment constraint on households

So far, our discussion of the labour supply decision has proceeded as if households were free to choose how much to work each period. If a household member decides to work five additional hours per week at the current wage rate, we have assumed that the person *can* work five hours more – that work is available. If someone who has not been working decides to work at the current wage rate, we have assumed that the person *can find a job*.

There are times when these assumptions do not hold. For example, during the Great Depression, unemployment rates in the USA reached 25% of the labour force. (Incidentally, this event led to the birth of macroeconomics in the 1930s.) Spain reached similar unemployment rates in the 1990s. And some 4 million people are currently looking for work in Germany alone.

All households face a budget constraint, regardless of the state of the economy. This budget constraint determines which bundles of goods are available to a household and which are not. It is determined by income, wealth and prices. When there is unemployment, some households feel an additional constraint. Some people may want to work 40 hours per week at the current wage rates yet only find part-time work. Others may find no work at all.

How does a household respond when it cannot work as much as it would like? It consumes less. If your current wage rate is €10 per hour, you normally work 40 hours a week and your average tax rate is 20%, your after-tax wage income is €340 per week. You are likely to spend much of this income during the week. If you are out of work, this income is not available, and you have less to spend.

You will spend something out of non-labour income, or perhaps from assets that can be withdrawn or sold, such as savings deposits or stocks and bonds. You may also be able to borrow. Even though you will spend something during the week, it is almost

Figure 33.2 The effects of government on household consumption and labour supply

The effects are larger if they are expected to be permanent rather than temporary.

	Tax rates		Transfer payments	
	Increase	Decrease	Increase	Decrease
Effect on consumption	Negative	Positive	Positive	Negative
Effect on labour supply	Negative*	Positive*	Negative	Positive

*If the substitution effect dominates.

certain that you spend less than you would have at your usual income of €340 in after-tax wages.

> Households consume less if they are constrained from working.

unconstrained supply of labour

The amount that a household would like to work at the current wage rate if it could find the work is called its **unconstrained supply of labour**. The amount that the household actually works in a given period at current wage rates is called its **constrained supply of labour**.

A household's constrained supply of labour is not a variable over which it has any control. The amount of labour the household supplies is imposed on it by the workings of the economy. However, the household's consumption *is* under its control. We have just seen that the less a household works – that is, the smaller the household's constrained supply of labour – the lower its consumption. Constraints on the supply of labour are an important determinant of consumption when there is unemployment.

Keynesian theory revisited

Recall the Keynesian theory that current income determines current consumption. We now know that the consumption decision is made jointly with the labour supply decision and that the two depend on the real wage rate. It is incorrect to think consumption depends only on income, at least when there is full employment. But when there is unemployment, Keynes is closer to being correct because income is not determined by households. When there is unemployment, the level of income (at least, workers' income) depends exclusively on the employment decisions made by firms. There are unemployed workers willing to work at the current wage rate, and their income is in effect determined by firms' hiring decisions. This income affects current consumption, which is consistent with Keynes's theory. Keynesian theory is considered to apply to periods of unemployment. It was, of course, developed during such a period.

A summary of household behaviour

Clearly, household consumption depends on more than current income. Households determine consumption and labour supply simultaneously, and they look ahead when making their decisions.

> The following factors affect household consumption and labour supply decisions:
>
> - current and expected future real wage rates
> - the initial value of wealth
> - current and expected future non-labour income
> - interest rates
> - current and expected future tax rates and transfer payments

If households are constrained in their labour supply decisions, income is directly determined by firms' hiring decisions. In this case, 'income' affects consumption in the traditional, Keynesian way.

Household behaviour in the UK

Let's look at UK data on some key aspects of household behaviour during the last three decades to illustrate and gauge the relevance of our discussion.

Household spending

Data on total consumption of households are recorded in the national income accounts. Figure 33.3a presents data for real GDP and private consumption expenditure. We find that consumption spending is somewhat smoother over time than

---

unconstrained supply of labour
The amount a household would like to work within a given period at the current wage rate if it could find the work.

constrained supply of labour
The amount a household actually works in a given period at the current wage rate.

Applications

Can one size fit all?

After EMU is launched on January 1st 1999, all member countries will share a common short-term interest rate. Some economists warn that a single monetary policy may be unwise if growth rates and hence inflationary pressures differ across Europe. For example, Ireland's economy grew by 10% last year; Germany's grew by 2.5%. This suggests that Ireland needs higher interest rates than Germany. But even if all countries were at the same point in the economic cycle, Europe's central bank would still have a problem. Differences in the way interest rates affect output across Europe mean that a given rise in rates would depress some economies more than others.

It has long been argued that British consumers are more sensitive to changes in interest rates than their counterparts in continental Europe, and that this is one good reason for the country to stay out of the single currency for now. But two recent studies find that there are also big differences in the way the expected EMU members respond to interest rates.

The first study . . . finds that in Austria, Belgium, Finland, Germany and The Netherlands the full effect of a rise in rates on output takes twice as long to happen as in France, Italy, Portugal and Spain. However, the final impact on output is twice as big in the first group of economies as in the second.

Another study . . . looks at just four likely EMU members. It concludes that the initial impact of a rise

in short-term interest rates is twice as high in Italy as in Germany and France and three times as high as in Spain. After two years, the gap between the countries narrows, but the output effect remains bigger in Italy. Thus although the two studies agree that interest-rate increases hurt some economies more than others, they disagree about which economies are most sensitive. . . .

Why do interest-rate changes affect countries' output differently? Higher rates influence economies in three main ways. First, they raise the cost of borrowing and so deter new investment or purchases of consumer durables on credit. Second, there is an 'income effect': debtors feel poorer because their debt-service costs are higher, whereas savers feel richer because their interest-income has gone up. Third, there is an exchange-rate effect: a rise in interest rates pushes up the currency and so squeezes exports.

Several things follow:

■ The higher the proportion of borrowing that is short term or at variable interest rates, the bigger the income effect and hence the bigger the drop in spending when interest rates rise. Lending on such terms is most popular in Austria, Britain and Italy (see chart). In contrast, in France, Germany, and the Netherlands, borrowing is mostly long term and at fixed interest rates.

■ Banks vary in the speed with which they pass on

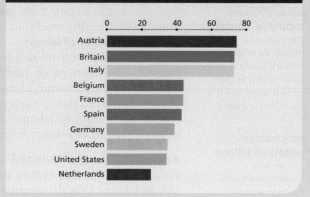

Figure 1 Drawing the short straw: lending to households and firms (% at short-term or variable interest rates)

Source: Bank for International Settlement.

rises in official interest rates to their customers. In Britain, The Netherlands and Spain short-term bank-lending rates are almost fully adjusted within three months. At the other extreme, even after 12 months French banks pass on only three-fifths of any increase in rates and German banks only three-quarters. . . .

■ The shape of firms' and households' balance sheets is important. Countries with lower levels of private-sector debt, like Italy, Germany and Belgium, will be hit less hard by a rise in interest rates than heavily indebted countries.

■ The more open an economy, the bigger will be the impact on output of an appreciation of the euro against the dollar as a result of higher interest rates. Ireland and Belgium are the most exposed: their exports outside the expected EMU area account for 34% and 21% of GDP respectively, compared with around 10% less in France, Germany, Italy and Spain.

. . . This analysis . . . suggests that when the European Central Bank (ECB) tightens monetary policy, the pain is likely to be distributed unevenly across the . . . 11 member countries. Germany has low levels of variable interest-rate debt, its banks are slow to pass on changes in official interest rates, and few of its exports are destined for countries outside the EMU area. In theory, it should slow by less in response to higher interest rates (and thus its inflation may stay higher) than a more open economy such as Ireland, or one with more borrowing at variable interest rates, such as Italy. . . .

Source: The Economist, 28 March 1998. The two studies mentioned in the extract are, first, R. Ramaswamy and T. Sloek, 'The real effects of monetary policy in the European Union: what are the differences?', IMF Working Paper No. 160, December 1997; and, second, R. Dornbusch and F. Giavazzi, 'A red letter day?', CEPR Discussion Paper No. 1804, February 1998.

Figure 33.3 UK GDP and consumption expenditures, 1970–1998

a. Income falls (by definition) during recessions. Consumption mirrors the movement of income. It fluctuates less than income, however.

b. Investment categories such as housing investment or car purchases are much more volatile over the business cycle than income itself. During recessions they fall dramatically.

Source: OECD.

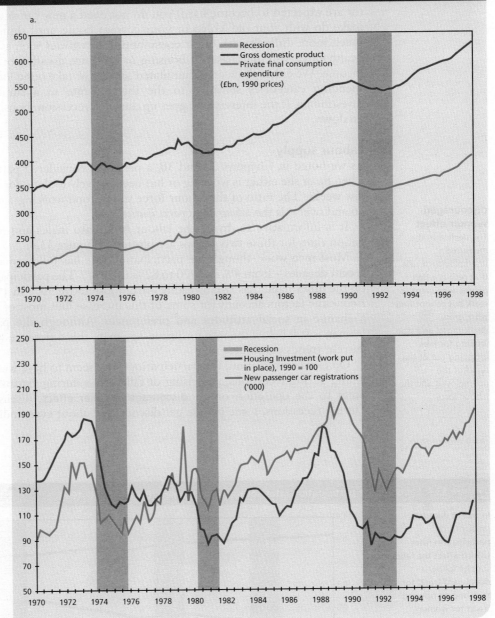

income. By and large, consumption spending reflects movements in income, though damped. In particular, consumption appears to fall much less, if at all, during recessions (shaded grey in the graph) than income. This is what we expect according to the permanent income hypothesis if households consider income sacrifices incurred during recessions as temporary.

Purchases of vehicles and housing

Not all categories of household spending are equally resistant during recessions. Figure 33.3b makes this point by plotting housing investment and new passenger car registrations. What makes these two categories special is that the items purchased are durable. In fact, purchases of new housing are considered an investment (included in I) from a macroeconomic perspective, even though they are undertaken by households. Although it has a strong investment component, the purchase of a new car is considered to be consumption spending (included in C).

Evidently, housing investment and car purchases fluctuate strongly, falling markedly on the advent of, and during, recessions. Why is this? When times are hard (or are expected to become hard) you do not need a new car or a new house; you can make do with your old Volvo or your current home until things get better. This is much more difficult with other consumption categories such as food, schooling and health care. Also, purchases of housing or a car are usually not made out of current income. We either draw on accumulated savings or take out a loan. That makes these spending categories sensitive to the interest rate in a similar way to business investments. If the interest rate goes up during a recession, housing and car purchases go down.

Labour supply

As we noted in Chapters 22 and 30, a person is considered part of the labour force when he or she either is working or has been actively looking for work during the past few weeks. The ratio of the labour force to the total working-age population – those 16 and over – is the *labour-force participation rate*.

It is informative to divide the labour force into males and females. The participation rates for these two groups are plotted in Figure 33.4.

Most men work, though the participation rate has followed a downward trend in recent decades – from 4% in 1970 to 82% in 1997.[3] The participation rate for women, on the other hand, has risen steadily – from just above 50% in 1970 to 71% in 1997. Economic factors account for some of this increase, but most of it is probably due to a change in social attitudes and preferences. Although the participation rate for women is still below the rate for prime-age men, this difference will narrow further if current trends continue.

On close examination, the participation rates seem to have weak cyclical features – falling during recessions, and rising or falling less during expansions. These features point to the operation of the **discouraged-worker effect**, discussed in Chapter 22. During recessions, some people get discouraged about ever finding a job. They stop

---

discouraged-worker effect

The decline in the measured unemployment rate that results when people who want to work but cannot find work grow discouraged and stop looking for jobs, dropping out of the ranks of the unemployed and the labour force.

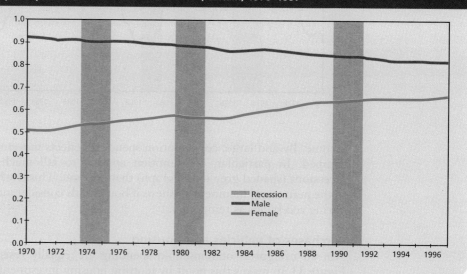

Figure 33.4 Labour-force participation rates for men and women, Britain, 1970–1997

In recent decades, labour force participation rates (which affect the labour supply) follow a downward trend for men and an upward trend for women. Many other countries experience the same.
Source: OECD.

[3]*A rate of 83% means that 83% of active men aged 15 to 64 were in the labour force.*

looking, and are not considered a part of the labour force. During expansions, people become encouraged. Once they begin looking for jobs, they are again considered a part of the labour force. If it exists at all, the discouraged-worker effect appears to be quite small. Certainly, the big picture is dominated by the long-run trends in society.

Firms: investment and employment decisions

We now turn to the behaviour of firms – the other major decision-making unit in the economy. When discussing firm behaviour in earlier chapters, we assumed that planned investment depends only on the interest rate. However, there are several other determinants of planned investment. We now discuss them as well as the factors that affect firms' employment decisions. Once again, microeconomic theory helps us gain some insights into the working of the macroeconomy.

In a market economy, firms determine which goods and services are available to consumers today and which will be available in the future, how many workers are needed for what kinds of jobs, and how much investment will be undertaken. In macroeconomic terms, the decisions of firms, taken together, determine output, labour demand and investment.

In this section, we concentrate on the input choices made by firms. By **inputs**, we mean all goods and services that firms purchase and turn into output. Two important inputs that firms use are capital and labour. These are often called **production factors**. (Other inputs are energy, raw materials and semi-finished goods.) Each period, firms must decide how much capital and labour to use in producing output. Let us first look at the decision about how much capital to use.

inputs The goods and services that firms purchase and turn into output.

production factors
A commonly used term for the inputs capital and labour.

Investment decisions

At any point in time, a firm has a certain stock of capital on hand. *Stock of capital* includes the factories and buildings (or 'plant') firms own, the equipment they need for production, and their inventories of partly or wholly finished goods. There are two basic ways a firm can add to its capital stock. One is by buying more machinery or building new factories or buildings. This kind of addition to the capital stock is **plant-and-equipment investment**.

The other way is to increase its inventories. When a firm produces more than it sells in a given period, the firm's stock of inventories increases.[4] This addition to the capital stock is **inventory investment**. Recall from Chapter 24 that unplanned inventory investment is different from planned inventory investment. When a firm sells less than it expected to, it experiences an unplanned increase in its inventories and is forced to invest more than it planned to. Unplanned increases in inventories result from factors beyond the firm's control. (We take up inventory investment in detail later in this chapter.)

plant-and-equipment investment
Purchases by firms of additional machines, factories or buildings within a given period.

inventory investment
Occurs when a firm produces more output than it sells within a given period.

Employment decisions

In addition to investment decisions, firms make *employment* decisions. At the beginning of each period, a firm has a certain number of workers on its payroll. Based on its current circumstances and production plans, the firm must decide whether to employ additional workers, keep the same number, or reduce its workforce by laying off some employees.

In Chapter 23, we argued that firms increase production when they experience unplanned decreases in inventory and reduce production when they experience

[4]*The change in inventories is exactly equal to the difference between production and sales. If a firm sells 20 units more than it produces in the course of a month, its inventories fall by 20 units; if it produces 20 units more than it sells, its inventories rise by 20 units.*

unplanned increases in inventory. We also alluded to increasing demand for labour when output grows. In reality, the set of decisions facing firms is more complex. The decision to produce more output is likely to involve additional demand for both labour *and* capital.

The demand for labour is very important in macroeconomics. If the demand for labour increases at times of less than full employment, the unemployment rate will fall. If the demand for labour increases when there is full employment, wage rates will rise. The demand for capital (which is partly determined by the interest rate) is important too. Remember that planned investment spending, I, is a component of planned aggregate expenditure. When planned investment spending increases, the result is additional output (income). We discussed the underlying investment multiplier effect in Chapter 23. Another aspect is that more capital increases labour's productivity and leads to growth.

Decision making and profit maximization

To understand the complex behaviour of firms in input markets, we must remember that firms' decisions always aim to maximize profits. The most important profit-maximizing decision that a firm faces is how to produce its output. In most cases, a firm must choose among alternative methods of production, or *technologies*. Different technologies generally require different combinations of capital and labour.

Consider a factory that manufactures shirts. The shirts could be made entirely by hand, with workers cutting the pieces of fabric and sewing them together. Or exactly the same shirt could be produced on complex machines that cut and sew hundreds of shirts per hour with very little human supervision. Between these two extremes lie dozens of alternative technologies.

Firms' decisions regarding the amount of capital and labour needed for production are closely related. If firms maximize profits, they will choose the technology that minimizes the cost of production. Logically, firms will choose the technology that is most efficient.

The efficiency of technology depends on the relative prices of capital and labour. A shirt factory in the Philippines wanting to increase production faces a large supply of relatively inexpensive labour. Wage rates in the Philippines are fairly low, whereas capital equipment must be imported and is very expensive. A shirt factory in the Philippines will probably choose a **labour-intensive technology** – one that requires a large amount of labour relative to capital. When labour-intensive technologies are used, expansions increase the demand for labour substantially but the demand for capital only modestly.

A shirt factory in Germany that decides to expand production is likely to buy a large amount of capital equipment and hire relatively few new workers. It will probably choose a **capital-intensive technology** – one that requires a large amount of capital relative to labour. German wage rates are quite high, wheras capital is plentiful.

> **labour-intensive technology**
>
> A production technique that uses a large amount of labour relative to capital.

> **capital-intensive technology**
>
> A production technique that uses a large amount of capital relative to labour.

Firms' decisions about labour demand and investment depend on the relative costs of labour and capital. The relative impact of an expansion of output on employment and on investment demand depends on the wage rate and the cost of capital.

Expectations and animal spirits

In addition to the cost of capital and the cost of labour, firms' expectations about the future play a big role in investment and employment decisions.

Time is a key factor in investment decisions. Capital has a life that typically extends over many years. A developer who builds an office tower is making an investment that will last (barring earthquakes or wars) for several decades. In deciding where to build a plant, a manufacturing firm is committing a large amount of resources to purchase capital that is expected to yield services over a long time. Furthermore, the decision to build a plant or to purchase large equipment must often be made years before the actual project is completed. While acquiring a small business computer may take only a few days, the planning process for developments in the centres of large cities is known to take decades.

For these reasons, investment decisions mean anticipating the future and forming expectations. Firms' expectation-formation involves numerous factors. At a minimum, a firm gathers information about the demand for its products, about what competitors are planning, about buyers and about the macroeconomy's overall health. A firm will hardly increase its production capacity if it does not expect to sell more in the future. Hilton will not put up a new hotel if it does not expect to fill the rooms at a profitable rate. Fiat will not build a new plant if it expects the Italian economy and other economies where it hopes to sell cars to enter a long recession.

Forecasting the future is fraught with dangers. Many events cannot be foreseen. Investments are always made on the basis of imperfect knowledge. Keynes pointed this out in 1936.

The outstanding fact is the extreme precariousness of the basis of knowledge on which our estimates of prospective yield have to be made. Our knowledge of the factors that will govern the yield of an investment some years hence is usually very slight, and often negligible. If we speak frankly, we have to admit that our basis of knowledge for estimating the yield ten years hence of a railway, a copper mine, a textile factory, a patent medicine, a cruise liner or a building in the City of London amounts to little and sometimes nothing.

Keynes concludes from this that much investment activity depends on psychology and on what he termed the **animal spirits of entrepreneurs**:

animal spirits of entrepreneurs
A phrase coined by Keynes to describe investors' feelings that have no objective relation with the economy.

Our decisions . . . can only be taken as a result of animal spirits. In estimating the prospects of investment, we must have regard, therefore, to nerves and hysteria and even the digestions and reactions to the weather of those upon whose spontaneous activity it largely depends.[5]

Because expectations about the future are subject to great uncertainty, they may change often. Thus animal spirits help to make investment a volatile component of GDP.

The accelerator effect

Expectations, at least in part, determine the level of planned investment spending. If businesses are optimistic, the level of investment is likely to be higher at any interest rate. If they are pessimistic, the level of planned investment will be lower. But what determines expectations?

One possibility borne out empirically is that expectations are optimistic when aggregate output (Y) is rising and pessimistic when aggregate output is falling.

accelerator effect
The tendency for investment to increase when aggregate output increases and to decrease when aggregate output decreases, accelerating the growth or decline of output.

At any given level of the interest rate, expectations are likely to be more optimistic and planned investment is likely to be higher when output is growing rapidly than when it is growing slowly or falling.

It is easy to see why. If firms expect future output to grow, they must plan now to add productive capacity. One indicator of future prospects is the current growth rate.

If this is true in reality, and evidence indicates that it is, the ultimate result will be an **accelerator effect**. If aggregate output (income) (Y) is rising, investment will increase even though the level of Y may be low. Higher investment spending leads to

[5]John Maynard Keynes, The General Theory of Employment, Interest, and Money (1936), First Harbinger edn (New York: Harcourt Brace Jovanovich, 1964), pp. 149, 152.

an added increase in output, further 'accelerating' the growth of aggregate output. If Y is falling, expectations are dampened, and investment spending will be cut even though the level of Y may be high, accelerating the decline.

Excess labour and excess capital effects

excess labour, excess capital
Labour and capital that are not needed to produce the firm's current level of output.

We must make one more point about firms' investment and employment decisions. Firms may sometimes choose to hold **excess labour** and/or **excess capital**. A firm holds excess labour (or capital) if it could reduce the amount of labour it employs (or capital it holds) and still produce the same amount of output.

Why would a firm want to employ more workers or have more capital on hand than it needs? Both labour and capital are costly – a firm must pay wages, and it forgoes interest on funds tied up in machinery or buildings. Why would a firm want to incur costs that yield no revenue?

To see why, suppose a firm suffers a sudden and large drop in sales, but it expects the low sales level to last only a few months, after which it believes they will pick up again. To avoid too large an increase in its stock of inventories the firm is likely to lower production in response to the sales change. With lower production the firm could get rid of some workers and machines, because it now needs less labour and less capital to produce the now lower level of output.

Alas things are not this simple. Decreasing its workforce and capital stock quickly can be costly for a firm. Abrupt cuts in the workforce hurt worker morale and increase personnel administration costs. Abrupt reductions in capital stock may be disadvantageous because of the difficulty of selling used machines. These types of costs are called **adjustment costs**, because they reflect the costs of adjusting to a new level of output. There are adjustment costs of increasing output as well. For example, it is usually costly to recruit and train new workers.

adjustment costs
The costs that a firm incurs when it changes its production level – for example, the administration costs of laying off employees or the training costs of hiring new workers.

Adjustment costs may be so large that a firm chooses not to decrease its workforce and capital stock when reducing production. The firm may choose to have more labour and capital on hand than is necessary to produce its current output, simply because getting rid of them would be more costly than keeping them. In practice, excess labour means workers are not working at their normal level of activity (more tea breaks and more idle time, for instance). Some of this excess labour may be trained so as to increase productivity once production picks up again.

The existence of excess labour and capital at any given moment will affect future employment and investment decisions. Suppose a firm has excess labour and capital resulting from a fall in sales and production. When production picks up again, the firm does not need to hire as many new workers or acquire as much new capital as it would otherwise need to.

The more excess capital a firm already has, the less likely it is to invest in new capital in the future. The more excess labour it has, the less likely it is to hire new workers in the future. In fact, if the firm finds itself holding excess capital, it may try to decrease its capital stock in the future, even if demand is actually increasing. The same is true for excess labour.

Inventory investment

We now turn briefly to the inventory-investment decision. This decision is quite different from the plant-and-equipment investment decision.

The role of inventories

Recall the distinction between a firm's sales and its output. If a firm can hold goods in inventory, then within a given period it can sell a quantity of goods different from the quantity of goods it produces. When a firm sells more (less) than it produces, its stock of inventories decreases (increases).

$$\text{Stock of inventories (end of period)} = \text{Stock of inventories (beginning of period)} + \text{Production} - \text{Sales}$$

Let a firm start the period with 100 umbrellas in inventory. If it produces 15 umbrellas during the period and sells 10 umbrellas, it will have 105 umbrellas (100 + 15 − 10) in inventory at the end of the period. A change in inventories is actually investment because inventories are counted as part of a firm's capital stock. In our example, inventory investment is a positive number: 5 umbrellas (105 − 100). When the number of goods produced is less than the number of goods sold, inventory investment is negative.

The optimal inventory policy

Let's examine consider firms' inventory decisions. Firms are concerned with what they are selling and producing now and in the future. At each point in time, a firm has some idea of how much it is going to sell in the current period and in future periods. Given these expectations and its knowledge of how much it has in stock, a firm must decide how much to produce in the current period.

Inventories are costly to a firm because they take up space and tie up funds that could be earning interest. However, if a firm's stock of inventories gets too low, the firm may have difficulty meeting the demand for its product. If demand increases unexpectedly, the firm may lose sales. The point between too low and too high a stock of inventory is called the **desired, or optimal, level of inventories**. At this level the extra cost (in lost sales) from slightly decreasing inventories is just equal to the extra gain (in interest revenue and decreased storage costs).

With no costs other than inventory costs, a firm would always aim to produce exactly the volume of goods necessary to meet its optimal stock of inventories at the end of the period. If the stock of inventory fell lower than desired, the firm would produce more than it expected to sell to bring the stock up. If the stock of inventory grew above the desired level, the firm would produce less than it expected to sell to reduce the stock.

There are other costs besides inventory costs. Large and abrupt changes in production can lead to costly adjustment. Production increases may lead to adjustment costs for hiring more labour and increasing the capital stock. If production decreases, there may be adjustment costs for laying off workers and decreasing the capital stock.

Because both holding inventories and changing production levels are costly, firms face a trade-off. Adjustment costs will lead a firm to smooth its production path relative to its sales path. This means production fluctuates less than sales, with changes in inventories to absorb the difference each period. However, there are also incentives not to stray too far from the optimal level of inventories, so fluctuations in production will not be eliminated completely.

Production will still fluctuate, though not as much as sales.

There are two other points. First, if a firm's stock of inventories is unusually or unexpectedly high, the firm is likely to produce less in the future than it would have, in order to decrease its high stock of inventories. In other words, although the stock of inventories fluctuates over time because production is smoothed relative to sales, at any point in time inventories may be unexpectedly high (low) because sales have been unexpectedly low (high).

An unexpected increase in inventories has a negative effect on future production, and an unexpected decrease in inventories has a positive effect on future production.

Second, firms can not know their future sales exactly. They have expectations of future sales, though these expectations will seldom turn out to be exactly right.

desired, or optimal, level of inventories
The level of inventory at which the extra cost (in lost sales) from reducing inventories by a small amount is just equal to the extra gain (in interest revenue and decreased storage costs).

This has important consequences. If sales turn out to be less than expected, inventories will be higher than expected, and there will be less production in the future. Furthermore, *future* sales expectations are likely to have an important effect on *current* production. If a firm expects its sales to be high in the future, it will adjust its planned production path accordingly. Even though a firm smooths production relative to sales, over a long period it must produce as much as it sells. If it did not, it would have an indefinitely falling stock of inventories.

> The level of a firm's planned production path depends on the level of its expected future sales path. If a firm's expectations of the level of its future sales path decrease, the firm is likely to decrease the level of its planned production path, including its production in the current period. Current production depends on expected future sales.

Because production is likely to depend on expectations of the future, animal spirits may play a role. If firms become more optimistic about the future, they are likely to produce more now. Keynes's view that animal spirits affect investment is also likely to apply to output.

A summary of firm behaviour

> The following factors affect firms' investment and employment decisions:
>
> ■ The wage rate and the cost of capital. (An important component of the cost of capital is the interest rate.)
> ■ Firms' expectations of future output.
> ■ The amount of excess labour and excess capital on hand.
>
> The most important points to remember about the relationship between production, sales, and inventory investment are:
>
> ■ Inventory investment (that is, the change in the stock of inventories) equals production minus sales.
> ■ An unexpected increase in the stock of inventories has a negative effect on future production.
> ■ Current production depends on expected future sales.

Firms in the UK

To close our discussion of firm behaviour, we now examine some aggregate investment and employment variables for Britain in the period from 1970 to 1998.

Investment

Gross investment and gross fixed capital formation are plotted in Figure 33.5a. Investment fared poorly during the three recessions after 1970. This observation is consistent with the observation that investment depends in part on output. An examination of the plot of real GDP in Figure 33.3 and the plot of investment in Figure 33.5a shows that investment generally tends to do poorly when GDP does poorly and does well when GDP does well.

Figure 33.5a also shows that investment fluctuates greatly. This is not surprising. The animal spirits of entrepreneurs are volatile by definition, and if they affect investment, it too will be volatile.

Employment

Employment in the private sector, plotted in Figure 33.5b, shows that employment fell in all three recessionary periods. This is consistent with the theory that

Figure 33.5 Investment and employment in Britain, 1970–1998

a. Investment (measured by gross investment or gross fixed capital formation) falls during recessions. It seems to depend in part on output.

b. Employment also falls during recessions. This reveals the link between employment and output. The fact that at the end of recessions investment returns while employment continues to fall may indicate rationalization efforts by firms while they move out of the recession.

Source: OECD.

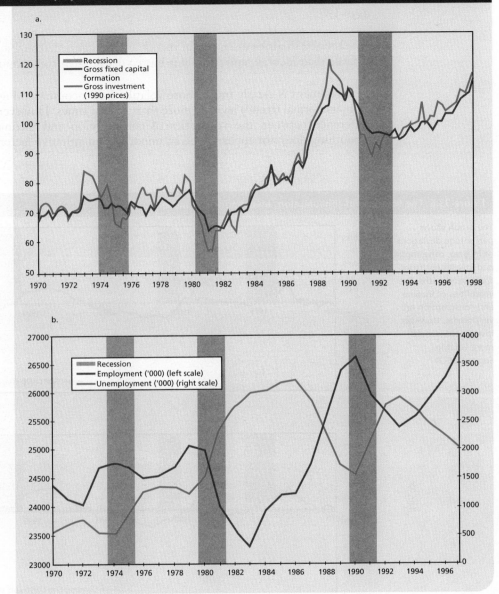

employment depends in part on output. Unemployment and employment usually move in opposite directions. Unemployment rises substantially during recessions, when output falls. This reflects *Okun's Law*. In the larger picture, though, unemployment rose substantially from 1974 to 1986, while employment fell very little.

The volatility of consumption, investment and income

Because there is saving, the marginal propensity to consume is less than 1. This means that when income moves, consumption moves along with it, but less so. Consumption smoothing, as suggested by the permanent income hypothesis, suppresses movements of consumption further, relative to movements of income. We therefore expect consumption to be less volatile than income.

The opposite is expected for investment. According to the accelerator hypothesis, investment is related to income growth $\Delta\%Y$. To take a numerical example, let $I = 5$

$\times \Delta\%Y$. If income grows by 1% in 1995 from 80 to 80.8, investment is 5 (= 5 × 1). If income grows by 2% in 1999 from 100 to 102, investment is 10 (= 5 × 2), twice as high as in 1995.

> The refined theories discussed in this chapter suggest that investment is more volatile than income, and income is more volatile than consumption.

Investment is clearly much more volatile than income (see Figure 33.6), deviating from its normal (trend) level by more than 25% at times. However, there is hardly any difference between the volatilities of consumption and income. So consumption smoothing does not appear to be an important quantitative factor in Britain.

Figure 33.6 The volatility of consumption, investment and income

The graph shows percentage deviations of income, consumption and investment from their trend paths. The volatilities of income and consumption are very similar. However, investment is much more volatile.
Source: OECD.

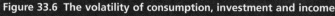

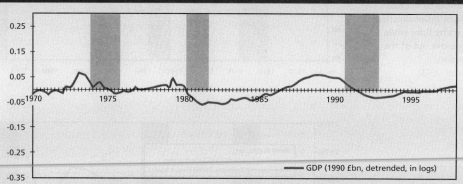

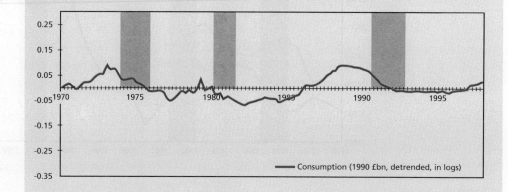

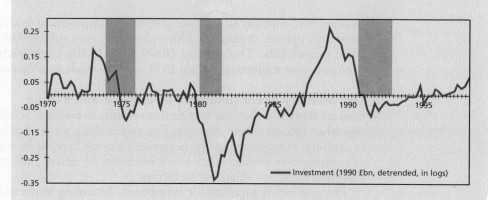

Productivity and the business cycle

We can use what we have just learned about firm behaviour to analyse movements in productivity. Productivity, sometimes called **labour productivity**, is defined as output per worker hour. If output is Y and the number of hours worked in the economy is H, then productivity is Y/H. Simply stated, productivity measures how much output an average worker produces in one hour.

Productivity fluctuates over the business cycle, tending to rise during expansions and to fall during contractions. The fact that firms sometimes hold excess labour helps to explain why productivity fluctuates in the same direction as output.

Figure 33.7 shows a hypothetical pattern of employment and output over time. Employment does not fluctuate as much as output over the business cycle. It is this pattern that creates the productivity fluctuations. During expansions in the economy, output rises by a larger percentage than employment and the ratio of output to workers rises. During downswings, output falls faster than employment and the ratio of output to workers falls.

The existence of excess labour when the economy is in a slump makes productivity as measured by the ratio Y/H fall. Is labour actually 'less productive' during recessions than before? Not really: a low Y/H merely reflects that firms choose to employ more labour than they need to. Some workers are in effect idle some of the time, even though they are considered as employed. They are not less productive in the sense of having less potential to produce output; it is just that they are not producing for part of the time that they are *counted* as working.

Productivity in the long run

Theories of long-run economic behaviour, which attempt to explain how and why economies grow over time, focus on productivity. *Output per worker* (or its closely related measure *GDP per capita*) is the key index of an economy's long-run performance. For example, in comparing how the economies of Britain and Japan performed over the past 98 years, we would begin by noting that Britain had a substantially higher income per person in 1900, while income per person in Japan is now clearly higher. As we shall see in Chapter 35, the growth of output per worker depends on technological progress and on the growth of the capital stock, both of which have been more rapid in Japan than in Britain.

Figure 33.7 Employment and output over the business cycle

In general, employment does not fluctuate as much as output over the business cycle. As a result, measured productivity (the output-to-labour ratio) tends to rise during expansionary periods and decline during contractionary periods.

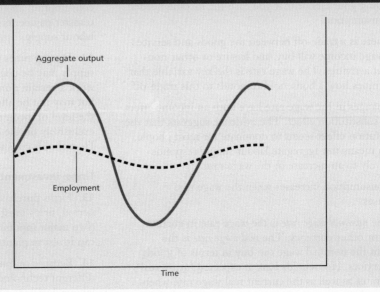

Aggregate output

Employment

Time

For now, the crucial point is this:

> Productivity figures can be misleading when used to diagnose the short-run health of the economy, because business cycles distort productivity measurements. Output per worker falls in recessions simply because firms hold excess labour. Output per worker rises in expansions because firms put the excess labour back to work. Neither of these conditions has anything to do with the economy's long-run potential to produce output.

Summary

Households: consumption and labour supply decisions

1. The Keynesian theory of consumption holds that household consumption (C) is positively related to income: the more you earn, the more you are likely to consume. Keynes also believed that high-income households consume a smaller proportion of their income than low-income households. The proportion of income households spend on consumption is measured by the *average propensity to consume (APC)*, which is equal to consumption divided by income (C/Y).

2. The *life-cycle theory of consumption* says that households make lifetime consumption decisions based on their expectations of lifetime income. Generally, households consume an amount less than their incomes during their prime working years, and an amount greater than their incomes during their early working years and after they have retired.

3. Households make consumption and labour supply decisions simultaneously. Consumption cannot be considered separately from labour supply, because it is by selling your labour that you earn the income needed for consumption.

4. There is a trade-off between the goods and services that wage income will buy, and leisure or other non-market activities. The wage rate is the key variable that determines how a household responds to this trade-off.

5. Changes in the wage rate have both an income effect and a substitution effect. The evidence suggests that the substitution effect seems to dominate for most people, which means the aggregate labour supply responds positively to an increase in the wage rate.

6. Consumption increases when the wage rate increases.

7. The *nominal wage rate* is the wage rate in current euros or other currency. The *real wage rate* is the amount the nominal wage can buy in terms of goods and services. Households look at expected future real wage rates as well as the current real wage rate when making their consumption and labour supply decisions.

8. Holding all else constant (including the stage in the life cycle), the more wealth a household has, the more it will consume, both now and in the future.

9. An unexpected increase in *non-labour income* (any income received from sources other than working, such as inheritances, interest and dividends) will have a positive effect on a household's consumption and will lead to a decrease in labour supply.

10. The interest rate also affects consumption, though the direction of the total effect depends on the relative sizes of the income and substitution effects. There is some evidence that the income effect is larger now than it was, making monetary policy less effective than it used to be.

11. The government influences household behaviour mainly through tax rates and transfer payments. If the substitution effect dominates, an increase in tax rates lowers after-tax income, decreases consumption and decreases the labour supply; a decrease in tax rates raises after-tax income, increases consumption and increases labour supply. Increases in transfer payments increase consumption and decrease labour supply; decreases in transfer payments decrease consumption and increase labour supply.

12. During times of unemployment, households' labour supply may be constrained. Households may wish to work a certain number of hours at current wage rates but may not be allowed to do so by firms. In this case, the level of income (at least workers' incomes) depends exclusively on the employment decisions made by firms. Households consume less if constrained from working.

Firms: investment and employment decisions

13. Firms purchase *inputs* to produce outputs. Each period, firms must decide how much capital and labour (two major inputs) to use in producing output. Firms can invest in plants and equipment or in inventory.

14. Because output can be produced using many different technologies, firms must make capital and labour decisions simultaneously. A *labour-intensive* *technique* uses a large amount of labour relative to capital. A *capital-intensive technique* uses a large amount of capital relative to labour. Which technology is used depends on the wage rate and the cost of capital.

15. Expectations affect investment and employment decisions. Keynes used the term *animal spirits of entrepreneurs* to refer to investors' feelings.

16. At any level of the interest rate, expectations are likely to be more optimistic and planned investment is likely to be higher when output is growing rapidly than when it is growing slowly or falling. The result is an *accelerator effect* that can cause the economy to expand more rapidly during an expansion and contract more quickly during a recession.

17. *Excess labour and capital* are labour and capital not needed to produce a firm's current level of output. Holding excess labour and capital may be more efficient than laying off workers or selling used equipment. The more excess capital a firm has, the less likely it is to invest in new capital in the future. The more excess labour it has, the less likely it is to hire new workers in the future.

18. Holding inventories is costly to a firm because they take up space and they tie up funds that could be earning interest. Not holding inventories can cause a firm to lose sales if demand increases. The *desired*, or *optimal, level of inventories* is the level at which the extra cost (in lost sales) from lowering inventories by a small amount is equal to the extra gain (in interest revenue and decreased storage costs).

19. An unexpected increase in inventories has a negative effect on future production, and an unexpected decrease in inventories has a positive effect on future production.

20. The level of a firm's planned production path depends on the level of its expected future sales path. If a firm's expectations of its future sales path decrease, the firm is likely to decrease the level of its planned production path, including its actual production in the current period.

21. *Productivity, or labour productivity*, is output per worker – the amount of output produced by an average worker in one hour. Productivity fluctuates over the business cycle, tending to rise during expansion and fall during contractions. Although workers are less productive during contractions this does not mean that they have less potential to produce output; it means that excess labour exists and workers are not working at their capacity.

Review Terms and Concepts

accelerator effect
adjustment costs
animal spirits of entrepreneurs
capital-intensive technology
constrained supply of labour
desired, or optimal, level of inventories
discouraged-worker effect
excess capital
excess labour
inputs
inventory investment

labour productivity
labour-intensive technology
life-cycle theory of consumption
nominal wage rate
non-labour, or non-wage, income
permanent income
plant-and-equipment investment
production factors
real wage rate
unconstrained supply of labour

Problem Set

1. In 1998, wage increases averaged 5% in Norway, but consumer prices rose by only 2.6%. How much has the real wage increased? What effect would rising wages probably have on the labour supply? Explain your answer using income and substitution effects.

2. In June 1998, the Bank of England raised interest rates in an effort to slow the British economy's rate of growth. Its goal: to prevent inflation.
a. What direct effects do higher interest rates have on household and firm behaviour?

b. Explain why higher interest rates would reduce the value of existing fixed rate bonds held by the public.
c. Some economists argue that the wealth effect of higher interest rates on consumption is as important as the direct effect of higher interest rates on consumption. Explain what economists mean by 'wealth effect on consumption' and illustrate with *AS/AD* curves.

3. In 1993, President Clinton proposed and Congress enacted an increase in US taxes. One of the increases was in the income tax rate for higher-income wage earners. The Republicans claimed that reducing the rewards for working (the net after-tax wage rate) would lead to less work effort and a lower labour supply. Supporters of the increase replied that this criticism was baseless because it 'ignored the income effect of the tax increase (net wage reduction)'. Explain what these supporters meant.

4. Graph the following two consumption functions:

$$C = 300 + 0.5Y$$
$$C = 0.5Y$$

a. For each function, calculate and graph the average propensity to consume (*APC*) when income is €100, €400 and €800.

b. In both examples, what happens to the *APC* as income rises?

c. In both examples, what is the relationship between the *APC* and the marginal propensity to consume?

d. Under consumption function (1), a family with an income of €50,000 consumes a smaller proportion of its income than a family with an income of €20,000; yet if we take a euro of income away from the rich family and give it to the poor family, total consumption by the two families does not change. Explain how this could be.

5. During the late 1990s, the price of houses in Ireland increased rapidly. What impact would you expect increases and decreases in home value to have on the consumption behaviour of home owners? Explain. In what ways might events in the housing market influence the rest of the economy through their effects on consumption spending? Be specific.

6. Adam Smith is 45 years old. He has assets (wealth) of €20,000 and has no debts or liabilities. He knows he will work for 20 more years, and will live for five years after that during which he will earn nothing. His salary each year for the rest of his working career is €14,000. (There are no taxes.) He wants to distribute his consumption over the rest of his life in such a way that he consumes the same amount each year. He cannot consume in total more than his current wealth plus the sum of his income for the next 20 years. Assume that the rate of interest is zero and that Adam decides not to leave any inheritance to his children.

a. How much will Adam consume this year? Next year? How did you arrive at your answer?

b. Plot on a graph Adam's income, consumption and wealth from the time he is 45 until he is 70 years old. What is the relationship between the annual increase in his wealth and his annual saving (income minus consumption)? In what year does Adam's wealth start to decline? Why? How much wealth does he have when he dies?

c. Suppose Adam receives a tax rebate of €100 per year, so his income is €14,100 per year for the rest of his working career. By how much does his consumption increase this year? Next year?

d. Now suppose that Adam receives a one-year-only tax refund of €100. That is, his income this year is €14,100, but in all succeeding years his income is back to €14,000. What happens to his consumption this year? In succeeding years?

7. Explain why a household's consumption and labour supply decisions are interdependent. What impact does this interdependence have on the way in which consumption and income are related?

8. Why do expectations play such an important role in investment demand? How, if at all, does this explain why investment is so volatile?

9. Can you think of any reasons why the price of a company's shares might be related to its level of investment? How might both respond after the announcement that the firm has made a major technological breakthrough in the development of a new product?

10. How can a firm maintain a smooth production schedule even when sales are fluctuating? What are the benefits of a smooth production schedule? What are the costs?

34

Debates in Macroeconomics: Monetarism, New Classical Theory and Supply-side Economics

Macroeconomics is about understanding the real world: unemployment and inflation, budget and trade deficits, income and growth. New developments often challenge current thinking, sending macroeconomists back to the drawing board to rethink or refine the views they hold. As a new view becomes accepted, policy making can tackle current issues in a new way, and perhaps overcome them, until new issues arise. This interaction between the issues posed by reality and how economists conceive the working of the macroeconomy is the key to how macroeconomics has evolved.

While the macroeconomic model developed in previous chapters has its roots in the Keynesian view of the economy, many of its features are drawn from other schools of thought that have made an impact on the development of macroeconomics.

We have not made a point of the differences between competing schools. Instead, we silently emphasized their similarities, and how they may be combined into a modern, pragmatic view of how the macroeconomy works. This chapter provides a history of macroeconomic thought in a nutshell, tracing the debate from Keynesian beginnings to the views of today. The time line shown in Figure 34.1 provides an orientation and crude illustration of how macreconomic thinking and reality interact.

schools of thought
Alternative views of the workings of the macroeconomy that have evolved since the beginning of the discipline of macroeconomics.

Keynesian economics

John Maynard Keynes's *General Theory of Employment, Interest and Money*, published in 1936 in the aftermath of the Great Depression at a time of falling incomes and high unemployment, remains one of the most important works in economics. While a great deal of the material in the previous chapters is drawn from modern research that postdates Keynes, much of it is built around a framework that Keynes constructed.

But what exactly is *Keynesian economics*? In one sense, it is the origin of macroeconomics. Keynes was the first to stress aggregate demand and the links between the money market and the goods market. And it was Keynes who pointed to the problem of sticky wages. Virtually all debates in this chapter can be understood in terms of the aggregate output / aggregate expenditure framework suggested by Keynes.

In recent years, the term 'Keynesian' has been used narrowly. Keynes believed in an activist government. He believed the government had a role to play in fighting inflation and unemployment, and he believed monetary and fiscal policy should be used to manage the macroeconomy. Thus, the term 'Keynesian' is sometimes used to refer to economists who advocate active government intervention in the macroeconomy.

Figure 34.1 The time line of macroeconomic events and thought

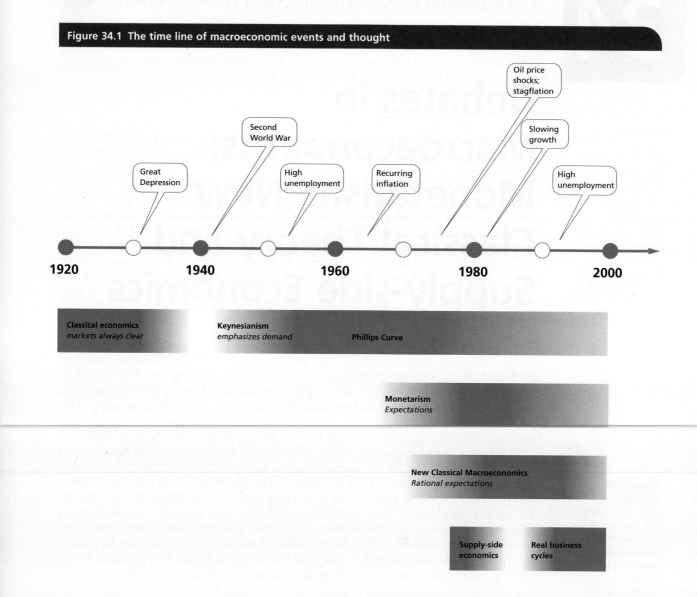

During the 1970s and 1980s, it became clear that managing the macroeconomy was more easily accomplished on paper than in practice. The inflation problems of the 1970s and early 1980s, the seriousness of the recessions of 1974–75 and 1980–82 led many economists to challenge the idea of active government intervention in the economy. Some of these challenges were simple attacks on the bureaucracy's ability to act in a timely manner. Others were theoretical assaults that claimed to show that monetary and fiscal policy could have *no effect whatsoever* on the economy, even if it were efficiently managed.

Two major schools decidedly *against* government intervention have played a major role in this debate: monetarism and new classical economics.

Monetarism

The debate between 'monetarist' and 'Keynesian' economics takes place along a broad spectrum. The terms mean different things to different people. Almost all economists would agree that the main monetarist message is 'money matters'. In the *AS/AD* story, for example, an increase in the money supply shifts the *AD* curve to the right, leading to an increase in both aggregate output (*Y*) and the price level (P). Monetary policy thus has an effect on output and the price level. **Monetarism**, however, is usually considered to go beyond this notion that money matters.

monetarism
A group of macroeconomic theories that hold that money supply is of primary importance, and that government intervention in the economy is ineffective or even harmful.

velocity of money
The number of times a euro note changes hands, on average, during the course of a year; the ratio of nominal GDP to the stock of money.

The velocity of money

To understand monetarist reasoning, you must understand the **velocity of money**. Think of velocity as the number of times a euro note changes hands, on average, during a year.

Suppose on 1 January you buy a new pen with a €5 note. The owner of the stationery shop does not spend your €5 right away. She may hold it until, say, 2 May, when she uses it to buy a dozen croissants. The baker does not spend the €5 he receives until 1 July, when he uses it (along with other cash) to buy 2000 litres of heating oil for winter. The oil distributor uses the bill to buy an engagement ring for his fiancée on 1 September. The €5 note is not used again in the remaining three months of the year. Because this €5 note has changed hands four times during the year, its velocity of circulation is four. A velocity of four means the €5 note stays with each owner for an average of three months, or for one quarter of a year.

In practice, we use GDP, rather than the total value of all transactions in the economy, to measure velocity,[1] because GDP data are more readily available. The income velocity of money (*V*) is the ratio of nominal GDP to the stock of money (*M*):

$$V \equiv \frac{GDP}{M}$$

If €6 trillion worth of final goods and services are produced in a year and if the money stock is €2 trillion, then the velocity of money is €6 trillion ÷ €2 trillion = 3.

We can expand this definition by noting that nominal income (nominal GDP) is equal to real income (real GDP or *Y*) times the overall price level (*P*):

$$GDP \equiv P \times Y$$

Substituting this into the above equation we obtain

$$V \equiv \frac{P \times Y}{M}$$

or

$$M \times V \equiv P \times Y$$

At this point, it is worth asking if this definition has provided us with any insights into the workings of the economy. The answer is no. Because we defined *V* as the ratio of GDP to the money supply, the statement $M \times V \equiv P \times Y$ is an identity – it is true by definition. It contains no more useful information than the statement 'A bachelor is an unmarried man'. The definition does not, for example, say anything about what will happen to $P \times Y$ when *M* changes. The final value of $P \times Y$ depends on what happens to *V*. If *V* falls when *M* increases, the product $M \times V$ could stay the same, in

---

[1] *Remember that GDP does not include transactions in intermediate goods (such as flour sold to a baker to make bread) or in existing assets (like the sale of a used car). If money is used in these transactions, however, they do influence the number of times money changes hands during the course of a year. GDP is an imperfect measure of transactions to use when calculating the velocity of money.*

which case the change in M would have had no effect on nominal income. To give monetarism some economic content, we turn to a simple version of monetarism known as the quantity theory of money.

The quantity theory of money

quantity theory of money

The theory based on the identity $M \times V \equiv P \times Y$ and the assumption that the velocity of money (V) is constant (or virtually constant).

The key assumption of the **quantity theory of money** is that the velocity of money is constant (or virtually constant) over time. If we let $\bar{V}$ denote the constant value of V, the equation for the quantity theory can be written:

$$M \times \bar{V} = P \times Y$$

Note that the normal equal sign has replaced the 'triple equal' identity sign because the equation is no longer an identity. The equation is true if velocity is constant (and equal to $\bar{V}$), but not otherwise. If the equation is true, it provides an easy way to explain nominal GDP. Given M, which can be considered a policy variable set by the central bank, nominal GDP is just $M \times V$. In this case, the effects of monetary policy are clear. Changes in M cause equal percentage changes in nominal GDP. For example, if the money supply doubles, nominal GDP also doubles. If the money supply remains unchanged, nominal GDP remains unchanged.

The key is whether the velocity of money is really constant. Early economists believed the velocity of money was determined largely by institutional considerations, such as how often people are paid and how the banking system clears transactions between banks. Because these factors change gradually, early economists believed velocity was essentially constant.

If there is equilibrium in the money market, then the quantity of money supplied is equal to the quantity of money demanded. That would mean M in the quantity-theory equation equals both the quantity of money supplied and the quantity of money demanded. If the quantity-theory equation is viewed as a demand-for-money equation, it says that the demand for money depends on nominal income (GDP, or $P \times Y$), but *not* on the interest rate.[2] If the interest rate changes and nominal income does not, the equation says that the quantity of money demanded will not change. This is contrary to the theory of the demand for money discussed in Chapter 27, which regarded the demand for money as depending on both income and the interest rate.

Testing the quantity theory of money

One way to test the validity of the quantity theory of money is to look at the demand for money using real data. The key is: does money demand depend on the interest rate? Most empirical work says yes. When demand-for-money equations are estimated (or 'fitted to the data'), the interest rate usually turns out to be a factor. The demand for money does not appear to depend only on nominal income.

Another way of testing the quantity theory is to plot velocity over time and see how it behaves. Figure 34.2 plots the velocity of money in Austria for the 1960–1997 period. The data show that velocity is far from constant. On average, velocity was greater during the 1980s than during the 1970s. A large shift occurred in the late 1970s, with velocity rising from 5.1 in 1978 to 6.3 in 1981. During the 1990s, it seems to be on a downward trend again. It also exhibits considerable short-term fluctuations. For instance, velocity rose from 4.7 in 1972 to 5.4 in 1974, then fell to 4.9 in 1975 before rising again to 5.2 in 1977. Changes of a few tenths of a point may seem small, but they are actually large. For example, the money supply in 1983 was 202.6 billion schillings (ATS). If velocity falls by 0.3 with a money supply constant at this amount,

[2]*In terms of the Appendix to Chapter 28, this means the LM curve is vertical.*

Figure 34.2 The velocity of money in Austria, 1960–1997

The velocity of money is not a constant. In Austria it varied between 4.8 and 6.4 since 1960. Its 1997 value, though, is very close to its 1960 value. This makes the quantity theory a useful tool for the explanation of the long-run relationship between money and prices. Substantial short-run deviations from the theory result from the fluctuations of velocity, however.

Source: OECD; Austrian Central Statistical Office.

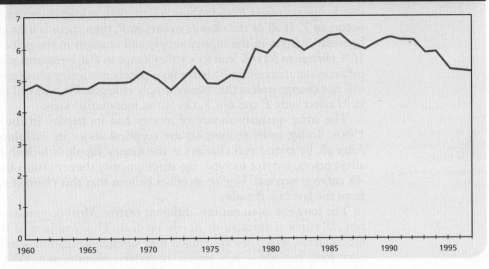

we have a change in nominal GDP ($P \times Y$) of ATS 60.8 billion (0.3 × 202.6 billion), which was about 5% of GDP for that year.

The debate over monetarist theories is more subtle than our discussion indicates so far. First, there are many definitions of the money supply. M1 is the money supply variable used in Figure 34.2, but there are other measures of the money supply that would lead to a smoother plot. For example, many people shifted their funds from cheque accounts to money market accounts when the latter became available in the late 1970s. GDP did not change as a result of this shift though M1 decreased, raising velocity – the ratio of GDP to M1. Suppose instead that we measure the supply of money by M2 (which includes both cheque accounts and money market accounts).

In this case, the decrease in cheque account deposits would be exactly offset by the rise in money market account deposits, and M2 would not change. With no change in GDP and no change in M2, the velocity of money stays constant. Fluctuations in velocity depend partly on how we measure the money supply.

There may also be a time lag between a change in the money supply and its effects on nominal GDP. Suppose we experience a 10% increase in the money supply today, but it takes one year for nominal GDP to increase by 10%. If we measured the ratio of today's money supply to today's GDP, it would seem that velocity had fallen by 10%. But if we measured today's money supply against GDP one year from now, when the increase in the supply of money had its full effect on income, then velocity would turn out to have been constant.

The debate over the usefulness of monetarist theory is primarily an empirical one. It is a debate that can be resolved by looking at facts about the real world and seeing whether they are in accord with the predictions of theory. Is there a measure of the money supply and a choice of the time lag between a change in the money supply and its effects on nominal GDP such that V is effectively constant? If so, then the monetarist theory is a useful approach to understanding how the macroeconomy works. If not, then some other theory is likely to be more appropriate. (We discuss the testing of alternative theories at the end of this chapter.)

Inflation as a purely monetary phenomenon

So far, we have talked only about nominal output ($P \times Y$). We have said nothing about how a monetarist would break down a change in nominal output (due to a money-supply change) into a change in P and a change in Y. Here again it is not possible to make a general statement about what all monetarists believe. Some believe that all of the change occurs in P, and others believe that, at least sometimes, some of the change occurs in Y. If all of the change occurs in P, then there is a proportional relationship between changes in the money supply and changes in the price level. For example, a 10% change in M will lead to a 10% change in P if Y remains unchanged. In this case, inflation (an increase in P) is always a purely monetary phenomenon. The price level will not change unless the money supply changes. We will call this view, that changes in M affect only P and not Y, the 'strict monetarist' view.

The strict quantity theory of money had its heyday in the late 1970s and early 1980s. Today, most economists are sceptical about its usefulness for the short run. After all, by saying that changes in the money supply (which shift the AD curve) only affect prices, but not income, the strict quantity theory claims that even the short-run AS curve is vertical. Few economists believe that this claim is supported by the data from the last two decades.

The long run is an entirely different matter. Most economists agree that the long-run AS curve is vertical, or nearly vertical. This was part of the national economy model, from which we concluded that sustained inflation – inflation that continues over long periods – is a purely monetary phenomenon. We pointed this out in Chapter 31 in the context of the AS/AD framework, arguing that inflation cannot continue indefinitely unless the central bank 'accommodates' it by increasing the money supply. It may be useful to review this.

Take the global economy model. Consider a continuously increasing level of government spending (G) without any corresponding increase in taxes. The increases in G keep shifting the AD curve to the right, which leads to a rising price level (P). (You may find it useful to draw a graph here.) With a fixed money supply, the increases in P lead to a higher and higher interest rate, but there is a limit to how far this can go. Because taxes are unchanged, the government must finance the increases in G by issuing bonds, and there is a limit to how many bonds the public is willing to hold regardless how high the interest rate. At the point where the public cannot be induced to hold any more bonds, the government will be unable to borrow any more to finance its expenditures. Only if the central bank is willing to increase the money supply (buy some of the government bonds) can the government spending, with its inflationary consequences, continue.

> Inflation cannot continue indefinitely without increases in the money supply. The strict monetarist view is a good approximation of the relationship between the money supply and the price level in the long run.

The Keynesian–Monetarist debate

The leading spokesman for monetarism over the last few decades has been Professor Milton Friedman, formerly of the University of Chicago and currently at the Hoover Institute in California. Most monetarists, including Friedman, blame much of the instability in the economy on government, arguing that the inflation encountered over the years could have been avoided had central banks not expanded the money supply so rapidly.

Most monetarists do not advocate activist monetary stabilization policies. They are against expanding the money supply during bad times and slowing the growth of the money supply during good times.

For 'strict' monetarists, the reason is obvious: monetary policy cannot affect income. It is useless, because even the short-run AS curve is vertical. But even monetarists with a less strict view are sceptical of government's ability to 'manage' the economy. The argument most often voiced is the existence of 'long and varying' time lags. This means, first, that it takes time for the money supply to affect demand and income. Monetary policy achieves the intended effect with a lag. And, second, the length of this lag is unpredictable. We can never be sure whether an initiated monetary expansion hits the economy at the right moment (when it is in a recession) or at the wrong moment (when it is already booming). Attempts to manage the economy may well enlarge the swings of the business cycle rather than reduce them.

For many years, Friedman has advocated a policy of slow and steady money growth; specifically, that the money supply should grow at a rate equal to the average growth of real output (income) (Y). That is, the central bank should pursue a constant policy of accommodating real growth but not inflation.

Keynesianism and monetarism are at odds with each other. Many Keynesians advocate coordinated monetary and fiscal policy tools to reduce instability in the economy – to fight inflation and unemployment. But not all Keynesians advocate an activist government. Some reject the strict monetarist position that only money matters in favour of the view that both monetary and fiscal policies make a difference, but *at the same time* believe the best possible policy for government to pursue is basically non-interventionist.

Modern Keynesians concede after the experience of the 1970s that monetary and fiscal tools are not finely calibrated. The notion that monetary and fiscal expansions and contractions can 'fine tune' the economy is gone for ever. Still, many feel that the experiences with the oil shocks of the 1970s warrant 'crude tuning' to help prevent even bigger economic disasters. Central banks that responded to the adverse supply shock by expanding the money supply managed to keep the recessions of those years much smaller than those central banks that didn't. Also, the contractionary fiscal and monetary policies of the mid- and late 1990s in many EU countries have clearly put strains on labour markets and income growth, at least in the short run.

Thirty years ago, the debate between Keynesians and monetarists was the central controversy in macroeconomics. That controversy, while still alive today, is no longer at the forefront. For the past two decades, the focus of current thinking in macroeconomics has turned to the new classical macroeconomics.

New classical macroeconomics

new classical macroeconomics
An approach to economics that grew out of the stagflations of the 1970s. Theorists hold that the 'rational expectations' of households and firms allow them to predict policy measures, allowing little scope for government intervention in the economy.

In the 1970s and 1980s, a new challenge to Keynesian and related theories emerged from a school sometimes referred to as the new classical macroeconomics.[3] Like 'monetarism' and 'Keynesianism', this term is vague. No two new classical macroeconomists think exactly alike, and no single model completely represents this school. The following discussion, however, conveys the flavour of the new classical views.

The development of new classical macroeconomics

New classical macroeconomics developed from two different, though related, sources. These sources are the theoretical and the empirical critiques of existing, or traditional, macroeconomics.

[3] *The term 'new classical' is used because many of the assumptions and conclusions of this group of economists resemble those of the classical economists – that is, those who wrote before Keynes.*

On the theoretical level, there was growing dissatisfaction with the way traditional models treat expectations. Keynes himself recognized that expectations (in the form of 'animal spirits') play a big part in economic behaviour. Friedman, in his critique of the orthodox Phillips curve, introduced inflation expectations as a variable determining the position of the short-run Phillips curve. The problem is that these and other traditional models assume that expectations are formed in naive ways. For example, a common assumption is that people form their expectations of future inflation adaptively, say by assuming that present inflation will continue. If they turn out to be wrong, they adjust their expectations by some fraction of the difference between their original forecast and the actual inflation rate. Suppose I expect 10% inflation next year. When next year comes and the inflation rate turns out to be only 5%, I have made an error of 5%. I might then predict an inflation rate of 7.5% for the following year, halfway between my earlier expectation (10%) and actual inflation last year (5%).

The problem with adaptive expectation is that it is not consistent with the assumptions of microeconomics. It implies that people systematically overlook information that would allow them to make better forecasts. There are costs to being wrong. If, as microeconomic theory assumes, people maximize their satisfaction and firms maximize profits, they should form their expectations in a cleverer way. Instead of naively assuming that the future will be like the past, they should actively seek to forecast the future. Any other behaviour violates the microeconomic view of households and firms as forward-looking and rational.

On the empirical level, many European economies experienced stagflation during the 1970s. Remember: stagflation is unemployment and inflation rising at the same time. The Phillips curve theory of the 1960s predicted that demand pressure pushes up prices, so that when demand is weak – in times of high unemployment, for example – prices should be stable (or perhaps even falling). The new classical theories were an attempt to explain the apparent breakdown in the 1970s of the simple inflation–unemployment trade-off predicted by the Phillips curve or by its mirror image, the *AS* curve. Just as the Great Depression of the 1930s motivated the development of Keynesian economics, the stagflation of the 1970s helped motivate the formulation of new classical macroeconomics.

Rational expectations

In previous chapters we stressed trades unions', households' and firms' expectations about the future. The money wage rate a trade union demands during collective bargaining depends on the expected price level. A firm's decision to build a new plant depends on its expectations of future sales. The amount of saving a household undertakes today depends on its expectations about future interest rates, wages and prices.

How are expectations formed? Do people assume that things will continue as they are at present (predicting rain tomorrow because it is raining today, say)? What information do people use to make their guesses about the future? Questions like these have become central to current macroeconomic thinking and research. One theory, the rational-expectations hypothesis, offers a powerful way of thinking about expectations.

Suppose we want to forecast inflation. What does it mean to say that inflation expectations are 'rational'? The rational-expectations hypothesis assumes that people know the 'true model' that generates inflation – they know exactly how inflation is determined in the economy – and they use this model to forecast future inflation rates. If there are no random, unpredictable events in the economy, and if people knew the true model generating inflation, then their forecasts of future inflation rates would be

rational-expectations hypothesis
The hypothesis that people know the 'true model' of the economy and that they use this model to form their expectations of the future.

perfect. Because it is true, the model does not permit mistakes, and thus the people using it make no mistakes.

Yet many events that affect the inflation rate are not predictable – they are random. By 'true' model, then, we can at best mean a model that is on average correct when forecasting inflation. Sometimes random events have a positive effect on inflation, which means the model underestimates inflation, and sometimes they have a negative effect, meaning the model overestimates the inflation rate. *On average*, the model is correct. Accordingly, rational expectations are correct on average, even though their predictions are not exactly right all the time.

To see this, suppose you have to forecast how many times a fair coin will come up heads out of 100 tosses. The true model in this case is that the coin has a 50–50 chance of coming up heads on any one toss. Because the outcome of the 100 tosses is random, you cannot be sure of guessing correctly. If you know the true model – that the coin is fair – your rational expectation of the outcome of 100 tosses is 50 heads. You are not likely to be exactly right – the actual number of heads may well be slightly higher or slightly lower than 50 – but *on average* you will be correct.

Sometimes people are said to have rational expectations if they use 'all available information' in forming their expectations. This definition is vague, because it is not always clear what 'all available information' means. The definition is precise, if by 'all available information' we mean that people know and use the true model. We cannot have more or better information than the true model.

If information can be obtained at no cost, then someone is not behaving rationally if they fail to use all available information. There are almost always costs to making a wrong forecast. It is therefore not rational to overlook information that can help to improve the accuracy of forecast, as long as the costs of acquiring that information do not outweigh the benefits of improving its accuracy.

Rational expectations and market clearing

If firms set prices and wages based on rational expectations, then, on average, those prices and wages will ensure equilibrium in the goods and labour markets. When a firm has rational expectations, it knows the demand curve for its output and the supply curve of labour that it faces, except when random shocks disrupt those curves. On average, the firm will set market-clearing prices and wages. It knows the true model, and will not set wages different from those expected to attract the number of workers it wants. If all firms behave this way, then wages will be such that on average the total amount of labour supplied will equal the total amount of labour that firms demand. In other words, on average there will be no unemployment.

In Chapter 30, we argued that there might be disequilibrium in the labour market (in the form of unemployment or excess demand for workers) because firms and trades unions make mistakes in their wage-setting behaviour due to expectation errors. If, on average, firms or unions do not make errors, then, on average, there is equilibrium. When expectations are rational, disequilibrium exists only temporarily as a result of random, unpredictable shocks – an important conclusion. If this is true, it means disequilibrium in any market is only temporary, because firms and trades unions, on average, set market-clearing wages and prices.

The assumption of rational expectations radically changes the way we view the economy. It takes us from a world where involuntary unemployment can exist for substantial periods of time and where the multiplier can operate, to a world in which (on average) all markets clear and there is full employment. In this world there is no need for government stabilization policies. Unemployment is not a problem; if it exists at all, it is due to unpredictable shocks that average out to zero. There is no more reason for the government to try to change the outcome in the labour market than there is for it to change the outcome in the banana market.

The Lucas supply function

The Lucas supply function, named after Robert E. Lucas of the University of Chicago, is an important component of a number of new classical macroeconomic theories. It is a deceptively simple function that yields a surprising policy conclusion. Real output (Y) is modelled to depend on (is a function of) the difference between the actual price level (P) and the expected price level (P^e):

$$Y = f(P - P^e)$$

This ought to look familiar. Without naming it, we actually derived a Lucas supply function in Chapter 30 when discussing the short-run *AS* curve. The actual price level minus the expected price level ($P - P^e$) is the **price surprise**. Before considering the policy implications of this function, we should look at the theory behind it, because it differs from the arguments on which we based the short-run *AS* curve.

Lucas begins by assuming that people and firms are specialists in production but generalists in consumption. If someone you know is a manual labourer, the chances are she sells only one thing – labour. If she is a lawyer, she sells only legal services. In contrast, people buy a large bundle of goods – ranging from petrol to ice cream and bread – on a regular basis. The same is true for firms. Most companies concentrate on producing a small range of products, but they typically buy a larger range of inputs – raw materials, labour, energy, capital. According to Lucas, this divergence between buying and selling creates an asymmetry. People know much more about the prices of the things they sell than they do about the prices of the things they buy.[4]

At the beginning of each period, a firm has some expectation of the average price level for that period. If the actual price level turns out to be different from what the firm expected, there is a price surprise. Say the average price level is higher than expected. Because the firm learns about the actual price level slowly, some time goes by before it realizes that all prices have gone up. The firm *does* learn *quickly* that the price of its *output* has gone up. Because at first it sees only the higher price for its product, the firm perceives – incorrectly, it turns out – that its price has risen relative to other prices, leading it to produce more.

A similar argument holds for workers. When there is a positive price surprise, workers at first believe that their 'price' – their wage rate – has increased relative to other prices: workers believe their real wage rate has risen. We know from theory that an increase in real wage is likely to encourage workers to work more hours.[5] The real wage has not actually risen, but it takes workers a while to work this out. In the meantime, they supply more hours of work than they would have. This means the economy produces more when prices are unexpectedly higher than when prices are at their expected level.

This is the rationale for the Lucas supply function. Unexpected increases in the price level can fool workers and firms into thinking that relative prices have changed, causing them to alter the amount of labour or goods they choose to supply.

Policy implications of the Lucas supply function

Combined with rational expectations the Lucas supply function implies that anticipated policy changes have no effect on real output. Consider a change in monetary policy. In general, the change will have some effect on the average price level. If the policy change is announced to the public, then people know how the price level will change, because they have rational expectations (and know the way changes in

---

[4] *It is not entirely obvious why this should be true. Some critics of the new classical school have argued that this is unrealistic and that Lucas supply function is too simple, because things other than price surprises affect aggregate output.*

[5] *This is true if we assume that the substitution effect dominates the income effect (see Chapter 33).*

monetary policy affect the price level). This means that the change in monetary policy affects both the actual price level and the expected price level in the same way. The new price level minus the new expected price level is zero – there is no price surprise. Since the Lucas supply function states that real output can change from its fixed level only if there is a price surprise, there will be no change in real output.

The general conclusion is that *any* announced policy change – monetary, fiscal or any other policy – has no effect on real output, because such a policy change affects both actual and expected price levels in the same way. Given rational expectations, announced policy changes produce no price surprises – and no increases in real output. The only way government policy can affect real output is if it comes from behind closed doors. Government policy affects real output only if it surprises people. Rational-expectations theory combined with the Lucas supply function proposes a very small role for government policy in the economy. If the government resorts to the same 'surprise' policy measures again and again, the economy learns to look through this pattern and the effect on output wears off.

Evaluating rational-expectations theory

What should we make of all this? The key question regarding the new classical macroeconomics is how realistic the assumption of rational expectations is. If it approximates the way expectations are actually formed, then it questions any theory that relies at least in part on expectation errors for the existence of disequilibrium. The arguments in favour of the rational-expectations assumption sound persuasive from the perspective of microeconomic theory. If expectations are not rational, there are likely to be unexploited profit opportunities – and most economists believe such opportunities are rare and short-lived.

One argument *against* the concept of rational expectations is that it requires too much knowledge on the part of trades unions, households and firms. People must know the true model (at least a good approximation of it) to form rational expectations, and this is a lot to expect. Even if firms and households are capable of learning the true model, it may be costly to take the time and gather the relevant information to learn it. The gain from learning the true model may not be worth the cost. In this sense, the unexploited profit opportunities vanish. Gathering information and learning economic models may not be worth the expected gain from improved forecasts.

Consider a firm engaged in maximizing profits. Somehow it forms expectations of the relevant future variables. Given these expectations, it works out what to do to maximize profits. Given a set of expectations, maximizing profits may not be too difficult. But what is difficult is *forming* accurate expectations in the first place. This may require firms to know much more about the overall economy than they possibly can, so the assumption that their expectations are rational becomes unrealistic. Firms, like the rest of us – so the argument goes – grope around in a world that is difficult to understand, trying to do their best but not always understanding enough to avoid mistakes.

A second argument, not against the concept of rational expectations but against its implications when combined with the Lucas supply curve, is of an empirical nature. The central implication that policies only affect income if they come as a surprise is inconsistent with what we observe in the real world. There are many examples of anticipated policy measures having real effects on income.[6] There is no agreement about why this is so. But in a pragmatic fashion, we can state that real-world economies behave much more like our national economy model with its *adaptive* expectations (which make shocks last) than a model incorporating rational expectations.

[6] *One source of evidence is that disinflation – the gradual reduction of high inflation rates to low ones through restrictive monetary policy – always causes income losses. See T. Jordan, 'Disinflation costs, accelerating inflation gains, and central bank independence', Weltwirtschaftliches Archiv 133 (1997), pp. 1–21.*

Real business cycle theory

Recent work in new classical macroeconomics has been concerned with whether there is a way to explain the existence of business cycles under the assumptions of complete price and wage flexibility (market clearing) and rational expectations. This work is called **real business cycle theory**. As we discussed in Chapter 30, if prices and wages are completely flexible, then the *AS* curve is vertical, even in the short run. If the *AS* curve is vertical, then events or phenomena that shift the *AD* curve (such as changes in the money supply or government spending, or shocks to consumer and investor behaviour) have no effect on real output. Since real output does fluctuate over time, the puzzle is to explain these fluctuations if they are not the result of policy changes or other shocks that shift the *AD* curve. Solving this puzzle is one of the main missions of real business cycle theory.

If shifts of the *AD* curve cannot account for real output fluctuations (because the *AS* curve is vertical), then shifts of the *AS* curve must be responsible. The task is to come up with convincing stories as to what causes these shifts and why they persist over a number of periods. This is particularly difficult when it comes to the labour market. If prices and wages are completely flexible, there is never any unemployment, apart from frictional unemployment. An example: the measured British unemployment rate was 11.5% in 1986 and 7.0% in 1990, so how do theorists explain why so many more people chose not to work in 1986 than in 1990?

Early real business cycle theorists emphasized shocks to the production technology. Say there is a negative shock that causes the marginal product of labour to decline. This leads to a fall in the real wage, which decreases the labour supply. People choose to work less because the negative technology shock has lowered the return from working. The opposite happens when there is a positive shock: the marginal product of labour rises, the real wage rises, and people choose to work more. The early theory was not as successful as some had hoped, because it required what seemed to be unrealistically large shocks to explain the observed movements in labour supply over time.

Different types of shocks have since been introduced, and work is progressing in this area to refine our understanding of the economy's supply side. To date, fluctuations of some variables, but not all, have been explained fairly well. It appears that supply-side shocks contribute more to the business cycle than was previously thought. But it also seems that important features of the business cycle cannot be explained in this way. Some recent work adds sticky prices to real business cycle models, creating a role for government demand policies again.

Supply-side economics

From our discussion of equilibrium in the goods market, beginning with the simple multiplier in Chapter 23 and continuing to Chapter 29, we have focused primarily on *demand*. Supply increases and decreases in response to changes in aggregate expenditure (which is closely linked to aggregate demand). Fiscal policy works by influencing aggregate expenditure through tax policy and government spending. Monetary policy works by influencing net exports through increases and decreases in the exchange rate. The models we have developed are 'demand orientated'.

The 1970s and their stagflation were difficult times for most economies. When the late 1970s saw inflation return to the high levels of 1974–75, it began to look as though policy makers were incapable of controlling the business cycle.

As a result of these seeming failures, academic economics came under fire. One assault came from a group of economists who expounded **supply-side economics**. The argument of the supply-siders was simple: all the attention to demand in orthodox macroeconomic theory distracted attention away from the real problem of modern economies. The real problem, said supply-siders, was that high rates of taxation and heavy regulation had reduced the incentive to work, save and invest. It was not a demand stimulus that was needed but better incentives to stimulate *supply*.

real business cycle theory

An attempt to explain business-cycle fluctuations under the assumptions of complete price and wage flexibility and rational expectations. It emphasizes shocks to technology and other shocks.

supply-side economics

A group of economic theorists who claim problems in modern economies are best solved by stimulating the supply side, for example by heavy tax cuts and deregulation.

If taxes are cut, people take home more of their pay, the argument continued, so they will work harder and save more. If businesses keep more of their profits and can be freed of government regulations, they will invest more. The added labour supply and investment, or capital supply, will lead to an expansion of the supply of goods and services. This will in turn reduce inflation and unemployment at the same time. The ultimate solution to the economy's woes, the supply-siders concluded, was on the *supply side* of the economy.

At their most extreme, supply-siders argued that the incentive effects of supply-side policies were likely to be so great that a major cut in tax rates would actually *increase* tax revenues. At lower tax *rates*, more people would be working and earning income and firms would earn more profits. This would sufficiently increase the *tax base* (profits, sales and income) to outweigh the decreases in rates, resulting in higher government revenues.

The Laffer curve

Figure 34.3 presents a key diagram of supply-side economics. The tax rate is measured on the vertical axis, and tax revenue is measured on the horizontal axis. The assumption behind this curve is that there exists some tax rate beyond which the supply response is large enough to lead to a decrease in tax revenue for further increases in the tax rate. Obviously, at some tax rate between zero and 100%, tax revenue is at a maximum. At a tax rate of zero, work effort is high but there is no tax revenue. At a tax rate of 100, the labour supply is presumably zero because no one can keep any income. Somewhere between zero and 100 lies the maximum-revenue rate.

The big debate in the 1980s was whether tax rates put the country on the upper or lower part of the curve in Figure 34.3. The supply-side school claimed that countries like Britain or the United States were at about point *A*, where tax cuts raise tax revenue; others argued that they were nearer *B*, where tax cuts reduce tax revenue.

The diagram in Figure 34.2 is known as the **Laffer curve**, after Arthur Laffer, who – so the legend goes – first sketched it on a napkin at a cocktail party. The Laffer curve influenced a tax package put forward by the Reagan administration in the United States that brought substantial cuts in both personal and business taxes. The individual income tax was cut by 25% over the course of three years. Corporate taxes were cut sharply so as to stimulate capital investment. The new law allowed firms to depreciate their capital at a rapid rate for tax purposes, the bigger deductions leading to significantly lower taxes.

Laffer curve A graph with the tax rate on the vertical axis and tax revenue on the horizontal axis. The Laffer curve shows that there is some tax rate beyond which the supply response is large enough to lead to a decrease in tax revenue for further increases in the tax rate.

Figure 34.3 The Laffer curve

The Laffer curve shows that the amount of revenue the government collects is a function of the tax rate. It also shows that when tax rates are very high, an increase in the tax rate could cause tax revenues to fall. Similarly, under the same circumstances, a cut in the tax rate could generate enough additional economic activity to cause tax revenues to rise.

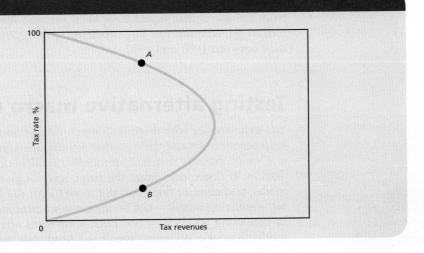

Evaluating supply-side economics

Supporters of supply-side economics claim that Reagan's tax policies were successful in stimulating the economy. They point to the fact that almost immediately after the tax cuts of 1981, the economy expanded to end the recession of 1980–82. At the same time, inflation rates fell sharply from the high rates of 1980 and 1981. And, except for one year, federal receipts continued to rise throughout the 1980s, despite the cut in tax rates.

Critics of supply-side policies do not dispute these facts but offer an alternative explanation of how the economy recovered. The Reagan tax cuts were enacted just as the US economy was in the middle of its deepest recession since the Great Depression. The unemployment rate stood at 10.8% in the fourth quarter of 1982. It was the recession, critics argue, that was responsible for the reduction in inflation – not the supply-side policies. And in theory, a tax cut could just as well lead to a *reduction* in labour supply. Recall our discussion of income and substitution effects in Chapter 33. While a higher after-tax wage rate provides a higher reward for each hour of work and thus a greater incentive to work, a tax cut also means that households receive more income for a given number of hours of work. Because they can earn the same amount of income while working fewer hours, households might actually choose to work *less*. They may prefer to spend some of their added income on leisure. Research done during the 1980s suggests that tax cuts modestly increase the supply of labour.

What about the recovery from the recession? Why did real output begin to grow rapidly in late 1982, precisely when the supply-side tax cuts were taking effect? Two reasons have been suggested. First, the supply-side tax cuts had large *demand*-side effects that stimulated the economy. Second, the Federal Reserve pumped up the money supply and drove interest rates down just when the tax cuts were being put into effect. The money supply expanded about 20% between 1981 and 1983, and interest rates tumbled. In 1981, the average three-month US Treasury bill paid 14% interest; in 1983, that figure had dropped to 8.6%.

Traditional theory also suggests that a huge tax cut will increase disposable income and, in turn, consumption spending (a component of aggregate expenditure). In addition, although higher planned investment (brought about by a lower interest rate) expands long-run productive capacity and supply, it also increases short-run expenditures on capital goods (new plant and equipment investment).

Whether the recovery from the 1981–82 recession was the result of supply-side expansion or supply-side policies with demand-side effects, one thing is clear: the extreme promises of the supply-siders did not materialize. President Reagan argued that because of the effect depicted in the Laffer curve, the government could maintain expenditures (and even increase defence expenditures sharply), cut tax rates *and* balance the budget. This was clearly not the case. Government revenues fell sharply from the levels that would have been realized without the tax cuts. After 1982, the federal government ran huge deficits, with nearly $2 trillion added to the national debt between 1983 and 1992.

Testing alternative macro models

You may wonder why there is so much disagreement in macroeconomics. Why can't macroeconomists test their models against one another to see which performs best?

One problem is that macroeconomic models differ in ways that are hard to standardize. If one model takes the price level as given, or as not explained within the model, and another does not, the model with the given price level may do better in, say, predicting output – not because it is a better model but simply because the errors in predicting prices have not been allowed to affect the predictions of output. The model that takes prices as given has a head start, so to speak.

Applications

The supply-siders ride again

Economic theory suggests that lower tax rates could boost growth in several ways. Reducing marginal tax rates might encourage people to work harder. This should boost both the labour supply and productivity. . . .

So much for theory. Is there empirical evidence to support it? American supply-siders like to point to the 'growth spurts' that have often followed big tax cuts. Ronald Reagan's tax reductions in the early 1980s, they argue, led to seven years of rapid growth between 1983 and 1989. But this is misleading: over relatively short periods, growth rates are affected by any number of things, notably the timing of the business cycle. This makes it hard to draw firm conclusions about how much tax cuts might boost growth.

To get a more accurate picture, economists can . . . [look] at the impact of specific tax changes, or . . . [seek] to measure the relationship between tax rates and growth over time and in different countries. On the face of it, the Reagan period should provide an ideal laboratory for . . . research in America: the top federal income-tax rate fell from 70% in 1980 to 28% in 1988.

Yet calculating the impact of this change on people's work . . . is extremely tricky. For one thing, marginal tax rates fell by different amounts across income groups, with much bigger cuts for the rich than for the poor. Nor were taxes cut consistently. The first big tax changes in 1981 sharply reduced taxes on income and capital; but some taxes were later raised. And the 1986 tax reforms cut top income-tax rates, but partly increased those on capital and left the overall tax burden unchanged.

In spite of this, most economists agree that the 1980s tax changes brought a small, but real, increase in the labour supply. This was largely thanks to more women working longer hours, with the biggest effect coming among those with relatively high incomes. The reforms' effect on taxable incomes was bigger than this suggests, however, partly because lower rates meant that the rich had less incentive to disguise income as tax-free corporate perks such as health insurance. Much of the increase in reported income over the period was due to the unravelling of such tax dodges. So it is hard to work out whether cutting marginal income-tax rates really led to higher growth.

. . . Nor do cross-country comparisons provide much evidence that tax cuts boost growth. Compare average growth rates and average tax burdens of OECD countries in the chart: in general, the countries with lower tax rates appear to have grown faster. Unfortunately, this simple correlation does not mean much, because so many factors influence a country's growth rate, notably initial income levels. Poorer countries are likely to grow faster than richer ones.

Such international studies also have a big drawback: they typically measure a country's average tax burden, whereas it is changes in marginal tax rates that matter most for incentives. So evidence of only a weak link between average tax burdens and growth rates does not mean that cutting punitively high marginal tax rates might not induce people to work . . . more.

Source: The Economist, 24 August 1996.

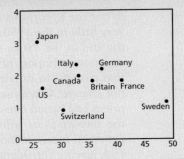

Figure 1 Unhappy returns: tax revenue and growth

Source: OECD.

Another problem arises when testing the rational-expectations assumption. Remember: if people have rational expectations, they are using the true model to form their expectations. To test this assumption we need the true model. But there's no way to be sure that whatever model is taken to be the true model is in fact the true one. Any test of the rational-expectations hypothesis is therefore a *joint* test (1) that expectations are formed rationally, and (2) that the model being used is the true one. If the test rejects the hypothesis, it may be that individuals have been using a different model from the really true one, rather than that expectations are not rational.

A further problem for macroeconomists is the small amount of data available. Most empirical work uses data beginning in about 1950, which in 1998 was 49 years' (196 quarters') worth of data. While this may seem like a lot, it is not. Macroeconomic data are fairly 'smooth', which means a typical variable does not vary much from quarter to quarter or from year to year. The typical number of business cycles within this 46-year period is small – about half a dozen. Testing various macroeconomic hypotheses on the basis of seven business cycle observations is not easy, and any conclusions must be interpreted with caution.

As an example of the problem of a small number of observations, consider trying to test the hypothesis that import prices affect domestic prices. Import prices changed very little in the 1950s and 1960s. Because of this, it would have been very difficult at the end of the 1960s to estimate the effect of import prices on domestic prices. The variation in import prices was too small to show any effects. We cannot demonstrate that changes in import prices explain changes in domestic prices if import prices do not change! Circumstances were different by the end of the 1970s; by then, import prices had varied considerably. By the end of the 1970s, there were good estimates of the import price effect. This kind of problem is encountered time and again in empirical macroeconomics. Often, there are not enough observations for much to be said, leaving considerable room for disagreement.

We said in Chapter 1 that it is difficult in economics to perform controlled experiments. Economists are at the mercy of historical data. If we were able to perform experiments, we could probably learn more about the economy in a shorter time. Alas, we must wait. In time, the current range of disagreements in macroeconomics should be narrowed.

Summary

Keynesian economics

1. In a broad sense, Keynesian economics is the foundation of modern macroeconomics. In a narrower sense, 'Keynesian' is used to refer to economists who advocate active government intervention in the economy.

Monetarism

2. The monetarist analysis of the economy places a great deal of emphasis on the velocity of money, defined as the number of times a euro note changes hands, on average, during the course of a year. The velocity of money is the ratio of nominal GDP to the stock of money, or $V \equiv GDP/M \equiv P \times Y/M$. Alternately, $M \times V \equiv P \times Y$.

3. The *quantity theory of money* assumes that velocity is constant (or virtually constant). This implies that changes in the supply of money will lead to equal percentage changes in nominal GDP. The quantity theory of money equation is $M \times \bar{V} = P \times Y$. According to the equation, the demand for money does not depend on the interest rate.

4. Most economists believe sustained inflation is a purely monetary phenomenon. Inflation cannot continue indefinitely unless the central bank 'accommodates' it by expanding the money supply.

5. Generally, monetarists blame most of the economy's instability on the government and are sceptical of the government's ability to manage the macroeconomy. They argue that the money supply should grow at a rate equal to the average growth of real output (income) (Y) – the central bank should expand the money supply to accommodate real growth but not inflation.

New classical macroeconomics

6. The *new classical macroeconomics* developed from two different though related sources: the theoretical and the empirical critiques of traditional macroeconomics. On the theoretical level, there was growing dissatisfaction with the way traditional models treat expectations. On the empirical level, the stagflation during the 1970s caused many people to look for alternative theories to explain the breakdown of the Phillips curve.

7. The *rational-expectations hypothesis* assumes people know the 'true model' that generates economic variables. For example, rational expectations assume that economists know how inflation is determined in the economy and use this model to forecast future inflation rates.

8. The *Lucas supply function* assumes that real output (Y) depends on the actual price level minus the expected price level, or the *price surprise*. This function combined with the assumption that expectations are rational implies that anticipated policy changes have no effect on real output.

9. *Real business cycle theory* is an attempt to explain business-cycle fluctuations under the assumptions of complete price and wage flexibility and rational expectations. It emphasizes shocks to technology and preferences.

Supply-side economics

10. *Supply-side economics* focuses on incentives to stimulate supply. Supply-side economists believe that if we lower taxes, workers work harder and save more and firms invest more and produce more. At their most extreme, supply-siders argue that incentive effects are so great that a major cut in taxes will increase tax revenues.

11. The *Laffer curve* shows the relationship between tax rates and tax revenues. Supply-side economists use it to argue that higher revenues can be generated by cutting tax rates. Evidence does not appear to support this. In the USA, the lower tax rates under the Reagan administration decreased tax revenues significantly and contributed to the massive increase in the federal debt during the 1980s.

Testing alternative macro models

12. Economists disagree about which macroeconomic model is best, for several reasons: (1) macroeconomic models differ in ways that are hard to standardize; (2) when testing the rational-expectations assumption, we can never be sure that the model taken to be the true model is actually the true one; (3) the amount of data available is fairly small.

Review Terms and Concepts

Laffer curve
Lucas supply function
monetarism
new classical macroeconomics
price surprise
quantity theory of money
rational-expectations hypothesis
real business cycle theory
schools of thought

supply-side economics
velocity of money (*V*)

Equations

$$V \equiv \frac{GDP}{M}$$

$$M \times V \equiv P \times Y$$

$$M \times \bar{V} = P \times Y$$

Problem Set

Table 1		
	Rate of growth of money supply, M1 (%)	Rate of growth of real GDP (%)
Britain	+6.1	+3.9
Canada	+13.8	+3.7
Japan	+8.1	−0.3
Netherlands	+9.8	+3.1
Spain	+12.8	+3.1
United States	−2.1	+4.0

Source: The Economist, 22–28 November 1997, p. 118; figures are for the latest full year for which data were available.

1. Table 1 gives the rate of money supply growth and the rate of real GDP growth for six countries in 1997.
a. If you were a pure monetarist, what would you predict about the rate of inflation across the six countries?
b. If you were a Keynesian, and assuming activist central banks, how might you interpret the same data?

2. The three diagrams in Figure 1 represent in a simplified way the predictions of the three theories presented in this chapter about the likely effects of a major tax cut.
a. Match each of the following three theories with a graph: (1) Keynesian economics, (2) supply-side economics, (3) rational expectations/monetarism. Briefly explain the logic behind the three graphs.
b. Which of the three theories do you find the most convincing? Explain your choice.

Figure 1

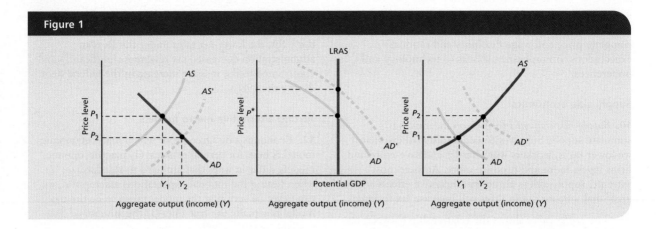

3. In 1998, a well-known economist was heard to say, 'The problem with supply-side economics is that when you cut taxes, they have both supply and demand side effects and you can't separate them'. Explain what he meant.

4. A cornerstone of new classical economics is the notion that expectations are 'rational'.
a. Does this mean that expectations must never be wrong?
b. What do you think will happen to the prices of single-family homes in your community over the next several years? On what do you base your expectations? Is your thinking consistent with the notion of rational expectations? Explain.

5. You are a monetarist, and you are given the following information. The money supply is €1000. The velocity of money is five.
a. What is nominal income? What is real income?
b. What happens to nominal income if the money supply is doubled? What happens to real income?

6. When US President Bill Clinton took office in January 1993, he faced two major economic problems: a large federal budget deficit and high unemployment resulting from a very slow recovery from the recession of 1990–91. In his first State of the Union message, the President called for spending cuts and substantial tax increases to reduce the deficit. Most of these proposed spending cuts were in the defence budget. The following day, Alan Greenspan, chair of the Federal Reserve Board of Governors, signalled his support for the President's plan. Many elements of the President's original plan were later incorporated into the deficit reduction bill passed in 1993.
a. Some said at the time that without the Fed's support, the Clinton plan would be a disaster. Explain this argument.
b. Supply-side economists and monetarists were very worried about the plan and the support it received from the Fed. What specific problems might a monetarist worry about? And what might worry a supply-side economist?

c. Suppose you had to report on the events of 1995 and 1996. What specific evidence would you look for to see if the Clinton plan was effective or whether the critics were right to be sceptical?

7. 'In an economy with reasonably flexible prices and wages, full employment is almost always maintained.' Explain why this is true.

8. The most famous monetarist policy experiment was conducted in Britain during the first half of the 1980s. At the time of Margaret Thatcher's first election victory in 1979, inflation was running in double digits. One of the Conservative party's election promises had been to reduce inflation. The proposed strategy was to set numerical targets for money growth, and to announce these well in advance to the public. Workers, it was argued, would understand this strategy and reduce their wage demands accordingly, and thus inflation would be reduced without higher unemployment. Although inflation came down from 18% in 1980 to 4% in 1986, this was accompanied by a huge rise in unemployment (from 5.4% in 1979 to 11% in 1986).
a. Use an *AS–AD* diagram to illustrate what happened.
b. Did the monetarist strategy of the Thatcher government fail because people's expectations were not rational? (Remember the discussion of policy makers' preferences in Chapter 32.)

During the same period, the Conservative Tory government also severely cut the influence of trades unions and passed legislation to increase labour market flexibility.
c. Explain why this was a supply-side policy. Why was it deemed important for the success of the monetarist strategy?
d. The Conservatives gave up targeting the money supply during the second part of the 1980s, but joined the ERM in 1990. Why?
e. What is the monetary strategy of the European Central Bank?

9. In a hypothetical economy there is a simple proportional tax on wages imposed at a rate *t*. And there are plenty of jobs, so if people enter the labour force they can find work. We define total government receipts from the tax as:

$$T = t \times W \times L$$

where t = tax rate, W = gross wage rate and L = total supply of labour. The net wage rate is:

$$W_n = (1 - t) \times W$$

The elasticity of labour supply is defined as:

$$\frac{\text{Percentage change in } L}{\text{Percentage change in } W_n} = \frac{\Delta L/L}{\Delta W_n/W_n}$$

a. Suppose t is cut from 0.25 to 0.20. How elastic must the supply of labour be for this cut to *increase* total government receipts from the tax? (Assume a constant gross wage and full employment.)

b. What does your answer imply about the supply-side assertion that a cut in taxes can increase tax revenues?

Economic Growth

When you travel abroad, whether in Europe or elsewhere, you can't help but notice that the material well-being of people differs substantially between countries. Differences are often so striking that they are way beyond the range within which booms and recessions make income fluctuate around its potential (the level of income produced when factors of production are employed at 'normal' levels). The reason why you find, say, Tunisia so much poorer than your own country is highly unlikely to be because your country is enjoying a boom while Tunisia is moving through a recession. So what is the explanation? In terms of the aggregate supply / aggregate demand model assembled in previous chapters, **potential income** does not appear to be the same in the two countries. Why? This brings us to one of two key questions asked when economists discuss **economic growth**. Why are some countries poor and other countries rich?

This question focuses on an international comparison of *income levels* at a specific point in time. The second key question looks at the *development* within a country over time. An illustrative measure of how much incomes change over time is provided by how many minutes we have to work to be able to purchase certain standardized items. Table 35.1 provides some examples.

In 1960, the average German had to work 46 minutes to earn enough to buy 10 eggs. In 1996 a bare 7 minutes sufficed. So, in terms of eggs, work in 1996 was 6.5 times as productive as it was in 1960. Gauging progress in terms of other goods and services gives similar, though usually less dramatic, results. Even goods we consider quite expensive, such as petrol, are much cheaper in terms of work time than they were in 1960. Common exceptions are services, such as restaurant meals, hotel rooms or having your hair washed at a hairdresser's, where measured productivity gains are small. Interestingly, even some fairly standardized items like toothpaste and Coca Cola did not become much cheaper in terms of work time. In general, however, and despite exceptions, the examples given in Table 35.1 motivate our second key question about economic growth: why do economies grow? And why do some countries grow faster than others?

In tackling the two key questions of this chapter, we first look at the *facts*, what the numbers tell us about comparative income levels and growth rates. We then we move on to gain an *understanding* of the facts, first in the context of **growth accounting**, which *describes* a country's growth experience rather than *explains* it. Then we learn about **growth theory**, which attempts to *explain* why incomes are where they are and develop the way they do.

Income comparisons and growth: the facts

GDP is a useful measure of the size of a country's economy, and of its economic weight in the world economy. However, the fact that China's GDP is 50 times larger than Luxemburg's says little about how living standards compare. For economic growth to increase the material well-being of the average citizen, the rate of GDP growth must exceed the rate of population increase. Thus, growth is usually discussed and income comparisons are made in terms of *GDP per capita*. Recent per capita GDPs are shown in Figure 35.1. Note that in such comparisons it would be misleading to simply use national GDPs converted into a common currency such as the pound, the euro or the dollar on the basis of this year's exchange rate. Why? Suppose you want to compare

---

potential income
The level of income produced when factors of production are employed at 'normal' levels.

economic growth
An increase in the total output of an economy. Defined by some economists as an increase of real GDP per capita.

growth accounting The *descriptive* study of economic growth. Growth accounting tries to determine how much changes in each factor of production or productivity increases have contributed to income growth.

growth theory
The attempt to *understand* economic growth. Growth theory sets out to *explain* why a country has the capital stock it has and produces the output it does.

Table 35.1 The purchasing power of work time, past and present

	Work time (minutes)		Productivity growth ratio
Germany	**1960**	**1996**	
10 eggs	46	7	6.5
1 litre of petrol	14	4	3.5
Hair wash (by hairdresser)	88	70	1.25
France	**1971**	**1997**	
Women's clothing	7,347	4,373	1.68
Toothpaste	26.3	24.6	1.07
Cinema ticket	140	110	1.28
Italy	**1971**	**1997**	
Spaghetti (1 kg)	24.6	18.6	1.32
Toothpaste	48.7	30.2	1.62
Restaurant meal	156.7	236.4	0.66
Britain	**1971**	**1997**	
Coca Cola (can)	6.9	7.1	0.96
Toothpaste	54.1	26.4	2.05
Hotel room	3,241	3,237	1.00
Switzerland	**1950**	**1990**	
Electricity (1 kWh)	7.4	0.4	18.5
Small car	12.2 (months)	4.6 (months)	2.65
Hospital (per day)	149	566	0.26

Sources: Britain, France and Italy: UBS, *Prices and Earnings around the Globe*, and unpublished data. Germany: Institut der deutschen Wirtschft, Zahlen zur wirtschaftlichen Entwicklung der Bundesrepublik Deutschland, 1997. Switzerland: Bundesamt für Statistik, Zahlen erzählen (NZZ-Verlag, 1994).

French and US per capita incomes for two consecutive years. Assume now that per capita incomes expressed in national currencies (that is, in francs and dollars) have not changed, and neither have domestic prices. Then real per capita GDP in France has not changed, since it buys the same amount of goods and services in both years. Now suppose you want to express it in dollars to be able to compare it with per capita income in the United States. Suppose further that the franc has depreciated by 20% relative to the dollar. Then French per capita income expressed in dollars has risen by 20%, but material well-being has not. French citizens can still buy exactly the same amount of goods and services that they could buy in the previous year.

For international comparisons of income levels to be meaningful, adjustments must be made for purchasing power. In the calculation of Figure 35.1, for example, French per capita income was 134,384 French francs. At the average $/franc exchange rate for 1996 this was equivalent to 26,270 US dollars. To take into account that dollar-denominated prices were not the same in both countries, it was noted that $1.22 bought the same amount of goods and services in France that $1.00 bought in the

Figure 35.1 International income levels in 1996

Per capita incomes (adjusted for differences in purchasing power) in European countries range from $34,480 in Luxemburg to $12,730 in Greece. Japan and the USA are near Europe's upper end. The four Asian tigers cover the full European spectrum. Many developing countries, such as Burundi and Tanzania, have to make do with much lower incomes.
Source: World Bank Atlas, 1998 (own estimate for Taiwan).

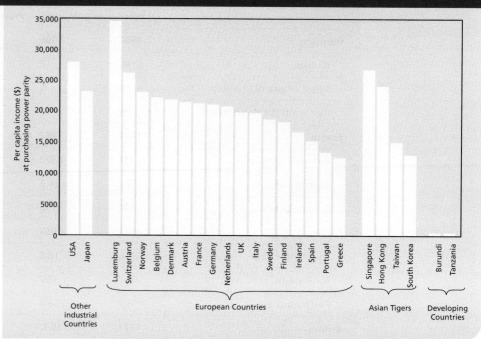

United States. In order to make French purchasing power comparable to US purchasing power, the per capita income of $26,270 had to be divided by 1.22 to yield 21,510. The purchasing power adjusted per capita incomes were obtained for all the other countries in the same way.

Figure 35.1 shows that per capita incomes differ substantially. The world's first division is made up of the European countries and a number of other industrialized countries, together with Japan and the United States, and the four Asian 'tiger' states whose growth rates have received so much attention in recent years. Per capita incomes in the world's poorest nations are about one-fiftieth of what the richest nations produce. The two examples shown are Burundi and Tanzania, where per capita incomes remain well below $1000.

Figure 35.2 shows GDP growth rates for the same countries. Note that growth rates achieved during a specific year say nothing about a country's growth record. Even in a generally quite healthily growing country, a recession may temporarily drive this rate below zero. Or a boom may make this year's growth look impressive even though today's income is scarcely higher than it was ten years ago. To prevent the business cycle from blurring the picture, Figure 35.2 shows *average* growth rates for the period from 1960 to 1992.

Long-run growth rates also exhibit substantial variation across countries. Hong Kong, Singapore, Taiwan and South Korea have taken the lead with growth rates of between 6% and 7% annually. Japan is not far behind. Other industrial countries, with the exception of Portugal, averaged more modest growth between 2% and 4%. These differences may appear small, but a 7% growth rate doubles GDP in 10 years. At Tanzania's 2% growth rate it takes almost 40 years to double income.

Figure 35.2 also shows income levels. This time it is those of 1960, the start of the recorded growth period. The group of European economies reveals a negative relationship between the initial income level and growth.

Within groups of similar countries those countries with lower income levels grow faster.

Figure 35.2 Income levels in 1960, and growth, 1960–1992

Here average growth rates between 1960 and 1992 are compared with per capita incomes in 1960. There is a negative correlation for the European countries. Those with low incomes in 1960 enjoyed high growth rates after. Japan, the USA and the tigers also fit into this picture. Burundi and Tanzania do not fit in. With their low income levels they should have had much higher growth rates.
Source: Penn World Table 5.6.

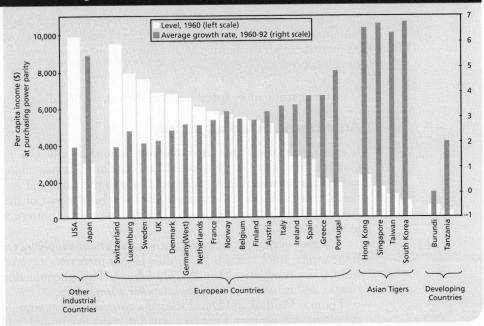

This means that incomes tend to converge: lower incomes gain ground on higher incomes. The United States and Japan fit this picture. So do the tigers, though their growth rates are somewhat higher than those of their European counterparts with similarly low initial incomes. Countries in other parts of the world with low 1960 incomes do not show any convergence at all. Tanzania did not grow faster than the United States or Switzerland. Neither did Burundi, whose 1992 income was the same as in 1960. Thus

> Across continents and cultures, many poor countries do not grow fast enough to catch up with the richer countries.

These countries appear to be trapped in poverty.

We now set out to *understand* the facts documented in Figures 35.1 and 35.2, in order to answer the questions arising from them. Why do incomes differ? Why do growth rates differ? Why do some countries appear to be left behind in the growth process, and what can be done to help them?

Growth accounting

All thinking about economic growth and about long-run income levels starts from the **aggregate production function**. As we learned in Chapter 30, the aggregate production function links total output produced in an economy to the factors used in the production process. An individual firm's production function is a mathematical representation of the relationship between the firm's inputs and its output. Output in an aggregate production function is national output, or gross domestic product. Stated simply, gross domestic product (output) (Y), depends upon the amount of labour (L) and the amount of capital (K) available in the economy (assuming that the amount of land is fixed).[1]

aggregate production function

The mathematical representation of the relationship between inputs and national output, or gross domestic product.

[1]The numbers in the tables that follow were derived from the production function $Y = 3 \times K^{1/3}L^{2/3}$.

If GDP is a function of labour and capital, then:

An increase in GDP can come about in three ways: (1) through an increase in the labour supply, (2) through an increase in physical or human capital, or (3) through an increase in productivity (the amount of product produced by each unit of capital or labour).

Before getting more specific and analytical, we first discuss these factors informally.

An increase in labour supply

It stands to reason that an increasing labour supply can generate more output. Consider, for example, what would happen if another person joined Robinson Crusoe and Friday on their island. He would join in the work and produce, so GDP would rise. Or suppose that a person who had not been a part of the labour force were to begin to work and use her time and energy to produce pottery. Real output would rise in this case too.

Whether output *per capita* rises when the labour supply increases is another matter. If the capital stock remains fixed while labour increases, it is likely that the new labour will be less productive than the old labour. This phenomenon is called *diminishing returns*, and it has worried economists for a long time.

Thomas Malthus and David Ricardo, two economists who lived in England during the nineteenth century, were concerned that the fixed supply of land would ultimately lead to diminishing returns. Land was in strictly limited supply and the population was expanding steadily; to increase agricultural output, people would be forced either to farm less productive land or to farm existing plots more intensively. In either case, the returns to successive increases in population would diminish. Both Malthus and Ricardo predicted a gloomy future as population outstripped the land's capacity to produce. What these economists omitted from their calculations, however, was technological change and capital accumulation. The twentieth century brought new and better farming techniques that raised agricultural productivity so dramatically that less than 5% of the EU labour force now provides more than enough food for the EU's entire population.

Diminishing returns can also set in when a nation's capital stock grows more slowly than its workforce. Capital enhances workers' productivity. A person with a spade digs a bigger hole than a person without one, and a person with a mechanical excavator outdigs them both. If a society's stock of plant and equipment does not grow and the technology of production does not change, then additional workers will not be as productive, because they have no additional machines to work with.

Table 35.2 illustrates how growth in the labour force, without a corresponding increase in the capital stock or technological change, might lead to growth of output but declining productivity and a lower standard of living. As labour increases, output

Table 35.2 Economic growth from an increase in labour: more output, but diminishing returns and lower labour productivity

Period	Quantity of labour (L) (hours)	Quantity of capital (K) (units)	Total output (Y) (units)	Measured labour productivity (Y/L)
1	100	100	300	3.0
2	110	100	320	2.9
3	120	100	339	2.8
4	130	100	357	2.7

rises from 300 units in Period 1 to 320 in Period 2, to 339 in Period 3, and so forth, but **labour productivity** (output per worker hour) falls. Output per worker hour, Y/L, is a measure of labour's productivity.

labour productivity

Output per worker hour; the amount of output produced by an average worker in one hour.

Increases in physical capital

An increase in the stock of capital can also increase output, even if it is not accompanied by an increase in the labour force. Physical capital both enhances the productivity of labour and provides valuable services directly.

It is easy to see how capital provides services directly. In the first few years on the island Robinson and Friday built a house, putting many hours of work into it that could have gone into producing things for immediate consumption. With the house for shelter, they live in relative comfort and can thus spend time on other things. In the same way, capital equipment produced in one year can add to the value of a product over many years. For example, we use and value bridges and tunnels built decades ago.

It is also easy to see how capital employed in production enhances the productivity of labour. Computers enable us to do almost instantly tasks that were once impossible or that might have taken years to complete. A plane can transport hundreds of people thousands of miles in a few hours with a relatively small crew. A bridge at a critical location may save thousands of labour hours that would otherwise be spent transporting materials and people the long way around. It is precisely this yield in terms of future valuable services that provides both private and public investors with the incentive to devote resources to capital production.

Table 35.3 shows how an increase in capital without a corresponding increase in labour can increase output. Several aspects about these numbers are noteworthy. First, additional capital increases measured productivity; output per worker hour (Y/L) increases from 3.0 to 3.1, to 3.19, and finally to 3.27 as the quantity of capital (K) increases. Second, there are diminishing returns to capital. Increasing capital by 10 units first increases output by 10 units – from 300 in Period 1 to 310 in Period 2. But the second increase of 10 units yields only 9 units of output, while the third increase yields only 8 units.

Increases in human capital

human capital

The skills and knowledge which determine the productivity of a worker.

Investment in **human capital** is another important source of economic growth. People in good health are more productive than people in poor health; people with skills are more productive than people without them.

Human capital is produced in a number of ways. Individuals invest in themselves by studying at universities, or following vocational training courses or apprenticeships. Firms invest in human capital through on-the-job training. The government invests in human capital through programmes that improve health or provide schooling and job training.

Table 35.3 Economic growth from an increase in capital: more output, diminishing returns to added capital, and higher measured labour productivity

Period	Quantity of labour (L) (hours)	Quantity of capital (K) (units)	Total output (Y) (units)	Measured labour productivity (Y/L)
1	100	100	300	3.0
2	100	110	310	3.1
3	100	120	319	3.2
4	100	130	327	3.3

Increases in productivity

productivity of an input
The amount of output produced per unit of an input.

Growth that cannot be explained by increases in the *quantity* of inputs can only be explained by an increase in the productivity of those inputs. In this case, each unit of input *produces* more output. The **productivity of an input** can be affected by several factors, including technological change, other advances in knowledge and economies of scale.

Technological change

The Industrial Revolution was in part sparked off by important new technological developments. The development of new techniques of spinning and weaving – the invention of the 'mule' and the 'spinning jenny', for example – were critical. And the high-tech boom that swept the world in the early 1980s was driven by the rapid development and dissemination of semiconductor technology.

invention
An advance in knowledge.

Technological change affects productivity in two stages. First, there is an advance in knowledge, or an **invention**. But knowledge by itself does nothing unless it is used. When new knowledge leads to the production of a new product or to more efficient production of an existing product, there is **innovation**.

innovation The use of new knowledge to produce a new product or to produce an existing product more efficiently.

Technological change cannot be measured directly. Some studies have attempted to present data on 'indicators' of the rate of technical change – the number of new patents or spending on research and development, for example – but none of these is very satisfactory. Still, witness the technological changes and improved productivity all around us. Computer technology has revolutionized the office environment, hybrid seeds have dramatically increased the productivity of land, and more efficient and powerful aircraft have made air travel routine and relatively inexpensive.

Other advances in knowledge

Over and above invention and innovation, advances in other kinds of knowledge can also improve productivity. An important category of knowledge is what we might call 'managerial knowledge'. For example, due to the very high cost of capital during the early 1980s, firms learned to keep production lines and distribution lines flowing with a much lower stock of inventories. Because inventories are part of a firm's capital stock, trimming them reduces costs and raises productivity. This is an example of a *capital-saving* innovation. Many of the advances that we commonly think about, such as the introduction of robots, replace manual tasks and are thus called *labour-saving*.

In addition to managerial knowledge, improved personnel management techniques, accounting procedures, data management and the like can also make production more efficient, reduce costs and increase measured productivity.

Economies of scale

External economies of scale are cost savings that result from increases in the size of industries. The economies that accompany growth in size may arise from a variety of causes. For example, as firms in a growing industry build plants at new locations, they may reduce transport costs. There may also be some economies of scale associated with research and development spending and job-training programmes. The wave of large-scale corporate mergers in the 1990s may reflect expectations of such cost savings.

Other influences on productivity

In addition to technological change, other advances in knowledge and economies of scale, there are other forces that affect productivity. During the 1970s and 1980s, for example, many governments required firms to reduce the air and water pollution they were producing. These requirements diverted capital and labour from the production of measured output and thus reduced measured productivity. Similarly, in recent years requirements imposed by occupational safety and health acts have required firms to improve the protection of workers from accidental injuries and potential health

Applications

Can we really measure productivity changes?

When the government publishes numbers like those presented in Figure 35.3, most people take them as 'true'. Even though we don't really know much about how they are constructed, we assume that they are the best measurements we can get.

Yet such data are often the source of great controversy. In fact, some have argued that the mix of products produced in the United States and the increased pace of technological change in recent years have made it increasingly difficult to measure productivity changes accurately. The observed productivity decline in recent decades may thus simply be measurement error.

These arguments make a certain amount of sense at an intuitive level. Even in agriculture, where it is relatively easy to measure productivity growth, the possibility of mismeasurement exists. The output of a soybean farm can be measured in bushels, and labour, capital,

and land inputs present no serious measurement problems. So, over time, as farming techniques improved and farmers acquired new and better machinery, output per acre and output per worker rose and have continued to rise. But today we have biotechnology. Genetic engineering now makes it possible to make soybeans higher in protein and more disease resistant. Clearly, technology has improved and 'output' has increased, but these increases do not show up in the data because of our relatively crude measures of output.

A similar problem exists with computers. If you simply counted the number of personal computers produced and measured the cost of the inputs used in their production, you would no doubt see some productivity advances. But computers being produced for $1300 in 1995 contained processors capable of performing tasks literally thousands of times faster than computers produced a few

years earlier. If we were to measure computer outputs not in terms of units produced but in terms of the actual 'services' they provide to users, we would find massive productivity advances. Most new PCs now contain CD-ROM slots and can be easily connected to the new and growing 'information superhighway', a source of cheap and plentiful information. In short, the problem is that many of the products that we now use are qualitatively different than the comparable products that we used only a few years ago, and the standard measures of productivity miss much of these quality changes.

The problems are even greater in the service sector, where output is extremely difficult to measure. It is easy to understand the problem if you think of what information technology has done for legal services. As recently as 10 years ago, a lawyer doing research to support a legal case might

spend hundreds of hours looking through old cases and public documents. Today's lawyers can log on to a computer and in seconds do a key word search on a massive legal database. Such time- and labour-saving productivity advances are not counted in the official data.

One of the leading experts on technology and productivity estimates that we have reasonably good measures of output and productivity in only about 31% of the U.S. economy. Does this mean that productivity is not a problem? On this topic economists have agreed to disagree.*

*This argument was described most clearly by Professor Zvi Grilliches of Harvard in his Presidential Address to the American Economic Association in January of 1994. The full text, entitled 'Productivity, R&D, and the Data Constraint', is published in the American Economic Review, March 1994. The counterargument is best advanced by Professor Dale Jorgenson in Productivity (Harvard University Press, 1995).

---

problems. These laws also divert resources from measured output. For attempts to adjust national income measures for pollution and resource depletion, see the Application 'Environmental accounting'.

It is important to understand that negative effects such as these are more a problem of *measurement* than of truly declining productivity. In the United States, for example, the EPA (Environmental Protection Agency) regulates air and water quality because clean air and water presumably have a value to US society. Thus, the resources diverted to produce that value are not wasted. A perfect measure of output produced that is of value to society would include environmental quality and good health.

The specifics of growth accounting

Growth accounting is not content with a general description of the growth process and the factors that drive it. As the word 'accounting' insinuates, it wants to arrive at some hard numbers. We introduce the approach with a stylized example, then add real-world findings and refinements to round out the picture.

Suppose output, Y, depends on the employed amounts of two factors of production, capital, K, and labour, L, according to the equation

$$Y = 3 \times K^{1/3}L^{2/3}$$

We already encountered this kind of *production function* when discussing the labour market in Chapter 30. Graphically, the function looks like the 'hill' shown in Figure 35.3. Income increases (you gain height) in two ways: as you walk up the hill in the direction of more labour, or in the direction of more capital.

Figure 35.3 Production function, labour and capital inputs

a. With unchanged 1950 technology the production function (or surface) remains the same. Income rises only if growth of the labour force or of the capital stock moves the economy up the production function.
b. An improvement in technology between 1950 and 2000 tilts the production function upwards. Income would rise even if labour and the capital stock remained unchanged.

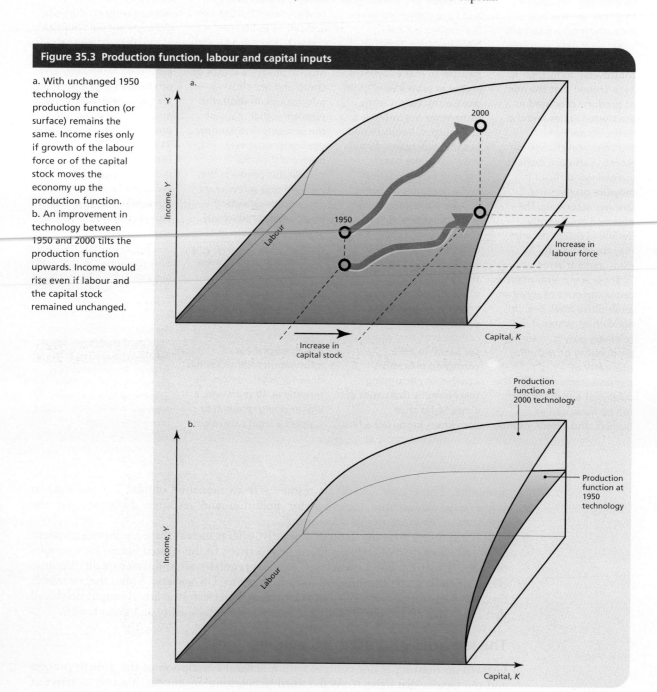

Growth accounting 'explains' income changes in terms of this production function. Figure 35.3 illustrates the two basic ways for economic growth to occur. In Figure 35.3a, we let a country operate with an unchanged technology from 1950 to the year 2000. Income growth during those five decades is achieved through population growth and a rising capital stock; these move the economy up the 3D production function along the bold red path.

Alternatively, growth may result from an improved production technology that permits a more efficient use of available inputs. This is illustrated in Figure 35.3b. Technological progress tilts the production function up from the blue into the yellow position. As a consequence GDP rises at any combination of capital and labour employed.

> Economic growth occurs when (a) society increases the use of one or more factors of production, or (b) society discovers ways of using available factors of production more efficiently.

The two motors of economic growth featured in the two panels of Figure 35.3 usually operate simultaneously. Growth accounting tries to identify their quantitative impacts. Its goal is to link observed income changes to observed movements of the production factors. It does not ask why, for example, Italy has a much larger capital stock than Turkey, but simply takes such observations as facts.

A stylized illustration

Let us be a little more specific about how growth accounting works. Suppose your country's income grew during the second half of the twentieth century along the red bold line shown in Figure 35.4.

Growth accounting assumes that this development of GDP is linked to movements of labour, L, capital, K, and technology, T, through a production function, $Y = T \times K^{\alpha} L^{1-\alpha}$, a general version of the production function introduced previously. First,

Figure 35.4 An illustration of growth accounting

Growth accounting uses statistical methods to attribute observed income growth to a limited number of production factors. The graph shows a hypothetical example.

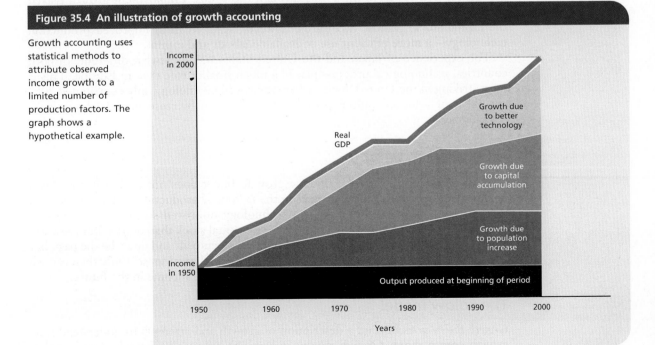

Table 35.4 Sources of growth in six OECD countries

	Percentage of income growth attributable to each source		
	Growth of capital stock (K)	Growth of employment (L)	Improvement of technology (T)
Britain	38	0	61
Germany	45	0	55
France	33	4	63
Italy	32	2	65
Japan	44	11	45
USA	37	42	20

Source: Steven A. Englander and Andrew Gurney, 'Medium-term determinants of OECD productivity growth', *OECD Economic Studies*, 22 (Spring 1994).

statistical methods are used to determine α. Suppose this yields $\alpha = 1/3$, close to where it is for many countries. Then $1 - \alpha = 2/3$. With this information and the knowledge of how L and K developed (T cannot be observed directly), we can compute the contribution of changes in L and K to an observed change of income. Whatever L and K do not account for must be the result of a change of technology, T. In the end, we are able to attribute income growth to its three sources (in our stylized example), as suggested in Figure 35.4.

When following the procedure described above, researchers break the factors of production down into finer components or add categories such as public infrastructure (roads, bridges, etc.) or human capital (the average education and skills of the labour force). Table 35.4 presents some results obtained in accordance with the above example.

One interesting result is that the four largest European economies had very similar growth experiences from the 1960s through the 1980s. Employment growth played no role at all. About one-third of the achieved output increase is due to an increase of the capital stock. Almost two-thirds, however, resulted from improved production technology – a more efficient use of available labour and capital.

The experience of Japan and the United States was somewhat different. In both countries, technological progress played a much smaller role than in Europe. This is most striking in the United States, where improved technology only contributed 20% and 42% of achieved output growth came from an increase in the labour force (employment).

Growth theory

Growth accounting *describes* economic growth, but it does not *explain* it. Observed income changes are linked to changes in the factors of production and in technology. Growth accounting does not ask *why* technology improved so much faster in one country, or *why* some country employs a larger capital stock than others. But these are important questions. If we are not content just to document and describe the past, but want to learn from it, we must understand it in an analytical sense. Only then can we hope to conceive policies that enhance growth and raise income in the future.

The Solow model

Growth theory goes beyond a description of growth and attempts to understand how growth comes about. Growth theory and growth accounting have in common that

Figure 35.5 The 3D production function from another perspective

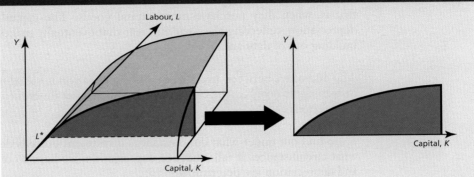

Output Y depends on capital K, labour L, and technology. For given technology we may draw a 3D production function (left) showing Y to rise as K or L increases. With L given at L^*, if K grows we move up the blue path on the production function. This partial production function may be displayed in a two-dimensional Y–K diagram (right).

their central building block is the macroeconomic production function, shown again in Figure 35.5. In Chapter 30, the 3D production function was the starting point of our discussions of the labour market. There we were interested in the short-run fluctuations of income. In the short run – say, in a given year – a country's capital stock (its factories, roads, airports, telephone lines, computers) are more or less given. But if the capital stock is a given (or is changing only very slowly), fluctuations of income had to be the result of fluctuations in employment. So when we were analysing the business cycle and the labour market, the capital stock was considered as fixed at the current level, whereas employment was considered to flexible, following short-run movements in demand and supply.

This view is reversed in the analysis of economic growth. In the long run, temporary fluctuations of employment even out. They may be ignored. On average, employment is at its normal level. This **potential employment** is determined by demographic and sociological factors. Let L^* stand for potential employment and assume it is constant.[2] When employment is fixed at L^*, only one variable input remains: the capital stock. To show how income changes when the capital stock changes, we no longer need the third dimension. To get rid of the L-dimension, simply cut a vertical slice out of the 3D production function parallel to the K axis at employment L^*. Move the slice out into a diagram with Y and K on the axes, and you have a new partial production function.

The partial production function showing how output moves with the capital stock when employment is given is the key building block of the **Solow model**. In itself, this function merely describes a menu of possibilities. What the Solow model adds to this production function is an explanation of what capital stock and what income level a country will eventually have. Explaining capital formation in the macroeconomy is the important contribution of the Solow model. Let us see how it is done.

Saving and investment

In order to focus on essential arguments we start by looking at the global economy model with no government. The reason why this makes things easier is because then investment equals saving, $I = S$, as we showed back in Chapter 23. Including the government complicates things because it may run a budget deficit, sucking up some private saving that is not available to finance investment projects any more. Including the possibility of capital exports or imports – the national economy case – also complicates things, because savings are free to flow abroad and are hence no longer available to finance investment projects at home. These complications are important. But we postpone dealing with them until later.

potential employment

A relatively constant level of employment, determined by demographic and sociological factors, at which temporary fluctuations are evened out.

Solow model

Explains the long-run equilibrium levels of the capital stock and income, and how the economy approaches this equilibrium.

[2]*This amounts to assuming a constant population. We look at the effects of population growth below.*

What affects the size of the capital stock? This is easy: anything that adds to or takes away from the capital stock. Firms add to the capital stock when they *invest* – that is, when they purchase more capital goods. The capital stock shrinks due to depreciation, reflecting the wear and tear that eventually makes a machine, a car or a building out of date and obsolete.

> The difference between investment and depreciation is called *net investment*. If net investment is positive, the capital stock grows. If net investment is negative, the capital stock falls.

To find out under what circumstances investment exceeds depreciation, and under what circumstances it falls short of depreciation, we have to discuss how investment and depreciation are determined.

■ **Determining investment** We noted above that:

> In the global economy with no government, investment equals saving: $I = S$.

If this holds, then one way to determine investment is to determine saving. We did this in Chapter 23, where we noted that in the absence of taxes, people either consume their income or save it: $Y = C + S$. If consumption is a fraction of income ($C = cY$), then saving must also be a fraction of income: $S = sY$. Note that if, say, 80% of income is consumed ($c = 0.8$), then 20% (= 100% – 80%) is saved ($s = 1 - c = 1 - 0.8 = 0.2$).

> In the global economy with no government investment, saving is proportional to income.

This lets us display investment on the same diagram as the production function. In Figure 35.6 the production function is shown in blue. If the saving rate is $s = 0.3$, saving and investment is 30% as high as income at any capital stock. In the numerical

---

Figure 35.6 The saving-and-investment function

The production function shows how income is related to the capital stock. If people save a given share of income, saving is related to the capital stock as indicated by the saving line. In the global economy with no government all saving is investment. Thus the saving line is also the investment line.

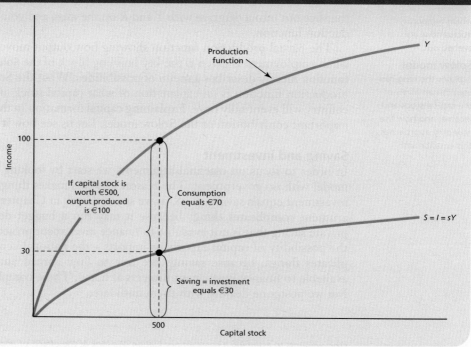

Figure 35.7 The depreciation function

Each year part of the capital stock wears out – a process called depreciation. If the rate of depreciation is 10%, 50 units worth of capital wear out if the capital stock is 500, and 100 units wear out if the capital stock is 1,000. Generally, the depreciation line is a straight line. Its slope equals the rate of depreciation.

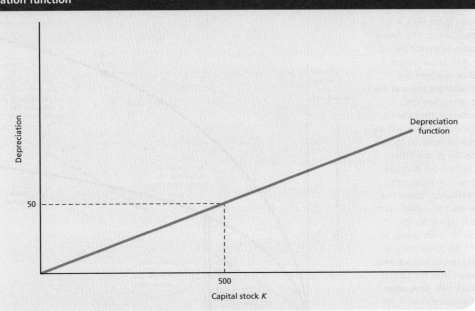

example shown in the graph, €500 worth of capital combined with potential employment L^* produce €100 worth of output (and income). €70 are spent on consumption goods and services; the remaining €30 are saved and invested. The investment function (shown in red) has the same properties as the production function: because it equals $I = sY$, it is steep when the capital stock is small, and becomes flatter and flatter as the capital stock increases.

■ **Determining depreciation**   Depreciation means that a capital good gradually loses its value through the normal wear and tear of being used. Each period, this eats up a certain fraction, d, of the existing capital stock

> Each period, depreciation eats up a given fraction, d, of the existing capital stock:
> depreciation = $d \times K$

In a graph with the capital stock measured along the horizontal axis and depreciation along the vertical axis, the depreciation function is a straight line. It passes through the origin (there is no depreciation if there is no capital) and has slope d. If $d = 0.1$, €50 worth of capital goods are lost this year if the capital stock is €500 (see Figure 35.7).

The steady state

To see under what conditions the capital stock rises and under what conditions it falls, we project the investment function (which shows what is added to the capital stock) and the depreciation function (which shows how much capital is lost) into the same graph (Figure 35.8). The red line shows depreciation. The blue line shows investment (which equals saving).

To get a feel for when and how the capital stock moves, we consider two specific cases. First, suppose the capital stock is small, worth €250 only. Then depreciation is small, equal to the length of the vertical red line. Investment is also small, equal to the vertical blue line, but higher than depreciation. So investment suffices to replace the part of the capital stock lost due to depreciation, and still add something to the existing capital stock. This *net investment* is equal to the length of the green line. Next period, the capital stock is higher, at €250 plus the quantity of euros measured by the green line.

Figure 35.8 The equilibrium or steady-state capital stock

The capital stock is in equilibrium, in a *steady state*, when it does not rise or fall any more. It obtains where the investment line and the depreciation line intersect. Here capital goods that wear out are exactly replaced by new capital goods. If the capital stock is at 250, firms purchase more new capital goods than needed to replace worn out capital. So the capital stock grows. At $K = 800$ investment is too low to replace what wears out. The capital stock falls. Only when the capital stock is 500 does it not change any more.

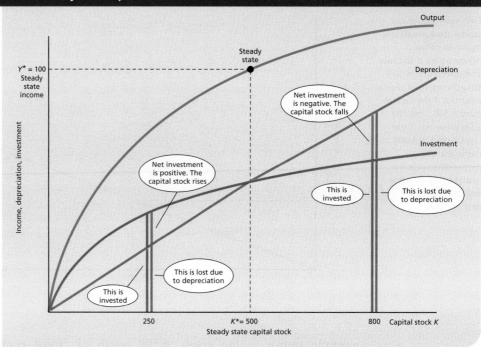

The constellation just encountered obtains in the entire range between 0 and 500. Whenever the capital stock exceeds 0 and is smaller than 500, the investment function lies above the depreciation line. Thus gross investment exceeds depreciation and the capital stock grows. So if the country starts out with a capital stock between zero and 500, the economy moves to the right. Having a higher capital stock each period, output produced is higher each period. The economy grows. This can be read off the production function, along which the economy moves 'north-east'.

Next, suppose the capital stock is initially high, worth €800. Then depreciation is high, equal to the length of the vertical red line. Investment is also quite high, equal to the vertical blue line, but this time it falls short of depreciation. So investment during each period is too small to replace the part of the capital stock that is worn out. This net loss equals the length of the green line. Next period, the capital stock is below €800 by the quantity of euros indicated by the length of the green line.

You can see from a comparison between the depreciation function and the investment function that net investment is always negative when the capital stock exceeds €500. The willingness of domestic residents to save and invest does not suffice to maintain such high capital stocks. So the capital stock falls, and income falls as well, as indicated by a 'south-eastward' movement along the production function.

Now if the capital stock rises when it falls short of €500 and falls when it exceeds €500, does it ever come to rest? Yes, at the level of exactly €500. At this level, and only at this level, do people save and firms invest just enough to replace all capital lost due to depreciation. This leaves the capital stock in equilibrium when K is €500. We denote this capital stock by $K^* = 500$ because it is a special kind of equilibrium, called a *steady state*.

Empirical research found that it takes decades for a country to move back towards the steady state after a destruction of parts of the capital stock, say in the course of a war. Therefore the steady state is an equilibrium concept for the very long run. The level of output produced when a country's capital stock is in the steady state is called **steady state output** (or income). It equals €100 in our graph, as can be determined by moving up vertically from $K^* = 500$ to the production function.

steady state output

The level of output produced when a country's capital stock is in the steady state.

Why do incomes differ between countries?

We can now draw on the Solow model to explain why incomes can differ, and often substantially so, between countries. Because such comparisons are usually based on income per capita, suppose for now that we are comparing two countries with the same population and labour force. Then a higher GDP translates directly into higher GDP per capita or per worker, and we can work with the graph shown in Figure 35.8.

Suppose that the two countries are Belgium and Portugal. They each have a population of about 10 million. But Belgium's GDP (and GDP per capita) is about twice as high as Portugal's. Why may that be?

Different saving rates

Let's start with the most straightforward reason in terms of Figure 35.8: the two countries have different capital stocks. This may be because one country suffered from wartime destruction or a major natural disaster but the other country did not. Then reasons outside the realm of economics are responsible for the differences in the capital stock and the differences in income. If no such extraordinary events struck in recent years or decades, however, we may presume that each country operates in, or close to, its steady state. What we are asked to explain, then, is why the steady state capital stock in the one country is higher than in the other.

The previous section taught us that the steady state capital stock obtains where the investment function and the depreciation function intersect. The blue lines in Figure 35.9 identify one such steady state. Let it be Portugal's.

For Belgium's steady state capital stock to be higher, the depreciation and investment functions must intersect further to the right. This could happen if the Belgium depreciation curve were flatter. But why should that be? Why should a computer, a car, a cooker or a steel mill wear out faster in Portugal than in Belgium? There is no obvious reason for this, so it is not plausible. Alternatively, Belgium's investment (or saving) curve could be higher, say in the red position. If Belgium's capital stock equalled Portugal's steady state capital stock, Belgians would save and invest more each period than is lost through depreciation. Net investment would add to the existing capital stock until the higher, red steady state is reached.

Figure 35.9 The saving rate and steady state income

The higher a country's saving rate, the more it invests at any given capital stock. Hence it can replace more capital that wears out each year. So even if Belgium and Portugal operated on the same production function, Belgium could afford a higher steady state capital stock and enjoy higher income if it had a higher saving rate.

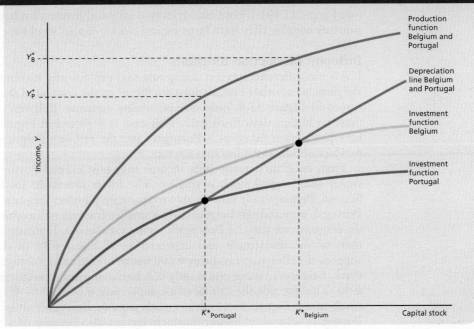

Figure 35.10 The global relationship between saving and income per capita

The higher a country's investment rate, the higher its income (per capita). The graph underscores this prediction of our model for a large number of the world's economies. *Source*: R. Barro and J. Lee: http://www.nuff.ox.ac.uk/Economics/Growth/barlee.htm

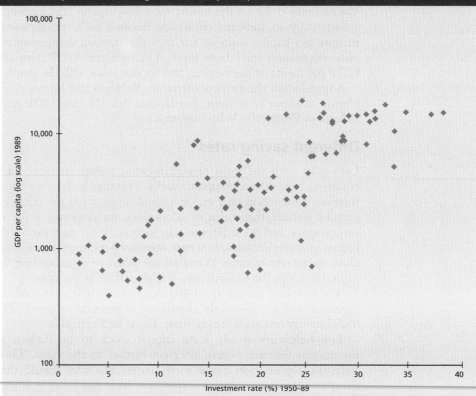

Do Belgians really save more than Portuguese? Well, actually not. On the contrary, Belgium's savings rate averaged only 17% between 1980 and 1989, whereas Portugal's stood at 23%, one of the highest among industrial countries. So we must rethink the Belgium–Portugal story in order to refine it. The big picture, however, including all the world's economies for which data are available, supports the proposed relationship (see Figure 35.10). Those countries that save and invest a lot have high incomes (presumably because they have large capital stocks; capital stocks are difficult to measure).

Different production functions

If it is not differences in the saving rate that explain why income is so much higher in Belgium, what other explanations are there? In the context of the Solow model as portrayed in Figure 35.8, only one possibility remains: Belgium's production function must be higher than Portugal's. This case is depicted in Figure 35.11, in which the blue production function is Portugal's and the red one Belgium's. The difference in production functions has two effects.

First, Belgium's steady state income may now exceed Portugal's even if Belgium's steady state capital stock is smaller. The lower threshold for this to be true is K_L. Second, Belgium may now be able to maintain a higher steady state capital stock than Portugal, even though Belgians save a smaller fraction of income than the Portuguese. To demonstrate this, let Portugal's saving rate be 0.3. If steady state income is €100, then saving, investment and depreciation all equal €30 in the steady state. Now suppose that Belgium produces €200 worth of output at Portugal's steady state capital stock. Belgium's saving rate is only 0.2, but saving and investment equal 0.2 × €200 = €40. This exceeds the capital stock depreciation of €30 by €10, making the capital stock grow. Figure 35.11 shows such a case: Belgium's income not only exceeds Portugal's because of higher productivity, but also because of a higher capital stock.

Figure 35.11 Different production functions and the steady state

When the production technology improves, the production function shifts upwards. If people still save the same fraction of income, the investment line tilts upwards too. This raises the steady-state capital stock. Steady-state income is higher for two reasons: (1) because of the higher capital stock we would even have moved up on the old production function; (2) because of better technology we make better use of the increased capital stock.

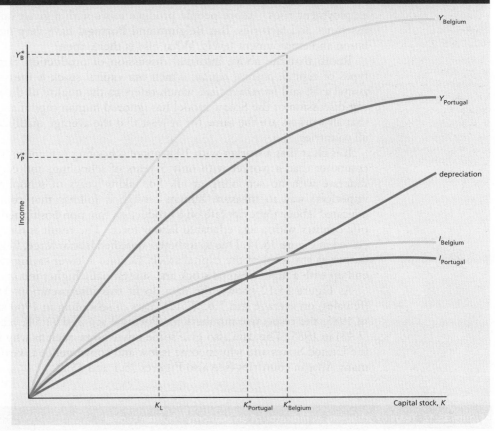

Differences in human capital

The above explanation for why Belgium's income may exceed Portugal's works well formally, but we still need an intuitive foundation. In our current view, Belgium's production function will be higher than Portugal's because Belgium employs better production technologies. How could that be? Granted, companies do have little secrets they like to keep to themselves. Otherwise industrial espionage would not exist. But does this matter much in the era of globalization when companies like Volkswagen are building cars in Brazil, the Czech Republic, Germany, Mexico and Spain, when any company with an innovative product in manufacturing or electronics, hardware or software, can flood the world market in no time? It is, therefore, plausible to assume that all countries have access to the same technology, and thus ought to be operating on the same production function.

This must not be confused with the question of whether a country is really able to buy the latest technology. A Ukrainian farmer may not work the fields with equipment as advanced and sophisticated as his French counterpart. This is only because current income and saving is so low in the Ukraine. In principle, the same equipment and technology is available to Ukraine's farmers in the international markets, but currently they lack the means to acquire it. Because the Ukrainian capital stock is worth very little, the country operates far to the left on its production function.

But if the availability of production technologies is universal, how can there still be different partial production functions for different countries? The key word here is *partial*, meaning that the function is drawn in the *Y/K* diagram while holding technology and other factors production unchanged: the function turns upwards when technology improves. But we have just argued that this is no plausible explanation of income differences between countries. The function also turns upwards if employment rises – more people produce more with a given number of computers, machines and factories. But Belgium and Portugal have very much the same population and employment levels. What else is there, then?

Recall that the above informal discussion of production factors mentioned two types of capital: *physical capital*, which our capital stock K measures along the horizontal axis; and *human capital*, which refers to the quality of the labour force. So far, our discussion of the Solow model has ignored human capital and assumed implicitly that all workers are the same (or at least that the average qualification is the same) in all countries.

It is clear that a worker with 10 years of schooling gets more out of working with a computer than a worker with only 5 years of schooling, and certainly more than an illiterate with no schooling at all. So, taking years of schooling as one (certainly imperfect) way to measure human capital, it follows that countries with a better educated labour force operate on a production function positioned further up than that of a country with a less educated labour force. The result is the same as the one discussed in Figure 35.11. Due to its better qualified labour force, Belgium produces more output at any level of the capital stock. Despite a lower saving rate, it may therefore end up with a higher capital stock and substantially higher income than Portugal.

As Figure 35.12 shows, the data do fit this interpretation. While Belgian males (females) on average had 7.62 (7.12) years of schooling in 1960 and 9.55 (8.79) years in 1985, the respective numbers for Portugal are 2.41 (1.54) years in 1960 and 4.29 (3.43) in 1985. The data also give some other hints, such as why income is so high in the United States and why income is low and convergence is virtually non-existent in many African countries (see also Figures 35.1 and 35.2).

Figure 35.12 Years of schooling as indicator of an economy's human capital

The higher a country's human capital, the higher its income (per capita). The graph underscores this prediction of our model for a large number of the world's economies. *Source*: R. Barro and J. Lee: http://www.nuff.ox. ac.uk/Economics/ Growth/barlee.htm

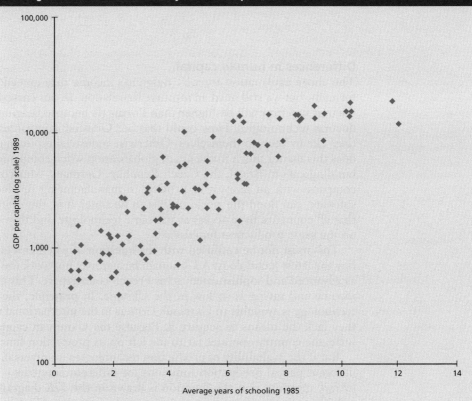

Income growth in the Solow model

We have acquired an understanding of how a country's income is determined in the long run, and why incomes may differ substantially between countries. You may have noticed during our discussions that in these steady states incomes no longer grow. In the Solow model, incomes grow only temporarily while they rise towards the steady state. For example, after a war destroys part of the capital stock, several decades of capital accumulation follow and hence a period of growing incomes. Or if a country's citizens suddenly save more than they previously did, positive net investment adds to the capital stock, driving income up too. But all this eventually peters out and income stagnates because the capital stock has stopped growing.

Just as in our discussion of growth accounting, only two things can make income grow further: (1) an increase in the labour force (or the population), or (2) an increase in productivity. Both tilt the partial production function upwards. The Solow model can *trace* what happens to income if technology improves or the labour force grows, but it does not *explain* why and how quickly this occurs. Explaining *growth*, and not just income levels, is the focus of recent research by growth economists. We will turn to some policy suggestions derived from this research towards the end of the chapter.

Per capita income and population growth

We have seen that improvements in production technology or in human capital, a rise in the saving rate or a larger labour force all raise a country's income. All except the last one not only raise income but also per capita income, the ultimate measure of the well-being of a country's population. This follows directly from the fact that in these cases income rises even if the population remains constant.

When income rises because the population grows, it is not obvious what happens to per capita income. After all, both numerator and denominator in the fraction Y/L rise. To sort out what happens, consider the following numerical example. Suppose the economy begins in a steady state with income 100, a capital stock of 500, and a labour force of 20 that does not grow. Income per capita is 5 and the capital stock per worker is 25. Since the rate of depreciation is 0.1 (10%), €50 need to be, and are, saved and invested each year to keep the capital stock at its steady state level of 500.

Now suppose employment (and the population) starts to grow by 5% each year, so that employment rises to 21 next year. What does this do to per capita income? First, the capital stock is still at 500, since €50 were invested and €50 worth of capital was lost through depreciation. We could leave each one of the initial 20 workers equipped with €25 worth of capital goods. The new worker would have no capital to work with and wouldn't produce anything. Or we could spread the capital stock over more workers. In the first year, the capital stock per worker is $500 \div 21 = 23.81$. This is less than each worker had before the population began growing. With less capital, each worker produces less though more workers work. Output per worker and per capita falls. This example can be generalized:

> In a growing population, not all investment is available to replace capital lost through depreciation. Some investment is needed to equip new workers with the same capital as the old workers already have. This causes capital per worker, and therefore income per worker, to fall.

The faster the population grows, the stronger is the described effect. If 10% new workers need to be equipped with new capital each period, less investment is left as a replacement for depreciated capital than if only 5% new workers enter employment. This yields the proposition:

> The higher a country's population growth rate, the lower its income per capita in the steady state.

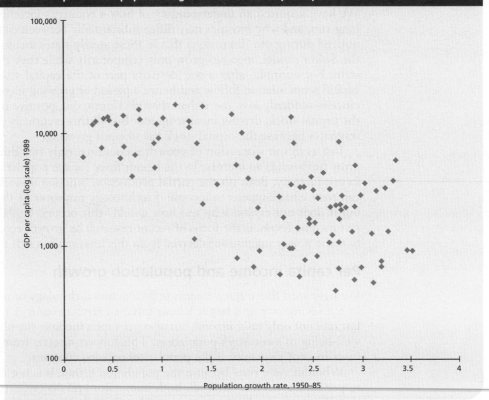

Figure 35.13 The global relationship between population growth and income per capita

The higher a country's rate of population growth, the lower its income per capita. This prediction of our model also holds for a large number of the world's economies, though less clearly so than the other predictions.
Source: R. Barro and J. Lee: http://www.nuff.ox. ac.uk/Economics/ Growth/barlee.htm

GDP per capita (log scale) 1989

Population growth rate, 1950–85

This proposition receives empirical support, as Figure 35.13 shows.

The role of the government in the Solow model

Now that we understand the basics of the Solow model, let's add realism. Our first step is to introduce the government. This can be done in a straightforward way. Remember that in the global economy with no government, investment equals saving, $I = S$. This permitted us to use the saving function and the investment function interchangeably in the last few diagrams, making life quite easy. By adding the government (but no foreign trade yet), we must remember the identity $(S - I) + (T - G) = 0$ (instead of $I - S = 0$) (see Chapter 24). Solving this for I, the investment function, yields

$$I = S - (G - T)$$

This equation shows that introducing the government drives a wedge between saving, S, and investment, I. Only if the government balances its budget ($G = T$) do we get $I = S$ as before, meaning that firms can draw on the entire saving of the private sector to invest. If $G > T$, the government runs a deficit. Let it be €10 billion. Then the government soaks up €10 billion worth of private saving in the capital market. This drives investment below the level of private saving, to exactly $I = S - 10$. If the government continues to run deficits year after year, investment falls short of what it could be each year, and the country ends up with a smaller capital stock. Figure 35.14 shows this effect on the by now familiar diagram.

In a world without government, the investment function equals the blue saving function. The steady state capital stock is 500 (billion €). Steady state income is 100. A government budget deficit drives the investment function down below the saving

Figure 35.14 Budget deficits and steady state income

Government budget deficits drive a wedge between private saving and investment. The reason is that the government absorbs part of private saving to finance the budget deficit. As a result, less saving is left for firms to finance investment. The lower investment line leads to a lower capital stock and lower steady state income.

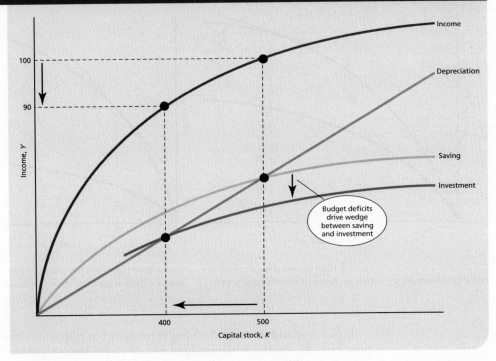

function, say into the red position. With reduced investment spending, it is impossible to keep the capital stock at 500. It declines until eventually reaching its new, lower steady state of 400. There the country produces a steady state income of 90.

This gives a new perspective to our previous results on expansionary fiscal policy. This long-run view is the main motivation behind the Maastricht treaty's deficit criterion.

> Expansionary fiscal policy temporarily stimulates demand and income. If expansionary fiscal policy is maintained for some time, its long-run consequences may be lower income in the steady state.

This is an important result, but we must qualify it. So far, we have assumed government spending on goods and services to constitute consumption. But governments build roads, waterways, telephone lines, schools and universities. These are clearly investment projects that add to a nation's capital stock. To the extent that the government runs deficits in order to finance urgent and productive public investment projects, the negative effects on steady state income are reduced or even eliminated.

International capital markets and the Solow model

A final step is needed to bring the growth model into line with our previous national economy model. We must allow for an individual country to have links with the rest of the world – via trade and via capital flows. The feature we focus on here, because of its dramatic consequences for a country's income level, is the presence of international capital flows. Global capital markets give everyone the opportunity to invest their savings anywhere in the world – the world is the limit, not the domestic economy.

To see the consequences, suppose you live in one of the world's rich countries, one with a large capital stock generating high income. Figure 35.15a depicts this high-income steady state.

Figure 35.15 Global capital markets and income

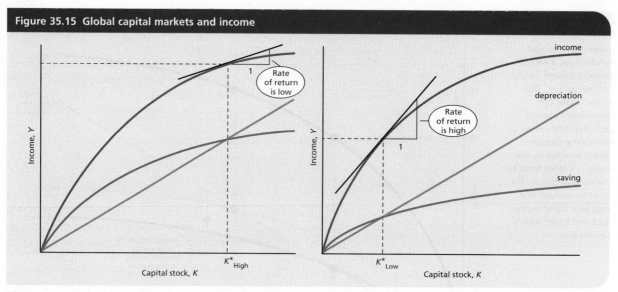

a. High-saving-and-income country: Here the marginal product of capital (which equals the return on financial investments) is small.

b. Low-saving-and-income country: Here the marginal product of capital (which equals the return on financial investments) is high.

If you save and invest that saving at home, what return can you expect? Well, compensation for capital is determined just like the compensation for labour, the wage rate. In equilibrium, the wage rate equals the marginal product of labour. The marginal product of labour is given by the slope of the partial production function on an output–labour diagram.

Analogously, the return to capital equals the marginal product of capital. The marginal product of capital is given by the slope of the partial production function on an output–capital-stock diagram. So the slope of the production function at the steady state capital stock of €500 tells you how much interest per period to expect for one euro of your saving invested at home.

Figure 35.15b shows a low income country with the same size population operating on the same production function as your country. Because of a low saving rate, this country's capital stock is small. This makes capital scarce. Therefore, the marginal productivity of capital is high. The graph illustrates this by the steep slope of the production function at this country's low steady state capital stock.

Global capital markets give you the option to invest your saving at home or in the low-income country. What will you do? If you see no particular risks in investing in the low-income country, you will certainly invest there. Returns are much higher. But this means that investment in your country falls below saving, and investment in the low-income country exceeds domestic saving. Thus capital stocks begin to move. The capital stock falls in your country, and it rises in the low-income country. In theory, this process continues until both countries have the same capital stock, the same income level and the same marginal product of capital.

In reality, investors often consider investments in developing countries riskier than those at home. This puts a brake on the convergence of capital stock and incomes. But the process is under way, especially where political, legal and economic stability guarantee that risks incurred by international investors are not completely out of line with risks taken by investing at home or in other industrial countries.

Economic growth and public policy

Most industrial countries experienced a serious slowdown in economic growth after the first oil price shock in the mid-1970s. Europe's performance looked particularly bleak in comparison with many Asian economies, notably the 'tigers' – Hong Kong, Singapore, Taiwan and South Korea. Insufficient growth is commonly considered to be a cause of Europe's high unemployment (remember Okun's Law?).

Several strategies for revitalizing growth in Europe and other established industrial countries have been suggested. Some have even been enacted into national law or international treaties, such as the EU's pact for stability and growth. Most measures discussed can be directly derived from our generalized Solow model. This suggests that a country's income per capita grows if (1) the capital stock grows (due to rising investment rates), (2) human capital improves, or (3) production technology improves.

Policies to increase the saving rate

In the global economy, capital accumulation is ultimately constrained by the rate of saving. The more saving, the more funds are available for investment. This also holds for national economies, despite the opening of capital markets. The national saving rate in Japan is twice as high as it is in the United States. Most European countries lie in between. The same holds for investment, which is a much higher fraction of GDP in Japan than in most of Europe, which in turn fares better than the United States. In the wake of the globalization of capital markets, the link between a country's saving and its investment has become weaker: funds for domestic investment projects may come from abroad if they are not supplied by domestic saving. But the link is still there. Countries with high saving still invest more than countries with low saving.

Some economists favour shifting to a system of consumption taxation rather than income taxation to reduce the tax burden on saving. Others claim that the social security system, by providing guaranteed retirement incomes, reduces the incentive for people to save. Private pension plans make deposits to workers' accounts, the balances of which are invested in the stock market and bond market and are thus available to firms for capital investment. Social security benefits, in contrast, are often paid out of current tax receipts, and no such accumulations are available for investment. Thus, the argument goes, if social security substitutes for private saving, the national saving rate is reduced. Evidence on the extent to which taxes and social security reduce the saving rate is not decisive.

Policies to stimulate investment

The capital stock in the national economy ultimately depends on the rate of investment. As we said above, this can be raised by stimulating the saving rate. But it can also be raised by attracting more investment from abroad. This works if the domestic economy is considered an attractive place to invest and operate in, and the particular investment project under consideration is received with a level of goodwill (material and non-material) not matched by other countries. The general investment climate can only be changed in the longer run. It reflects things like the working of the bureaucracy, the availability of workers with certain qualifications, labour relations and costs, infrastructure, the legal system, and political stability. This makes competition among countries, states or regions for new, large-scale investment projects particularly fierce. Examples that made headlines are the competition between Alsace and Baden Wurttemberg for Daimler-Benz's Smart car plant, or the competition among several southern US states for the first BMW plant in North America. On a larger scale, Ireland was extremely successful in attracting high-quality investment by renowned companies during the 1980s.

Policies to improve the quality of education

We learned above that human capital is another key determinant of a country's income level. Empirical studies lend support to this proposition, finding that years of schooling or the level of government spending on education affects income and growth positively.

Applications

Environmental accounting

If national income accounts ignore environmental considerations why not modify the accounts? Alas it is easier said than done.

The difficulties of creating environmental statistics that are comparable to national income and wealth statistics are serious. GDP is measured in money, but putting monetary values on environmental assets is a black art. Some assets, such as timber, may have a market value, but that value does not encompass the trees' role in harbouring rare beetles say, or their sheer beauty. Methods for valuing such benefits are controversial. To get round these problems, the UN guidelines suggest measuring the cost of repairing environmental damage. But some kinds of damage, such as extinction, are beyond costing, and others are hard to estimate.

For economists, the average value of a good or service is usually less important than the

marginal value – the cost or benefit of one more unit. Marginal value, however, is a tricky concept to bring into environmental analysis. It may be clear that the cost of wiping out an entire species of beetle would be high, but what value should be attached to the extermination of a few hundred bugs?

Putting environmental concepts into economic terms raises other difficulties as well. Geography weighs differently: a tonne of sulphur dioxide emitted in a big city may cause more harm than the same tonne emitted in a rural area, while a dollar's worth of output counts the same wherever it is produced. And the exploitation of natural resources may not always have a cost. Is a country depleting resources if it mines a tonne of coal? All other things equal, the mining of that tonne might raise the value of the coal that remains in the ground, leaving the value of coal assets unchanged.

In addition to these conceptual problems, Steven Keuning, head of the Dutch national accounts department, points out that the entire attempt to attach cash values to environmental goods and bads is a bit nonsensical. The reason is that, had the environment been priced in the way that statisticians might value it, people would have behaved differently. The valuation exercise, he says, postulates a situation that could never have existed.

Faced with such objections, government statisticians in Europe and Canada have concentrated on a different approach, advocated by Mr Keuning and by Eurostat, the statistical arm of the European Union. The idea is to relate economic activity, measured in cash terms, to environmental magnitudes in physical units. So the accounts try to show, for instance, how many tonnes of carbon dioxide are emitted by which sectors of an economy, and how those

We all think the environment is important but placing a value on it is very difficult.

amounts are changing. This describes the relationship between the economy and the environment, but it does not adjust economic figures to take account of the degradation of environmental assets. It therefore does not meet the clamour of environmentalists for a measure that will change the way governments look at economic growth.

Source: 'An invaluable environment', The Economist, April 18, 1998, p. 105.

Policies to increase research and development (R&D)

Research shows that the rate of return on investment in R&D is quite high. Estimates place the rate of return at about 30%.[3] R&D is similar to investment in human capital. Both increase our knowledge of how to do things and are readily subsumed under 'improvement of technology'. There is an important difference, however. Human capital is tied directly to the labour force. As long as workers stay in a country, their human capital stays, and with them the production techniques.

By contrast, new knowledge achieved in the context of R&D is like a public good. Although the industrialized world has a patent system to protect gains of R&D for

[3]See M. Nadiri, 'Contributions and determinants of research and development expenditures in the US manufacturing industries', in George M. von Furstenberg (ed.), Capital Efficiency and Growth (Cambridge, MA: Ballinger Press, 1980).

inventors and innovators, many of the benefits flow to imitators and others, including the public. This logic has been used to justify public subsidization of R&D spending, but also to argue that investment in R&D may be less crucial than investment in human capital.

Reduced regulations

One of the cornerstones of the Reagan and Bush administrations in the United States and of the Thatcher government in the UK was a commitment to reduced government regulation, which many believed stood in the way of investment and production. If only because they are feeling the pressure of global competition, many European countries are following this path.

Critics of these policies argue that many regulations serve perfectly legitimate economic purposes. For example, environmental regulations, if properly administered, improve efficiency. Judicious use of fair competition laws can also improve the allocation of resources and stimulate investment and production.

Industrial policy

industrial policy
Government involvement in the allocation of capital across manufacturing sectors.

The Solow model assumes that perfect competition directs investment to its best use. Arguing that competition is imperfect or distorted in many industries, a number of economists have called for more government involvement in the allocation of capital across manufacturing sectors, a practice known as industrial policy. They argue that because governments of other countries are 'targeting' industries for special subsidies and rapid investment, Europe should follow suit to avoid losing out in international competition. The Japanese Ministry of Trade and Industry, for example, targeted the car industry very early on and decided to expand its role in world markets. The strategy succeeded very well – at the expense of the European and US car industry. A European example is Airbus Industrie. Floated and still nurtured by large government subsidies – purportedly necessary to counterbalance the indirect subsidies that US plane makers received via defence contracts – Airbus has established itself as a major force on the world market for commercial aircraft, which might otherwise have placed European carriers at the mercy of US monopolies.

Control of government budget deficits

As the EU's pact for stability and growth conveys and our analysis above showed, cautious and responsible government spending also fosters growth. The pact tries to ensure this by requiring deficit ratios to remain below 3% of GDP during normal times. While this may serve its purpose as a rule of thumb, it is important that governments do not sacrifice those spending items essential to promoting growth in order to meet the criterion. Such items are spending on education, on R&D and on public infrastructure in general. This reveals that more often than not there is a trade-off between different policies to encourage growth: one policy may not be pushed without sacrificing some other.

Growth policy: a long-run proposition

Fiscal and monetary policies designed to counteract the cyclical up-and-down swings in the economy can produce measurable results in a short period of time. By contrast, the effects of policies designed to increase growth may not be observed for many years. For example, a policy that succeeded in raising the rate of growth by one percentage point, say from 2.5% to 3.5%, would be viewed as a tremendous success. Yet it would be almost a decade before such a policy raised GDP by 10%.

But even though pro-growth policies work only in the long run, are they worth pursuing? Not everyone agrees that the top priority in a developed economy should be continued growth. To close the chapter, we now turn to this debate.

The pros and cons of growth

Views on economic growth are divided: some believe that growth should be the primary objective of any society, and some believe that the costs of growth are too great.

The pro-growth argument

To advocates of growth, growth is progress. In a market economy, resources are used to produce what people want. Even in a centrally planned economy, resources are targeted to fulfil needs and wants. If a society is able to produce those things more efficiently and at less cost, how can that be bad?

One way to think about the benefits of growth is to compare two time periods, say 1950 and 1995. In 1995, real GDP per capita in most industrial countries was more than twice what it was in 1950. This means that incomes have grown twice as fast as prices, so we can buy that much more. Table 35.1 gave some specific examples.

Although it is true that the goods available in each time period were not exactly the same, growth has given us *more* choice, not less. Consider transport. In the 1950s, the European road system (social capital) was a far cry from what it is today. Driving from Copenhagen to Barcelona took more than twice as long as it does now, not to speak of advances in air travel. In the late 1990s, it is cheaper to get from Copenhagen to Barcelona than it was in the 1950s and it takes a fraction of the time.

Do these changes improve the quality of life? Yes, because we can travel more frequently, and spend less time getting where we want to go so we can spend more time there. People are able to get to more places for less money.

What about consumer durables – dishwashers, microwave ovens, compact disc players, powered lawn mowers, and so forth? Do they really enhance the quality of life? If they do not, why do we buy them? Few of these things were around in the 1950s.

What makes a dishwasher worthwhile? It saves the most valuable commodity of all: *time*. Many consumer durables have no intrinsic value – that is, they don't provide satisfaction directly. They do allow us to perform boring tasks and chores more easily and quickly, however, giving us more time for other things.

And think of the improvement in *quality*. Gramophones in the 1950s reproduced sound very imperfectly; high fidelity was just being developed, and stereo was in the future. Today you can get a compact disc player for under €50 that sounds far better than the best machines available in the 1950s.

Growth also makes it possible to improve conditions for the less fortunate in society. With higher incomes, we can better afford the sacrifices needed to help the poor. Growth also produces jobs. When population growth is not accompanied by growth in output and, therefore, in jobs, unemployment and poverty increase.

It is easy for advanced societies to be complacent or even critical about growth. But developing countries understand its benefits well. When 75% of the population is poor, redistributing *existing* incomes does not do much. The only hope for improvement is economic growth.

The anti-growth argument

Those who argue against economic growth generally make four major points.

Growth has negative effects on the quality of life

Any measure of output measures only the value of those things that are exchanged in the market. Many things that affect the quality of life are not traded in the market, and those things generally lose value when growth occurs.

Perhaps the most dramatic 'unmeasurable' changes affecting the quality of life occur in the early stages of growth when societies become industrialized. It is true that more is produced. But most people are crowded into cities, and their lives change drastically.

There are other consequences of growth that are not counted in the growth calculation. Perhaps the most significant is environmental damage. As the industrial engine is fed, waste is produced; often, both this feeding and the waste cause massive environmental damage. Well-known consequences are acid rain, global warming, the pollution of the world's oceans and the destruction of rain forests.

Growth-related problems are by no means confined to Europe. Japan, for example, paid little attention to the environment during the early years of its rapid economic growth. Many of the results were disastrous. The best known of these results were the horrifying birth defects following the dumping of industrial mercury into the waters of Minamata Bay. In addition to birth defects, thousands of cases of 'Minamata disease' in adults have been documented, and hundreds have died.

Growth encourages the creation of artificial needs

For growth to occur, industry must cause consumers to develop new tastes and preferences. Therefore, we have no real need for many of the things we now consume. Wants are created, and consumers have become the servants, rather than the masters, of the economy.

This contrasts with the orthodox view, which lies at the heart of modern welfare economics, that preferences exist among consumers and that the economy's purpose is to serve those needs. According to the notion of **consumer sovereignty**, people are free to choose, and things that people do not want will not sell.

consumer sovereignty
The notion that people are free to choose, and that things people do not want will not sell. Thus, 'the customer rules'.

Growth means the rapid depletion of a finite quantity of resources

The world has a finite quantity of resources, and rapid growth is consuming them at a rate that cannot continue. Because the available resources impose limits to growth, we should begin now to plan for the future, when growth will be impossible.

In 1972, the Club of Rome published *The Limits to Growth*.[4] This report presented the results of computer simulations that extrapolated present growth rates of population, food, industrial output and resource exhaustion. According to these data, sometime after the year 2000 the limits would be reached, and the entire world economy would come crashing down. This argument is similar to one offered almost 200 years ago by Thomas Malthus, whom we mentioned earlier in this chapter.

In the 1970s, many thought that the Club of Rome's predictions had come true. It seemed as if we were starting to run up against the limits of world energy supplies; energy prices products shot up, and there were serious shortages. But dramatic changes have occurred since. New reserves have been found, new sources of energy have been discovered and developed, and conservation measures have been tremendously successful (for example, car fuel consumption has been reduced to levels that were inconceivable in the 1970s). Energy prices have fallen to levels that in real terms are about the same as they were before the oil price shocks of the 1970s.

A variation of the depletion-of-resources argument stops short of predicting doomsday. It does point out, however, that unchecked growth in the developed world may have very undesirable distributional consequences. To fuel our growth, we buy vast quantities of minerals and other resources from developing countries, which have become dependent on those sales to buy food and other commodities on world markets. By the time these countries have grown to the point of needing mineral resources, their resources may be gone.

Growth requires an unfair income distribution, and propagates it

One of the principal causes of growth is capital accumulation. Capital investment requires saving. Certainly, the rich save more than the poor, and in the developing countries most people are poor and need to use whatever income they have for survival.

[4]*Dennis L. Meadows*, et al., The Limits to Growth *(Washington, DC: Potomac Associates, 1972).*

Generally, critics claim, the real beneficiaries of growth are the rich. Choices open to the 'haves' in society are greatly enhanced, but the choices open to the 'have-nots' remain severely limited. If the benefits of growth trickle down to the poor, why are there more homeless today in the streets of Europe or North America than there were 20 years ago?

No 'right answer'

We have presented the arguments for and against economic growth in simple and categorical terms. In reality, even those who take extreme positions acknowledge that there is no 'right answer'. To suggest that all economic growth is bad is wrong; to suggest that economic growth should run unchecked is equally wrong. The real question for society is: how can we derive the benefits of growth while minimizing its undesirable consequences?

Society must make choices in the face of trade-offs. For example, we can grow faster if we pay less attention to environmental concerns. But how much environmental damage should we accept to spur growth? There is also a trade-off between growth and the distribution of income. More financial inequality probably leads to more saving, more capital and faster growth. Using taxes and income transfers to redistribute some of the benefits of growth to the poor probably slows the rate of growth. Society must decide how much inequality is desirable.

As long as these trade-offs exist, people will disagree. The debate in contemporary politics is largely about the costs and benefits of shifting more effort towards the goal of economic growth and away from environmental and social welfare goals.

Summary

Income comparisons and growth: the facts

1. Per capita incomes differ substantially between countries. In the world's richest nations they are more than 50 times higher than in the poorest.

2. Income growth rates also vary substantially across countries. Within similar groups of countries, such as in Europe, there is convergence of income levels. This means that those countries grow faster who currently have lower income levels. This tendency does not hold worldwide. In particular, Sub-Saharan African countries show no signs of convergence.

Growth accounting

3. If growth in output outpaces population growth, and if the economic system is producing what people want, growth increases the standard of living. Growth occurs either when (1) society acquires more inputs (factors of production), or (2) society discovers ways of using available inputs more efficiently.

4. An aggregate production function embodies the relationship between inputs – the labour force and the stock of capital – and aggregate output.

5. A number of factors contribute to economic growth: (1) an increase in the labour supply; (2) an increase in physical capital – plant and equipment – and/or human capital – education, training and health; (3) an increase

in productivity brought about by technological change, other advances in knowledge (managerial skills and so forth), and/or economies of scale.

6. Growth accounting tries to determine how much changes in each factor of production or productivity increases have contributed to income growth. Income growth in European economies has tended to stem from productivity increase, while most of income growth in the USA came from growth of employment. Between 30 and 45% of income growth resulted from capital accumulation.

Growth theory

7. Growth theory is not satisfied with a *description* of growth and how it relates to its determinants. It sets out to *explain* why a country has the capital stock it has and produces the output it does. The basic model assumes a global economy without government. In such an economy investment always equals saving.

8. The key for understanding capital accumulation is, first, that investment adds to the capital stock, and, second, depreciation takes away from the capital stock. When the capital stock is small, investment exceeds depreciation and the capital stock grows. When the capital stock is large, depreciation exceeds investment and the capital stock falls. In between these case, the single level of the capital stock where depreciation exactly equals investment is the steady state capital stock.

9. A country's income rises if productivity improves, human capital improves, the labour force increases or the saving rate rises. In the last case, countries can maintain a higher capital stock in the steady state.

10. The Solow model explains income levels, and why they may differ between countries. It does not explain long-run growth.

11. An improvement in productivity or human capital, or a rise in the saving rate, raises income per capita. A higher population growth rate lowers per capita income. The reason is that each new entrant into the labour market must be equipped with capital. They absorb investment that would otherwise be used to maintain a higher capital stock for each of the original workers.

The role of the government in the Solow model

12. A government budget deficit drives investment below saving, reducing the capital stock and steady state income. This effect is reduced if the government spends on investment projects.

International capital markets and the Solow model

13. The globalization of capital markets permits investors to invest their saving in low-income countries, which promise higher returns on capital than the industrial countries. This should propel the worldwide convergence of incomes.

Economic growth and public policy

14. A number of public policies have been pursued with the aim of improving the level and growth of real output. These policies include efforts to improve the quality of education, to encourage saving, to stimulate investment, to increase research and development, and to reduce regulation. Some economists also argue in favour of increased government involvement in the allocation of capital across manufacturing sectors, a practice known as *industrial policy*.

The pros and cons of growth

15. Advocates of growth argue that growth is progress. Growth gives us more freedom – that is, more choices. It saves time, improves the standard of living, and is the only way to improve conditions for the poor. Growth creates jobs and increases income simply because there is more to go round.

16. Those who argue against growth generally make four major points. First, many things that affect the quality of life are not traded in the market. These things often lose value when there is growth. Second, to have growth, industry must cause consumers to develop new tastes and preferences for many things they do not really need. Third, the world has a finite quantity of resources. Rapid growth is eating them up at a rate that cannot continue. Fourth, growth requires that income be distributed inequitably.

Review Terms and Concepts

aggregate production function
consumer sovereignty
economic growth
growth accounting
growth theory
human capital
industrial policy
innovation

invention
labour productivity
potential employment
potential income
productivity of an input
Solow model
steady state output

Problem Set

1. During 1997 and early 1998, real GDP in the United States was growing at a rate of about 4% per year. The Federal Reserve was contemplating a rise in interest rates to slow the growth rate to about 2.5% per year. If growth is a good thing for an economy, why would the Fed try to slow it down?

2. Tables 1, 2, and 3 present some data on three hypothetical economies. Complete the tables by calculating the measured productivity of labour and the rate of output growth. What do the data tell you about the causes of economic growth? (*Hint*: How fast are *L* and *K* growing?)

Table 1

Period	L	K	Y	Y/L	Growth rate of output
1	1052	3065	4506		
2	1105	3095	4674		
3	1160	3126	4842		
4	1218	3157	5019		

Table 2

Period	L	K	Y	Y/L	Growth rate of output
1	1052	3065	4506		
2	1062	3371	4683		
3	1073	3709	4866		
4	1084	4079	5055		

Table 3

Period	L	K	Y	Y/L	Growth rate of output
1	1052	3065	4506		
2	1062	3095	4731		
3	1073	3126	4967		
4	1084	3157	5216		

3. Productivity in France has grown at about 2.4% annually on average since 1973, but in the United States annual productivity growth is only about 1.1%. Yet, output growth has averaged 2.4% in the United States compared to 2.1% in France. Explain this seeming paradox. Be specific. Can you provide statistical evidence to support your theory?

4. In earlier chapters, you learned that aggregate expenditure must be equal to aggregate output for the economy to be in equilibrium. You also saw that when consumption spending rises, aggregate expenditure increases, inventories fall and aggregate output rises. Thus, policies that simultaneously increase consumer spending and reduce saving would lead to a higher level of GDP. In this chapter, it was argued that a higher saving rate, even with lower consumption spending, leads to a higher level of GDP. How can both arguments be correct?

5. According to Angus Maddison, in *Dynamic Forces in Capitalist Development* (Oxford: Oxford University Press, 1991), in about AD 1400 China's GDP per capita was approximately 15% higher than Western Europe's. By 1950, Western Europe's average GDP per capita was more than 10 times as large as China's. Can you suggest any explanations for these developments?

6. Some countries allow firms to partly offset the depreciation of their capital stock against tax payments.
a. How does this affect the effective depreciation function from the point of view of firms?
b. What is the effect of such a policy on the long-term rate of growth? On income?

7. Look back at Figure 35.11. If we assume that knowledge and technology are public goods and thus freely available to every country, why might countries operate on different production functions?

8. Suppose you have just been elected to your national parliament and that you find yourself on the Ways and Means Committee – the committee that decides on tax matters. The committee is debating a bill that would make major changes in tax policy. First, the corporate tax would be lowered substantially in an effort to stimulate investment. The bill contains a 15% investment tax credit – firms would be able to reduce their taxes by 15% of the value of investment projects that they undertake. To keep revenues constant, the bill would impose a national sales tax that would raise the price of consumer goods and reduce consumption. What trade-offs do you see in this bill? What are the pros and cons? How would you vote?

9. Labour is a factor of production. Since the marginal product of labour is positive, more workers will produce more output, *ceteris paribus*. Why, then, does faster population growth lead to lower steady state income in the Solow model?

10. In a recent article, Nobel Prize winner Robert Lucas asked the following question: 'Why doesn't capital flow from rich to poor countries?'
a. Use the Solow model to explain why we might expect that capital *should* flow from rich to poor countries.
b. Can you suggest any answers to Lucas's question?

11. Many economists argue that high government budget deficits today will reduce the growth rate of the economy in the future. Why? Do the reasons for the high budget deficit matter? In other words, does it matter whether the deficit is caused by lower taxes, increased defence spending, more job-training schemes, and so on?

International Economics

36

International Trade, Comparative Advantage and Protectionism

Over the last 25 years, international transactions have become increasingly important to the world economy. World trade has grown much faster than world output. The 'internationalization' or 'globalization' of economies has occurred in the private and public sectors, in input and output markets, and in business firms and households. In most countries, foreign products are now everywhere, from the utensils in our kitchens to the cars we drive. Although it varies in extent, all countries rely on international trade in goods and services (see Table 36.1). Goods and services move freely across the world. At the same time, financial capital flows swiftly across international boundaries in search of high returns. In 1997–98, for example, the deep recession in some Asian economies, including Korea and Thailand, caused an outflow of international capital and a sharp decline in stock market prices.

The inextricable connection of the European economy to the economies of the rest of the world has had a profound impact on the discipline of economics and is the basis of one of its most important insights:

All economies, regardless of their size, depend to some extent on other economies and are affected by events outside their borders.

We have already spent time examining international economic relationships, but here we explore the underlying logic of trade. Why should a country engage in international trade? Then we address the controversial issue of protectionism. Should a country provide certain industries with protection in the form of import quotas, tariffs, or subsidies? Whenever international trade is encouraged there are winners and losers. The losers frequently complain.

For hundreds of years, industries have petitioned governments for protection and societies have debated the pros and cons of free and open trade. For the last century and a half, the principal argument used against protection has been the theory of comparative advantage, which we first discussed in Chapter 2.

The economic basis for trade: comparative advantage

Corn Laws The tariffs, subsidies and restrictions enacted by the British parliament in the early nineteenth century to discourage imports and encourage exports of grain.

Perhaps the best-known debate on the issue of free trade took place in the British parliament during the early years of the nineteenth century. At that time, the landed gentry – the landowners – controlled parliament. For a number of years, imports and exports of grain had been subject to a set of tariffs, subsidies and restrictions collectively called the **Corn Laws**. Designed to discourage imports of grain and encourage exports, the Corn Laws' purpose was to keep the price of food high. The landlords' incomes, of course, depended on the prices they got for what their land produced. The Corn Laws clearly worked to the advantage of those in power.

Table 36.1 Proportion of GDP accounted for by international trade in selected economies

	Trade (% of GDP)	
	1980	**1995**
Low-income economies		
Ethiopia	27	39
Bangladesh	24	37
India	17	27
China	13	40
Lower-middle-income economies		
Bolivia	38	47
Philippines	52	80
Bulgaria	66	94
Turkey	17	45
Upper-middle-income economies		
South Africa	64	44
Mexico	24	48
Uruguay	36	41
Greece	47	57
High-income economies		
Spain	34	47
New Zealand	62	62
Australia	34	40
Sweden	61	77

Source: World Bank, *World Development Report*, 1997.

With the Industrial Revolution, a class of wealthy industrial capitalists began to emerge. The industrial sector had to pay workers at least enough to live on, and a living wage depended greatly on the price of food. Tariffs on grain imports and export subsidies that kept grain and food prices high increased the wages that capitalists had to pay, cutting into their profits. The political battle raged for years. But as time went by, the power of the landowners in the House of Lords was significantly reduced. When the conflict ended in 1848, the Corn Laws were repealed.

On the side of repeal was David Ricardo, a businessman, economist, member of parliament and one of the fathers of modern economics. Ricardo's main work, *Principles of Political Economy and Taxation*, was published in 1817, two years before he entered parliament. Ricardo's **theory of comparative advantage**, which he used to argue against the Corn Laws, claimed that trade enables countries to specialize in producing the products they produce best. According to the theory:

theory of comparative advantage
Ricardo's theory that specialization and free trade will benefit all trading partners (real wages will rise), even those that may be absolutely less efficient producers.

> Specialization and free trade will benefit all trading partners (real wages will rise), even those that may be absolutely less efficient producers.

This basic argument remains at the heart of free-trade debates even today.

Specialization and trade: the two-person case

The easiest way to understand the theory of comparative advantage is to examine a simple two-person society. Suppose David and Anna, who we left stranded on a deserted island in Chapter 2, have only two tasks to accomplish each week: gathering food to eat and cutting logs that will be used in constructing a house. If Anna could cut more logs than David in a day and David could gather more berries and fruits, specialization would clearly benefit both of them.

But suppose David is slow and clumsy and Anna is better at both cutting logs *and* gathering food. Ricardo's point is that it still pays for them to specialize. They can produce more in total by specializing than they can by sharing the work equally. (It may be helpful to review the discussion of comparative advantage in Chapter 2 before proceeding.)

Absolute advantage versus comparative advantage

absolute advantage

The advantage in the production of a product enjoyed by one country over another when it uses fewer resources to produce that product than the other country does.

comparative advantage

The advantage in the production of a product that one country enjoys over another when that product can be produced at lower cost in terms of other goods than it could be in the other country.

A country enjoys an **absolute advantage** over another country in the production of a product if it uses fewer resources to produce that product than the other country does. Suppose country A and country B produce wheat, but A's climate is more suited to wheat and its labour is more productive. Country A will produce more wheat per hectare than country B and use less labour to grow it and bring it to market. Country A enjoys an absolute advantage over country B in the production of wheat.

A country enjoys a **comparative advantage** in the production of a good if that good can be produced at lower cost *in terms of other goods*. Suppose countries C and D both produce wheat and maize and C enjoys an absolute advantage in the production of both – that is, C's climate is better than D's, and fewer of C's resources are needed to produce a given quantity of both wheat and maize. Now C and D must each choose whether they plant their land with wheat or corn. For C or D to produce more wheat, it must transfer land from maize production; to produce more maize, it must transfer land from wheat production. The cost of wheat in each country can be measured in tonnes of maize, and the cost of maize can be measured in tonnes of wheat.

Suppose that in country C, a tonne of wheat has an opportunity cost of two tonnes of maize. That is, to produce an additional tonne of wheat, C must give up two tonnes of maize. At the same time, producing a tonne of wheat in country D requires the sacrifice of only one tonne of maize. Even though C has an *absolute* advantage in the production of both products, D enjoys a *comparative* advantage in the production of wheat because the *opportunity cost* of producing wheat is lower in D. Under these circumstances, Ricardo claims, D can benefit from trade if it specializes in the production of wheat.

Gains from mutual absolute advantage

To illustrate Ricardo's logic in more detail. Suppose Australia and New Zealand each have a fixed amount of land and do not trade with the rest of the world. There are only two goods – wheat to produce bread, and cotton to produce clothing. This kind of two-country/two-good world does not exist, but its operations can be generalized to many countries and many goods.

To proceed, we have to make some assumptions about the preferences of the people living in New Zealand and the people living in Australia. If the citizens of both countries go around naked, there is no need to produce cotton; all the land can be

Table 36.2 Yield per hectare of wheat and cotton		
	New Zealand	**Australia**
Wheat	6 tonnes	2 tonnes
Cotton	2 bales	6 bales

Table 36.3 Total production of wheat and cotton assuming no trade, mutual absolute advantage, and 100 available hectares

	New Zealand	Australia
Wheat	25 hectares × 6 tonnes/hectare = 150 tonnes	75 hectares × 2 tonnes/hectare = 150 tonnes
Cotton	75 hectares × 2 bales/hectare = 150 bales	25 hectares × 6 bales/hectare = 150 bales

used to produce wheat. However, assume that people in both countries have similar preferences with respect to food and clothing: the populations of both countries use both cotton and wheat. And preferences for food and clothing are such that both countries consume equal amounts of wheat and cotton.

Finally, we assume that each country has only 100 hectares of land for planting and that land yields are as given in Table 36.2. New Zealand can produce three times the wheat that Australia can on one hectare of land, and Australia can produce three times the cotton that New Zealand can in the same space. New Zealand has an absolute advantage in the production of wheat, and Australia has an absolute advantage in the production of cotton. In cases like this, we say the two countries have *mutual absolute advantage.*

If there is no trade and each country divides its land to obtain equal units of cotton and wheat production, each country produces 150 tonnes of wheat and 150 bales of cotton. New Zealand puts 75 hectares into cotton but only 25 hectares into wheat, while Australia does the reverse. (See Table 36.3.)

We can organize the same information in graphical form by constructing production possibilities frontiers for each country. In Figure 36.1, which presents the positions of the two countries before trade, each country is constrained by its own resources and productivity. If Australia put all its land into cotton, it would produce 600 bales of cotton (100 hectares × 6 bales/hectare) and no wheat; if it put all its land into wheat, it would produce 200 tonnes of wheat (100 hectares × 2 tonnes/hectare) and no cotton. The opposite is true for New Zealand. Recall from Chapter 2 that a country's production possibilities frontier represents all combinations of goods that

Figure 36.1 Production possibility frontiers for Australia and New Zealand, before trade

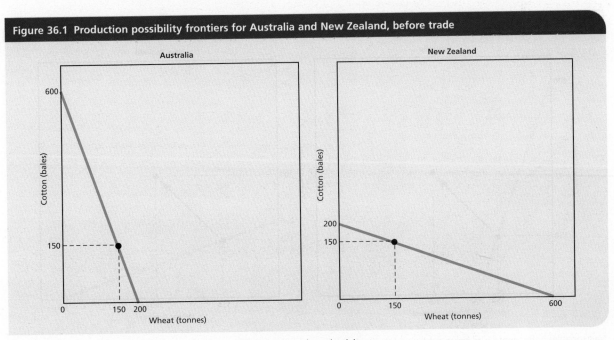

Without trade, countries are constrained by their own resources and productivity.

Table 36.4 Production and consumption of wheat and cotton after specialization

Production	New Zealand	Australia
Wheat	100 hectares × 6 tonnes/hectare = 600 tonnes	0 hectares = 0
Cotton	0 hectares = 0	100 hectares × 6 bales/hectare = 600 bales
Consumption	**New Zealand**	**Australia**
Wheat	300 tonnes	300 tonnes
Cotton	300 bales	300 bales

can be produced, given the country's resources and state of technology. Each country must pick a point along its own production possibilities curve.

Because both countries have an absolute advantage in the production of one product, specialization and trade will benefit both. Australia should produce cotton, New Zealand should produce wheat. Transferring all land to wheat production in New Zealand yields 600 tonnes; transferring all land to cotton production in Australia yields 600 bales. An agreement to trade 300 tonnes of wheat for 300 bales of cotton would double both wheat and cotton consumption in both countries. (Remember: before trade both countries produced 150 tonnes of wheat and 150 bales of cotton. After trade, each country will have 300 tonnes of wheat and 300 bales of cotton to consume. The final production and trade figures appear in Table 36.4 and Figure 36.2.)

Trade enables both countries to move out beyond their previous resource and productivity constraints.

The advantages of specialization and trade seem obvious when one country is technologically superior at producing one product and another country is technologically superior at producing another product. But let us turn to the case in which one country has an absolute advantage in the production of *both* goods.

Figure 36.2 Expanded possibilities after trade

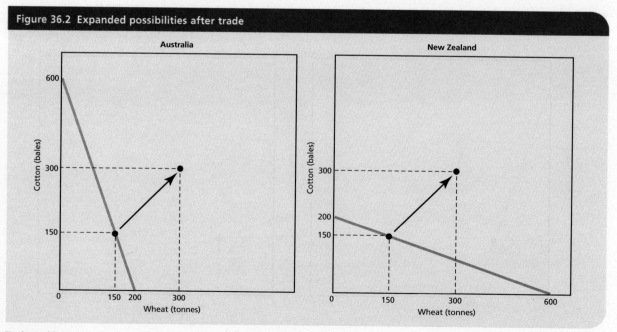

Trade enables both countries to move out beyond their own resource constraints – beyond their individual production possibility frontiers.

Table 36.5 Yield per hectare of wheat and cotton

	New Zealand	Australia
Wheat	6 tonnes	1 tonne
Cotton	6 bales	3 bales

Gains from comparative advantage

Table 36.5 contains different land yield figures for New Zealand and Australia. Now, New Zealand has a considerable absolute advantage in the production of both cotton and wheat, with one hectare of land yielding six times as much wheat and twice as much cotton as one hectare in Australia. Ricardo would argue that *specialization and trade are still mutually beneficial.*

Again, preferences imply consumption of equal units of cotton and wheat in both countries. With no trade, New Zealand would divide its 100 available hectares evenly, or 50/50, between the two crops. The result would be 300 bales of cotton and 300 tonnes of wheat. Australia would divide its land 75/25. Table 36.6 shows that final production in Australia would be 75 bales of cotton and 75 tonnes of wheat. (Remember: we are assuming that in each country, people consume equal amounts of cotton and wheat.) Again, before any trade takes place each country is constrained by its own domestic production possibilities curve.

Imagine we are at a meeting of trade representatives of both countries. As a special adviser, David Ricardo is asked to demonstrate that trade can benefit both countries. He divides his demonstration into three stages, which you can follow in Table 36.7.

Table 36.6 Total production of wheat and cotton, assuming no trade and 100 available hectares

	New Zealand	Australia
Wheat	50 hectares × 6 tonnes/hectare = 300 tonnes	75 hectares × 1 tonne/hectare = 75 tonnes
Cotton	50 hectares × 6 bales/hectare = 300 bales	25 hectares × 3 bales/hectare = 75 bales

Table 36.7 Realizing a gain from trade when one country has a double absolute advantage

Stage 1	New Zealand	Australia
Wheat	50 hectares × 6 tonnes/hectare = 300 tonnes	0 hectares = 0
Cotton	50 hectares × 6 bales/hectare = 300 bales	100 hectares × 3 bales/hectare = 300 bales
Stage 2	**New Zealand**	**Australia**
Wheat	75 hectares × 6 tonnes/hectare = 450 tonnes	0 hectares = 0
Cotton	25 hectares × 6 bales/hectare = 150 bales	100 hectares × 3 bales/hectare = 300 bales
Stage 3	**New Zealand Australia**	
Wheat	100 tonnes (trade) 350 tonnes ——▶ 100 tonnes (after trade)	
Cotton	200 bales (trade) 350 bales ◀—— 100 bales (after trade)	

In Stage 1, Australia transfers all its land into cotton production. It will have no wheat and 300 bales of cotton. New Zealand cannot completely specialize in wheat because it needs 300 bales of cotton and will not be able to get enough cotton from Australia. This is because we are assuming that each country wants to consume equal amounts of cotton and wheat. In Stage 2, New Zealand transfers 25 hectares out of cotton and into wheat. Now New Zealand has 25 hectares in cotton that produce 150 bales and 75 hectares in wheat that produce 450 tonnes.

Finally, the two countries trade. We assume New Zealand ships 100 tonnes of wheat to Australia in exchange for 200 bales of cotton. After the trade, New Zealand has 350 bales of cotton and 350 tonnes of wheat; Australia has 100 bales of cotton and 100 tonnes of wheat. Both countries are better off than they were before the trade (Table 36.6), and both have moved beyond their own production possibilities frontiers.

Why does Ricardo's plan work?

To understand why Ricardo's scheme works, let us return to the definition of comparative advantage.

The real cost of producing cotton is the wheat that must be sacrificed to produce it. *When we think of cost this way, it is less costly to produce cotton in Australia than to produce it in New Zealand, even though a hectare of land produces more cotton in New Zealand.* Consider the 'cost' of three bales of cotton in the two countries. In terms of opportunity cost, three bales of cotton in New Zealand cost three tonnes of wheat; in Australia, three bales of cotton cost only one tonne of wheat. Because three bales are produced by one hectare of Australian land, to get three bales an Australian must transfer one hectare of land from wheat to cotton production. And because a hectare of land produces a tonne of wheat, losing one hectare to cotton implies the loss of one tonne of wheat. *Australia has a comparative advantage in cotton production* because its opportunity cost, in terms of wheat, is lower than New Zealand's. This is illustrated in Figure 36.3.

Conversely, New Zealand has a comparative advantage in wheat production. A unit of wheat in New Zealand costs one unit of cotton; a unit of wheat in Australia costs three units of cotton.

Figure 36.3 Comparative advantage means lower opportunity cost

The real cost of cotton is the wheat sacrificed to obtain it. The cost of three bales of cotton in New Zealand is three tonnes of wheat (half a hectare of land must be transferred from wheat to cotton – refer to Table 36.5). But the cost of three bales of cotton in Australia is only one tonne of wheat (one hectare of land must be transferred). Thus, Australia has a comparative advantage over New Zealand in cotton production, and New Zealand has a comparative advantage over Australia in wheat production.

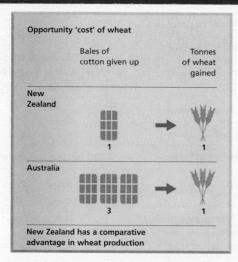

Opportunity 'cost' of wheat

Bales of cotton given up → Tonnes of wheat gained

New Zealand: 1 → 1

Australia: 3 → 1

New Zealand has a comparative advantage in wheat production

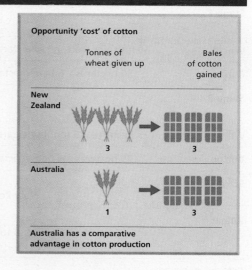

Opportunity 'cost' of cotton

Tonnes of wheat given up → Bales of cotton gained

New Zealand: 3 → 3

Australia: 1 → 3

Australia has a comparative advantage in cotton production

When countries specialize in producing goods in which they have a comparative advantage, they maximize their combined output and allocate their resources more efficiently.

Terms of trade

Ricardo might suggest a number of options that are open to the trading partners. The one we just examined benefited both partners; in percentage terms, Australia was slightly better off. Other deals might have been more advantageous to New Zealand.

The ratio at which a country can trade domestic products for imported products is the **terms of trade**. The terms of trade determine how the gains from trade are distributed among trading partners. In the case just considered, the agreed-upon terms of trade were one tonne of wheat for two bales of cotton. Such terms of trade benefit New Zealand, which can get two bales of cotton for each tonne of wheat. If it were to transfer its own land from wheat to cotton, it would get only one bale. The same terms of trade benefit Australia, which can get one tonne of wheat for two bales of cotton. A direct transfer of its own land would force it to give up three bales of cotton for one tonne of wheat.

If the terms of trade changed to three bales of cotton for every tonne of wheat, only New Zealand would benefit. At those terms of trade *all* the gains from trade would flow to New Zealand. Such terms do not benefit Australia at all, because the opportunity cost of producing wheat domestically is *exactly the same* as the trade cost: one tonne of wheat costs three bales of cotton. If the terms of trade went the other way – one bale of cotton for each tonne of wheat – only Australia would benefit. New Zealand gains nothing, because it can already substitute cotton for wheat at that ratio. To get a tonne of wheat domestically, however, Australia must give up three bales of cotton, and one-for-one terms of trade would make wheat much less costly for Australia.

Both parties must have something to gain for trade to take place. In this case, you can see that both Australia and New Zealand will gain when the terms of trade are set between 1:1 and 3:1, cotton to wheat.

Exchange rates

The examples we have used thus far have shown that trade can result in gains to both parties. We have not yet discussed how trade actually comes about.

When trade is free – that is, unimpeded by government-instituted barriers – patterns of trade and trade flows result from the independent decisions of thousands of importers and exporters and millions of private households and firms.

Private households decide whether to buy Toyotas or BMWs, and private firms decide whether to buy machine tools made in Europe or machine tools made in Taiwan, raw steel produced in Germany or raw steel produced in the UK.

Before a citizen of one country can buy a product made in, or sold by, someone in another country, a currency swap must take place. Consider Andrew, who buys a Volkswagen from a dealer in the UK. He pays in sterling, but the German workers who made the car receive their salaries in deutschemarks. Somewhere between the buyer of the car and the producer, a currency exchange must be made. The regional distributor probably takes payment in sterling and converts them into marks before remitting the proceeds back to Germany.

To buy a foreign-produced good, then, I in effect have to buy foreign currency. The price of Andrew's Volkswagen in sterling depends on both the price of the car stated in deutschemarks and the price of deutschemarks. The attractiveness of foreign goods depends in part on **exchange rates**. (You will recall that the exchange rate is the ratio at which two currencies are traded.)

terms of trade
The ratio at which a country can trade domestic products for imported products.

exchange rate
The ratio at which two currencies are traded for each other. The price of one currency in terms of another.

To understand the patterns of trade that result from the actions of hundreds of thousands of independent buyers and sellers – households and firms – we must know something about the factors that determine exchange rates. We have already examined exchange rates in earlier chapters. Here, however, we can demonstrate two things:

First, for any pair of countries, there is a range of exchange rates that can lead automatically to both countries realizing the gains from specialization and comparative advantage. Second, within that range, the exchange rate will determine which country gains the most from trade. In short, exchange rates determine the terms of trade.

Trade and exchange rates in a two-country/two-good world

Consider first a simple two-country/two-good model. Suppose both the United States and Germany produce only two goods – raw timber and rolled steel. Table 36.8 gives the current prices of both goods as domestic buyers see them. In Germany, timber is priced at 3 deutsche marks (DM) per foot and steel is priced at 4 DM per metre. In the United States, timber costs $1 per foot and steel costs $2 per metre.

Suppose US and German buyers have the option of buying at home or importing to meet their needs. The options they choose will depend on the exchange rate. For the time being, we will ignore transport costs between countries and assume that German and US products are of equal quality.

Let us start with the assumption that the exchange rate is $1 = 1 DM. From the standpoint of US buyers, neither German steel nor German timber is competitive at this exchange rate. A dollar buys a foot of timber in the United States, but if converted into a mark it will buy only one-third of a foot. The price of German timber to an American is $3 because it will take $3 to buy the necessary 3 DM. Similarly, $2 buys a metre of rolled steel in the United States, but the same $2 buys only half a metre of German steel. The price of German steel to an American is $4, twice the price of domestically produced steel.

At this exchange rate, however, Germans find that US-produced steel and timber are both less expensive than steel and timber produced in Germany. Timber at home – Germany – costs 3 DM, but 3 DM buys $3, which buys three times as much timber in the United States. Similarly, steel costs 3 DM at home, but 4 DM buys $4, which buys twice as much US-made steel. At an exchange rate of $1 = 1 DM, Germany will import steel and timber and the United States will import nothing.

But now suppose the exchange rate is 1 DM = $0.25. We could say the 'price' of a DM is $0.25. This means that a dollar buys 4 DM. At this exchange rate, the Germans buy timber and steel at home and the Americans import both goods. At this exchange rate, Americans must pay a dollar for a foot of US timber, but the same amount of timber can be had in Germany for the equivalent of $0.75. (Since one DM costs $0.25, 3 DM can be purchased for $0.75.) Similarly, steel that costs $2 per metre in the United States costs an American half as much in Germany, because $2 buys 8 DM, which buys two metres of German steel. At the same time, Germans are not interested in importing, because both goods are cheaper when purchased from a German producer. In this case, the United States imports both goods and Germany imports nothing.

Table 36.8 Domestic prices of timber (per foot) and rolled steel (per metre) in the United States and Germany

	United States	Germany
Timber	$1	3 DM
Rolled steel	$2	4 DM

Table 36.9 Trade flows determined by exchange rates

Exchange rate	Price of DM	Result
$1 = 1 DM	$1.00	Germany imports timber and steel
$1 = 2 DM	$0.50	Germany imports timber
$1 = 2.1 DM	$0.48	Germany imports timber; United States imports steel
$1 = 2.9 DM	$0.34	Germany imports timber; United States imports steel
$1 = 3 DM	$0.33	United States imports steel
$1 = 4 DM	$0.25	United States imports timber and steel

So far, we can see that at exchange rates of $1 = 1 DM and $1 = 4 DM we get trade flowing in only one direction. Let us now try an exchange rate of $1 = 2 DM, or 1 DM = $0.50. First, Germans will buy timber in the United States. German timber costs 3 DM per foot, but 3 DM buys $1.50, which is enough to buy one and a half feet of US timber. Buyers in the United States will find German timber too expensive, but Germany will import timber from the United States. At this same exchange rate, however, both German and US buyers will be indifferent between German and US steel. To US buyers, domestically produced steel costs $2. Since $2 buys 4 DM, a metre of imported German steel also costs $2. German buyers also find that steel costs 4 DM, whether domestically produced or imported. Thus, there is likely to be no trade in steel.

But what happens if the exchange rate rises so that $1 buys 2.1 DM? While US timber is still cheaper to both Germans and Americans, German steel begins to look good to US buyers. Steel produced in the United States costs $2 per metre, but $2 buys 4.2 DM, which buys more than a metre of steel in Germany. When the exchange rate rises above $1 = 2 DM, trade begins to flow in both directions: Germany will import timber and the United States will import steel.

If you examine Table 36.9 carefully, you will see that trade flows in both directions as long as the exchange rate settles between $1 = 2 DM and $1 = 3 DM. Stated the other way around, trade will flow in both directions if the price of a deutschemark is between $0.33 and $0.50.

Exchange rates and comparative advantage

If the foreign exchange market drives the exchange rate to anywhere between 2 and 3 DM per dollar, the countries will automatically adjust and comparative advantage will be realized. At these exchange rates, US buyers begin buying all their steel in Germany. The US steel industry finds itself in trouble. Plants close, and US workers begin to lobby for tariff protection against German steel. At the same time, the US timber industry does well, fuelled by strong export demand from Germany. The timber-producing sector expands. Resources, including capital and labour, are attracted into timber production.

The opposite occurs in Germany. The German timber industry suffers losses as export demand dries up and Germans turn to cheaper US imports. In Germany, timber companies turn to the government and ask for protection from cheap US timber. But steel producers in Germany are happy. Not only are they supplying 100% of the domestically demanded steel, but they are selling to US buyers as well. The steel industry expands, and the timber industry contracts. Resources, including labour, flow into steel.

With this expansion-and-contraction scenario in mind, let us look again at our original definition of comparative advantage. If we assume that prices reflect resource use and that resources can be transferred from sector to sector, we can calculate the opportunity cost of steel/timber in both countries. In the United States, the production of a metre of rolled steel consumes twice the resources that the production of a foot of timber consumes. Assuming that resources can be transferred, the opportunity cost of a metre of steel is two feet of timber. (Refer again to Table 36.8.) In Germany, a metre of steel uses resources costing 4 DM, while a unit of timber costs 3 DM. To produce a metre of steel means the sacrifice of only four thirds, or one and a third, feet of timber. Because the opportunity cost of a metre of steel (in terms of timber) is lower in Germany, we say Germany has a comparative advantage in steel production.

Conversely, consider the opportunity cost of timber in the two countries. Increasing timber production in the United States requires the sacrifice of half a metre of steel for every foot of timber – producing a metre of steel uses $2 worth of resources, while producing a foot of timber requires only $1 worth of resources. But each foot of timber production in Germany requires the sacrifice of three-quarters of a metre of steel. Because the opportunity cost of timber is lower in the United States, the United States has a comparative advantage in the production of timber.

If exchange rates end up in the right ranges, the free market will drive each country to shift resources into those sectors in which it enjoys a comparative advantage. Only those products in which a country has a comparative advantage will be competitive in world markets.

The sources of comparative advantage

Specialization and trade can benefit all trading partners, even those that may be inefficient producers in an absolute sense. If markets are competitive, and if foreign exchange markets are linked to goods-and-services exchange, countries will specialize in producing products in which they have a comparative advantage.

So far, we have said nothing about the sources of comparative advantage. What determines whether a country has a comparative advantage in heavy manufacturing or in agriculture? What explains the actual trade flows observed around the world? Various theories and empirical work on international trade have provided some answers. Most economists look to **factor endowments** – to the quantity and quality of labour, land and natural resources – as the principal sources of comparative advantage. Factor endowments seem to explain a significant portion of actual world trade patterns.

The Heckscher–Ohlin theorem

Eli Heckscher and Bertil Ohlin, two Swedish economists who wrote in the first half of the twentieth century, expanded and elaborated on Ricardo's theory of comparative advantage. The **Heckscher–Ohlin theorem** ties the theory of comparative advantage to factor endowments. It assumes that products can be produced using differing proportions of inputs and that inputs are mobile between sectors in each economy, but that factors are not mobile *between* economies. According to this theorem:

A country has a comparative advantage in the production of a product if that country is relatively well endowed with inputs used intensively in the production of that product.

This idea is simple. A country with a lot of good fertile land is likely to have a comparative advantage in agriculture. A country with a large amount of accumulated capital is likely to have a comparative advantage in heavy manufacturing. A country with a lot of human capital is likely to have a comparative advantage in highly technical goods.

factor endowments
The quantity and quality of labour, land and natural resources of a country.

Heckscher–Ohlin theorem
A theory that explains the existence of a country's comparative advantage by its factor endowments. A country has a comparative advantage in the production of a product if that country is relatively well endowed with inputs used intensively in the production of that product.

After an extensive study, US economist Edward Leamer has concluded that a short list of factors accounts for a large portion of world trade patterns. Natural resources, knowledge capital, physical capital, land, and skilled and unskilled labour, Leamer believes, explain 'a large amount of the variability of net exports across countries'.[1]

Other explanations for observed trade flows

Comparative advantage is not the only reason for trade between countries. It does not explain why many countries both import and export the same kinds of goods. Many European countries, for example, both export and import cars.

And just as industries within a country differentiate their products to capture a domestic market, so too they differentiate their products to please the wide variety of tastes that exists worldwide. The Japanese car industry, for example, began producing small, fuel-efficient cars long before car industries in other countries. In doing so, they developed expertise in creating products that attracted a devoted following and considerable brand loyalty. BMWs, made only in Germany, and Volvos, made only in Sweden, also have their champions in many countries. Just as product differentiation is a natural response to diverse preferences within an economy, it is also a natural response to diverse preferences across economies.

This idea is not inconsistent with the theory of comparative advantage. If the Japanese have developed skills and knowledge that gave them an edge in the production of fuel-efficient cars, that knowledge can be thought of as a very specific kind of capital not currently available to other producers. The Volvo company invested in

Applications

The fallacies of competitiveness

Are emerging economies a threat to EU and US well-being? The answer is no. Samuel Brittan explains in this review of Professor Krugman's book, *Pop Internationalism*, published by MIT Press.

The conventional political wisdom assumes that the US and Europe face a 'competitiveness' threat from the emerging countries. They assert the low wages paid in the latter will undermine prosperity and destroy jobs unless we engage in activities ranging from industrial policy to back door protectionism.

The crisis that has hit east Asian economies and Japan is not, unfortunately, likely to put a stop to this nonsense. The devaluation of their currencies could generate even more blood-curdling stories of their threat to western jobs.

Prof. Krugman's riposte consists of a series of separate essays mostly written in the early and middle 1990s. The theme is simple. Countries are not entities like Coca-Cola and PepsiCo that compete with each other in essentially a zero sum game. The growth of the new economies is not a threat but an opportunity.

If the emerging countries attract extensive investment from the west, they cannot at the same time have large export surpluses. By definition the gap between exports and imports equals the gap between savings and investment. The emerging countries may attract inward investment, in which case they will run trade deficits not surpluses. Or they will run surpluses, but then they will export capital to, and not import it from, the west.

In addition, trade does not depend on one country being absolutely better in producing a given product. It would pay Norway to export fish and import bananas, even if hothouse technology allowed bananas to be grown more efficiently in the Arctic than on the equator.

What about the low wages in emerging countries? Aren't they a threat to western nations? No. Wages reflect, at a first approximation, the average level of efficiency in an economy. If wages are low in a high-tech Chinese factory, it is because the average level of productivity in China is low. There will be plenty of sectors left where higher US wages are offset by greater efficiency.

Source: Samuel Brittan, 'The fallacies of competitiveness', Financial Times, 15 January 1998.

---

[1]*Edward E. Leamer*, Sources of International Comparative Advantage: Theory and Evidence *(Cambridge, MA: MIT Press, 1984), p. 187.*

a form of intangible capital that we call *goodwill*. That goodwill, which may come from establishing a reputation for safety and quality over the years, is one source of the comparative advantage that keeps Volvos selling on the international market. Some economists distinguish between gains from *acquired comparative advantages* and those acquired from *natural comparative advantages*.

Another explanation for international trade is that some economies of scale may be available when producing for a world market that would not be available when producing for a more limited domestic market. But because the evidence suggests that economies of scale are exhausted at relatively small size in most industries, it seems unlikely that they constitute a valid explanation of world trade patterns.

Trade barriers: tariffs, export subsidies and quotas

protection The practice of shielding a sector of the economy from foreign competition.

Trade barriers – also called *obstacles to trade* – take many forms, the three most common are tariffs, export subsidies and quotas. All are forms of **protection**, shielding some sector of the economy from foreign competition.

tariff A tax on imports.

A **tariff** is a tax on imports. The average tariff on manufactured imports is about 5–6%. Some protected items in certain countries have much higher tariffs. For example, the tariff rate on some agricultural goods imported into Europe can be over 100%.

export subsidies Government payments made to domestic firms to encourage exports.

Export subsidies – government payments made to domestic firms to encourage exports – can also act as a barrier to trade. One of the provisions of the Corn Laws that stimulated Ricardo's musings was an export subsidy automatically paid to farmers by the British government when the price of grain fell below a specified level. The subsidy served to keep domestic prices high, but it flooded the world market with cheap subsidized grain. Foreign farmers who were not subsidized were driven out of the international marketplace by the artificially low prices.

Farm subsidies remain a part of the international trade landscape today. Many countries, especially in Europe, continue to appease their farmers by heavily subsidizing exports of agricultural products. The political power of the farm lobby in many countries has had an important effect on recent international trade negotiations aimed at reducing trade barriers.

dumping Takes place when a firm or industry sells products on the world market at prices below the cost of production.

Closely related to subsidies is **dumping**. Dumping takes place when a firm or an industry sells products on the world market at prices *below* the cost of production. The charge has been levelled against several specific Japanese industries, including cars, consumer electronics and silicon computer chips.

Generally, a company dumps when it wants to dominate a world market. After the lower prices of the dumped goods have succeeded in driving out all the competition, the dumping company can exploit its position by raising the price of its product.

quota A limit on the quantity of imports.

A **quota** is a limit on the quantity of imports. Quotas can be mandatory or voluntary, and they may be legislated or negotiated with foreign governments. The best-known voluntary quota, or 'voluntary restraint', was negotiated with the Japanese government. Both European and US governments limited the import of Japanese cars with the agreement of the Japanese government. Many Japanese cars are now produced by Japanese factories located in Europe.

GATT: a new world trade agreement

General Agreement on Tariffs and Trade (GATT) A body formed to promote the liberalization of foreign trade.

In 1947, an agreement signed by 23 nations established an organization, the **General Agreement on Tariffs and Trade (GATT)**, to promote the liberalization of foreign trade. The most recent round of trade talks sponsored by GATT was the 'Uruguay Round' of multinational trade negotiations, launched in Punta del Este, Uruguay, in 1986, and concluded in Geneva on 15 December 1993, when 116 nations initialled what was called the 'Final Act'.

The Final Act is a document of over 26,000 pages – the most comprehensive and complex trade agreement in history. Proponents say its implementation will increase the volume of world merchandise trade by between 9 and 24% above what it would have been without the agreement.[2]

The Final Act's first objective is to reduce tariffs and protection for agricultural products. Throughout history, agricultural goods have been the target of high import duties, large domestic subsidies and outright trade restrictions. In many cases, this was due to the farmers' political power. Talk of reducing subsidies to agriculture in France led on several occasions during the 1980s and 1990s to blockaded roads and violent demonstrations by French farmers. The agreement calls for an end to many agricultural subsidies, an end to non-tariff barriers, such as quantitative restrictions and bans, and an average tariff reduction of 37% on agricultural imports. In general, developed countries have agreed to reduce tariffs on 64% of their imports by about 40%, from an average rate of 6.3% to 3.8%. The percentage of industrial imports allowed to enter the developed countries with no duties at all will increase from 20% to 44%. The developing countries have agreed to lower tariffs on about 33% of their imports.

Second, the Uruguay round is the first multilateral negotiation to reach a comprehensive agreement on international trade in services. It outlaws restrictions on the import of services such as banking, legal services, insurance, accounting and computer consulting.

Third, the Final Act makes provisions for the protection of intellectual property. Although existing patent and copyright laws usually protect artists, designers, computer software producers, authors and the like from 'theft' within their own countries, foreign pirating is common. It is usually illegal to reproduce and sell pirated CDs, videotapes, books and computer software packages produced within a country, but there were no internationally applicable rules about pirating across borders before the new agreement was signed. The new trade agreement requires all signatory countries to apply copyright and patent laws equally to foreign owners of intellectual property.

In addition, the Final Act established a Dispute Settlement Body designed to ensure compliance and to resolve conflicts between member countries.

A further outcome of the deal was the setting up in 1995 of the **World Trade Organization (WTO)** as a successor to GATT. The WTO was given stronger powers than its predecessor to settle disputes and to enforce its rulings. However, the outlook is uncertain for further mutually agreed reductions in trade barriers. By late 1998 fears of a world recession spreading from South East Asia were strengthening the hands of the protectionists.

Widespread breaching of WTO rules had not occurred but some countries had begun to restrict imports in other ways. South Korea raised duties on luxury goods. Some countries raised tariffs from levels which were below the maximum WTO agreed rate. Malaysia introduced capital controls, impeding trade by making it harder for importers to obtain foreign currency.

Nevertheless these moves were small compared with the substantial reduction in trade barriers achieved over the previous thirty five years.

Economic integration

Economic integration occurs when two or more nations join to form a *free-trade zone*. The **European Union (EU)**, to which we have given much attention in earlier chapters, is only one of the world's free-trade zones. In 1988, for example, the United States (under President Reagan) and Canada (under Prime Minister Mulroney) signed the **US–Canadian Free-Trade Agreement**, which undertook to remove all barriers to trade, including tariffs and quotas, between the two countries by 1998.

World Trade Organization (WTO)

The successor to GATT. An international body aimed at reducing trade barriers.

economic integration Occurs when two or more nations join to form a free-trade zone.

European Union (EU)

The European trading bloc composed of Austria, Belgium, Denmark, Finland, France, Germany, Greece, Ireland, Italy, Luxemburg, The Netherlands, Portugal, Spain, Sweden and the United Kingdom.

US–Canadian Free-Trade Agreement

An agreement in which the United States and Canada agreed to eliminate all barriers to trade between the two countries by 1998.

---

[2]*See Norman S. Fieleke, 'The Uruguay Round of trade negotiations: an overview', New England Economic Review (May–June, 1995).*

During the last days of the administration of US President Bush, the United States, Mexico and Canada signed the **North American Free-Trade Agreement (NAFTA)**, under which the three countries agree to establish all of North America as a free-trading zone. The North American free-trade area will include 360 million people and a total output of over $7 trillion – larger than the output of the European Union. The agreement will eliminate all tariffs over a 10- to 15-year period and remove restrictions on most investments.

During the US presidential campaign of 1992, NAFTA was hotly debated. Candidates Bill Clinton and George Bush both supported the agreement. Industrial trades unions that might be affected by increased imports from Mexico (like those in the car industry) opposed the agreement, while industries whose exports to Mexico might increase as a result of the agreement (for example, the machine tool industry) supported it. Another concern was that Mexican companies were not subject to the same environmental regulations as US firms, so US firms might move to Mexico for this reason.

NAFTA was ratified by the US Congress in late 1993 and went into effect on the first day of 1994. The US Department of Commerce has estimated that as a result of NAFTA, trade between the United States and Mexico increased by nearly $16 billion in 1994. In addition, exports from the United States to Mexico outpaced imports from Mexico during 1994. By 1998, a general consensus emerged among economists that NAFTA had led to expanded employment opportunities in both the United States and Mexico.

Free trade or protection?

One of the great economic debates of all time revolves around the free-trade-versus-protection controversy. Here we briefly summarize the arguments in favour of each.

The case for free trade

In one sense, the theory of comparative advantage *is* the case for free trade. Trade has potential benefits for all nations. A good is not imported unless its net price to buyers is below the net price of the domestically produced alternative. When the Germans in our earlier example found US timber less expensive than their own, they bought it, yet they continued to pay the same price for home-made steel. Americans bought less-expensive German steel, but they continued to buy domestic timber at the same lower price. Under these conditions, *both Americans and Germans ended up paying less and consuming more.*

At the same time, resources (including labour) move out of steel production and into timber production in the United States. In Germany, resources (including labour) move out of timber production and into steel production. The resources in both countries are more efficiently used. Tariffs, export subsidies and quotas, which interfere with the free movement of goods and services around the world, reduce or eliminate the gains of comparative advantage.

We can use supply and demand curves to illustrate this. Suppose that Figure 36.4a shows domestic supply and demand for textiles. In the absence of trade, the market clears at price of €4.20. At equilibrium, 450 million metres of textiles are produced and consumed.

Assume that textiles are available at a world price of €2. This is the price in euros that Europeans must pay for textiles from foreign sources. If we assume that an unlimited amount of textiles is available at €2 and that there is no difference in quality between domestic and foreign textiles, no domestic producer will be able to charge more than €2. In the absence of trade barriers, the world price sets the price in Europe. As the price in Europe falls from €4.20 to €2.00, the quantity demanded by consumers increases from 450 million metres to 700 million metres, but the quantity supplied by domestic producers drops from 450 million metres to 200 million metres. The difference, 500 million metres, is the quantity of textiles imported.

The argument for free trade is that each country should specialize in producing the goods and services in which it enjoys a comparative advantage. If foreign producers can produce textiles at a much lower price than domestic producers, they have a comparative advantage. As the world price of textiles falls to €2, domestic (European) supply drops and resources are transferred to other sectors. These other sectors, which may be export industries or domestic industries, are not shown in Figure 36.4a. It is clear that the allocation of resources is more efficient at a price of €2. Why should Europe use domestic resources to produce what foreign producers can produce at a lower cost? Europe's resources should move into the production of the things it produces best.

Consider what happens to the domestic price of textiles when a trade barrier is imposed. Figure 36.4b shows the effect of a set tariff of €1 per metre imposed on imported textiles. The tariff raises the domestic price of textiles to €2 + €1 = €3. The result is that some of the gains from trade are lost. First, consumers are forced to pay a higher price for the same good; the quantity of textiles demanded drops from 700 million metres under free trade to 600 million metres because some consumers are not willing to pay the higher price.

At the same time, the higher price of textiles draws some marginal domestic producers who could not make a profit at €2 into textile production. (Recall: domestic producers do not pay a tariff.) As the price rises to €3, the quantity supplied by producers rises from 200 million to 300 million metres. The result is a decrease in imports from 500 million to 300 million metres.

Finally, the imposition of the tariff means the government collects revenue equal to the shaded grey area in Figure 36.4b. This shaded area is equal to the tariff rate per unit (€1) times the number of units imported after the tariff is in place (300 million metres). Thus, receipts from the tariff are €300 billion.

What is the final result of the tariff? Domestic producers receiving revenues of only €2 per unit before the tariff was imposed now receive a higher price and earn higher profits. But these higher profits are achieved at a loss of efficiency.

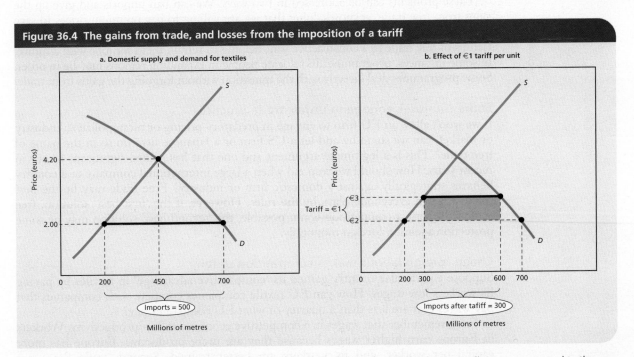

Figure 36.4 The gains from trade, and losses from the imposition of a tariff

A tariff of €1 increases the market price facing consumers from €2 to €3 per metre. The government collects revenues equal to the grey shaded area. The loss of efficiency has two components. First, consumers must pay a higher price for goods that could be produced at lower cost. Second, marginal producers are drawn into textiles and away from other goods, resulting in inefficient domestic production.

> Trade barriers prevent a nation from reaping the benefits of specialization, push it to adopt relatively inefficient production techniques, and force consumers to pay higher prices for protected products than they would otherwise pay.

The case for protection

Arguments can also be made in favour of tariffs and quotas. Over the course of time, these arguments have been made so many times by so many industries that it seems all pleas for protection share the same themes. Here we describe the most frequently heard pleas.

Protection saves jobs

The main argument for protection is that foreign competition costs jobs in the domestic economy. When Europeans buy Toyotas made in Japan, European cars go unsold. This leads to layoffs in the domestic car industry. When Europeans buy Japanese steel, steelworkers in Europe lose their jobs. When Europeans buy shoes or textiles from Korea or Taiwan, millworkers in Europe lose their jobs.

It is true that when we buy goods from foreign producers, domestic producers suffer. But there is no reason to believe that the workers laid off in the contracting sectors will not be ultimately re-employed in other expanding sectors. Foreign competition in textiles, for example, has meant the loss of EU jobs in that industry. However, in the longer term, expanding industries have taken up some of these displaced workers whose output is now more highly valued.

The adjustment is far from costless. The knowledge that some other industry, perhaps in some other part of the country, may be expanding is of little comfort to the person whose skills become obsolete or whose pension benefits are lost when his or her company abruptly closes a plant or goes bankrupt. The social and personal problems brought about by industry-specific unemployment, obsolete skills and bankruptcy as a result of foreign competition are significant.

These problems can be addressed in two ways. We can ban imports and give up the gains from free trade, acknowledging that we are willing to pay premium prices to save domestic jobs in industries that can produce more efficiently abroad. Or we can aid the victims of free trade in a constructive way, helping to retrain them for jobs with a future. In some instances, programmes to relocate people in expanding regions may be in order. Some programmes deal directly with the transition without forgoing the gains from trade.

Some countries engage in unfair trade practices

If we won't allow an EU firm to engage in predatory pricing or monopolize an industry or market, can we stand by and let a US firm or a Japanese firm do so in the name of free trade? This is a legitimate argument and one that has gained significant favour in recent years. How should we respond when a large international company or a country behaves strategically against a domestic firm or industry? Free trade may be the best solution when everybody plays by the rules. However, if the 'first best' solution, free trade with perfect competition is not possible, the 'second best' solution may be some protection against a foreign monopoly.

Cheap foreign labour makes competition unfair

Suppose a particular country gained its 'comparative advantage' in textiles by paying its workers low wages. How can EU textile companies compete with companies that pay wages that are less than a quarter of what EU companies pay?

First, remember that wages in a competitive economy reflect productivity. Workers in Europe earn higher wages because they are more productive. Europe has more capital per worker, and its workers are better trained. Second, trade flows not according to *absolute* advantage but according to *comparative* advantage: all countries benefit, even if one country is more efficient at producing everything.

Protection safeguards national security

Beyond saving jobs, certain sectors of the economy may appeal for protection for other reasons. The agriculture industry argues that it is vital to national defence. In the event of a war, we would not want to depend on foreign countries for products as vital as foodstuffs. Even if we acknowledge another country's comparative advantage, we may want to protect our own resources.

Protection discourages dependency

Closely related to the national defence argument is the claim that countries, particularly small or developing countries, may come to rely too heavily on one or more trading partners for many items. If Lilliput comes to rely on a major power for food or energy or some important raw material in which the large nation has a comparative advantage, it may be difficult for the smaller nation to remain politically neutral. Some critics of free trade argue that the superpowers have consciously engaged in trade with smaller countries to create these kinds of dependencies.

Therefore, should small independent countries consciously avoid trading relationships that might lead to political dependence? This may involve developing domestic industries in areas where a country has a comparative disadvantage. To do so would mean protecting that industry from international competition.

Protection safeguards infant industries

Young industries in a given country may have a difficult time competing with established industries in other countries. And in a dynamic world, a protected **infant industry** might mature into a strong one worldwide because of an acquired, but real, comparative advantage. If such an industry is undercut and driven out of world markets at the beginning of its life, that comparative advantage might never develop.

infant industry

A young industry that may need temporary protection from competition from the established industries of other countries in order to develop an acquired comparative advantage.

Yet efforts to protect infant industries can backfire. In July 1991, the US government imposed a 62.67% tariff on imports from Japan of active-matrix liquid crystal display screens (or 'flat panel displays'), primarily used for laptop computers. The US Commerce Department and the International Trade Commission agreed that Japanese producers were selling their screens in the US market at a price below cost and that this 'dumping' threatened the survival of domestic laptop screen producers. The tariff was meant to protect the infant US industry until it could compete head-on with the Japanese.

Unfortunately for US producers of laptop computers and for consumers who purchase them, the tariff had an unintended (though predictable) effect on the industry. Because US laptop screens were generally recognized to be of lower quality than their Japanese counterparts, the imposition of the tariff left US computer manufacturers with three options: (1) they could use the screens available from US producers and watch sales of their final product decline in the face of *higher quality* competition from abroad; (2) they could pay the tariff for the higher quality screens and watch sales of their final product decline in the face of *lower priced* competition from abroad; or (3) they could do what was the most profitable for them to do – move their production facilities abroad to avoid the tariff completely. The last is exactly what both Apple and IBM announced they would do. In the end, not only were the laptop industry and its consumers hurt by the imposition of the tariff (through higher production cost and higher laptop computer prices), but the loss of buyers for its product mean that the US screen industry was hurt too – by a policy specifically designed to help it.

An economic consensus

Critical to our study of international economics is the debate between free-traders and protectionists. On one side is the theory of comparative advantage, formalized by David Ricardo in the early part of the nineteenth century. According to this view, all countries benefit from specialization and trade. The gains from trade are real, and they can be large: free international trade raises real incomes and improves the standard of living.

On the other side are the protectionists, who point to the loss of jobs and argue for the protection of workers from foreign competition. But although foreign competition can cause job loss in specific sectors, it is unlikely to cause net job loss in an economy, and over time workers will be absorbed into expanding sectors.

> Foreign trade and full employment can be pursued simultaneously. Although economists disagree about many things, the vast majority of them favour free trade.

Summary

1. All economies, regardless of their size, depend to some extent on other economies and are affected by events outside their borders.

2. For most countries, dependence on international trade has increased in the last 15–20 years.

The economic basis for trade: comparative advantage

3. The *theory of comparative advantage*, first proposed by David Ricardo in the nineteenth century, holds that specialization and free trade will benefit all trading partners, even those that may be less efficient producers in the absolute sense.

4. A country enjoys an *absolute advantage* over another country in the production of a product if it uses fewer resources to produce that product than the other country does. A country has a *comparative advantage* in the production of a product if that product can be produced at a lower cost in terms of other goods.

5. Trade enables countries to move beyond their previous resource and productivity constraints. When countries specialize in producing those goods in which they have a comparative advantage, they maximize their combined output and allocate their resources more efficiently.

6. When trade is free, patterns of trade and trade flows result from the independent decisions of thousands of importers and exporters, and millions of private households and firms.

7. The relative attractiveness of foreign goods to EU buyers and of EU goods to foreign buyers depends in part on *exchange rates*, the ratios at which two currencies are traded for each other.

8. For any pair of countries, there is a range of exchange rates that will lead automatically to both countries realizing the gains from specialization and comparative advantage. Within that range, the exchange rate will determine which country gains the most from

trade. This leads us to conclude that exchange rates determine the *terms of trade*.

9. If exchange rates end up in the right range (that is, in a range that facilitates the flow of goods between nations), the free market will drive each country to shift resources into those sectors in which it enjoys a comparative advantage. Only those products in which a country has a comparative advantage will be competitive in world markets.

The sources of comparative advantage

10. The *Heckscher–Ohlin theorem* looks to relative *factor endowments* to explain comparative advantage and trade flows. According to the theorem, a country has a comparative advantage in the production of a product if that country is relatively well endowed with the inputs that are used intensively in the production of that product.

11. A relatively short list of inputs – natural resources, knowledge capital, physical capital, land, and skilled and unskilled labour – explains a surprisingly large portion of world trade patterns. But the simple version of the theory of comparative advantage cannot explain why many countries import and export the same goods.

12. Some theories argue that comparative advantage can be acquired. Just as industries within a country differentiate their products to capture a domestic market, so too they differentiate their products to please the wide variety of tastes that exists worldwide. This theory is not inconsistent with the theory of comparative advantage.

Trade barriers: tariffs, export subsidies and quotas

13. Trade barriers take many forms; the three most common are *tariffs*, *export subsidies* and *quotas*. All are forms of *protection* through which some sector of the economy is shielded from foreign competition.

14. The general movement has been away from tariffs and quotas. The purpose of the *General Agreement on Tariffs and Trade (GATT)*, and subsequently the World Trade Organization (WTO) is to reduce barriers to world trade and keep them down.

15. Important examples of economic integration are the *European Union (EU)*, the *US–Canadian Free-Trade Agreement* and the *North American Free-Trade Agreement*.

Free trade or protection?

16. In one sense, the theory of comparative advantage *is* the case for free trade. Trade barriers prevent a nation from reaping the benefits of specialization, push it to adopt relatively inefficient production techniques, and force consumers to pay higher prices for protected products than they would otherwise pay.

17. The case for protection rests on a number of propositions, one of which is that foreign competition results in a loss of domestic jobs. But there is no reason to believe that the workers laid off in the contracting sectors will not be ultimately re-employed in other expanding sectors. This adjustment process is far from costless, however.

18. Other arguments for protection hold that cheap foreign labour makes competition unfair; that some countries engage in unfair trade practices; that it protects national security and discourages dependency; and that it protects *infant industries*. Despite these arguments, most economists favour free trade.

Review Terms and Concepts

absolute advantage
comparative advantage
Corn Laws
dumping
economic integration
European Union (EU)
exchange rate
export subsidies
factor endowments
General Agreement on Tariffs and Trade (GATT)

Heckscher–Ohlin theorem
infant industry
North American Free-Trade Agreement (NAFTA)
protection
quota
tariff
terms of trade
theory of comparative advantage
US–Canadian Free-Trade Agreement
World Trade Organization (WTO)

Problem Set

1. Suppose Belgium and Denmark each only produce two goods: guns and butter. Both are produced using labour alone, and the value of a good is equal to the number of labour units required to produce it. Assuming both countries are at full employment, you are given the information summarized in Table 1.

Table 1	
Belgium	10 units of labour are required to produce 1 gun
	5 units of labour are required to produce 1 kg of butter
	Total labour force: 1,000,000 units
Denmark	15 units of labour are required to produce 1 gun
	10 units of labour are required to produce 1 kg of butter
	Total labour force: 750,000 units

a. Draw the production possibility frontiers for each country in the absence of trade.
b. If transport costs are ignored and trade is allowed, will Belgium and Denmark engage in trade? Explain.
c. If a trade agreement were negotiated, at what rate (number of guns per unit of butter) would they agree to exchange?

2. The United States and Russia each produce only bearskin caps and wheat. Domestic prices are given in Table 2 (Ru = roubles). On 1 April, the exchange rate is $1 = 1 Ru.
a. Which country has an absolute advantage in the production of bearskin caps? The production of wheat?

Table 2		
	Russia	**USA**
Bearskin caps (cost per cap)	10 Ru	$7
Wheat (cost per kilo)	15 Ru	$10

b. Which country has a comparative advantage in the production of bearskin caps? The production of wheat?
c. If the USA and Russia were the only two countries engaging in trade, what adjustments would you predict, assuming exchange rates are freely determined by the laws of supply and demand?

3. Europe is said to have a comparative disadvantage in the production of agricultural goods. How would you go about testing this proposition? What data would you need? How does the Common Agricultural Policy affect international trade in agricultural products?

4. Table 3 gives recent yield figures (in bushels per acre) from the US states of Illinois and Kansas.

Table 3

	Wheat	Soybeans
Illinois	48	39
Kansas	40	24

Source: US Department of Agriculture crop production statistics.

a. If we assume that farmers in Illinois and Kansas use the same amount of labour, capital and fertilizer, which state has an absolute advantage in wheat production? Soybean production?
b. If we transfer land out of wheat into soybeans, how many bushels of wheat do we give up in Illinois per additional bushel of soybeans produced? In Kansas?
c. Which state has a comparative advantage in wheat production? In soybean production?
d. Table 4 gives the distribution of land (millions of acres) planted for each state in the same year. Are these data consistent with your answer to part (c)? Explain.

Table 4

Land under cultivation		Wheat	Soybeans
Illinois	22.9	1.9 (8.3%)	9.1 (39.7%)
Kansas	20.7	11.8 (57.0%)	1.9 (9.2%)

5. The EU is composed of a number of separate economies – i.e. member countries – with no trade barriers. In such an open environment, each country specializes in the products that it produces best.
a. What product or products does your country specialize in?
b. Can you identify the source of the comparative advantage that lies behind the production of one or more of these products (a natural resource, plentiful cheap labour, a skilled labour force, etc.)?
c. Do you think that the theory of comparative advantage and the Heckscher–Ohlin theorem help to explain why your country specializes in the way that it does?

6. Germany and France produce white and red wines. Suppose that current domestic prices are as given in Table 5, and that the exchange rate is 1 DM = 1 franc (F).

Table 5

	Germany	France
White wine	5 DM	10 F
Red wine	10 DM	15 F

a. If the price ratios within each country reflect resource use, which country has a comparative advantage in the production of red wine? White wine?
b. Assume that there are no other trading partners and that the only motive for holding foreign currency is to buy foreign goods. Will the current exchange rate lead to trade flows in both directions between the two countries?
c. What adjustments might you expect in the exchange rate? Be specific.
d. What would you predict about trade flows between Germany and France in the long run?

7. The EU is scheduled to remove all trade barriers within its member countries soon after the millennium. Its goal is to become one common market with one uniform currency. Explain the probable benefits and costs to the EU's member countries. Should other countries such as Switzerland be concerned about these developments? Why, or why not?

37

Economic Growth in Developing Nations

Our primary focus in this text has been on economic issues facing Europe. Welfare reform, slow economic growth in recent years and worries about unemployment are familiar to Europeans. But the economics we have been studying also applies to other countries: welfare reform is a big issue in the United States, and Japan is facing major fiscal deficits. We can analyse these and other issues in the United States and Japan with some confidence because these countries have so much in common with Europe. In spite of differences in languages and cultures, all these countries have modern industrialized economies that rely heavily on markets to allocate resources. But what about the economic problems facing Somalia or Haiti? Can we apply the same economic principles that we have been studying to these less-developed countries (sometimes called LDCs)?

The answer is yes. All economic analysis deals with the basic problem of making choices under conditions of scarcity, and the problem of satisfying their citizens' wants and needs is certainly as real for Somalia and Haiti as it is for The Netherlands, the United Kingdom and Japan. The universality of scarcity is what makes economic analysis relevant to all nations, regardless of their level of material well-being or ruling political ideology.

The basic tools of supply and demand, theories about consumers and firms, and theories about the structure of markets all contribute to an understanding of the economic problems confronting the world's developing nations. However, these nations often face economic problems quite different from those faced by richer, more developed countries. In the developing nations, the economist may have to worry about chronic food shortages, explosive population growth, and hyperinflations that reach triple or even quadruple digits. Europe and other industrialized economies rarely encounter such difficulties.

The instruments of economic management also vary from nation to nation. Europe has well-developed financial market institutions and strong central banks through which the government can control the macroeconomy to some extent. But even limited intervention is impossible in some of the developing countries. In Europe, tax laws can be changed to stimulate saving, to encourage particular kinds of investments, or to redistribute income. In most developing countries, there are neither meaningful personal income taxes nor effective tax policies.

But even though economic problems and the policy instruments available to tackle them vary across nations, economic thinking about these problems can be transferred quite easily from one setting to another. In this chapter we discuss several of the economic problems specific to developing nations in an attempt to capture some of the insights that economic analysis can offer.

Life in the developing nations: population and poverty

By the year 2000, the population of the world will reach over 6.1 billion people. Most of the world's 200-plus nations belong to the developing world, in which about three-quarters of the world's population lives.

In the early 1960s, the nations of the world could be assigned rather easily to categories: the *developed countries* included most of Europe, North America, Japan, Australia and New Zealand; the *developing countries* included the rest of the world. The developing nations were often referred to as the 'Third World' to distinguish them from the Western industrialized nations (the 'First World') and the former Socialist bloc of Eastern European nations (the 'Second World').

By the 1990s, however, the world no longer divided into three neat parts as easily as it once did. Rapid economic progress has brought some developing nations closer to developed economies. Countries such as Argentina and Korea, while still considered to be 'developing', are often referred to as middle-income, or newly industrialized, countries. Meanwhile, other countries, such as much of sub-Saharan Africa and some of South Asia, have stagnated and fallen so far behind the economic advances of the rest of the world that a new designation, the 'Fourth World', has been coined to describe them. It is not clear yet where the republics of the former Soviet Union and other formerly Communist countries of Eastern Europe will end up. Production has fallen sharply in many of them. For example, between 1990 and 1998, real GDP fell about 40% in the transition economies and by over 50% in Russia and Central Asia. One estimate puts current per capita GDP in Russia at less than $2500. Some of the new republics now have more in common with developing countries than with developed countries.

Although the countries of the developing world exhibit considerable diversity, both in their standards of living and in their particular experiences of growth, marked differences continue to separate them from the developed nations. To begin with, the developed countries have a higher average level of material well-being. By material well-being, we mean the amounts of food, clothing, shelter and other commodities consumed by the average person. Comparisons of gross national product (GNP) per capita – that is, of the value of goods and services produced per person in an economy – are often used as a crude index of the level of material well-being across nations. As you can see from Table 37.1, GNP per capita in the industrial market economies significantly exceeds that of both the low- and middle-income developing economies.

Other characteristics of economic development include improvements in basic health and education. The degree of political and economic freedom enjoyed by individual citizens might also be part of a comprehensive definition of what it means to be a developed nation. Some of these criteria are easier to quantify than others; Table

Table 37.1 Indicators of economic development

Country group	Population, 1995 (millions)	GNP per capita, 1995 (US$)	Life expectancy, 1995 (years)	Infant mortality, 1995 (deaths before age 1 per 1000 births)	Percentage of population in urban areas, 1992
Low-income (e.g. China, Ethiopia, Haiti, India)	3,180	430	63	69	29
Lower middle-income (e.g. Guatemala, Poland, Philippines, Thailand)	1,153	1,670	67	41	56
Upper middle-income (e.g. Brazil, Malaysia, Mexico)	438	4,260	69	35	73
Industrial market economies (e.g. Japan, Germany, New Zealand, United States)	902	24,930	77	7	75

Note: GDP data not reported.

Source: World Bank, *World Development Report* (1997). Note that all numbers refer to weighted averages for each country group, where the weights equal the populations of each nation in a specific country group.

37.1 presents data for different types of economies according to some of the more easily measured indexes of development. As you can see, the industrial market economies enjoy higher standards of living according to whatever indicator of development is chosen.

Applications

The challenge of development

The following is an excerpt from a speech given by World Bank President James D. Wolfensohn on the challenge facing the world in 1997.

. . . Our goal must be to reduce these disparities across and within countries, to bring more and more people into the economic mainstream, to promote equitable access to the benefits of development regardless of nationality, race or gender. This – the *Challenge of Inclusion* – is the key development challenge of our time.

You and I, and all of us in this room – the privileged of the developing world – can choose to ignore it. We can focus only on the successes. We can live with a little more crime, a few more wars, air that is a little bit dirtier. We can insulate ourselves from whole sections of the world for which crisis is real and daily but which to the rest of us is largely invisible. But we must recognize that we are living with a time bomb, and unless we take action now, it could explode in our children's faces.

If we do not act, in thirty years the inequities will be greater. With population growing at 80 million a year, instead of 3 billion living on under $2 a day, it

could be as high as 5 billion. In thirty years, the quality of our environment will be worse. Instead of 4% of tropical forests lost since Rio, it could be 24%.

In thirty years, the number of conflicts may be higher. Already, we live in a world which last year alone saw twenty-six interstate wars and 23 million refugees. One does not have to spend long in Bosnia or Gaza or the Lakes District in Africa to know that without economic hope, we will not have peace. Without equity, we will not have global stability. Without a better sense of social justice our cities will not be safe, and our societies will not be stable. Without inclusion, too many of us will be condemned to live separate, armed, and frightened lives.

And economics is fundamentally changing the relationships between the rich and poor nations. Over the next twenty-five years, growth in China, India, Indonesia, Brazil and Russia will likely redraw the economy map of the world as the share in global output of the developing and transition economies doubles. Today, these counties represent 50% of the world's population but only 8% of its GDP. Their share in world trade is a

quarter that of the European Union. By the year 2020, their share in world trade could be 50% more than Europe's.

We share the same world and we share the same challenge. The fight against poverty is the fight for peace, security and growth for us all.

How then do we proceed? This much we know: no country has been successful in reducing poverty without sustained economic growth. Those countries that have been most successful – including, most notably, many here in East Asia – have also invested heavily in their people, have put in place the right policy fundamentals, and have not discriminated against their rural sectors. The results have been dramatic: large private capital inflows, rapid growth and substantial poverty reduction.

The message for countries is clear: educate your people; ensure their health; give them voice and justice; financial systems that work, and sound economic policies; and they will respond, and they will save, and they will attract the investment, both domestic and foreign, that is needed to raise living standards and fuel development.

World Bank president James Wolfensohn.

But another message is also emerging from recent developments. We have seen in recent months how financial markets are demanding more information disclosure, and how they are making swift judgements about the quality and sustainability of government policies based on that information. We have seen that without sound organization and supervision, a financial system can falter with the poor hurt the most. We have seen how corruption flourishes in the dark, how it prevents growth and social equity, and how it creates the basis for social and political instability. . . .

Source: 'The challenge of inclusion', address by James D. Wolfensohn, President of the World Bank Group, to the Board of Governors, Hong Kong, China, 23 September 1997.

Behind these statistics lies the reality of the very difficult life facing the people of the developing world. For most, meagre incomes provide only the basic necessities of life. Most meals are the same, consisting of the region's food staple – typically rice, wheat or maize. Shelter is primitive. Many people share a small room, usually with an earthen floor and no sanitary facilities. The great majority of the population lives in rural areas where agricultural work is hard and extremely time-consuming. Productivity (output produced per worker) is low because household plots are small and only the crudest of farm implements are available. Low productivity means that farm output per person is at levels barely sufficient to feed a farmer's own family, with nothing left over to sell to others. School-age children may receive some formal education, but illiteracy remains chronic for young and old alike. Infant mortality runs ten times higher than in the industrial market economies. Although parasitic infections are common and debilitating, there is only one doctor for every 5000 people.

Life in the developing nations is a continual struggle against the circumstances of poverty, and prospects for dramatic improvements in living standards for most people are poor. However, as with all generalizations, there are important exceptions. Some nations are better off than others, and in any given nation an elite group always lives in considerable luxury. Just as in any advanced economy, income is distributed in a fashion that allows a small percentage of households to consume a disproportionately large share of national income. Income distribution in developing countries is often so skewed that the richest households surpass the living standards of many high-income families in the advanced economies. Table 37.2 presents data on the distribution of income in some developing countries.

Clearly, poverty – not affluence – dominates the developing world. Recent studies suggest that 40% of the population of the developing nations have annual incomes insufficient to provide for adequate nutrition.

While the developed nations account for only about a quarter of the world's population, they are estimated to consume three-quarters of the world's output. This leaves the developing countries with about three-quarters of the world's people, but only a quarter of the world's income. The simple result is that most of our planet's population is poor.

In a typical EU country, the poorest one-fifth (bottom 20%) of the families receive around 7% of total income, while the richest one-fifth receive over 40% of the income. But the inequality in the world distribution of income is much greater. When we look at the population of the world, the poorest one-fifth of the families earns about 0.5% of the total world income, and the richest one-fifth earn 79% of world income!

Table 37.2 Income distribution in some developing countries (percentages)

	Sri Lanka	Brazil	Pakistan	Indonesia
Per capita GNP, 1995	$700.0	$3640.0	$460.0	$980.0
Bottom 20%	8.9	8.9	8.4	8.7
Second 20%	13.1	4.9	12.9	12.3
Third 20%	16.9	8.9	16.9	16.3
Fourth 20%	21.7	16.8	22.2	21.1
Top 20%	39.3	67.5	39.7	40.7
Top 10%	25.2	51.3	25.2	25.6

Source: World Bank, *World Development Report* (1997).

Economic development: sources and strategies

Economists have been trying to understand the process of economic growth and development since the days of Adam Smith and David Ricardo in the eighteenth and nineteenth centuries, but the study of development economics as it applies to the developing nations has a much shorter history. The geopolitical struggles that followed the Second World War brought increased attention to the developing nations and their economic problems. During this period, the central question of the new field of development economics was simply: why are some nations poor and others rich? If economists could understand the barriers to economic growth that prevent nations from developing and the prerequisites that would help them to develop, then they could prescribe suitable strategies for achieving economic advancement.

The sources of economic development

While a general theory of economic development applicable to all nations has not emerged and probably never will, some basic factors that limit a poor nation's economic growth have been suggested. These include insufficient capital formation, a shortage of human resources and entrepreneurial ability, a lack of social overhead capital, and the constraints imposed by dependency on the already developed nations.

Capital formation

One explanation for low levels of output in developing nations is the absence of sufficient quantities of necessary inputs. Developing nations have diverse resource endowments – Congo, for instance, is abundant in natural resources, while Bangladesh is resource poor. Almost all developing nations have a scarcity of physical capital relative to other resources, especially labour. The small stock of physical capital (including factories, machinery, farm equipment and other types of productive capital) constrains labour's productivity and holds back national output.

But citing capital shortages as the cause of low productivity does not really explain much. To get to the heart of the matter, we need to know why capital is in such short supply in developing countries. Many explanations have been offered. One, the **vicious-circle-of-poverty hypothesis**, suggests that a poor nation must consume most of its income just to maintain its already low standard of living. Just like a poor family, a poor nation finds that the opportunity cost of forgoing current consumption (that is, saving instead of consuming) is too high. Consuming most of national income implies limited saving, and this in turn implies low levels of investment. Without investment, the capital stock does not grow, income remains low, and the vicious circle is complete. Poverty becomes self-perpetuating.

The difficulty with the vicious-circle argument is that if it were true, no nation could ever develop. For example, Japanese GDP per capita at the beginning of the twentieth century was well below that of many of today's developing nations. If the vicious-circle explanation were completely correct, Japan could never have grown into the industrial power it is today. The vicious-circle argument fails to recognize that every nation has some surplus above consumption needs that is available for investment. Often, this surplus is most visible in the conspicuous-consumption habits of the nation's richest families. In short:

> Poverty alone cannot explain capital shortages, nor is poverty necessarily self-perpetuating.

In a developing economy, scarcity of capital may have more to do with a lack of incentives for citizens to save and invest productively than with any absolute scarcity of income available for capital accumulation. The inherent riskiness and uncertainty

vicious-circle-of-poverty hypothesis Suggests that poverty is self-perpetuating because poor nations are unable to save and invest enough to accumulate the capital stock that would help them grow.

that surround a developing nation's economy and its political system tend to reduce incentives to invest in any activity, especially those that require long periods of time to yield a return. Many of the rich in developing countries take their savings and invest them in Europe or in the United States rather than risk holding them in what is often an unstable political climate. Savings transferred to Europe do not lead to physical capital growth in the developing countries. The term **capital flight** is often used to refer to the fact that both human capital and financial capital (domestic savings) often leave developing countries in search of higher rates of return elsewhere. In addition, a range of government policies in the developing nations – including price ceilings, import controls, and even outright appropriation of private property – tend to discourage investment activity.

capital flight
The tendency for both human capital and financial capital to leave developing countries in search of higher rates of return elsewhere.

Whatever the causes of capital shortages, it is clear that the absence of productive capital prevents income from rising in any economy. The availability of capital is a necessary, but not a *sufficient*, condition for economic growth. Many developing countries are littered with idle factories and abandoned machinery. Clearly, other ingredients are required to achieve economic progress.

Human resources and entrepreneurial ability

Capital is not the only factor of production required to produce output. Labour is an equally important input. But the quantity of available labour rarely constrains a developing economy. In most developing nations, rapid population growth through several decades has resulted in rapidly expanding labour supplies. The *quality* of available labour, however, may pose a serious constraint on the growth of income. Or, to put it another way, the shortage of *human capital* – the stock of knowledge and skill embodied in the workforce – may act as a barrier to economic growth.

Human capital may be developed in a number of ways. Because malnutrition and the lack of basic health care can substantially reduce labour productivity, programmes to improve nutrition and health represent one kind of human capital investment that can lead to increased productivity and higher incomes. The more familiar forms of human capital investment, including formal education and on-the-job training, may also play an important role. Basic literacy, as well as specialized training in farm management, for example, can yield high returns to both the individual worker and the economy. Education has grown to become the largest category of government expenditure in many developing nations, in part because of the belief that human resources are the ultimate determinant of economic advance.

Unfortunately, those lucky enough to get an education often leave developing countries because they can do better financially in the developed world. Just as financial capital seeks the highest and safest return, so does human capital. Thousands of students from developing countries, many of whom were supported by their governments, graduate every year from European colleges and universities as engineers, doctors, scientists, economists and the like. After graduation, these people face a difficult choice: to remain in Europe and earn a high salary or to return home and accept a job at a much lower salary. Many people choose to remain in Europe. This **brain drain** siphons off many of the most talented minds from developing countries.

brain drain The tendency for talented people from developing countries to become educated in a developed country and remain there after they graduate.

Another frequently cited barrier to economic development is the apparent shortage of entrepreneurial activity in developing nations. Innovative entrepreneurs who are willing to take risks are an essential human resource in any economy. In a developing nation, new techniques of production rarely need to be invented, since they can usually be adapted from the technology already developed by the technologically advanced nations. But entrepreneurs who are willing and able to organize and carry out economic activity appear to be in short supply. Family and political ties often seem to be more important than ability when it comes to securing positions of authority. Whatever the explanation:

Development cannot proceed without human resources capable of initiating and managing economic activity.

Social overhead capital

Anyone who has spent time in a developing nation knows how difficult it can be to send a letter, make a local phone call, or travel within the country itself. Add to this list of obstacles problems with water supplies, frequent electrical power failures – in the few areas where electricity is available at all – and often ineffective mosquito and pest control, and you soon realize how deficient even the simplest, most basic government-provided goods and services can be.

For example, in 1995, Nepal had a population of 22 million and a per capita GDP of just $200. Only 48% of the population had access to safe water and just 6% had access to sanitation, according to the World Bank Development Report.

In any economy, developing or otherwise, the government has considerable opportunity and responsibility for involvement where conditions encourage natural monopoly (as in the utilities industries) and where public goods (such as roads and pest control) must be provided. In a developing economy, the government must place particular emphasis on creating a basic infrastructure – roads, power generation, irrigation systems. There are often good reasons why such projects, referred to as **social overhead capital**, cannot successfully be undertaken by the private sector. First, many of these projects operate with economies of scale, which means that they can be efficient only if they are very large. In that case, they may be simply too large for any private company, or even a group of such companies, to carry out.

Second, many socially useful projects cannot be undertaken by the private sector because there is no way for private agents to capture enough of the returns to make such projects profitable. This so-called *free-rider problem* is common in the economics of the developed world. Consider as an example national defence. Because everyone in a country benefits from national defence, whether they have paid for it or not, anyone who attempted to go into the private business of providing national defence would quickly go broke. Why should I buy any national defence at all if your purchase of defence will also protect me? Why should you buy any if my purchase will also protect you?

The governments of developing countries can do important and useful things to encourage development, but many of their efforts must be concentrated in areas that the private sector would never touch. If government action in these realms is not forthcoming, economic development may be curtailed by a lack of social overhead capital.

Dependency theories

In trying to understand why some nations are rich and others poor, some economists find the explanation within the developing nations themselves. In advanced industrial economies, these economists explain, the early merchant classes were responsible for breaking down traditional feudalism and replacing it with a market economy orientated towards growth and development. In many developing nations, however, the class that could foster capitalism has not followed the same path, perhaps out of fear of a socialist takeover. In the view of some analysts, potential capitalists have not transformed traditional societies but have instead acted to maintain the status quo and have thus retarded economic advancement.

Another position, **dependency theory**, holds that the poverty of the developing nations is due to the 'dependence' of the developing world on nations that are already developed. (A *dependent country* is one whose economy is dependent on the development and expansion of another country's economy.) During the colonial period, European powers dominated much of the political and economic life of what is today the developing world. Colonial powers sometimes directly destroyed local industries, either by prohibiting certain economic activities or by flooding the colony's markets with manufactured goods from the parent country. Furthermore, by not developing basic physical infrastructure or local human capital and by draining mineral wealth

---

social overhead capital
Basic infrastructure projects such as roads, power generation and irrigation systems.

dependency theory
The theory that the poverty of the developing nations is due to the 'dependence' of the developing world on nations that are already developed; it suggests that even after the end of colonialism, this dependence is maintained because developed countries are able to use their economic power to determine to their own advantage (and to the disadvantage of others) the relative prices and conditions under which the international exchange of goods takes place.

from the colonies, colonialism created countries that had become helpless and economically dependent by the time they achieved political independence.

Some economists contend that economic dependency is maintained today, even though colonialism is long past, through the structure of international trade relations. Developed economies provide important markets for the exports of developing nations and are often their only sources of critical inputs. Industrialized economies also influence world interest rates, capital flows and exchange rates. Through their economic power, it is argued, industrialized nations often determine to their own advantage (and the disadvantage of others) the relative prices and conditions under which the international exchange of goods takes place.

Dependency theorists argue that the unequal relationship between rich and poor nations in world markets works to the detriment of the developing world. This view has led many leaders in the developing countries to call for a *new international economic order*. Such an arrangement would require agreements between developed and developing nations that would increase the gains that accrue to the developing world from international exchange. Plans for such a set of agreements have been widely discussed in the developing world. But because of divisions among the developing nations and a lack of cooperation from most developed countries there has been virtually no progress in reaching any sort of accord.

Strategies for economic development

Just as no single theory appears to explain lack of economic advancement, so too is it unlikely that one development strategy will succeed in all nations. In fact, many alternative development strategies have been proposed over the past 30 or 40 years. Although these strategies have been very different, they all share the recognition that a developing economy faces certain basic trade-offs. An insufficient amount of both human and physical resources dictates that choices must be made. Some of the basic trade-offs that underlie any development strategy include those between agriculture and industry, exports and import substitution, and central planning and free markets.

Agriculture or industry?

Most developing countries World countries began to gain political independence just after the Second World War. The tradition of promoting industrialization as the solution to the problems of the developing world dates from this time. The early five-year development plans of India called for promoting manufacturing; the current government in Ethiopia (an extremely poor country) has similar intentions.

Industry has several apparent attractions over agriculture. First, if it is true that capital shortages constrain economic growth, then the building of factories is an obvious step towards increasing a nation's stock of capital. Second, and perhaps most important, one of the primary characteristics of more developed economies is their structural transition away from agriculture and towards manufacturing and modern services. As Table 37.3 shows, agriculture's share in GDP declines substantially as per capita incomes increase. The share of services increases correspondingly, especially in the early phases of economic development.

Many economies have pursued industry at the expense of agriculture. In many countries, however, industrialization has been either unsuccessful or disappointing – that is, it has not brought the benefits that were expected. Experience suggests that simply trying to replicate the structure of developed economies does not in itself guarantee, or even promote, successful development.

Since the early 1970s, the agricultural sector has received considerably more attention. Agricultural strategies have had numerous benefits. Although some agricultural projects (such as the building of major dams and irrigation networks) are very capital intensive, many others (such as services to help teach better farming techniques and small-scale fertilizer programmes) have low capital and import requirements. Programmes like these can affect large numbers of households, and because their

Table 37.3 The structure of production in selected developed and developing economies, 1995

Country	Per capita income (US$)	Percentage of GDP		
		Agriculture	Industry	Services
Tanzania	120	58	17	24
Bangladesh	240	31	18	52
China	620	21	48	31
Colombia	1,910	14	32	54
Thailand	2,740	11	40	49
Brazil	3,640	14	37	49
Korea (Republic)	9,700	7	43	50
Japan	39,640	2	38	60

Source: World Bank, *World Development Report* (1997), Tables 1 and 12.

benefits are directed at rural areas, they are most likely to help a country's poorest families.

Experience over the last three decades suggests that some balance between these approaches leads to the best outcome – that is, it is important and effective to pay attention to both industry and agriculture. The Chinese have referred to this dual approach to development as 'walking on two legs'.

Exports or import substitution?

As developing nations expand their industrial activities, they must decide what type of trade strategy to pursue. The choice usually boils down to one of two major alternatives: import substitution or export promotion.

Import substitution is an industrial trade strategy that favours developing local industries that can manufacture goods to replace imports. For example, if fertilizer is currently imported, import substitution calls for establishment of a domestic fertilizer industry to produce replacements for fertilizer imports. This strategy gained prominence throughout South America in the 1950s. At that time, most developing nations exported agricultural and mineral products, goods that faced uncertain and often unstable international markets. Furthermore, the *terms of trade* for these nations – the ratio of export to import prices – seemed to be on a long-run decline.[1] A decline in a country's terms of trade means that its imports of manufactured goods become relatively expensive in the domestic market, while its exports – mostly primary goods such as rubber and wheat and oil – become relatively inexpensive in the world market.

Under these conditions, the call for import-substitution policies was understandable. Special government actions, including tariff and quota protection and subsidized imports of machinery, were set up to encourage new domestic industries. Multinational corporations were also invited into many countries to begin domestic operations.

Most economists believe that import-substitution strategies have failed almost everywhere they have been tried. With domestic industries sheltered from international

import substitution
An industrial trade strategy that favours developing local industries that can manufacture goods to replace imports.

[1] *It now appears that the terms of trade for developing countries as a group were not actually on a long-run decline. Of course, the prices of commodities have changed, with some doing very well and others doing quite poorly. During the 1950s, however, many policy makers believed that the purchasing power of developing-country exports was in a permanent slump.*

competition by high tariffs (often as high as 200%), major economic inefficiencies were created. For example, Peru has a population of just over 24 million, only a tiny fraction of whom could ever afford to buy a car. Yet at one time the country had five or six different car manufacturers, each of which produced only a few thousand cars per year. Since there are substantial economies of scale in car production, the cost per car was much higher than it needed to be, and valuable resources that could have been devoted to another, much more productive, activity were squandered producing cars.

Furthermore, policies designed to promote import substitution often encouraged capital-intensive production methods, which limited the creation of jobs and hurt export activities. Obviously, a country like Peru could not export cars, because it could produce them only at a cost far greater than their price on the world market. Worse still, import-substitution policies encouraged the use of expensive domestic products, such as tractors and fertilizer, instead of lower-cost imports. These policies thus served to tax the very sectors that might have successfully competed in world markets. To the extent that the Peruvian sugar industry had to rely on domestically produced high-cost fertilizer, for example, its ability to compete in international markets was reduced, because its production costs were artificially raised.

export promotion
A trade policy designed to encourage exports.

As an alternative to import substitution, some nations have pursued strategies of export promotion. **Export promotion** is simply the policy of encouraging exports. As an industrial market economy, Japan is a striking example to the developing world of the economic success that exports can provide. With an average annual per capita real GDP growth rate of roughly 6% since 1960, Japan's achievements have been in part based on industrial production orientated towards foreign consumers.

Several countries in the developing world have emulated Japan's success. Starting in about 1970, Hong Kong, Singapore, Korea and Taiwan (sometimes called the 'four little dragons' between the two big dragons, China and Japan) all began to pursue export promotion of manufactured goods. At one stage their growth rates surpassed even Japan's. Other nations, including Brazil, Colombia and Turkey, have also had some success at pursuing a more outward-looking trade policy.

Government support of export promotion has often taken the form of maintaining an exchange rate that is favourable enough to permit exports to compete with products manufactured in developed economies. For example, many people believe that the Japanese kept the value of the yen artificially low during the 1970s. Because a 'cheap' yen means inexpensive Japanese goods in Europe and the United States, sales of Japanese goods (especially cars) increased dramatically. Governments have also provided subsidies to export industries.

In 1997–98, Japan was in a serious recession. Overall, Japan's performance since 1990 has not been as strong as its pre-1990 performance. But its recent troubles do not diminish the incredible performance of the Japanese economic machine between 1960 and 1990.

Central planning or the market?

As part of its strategy for achieving economic development, a nation must decide how its economy will be directed. Its basic choices lie between a market-orientated economic system and a centrally planned one.

In the 1950s and into the 1960s, development strategies that called for national planning commanded wide support. The rapid economic growth of the Soviet Union, a centrally planned economy, provided a historical example of the speed with which a less developed agrarian nation could be transformed into a modern industrial power. (The often appalling costs of this strategy – namely severe discipline, gross violation of human rights, and environmental damage – were less widely known.) In addition, the underdevelopment of many commodity and asset markets in developing countries led many experts to believe that market forces could not direct an economy reliably and that major government intervention was therefore necessary.

Today, planning takes many forms in the developing nations. In some settings, central planning has replaced market-based outcomes with direct, administratively determined controls over such economic variables as prices, output and employment. In other situations, national planning amounts to little more than the formulation of general five- or ten-year goals that serve as rough blueprints for a nation's economic future.

The economic appeal of planning lies theoretically in its ability to channel savings into productive investment and to coordinate economic activities that private actors in the economy might not otherwise undertake. The reality of central planning, however, is that it is technically difficult, highly politicized and a nightmare to administer. Given the scarcity of human resources and the unstable political environment in many developing nations, planning itself – let alone the execution of the plan – becomes a formidable task.

The failure of many central planning efforts has brought increasing calls for less government intervention and more market orientation in developing economies. The elimination of price controls, privatization of state-run enterprises and reductions in import restraints are examples of market-orientated reforms that are frequently recommended by such international agencies as the **International Monetary Fund**, whose primary goals are to stabilize international exchange rates and to lend money to countries that have problems financing their international transactions, and the **World Bank**, which lends money to individual countries for projects that promote economic development.

Members' contributions to both organizations are determined by the size of their economies. Only 20% of the World Bank's funding comes from contributions; the other 80% comes from retained earnings and investments in capital markets. Throughout the developing world, a recognition of the value of market forces in determining the allocation of scarce resources appears to be increasing. Nonetheless, government still has a major role to play. In the decades ahead, the governments of developing nations will need to determine those cases where planning is superior to the market and those where the market is superior to planning.

Growth versus development: the policy cycle

Until now, we have used the words 'growth' and 'development' as if they meant essentially the same thing. But this may not always be the case. One can easily imagine instances in which a country has achieved higher levels of income (growth) with little or no benefit accruing to most of its citizens (development). Thus, one central question in evaluating alternative strategies for achieving economic development is whether economic growth necessarily brings about economic development.

In the past, most development strategies were aimed at increasing the growth rate of income per capita. Many still are, based on the theory that benefits of economic growth will 'trickle down' to all members of society. If this theory is correct, then growth should promote development.

By the early 1970s, however, the relationship between growth and development was increasingly being questioned. A major study by the World Bank in 1974 concluded that

it is now clear that more than a decade of rapid growth in underdeveloped countries has been of little or no benefit to perhaps a third of their population . . . Paradoxically, while growth policies have succeeded beyond the expectations of the first development decade, the very idea of aggregate growth as a social objective has increasingly been called into question.

The World Bank study indicated that increases in GDP per capita did not guarantee significant improvements in such development indicators as nutrition, health and education. Although GDP per capita did indeed rise, its benefits trickled down to only a small minority of the population. This realization prompted a call for new development strategies that would directly address the problems of poverty. Such new

International Monetary Fund An international agency whose primary goals are to stabilize international exchange rates and to lend money to countries that have problems financing their international transactions.

World Bank An international agency that lends money to individual countries for projects that promote economic development.

strategies favoured agriculture over industry, called for domestic redistribution of income and wealth (especially land), and encouraged programmes to satisfy such basic needs as food and shelter.

In the late 1970s and early 1980s, the international macroeconomic crises of high oil prices, worldwide recession and developing-country debt forced attention away from programmes designed to eliminate poverty directly. Then, during the 1980s and 1990s, the policy focus turned through 180 degrees. The World Bank began demanding 'structural adjustment' in the developing countries as a prerequisite for sending aid to them. **Structural adjustment** programmes entail reducing the size of the public sector through privatization and/or expenditure reductions, substantially cutting budget deficits, reigning in inflation, and encouraging private saving and investment with tax reforms. These pro-market demands were an attempt to stimulate growth; distributional consequences took a back seat. (See the Application 'Do we really need the World Bank?')

structural adjustment A series of programmes in developing nations designed to (1) reduce the size of their public sectors through privatization and/or expenditure reductions, (2) decrease their budget deficits, (3) control inflation, and (4) encourage private saving and investment through tax reform.

Applications

Do we really need the World Bank?

Professor Rud Dornbusch argues that what the World Bank does, private capital can do more efficiently.

There is nothing new in the idea of lending to risky, emerging markets. International finance of the 19th century did just that. The US was developed with the help of British money, as were Australia, Canada, and Latin America. The late 19th century was a golden age of international bond markets financing ports, railroads, power plants, and waterworks. The process was briefly suspended in the late 1920s when the global capital market collapsed and debtors defaulted world-wide.

In the post-war years, lending got under way once again, with commercial banks providing much of the credit. The debt crisis of the early 1980s, brought about

by overlending and dramatically high US rates, made no lasting impression. The next lending wave was composed of equity capital, bonds, and increasingly direct investment. Mexico's crisis of 1995 curbed the flows only temporarily.

What drives the current round of investment? Two financial strategies. Investors are searching for higher yields offshore while, at the same time, diversifying their risks. Asset prices around the world are low. There are plenty of bargains. Most important, genuine reform and a farewell to big-government policies world-wide are turning economies from statist-stagnant to private-dynamic. That has opened up profitable opportunities. The emergence of a vibrant private economy in the developing world is the single most important

reason for the large increase in resource flows.

The market economy is here to stay, and its roots are growing deeper by the day. Take Brazil: it has always been the country of the future. Even if the government is still bungling its programme to stabilize inflation, the private economy is vigorously at work restructuring itself to become more competitive. In Argentina, the reform process has deeply changed the economy and is already paying off. The country has embarked on a course of economic reform similar to the one Chile has experienced over the past decade. And the same can be said of Poland and Vietnam. We have moved to the point where money is simply not the issue. If the prospects are right, capital will go to the ends of the earth for a little extra return.

How might this optimistic view of a world-wide capital market go sour? Pessimists wait for a stock market crash. In that event, emerging markets will sell off with a vengeance and capital will flee to safe havens. But not for long. The very fact that there has been a sell-off will bring investors back in no time to pick up the pieces at bargain prices, just as happened in 1995 in the aftermath of Mexico. The opportunities are there, and a reform process is moving forward that makes Argentina more plausible than Spain. Foreign investors won't miss out on making a bundle. The occasional setbacks are certainly painful, but they won't discourage this hot line of finance.

Source: Rud Dornbusch, 'Do we really need the World Bank any more?' Business Week, European edn, 24 February 1997, p. 10.

Issues in economic development

Every developing nation has a unique cultural, political and economic history and therefore confronts a correspondingly unique set of problems. Still, it is possible to discuss common economic issues that each nation must face in its own particular way. These issues include rapid population growth, food shortages, agricultural output and pricing policies, and the developing-country debt problem.

Population growth

The populations of the developing nations are estimated to be growing at a rate of about 1.7% per year. (Compare this with a population growth rate of only 0.5% per year in the industrial market economies.) If the developing-country population growth rate remains at 1.7%, it will take only 41 years for the population of the developing world to double from its 1990 level of 4.1 billion to over 8 billion by the year 2031. It will take the industrialized nations 139 years to double their populations. What is so immediately alarming about these numbers is that given the developing nations' current economic problems, it is hard to imagine how they can possibly absorb so many more people in such a relatively short period.

Concern over world population growth is not new. The Reverend Thomas Malthus (who would one day become England's first professor of political economy) expressed his fears about the population increases he observed 200 years ago. Malthus believed that populations grow geometrically (that is, at a constant growth rate: thus the absolute size of the increase each year gets larger and larger), but that food supplies grow much more slowly because of the diminishing marginal productivity of land.[2] These two phenomena led Malthus to predict the increasing impoverishment of the world's people unless population growth could be slowed.

Malthus' fears for Europe and America proved unfounded, because he anticipated neither the technological changes that revolutionized agricultural productivity nor the eventual decrease in population growth rates in Europe and North America. But Malthus' prediction may have been premature rather than wrong. Do the circumstances in the developing world now fit his predictions? While some contemporary observers believe that the Malthusian view is correct and that the earth's population will eventually grow to a level that the world's resources will be unable to support, others argue that technological change and demographic transitions (to slower population growth rates) will permit further increases in global welfare.

The consequences of rapid population growth

Surprisingly, we know far less about the economic consequences of rapid population growth than you might expect. Conventional wisdom warns that dire economic consequences will follow the developing nations' 'population explosion', but these predictions are difficult to substantiate using the available evidence. The rapid economic growth of the United States, for example, was accompanied by relatively rapid population growth by historical standards. Nor has any slowing of population growth been necessary for the economic progress achieved by many of the newly industrialized countries. Nonetheless, population expansion in many of today's poorest nations is of a magnitude unprecedented in world history, as Figure 37.1 clearly shows. From AD 1 until the mid-1600s, populations grew slowly, at rates of only about 0.04% per year. Since then, and especially since 1950, population growth rates have skyrocketed. Today, populations are growing at rates of 1.5% to 4.0% per year throughout the developing world.

---

[2]*The law of diminishing marginal productivity says that with a fixed amount of some resource (land), additions of more and more of a variable resource (labour) will produce smaller and smaller gains in output.*

Figure 29.1 A situation in which no overall equilibrium exists in the national economy

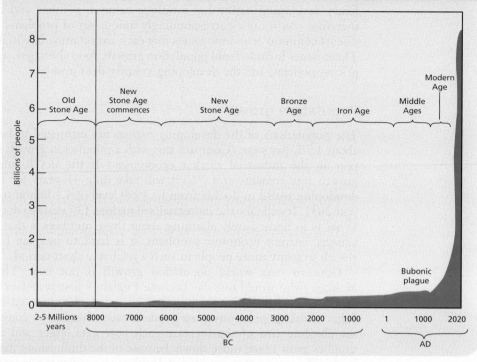

Because growth rates like these have never occurred before the twentieth century, no one knows what impact they will have on future economic development. But a basic economic concern is that such rapid population growth may limit investment and restrain increases in labour productivity and income. Rapid population growth changes the age composition of a population, generating many dependent children relative to the number of productive working adults. Such a situation may diminish saving rates, and hence investment, as the immediate consumption needs of the young take priority over saving for the future.

Even if low saving rates are not a necessary consequence of rapid population growth, as some authorities contend, other economic problems remain. The ability to improve human capital through a broad range of programmes, from infant nutrition to formal secondary education, may be severely limited if the population explosion continues. Such programmes are most often the responsibility of the state, and governments that are already weak cannot be expected to improve their services under the burden of population pressures that rapidly increase demands for all kinds of public goods and services.

For example, Mozambique's population growth rate – 3.7% – is one of the highest in the world. It is likely that its 1997 population of over 17 million people will grow by about 3.4 million in the following five years and by 7.5 million in the next decade. This is a daunting prospect, and it is hard to imagine how, in so little time, Mozambique with its per capita GDP under $100 will be able to provide its population with the physical and human capital needed to maintain, let alone improve, already low standards of living.

Causes of rapid population growth

Population growth is determined by the relationship between births and deaths – that is, between **fertility rates** and **mortality rates**. The **natural rate of population increase** is defined as the difference between the birth rate and the death rate. If the birth rate is 4%, for example, and the death rate is 3%, the population is growing at a rate of 1% per year.

fertility rate The birth rate. Equal to (the number of births per year divided by the population) × 100.

mortality rate The death rate. Equal to (the number of deaths per year divided by the population) × 100.

natural rate of population increase The difference between the birth rate and the death rate. It does not take migration into account.

Historically, low rates of population growth were maintained because of high mortality rates despite high levels of fertility. That is, families had many children, but average life expectancies were low, and many children (and adults) died young. In Europe and North America, improvements in nutrition, in public health measures (especially those concerned with drinking water and sanitation services), and in medical practices have led to a drop in the mortality rate and hence to more rapid population growth. Eventually, fertility rates also fell, returning population growth to a low and stable rate.

Public health programmes and improved nutrition over the past 30 years have brought about precipitous declines in mortality rates in the developing nations too. But fertility rates have not declined as quickly, and the result has been high natural rates of population growth. Reduced population growth depends to some extent on decreased birth rates, but attempts to lower fertility rates must take account of how different cultures feel and behave with regard to fertility.

Family planning and modern forms of birth control are important mechanisms for decreasing fertility, but by themselves such programmes have had rather limited success in most countries where they have been tried. If family planning strategies are to be successful, they must make sense to the people who are supposed to benefit from them. The planners of such strategies must therefore understand why families in developing nations have so many children.

To a great extent, in developing countries people want large families because they believe they need them. Economists have attempted to understand fertility patterns in the developing countries by focusing on the determinants of the demand for children. In agrarian societies, children are important sources of farm labour, and they may thus make significant contributions to household income. In societies without public old-age welfare programmes, children may also provide a vital source of income for parents who are too old to support themselves. With the high value of children enhanced by high rates of infant mortality, it is no wonder that families try to have many children to ensure that a sufficient number will survive into adulthood.

Cultural and religious values also affect the number of children families want to have, but the economic incentives to have large families are extremely powerful. Only when the relationship between the costs and benefits of having children changes will fertility rates decline. Expanding the opportunities for women in an economy increases the opportunity costs of child rearing (by giving women a more highly valued alternative to bringing up children) and often leads to lower birth rates. Government incentives for smaller families, such as subsidized education for families with fewer than three children, can have a similar effect. In general, rising incomes appear to decrease fertility rates, indicating that economic development itself reduces population growth rates.

Economic theories of population growth suggest that fertility decisions made by poor families should not be viewed as uninformed and uncontrolled. An individual family may find that having many children is a rational strategy for economic survival, given the conditions in which it finds itself. This does not mean, however, that having many children is a net benefit to society as a whole. When a family decides to have a large number of children, it imposes costs on the rest of society; the children must be educated, their health provided for, and so forth. In other words, what makes sense for an individual household may create negative effects for the nation as a whole. Thus:

Any nation that wants to slow its rate of population growth will probably find it necessary to have in place economic incentives for fewer children as well as family planning programmes.

Food shortages: acts of nature or human mistakes?

Television news and newspaper reports portraying victims of the famine in Somalia burned indelible images of starving people into the minds of most Europeans. No other event in recent memory so forcefully dramatized the ongoing food crisis in many of the developing nations. The famines that have struck various parts of Africa and Asia in the past 15 years represent the most acute form of the chronic food shortage confronting the developing nations.

Pictures of the parched Somalian countryside might lead a casual observer to conclude that famines are ultimately acts of nature. After all, if the rains do not come or the locusts do, human beings can do little but sit and wait. But this simplistic view of food shortages fails to recognize the extent to which contemporary food crises are the result of human behaviour. Even such natural events as severe flooding can often be traced to the overharvesting of firewood, which denudes the landscape, increases soil erosion and exacerbates spring floods.

Human behaviour is indeed a very strong factor in the inadequate distribution of available food to those who need it. India now grows enough grains to feed its vast population, for example, but malnutrition remains widespread because many people cannot afford to feed themselves. Other parts of the distribution problem involve failures to stockpile adequate food reserves in years of good harvests, and transport and communication barriers that prevent supplies from reaching those in need. World and domestic politics also heavily influence where, how and whether food is available. During the Ethiopian famine in 1988, for example, the Ethiopian government blocked relief agencies from delivering food and medical supplies to the famine area because a civil war was being waged there. Similar events occurred when the United Nations attempted to aid Somalia in 1992. This led to US military intervention in 1992 and 1993. War between the Hutu and the Tutsis in Rwanda in 1994 led to a mass exodus into Zaire, loss of crops, and starvation. In 1997, a civil war led to a bitter struggle in the Congo (formerly Zaire) that left millions in refugee camps.

Even though food shortages are recognized chronic problems, developing nations often pursue farm policies that actually discourage agricultural production. Agricultural production in sub-Saharan Africa today is lower than it was 20 years ago. Economists believe that misguided agricultural policies are responsible for much of this decline.

Agricultural output and pricing policies

Few governments in either industrialized or developing nations have permitted market forces alone to determine agricultural prices. In Europe and in the United States, farm subsidies often encourage production that results in food surpluses rather than shortages. Some developing nations follow similar policies, maintaining high farm prices both to increase agricultural production and to maintain farm incomes. However, many developing nations follow a different route, offering farmers low prices for their output.

To appreciate the motives behind different pricing policies, you need to understand several things about the structure of agricultural markets in many developing nations. Often, the government is the primary purchaser of both basic foodstuffs and export crops. Through **produce-marketing boards**, the governments of some developing countries buy farm output and sell it to urban residents at government-controlled prices. By setting the prices they pay to farmers at low levels, the government can afford to sell basic foodstuffs to urban consumers at low prices. Governments often find this an attractive course of action because the direct political influence of the relatively small urban population typically far outweighs the influence of the majority who live in the countryside. Because most city dwellers spend about half their incomes on food, low consumer prices bolster the real incomes of the urban residents and help keep them content. Urban food riots have been common in developing nations over the years, and whether a government is allowed to exist may hinge on its food-pricing strategy.

Although we can easily appreciate the political motives behind food pricing, policies that set artificially low prices have significant pitfalls. Farmers react to these

produce-marketing boards
The channels through which the governments of some developing countries buy domestic farm output and then sell it to urban residents at government-controlled prices.

prices – which are often set so low that farmers cannot cover their production costs – by reducing the amount of output they produce. In the city, meanwhile, excess demand for food at the artificially low ceiling prices imposed by the government may promote the emergence of black markets.

Many developing economies that have followed low agricultural pricing policies have experienced exactly these results. Until recently, for example, Mexico kept maize prices low in order to hold down the price of tortillas, made from maize flour, which are the staple diet of much of Mexico's urban population. As a result, maize production fell as farmers switched to crops whose prices the government did not control. Domestic maize shortages became widespread, and maize had to be imported to sustain urban demand.

Agricultural output: the supply side

In 1998, a single US farmer could provide enough food to feed 80 people. Productivity in most EU farms is somewhat less. In most developing economies, a single farmer can provide barely enough food to feed his or her own family. While differences in agricultural pricing policies account for a part of this gap, other factors are also at work. Traditionally, low agricultural productivity in the developing world was blamed on the ignorance and laziness of peasant farmers. Today's more enlightened view traces the problem to a shortage of inputs, including land, fertilizer, irrigation, machinery, new seed varieties and agricultural extension services (which provide credit and technical advice to farmers).

Green Revolution

The agricultural breakthroughs of modern science, such as the development of new, high-yield crop varieties.

Modern agricultural science has created a so-called **Green Revolution** (not to be confused with the 'environmental revolution') based on new, high-yield varieties of wheat, rice and other crops. Using new, faster-growing varieties instead of the single-crop plants they have relied upon for centuries, some farmers can now grow three crops of rice a year. In Mexico, under ideal conditions, 'miracle' wheat has produced yields ten times as high as traditional varieties.

If the Green Revolution suggests that science can, in principle, solve world food shortages, the often disappointing history of developing countries' experiments with scientific agriculture offers a less optimistic outlook. Economic factors have greatly limited the adoption of Green Revolution techniques in developing countries. New seeds are expensive, and their cultivation requires the presence of many complementary inputs, including fertilizers and irrigation. With poorly developed rural credit markets, farmers often face interest rates so high that new technologies, regardless of their promise of higher crop yields, are out of reach or ultimately unprofitable. Although the reluctance of peasant farmers to adopt new agricultural techniques has often been blamed on superstition or lack of education, such decisions typically reflect a rational choice. Given the costs and benefits of new inputs and the inherent riskiness of any new method of cultivation, it is not surprising that it has been difficult to get farmers in the developing nations to accept the advances of the Green Revolution.

Peasant farmers in developing nations are also constrained by the amount of land they have to work. In some countries, high population density in the rural areas requires highly labour-intensive cultivation. In other countries, poor distribution of land decreases agricultural output. Throughout Latin America, for example, it is estimated that less than 2% of all landowners control almost 75% of the land under cultivation. Improved crop yields often follow land reforms that redistribute holdings, because owner households are often more productive than tenant farmers. Land reform has had positive effects on output in countries with economic systems as diverse as those of Korea and the People's Republic of China.

In sum:

Although acts of nature will always threaten agricultural production, human actions, especially policies designed to support the agricultural sector, can have a major impact on reducing the food problems of the developing world.

Third world debt

In the 1970s, development experts worried about many crises facing the developing world, but the debt crisis was not among them. Within a decade, this situation changed dramatically. The financial plight of nations such as Brazil, Mexico and the Philippines became front-page news. What alarmed those familiar with the debt problem was not only its potential impact on the developing nations, but a belief that it threatened the economic welfare of the developed nations as well.

Between 1970 and 1984, developing nations, encouraged by low interest rates, borrowed so much money from other nations that their combined debt increased by 1000%, to almost $700 billion. As recession took hold in the economically advanced countries during the early 1980s, growth in the exports of the debtor countries slowed, and many found they could no longer pay back the money they owed. And the problem was made much worse, because a principal cause of the recession was a sharp increase in interest rates in advanced economies.

As the situation continued to deteriorate, many feared that debtor nations might simply repudiate their debts outright and default on their outstanding loans. When *default* (non-payment) occurs with domestic loans, some collateral is usually available to cover all or part of the remaining debt. For loans to another country, however, such collateral is virtually impossible to secure. Given their extensive involvement with developed-country borrowers, Western banks did not want to set in motion a pattern of international default. Nor did borrowers want to default. Leaders of the developing nations recognized that default might result in the denial of access to developed-country banking facilities and to markets in the industrial countries, creating major obstacles to further development efforts.

Various countries rescheduled their debt as an interim solution. Under a **debt rescheduling** agreement, banks and borrowers negotiate a new schedule for the repayment of existing debt, often with some of the debt written off and with repayment periods extended. In return, borrowing countries are expected to sign an agreement with the International Monetary Fund to revise their economic policies to provide incentives for higher export earnings and lower imports. This kind of agreement is often referred to as a **stabilization programme**, and it usually requires painful austerity measures such as currency devaluations, a reduction in government expenditures and an increase in tax revenues.

By the early 1990s, the debt crisis was not over but it had lessened, largely as a result of macroeconomic events that led to reduced interest rates. The international economy had revived somewhat, helping some nations to increase their export earnings. Several nations have benefited from new domestic policies. However, other countries, including Panama and many African nations, continue to face debt burdens that are unmanageable in the short run. Table 37.4 presents figures for a selected group of countries in 1995.

Of concern in recent years has been Mexico's monetary and debt problems. Mexico's total external debt in 1995, $166 billion, was the highest in the world. Following approval of the North American Free Trade Agreement (NAFTA), there was great optimism about Mexico, and massive amounts of capital flowed to Mexico to take advantage of the relatively high interest rates available on Mexican debt. As a result, Mexico's total external debt increased dramatically. Although the flow of capital pushed up the value of the peso during 1993 and early 1994, by mid-1994 investors had become nervous about the possibility of a decline in the peso's value and began to pull out of Mexico. The peso's value finally collapsed in early 1995, and the Mexican government's inability to get investors to buy Mexican bonds pushed it to the brink of defaulting on its obligations. A loan guarantee of $37 billion from the United States and the International Monetary Fund at least temporarily restored confidence and probably saved Mexico the embarrassment of a default in 1995.

In 1997, several Asian countries including Korea and Thailand, had financial problems that led to loan guarantee funds from the International Monetary Fund (IMF). Korea's package totalled more than $50 billion. In 1998 Russia's problems

debt rescheduling
An agreement between banks and borrowers through which a new schedule of repayments of the debt is negotiated; often, some of the debt is written off and the repayment period is extended.

stabilization programme An agreement between a borrower country and the International Monetary Fund in which the country agrees to revise its economic policies to provide incentives for higher export earnings and lower imports.

Table 37.4 Total (public and private) external debt for selected countries, 1995

Country	Total external debt (US$ billion)	Total debt as a percentage of GDP (US$ billion)
Mexico	165.7	69.9
Brazil	159.1	24.0
Russian Federation	120.5	37.6
China	118.1	17.2
Indonesia	107.8	56.9
India	93.8	28.2
Argentina	89.7	33.1
Turkey	73.6	44.1
Thailand	56.8	34.9
Peru	30.8	54.1
Nicaragua	9.3	589.7

Source: World Bank, *World Development Report*, (1997).

deepened. However the IMF was reluctant to increase its loans there when evidence began to emerge, indicating that previous loans had been stolen or wasted.

One of the major economic lessons of the last two decades is that proper management of foreign capital in developing countries is essential. Much foreign borrowing was wasted on projects that had little chance of generating the returns necessary to pay back their initial costs. In other cases, domestic policies that used debt as a substitute for adjusting to new economic circumstances proved to be harmful in the long run. And, overall, much of the optimism about the prospects of the developing economies was inappropriate. Whatever else we may have learned from these mistakes, the debt crisis underscored the growing interdependence of all economies – rich and poor, large and small.

Summary

1. The economic problems facing the developing countries are often quite different from those confronting industrialized nations. The policy options available to governments may also differ. Nonetheless, the tools of economic analysis are as useful in understanding the economies of less developed countries as in understanding the European economy.

Life in the developing nations: population and poverty

2. The central reality of life in the developing countries is poverty. Although there is considerable diversity across the developing nations, most of the people in most developing countries are extremely poor by European standards.

Economic development: sources and strategies

3. Almost all developing nations have a scarcity of physical capital relative to other resources, especially labour. The *vicious-circle-of-poverty hypothesis* argues that poor countries cannot escape from poverty because they cannot afford to postpone consumption (that is, they cannot afford to save) in order to make investments. In its crude form, the hypothesis is wrong inasmuch as

some prosperous countries were at one time poorer than many developing countries are today. However, it is often difficult to mobilize savings efficiently in many developing nations.

4. Human capital – the stock of education and skills embodied in the workforce – plays a vital role in economic development.

5. Developing countries are often burdened by inadequate *social overhead capital*, ranging from poor public health and sanitation facilities to inadequate roads, telephones and court systems. Such social overhead capital is often expensive to provide, and many governments are simply not in a position to undertake many useful projects because they are too costly.

6. *Dependency theory* argues that the reason for the poverty of the developing nations is the relationship between the advanced industrial nations and the developing countries, a relationship designed by the former to work to their own advantage at the expense of the latter.

7. Because developed economies are characterized by a large share of output and employment in the industrial sector, many developing countries seem to believe that development and industrialization are synonymous. In many cases, developing countries have pursued industry at the expense of agriculture, with mixed results. Recent evidence suggests that some balance between industry and agriculture leads to the best outcome.

8. *Import substitution* policies, a trade strategy that favours developing local industries that can manufacture goods to replace imports, were once very common in the developing nations. In general, such policies have not succeeded as well as those promoting open export-orientated economies.

9. The failure of many central planning efforts has brought increasing calls for less government intervention and more market orientation in developing economies.

Issues in economic development

10. Rapid population growth is characteristic of many developing countries. Large families can be economically rational for parents who need support in their old age, or because children offer an important source of labour. But the fact that parents find it in their interests to have large families does not mean that having many children is a net benefit to society as whole. Rapid population growth can put a strain on already overburdened public services, such as education and health.

11. Food shortages in developing countries are not simply the result of bad weather. Public policies that depress the prices of agricultural goods, thereby lowering farmers' incentives to produce, are common throughout the developing nations, and human behaviour is very much behind the inadequate distribution of available food to those who need it. While acts of nature will always threaten agricultural production, human actions, especially policies designed to support the agricultural sector, can have a major impact on reducing the food problems of the developing world.

12. Between 1970 and 1984, the debts of the developing countries grew tenfold. As recession took hold in the advanced countries during the early 1980s, growth in the exports of the debtor countries slowed, and many found they could no longer pay back money they owed. The prospect of loan defaults by developing nations threatened the entire international financial system and transformed the debt crisis into a global problem. The size of the debt for many poor nations is still far too large to be manageable without Western help.

Review Terms and Concepts

brain drain
capital flight
debt rescheduling
dependency theory
export promotion
fertility rate
Green Revolution
import substitution

International Monetary Fund
mortality rate
natural rate of population increase
produce-marketing boards
social overhead capital
stabilization programme
structural adjustment
vicious-circle-of-poverty hypothesis
World Bank

Problem Set

1. Two developing countries that have been in the news lately are Thailand and Indonesia. Both countries were experiencing excellent growth during the early 1990s, but fell on hard times in 1997. Choose either country and using indexes to the popular press write a chronology of events starting in mid-1997.
a. Using what you have learned in economics, what explanations can you offer for what happened?
b. Were the problems that arose the result of mismanagement by governments, or of the way the markets worked (or failed to work)? What lessons have we learned?

2. 'Famines are acts of God, resulting from bad weather or other natural disasters. There is nothing we can do about them except to send food relief after they occur.' Explain why this position is inaccurate. Concentrate on agricultural pricing policies and distributional issues.

3. Financial markets have become increasingly international. Savings flow between countries very quickly as investment opportunities arise or expectations change. International investors are reluctant to invest in countries where there is political or economic instability, and domestic investors, faced with uncertainty at home, are likely to protect their wealth by investing it in safe countries. During 1997 and 1998, there was much uncertainty and instability in many parts of the developing world. At the same time, the European economy remained relatively stable.
a. What effect was this likely to have had on the value of european currencies? Explain.
b. Verify what actually happened to the value of european currencies during 1997.
c. What are the short- and long-term implications for the developing countries?

4. The GDP of any country can be divided into two kinds of goods: capital goods and consumption goods. The proportion of national output devoted to capital goods determines, to some extent, the nation's growth rate.

a. Explain how capital accumulation leads to economic growth.
b. Briefly describe how a market economy determines how much investment will be undertaken during each period.
c. 'Consumption versus investment is a more painful conflict to resolve for developing countries.' Comment.
d. If you were the benevolent dictator of a developing country, what plans would you implement to increase per capita GDP?

5. 'The main reason developing countries are poor is that they don't have enough capital. If we give them machinery, or build factories for them, we can greatly improve their condition.' Comment.

6. 'Poor countries are trapped in a vicious circle of poverty. For output to grow, they must accumulate capital. To accumulate capital, they must save (consume less than they produce). But because they are poor, they have little or no extra output available for savings – it must all go to feed and clothe the present generation. Thus they are doomed to stay poor for ever.' Comment on each step in this argument.

7. If children are an 'investment in the future', why do some developing nations offer incentives to households that limit the size of their families? Why are these incentives often ignored?

8. If you were in charge of economic policy for a developing country and wanted to promote rapid economic growth, would you choose to favour industry over agriculture? What about exports versus import substitution? In each case, briefly explain your reasoning. How do you explain the fact that many countries have chosen industry and a protectionist import-substitution policy?

38

Economies in Transition and Alternative Economic Systems

For 40 years, between the end of the Second World War and the mid-1980s, a powerful rivalry existed between the Soviet Union and the United States. This 'cold war' pitted the two superpowers against each other in a bitter struggle for influence and fuelled the nuclear arms race. Indeed, at one time the mutual distrust between the United States and the Soviet Union was so strong that the concept of 'mutually assured destruction' became a dominant theme in international relations.

But the world began to change in the mid-1980s as the political and economic structures of the Soviet Union and the Eastern European communist countries started to crumble. In 1989, relatively peaceful revolutions took place in rapid succession in Poland, Hungary and Czechoslovakia (now the Czech Republic). A bloody revolution in Romania toppled Nicolae Ceausescu, who had ruled with an iron fist for 24 years. The Berlin Wall, which had separated the two halves of Germany since 1961, was knocked down and the country reunited. Then, in August 1991, after a failed coup attempt by hard-line communists, the Soviet Union itself began to come apart. By the end of 1991, the Soviet Union had dissolved into 15 independent states, the largest of which is the Russian Republic. Ten of these 15 republics formed the Commonwealth of Independent States (CIS) in December 1991. The Cold War was over.

Why do we reflect on historical political rivalries in an economics text? There are two reasons. First, the 40-year struggle between the United States and the Soviet Union was fundamentally a struggle between two economic systems: market-based capitalism (the US system) and centrally planned socialism (the Soviet system). Second, the Cold War ended so abruptly in the late 1980s because the Soviet and Eastern European economies virtually collapsed during that period. In a sense, one could say that 1991 was the year that the market triumphed.

But what now? The independent states of the former Soviet Union and the other former communist economies of Eastern Europe are struggling to make the transition from centrally planned socialism to some form of market-based capitalism. In some countries, such as Serbia and Bosnia-Herzegovina, economic reforms have taken a back seat to bitter and violent ethnic and political rivalries that have been simmering for decades. In other countries, like Poland and Russia, the biggest issue continues to be economic transformation.

The success or failure of this transition from centrally planned socialism to market-based capitalism will determine the course of history, yet it has no historical precedent. Although many countries have made the transition from a market-based system to a centrally planned system, the opposite has never occurred. Undoubtedly, the process has been and will continue to be painful and filled with ups and downs. Between 1989 and 1997, industrial production fell more than 40% in countries like the former East Germany, Albania, Poland and Romania. In Russia, production decreased about 30%. In all these nations, fairly prosperous people suddenly found themselves with annual real incomes closer to those of people in developing countries. For many, the issue became survival: how to obtain enough food and fuel to get through the winter.

By 1995, things had turned around, and while much uncertainty and many problems remained, output was rising in much of Eastern and Central Europe. A growing sense of optimism seemed to be spreading slowly. The biggest success story was in the former East Germany, where real output in 1994 grew by over 9%, the fastest growth rate of any region of Europe. A construction boom, rapid development of infrastructure, low inflation, and rising exports all contributed to the region's success. But East Germany's situation is unique because it was absorbed by a prosperous, fully developed and modern West Germany that has made development in the East its primary goal.

The countries of Central Europe, including Hungary, Poland, the Czech Republic, Bulgaria and Romania, also achieved basic macroeconomic stability and began to grow in 1993 and 1994. Poland enjoyed the most rapid economic growth in the group (around 4.5%). Fuelled by foreign investment, privatization and entrepreneurship, the

Applications

The challenge to private enterprise in Poland

Since 1991, the private sectors of most of the countries of the former Soviet Union and the formerly communist countries of Central and Eastern Europe have expanded dramatically. Apart from East Germany, Poland's private sector has expanded the most, and it now accounts for well over a third of the economy's production.

This private expansion comes from four sources:

■ Thousands of entrepreneurs have started new businesses. An estimated 2 million or more Polish entrepreneurs have formed businesses, and small business in Poland is growing at about 10% per year.
■ Foreign investment is flowing into the region, though not at the pace once anticipated.
■ 'Spontaneous privatizations', initiated by managers of state-owned enterprises, have converted many firms to private ownership without a great deal of state participation. The earliest forms of spontaneous privatization in Russia took the form of

managers setting up parallel private firms opposite or even inside state-owned enterprises. The new private firm would buy the product of the state-owned enterprise at a controlled price and then resell it at the market price.
■ Most countries have been selling off state-owned private enterprises directly or indirectly to private shareholders.

Because the process of selling off state-owned assets has been slow, much of the economic action has occurred in entrepreneurial businesses.

Start-ups are the engine of Poland's post-communist boom. A book [*Poland to 2005*, by Louisa Vinton] published . . . by the Economist Intelligence Unit, a sister company of the *Economist*, calculates that private firms have trebled their share in industrial output since the transition began, from 16% of gross sales at the end of 1989 to 45% in 1995 – an annual growth rate of more than a fifth. Since small businesses have every incentive to understate their

performance, the real picture is probably even brighter.

Of course, not every post-communist start-up is successful. Mr Kunsch at Creditanstalt in Budapest reckons that the failure rate in Hungary is around 30% – one reason why his own and other banks are so cautious about lending money to them. But all the post-communist economies have their quota of success stories in both manufacturing and service industries. Euronet, a Hungarian operator of bank teller machines, is already listed on Nasdaq, America's small-company stock exchange. PCS, a software developer which started in Prague with $3000 in 1990, now has over 100 employees and sales of $30 million.

The success of these companies (some of which have annual rates of return on capital of several hundred percent) is all the more remarkable seen against the uphill struggle of their early years. Premises were cramped, working capital scarce, infrastructure fragile and the bureaucracy tiresome.

Many entrepreneurs say that it is only now – with finance becoming easier and their credibility with foreign partners rising – that their business can really take off.

The start-ups have done so well for two main reasons. First, they were expanding into a vacuum. The collapse of communism created new markets overnight. Even when competing products or services existed, the locals often turned out to be more knowledgeable, hard-working, flexible and cost-effective. The second reason has to do with human nature. For Eastern Europeans who had seen large chunks of their working lives wasted by communism, starting a business offered the chance to catch up. Self-employment, therefore, has attracted a large number of Eastern Europe's brightest and best, with impressive results.

Sources: 'Survey: business Eastern Europe', The Economist (22–28 November 1997), p. 10; Olivier Jean Blanchard, Kenneth A. Froot and Jeffrey D. Sachs (eds), The Transition in Eastern Europe (Chicago: University of Chicago Press, 1994).

Polish private sector by 1992 accounted for well over a third of the nation's total output, though many problems persist. (For more details, see the Application 'The challenges to private enterprise in Poland'.) Russia and some of the countries of the former Soviet Union have achieved less through 1997 and 1998. Russia, in particular was again in deep crisis by 1998. The crisis in South East Asia reduced demand for commodities causing prices to fall sharply. This included the price of oil and gold, vital exports for Russia. As a result the value of the rouble fell by over 50% during 1998 sharply increasing Russian inflation and causing output to contract yet again.

In this chapter, we focus on the ongoing debate over economic reform. What can be done to make the transition from socialism to capitalism successful? In what sequence should changes be made? How quickly can market institutions be established? How much help from Europe and the rest of the world will be required?

To understand the transformation process, it is necessary to begin with some history. From what are these countries making a transition? Our chapter starts with a discussion of alternative economic systems, the vision of communism, and a brief description of the economic structure of the former Soviet Union. We then turn to the current debate over the transition process, focusing on the experiences of Poland and Russia. We end the chapter by examining a different kind of economic transformation that has been going on for some time in China and finally by discussing the performance of the Japanese economy since the Second World War.

Political systems and economic systems: socialism, capitalism and communism

Every society has both a political system and an economic system. Unfortunately, the political and economic dimensions of a society are often confused.

The terms 'democracy' and 'dictatorship' refer to *political* systems. A *democracy* is a system of government in which ultimate power rests with the people, who make governmental decisions either directly through voting or indirectly through representatives. A *dictatorship* is a political system in which ultimate power is concentrated either in a small elite group or a single person.

Historically, two major alternative economic systems have existed: socialism and capitalism. A **socialist economy** is one in which most capital – factories, equipment, buildings, railways and so forth – is owned by the government rather than by private citizens. *Social ownership* is another term that is often used to describe this kind of system. A **capitalist economy** is one in which most capital is privately owned. Beyond these systems is a purely theoretical economic system called *communism*.

Communism is an economic system in which the people control the means of production (land and capital) directly, without the intervention of a government or state. In the world envisioned by communists, the state would wither away and society would plan the economy in much the same way that a collective would. In fact, although some countries still consider themselves communist – including China, North Korea, Cuba and Tanzania – economic planning is done by the government in all of them. Thus:

> In terms of comparing economies today, the real distinction is between centrally planned socialism and capitalism, not between capitalism and communism.

No pure socialist economies and no pure capitalist economies exist. Even the Soviet Union, which was basically socialist, had a large private sector. Fully one-quarter of agricultural output in what was the USSR was legally produced on private plots and sold, and in a large 'second economy' private citizens provided goods and services to each other, sometimes in violation of the law. Conversely, the strongly capitalistic Switzerland supports many government enterprises. Nonetheless, public ownership is the exception in much of Western Europe and private ownership was the exception in the Soviet Union.

socialist economy
An economy in which most capital is owned by the government rather than by private citizens. Also called social ownership.

capitalist economy
An economy in which most capital is privately owned.

communism An economic system in which the people control the means of production (capital and land) directly, without the intervention of a government or state.

Whether particular kinds of political systems tend to be associated with particular kinds of economic systems is hotly debated. Switzerland and Japan are examples of countries with essentially capitalist economic systems and essentially democratic political institutions. China and North Korea have basically socialist economies with political power highly concentrated in a single political party. These observations do not imply that all capitalist countries have democratic political institutions, however, or that all socialist countries are subject to totalitarian party rule.

Many countries – Indonesia, for example – have basically capitalist economies without democratic political systems. Many other countries that are much closer to the socialist end of the economic spectrum also maintain strong democratic traditions. The people of France, for instance, elected the socialist government of François Mitterrand in 1981, and that government promptly nationalized several major industries. Great Britain and Sweden are other examples of democratic countries that support certain strong socialist institutions.

But do certain kinds of economic systems lead to repressive governments? Austrian economist Friedrich Hayek argues that the answer is yes:

Economic reforms and government coercion are the road to serfdom. . . . Personal and economic freedoms are inseparable. Once you start down the road to government regulation and planning of the economy, the freedom to speak minds and select political leaders will be jeopardized.[1]

The recent events in Eastern Europe and Russia seem to support Hayek's thesis. There, economic and political reforms are proceeding side by side, and the evidence is mounting that the heart of both the market system and democracy is individual freedom.

Nonetheless, some counter Hayek's argument by claiming that social reform and active government involvement in the economy are the only ways to prevent the rise of a totalitarian state. They argue that free and unregulated markets lead to inequality and the accumulation of economic power. Accumulated economic power, in turn, leads to political power that is inevitably used in the interests of the wealthy few, not in the interests of all.

Central planning versus the market

In addition to the degree to which capital is owned by private citizens rather than the government, economic systems also differ significantly in the extent to which economic decisions are made through central planning rather than through a market system. In some socialist economies, the allocation of resources, the mix of output and the distribution of output are determined centrally according to a plan. The former Soviet Union, for example, generated one-year and five-year plans laying out specific production targets in virtually every sector of the economy. In market economies, decisions are made independently by buyers and sellers responding to market signals. Producers produce only what they expect to sell. Labour is attracted into and out of various occupations by wages that are determined by the forces of supply and demand.

Just as there are no pure capitalist and no pure socialist economies, so there are no pure market economies and no pure planned economies. Even in the former Soviet Union, markets existed and determined, to a large extent, the allocation of resources. Production targets in Europe are set by many agencies.

Generally, socialist economies favour central planning over market allocation, while capitalist economies rely to a much greater extent on the market. Nonetheless, some variety exists. The former Yugoslavia, for example, was a socialist country that made extensive use of the market. While ownership of capital and land rested with the government, individual firms determined their own output levels and prices and made their own investment plans. Yugoslavian firms borrowed from banks to

[1]*Friedrich Hayek,* The Road to Serfdom *(Chicago: University of Chicago Press, 1944).*

finance investments and paid interest on their loans. This type of system, which combines government ownership with market allocation, is often referred to as a market-socialist economy.

market-socialist economy

An economy that combines government ownership with market allocation.

The economic theories of Karl Marx

The conflict between economic systems has taken place on two levels. On one hand, there are alternative economic *theories* that lead to dramatically different conclusions about the relative merits of market-capitalist and planned socialist systems. On the other hand, the actual *performance* of these differently organized economies must be considered.

The events of the early 1990s in Eastern Europe provide strong evidence that central planning loses on the basis of performance. Why, then, should we spend time studying the theoretical underpinnings of communism and socialism? There are at least four reasons. First, for over 70 years in the Soviet Union, and for over 40 years in most parts of Eastern Europe and China, socialist ideology was dominant. Until very recently, about one-third of the world's population lived in countries whose economies were based on socialist and communist philosophies. Second, even though the economies of the republics of the former Soviet Union and the economies of Eastern Europe have been moving rapidly towards a market-based system, a number of other countries remain firmly committed to the ideas of centrally planned socialism. Third, the problems which Russia has found in moving to a market economy are severe enough to make many there want to move back towards the system they once had. Finally, to understand the capitalist system, one must understand the criticisms that have been levelled against it.

Marxian economics: an overview

Perhaps no single modern thinker has had a greater impact on the world in the twentieth century than Karl Marx, whose work is the basis of the communist ideology. Stated simply, Marxian economic analysis concludes that the capitalist system is morally wrong and doomed to ultimate failure.

The most common misconception about Marx's work is that it contains a blueprint for the operation of a socialist or communist economy. In fact, Marx did not write much about socialism; he wrote about capitalism. Published mostly after his death in 1883, his major work, the three-volume *Das Kapital*, is an extensive analysis of how capitalist economies function and how they are likely to develop over time. *The Communist Manifesto* (written with Friedrich Engels and published in 1848) and his other writings contain only a rough sketch of the socialist and communist societies that Marx predicted would ultimately replace capitalism.

Marx's economic theories lie at the root of his interpretation of history. In examining his work, let us begin with what might be called 'Marxian microeconomics' and then turn to the macroeconomic conclusions that emerge from it.

The labour theory of value

labour theory of value

Marx's theory that the value of a commodity depends exclusively upon the amount of labour required to produce it. A commodity is the physical embodiment of the past labour used to produce it.

The centrepiece of Marx's economic theories is the labour theory of value. Marx argued that the value of a commodity depends exclusively upon the amount of labour required to produce it. Commodities are thus the physical embodiment of the labour that produced them:

A commodity has value, because it is a crystallization of social labour. The greatness of its value, of its relative value, depends upon the greater or less amount of that social substance contained in it . . . The relative values of commodities are, therefore, determined by the respective quantities or amounts of labour, worked up, realized, fixed in them.[2]

[2]*Karl Marx*, Wages, Price and Profit *(Beijing: Foreign Languages Press, 1975), pp. 34–5.*

The labour theory of value also addresses the nature and uses of capital. As you know, goods can be produced with a variety of combinations of capital and labour. Are goods produced with a lot of capital and little labour worth less than those produced with a lot of labour and little capital? The answer is no. Capital, according to Marx, is the physical embodiment of the *past labour* that was used to produce it. When used in production, capital contributes value by passing that past labour through to the final product. A machine that took 100 hours to build contributes 100 hours of value to final products over its lifetime. The value of a commodity is thus the sum of the values contributed by present labour and past labour (capital).

The nature of profit: the marxian view

If, as Marx believed, commodity values depend only on labour's contribution, where does profit come in? The answer is simple. Capitalists own the **means of production**, Marx's term for land and capital. They hire individual workers who have no way to make a living except by selling their labour power. Capitalists make a profit by paying workers a daily wage that is less than the value that workers contribute to final products in a day.

The wage rate is the **value of labour power**, and it is determined in the same way as the value of any other commodity. That is, the value of labour power depends on the amount of labour required to 'produce' it. To produce and sustain labour power requires food, clothing, shelter, basic education, medical care and so on. The value of labour power, then, is determined by the amount of labour it takes to produce those things necessary to sustain a worker and his or her family. In essence, Marx was proposing a *subsistence theory of wages*: capitalists will pay a wage that is just enough for labourers to live on.

Let's suppose that it takes four hours to produce everything necessary to sustain a worker for a day. Marx would argue in this case that a day's wage paid by capitalists will be the equivalent of four hours' worth of value. If a worker is employed for 12 hours, the capitalist ends up with a final product containing 12 hours of value, but needs to give only four hours' worth of value – or wages – to the worker. The difference (eight hours), which Marx called **surplus value**, is profit.

Profit is thus value created by workers but 'expropriated' by capitalists. Capitalists are able to expropriate surplus value because they own the means of production and control access to them. Profit is not a reward for any productive activity; it is extracted solely by virtue of ownership. Marx referred to the ratio of surplus value to the value of labour power as the **rate of exploitation**.

The nature of profit: the neoclassical view

The bulk of this text has presented mainstream, or neoclassical, economic theory, with its deep roots in nineteenth-century philosophy. At this point we should reflect briefly on the nature of profit in that model, because it is so different from the Marxian notion of surplus value.

Neoclassical economics views both capital and labour as productive factors of production. If you have one worker digging a hole and you want a bigger hole faster, you can accomplish your goal by hiring a second worker *or* by giving the first worker a better spade. Add labour and you get more product; add capital and you also get more product. According to neoclassical theory, every factor of production in a competitive market economy ends up being paid in accordance with the market value of its product. Profit-maximizing firms hire labour and capital as long as both contribute more to the final value of a product than they cost.

In sum:

Neoclassical theory views profit as the legitimate return to capital. Marx, however, saw profit as value created by labour and unjustly expropriated by non-productive capitalists, who own the means of production and thus are able to exploit labour.

---

means of production

Marx's term for land and capital.

value of labour power

The wage rate, dependent on the amount of clothing, shelter, basic education, medical care, and so on required to produce and sustain labour power.

surplus value

The profit a capitalist earns by paying workers less than the value of what they produce.

rate of exploitation The ratio of surplus value to the value of labour power.

Marx's predictions

The labour theory of value led Marx to conclude that capitalism was doomed. The essence of his argument was that the rate of profit has a natural tendency to fall over time. With the rate of profits falling, capitalists increase the rate of exploitation, pushing workers deeper and deeper into misery. At the same time, the ups and downs of business cycles become more and more extreme. Ultimately, Marx believed, workers would rise up and overthrow the repressive capitalist system.

The theory that capitalism would ultimately collapse under its own weight was part of Marx's longer view of history. Capitalism had emerged naturally from a previous stage (*feudalism*) that had emerged from an even earlier stage (*ancient slavery*), and so forth. In the economic evolutionary process, Marx believed, capitalism would come to be replaced by socialism, which ultimately would be replaced by communism.

At each stage of economic evolution, Marx said, a set of rules called the *social relations of production* defines the economic system. Contradictions and conflicts inevitably arise at each stage, and these problems are ultimately resolved in the establishment of a new set of social relations. The conflicts in capitalism include alienation, increasing exploitation, misery (or, as Marx called it, 'emiserization'), and deeper and deeper business cycles.

It is clear that Marx was eager for the demise of capitalism. He advocated strong and powerful trades unions for two reasons. First, unions would push wages above subsistence and transfer some surplus value back to workers. Second, unions were a way of raising the consciousness of workers about their condition. Only through class consciousness, Marx believed, would workers be empowered to throw off the shackles of capitalism.

At the heart of Marx's ideas is the argument that private ownership and profit are unfair and unethical. Even if it could be demonstrated that the incentives provided by the institution of private property result in faster economic growth or improved living standards, anyone who accepts Marx's interpretation has to reject capitalism on moral grounds, on ideological grounds, or on both.

Economies in transition: experiences of Russia and Eastern Europe

The Eastern European nations' transitions to market systems were in large measure the result of the economic failures of centrally planned socialism, which had ultimately failed to 'deliver the goods'. To understand the failure of the Eastern European socialist economies and the difficult process of transition that lies ahead for them, students of economics must be aware of these countries' economic histories. In this section, we briefly describe the Soviet system as it existed for nearly 75 years and the changes taking place today.

The Soviet Union: history and reform

Marx believed that socialist revolution would occur in advanced capitalist states where a repressive industrial society would push workers to unite and rise up against their industrialist masters. The Russian nation in 1913 had experienced the beginnings of modern economic growth, but it could hardly have been called an advanced capitalist system. Table 38.1 shows that its relative position in terms of per capita income had improved in the half century prior to 1913, but that it still lagged far behind the other industrial countries of the world.

When the Bolsheviks took power after the October Revolution in 1917, they found themselves without the advanced industrial base that Marx had envisioned and with no real blueprint for running a socialist or communist state. Marx's writings provided

Table 38.1 Per capita income in selected countries, 1861 and 1913 (roubles)

	1861	1913
Russia	71	119
UK	323	580
France	150	303
Germany	175	374
USA	450	1,033
Netherlands	–	366
Norway	166	659
Sweden	112	340
Italy	183	261
Spain	–	199
Austria/Hungary	–	190

Source: Paul Gregory and Robert Stuart, *Soviet Economic Structure and Performance*, 2nd edn (New York: Harper & Row, 1981), p. 20.

only the broadest guidelines. Undaunted, the new government immediately abolished private land ownership and ordered that the land be distributed to those who worked on it. It also established worker control of industry and nationalized the banks. Sweeping nationalization of industry began in June 1918. Money, private trade, and wage differentials were abolished. All decisions were made centrally.

The headlong rush into uncharted waters was too much too soon, and between 1921 and 1928 Soviet leaders retreated from their initial hard line back towards a market orientation. The **New Economic Policy** of the period was characterized by decentralization. Most smaller industrial enterprises were denationalized, though the peasants remained in control of agriculture. State control of production was replaced by market links between consumers and industry and between industry and agriculture.

The relative merits and demerits of these two periods, 1917–21 and 1921–28, were debated at length among the Soviet leadership. Finally, in 1928, the Soviet Union settled on an economic structure that lasted into the 1980s: comprehensive central planning and the collectivization of agriculture. In 1928, under the leadership of Joseph Stalin, the first of many **five-year plans** was approved. The plan emphasized rapid industrialization and the production of industrial capital; in fact, the plan called for a doubling of the fixed capital stock of the Soviet Union in five years. Consumer goods were to be produced only when all other needs of the new industrial structure had been met.

The industrialization programme depended on a steady flow of food and agricultural raw materials from the countryside, and that did not come easily. As a result, Stalin was forced to rely more and more on coercion. In 1929, the land holdings of the peasants were organized into collective farms that were required to deliver state-ordered quotas of farm products. Repression was severe, and millions of peasants perished.[3]

New Economic Policy

The Soviet economic policy in effect between 1921 and 1928, and characterized by decentralization and a retreat to a market orientation.

five-year plans

Plans developed in the Soviet Union that provided general guidelines and directions for the following five years.

[3]*George Orwell's novel* Animal Farm *is a parable on this period in Soviet history.*

No serious debate about economic matters took place in the Soviet Union until after Stalin's death in 1953. In 1965, official reforms were introduced by the government of Alexei Kosygin. Later, Mikhail Gorbachev announced a series of reforms in 1986 and more dramatic reforms in 1987, but the structure of the economy was not changed fundamentally on either of these occasions.

In 1991, Boris Yeltsin became president of the Russian Republic and the champion of reform. Yeltsin deregulated most prices, begun the privatization process, and attempted to stabilize the macroeconomy. By 1995 progress had been slow but significant. Privatization had made steady progress, reaching a point in 1994 where the private sector was generating 60% of personal income. Inflation was down, and a new 'economic constitution' in the form of revised laws to establish property rights and stimulate economic activity went into effect in 1995. But things were not going well across the board. Most observers estimate that Russian GDP began to grow in the spring of 1997 after falling by about 50% from its 1989 level. However, problems remained severe into 1998. The collapse in the external value of the rouble made it extremely difficult to attract investment. Crime and corruption remained as a huge problem. The Russian government was finding it very difficult to enforce the rule of law. The term *cowboy capitalism* is often used to describe the situation in Russia today.

Economic performance

The Stalinist/Soviet strategy to achieve high rates of growth worked for many years. The highest rates of growth in Soviet GNP were during the 1950s. Official Soviet statistics put the real growth rate during that decade at over 10%, an extraordinary rate at which real output would double every seven years. Even the CIA's more conservative estimates, shown in Table 38.2, estimated the Soviet growth rate at 5.7%, nearly 80% above the US average for the decade.

In 1957, the Soviet Union's GNP stood at about 39% of the United States' GNP. A year later, Soviet GNP had jumped to nearly 44% of US GNP. The rate at which the Soviet Union was catching up was so remarkable that it prompted Soviet Premier Nikita Khrushchev to promise 'We will bury you!' If the Soviet growth rate estimates had been correct, and if both countries had continued to grow at the same rates that they did during the 1950s, Soviet GNP would indeed have surpassed US GNP by 1970.

Table 38.2 Economic growth and investment in the Soviet Union and the United States, 1950–1990

	Annual average rate of growth				
	USSR net material product (USSR, official figures)	USSR real GNP (CIA)	USA real GNP	USSR capital stock	USA capital stock
1950–1960	10.3	5.7	3.2	9.5	3.6
1960–1970	7.1	5.1	4.0	8.0	4.0
1970–1975	5.7	3.7	2.6	7.9	4.0
1975–1980	4.3	2.7	3.7	6.8	3.9
1980–1984	–	2.6	2.7	6.3*	3.6
1984–1987	–	1.8	2.4	NA	NA
1988–1990	–	0.0	2.4	NA	NA

Note: *1980–1983; NA = not available; GDP data not available.

Sources: Abram Bergson, 'Gorbachev calls for intensive growth', Challenge (November–December 1985); for the United States, *Statistical Abstract of the United States*, 1986 and 1990, *Historical Statistics of the United States*, and *Economic Report of the President*, 1990.

The primary force behind Soviet growth was capital accumulation. During the 1950s, the capital stock of the USSR grew at 9.5% annually; in the United States, the corresponding figure was only 3.6%. Through 1975, Soviet capital stocks grew at twice the rate of capital accumulation in the United States. But these growth rates did not continue, and during the late 1970s they slowed down. Between 1975 and 1985, even the slowly growing US economy outperformed the Soviet Union. In 1975, per capita GNP in the Soviet Union stood at 48.2% of per capita GNP in the United States. In 1985 the figure was 48.1%.

Gorbachev and perestroika

In March 1985, Mikhail Gorbachev became general secretary of the Soviet Communist party and almost immediately began to press for reforms that had an enormous impact on the world. In 1990, Gorbachev won the Nobel Peace Prize for ending the Cold War and was named 'Man of the Decade' by *Time* magazine. Yet despite his enormous popularity around the world and his political successes, one prize continued to elude Gorbachev: improved economic performance in the Soviet Union.

Gorbachev's reforms fell into two broad categories: *glasnost* ('openness') and *perestroika* ('restructuring'). *Glasnost* led to the almost completely open discussion of virtually every aspect of political and economic reform in the Soviet Union. It also led to a new set of political institutions, including an end to the power monopoly of the Communist party[4] and more free elections. Glasnost was relatively easy to achieve, but the establishment of new economic structures – the key element of Gorbachev's *perestroika* – proved much more difficult.

The initial goal of *perestroika* was to increase workers' responsibilities and discipline by attacking corruption and alcoholism. In these arenas, Gorbachev met with some success. Numerous bureau chiefs were replaced, alcoholism was reduced through strict law enforcement, absenteeism declined and productivity increased. Then, in 1986, the focus of reform shifted to the performance of agriculture. In that year, Gorbachev announced a major restructuring of the agricultural sector that gave local farm units and the peasantry significant new freedoms. Local farm units, for example, were allowed to use the market to dispose of any surplus over five-year plan levels. Payments to state and collective farm workers were tied to productivity and profits, and local directors were given much more authority over management and investment decisions.

But the best was yet to come. In June of 1987, Gorbachev announced yet another series of reforms. The package included some surprising changes. First, price subsidies were to be drastically reduced or eliminated, even on such staple items as meat, bread, dairy products and housing. Second, all limits on what workers could earn were to be removed, and salaries were to be tied directly to performance. Third, the decision-making authority of the farms and enterprises was to be greatly expanded. Central plans were to contain far less detail than in previous years. At the same time, Gorbachev called for sharp increases in small-scale family farming and for a 'competitive atmosphere' among enterprises to ensure that goods were sold to consumers at the lowest possible prices that would still cover costs of production.

---

[4]*For many years, membership in and loyalty to the Communist party were the ticket to the good life in the Soviet Union. Under the nomenclature party patronage system, Communist party leaders received power and privilege in exchange for loyalty to the party. In addition to determining the staffing of government and industrial posts (a practice that led to a good deal of favouritism and nepotism), party members also enjoyed the right to shop at special state-run stores. These stores stocked luxury items that were not available to the general public. Travel privileges, admissions to the best colleges and universities, better housing and bigger cars also went to members of the nomenclature. In 1990, the Central Committee of the Soviet Communist party approved a proposal by President Gorbachev calling for an end to the party's constitutional guarantee of power and thus an end to the nomenclature. After the failed August 1991 coup, the Communist party was completely dismantled.*

Perhaps the most radical of the 1987 reforms, however, was that job security, a sacred tenet of the Soviet system, would be reduced. For the first time, enterprises could actually fire lazy workers, and unproductive enterprises could be shut down.

Economic crisis and collapse

Although many of Gorbachev's ideas seemed promising, the situation in the Soviet Union deteriorated sharply after 1987. The attempted transition from central planning to a partly free-market system caused major problems. Growth of output slowed to a crawl in 1989 and 1990, and in 1991 the economic system collapsed. Industrial production dropped sharply, food shortages grew worse, inflation became a serious problem and external debt increased rapidly.

Gorbachev ran out of time in August of 1991 as the struggle between the hard-liners and the radical reformers came to a head. The hard-liners took Gorbachev prisoner and assumed control of the government. The coup lasted only three days. People took to the streets of Moscow and resisted the tanks, the Soviet army refused to obey orders, and the hard-liners were ousted.

But the end was near for both Gorbachev and the Soviet Union. In December 1991, the Soviet Union was dissolved, ten of the former Soviet republics came together to form the Commonwealth of Independent States (CIS), and Boris Yeltsin became president of the Russian Republic as Gorbachev became part of history. From the beginning, Yeltsin showed himself to be a reformer committed to converting the Russian economy rapidly into a market system while maintaining hard-won political freedoms for the people. His reform plan called for deregulating prices, privatizing public enterprises and stabilizing the macroeconomy.

The transition to a market economy

The reforms under way in the Russian Republic and in the other formerly communist countries of Eastern Europe have taken shape very slowly and amid a great deal of debate about how best to proceed. It is important to remember that there is absolutely no historical precedent to provide lessons. Despite this lack of precedent, however, there is substantial agreement among economists about what needs to be done. Specifically:

> Economists generally agree on six basic requirements for a successful transition from socialism to a market-based system: (1) macroeconomic stabilization; (2) deregulation of prices and liberalization of trade; (3) privatization of state-owned enterprises and development of new private industry; (4) the establishment of market-supporting institutions, such as property and contract laws, accounting systems and so forth; (5) a social safety net to deal with unemployment and poverty; and (6) external assistance.

We discuss each of these components in the sections that follow. Although we focus on the experience of the Russian Republic, keep in mind that these principles apply to all economies in transition.

Macroeconomic stabilization

Virtually every one of the countries in transition has had a problem with inflation, but nowhere has it been worse than in Russia. As economic conditions worsened, the government found itself with serious budget problems. As revenue flows slowed and expenditure commitments increased, large budget deficits resulted. At the same time, each of the new republics established its own central bank. Each central bank began issuing 'rouble credits' to keep important enterprises afloat and to pay the government's bills. The issuance of these credits, which were generally accepted as a means of payment throughout the country, led to a dramatic expansion of the money supply.

Almost from the beginning, the expanded money supply meant that too much money was chasing too few goods. This situation was made worse by government-controlled prices set substantially below market-clearing levels. The combination of monetary expansion and price control was deadly. Government-run shops that sold goods at controlled prices were empty. People queued for days and often became violent when their efforts to buy goods at low official prices were thwarted. At the same time, suppliers found that they could charge much higher prices for their products on the black market – which grew bigger by the day, further exacerbating the shortage of goods at government shops. Over time, the rouble became worth less and less as black market prices continued to rise ever more rapidly. As a result, Russia found itself with near hyperinflation in 1992. Between 1992 and 1998 inflation was brought under some measure of control. However, the sharp fall in the external value of the rouble in late 1998 gave a sharp twist to the country's inflationary problems.

To achieve a properly functioning market system, prices must be stabilized. To do so, the government must find a way to move towards a balanced budget and to bring the supply of money under control.

Deregulation of prices and liberalization of trade

To move successfully from central planning to a market system, individual prices must be deregulated. A system of freely moving prices forms the backbone of a market system. When people want more of a good than is currently being produced, its price will rise. This higher price increases producers' profits and provides an incentive for existing firms to expand production and for new firms to enter the industry. Conversely, if an industry is producing a good for which there is no market or a good that people no longer want in the same quantity, the result will be excess supply and the price of that good will fall. This reduces profits or creates losses, providing an incentive for some existing firms to cut back on production and for others to go out of business. In short, an unregulated price mechanism ensures an efficient allocation of resources across industries. Until prices are deregulated, this mechanism cannot function.

Trade barriers must also be removed. To achieve a successful transition, reform-minded countries must be able to import capital, technology and ideas from abroad. In addition, it makes no sense to continue to subsidize industries that cannot be competitive on world markets. If it is cheaper to buy steel from an efficient West German steel mill than to produce it in a subsidized antiquated Russian mill, the Russian mill should be modernized or shut down. Ultimately, as the theory of comparative advantage suggests, liberalized trade will push each country to produce those products that it produces best.

Deregulating prices and eliminating subsidies can bring serious political problems. Many products in Russia and the rest of the socialist world were priced below market-clearing levels for equity reasons. Housing, food and clothing were considered by many to be entitlements. Making them more expensive, at least relative to their prices in previous times, is not likely to be popular. In addition, forcing inefficient firms to operate without subsidies will lead many to go out of business, and jobs will be lost. In the longer term these resources may be used in other industries where they are more productive. In the short term, resources are not highly mobile. So while price deregulation and trade liberalization are necessary, they are very difficult politically.

Privatization

One problem with a system of central ownership is a lack of accountability. Under a system of private ownership, owners reap the rewards of their successes and suffer the consequences of their failures. Private ownership provides a strong incentive for efficient operation, innovation and hard work that is lacking when ownership is centralized and profits are distributed to the people.

The classic story used to illustrate this point is called the **tragedy of commons**. Suppose that an agricultural community has 10,000 hectares of grazing land. If the land were held in common so that all farmers had unlimited rights to graze their animals, each farmer would have an incentive to overgraze. He or she would reap the

tragedy of commons The idea that collective ownership may not provide the proper private incentives for efficiency because individuals do not bear the full costs of their own decisions but do enjoy the full benefits.

full benefits from grazing additional calves while the costs of grazing the calves would be borne collectively. The system provides no incentive to manage the land efficiently. Similarly, if the efficiency and benefits of my hard work and managerial skills accrue to others or to the state, what incentive do I have to work hard or to be efficient?

One response to the tragedy of commons attempted in eighteenth-century Britain was to divide up common land into private holdings. Today, many economists argue, the solution to the incentive problem encountered in state-owned enterprises is to privatize them and let the owners compete.

In addition to increasing accountability, privatization means creating a climate in which new enterprises can flourish. If there is market demand for a product not currently being produced, individual entrepreneurs should be free to set up a business and make a profit. During the last months of the Soviet Union's existence, private enterprises such as taxi services, car repair services, restaurants and even hotels began to spring up all over the country.

Like deregulation of prices, privatization is difficult politically. Privatization means that many protected enterprises will go out of business because they cannot compete at world prices. Going out of business means a loss of jobs, at least temporarily.

Market-supporting institutions

Between 1991 and 1995, Western European and US firms raced to Eastern Europe in search of markets and investment opportunities and immediately became aware of a major obstacle. The institutions that make the market function relatively smoothly in Western Europe and the United States do not exist in Eastern Europe.

For example, the capital market, which channels private saving into productive capital investment in developed capitalist economies, is made up of hundreds of different institutions. The banking system, venture capital funds, the stock market, the bond market, the commodity exchanges, brokerage houses, investment banks and the like have all developed in Western market economies over a period of hundreds of years, and they will not simply be replicated overnight in the formerly communist world.

Many market-supporting institutions are so basic that we take them for granted. The institution of private property, for example, is a set of rights that must be protected by laws that the government must be willing to enforce. Suppose that the French hotel chain Novotel decides to build a new hotel in Moscow. Novotel must first acquire land. Then it will construct a building based on the expectation of renting hotel rooms to customers. These investments are made with the expectation that the owner has a right to use them and a right to the profits that they produce. For such investments to be undertaken, these rights must be guaranteed by a set of property laws. This is equally true for large business firms and for Russian entrepreneurs who want to start their own enterprises.

Similarly, the law must provide for the enforcement of contracts. In Europe, a huge body of law determines what happens to you if you break a formal promise made in good faith. Businesses exist on promises to produce and promises to pay. Without recourse to the law when a contract is breached, contracts will not be entered into, goods will not be manufactured, and services will not be provided.

Another seemingly simple matter that turns out to be quite complex is the establishment of a set of accounting principles. In European countries, the rules of the accounting game are embodied in a set of accounting principles that carry the force of law. Companies are required to keep track of their receipts, expenditures and liabilities so that their performance can be observed and evaluated by shareholders, taxing authorities and others who have an interest in the company. If you have ever taken a course in accounting, you know how detailed these rules have become. Imagine trying to do business in a country operating under hundreds of different sets of rules and you can imagine what has been happening in Russia.

Another institution worthy of mention is insurance. Whenever a venture undertakes a high-risk activity, it buys insurance to protect itself. Several years ago,

Amnesty International (a non-profit organization that works to protect civil liberties around the world) sponsored a worldwide concert tour with a number of well-known rock bands and performers. The most difficult part of organizing the tour was obtaining insurance for the artists and their equipment when they played in the then-communist countries of Eastern Europe.

Social safety net

In a centrally planned socialist economy, the labour market does not function freely. Everyone who wants a job is guaranteed one somewhere. The number of jobs is determined by a central plan to match the number of workers, so in centrally planned economies there is essentially no such thing as unemployment. This, it has been argued, is one of the great advantages of a planned system. In addition, a central planning system provides basic housing, food and clothing at very affordable levels for all. With no unemployment, and with necessities available at very low prices, there is no need for unemployment or welfare benefits or other social programmes.

Transition to a free labour market and liberalization of prices means that some workers will end up unemployed and everyone will pay higher prices for necessities. Indeed, during the early phases of the transition process, unemployment will be high. Inefficient state-owned enterprises will go out of business; some sectors will contract while others expand. As more people experience unemployment, popular support for reform is likely to drop unless some sort of social safety net is erected to ease the transition. This social safety net might include unemployment benefits, aid for the poor, and food and housing assistance. The experiences of the developed world have shown that such measures are expensive.

External assistance

Very few believe that the transition to a market system can be achieved without outside support and some outside financing. Knowledge of and experience with capitalist institutions that exist in Western Europe, the United States, Japan and other developed economies are of vital interest to the Eastern European nations. The basic skills of accounting, management and enterprise development can be taught to Eastern Europe, and many argue that it is in everyone's best interest to do so. Many also argue that the world's biggest nightmare is an economically weak or desperate Russia armed with nuclear weapons giving up on reform or falling into the hands of a dictator.

There is little agreement about the extent of *financial* support that should be given, however. Aid, many argue, will help Russia stabilize its macroeconomy and buy desperately needed goods from abroad. However, critics in potential donor countries argue that pouring money into Russia now is like pouring it into a black hole. No matter how much money we donate, they say, it will have little impact on the ultimate success or failure of the reforms.

Shock therapy or gradualism?

Although economists generally agree on what the former socialist economies need to do, there is much debate about the sequence and timing of specific reforms.

The popular press describes the debate as one between those who believe in 'shock therapy' (sometimes called the 'Big Bang' approach) and those who prefer a more gradual approach. Advocates of **shock therapy** believe that the economies in transition should proceed immediately on all fronts. That is, they should deregulate prices and liberalize trade, stop printing money, privatize, develop market institutions, build a social safety net and acquire external aid – all as quickly as possible. The pain will be severe, the argument goes, but in the end it will be forgotten as the transition raises living standards. Advocates of a *gradualist* approach believe the best course of action is to build up market institutions to begin with, to gradually decontrol prices, and to privatize only the most efficient government enterprises first.

shock therapy The approach to transition from socialism to market capitalism that advocates rapid deregulation of prices, liberalization of trade, and privatization.

Those who favour moving quickly point to the apparent success of Poland, which moved quite rapidly through the first phases of reform. Russia's experience during the first years of its transition have demonstrated that, at least in that country, change must be to some extent gradual. In theory, stabilization and price liberalization can be achieved instantaneously. But to enjoy the benefits of liberalization, a good deal of privatization must have taken place – and that will take more time. As one analyst has said, privatization means 'selling assets with no value to people with no money'. Some estimates suggest that as many as half of Russian state-owned enterprises are incapable of making a profit at world prices. Simply cutting them loose would create chaos. In a sense, Russia has no choice but to move slowly.

Alternative economic systems

We now turn to a discussion of two alternative economic systems: that of China and that of Japan.

The People's Republic of China

Continuing around the globe eastwards from the Russian Republic lies China, the world's most populous country. With 1.2 billion people, mainland China accounts for one out of every five people in the world. And China is very poor, with a per capita GDP of about US$850 in 1998.

China remains a country in which political dissent is not tolerated and the economic system remains communist, but in which private enterprise is permitted and even encouraged. This seemingly incongruous system is performing, at least for now, as well as any economy in the world. China, like Russia, is an enormously important power in the world, and understanding its history and the nature of its economic institutions is an essential part of understanding economics.

Compared to the European average, the People's Republic of China is very large and very poor. Per capita income in China is about one-fifteenth of per capita income in Europe. The history of the People's Republic, established after the communist victory in the revolution of 1949, has been marked by wild gyrations of policy and some extraordinary economic experiments.

Socialization under Mao Zedong

Soon after gaining power, the Chinese communists, under the leadership of Chairman Mao Zedong, became involved in the Korean War and found themselves heavily dependent on the Soviet Union. Not surprisingly, then, the early structure of the Chinese economic system was built on the Soviet-Stalinist model. China's first five-year plan, from 1953 to 1957, focused on developing capital-intensive heavy industries. Agriculture was collectivized, household farming was eliminated, and compulsory output quotas were put in place.

In 1958 China departed sharply from the Soviet model and launched a new economic strategy called the **Great Leap Forward**. The focus of production shifted from large-scale, capital-intensive industry to small-scale, labour-intensive industry scattered across the countryside. In addition, material incentives were reduced and replaced by the motivating power of revolutionary ideology and inspiration. Although initially successful, the strategy ultimately failed. In the early 1960s, output fell below 1958 levels. Between 1961 and 1965, material incentives were restored and a period of relative calm followed.

During the late 1960s and 1970s, economic development in China suffered a heavy blow from the **Great Proletarian Cultural Revolution** which began in 1966. For almost a decade, the rule was ideological purity. The faithful – which included almost everyone – denounced those who favoured material incentives and reform, and scientists, engineers, managers and scholars whose views were out of favour were sent to the

Great Leap Forward

The economic strategy in the People's Republic of China that began in 1958 when it departed from the Soviet model and shifted from large-scale, capital-intensive industry to small-scale, labour-intensive industry scattered across the countryside. Material incentives were reduced and replaced by the motivating power of revolutionary ideology and inspiration.

Great Proletarian Cultural Revolution (1966–1976)

A period of ideological purity in the People's Republic of China. Material incentives and reforms were denounced and highly trained specialists were sent to work in the fields. The effect of the Cultural Revolution on the Chinese economy was catastrophic.

countryside to work in the fields. The universities were essentially closed down. Untrained revolutionary *cadres* (small groups of leaders) replaced trained specialists in almost all jobs, and the economy suffered terribly. Most estimates place per capita income and consumption in the late 1970s at levels only slightly above the levels of 1956–57.[5]

The reforms of Deng Xiaoping

When Chairman Mao died in September 1976, the Cultural Revolution formally ended. In the meantime, China watched as its once poor neighbours – Japan, South Korea, Taiwan and Singapore – enjoyed extraordinary growth and prosperity.

In December 1978, the Chinese Central Committee, under the leadership of Deng Xiaoping, announced sweeping reforms. These early reforms focused on agriculture, and they signalled the beginning of profound changes in the Chinese economy that would continue over the next ten years.

Prior to 1978, each agricultural commune had distributed the harvest equally among its members. Incentives were purely collective, with everything done for the glory of the revolution. Because the cadres often overstated harvests, the state raised local delivery quotas, leaving the peasants with barely enough to go around. The new system begun under Deng Xiaoping gave individual families, through a 15-year family contract, formal rights to the land that they worked. Families were also given the rights to dispose of any surpluses and to hire out part of the family labour force to enterprises outside the family plot. Deng gave the Chinese peasants permission to enrich themselves, and they did.

The results were extraordinary. Output of grain and other basic necessities, such as cotton, increased substantially. More importantly, rural industry grew dramatically, employing over 20% of the rural labour force by 1985. From 1978 to 1983, wheat production increased at an annual rate of 8.6%, rice at 4.3% and cotton at 16.4%. From 1981 to 1984, the growth rate of all agricultural output reached 11.0% annually. In 1984, China actually became an exporter of food, despite a population of over one billion. Peasant income more than doubled in less than a decade, and private consumption and house building increased sharply.[6]

Similar reforms were implemented in Chinese industry on an experimental basis. Initially, enterprises were able to retain 15% to 25% of any profits over and above those specified by the plan. By 1984, Chinese enterprises across the country were retaining over 85% of increased profits. As with agricultural reform, the goals of industrial reform were to increase the role of the producing unit, to increase individual incentives, and to reduce the role of the state and the central planners.

The most significant element of all these reforms, however, was the movement by the Chinese government to support the expansion of enterprise rights. In the spirit of the Soviet New Economic Policy of the 1920s, the Chinese are actively encouraging small private trade and manufacturing. Today, there is an increasingly important Chinese private sector competing with state stores in style, service, quality and even price. By 1986, 480,000 'new economic associations' were employing 4.2 million people.[7] China is also now encouraging foreign investment. Initially, only joint ventures with the government were permitted, but now foreigners retain 100% ownership in several projects.

[5]See Nicholas Lardy, 'Agricultural reform', Journal of International Affairs *(Winter 1986).*

[6]China: Economic Performance in 1985: A Report to the Subcommittee on Economic Resources, Competitiveness and Security of the Joint Economic Committee *(US Central Intelligence Agency (CIA), Washington, DC, 17 March 1986), mimeo, p. 2.*

[7]Beijing Review, *25 (23 June 1986).*

China after Tiananmen Square

Despite the economic advances that China has made in the last decades, there is a great deal of political unrest in the country. In May 1989, thousands of university students openly challenged the authority of the government by occupying Tiananmen Square in Beijing. Many went on hunger strikes to protest China's lack of democracy. The 'democracy movement' was crushed on 3 June 1989, when the government cleared the square with troops and tanks as the world watched in horror.

The events of 1989 turned the tide of world opinion against the Chinese and at least temporarily slowed the movement towards economic reform. A number of joint ventures were cancelled, and the amount of direct aid flowing into China was reduced. But even before Tiananmen Square, Chinese economic reforms were beginning to encounter difficulty.

In 1988, China experienced serious inflation for the first time. By late 1988, prices were rising by historically unprecedented amounts, at nearly 30% per year. In September, the government began implementing an austerity programme that included strict price controls, reduced state investment and reduced imports. The rate of inflation had dropped by 1989, but output of goods and services in China fell in 1989 and grew only slightly in 1990.

One of the engines of recent Chinese growth has been exports. But the huge fall in the value of the Korean and Thai currencies in 1997 makes them more competitive with China. Some fear a further slowdown for China as the country's neighbours recover.

The years 1991–1995 saw a dramatic turnaround for China. Although the current Communist government has retained power and maintained a hard line on the political front, economic freedoms have been extended into every sphere. Private enterprise continues to be encouraged (see the Global Perspective 'China: Free Enterprise in a Communist Country'). A stock market was established and stock prices have boomed dramatically. Everyone in China, it seems, wants to share in this success. For example, in October 1992, First Boston Corporation, Merrill Lynch and Co. and Salomon Brothers offered five million shares in and raised more than US$75 million

Global Perspectives

China: free enterprise in a communist country

The following excerpt from a New York newspaper article nicely summarizes the rise of free enterprise in the rapidly changing China of the early 1990s.

Qiaotou, China – For a glimpse into China's economic revolution, it is useful to stroll down the main street of this humble little town. . . . [which] has propelled itself over the last dozen years into the button capital of the world.

Each year, the privately run factories of Qiaotou produce about 12 billion buttons . . . This button boom, amounting to two buttons annually per inhabitant on earth, has transformed rice paddies into factory districts, and peasants into tycoons.

One of them is Zhan Yusheng, a 27-year-old who began making buttons in his home 10 years ago. Today he owns a button factory with 100 employees, and last year he had sales of nearly $200,000.

'Now we need to upgrade our quality and produce more high-quality buttons', said Chen Jianlin, Qiaotou's Communist party secretary. 'Then we can expand on the international market.' . . . Mr Chen sees his mission primarily as promoting private enterprise.

'My most important job is building up the economy', Mr. Chen said as he sipped tea at the conference table in his office. 'People here say: "If you push the economy along, you're a good leader. Otherwise, you're not".'

While his salary is only $20 a month, about a third as much as the 20,000 migrant workers employed in Qiaotou's factories, . . .

the party covers most of his expenses, supplies him with a house, a chauffeured Audi, a phone with international direct dialling, a beeper, and a Mastercard.

'A lot of people here now carry credit cards when they travel', Mr. Chen said, beaming as he passed around his Mastercard for inspection. 'Credit cards are very convenient and you don't have to carry so much cash.'

Source: Nicholas D. Kristof, 'Free enterprise encouraged', New York Times, 18 January 1993.

for the JinBei Vehicle Manufacturing Company in the city of Shenyang. Hundreds of billions of euros in foreign investment are now flowing into China from Europe, the United States, Japan, Singapore, Taiwan and Korea.

Some problems and challenges remain. First, many fear that food shortages are imminent. While the Chinese population has continued to grow, the country's expanding industrial and housing sectors have led to a declining amount of land under cultivation. (In fact, China contains 20% of the world's population but only 7% of the world's arable land.) Second, over 50,000 state-owned enterprises continue to operate, though the process of selling these enterprises to foreign investors and allowing them to go into a form of bankruptcy continues.

In July 1997, Hong Kong, previously a British colony, was returned to China with great ceremony. Hong Kong, boasting one of the most successful capitalist economies in the world, would continue to exist as a capitalist enclave, albeit under rule of a communist government. No one knows what the future holds for Hong Kong, though most analysts are optimistic. At the end of 1997, however, there were some signs of potential trouble for the former colony. The Hong Kong stock market fell over 20% during the year and property values, which had been bid up wildly before the handover, fell significantly.

In China as a whole, growth cooled to under 8% during 1997, but the economy seemed to hold its own amid deep troubles around Asia in countries like Korea, Thailand and Japan. But while China continues to grow, it is important to remember that in per capita GDP terms it remains very poor.

Japan

No discussion of alternative economic systems would be complete without a few words about Japan. No country in history has accomplished what the Japanese economy has during the period since the Second World. Japan's economic progress over the last several decades is, with good reason, called the 'Japanese economic miracle'.

Since 1950, per capita GNP in Japan has grown from less than 20% of US GNP to over 70%. Between 1951 and 1973, real GNP in Japan grew at an average annual rate of over 10% – in just over two decades, a seven-and-a-half-fold increase. Since the mid-1970s, economic growth in Japan has slowed, but until the sharp recession of the 1990's the Japanese economy still significantly outperformed the European economy.

What led to the Japanese 'miracle'? Was it simply a matter of culture? Japan is a very disciplined society with a strong work ethic and a long tradition of cooperation. But although cultural differences may be part of the story, there is far more to it than that.

Structurally, Japan's is essentially a free-market capitalist economy. No industrialized country in the world has a smaller public sector, and none has a more 'pro-business' government. To a very large extent, the private decisions of households and firms produced the miracle.

To explain Japan's success more specifically, analysts point to four major factors: (1) very high rates of saving and investment, (2) a highly trained labour force, (3) rapid absorption and effective utilization of technology, much of it imported, and (4) a pro-growth government policy.[8] Of these, perhaps the single most important cause of Japan's growth has been its incredible rate of investment. Between 1951 and 1973, the capital stock of Japan grew by more than 9% per year, and for a substantial period investment approached 40% of GNP. As a comparison, between 1960 and 1980 the capital stock in the average EU country increased at about 4% per year, while gross investment fluctuated between 15% and 17% per year. Virtually all of Japan's investment was financed with domestic saving. Japan's rate of saving by households has been the highest in the world.

[8]This discussion owes much to an excellent paper by Hugh Patrick and Henry Rosovsky, 'Japan's economic performance: an overview', in Hugh Patrick and Henry Rosovsky (eds), Asia's New Giant (The Brookings Institution, 1976).

Until recent years, rates of return on new investment in Japan were high. But today Japan faces a new problem. Its high rates of investment have virtually exhausted the investment opportunities in the nation and have pushed rates of return on saving to very low levels. The saving rate has remained high, however, and this has led many Japanese citizens to look abroad for a place to put their savings. A significant part of those savings flowed to the United States during the 1980s. Real interest rates are much higher in the United States than in Japan, and a considerable number of new US government bonds are now being sold to the Japanese. The Japanese are investing billions of dollars in US common stocks and real estate. There are large Japanese investments in plant and equipment in Europe, notably in cars and high-tech products. Substantial sums are also going into European stock markets.

The second factor contributing to Japan's economic success is the quality of the Japanese labour force. As early as 1950, Japan had an education level comparable to that of Europe, despite a much lower level of economic development. Most Japanese workers were employed in jobs that demanded extremely low productivity relative to the education and training of those holding them. As the country's capital stock grew, workers moved easily into higher-productivity jobs.

Japan also consciously adopted the most advanced industrial technologies in the world. Much of the knowledge necessary to do this was available in technical journals or obtainable in graduate institutions abroad, and some came embodied in machinery and equipment imported into Japan. The Japanese were extremely effective at improving upon and commercializing what they imported. By importing technology, Japan did not have to develop it on its own; and, until recently, Japan devoted a smaller portion of its GNP to research and development than did many European countries.

The role of government in the Japanese economy is certainly different from the role of government in much of Europe. There is disagreement among economists about the importance of government as an instrument of growth in Japan. It is clear that the main source of growth has been the private sector but that the government has played a supportive role. For example, after the Second World War the Japanese government, through the **Ministry of Trade and Industry (MITI)**, used tariffs and quotas to protect and subsidize a number of key industries, including coal, steel, electric power and shipbuilding. During the 1960s, chemicals and machinery were added to the list. In the mid-1980s, the government and the private sector launched a partnership designed to develop and market the next generation of computers. MITI also helps some sectors of the economy plan orderly reductions in capacity. In short, the Japanese government is actively involved in the allocation process and has much to say about which industries will grow and which will not.

Ministry of Trade and Industry (MITI)
The agency of the Japanese government responsible for industrial policy. It uses tariffs and subsidies to protect and subsidize key industries and helps some sectors plan orderly reductions in capacity.

Japan in the 1990s
The enormous success of the Japanese economy led to seemingly unbounded optimism at the end of the 1980s. Spurred on by the profitability of Japanese firms, the market prices of Japanese stocks raced to unprecedented levels. At the same time, Japanese land values boomed.

Then, in 1992, the bottom fell out of the Japanese stock market and land prices began to fall. For the first time in the history of modern Japan, confidence in the future was shaken. During 1992 and 1993, Japan slipped into a recession, which continued into 1994, and real GDP fell. People in Japan began referring to the 1980s as the period of the 'bubble economy'. Late 1994 saw a return to growth, but 1995 brought a series of setbacks, including a devastating earthquake in the city of Kobe as well as a tremendous increase in the value of the yen. A more expensive yen made Japanese products look much more expensive to the rest of the world and threatened to choke off demand and plunge the Japanese economy back into recession.

1997 and 1998 were miserable years for Japan. The economy continued in deep recession. It became ever clearer that most leading banks had operated disastrous lending policies and many were on the verge of bankruptcy. The stock market continued to fall and consumer spending remained depressed. No clear government policy towards the economy emerged.

Despite these substantial setbacks, Japan remains an enormous economic power. As the economy becomes ever more globalized in the coming years, it will be even more important to understand fully the successes and failures of Japanese industrial policy.

Conclusion

This chapter has introduced very briefly the structure, history and performance of several different economic systems. It has also discussed the enormous problems of transforming a socialist economy into a market-based economy. So brief a description and analysis, we acknowledge, must be somewhat frustrating. After all, many volumes have been written on these topics. But a study of basic economics without such a 'tour', however hasty, would be incomplete.

Studying alternative economic systems is a fitting way to conclude an introduction to economics. One of the themes running through this book has been the role of government in a market economy. We have tried to present a balanced description of how economies function, both in theory and in the real world. Throughout, we have focused on the potential benefits and problems associated with public-sector involvement. Eastern Europe, Russia, China and Japan present very different perspectives on the interaction between the private and public sectors.

Concluding with this chapter is also, we hope, an enticement to further study. This is an exciting time in the world's economic history. Never before have systems changed so dramatically in such a short time. Many believe that the reforms in China, Eastern Europe and Russia have brought the world much closer together and that the time is ripe for a significant reduction in world political tensions. Others believe that the problems of transition are so difficult that the whole process will disintegrate into chaos. Only time will tell.

Summary

Political systems and economic systems: socialism, capitalism and communism

1. A *socialist economy* is one in which most capital is owned by the government rather than by private citizens. A *capitalist economy* is one in which most capital is privately owned. *Communism* is a theoretical economic system in which the people directly control the means of production (capital and land) without the intervention of a government or state.

2. Economies differ in the extent to which decisions are made through central planning rather than through a market system. Generally, socialist economies favour central planning over market allocation, and capitalist economies rely to a much greater extent on the market.

Nonetheless, there are markets in all societies, and planning takes place in all economies.

The economic theories of Karl Marx

3. According to Marxian thought, private ownership and profit are both unfair and unethical. Profit is value that is created by labour but expropriated by non-productive capitalists, who are able to exploit labour by virtue of their ownership of the means of production (land and capital).

4. Marx predicted that falling rates of profit, increasing exploitation and deeper business cycles would eventually cause capitalism to collapse.

5. Neoclassical economics sees profit as a return to a productive factor (capital) just as wages are the return to another productive factor (labour).

Economies in transition: the experiences of Russia and Eastern Europe

6. When the Bolsheviks took power in Russia after the October Revolution in 1917, they found themselves without the advanced industrial base that Marx had envisioned and with no real blueprint for running a socialist or communist state. Marx had written mainly about capitalism, not socialism.

7. In 1928, the Soviet Union settled into comprehensive central planning and collectivization of agriculture, an economic structure that lasted into the 1980s. Virtually all productive assets, including most land and capital, were publicly owned. There was no formal private business sector, no market for capital goods and no income from property.

8. The Soviet Union grew rapidly through the mid-1970s. During the late 1950s, the Soviet Union's economy was growing much faster than that of Europe. The key to early Soviet success was rapid planned capital accumulation. The late 1970s saw things begin to deteriorate. Dramatic reforms were finally introduced by Mikhail Gorbachev after his rise to power in 1985. Nonetheless, the Soviet economy collapsed in 1991. The Soviet Union was dissolved, and the new president of the Russian Republic, Boris Yeltsin, was left to start the difficult task of transition to a market system.

9. Economists generally agree on six requirements for a successful transition from socialism to a market-based system: (1) macroeconomic stabilization, (2) deregulation of prices and liberalization of trade, (3) privatization, (4) the establishment of market-supporting institutions, (5) a social safety net, and (6) external assistance.

10. There is much debate about the sequence and timing of specific reforms. The idea of *shock therapy* is to proceed immediately on all six fronts, including rapid deregulation of prices and privatization. The gradualist approach is to build up market institutions to start with, gradually decontrol prices, and privatize only the most efficient government enterprises first.

Alternative economic systems

11. China, the largest country in the world, became communist following the revolution of 1949. In its early years under Chairman Mao Zedong, China organized under the Soviet model of central planning and rapid capital accumulation in heavy industry. In 1958, China departed sharply from the Soviet model, emphasizing small-scale, labour-intensive industry scattered around the countryside.

12. In 1978, Deng Xiaoping instituted sweeping reforms in the organization of the Chinese economy, particularly in agriculture. These reforms moved China away from central planning towards a system driven by market incentives.

13. China remains a country in which political dissent is not tolerated and the economic system remains communist, but in which private enterprise is permitted and even encouraged. In the last several years the country has enjoyed rapid growth and substantial outside investment. However, inflation has been a problem, a fear of food shortages remain, and more than 50,000 state-owned enterprises continue to operate.

14. No country in history has accomplished what the Japanese economy has during the post-war period. Analysts point to four major factors to explain Japan's success: (1) a very high rate of saving and investment, (2) a highly trained labour force, (3) rapid absorption and effective utilization of technology, much of it imported, and (4) a pro-growth government policy. Despite some severe setbacks in the 1990s, Japan remains an important economic power.

Review Terms and Concepts

capitalist economy
communism
five-year plans
Great Leap Forward
Great Proletarian Cultural Revolution
labour theory of value
market-socialist economy
means of production

Ministry of Trade and Industry (MITI)
New Economic Policy
rate of exploitation
shock therapy
socialist economy
surplus value
tragedy of commons
value of labour power

Problem Set

1. Choose one of the transitional economies of Central Europe (Poland, Hungary, Bulgaria, the Czech Republic or Romania), or one of the ten countries of the Commonwealth of Independent States (Armenia, Azerbaijan, Ukraine, Uzbekistan, Russia, etc.). Write a brief paper on how the transition to a market economy was proceeding in 1998 and 1999. Has the economy (prices, employment, etc.) stabilized? Has there been economic growth? How far has privatization progressed? What problems have been encountered? (A good source of information would be the chronological index to a publication like *The Economist*.)

2. 'The difference between Europe and the Soviet Union is that European countries have a capitalist economic system and the Soviet Union had a totalitarian government.' Explain how this comparison confuses the economic and political aspects of the two societies. What words describe the former economic system of the Soviet Union?

3. In 1998, Japan seemed on the brink of a major collapse. Real GDP in Japan continued to fall. Most of Japan's twenty largest banks were reporting big losses. The yen had declined sharply. With the recession, Japan's imports from Europe fell and the cheap yen caused imports to Europe to rise, increasing Japan's trade surplus with Europe.
a. What has happened to the Japanese economy since 1997? Has real GDP increased or decreased? At what rate?
b. What has happened to the value of the yen?
c. What steps have the Japanese taken to 'restructure' their economy?

Again, a good source for such information is *The Economist*. Another source is the web site of the Organization for Economic Cooperation and Development (OECD).

4. You are assigned the task of debating the strengths of a socialist economy (regardless of your own viewpoint). Outline the points that you would make in the debate. Be sure to define socialism carefully in your presentation.

5. What is the 'tragedy of commons'? Suppose that all workers in a factory are paid the same wage and have no chance of being fired. Use the logic of the 'tragedy of commons' to predict the result. How would you expect workers to behave?

6. 'European governments should institute a policy of subsidizing those firms that are likely to be successful competitors in the international economic wars! Such an "industrial policy" should have the authority to override any fair competition or antitrust laws.' Do you agree or disagree? Explain your answer.

7. Explain why Karl Marx thought profit was unjustified. Be sure to define the labour theory of value. Contrast the Marxian view with the neoclassical view of profit.

8. Do you agree or disagree with each of the following statements? Explain your answers.
a. Over time, the Chinese have shifted from a decentralized approach to economic development to a more centrally planned system. Since the events of 1989 in Tiananmen Square, there has been a severe crackdown on private businesses.
b. Both Japan and the Soviet Union grew rapidly during the 1950s and 1960s. Growth in the Soviet Union was based on rapid accumulation of capital forced by the central plan under Stalin and Khrushchev. In Japan, the growth was not due to capital accumulation.
c. Although economists generally agree that transition from socialism to a market-based system must proceed rapidly, there is little agreement about what must be done to make the transition successful.

9. The distribution of income in a capitalist economy is likely to be more unequal than it is in a socialist economy. Why is this so? Is there a tension between the goal of limiting inequality and the goal of motivating risk taking and hard work? Explain your answer in detail.

10. 'There is no doubt that a centrally planned socialist system has the potential to grow faster than a market-orientated capitalist system.' Do you agree or disagree? What are some of the trade-offs facing socialist planners who set target growth rates?

11. In the 1990s, the world witnessed the rapid decline of several Eastern European governments (East Germany, Poland and Romania, to name just a few). Poland immediately began moving its socialist economy towards a capitalist economy. Some of the effects of this transition have been increased unemployment and price inflation. Can you explain why? (*Hint*: focus on differences between socialist and capitalist systems regarding the determination of prices and production levels.)

Solutions

Chapter 1

2. a, b, c and f are examples of positive economics; d and e are examples of normative economics because they make value judgements about the outcomes.

4. Average cost: €0.59. Marginal cost: 0.

6. a. Shopkeepers would gain through greater access to customers and higher profits. All city residents would gain, because greater access will generate higher sales and greater sales tax revenues. Consumers gain as a result of the opportunity cost of time not spent waiting in traffic jams.

   b. Losers would include shopkeepers closer to the other, older bridge whose customers choose to shop closer to the new bridge. Any taxpayers for whom the extra taxes exceed the added benefit of the new bridge would also lose.

   c. The gains/losses could be measured by adding up the value of all the time saved not waiting in queues. We might say the bridge is efficient if the value of the time saved were greater than the cost of building the bridge.

8. a. Because gambling is not mandatory, only those who want to do so will gamble. The state should allow the market to provide what people want.

   b. It has been argued that gambling casinos bring with them higher crime and 'undesirable' types of people. In addition, gambling can be addictive, and it often leads some who can least afford it into poverty and bankruptcy. Thus, opponents argue that wanting to gamble may not be strictly voluntary. Clearly, lotteries may produce more than just the enjoyment of gambling.

   c. The most frequent argument against lotteries is that lower-income households tend to gamble away more of their incomes than do higher-income households. Thus, the taxes collected from gambling come predominantly from lower-income households, and often from gambling addicts.

Appendix

2. a. Negative slope. As price rises, quantity of apples purchased falls.

   b. Positive (and declining) slope. As income rises, taxes rise, but the rise in taxes is less at higher incomes than at lower incomes.

   c. Negative (and declining) slope. As mortgage rates fall, home sales increase, but the increase in home sales is more at lower mortgage rates than at higher mortgage rates.

   d. Negative, then positive, slope. As young children get older, they run faster, but as adults get older (beyond a certain age), they run slower.

   e. Positive slope. Greater sunshine leads to greater corn yield.

   f. Positive, then negative, slope. Up to a point, more fertilizer increases corn yield, but, beyond a certain point, adding more fertilizer actually decreases the yield.

Chapter 2

2. Both land and capital are inputs, but capital is something that is produced by human beings. Trees growing wild are like land; they are not produced by human beings. However, an orchard that is planted by human beings can be classified as capital. It took time, labour and perhaps machinery to plant the orchard and to prune the trees.

4. a. For Kristen the 'cost' of a potholder is 5 wristbands; for Anna the cost of a potholder is 6 wristbands. Kristen has a comparative advantage in potholders.

   b. Anna has a comparative advantage in the production of wristbands because the opportunity cost (1/6 potholder) is lower for Anna than it is for Kristen (1/5 potholder).

   c.

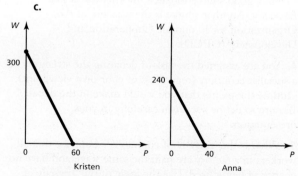

   d. Kristen: 150 wristbands and 30 potholders. Anna: 120 wristbands and 20 potholders. Total wristbands = 270. Total potholders = 50.

   e. 285 wristbands and 51 potholders.

   f. Kristen should completely specialize in potholder production and earn 60 × €5.50 = €330. Anna should completely specialize in wristband production and earn 240 × €1 = €240. Maximum joint revenue is €570.

6. a. A straight-line ppf curve intersecting the Y axis at 1000 units of music and merriment and intersecting the X axis at 500 units of food. These are the limits of production if all resources are used to produce only one good.

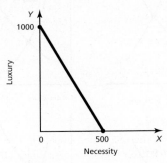

b. Unemployment or underemployment of labour would put the society inside the ppf – as would any inefficient use of resources. Full employment would move the society to some point on the ppf.

c. Answers will vary, but the decision should be based on the relative values of food and of music and merriment, and the degree of concern that all fellow citizens have enough of basic commodities such as food.

d. If left to the free market, prices would (at least ideally) be determined by market forces; incomes would be determined by a combination of ability, effort and inheritance. It would be up to each individual to find a job and determine how to spend the income.

8. a. 3.

b. 1, 4, 5, 6.

d. 5.

e. 2, 3, 4, 5, 6.

f. 2.

Chapter 3

2. Firms and unions in industries vulnerable to foreign competition (for example, from South-east Asia) are opposed to their removal. Export industries favour increased competition. Their reason: the theory of comparative advantage. (See Chapter 2.) Consumers will also gain.

4. Answers will vary between countries, but check government expenditure as a percentage of GDP. Also check government *employment* as a percentage of total employment. And note that government purchases of goods and services may have changed as a percentage of GDP.

6. Disagree. Change the word *corporations* to *sole proprietorships* and the statement is true.

8. Some is paid to government as taxes; some is retained by companies, mostly for investment but also as a cushion against possible bad times ahead.

10. No matter how much the firm produces, it is so small relative to the total market that its output has no effect on the market price. Therefore, the firm must be a 'price taker'; it accepts the market-determined price charged by all other firms as a given that it cannot influence.

12. Government spending could increase while taxes are decreasing due to deficit spending (borrowing). Government spending could increase while government employment is decreasing, if government is purchasing goods and services from the private sector that it formerly produced itself.

14. The rationale for awarding patents is that it provides an incentive for research, invention and innovation. If anyone can simply use my ideas and copy exactly what I produce, what incentive do I have to innovate? I would not be a monopolist if I invented a new perfume, because there are many substitutes available for my product.

Chapter 4

2. a. Disagree. They are complements.

b. Agree.

c. Disagree. A rise in income will cause the demand for inferior goods to fall, pushing prices down.

d. Disagree. Yes, they can – steak and lobster are both normal goods, for example.

e. Disagree. Price could go down if the shift of supply is larger than the shift of demand.

f. Disagree. They are substitutes.

4. a.

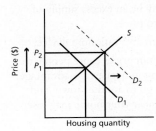

b.

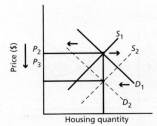

c.

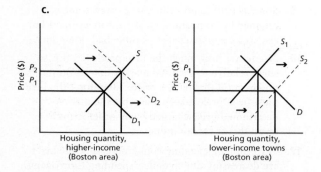

d.

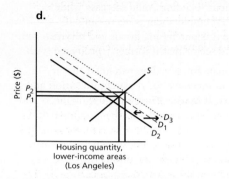

6. a.

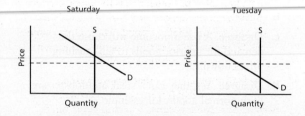

Note the vertical supply curve.

b. Possibly. In the diagram for Tuesday there is a (lower) price at which $Q_S = Q_D$. However, if D is very low there may be an excess supply of spaces, even at a zero price.

c. Queues are the alternative rationing device.

d. Advantage: equilibrium prices cause people to waste less time sitting in queues. Disadvantage: some shoppers may go to another town, and traders in the town near your home may lose out.

8.

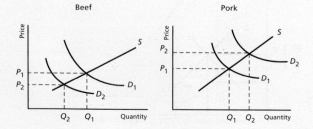

10.

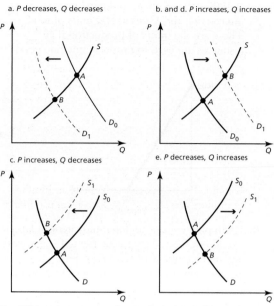

12. This sequence confuses changes in demand (*shifts of* the demand curve) with changes in quantity demanded (*movements along* a demand curve). First, a demand *shift* does cause price to rise. As price rises, the *quantity supplied* increases along the supply curve, and the *quantity demanded* declines along the demand curve as the market moves to re-establish equilibrium. Nothing here suggests that demand shifts back down.

14. a. $P = 35$; b. $Q = 70$, when price is zero.

Chapter 5

2. Answers will vary. But this process – regardless of its morality – helps to eliminate shortages by creating a 'market' where the price can rise to its equilibrium value. Anyone willing to pay the equilibrium price should be able to obtain a ticket. Also, by allowing price rationing to work to some extent, touts reduce the need for queuing, which results in less wasted time.

4. a.

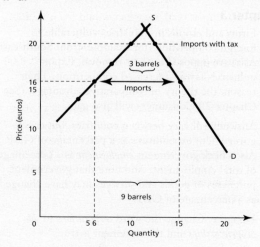

b. The equilibrium price is €16 per barrel, and the equilibrium quantity is 70 million barrels per day.

c. With free trade in oil, Europeans would pay the same price for oil as everyone else: €16 per barrel. At this price, the European demand schedule shows that Europeans would buy 15 million barrels per day. The European supply schedule shows that European producers would supply 6 million barrels per day, with the remainder – 9 million barrels – imported from foreign sources.

d. With a tax of €4 per barrel, Europeans would have to pay €20 for imported oil. Quantity demanded would decrease from 15 million to 13 million barrels. Of this, European producers would supply 10 million barrels, while imports would be cut back from 9 million to 3 million barrels. The European governments would collect a tax of €4 × 3 million = €12 million per day.

e. European oil consumers are harmed by the tax; they are paying a higher price for oil. European oil producers are helped by the tax; they receive a higher price for oil, and this induces them to produce more oil. Foreign oil producers are harmed, because Europeans buy less imported oil. Finally, European governments and European taxpayers (generally) benefit from the tax revenue.

6. The subsidy does increase the 'cost' of planting – there is now an opportunity cost. (By planting, the farmers will have to give up the subsidy.) The subsidy will clearly lead to fewer hectares under production, and higher farm prices. In effect, it shifts the supply curve to the left.

8. Absolutely not. This statement confuses a shift of demand with change in quantity demanded along a demand curve. The demand for jeans shifted upwards, causing price to rise.

10. a. Between points A and B: –3.666. Between points C and D: –1. Between points E and F: –0.273.

b. Starting at €50, revenues would fall by €4000, from €10,000 to €6000. Starting at €30, revenues would remain constant at €12,000. Starting at €10, revenues would rise by €4000, from €6000 to €10,000.

c. When demand is elastic (e.g. between points A and B), a price increase will lead to a revenue decline. When elasticity is unitary (e.g. between points C and D), a price increase will leave revenues unchanged. When demand is inelastic (e.g. between points E and F), a price increase will increase revenue.

12. a. –1.2.

b. +10%.

c. +15%.

d. +12%.

e. +0.67.

14. a. $\%\Delta Q \div \% \Delta P = 0.2$.

Thus, $\% \Delta P = \% \Delta Q \div 0.2 = 10\% \div 0.2 = 50\%$.

b. A price ceiling at €1.40 per gallon would create a shortage of petrol. The result might be long queues at petrol stations, and perhaps a black market in petrol.

16. Before advertising, elasticity of demand is –0.176. After advertising, demand elasticity is –0.093. Advertising can be designed to shift the demand curve outwards and/or to make demand less elastic (build up brand loyalty). Here advertising is successful as demand is now less elastic.

Chapter 6

2. a. She can no longer afford to buy the same combination of things that she bought last year. Her real income is lower. Something has to give – her budget constraint changed. So, she must cut back on some things, and her preferences dictated that these would be concerts and CDs.

b. She is worse off: her real income is lower. She will reduce consumption of normal goods, including air trips home; this is the income effect. In addition, the opportunity cost of a trip home increases from €350 to €600. Thus, Dominique will be pushed to substitute other goods for air travel. This is the substitution effect.

4. The substitution effect is that leisure was less costly – each hour of leisure requires a smaller sacrifice of income because working gains only $0.20 on the dollar. Thus you would tend to work less after the cuts. However, the decline in welfare benefits also causes a decrease in purchasing power (for any given amount of leisure, you have less income than before). If leisure is a normal good, you would buy less of it. The income effect thus suggests working more. The two effects work in opposite directions, and the net result is ambiguous.

6.

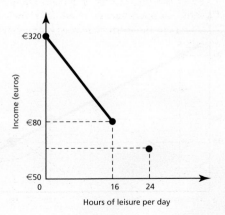

8. Supply remains stable and demand shifts to the left, causing price to fall. As the price of airline tickets falls, the substitution effect works to increase the demand for air travel. If air travel is a normal good (which is likely), the income effect also will increase the demand for travel.

10. **a.** Disagree. If the income effect of a wage change dominates the substitution effect, we know that wage increases will cause additional consumption of leisure and less work, and that lower wages will cause additional work and an increased labour supply. Thus, if our household works more it must have a wage cut.

b. Disagree. In product markets, a price cut makes households better off: they have a higher real income. Thus, for normal goods, the income effect leads to *greater* consumption of the good.

12. The Dutch auction is probably more effective in reducing consumer surplus, since a bidder – to be sure of getting the good – will have to bid the highest price he or she is willing to pay for it. By definition, this eliminates all consumer surplus. In a normal auction, the individual would begin the bidding at a price less than the highest price he or she is willing to pay. Unless other bidders force the price up to this maximum, he or she will be able to purchase at a lower price, gaining some consumer surplus.

14. **a.** $TU = 224$.

b. $TU = 384$.

c. $MU = 64 - 4Q$.

d. MU declines at a constant rate.

e. MU is zero where $64 - 4Q = 0$, so $Q = 16$.

Appendix

2. $I/P_{x1} = 100$ and $I = 100$, thus $P_{x1} = €1.00$ (point A on the demand curve).

$I/P_{x2} = 200$ and $I = 100$, thus $P_{x2} = €0.50$ (point B on the demand curve).

$I/P_{x3} = 300$ and $I = 100$, thus $P_{x3} = €0.33$ (point C on the demand curve).

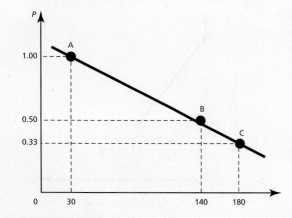

4. **a.** We know that $P_A A + P_N N = 100 \rightarrow 5N + 10A = 100$. We also know that $MU_N/MU_A = A/N = P_N/P_A = 5/10 \rightarrow N = 2A$. Substituting, we find that $5(2A) + 10A = 100 \rightarrow A = 5$; $N = 10$.

b. If $P_N = 10$, $N = 5$, and if $P_N = 2$, $N = 25$.

c. Answers will vary, but the graph should show an indifference curve tangent to a budget constraint drawn for $P_A = £10$ and P_N equal to one of the prices given in the answer to b.

Chapter 7

2. The size of the theatre is the fixed factor. Decisions include how to divide up the tickets, what price to charge, what shows to put on, and what kind of stage sets to use. All are constrained by the scale of the theatre. In the long run, you might be able to raise money and build or acquire a bigger theatre. There is no fixed factor in the long run; you can think big!

4. **a.** The marginal product decreases as a single variable factor increases, holding all other factors constant.

b. The table does exhibit diminishing returns because the marginal product of labour falls as labour increases:

L	TP	MP
0	0	–
1	5	5
2	9	4
3	12	3
4	14	2
5	15	1

6. **a.** Technology B in all three cases.

b. When $Q = 1$: €6; $Q = 2$: €10; $Q = 3$: €13.

c. When $Q = 1$, $K = 5$ and $L = 1$. When $Q = 2$, $K = 8$ and $L = 2$. When $Q = 3$, $K = 10$ and $L = 3$.

d. Technology A in all three cases. When $Q = 1$: €9; $Q = 2$: €16; $Q = 3$: €21. When $Q = 1$, $K = 2$ and $L = 5$. When $Q = 2$, $K = 3$ and $L = 10$. When $Q = 3$, $K = 4$ and $L = 13$.

8. **a.** Tall buildings – skyscrapers.

b. Product usually has to move along an assembly line and out into a warehouse. An assembly line usually takes a lot of space on a single floor. (Can you imagine a vertical assembly line?)

c. Offices can be 'stacked up'. People can easily move by stairs or lifts.

d. Accessibility!

e. The area of land increases with the square of distance from the centre: When a city grows out by 5 miles, area (Br^2) increases by 25 times!

10. a. The first step is to calculate the cost for each level of output using each of the three technologies. With capital costing €100 per day, and labour costing €80 per day, the results are as follows:

Daily output	Technology 1	Technology 2	Technology 3
100	860	800	820
150	1,100	960	900
200	1,280	1,140	1,080
250	1,540	1,400	1,340

From the table, we can see that for an output of 100, Technology 2 is the cheapest. For output levels of 150, 200 and 250, Technology 3 is cheapest.

b. In a low-wage country, where capital costs €100 per day and labour costs only €40 per day, the cost figures are as follows:

Daily output	Technology 1	Technology 2	Technology 3
100	580	600	660
150	700	680	700
200	840	820	840
250	1,020	1,000	1,020

From the table, we can see that for an output of 100, Technology 1 is now cheapest. For output levels of 150, 200 or 250, Technology 2 is now cheapest.

c. If the firm moves from a high-wage to a low-wage country and continues to produce 200 units per day, it will change from Technology 3 (with 6 workers) to Technology 2 (with 8 workers). Employment increases by two workers.

Appendix

2. At A, $MP_L/MP_K > P_L/P_K$ because the slope of the isoquant is greater than the slope of the isocost. That means that $MP_L/P_L > MP_K/P_K$; thus the firm can cut costs by hiring more labour and less capital. At B, $MP_L/MP_K < P_L/P_K$ because the slope of the isoquant is less than the slope of the isocost.

That means that $MP_K/P_K > MP_L/P_L$; thus the firm can cut costs by hiring more capital and less labour.

Chapter 8

2. a. False. MC may be rising, but if it is below AC then AC will still be falling.

b. False. At the level of output where ATC is minimized, if $P > MC$, the firm should increase production even if this decision raises ATC. As long as $P > MC$ a competitive firm will increase its profits by increasing production (with one exception, as explained in Chapter 9).

c. False. AFC = Total fixed cost/Output = TFC/q. As q rises, fixed cost remains constant, so AFC must decrease.

4. a. Marginal cost is a constant 1 guilder from one unit of output up to 100 units, since the most efficient machine will be used. From the 101st unit to the 300th unit, MC is constant at 2 guilders. From the 301st unit to the 800th unit, MC is constant at 3 guilders.

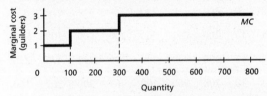

Total cost is 100 guilders at zero units of output and rises by 1 guilder per unit up to a total of 200 guilders at 100 units of output. From 101 units of output up to 300 units, total cost increases by 2 per unit up to a total of 600 guilders. After that it rises at 3 guilders per unit to a total of 2100 guilders at 800 units of output.

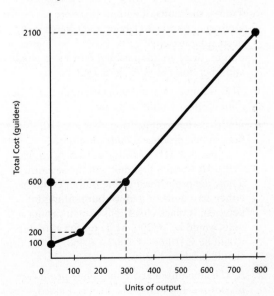

b. At a price of 2.50 guilders, the company should produce 300 books. $TR = 750$, $TC = 600$, so profit = 150 guilders.

6. a. The table gives the marginal product from each day's efforts: 100, 80, 60, and 40 kg.

b. Marginal cost of a kilogram of fish is the change in cost divided by the change in q. During prime season, each day brings in 100 kg of fish at a cost of 6000 leva, or $MC = 6000/100 = 60$ leva. During month 7, it's $6000/80 = MC = 75$ leva. During month 8, it's $6000/60 = MC = 100$ leva. During the rest of the year it's $6000/40 = 150$ leva.

c. Produce as long as price, which is marginal revenue (80 leva), is greater than MC. Thus, the boat should be in the water and fishing during prime season and month 7, but should not fish during month 8 or during the rest of the year.

8. a.

Q	L	TFC	TVC	TC	AFC	AVC	ATC	MC
0	0	200	0	200	–	–	–	–
1	10	200	500	700	200	500	700	500
2	15	200	750	950	100	375	475	250
3	18	200	900	1,100	67	300	367	150
4	22	200	1,100	1,300	50	275	325	200
5	28	200	1,400	1,600	40	280	320	300
6	36	200	1,800	2,000	33	300	333	400
7	48	200	2,400	2,600	29	343	372	600

b. Student verification.

c. From 0 to 3 units of output, there are increasing returns to labour and (therefore) decreasing marginal costs. From 3 to 7 units of output, there are diminishing returns to labour and (therefore) increasing marginal costs.

d. AVC is minimized at 4 units of output. ATC is minimized at 5 units of output.

e. Under perfect competition, $MR = €410$, so the firm should produce 6 units of output.

(Note that $MR > MC$ for units 2–6, while $MR < MC$ for the first unit and the seventh. Thus, the profit-maximizing output could be either zero units or 6 units, but nothing in between. A quick check tells us that profits at 0 units would be $−€200$, while profits at 6 units would be $€410(6) − €2000 = €460$. So the firm should produce 6 units.)

f. ATC is minimized at 5 units, while profits are maximized at 6 units. The firm is, indeed,

'minimizing costs' in the sense that it is producing any given level of output at the lowest possible cost. But its goal in choosing among different output levels is to maximize profits, not to minimize average costs. Since $MR > MC$ for the sixth unit, producing the sixth units adds to profits, even though it also raises ATC.

*10. a. $TR = 104 \times 20 = 2080$.

b. $TFC = 10$.

c. $TVC = (4 \times 10) + (2 \times 10^2) = 240$.

d. $TC = TFC + TVC = 250$.

e. Profits are maximized where $MC = MR$.
$MR = 104$.
$MC = 4 + 4Q = 104$.
$Q = 25$.

f. $TC = 1360$.

g. $TR = 2600$.

h. Profit = 1240.

Chapter 9

2. One could make a case that some economies probably exist in all seven, but the case is much stronger in electric power (needs a large power plant or dam) and aircraft manufacturing (requires a big assembly line and a great deal of cooperation).

House building: House building is often undertaken by very small independent contractors, though there are some large developers that produce tens of thousands of homes each year. They practise quantity buying and use mass-produced parts.

Higher education: This one is tricky. Although big institutions can have larger classes and larger staff–student ratios, they often produce a different product from smaller institutions.

It is hard to find economies of much significance in *software development*, *market gardening* and *accounting*. Although some firms in those industries are large, many are fairly small and quite competitive.

4. a. Not true. A firm will never sell its output for less than the *marginal* cost of producing it, though it may indeed sell at less than *average* total cost as long as it can earn an operating profit.

b. Not true. The short-run marginal cost curve assumes at least one input is fixed. The long-run average cost curve allows all inputs to vary. For example, the short-run MC curve for each fixed level of capital could be U-shaped, and yet the $LRAC$ curve could be flat (constant returns to scale).

6. a. Disagree. Constant returns to scale means that the long-run average cost curve is flat over most of its range.

  b. Disagree. Firms earning profits will produce to the right of the minimum point on the average total cost function.

  c. Disagree. The supply curve of a competitive firm is its marginal cost curve above the average *variable* cost curve. At any point above *AVC*, total revenue is greater than total variable cost and firms will choose to operate.

  d. Disagree. A firm suffering losses will continue to operate as long as total revenue covers *variable* cost.

8. The enterprise is suffering a €1000 loss: *TR* = €30,000, *TC* = €29,000, accounting profit = €1000. But the opportunity cost of capital is 10% or €2000. When this €2000 is added to cost, the result is a €1000 economic loss.

*10. a. $6 + 3Q^2 = 18$, so $Q = 2$.

  b. Produce and profit = −8. Shut down, and short-run loss is fixed costs. So profit is −24.
    Hence it is better in the short run to continue producing.

12. a. Fixed costs = €100 per day. Variable costs = $7q$. Total costs = €100 + $7q$.

  $MC = 7$.

  $ATC = TC/q = (100 + 7q)/q$

  $AVC = TVC/q = 7$.

  $AFC = 100/q$.

  b.

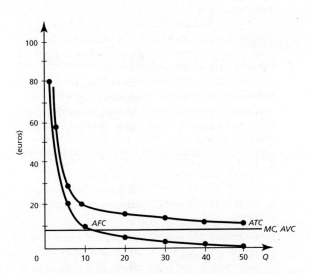

  c. Adam should produce 50 pies (the maximum) each day. Profit will be €400 − €450 = −50, or a loss of €50 per day.

  d. In the long run, Adam should produce zero pies (he should exit the industry), since he cannot make an economic profit at a price of €8 and, given the assumption in the problem, he must operate with only one oven.

  e. In the short run, Adam should operate at any price of €7 or greater. In the long run, Adam needs a price of €9 to break even (at 50 pies per day).

Appendix

2. See the story in the appendix to this chapter and figure 9A.2, for an increasing-cost industry.

Chapter 10

2.

Workers	Kilos	MP	MRP (fr)
0	0	–	–
1	40	40	80
2	70	30	60
3	90	20	40
4	100	10	20
5	105	5	10
6	102	−3	−6

The firm should hire workers as long as *MRP* > *W*. When *W* = 30 francs, the firm should hire three workers. If *W* increases to 50 francs, the firm should cut back to only two workers, since the *MRP* of the third worker (40 francs) is now less than the cost of hiring him/her (50 francs).

4. a. Demand curve for construction workers shifts leftwards: wage decreases; employment decreases.

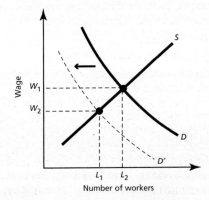

  b. and c. Demand curve for construction workers shifts rightwards; wage increases; employment increases.

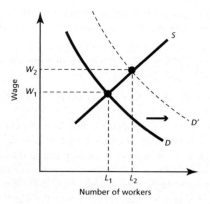

Wage — W_2, W_1 — Number of workers — L_1, L_2 — S, D', D

6. Investment subsidies reduce the cost of capital relative to the cost of labour. To the extent that capital is a substitute for labour, these subsidies can lead to layoffs and slower employment growth.

8. It is possible. Demand for executive salaries is derived from the demand for electricity. Demand was rising. Much of the compensation is in the form of stock options. The value of these options is directly tied to the market price of the shares, which did very well during that period as costs were cut and profits increased. In a sense, the executives were being paid their marginal revenue product.

   On the other hand, it is difficult to show that the share performance and electricity profits were due to their efforts and skills rather than the market power of the products they were producing.

10. You would weigh the benefits with the costs. The costs are €20 per week, but the benefits depend on the value of the housemates' time and the displeasure that each gets from mowing. It also depends on their incomes and wealth. There could easily be disagreement.

12. **a.** Even though the ratios MRP_L/P_L and MRP_K/P_K are equal, we still have $MRP_L > P_L$ and $MRP_K > PK_K$.

    b. The firm could increase profits by either purchasing more capital or hiring more workers. Either action would add more to revenue than it would add to costs.

Chapter 11

2. No. The total capital costs of the petrol station is 1 million francs. With revenues of 420,000 francs and costs of 360,000 francs, profit is just 60,000 which is a 6% yield on an investment of 1 million francs. If I can get 7.5% by investing in perfectly safe government securities, why buy a petrol station?

4. **a.** Laura is saving. Jim is dissaving. There is no investment going on; assets are simply being exchanged.

   b. Saving of £1000. (Also investment of £1000 if Reuters uses this money to purchase new capital.)

c. Investment of F 350 million by Paris developer. The savers are the bank's depositors.

d. Dissaving (negative saving) of DM 5000 by grandmother. No investment. Saving is being done by whoever is financing the bond dealer.

e. Saving by Peter of €10,000. Investment of €10,000 by Luxemburg government.

6. Savings can be borrowed by business firms, which can purchase new technology, engage in research to develop new technology, expand existing plants, or build new plants. Savings can be borrowed by individuals, who can invest in human capital (higher education, professional or technical training) or purchase newly constructed houses.

   Investment is what enables a nation's average standard of living to grow. With more capital, labour is more productive, output is greater and real incomes rise. But investment requires that productive resources be diverted from consumer goods. Thus, investment requires a sacrifice of current consumption.

8. Stockholders have put up €100,000 and receive dividends of €30,000. With an interest rate of 10%, €10,000 of this is the normal rate of return. The other €20,000 is economic profit, earned by the stockholders.

10. There were just enough buyers of Eurotunnel shares in 1987 willing to pay £3.50 per share because they believed that, given the projected costs and revenues, this represented at least as good a way to save as any other of similar risk. Because building the tunnel turned out to be vastly more expensive than originally estimated, the revenues would have to be shared out among more investors, making each share worth less.

Appendix

2. Disagree. The bridge cannot be justified on efficiency grounds, because simply investing the 25,000 kroner in the financial markets would generate a stream of income worth more to citizens than the benefits from the bridge. However, at substantially lower interest rates, the present value of the benefits would be higher and might exceed 25,000 kroner. In that case, the bridge should be built.

4. **a.** €3,000/(1.05) = €2,857.14.

   b. €3,000/(1.05)^2 = €2,721.09.

   c. €1,000/(1.05) + €1,000/(1.05)^2 + €1,000/(1.05)^3 = €2,723.24.

6. **a.** is false; **b.** is true.

Chapter 12

2. **a.** First, calculate MP and $P \times MP$:

Workers	Loaves of bread	MP	P × MP
0	0	–	–
1	15	15	210
2	30	15	210
3	42	12	168
4	52	10	140
5	60	8	112
6	66	6	84
7	70	4	56

At a wage of 119 koruna per hour, four workers should be hired. The fifth worker would produce less value in an hour (112 koruna) than his/her wage.

   b. When the price of bread rises to 20 koruna, the last column must be recalculated:

Workers	P × MP
0	–
1	300
2	300
3	240
4	200
5	160
6	120
7	80

Now, six workers should be employed.

   c. If the wage rises to 125 koruna per hour then, assuming bread still costs 20 koruna, only five workers should be hired. (If bread still costs 14 koruna, as in the first example, only four workers would be taken on.)

   d. Yes, the allocation of labour would be efficient, because each firm would hire labour until the wage were equal to the value of the marginal product of output. If all firms paid the same wage, they would all have the same marginal product of labour, and no reallocation of labour could increase total output.

4. a. Disagree. The enjoyment of housing can be limited to those who pay for it. Therefore, the private market will supply it.

   b. Disagree. Monopolies produce too little product and charge an artificially high price.

   c. Agree. It is difficult for consumers to evaluate the skills of a doctor or to judge the advice that a doctor gives them.

6. The coin toss is more 'equitable', because both parties have the same chance of winning, regardless of their income. But with the coin toss, there is no guarantee that the party who values the ticket most would get it. Selling the ticket to the higher bidder is more 'efficient', since whoever places the higher money-value on the ticket will get it, but is less equitable since it favours those with larger incomes.

8. a. Pareto efficient. Both you and the street vendor benefit.

   b. Pareto efficient. You are better off (you don't die) and the vagabond is better off (by €10,000). Given your circumstances, this is a voluntary exchange.

   c. Not Pareto efficient. Not a voluntary exchange, and you are worse off.

   d. Not Pareto efficient. You and the taxi driver are better off, but you are also adding to traffic congestion that will make other rush-hour travellers worse off.

10. The allocation of labour is inefficient. Because each factory is hiring the profit-maximizing number of workers (where $W = P_X \times MP_L$), the value of the marginal product of labour in factory A is €10, while that in factory B is only €6. If workers were moved from factory B to factory A, the value of total output would rise.

Chapter 13

2. A competitive firm can sell all the output it wants without having any impact on market price. For each additional unit sold, its revenue will rise by the market price. Hence, MR is the same at all levels of output.

Each time a monopolist increases output by one unit, the market price falls. The additional revenue the monopolist receives is actually less than the price, because consumers who were already buying the output get a price break too. MR is thus lower than price, and as output increases, both price and MR decline.

4. a. 0–5: 90; 5–10: 70; 10–15: 50; 15–20: 30; 20–25: 10; 25–30: –10; 30–35: –30; 35–40: –50

   b. $Q = 20$; economic profits are 700.

   c. $Q = 15$; economic profits are 350.

6. a. and b.

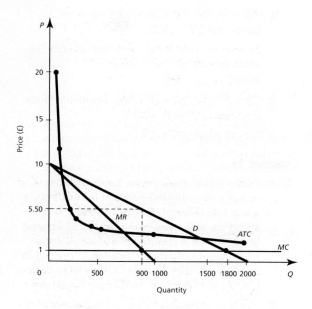

c. Profit-maximizing output is 900; profit-maximizing price is £5.50.

d. Efficient price would be £1, where the demand curve intersects the marginal cost curve. At this price, Q = 1800.

e. Long-run output would be zero, because losses would cause the monopoly to exit the industry.

f. Alternatively, regulators could require the monopoly to charge a price equal to marginal cost and then subsidize the monopoly's loss.

*8. a. Price is *AR* at 8 units of output = 24.

b. Price is *AR* at 6 units of output = 28.

c. Monopoly profit is *TR – TC* = 134.

d. 64.

e. 36.

f. 12.

Chapter 14

2. a. Monopolistic competition: free entry, lots of firms, product differentiation, close substitutability.

b. As new establishments open, demand curves for existing firms shift leftwards. Price of admission falls and profits drop to zero at the tangency of demand and *ATC*. (See Figure 14.3.)

4. a. Disagree. Product differentiation should decrease elasticity. The more differentiated the product, the fewer customers are gained or lost when price changes.

b. Disagree. Because there is ordinarily no free entry in monopoly, above-normal profits are possible in the long run. Under monopolistic competition, above-normal profits lead to entry, which eliminates the above-normal profits.

c. Disagree. Monopolistically competitive industries do have some market power (they are not price-takers), but this comes from differentiating their product, not from their size. If a firm is large relative to the market, the industry is an oligopoly.

6. Both A's and B's potential losses are minimized by cheating. To minimize the maximum loss, A should cheat, because it yields higher profit regardless of what B does. The same is true for B. If A cheats, so will B; and if B cheats, so will A. Most likely outcome: both will cheat.

8. a. 30 units.

b. *P* = €14.

c. *TR* = 30 × €14 = €420.

TC = €9 × 30 = €270.

Profit = €420 – €270 = €150.

d. In the long run, entry will shift the demand and marginal revenue curves leftwards until normal profit is earned at the profit-maximizing output level. This occurs when the demand curve is tangent to the *ATC* curve.

10. a. Both have dominant strategies in Game 1 – charge the low price. Neither has a dominant strategy in Game 2.

b. You might try tit for tat (match the competitor's move) to signal to the opposition that if she prices high, you might do so too.

c. If you are risk averse, you would probably swerve to guarantee a gain of 3. This minimizes your losses from the worst thing that can happen to you (a *maximin* strategy).

Chapter 15

2. a. Jobs might go because the motive for such mergers is economies of scale. The same output can then be produced for fewer inputs (less costs) including labour. If the motive for the merger is to increase market power, prices will rise. Although this will increase profits it will reduce output (the demand curve will be downward sloping). Less output means a lower quantity of resources demanded, including labour.

b. Where there are economies of scale the merger may well increase welfare, because it is now possible to produce more output for a given level of inputs. However, some will lose out in the short run until they have found jobs in other industries. (For some people, this might take a long time.) If the motive for the merger is increased market power, it is socially inefficient.

4. a. In Europe it may or may not be allowed, depending upon the perceived costs (increased

market power) and benefits (more efficient use of resources can lead to lower prices).

b. In the USA it would almost certainly not be allowed, since it leads to an unacceptable increase in market power as measured by the HHI.

The HHI for this market is $5(15^2) + 5(5^2) = 1125 + 125 = 1250$.

Increase in HHI due to merger: $(30^2) - 2(15^2) = 450$.

Under current guidelines, the US Justice Department will challenge any merger in an industry with an HHI between 1000 and 1800 that increases the HHI by more than 100 points. Since this merger does so, the Justice Department will challenge it.

6. Defining market share is a problem. Products of different firms may be slightly or greatly differentiated, and an arbitrary line must be drawn to define 'the market'. One must also (arbitrarily) decide the geographical size of the market. A firm might dominate the market within a single city or region, yet have a small share of the national market. Mergers that would be forbidden with one definition of the product or the market size might be permitted under alternative definitions. In addition, there is a special problem for multiproduct firms: the HHI criterion might forbid merger for some product lines and permit it for others. In this case, there is no clearly defined criterion for allowing a merger even if there is agreement on how to calculate market share.

A further problem occurs, because these measures focus on the concentration of market power rather than its dispersal.

8. See Figure 13.9 in the text. In the competitive industry, output expands until $P = MC$. Under monopoly, output is smaller, and $P > MC$.

10.

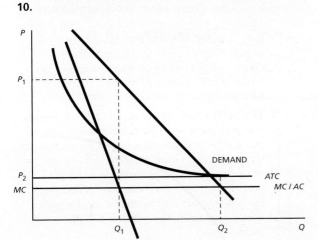

a. P_1.

b. $TR = P_1 \times Q_1$; $TC = Q_1 \times MC$ (where MC is horizontal $MC = AC$). ← fel

Economic profit is the difference between these areas, namely $Q_1 \times (P_1 - MC)$.

c. Where price = MC.

d. $TR = P_2 \times Q_2$; $TC = Q_2 \times MC$. Economic profit is negative: $Q_2 \times (P_2 - MC)$

e. Price at which $AC = AR$.

Chapter 16

2. a. With private goods, we each get to choose what quantity of each good we want. If I don't like a good, I don't buy it. But with public goods, we all get the same level of output. We all breathe better air if it is cleaned up, and we all get the same amount of national defence. When public goods are produced locally we have more choice. (See the discussion of the Tiebout hypothesis.)

b. Representative democracy is not guaranteed to produce the socially optimal mix of public goods. Some problems are logrolling, a poorly informed electorate, poor incentives for people to become informed and vote, and the fact that votes are limited to *bundles* of public goods. Also, Arrow's theorem implies that there is no consistent, non-arbitrary way to agree on what the socially optimal mix is. The voting paradox is an example of why majority voting does not provide a consistent social choice mechanism.

c. An example might be a bureaucrat who is motivated just to increase the power, prestige and budget of her department. This might lead to bloated bureaucracies.

4. a. *Elementary and secondary education*: Private aspects – substantial benefits accrue to the individual, and those who do not pay could, in theory, be excluded from receiving them. Also rivalry, in that there is a limited number of students that one teacher can effectively teach. Public aspects – there are substantial benefits to the public at large (more informed voting, more socialized behaviour). It is impossible to limit these benefits to those who pay.

b. *Higher education*: Same as above, but here even more of the benefits accrue to the individual, and the costs are often borne by those who benefit.

c. *Medical care*: Private aspects – most of the benefits of good health are enjoyed by the individual, and in theory we could exclude those who won't or can't pay. Also, high degree of rivalry. Public aspects – substantial public benefits when communicable diseases are reduced or public health is improved.

d. *Air-traffic control*: Private aspects – there is certainly rivalry, as shown by the congested skies over urban airports and the ulcers suffered by overworked air-traffic controllers. Public aspects – all air traffic in a given area must be controlled by a single set of controllers. Competing firms would not be able to supply this service effectively. Also, substantial benefits to the public at large, which are non-excludable (e.g. reduced probability of a plane crashing into one's home).

6. **a.** People disagree about this. There are private aspects of housing for the poor: excludability and rivalry. There may also be substantial benefits for society at large when everyone has a place to sleep at night.

   b. Disagree. An unregulated market economy tends to *under*produce public goods, because non-excludability and the free-rider problem prevent the private sector from charging for these goods.

8. **a.** and **b.** Most economists would argue that the patent system is, on balance, a good thing. True, patent holders – as monopolies – charge a higher-than-efficient price for the technology. But without such monopolies, the new technologies would not have been developed in the first place. Still, government involvement in research may be justified on several grounds. It might be better to have the government fund the research and make the results widely available than to encourage research via patents that impart monopoly control over new ideas. Also, patents may not be sufficient to keep new technology from being imitated once developed. In this case, the private sector has little incentive to develop the new technology.

10. **a.** *Imperfect information*: It is impossible to verify who is faking. Also, *moral hazard*: There is less reason to avoid injury, due to benefits received.

    b. *Adverse selection*: A disproportionate number of damaged computers will be sold.

    c. *Imperfect information*: It is difficult to know how well a company's system will work until after it is in place. Hard to evaluate competing bids.

    d. *Adverse selection*: The worst drivers will buy more insurance, forcing up rates and causing better drivers to choose between subsidizing bad drivers or doing without insurance. Also, *moral hazard*: Less reason to avoid collisions if insurance company will bear the costs.

Chapter 17

2. The justification would be that equilibrium wage rates for women are lower. Reasons for this include the following. Women on average may have less education and training than men. Employers are afraid to employ women who may leave to begin a family. A higher proportion of women are in non-unionized jobs. Prejudice. However, if employers give jobs to men for such reasons their profits will be lower. In competitive markets this would be difficult.

   Evidence suggests that legislation in this area meets with limited success because it is relatively easy to avoid the legislation. It would be very difficult to prove that a woman who didn't get the job really was better, and should have been employed.

4. Disagree. The statement ignores different working conditions, different holidays, and differing time available for other income opportunities (writing books, consulting). Also, choices reveal preferences for various jobs. Academic jobs must yield more utility to some, or no one would be an academic.

6. Answers will vary. Cost-of-living differences would imply that they should be different. The concept of 'horizontal equity' (equal treatment of equals), would argue for similar benefits after adjusting for cost-of-living differences. On the other hand, it may well be true that people tend to move to higher-benefit areas and away from low-benefit areas. This could result in concentrations of poverty. Mobility between countries is clearly more difficult than between areas of one country.

8. Answers will vary. Philosophical arguments might include the importance of shelter to human survival and dignity, and the values of a humanitarian society. Practical arguments might stress the public goods aspects of reducing homelessness – we all benefit from reduced homelessness, whether we contribute to the effort or not.

Chapter 18

2.

Income	25,000	35,000	45,000	60,000	80,000	100,000
Tax paid	0	2,500	5,000	8,750	13,750	18,750
Average tax rate (%)	–	7.1	11.1	14.6	17.2	18.2

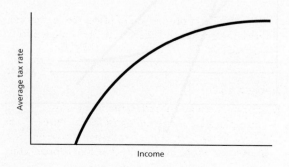

The tax is progressive because the first €25,000 is taxed at a marginal rate of zero. As income rises, the part subject to the 0% rate shrinks as a percentage of total income and the part subject to the 25% marginal rate rises as a percentage of total income.

4. Disagree. Excess burdens come about because of distortions in behaviour. If a good has a low demand elasticity, the tax will have a relatively small effect on quantity demanded, and the excess burden will be relatively small.

6. If one thinks of the social security tax as a payment for future entitlements, it would be correct to list it as part of employee compensation. However, one could always change the law so that those 'entitlements' aren't received, and staff may prefer to receive cash rather than future benefits; to this extent, the full value of the payroll tax should not be counted as compensation. Also, it must be pointed out that the imposition of tax does not raise overall employee compensation. If it really is just another form of compensation, wages will simply fall by the amount of the tax. To the extent that it is a tax because workers prefer to be compensated in a different way, if the supply of labour is inelastic workers will bear the burden of the tax and their compensation will be reduced.

8. If the cost of one's car is proportional to one's income, then the tax would be proportional. If high-income people spend a smaller (larger) *percentage* of their income on cars, then the tax would be regressive (progressive). The tax would distort by discouraging car ownership (especially ownership of expensive cars) but might also correct for existing externalities (congestion, air pollution, noise).

10.

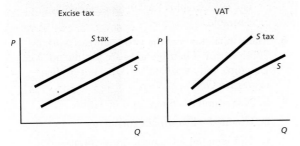

Excise tax   VAT

Since VAT is a proportion of price, the higher the price the greater the effect of the tax on quantity supplied.

Chapter 19

2. The unemployment rate is the number of unemployed as a fraction of the labour force. To be in the *labour force*, one has to have a job or be *looking* for a job. In essence, the labour force is the supply of labour. If the labour force expands by more than the number of employed expands, the unemployment rate rises!

4. **a.** Total money cost = two years' forgone salary + 2 years' tuition = €21,000 + €21,000 + €15,000 + €15,000 = €72,000 (ignoring discounting of the second year's costs).

b. Loss of seniority in present job; possible summer employment to partially offset lost annual income of €21,000; loss of work experience; etc.

c. Rate of return = €5,000/€72,000 = 0.69 or 6.9%. With an increase in net wage of €15,000, rate of return = €15,000/€72,000 = 0.208 or 20.8%.

d. Jane should look at the interest rate and see if she could earn a higher rate of return by investing her money in a financial asset. She should also consider the non-monetary rewards of a job that requires an MBA and how much she would enjoy (or dislike) business school.

6. When you work, you lose some of your income. Thus, when I earn a euro, I don't get to keep a full euro. The existence of taxes affects the opportunity cost of leisure and can thus affect work effort.

8.

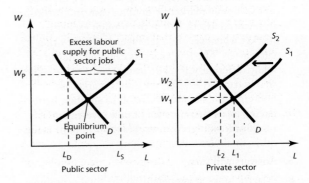

Public sector   Private sector

10. Your answer should include compensating differentials, differences in human capital (which explains the lower wages of teenagers), occupational segregation (which explains in part the lower wages of women), and labour market discrimination.

*12. **a.** $W = 5$.

b. $W = 75$.

c. Transfer earnings = 33.3; economic rent = 16.7 (transfer earnings plus economic rent).

d. Total wages paid = 50.

e. 25.

Chapter 20

2. The unemployed are those people in the labour force who do not work. No: only those jobless actually willing to work are considered unemployed.

900

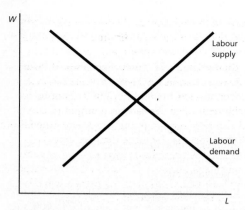

The Labour Market

The figure depicts the labour market. The demand for labour curve shows how much labour firms are willing to employ at each wage. The demand for labour depends on the wage and the marginal product of labour. The supply of labour curve shows how much labour workers are willing to supply at each wage. The supply of labour depends on the wage and (inversely) on the utility of leisure. The utility of leisure forgone is the opportunity cost of holding a job.

4. Marie-Therese participates in the goods market as a consumer, in the labour market as an employee, in the money market by holding cash and investing in financial assets, and in the foreign exchange market whenever she exchanges euros for other currencies. The four markets can affect her in many different ways. For instance, the value of her shares could rise when the goods market is booming. Or she may move on to another, better-paying job if there is a lot of new investment as a result of low interest rates. You can think of many other examples.

6. Answers will vary.

8. 'Macro' looks at aggregates in the total economy, while 'micro' looks at individual markets and individual economic agents. It is often helpful (and more accurate) to base macroeconomic theories on the behaviour of the individuals who make up the macroeconomy.

10. Wrong. Incomes have actually risen faster than prices, so that the purchasing power of the average citizen has increased.

Chapter 21

2. Every payment made by a buyer becomes income for the seller. Thus, the euro value of the purchases of new goods and services in a year must be the euro value of the income generated in that year.

4 a. 1998: 100; 1999: 142; percentage change: 42%.
   b. 1998: 100; 1999: 123.89; percentage change: 23.89%.
   c. 1998: 100; 1999: 144; percentage change: 44%.
   d. 1998: 100; 1999: 125.63; percentage change: 25.63%.
   e. With fixed-weight indexes, the percentage change in the index from year to year depends on the weights chosen and thus on the base year. We can see that the answers to (a) and (b) vary widely, as do those to (c) and (d).

   There are reasons to feel that the index in (a) overstates the change in real output and that the index in (b) understates it. Goods whose output decreases (or increases slowly) because of slowly or backward shifting supply curves (in our example, peaches) will have their relative prices increase. If we use the old prices as weights, we will tend to understate the importance of this decrease. Implicitly, we are assuming that all of the peaches given up are valued at the old price, which is not true. Likewise, if we use the new prices as weights, we overstate the importance of the production decline, because this says that all the units of peaches given up were valued at the new high price.

   Fixed-weight price indexes that use old quantities as weights are generally taken as overestimates of the increase in the price level, because these indexes ignore consumers' opportunities to find substitutes for goods whose relative prices rise. Those that use current-year quantities as weights are taken to underestimate changes in the price level because they implicitly assume that the substitutes people chose for the goods whose relative prices rose are considered just as good as the 'real thing'.

   The use of fixed-weight indexes poses special problems when used to make measurements over long periods of time, because the use of, say, 1950 weights for 1995's economy is not desirable.

6. Many inhabitants of the two countries work in South Africa. Their incomes are not included in Lesotho's and Swaziland's GDPs, but in their respective GNPs.

8. a. Not counted – financial transaction.
   b. Counted – investment spending.
   c. Not counted – financial transaction.
   d. Not counted – financial transfer.
   e. Counted – consumption spending.
   f. Not counted – used goods (unless you are in the second-hand book business, and declare your income to the government).
   g. Not counted – transfer payment.
   h. Counted – investment spending
   i. Counted – consumption (the cheese is part of the value of the final good).

j. Not counted – non-market activity.

k. Not counted – illegal goods.

10. Imports are included with the final purchases of consumption, investment, and government goods. If they were not subtracted, they would be incorrectly included as domestic production.

Chapter 22

2. As the data in the chapter show, especially the young but also women tend to be more affected by unemployment. There can also be sectoral differences. In some areas, racial minorities experience higher unemployment rates. Possible reasons range from a mismatch of skills offered and required, lack of experience, wage rigidities and labour immobility, to discrimination (this is the reason why most countries have *equal opportunity* legislation).

4. Answers will vary.

6. Yes, inflation would still be a problem. There are other costs of inflation besides the redistribution of income that occurs when incomes are not indexed. These include the waste of time and resources spent coping with inflation, and the higher risk on financial assets in an inflationary environment. See the section on 'Administrative costs and inefficiencies' under the heading 'Costs of inflation'.

8. In this case, the price of humbugs would have increased, and the quantity purchased decreased, between years 1 and 2. The opposite would have happened for lemon drops. The CPI keeps quantities constant in measuring the rise in the cost of living. This will overstate the rise in the cost of living, because it places too much weight on the good whose price increased.

10. In the short run, this could be due to a higher participation rate – that is, employment may be rising faster than the workforce. In the long run, it is only possible with productivity growth.

Chapter 23

2. The economy is described by the following equations:

Consumption: $C = 0.75Y$

Investment: $I = 75$

Aggregate expenditure: $AE = 75 + 0.75Y$

Initially, $Y = 200$, so $AE = 75 + 0.75(200) = 75 + 150 = 225$. Since $AE > Y$, the economy is in disequilibrium. To meet the excess demand, firms will run down their inventories. Then, to subsequently replenish their inventories, firms will increase production, raising total output. This process will continue until $I = S$. Since $S = 0.25Y$, equilibrium implies that $75 = 0.25Y$. Solving for Y gives $0.75/0.25 = 300$. Thus things will stop changing when $Y = 300$.

4. Think of the adjustment that occurs when, with the economy at the equilibrium level of output, an increase in planned investment occurs. Inventories are drawn down, and output increases. If firms increase output by the amount of the increase in planned investment, equilibrium will not be re-established, since the increased output (income) will also raise consumption. Aggregate expenditure will therefore rise by more than the extra investment. Output must increase further to re-establish equilibrium. The total effect on output is finite because a fraction of the extra income is saved at each successive stage. The new equilibrium will be reached when saving has risen enough to exactly match the higher level of planned investment. Formally, $\Delta S = \Delta I$. Since $\Delta S = MPS \times \Delta Y$, we can solve for ΔY:

$$\Delta Y = \frac{1}{MPS} \times \Delta I$$

6 a. $MPC = 0.8$; $MPS = 0.2$.

  b.

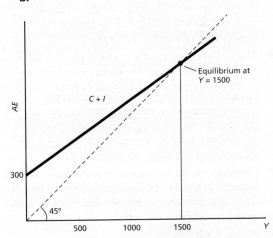

  c. $\Delta Y = (1/MPS) \times \Delta I$. Multiplier $= 1/MPS = 1/0.2 = 5$. In this case, with the multiplier equal to 5 and an increase in investment of 10, $\Delta Y = (5)(10) = 50$. Equilibrium Y increases from 1500 to 1550.

  d. $S = Y - C$

  $= Y - (200 + 0.8Y)$

  $= -200 + 0.2Y$

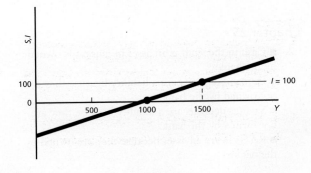

The equilibrium must be the same in both graphs because $Y = C + I$ and $S = I$ are the same condition. To see this, remember that $Y = C + S$ always. Substitute $C + S$ for Y in the equilibrium condition $Y = C + I$ to obtain $C + S = C + I$, which simplifies to $S = I$.

8. No. *AE* is planned aggregate expenditure. If you add unplanned changes in inventory to it, the sum equals aggregate output (income).

Chapter 24

2 a. $Y = 1000$, $Y_d = 800$, $C = 600$, $S = 200$, $I = 100$, $G = 200$. Since total spending $C + I + G = 600 + 100 + 200 = 900$ is less than the total output of 1000, one would predict that inventories will pile up, and firms will decide to reduce output.

b. Y would settle at 600. At this level of output, we would have $C = 300$, $I = 100$ and $G = 200$ so that $Y = C + I + G = 600$.

c. Cutting government purchases would make the fall in output worse! In particular, a cut of 25 would cause equilibrium Y to decline by $25(1/MPS) = (25)(4) = 100$. This would mean Y would decline to 500 instead of 600.

4. This statement is true if one only cares about the budget deficit. But there are also political controversies about the efficiency and the appropriate size of the government sector that would lead some to favour the tax cuts even though they raise the deficit by more.

6. There would be no automatic stabilizers. (At least, none that have been presented in the text thus far. In future chapters, we will see that interest rate changes and price level changes also act as automatic stabilizers).

There would be no distinction between the actual and full-employment deficits, because changes in income would have no impact on the budget deficit.

8. The debt is the accumulation of all past deficits (minus any surpluses). If the deficit were zero – including the government expense of interest on the national debt – there would be no increase in the debt.

Chapter 25

2. ■ Cash in the vault is an asset because it is owned by the bank.

■ Demand deposits are a liability because they are not owned by the bank.

■ Savings deposits are a liability because they are not owned by the bank.

■ Reserves are an asset because they are owned by the bank.

■ Loans are an asset because their financial worth is owned by the bank.

■ Deposits at the central bank are an asset because they are owned by the bank.

4. Before the change, the banks are holding $67.2 billion (10% of demand deposits) in reserve assets against demand deposits. Changing the reserve requirement does not increase or decrease the quantity of reserves. Rather, it changes the volume of deposits that can be held for each dollar of reserves. At an 11% reserve requirement, $67.2 billion can support only about $611 billion in demand deposits. Thus, the money supply would have to shrink by $61 billion ($672 billion – $611 billion) to restore banks to compliance with the reserve requirement.

6. M2 includes everything in M1, plus savings accounts, money market accounts, and some other categories. A shift of funds between, say, savings accounts and cheque accounts will affect M1 but not M2, because both savings accounts and cheque accounts are part of M2.

8 a. Money injected through open market operations results in a multiple expansion of the money supply only if it leads to loans, and loans can be made only if the new money ends up in banks as reserves. If the ECB buys a bond from James Q. Public, who immediately deposits the proceeds into a euro-denominated Swiss bank account, the EMU countries' money supply won't expand at all. If the money ends up in his pockets or in his mattress, the expansion of the money supply will stop right there. If he had deposited the proceeds in an EMU country's bank, excess reserves would have been created, stimulating lending and further money creation.

b. Reserves will increase by €750 (75% of 1000) and the multiplier is 1/(required reserve ratio) = 1/0.12 = 8.333. €750 × 8.333 = €6250. Thus, the money multiplier is reduced to 6.25.

10. In addition to controlling the money supply, central banks clear interbank payments, are responsible for many of the regulations governing banking practices and standards, and are the lender of last resort for the banking system. They are also responsible for managing exchange rates and the nation's foreign exchange reserves.

Answers to the second part of the question will vary.

Chapter 26

2. If households believe that interest rates will rise, why should they lend money now? They will desire to hold more of their wealth as money for the time being, betting that they can get a higher interest rate if they wait. If they buy bonds now, they risk a capital loss (a decrease in the value of their assets), because bond prices fall when interest rates rise. When households hold money to speculate in this way, we call their motive for holding money the 'speculation motive'.

4 a.

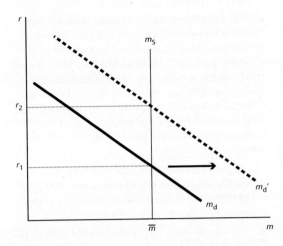

b.

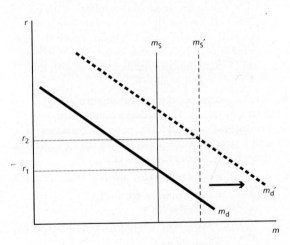

6. A recession is a decline in real GDP. When output falls, there is less economic activity and fewer transactions. Fewer transactions means that (*ceteris paribus*) money demand will fall. This will cause a leftward shift in the M_d curve, which results in a lower equilibrium interest rate (assuming that the money supply remains fixed).

Chapter 27

2. Consider the next *IS–LM* diagram. The increase in taxes would shift the *IS* curve to the left, lowering income from Y_0 to Y_1, and the interest rate from r_0 to r_1. The Japanese central bank could respond by raising the money supply, if it wanted to maintain output at its original level. In this case, the *LM*

curve would shift to the right to LM_1. The interest rate would be even lower (at r_2) as a result of this expansionary monetary policy. Investment would be stimulated.

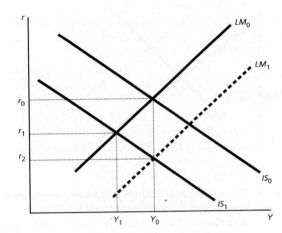

4 a.

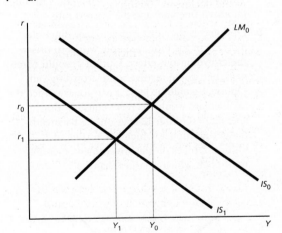

b.

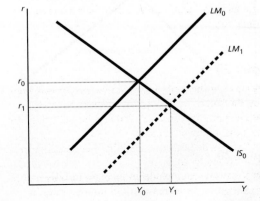

c.

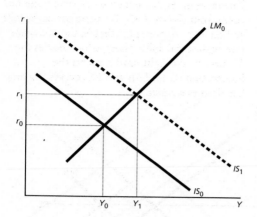

6 a. The decline in investment would be a reduction in aggregate expenditure, causing equilibrium output (income) to decrease in the goods market. In the money market, the drop in income would decrease the demand for money (shifting the M_d curve to the left), causing the interest rate to fall and investment spending to rise back up somewhat. But the net effect would be a decline in output (income) and the interest rate.

b. Option 3 is the most expansionary, since the increase in the money supply works to offset the crowding-out effect. Option 2 would come next, but would involve some crowding out. Option 1 would be least expansionary, since the tax increase would decrease consumption spending. (Option 1 relies on the balanced-budget multiplier, which has a value of 1. Option 2 relies on the government spending multiplier, which is larger than 1.)

8.

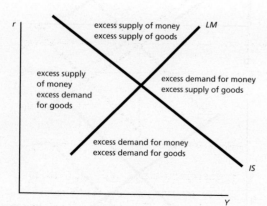

Chapter 28

2 a. Answers can include an increase in UK incomes, an increase in US interest rates, a decrease in UK interest rates, a decrease in the US price level, and an increase in the UK price level.

b. All of the above, except for the increase in UK incomes, would also cause the supply curve to shift to the left.

c. If the exchange rate is flexible, none of them will affect the balance of payments. However, the two changes in interest rates listed in (a) and (b) above – which would raise the value of the dollar without any other simultaneous change in import or export demand – would make US goods relatively more expensive and decrease the US trade balance (shrink the surplus, or increase the deficit).

4 a. The expansionary fiscal policy increased incomes and the demand for money. This in itself would cause US interest rates to rise. In addition, the contractionary monetary policy caused interest rates to rise further.

b. The supply curve for dollars would shift to the left, and the demand curve would shift to the right. The value of the dollar would rise.

c. The rise in the value of the dollar – with no other changes in the desire to buy imports or exports – would make US goods relatively more expensive. The US trade deficit would worsen, and other countries' trade balances with the United States would rise.

6. A strong currency means that imports are relatively cheap. This reduces inflationary pressures. Psychologically, people sometimes feel that a stronger currency reflects a strong economy, though this is not always the case.

8 a.
$$Y = C + I + G + (EX - IM)$$
$$= 100 + 0.8(Y - 40) + 38 + 75 + 25 - 0.05(Y - 40)$$
$$= 238 + 0.8Y - 0.8(40) - 0.05Y + 0.05(40)$$
$$= 208 + 0.75Y$$
$$0.25Y = 208$$
$$Y = 832$$

Government deficit = $G - T = 75 - 40 = 35$

Current account balance $= EX - IM$
$$= 25 - 0.05(832 - 40)$$
$$= 214.6$$

b. The multiplier $= 1/[1 - (MPC - MPM)]$
$$= 1/[1 - (0.8 - 0.05)]$$
$$= 4$$

When G increases from 75 to 80, Y will increase by $5 \times 4 = 20$. Imports will rise by $0.05 \times 20 = 1$. With the quota, the MPM is zero, so the multiplier $= 1/(1 - 0.8) = 5$. Y will rise by $5 \times 5 = 25$. (This assumes that IM is greater than or equal to 40 without the quota, before the increase in G. Actually it is 39.6, but assuming $MPM = 0$ is a very close approximation.) Imports that rise with income act as a leakage and reduce the size of the multiplier.

c. With $EX = 25$, we need $IM = 0.05(Y - 40) = 25$. This implies $Y = 540$. Income is currently 832, so it must be decreased by $832 - 540 = 292$. With a multiplier of 4, this will require a decrease in government spending of $292/4 = 73$.

Chapter 29

2 a. As explained in the chapter, the central bank that issues the nth currency is free to choose its monetary policy.

b. (See the figure.) The reduction in German interest rates lowers the Dutch FE line from FE_0 to FE_1. This leads to an inflow of foreign currency which raises the Dutch money supply. This process will continue until the Dutch LM curve passes through the intersection of FE_1 and IS_0 curves.

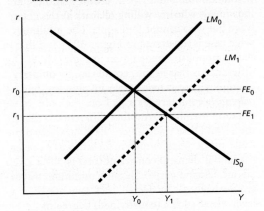

c. Answers will vary.

4. In the global economy model, an increase in government spending raises interest rates and thus reduces investment spending. In the national economy model, interest rates are determined by interest rates abroad. An increase in government spending under flexible exchange rates leads to an increase in the demand for domestic currency, which leads to an appreciation. As a result, domestically produced goods become relatively more expensive, compared to goods produced abroad. This leads to a deterioration of the trade balance.

6. Since all eleven countries were members of the ERM during the preceding years, their exchange rates had already been fixed. Monetary policy had thus already been ineffective (except in the nth currency country). However, in joining the monetary union, they have also committed themselves not to run excessive deficits. Thus, in addition to giving up monetary policy, they also face constraints on the use of fiscal policies.

8 a. If interest rates are determined by those abroad (here, the United States), they will not change. The increase in the money supply shifts the LM curve from LM_0 to LM_1. Demand for euros falls and the euro depreciates (that is, the exchange rate against the dollar rises), which moves the IS curve to the right until it meets the intersection of the LM_1 and FE_0 curves. Income has risen as a result.

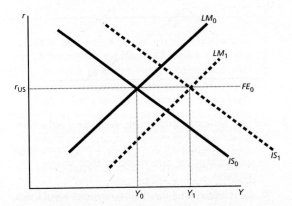

b. If the Fed also raises the money supply, the FE line drops from FE_0 to FE_1. Depending on the relative size of the money supply increases, the new equilibrium (where FE_1 and LM_1 intersect) can lead to a higher or lower income, and make the exchange rate depreciate or appreciate. In the next diagram the domestic money supply effect dominates, and because the euro depreciates, income rises. Interest rates will always be lower than before.

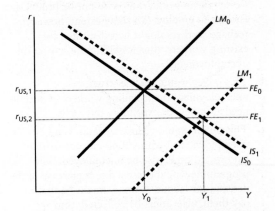

c. When the Fed reduces the money supply, interest rates rise, shifting the FE curve upwards to FE_1. The excess supply of domestic currency is even greater now than in case (a), leading to a bigger depreciation of the euro. Net exports rise, shifting the IS curve to the right until it meets the LM_1 and FE_1 curves at their intersection. Again, income has risen.

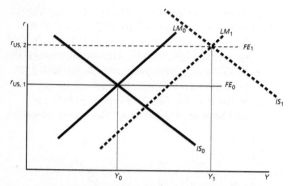

10 **a.** Their interest rates will be below that in the monetary union. Demand for their currencies falls, leading to a depreciation of their respective currencies (assuming they do not fix their respective exchange rates against the euro). The result is an improvement in their net exports, leading to higher levels of output.

   b. They would need to keep their currencies from depreciating by also reducing their money supplies.

   c. (a) The demand for their currencies would rise, leading to a leftward shift of their *LM* curves. Output would fall. (b) Use expansionary fiscal policies which shift the *IS* curve to the right.

Chapter 30

2. These factors indicate that Japan probably has a low rate of frictional unemployment. One part of the natural unemployment rate is made up of movers and workers changing jobs.

4 **a.** This policy would decrease structural unemployment by making it profitable to hire workers who would otherwise not be productive enough to employ. (To some extent, however, teenage workers might be substituted for existing workers, thus lessening the impact on unemployment.)

   b. This policy would reduce structural unemployment by providing workers with skills needed in new or expanding industries.

   c. This policy would reduce structural and cyclical unemployment by providing jobs for people who would otherwise be unemployed. The programme would cause a direct increase in the demand for labour. A worry might be that to pay them, taxes must be collected, thus reducing demand in the private sector and eliminating some private-sector jobs.

   d. This reduces frictional unemployment by aiding workers in their job hunts.

6 **a.** The effect of a higher wage tax on household labour force behaviour is ambiguous. Workers may respond to the decrease in after-tax income by consuming more leisure, which now has a lower opportunity cost, so that labour supply

will fall. However, workers are worse off. Since leisure is a normal good, consumption of it might fall and thus labour supply might rise.

   b. Improved child care reduces the opportunity cost of working. It is likely to attract more parents to the workforce, increasing the labour force and labour supply. It would also reduce the demand for labour by increasing the full costs of employing a worker. Over the short run, during which some wage rigidity is likely, the effect of an increase in labour supply and a decrease in labour demand would be an increase in the unemployment rate.

   c. Increased immigration will increase labour supply at a given wage rate without a corresponding increase in jobs. With short-run wage rigidity, unemployment will rise.

   d. Labour supply (and the labour force) should increase as more workers begin to seek even low-paid work to support themselves. With short-run wage rigidity, unemployment will rise.

8. Involuntary unemployment means that there are individuals who are willing to work at the going wage but who cannot find a job. The minimum wage case is illustrated in Figure 30.5, and that of the monopolistic trade union in Figure 30.8. One difference is that in the second case involuntary unemployment is *individually* involuntary, but *collectively* voluntary (at least from the point of view of union members). Another difference is that in the second case trade unions have maximized the trade-off between employment and wages, given the labour demand constraint (that is, for a given labour demand curve). Because minimum wages are normally set by decree, they may not be at a level where such a (constrained) degree of optimality prevails.

10. When expectations are fulfilled, $P = P^e$, and thus the equation becomes $0 = 1/b \, (Y - Y^*)$, which can only hold when $Y = Y^*$.

Chapter 31

2. Under flexible exchange rates, equilibrium in the *IS–LM* model is determined by the intersection of *FE* and *LM* curves.

   a. A decrease in the money supply shifts the *LM* curve to the left, reducing aggregate expenditure (at a given price level). The *AD* curve also shifts to the left.

   b. An increase in the world interest rate depreciates the domestic currency leading to an increase in aggregate expenditure (at a given price level). The *AD* curve shifts to the right.

   c. Increased demand for exports shifts the *IS* curve to the right. However, this increases the demand for domestic currency, leading to an appreciation, which in turn reduces net exports again. Overall, aggregate expenditure (at a given price level) remains unchanged. The *AD* curve does not shift.

4 a. A tax cut (under fixed exchange rates) raises aggregate demand, leading to higher output and prices in the short run (see the next figure).

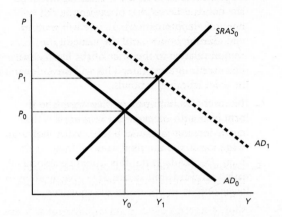

b. An increase in the money supply (under flexible exchange rates) raises aggregate demand, leading to higher output and prices in the short run (again, see figure).

c. An increase in the price of oil raises production costs, shifting the aggregate supply curve upwards. This leads to lower output and higher prices in the short run (see the next figure).

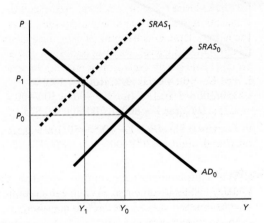

6. Under fixed exchange rates, countries cannot pursue independent monetary policies. This implies that the rate of money growth is determined by monetary policies abroad. Thus the rate of inflation is 'imported' from abroad. It is for this reason that fixed exchange rates are sometimes used to contain domestic inflation.

8. The difference between the two countries was that Finland, a future EMU participant, had a fixed exchange rate, whereas Norway had a flexible exchange rate. The next diagram illustrates their common initial position. In both countries a high

level of aggregate demand had pushed the level of output above the natural level, Y^*. To control inflation, the authorities would have had to reduce aggregate demand back to AD_0. In the Finnish case, this would have been possible through a reduction in government expenditure or an increase in taxes. The Norwegian authorities would have needed to reduce the money supply.

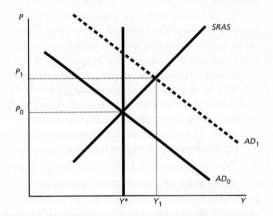

10 a. A vertical *AS* curve implies a vertical Phillips curve.

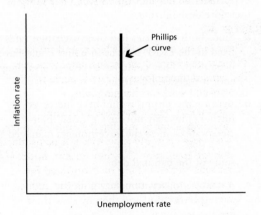

b. Accelerating inflation expectations shift the short-run Phillips curve upwards.

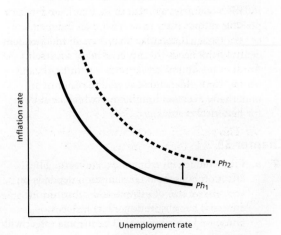

Chapter 32

2. The criteria are shown in Table 32.1. The first two aim at disciplining fiscal policy. The deficit criterion imposes a lid on public spending. The debt criterion applies to excessive fiscal spending in the past, ensuring that countries with a tradition of deficit spending would not be able to join. In practice, because it takes a long time to reduce the debt, this criterion was applied less stringently.

   The remaining three are aimed at disciplining monetary policy. The inflation criterion outlaws expansionary monetary policies in the run-up to EMU, while the interest rate criterion requires countries to be at similar stages of their business cycles. The last criterion is somewhat redundant, since only countries that also satisfy the third and fourth criteria are likely to be ERM members. However, it may stabilize the expectations of foreign exchange dealers, preventing speculative fluctuations in exchange rates.

4. If governments must have balanced budgets they are unable to use spending and taxing to offset economic shocks. Moreover, an adverse shock that sends budgets into deficit requires the government to raise taxes or cut spending, which will exacerbate the impact of the shock. The effect is therefore destabilizing.

6 a. Since both countries had their exchange rates fixed in the ERM, only fiscal policy could have been used. They could have reduced spending and/or increased taxation.

   b. Because the surplus would have increased further. This may not have pleased their electorates, unless the governments managed to convince voters that it was worthwhile to repay some of the national debt.

   c. A contractionary monetary policy to reduce aggregate demand and thereby slow their economies down.

8. The causality may run from low inflation to greater central bank independence if the low-inflation countries are also those that bear the least possible output costs from having an independent central bank. (Remember that even an independent central bank needs to earn credibility for itself.) Another possibility is that both low inflation and central bank independence are the result of an underlying aversion to inflation (which could be for historical reasons).

Chapter 33

2 a. Firms reduce investment expenditure. The effect on household consumption depends on the relative size of income and substitution effects. The substitution effect reduces household consumption. The income effect will be positive if households are net asset holders. The data suggest that the substitution effect dominates the income effect. This implies that higher interest rates reduce consumption expenditures.

   b. Since higher interest rates mean that the coupon value (that is, the regular payment) on new bonds exceeds that of existing bonds (with the same denomination), no one will want to hold existing bonds until the value of the coupon relative to the price of the bond equals the current interest rate. This will drive down the price of existing bonds.

   c. If households hold part of their wealth in the form of bonds, the answer to (b) implies that higher interest rates will be associated with a reduction in the nominal value of their wealth. In an *AS–AD* diagram, this would be associated with a leftward shift of the *AD* curve, leading to lower output and prices in the short run.

4.

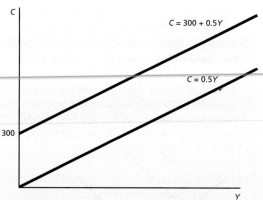

   a. For $C = 300 + 0.5Y$: APC (for $Y = 100$) = $350/100 = 3.5$; APC (for $Y = 400$) = $500/400 = 1.25$; APC (for $Y = 800$) = $700/800 = 0.875$.

   For $C = 0.5Y$: APC ($Y = 100$) = $50/100 = 0.5$; APC ($Y = 400$) = $200/400 = 0.5$; APC ($Y = 800$) = $400/800 = 0.5$.

   b. When autonomous consumption is positive, the *MPC* falls as income rises. When autonomous consumption is zero, the *MPC* is constant.

   c. For $C = 300 + 0.5Y$, the *APC* approaches the *MPC* as income rises. For $C = 0.5Y$, *APC* equals *MPC*.

   d. Since their *MPC*s are equal, a change in income will affect each family in the same way. An income reduction of one euro reduces consumption of the richer family by half a euro; an income increase of one euro increases consumption of the poorer family by half a euro.

6 a. His total lifetime wealth equals €300,000 = €20,000 + (20 × €14,000). He will consume €300,000/25 = €12,000 each year.

   b. See the diagram. Change in wealth = Income − Consumption. His wealth starts to decline when he stops working. His has zero wealth when he dies.

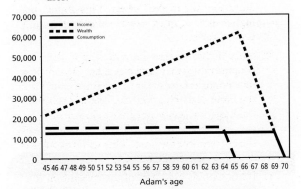

c. His total lifetime wealth is now €302,000 = €20,000 + (20 × €14,100). He will consume €302,000/25 = €12,080 each year. His consumption increases by €80 each year.

d. In this case, his total lifetime wealth equals €300,100 = €20,000 + (1 × €14,100) + (19 × €14,000) now. He will consume €300,100/25 = €12,004 each year. His consumption increases by only €4 each year.

8. Expectations of future sales determine how much capital a firm will want to have in place in the future. To have this capital when it is needed, investment spending must take place in earlier periods. Since expectations of future sales are affected by government policy announcements, the release of economic data, and 'animal spirits' – all of which can change rapidly – the resulting investment spending is quite volatile.

10. Maintaining inventory stocks helps a firm maintain a smooth production level. When sales unexpectedly increase, goods can be sold out of inventory. When sales unexpectedly decrease, goods can be added to inventories. By smoothing production, a firm can save on the adjustment costs associated with frequent changes in capital stock and employment levels. The cost of this policy is the forgone interest from investing funds in inventory stocks instead of lending out the money in financial markets.

Chapter 34

2 a. Graph 1: *Supply-side economics*. It focuses on the supply-side effects of a tax cut and tends to ignore the demand-side impacts. Tax cuts should increase the incentive to work, save and invest. If work effort, saving and investment all increase, the *AS* curve will shift to the right, increasing output and reducing the price level. The extent to which the supply curve is likely to shift depends on the responsiveness of behaviour to the tax cuts. This is the subject of much controversy.

Graph 2: *Monetarism/New classical economics*. Both schools believe that fiscal policy cannot

have an impact on the level of real output. Monetarism believes that nominal GDP cannot change as long as the money supply and the velocity of money remain constant. Thus real GDP will not respond to a tax cut. New classical theories predict that 'anticipated' fiscal policies will have no effect on real GDP, which remains at the potential output level determined in the long run in markets such as the labour market.

Graph 3: *Keynesian economics*. As long as the economy is not operating at capacity, and as long as the central bank accommodates somewhat by increasing the money supply, a permanent tax cut can increase the level of GDP and is likely to be inflationary. The impact on the price level is determined by how close to capacity the economy is operating.

b. Answers will vary.

4 a. No, it only means that individuals do not make systematic errors when they form their expectations.

b. Answers will vary.

6 a. Clinton's tax increases and spending cuts would be a fiscal contraction. With no change in Fed policy, output would decrease and unemployment would increase. If the Fed matches the fiscal contraction with a monetary expansion, reducing interest rates to stimulate investment, the decline in output could be avoided.

b. Monetarists would worry about imperfect policy timing. Fed stimulation might take effect at the wrong time (for example, after the economy has recovered from the impact of the fiscal contraction). Supply-siders would worry that higher tax rates would decrease the incentive to work and invest. Extreme supply-siders might worry that an increase in tax rates would decrease tax revenue and result in an even larger budget deficit.

c. To evaluate the supply-side argument, you would need to see what happened to tax revenues and labour supply after the tax-rate increases. An increase in tax revenues, *ceteris paribus*, would contradict the view of extreme supply-siders. If labour supply did not decrease much, general supply-side arguments would be weakened. To evaluate the monetarist argument, you would need to see if investment spending increased as consumption spending declined (proper policy timing), or only after consumption began to recover (poor timing).

8 a. As the next diagram shows, the contractionary monetary policy shifted the *AD* curve downwards, leading to lower prices and output. The position of the *AS* curve is partly determined by people's price expectations. Because expectations seemed to change very little, the economy experienced a large fall in output.

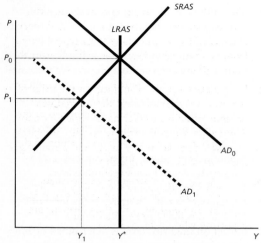

P_0

P_1

SRAS

LRAS

AD_0

AD_1

Y_1 Y^* Y

b. Not necessarily. The likely problem was a lack of credibility. Given the UK's inflation record, it may have been rational to expect the government not to stick to its promises. A second reason for the large rise in unemployment could have been sticky wages and prices, if contracts had been set in advance.

c. *Ceteris paribus*, this should lead to more employment (recall the monopolistic traded union model from Chapter 30) if the trade unions were no longer able to set wages above the market-clearing level, and hence to a higher level of output. It was also hoped that these changes would increase wage flexibility, thus allowing workers to respond more quickly to the new monetary policy.

d. When exchange rates are fixed, the domestic monetary policy is determined by monetary policies abroad. It was hoped that fixing Sterling to the DM zone (remember that the DM was the nth currency in the ERM) would therefore lead to lower inflation.

e. The ECB has a monetary strategy very similar to that of the Bundesbank. That is, its prime objective is to ensure price stability through a conservative monetary policy.

Chapter 35

2.

Table 1

Period	L	K	Y	Y/L	Growth rate of output
1	1052	3065	4506	4.28	–
2	1105	3095	4674	4.23	3.7
3	1160	3126	4842	4.17	3.6
4	1218	3157	5019	4.12	3.7

Table 2

Period	L	K	Y	Y/L	Growth rate of output
1	1052	3065	4506	4.28	–
2	1062	3371	4683	4.41	3.9
3	1073	3709	4866	4.53	3.9
4	1084	4079	5055	4.66	3.9

Table 3

Period	L	K	Y	Y/L	Growth rate of output
1	1052	3065	4506	4.28	–
2	1062	3095	4731	4.45	5.0
3	1073	3126	4967	4.63	5.0
4	1084	3157	5216	4.81	5.0

In Table 1, L is increasing faster than K and Y, so productivity is falling. In Table 2, K and Y are increasing faster than L, so productivity is growing. The productivity increase is due to more capital per worker. In Table 3, K and L are increasing at the same slow rate, but technology is pushing Y up faster than either is growing.

4. In the short run, output responds to aggregate expenditure, and an increase in consumption will cause output and employment to increase. In the long run, output will gravitate to potential output, so fluctuations in aggregate expenditure are less relevant. But higher levels of consumption spending in the long run use up funds and resources that would otherwise be available for the purchase of capital equipment by business firms. The savings function would shift downwards, resulting in a lower level of income.

6 a. Effective depreciation is now $d(1 - t)$ where t is the rate at which depreciation can be offset against tax payments. The depreciation function becomes flatter.

b. Income would be higher, since the depreciation function intersects the saving function further to the right. Growth will change in the transition, but not at the new steady state.

8. Assuming that the economy stays at full employment, the bill would cause the economy to produce more capital goods and fewer consumption goods. This would lead to higher growth in the transition to the new steady state. The trade-off is less consumption today. There are also distributional consequences. Capital income earners (who have higher incomes on average) would benefit. The members of the higher-income households (who spend a smaller fraction of their incomes) would bear relatively less of the consumption-tax burden, while the members of the low-income households (who spend a higher fraction of their incomes) would bear relatively more of the consumption-tax burden.

10 **a.** Figure 35.15 shows that, in countries with a low level of capital (the poorer countries), the return to capital (that is, its marginal product) is higher than in those with a large capital stock, *ceteris paribus*. Investors in rich countries thus have an incentive to reallocate some of their capital to poorer countries.

   b. Investors often consider investments in developing countries riskier than those at home.

Chapter 36

2. **a.** Bearskin caps: USA.
    Wheat: USA.

   b. Bearskin caps: USA.
   Wheat: Russia.

   c. The USA will export bearskin caps and import wheat. Russia will import bearskin caps and export wheat. At the current exchange rate, Russia's consumers would wish to buy all goods from the USA. This will raise the dollar price and depress the rouble price.

4. **a.** Illinois would have an absolute advantage in both wheat and soybeans.

   b. In Illinois, taking one acre out of wheat and moving it into soybeans sacrifices 48 bushels of wheat for 39 bushels of soybeans. This is 48/39 = 1.23 bushels of wheat for each bushel of soybeans. In Kansas, the sacrifice is 40/24 = 1.66 bushels of wheat for each bushel of soybeans.

   c. Based on the calculations in b. above, Kansas has a comparative advantage in wheat, and Illinois has a comparative advantage in soybeans.

   d. Yes, the data are consistent with the conclusions in c. above. Kansas has more land devoted to wheat than to soybeans, while in Illinois there is more land devoted to soybeans than to wheat. Although neither state completely 'specializes', each state seems to be devoting more of its resources to producing the good in which it has a comparative advantage.

6. **a.** The opportunity cost of a bottle of red wine is 1.5 bottles of white in France and 2 bottles of white in Germany. France, therefore, has a comparative advantage in red wine.

   The opportunity cost of a bottle of white wine is 0.66 bottles of red in France and 0.5 bottles of white wine in Germany. Germany, therefore, has a comparative advantage in white wine.

   b. No. At the current exchange rate, both white and red wine are cheaper in Germany. French citizens will want to import both types of wine from Germany, but Germans will not want to import French wine.

   c. In this situation, we would expect the price of the franc to decrease until French red wine became attractive to Germans while German white wine was still attractive to the French. (An exchange rate between 1.5 and 2 francs per mark would accomplish this.)

   d. In the long run, we would expect exchange rates to adjust until the French are exporting red wine to Germany, and the Germans are exporting white wine to France.

Chapter 37

2. Many recent famines have resulted from government polices. In some cases, keeping farm prices artificially low has led to a decrease in production. In other cases, a failure to invest in a distributional infrastructure has led to a famine in outlying rural areas.

4. **a.** Capital increases the productivity of labour. A given-sized labour force can produce more output, and output per capita rises.

   b. In a market economy, individual household savings decisions determine the pool of aggregate savings. Aggregate savings, in turn, is the amount made available for firms to purchase capital. Savings are matched to investment projects in financial markets, where the interest rate adjusts to equate total desired investment with total desired savings.

   c. In developing countries, a greater fraction of output is needed just to ensure the current population's survival. An increase in investment requires a decrease in current consumption, and at a minimum causes more discomfort than it would in developed countries.

   d. Answers will vary. Market-orientated economists would stress increased incentives for private investment (political stability, lower government budget deficit, and perhaps loans from abroad). Planning-orientated economists might stress government-directed projects, taxes on luxury goods, and capital controls designed to prevent capital flight to developed countries.

6. It is true that poor countries must accumulate capital in order to grow. But many poor countries do indeed have extra output available for savings. The problem is often that the available savings goes abroad (capital flight). Increased political stability and a more stable investment climate would help investment in the domestic economy.

In addition, poor countries can get loans and other assistance from developed countries to help them accumulate capital.

8. A country should work to develop both its agricultural and its industrial sectors. Development of the agricultural sector can have high payoffs because it often requires little capital investment and directly benefits the poorest (rural) segment of society. Experience has shown that import substitution is a poor development policy. Its disadvantages include reduced competition in the domestic market, fewer jobs created, and expensive inputs for domestic industries.

Many countries favour industry as a more direct route to growth in the capital stock, and also to emulate the production pattern of already developed countries. Import substitution is attractive because it reduces dependence on unstable foreign demand for exports.

Chapter 38

2. The speaker confuses political systems with economic systems. The Soviet economic system was one of socialism (government ownership of land and capital) and central planning (government direction of resource allocation). Totalitarianism is a political – not an economic – system in which the ruler exercises authoritarian control without the consent of those governed.

4. Socialism is an economic system in which the 'means of production' (land and capital) are owned and controlled by government. The possible strengths: rapid growth from planned capital accumulation, internalization of external costs, a fairer distribution of income (because no property income).

6. Most economists would disagree with the need for subsidies. If companies have a comparative

advantage in production they will be able to survive without subsidies. Some would argue, however, that in the short term subsidies can be efficient on an 'infant industry' basis. Young companies may need protection until they 'grow up' and can stand without government help.

There is certainly a case for allowing mergers that raise concentration in the domestic market if there is significant international competition which will prevent the exploitation of monopoly power.

8. a. Disagree. Exactly the opposite has occurred. Since 1958, China has moved towards a decentralized industrial base. Since Tiananmen Square, China has cracked down on political dissent but it has encouraged private enterprise.

b. The first two sentences are correct, the third is not. Japan's growth was primarily due to very high rates of saving and investment – capital accumulation.

c. Disagree. The opposite is true. Economists agree about the six components of transition, but disagree about the sequencing and speed.

10. Disagree. While it is true that central planners can command a higher rate of national saving and capital accumulation, central planning requires keen and virtuous planners to ensure that scarce capital flows to where it is needed most. In a capitalist market economy, the self-interest of capital owners steers capital to those sectors where it is needed most – that is, those sectors offering the highest rate of return. Thus, while under central planning there might be more capital accumulation, it will not necessarily be the right kind of capital and will not necessarily find its way to the right places. Empirically, European market economies grew faster than the USSR in the 1970s and 1980s.

Index